NINETY-EIGHTH EDITION
SINCE 1912

WHO'S WHO
IN BASEBALL
2013

Official Lifetime Records
Of Major League Players

Editor
Pete Palmer

Associate Editor
Stuart Shea

Managing Editor
Rory S. Slifkin

Cover Photo: ICON Sports Media

EDITOR'S NOTE: *Denotes League Leader throughout the publication.

WHO'S WHO IN BASEBALL is published annually by Who's Who in Baseball Magazine Co., Inc., 1115 Broadway, New York, New York 10010. Single copy price: $9.95. Submissions of manuscripts, illustrations and/or photographs must be accompanied by a stamped, self-addressed envelope. The publisher assumes no responsibility for unsolicited material. Copyright © 2013 by Who's Who in Baseball Magazine Co., Inc. All rights reserved under International and Pan American Copyright Conventions. Reproduction in whole or in part without written permission of the publisher is strictly prohibited. Printed in U.S.A.

BATTERS

ABREU, BOB KELLY (BOBBY)

Born, Maracay, Venezuela, March 11, 1974.
Bats Left. Throws Right. Height, 6 feet. Weight, 210 pounds.

Year	Club	Lea	Pos	G	AB	R	H	2B	3B	HR	RBI	SB	Avg
1991 Astros	Gulf Coast	OF-SS	56	183	21	55	7	3	0	20	10	.301
1992 Asheville	So. Atl.	OF	135	480	81	140	21	4	8	48	15	.292
1993 Osceola	Fla. St.	OF	129	474	62	134	21	17	5	55	10	.283
1994 Jackson	Texas	OF	118	400	61	121	25	9	16	73	12	.303
1995 Tucson	P.C.	OF-2B	114	415	72	126	24	17	10	75	16	.304
1996 Tucson	P.C.	OF	132	484	86	138	14	16	13	68	24	.285
1996 Houston	N.L.	OF	15	22	1	5	1	0	0	1	0	.227
1997 Jackson	Texas	OF	3	12	2	2	1	0	0	0	0	.167
1997 New Orleans	A.A.	OF	47	194	25	52	9	4	2	22	7	.268
1997 Houston a-b-c	N.L.	OF	59	188	22	47	10	2	3	26	7	.250
1998 Philadelphia	N.L.	OF	151	497	68	155	29	6	17	74	19	.312
1999 Philadelphia	N.L.	OF	152	546	118	183	35	*11	20	93	27	.335
2000 Philadelphia	N.L.	OF	154	576	103	182	42	10	25	79	28	.316
2001 Philadelphia	N.L.	OF	*162	588	118	170	48	4	31	110	36	.289
2002 Philadelphia	N.L.	OF	157	572	102	176	*50	6	20	85	31	.308
2003 Philadelphia	N.L.	OF	158	577	99	173	35	1	20	101	22	.300
2004 Philadelphia	N.L.	OF	159	574	118	173	47	1	30	105	40	.301
2005 Philadelphia	N.L.	OF	*162	588	104	168	37	1	24	102	31	.286
2006 Philadelphia	N.L.	OF	98	339	61	94	25	2	8	65	20	.277
2006 New York d	A.L.	OF	58	209	37	69	16	0	7	42	10	.330
2007 New York	A.L.	OF	158	605	123	171	40	5	16	101	25	.283
2008 New York e	A.L.	OF	156	609	100	180	39	4	20	100	22	.296
2009 Los Angeles	A.L.	OF	152	563	96	165	29	3	15	103	30	.293
2010 Los Angeles	A.L.	OF	154	573	88	146	41	1	20	78	24	.255
2011 Los Angeles	A.L.	DH-OF	142	502	54	127	30	1	8	60	21	.253
2012 Albuquerque	P.C.	OF	5	17	2	6	1	0	0	0	0	.353
2012 Los Angeles	A.L.	OF	8	24	1	5	3	0	0	5	0	.208
2012 Los Angeles f-g	N.L.	OF	92	195	28	48	8	1	3	19	6	.246
Major League Totals		17 Yrs.	2347	8347	1441	2437	565	59	287	1349	399	.292
Division Series												
1997 Houston	N.L.	PH	3	3	0	1	0	0	0	0	1	.333
2006 New York	A.L.	OF	4	15	2	5	1	0	0	4	0	.333
2007 New York	A.L.	OF	4	15	1	4	1	0	1	2	1	.267
2009 Los Angeles	A.L.	OF	3	9	4	5	2	0	0	1	0	.556
Division Series Totals			14	42	7	15	4	0	1	7	2	.357
Championship Series												
2009 Los Angeles	A.L.	OF	6	25	2	4	2	0	0	2	0	.160

a On disabled list from May 25 to July 1, 1997.
b Selected in expansion draft by Tampa Bay Devil Rays, November 18, 1997.
c Traded to Philadelphia Phillies for infielder Kevin Stocker, November 19, 1997.
d Traded to New York Yankees with pitcher Cory Lidle for infielder C.J. Henry, pitcher Matt Smith, catcher Jesus Sanchez and pitcher Carlos Monasterios, July 30, 2006.
e Filed for free agency, October 30, 2008. Signed with Los Angeles Angels, February 12, 2009.
f Released by Los Angeles Angels, April 28, 2012. Signed with Los Angeles Dodgers, May 4, 2012.
g Filed for free agency, November 3, 2012.

ACKLEY, DUSTIN MICHAEL

Born, Winston-Salem, North Carolina, February 26, 1988.
Bats Left. Throws Right. Height, 6 feet, 1 inch. Weight, 185 pounds.

Year	Club	Lea	Pos	G	AB	R	H	2B	3B	HR	RBI	SB	Avg
2010 Tacoma	P.C.	2B	52	212	37	58	12	4	5	23	2	.274
2010 West Tenn	Southern	2B	82	289	42	76	21	4	2	28	8	.263
2011 Tacoma	P.C.	2B	66	271	57	82	17	3	9	35	7	.303
2011 Seattle	A.L.	2B-1B	90	333	39	91	16	7	6	36	6	.273
2012 Seattle	A.L.	2B-1B	153	607	84	137	22	2	12	50	13	.226
Major League Totals		2 Yrs.	243	940	123	228	38	9	18	86	19	.243

ALONSO, YONDER

Born, Havana, Cuba, April 8, 1987.
Bats Left. Throws Right. Height, 6 feet, 2 inches. Weight, 240 pounds.

Year	Club	Lea	Pos	G	AB	R	H	2B	3B	HR	RBI	SB	Avg
2008 Sarasota		Fla.St.	1B	6	19	1	6	1	0	0	2	0	.316
2009 Reds		Gulf Coast	1B	6	15	0	2	0	0	0	0	0	.133
2009 Sarasota		Fla.St.	1B	49	175	21	53	13	0	7	38	0	.303
2009 Carolina		Southern	1B	29	105	12	31	11	0	2	14	1	.295
2010 Carolina		Southern	1B-OF	31	101	19	27	5	0	3	13	4	.267
2010 Louisville		Int.	1B-OF	101	406	50	120	31	2	12	56	9	.296
2010 Cincinnati		N.L.	1B	22	29	2	6	2	0	0	3	0	.207
2011 Louisville		Int.	OF-1B	91	358	46	106	24	4	12	56	6	.296
2011 Cincinnati a		N.L.	OF-1B-3B	47	88	9	29	4	0	5	15	0	.330
2012 San Diego		N.L.	1B	155	549	47	150	39	0	9	62	3	.273
Major League Totals			3 Yrs.	224	666	58	185	45	0	14	80	3	.278

a Traded to San Diego Padres with pitcher Edinson Volquez, pitcher Brad Boxberger and catcher Yasmani Grandal for pitcher Mat Latos, December 17, 2011.

ALTUVE, JOSE CARLOS

Born, Maracay, Venezuela, May 6, 1990.
Bats Right. Throws Right. Height, 5 feet, 7 inches. Weight, 170 pounds.

Year	Club	Lea	Pos	G	AB	R	H	2B	3B	HR	RBI	SB	Avg
2008 Greeneville		Appal.	2B-3B	40	141	26	40	9	3	2	21	8	.284
2009 Greeneville		Appal.	2B	45	179	45	58	20	2	3	18	21	.324
2009 Tri-City		N.Y.-Penn.	2B	21	76	13	19	5	0	0	7	7	.250
2010 Lexington		So.Atl.	2B-3B	94	393	75	121	15	3	11	45	39	.308
2010 Lancaster		Calif.	2B-3B	31	116	18	32	5	2	4	22	3	.276
2011 Lancaster		Calif.	2B	52	213	38	87	13	7	5	34	19	.408
2011 Corpus Christi		Texas	2B-3B	35	144	21	52	9	3	5	25	5	.361
2011 Houston		N.L.	2B	57	221	26	61	10	1	2	12	7	.276
2012 Houston		N.L.	2B	147	576	80	167	34	4	7	37	33	.290
Major League Totals			2 Yrs.	204	797	106	228	44	5	9	49	40	.286

ALVAREZ, PEDRO MANUEL

Born, New York, New York, February 6, 1987.
Bats Left. Throws Right. Height, 6 feet, 3 inches. Weight, 225 pounds.

Year	Club	Lea	Pos	G	AB	R	H	2B	3B	HR	RBI	SB	Avg
2009 Lynchburg		Carolina	3B	66	243	38	60	14	1	14	55	1	.247
2009 Altoona		Eastern	3B	60	222	42	74	18	0	13	40	1	.333
2010 Indianapolis		Int.	3B	66	242	42	67	15	4	13	53	4	.277
2010 Pittsburgh		N.L.	3B	95	347	42	89	21	1	16	64	0	.256
2011 Pirates		Gulf Coast	3B	1	1	0	0	0	0	0	0	0	.000
2011 Bradenton		Fla.St.	3B	6	16	2	3	0	0	1	2	0	.188
2011 Indianapolis		Int.	3B	35	125	16	32	5	1	5	19	0	.256
2011 Pittsburgh a		N.L.	3B	74	235	18	45	9	1	4	19	1	.191
2012 Pittsburgh		N.L.	3B	149	525	64	128	25	1	30	85	1	.244
Major League Totals			3 Yrs.	318	1107	124	262	55	3	50	168	2	.237

a On disabled list from May 20 to July 9, 2011.

AMARISTA (AZOCAR), ALEXI JOSE

Born, Barcelona, Venezuela, April 6, 1989.
Bats Left. Throws Right. Height, 5 feet, 8 inches. Weight, 150 pounds.

Year	Club	Lea	Pos	G	AB	R	H	2B	3B	HR	RBI	SB	Avg
2008 Angels		Arizona	OF-2B	51	202	46	67	6	4	2	21	22	.332
2008 Cedar Rapids		Midwest	SS-OF	1	2	0	0	0	0	0	0	0	.000
2009 Cedar Rapids		Midwest	2B	125	477	84	152	39	10	4	49	38	.319
2010 Rancho Cucamonga		Calif.	2B	72	297	39	90	19	6	4	39	17	.303
2010 Salt Lake		P.C.	2B-SS	15	65	13	26	6	3	0	9	4	.400
2010 Arkansas		Texas	2B	48	191	25	55	2	1	1	20	4	.288
2011 Salt Lake		P.C.	2B-OF-SS	86	363	49	106	24	5	4	50	15	.292
2011 Los Angeles		A.L.	2B-OF-SS	23	52	2	8	3	1	0	5	0	.154
2012 Tucson		P.C.	2B-SS-3B	11	49	6	14	1	0	1	6	3	.286
2012 Salt Lake		P.C.	2B-3B-SS-OF	18	77	11	21	6	2	0	12	1	.273
2012 Los Angeles		A.L.	DH	1	0	0	0	0	0	0	0	0	.000
2012 San Diego a		N.L.	2B-OF-SS-3B	105	275	35	66	15	5	5	32	8	.240
Major League Totals			2 Yrs.	129	327	38	74	18	6	5	37	8	.226

a Traded to San Diego Padres with pitcher Donn Roach for pitcher Ernesto Frieri, May 3, 2012.

ANDINO, ROBERT LAZARO

Born, Miami, Florida, April 25, 1984.
Bats Right. Throws Right. Height, 6 feet. Weight, 195 pounds.

Year	Club	Lea	Pos	G	AB	R	H	2B	3B	HR	RBI	SB	Avg
2002	Marlins	Gulf Coast	SS	9	27	2	7	0	0	0	2	3	.259
2002	Jamestown	N.Y.-Penn.	SS	9	36	2	6	1	1	0	3	1	.167
2003	Greensboro	So.Atl.	SS	119	416	45	78	17	2	2	27	6	.188
2004	Jupiter	Fla.St.	SS-2B	48	196	18	55	7	2	0	15	6	.281
2004	Greensboro	So.Atl.	SS	76	295	27	83	10	1	8	46	9	.281
2005	Carolina	Southern	SS-2B	127	516	63	139	30	0	5	48	22	.269
2005	Florida	N.L.	SS	17	44	4	7	4	0	0	1	1	.159
2006	Albuquerque	P.C.	SS-2B	120	498	70	127	18	6	8	46	13	.255
2006	Florida	N.L.	SS	11	24	0	4	1	0	0	2	1	.167
2007	Albuquerque	P.C.	SS-2B	142	598	85	166	25	13	13	50	21	.278
2007	Florida	N.L.	SS	7	13	0	5	1	0	0	0	0	.385
2008	Albuquerque	P.C.	SS-2B	43	181	28	52	14	3	6	26	9	.287
2008	Florida	N.L.	2B-SS-3B-OF	44	63	7	13	2	0	2	9	0	.206
2009	Baltimore a	A.L.	SS-2B-3B-OF	78	198	31	44	7	0	2	10	3	.222
2010	Norfolk	Int.	SS-2B	132	546	72	144	30	4	13	76	16	.264
2010	Baltimore	A.L.	2B-SS-3B	16	61	6	18	4	0	2	6	1	.295
2011	Baltimore	A.L.	2B-SS-3B-OF	139	457	63	120	22	0	5	36	13	.263
2012	Norfolk	Int.	2B	2	9	1	3	0	0	0	2	0	.333
2012	Baltimore b-c-d	A.L.	2B-3B-SS-OF	127	384	41	81	13	1	7	28	5	.211
Major League Totals			8 Yrs.	439	1244	152	292	54	1	18	92	24	.235
Wild Card Playoff													
2012 Baltimore		A.L.	2B	1	1	2	1	1	0	0	0	0	1.000
Division Series													
2012 Baltimore		A.L.	2B	5	11	1	4	0	0	0	0	0	.364

a Traded to Baltimore Orioles for pitcher Hayden Penn, April 1, 2009.
b On disabled list from July 16 to July 31, 2012.
c Traded to Seattle Mariners for outfielder Trayvon Robinson, November 20, 2012.
d Not offered contract, November 30, 2012, re-signed with Seattle Mariners, November 30, 2012.

ANDRUS (TORRES), ELVIS AUGUSTO

Born, Maracay, Venezuela, August 26, 1988.
Bats Right. Throws Right. Height, 6 feet. Weight, 185 pounds.

Year	Club	Lea	Pos	G	AB	R	H	2B	3B	HR	RBI	SB	Avg
2005	Danville	Appal.	SS	6	18	3	5	1	0	0	1	1	.278
2005	Braves	Gulf Coast	SS-2B	46	166	26	49	6	1	3	20	7	.295
2006	Rome	So.Atl.	SS	111	437	67	116	25	4	3	50	23	.265
2007	Bakersfield	Calif.	SS	27	110	19	33	2	0	2	12	15	.300
2007	Myrtle Beach a	Carolina	SS	99	385	59	94	20	3	3	37	25	.244
2008	Frisco	Texas	SS	118	482	82	142	19	2	4	65	54	.295
2009	Texas	A.L.	SS	145	480	72	128	17	8	6	40	33	.267
2010	Texas	A.L.	SS	148	588	88	156	15	3	0	35	32	.265
2011	Texas	A.L.	SS	150	587	96	164	27	3	5	60	37	.279
2012	Texas	A.L.	SS	158	629	85	180	31	9	3	62	21	.286
Major League Totals			4 Yrs.	601	2284	341	628	90	23	14	197	123	.275
Wild Card Playoff													
2012 Texas		A.L.	SS	1	4	0	2	0	0	0	0	0	.500
Division Series													
2010 Texas		A.L.	SS	5	24	2	8	1	0	0	1	3	.333
2011 Texas		A.L.	SS	4	14	1	2	0	0	0	0	0	.143
Division Series Totals				9	38	3	10	1	0	0	1	3	.263
Championship Series													
2010 Texas		A.L.	SS	6	27	4	9	2	0	0	2	4	.333
2011 Texas		A.L.	SS	6	25	4	6	0	0	0	1	1	.240
Championship Series Totals				12	52	8	15	2	0	0	3	5	.288
World Series Record													
2010 Texas		A.L.	SS	5	17	2	3	0	0	0	1	1	.176
2011 Texas		A.L.	SS	7	29	5	8	1	0	0	0	0	.276
World Series Totals				12	46	7	11	1	0	0	1	1	.239

a Traded by Atlanta Braves to Texas Rangers with catcher Jarrod Saltalamacchia, pitcher Neftali Feliz, pitcher Matt Harrison and pitcher Beau James for infielder Mark Teixeira and pitcher Ron Mahay, July 31, 2007.

AOKI, NORICHIKA

Born, Hyuga City, Japan, January 5, 1982.
Bats Left. Throws Right. Height, 5 feet, 9 inches. Weight, 180 pounds.

Year	Club	Lea	Pos	G	AB	R	H	2B	3B	HR	RBI	SB	Avg
2004 Yakult	Japan	Pac.	OF	10	15	1	3	0	0	0	0	1	.200
2005 Yakult	Japan	Pac.	OF	144	588	100	202	26	4	3	28	29	.344
2006 Yakult	Japan	Pac.	OF	146	599	112	192	26	3	13	62	41	.321
2007 Yakult	Japan	Pac.	OF	143	557	114	193	26	2	20	58	17	.346
2008 Yakult	Japan	Pac.	OF	112	444	85	154	29	5	14	64	31	.347
2009 Yakult	Japan	Pac.	OF	142	531	87	161	23	2	16	66	18	.303
2010 Yakult	Japan	Pac.	OF	144	583	92	209	44	1	14	63	19	.358
2011 Yakult	Japan	Pac.	OF	144	583	73	170	18	5	4	44	8	.292
2012 Milwaukee a	N.L.		OF	151	520	81	150	37	4	10	50	30	.288

a Signed with Milwaukee Brewers, January 17, 2012.

ARENCIBIA, JONATHAN PAUL (J.P.)

Born, Miami, Florida, January 5, 1986.
Bats Right. Throws Right. Height, 6 feet, 1 inch. Weight, 210 pounds.

Year	Club	Lea	Pos	G	AB	R	H	2B	3B	HR	RBI	SB	Avg
2007 Auburn	N.Y.-Penn.		C	63	228	31	58	17	1	3	25	0	.254
2008 Dunedin	Fla.St.		C	59	248	38	78	22	0	13	62	0	.315
2008 New Hampshire	Eastern		C	67	262	32	74	14	0	14	43	0	.282
2009 Las Vegas	P.C.		C	116	466	67	110	32	1	21	75	0	.236
2010 Las Vegas	P.C.		C	104	412	76	124	36	1	32	85	0	.301
2010 Toronto	A.L.		C	11	35	3	5	1	0	2	4	0	.143
2011 Toronto	A.L.		C	129	443	47	97	20	4	23	78	1	.219
2012 Dunedin	Fla.St.		DH	1	5	0	1	1	0	0	0	0	.200
2012 Toronto a	A.L.		C	102	347	45	81	16	0	18	56	1	.233
Major League Totals		3 Yrs.		242	825	95	183	37	4	43	138	2	.222

a On disabled list from July 26 to September 7, 2012.

ARIAS, JOAQUIN

Born, Santo Domingo, Dominican Republic, September 21, 1984.
Bats Right. Throws Right. Height, 6 feet, 1 inch. Weight, 170 pounds.

Year	Club	Lea	Pos	G	AB	R	H	2B	3B	HR	RBI	SB	Avg
2002 Yankees	Gulf Coast		2B-SS-3B	57	203	29	61	7	6	0	21	2	.300
2003 Battle Creek	Midwest		SS	130	481	60	128	12	8	3	48	12	.266
2004 Stockton a	Calif.		SS	123	500	77	150	20	8	4	62	30	.300
2005 Frisco	Texas		SS	120	499	65	157	23	8	5	56	20	.315
2006 Oklahoma	P.C.		SS	124	493	56	132	14	10	4	49	26	.268
2006 Texas	A.L.		SS-3B	6	11	4	6	1	0	0	1	0	.545
2007 Rangers	Arizona		SS	2	7	1	2	1	0	0	1	0	.286
2007 Oklahoma b	P.C.		SS	3	11	3	2	0	0	0	1	1	.182
2008 Oklahoma	P.C.		SS-2B	104	432	59	128	15	9	7	49	23	.296
2008 Texas	A.L.		2B	32	110	15	32	7	3	0	9	4	.291
2009 Texas	A.L.		2B-3B	3	8	0	0	0	0	0	0	0	.000
2009 Oklahoma	P.C.		SS	118	504	63	134	14	3	5	52	24	.266
2010 Frisco	Texas		1B-SS-2B-3B	8	31	4	6	0	0	0	1	0	.194
2010 Texas	A.L.		2B-1B-SS	50	98	18	27	5	1	0	9	1	.276
2010 New York c-d-e	N.L.		2B-SS-OF	22	30	5	6	1	0	0	4	0	.200
2011 Omaha f	P.C.		3B-1B-SS-2B	69	241	37	56	12	4	3	25	7	.232
2012 Fresno	P.C.		SS	18	70	14	28	5	0	2	17	0	.400
2012 San Francisco	N.L.		3B-SS-2B	112	319	30	86	13	5	5	34	5	.270
Major League Totals		5 Yrs.		225	576	72	157	27	9	5	57	10	.273
Division Series													
2012 San Francisco	N.L.		SS-3B	4	6	3	3	2	0	0	0	0	.500
Championship Series													
2012 San Francisco	N.L.		3B-SS	4	2	0	0	0	0	0	0	0	.000
World Series Record													
2012 San Francisco	N.L.		3B	4	0	0	0	0	0	0	0	0	.000

a Sent to Texas Rangers as player to be named later for infielder Alex Rodriguez, March 23, 2004.
b On disabled list from March 23 to October 15, 2007.
c On disabled list from April 30 to May 16 and July 31 to August 16, 2010.
d Traded to New York Mets for outfielder Jeff Francoeur, September 1, 2010.
e Claimed on waivers by Kansas City Royals, November 4, 2010.
f Filed for free agency, November 2, 2011. Signed with San Francisco Giants organization, December 25, 2011.

AVILA, ALEXANDER THOMAS (ALEX)

Born, Hialeah, Florida, January 29, 1987.
Bats Left. Throws Right. Height, 5 feet, 11 inches. Weight, 210 pounds.

Year Club	Lea	Pos	G	AB	R	H	2B	3B	HR	RBI	SB	Avg
2008 West Michigan . . . . . Midwest		C	58	213	21	65	14	0	1	22	0	.305
2009 Erie. . . . . Eastern		C-1B	93	329	52	87	23	1	12	55	2	.264
2009 Detroit . . . . A.L.		C	29	61	9	17	4	0	5	14	0	.279
2010 Detroit . . . . A.L.		C	104	294	28	67	12	0	7	31	2	.228
2011 Detroit . . . . A.L.		C-3B	141	464	63	137	33	4	19	82	3	.295
2012 Toledo . . . . Int.		C	3	7	0	3	0	0	0	1	0	.429
2012 Detroit a . . . . A.L.		C	116	367	42	89	21	2	9	48	2	.243
Major League Totals	4 Yrs.		390	1186	142	310	70	6	40	175	7	.261
Division Series												
2011 Detroit . . . . A.L.		C	5	16	0	1	0	0	0	1	0	.06
2012 Detroit . . . . A.L.		C	4	12	2	3	1	0	1	1	0	.250
Division Series Totals			9	28	2	4	1	0	1	2	0	.143 3
Championship Series												
2011 Detroit . . . . A.L.		C	6	25	1	2	0	0	1	1	0	.080
2012 Detroit . . . . A.L.		C	3	10	0	2	0	0	0	0	0	.200
Championship Series Totals			9	35	1	4	0	0	1	1	0	.114
World Series Record												
2012 Detroit . . . . A.L.		C	2	7	0	1	0	0	0	0	0	.143

a On disabled list from June 6 to June 21, 2012.

AVILES, MICHAEL ANTHONY (MIKE)

Born, New York, New York, March 13, 1981.
Bats Right. Throws Right. Height, 5 feet, 9 inches. Weight, 195 pounds.

Year Club	Lea	Pos	G	AB	R	H	2B	3B	HR	RBI	SB	Avg
2003 Royals 1 . . . . Arizona		SS	52	212	51	77	19	5	6	39	11	.363
2004 Wilmington . . . Carolina		SS	126	463	66	139	40	4	6	68	2	.300
2005 Wichita . . . . Texas		SS-3B-2B	133	521	79	146	33	6	14	80	11	.280
2006 Omaha . . . . P.C.		3B-SS-2B	129	469	52	124	21	3	8	47	14	.264
2007 Omaha . . . . P.C.		SS-3B-2B	133	538	78	159	27	6	17	77	5	.296
2008 Omaha . . . . P.C.		2B-SS	51	214	42	72	21	6	10	42	3	.336
2008 Kansas City . . . . . . A.L.		SS-2B-3B	102	419	68	136	27	4	10	51	8	.325
2009 Kansas City a . . . , . A.L.		SS-3B	36	120	10	22	3	1	1	8	1	.183
2010 Omaha . . . . P.C.		SS-2B	17	70	8	19	3	1	1	8	0	.271
2010 Kansas City . . . . . . A.L.		2B-SS-3B	110	424	63	129	16	3	8	32	14	.304
2011 Omaha . . . . P.C.		SS-2B	35	140	21	43	8	2	9	25	6	.307
2011 Kansas City-Boston b A.L.		3B-2B-SS-OF	91	286	31	73	17	3	7	39	14	.255
2012 Boston c-d . . . . A.L.		SS-2B-3B	136	512	57	128	28	0	13	60	14	.250
Major League Totals	5 Yrs.		475	1761	229	488	91	11	39	190	51	.277

a On disabled list from May 24 to November 16, 2009.
b Traded to Boston Red Sox for infielder Yamaico Navarro and pitcher Kendal Volz, July 30, 2011.
c Traded to Toronto Blue Jays for manager John Farrell and pitcher David Carpenter, October 21, 2012.
d Traded to Cleveland Indians with catcher Yan Gomes for pitcher Esmil Rogers, November 3, 2012.

AYBAR, ERICK JOHAN

Born, Bani, Dominican Republic, January 14, 1984.
Bats Both. Throws Right. Height, 5 feet, 10 inches. Weight, 170 pounds.

Year Club	Lea	Pos	G	AB	R	H	2B	3B	HR	RBI	SB	Avg
2002 Provo . . . . Pioneer		SS	67	273	64	89	15	6	4	29	15	.326
2003 Cedar Rapids . . . . . . Midwest		SS	125	496	83	153	30	10	6	57	32	.308
2004 Rancho Cucamonga . . . . Calif.		SS-2B	136	573	102	189	25	11	14	65	51	.330
2005 Arkansas . . . . Texas		SS	134	535	101	162	29	10	9	54	49	.303
2006 Salt Lake . . . . P.C.		SS	81	339	63	96	20	3	6	45	32	.283
2006 Los Angeles . . . . A.L.		SS-2B	34	40	5	10	1	1	0	2	1	.250
2007 Rancho Cucamonga . . . . Calif.		SS	2	5	3	2	0	0	0	0	3	.400
2007 Salt Lake . . . . P.C.		SS-2B	3	12	2	4	0	0	0	2	2	.333
2007 Los Angeles a . . . . A.L.		2B-SS-OF-3B	79	194	18	46	5	1	1	19	4	.237
2008 Rancho Cucamonga . . . . Calif.		SS	3	10	2	4	1	0	0	3	2	.400
2008 Los Angeles b . . . . A.L.		SS-2B	98	346	53	96	18	5	3	39	7	.277
2009 Los Angeles . . . . A.L.		SS	137	504	70	157	23	9	5	58	14	.312
2010 Los Angeles . . . . A.L.		SS	138	534	69	135	18	4	5	29	22	.253
2011 Salt Lake . . . . P.C.		SS	1	4	1	1	0	0	0	0	0	.250
2011 Los Angeles c . . . . A.L.		SS	143	556	71	155	33	8	10	59	30	.279

6

Year	Club	Lea	Pos	G	AB	R	H	2B	3B	HR	RBI	SB	Avg
2012 Los Angeles d	A.L.	SS	141	517	67	150	31	5	8	45	20	.290
Major League Totals		7 Yrs.	770	2691	353	749	129	33	32	251	98	.278
Division Series												
2007 Los Angeles	A.L.	OF	1	1	0	0	0	0	0	0	0	.000
2008 Los Angeles	A.L.	SS	4	18	0	2	0	0	0	1	0	.111
2009 Los Angeles	A.L.	SS	3	11	2	4	1	1	0	2	0	.364
Division Series Totals			8	30	2	6	1	1	0	3	0	.200
Championship Series												
2009 Los Angeles	A.L.	SS	6	20	2	5	1	0	0	1	3	.250

a On disabled list from July 2 to August 6 and August 20 to September 5, 2007.
b On disabled list from May 21 to June 18, 2008.
c On disabled list from April 3 to April 20, 2011.
d On disabled list from July 22 to August 6, 2012.

BAKER, JEFFREY GLEN (JEFF)

Born, Bad Kissingen, West Germany, June 21, 1981.
Bats Right. Throws Right. Height, 6 feet, 2 inches. Weight, 210 pounds.

Year	Club	Lea	Pos	G	AB	R	H	2B	3B	HR	RBI	SB	Avg
2003 Asheville.........	So.Atl.	3B	70	263	44	76	17	0	11	44	4	.289
2004 Visalia	Calif.	3B-SS	73	271	60	88	23	1	11	64	1	.325
2004 Tulsa	Texas	3B	24	91	10	27	5	1	4	20	1	.297
2005 Colorado	N.L.	3B	12	38	6	8	4	0	1	4	0	.211
2005 Colorado Springs...	P.C.	3B	61	228	40	69	16	1	10	41	3	.303
2006 Colorado Springs...	P.C.	OF-3B	128	482	71	147	30	4	20	108	7	.305
2006 Colorado	N.L.	OF-1B	18	57	13	21	7	2	5	21	2	.368
2007 Colorado Springs...	P.C.	1B-OF	7	26	3	6	1	0	1	2	0	.231
2007 Colorado a........	N.L.	1B-OF-3B	85	144	17	32	2	2	4	12	0	.222
2008 Colorado	N.L.	2B-1B-3B-OF	104	299	55	80	22	1	12	48	4	.268
2009 Modesto.........	Calif.	2B-3B	2	5	1	2	1	0	0	1	0	.400
2009 Colorado Springs...	P.C.	2B-3B	7	23	3	5	2	0	1	1	0	.217
2009 Colorado-Chicago b-c	N.L.	2B-3B-1B	81	226	27	65	15	2	4	24	1	.288
2010 Chicago	N.L.	3B-2B-1B-OF	79	206	29	56	13	2	4	21	1	.272
2011 Iowa.............	P.C.	2B-OF	3	10	1	3	1	1	0	1	0	.300
2011 Chicago d........	N.L.	1B-2B-3B-OF	81	201	20	54	12	1	3	23	0	.269
2012 Detroit	A.L.	OF-3B	15	35	1	7	2	0	0	4	0	.200
2012 Chicago-Atlanta e-f-g	N.L.	1B-OF-2B	68	153	17	38	10	1	4	21	4	.248
Major League Totals		8 Yrs.	543	1359	185	361	87	11	37	178	12	.266
Division Series												
2007 Colorado	N.L.	PH	1	1	0	1	0	0	0	1	0	1.000
Championship Series												
2007 Colorado	N.L.	PH	2	2	0	1	0	0	0	0	0	.500
World Series Record												
2007 Colorado	N.L.	PH	1	1	0	0	0	0	0	0	0	.000

a On disabled list from August 12 to September 1, 2007.
b Traded to Chicago Cubs for pitcher Al Alburquerque, July 2, 2009.
c On disabled list from April 27 to July 2, 2009.
d On disabled list from May 30 to June 13, 2011.
e Traded to Detroit Tigers for player to be named later and cash, August 5, 2012. Chicago Cubs received pitcher Marcelo Carreno to complete trade, October 16, 2012.
f Traded to Atlanta Braves for player to be named later, August 31, 2012. Detroit Tigers received pitcher Greg Ross to complete trade, September 25, 2012.
g Filed for free agency, November 3, 2012.

BAKER, JOHN DAVID

Born, Alameda, California, January 20, 1981.
Bats Left. Throws Right. Height, 6 feet, 1 inch. Weight, 220 pounds.

Year	Club	Lea	Pos	G	AB	R	H	2B	3B	HR	RBI	SB	Avg
2002 Vancouver	Northwest	C	39	115	15	27	5	0	1	13	2	.235
2003 Kane County.......	Midwest	C	82	304	42	94	23	2	6	49	1	.309
2003 Midland	Texas	C	43	150	16	36	3	0	1	21	0	.240
2004 Sacramento	P.C.	C	14	49	11	17	3	0	0	10	0	.347
2004 Midland	Texas	C-1B	117	439	67	123	32	5	15	78	0	.280
2005 Sacramento a.........	P.C.	C	103	346	43	81	24	3	5	41	1	.234
2006 Sacramento b.........	P.C.	C	83	293	49	80	19	1	4	38	6	.273
2007 Albuquerque c	P.C.	C-1B	89	270	35	77	15	0	8	41	2	.285
2008 Albuquerque..........	P.C.	C-1B	59	193	35	62	14	1	6	31	1	.321
2008 Florida	N.L.	C	61	197	32	59	14	0	5	32	0	.299
2009 Florida	N.L.	C	112	373	59	101	25	0	9	50	0	.271

Year	Club	Lea	Pos	G	AB	R	H	2B	3B	HR	RBI	SB	Avg
2010 Florida	N.L.		C	23	78	7	17	3	1	0	6	0	.218
2010 Jupiter d...........	Fla.St.		C	3	6	2	2	0	0	0	0	0	.333
2011 Jacksonville	Southern		C	3	9	0	1	1	0	0	0	0	.111
2011 Jupiter	Fla.St.		C	12	28	8	8	2	2	0	1	0	.286
2011 Florida e-f...........	N.L.		C	16	13	0	2	0	0	0	1	0	.154
2012 San Diego	N.L.		C	63	193	17	46	8	0	0	14	2	.238
Major League Totals		5 Yrs.		275	854	115	225	50	1	14	103	2	.263

a Claimed on waivers by Florida Marlins from Oakland Athletics, December 15, 2005.
b Claimed on waivers by Oakland Athletics, January 5, 2006.
c Traded to Florida Marlins for infielder Jason Stokes, March 30, 2007.
d On disabled list from May 14 to November 5, 2010.
e On disabled list from March 30 to September 5, 2011.
f Traded to San Diego Padres for pitcher Wade LeBlanc, November 22, 2011.

BARAJAS, RODRIGO RICHARD (ROD)
Born, Ontario, California, September 5, 1975.
Bats Right. Throws Right. Height, 6 feet, 2 inches. Weight, 245 pounds.

Year	Club	Lea	Pos	G	AB	R	H	2B	3B	HR	RBI	SB	Avg
1996 Visalia	Calif.		C	27	74	6	12	3	0	0	8	0	.162
1996 Lethbridge a.......	Pioneer		C-1B	51	175	47	59	9	3	10	50	2	.337
1997 High Desert	Calif.		C-1B	57	199	24	53	11	0	7	30	0	.266
1998 High Desert	Calif.		C	113	442	67	134	26	0	23	81	1	.303
1999 El Paso	Texas		C-1B	127	510	77	162	41	2	14	95	2	.318
1999 Arizona..............	N.L.		C	5	16	3	4	1	0	1	3	0	.250
2000 Tucson	P.C.		C-1B-3B	110	416	43	94	25	0	13	75	4	.226
2000 Arizona..............	N.L.		C	5	13	1	3	0	0	1	3	0	.231
2001 Arizona..............	N.L.		C	51	106	9	17	3	0	3	9	0	.160
2001 Tucson	P.C.		1B-C-3B	45	162	23	52	13	0	9	32	3	.321
2002 Arizona..............	N.L.		C-1B	70	154	12	36	10	0	3	23	1	.234
2002 Tucson	P.C.		C-1B	5	16	2	7	1	0	1	1	0	.438
2003 Tucson	P.C.		C	4	16	3	7	1	0	1	4	0	.438
2003 Lancaster............	Calif.		C	3	12	2	5	0	0	0	3	0	.417
2003 Arizona b-c...........	N.L.		C	80	220	19	48	15	0	3	28	0	.218
2004 Texas d.............	A.L.		C-1B	108	358	50	89	26	1	15	58	0	.249
2005 Texas	A.L.		C-1B	120	410	53	104	24	0	21	60	0	.254
2006 Texas e.............	A.L.		C-1B	97	344	49	88	20	0	11	41	0	.256
2007 Reading	Eastern		C	2	5	0	1	0	0	0	0	0	.200
2007 Lakewood...........	So.Atl.		C	6	16	0	6	2	0	0	2	0	.375
2007 Philadelphia f-g	N.L.		C-1B	48	122	16	28	8	0	4	10	0	.230
2008 Toronto	A.L.		C-1B	104	349	44	87	23	0	11	49	0	.249
2009 Toronto	A.L.		C	125	429	43	97	19	0	19	71	1	.226
2010 Mets..........	Gulf Coast		DH	1	4	1	1	0	0	1	3	0	.250
2010 St. Lucie............	Fla.St.		C	4	17	1	4	0	0	0	2	0	.235
2010 New York-LA h-i-j-k	N.L.		C	99	313	39	75	14	0	17	47	0	.240
2011 Rancho Cucamonga....	Calif.		C	4	18	4	7	2	0	1	2	0	.389
2011 Los Angeles l-m.......	N.L.		C	98	305	29	70	13	0	16	47	0	.230
2012 Pittsburgh n.........	N.L.		C-1B	104	321	29	66	11	0	11	31	0	.206
Major League Totals		14 Yrs.		1114	3460	396	812	187	1	136	480	2	.235
Division Series													
2001 Arizona..............	N.L.		C	1	0	0	0	0	0	0	0	0	.000
2002 Arizona..............	N.L.		C	2	4	1	1	0	0	1	1	0	.250
Division Series Totals				3	4	1	1	0	0	1	1	0	.250
World Series Record													
2001 Arizona..............	N.L.		C	2	5	1	2	0	0	1	1	0	.400

a Loaned to Oakland A's organization, April 5 to June 16, 1996.
b On disabled list from April 7 to April 28, 2003.
c On disabled list from July 5 to July 23, 2003.
d Not offered contract, December 21, 2003. Signed with Texas Rangers organization, January 12, 2004.
e Filed for free agency, October 28, 2006. Signed with Philadelphia Phillies organization, December 21, 2006.
f On disabled list from August 3 to September 1, 2007.
g Filed for free agency, October 30, 2007. Signed with Toronto Blue Jays, January 24, 2008.
h Filed for free agency, November 9, 2009. Signed with New York Mets, February 24, 2010.
i On disabled list from July 25 to August 19, 2010.
j Claimed on waivers by Los Angeles Dodgers, August 22, 2010.
k Filed for free agency, November 1, 2010, re-signed with Los Angeles Dodgers, December 3, 2010.
l On disabled list from June 19 to July 14, 2011.
m Filed for free agency, October 30, 2011. Signed with Pittsburgh Pirates, November 10, 2011.
n Filed for free agency, November 3, 2012.

BARMES, CLINT HAROLD

Born, Vincennes, Indiana, March 6, 1979.
Bats Right. Throws Right. Height, 6 feet. Weight, 210 pounds.

Year	Club	Lea	Pos	G	AB	R	H	2B	3B	HR	RBI	SB	Avg
2000	Portland	Northwest	SS-OF	45	181	37	51	6	4	2	16	12	.282
2000	Asheville	So.Atl.	2B-SS-3B-OF	19	81	11	14	4	0	0	4	4	.173
2001	Salem	Carolina	SS	38	121	17	30	3	3	0	9	4	.248
2001	Asheville	So.Atl.	SS	74	285	40	74	14	1	5	24	21	.260
2002	Carolina	Southern	SS	103	438	62	119	23	2	15	60	15	.272
2003	Colorado Springs	P.C.	SS-2B	136	493	63	136	35	1	7	54	12	.276
2003	Colorado	N.L.	SS	12	25	2	8	2	0	0	2	0	.320
2004	Colorado Springs	P.C.	SS-2B	125	533	104	175	42	2	16	51	20	.328
2004	Colorado	N.L.	2B-SS	20	71	14	20	3	1	2	10	0	.282
2005	Tulsa	Texas	SS	8	34	6	11	1	0	0	0	1	.324
2005	Colorado a	N.L.	SS	81	350	55	101	19	1	10	46	6	.289
2006	Colorado	N.L.	SS-2B	131	478	57	105	26	4	7	56	5	.220
2007	Colorado Springs	P.C.	SS-OF-2B-3B	108	428	68	128	20	6	11	44	8	.299
2007	Colorado	N.L.	SS-2B-OF-3B	27	37	5	8	3	0	0	1	0	.216
2008	Colorado Springs	P.C.	2B-SS	5	18	2	5	0	0	0	3	0	.278
2008	Colorado b	N.L.	2B-SS-3B-OF	107	393	47	114	25	6	11	44	13	.290
2009	Colorado	N.L.	2B-SS	154	550	69	135	32	3	23	76	12	.245
2010	Colorado c	N.L.	2B-SS-3B	133	387	43	91	21	0	8	50	3	.235
2011	Corpus Christi	Texas	SS	2	9	2	4	0	0	0	2	0	.444
2011	Oklahoma	P.C.	SS	2	6	2	2	1	0	0	1	0	.333
2011	Houston d-e	N.L.	SS	123	446	47	109	27	0	12	39	3	.244
2012	Pittsburgh	N.L.	SS-1B	144	455	34	104	16	1	8	45	0	.229
Major League Totals			10 Yrs.	932	3192	373	795	174	16	81	369	42	.249
Division Series													
2009	Colorado	N.L.	2B	4	14	0	0	0	0	0	0	0	.000

a On disabled list from June 6 to September 2, 2005.
b On disabled list from May 24 to June 23, 2008.
c Traded to Houston Astros for pitcher Felipe Paulino, November 18, 2010.
d On disabled list from March 26 to April 29, 2011.
e Filed for free agency, October 30, 2011. Signed with Pittsburgh Pirates, November 21, 2011.

BARNEY, DARWIN JAMES KUNANE

Born, Portland, Oregon, November 8, 1985.
Bats Right. Throws Right. Height, 5 feet, 10 inches. Weight, 180 pounds.

Year	Club	Lea	Pos	G	AB	R	H	2B	3B	HR	RBI	SB	Avg
2007	Cubs	Arizona	SS	5	18	6	8	3	0	0	2	0	.444
2007	Peoria	Midwest	SS	44	176	27	48	9	3	2	21	5	.273
2008	Daytona	Fla.St.	SS	123	409	46	107	22	4	3	51	8	.262
2009	Tennessee	Southern	SS-2B-3B	74	252	30	80	12	0	3	32	5	.317
2009	Iowa	P.C.	SS-2B	63	212	25	56	12	1	0	17	4	.264
2010	Iowa	P.C.	SS-2B	114	479	72	143	24	4	2	49	11	.299
2010	Chicago	N.L.	SS-2B-3B	30	79	12	19	4	0	0	2	0	.241
2011	Iowa	P.C.	2B	4	14	3	5	1	0	1	3	1	.357
2011	Chicago a	N.L.	2B-SS	143	529	66	146	23	6	2	43	9	.276
2012	Chicago	N.L.	2B-SS	156	548	73	139	26	4	7	44	6	.254
Major League Totals			3 Yrs.	329	1156	151	304	53	10	9	89	15	.263

a On disabled list from June 15 to June 29, 2011.

BAUTISTA, JOSE ANTONIO

Born, Santo Domingo, Dominican Republic, October 19, 1980.
Bats Right. Throws Right. Height, 6 feet. Weight, 190 pounds.

Year	Club	Lea	Pos	G	AB	R	H	2B	3B	HR	RBI	SB	Avg
2001	Williamsport	N.Y.-Penn.	3B-OF	62	220	43	63	10	3	5	30	8	.286
2002	Hickory	So.Atl.	3B-SS	129	438	72	132	26	3	14	57	3	.301
2003	Lynchburg	Carolina	3B-2B	51	165	28	40	14	2	4	20	1	.242
2003	Pirates a	Gulf Coast	3B	7	23	5	8	1	0	1	3	0	.348
2004	Pittsburgh	N.L.	OF	23	40	1	8	2	0	0	0	0	.200
2004	Baltimore-T.B.-K.C. b-c-d-e.	A.L.	3B-OF	41	48	5	10	1	0	0	2	0	.208
2005	Altoona	Eastern	3B	117	445	63	126	27	1	23	90	7	.283
2005	Indianapolis	Int.	3B	13	51	6	13	3	0	1	4	1	.255
2005	Pittsburgh	N.L.	3B	11	28	3	4	1	0	0	1	1	.143
2006	Indianapolis	Int.	3B-OF-2B	29	101	12	28	9	0	2	9	2	.277
2006	Pittsburgh	N.L.	OF-3B-2B	117	400	58	94	20	3	16	51	2	.235
2007	Pirates	Gulf Coast	3B	2	8	1	3	2	0	0	1	0	.375

Year	Club	Lea	Pos	G	AB	R	H	2B	3B	HR	RBI	SB	Avg
2007 Pittsburgh f	N.L.	3B-OF	142	532	75	135	36	2	15	63	6	.254
2008 Indianapolis	Int.	OF-2B	5	20	6	6	2	0	2	8	1	.300
2008 Pittsburgh	N.L.	3B	107	314	38	76	15	0	12	44	1	.242
2008 Toronto g	A.L.	3B-1B-2B	21	56	7	12	2	0	3	10	0	.214
2009 Toronto	A.L.	OF-3B	113	336	54	79	13	3	13	40	4	.235
2010 Toronto	A.L.	OF-3B-1B	161	569	109	148	35	3	*54	124	9	.260
2011 Toronto	A.L.	OF-3B	149	513	105	155	24	2	*43	103	9	.302
2012 Blue Jays	Gulf Coast	DH	1	3	0	0	0	0	0	0	0	.000
2012 New Hampshire	Eastern	OF	1	4	2	2	0	0	2	5	0	.500
2012 Toronto h	A.L.	OF-1B-3B	92	332	64	80	14	0	27	65	5	.241
Major League Totals			9 Yrs.	977	3168	519	801	163	13	183	503	37	.253

a Selected by Baltimore Orioles from Pittsburgh in Rule V draft, December 15, 2003.
b Claimed on waivers by Tampa Bay Devil Rays, June 3, 2004.
c Sold to Kansas City Royals, June 28, 2004.
d Traded to New York Mets for catcher Justin Huber, July 30, 2004.
e Traded to Pittsburgh Pirates with infielder Ty Wigginton and pitcher Matt Peterson for pitcher Kris Benson and infielder Jeff Keppinger, July 30, 2004.
f On disabled list from July 15 to August 1, 2007.
g Traded to Toronto Blue Jays for player to be named later, August 21, 2008. Pittsburgh Pirates received infielder Robinzon Diaz to complete trade, August 25, 2008.
h On disabled list from July 17 to August 24 and August 26 to October 4, 2012.

BAXTER, MICHAEL JOSEPH (MIKE)
Born, Queens, New York, December 7, 1984.
Bats Left. Throws Right. Height, 6 feet. Weight, 195 pounds.

Year	Club	Lea	Pos	G	AB	R	H	2B	3B	HR	RBI	SB	Avg
2005 Fort Wayne	Midwest	1B	45	183	11	40	12	1	1	17	4	.219
2006 Fort Wayne	Midwest	OF-1B-2B	117	476	67	122	28	7	3	40	13	.256
2007 Lake Elsinore	Calif.	OF	111	417	74	115	21	6	7	44	12	.276
2007 Portland	P.C.	OF	10	29	1	6	2	1	0	7	1	.207
2008 Lake Elsinore	Calif.	OF-1B	24	92	13	22	4	1	1	17	3	.239
2008 San Antonio	Texas	OF-1B	100	324	41	88	18	4	8	48	2	.272
2009 Portland	P.C.	OF-1B	82	303	38	84	17	4	5	34	9	.277
2009 San Antonio	Texas	OF-1B	51	202	38	76	23	1	4	45	5	.376
2010 Portland	P.C.	OF-1B-3B	136	482	89	145	30	10	18	72	22	.301
2010 San Diego	N.L.	1B	9	8	0	1	0	0	0	1	0	.125
2011 Lake Elsinore	Calif.	OF-1B	11	36	5	10	1	0	0	2	0	.278
2011 St. Lucie	Fla.St.	OF	4	16	2	7	2	0	0	4	0	.438
2011 Buffalo	Int.	OF-1B	18	64	4	12	0	2	1	7	1	.188
2011 New York a-b-c	N.L.	OF	22	34	6	8	2	1	1	4	0	.235
2012 St. Lucie	Fla.St.	DH	4	15	1	4	3	0	0	4	0	.267
2012 Binghamton	Eastern	OF	3	10	1	3	0	0	0	1	0	.300
2012 Buffalo	Int.	OF	6	24	2	9	1	0	0	3	0	.375
2012 New York d	N.L.	OF	89	179	26	47	14	2	3	17	5	.263
Major League Totals			3 Yrs.	120	221	32	56	16	3	4	22	5	.253

a On disabled list from March 28 to July 22, 2011.
b Claimed on waivers by New York Mets, July 22, 2011.
c Not offered contract, December 12, 2011, re-signed with New York Mets organization, January 3, 2012.
d On disabled list from June 2 to July 30, 2012.

BAY, JASON RAYMOND
Born, Trail, British Columbia, Canada, September 20, 1978.
Bats Right. Throws Right. Height, 6 feet, 2 inches. Weight, 205 pounds.

Year	Club	Lea	Pos	G	AB	R	H	2B	3B	HR	RBI	SB	Avg
2000 Vermont	N.Y.-Penn.	OF	35	135	17	41	5	0	2	12	17	.304
2001 Jupiter	Fla.St.	OF-2B	38	123	12	24	4	1	1	10	10	.195
2001 Clinton	Midwest	OF	87	318	67	115	20	4	13	61	15	.362
2002 St. Lucie	Fla.St.	OF	69	261	48	71	12	2	9	54	22	.272
2002 Binghamton	Eastern	OF	34	107	17	31	4	2	4	19	13	.290
2002 Mobile a-b	Southern	OF	23	81	16	25	5	2	4	12	4	.309
2003 Portland	P.C.	OF	91	307	64	93	11	1	20	59	23	.303
2003 San Diego-Pittsburgh c-d-e	N.L.	OF	30	87	15	25	7	1	4	14	3	.287
2004 Nashville	P.C.	OF	4	10	3	4	2	0	1	3	0	.400
2004 Pittsburgh f-g	N.L.	OF	120	411	61	116	24	4	26	82	4	.282
2005 Pittsburgh	N.L.	OF	*162	599	110	183	44	6	32	101	21	.306
2006 Pittsburgh	N.L.	OF	159	570	101	163	29	3	35	109	11	.286
2007 Pittsburgh	N.L.	OF	145	538	78	133	25	2	21	84	4	.247

Year Club	Lea	Pos	G	AB	R	H	2B	3B	HR	RBI	SB	Avg
2008 Pittsburgh .... N.L.		OF	106	393	72	111	23	2	22	64	7	.282
2008 Boston h .... A.L.		OF	49	184	39	54	12	2	9	37	3	.293
2009 Boston i .... A.L.		OF	151	531	103	142	29	3	36	119	13	.267
2010 New York j .... N.L.		OF	95	348	48	90	20	6	6	47	10	.259
2011 St. Lucie ....Fla.St.		OF	4	12	5	6	0	0	2	4	0	.500
2011 New York k .... N.L.		OF	123	444	59	109	19	1	12	57	11	.245
2012 St. Lucie............Fla.St.		OF	5	15	0	2	0	0	0	1	1	.133
2012 Buffalo ....Int.		OF	3	10	2	3	0	0	0	0	1	.300
2012 New York l-m .... N.L.		OF	70	194	21	32	2	0	8	20	5	.165
Major League Totals	10 Yrs.		1210	4299	707	1158	234	30	211	734	92	.269
Division Series												
2008 Boston .... A.L.		OF	4	17	3	7	2	0	2	5	0	.412
2009 Boston .... A.L.		OF	3	8	0	1	0	0	0	0	0	.125
Division Series Totals			7	25	3	8	2	0	2	5	0	.320
Championship Series												
2008 Boston .... A.L.		OF	7	24	3	7	1	0	1	4	0	.292

a Traded by Montreal Expos to New York Mets with pitcher Jim Serrano for infielder Lou Collier, March 26, 2002.
b Traded to San Diego Padres with pitcher Bobby M. Jones and pitcher Josh Reynolds for pitcher Jason Middlebrook and pitcher Steve Reed, July 31, 2002.
c On disabled list from May 26 to July 8, 2003.
d Traded to Pittsburgh Pirates with pitcher Oliver Perez and player to be named later for outfielder Brian Giles, August 26, 2003.
e Pittsburgh Pirates received pitcher Cory Stewart to complete trade, October 2, 2003.
f On disabled list from March 26 to May 7, 2004.
g Selected Rookie of the Year in National League for 2004.
h Traded to Boston Red Sox for outfielder Manny Ramirez, outfielder Brandon Moss and pitcher Craig Hansen, July 31, 2008.
i Filed for free agency, November 5, 2009. Signed with New York Mets, December 29, 2009.
j On disabled list from July 26 to November 2, 2010.
k On disabled list from March 25 to April 21, 2011.
l On disabled list from April 24 to June 6 and June 16 to July 17, 2012.
m Released by New York Mets, November 7, 2012. Signed with Seattle Mariners, December 8, 2012.

BECKHAM, JAMES GORDON (GORDON)

Born, Atlanta, Georgia, September 16, 1986.
Bats Right. Throws Right. Height, 6 feet. Weight, 190 pounds.

Year Club	Lea	Pos	G	AB	R	H	2B	3B	HR	RBI	SB	Avg
2008 Kannapolis .... So.Atl.		SS	14	58	11	18	2	0	3	8	0	.310
2009 Birmingham ...... Southern		SS-2B-3B	38	147	23	44	17	0	4	22	1	.299
2009 Charlotte .... Int.		3B-SS	7	28	6	13	6	0	0	3	1	.464
2009 Chicago .... A.L.		3B	103	378	58	102	28	1	14	63	7	.270
2010 Chicago .... A.L.		2B	131	444	58	112	25	2	9	49	4	.252
2011 Chicago .... A.L.		2B	150	499	60	115	23	0	10	44	5	.230
2012 Chicago .... A.L.		2B	151	525	62	123	24	0	16	60	5	.234
Major League Totals	4 Yrs.		535	1846	238	452	100	3	49	216	21	.245

BELT, BRANDON KYLE

Born, Nacogdoches, Texas, April 20, 1988.
Bats Left. Throws Left. Height, 6 feet, 5 inches. Weight, 220 pounds.

Year Club	Lea	Pos	G	AB	R	H	2B	3B	HR	RBI	SB	Avg
2010 San Jose ....Calif.		1B	77	269	62	103	28	4	10	62	18	.383
2010 Richmond .... Eastern		1B-OF	46	175	26	59	11	6	9	40	2	.337
2010 Fresno .... P.C.		OF-1B	13	48	11	11	4	0	4	10	2	.229
2011 San Jose ....Calif.		1B	4	13	3	6	1	0	0	4	1	.462
2011 Fresno .... P.C.		OF-1B	49	165	32	51	12	0	8	32	4	.309
2011 San Francisco a .... N.L.		OF-1B	63	187	21	42	6	1	9	18	3	.225
2012 San Francisco .... N.L.		1B-OF	145	411	47	113	27	6	7	56	12	.275
Major League Totals	2 Yrs.		208	598	68	155	33	7	16	74	15	.259
Division Series												
2012 San Francisco ...... N.L.		1B	5	13	0	1	0	0	0	0	0	.077
Championship Series												
2012 San Francisco ...... N.L.		1B	6	23	6	7	1	1	1	2	1	.304
World Series Record												
2012 San Francisco .... N.L.		1B	4	13	1	1	0	1	0	1	0	.077

a On disabled list from June 1 to July 7, 2011.

BELTRAN, CARLOS IVAN
Born, Manati, Puerto Rico, April 24, 1977.
Bats Both. Throws Right. Height, 6 feet. Weight,200 pounds.

Year	Club	Lea	Pos	G	AB	R	H	2B	3B	HR	RBI	SB	Avg
1995 Royals	Gulf Coast		OF	52	180	29	50	9	0	0	23	5	.278
1996 Lansing	Midwest		OF	11	42	3	6	2	0	0	0	1	.143
1996 Spokane	Northwest		OF	59	215	29	58	8	3	7	29	10	.270
1997 Wilmington	Carolina		OF	120	419	57	96	15	4	11	46	17	.229
1998 Wilmington	Carolina		OF	52	192	32	53	14	0	5	32	11	.276
1998 Wichita	Texas		OF	47	182	50	64	13	3	14	44	7	.352
1998 Kansas City	A.L.		OF	14	58	12	16	5	3	0	7	3	.276
1999 Kansas City a	A.L.		OF	156	663	112	194	27	7	22	108	27	.293
2000 GC Royals	Gulf Coast		PH	1	4	3	2	1	0	1	1	0	.500
2000 Wilmington	Carolina		OF	3	13	2	4	0	1	2	6	0	.308
2000 Omaha	P.C.		OF	5	18	4	6	1	0	2	2	1	.333
2000 Kansas City b	A.L.		OF	98	372	49	92	15	4	7	44	13	.247
2001 Kansas City	A.L.		OF	155	617	106	189	32	12	24	101	31	.306
2002 Kansas City	A.L.		OF	*162	637	114	174	44	7	29	105	35	.273
2003 Wichita	Texas		OF	3	9	3	3	2	0	0	1	1	.333
2003 Kansas City c	A.L.		OF	141	521	102	160	14	10	26	100	41	.307
2004 Kansas City	A.L.		OF	69	266	51	74	19	2	15	51	14	.278
2004 Houston d-e	N.L.		OF	90	333	70	86	17	7	23	53	28	.258
2005 New York	N.L.		OF	151	582	83	155	34	2	16	78	17	.266
2006 New York	N.L.		OF	140	510	127	140	38	1	41	116	18	.275
2007 New York f	N.L.		OF	144	554	93	153	33	3	33	112	23	.276
2008 New York	N.L.		OF	161	606	116	172	40	5	27	112	25	.284
2009 Brooklyn	N.Y.-Penn.		OF	5	18	1	3	0	0	0	2	0	.167
2009 New York g	N.L.		OF	81	308	50	100	22	1	10	48	11	.325
2010 St. Lucie	Fla.St.		OF	14	49	5	18	5	0	0	5	0	.367
2010 New York h	N.L.		OF	64	220	21	56	11	3	7	27	3	.255
2011 New York-San Fran. i-j-k	N.L.		OF	142	520	78	156	39	6	22	84	4	.300
2012 St. Louis	N.L.		OF	151	547	83	147	26	1	32	97	13	.269
Major League Totals		15 Yrs.		1919	7314	1267	2064	416	74	334	1243	306	.282
Wild Card Playoff													
2012 St. Louis	N.L.		OF	1	4	1	1	0	0	0	0	0	.250
Division Series													
2004 Houston	N.L.		OF	5	22	9	10	2	0	4	9	2	.455
2006 New York	N.L.		OF	3	9	2	2	0	0	0	1	1	.222
2012 St. Louis	N.L.		OF	5	18	5	8	3	0	2	4	1	.444
Division Series Totals				13	49	16	20	5	0	6	14	4	.408
Championship Series													
2004 Houston	N.L.		OF	7	24	12	10	1	0	4	5	4	.417
2006 New York	N.L.		OF	7	27	8	8	1	0	3	4	1	.296
2012 St. Louis	N.L.		OF	6	20	2	6	3	0	1	2	2	.300
Championship Series Totals				20	71	22	24	5	0	8	11	7	.338

a Selected Rookie of the Year in American League for 1999.
b On disabled list from July 4 to September 3, 2000.
c On disabled list from March 21 to April 18, 2003.
d Traded to Houston Astros for pitcher Octavio Dotel and catcher John Buck, June 24, 2004.
e Filed for free agency, October 28, 2004. Signed with New York Mets, January 11, 2005.
f On disabled list from July 25 to August 10, 2007.
g On disabled list from June 22 to September 8, 2009.
h On disabled list from March 26 to July 15, 2010.
i Traded to San Francisco Giants for pitcher Zack Wheeler, July 28, 2011.
j On disabled list from August 8 to August 23, 2011.
k Filed for free agency, October 30, 2011. Signed with St. Louis Cardinals, December 23, 2011.

BELTRE, ADRIAN
Born, Santo Domingo, Dominican Republic, April 7, 1979.
Bats Right. Throws Right. Height, 5 feet, 11 inches. Weight, 220 pounds.

Year	Club	Lea	Pos	G	AB	R	H	2B	3B	HR	RBI	SB	Avg
1995 LA-S.Domingo	Dominican		3B	62	218	56	67	15	3	8	40	2	.307
1996 Savannah	So.Atl.		3B-2B	68	244	48	75	14	3	16	59	4	.307
1996 San Berndno a	California		3B	63	238	40	62	13	1	10	40	3	.261
1997 Vero Beach	Fla.St.		3B-OF	123	435	95	138	24	2	26	104	25	.317
1998 San Antonio	Texas		3B	64	246	49	79	21	2	13	56	20	.321
1998 Los Angeles	N.L.		3B-SS	77	195	18	42	9	0	7	22	3	.215
1999 Los Angeles	N.L.		3B	152	538	84	148	27	5	15	67	18	.275
2000 Los Angeles b	N.L.		3B-SS	138	510	71	148	30	2	20	85	12	.290

Year	Club	Lea	Pos	G	AB	R	H	2B	3B	HR	RBI	SB	Avg
2001 Vero Beach	Fla.St.	3B	3	9	0	4	1	0	0	1	0	.444	
2001 Las Vegas	P.C.	3B	2	5	2	3	1	0	1	2	0	.600	
2001 Los Angeles c	N.L.	3B-SS	126	475	59	126	22	4	13	60	13	.265	
2002 Los Angeles	N.L.	3B	159	587	70	151	26	5	21	75	7	.257	
2003 Los Angeles	N.L.	3B-SS	158	559	50	134	30	2	23	80	2	.240	
2004 Los Angeles d	N.L.	3B-SS	156	598	104	200	32	0	*48	121	7	.334	
2005 Seattle	A.L.	3B	156	603	69	154	36	1	19	87	3	.255	
2006 Seattle	A.L.	3B-2B	156	620	88	166	39	4	25	89	11	.268	
2007 Seattle	A.L.	3B	149	595	87	164	41	2	26	99	14	.276	
2008 Seattle	A.L.	3B	143	556	74	148	29	1	25	77	8	.266	
2009 Seattle e-f	A.L.	3B	111	449	54	119	27	0	8	44	13	.265	
2010 Boston g	A.L.	3B	154	589	84	189	*49	2	28	102	2	.321	
2011 Round Rock	P.C.	3B	2	8	1	2	0	0	0	0	0	.250	
2011 Texas h	A.L.	3B	124	487	82	144	33	0	32	105	1	.296	
2012 Texas	A.L.	3B	156	604	95	194	33	·2	36	102	1	.321	
Major League Totals		15 Yrs.	2115	7965	1089	2227	463	30	346	1215	115	.280	
Wild Card Playoff													
2012 Texas	A.L.	3B	1	4	0	0	0	0	0	0	0	.000	
Division Series													
2004 Los Angeles	N.L.	3B	4	15	1	4	0	0	0	1	0	.267	
2011 Texas	A.L.	3B	4	15	5	4	0	0	3	4	0	.267	
Division Series Totals			8	30	6	8	0	0	3	5	0	.267	
Championship Series													
2011 Texas	A.L.	3B	6	27	4	6	3	0	0	2	0	.222	
World Series Record													
2011 Texas	A.L.	3B	7	30	5	9	2	0	2	3	0	.300	

a On disabled list from June 25 to July 2, 1996.
b On disabled list from May 28 to June 16, 2000.
c On disabled list from March 23 to May 12, 2001.
d Filed for free agency, October 29, 2004. Signed with Seattle Mariners, December 17, 2004.
e On disabled list from June 29 to August 4 and August 13 to September 1, 2009.
f Filed for free agency, November 5, 2009. Signed with Boston Red Sox, January 7, 2010.
g Filed for free agency, November 2, 2010. Signed with Texas Rangers, January 5, 2011.
h On disabled list from July 23 to September 1, 2011.

BERKMAN, WILLIAM LANCE (LANCE)

Born, Waco, Texas, February 10, 1976.
Bats Both. Throws Left. Height, 6 feet, 1 inch. Weight, 220 pounds.

Year	Club	Lea	Pos	G	AB	R	H	2B	3B	HR	RBI	SB	Avg
1997 Kissimmee	Fla.St.	OF	53	184	31	54	10	0	12	35	2	.293	
1998 Jackson	Texas	OF	122	425	82	130	34	0	24	89	6	.306	
1998 New Orleans	P.C.	OF	17	59	14	16	4	0	6	13	0	.271	
1999 New Orleans	P.C.	OF	64	226	42	73	20	0	8	49	7	.323	
1999 Houston a	N.L.	OF-1B	34	93	10	22	2	0	4	15	5	.237	
2000 New Orleans	P.C.	OF	31	112	18	37	4	2	6	27	4	.330	
2000 Houston	N.L.	OF-1B	114	353	76	105	28	1	21	67	6	.297	
2001 Houston	N.L.	OF	156	577	110	191	*55	5	34	126	7	.331	
2002 Houston	N.L.	OF	158	578	106	169	35	2	42	*128	8	.292	
2003 Houston	N.L.	OF	153	538	110	155	35	6	25	93	5	.288	
2004 Houston	N.L.	OF-1B	160	544	104	172	40	3	30	106	9	.316	
2005 Round Rock	P.C.	OF	4	14	2	4	1	0	0	1	0	.286	
2005 Houston b	N.L.	1B-OF	132	468	76	137	34	1	24	82	4	.293	
2006 Houston	N.L.	1B-OF	152	536	95	169	29	0	45	136	3	.315	
2007 Houston	N.L.	1B-OF	153	561	95	156	24	2	34	102	7	.278	
2008 Houston	N.L.	1B	159	554	114	173	*46	4	29	106	18	.312	
2009 Houston c	N.L.	1B	136	460	73	126	31	1	25	80	7	.274	
2010 Trenton	Eastern	DH	2	8	1	2	0	0	0	0	0	.250	
2010 Round Rock	P.C.	1B	2	6	3	3	2	0	1	3	0	.500	
2010 Houston	N.L.	1B	85	298	39	73	16	1	13	49	3	.245	
2010 New York d-e-f-g	A.L.	DH-1B	37	106	9	27	7	0	1	9	0	.255	
2011 St. Louis	N.L.	OF-1B	145	488	90	147	23	2	31	94	2	.301	
2012 Memphis	P.C.	1B	6	17	1	4	1	0	0	1	0	.235	
2012 St. Louis h-i	N.L.	1B	32	81	12	21	7	1	2	7	2	.259	
Major League Totals		14 Yrs.	1806	6235	1119	1843	412	29	360	1200	86	.296	
Division Series													
2001 Houston	N.L.	OF	3	12	0	2	0	0	0	0	0	.167	
2004 Houston	N.L.	OF	5	22	5	9	1	0	1	3	0	.409	
2005 Houston	N.L.	1B-OF	4	14	4	5	1	0	1	5	0	.357	

Year Club	Lea	Pos	G	AB	R	H	2B	3B	HR	RBI	SB	Avg
2010 New York	A.L.	DH	1	4	2	2	1	0	1	2	0	.500
2011 St. Louis	N.L.	OF	5	18	4	3	1	0	1	4	1	.167
Division Series Totals			18	70	15	21	4	0	4	14	1	.300
Championship Series												
2004 Houston	N.L.	OF	7	24	7	7	2	0	3	9	1	.292
2005 Houston	N.L.	1B-OF	6	21	2	6	2	0	1	3	0	.286
2010 New York	A.L.	1B-DH	4	12	1	3	0	1	0	2	0	.250
2011 St. Louis	N.L.	OF	6	20	4	6	0	0	0	2	1	.300
Championship Series Totals			23	77	14	22	4	1	4	16	2	.286
World Series Record												
2005 Houston	N.L.	OF-1B	4	13	0	5	2	0	0	6	1	.385
2011 St. Louis	N.L.	OF-DH	7	26	9	11	1	0	1	7	0	.423
World Series Totals			11	39	9	16	3	0	1	13	1	.410

a On disabled list from April 13 to May 14, 1999.
b On disabled list from March 25 to May 6, 2005.
c On disabled list from July 23 to August 12, 2009.
d On disabled list from March 26 to April 20, 2010.
e Traded to New York Yankees with cash for pitcher Mark Melancon and infielder Jimmy Paredes, July 31, 2010.
f On disabled list from August 16 to September 1, 2010.
g Filed for free agency, November 1, 2010. Signed with St. Louis Cardinals, December 4, 2010.
h On disabled list from April 19 to May 13 and May 20 to July 14 and August 3 to September 1, 2012.
i Filed for free agency, November 3, 2012. Signed with Texas Rangers, January 7, 2013.

BERNADINA, ROGEARVIN ARGELO (ROGER)

Born, Willemstad, Curacao, Netherlands Antilles, June 12, 1984.
Bats Left. Throws Left. Height, 6 feet, 1 inch. Weight, 200 pounds.

Year Club	Lea	Pos	G	AB	R	H	2B	3B	HR	RBI	SB	Avg
2002 Expos	Gulf Coast	OF	57	196	22	54	7	0	3	18	1	.276
2003 Savannah	So.Atl.	OF	77	278	36	66	12	3	4	39	11	.237
2004 Savannah	So.Atl.	OF	129	450	67	107	24	7	7	66	24	.238
2005 Savannah	So.Atl.	OF	122	417	64	97	15	3	12	54	35	.233
2006 Potomac.	Carolina	OF	123	434	60	117	19	3	6	42	28	.270
2007 Harrisburg	Eastern	OF	97	371	58	100	15	2	6	36	40	.270
2007 Columbus	Int.	OF	13	42	6	7	3	0	0	1	0	.167
2008 Harrisburg	Eastern	OF	73	266	47	86	11	7	5	38	26	.323
2008 Columbus	Int.	OF	47	191	33	67	13	3	4	16	15	.351
2008 Washington	N.L.	OF	26	76	10	16	1	1	0	2	4	.211
2009 Syracuse	Int.	OF	5	18	1	3	0	0	0	0	1	.167
2009 Washington	N.L.	OF	3	4	1	1	1	0	0	0	1	.250
2009 Nationals a	Gulf Coast	OF	2	4	0	1	0	0	0	0	0	.250
2010 Syracuse	Int.	OF	14	61	8	23	2	1	2	8	7	.377
2010 Washington	N.L.	OF	134	414	52	102	18	3	11	47	16	.246
2011 Syracuse	Int.	OF	46	164	26	41	9	0	6	14	14	.250
2011 Washington	N.L.	OF	91	309	40	75	12	2	7	27	17	.243
2012 Washington	N.L.	OF	129	227	25	66	11	0	5	25	15	.291
Major League Totals	5 Yrs.		383	1030	128	260	43	6	23	101	53	.252
Division Series												
2012 Washington	N.L.	PH	4	2	0	0	0	0	0	0	0	.000

a On disabled list from April 19 to November 8, 2009.

BERRY, QUINTON LONELL (QUINTIN)

Born, San Diego, California, November 21, 1984.
Bats Left. Throws Left. Height, 6 feet. Weight, 175 pounds.

Year Club	Lea	Pos	G	AB	R	H	2B	3B	HR	RBI	SB	Avg
2006 Batavia	N.Y.-Penn.	OF	62	210	34	46	2	2	0	13	19	.219
2007 Lakewood	So.Atl.	OF	126	487	86	152	19	4	3	44	55	.312
2008 Clearwater	Fla.St.	OF	134	511	63	139	24	1	3	43	51	.272
2009 Reading	Eastern	OF	135	516	89	137	17	2	5	28	48	.266
2010 Reading	Eastern	OF	66	238	35	50	10	2	2	25	23	.210
2010 San Antonio a-b	Texas	OF	33	110	11	23	1	1	1	8	4	.209
2011 Louisville	Int.	OF	4	18	2	1	0	0	0	0	2	.056
2011 Carolina c-d	Southern	OF	93	320	64	95	16	1	6	41	40	.297
2012 Toledo	Int.	OF	39	159	18	43	8	0	0	11	19	.270
2012 Detroit	A.L.	OF	94	291	44	75	10	6	2	29	21	.258
Division Series												
2012 Detroit	A.L.	OF	4	10	1	3	1	0	0	0	1	.300

Championship Series

Year	Club	Lea	Pos	G	AB	R	H	2B	3B	HR	RBI	SB	Avg
2012 Detroit	A.L.	OF	3	8	2	2	1	0	0	0	1	.250

World Series Record

Year	Club	Lea	Pos	G	AB	R	H	2B	3B	HR	RBI	SB	Avg
2012 Detroit	A.L.	OF	4	8	0	0	0	0	0	0	0	.000

a Claimed on waivers from Philadelphia Phillies by San Diego Padres, July 14, 2010.
b Selected by New York Mets in Rule V draft, December 9, 2010.
c Released by New York Mets, April 1, 2011. Signed with Cincinnati Reds organization, April 21, 2011.
d Filed for free agency, November 2, 2011. Signed by Detroit Tigers organization, November 9, 2011.

BETEMIT, WILSON

Born, Santo Domingo, Dominican Republic, November 2, 1981.
Bats Both. Throws Right. Height, 6 feet, 2 inches. Weight, 220 pounds.

Year	Club	Lea	Pos	G	AB	R	H	2B	3B	HR	RBI	SB	Avg
1997 Braves	Gulf Coast	SS	32	113	12	24	6	1	0	15	0	.212
1998 Braves	Gulf Coast	SS	51	173	23	38	8	4	5	16	6	.220
1999 Danville	Appal.	SS	67	259	39	83	18	2	5	53	6	.320
2000 Jamestown...	N.Y.-Penn.	SS	69	269	54	89	15	2	5	37	3	.331
2001 Myrtle Beach ..	Carolina	SS	84	318	38	88	20	1	7	43	8	.277
2001 Greenville.....	Southern	SS	47	183	22	65	14	0	5	19	6	.355
2001 Atlanta	N.L.	SS	8	3	1	0	0	0	0	0	1	.000
2002 Braves	Gulf Coast	SS	7	19	2	5	4	0	0	2	1	.263
2002 Richmond	Int.	SS	93	343	43	84	17	1	8	34	8	.245
2003 Richmond	Int.	3B-SS	127	478	55	125	23	13	8	65	8	.262
2004 Richmond	Int.	3B-SS	105	356	48	99	24	2	13	59	3	.278
2004 Atlanta	N.L.	SS-3B	22	47	2	8	0	0	0	3	0	.170
2005 Atlanta	N.L.	3B-SS-2B	115	246	36	75	12	4	4	20	1	.305
2006 Atlanta-LA a	N.L.	3B-SS-2B	143	373	49	98	23	0	18	53	3	.263
2007 Los Angeles	N.L.	3B-SS-2B-OF	84	156	22	36	8	0	10	26	0	.231
2007 New York b......	A.L.	1B-3B-SS-2B	37	84	11	19	4	0	4	24	0	.226
2008 Scranton/WB	Int.	1B-3B-2B-SS	8	27	5	9	4	0	1	5	0	.333
2008 New York c-d ..	A.L.	1B-3B-SS-2B	87	189	24	50	13	0	6	25	0	.265
2009 Chicago	A.L.	1B-3B	20	45	2	9	5	0	0	3	0	.200
2009 Charlotte e	Int.	3B-1B-SS	72	261	36	63	19	0	11	49	2	.241
2010 Omaha	P.C.	SS-1B-3B	29	113	9	30	6	2	2	17	1	.265
2010 Kansas City	A.L.	3B-1B-2B	84	276	36	82	20	0	13	43	0	.297
2011 Kansas City-Detroit f-g	A.L.	3B-1B-2B	97	323	40	92	22	4	8	46	4	.285
2012 Bowie........	Eastern	1B-3B	2	8	1	2	0	0	1	4	0	.250
2012 Baltimore h	A.L.	3B-1B-OF	102	341	41	89	19	0	12	40	0	.261
Major League Totals		10 Yrs.	799	2083	264	558	126	8	75	283	9	.268

Division Series

Year	Club	Lea	Pos	G	AB	R	H	2B	3B	HR	RBI	SB	Avg
2004 Atlanta	N.L.	PH	1	0	0	0	0	0	0	0	0	.000
2005 Atlanta	N.L.	PH	2	2	0	1	0	0	0	0	0	.500
2006 Los Angeles	N.L.	3B	3	8	3	4	1	0	1	1	0	.500
2011 Detroit	A.L.	3B	3	8	0	0	0	0	0	0	0	.000
Division Series Totals			9	18	3	5	1*	0	1	1	0	.278

Championship Series

Year	Club	Lea	Pos	G	AB	R	H	2B	3B	HR	RBI	SB	Avg
2011 Detroit	A.L.	PH	1	1	0	0	0	0	0	0	0	.000

a Traded to Los Angeles Dodgers for pitcher Danys Baez, infielder Willy Aybar and cash, July 28, 2006.
b Traded to New York Yankees for pitcher Scott Proctor, July 31, 2007.
c On disabled list from April 14 to May 6 and May 11 to May 26, 2008.
d Traded to Chicago White Sox with pitcher Jeff Marquez and pitcher Jhonny Nunez for infielder Nick Swisher and pitcher Kaneoka Texeira, November 13, 2008.
e Filed for free agency, October 5, 2009. Signed with Kansas City Royals organization, November 12, 2009.
f Traded to Detroit Tigers for pitcher Antonio Cruz and catcher Julio Rodriguez, July 20, 2011.
g Filed for free agency, October 30, 2011. Signed with Baltimore Orioles organization, January 24, 2012.
h On disabled list from August 12 to September 1, 2012.

BLANCO (PEDRAZA), GREGOR MIGUEL

Born, Caracas, Venezuela, December 24, 1983.
Bats Left. Throws Left. Height, 5 feet, 11 inches. Weight, 185 pounds.

Year	Club	Lea	Pos	G	AB	R	H	2B	3B	HR	RBI	SB	Avg
2002 Macon	So.Atl.	OF	132	468	87	127	14	9	7	36	40	.271
2003 Myrtle Beach	Carolina	OF	126	461	66	125	19	7	5	36	34	.271
2004 Myrtle Beach	Carolina	OF	119	435	73	117	17	9	8	41	25	.269
2005 Mississippi.......	Southern	OF	123	401	64	101	11	12	6	37	28	.252
2006 Richmond	Int.	OF	73	269	43	79	12	1	0	19	14	.294
2006 Mississippi.......	Southern	OF	66	251	45	72	16	3	0	9	17	.287

Year	Club	Lea	Pos	G	AB	R	H	2B	3B	HR	RBI	SB	Avg
2007 Richmond	Int.		OF	124	464	81	131	18	5	3	35	23	.282
2008 Atlanta	N.L.		OF	144	430	52	108	14	4	1	38	13	.251
2009 Atlanta	N.L.		OF	24	43	5	8	0	1	0	1	2	.186
2009 Gwinnett	Int.		OF	90	333	54	76	9	1	2	30	10	.228
2010 Atlanta	N.L.		OF	36	58	9	18	1	1	0	3	1	.310
2010 Gwinnett	Int.		OF	44	154	26	44	8	0	1	11	9	.286
2010 Kansas City a	A.L.		OF	49	179	22	49	8	3	1	11	10	.274
2011 Syracuse	Int.		OF	51	143	28	29	7	2	3	10	15	.203
2011 Omaha b-c	P.C.		OF	23	56	13	11	5	0	0	4	9	.196
2012 San Francisco	N.L.		OF	141	393	56	96	14	5	5	34	26	.244
Major League Totals	4 Yrs.			394	1103	144	279	37	14	7	87	52	.253
Division Series													
2012 San Francisco	N.L.		OF	5	14	3	4	1	0	1	2	0	.286
Championship Series													
2012 San Francisco	N.L.		OF	7	22	6	4	1	1	0	2	0	.182
World Series Record													
2012 San Francisco	N.L.		OF	4	15	1	4	0	1	0	1	0	.267

a Traded to Kansas City Royals with pitcher Jesse Chavez and pitcher Tim Collins for outfielder Rick Ankiel, pitcher Kyle Farnsworth and cash, July 31, 2010.

b Sold to Washington Nationals, May 8, 2011.

c Filed for free agency, November 2, 2011. Signed with San Francisco Giants organization, November 16, 2011.

BLOOMQUIST, WILLIAM PAUL (WILLIE)

Born, Bremerton, Washington, November 27, 1977.

Bats Right. Throws Right. Height, 5 feet, 11 inches. Weight, 195 pounds.

Year	Club	Lea	Pos	G	AB	R	H	2B	3B	HR	RBI	SB	Avg
1999 Everett	Northwest		2B	41	178	35	51	10	3	2	27	17	.287
2000 Lancaster	California		2B-SS	64	256	63	97	19	6	2	51	22	.379
2000 Tacoma a	P.C.		2B	51	191	17	43	5	1	1	23	5	.225
2001 San Antonio	Texas		SS-2B	123	491	59	125	23	2	0	28	34	.255
2002 Tacoma	P.C.		OF-2B-3B-SS	104	337	47	91	14	3	6	47	20	.270
2002 Seattle b	A.L.		OF-2B	12	33	11	15	4	0	0	7	3	.455
2003 Seattle	A.L.		3B-SS-OF	89	196	30	49	7	2	1	14	4	.250
2004 Tacoma	P.C.		SS-OF	3	12	2	5	0	0	1	3	1	.417
2004 Seattle c	A.L.		3B-SS-1B-OF	93	188	27	46	10	0	2	18	13	.245
2005 Seattle d	A.L.		2B-SS-OF-3B	82	249	27	64	15	2	0	22	14	.257
2006 Seattle	A.L.		OF-SS-2B-3B	102	251	36	62	6	2	1	15	16	.247
2007 Seattle	A.L.		OF-2B-3B-SS	91	173	28	48	3	0	2	13	7	.277
2008 Seattle e-f	A.L.		OF-2B-3B	71	165	32	46	1	0	0	9	14	.279
2009 Kansas City	A.L.		OF-SS-2B-1B	125	434	52	115	11	8	4	29	25	.265
2010 Kansas City	A.L.		OF-3B-2B	72	170	31	45	10	1	3	17	8	.265
2010 Cincinnati g-h	N.L.		OF-2B	11	17	0	5	0	0	0	0	0	.294
2011 Arizona i-j	N.L.		SS-OF-2B	97	350	44	93	10	2	4	26	20	.266
2012 D-Backs	Arizona		SS	4	9	3	3	1	1	0	4	0	.333
2012 Arizona k	N.L.		SS-3B-OF-2B	80	324	47	98	21	5	0	23	7	.302
Major League Totals	11 Yrs.			925	2550	365	686	98	22	17	193	131	.269
Division Series													
2011 Arizona	N.L.		SS	5	22	3	7	0	0	0	1	3	.318

a On disabled list from August 6 to September 29, 2000.

b On disabled list from April 22 to May 3 and June 6 to 18, 2002.

c On disabled list from May 2 to May 21, 2004.

d On disabled list from August 30 to October 31, 2005.

e On disabled list from August 10 to September 29, 2008.

f Filed for free agency, October 30, 2008. Signed with Kansas City Royals, January 9, 2009.

g Sold to Cincinnati Reds, September 13, 2010.

h Filed for free agency, November 1, 2010. Signed with Arizona Diamondbacks, January 18, 2011.

i On disabled list from April 22 to May 18, 2011.

j Filed for free agency, October 31, 2011, re-signed with Arizona Diamondbacks, November 9, 2011.

k On disabled list from August 9 to September 1, 2012.

BOESCH, BRENNAN PHILIP

Born, Santa Monica, California, April 12, 1985.

Bats Left. Throws Left. Height, 6 feet, 4 inches. Weight, 235 pounds.

Year	Club	Lea	Pos	G	AB	R	H	2B	3B	HR	RBI	SB	Avg
2006 Oneonta	N.Y.-Penn.		OF	70	292	27	85	15	6	5	54	3	.291
2007 West Michigan	Midwest		OF	126	513	52	137	19	4	10	86	15	.267
2008 Lakeland	Fla.St.		OF	111	417	46	104	17	8	7	64	3	.249

Year	Club	Lea	Pos	G	AB	R	H	2B	3B	HR	RBI	SB	Avg
2009 Erie.	Eastern	OF	131	527	89	145	26	7	28	93	11	.275
2010 Toledo	Int.	OF	15	58	6	22	3	1	3	17	2	.379
2010 Detroit	A.L.	OF	133	464	49	119	26	3	14	67	7	.256
2011 Detroit a	A.L.	OF	115	428	75	121	25	1	16	54	5	.283
2012 Detroit	A.L.	OF	132	470	52	113	22	2	12	54	6	.240
Major League Totals		3 Yrs.	380	1362	176	353	73	6	42	175	18	.259

a On disabled list from September 9 to October 21, 2011.

BOGUSEVIC, BRIAN THOMAS

Born, Palos Heights, Illinois, February 18, 1984.
Bats Left. Throws Left. Height, 6 feet, 3 inches. Weight, 220 pounds.

Year	Club	Lea	Pos	G	AB	R	H	2B	3B	HR	RBI	SB	Avg
2007 Corpus Christi a	Texas	PH	2	2	0	1	0	0	0	0	0	.500
2008 Salem.	Carolina	OF	8	23	4	5	2	0	1	6	1	.217
2008 Corpus Christi	Texas	OF	42	124	21	46	10	2	3	20	8	.371
2009 Round Rock.	P.C.	OF	138	520	68	141	25	3	6	53	22	.271
2010 Round Rock.	P.C.	OF-1B	131	502	91	139	26	2	13	57	23	.277
2010 Houston.	N.L.	OF	19	28	5	5	3	0	0	3	1	.179
2011 Oklahoma.	P.C.	OF-1B	58	218	27	57	11	5	3	35	20	.261
2011 Houston	N.L.	OF	87	164	22	47	14	1	4	15	4	.287
2012 Houston b	N.L.	OF-P	146	355	39	72	9	2	7	28	15	.203
Major League Totals		3 Yrs.	252	547	66	124	26	3	11	46	20	.227

a Pitched in Houston Astros organization from 2005 through 2008.
b Filed for free agency, November 3, 2012. Signed with Chicago Cubs organization, November 14, 2012.

BONIFACIO, EMILIO JOSE

Born, Santo Domingo, Dominican Republic, April 23, 1985.
Bats Both. Throws Right. Height, 5 feet, 11 inches. Weight, 195 pounds.

Year	Club	Lea	Pos	G	AB	R	H	2B	3B	HR	RBI	SB	Avg
2003 Missoula	Pioneer	2B	54	146	20	29	1	1	0	16	15	.199
2004 South Bend . . .	Midwest	2B	120	411	59	107	9	6	1	37	40	.260
2005 South Bend . . .	Midwest	2B	127	522	81	141	14	7	1	44	55	.270
2006 Lancaster	Calif.	2B	130	546	117	175	35	7	7	50	61	.321
2007 Mobile	Southern	2B-SS	132	551	84	157	21	5	2	40	41	.285
2007 Arizona.	N.L.	2B	11	23	2	5	1	0	0	2	0	.217
2008 Tucson.	P.C.	2B-OF-SS	85	367	49	111	18	5	1	29	17	.302
2008 Columbus.	Int.	2B	8	31	9	14	2	0	0	3	4	.452
2008 Arizona-Washington a-b	N.L.	2B-OF	49	169	29	41	6	5	0	14	7	.243
2009 Florida	N.L.	3B-SS-OF-2B	127	461	72	116	11	6	1	27	21	.252
2010 New Orleans.	P.C.	2B-SS	40	164	19	45	8	3	0	11	8	.274
2010 Florida	N.L.	OF-SS-3B-2B	73	180	30	47	6	3	0	10	12	.261
2011 Florida	N.L.	SS-OF-3B-2B	152	565	78	167	26	7	5	36	40	.296
2012 Jupiter	Fla.St.	OF	9	30	6	5	1	0	0	4	3	.167
2012 Miami c-d	N.L.	OF-2B	64	244	30	63	3	4	1	11	30	.258
Major League Totals		6 Yrs.	476	1642	241	439	53	25	7	100	110	.267

a Traded to Washington Nationals for pitcher Jon Rauch, July 22, 2008.
b Traded to Florida Marlins with pitcher P.J. Dean and infielder Jake Smolinski for pitcher Scott Olsen and outfielder Josh Willingham, November 11, 2008.
c On disabled list from May 19 to July 13 and August 4 to August 19 and August 22 to October 31, 2012.
d Traded to Toronto Blue Jays with catcher John Buck, pitcher Mark Buehrle, pitcher Josh Johnson and infielder Jose Reyes for pitcher Henderson Alvarez, infielder Yunel Escobar, infielder Adeiny Hechavarria, catcher Jeff Mathis, pitcher Anthony De Sclafani, outfielder Jake Marisnick and pitcher Justin Nicolino, November 19, 2012.

BOURJOS, PETER CHRISTOPHER

Born, Park Ridge, Illinois, March 31, 1987.
Bats Right. Throws Right. Height, 6 feet, 1 inch. Weight, 180 pounds.

Year	Club	Lea	Pos	G	AB	R	H	2B	3B	HR	RBI	SB	Avg
2006 Orem	Pioneer	OF	65	250	42	73	16	7	5	28	13	.292
2007 Angels	Arizona	OF	4	16	3	5	0	1	0	2	0	.313
2007 Cedar Rapids	Midwest	OF	63	237	37	65	9	6	5	29	19	.274
2008 Rancho Cucamonga. . . .	Calif.	OF	121	509	83	150	29	10	9	51	50	.295
2009 Arkansas	Texas	OF	110	437	72	123	16	14	6	51	32	.281
2010 Salt Lake	P.C.	OF	102	414	85	130	13	12	13	52	27	.314
2010 Los Angeles	A.L.	OF	51	181	19	37	6	4	6	15	10	.204
2011 Los Angeles a	A.L.	OF	147	502	72	136	26	*11	12	43	22	.271

Year Club	Lea	Pos	G	AB	R	H	2B	3B	HR	RBI	SB	Avg
2012 Salt Lake . . . . .P.C.		OF	7	29	4	9	1	3	0	3	0	.310
2012 Los Angeles b . . . . . A.L.		OF	101	168	27	37	7	0	3	19	3	.220
Major League Totals	3 Yrs.		299	851	118	210	39	15	21	77	35	.247

a On disabled list from July 8 to July 23, 2011.

b On disabled list from August 19 to September 3, 2012.

BOURN, MICHAEL RAY

Born, Houston, Texas, December 27, 1982.
Bats Left. Throws Right. Height, 5 feet, 11 inches. Weight, 180 pounds.

Year Club	Lea	Pos	G	AB	R	H	2B	3B	HR	RBI	SB	Avg
2003 Batavia . . . . N.Y.-Penn.		OF	35	125	12	35	0	1	0	4	23	.280
2004 Lakewood. . . . . So.Atl.		OF	109	413	92	130	20	14	5	53	58	.315
2005 Reading . . . . Eastern		OF	135	544	80	146	18	8	6	44	38	.268
2006 Reading . . . . Eastern		OF	80	318	62	87	5	6	4	26	30	.274
2006 Scranton-WB . . . . Int.		OF	38	152	34	43	5	7	1	15	15	.283
2006 Philadelphia . . . . N.L.		OF	17	8	2	1	0	0	0	0	1	.125
2007 Philadelphia a-b . . . . . . N.L.		OF	105	119	29	33	3	3	1	6	18	.277
2008 Houston . . . . N.L.		OF	138	467	57	107	10	4	5	29	41	.229
2009 Houston . . . . N.L.		OF	157	606	97	173	27	12	3	35	*61	.285
2010 Houston . . . . N.L.		OF	141	535	84	142	25	6	2	38	*52	.265
2011 Houston-Atlanta c . . . . . N.L.		OF	158	656	94	193	34	10	2	50	*61	.294
2012 Atlanta d. . . . . N.L.		OF	155	624	96	171	26	10	9	57	42	.274
Major League Totals	7 Yrs.		871	3015	459	820	125	45	22	215	276	.272
Wild Card Playoff												
2012 Atlanta . . . . N.L.		OF	1	5	0	1	0	0	0	1	0	.200
Division Series												
2007 Philadelphia . . . . N.L.		PH	2	1	0	0	0	0	0	0	0	.000

a On disabled list from July 31 to September 10, 2007.

b Traded to Houston Astros with pitcher Geoff Geary and infielder Mike Costanzo for infielder Eric Bruntlett and pitcher Brad Lidge, November 12, 2007.

c Traded to Atlanta Braves with cash for outfielder Jordan Schafer, pitcher Juan Abreu, pitcher Paul Clemens and pitcher Brett Oberholtzer, July 31, 2011.

d Filed for free agency, November 3, 2012.

BRANTLEY, MICHAEL CHARLES JR.

Born, Bellevue, Washington, May 15, 1987.
Bats Left. Throws Left. Height, 6 feet, 2 inches. Weight, 200 pounds.

Year Club	Lea	Pos	G	AB	R	H	2B	3B	HR	RBI	SB	Avg
2005 Brewers . . . . Arizona		OF	44	173	34	60	3	1	0	19	14	.347
2005 Helena . . . . Pioneer		OF	10	34	8	11	2	0	0	3	2	.324
2006 West Virginia . . . . So.Atl.		OF	108	360	47	108	10	2	0	42	24	.300
2007 West Virginia . . . . So.Atl.		1B-OF	56	218	41	73	15	1	2	32	18	.335
2007 Huntsville . . . . Southern		OF-1B	59	187	28	47	6	1	0	21	17	.251
2008 Huntsville a . . . . . . Southern		OF-1B	106	420	80	134	17	2	4	40	28	.319
2009 Columbus. . . . . Int.		OF	116	457	80	122	21	2	6	37	46	.267
2009 Cleveland . . . . A.L.		OF	28	112	10	35	4	0	0	11	4	.313
2010 Columbus. . . . . Int.		OF	67	273	54	87	13	2	4	29	13	.319
2010 Cleveland . . . . A.L.		OF	72	297	38	73	9	3	3	22	10	.246
2011 Cleveland b . . . . A.L.		OF	114	451	63	120	24	4	7	46	13	.266
2012 Cleveland . . . . A.L.		OF	149	552	63	159	37	4	6	60	12	.288
Major League Totals	4 Yrs.		363	1412	174	387	74	11	16	139	39	.274

a Sent by Milwaukee Brewers to Cleveland Indians as player to be named later for pitcher C.C. Sabathia, October 3, 2008.

b On disabled list from August 23 to November 2, 2011.

BRANTLY, ROBERT JACOB (ROB)

Born, San Diego, California, July 14, 1989.
Bats Left. Throws Right. Height, 6 feet, 2 inches. Weight, 205 pounds.

Year Club	Lea	Pos	G	AB	R	H	2B	3B	HR	RBI	SB	Avg
2010 West Michigan . . . . . Midwest		C	52	188	26	48	10	1	1	21	2	.255
2011 Lakeland. . . . . Fla.St.		C	39	146	16	32	6	0	3	18	0	.219
2011 West Michigan . . . . . Midwest		C	75	284	42	86	16	1	7	44	2	.303
2012 Erie. . . . . Eastern		C	46	180	16	56	16	1	3	24	0	.311
2012 New Orleans. . . . . P.C.		C	14	52	7	19	4	0	2	11	0	.365
2012 Toledo . . . . Int.		C	36	130	11	33	4	0	0	6	0	.254
2012 Miami. . . . . N.L.		C	31	100	14	29	8	0	3	8	1	.290

BRAUN, RYAN JOSEPH
Born, Mission Hills, California, November 17, 1983.
Bats Right. Throws Right. Height, 6 feet, 2 inches. Weight, 200 pounds.

Year	Club	Lea	Pos	G	AB	R	H	2B	3B	HR	RBI	SB	Avg
2005 Helena	Pioneer		3B	10	41	6	14	2	1	2	10	2	.341
2005 West Virginia	So.Atl.		3B	37	152	21	54	16	2	8	35	2	.355
2006 Brevard County	Fla.St.		3B	59	226	34	62	12	2	7	37	14	.274
2006 Huntsville	Southern		3B	59	231	42	70	19	1	15	40	12	.303
2007 Nashville	P.C.		3B	34	117	28	40	12	0	10	22	4	.342
2007 Milwaukee a	N.L.		3B	113	451	91	146	26	6	34	97	15	.324
2008 Milwaukee	N.L.		OF	151	611	92	174	39	7	37	106	14	.285
2009 Milwaukee	N.L.		OF	158	635	113	*203	39	6	32	114	20	.320
2010 Milwaukee	N.L.		OF	157	619	101	188	45	1	25	103	14	.304
2011 Milwaukee b	N.L.		OF	150	563	109	187	38	6	33	111	33	.332
2012 Milwaukee	N.L.		OF	154	*598	108	191	36	3	*41	112	30	.319
Major League Totals	6 Yrs.			883	3477	614	1089	223	29	202	643	126	.313
Division Series													
2008 Milwaukee	N.L.		OF	4	16	0	5	2	0	0	2	0	.313
2011 Milwaukee	N.L.		OF	5	18	5	9	4	0	1	4	1	.500
Division Series Totals				9	34	5	14	6	0	1	6	1	.412
Championship Series													
2011 Milwaukee	N.L.		OF	6	24	2	8	3	0	1	6	0	.333

a Selected Rookie of the Year in National League for 2007.
b Selected Most Valuable Player in National League for 2011.

BROWN, DOMONIC LARUN
Born, Lithonia, Georgia, September 3, 1987.
Bats Left. Throws Left. Height, 6 feet, 5 inches. Weight, 200 pounds.

Year	Club	Lea	Pos	G	AB	R	H	2B	3B	HR	RBI	SB	Avg
2006 Phillies	Gulf Coast		OF	34	117	13	25	3	0	1	7	13	.214
2007 Clearwater	Fla.St.		OF	3	9	2	4	1	0	1	7	0	.444
2007 Williamsport	N.Y.-Penn.		OF	74	285	43	84	11	5	3	32	14	.295
2008 Lakewood	So.Atl.		OF	114	444	77	129	23	3	9	54	22	.291
2009 Reading	Eastern		OF	37	147	20	41	9	4	3	20	8	.279
2009 Clearwater	Fla.St.		OF	66	238	41	72	12	3	11	44	15	.303
2009 Phillies	Gulf Coast		OF	3	10	4	5	0	2	0	0	0	.500
2010 Reading	Eastern		OF	65	236	50	75	16	3	15	47	12	.318
2010 Lehigh Valley	Int.		OF	28	107	15	37	6	1	5	21	5	.346
2010 Philadelphia	N.L.		OF	35	62	8	13	3	0	2	13	2	.210
2011 Clearwater	Fla.St.		OF	5	19	4	7	1	0	2	4	0	.368
2011 Lehigh Valley	Int.		OF	41	138	22	36	6	0	3	15	12	.261
2011 Philadelphia a	N.L.		OF	56	184	28	45	10	1	5	19	3	.245
2012 Phillies	Gulf Coast		OF	5	19	4	11	7	0	0	4	1	.579
2012 Lehigh Valley	Int.		OF	60	220	33	63	13	2	5	28	4	.286
2012 Philadelphia	N.L.		OF	56	187	21	44	11	2	5	26	0	.235
Major League Totals	3 Yrs.			147	433	57	102	24	3	12	58	5	.236
Division Series													
2010 Philadelphia	N.L.		PH	1	1	1	0	0	0	0	0	0	.000
Championship Series													
2010 Philadelphia	N.L.		PH	2	2	0	0	0	0	0	0	0	.000

a On disabled list from March 22 to May 2, 2011.

BRUCE, JAY ALLEN
Born, Beaumont, Texas, April 3, 1987.
Bats Left. Throws Left. Height, 6 feet, 3 inches. Weight, 205 pounds.

Year	Club	Lea	Pos	G	AB	R	H	2B	3B	HR	RBI	SB	Avg
2005 Reds	Gulf Coast		OF	37	122	29	33	9	2	5	25	4	.270
2005 Billings	Pioneer		OF	17	70	16	18	2	0	4	13	2	.257
2006 Dayton	Midwest		OF	117	444	69	129	42	5	16	81	19	.291
2007 Sarasota	Fla.St.		OF	67	268	49	87	27	5	11	49	4	.325
2007 Louisville	Int.		OF	50	187	28	57	12	2	11	25	2	.305
2007 Chattanooga	Southern		OF	16	66	10	22	7	1	4	15	2	.333
2008 Louisville	Int.		OF	49	184	34	67	9	5	10	37	8	.364
2008 Cincinnati	N.L.		OF	108	413	63	105	17	1	21	52	4	.254
2009 Louisville	Int.		OF	5	18	3	5	0	0	0	0	2	.278
2009 Cincinnati a	N.L.		OF	101	345	47	77	15	2	22	58	3	.223
2010 Cincinnati	N.L.		OF	148	509	80	143	23	5	25	70	5	.281

Year Club	Lea	Pos	G	AB	R	H	2B	3B	HR	RBI	SB	Avg
2011 Cincinnati	N.L.	OF	157	585	84	150	27	2	32	97	8	.256
2012 Cincinnati	N.L.	OF	155	560	89	141	35	5	34	99	9	.252
Major League Totals	5 Yrs.		669	2412	363	616	117	15	134	376	29	.255
Division Series												
2010 Cincinnati	N.L.	OF	3	8	1	2	0	0	1	1	0	.250
2012 Cincinnati	N.L.	OF	5	19	2	5	2	0	1	4	0	.263
Division Series Totals			8	27	3	7	2	0	2	5	0	.259

a On disabled list from July 12 to September 14, 2009.

BUCK, JOHNATHAN RICHARD (JOHN)

Born, Kemmerer, Wyoming, July 7, 1980.
Bats Right. Throws Right. Height, 6 feet, 3 inches. Weight, 220 pounds.

Year Club	Lea	Pos	G	AB	R	H	2B	3B	HR	RBI	SB	Avg
1998 Astros	Gulf Coast	C	36	126	24	36	9	0	3	15	2	.286
1999 Auburn	N.Y.-Penn.	C	63	233	36	57	17	0	3	29	7	.245
1999 Michigan	Midwest	C	4	10	1	1	1	0	0	0	0	.100
2000 Michigan	Midwest	C	109	390	57	110	33	0	10	71	2	.282
2001 Lexington	So.Atl.	C	122	443	72	122	24	1	22	73	4	.275
2002 Round Rock	Texas	C	120	448	48	118	29	3	12	89	2	.263
2003 New Orleans	P.C.	C	78	274	32	70	18	2	2	39	1	.255
2004 New Orleans	P.C.	C	65	227	31	68	11	0	12	35	0	.300
2004 Kansas City a	A.L.	C	71	238	36	56	9	0	12	30	1	.235
2005 Kansas City	A.L.	C	118	401	40	97	21	1	12	47	2	.242
2006 Kansas City	A.L.	C	114	371	37	91	21	1	11	50	0	.245
2007 Kansas City	A.L.	C	113	347	41	77	18	0	18	48	0	.222
2008 Kansas City	A.L.	C	109	370	48	83	23	1	9	48	0	.224
2009 Omaha	P.C.	C	7	27	3	7	1	0	2	4	0	.259
2009 Kansas City b-c	A.L.	C	59	186	16	46	12	4	8	36	1	.247
2010 New Hampshire	Eastern	C	3	11	2	3	0	0	2	6	0	.273
2010 Toronto d-e	A.L.	C	118	409	53	115	25	0	20	66	0	.281
2011 Florida	N.L.	C	140	466	41	106	15	1	16	57	0	.227
2012 Miami f-g	N.L.	C	106	343	29	66	15	1	12	41	0	.192
Major League Totals	9 Yrs.		948	3131	341	737	159	9	118	423	4	.235

a Traded by Houston Astros to Kansas City Royals with pitcher Octavio Dotel for outfielder Carlos Beltran, June 24, 2004.

b On disabled list from May 31 to July 6, 2009.

c Not offered contract, December 12, 2009. Signed with Toronto Blue Jays, December 16, 2009.

d On disabled list from August 5 to August 20, 2010.

e Filed for free agency, November 1, 2010. Signed with Florida Marlins, November 16, 2010.

f Traded to Toronto Blue Jays with outfielder Emilio Bonifacio, pitcher Mark Buehrle, pitcher Josh Johnson and infielder Jose Reyes for pitcher Henderson Alvarez, infielder Yunel Escobar, infielder Adeiny Hechavarria, catcher Jeff Mathis, pitcher Anthony De Sclafani, outfielder Jake Marisnick and pitcher Justin Nicolino, November 19, 2012.

g Traded to New York Mets with pitcher Noah Syndergaard, catcher Travis D'Arnaud and outfielder Wuilmer Becerra for catcher Josh Thole, catcher Mike Nickeas and pitcher R.A. Dickey, December 17, 2012.

BURRISS, EMMANUEL ALLEN

Born, Washington, District of Columbia, January 17, 1985.
Bats Both. Throws Right. Height, 6 feet. Weight, 205 pounds.

Year Club	Lea	Pos	G	AB	R	H	2B	3B	HR	RBI	SB	Avg
2006 Salem-Keizer	Northwest	SS	65	254	50	78	8	2	1	27	35	.307
2007 San Jose	Calif.	SS	36	139	23	23	2	0	0	8	17	.165
2007 Augusta	So.Atl.	SS	89	365	64	117	14	4	0	38	51	.321
2008 Fresno	P.C.	2B-SS	14	62	6	16	1	1	0	6	2	.258
2008 San Francisco	N.L.	SS-2B-OF	95	240	37	68	6	1	1	18	13	.283
2009 San Francisco	N.L.	2B	61	202	18	48	6	0	0	13	11	.238
2009 Fresno a	P.C.	2B	17	71	9	19	2	1	1	7	6	.268
2010 San Jose	Calif.	SS	5	14	2	3	0	0	0	1	1	.214
2010 Fresno	P.C.	SS-2B	67	273	32	77	11	2	0	22	11	.282
2010 San Francisco b	N.L.	2B	7	5	3	2	0	0	0	0	0	.400
2011 Fresno	P.C.	2B-SS-OF	45	175	31	52	8	1	2	10	24	.297
2011 San Francisco	N.L.	2B-SS-1B-3B	59	137	14	28	1	0	0	4	11	.204
2012 Fresno	P.C.	2B-OF-SS-3B	29	106	12	29	7	2	0	3	5	.274
2012 San Francisco c	N.L.	2B-3B-SS-OF	60	136	15	29	1	0	0	7	5	.213
Major League Totals	5 Yrs.		282	720	87	175	14	1	1	42	40	.243

a On disabled list from September 1 to November 10, 2009.

b On disabled list from March 26 to June 25, 2010.

c Filed for free agency, November 8, 2012. Signed with Cincinnati Reds organization, November 14, 2012.

BUTLER, BILLY RAY

Born, Orange Park, Florida, April 18, 1986.
Bats Right. Throws Right. Height, 6 feet, 1 inch. Weight, 240 pounds.

Year Club	Lea	Pos	G	AB	R	H	2B	3B	HR	RBI	SB	Avg
2004 Idaho Falls	Pioneer	3B	72	260	74	97	22	3	10	68	5	.373
2005 High Desert	Calif.	3B-OF	92	379	70	132	30	2	25	91	0	.348
2005 Wichita	Texas	OF	29	112	14	35	9	0	5	19	0	.313
2006 Wichita	Texas	OF	119	477	82	158	33	1	15	96	1	.331
2007 Omaha	P.C.	OF-1B	57	203	40	59	10	1	13	46	1	.291
2007 Kansas City	A.L.	DH-1B-OF	92	329	38	96	23	2	8	52	0	.292
2008 Omaha	P.C.	1B	26	101	18	34	6	1	5	13	0	.337
2008 Kansas City	A.L.	DH-1B	124	443	44	122	22	0	11	55	0	.275
2009 Kansas City	A.L.	1B	159	608	78	183	51	1	21	93	1	.301
2010 Kansas City	A.L.	1B	158	595	77	189	45	0	15	78	0	.318
2011 Kansas City	A.L.	DH-1B	159	597	74	174	44	0	19	95	2	.291
2012 Kansas City	A.L.	DH-1B	161	614	72	192	32	1	29	107	2	.313
Major League Totals		6 Yrs.	853	3186	383	956	217	4	103	480	5	.300

CABRERA, ASDRUBAL JOSE

Born, Puerto La Cruz, Venezuela, November 13, 1985.
Bats Both. Throws Right. Height, 6 feet. Weight, 170 pounds.

Year Club	Lea	Pos	G	AB	R	H	2B	3B	HR	RBI	SB	Avg
2004 Everett	Northwest	SS-2B-3B	63	239	44	65	16	3	5	41	7	.272
2005 Inland Empire	Calif.	SS	55	225	31	64	15	6	1	26	3	.284
2005 Wisconsin	Midwest	2B-SS-3B	51	192	26	61	12	3	4	30	2	.318
2005 Tacoma	P.C.	SS	6	23	4	5	0	1	0	3	0	.217
2006 Buffalo a	Int.	SS	52	190	26	50	11	0	1	14	5	.263
2006 Tacoma a	P.C.	SS	60	203	27	48	12	2	3	22	7	.236
2007 Akron	Eastern	SS-2B	96	368	78	114	23	3	8	54	23	.310
2007 Buffalo	Int.	SS-2B	9	38	6	12	3	0	0	3	2	.316
2007 Cleveland	A.L.	2B-SS-3B	45	159	30	45	9	2	3	22	0	.283
2008 Buffalo	Int.	SS-2B	34	141	25	46	7	1	4	13	2	.326
2008 Cleveland	A.L.	2B-SS	114	352	48	91	20	0	6	47	4	.259
2009 Akron	Eastern	SS	4	16	5	4	1	0	0	0	2	.250
2009 Cleveland b	A.L.	SS-2B	131	523	81	161	42	4	6	68	17	.308
2010 Mahoning Valley	N.Y.-Penn.	SS	2	6	0	2	1	0	0	2	0	.333
2010 Akron	Eastern	SS	4	14	4	5	2	0	1	1	2	.357
2010 Cleveland c	A.L.	SS	97	381	39	105	16	1	3	29	6	.276
2011 Cleveland	A.L.	SS	151	604	87	165	32	3	25	92	17	.273
2012 Cleveland	A.L.	SS	143	555	70	150	35	1	16	68	9	.270
Major League Totals		6 Yrs.	681	2574	355	717	154	11	59	326	53	.279
Division Series												
2007 Cleveland	A.L.	2B	4	17	3	3	0	0	1	2	0	.176
Championship Series												
2007 Cleveland	A.L.	2B	7	29	2	7	0	0	0	4	0	.241

a Traded to Cleveland Indians by Seattle Mariners for outfielder Eduardo Perez, June 30, 2006.
b On disabled list from June 3 to June 28, 2009.
c On disabled list from May 18 to July 20, 2010.

CABRERA, EVERTH

Born, Nandaime, Nicaragua, November 17, 1986.
Bats Both. Throws Right. Height, 5 feet, 10 inches. Weight, 175 pounds.

Year Club	Lea	Pos	G	AB	R	H	2B	3B	HR	RBI	SB	Avg
2006 Casper	Pioneer	2B	54	185	30	47	4	2	0	14	18	.254
2007 Modesto	Calif.	2B	4	15	3	4	0	1	0	2	1	.267
2007 Tri-City	Northwest	2B-SS	42	150	29	45	8	3	1	23	12	.300
2008 Asheville a	So.Atl.	2B-SS	121	479	80	136	25	6	6	38	73	.284
2009 Lake Elsinore	Calif.	SS-2B	7	23	7	9	1	1	0	4	4	.391
2009 Portland	P.C.	SS	7	27	5	9	2	0	0	0	1	.333
2009 San Diego b	N.L.	SS	103	377	59	96	18	8	2	31	25	.255
2010 Lake Elsinore	Calif.	SS	3	10	1	3	0	0	0	1	1	.300
2010 Portland	P.C.	SS	8	31	7	8	1	0	0	3	3	.258
2010 San Diego c	N.L.	SS-2B	76	212	22	44	6	3	1	22	10	.208
2011 San Diego	N.L.	SS	2	8	1	1	0	0	0	0	2	.125
2011 Tucson	P.C.	SS	58	246	52	73	12	4	2	15	29	.297
2012 Tucson	P.C.	SS-3B-OF-2B	34	144	27	48	9	1	0	15	15	.333
2012 San Diego	N.L.	SS-2B-3B	115	398	49	98	19	3	2	24	*44	.246
Major League Totals		4 Yrs.	296	995	131	239	43	14	5	77	81	.240

a Selected by San Diego Padres from Colorado Rockies in Rule V draft, December 11, 2008.
b On disabled list from April 20 to June 19, 2009.
c On disabled list from April 27 to May 14 and May 24 to June 25, 2010.

CABRERA, JOSE MIGUEL (MIGUEL)

Born, Maracay, Venezuela, April 18, 1983.
Bats Right. Throws Right. Height, 6 feet, 2 inches. Weight, 240 pounds.

Year	Club	Lea	Pos	G	AB	R	H	2B	3B	HR	RBI	SB	Avg
2000 Marlins	Gulf Coast		SS	57	219	38	57	10	2	2	22	1	.260
2000 Utica	N.Y.-Penn		SS	8	32	3	8	2	0	0	6	0	.250
2001 Kane County	Midwest		SS	110	422	61	134	19	4	7	66	3	.318
2002 Jupiter	Fla.St.		3B	124	478	77	134	43	1	9	75	10	.274
2003 Carolina	Southern		3B-OF	69	266	46	97	29	3	10	59	9	.365
2003 Florida	N.L.		OF-3B	87	314	39	84	21	3	12	62	0	.268
2004 Florida	N.L.		OF	160	603	101	177	31	1	33	112	5	.294
2005 Florida	N.L.		OF-3B	158	613	106	198	43	2	33	116	1	.323
2006 Florida	N.L.		3B	158	576	112	195	50	2	26	114	9	.339
2007 Florida a	N.L.		3B	157	588	91	188	38	2	34	119	2	.320
2008 Detroit	A.L.		1B-3B	160	616	85	180	36	2	*37	127	1	.292
2009 Detroit	A.L.		1B	160	611	96	198	34	0	34	103	6	.324
2010 Detroit	A.L.		1B	150	548	111	180	45	1	38	*126	3	.328
2011 Detroit	A.L.		1B	*161	572	111	197	*48	0	30	105	2	*.344
2012 Detroit b	A.L.		3B-1B	161	622	109	205	40	0	*44	*139	4	*.330
Major League Totals		10 Yrs.	1512	5663	961	1802	386	13	321	1123	33	.318	
Division Series													
2003 Florida	N.L.		3B	4	14	1	4	2	0	0	3	0	.286
2011 Detroit	A.L.		1B	5	15	2	3	0	0	1	3	1	.200
2012 Detroit	A.L.		3B	5	20	1	5	2	0	0	1	0	.250
Division Series Totals				14	49	4	12	4	0	1	7	1	.245
Championship Series													
2003 Florida	N.L.	OF-3B-SS	7	30	9	10	0	0	3	6	0	.333	
2011 Detroit	A.L.		1B	6	20	5	8	4	0	3	7	1	.400
2012 Detroit	A.L.		3B	4	16	3	5	1	0	1	4	0	.313
Championship Series Totals				17	66	17	23	5	0	7	17	1	.348
World Series Record													
2003 Florida	N.L.		OF	6	24	1	4	0	0	1	3	0	.167
2012 Detroit	A.L.		3B	4	13	1	3	0	0	1	3	0	.231
World Series Totals				10	37	2	7	0	0	2	6	0	.189

a Traded to Detroit Tigers with pitcher Dontrelle Willis for pitcher Burke Badenhop, pitcher Eulogio De La Cruz, pitcher Andrew Miller, catcher Mike Rabelo and outfielder Cameron Maybin, December 5, 2007.
b Selected Most Valuable Player in American League for 2012.

CABRERA, MELKY

Born, Santo Domingo, Dominican Republic, August 11, 1984.
Bats Both. Throws Left. Height, 5 feet, 11 inches. Weight, 200 pounds.

Year	Club	Lea	Pos	G	AB	R	H	2B	3B	HR	RBI	SB	Avg
2003 Staten Island	N.Y.-Penn.		OF	67	279	34	79	10	2	2	31	13	.283
2004 Tampa	Fla.St.		OF	85	333	48	96	20	3	8	51	3	.288
2004 Battle Creek	Midwest		OF	42	171	35	57	16	3	0	16	7	.333
2005 New York	A.L.		OF	6	19	1	4	0	0	0	0	0	.211
2005 Columbus	Int.		OF	26	101	15	25	3	0	3	17	2	.248
2005 Trenton	Eastern		OF	106	426	57	117	22	3	10	60	11	.275
2006 Columbus	Int.		OF	31	122	19	47	6	2	4	24	3	.385
2006 New York	A.L.		OF	130	460	75	129	26	2	7	50	12	.280
2007 New York	A.L.		OF	150	545	66	149	24	8	8	73	13	.273
2008 Scranton-WB	Int.		OF	15	57	8	19	2	0	0	5	1	.333
2008 New York	A.L.		OF	129	414	42	103	12	1	8	37	9	.249
2009 New York a	A.L.		OF	154	485	66	133	28	1	13	68	10	.274
2010 Atlanta b	N.L.		OF	147	458	50	117	27	3	4	42	7	.255
2011 Kansas City c	A.L.		OF	155	658	102	201	44	5	18	87	20	.305
2012 San Francisco d	N.L.		OF	113	459	84	159	25	10	11	60	13	.346
Major League Totals		8 Yrs.	984	3498	486	995	186	30	69	417	84	.284	
Division Series													
2006 New York	A.L.		OF	2	3	0	0	0	0	0	0	0	.000
2007 New York	A.L.		OF	4	16	2	3	0	0	1	2	0	.188
2009 New York	A.L.		OF	3	12	1	2	0	0	0	0	0	.167
2010 Atlanta	N.L.		OF	3	8	1	0	0	0	0	1	0	.000

22

Year	Club	Lea	Pos	G	AB	R	H	2B	3B	HR	RBI	SB	Avg
Division Series Totals				12	39	4	5	0	0	1	3	0	.128
Championship Series													
2009 New York	A.L.		OF	6	23	3	9	2	0	0	4	0	.391
World Series Record													
2009 New York	A.L.		OF	4	13	1	2	0	0	0	0	0	.154

a Traded to Atlanta Braves with pitcher Arodys Vizcaino, pitcher Michael Dunn and cash for pitcher Javier Vazquez and pitcher Boone Logan, December 22, 2009.
b Released by Atlanta Braves, October 18, 2010. Signed with Kansas City Royals, December 10, 2010.
c Traded to San Francisco Giants for pitcher Jonathan Sanchez and pitcher Ryan Verdugo, November 7, 2011.
d Filed for free agency, November 3, 2012. Signed with Toronto Blue Jays, November 19, 2012.

CAIN, LORENZO LAMAR

Born, Valdosta, Georgia, April 13, 1986.
Bats Right. Throws Right. Height, 6 feet, 2 inches. Weight, 200 pounds.

Year	Club	Lea	Pos	G	AB	R	H	2B	3B	HR	RBI	SB	Avg
2005 Brewers	Arizona		OF	50	205	45	73	18	5	5	37	12	.356
2005 Helena	Pioneer		OF	6	24	4	5	0	0	0	1	0	.208
2006 West Tenn	So.Atl.		OF	132	527	91	162	36	4	6	60	34	.307
2007 Brevard County	Fla.St.		OF	126	482	67	133	21	3	2	44	24	.276
2008 Brevard County	Fla.St.		OF	80	317	50	91	22	4	7	41	19	.287
2008 Nashville	P.C.		OF	6	19	0	3	0	0	0	2	0	.158
2008 Huntsville.......	Southern		OF	40	148	21	41	9	5	4	17	6	.277
2009 Brewers	Arizona		OF	3	9	1	4	1	0	0	1	0	.444
2009 Wisconsin	Midwest		OF	15	52	3	10	4	0	0	3	0	.192
2009 Huntsville.......	Southern		OF	42	145	17	31	6	0	4	15	3	.214
2010 Huntsville.......	Southern		OF	62	244	45	79	6	6	3	18	21	.324
2010 Nashville	P.C.		OF	22	87	13	26	5	3	0	9	5	.299
2010 Milwaukee a	N.L.		OF	43	147	17	45	11	1	1	13	7	.306
2011 Omaha	P.C.		OF	128	487	84	152	28	7	16	81	16	.312
2011 Kansas City	A.L.		OF	6	22	4	6	1	0	0	1	0	.273
2012 NW Arkansas	Texas		OF	7	24	4	5	1	0	1	1	0	.208
2012 Omaha	P.C.		OF	7	28	4	9	3	0	1	6	0	.321
2012 Kansas City b	A.L.		OF	61	222	27	59	9	2	7	31	10	.266
Major League Totals		3 Yrs.		110	391	48	110	21	3	8	45	17	.281

a Traded to Kansas City Royals with infielder Alcides Escobar, pitcher Jeremy Jeffress and pitcher Jake Odorizzi for outfielder Yuniesky Betancourt and pitcher Zack Greinke, December 19, 2010.
b On disabled list from April 11 to July 9, 2012.

CAIRO, MIGUEL JESUS

Born, Anaco, Venezuela, May 4, 1974.
Bats Right. Throws Right. Height, 6 feet, 1 inch. Weight, 225 pounds.

Year	Club	Lea	Pos	G	AB	R	H	2B	3B	HR	RBI	SB	Avg
1992 Dodgers	Gulf Coast		SS-3B	21	76	10	23	5	2	0	9	1	.303
1992 Vero Beach	Fla.St.		2B-SS	36	125	7	28	0	0	0	7	5	.224
1993 Vero Beach	Fla.St.		2B-SS-3B	90	346	50	109	10	1	1	23	23	.315
1994 Bakersfield	Calif.		2B-SS	133	533	76	155	23	4	2	48	44	.291
1995 San Antonio a....	Texas		2B-SS	107	435	53	121	20	1	1	41	33	.278
1996 Syracuse	Int.		2B-3B-SS	120	465	71	129	14	4	3	48	27	.277
1996 Toronto b	A.L.		2B	9	27	5	6	2	0	0	1	0	.222
1997 Iowa	A.A.		2B-SS	135	569	82	159	35	4	5	46	40	.279
1997 Chicago c	N.L.		2B-SS	16	29	7	7	1	0	0	1	0	.241
1998 Tampa Bay	A.L.		2B	150	515	49	138	26	5	5	46	19	.268
1999 Tampa Bay	A.L.		2B	120	465	61	137	15	5	3	36	22	.295
1999 Orlando	Southern		2B	3	13	1	5	2	0	0	1	0	.385
1999 St. Petersburg d..	Fla.St.		2B	3	13	2	5	0	0	0	0	1	.385
2000 Tampa Bay	A.L.		2B	119	375	49	98	18	2	1	34	28	.261
2001 Iowa	P.C.		2B-SS-3B	34	123	22	37	7	1	3	14	3	.301
2001 Chicago-St. Louis e-f-g	N.L.		3B-2B-OF-SS	93	156	25	46	8	1	3	16	2	.295
2002 St. Louis........	N.L.		OF-2B-3B-SS	108	184	28	46	9	2	2	23	1	.250
2003 Memphis	P.C.		2B	3	13	2	3	1	0	0	0	0	.231
2003 St. Louis h-i	N.L.		2B-OF-3B-SS	92	261	41	64	15	2	5	32	4	.245
2004 New York	A.L.		2B-3B-SS-1B	122	360	48	105	17	5	6	42	11	.292
2005 St. Lucie........	Fla.St.		DH	1	4	0	1	0	0	0	0	0	.250
2005 Mets........	Gulf Coast		2B	3	13	3	4	1	0	0	0	0	.308
2005 New York j-k.....	N.L.		2B-1B-3B-OF	100	327	31	82	18	0	2	19	13	.251
2006 New York l-m.....	A.L.		2B-1B-SS-3B	81	222	28	53	12	3	0	30	13	.239
2007 New York	A.L.		1B-SS-3B-2B	54	107	12	27	7	0	0	10	8	.252

23

Year Club	Lea	Pos	G	AB	R	H	2B	3B	HR	RBI	SB	Avg
2007 Memphis	P.C.	3B-SS-OF-1B	9	31	8	9	2	0	0	3	2	.290
2007 St. Louis n-o	N.L.	3B-2B-1B-OF	28	67	8	17	2	2	0	5	2	.254
2008 Seattle p	A.L.	1B-3B-2B-OF	108	221	34	55	14	2	0	23	5	.249
2009 Lehigh Valley	Int.	SS-2B-3B-1B	78	296	44	85	12	2	5	33	8	.287
2009 Philadelphia q-r	N.L.	2B-SS-3B	27	45	6	12	2	1	1	2	0	.267
2010 Cincinnati s	N.L.	3B-1B-2B-SS	91	200	30	58	12	0	4	28	4	.290
2011 Cincinnati	N.L.	3B-2B-1B	102	245	33	65	8	2	8	33	3	.265
2012 Dayton	Midwest	3B	3	10	0	0	0	0	0	0	0	.000
2012 Cincinnati t-u	N.L.	1B-3B-2B	70	150	9	28	7	2	1	13	4	.187
Major League Totals	17 Yrs.		1490	3956	504	1044	193	34	41	394	139	.264
Division Series												
2001 St. Louis	N.L.	OF	3	5	0	1	0	0	0	0	1	.200
2002 St. Louis	N.L.	3B	2	4	2	4	1	0	0	3	0	1.000
2004 New York	A.L.	2B	4	14	3	3	1	0	0	1	0	.214
2009 Philadelphia	N.L.	OF-3B	2	3	0	0	0	0	0	0	0	.000
2010 Cincinnati	N.L.	PH	3	3	0	0	0	0	0	0	0	.000
2012 Cincinnati	N.L.	1B	3	2	0	0	0	0	0	0	0	.000
Division Series Totals			17	31	5	8	2	0	0	4	1	.258
Championship Series												
2002 St. Louis	N.L.	3B	3	13	2	5	0	0	1	2	0	.385
2004 New York	A.L.	2B	7	25	4	7	3	0	0	0	1	.280
2009 Philadelphia	N.L.	PH	2	2	0	0	0	0	0	0	0	.000
Championship Series Totals			12	40	6	12	3	0	1	2	1	.300

a Traded to Toronto Blue Jays with pitcher Bill Risley for pitcher Edwin Hurtado and pitcher Paul Menhart, December 18, 1995.
b Traded to Chicago Cubs for pitcher Jason Stevenson, November 20, 1996.
c Selected by Tampa Bay Devil Rays in expansion draft. November 18, 1997.
d On disabled list from April 24 to May 17 and July 26 to August 11, 1999.
e Released by Tampa Bay Devil Rays, November 27, 2000. Signed with Oakland Athletics organization, January 11, 2001.
f Traded to Chicago Cubs with pitcher Scott Chiasson for infielder Eric Hinske, March 28, 2001.
g Claimed on waivers by St. Louis Cardinals, August 10, 2001.
h On disabled list from June 19 to July 29, 2003.
i Filed for free agency, October 26, 2003. Signed with New York Yankees, December 19, 2003.
j Filed for free agency, October 28, 2004. Signed with New York Mets, January 10, 2005.
k On disabled list from June 15 to July 2, 2005.
l Filed for free agency, October 28, 2005. Signed with New York Yankees, January 5, 2006.
m On disabled list from August 6 to September 11, 2006.
n Filed for free agency, October 28, 2006, re-signed with New York Yankees, January 26, 2007.
o Released by New York Yankees, August 15, 2007. Signed with St. Louis Cardinals organization, August 19, 2007.
p Filed for free agency, October 29, 2007. Signed with Seattle Mariners organization, January 8, 2008.
q Filed for free agency, October 30, 2008. Signed with Philadelphia Phillies organization, February 15, 2009.
r Filed for free agency, November 6, 2009. Signed with Cincinnati Reds organization, January 27, 2010.
s Filed for free agency, November 1, 2010. Signed with Cincinnati Reds, December 8, 2010.
t On disabled list from April 17 to May 7, 2012.
u Filed for free agency, November 3, 2012.

CALLASPO, ALBERTO JOSE

Born, Maracay, Venezuela, April 19, 1983.
Bats Both. Throws Right. Height, 5 feet, 10 inches. Weight, 180 pounds.

Year Club	Lea	Pos	G	AB	R	H	2B	3B	HR	RBI	SB	Avg
2002 Provo	Pioneer	2B-SS	70	299	70	101	16	10	3	60	13	.338
2003 Cedar Rapids	Midwest	2B-SS	133	514	86	168	38	4	2	67	20	.327
2004 Arkansas	Texas	SS-2B	136	550	76	156	29	2	6	48	15	.284
2005 Salt Lake	P.C.	2B	50	212	28	67	21	2	1	31	2	.316
2005 Arkansas	Texas	2B	89	350	53	104	8	0	10	49	9	.297
2006 Tucson	P.C.	2B-SS-3B-OF	114	490	93	165	24	12	7	68	8	.337
2006 Arizona a	N.L.	SS-2B-3B	23	42	2	10	1	1	0	6	0	.238
2007 Tucson	P.C.	SS-2B-3B	59	226	48	77	15	2	5	30	1	.341
2007 Arizona b	N.L.	3B-2B-OF-SS	56	144	10	31	8	0	0	7	1	.215
2008 Omaha	P.C.	2B	4	16	5	3	0	0	0	0	0	.188
2008 Kansas City c	A.L.	2B-SS-OF-3B	74	213	21	65	8	3	0	16	2	.305
2009 Kansas City	A.L.	2B-3B-SS	155	576	79	173	41	8	11	73	2	.300
2010 Kansas City-LA d	A.L.	3B-2B-OF	146	562	61	149	27	2	10	56	5	.265
2011 Los Angeles	A.L.	3B	141	475	54	137	23	0	6	46	8	.288
2012 Los Angeles	A.L.	3B	138	457	55	115	20	0	10	53	4	.252
Major League Totals	7 Yrs.		733	2469	282	680	128	14	37	257	22	.275

Year	Club	Lea	Pos	G	AB	R	H	2B	3B	HR	RBI	SB	Avg
Championship Series													
2007 Arizona..........	N.L.		PH	2	2	0	0	0	0	0	0	0	.000

a Traded by Los Angeles Angels to Arizona Diamondbacks for pitcher Jason Bulger, February 28, 2006.
b Traded to Kansas City Royals for pitcher Billy Buckner, December 14, 2007.
c On disabled list from June 28 to August 23, 2008.
d Traded to Anaheim Angels for pitcher Sean O'Sullivan and pitcher Will Smith, July 22, 2010.

CAMPANA, ANTHONY EDWARD (TONY)

Born, Kettering, Ohio, May 30, 1986.
Bats Left. Throws Left. Height, 5 feet, 8 inches. Weight, 165 pounds.

Year	Club	Lea	Pos	G	AB	R	H	2B	3B	HR	RBI	SB	Avg
2008 Cubs.............	Arizona	OF	24	83	17	23	0	0	0	10	22	.277
2008 Boise..........	Northwest	OF	1	3	0	0	0	0	0	0	0	.000
2009 Daytona...........	Fla.St.	OF	108	430	56	122	8	2	0	25	55	.284
2009 Peoria...........	Midwest	OF	18	53	14	15	1	1	0	5	11	.283
2010 Tennessee.......	Southern	OF	131	489	76	156	22	5	0	39	48	.319
2011 Iowa................	P.C.	OF	30	120	27	41	8	2	0	9	8	.342
2011 Chicago.............	N.L.	OF	95	143	24	37	3	0	1	6	24	.259
2012 Iowa...............	P.C.	OF	37	143	24	40	2	1	1	4	18	.280
2012 Chicago.............	N.L.	OF	89	174	26	46	6	0	0	5	30	.264
Major League Totals............		2 Yrs.	184	317	50	83	9	0	1	11	54	.262

CANO (MERCEDES), ROBINSON JOSE

Born, San Pedro de Macoris, Dominican Republic, October 22, 1982.
Bats Left. Throws Right. Height, 6 feet. Weight, 200 pounds.

Year	Club	Lea	Pos	G	AB	R	H	2B	3B	HR	RBI	SB	Avg
2001 Yankees........	Gulf Coast	2B-SS-3B	57	200	37	46	14	2	3	34	11	.230
2001 Staten Island....	N.Y.-Penn.	3B-SS	2	8	0	2	0	0	0	2	0	.250
2002 Staten Island....	N.Y.-Penn.	2B-SS	22	87	11	24	5	1	1	15	6	.276
2002 Greensboro........	So.Atl.	SS-2B	113	474	67	131	20	9	14	66	2	.276
2003 Trenton...........	Eastern	2B-SS-C	46	164	21	46	9	1	1	13	0	.280
2003 Tampa.............	Fla.St.	2B	90	366	50	101	16	3	5	50	1	.276
2004 Trenton...........	Eastern	2B-3B	74	292	43	88	20	8	7	44	2	.301
2004 Columbus...........	Int.	2B	61	216	22	56	9	2	6	30	0	.259
2005 Columbus............	Int.	2B-3B	24	108	19	36	8	3	4	24	0	.333
2005 New York.........	A.L.	2B	132	522	78	155	34	4	14	62	1	.297
2006 Yankees........	Gulf Coast	DH	1	5	0	2	0	0	0	1	0	.400
2006 Trenton...........	Eastern	2B	3	10	1	5	2	0	0	2	0	.500
2006 New York a.......	A.L.	2B	122	482	62	165	41	1	15	78	5	.342
2007 New York.........	A.L.	2B	160	617	93	189	41	7	19	97	4	.306
2008 New York.........	A.L.	2B	159	597	70	162	35	3	14	72	2	.271
2009 New York.........	A.L.	2B	*161	637	103	204	48	2	25	85	5	.320
2010 New York.........	A.L.	2B	160	626	103	200	41	3	29	109	3	.319
2011 New York.........	A.L.	2B	159	623	104	188	46	7	28	118	8	.302
2012 New York.........	A.L.	2B	161	627	105	196	48	1	33	94	3	.313
Major League Totals............		8 Yrs.	1214	4731	718	1459	334	28	177	715	31	.308
Division Series													
2005 New York.........	A.L.	2B	5	19	3	5	3	0	0	5	0	.263
2006 New York.........	A.L.	2B	4	15	0	2	0	0	0	0	0	.133
2007 New York.........	A.L.	2B	4	15	3	5	1	0	2	3	0	.333
2009 New York.........	A.L.	2B	3	12	1	2	0	0	0	1	0	.167
2010 New York.........	A.L.	2B	3	12	3	4	0	1	0	1	0	.333
2011 New York.........	A.L.	2B	5	22	2	7	2	0	2	9	0	.318
2012 New York.........	A.L.	2B	5	22	1	2	2	0	0	4	0	.091
Division Series Totals............			29	117	13	27	8	1	4	23	0	.231
Championship Series													
2009 New York.........	A.L.	2B	6	23	4	6	1	2	0	4	0	.261
2010 New York.........	A.L.	2B	6	23	5	8	1	0	4	5	0	.348
2012 New York.........	A.L.	2B	4	18	0	1	0	0	0	0	0	.056
Championship Series Totals......			16	64	9	15	2	2	4	9	0	.234
World Series Record													
2009 New York.........	A.L.	2B	6	22	0	3	0	0	0	1	0	.136

a On disabled list from June 26 to August 8, 2006.

CARPENTER, MATT MARTIN
Born, Sugar Land, Texas, November 26, 1985.
Bats Left. Throws Right. Height, 6 feet, 3 inches. Weight, 200 pounds.

Year Club	Lea	Pos	G	AB	R	H	2B	3B	HR	RBI	SB	Avg
2009 Palm Beach	Fla.St.	3B	32	114	13	25	6	1	2	9	1	.219
2009 Quad Cities	Midwest	3B	29	105	11	31	6	2	0	10	2	.295
2009 Batavia	N.Y.-Penn.	3B-1B	9	32	9	15	3	0	0	3	0	.469
2010 Palm Beach	Fla.St.	3B	28	99	17	28	5	2	1	16	0	.283
2010 Springfield	Texas	3B	105	396	76	125	26	3	12	53	11	.316
2011 Memphis	P.C.	3B	130	434	61	130	29	3	12	70	5	.300
2011 St. Louis	N.L.	3B	7	15	0	1	1	0	0	0	0	.067
2012 Springfield	Texas	1B-OF	3	10	3	3	0	0	1	3	0	.300
2012 Memphis	P.C.	OF-3B	3	7	1	1	0	0	0	0	0	.143
2012 St. Louis a	N.L.	1B-3B-OF-2B	114	296	44	87	22	5	6	46	1	.294
Major League Totals		2 Yrs.	121	311	44	88	23	5	6	46	1	.283
Wild Card Playoff												
2012 St. Louis	N.L.	3B	1	1	0	1	0	0	0	1	0	1.000
Division Series												
2012 St. Louis	N.L.	3B	5	4	0	0	0	0	0	0	0	.000
Championship Series												
2012 St. Louis	N.L.	1B-OF	3	9	3	3	1	0	1	2	0	.333

a On disabled list from May 23 to June 22, 2012.

CARRERA (REYES), EZEQUIEL MANUEL
Born, Guiria, Venezuela, June 11, 1987.
Bats Left. Throws Left. Height, 5 feet, 10 inches. Weight, 185 pounds.

Year Club	Lea	Pos	G	AB	R	H	2B	3B	HR	RBI	SB	Avg
2007 Mets	Gulf Coast	OF	45	179	41	61	8	3	1	26	16	.341
2007 Brooklyn	N.Y.-Penn.	OF	20	70	11	21	2	0	0	6	6	.300
2008 St. Lucie a	Fla.St.	OF	114	430	61	113	11	12	7	29	28	.263
2009 West Tenn	Southern	OF	91	329	68	111	12	4	2	38	27	.337
2010 Indians	Arizona	OF	4	14	2	6	1	0	0	4	0	.429
2010 Columbus	Int.	OF	41	161	19	46	7	3	1	16	11	.286
2010 Tacoma b	P.C.	OF	64	213	24	57	6	2	0	18	9	.268
2011 Columbus	Int.	OF	82	328	63	94	8	3	2	25	35	.287
2011 Cleveland	A.L.	OF	68	202	27	49	8	3	0	14	10	.243
2012 Columbus	Int.	OF	97	394	65	116	19	6	6	42	26	.294
2012 Cleveland	A.L.	OF	48	147	20	40	6	3	2	11	8	.272
Major League Totals		2 Yrs.	116	349	47	89	14	6	2	25	18	.255

a Traded by New York Mets to Seattle Mariners with pitcher Aaron Heilman, outfielder Endy Chavez, pitcher Jason Vargas, infielder Mike Carp, pitcher Maikel Cleto and pitcher Joe Smith for pitcher J.J. Putz, pitcher Sean Green and outfielder Jeremy Reed, December 10, 2008.

b Traded to Cleveland Indians with infielder Juan Diaz for infielder Russell Branyan, June 26, 2010.

CARROLL, JAMEY BLAKE
Born, Evansville, Indiana, February 18, 1974.
Bats Right. Throws Right. Height, 5 feet, 9 inches. Weight, 170 pounds.

Year Club	Lea	Pos	G	AB	R	H	2B	3B	HR	RBI	SB	Avg
1996 Vermont	N.Y.-Penn.	SS-2B-3B	54	203	40	56	6	1	0	17	16	.276
1997 Wst Plm Bch	Fla.St.	SS-2B-3B	121	407	56	99	19	1	0	38	17	.243
1998 Jupiter	Fla.St.	2B-SS	55	222	40	58	5	0	0	14	11	.261
1998 Harrisburg	Eastern	2B-SS	75	261	43	66	11	3	0	20	11	.253
1999 Harrisburg	Eastern	2B	141	561	78	164	34	5	5	63	21	.292
2000 Harrisburg	Eastern	3B-SS-2B	45	169	23	49	5	3	0	18	8	.290
2000 Ottawa	Int.	2B-SS-3B	91	349	53	97	17	2	2	23	6	.278
2001 Ottawa	Int.	2B-SS-3B	83	267	26	64	8	2	0	16	5	.240
2002 Harrisburg	Eastern	2B	3	9	1	4	0	0	0	1	0	.444
2002 Ottawa	Int.	3B-2B-SS	117	421	57	118	19	2	8	49	6	.280
2002 Montreal	N.L.	3B-SS-2B	16	71	16	22	5	3	1	6	1	.310
2003 Montreal	N.L.	3B-SS-2B	105	227	31	59	10	1	1	10	5	.260
2004 Montreal	N.L.	2B-3B-SS-OF	102	218	36	63	14	2	0	16	5	.289
2005 Washington	N.L.	2B-SS-3B	113	303	44	76	8	1	0	22	3	.251
2006 Colorado a	N.L.	2B-SS-3B	136	463	84	139	23	5	5	36	10	.300
2007 Colorado b	N.L.	2B-3B-SS-OF	108	227	45	51	9	1	2	22	6	.225
2008 Cleveland	A.L.	2B-3B-OF	113	347	60	96	13	4	1	36	7	.277
2009 Columbus	Int.	2B-3B	3	11	2	3	1	0	0	0	0	.273
2009 Cleveland c-d	A.L.	2B-3B-OF	93	315	53	87	10	2	2	26	4	.276
2010 Los Angeles	N.L.	SS-2B-3B-OF	133	351	48	102	15	1	0	23	12	.291

Year	Club	Lea	Pos	G	AB	R	H	2B	3B	HR	RBI	SB	Avg
2011 Los Angeles e......N.L.			2B-SS	146	452	52	131	14	6	0	17	10	.290
2012 Minnesota ........A.L.			2B-3B-SS	138	470	65	126	18	1	1	40	9	.268
Major League Totals			11 Yrs.	1203	3444	534	952	139	27	13	254	72	.276
Division Series													
2007 Colorado .........N.L.			2B	1	0	0	0	0	0	0	0	0	.000
Championship Series													
2007 Colorado .........N.L.			3B	2	1	0	0	0	0	0	0	0	.000
World Series Record													
2007 Colorado .........N.L.			2B	1	1	0	0	0	0	0	0	0	.000

a Sold to Colorado Rockies, February 11, 2006.

b Traded to Cleveland Indians for player to be named later, December 8, 2007. Colorado Rockies received pitcher Sean Smith to complete trade, April 22, 2008

c On disabled list from April 5 to May 12, 2009.

d Filed for free agency, November 5, 2009. Signed with Los Angeles Dodgers, December 16, 2009.

e Filed for free agency, October 30, 2011. Signed with Minnesota Twins, November 16, 2011.

CARTER, VERNON CHRISTOPHER (CHRIS)

Born, Redwood City, California, December 18, 1986.
Bats Right. Throws Right. Height, 6 feet, 5 inches. Weight, 245 pounds.

Year	Club	Lea	Pos	G	AB	R	H	2B	3B	HR	RBI	SB	Avg
2005 Bristol ....Appal.			3B-1B-SS	65	233	33	66	17	0	10	37	2	.283
2006 Great Falls .....Pioneer			1B	69	251	37	75	21	1	15	59	4	.299
2006 Kannapolis ....So.Atl.			1B	13	46	4	6	3	0	1	5	0	.130
2007 Kannapolis a-b..So.Atl.			1B	126	467	84	136	27	3	25	93	3	.291
2008 Stockton........Calif.			1B-3B-OF	137	506	101	131	32	4	39	104	4	.259
2009 Sacramento .......P.C.			1B-OF	13	54	7	14	2	0	4	14	0	.259
2009 Midland ....Texas			1B-OF-3B	125	490	108	165	41	2	24	101	13	.337
2010 Sacramento .......P.C.			1B-OF	125	465	92	120	29	2	31	94	1	.258
2010 Oakland .........A.L.			OF	24	70	8	13	1	0	3	7	1	.186
2011 Stockton........Calif.			1B	6	24	3	8	0	0	3	7	0	.333
2011 Sacramento .......P.C.			1B-OF-3B	75	296	55	81	18	2	18	72	5	.274
2011 Oakland .........A.L.			1B	15	44	2	6	0	0	0	0	0	.136
2012 Sacramento .......P.C.			1B	72	276	48	77	19	1	12	53	5	.279
2012 Oakland .........A.L.			1B	67	218	38	52	12	0	16	39	0	.239
Major League Totals			3 Yrs.	106	332	48	71	13	0	19	46	1	.214

a Traded by Chicago White Sox to Arizona Diamondbacks for outfielder Carlos Quentin, December 3, 2007.

b Traded to Oakland Athletics with pitcher Brett Anderson, pitcher Dana Eveland, pitcher Greg Smith, outfielder Aaron Cunningham and outfielder Carlos Gonzalez for pitcher Danny Haren and pitcher Connor Robertson, December 14, 2007.

CASILLA (LORA), ALEXI

Born, San Cristobal, Dominican Republic, July 20, 1984.
Bats Both. Throws Right. Height, 5 feet, 9 inches. Weight, 180 pounds.

Year	Club	Lea	Pos	G	AB	R	H	2B	3B	HR	RBI	SB	Avg
2004 Angels ....Arizona			2B-SS	45	163	29	42	1	4	0	10	24	.258
2004 Cedar Rapids ..Midwest			2B	9	29	6	9	2	1	0	1	1	.310
2004 Provo.........Pioneer			2B-3B	4	12	4	4	1	1	0	1	1	.333
2005 Cedar Rapids ..Midwest			SS-2B	78	308	62	100	11	3	3	17	47	.325
2005 Salt Lake .........P.C.			2B-SS	13	39	3	10	0	0	0	1	1	.256
2005 Arkansas a......Texas			SS-2B	7	19	4	4	0	0	0	4	1	.211
2006 Fort Myers .....Fla.St.			2B-SS	78	323	56	107	12	6	0	33	31	.331
2006 New Britain ....Eastern			SS	45	170	28	50	10	1	1	13	19	.294
2006 Minnesota ........A.L.			2B-SS	9	4	1	1	0	0	0	0	0	.250
2007 Rochester.........Int.			2B-SS	84	320	53	86	13	1	3	20	24	.269
2007 Minnesota ........A.L.			2B-SS	56	189	15	42	5	1	0	9	11	.222
2008 Beloit ....Midwest			2B	2	7	2	4	0	0	0	1	0	.571
2008 Rochester.........Int.			SS-2B	32	96	11	21	3	0	0	2	4	.219
2008 Minnesota b......A.L.			2B-SS	98	385	58	108	15	0	7	50	7	.281
2009 Rochester.........Int.			2B	40	156	21	53	3	4	2	17	9	.340
2009 Minnesota ........A.L.			2B-SS	80	228	25	46	7	3	0	17	11	.202
2010 Twins ....Gulf Coast			2B	5	14	1	2	1	0	0	0	0	.143
2010 Fort Myers .....Fla.St.			2B-SS	3	12	0	2	0	0	0	1	1	.167
2010 New Britain ....Eastern			2B-3B-SS	6	20	1	7	0	0	0	0	1	.350
2010 Minnesota c.......A.L.			SS-2B-3B-OF	69	152	26	42	7	4	1	20	6	.276
2011 Fort Myers .....Fla.St.			2B	1	2	0	0	0	0	0	0	0	.000
2011 Minnesota d.......A.L.			2B-SS	97	323	52	84	21	4	2	21	15	.260

Year Club	Lea	Pos	G	AB	R	H	2B	3B	HR	RBI	SB	Avg
2012 Minnesota	A.L.	2B-3B	106	299	33	72	17	2	1	30	21	.241
Major League Totals		7 Yrs.	515	1580	210	395	72	14	11	147	71	.250

a Traded to Minnesota Twins for pitcher J.C. Romero, December 9, 2005.
b On disabled list from July 29 to August 21, 2008.
c On disabled list from June 1 to July 22, 2010.
d On disabled list from July 28 to August 12 and August 13 to October 14, 2011.

CASTILLO, WELINGTON ANDRES
Born, San Isidro, Dominican Republic, April 24, 1987.
Bats Right. Throws Right. Height, 5 feet, 10 inches. Weight, 210 pounds.

Year Club	Lea	Pos	G	AB	R	H	2B	3B	HR	RBI	SB	Avg
2006 Cubs.............	Arizona	C-1B	7	26	4	5	0	0	0	0	0	.192
2006 Boise	Northwest	C	3	6	1	1	0	0	0	0	0	.167
2007 Peoria.........	Midwest	C	98	317	41	86	11	2	11	44	1	.271
2008 Daytona	Fla.St.	C	33	121	15	33	8	0	0	12	1	.273
2008 Iowa.................	P.C.	C	1	5	0	1	0	0	0	1	0	.200
2008 Tennessee	Southern	C	57	198	25	59	11	0	4	24	0	.298
2009 Tennessee	Southern	C	95	319	27	74	16	0	11	39	1	.232
2010 Iowa.................	P.C.	C	69	239	35	61	17	1	13	59	0	.255
2010 Chicago	N.L.	C	7	20	3	6	4	0	1	5	0	.300
2011 Daytona	Fla.St.	C	12	42	6	10	3	0	1	7	0	.238
2011 Chicago	N.L.	C	4	13	0	2	0	0	0	0	0	.154
2011 Cubs.............	Arizona	C	2	6	2	4	3	0	0	0	0	.667
2011 Iowa.................	P.C.	C	61	227	38	65	9	0	15	35	0	.286
2012 Tennessee	Southern	C-1B	5	11	3	4	0	0	2	6	0	.364
2012 Iowa.................	P.C.	C	44	146	22	38	6	0	6	22	0	.260
2012 Chicago a............	N.L.	C-1B	52	170	16	45	11	0	5	22	0	.265
Major League Totals		3 Yrs.	63	203	19	53	15	0	6	27	0	.261

a On disabled list from May 19 to June 14, 2012.

CASTRO, JASON MICHAEL
Born, Castro Valley, California, June 18, 1987.
Bats Left. Throws Right. Height, 6 feet, 3 inches. Weight, 215 pounds.

Year Club	Lea	Pos	G	AB	R	H	2B	3B	HR	RBI	SB	Avg
2008 Tri-City	N.Y.-Penn.	C	39	138	10	38	9	0	2	12	0	.275
2009 Lancaster...........	Calif.	C	56	207	27	64	20	1	7	44	1	.309
2009 Corpus Christi	Texas	C	63	239	38	70	11	1	3	29	2	.293
2010 Round Rock..........	P.C.	C	57	211	31	56	7	0	4	26	1	.265
2010 Houston.............	N.L.	C	67	195	26	40	8	1	2	8	0	.205
2011 Houston a	N.L.		INJURED—Did Not Play									
2012 Corpus Christi	Texas	C	3	5	1	4	2	0	0	0	0	.800
2012 Oklahoma.............	P.C.	C	4	13	1	6	1	0	1	2	0	.462
2012 Houston b	N.L.	C	87	257	29	66	15	2	6	29	0	.257
Major League Totals		2 Yrs.	154	452	55	106	23	3	8	37	0	.235

a On disabled list from March 22 to October 31, 2011.
b On disabled list from July 8 to August 13, 2012.

CASTRO, STARLIN DE JESUS
Born, Monte Cristi, Dominican Republic, March 24, 1990.
Bats Right. Throws Right. Height, 6 feet. Weight, 190 pounds.

Year Club	Lea	Pos	G	AB	R	H	2B	3B	HR	RBI	SB	Avg
2008 Cubs..........	Arizona	SS-2B-3B-OF	51	196	33	61	11	5	3	22	6	.311
2009 Daytona	Fla.St.	SS	96	358	45	108	17	3	3	35	22	.302
2009 Tennessee ....Southern		SS	31	111	11	32	6	3	0	14	6	.288
2010 Tennessee ....Southern		SS	26	109	20	41	8	5	1	20	4	.376
2010 Chicago ..........N.L.		SS	125	463	53	139	31	5	3	41	10	.300
2011 Chicago ..........N.L.		SS	158	*674	91	*207	36	9	10	66	22	.307
2012 Chicago ..........N.L.		SS	*162	*646	78	183	29	12	14	78	25	.283
Major League Totals		3 Yrs.	445	1783	222	529	96	26	27	185	57	.297

CEDENO, RONNY ALEXANDER

Born, Puerto Cabello, Venezuela, February 2, 1983.
Bats Right. Throws Right. Height, 6 feet. Weight, 180 pounds.

Year Club	Lea	Pos	G	AB	R	H	2B	3B	HR	RBI	SB	Avg
2001 Cubs.........	Arizona	SS-2B-OF	52	206	36	72	13	4	1	17	17	.350
2001 Lansing	Midwest	2B-SS-3B	17	56	9	11	4	1	1	2	0	.196
2002 Lansing	Midwest	SS-2B	98	376	44	80	17	4	2	31	14	.213
2002 Boise	Northwest	SS-2B	29	110	17	24	5	2	0	6	8	.218
2003 Daytona	Fla.St.	SS-2B	107	380	43	80	18	1	4	36	19	.211
2004 West Tenn	Southern	SS	116	384	39	107	19	5	6	48	10	.279
2005 Iowa...........	P.C.	SS	65	245	42	87	14	1	8	36	11	.355
2005 Chicago	N.L.	SS-2B	41	80	13	24	3	0	1	6	1	.300
2006 Chicago	N.L.	SS-2B	151	534	51	131	18	7	6	41	8	.245
2007 Iowa...........	P.C.	SS	75	287	52	103	15	3	10	37	6	.359
2007 Chicago	N.L.	SS-2B	38	74	6	15	2	0	4	13	2	.203
2008 Chicago	N.L.	2B-SS-3B-OF	99	216	36	58	12	0	2	28	4	.269
2009 Seattle	A.L.	SS-2B-OF-3B	59	186	15	31	4	2	5	17	3	.167
2009 Pittsburgh a-b	N.L.	SS	46	155	17	40	4	1	5	21	2	.258
2010 Pittsburgh	N.L.	SS	139	468	42	120	29	3	8	38	12	.256
2011 Indianapolis	Int.	SS	4	15	2	4	1	1	0	1	0	.267
2011 Pittsburgh c-d	N.L.	SS-2B	128	413	43	103	25	3	2	32	2	.249
2012 St. Lucie.......	Fla.St.	SS	1	4	0	0	0	0	0	0	0	.000
2012 Buffalo...........	Int.	SS-2B	7	29	2	5	0	0	0	1	0	.172
2012 New York e-f	N.L.	2B-SS-3B	78	166	18	43	11	1	4	22	0	.259
Major League Totals		8 Yrs.	779	2292	241	565	108	17	37	218	34	.247
Division Series												
2007 Chicago	N.L.	PH	2	0	0	0	0	0	0	0	0	.000
2008 Chicago	N.L.	PH	1	0	0	0	0	0	0	0	1	.000
Division Series Totals			3	0	0	0	0	0	0	0	1	.000

a Traded to Seattle Mariners with pitcher Garrett Olson for pitcher Aaron Heilman, January 28, 2009.
b Traded to Pittsburgh Pirates with outfielder Jeff Clement, pitcher Aaron Pribanic, pitcher Brett Lorin and pitcher Nathan Adcock for infielder Jack Wilson and pitcher Ian Snell, July 29, 2009.
c On disabled list from July 2 to July 22, 2011.
d Filed for free agency, October 31, 2011. Signed with New York Mets, January 10, 2012.
e On disabled list from April 21 to May 11 and May 27 to June 22, 2012.
f Filed for free agency, November 3, 2012.

CESPEDES (MILANES), YOENIS

Born, Granma, Cuba, October 18, 1985.
Bats Right. Throws Right. Height, 5 feet, 10 inches. Weight, 210 pounds.

Year Club	Lea	Pos	G	AB	R	H	2B	3B	HR	RBI	SB	Avg
2012 Sacramento	P.C.	OF	3	9	1	3	0	0	0	0	0	.333
2012 Oakland a-b-c.........	A.L.	OF	129	487	70	142	25	5	23	82	16	.292
Division Series												
2012 Oakland	A.L.	OF	5	19	1	6	1	0	0	2	2	.316

a Played in Cuba 2003-2011.
b Signed with Oakland Athletics, March 3, 2012.
c On disabled list from May 7 to June 1, 2012.

CHAVEZ, ENDY DE JESUS

Born, Valencia, Venezuela, February 7, 1978.
Bats Left. Throws Left. Height, 6 feet. Weight, 170 pounds.

Year Club	Lea	Pos	G	AB	R	H	2B	3B	HR	RBI	SB	Avg
1997 Mets..........	Gulf Coast	OF	33	119	26	33	6	3	0	15	1	.277
1997 Kingsport..........	Appal.	OF	19	73	16	22	4	0	0	4	5	.301
1998 Kingsport..........	Appal.	OF	33	114	26	33	8	4	0	16	10	.289
1999 St. Lucie............	Fla.St.	OF	45	183	33	57	8	3	2	18	9	.311
1999 Columbia	So.Atl.	OF	73	253	40	64	8	1	0	15	20	.253
2000 St. Lucie a	Fla.St.	OF	111	433	84	129	20	2	1	43	38	.298
2001 Wichita............	Texas	OF	43	168	27	50	6	1	1	13	11	.298
2001 Kansas City	A.L.	OF	29	77	4	16	2	0	0	5	0	.208
2001 Omaha b-c............	P.C.	OF	23	104	18	35	6	0	0	4	4	.337
2002 Ottawa	Int.	OF	103	405	67	139	28	5	4	41	21	.343
2002 Montreal d-e	N.L.	OF	36	125	20	37	8	5	1	9	3	.296
2003 Montreal............	N.L.	OF	141	483	66	121	25	5	5	47	18	.251
2004 Edmonton	P.C.	OF	14	61	9	21	3	2	0	7	5	.344
2004 Montreal............	N.L.	OF	132	502	65	139	20	6	5	34	32	.277
2005 New Orleans...........	P.C.	OF	23	87	11	22	4	0	1	4	6	.253

Year	Club	Lea	Pos	G	AB	R	H	2B	3B	HR	RBI	SB	Avg
2005 Washington-Philadelphia f-g.	N.L.	OF	98	116	19	25	4	3	0	11	2	.216
2006 New York	N.L.	OF	133	353	48	108	22	5	4	42	12	.306
2007 Mets	Gulf Goast	OF	2	8	2	5	0	0	0	4	0	.625
2007 St. Lucie	Fla.St.	OF	4	16	3	8	1	0	0	2	0	.500
2007 Binghamton	Eastern	OF	1	3	0	0	0	0	0	0	0	.000
2007 New York h	N.L.	OF	71	150	20	43	7	2	1	17	5	.287
2008 New York i	N.L.	OF	133	270	30	72	10	2	1	12	6	.267
2009 Seattle j	A.L.	OF	54	161	17	44	3	1	2	13	9	.273
2010 Rangers	Arizona	OF	3	11	3	6	0	0	0	1	3	.545
2010 Oklahoma	P.C.	OF	1	5	2	1	1	0	0	0	0	.200
2010 Frisco k	Texas	OF	4	15	3	5	0	0	0	1	2	.333
2011 Round Rock	P.C.	OF	30	128	16	39	8	2	2	17	6	.305
2011 Texas l	A.L.	OF	83	256	37	77	11	3	5	27	10	.301
2012 Orioles	Gulf Coast	OF	1	4	0	0	0	0	0	0	0	.000
2012 Delmarva	So.Atl.	OF	3	9	2	1	0	0	0	1	0	.111
2012 Bowie	Eastern	OF	3	10	3	2	0	0	0	0	0	.200
2012 Norfolk	Int.	OF	15	47	2	7	3	0	0	4	0	.149
2012 Baltimore m-n	A.L.	OF	64	158	15	32	6	0	2	12	3	.203
Major League Totals	11 Yrs.		974	2651	341	714	118	32	26	229	100	.269
Wild Card Playoff												
2012 Baltimore	A.L.	OF	1	0	0	0	0	0	0	0	0	.000
Division Series												
2006 New York	N.L.	OF	3	8	1	3	0	0	0	0	0	.375
2012 Baltimore	A.L.	OF	3	1	0	0	0	0	0	0	0	.000
Division Series Totals			6	9	1	3	0	0	0	0	0	.333
Championship Series												
2006 New York	N.L.	OF	7	27	1	5	2	0	0	0	0	.185
2011 Texas	A.L.	OF	2	4	0	0	0	0	0	0	0	.000
Championship Series Totals			9	31	1	5	2	0	0	0	0	.161
World Series Record												
2011 Texas	A.L.	OF	3	1	0	0	0	0	0	0	0	.000

a Selected by Kansas City Royals from New York Mets in Rule V draft, December 11, 2000.
b Retained by Kansas City Royals in trade for outfielder Michael Curry, March 30, 2001.
c Claimed on waivers by Detroit Tigers, December 20, 2001.
d Claimed on waivers by New York Mets, February 1, 2002.
e Claimed on waivers by Montreal Expos, February 22, 2002.
f Traded to Philadelphia Phillies for outfielder Marlon Byrd, May 14, 2005.
g Not offered contract, December 21, 2005. Signed with New York Mets, December 23, 2005.
h On disabled list from June 7 to August 28, 2007.
i Traded to Seattle Mariners with pitcher Aaron Heilman, pitcher Jason Vargas, infielder Mike Carp, outfielder Ezequiel Carrera, pitcher Maikel Cleto and pitcher Joe Smith for pitcher J.J. Putz, pitcher Sean Green and outfielder Jeremy Reed, December 10, 2008.
j On disabled list from June 20 to November 6, 2009.
k Filed for free agency, November 6, 2009. Signed with Texas Rangers organization, February 15, 2010.
l Filed for free agency, October 30, 2011. Signed with Baltimore Orioles, December 20, 2011.
m On disabled list from May 10 to May 29 and June 13 to July 13, 2012.
n Filed for free agency, November 3, 2012. Signed with Kansas City Royals organization, December 31, 2012.

CHAVEZ, ERIC CESAR
Born, Los Angeles, California, December 7, 1977.
Bats Left. Throws Right. Height, 6 feet. Weight, 215 pounds.

Year	Club	Lea	Pos	G	AB	R	H	2B	3B	HR	RBI	SB	Avg
1997 Visalia	Calif.	3B	134	520	67	141	30	3	18	100	13	.271
1998 Huntsville	Southern	3B	88	335	66	110	27	1	22	86	12	.328
1998 Edmonton	P.C.	3B	47	194	38	63	18	0	11	40	2	.325
1998 Oakland	A.L.	3B	16	45	6	14	4	1	0	6	1	.311
1999 Oakland a	A.L.	3B-SS	115	356	47	88	21	2	13	50	1	.247
2000 Oakland	A.L.	3B-SS	153	501	89	139	23	4	26	86	2	.277
2001 Oakland	A.L.	3B-1B-SS	151	552	91	159	43	0	32	114	8	.288
2002 Oakland	A.L.	3B-OF	153	585	87	161	31	3	34	109	8	.275
2003 Oakland	A.L.	3B	156	588	94	166	39	5	29	101	8	.282
2004 Sacramento	P.C.	3B	3	13	2	4	1	0	0	0	0	.308
2004 Oakland b	A.L.	3B-OF	125	475	87	131	20	0	29	77	6	.276
2005 Oakland	A.L.	3B	160	625	92	168	40	1	27	101	6	.269
2006 Oakland	A.L.	3B	137	485	74	117	24	2	22	72	3	.241
2007 Oakland c	A.L.	3B	90	341	43	82	21	2	15	46	4	.240
2008 Sacramento	P.C.	3B	9	30	7	11	3	0	2	3	0	.367
2008 Oakland d	A.L.	3B	23	89	10	22	7	0	2	14	0	.247

Year Club	Lea	Pos	G	AB	R	H	2B	3B	HR	RBI	SB	Avg
2009 Oakland e ........A.L.		3B	8	30	0	3	1	0	0	1	0	.100
2010 Athletics.......	Arizona	DH	1	3	0	1	0	0	0	0	0	.333
2010 Oakland f	A.L.	DH-1B	33	111	10	26	8	0	1	10	0	.234
2011 Tampa	Fla.St.	3B	6	21	4	7	2	0	1	3	0	.333
2011 New York g-h-i .....A.L.		3B-1B	58	160	16	42	7	1	2	26	0	.262
2012 New York j-k.......A.L.		3B-1B	113	278	36	78	12	0	16	37	0	.281
Major League Totals		15 Yrs.	1491	5221	782	1396	301	21	248	850	47	.267
Division Series												
2000 Oakland ..........A.L.		3B	5	21	4	7	3	0	0	4	0	.333
2001 Oakland ..........A.L.		3B	5	21	0	3	1	0	0	0	0	.143
2002 Oakland ..........A.L.		3B	5	21	3	8	0	0	1	5	0	.381
2003 Oakland ..........A.L.		3B	5	22	1	1	1	0	0	1	0	.045
2006 Oakland ..........A.L.		3B	3	10	2	2	1	0	1	1	0	.200
2011 New York ........A.L.		PH	1	1	0	0	0	0	0	0	0	.000
2012 New York .........A.L.		3B	3	8	0	0	0	0	0	0	0	.000
Division Series Totals			27	104	10	21	6	0	2	10	1	.202
Championship Series												
2006 Oakland ..........A.L.		3B	4	13	1	3	1	0	1	2	0	.231
2012 New York ........A.L.		3B	3	8	0	0	0	0	0	0	0	.000
Championship Series Totals			7	21	1	3	1	0	1	2	0	.143

a On disabled list from August 21 to September 19, 1999.
b On disabled list from June 2 to July 9, 2004.
c On disabled list from July 27 to October 8, 2007.
d On disabled list from March 19 to May 29 and from July 2 to November 14, 2008.
e On disabled list from April 25 to November 6, 2009.
f On disabled list from May 21 to November 2, 2010.
g Filed for free agency, November 3, 2010. Signed with New York Yankees organization, February 11, 2011.
h On disabled list from May 6 to July 26, 2011.
i Filed for free agency, October 30, 2011, re-signed with New York Yankees, February 27, 2012.
j On disabled list from May 3 to May 11, 2012.
k Filed for free agency, November 3, 2012. Signed with Arizona Diamondbacks, December 8, 2012.

CHISENHALL, LONNIE DAVID
Born, Morehead City, North Carolina, October 4, 1988.
Bats Left. Throws Right. Height, 6 feet, 1 inch. Weight, 200 pounds.

Year Club	Lea	Pos	G	AB	R	H	2B	3B	HR	RBI	SB	Avg
2008 Mahoning Valley..	N.Y.-Penn.	SS	68	276	38	80	20	3	5	45	7	.290
2009 Kinston	Carolina	3B	99	388	59	107	26	2	18	79	2	.276
2009 Akron.............	Eastern	3B	24	93	13	17	5	1	4	13	1	.183
2010 Akron.............	Eastern	3B	117	460	81	128	22	3	17	84	3	.278
2011 Columbus.........	Int.	3B	66	255	45	68	15	3	7	45	0	.267
2011 Cleveland	A.L.	3B-OF	66	212	27	54	13	0	7	22	1	.255
2012 Columbus.............	Int.	3B	30	118	16	37	12	0	4	17	0	.314
2012 Cleveland a	A.L.	3B	43	142	16	38	6	1	5	16	2	.268
Major League Totals		2 Yrs.	109	354	43	92	19	1	12	38	3	.260

a On disabled list from June 30 to September 9, 2012.

CHOO, SHIN-SOO
Born, Pusan, South Korea, July 13, 1982.
Bats Left. Throws Left. Height, 5 feet, 11 inches. Weight, 200 pounds.

Year Club	Lea	Pos	G	AB	R	H	2B	3B	HR	RBI	SB	Avg
2001 Mariners..........	Arizona	OF	51	199	51	60	10	10	4	35	12	.302
2001 Wisconsin	Midwest	OF	3	13	1	6	0	0	0	3	2	.462
2002 San Bernardino	Calif.	OF	11	39	14	12	5	1	1	9	3	.308
2002 Wisconsin	Midwest	OF	119	420	69	127	24	8	6	48	34	.302
2003 Inland Empire........	Calif.	OF	110	412	62	118	18	13	9	55	18	.286
2004 San Antonio	Texas	OF	132	517	89	163	17	7	15	84	40	.315
2005 Tacoma	P.C.	OF	115	429	73	121	21	5	11	54	20	.282
2005 Seattle	A.L.	OF	10	18	1	1	0	0	0	1	0	.056
2006 Tacoma	P.C.	OF	94	375	71	121	21	3	13	48	26	.323
2006 Seattle-Cleveland a.....	A.L.	OF	49	157	23	44	12	3	3	22	5	.280
2007 Cleveland	A.L.	OF	6	17	5	5	0	0	0	5	0	.294
2007 Indians	Gulf Coast	OF	2	5	0	1	1	0	0	2	0	.200
2007 Buffalo	Int.	OF	59	208	34	54	11	2	3	26	10	.260
2008 Buffalo	Int.	OF	12	42	1	11	2	0	1	3	1	.262
2008 Cleveland b	A.L.	OF	94	317	68	98	28	3	14	66	4	.309

Year	Club	Lea	Pos	G	AB	R	H	2B	3B	HR	RBI	SB	Avg
2009 Cleveland............	A.L.	OF	156	583	87	175	38	6	20	86	21	.300
2010 Akron.............	Eastern	OF	3	11	1	1	0	0	0	0	1	.091
2010 Cleveland c........	A.L.	OF	144	550	81	165	31	2	22	90	22	.300
2011 Lake County......	Midwest.	OF	3	8	0	0	0	0	0	0	1	.000
2011 Cleveland d.........	A.L.	OF	85	313	37	81	11	3	8	36	12	.259
2012 Cleveland e........	A.L.	OF	155	598	88	169	43	2	16	67	21	.283
Major League Totals...........		8 Yrs.	699	2553	390	738	163	19	83	373	85	.289	

a Traded to Cleveland Indians with player to be named later for infielder Ben Broussard and cash, July 27, 2006. Cleveland Indians received pitcher Shawn Nottingham to complete trade, August 24, 2006.
b On disabled list from March 21 to May 30, 2008.
c On disabled list from July 3 to July 23, 2010.
d On disabled list from June 25 to August 12 and September 1 to September 15 and September 16 to November 2, 2011.
e Traded to Cincinnati Reds with infielder Jason Donald for infielder Didi Gregorius and outfielder Drew Stubbs, December 11, 2012.

CIRIACO, PEDRO

Born, San Pedro de Macoris, Dominican Republic, September 27, 1985.
Bats Right. Throws Right. Height, 6 feet. Weight, 170 pounds.

Year	Club	Lea	Pos	G	AB	R	H	2B	3B	HR	RBI	SB	Avg
2005 Missoula......	Pioneer	SS	69	254	28	61	9	4	2	31	7	.240
2006 South Bend...	Midwest	SS	128	550	77	145	15	5	2	32	19	.264
2007 Visalia.........	Calif.	SS	119	463	61	116	14	5	3	39	20	.251
2008 Visalia.........	Calif.	SS-2B	124	520	85	161	26	5	5	61	40	.310
2009 Mobile......	Southern	SS-2B	121	469	56	139	15	3	4	54	38	.296
2010 Reno...........	P.C.	SS-2B	87	355	44	92	15	7	6	51	14	.259
2010 Indianapolis.......	Int.	SS	32	121	19	34	9	1	0	6	5	.281
2010 Pittsburgh a......	N.L.	SS	8	6	3	3	1	1	0	1	0	.500
2011 Indianapolis......	Int.	SS-2B-OF-3B	71	277	31	64	7	3	2	24	13	.231
2011 Pittsburgh......	N.L.	SS-3B-OF	23	33	4	10	2	1	0	6	2	.303
2012 Pawtucket........	Int.	SS-2B-3B	64	276	41	83	13	2	4	21	14	.301
2012 Boston b.........	A.L.	3B-2B-SS	76	259	33	76	15	2	2	19	16	.293
Major League Totals...........		3 Yrs.	107	298	40	89	18	4	2	26	18	.299	

a Traded by Arizona Diamondbacks to Pittsburgh Pirates with catcher Chris Snyder and cash for infielder Bobby Crosby, outfielder Ryan Church and pitcher D.J. Carrasco, July 31, 2010.
b Not offered contract, December 12, 2011. Signed with Boston Red Sox organization, January 3, 2012.

CLEVENGER, STEVEN SCOTT (STEVE)

Born, Baltimore, Maryland, April 5, 1986.
Bats Left. Throws Right. Height, 6 feet. Weight, 195 pounds.

Year	Club	Lea	Pos	G	AB	R	H	2B	3B	HR	RBI	SB	Avg
2006 Boise..........	Northwest	2B	63	220	35	63	8	1	2	21	5	.286
2007 Daytona............	Fla.St.	1B-C	43	164	21	53	8	1	2	24	0	.323
2007 Boise..........	Northwest	C-1B	22	83	10	31	9	0	0	18	0	.373
2008 Daytona..........	Fla.St.	C-1B	84	284	36	89	20	0	2	39	7	.313
2008 Tennessee.......	Southern	C-1B	29	89	5	22	5	1	1	15	0	.247
2009 Iowa............	P.C.	C-1B-3B	68	230	21	61	12	1	0	26	4	.265
2009 Tennessee.......	Southern	C-3B	26	77	12	28	4	3	1	10	0	.364
2010 Tennessee.......	Southern	C-3B	88	271	37	86	24	0	5	47	0	.317
2011 Iowa............	P.C.	C	25	86	9	35	3	1	3	15	1	.407
2011 Tennessee.......	Southern	C-1B-3B	95	312	42	92	27	3	5	39	1	.295
2011 Chicago........	N.L.	C	2	4	1	1	1	0	0	0	0	.250
2012 Iowa............	P.C.	C	5	13	5	6	2	0	1	3	0	.462
2012 Chicago a............	N.L.	C-1B-3B	69	199	16	40	12	0	1	16	0	.201
Major League Totals...........		2 Yrs.	71	203	17	41	13	0	1	16	0	.202	

a On disabled list from April 26 to May 29, 2012.

COLVIN, TYLER EUGENE

Born, Augusta, Georgia, September 5, 1985.
Bats Left. Throws Left. Height, 6 feet, 3 inches. Weight, 210 pounds.

Year	Club	Lea	Pos	G	AB	R	H	2B	3B	HR	RBI	SB	Avg
2006 Boise..........	Northwest	OF	64	265	50	71	12	6	11	53	12	.268
2007 Daytona............	Fla.St.	OF	63	245	38	75	24	3	7	50	10	.306
2007 Tennessee.......	Southern	OF	62	247	34	72	11	2	9	31	7	.291
2008 Tennessee.......	Southern	OF	137	540	68	138	27	11	14	80	7	.256
2009 Daytona............	Fla.St.	OF	32	112	18	28	5	2	1	10	3	.250

Year	Club	Lea	Pos	G	AB	R	H	2B	3B	HR	RBI	SB	Avg
2009 Tennessee	Southern	OF	84	307	51	92	13	7	14	50	5	.300
2009 Chicago	N.L.	OF	6	17	1	3	0	0	0	2	0	.176
2010 Chicago a	N.L.	OF	135	358	60	91	18	5	20	56	6	.254
2011 Iowa	P.C.	OF-1B	50	203	32	52	12	6	7	32	1	.256
2011 Chicago b	N.L.	OF-1B	80	206	17	31	8	3	6	20	0	.150
2012 Colorado	N.L.	OF-1B	136	420	62	122	27	10	18	72	7	.290
Major League Totals	4 Yrs.		357	1001	140	247	53	18	44	150	13	.247

a On disabled list from September 20 to October 6, 2010.
b Traded to Colorado Rockies with infielder D.J. Le Mahieu for pitcher Casey Weathers and infielder Ian Stewart, December 8, 2011.

COOPER, DAVID FLETCHER
Born, Stockton, California, February 12, 1987.
Bats Left. Throws Left. Height, 6 feet. Weight, 200 pounds.

Year	Club	Lea	Pos	G	AB	R	H	2B	3B	HR	RBI	SB	Avg
2008 Dunedin	Fla.St.	1B	24	92	10	28	9	0	1	13	0	.304
2008 Lansing	Midwest	1B	24	96	15	34	10	0	2	17	0	.354
2008 Auburn	N.Y.-Penn.	1B	21	85	10	29	10	1	2	21	0	.341
2009 New Hampshire	Eastern	1B	128	473	62	122	32	0	10	66	0	.258
2010 New Hampshire	Eastern	1B	132	498	59	128	30	1	20	78	0	.257
2011 Las Vegas	P.C.	1B	120	467	77	170	51	1	9	96	1	.364
2011 Toronto	A.L.	1B	27	71	9	15	7	0	2	12	0	.211
2012 Las Vegas	P.C.	1B	68	261	45	82	27	1	10	52	0	.314
2012 Toronto a	A.L.	1B	45	140	16	42	11	0	4	11	0	.300
Major League Totals	2 Yrs.		72	211	25	57	18	0	6	23	0	.270

a On disabled list from August 23 to October 4, 2012.

COZART, ZACHARY WARREN (ZACK)
Born, Memphis, Tennessee, August 12, 1985.
Bats Right. Throws Right. Height, 6 feet. Weight, 195 pounds.

Year	Club	Lea	Pos	G	AB	R	H	2B	3B	HR	RBI	SB	Avg
2007 Dayton	Midwest	SS-2B	53	184	28	44	7	2	2	18	3	.239
2008 Dayton	Midwest	SS-2B	109	418	57	117	20	6	14	49	3	.280
2009 Carolina	Southern	SS	131	462	72	121	29	2	10	59	10	.262
2010 Louisville	Int.	SS	136	553	91	141	30	4	17	67	30	.255
2011 Louisville	Int.	SS	77	323	57	100	26	2	7	32	9	.310
2011 Cincinnati a	N.L.	SS	11	37	6	12	0	0	2	3	0	.324
2012 Cincinnati	N.L.	SS	138	561	72	138	33	4	15	35	4	.246
Major League Totals	2 Yrs.		149	598	78	150	33	4	17	38	4	.251
Division Series												
2012 Cincinnati	N.L.	SS	5	21	2	5	0	0	0	0	0	.238

a On disabled list from July 24 to November 2, 2011.

CRAIG, ALLEN THOMAS
Born, Mission Viejo, California, July 18, 1984.
Bats Right. Throws Right. Height, 6 feet, 2 inches. Weight, 210 pounds.

Year	Club	Lea	Pos	G	AB	R	H	2B	3B	HR	RBI	SB	Avg
2006 State College	N.Y.-Penn.	3B-SS-2B	48	175	21	45	13	0	4	29	0	.257
2007 Palm Beach	Fla.St.	3B-1B	112	423	77	132	25	2	21	77	8	.312
2007 Springfield	Texas	3B	7	24	5	7	2	0	3	3	0	.292
2008 Springfield	Texas	3B-OF-1B	129	506	84	154	30	0	22	85	2	.304
2009 Memphis	P.C.	OF-1B-3B	126	472	78	152	26	1	26	83	3	.322
2010 Memphis	P.C.	OF-1B	83	306	57	98	24	2	14	81	1	.320
2010 St. Louis	N.L.	OF-1B-3B-2B	44	114	12	28	7	0	4	18	0	.246
2011 Springfield	Texas	OF	2	6	0	0	0	0	0	1	0	.000
2011 Memphis	P.C.	OF-2B	10	35	9	10	2	1	1	5	0	.286
2011 St. Louis a	N.L.	OF-2B-1B-3B	75	200	33	63	15	0	11	40	5	.315
2012 Palm Beach	Fla.St.	DH	3	11	1	4	0	0	1	1	0	.364
2012 Memphis	P.C.	1B	4	17	3	6	0	0	2	7	0	.353
2012 St. Louis b	N.L.	1B-OF	119	469	76	144	35	0	22	92	2	.307
Major League Totals	3 Yrs.		238	783	121	235	57	0	37	150	7	.300
Wild Card Playoff												
2012 St. Louis	N.L.	1B	1	4	1	2	1	0	0	1	0	.500

Year Club	Lea	Pos	G	AB	R	H	2B	3B	HR	RBI	SB	Avg
Division Series												
2011 St. Louis.........N.L.		OF	3	10	3	1	0	1	0	0	0	.100
2012 St. Louis.........N.L.		1B	5	19	2	6	2	0	1	3	0	.316
Division Series Totals			8	29	5	7	2	1	1	3	0	.241
Championship Series												
2011 St. Louis.........N.L.		OF	5	8	1	3	0	0	1	3	0	.375
2012 St. Louis.........N.L.		1B-OF	7	24	1	3	1	0	0	2	0	.125
Championship Series Totals			12	32	2	6	1	0	1	5	0	.188
World Series Record												
2011 St. Louis.........N.L.		OF	7	19	5	5	0	0	3	5	0	.263

a On disabled list from April 17 to May 2 and June 8 to August 10, 2011.
b On disabled list from March 26 to May 1 and May 17 to June 1, 2012.

CRAWFORD, BRANDON MICHAEL

Born, Mountain View, California, January 21, 1987.
Bats Left. Throws Right. Height, 6 feet, 2 inches. Weight, 215 pounds.

Year Club	Lea	Pos	G	AB	R	H	2B	3B	HR	RBI	SB	Avg
2008 Giants............Arizona		SS	4	14	3	6	1	1	0	3	0	.429
2008 Salem-Keizer .... Northwest		SS	1	2	0	0	0	0	0	0	0	.000
2009 San Jose ....Calif.		SS	25	105	21	39	2	2	6	17	2	.371
2009 Connecticut ....Eastern		SS	108	392	38	101	26	2	4	31	11	.258
2010 San Jose ....Calif.		3B-SS	5	18	4	3	1	0	0	1	0	.167
2010 Richmond ....Eastern		SS	79	291	43	70	12	3	7	22	4	.241
2011 San Jose ....Calif.		SS	14	59	14	19	5	1	3	15	0	.322
2011 Fresno ..............P.C.		SS	29	107	13	25	5	1	1	9	5	.234
2011 San Francisco ........N.L.		SS	66	196	22	40	5	2	3	21	1	.204
2012 San Francisco ........N.L.		SS	143	435	44	108	26	3	4	45	1	.248
Major League Totals	2 Yrs.		209	631	66	148	31	5	7	66	2	.235
Division Series												
2012 San Francisco ........N.L.		SS	5	11	1	2	0	1	0	1	0	.182
Championship Series												
2012 San Francisco ........N.L.		SS	7	23	2	5	1	0	0	5	0	.217
World Series Record												
2012 San Francisco ........N.L.		SS	4	12	0	3	0	0	0	1	1	.250

CRAWFORD, CARL DEMONTE

Born, Houston, Texas, August 5, 1981.
Bats Left. Throws Left. Height, 6 feet, 2 inches. Weight, 220 pounds.

Year Club	Lea	Pos	G	AB	R	H	2B	3B	HR	RBI	SB	Avg
1999 Princeton ....Appal.		OF	60	260	62	83	14	4	0	25	17	.319
2000 Charleston-SC ......So.Atl.		OF	135	564	99	170	21	11	6	57	55	.301
2001 Orlando .... Southern		OF	132	537	64	147	24	3	4	51	36	.274
2002 Durham ....Int.		OF	85	353	59	105	17	9	7	52	26	.297
2002 Tampa Bay ...........A.L.		OF	63	259	23	67	11	6	2	30	9	.259
2003 Tampa Bay ...........A.L.		OF	151	630	80	177	18	9	5	54	*55	.281
2004 Tampa Bay ...........A.L.		OF	152	626	104	185	26	*19	11	55	*59	.296
2005 Tampa Bay ...........A.L.		OF	156	644	101	194	33	*15	15	81	46	.301
2006 Tampa Bay ...........A.L.		OF	151	600	89	183	20	*16	18	77	*58	.305
2007 Tampa Bay a..........A.L.		OF	143	584	93	184	37	9	11	80	*50	.315
2008 Tampa Bay ...........A.L.		OF	109	443	69	121	12	10	8	57	25	.273
2009 Tampa Bay ...........A.L.		OF	156	606	96	185	28	8	15	68	60	.305
2010 Tampa Bay b..........A.L.		OF	154	600	110	184	30	*13	19	90	47	.307
2011 Pawtucket ....Int.		OF	2	5	1	1	0	0	0	1	0	.200
2011 Boston c.............A.L.		OF	130	506	65	129	29	7	11	56	18	.255
2012 Red Sox .... Gulf Coast		OF	5	14	2	3	1	0	0	0	0	.214
2012 Portland ....Eastern		OF	3	10	2	4	0	1	0	1	1	.400
2012 Pawtucket ....Int.		OF	3	12	2	4	0	0	0	1	1	.333
2012 Boston d-e............A.L.		OF	31	117	23	33	10	2	3	19	5	.282
Major League Totals	11 Yrs.		1396	5615	853	1642	254	114	118	667	432	.292
Division Series												
2008 Tampa Bay ...........A.L.		OF	4	14	2	3	0	0	0	2	3	.214
2010 Tampa Bay ...........A.L.		OF	5	21	1	3	0	0	1	1	1	.143
Division Series Totals			9	35	3	6	0	0	1	3	4	.171
Championship Series												
2008 Tampa Bay ...........A.L.		OF	7	29	3	10	2	1	0	4	3	.345

| World Series Record | | | | | | | | | | | | | |
| 2008 Tampa Bay........... | | A.L. | OF | 5 | 19 | 4 | 5 | 1 | 0 | 2 | 2 | 1 | .263 |

a On disabled list from August 10 to September 26, 2008.
b Filed for free agency, November 1, 2010. Signed with Boston Red Sox, December 11, 2010.
c On disabled list from June 18 to July 18, 2011.
d On disabled list from March 26 to July 16 and August 20 to October 29, 2012.
e Traded to Los Angeles Dodgers with infielder Adrian Gonzalez, pitcher Josh Beckett, infielder Nick Punto and cash for infielder James Loney, infielder Ivan DeJesus, pitcher Allen Webster and player to be named later, August 25, 2012. Boston Red Sox received pitcher Rubby De La Rosa to complete trade, October 4, 2012.

CRISP, COVELLI LOYCE (COCO)

Born, Los Angeles, California, November 1, 1979.
Bats Both. Throws Right. Height, 6 feet. Weight, 180 pounds.

Year	Club	Lea	Pos	G	AB	R	H	2B	3B	HR	RBI	SB	Avg
1999 Johnson City........	Appal.		2B	65	229	55	59	5	4	3	22	27	.258
2000 New Jersey.....	N.Y.-Penn.		OF-2B	36	134	18	32	5	0	0	14	25	.239
2000 Peoria...........	Midwest		OF	27	98	14	27	9	0	0	7	7	.276
2001 Potomac.........	Carolina		OF	139	530	80	162	23	3	11	47	39	.306
2002 New Haven........	Eastern		OF	89	355	61	107	16	1	9	47	26	.301
2002 Akron.........	Eastern		OF	7	32	9	13	1	0	1	4	4	.406
2002 Buffalo..............	Int.		OF	4	21	3	5	1	0	0	2	1	.238
2002 Cleveland a........	A.L.		OF	32	127	16	33	9	2	1	9	4	.260
2003 Buffalo..............	Int.		OF	56	225	42	81	19	6	1	24	20	.360
2003 Cleveland.........	A.L.		OF	99	414	55	110	15	6	3	27	15	.266
2004 Cleveland..........	A.L.		OF	139	491	78	146	24	2	15	71	20	.297
2005 Cleveland b........	A.L.		OF	145	594	86	178	42	4	16	69	15	.300
2006 Pawtucket..........	Int.		OF	1	3	0	1	0	0	0	2	0	.333
2006 Boston c-d........	A.L.		OF	105	413	58	109	22	2	8	36	22	.264
2007 Boston...........	A.L.		OF	145	526	85	141	28	7	6	60	28	.268
2008 Boston e..........	A.L.		OF	118	361	55	102	18	3	7	41	20	.283
2009 Kansas City f-g.....	A.L.		OF	49	180	30	41	8	5	3	14	13	.228
2010 Stockton...........	Calif.		OF	2	6	2	5	0	1	1	3	0	.833
2010 Sacramento.........	P.C.		OF	6	22	7	13	2	1	0	5	2	.591
2010 Oakland h.........	A.L.		OF	75	290	51	81	14	4	8	38	32	.279
2011 Oakland i..........	A.L.		OF	136	531	69	140	27	5	8	54	*49	.264
2012 Oakland j.........	A.L.		OF	120	455	68	118	25	7	11	46	39	.259
Major League Totals...........		11 Yrs.		1163	4382	651	1199	232	47	86	465	257	.274
Division Series													
2007 Boston..............	A.L.		OF	3	10	0	2	0	0	0	2	1	.200
2008 Boston..............	A.L.		OF	2	4	2	1	0	0	0	0	1	.250
2012 Oakland..............	A.L.		OF	5	22	3	4	0	0	1	2	0	.182
Division Series Totals...........				10	36	5	7	0	0	1	4	2	.194
Championship Series													
2007 Boston..............	A.L.		OF	7	21	2	3	1	0	0	0	1	.143
2008 Boston..............	A.L.		OF	5	20	2	9	2	0	0	1	0	.450
Championship Series Totals......				12	41	4	12	3	0	0	1	1	.293
World Series Record													
2007 Boston..............	A.L.		OF	3	2	1	1	0	0	0	0	0	.500

a Sent by St. Louis Cardinals to Cleveland Indians as player to be named later for pitcher Chuck Finley, August 6, 2002.
b On disabled list from May 18 to June 2, 2005.
c Traded to Boston Red Sox with pitcher David Riske and catcher Josh Bard for infielder Andy Marte, catcher Kelly Shoppach and pitcher Guillermo Mota, January 27, 2006.
d On disabled list from April 9 to May 28, 2006.
e Traded to Kansas City Royals for pitcher Ramon Ramirez, November 19, 2008.
f On disabled list from June 13 to November 9, 2009.
g Filed for free agency, November 9, 2009. Signed with Oakland Athletics, December 23, 2009.
h On disabled list from April 3 to May 21 and May 26 to June 22, 2010.
i Filed for free agency, October 30, 2011, re-signed with Oakland Athletics, January 5, 2012.
j On disabled list from May 3 to May 21, 2012.

CRUZ (BOJORQUEZ), LUIS ALFONSO

Born, Navojoa, Mexico, February 10, 1984.
Bats Right. Throws Right. Height, 6 feet, 1 inch. Weight, 220 pounds.

Year	Club	Lea	Pos	G	AB	R	H	2B	3B	HR	RBI	SB	Avg
2001 Red Sox.....	Gulf Coast		SS-3B	53	197	18	51	9	0	3	18	1	.259
2002 Red Sox.....	Gulf Coast		SS	21	72	10	21	4	0	0	9	2	.292

Year Club	Lea	Pos	G	AB	R	H	2B	3B	HR	RBI	SB	Avg
2002 Augusta a........So.Atl.		SS	58	202	16	38	7	1	3	15	0	.188
2003 Fort Wayne....Midwest		SS-2B	129	481	55	111	24	1	8	53	2	.231
2004 Lake Elsinore.....Calif.		SS-3B	124	512	75	142	35	3	8	72	3	.277
2005 Mexico City...Mexican		SS	61	226	29	64	15	3	4	23	4	.283
2005 Mobile......Southern		SS-3B	44	151	14	24	2	1	3	6	0	.159
2006 Mobile......Southern		2B-SS-3B	130	499	65	130	35	3	12	65	8	.261
2007 Portland.........P.C.		SS-2B-3B	45	155	15	26	10	1	5	17	0	.168
2007 San Antonio b...Texas		SS	69	238	24	60	10	0	4	19	3	.252
2008 Altoona......Eastern		SS-2B-3B	105	375	41	99	24	1	6	46	3	.264
2008 Indianapolis......Int.		SS-2B-OF	32	120	19	39	10	0	3	15	2	.325
2008 Pittsburgh........N.L.		SS-2B	22	67	6	15	3	0	0	3	1	.224
2009 Indianapolis......Int.		SS-3B-OF-2B	66	229	28	58	15	0	3	23	3	.253
2009 Pittsburgh c......N.L.		SS-2B	27	70	5	15	1	0	0	2	0	.214
2010 Nashville.........P.C.		SS-3B-2B	129	488	54	137	29	3	10	68	0	.281
2010 Milwaukee........N.L.		SS	7	17	2	4	0	1	0	1	0	.235
2011 Mexico City...Mexican		SS	16	64	15	26	3	0	7	18	0	.406
2011 Round Rock d-e-f...P.C.		SS-2B-OF-3B	67	275	34	75	15	1	9	34	2	.273
2012 Albuquerque.....P.C.		SS-3B-2B-OF	74	289	46	92	31	3	8	46	1	.318
2012 Los Angeles.......N.L.		3B-SS-2B	78	283	26	84	20	0	6	40	2	.297
Major League Totals............		4 Yrs.	134	437	39	118	24	1	6	46	3	.270

a Traded by Boston Red Sox to San Diego Padres for infielder Cesar Crespo, December 16, 2002.
b Filed for free agency October 29, 2007. Signed with Pittsburgh Pirates organization, December 11, 2007.
c Claimed on waivers by Milwaukee Brewers, December 7, 2009.
d Filed for free agency, March 28, 2011. Signed with Texas Rangers organization, March 30, 2011.
e Loaned to Mexico City June 20 to September 2, 2011.
f   Filed for free agency, November 2, 2011. Signed with Los Angeles Dodgers organization, November 15, 2011.

CRUZ, NELSON RAMON

Born, Monte Cristi, Dominican Republic, July 1, 1980.
Bats Right. Throws Right. Height, 6 feet, 3 inches. Weight, 230 pounds.

Year Club	Lea	Pos	G	AB	R	H	2B	3B	HR	RBI	SB	Avg
2001 Athletics a.........Arizona		OF	23	88	11	22	3	1	3	16	6	.250
2002 Vancouver......Northwest		OF	63	214	23	59	14	0	4	25	12	.276
2003 Kane County.......Midwest		OF	119	470	65	112	26	2	20	85	10	.238
2004 Modesto...........Calif.		OF	66	261	54	90	27	1	11	52	8	.345
2004 Sacramento........P.C.		OF	4	13	4	3	1	0	1	2	0	.231
2004 Midland b..........Texas		OF	67	262	51	82	14	2	14	46	8	.313
2005 Huntsville.......Southern		OF	68	248	45	76	19	0	16	54	10	.306
2005 Nashville.........P.C.		OF	60	208	33	56	13	0	11	27	9	.269
2005 Milwaukee..........N.L.		OF	8	5	1	1	1	0	0	0	0	.200
2006 Nashville.........P.C.		OF	104	371	68	112	22	1	20	73	17	.302
2006 Texas c...........A.L.		OF	41	130	15	29	3	0	6	22	1	.223
2007 Oklahoma..........P.C.		OF	44	162	32	57	9	1	15	45	1	.352
2007 Texas.............A.L.		OF	96	307	35	72	15	2	9	34	2	.235
2008 Rangers.........Arizona		OF	1	4	1	1	1	0	0	1	0	.250
2008 Oklahoma..........P.C.		OF	103	383	93	131	18	3	37	99	24	.342
2008 Texas.............A.L.		OF	31	115	19	38	9	1	7	26	3	.330
2009 Oklahoma..........P.C.		OF	3	10	0	0	0	0	0	0	1	.000
2009 Texas d...........A.L.		OF	128	462	75	120	21	1	33	76	20	.260
2010 Frisco.............Texas		OF	3	11	1	4	1	0	0	1	1	.364
2010 Oklahoma..........P.C.		OF	5	19	1	4	1	0	0	4	0	.211
2010 Texas e...........A.L.		OF	108	399	60	127	31	3	22	78	17	.318
2011 Frisco.............Texas		OF	3	11	1	2	1	0	0	0	0	.182
2011 Round Rock.......P.C.		OF	3	11	3	5	0	0	3	4	0	.455
2011 Texas f...........A.L.		OF	124	475	64	125	28	1	29	87	9	.263
2012 Texas.............A.L.		OF	159	585	86	152	45	0	24	90	8	.260
Major League Totals............		8 Yrs.	695	2478	355	664	153	8	130	413	60	.268
Wild Card Playoff												
2012 Texas...............A.L.		OF	1	4	0	2	0	0	0	0	0	.500
Division Series												
2010 Texas..............A.L.		OF	5	20	5	8	2	0	3	3	1	.400
2011 Texas..............A.L.		OF	4	15	1	1	0	0	0	0	0	.067
Division Series Totals..........			9	35	6	9	2	0	3	3	1	.257
Championship Series												
2010 Texas..............A.L.		OF	6	20	6	7	3	0	2	5	0	.350
2011 Texas..............A.L.		OF	6	22	7	8	2	0	6	13	0	.364
Championship Series Totals......			12	42	13	15	5	0	8	18	0	.357

World Series Record

Year	Club	Lea	Pos	G	AB	R	H	2B	3B	HR	RBI
2010 Texas	A.L.		OF	5	20	2	4	2	0	1	
2011 Texas	A.L.		OF	7	25	5	5	0	0	2	
World Series Totals				12	45	7	9	2	0		

a Traded by New York Mets to Oakland Athletics for infielder Jorge Velandia, August 30, 2000.
b Traded to Milwaukee Brewers with pitcher Justin Lehr for infielder Keith Ginter, December 15, 20...
c Traded to Texas Rangers with outfielder Carlos Lee for pitcher Francisco Cordero, outfielder Ke...
   outfielder Laynce Nix and pitcher Julian Cordero, July 28, 2006.
d On disabled list from August 4 to August 20, 2009.
e On disabled list from April 27 to May 14 and May 29 to June 22 and August 15 to August 30, 2010.
f On disabled list from May 4 to May 23 and August 29 to September 13, 2011.

CUDDYER, MICHAEL BRENT

Born, Norfolk, Virginia, March 27, 1979.
Bats Right. Throws Right. Height, 6 feet, 2 inches. Weight, 220 pounds.

Year	Club	Lea	Pos	G	AB	R	H	2B	3B	HR	RBI	SB	Avg
1998 Fort Wayne....	Midwest	SS-2B	129	497	82	137	37	7	12	81	16	.276	
1999 Fort Myers......	Fla.St.	3B	130	466	87	139	24	4	16	82	14	.298	
2000 New Britain....	Eastern	3B	138	490	72	129	30	8	6	61	5	.263	
2001 New Britain....	Eastern	3B-1B-OF	141	509	95	153	36	3	30	87	5	.301	
2001 Minnesota........	A.L.	1B-3B	8	18	1	4	2	0	0	1	1	.222	
2002 Edmonton......	P.C.	OF-1B-3B	86	330	70	102	16	9	20	53	12	.309	
2002 Minnesota........	A.L.	OF-3B-1B	41	112	12	29	7	0	4	13	2	.259	
2003 Twins.......	Gulf Coast	OF	2	5	1	4	0	0	1	3	0	.800	
2003 Rochester........	Int.	OF-2B-3B-1B	53	186	25	57	17	0	3	34	5	.306	
2003 Minnesota........	A.L.	OF-3B-1B-2B	35	102	14	25	1	3	4	8	1	.245	
2004 Minnesota........	A.L.	2B-3B-OF-1B	115	339	49	89	22	1	12	45	5	.263	
2005 Rochester........	Int.	3B-1B	3	9	1	1	0	0	0	0	2	.111	
2005 Minnesota a.......	A.L.	3B-OF-2B-1B	126	422	55	111	25	3	12	42	3	.263	
2006 Minnesota........	A.L.	OF-1B	150	557	102	158	41	5	24	109	6	.284	
2007 Minnesota b.......	A.L.	OF-1B	144	547	87	151	28	5	16	81	5	.276	
2008 Rochester........	Int.	OF	4	10	3	3	2	0	0	1	0	.300	
2008 Minnesota c.......	A.L.	OF-1B	71	249	30	62	13	4	3	36	5	.249	
2009 Minnesota........	A.L.	OF-1B-2B	153	588	93	162	34	7	32	94	6	.276	
2010 Minnesota........	A.L.	1B-OF-3B-2B	157	609	93	165	37	5	14	81	7	.271	
2011 Minnesota d.......	A.L.	OF-1B-2B-P	139	529	70	150	29	2	20	70	11	.284	
2012 Colorado Springs...	P.C.	1B-OF	2	9	4	6	1	0	1	3	0	.667	
2012 Colorado e........	N.L.	OF-1B	101	358	53	93	30	2	16	58	8	.260	
Major League Totals		12 Yrs.	1240	4430	659	1199	269	37	157	638	60	.271	

Division Series

Year	Club	Lea	Pos	G	AB	R	H	2B	3B	HR	RBI	SB	Avg
2002 Minnesota........	A.L.	OF	5	13	1	5	1	0	0	1	0	.385	
2003 Minnesota........	A.L.	DH	1	4	0	1	0	0	0	1	0	.250	
2004 Minnesota........	A.L.	2B-1B	4	15	1	7	0	0	0	2	0	.467	
2006 Minnesota........	A.L.	OF	3	12	2	3	0	1	1	1	0	.250	
2009 Minnesota........	A.L.	1B	3	14	0	6	0	0	0	1	0	.429	
2010 Minnesota........	A.L.	1B	3	11	1	2	1	0	1	2	0	.182	
Division Series Totals			19	69	5	24	2	1	2	8	0	.348	

Championship Series

Year	Club	Lea	Pos	G	AB	R	H	2B	3B	HR	RBI	SB	Avg
2002 Minnesota........	A.L.	OF	3	5	0	1	0	0	0	0	0	.200	

a On disabled list from June 30 to July 17, 2005.
b On disabled list from July 19 to August 3, 2007.
c On disabled list from April 5 to April 25 and June 28 to September 13, 2008.
d Filed for free agency, October 30, 2011. Signed with Colorado Rockies, December 20, 2011.
e On disabled list from August 1 to August 16 and August 19 to October 5, 2012.

DAVIS, CHRISTOPHER LYN (CHRIS)

Born, Longview, Texas, March 17, 1986.
Bats Left. Throws Right. Height, 6 feet, 4 inches. Weight, 230 pounds.

Year	Club	Lea	Pos	G	AB	R	H	2B	3B	HR	RBI	SB	Avg
2006 Spokane.....	Northwest	OF-1B	69	253	38	70	18	1	15	42	2	.277	
2007 Bakersfield.......	Calif.	3B	99	386	69	115	28	3	24	93	3	.298	
2007 Frisco.........	Texas	3B	30	109	21	32	7	0	12	25	0	.294	
2008 Frisco.........	Texas	1B	46	186	43	62	14	0	13	42	5	.333	
2008 Oklahoma........	P.C.	1B	31	111	25	37	7	1	10	31	2	.333	
2008 Texas..........	A.L.	1B-3B	80	295	51	84	23	2	17	55	1	.285	
2009 Oklahoma..........	P.C.	3B-1B	44	165	27	54	12	1	6	30	0	.327	
2009 Texas	A.L.	1B-3B	113	391	48	93	15	1	21	59	0	.238	

Year	Club	Lea	Pos	G	AB	R	H	2B	3B	HR	RBI	SB	Avg
2010 Oklahoma.........P.C.			3B-1B-OF	103	398	67	130	31	2	14	80	3	.327
2010 Texas ............A.L.			1B-3B	45	120	7	23	9	0	1	4	3	.192
2011 Bowie........Eastern			1B-3B	2	6	2	3	1	0	0	0	0	.500
2011 Round Rock.......P.C.			3B-OF	48	193	39	71	14	1	24	66	1	.368
2011 Texas-Baltimore a-b A.L.			1B-3B	59	199	25	53	12	0	5	19	1	.266
2012 Baltimore.........A.L.			DH-OF-1B-P	139	515	75	139	20	0	33	85	2	.270
Major League Totals			5 Yrs.	436	1520	206	392	79	3	77	222	7	.258
Wild Card Playoff													
2012 Baltimore.........A.L.			OF	1	4	0	1	0	0	0	0	0	.250
Division Series													
2012 Baltimore.........A.L.			OF	5	20	1	4	0	0	0	2	0	.200

a Traded to Baltimore Orioles with pitcher Tommy Hunter for pitcher Koji Uehara and cash, July 30, 2011.
b On disabled list from August 15 to September 6, 2011.

DAVIS, ISAAC BENJAMIN (IKE)
Born, Edina, Minnesota, March 22, 1987.
Bats Left. Throws Left. Height, 6 feet, 4 inches. Weight, 215 pounds.

Year	Club	Lea	Pos	G	AB	R	H	2B	3B	HR	RBI	SB	Avg
2008 Brooklyn........N.Y.-Penn.			1B	58	215	17	55	15	0	0	17	0	.256
2009 Binghamton........Eastern			1B-OF	55	207	30	64	14	0	13	43	0	.309
2009 St. Lucie.........Fla.St.			1B	59	222	28	64	17	3	7	28	0	.288
2010 Buffalo..............Int.			1B	10	33	8	12	3	0	2	4	0	.364
2010 New York ...........N.L.			1B	147	523	73	138	33	1	19	71	3	.264
2011 New York a...........N.L.			1B	36	129	20	39	8	1	7	25	0	.302
2012 New York...........N.L.			1B	156	519	66	118	26	0	32	90	0	.227
Major League Totals			3 Yrs.	339	1171	159	295	67	2	58	186	3	.252

a On disabled list from May 11 to October 24, 2011.

DAVIS, RAJAI LAVAE
Born, Norwich, Connecticut, October 19, 1980.
Bats Right. Throws Right. Height, 5 feet, 11 inches. Weight, 195 pounds.

Year	Club	Lea	Pos	G	AB	R	H	2B	3B	HR	RBI	SB	Avg
2001 Pirates .... Gulf Coast			OF	26	84	19	22	1	0	0	4	11	.262
2001 Williamsport.....N.Y.-Penn.			OF-2B	6	12	1	1	0	0	0	0	0	.083
2002 Pirates .... Gulf Coast			OF	58	224	38	86	16	5	4	35	24	.384
2002 Williamsport.....N.Y.-Penn.			OF	1	4	0	0	0	0	0	0	0	.000
2002 Hickory............So.Atl.			OF	6	14	4	6	0	0	0	3	2	.429
2003 Hickory............So.Atl.			OF	125	478	84	146	21	7	6	54	40	.305
2004 Lynchburg .... Carolina			OF	127	509	91	160	27	7	5	38	57	.314
2005 Altoona...........Eastern			OF	123	499	82	140	22	5	4	34	45	.281
2006 Indianapolis ....Int.			OF	100	385	53	109	17	1	2	21	45	.283
2006 Pittsburgh ...........N.L.			OF	20	14	1	2	1	0	0	0	1	.143
2007 Indianapolis ....Int.			OF	53	211	31	67	12	4	4	30	27	.318
2007 Pittsburgh-San Francisco a N.L.			OF	75	190	32	53	11	2	1	9	22	.279
2008 San Francisco ........N.L.			OF	12	18	2	1	0	0	0	0	4	.056
2008 Oakland b.............A.L.			OF-2B	101	196	28	51	5	4	3	19	25	.260
2009 Oakland ...............A.L.			OF	125	390	65	119	27	5	3	48	41	.305
2010 Oakland c.............A.L.			OF	143	525	66	149	28	3	5	52	50	.284
2011 Dunedin ....Fla.St.			OF	2	5	1	2	0	0	1	1	0	.400
2011 New Hampshire .....Eastern			OF	4	10	1	3	1	0	0	0	0	.300
2011 Toronto d ............A.L.			OF	95	320	44	76	21	6	1	29	34	.237
2012 Toronto e ............A.L.			OF	142	447	64	115	24	3	8	43	46	.257
Major League Totals			7 Yrs.	713	2100	302	566	117	23	21	200	223	.270

a Traded to San Francisco Giants with player to be named later for pitcher Matt Morris, July 31, 2007. San Francisco Giants received pitcher Steve MacFarland to complete trade, August 27, 2007.
b Claimed on waivers by Oakland Athletics, April 23, 2008.
c Traded to Toronto Blue Jays for pitcher Daniel Farquhar and pitcher Trystan Magnuson, November 17, 2010.
d On disabled list from April 11 to April 29 and August 14 to November 1, 2011.
e Filed for free agency, October 31, 2012, re-signed with Toronto Blue Jays, October 31, 2012.

DE AZA (CEDA), ALEJANDRO ALBERTO

Born, Guaymate, Dominican Republic, April 11, 1984.
Bats Left. Throws Left. Height, 6 feet. Weight, 190 pounds.

Year Club	Lea	Pos	G	AB	R	H	2B	3B	HR	RBI	SB	Avg
2002 Dodgers	Gulf Coast	OF-C	39	128	27	29	6	1	1	14	16	.227
2003 Ogden	Pioneer	OF	55	208	36	48	11	1	2	24	15	.231
2004 Columbus a	So.Atl.	OF-1B	102	341	63	87	17	2	4	45	24	.255
2005 Jupiter	Fla.St.	OF	123	472	75	135	24	9	3	37	34	.286
2006 Jupiter	Fla.St.	OF	2	7	1	1	0	1	0	0	0	.143
2006 Marlins	Gulf Coast	OF	7	24	7	11	1	0	0	4	3	.458
2006 Carolina	Southern	OF	69	230	40	64	12	2	2	16	27	.278
2007 Marlins	Gulf Coast	OF	4	9	2	6	2	0	0	1	2	.667
2007 Jupiter	Fla.St.	OF	2	8	1	4	1	1	0	0	0	.500
2007 Carolina	Southern	OF	5	20	7	7	2	0	2	3	0	.350
2007 Florida	N.L.	OF	45	144	14	33	8	2	0	8	2	.229
2008 Florida b	N.L.			INJURED—Did Not Play								
2009 Florida	N.L.	OF	22	20	6	5	1	0	0	3	0	.250
2009 New Orleans c	P.C.	OF	87	267	45	80	21	5	8	34	11	.300
2010 Charlotte	Int.	OF	79	318	53	96	21	4	5	49	16	.302
2010 Chicago	A.L.	OF	19	30	7	9	3	0	0	2	2	.300
2011 Charlotte	Int.	OF	99	385	64	124	29	5	9	37	22	.322
2011 Chicago	A.L.	OF	54	152	29	50	11	3	4	23	12	.329
2012 Charlotte	Int.	OF	5	20	3	5	1	0	1	2	0	.250
2012 Chicago d	A.L.	OF	131	524	81	147	29	6	9	50	26	.281
Major League Totals		5 Yrs.	271	870	137	244	52	11	13	86	42	.280

a Selected Florida Marlins from Los Angeles Dodgers in Rule V draft, December 13, 2004.
b On disabled list from March 30 to October 1, 2008.
c Claimed on waivers by Chicago White Sox, October 21, 2009.
d On disabled list from August 18 to September 2, 2012.

DE JESUS, DAVID CHRISTOPHER

Born, Brooklyn, New York, December 20, 1979.
Bats Left. Throws Left. Height, 6 feet. Weight, 190 pounds.

Year Club	Lea	Pos	G	AB	R	H	2B	3B	HR	RBI	SB	Avg
2001 a				INJURED—Did Not Play								
2002 Wilmington	Carolina	OF	87	334	69	99	22	6	4	41	15	.296
2002 Wichita	Texas	OF	25	79	7	20	5	2	2	15	3	.253
2003 Wichita	Texas	OF	17	71	14	24	4	0	2	10	1	.338
2003 Omaha	P.C.	OF	59	215	49	64	16	3	5	23	8	.298
2003 Kansas City	A.L.	OF	12	7	0	2	0	1	0	0	0	.286
2004 Omaha	P.C.	OF	50	197	38	62	14	4	6	16	7	.315
2004 Kansas City	A.L.	OF	96	363	58	104	15	3	7	39	8	.287
2005 Kansas City	A.L.	OF	122	461	69	135	31	6	9	56	5	.293
2006 Omaha	P.C.	OF	3	13	0	5	0	0	0	2	0	.385
2006 Kansas City b	A.L.	OF	119	491	83	145	36	7	8	56	6	.295
2007 Kansas City	A.L.	OF	157	605	101	157	29	9	7	58	10	.260
2008 Kansas City	A.L.	OF	135	518	70	159	25	7	12	73	11	.307
2009 Kansas City	A.L.	OF	144	558	74	157	28	9	13	71	4	.281
2010 Kansas City c-d	A.L.	OF	91	352	46	112	23	3	5	37	3	.318
2011 Oakland e	A.L.	OF	131	442	60	106	20	5	10	46	4	.240
2012 Chicago	N.L.	OF	148	506	76	133	28	8	9	50	7	.263
Major League Totals		10 Yrs.	1155	4303	637	1210	235	58	80	486	58	.281

a On minor league disabled list from June 19 to September 17, 2001.
b On disabled list from April 19 to May 29, 2006.
c On disabled list from July 23 to November 10, 2010.
d Traded to Oakland Athletics for pitcher Vin Mazzaro and pitcher Justin Marks, November 10, 2010.
e Filed for free agency, October 30, 2011. Signed with Chicago Cubs, November 30, 2011.

DENORFIA, CHRISTOPHER ANTHONY (CHRIS)

Born, Bristol, Connecticut, July 15, 1980.
Bats Right. Throws Right. Height, 6 feet, 1 inch. Weight, 205 pounds.

Year Club	Lea	Pos	G	AB	R	H	2B	3B	HR	RBI	SB	Avg
2002 Reds	Gulf Coast	OF	57	200	38	68	9	2	0	19	18	.340
2002 Dayton	Midwest	OF	3	10	2	0	0	0	0	0	0	.000
2002 Chattanooga	Southern	OF	3	7	0	3	2	1	0	0	0	.429
2003 Potomac	Carolina	OF	128	470	60	111	10	5	4	39	20	.236
2004 Potomac	Carolina	OF	75	269	52	84	18	4	11	51	10	.312
2004 Chattanooga	Southern	OF	61	221	30	55	10	2	6	27	5	.249

Year Club	Lea	Pos	G	AB	R	H	2B	3B	HR	RBI	SB	Avg
2005 Chattanooga......	Southern	OF	46	188	40	62	17	3	7	26	4	.330
2005 Louisville	Int.	OF	91	323	50	100	12	6	13	61	8	.310
2005 Cincinnati...........	N.L.	OF	18	38	8	10	3	0	1	2	1	.263
2006 Louisville	Int.	OF	83	312	46	109	19	1	7	45	15	.349
2006 Cincinnati...........	N.L.	OF	49	106	14	30	6	0	1	7	1	.283
2007 Cincinnati...........	N.L.	INJURED—Did Not Play										
2007 Oakland a-b	A.L.	INJURED—Did Not Play										
2008 Stockton............	Calif.	OF	2	9	1	3	0	0	0	0	0	.333
2008 Sacramento	P.C.	OF	45	189	34	57	13	1	2	20	5	.302
2008 Oakland c............	A.L.	OF	29	62	10	18	3	0	1	9	2	.290
2009 Oakland	A.L.	OF	4	2	1	0	0	0	0	1	0	.000
2009 Sacramento d........	P.C.	OF	107	432	62	117	18	5	9	49	15	.271
2010 Portland	P.C.	OF	34	121	17	37	10	4	2	12	7	.306
2010 San Diego	N.L.	OF	99	284	41	77	15	2	9	36	8	.271
2011 Lake Elsinore	Calif.	OF	2	6	1	4	1	0	0	2	0	.667
2011 Tucson	P.C.	OF	7	17	0	2	1	0	0	0	0	.118
2011 San Diego e	N.L.	OF	111	307	38	85	13	2	5	19	11	.277
2012 San Diego	N.L.	OF	130	348	56	102	19	6	8	36	13	.293
Major League Totals	7 Yrs.		440	1147	168	322	59	10	25	110	36	.2815

a On disabled list from March 24 to October 15, 2007.
b Traded to Oakland Athletics for pitcher Marcus McBeth and player to be named later, April 27, 2007. Cincinnati Reds received pitcher Ben Jukich to complete trade, June 12, 2007.
c On disabled list from May 7 to July 19, 2008.
d Filed for free agency, November 9, 2009. Signed with San Diego Padres organization, December 17, 2009.
e On disabled list from August 4 to September 5, 2011.

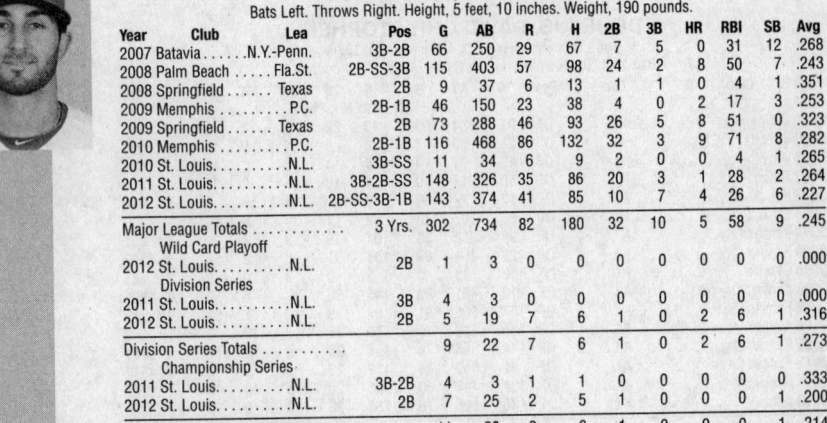

DESCALSO, DANIEL WILLIAM

Born, Redwood City, California, October 19, 1986.
Bats Left. Throws Right. Height, 5 feet, 10 inches. Weight, 190 pounds.

Year Club	Lea	Pos	G	AB	R	H	2B	3B	HR	RBI	SB	Avg
2007 Batavia......	N.Y.-Penn.	3B-2B	66	250	29	67	7	5	0	31	12	.268
2008 Palm Beach	Fla.St.	2B-SS-3B	115	403	57	98	24	2	8	50	7	.243
2008 Springfield	Texas	2B	9	37	6	13	1	1	0	4	1	.351
2009 Memphis	P.C.	2B-1B	46	150	23	38	4	0	2	17	3	.253
2009 Springfield	Texas	2B	73	288	46	93	26	5	8	51	0	.323
2010 Memphis	P.C.	2B-1B	116	468	86	132	32	3	9	71	8	.282
2010 St. Louis..........	N.L.	3B-SS	11	34	6	9	2	0	0	4	1	.265
2011 St. Louis..........	N.L.	3B-2B-SS	148	326	35	86	20	3	1	28	2	.264
2012 St. Louis..........	N.L.	2B-SS-3B-1B	143	374	41	85	10	7	4	26	6	.227
Major League Totals	3 Yrs.		302	734	82	180	32	10	5	58	9	.245
Wild Card Playoff												
2012 St. Louis..........N.L.		2B	1	3	0	0	0	0	0	0	0	.000
Division Series												
2011 St. Louis..........N.L.		3B	4	3	0	0	0	0	0	0	0	.000
2012 St. Louis..........N.L.		2B	5	19	7	6	1	0	2	6	1	.316
Division Series Totals			9	22	7	6	1	0	2	6	1	.273
Championship Series												
2011 St. Louis..........N.L.		3B-2B	4	3	1	1	0	0	0	0	0	.333
2012 St. Louis..........N.L.		2B	7	25	2	5	1	0	0	0	1	.200
Championship Series Totals			11	28	3	6	1	0	0	0	1	.214
World Series Record												
2011 St. Louis..........N.L.		3B-SS	5	3	2	2	0	0	0	0	0	.667

DESMOND, IAN M.

Born, Sarasota, Florida, September 20, 1985.
Bats Right. Throws Right. Height, 6 feet, 2 inches. Weight, 210 pounds.

Year Club	Lea	Pos	G	AB	R	H	2B	3B	HR	RBI	SB	Avg
2004 Expos.......	Gulf Coast	SS	55	216	28	49	11	0	1	27	13	.227
2004 Vermont.....	N.Y.-Penn.	SS	4	12	2	3	0	0	1	1	0	.250
2005 Potomac......	Carolina	SS	55	219	37	56	13	3	3	15	13	.256
2005 Savannah......	So.Atl.	SS	73	296	37	73	10	2	4	23	20	.247
2006 Potomac......	Carolina	SS	92	365	50	89	20	2	9	45	14	.244
2006 Harrisburg	Eastern	SS	37	121	8	22	4	1	0	3	4	.182
2007 Potomac......	Carolina	SS	129	458	69	121	30	4	13	45	27	.264
2008 Harrisburg	Eastern	SS	93	323	42	81	14	0	12	44	12	.251
2008 Nationals	Gulf Coast	SS	3	13	1	5	1	0	0	2	3	.385

Year Club	Lea	Pos	G	AB	R	H	2B	3B	HR	RBI	SB	Avg
2009 Harrisburg	Eastern	SS	42	170	29	52	12	1	6	18	13	.306
2009 Syracuse	Int.	SS-OF	55	178	25	63	12	2	1	14	8	.354
2009 Washington	N.L.	SS-2B-OF	21	82	9	23	7	2	4	12	1	.280
2010 Washington	N.L.	SS-OF	154	525	59	141	27	4	10	65	17	.269
2011 Washington	N.L.	SS	154	584	65	148	27	5	8	49	25	.253
2012 Washington a	N.L.	SS	130	513	72	150	33	2	25	73	21	.292
Major League Totals		4 Yrs.	459	1704	205	462	94	13	47	199	64	.271
Division Series												
2012 Washington	N.L.	SS	5	19	2	7	1	0	0	0	0	.368

a On disabled list from July 22 to August 17, 2012.

DICKERSON, CHRISTOPHER CHARLES (CHRIS)

Born, Hollywood, California, April 10, 1982.
Bats Left. Throws Left. Height, 6 feet, 3 inches. Weight, 225 pounds.

Year Club	Lea	Pos	G	AB	R	H	2B	3B	HR	RBI	SB	Avg
2003 Billings	Pioneer	OF	58	201	36	49	6	4	6	38	9	.244
2004 Potomac.	Carolina	OF	15	45	5	9	2	0	0	5	3	.200
2004 Dayton	Midwest	OF	84	314	50	95	15	3	4	34	27	.303
2005 Sarasota	Fla.St.	OF	119	436	68	103	17	7	11	43	19	.236
2006 Chattanooga	Southern	OF	115	389	65	94	21	7	12	48	21	.242
2007 Louisville	Int.	OF	104	354	58	92	11	6	13	44	23	.260
2007 Chattanooga	Southern	OF	30	114	11	31	4	1	1	11	7	.272
2008 Louisville	Int.	OF	97	349	65	100	16	9	11	53	26	.287
2008 Cincinnati	N.L.	OF	31	102	20	31	9	2	6	15	5	.304
2009 Louisville	Int.	OF	4	12	2	3	0	0	0	1	2	.250
2009 Cincinnati a	N.L.	OF	97	255	31	70	13	3	2	15	11	.275
2010 Louisville	Int.	OF	13	43	12	19	5	0	3	7	6	.442
2010 Cincinnati-Milwaukee b-c.	N.L.	OF	45	97	11	20	2	2	0	5	4	.206
2011 Scranton-WB	Int.	OF	57	212	33	51	10	1	2	16	18	.241
2011 New York d	A.L.	OF	60	50	9	13	2	0	1	7	4	.260
2012 Scranton-WB	Int.	OF	69	266	57	84	24	4	7	25	17	.316
2012 New York	A.L.	OF	25	14	5	4	0	0	2	5	3	.286
Major League Totals		5 Yrs.	258	518	76	138	26	7	11	47	27	.266
Division Series												
2011 New York	A.L.	OF	1	1	1	0	0	0	0	0	0	.000

a On disabled list from July 27 to August 11 and August 24 to September 30, 2009.
b On disabled list from April 30 to August 9, 2010.
c Traded to Milwaukee Brewers for outfielder Jim Edmonds, August 9, 2010.
d Traded to New York Yankees for pitcher Sergio Mitre, March 25, 2011.

DIRKS, ANDREW LEE (ANDY)

Born, Hutchinson, Kansas, January 24, 1986.
Bats Left. Throws Left. Height, 6 feet. Weight, 195 pounds.

Year Club	Lea	Pos	G	AB	R	H	2B	3B	HR	RBI	SB	Avg
2008 Tigers	Gulf Coast	OF	10	34	10	14	3	2	0	7	2	.412
2008 West Michigan	Midwest	OF	3	10	0	1	0	0	0	2	0	.100
2009 Erie	Eastern	OF	98	361	46	92	14	1	6	44	11	.255
2009 Lakeland	Fla.St.	OF	27	103	11	34	5	0	0	18	10	.330
2010 Erie	Eastern	OF	98	388	64	108	20	2	11	46	19	.278
2010 Toledo	Int.	OF	22	88	14	33	10	1	4	17	3	.375
2011 Toledo	Int.	OF	41	157	30	51	8	1	7	24	12	.325
2011 Detroit	A.L.	OF	78	219	34	55	13	0	7	28	5	.251
2012 Toledo	Int.	OF	10	37	4	8	1	0	2	5	2	.216
2012 Detroit a	A.L.	OF	88	314	56	101	18	5	8	35	1	.322
Major League Totals		2 Yrs.	166	533	90	156	31	5	15	63	6	.293
Division Series												
2012 Detroit	A.L.	OF	5	17	0	5	1	0	0	0	1	.294
Championship Series												
2011 Detroit	A.L.	OF	2	5	1	1	0	0	0	0	1	.200
2012 Detroit	A.L.	OF	4	18	0	4	1	0	0	1	0	.222
Championship Series Totals			6	23	1	5	1	0	0	1	1	.217
World Series Record												
2012 Detroit	A.L.	OF	4	9	0	1	0	0	0	0	0	.111

a On disabled list from May 31 to August 3, 2012.

DOBBS, GREGORY STUART (GREG)
Born, Los Angeles, California, July 2, 1978.
Bats Left. Throws Right. Height, 6 feet, 1 inch. Weight, 205 pounds.

Year	Club	Lea	Pos	G	AB	R	H	2B	3B	HR	RBI	SB	Avg
2001 San Bernardino	...	Calif.	OF	3	13	2	5	1	0	1	3	0	.385
2001 Everett	......	Northwest	1B-OF-3B	65	249	37	80	17	2	6	41	5	.321
2002 Wisconsin	....	Midwest	3B	86	320	43	88	16	2	10	48	13	.275
2002 San Antonio	....	Texas	OF-1B	27	96	13	35	2	0	5	15	1	.365
2003 San Antonio	....	Texas	3B	2	6	0	2	2	0	0	0	0	.333
2004 San Antonio	....	Texas	3B	51	203	25	66	14	4	5	34	5	.325
2004 Tacoma	....	P.C.	3B	67	255	28	69	9	2	8	31	4	.271
2004 Seattle	....	A.L.	3B	18	53	4	12	1	0	1	9	0	.226
2005 Tacoma	....	P.C.	1B-3B-OF	50	190	27	61	9	0	3	22	5	.321
2005 Seattle	....	A.L.	DH-1B-OF-3B	59	142	8	35	7	1	1	20	1	.246
2006 Tacoma	....	P.C.	3B-1B-OF	99	379	60	119	19	3	9	55	14	.314
2006 Seattle	....	A.L.	1B-OF-3B	23	27	4	10	3	1	0	3	0	.370
2007 Philadelphia a	......	N.L.	3B-OF-1B-2B	142	324	45	88	20	4	10	55	3	.272
2008 Philadelphia	......	N.L.	3B-OF-1B	128	226	30	68	14	1	9	40	3	.301
2009 Philadelphia b	......	N.L.	3B-OF-1B	97	154	15	38	6	0	5	20	1	.247
2010 Lehigh Valley	......	Int.	OF-3B	16	62	10	13	3	1	2	9	2	.210
2010 Philadelphia c	......	N.L.	3B-1B-OF	88	163	13	32	7	0	5	15	1	.196
2011 Florida d	....	N.L.	3B-OF-1B	134	411	38	113	23	0	8	49	0	.275
2012 Miami	....	N.L.	OF-3B-1B	120	319	26	91	13	2	5	39	4	.285
Major League Totals	....		9 Yrs.	809	1819	183	487	94	9	44	250	13	.268
Division Series													
2007 Philadelphia	......	N.L.	3B	3	3	0	0	0	0	0	0	0	.000
2008 Philadelphia	......	N.L.	3B	3	5	0	3	0	0	0	0	0	.600
2009 Philadelphia	......	N.L.	PH	3	3	0	0	0	0	0	0	0	.000
Division Series Totals	....			9	11	0	3	0	0	0	0	0	.273
Championship Series													
2008 Philadelphia	......	N.L.	3B	3	6	2	3	1	0	0	0	0	.500
2009 Philadelphia	......	N.L.	PH	2	1	0	0	0	0	0	0	0	.000
Championship Series Totals	......			5	7	2	3	1	0	0	0	0	.429
World Series Record													
2008 Philadelphia	......	N.L.	DH	2	3	0	1	0	0	0	0	0	.333

a Claimed by Philadelphia Phillies on waivers, January 16, 2007.
b On disabled list from August 22 to September 16, 2009.
c Filed for free agency, October 28, 2010. Signed with Florida Marlins organization, January 31, 2011.
d Filed for free agency, October 30, 2011, re-signed with Florida Marlins, January 5, 2012.

DONALDSON, JOSHUA ADAM (JOSH)
Born, Pensacola, Florida, December 8, 1985.
Bats Right. Throws Right. Height, 6 feet. Weight, 220 pounds.

Year	Club	Lea	Pos	G	AB	R	H	2B	3B	HR	RBI	SB	Avg
2007 Cubs	....	Arizona	C	4	11	1	2	2	0	0	0	0	.182
2007 Boise	......	Northwest	C	49	162	37	56	11	2	9	35	6	.346
2008 Stockton	....	Calif.	C-3B-1B	47	188	37	62	13	2	9	39	0	.330
2008 Peoria a	......	Midwest	C	63	235	27	51	13	0	6	23	7	.217
2009 Midland	......	Texas	C-3B-1B	124	455	67	123	37	1	9	91	7	.270
2010 Sacramento	......	P.C.	C-3B-1B-OF	86	294	52	70	14	1	18	67	3	.238
2010 Oakland	....	A.L.	C-1B	14	32	1	5	1	0	1	4	0	.156
2011 Sacramento	......	P.C.	C-3B-2B-OF	115	444	79	116	28	0	17	70	13	.261
2012 Sacramento	......	P.C.	3B-C-2B-SS	51	209	38	70	12	2	13	45	5	.335
2012 Oakland	....	A.L.	3B-C-1B	75	274	34	66	16	0	9	33	4	.241
Major League Totals	....		2 Yrs.	89	306	35	71	17	0	10	37	4	.232
Division Series													
2012 Oakland	....	A.L.	3B	5	17	1	5	1	0	0	0	0	.294

a Traded by Chicago Cubs to Oakland Athletics with pitcher Sean Gallagher, outfielder Matt Murton and outfielder Eric Patterson for pitcher Rich Harden and pitcher Chad Gaudin, July 8, 2008.

DOUMIT, RYAN MATTHEW
Born, Moses Lake, Washington, April 3, 1981.
Bats Both. Throws Right. Height, 6 feet. Weight, 200 pounds.

Year	Club	Lea	Pos	G	AB	R	H	2B	3B	HR	RBI	SB	Avg
1999 Pirates	....	Gulf Coast	C	29	85	17	24	5	0	1	7	4	.282
2000 Williamsport	.....	N.Y.-Penn.	C	66	246	25	77	15	5	2	40	2	.313
2001 Altoona	....	Eastern	C	2	4	0	1	0	0	0	2	0	.250

Year Club	Lea	Pos	G	AB	R	H	2B	3B	HR	RBI	SB	Avg
2001 Pirates	Gulf Coast	C	7	17	2	4	2	0	0	3	0	.235
2001 Hickory.	So.Atl.	C	39	148	14	40	6	0	2	14	2	.270
2002 Hickory.	So.Atl.	C	68	258	46	83	14	1	6	47	3	.322
2003 Lynchburg	Carolina	C	127	458	75	126	38	1	11	77	4	.275
2004 Altoona.	Eastern	C	67	221	31	58	20	0	10	34	0	.262
2005 Indianapolis	Int.	C-OF	51	165	41	57	11	0	12	35	1	.345
2005 Pittsburgh	N.L.	C-OF	75	231	25	59	13	1	6	35	2	.255
2006 Pirates	Gulf Coast	C-1B	5	14	1	0	0	0	0	0	0	.000
2006 Altoona.	Eastern	C-1B	4	15	4	5	3	0	0	4	0	.333
2006 Indianapolis	Int.	C	6	22	3	7	1	1	0	7	0	.318
2006 Pittsburgh a	N.L.	1B-C	61	149	15	31	9	0	6	17	0	.208
2007 Indianapolis	Int.	C	16	53	15	22	4	0	4	20	3	.415
2007 Pittsburgh b	N.L.	OF-C-1B	83	252	33	69	19	2	9	32	1	.274
2008 Altoona.	Eastern	C	3	7	0	3	0	0	0	0	0	.429
2008 Pittsburgh c	N.L.	C-1B	116	431	71	137	34	0	15	69	2	.318
2009 Pirates	Gulf Coast	C	2	7	0	0	0	0	0	0	0	.000
2009 Indianapolis	Int.	C	5	17	1	2	0	0	0	0	0	.118
2009 Pittsburgh d	N.L.	C-OF	75	280	31	70	16	0	10	38	4	.250
2010 Indianapolis	Int.	OF-C	4	12	2	2	1	0	1	2	0	.167
2010 Pittsburgh e	N.L.	C-OF-1B	124	406	42	102	22	1	13	45	1	.251
2011 Bradenton	Fla.St.	C	5	14	1	2	0	0	0	1	0	.143
2011 Indianapolis	Int.	C	8	26	4	6	1	1	0	3	0	.231
2011 Pittsburgh f-g	N.L.	C	77	218	17	66	12	1	8	30	0	.303
2012 Minnesota	A.L.	C-OF-1B	134	484	56	133	34	1	18	75	0	.275
Major League Totals	8 Yrs.		745	2451	290	667	159	6	85	341	10	.272

a On disabled list from April 12 to May 3 and June 5 to August 23, 2006.
b On disabled list from August 13 to September 8 and September 9 to November 13, 2007.
c On disabled list from May 14 to June 6, 2008.
d On disabled list from April 20 to July 10, 2009.
e On disabled list from July 22 to August 7, 2010.
f On disabled list from May 30 to August 3, 2011.
g Filed for free agency, October 31, 2011. Signed with Minnesota Twins, November 23, 2011.

DOWNS, RUSSELL MATT (MATT)

Born, Tuscaloosa, Alabama, March 19, 1984.
Bats Right. Throws Right. Height, 6 feet, 2 inches. Weight, 185 pounds.

Year Club	Lea	Pos	G	AB	R	H	2B	3B	HR	RBI	SB	Avg
2006 Giants.	Arizona	3B	46	168	34	52	16	4	0	29	6	.310
2007 Salem-Keizer .	Northwest	1B-2B-3B	73	287	68	97	33	0	8	48	16	.338
2008 San Jose	Calif.	2B-3B-SS-OF	109	437	74	133	30	1	17	75	24	.304
2008 Fresno	P.C.	2B-OF-SS	22	86	10	21	5	0	3	7	1	.244
2009 San Francisco	N.L.	2B	17	53	6	9	2	0	1	2	1	.170
2009 Fresno	P.C.	2B-3B-OF-SS	109	424	68	127	33	3	14	74	8	.300
2010 Fresno	P.C.	3B-2B-SS	56	197	37	50	9	1	7	28	3	.254
2010 Giants.	Arizona	3B-SS	2	7	1	2	1	0	0	2	0	.286
2010 Round Rock.	P.C.	2B	6	19	0	2	1	0	0	2	1	.105
2010 San Fran.-Houston a	N.L.	2B-3B-SS	40	97	8	21	7	0	1	7	0	.216
2011 Houston	N.L.	2B-3B-1B-OF	106	199	29	55	18	0	10	41	0	.276
2012 Oklahoma.	P.C.	1B-2B-3B-OF	24	90	14	24	2	0	3	15	3	.267
2012 Houston b	N.L.	1B-3B-OF-2B	91	178	15	36	4	1	8	16	2	.202
Major League Totals	4 Yrs.		254	527	58	121	31	1	20	66	3	.230

a Claimed on waivers by Houston Astros, August 25, 2010.
b Filed for free agency, November 1, 2012.

DREW, STEPHEN ORIS

Born, Hahira, Georgia, March 16, 1983.
Bats Left. Throws Right. Height, 6 feet, 1 inch. Weight, 185 pounds.

Year Club	Lea	Pos	G	AB	R	H	2B	3B	HR	RBI	SB	Avg
2005 Tennessee	Southern	SS	27	101	11	22	5	0	4	13	2	.218
2006 Tucson	P.C.	SS	83	342	55	97	16	3	13	51	5	.284
2006 Arizona.	N.L.	SS	59	209	27	66	13	7	5	23	2	.316
2007 Arizona.	N.L.	SS	150	543	60	129	28	4	12	60	9	.238
2008 Arizona.	N.L.	SS	152	611	91	178	44	11	21	67	3	.291
2009 Reno	P.C.	SS	2	9	0	3	0	1	0	1	0	.333
2009 Arizona a	N.L.	SS	135	533	71	139	29	12	12	65	5	.261
2010 Arizona.	N.L.	SS	151	565	83	157	33	12	15	61	10	.278
2011 Arizona b	N.L.	SS	86	321	44	81	21	5	5	45	4	.252

Year Club	Lea	Pos	G	AB	R	H	2B	3B	HR	RBI	SB	Avg
2012 Mobile .... Southern		SS	2	5	0	1	0	0	0	0	0	.200
2012 Reno	.P.C.	SS	9	36	6	9	1	1	2	5	0	.250
2012 Arizona...........	.N.L.	SS	40	135	17	26	8	1	2	12	0	.193
2012 Oakland c-d-e.....	.A.L.	SS	39	152	21	38	5	0	5	16	1	.250
Major League Totals		7 Yrs.	812	3069	414	814	181	52	77	349	34	.265
Division Series												
2007 Arizona...........	.N.L.	SS	3	14	4	7	1	1	2	4	1	.500
2012 Oakland	.A.L.	SS	5	19	0	4	2	0	0	1	0	.211
Division Series Totals			8	33	4	11	3	1	2	5	1	.333
Championship Series												
2007 Arizona...........	.N.L.	SS	4	17	2	5	0	0	0	0	0	.294

a On disabled list from April 25 to May 12, 2009.
b On disabled list from July 21 to October 31, 2011.
c On disabled list from March 26 to June 27, 2012.
d Traded to Oakland Athletics for infielder Sean Jamieson, August 21, 2012.
e Filed for free agency, November 3, 2012. Signed with Boston Red Sox, December 26, 2012.

DUDA, LUCAS CHRISTOPHER
Born, Fontana, California, February 3, 1986.
Bats Left. Throws Right. Height, 6 feet, 5 inches. Weight, 255 pounds.

Year Club	Lea	Pos	G	AB	R	H	2B	3B	HR	RBI	SB	Avg
2007 Brooklyn........	N.Y.-Penn.	1B-OF	67	234	32	70	20	3	4	32	3	.299
2008 St. Lucie...........	.Fla.St.	1B-OF	133	483	58	127	26	3	11	66	2	.263
2009 Binghamton	Eastern	1B-OF	110	395	49	111	29	1	9	53	2	.281
2010 Binghamton	Eastern	OF-1B	45	161	30	46	17	0	6	34	1	.286
2010 Buffalo	Int.	OF-1B	70	264	44	83	23	2	17	53	0	.314
2010 New York	.N.L.	OF	29	84	11	17	6	0	4	13	0	.202
2011 Buffalo	Int.	OF-1B	38	129	22	39	8	0	10	24	0	.302
2011 New York	.N.L.	OF-1B	100	301	38	88	21	3	10	50	1	.292
2012 Buffalo	Int.	OF-1B	25	96	12	25	4	0	3	8	0	.260
2012 New York	.N.L.	OF-1B	121	401	43	96	15	0	15	57	1	.239
Major League Totals		3 Yrs.	250	786	92	201	42	3	29	120	2	.256

DUNCAN, DAVID SHELLEY (SHELLEY)
Born, Tucson, Arizona, September 29, 1979.
Bats Right. Throws Right. Height, 6 feet, 5 inches. Weight, 225 pounds.

Year Club	Lea	Pos	G	AB	R	H	2B	3B	HR	RBI	SB	Avg
2001 Staten Island	N.Y.-Penn.	DH	70	273	43	67	17	2	8	39	5	.245
2002 Greensboro	So.Atl.	OF	101	356	58	95	23	2	14	56	15	.267
2003 Tampa	.Fla.St.	OF	91	330	42	87	19	2	8	47	5	.264
2004 Tampa	.Fla.St.	1B-OF	123	424	65	105	27	1	19	78	6	.248
2005 Trenton...........	Eastern	1B	142	537	86	129	28	2	34	92	3	.240
2006 Trenton...........	Eastern	1B-OF	92	351	47	90	24	0	19	61	3	.256
2006 Columbus...........	Int.	OF	12	43	1	8	1	0	1	4	0	.186
2007 Scranton/WB	Int.	OF-1B	91	336	58	99	18	1	25	79	2	.295
2007 New York	A.L.	DH-OF-1B	34	74	16	19	1	0	7	17	0	.257
2008 New York	A.L.	1B-OF	23	57	7	10	3	0	1	6	0	.175
2008 Yankees	Gulf Coast	DH	2	7	0	0	0	0	0	0	0	.000
2008 Scranton/WB	Int.	OF-1B	58	205	38	49	14	0	12	44	6	.239
2009 Scranton/WB	Int.	OF-1B	123	452	85	125	30	1	30	99	2	.277
2009 New York	A.L.	OF	11	15	1	3	0	0	0	1	0	.200
2010 Columbus...........	Int.	OF-1B	38	146	21	44	11	0	6	34	0	.301
2010 Cleveland a.........	A.L.	OF-1B	85	229	29	53	10	0	11	36	1	.231
2011 Columbus...........	Int.	OF-1B	33	109	20	22	3	0	5	19	1	.202
2011 Cleveland	A.L.	OF-1B	76	223	29	58	17	0	11	47	0	.260
2012 Cleveland	A.L.	OF-1B	81	232	29	47	10	0	11	31	1	.203
Major League Totals		6 Yrs.	310	830	111	190	41	0	41	138	2	.229
Division Series												
2007 New York	A.L.	1B	3	4	1	2	0	0	0	0	0	.500

a Filed for free agency, November 25, 2009. Signed with Cleveland Indians organization, January 4, 2010.

DUNN, ADAM TROY

Born, Houston, Texas, November 9, 1979.
Bats Left. Throws Right. Height, 6 feet, 6 inches. Weight, 275 pounds.

Year Club	Lea	Pos	G	AB	R	H	2B	3B	HR	RBI	SB	Avg
1998 Billings............Pioneer		OF	34	125	26	36	3	1	4	13	4	.288
1999 Rockford.........Midwest		OF	92	313	62	96	16	2	11	44	21	.307
2000 Dayton...........Midwest		OF	122	420	101	118	29	1	16	79	24	.281
2001 Chattanooga...... Southern		OF	39	140	30	48	9	0	12	31	6	.343
2001 Louisville.............Int.		OF	55	210	44	69	13	0	20	53	5	.329
2001 Cincinnati............N.L.		OF	66	244	54	64	18	1	19	43	4	.262
2002 Cincinnati...........N.L.		OF-1B	158	535	84	133	28	2	26	71	19	.249
2003 Cincinnati a..........N.L.		OF-1B	116	381	70	82	12	1	27	57	8	.215
2004 Cincinnati...........N.L.		OF-1B	161	568	105	151	34	0	46	102	6	.266
2005 Cincinnati...........N.L.		OF-1B	160	543	107	134	35	2	40	101	4	.247
2006 Cincinnati...........N.L.		OF-1B	160	561	99	131	24	0	40	92	7	.234
2007 Cincinnati...........N.L.		OF	152	522	101	138	27	2	40	106	9	.264
2008 Cincinnati-Arizona b-c . N.L.		OF-1B	158	517	79	122	23	0	40	100	2	.236
2009 Washington..........N.L.		OF-1B	159	546	81	146	29	0	38	105	0	.267
2010 Washington d.........N.L.		1B	158	558	85	145	36	2	38	103	0	.260
2011 Chicago.............A.L.		DH-1B-OF	122	415	36	66	16	0	11	42	0	.159
2012 Chicago.............A.L.		DH-1B-OF	151	539	87	110	19	0	41	96	2	.204
Major League Totals........... 12 Yrs.			1721	5929	988	1422	301	10	406	1018	61	.240

a On disabled list from August 16 to October 2, 2003.
b Traded to Arizona Diamondbacks for pitcher Dallas Buck and two players to be named later, August 12, 2008. To complete trade, Cincinnati Reds received catcher Wilkin Castillo on August 14, 2008 and pitcher Micah Owings on September 10, 2008.
c Filed for free agency, November 1, 2008. Signed with Washington Nationals, February 11, 2009.
d Filed for free agency, November 1, 2010. Signed with Chicago White Sox, December 3, 2010.

DYSON, JARROD MARTEL

Born, McComb, Mississippi, August 15, 1984.
Bats Left. Throws Right. Height, 5 feet, 9 inches. Weight, 165 pounds.

Year Club	Lea	Pos	G	AB	R	H	2B	3B	HR	RBI	SB	Avg
2006 Royals...........Arizona		OF	51	161	40	44	4	6	0	19	19	.273
2007 Burlington........Midwest		OF	10	37	6	10	1	0	0	0	3	.270
2008 Wilmington....... Carolina		OF	93	288	40	75	8	0	0	24	39	.260
2009 Burlington.......Midwest		OF	17	67	14	23	2	1	0	5	9	.343
2009 NW Arkansas....... Texas		OF	63	248	38	64	7	4	0	14	37	.258
2010 Royals...........Arizona		OF	6	25	4	13	1	1	0	6	3	.520
2010 Wilmington...... Carolina		OF	12	49	7	16	6	2	0	9	5	.327
2010 NW Arkansas....... Texas		OF	7	25	6	6	0	0	0	6	3	.240
2010 Omaha..............P.C.		OF	46	195	33	53	10	1	1	19	13	.272
2010 Kansas City.........A.L.		OF	18	57	11	12	4	2	1	5	9	.211
2011 Omaha..............P.C.		OF	83	319	69	89	10	3	3	26	38	.279
2011 Kansas City.........A.L.		OF	26	44	8	9	1	0	0	3	11	.205
2012 Omaha..............P.C.		OF	15	63	12	21	3	3	0	5	7	.333
2012 Kansas City.........A.L.		OF	102	292	52	76	8	5	0	9	30	.260
Major League Totals........... 3 Yrs.			146	393	71	97	13	7	1	17	50	.247

EATON, ADAM C.

Born, Springfield, Ohio, December 6, 1988.
Bats Left. Throws Left. Height, 5 feet, 8 inches. Weight, 185 pounds.

Year Club	Lea	Pos	G	AB	R	H	2B	3B	HR	RBI	SB	Avg
2010 Missoula.........Pioneer		OF	68	226	48	87	14	4	7	37	20	.385
2011 Visalia...........Calif.		OF	65	244	54	81	15	3	6	39	24	.332
2011 Mobile.......... Southern		OF	56	212	31	64	7	4	4	28	10	.302
2012 Mobile......... Southern		OF	11	40	11	12	1	0	0	3	6	.300
2012 Reno...............P.C.		OF	119	488	119	186	46	5	7	45	38	.381
2012 Arizona............N.L.		OF	22	85	19	22	3	2	2	5	2	.259

ELLIS, ANDREW JAMES (A.J.)

Born, Cape Girardeau, Missouri, April 9, 1981.
Bats Right. Throws Right. Height, 6 feet, 3 inches. Weight, 225 pounds.

Year	Club	Lea	Pos	G	AB	R	H	2B	3B	HR	RBI	SB	Avg
2003	South Georgia	So.Atl.	C-1B	3	6	0	0	0	0	0	0	0	.000
2004	Vero Beach	Fla.St.	C-1B	40	114	15	25	4	0	2	22	1	.219
2005	Vero Beach	Fla.St.	C	57	176	27	45	8	0	3	22	1	.256
2006	Jacksonville	Southern	C	81	252	34	63	9	1	0	21	2	.250
2007	Jacksonville	Southern	C-1B-OF	109	357	59	96	22	2	8	57	1	.269
2008	Las Vegas	P.C.	C-1B	84	274	44	88	17	4	4	59	0	.321
2008	Los Angeles	N.L.	C	4	3	1	0	0	0	0	0	0	.000
2009	Albuquerque	P.C.	C	90	283	48	89	13	2	0	39	2	.314
2009	Los Angeles	N.L.	C	8	10	0	1	0	0	0	1	0	.100
2010	Albuquerque	P.C.	C	18	61	11	16	5	1	0	7	1	.262
2010	Los Angeles	N.L.	C	44	108	6	30	5	0	0	16	0	.278
2011	Albuquerque	P.C.	C-1B	59	184	36	56	15	0	2	28	0	.304
2011	Los Angeles	N.L.	C	31	85	8	23	1	1	2	11	0	.271
2012	Los Angeles	N.L.	C	133	423	44	114	20	1	13	52	0	.270
Major League Totals			5 Yrs.	220	629	59	168	26	2	15	80	0	.267

ELLIS, MARK WILLIAM

Born, Rapid City, South Dakota, June 6, 1977.
Bats Right. Throws Right. Height, 5 feet, 11 inches. Weight, 195 pounds.

Year	Club	Lea	Pos	G	AB	R	H	2B	3B	HR	RBI	SB	Avg
1999	Spokane	Northwest	SS	71	281	67	92	14	0	7	47	21	.327
2000	Wilmington	Carolina	SS-2B	132	484	83	146	27	4	6	62	25	.302
2000	Wichita	Texas	2B	7	22	4	7	1	0	0	4	1	.318
2001	Sacramento a	P.C.	SS	132	472	71	129	38	0	10	53	21	.273
2002	Sacramento	P.C.	SS	21	84	14	25	10	1	0	5	4	.298
2002	Oakland	A.L.	2B-SS-3B	98	345	58	94	16	4	6	35	4	.272
2003	Oakland	A.L.	2B	154	553	78	137	31	5	9	52	6	.248
2004	Oakland b	A.L.					INJURED—Did Not Play						
2005	Oakland	A.L.	2B-SS-1B	122	434	76	137	21	5	13	52	1	.316
2006	Sacramento	P.C.	2B	4	12	1	2	0	0	0	2	0	.167
2006	Oakland c	A.L.	2B-1B	124	441	64	110	25	1	11	52	4	.249
2007	Oakland	A.L.	2B	150	583	84	161	33	3	19	76	9	.276
2008	Oakland d	A.L.	2B	117	442	55	103	20	3	12	41	14	.233
2009	Stockton	Calif.	2B	2	4	0	0	0	0	0	0	0	.000
2009	Sacramento	P.C.	2B	8	33	2	6	1	0	0	3	0	.182
2009	Oakland e	A.L.	2B	105	377	52	99	23	0	10	61	10	.263
2010	Stockton	Calif.	2B	2	5	0	1	0	0	0	1	0	.200
2010	Sacramento	P.C.	2B	1	4	0	1	0	0	0	0	0	.250
2010	Oakland f	A.L.	2B	124	436	45	127	24	0	5	49	7	.291
2011	Sacramento	P.C.	2B	3	10	0	2	1	0	0	1	0	.200
2011	Oakland	A.L.	2B-1B	62	217	21	47	11	1	1	16	7	.217
2011	Colorado g-h-i	N.L.	2B	70	263	34	72	13	0	6	25	7	.274
2012	Rancho Cucamonga	Calif.	2B	4	14	3	4	0	0	0	3	0	.286
2012	Los Angeles j	N.L.	2B	110	415	62	107	21	1	7	31	5	.258
Major League Totals			10 Yrs.	1236	4506	629	1194	238	23	99	490	74	.265
Division Series													
2002	Oakland	A.L.	2B	5	19	1	7	2	0	1	4	0	.368
2003	Oakland	A.L.	2B	5	17	2	2	0	0	0	0	0	.118
2006	Oakland	A.L.	2B	2	7	0	2	0	0	0	0	0	.286
Division Series Totals				12	43	3	11	2	0	1	4	0	.256

a Traded to Oakland Athletics by Kansas City Royals with outfielder Johnny Damon and player to be named later for pitcher Roberto Hernandez, catcher A.J. Hinch, infielder Angel Berroa and cash, January 8, 2001.
b On disabled list from March 26 to October 20, 2004.
c On disabled list from June 1 to June 30, 2006.
d On disabled list from September 21 to November 14, 2008.
e On disabled list from April 29 to June 28, 2009.
f On disabled list from April 21 to May 22, 2010.
g On disabled list from June 7 to June 22, 2011.
h Traded to Colorado Rockies for pitcher Bruce Billings, cash and player to be named later, June 30, 2011. Oakland Athletics received outfielder Eliezer Mesa to complete trade, September 30, 2011.
i Filed for free agency, October 30, 2011. Signed with Los Angeles Dodgers, November 14, 2011.
j On disabled list from May 19 to July 4, 2012.

ELLSBURY, JACOBY McCABE

Born, Madras, Oregon, September 11, 1983.
Bats Left. Throws Left. Height, 6 feet, 1 inch. Weight, 185 pounds.

Year	Club	Lea	Pos	G	AB	R	H	2B	3B	HR	RBI	SB	Avg
2005	Lowell	N.Y.-Penn.	OF	35	139	28	44	3	5	1	19	23	.317
2006	Wilmington	Carolina	OF	61	244	35	73	7	5	4	32	25	.299
2006	Portland	Eastern	OF	50	198	29	61	10	3	3	19	16	.308
2007	Portland	Eastern	OF	17	73	16	33	10	2	0	13	8	.452
2007	Pawtucket	Int.	OF	87	363	66	108	14	5	2	28	33	.298
2007	Boston	A.L.	OF	33	116	20	41	7	1	3	18	9	.353
2008	Boston	A.L.	OF	145	554	98	155	22	7	9	47	*50	.280
2009	Boston	A.L.	OF	153	624	94	188	27	*10	8	60	*70	.301
2010	Red Sox	Gulf Coast	OF	3	8	3	2	0	0	0	0	1	.250
2010	Portland	Eastern	OF	2	7	2	3	1	0	0	0	1	.429
2010	Pawtucket	Int.	OF	4	17	5	8	1	0	0	2	0	.471
2010	Boston a.	A.L.	OF	18	78	10	15	4	0	0	5	7	.192
2011	Boston	A.L.	OF	158	660	119	212	46	5	32	105	39	.321
2012	Red Sox	Gulf Coast	OF	4	10	3	2	1	0	1	3	0	.200
2012	Portland	Eastern	OF	2	9	1	2	1	0	0	0	0	.222
2012	Pawtucket	Int.	OF	2	8	1	1	0	0	0	0	0	.125
2012	Boston b	A.L.	OF	74	303	43	82	18	0	4	26	14	.271
Major League Totals		6 Yrs.		581	2335	384	693	124	23	56	261	189	.297
Division Series													
2007	Boston	A.L.	OF	2	1	1	0	0	0	0	0	0	.000
2008	Boston	A.L.	OF	4	18	2	6	3	0	0	6	3	.333
2009	Boston	A.L.	OF	3	12	2	3	0	1	0	0	0	.250
Division Series Totals				9	31	5	9	3	1	0	6	3	.290
Championship Series													
2007	Boston	A.L.	OF	5	8	3	2	0	0	0	1	1	.250
2008	Boston	A.L.	OF	4	14	0	0	0	0	0	1	0	.000
Championship Series Totals				9	22	3	2	0	0	0	2	1	.091
World Series Record													
2007	Boston	A.L.	OF	4	16	4	7	4	0	0	3	1	.438

a On disabled list from April 12 to May 22 and May 28 to August 4 and August 14 to November 8, 2010.
b On disabled list from April 14 to July 13, 2012.

ENCARNACION, EDWIN ELPIDIO

Born, La Romana, Dominican Republic, January 7, 1983.
Bats Right. Throws Right. Height, 6 feet, 1 inch. Weight, 215 pounds.

Year	Club	Lea	Pos	G	AB	R	H	2B	3B	HR	RBI	SB	Avg
2000	Rangers	Gulf Coast	3B	51	177	31	55	6	3	0	36	3	.311
2001	Dayton	Midwest	3B	9	37	2	6	2	0	1	6	0	.162
2001	Billings........	Pioneer	3B	52	211	27	55	8	2	5	26	8	.261
2001	Savannah a	So.Atl.	3B	45	170	23	52	9	2	4	25	3	.306
2002	Dayton	Midwest	3B-SS	136	517	80	146	32	4	17	73	25	.282
2003	Potomac......	Carolina	3B	58	215	40	69	15	1	6	29	7	.321
2003	Chattanooga...	Southern	3B-SS	67	254	40	69	13	1	5	36	8	.272
2004	Chattanooga...	Southern	3B	120	469	73	132	35	1	13	76	17	.281
2005	Louisville	Int.	3B	78	290	44	91	23	0	15	54	7	.314
2005	Cincinnati........	N.L.	3B	69	211	25	49	16	0	9	31	3	.232
2006	Louisville.........	Int.	3B-1B	10	36	6	11	3	0	1	1	0	.306
2006	Cincinnati b	N.L.	3B-1B	117	406	60	112	33	1	15	72	6	.276
2007	Louisville	Int.	3B	11	46	12	19	3	0	3	7	1	.413
2007	Cincinnati........	N.L.	3B	139	502	66	145	25	1	16	76	8	.289
2008	Cincinnati........	N.L.	3B	146	506	75	127	29	1	26	68	1	.251
2009	Louisville	Int.	3B	11	37	5	10	1	0	2	8	0	.270
2009	Cincinnati........	N.L.	3B	43	139	10	29	6	1	5	16	1	.209
2009	Toronto c-d-e	A.L.	3B	42	154	25	37	5	1	8	23	1	.240
2010	Dunedin	Fla.St.	3B	3	10	2	1	0	0	1	1	0	.100
2010	Las Vegas	P.C.	3B	7	32	9	14	2	0	3	13	0	.438
2010	Toronto f-g-h	A.L.	3B	96	332	47	81	16	0	21	51	1	.244
2011	Toronto	A.L.	DH-3B-1B	134	481	70	131	36	0	17	55	8	.272
2012	Toronto	A.L.	DH-1B-OF-3B	151	542	93	152	24	0	42	110	13	.280
Major League Totals		8 Yrs.		937	3273	471	863	190	5	159	502	42	.264

a Traded by Texas Rangers to Cincinnati Reds with outfielder Ruben Mateo for pitcher Rob Bell, June 15, 2001.
b On disabled list from June 7 to July 6, 2006.
c On disabled list from April 28 to July 3, 2009.
d Traded to Toronto Blue Jays with pitcher Josh Roenicke and pitcher Zach Stewart for infielder Scott Rolen, July 31, 2009.

e On disabled list from August 21 to September 5, 2009.
f On disabled list from April 15 to May 18 and August 29 to September 13, 2010.
g Claimed on waivers by Oakland Athletics, November 12, 2010.
h Not offered contract, December 2, 2010. Signed with Toronto Blue Jays, December 16, 2010.

ESCOBAR, ALCIDES
Born, Lasabana, Venezuela, December 16, 1986.
Bats Right. Throws Right. Height, 6 feet, 1 inch. Weight, 180 pounds.

Year Club	Lea	Pos	G	AB	R	H	2B	3B	HR	RBI	SB	Avg
2004 Helena	Pioneer	SS	67	231	38	65	8	0	2	24	20	.281
2005 West Virginia	So.Atl.	SS	127	520	80	141	25	8	2	36	30	.271
2006 Brevard County	Fla.St.	SS	87	350	47	90	9	1	2	33	28	.257
2007 Brevard County	Fla.St.	SS	63	268	37	87	8	3	0	25	18	.325
2007 Huntsville	Southern	SS	62	226	27	64	5	4	1	28	4	.283
2008 Huntsville	Southern	SS	131	546	95	179	24	5	8	76	34	.328
2008 Milwaukee	N.L.	SS	9	4	2	2	0	0	0	0	0	.500
2009 Nashville	P.C.	SS-2B	109	430	76	128	24	6	4	34	42	.298
2009 Milwaukee	N.L.	SS	38	125	20	38	3	1	1	11	4	.304
2010 Milwaukee a	N.L.	SS-OF	145	506	57	119	14	10	4	41	10	.235
2011 Kansas City	A.L.	SS	158	548	69	139	21	8	4	46	26	.254
2012 Kansas City	A.L.	SS	155	605	68	177	30	7	5	52	35	.293
Major League Totals		5 Yrs.	505	1788	216	475	68	26	14	150	75	.266

a Traded to Kansas City Royals with outfielder Lorenzo Cain, pitcher Jeremy Jeffress and pitcher Jake Odorizzi for outfielder Yuniesky Betancourt and pitcher Zack Greinke, December 19, 2010.

ESCOBAR, EDUARDO JOSE
Born, Villa de Cura, Venezuela, January 5, 1989.
Bats Both. Throws Right. Height, 5 feet, 10 inches. Weight, 165 pounds.

Year Club	Lea	Pos	G	AB	R	H	2B	3B	HR	RBI	SB	Avg
2008 Great Falls	Pioneer	SS	6	24	6	10	2	1	1	4	1	.417
2008 Kannapolis	So.Atl.	SS-2B	60	243	37	65	6	1	0	22	4	.267
2009 Kannapolis	So.Atl.	SS-2B	128	464	64	119	10	7	3	41	20	.256
2010 Winston-Salem	Carolina	SS	87	368	57	105	18	8	3	39	8	.285
2010 Birmingham	Southern	SS	49	202	22	53	8	3	3	22	3	.262
2011 Charlotte	Int.	SS-2B	137	489	55	130	23	4	4	49	13	.266
2011 Chicago	A.L.	SS-2B	9	7	0	2	0	0	0	0	0	.286
2012 Rochester	Int.	3B-SS-2B	35	138	19	30	3	3	1	9	3	.217
2012 Chicago-Minnesota a	A.L.	3B-2B-SS-OF	50	131	18	28	4	1	0	9	3	.214
Major League Totals		2 Yrs.	59	138	18	30	4	1	0	9	3	.217

a Traded to Minnesota Twins with pitcher Pedro Hernandez for pitcher Francisco Liriano, July 29, 2012.

ESCOBAR, YUNEL
Born, Havana, Cuba, November 2, 1982.
Bats Right. Throws Right. Height, 6 feet, 2 inches. Weight, 200 pounds.

Year Club	Lea	Pos	G	AB	R	H	2B	3B	HR	RBI	SB	Avg
2005 Danville	Appal.	SS	8	30	9	12	2	1	2	8	0	.400
2005 Rome	So.Atl.	SS	48	198	30	62	13	3	4	19	0	.313
2006 Mississippi	Southern	SS-3B-2B	121	428	55	113	21	4	2	45	7	.264
2007 Richmond	Int.	SS	46	180	20	60	10	3	2	29	7	.333
2007 Atlanta	N.L.	SS-3B-2B	94	319	54	104	25	0	5	28	5	.326
2008 Atlanta	N.L.	SS	136	514	71	148	24	2	10	60	2	.288
2009 Atlanta	N.L.	SS	141	528	89	158	26	2	14	76	5	.299
2010 Gwinnett	Int.	SS	1	3	1	2	0	0	0	0	0	.667
2010 Atlanta	N.L.	SS	75	261	28	62	12	0	0	19	5	.238
2010 Toronto a-b	A.L.	SS	60	236	32	65	7	0	4	16	1	.275
2011 Toronto c	A.L.	SS	133	513	77	149	24	3	11	48	3	.290
2012 Toronto d-e	A.L.	SS	145	558	58	141	22	1	9	51	5	.253
Major League Totals		6 Yrs.	784	2929	409	827	140	8	53	298	26	.282

a On disabled list from April 30 to May 15, 2010.
b Traded to Toronto Blue Jays with pitcher Jo-Jo Reyes for infielder Alex Gonzalez, pitcher Tim Collins and infielder Tyler Pastornicky, July 14, 2010.
c On disabled list from September 11 to September 29, 2011.
d Traded to Miami Marlins with pitcher Henderson Alvarez, infielder Adeiny Hechavarria, catcher Jeff Mathis, pitcher Anthony De Sclafani, outfielder Jake Marisnick and pitcher Justin Nicolino for outfielder Emilio Bonifacio, catcher John Buck, pitcher Mark Buehrle, pitcher Josh Johnson and infielder Jose Reyes, November 19, 2012.
e Traded to Tampa Bay Rays for infielder Derek Dietrich, December 4, 2012.

ESPINOSA, DANIEL RICHARD (DANNY)

Born, Santa Ana, California, April 25, 1987.
Bats Both. Throws Right. Height, 6 feet. Weight, 190 pounds.

Year	Club	Lea	Pos	G	AB	R	H	2B	3B	HR	RBI	SB	Avg
2008 Vermont	N.Y.-Penn.		SS	19	64	8	21	2	0	0	4	2	.328
2009 Potomac	Carolina		SS	133	474	90	125	31	4	18	72	29	.264
2010 Harrisburg	Eastern		SS	99	386	66	101	16	4	18	54	20	.262
2010 Syracuse	Int.		SS-2B	24	95	14	28	2	1	4	15	5	.295
2010 Washington	N.L.		2B-SS	28	103	16	22	4	1	6	15	0	.214
2011 Washington	N.L.		2B	158	573	72	135	29	5	21	66	17	.236
2012 Washington	N.L.		2B-SS	160	594	82	147	37	2	17	56	20	.247
Major League Totals		3 Yrs.		346	1270	170	304	70	8	44	137	37	.239
Division Series													
2012 Washington	N.L.		2B	5	15	0	1	0	0	0	0	0	.067

ETHIER, ANDRE EVERETT

Born, Phoenix, Arizona, April 10, 1982.
Bats Left. Throws Left. Height, 6 feet, 1 inch. Weight, 210 pounds.

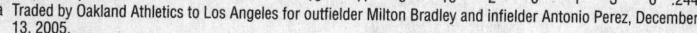

Year	Club	Lea	Pos	G	AB	R	H	2B	3B	HR	RBI	SB	Avg
2003 Kane County	Midwest		OF	40	162	23	44	10	0	0	11	2	.272
2003 Vancouver	Northwest		OF	10	41	7	16	4	1	1	7	2	.390
2004 Modesto	Calif.		OF	99	419	72	131	23	5	7	53	2	.313
2005 Sacramento	P.C.		OF	4	15	0	4	1	0	0	2	0	.267
2005 Midland a	Texas		OF	131	505	104	161	30	3	18	80	1	.319
2006 Las Vegas	P.C.		OF	25	86	15	30	4	3	1	12	2	.349
2006 Los Angeles	N.L.		OF	126	396	50	122	20	7	11	55	5	.308
2007 Los Angeles	N.L.		OF	153	447	50	127	32	2	13	64	0	.284
2008 Los Angeles	N.L.		OF	141	525	90	160	38	5	20	77	6	.305
2009 Los Angeles	N.L.		OF	160	596	92	162	42	3	31	106	6	.272
2010 Albuquerque	P.C.		OF	2	5	4	3	0	0	0	2	0	.600
2010 Los Angeles b	N.L.		OF-1B	139	517	71	151	33	1	23	82	2	.292
2011 Los Angeles	N.L.		OF	135	487	67	142	30	0	11	62	0	.292
2012 Rancho Cucamonga	Calif.		OF	2	4	0	0	0	0	0	1	0	.000
2012 Los Angeles c	N.L.		OF	149	556	79	158	36	1	20	89	2	.284
Major League Totals		7 Yrs.		1003	3524	499	1022	231	19	129	535	21	.290
Division Series													
2006 Los Angeles	N.L.		OF	2	1	0	0	0	0	0	0	0	.000
2008 Los Angeles	N.L.		OF	3	10	2	1	0	0	0	0	0	.100
2009 Los Angeles	N.L.		OF	3	12	5	6	2	1	2	3	0	.500
Division Series Totals				8	23	7	7	2	1	2	3	0	.304
Championship Series													
2008 Los Angeles	N.L.		OF	5	22	4	5	1	0	0	0	0	.227
2009 Los Angeles	N.L.		OF	5	19	2	5	1	0	1	3	0	.263
Championship Series Totals				10	41	6	10	2	0	1	3	0	.244

a Traded by Oakland Athletics to Los Angeles for outfielder Milton Bradley and infielder Antonio Perez, December 13, 2005.
b On disabled list from May 15 to May 31, 2010.
c On disabled list from June 28 to July 13, 2012.

FIELDER, PRINCE SEMIEN

Born, Ontario, California, May 9, 1984.
Bats Left. Throws Right. Height, 6 feet. Weight, 260 pounds.

Year	Club	Lea	Pos	G	AB	R	H	2B	3B	HR	RBI	SB	Avg
2002 Beloit	Midwest		1B	32	112	15	27	7	0	3	11	0	.241
2002 Ogden	Pioneer		1B	41	146	35	57	12	0	10	40	3	.390
2003 Beloit	Midwest		1B	137	502	81	157	22	2	27	112	2	.313
2004 Huntsville	Southern		1B-OF	136	497	70	135	29	1	23	78	11	.272
2005 Nashville	P.C.		1B	103	378	68	110	21	0	28	86	8	.291
2005 Milwaukee	N.L.		1B	39	59	2	17	4	0	2	10	0	.288
2006 Milwaukee	N.L.		1B	157	569	82	154	35	1	28	81	7	.271
2007 Milwaukee	N.L.		1B	158	573	109	165	35	2	*50	119	2	.288
2008 Milwaukee	N.L.		1B	159	588	86	162	30	2	34	102	3	.276
2009 Milwaukee	N.L.		1B	*162	591	103	177	35	3	46	*141	2	.299
2010 Milwaukee	N.L.		1B	161	578	94	151	25	0	32	83	1	.261
2011 Milwaukee a	N.L.		1B	*162	569	95	170	36	1	38	120	1	.299
2012 Detroit	A.L.		1B	*162	581	83	182	33	1	30	108	1	.313
Major League Totals		8 Yrs.		1160	4108	654	1178	233	10	260	764	17	.287

Year	Club	Lea	Pos	G	AB	R	H	2B	3B	HR	RBI	SB	Avg
Division Series													
2008 Milwaukee	N.L.		1B	4	14	1	1	0	0	1	2	0	.071
2011 Milwaukee	N.L.		1B	5	18	2	5	2	0	1	3	0	.278
2012 Detroit	A.L.		1B	5	21	1	4	0	0	1	2	0	.190
Division Series Totals				14	53	4	10	2	0	3	7	0	.189
Championship Series													
2011 Milwaukee	N.L.		1B	6	20	4	4	2	0	2	3	0	.200
2012 Detroit	A.L.		1B	4	17	1	4	0	0	0	1	0	.235
Championship Series Totals				10	37	5	8	2	0	2	4	0	.216
World Series Record													
2012 Detroit	A.L.		1B	4	14	0	1	0	0	0	0	0	.071

a Filed for free agency, October 30, 2011. Signed with Detroit Tigers, January 26, 2012.

FLAHERTY, RYAN EDWARD
Born, Portland, Maine, July 27, 1986.
Bats Left. Throws Right. Height, 6 feet, 3 inches. Weight, 210 pounds.

Year	Club	Lea	Pos	G	AB	R	H	2B	3B	HR	RBI	SB	Avg
2008 Boise	Northwest		SS	56	219	39	65	19	2	8	26	4	.297
2009 Peoria.......	Midwest		2B-SS-3B	131	485	81	134	24	5	20	81	7	.276
2010 Daytona........	Fla.St.		3B-2B-SS	108	420	65	120	34	3	9	63	6	.286
2010 Tennessee	Southern		2B-3B	23	71	10	13	2	0	1	9	1	.183
2011 Iowa	P.C.		2B-3B-OF	49	173	22	41	11	1	5	22	1	.237
2011 Tennessee a ...	Southern		2B-OF-SS-3B	83	302	52	92	20	2	14	66	4	.305
2012 Norfolk........	Int.		OF-1B-2B-3B	9	38	5	11	1	1	2	3	0	.289
2012 Baltimore b	A.L.		2B-OF-3B-1B	77	153	15	33	2	1	6	19	1	.216
Wild Card Playoff													
2012 Baltimore	A.L.		2B	1	3	0	1	0	0	0	0	0	.333
Division Series													
2012 Baltimore	A.L.		2B	3	8	1	2	0	0	1	1	0	.250

a Selected by Baltimore Orioles from Chicago Cubs in Rule V draft, December 8, 2011.

b On disabled list from August 2 to August 24, 2012.

FLORES, JESUS MIGUEL
Born, Carupano, Venezuela, October 26, 1984.
Bats Right. Throws Right. Height, 6 feet, 1 inch. Weight, 210 pounds.

Year	Club	Lea	Pos	G	AB	R	H	2B	3B	HR	RBI	SB	Avg
2004 Mets...........	Gulf Coast		C	45	141	16	45	12	3	4	25	1	.319
2004 Brooklyn........	N.Y.-Penn.		C	3	6	1	2	0	0	1	3	0	.333
2005 Hagerstown	So.Atl.		C	82	319	34	69	18	0	7	42	2	.216
2006 St. Lucie a	Fla.St.		C	120	429	66	114	32	0	21	70	2	.266
2007 Washington	N.L.		C	79	180	21	44	9	0	4	25	0	.244
2008 Columbus............	Int.		C-1B	17	59	8	9	3	0	1	7	0	.153
2008 Washington b........	N.L.		C	90	301	23	77	18	1	8	59	0	.256
2009 Harrisburg	Eastern		C	3	11	1	4	0	0	0	0	0	.364
2009 Washington c........	N.L.		C	29	93	13	28	3	2	4	15	0	.301
2010 Washington d........	N.L.		INJURED—Did Not Play										
2011 Syracuse	Int.		C	56	209	17	49	15	0	5	30	0	.234
2011 Washington	N.L.		C	30	86	5	18	6	0	1	2	0	.209
2012 Washington e........	N.L.		C	83	277	22	59	12	1	6	26	1	.213
Major League Totals		5 Yrs.		311	937	84	226	48	4	23	127	1	.241

a Selected by Washington Nationals from New York Mets in Rule V draft, December 7, 2006.

b On disabled list from September 15 to October 3, 2008.

c On disabled list from May 10 to September 4 and from September 18 to November 8, 2009.

d On disabled list from April 4 to November 10, 2010.

e Not offered contract, November 30, 2012. Signed with Los Angeles Dodgers, January 16, 2013.

FLORIMON, PEDRO ALEXANDER
Born, LaRomana, Dominican Republic, December 10, 1986.
Bats Both. Throws Right. Height, 6 feet, 2 inches. Weight, 180 pounds.

Year	Club	Lea	Pos	G	AB	R	H	2B	3B	HR	RBI	SB	Avg
2006 Bluefield........	Appal.		SS	33	120	23	40	6	1	1	8	7	.333
2006 Aberdeen	N.Y.-Penn.		SS	26	105	13	26	4	1	0	5	0	.248
2007 Delmarva	So.Atl.		SS	111	371	50	73	14	1	4	34	16	.197
2008 Delmarva	So.Atl.		SS-2B	81	269	28	60	18	1	0	19	13	.223
2009 Frederick	Carolina		SS	115	430	76	115	32	5	9	68	26	.267

Year	Club	Lea	Pos	G	AB	R	H	2B	3B	HR	RBI	SB	Avg
2009 Bowie	Eastern		SS	7	22	0	2	0	0	0	1	0	.091
2010 Frederick	Carolina		SS	62	222	32	64	10	4	4	33	8	.288
2010 Bowie	Eastern		SS	37	120	16	22	3	0	1	12	4	.183
2010 Aberdeen	N.Y.-Penn.		SS	5	19	1	3	0	0	0	0	0	.158
2011 Bowie	Eastern		SS-2B-OF	133	454	53	121	27	4	8	60	15	.267
2011 Baltimore a	A.L.		SS	4	8	1	1	1	0	0	2	0	.125
2012 New Britain	Eastern		SS	30	113	11	32	4	0	2	8	7	.283
2012 Rochester	Int.		SS	83	311	38	78	16	2	3	27	6	.251
2012 Minnesota	A.L.		SS	43	137	16	30	5	2	1	10	3	.219
Major League Totals			2 Yrs.	47	145	17	31	6	2	1	12	3	.214

a Claimed on waivers by Minnesota Twins, December 5, 2011.

FLOWERS, COLE TYLER (TYLER)

Born, Roswell, Georgia, January 24, 1986.
Bats Right. Throws Right. Height, 6 feet, 4 inches. Weight, 245 pounds.

Year	Club	Lea	Pos	G	AB	R	H	2B	3B	HR	RBI	SB	Avg
2006 Danville	Appal.		1B-C	34	129	24	36	9	0	5	16	0	.279
2007 Rome	So.Atl.		1B-C	106	389	65	116	34	2	12	70	3	.298
2008 Myrtle Beach a	Carolina		C-1B	122	413	72	119	32	1	17	88	8	.288
2009 Birmingham	Southern		C	77	248	54	75	18	2	13	43	3	.302
2009 Charlotte	Int.		C	31	105	13	30	10	0	2	13	0	.286
2009 Chicago	A.L.		C	10	16	3	3	1	0	0	0	0	.188
2010 Charlotte	Int.		C	100	346	43	76	22	2	16	53	2	.220
2010 Chicago	A.L.		C	8	11	2	1	0	0	0	0	0	.091
2011 Charlotte	Int.		C	65	222	36	58	8	0	15	32	2	.261
2011 Chicago	A.L.		C-1B	38	110	13	23	5	1	5	16	0	.209
2012 Chicago	A.L.		C-1B	52	136	19	29	6	0	7	13	2	.213
Major League Totals			4 Yrs.	108	273	37	56	12	1	12	29	2	.205

a Traded by Atlanta Braves to Chicago White Sox with infielder Jonathan Gilmore, infielder Brent Lillibridge and pitcher Santos Rodriguez for pitcher Javier Vazquez and pitcher Boone Logan, December 4, 2008.

FORSYTHE, JOHN LOGAN (LOGAN)

Born, Memphis, Tennessee, January 14, 1987.
Bats Right. Throws Right. Height, 6 feet, 1 inch. Weight, 205 pounds.

Year	Club	Lea	Pos	G	AB	R	H	2B	3B	HR	RBI	SB	Avg
2008 Eugene	Northwest		3B	3	9	2	3	1	0	0	0	0	.333
2008 Padres	Arizona		3B	9	26	2	6	0	0	0	0	0	.231
2009 Lake Elsinore	Calif.		3B	66	236	46	76	13	3	8	30	6	.322
2009 San Antonio	Texas		3B	66	244	37	68	9	3	3	31	5	.279
2010 San Antonio	Texas		2B-3B	107	392	66	99	22	1	3	38	17	.253
2011 Tucson	P.C.		2B-3B-SS	46	178	41	58	12	0	8	34	8	.326
2011 San Diego	N.L.		3B-2B-SS	62	150	12	32	9	1	0	12	3	.213
2012 Tucson	P.C.		3B-SS-2B	16	58	12	15	2	3	1	9	3	.259
2012 San Diego a	N.L.		2B-SS-3B	91	315	45	86	13	3	6	26	8	.273
Major League Totals			2 Yrs.	153	465	57	118	22	4	6	38	11	.254

a On disabled list from March 26 to June 3, 2012.

FOWLER, WILLIAM DEXTER (DEXTER)

Born, Atlanta, Georgia, March 22, 1986.
Bats Both. Throws Right. Height, 6 feet, 4 inches. Weight, 185 pounds.

Year	Club	Lea	Pos	G	AB	R	H	2B	3B	HR	RBI	SB	Avg
2005 Casper	Pioneer		OF	62	220	43	60	10	4	4	23	18	.273
2006 Asheville	So.Atl.		OF	99	405	92	120	31	6	8	46	43	.296
2007 Modesto	Calif.		OF	65	245	43	67	7	5	2	23	20	.273
2008 Tulsa	Texas		OF	108	421	92	141	31	9	9	64	20	.335
2008 Colorado	N.L.		OF	13	26	3	4	0	0	0	0	0	.154
2009 Tulsa	Texas		OF	3	10	3	4	2	0	0	3	1	.400
2009 Colorado a	N.L.		OF	135	433	73	115	29	10	4	34	27	.266
2010 Colorado Springs	P.C.		OF	27	106	23	36	10	4	2	13	1	.340
2010 Colorado	N.L.		OF	132	439	73	114	20	*14	6	36	13	.260
2011 Colorado Springs	P.C.		OF	24	97	17	23	6	1	2	9	2	.237
2011 Colorado b	N.L.		OF	125	481	84	128	35	15	5	45	12	.266
2012 Colorado	N.L.		OF	143	454	72	136	18	11	13	53	12	.300
Major League Totals			5 Yrs.	548	1833	305	497	102	50	28	168	64	.271

Year	Club	Lea	Pos	G	AB	R	H	2B	3B	HR	RBI	SB	Avg
Division Series													
2009 Colorado	N.L.		OF	4	14	1	3	0	0	0	2	0	.214

a On disabled list from August 25 to September 9, 2009.
b On disabled list from June 5 to June 20, 2011.

FRANCISCO (GONZALEZ), JUAN RAMON

Born, Bonao, Dominican Republic, June 24, 1987.
Bats Left. Throws Right. Height, 6 feet, 2 inches. Weight, 245 pounds.

Year	Club	Lea	Pos	G	AB	R	H	2B	3B	HR	RBI	SB	Avg
2006 Reds........	Gulf Coast	3B	45	182	24	51	14	0	3	30	2	.280	
2006 Billings.......	Pioneer	3B	9	36	6	12	3	0	0	2	2	.333	
2007 Dayton	Midwest	3B	135	534	69	143	21	4	25	90	12	.268	
2008 Sarasota........	Fla.St.	3B-OF	127	516	71	143	34	5	23	92	1	.277	
2009 Carolina	Southern	3B	109	437	64	123	26	2	22	74	6	.281	
2009 Louisville	Int.	3B-OF	22	92	17	33	5	1	5	19	0	.359	
2009 Cincinnati.........	N.L.	3B	14	21	4	9	1	0	1	7	0	.429	
2010 Louisville	Int.	3B-OF-1B	77	308	46	88	24	4	18	59	1	.286	
2010 Cincinnati.........	N.L.	3B	36	55	3	15	3	0	1	7	0	.273	
2011 Reds.........	Arizona	3B	5	18	3	9	3	0	1	3	0	.500	
2011 Louisville	Int.	3B-OF	74	300	46	92	13	1	15	50	0	.307	
2011 Cincinnati a	N.L.	3B	31	93	10	24	7	1	3	15	1	.258	
2012 Atlanta b.........	N.L.	3B	93	192	17	45	11	0	9	32	1	.234	
Major League Totals		4 Yrs.	174	361	34	93	22	1	14	61	2	.258		
Division Series													
2010 Cincinnati.........	N.L.	PH	1	1	0	0	0	0	0	0	0	.000	

a On disabled list from April 17 to May 17, 2011.
b Traded to Atlanta Braves for pitcher J.J Hoover, April 1, 2012.

FRANCISCO, LOUIS BEN (BEN)

Born, Santa Ana, California, October 23, 1981.
Bats Right. Throws Right. Height, 6 feet, 1 inch. Weight, 190 pounds.

Year	Club	Lea	Pos	G	AB	R	H	2B	3B	HR	RBI	SB	Avg
2002 Mahoning Valley..	N.Y.-Penn.	OF	58	235	55	82	23	2	3	23	22	.349	
2003 Lake County........	So.Atl.	OF	80	289	57	83	21	1	11	48	15	.287	
2004 Akron.............	Eastern	OF	133	497	72	126	29	3	15	71	21	.254	
2005 Akron.............	Eastern	OF	83	323	45	99	19	7	7	46	15	.307	
2005 Buffalo.............	Int.	OF	4	16	4	8	1	0	0	3	1	.500	
2006 Buffalo.............	Int.	OF	134	515	80	143	32	4	17	59	25	.278	
2007 Buffalo.............	Int.	OF	95	377	60	120	27	2	12	51	22	.318	
2007 Cleveland............	A.L.	OF	25	62	10	17	5	0	3	12	0	.274	
2008 Buffalo.............	Int.	OF	24	92	9	21	3	1	1	6	3	.228	
2008 Cleveland............	A.L.	OF	121	447	65	119	32	0	15	54	4	.266	
2009 Cleveland............	A.L.	OF	89	308	48	77	21	1	10	33	13	.250	
2009 Philadelphia a.......	N.L.	OF	37	97	10	27	9	0	5	13	1	.278	
2010 Philadelphia	N.L.	OF	88	179	24	48	13	0	6	28	8	.268	
2011 Philadelphia b.......	N.L.	OF	100	250	24	61	10	1	6	34	4	.244	
2012 Dunedin	Fla.St.	OF	2	6	0	0	0	0	0	0	0	.000	
2012 New Hampshire	Eastern	OF	9	36	2	8	3	0	0	2	0	.222	
2012 Houston	N.L.	OF	31	85	5	21	4	0	2	5	0	.247	
2012 Toronto-Tampa Bay c-d-e-f	A.L.	OF	51	107	9	25	10	1	2	10	0	.234	
Major League Totals		6 Yrs.	542	1535	195	395	104	3	49	189	30	.257		
Division Series													
2009 Philadelphia	N.L.	OF	3	1	0	0	0	0	0	0	0	.000	
2010 Philadelphia	N.L.	PH	1	0	0	0	0	0	0	0	0	.000	
2011 Philadelphia	N.L.	PH	2	2	1	1	0	0	1	3	0	.500	
Division Series Totals			6	3	1	1	0	0	1	3	0	.333		
Championship Series													
2009 Philadelphia	N.L.	OF	4	3	0	0	0	0	0	0	0	.000	
2010 Philadelphia	N.L.	OF	3	6	1	1	0	0	0	0	0	.167	
Championship Series Totals			7	9	1	1	0	0	0	0	0	.111		
World Series Record													
2009 Philadelphia	N.L.	OF	4	7	0	0	0	0	0	0	0	.000	

a Traded to Philadelphia Phillies with pitcher Cliff Lee for catcher Lou Marson, pitcher Jason Knapp, infielder Jason Donald and pitcher Carlos Carrasco, July 29, 2009.
b Traded to Toronto Blue Jays for pitcher Frank Gailey, December 12, 2011.
c On disabled list from May 21 to June 25, 2012.

d Traded to Houston Astros with pitcher Francisco Cordero, pitcher Joseph Musgrove, pitcher Asher Wojciechowski, pitcher David Rollins, catcher Carlos Perez and player to be named later for pitcher Brandon Lyon, pitcher J.A. Happ and pitcher David Carpenter, July 20, 2012. Houston Astros received pitcher Kevin Comer to complete trade, August 16, 2012.

e Traded to Tampa Bay Rays for player to be named later, August 31, 2012. Houston received pitcher Theron Keith to complete trade, September 20, 2012.

f Not offered contract, November 30, 2012.

FRANCOEUR, JEFFREY BRADEN (JEFF)

Born, Atlanta, Georgia, January 8, 1984.
Bats Right. Throws Right. Height, 6 feet, 4 inches. Weight, 220 pounds.

Year	Club	Lea	Pos	G	AB	R	H	2B	3B	HR	RBI	SB	Avg
2002	Danville	Appal.	OF	38	147	31	48	12	1	8	31	8	.327
2003	Rome	So.Atl.	OF	134	524	78	147	26	9	14	68	14	.281
2004	Myrtle Beach	Carolina	OF	88	334	56	98	26	0	15	52	10	.293
2004	Greenville	Southern	OF	18	76	8	15	2	0	3	9	1	.197
2005	Mississippi	Southern	OF	84	335	40	92	28	2	13	62	13	.275
2005	Atlanta	N.L.	OF	70	257	41	77	20	1	14	45	3	.300
2006	Atlanta	N.L.	OF	*162	651	83	169	24	6	29	103	1	.260
2007	Atlanta	N.L.	OF	*162	642	84	188	40	0	19	105	5	.293
2008	Mississippi	Southern	OF	3	13	3	7	1	0	1	2	0	.538
2008	Atlanta	N.L.	OF	155	599	70	143	33	3	11	71	0	.239
2009	Atlanta-New York a	N.L.	OF	157	593	72	166	32	4	15	76	6	.280
2010	New York	N.L.	OF	124	401	43	95	16	2	11	54	8	.237
2010	Texas b-c	A.L.	OF	15	53	9	18	2	0	2	11	0	.340
2011	Kansas City	A.L.	OF	153	601	77	171	47	4	20	87	22	.285
2012	Kansas City	A.L.	OF	148	561	58	132	26	3	16	49	4	.235
Major League Totals			8 Yrs.	1146	4358	537	1159	240	23	137	601	49	.266
Division Series													
2005	Atlanta	N.L.	OF	4	17	2	4	1	1	0	1	0	.235
2010	Texas	A.L.	OF	2	8	1	1	1	0	0	1	0	.125
Division Series Totals				6	25	3	5	2	1	0	2	0	.200
Championship Series													
2010	Texas	A.L.	OF	4	10	0	2	0	0	0	0	0	.200
World Series Record													
2010	Texas	A.L.	OF	3	6	0	0	0	0	0	0	0	.000

a Traded to New York Mets with cash for outfielder Ryan Church, July 10, 2009.

b Traded to Texas Rangers for infielder Joaquin Arias, September 1, 2010.

c Filed for free agency, November 10, 2010. Signed with Kansas City Royals, December 8, 2010.

FRANDSEN, KEVIN VINCENT

Born, San Jose, California, May 24, 1982.
Bats Right. Throws Right. Height, 6 feet. Weight, 185 pounds.

Year	Club	Lea	Pos	G	AB	R	H	2B	3B	HR	RBI	SB	Avg
2004	Salem-Keizer	Northwest	2B-SS	25	98	22	29	5	0	3	14	0	.296
2005	San Jose	Calif.	2B-SS	75	291	57	102	22	3	2	40	13	.351
2005	Norwich	Eastern	2B-SS-3B	33	129	22	37	8	0	2	20	7	.287
2005	Fresno	P.C.	2B	20	94	18	33	10	1	2	16	1	.351
2006	Fresno	P.C.	2B-3B-SS	71	293	46	89	25	3	3	30	7	.304
2006	San Jose	Calif.	SS	2	7	1	3	0	0	0	1	0	.429
2006	San Francisco a	N.L.	2B-SS	41	93	12	20	4	0	2	7	0	.215
2007	Fresno	P.C.	2B-SS-3B	19	67	13	27	5	0	1	7	4	.403
2007	San Francisco	N.L.	2B-SS-OF-3B	109	264	26	71	12	1	5	31	4	.269
2008	San Francisco b	N.L.	PH	1	1	0	0	0	0	0	0	0	.000
2009	Fresno	P.C.	SS-2B-1B-3B	110	427	67	126	18	2	13	55	3	.295
2009	San Francisco	N.L.	2B-SS	23	50	3	7	2	0	0	1	0	.140
2010	Pawtucket	Int.	SS-2B-3B	17	62	9	16	3	0	2	4	2	.258
2010	Salt Lake	P.C.	3B-2B-SS-1B	36	137	25	38	9	1	1	12	2	.277
2010	Los Angeles c-d	A.L.	3B-1B-2B-OF	54	160	24	40	11	0	0	14	2	.250
2011	Reading	Eastern	2B	1	4	1	2	0	0	1	2	0	.500
2011	Clearwater	Fla.St.	SS-2B	3	10	1	4	2	0	0	1	0	.400
2011	Lehigh Valley e-f-g	Int.	2B-SS-3B-1B	77	284	32	86	13	3	4	40	10	.303
2012	Lehigh Valley	Int.	2B-1B-3B-SS	99	391	38	118	34	0	1	33	2	.302
2012	Philadelphia	N.L.	3B	55	195	24	66	10	3	2	14	0	.338
Major League Totals			6 Yrs.	283	763	89	204	39	4	9	67	6	.267

a On disabled list from August 18 to September 2, 2006.

b On disabled list from March 21 to September 27, 2008.

c Sold to Boston Red Sox, March 26, 2010.

d Claimed on waivers by Los Angeles Angels, April 29, 2010.

53

e Not offered contract, December 2, 2010. Signed with San Diego Padres organization, January 6, 2011.
f Released by San Diego Padres, March 25, 2011. Signed with Philadelphia Phillies organization, April 1, 2011.
g Filed for free agency, November 2, 2011. Signed with Philadelphia Phillies organization, November 30, 2011.

FRAZIER, TODD B.
Born, Point Pleasant, New Jersey, February 12, 1986.
Bats Right. Throws Right. Height, 6 feet, 3 inches. Weight, 215 pounds.

Year Club	Lea	Pos	G	AB	R	H	2B	3B	HR	RBI	SB	Avg
2007 Dayton	Midwest	SS	6	22	4	7	3	0	2	5	0	.318
2007 Billings	Pioneer	SS	41	160	29	51	6	5	5	25	3	.319
2008 Sarasota	Fla.St.	SS-1B-3B-OF	100	366	62	103	20	3	12	54	8	.281
2008 Dayton	Midwest	SS-1B-3B-OF	30	112	25	36	10	0	7	20	4	.321
2009 Louisville	Int.	2B-OF	16	63	9	19	5	0	2	9	2	.302
2009 Carolina	Southern	OF-2B-1B-3B	119	451	59	131	40	2	14	68	7	.290
2010 Louisville	Int.	OF-3B-1B	130	480	71	124	32	4	17	66	14	.258
2011 Louisville	Int.	3B-1B-OF-2B	90	315	47	82	18	1	15	46	17	.260
2011 Cincinnati	N.L.	3B-OF-2B-SS	41	112	17	26	5	0	6	15	1	.232
2012 Louisville	Int.	3B-OF	10	39	4	9	2	0	1	7	3	.231
2012 Cincinnati	N.L.	3B-1B-OF	128	422	55	115	26	6	19	67	3	.273
Major League Totals		2 Yrs.	169	534	72	141	31	6	25	82	4	.264
Division Series												
2012 Cincinnati	N.L.	3B-1B	4	6	0	1	0	0	0	1	0	.167

FREEMAN, FREDERICK CHARLES (FREDDIE)
Born, Fountain Valley, California, September 12, 1989.
Bats Left. Throws Right. Height, 6 feet, 5 inches. Weight, 225 pounds.

Year Club	Lea	Pos	G	AB	R	H	2B	3B	HR	RBI	SB	Avg
2007 Braves	Gulf Coast	1B-3B	59	224	24	60	7	0	6	30	1	.268
2008 Rome	So.Atl.	1B	130	491	70	155	33	7	18	95	5	.316
2009 Myrtle Beach	Carolina	1B	70	255	43	77	19	0	6	34	1	.302
2009 Mississippi	Southern	1B	41	149	15	37	8	0	2	24	0	.248
2010 Gwinnett	Int.	1B	124	461	73	147	35	2	18	87	6	.319
2010 Atlanta	N.L.	1B	20	24	3	4	1	0	1	1	0	.167
2011 Atlanta	N.L.	1B	157	571	67	161	32	0	21	76	4	.282
2012 Atlanta	N.L.	1B	147	540	91	140	33	2	23	94	2	.259
Major League Totals		3 Yrs.	324	1135	161	305	66	2	45	171	6	.269
Wild Card Playoff												
2012 Atlanta	N.L.	1B	1	4	0	3	1	0	0	0	0	.750

FREESE, DAVID RICHARD
Born, Corpus Christi, Texas, April 28, 1983.
Bats Right. Throws Right. Height, 6 feet, 2 inches. Weight, 220 pounds.

Year Club	Lea	Pos	G	AB	R	H	2B	3B	HR	RBI	SB	Avg
2006 Fort Wayne	Midwest	3B	53	204	27	61	13	3	8	44	1	.299
2006 Eugene	Northwest	3B	18	58	19	22	8	0	5	26	0	.379
2007 Lake Elsinore a	Calif.	3B	128	503	104	152	31	6	17	96	6	.302
2008 Memphis	P.C.	3B	131	464	83	142	29	3	26	91	5	.306
2009 Cardinals	Gulf Coast	3B	4	11	2	5	2	0	1	6	0	.455
2009 Springfield	Texas	3B	4	16	3	6	1	0	1	5	0	.375
2009 Memphis	P.C.	3B-1B	56	200	34	60	15	0	10	37	1	.300
2009 St. Louis	N.L.	3B-1B-C	17	31	3	10	2	0	1	7	0	.323
2010 Springfield	Texas	DH	1	2	0	1	1	0	0	0	0	.500
2010 St. Louis b	N.L.	3B-1B	70	240	28	71	12	1	4	36	1	.296
2011 Memphis	P.C.	3B	4	13	1	3	1	0	0	1	0	.231
2011 St. Louis c	N.L.	3B-1B	97	333	41	99	16	1	10	55	1	.297
2012 St. Louis	N.L.	3B	144	501	70	147	25	1	20	79	3	.293
Major League Totals		4 Yrs.	328	1105	142	327	55	3	35	177	5	.296
Wild Card Playoff												
2012 St. Louis	N.L.	3B	1	2	0	0	0	0	0	1	0	.000
Division Series												
2011 St. Louis	N.L.	3B	5	18	1	5	2	0	1	5	0	.278
2012 St. Louis	N.L.	3B	5	19	3	8	3	0	1	1	0	.421
Division Series Totals			10	37	4	13	5	0	1	6	0	.351
Championship Series												
2011 St. Louis	N.L.	3B	6	22	7	12	3	0	3	9	0	.545

Year	Club	Lea	Pos	G	AB	R	H	2B	3B	HR	RBI	SB	Avg
2012 St. Louis.............	N.L.		3B	7	26	2	5	2	0	1	2	0	.192
Championship Series Totals				13	48	9	17	5	0	4	11	0	.354
World Series Record													
2011 St. Louis.............	N.L.		3B	7	23	4	8	3	1	1	7	0	.348

a Traded by San Diego Padres to St. Louis Cardinals for outfielder Jim Edmonds, December 15, 2007.
b On disabled list from June 28 to November 2, 2010.
c On disabled list from May 2 to June 27, 2011.

FULD, SAMUEL BABSON (SAM)
Born, Durham, New Hampshire, November 20, 1981.
Bats Left. Throws Left. Height, 5 feet, 10 inches. Weight, 180 pounds.

Year	Club	Lea	Pos	G	AB	R	H	2B	3B	HR	RBI	SB	Avg
2005 Peoria...........	Midwest	OF	125	443	82	133	32	6	5	37	18	.300
2006 Daytona	Fla.St.	OF	89	353	63	106	19	6	4	40	22	.300
2007 Iowa................	P.C.	OF	14	52	13	14	4	1	1	2	2	.269
2007 Tennessee	Southern	OF	90	335	56	97	23	2	2	27	10	.290
2007 Chicago	N.L.	OF	14	6	3	0	0	0	0	0	0	.000
2008 Iowa................	P.C.	OF	20	63	11	14	3	0	1	4	3	.222
2008 Tennessee	Southern	OF	85	339	48	92	16	3	5	48	7	.271
2009 Iowa................	P.C.	OF	84	328	62	93	17	10	2	33	23	.284
2009 Chicago	N.L.	OF	65	97	17	29	6	1	1	2	2	.299
2010 Iowa................	P.C.	OF	112	368	69	100	15	9	4	27	21	.272
2010 Chicago	N.L.	OF	19	28	3	4	1	0	0	3	0	.143
2011 Tampa Bay a......	A.L.	OF	105	308	41	74	18	5	3	27	20	.240
2012 Charlotte	Fla.St.	OF	5	13	0	2	0	0	0	0	0	.154
2012 Durham	Int.	OF	5	18	0	3	1	0	0	0	0	.167
2012 Tampa Bay b	A.L.	OF	44	98	14	25	3	2	0	5	7	.255

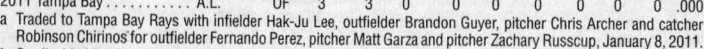

Major League Totals	5 Yrs.	247	537	78	132	28	8	4	37	29	.246
Division Series											
2011 Tampa Bay .... A.L.	OF	3	3	0	0	0	0	0	0	0	.000

a Traded to Tampa Bay Rays with infielder Hak-Ju Lee, outfielder Brandon Guyer, pitcher Chris Archer and catcher Robinson Chirinos for outfielder Fernando Perez, pitcher Matt Garza and pitcher Zachary Russcup, January 8, 2011.
b On disabled list from April 4 to July 24, 2012.

FURCAL, RAFAEL
Born, Loma de Cabrera, Dominican Republic, August 24, 1977.
Bats Both. Throws Right. Height, 5 feet, 8 inches. Weight, 195 pounds.

Year	Club	Lea	Pos	G	AB	R	H	2B	3B	HR	RBI	SB	Avg
1997 Braves	Gulf Coast	2B-OF	50	190	31	49	5	4	1	9	15	.258
1998 Danville	Appal.	2B	66	268	56	88	15	4	0	23	60	.328
1999 Myrtle Beach	Carolina	SS	43	184	32	54	9	3	0	12	23	.293
1999 Macon	So.Atl.	SS	83	335	73	113	15	1	1	29	73	.337
2000 Greenville........	Southern	SS	3	10	1	2	0	0	1	3	0	.200
2000 Atlanta a-b	N.L.	SS-2B	131	455	87	134	20	4	4	37	40	.295
2001 Atlanta c.............	N.L.	SS	79	324	39	89	19	0	4	30	22	.275
2002 Atlanta	N.L.	SS-2B	154	636	95	175	31	8	8	47	27	.275
2003 Atlanta	N.L.	SS	156	664	130	194	35	*10	15	61	25	.292
2004 Atlanta	N.L.	SS-2B	143	563	103	157	24	5	14	59	29	.279
2005 Atlanta d.............	N.L.	SS	154	616	100	175	31	11	12	58	46	.284
2006 Los Angeles	N.L.	SS	159	654	113	196	32	9	15	63	37	.300
2007 Inland Empire.........	Calif.	SS	2	6	0	1	0	0	0	0	1	.167
2007 Los Angeles e	N.L.	SS	138	581	87	157	23	4	6	47	25	.270
2008 Las Vegas.............	P.C.	SS	1	3	0	1	1	0	0	1	0	.333
2008 Los Angeles f-g	N.L.	SS	36	143	34	51	12	2	5	16	8	.357
2009 Los Angeles	N.L.	SS	150	613	92	165	28	5	9	47	12	.269
2010 Inland Empire.........	Calif.	SS	2	4	0	0	0	0	0	0	0	.000
2010 Albuquerque........	P.C.	SS	2	5	3	3	1	1	1	4	0	.600
2010 Los Angeles h	N.L.	SS	97	383	66	115	23	7	8	43	22	.300
2011 Rancho Cucamonga....	Calif.	SS	6	22	10	7	0	0	0	1	1	.318
2011 Albuquerque........	P.C.	SS	4	13	2	5	1	0	1	6	0	.385
2011 Los Angeles-St. Louis i-j-k.	N.L.	SS	87	333	44	77	15	0	8	28	9	.231
2012 St. Louis l.............	N.L.	SS	121	477	69	126	18	3	5	49	12	.264

Major League Totals	13 Yrs.	1605	6442	1059	1811	311	68	113	585	314	.281
Division Series											
2000 Atlanta .... N.L.	SS	3	11	2	1	0	0	0	0	1	.091
2002 Atlanta .... N.L.	SS	5	24	2	6	1	1	0	2	1	.250
2003 Atlanta .... N.L.	SS	5	19	3	4	0	0	0	0	1	.211

Year	Club	Lea	Pos	G	AB	R	H	2B	3B	HR	RBI	SB	Avg
2004 Atlanta	N.L.	SS	5	21	5	8	0	1	2	4	3	.381
2005 Atlanta	N.L.	SS	4	20	1	3	0	0	0	0	3	.150
2006 Los Angeles	N.L.	SS	3	11	1	2	0	0	0	1	2	.182
2008 Los Angeles	N.L.	SS	3	12	4	4	0	0	0	2	0	.333
2009 Los Angeles	N.L.	SS	3	12	2	6	0	1	0	2	0	.500
2011 St. Louis.	N.L.	SS	5	22	2	5	0	2	0	1	1	.227
Division Series Totals			36	152	22	39	1	5	2	12	12	.257
Championship Series												
2008 Los Angeles	N.L.	SS	5	19	5	4	0	0	1	1	0	.211
2009 Los Angeles	N.L.	SS	5	21	0	3	1	0	0	1	1	.143
2011 St. Louis.	N.L.	SS	6	27	5	5	2	0	1	1	0	.185
Championship Series Totals			16	67	10	12	3	0	2	3	1	.179
World Series Record												
2011 St. Louis.	N.L.	SS	7	28	1	5	1	0	0	1	0	.179

a On disabled list from June 13 to June 28, 2000.
b Selected Rookie of the Year in National League for 2000.
c On disabled list from July 7 to November 6, 2001.
d Filed for free agency, October 31, 2005. Signed with Los Angeles Dodgers, December 7, 2005.
e On disabled list from March 23 to April 13, 2007.
f On disabled list from May 6 to September 24, 2008.
g Filed for free agency, November 3, 2008, re-signed with Los Angeles Dodgers, December 19, 2008.
h On disabled list from April 28 to May 25 and August 3 to September 3, 2010.
i On disabled list from April 12 to May 22 and June 4 to July 3, 2011.
j Traded to St. Louis Cardinals with cash for outfielder Alex Castellanos, July 31, 2011.
k Filed for free agency, October 31, 2011, re-signed with St. Louis Cardinals, December 10, 2011.
l On disabled list from August 31 to October 26, 2012.

GALVIS, FREDDY JOSE

Born, Punto Fijo, Venezuela, November 14, 1989.
Bats Both. Throws Right. Height, 5 feet, 10 inches. Weight, 170 pounds.

Year	Club	Lea	Pos	G	AB	R	H	2B	3B	HR	RBI	SB	Avg
2007 Williamsport	N.Y.-Penn.	SS	38	143	20	29	5	1	0	7	9	.203
2008 Lakewood..........	So.Atl.	SS	127	458	59	109	12	1	3	42	14	.238
2009 Reading	Eastern	SS	16	61	6	12	0	0	1	5	0	.197
2009 Clearwater	Fla.St.	SS-3B	63	251	29	62	8	2	1	15	6	.247
2009 Phillies	Gulf Coast	SS	7	29	6	8	1	0	0	0	1	.276
2010 Reading	Eastern	SS	138	502	58	117	16	4	5	48	15	.233
2011 Reading	Eastern	SS	104	422	63	115	22	4	8	35	19	.273
2011 Lehigh Valley	Int.	SS	33	121	15	36	6	1	0	8	4	.298
2012 Philadelphia a.........	N.L.	2B-SS	58	190	14	43	15	1	3	24	0	.226

a On disabled list from June 6 to October 5, 2012.

GARDNER, BRETT MICHAEL

Born, Holly Hill, South Carolina, August 24, 1983.
Bats Left. Throws Left. Height, 5 feet, 10 inches. Weight, 185 pounds.

Year	Club	Lea	Pos	G	AB	R	H	2B	3B	HR	RBI	SB	Avg
2005 Staten Island	N.Y.-Penn.	OF-3B	73	282	62	80	9	1	5	32	19	.284
2006 Trenton...........	Eastern	OF	55	217	41	59	4	3	0	13	28	.272
2006 Tampa	Fla.St.	OF	63	232	46	75	12	5	0	22	30	.323
2007 Trenton...........	Eastern	OF	54	203	43	61	14	5	0	17	18	.300
2007 Scranton/WB	Int.	OF	45	181	37	47	4	3	1	9	21	.260
2008 Scranton/WB	Int.	OF	94	341	68	101	12	11	3	32	37	.296
2008 New York	A.L.	OF	42	127	18	29	5	2	0	16	13	.228
2009 Scranton/WB	Int.	OF	4	11	3	1	0	0	0	0	3	.091
2009 New York a...........	A.L.	OF	108	248	48	67	6	6	3	23	26	.270
2010 New York	A.L.	OF	150	477	97	132	20	7	5	47	47	.277
2011 New York	A.L.	OF	159	510	87	132	19	8	7	36	*49	.259
2012 Charleston	So.Atl.	OF	1	3	1	1	0	0	0	0	1	.333
2012 Scranton-WB	Int.	OF	2	5	1	3	0	1	0	0	0	.600
2012 New York b...........	A.L.	OF	16	31	7	10	2	0	0	3	2	.323
Major League Totals	5 Yrs.		475	1393	257	370	52	23	15	125	137	.266
Division Series												
2009 New York	A.L.	OF	3	0	0	0	0	0	0	0	1	.000
2010 New York	A.L.	OF	3	10	1	2	0	0	0	1	1	.200
2011 New York	A.L.	OF	5	17	3	7	1	0	0	5	0	.412

Year Club	Lea	Pos	G	AB	R	H	2B	3B	HR	RBI	SB	Avg
2012 New York	A.L.	OF	2	0	0	0	0	0	0	0	0	.000
Division Series Totals			13	27	4	9	1	0	0	6	2	.333
Championship Series												
2009 New York	A.L.	OF	6	3	2	2	0	0	0	0	0	.667
2010 New York	A.L.	OF	6	17	1	3	0	0	0	1	1	.176
2012 New York	A.L.	OF	3	8	0	0	0	0	0	0	2	.000
Championship Series Totals			15	28	3	5	0	0	0	1	3	.179
World Series Record												
2009 New York	A.L.	OF	5	10	1	0	0	0	0	0	0	.000

a On disabled list from July 26 to September 7, 2009.
b On disabled list from April 18 to September 25, 2012.

GENTRY, CRAIG ALAN

Born, Fort Smith, Arkansas, November 29, 1983.
Bats Right. Throws Right. Height, 6 feet, 2 inches. Weight, 190 pounds.

Year Club	Lea	Pos	G	AB	R	H	2B	3B	HR	RBI	SB	Avg
2006 Spokane	Northwest	OF	56	221	27	62	15	4	0	13	20	.281
2007 Rangers	Arizona	OF	3	11	4	3	0	0	0	1	2	.273
2007 Clinton	Midwest	OF	55	223	40	61	15	0	3	12	24	.274
2007 Bakersfield	Calif.	OF	51	213	31	58	16	1	1	18	16	.272
2008 Frisco	Texas	OF	76	301	43	83	17	0	4	33	16	.276
2008 Oklahoma	P.C.	OF	18	59	6	12	1	0	0	1	1	.203
2009 Frisco	Texas	OF	127	512	100	155	21	7	8	53	49	.303
2009 Texas	A.L.	OF	11	17	4	2	1	0	0	1	0	.118
2010 Texas	A.L.	OF	20	33	4	7	0	0	0	3	1	.212
2010 Oklahoma a	P.C.	OF	69	259	43	80	7	4	4	35	12	.309
2011 Round Rock	P.C.	OF	30	110	21	27	5	1	1	10	5	.245
2011 Texas b	A.L.	OF	64	133	26	36	5	1	1	13	18	.271
2012 Texas	A.L.	OF-P	122	240	31	73	12	3	1	26	13	.304
Major League Totals	4 Yrs.		217	423	65	118	18	4	2	43	32	.279
Wild Card Playoff												
2012 Texas	A.L.	OF	1	2	0	0	0	0	0	0	0	.000
Division Series												
2011 Texas	A.L.	OF	4	5	1	2	0	0	0	0	2	.400
Championship Series												
2011 Texas	A.L.	OF	3	5	0	2	0	0	0	1	0	.400
World Series Record												
2011 Texas	A.L.	OF	6	5	1	1	0	0	0	0	0	.200

a On disabled list from August 30 to November 5, 2010.
b On disabled list from July 28 to August 11, 2011.

GETZ, CHRISTOPHER RYAN (CHRIS)

Born, Southfield, Michigan, August 30, 1983.
Bats Left. Throws Right. Height, 6 feet. Weight, 185 pounds.

Year Club	Lea	Pos	G	AB	R	H	2B	3B	HR	RBI	SB	Avg
2005 Great Falls	Pioneer	SS-2B	6	24	3	8	1	0	0	4	2	.333
2005 Kannapolis	So.Atl.	2B-SS	55	214	38	65	13	2	1	28	11	.304
2006 Birmingham . . .	Southern	2B-SS	130	508	67	130	15	6	2	36	19	.256
2007 Birmingham . . .	Southern	2B	72	278	40	83	10	2	3	29	13	.299
2008 Charlotte	Int.	2B-SS-OF-3B	111	404	60	122	24	1	11	52	11	.302
2008 Chicago	A.L.	2B	10	7	2	2	0	0	0	1	1	.286
2009 Charlotte	Int.	2B	5	15	4	4	0	0	0	0	2	.267
2009 Chicago a-b	A.L.	2B	107	375	49	98	18	4	2	31	25	.261
2010 Omaha	P.C.	2B	2	6	3	2	0	0	0	0	0	.333
2010 Kansas City c	A.L.	2B-3B	72	224	23	53	9	0	0	18	15	.237
2011 Kansas City	A.L.	2B-SS	118	380	50	97	6	3	0	26	21	.255
2012 Omaha	P.C.	2B	11	43	7	12	2	1	0	8	1	.279
2012 Kansas City d	A.L.	2B	64	189	22	52	10	3	0	17	9	.275
Major League Totals	5 Yrs.		371	1175	146	302	43	10	2	93	71	.257

a On disabled list from August 12 to September 1, 2009.
b Traded to Kansas City Royals with infielder Josh Fields for infielder Mark Teahen, November 6, 2009.
c On disabled list from April 15 to April 30, 2010.
d On disabled list from May 22 to June 12 and June 18 to July 9 and August 18 to October 16, 2012.

GIAMBI, JASON GILBERT

Born, West Covina, California, January 8, 1971.
Bats Left. Throws Right. Height, 6 feet, 3 inches. Weight, 230 pounds.

Year	Club	Lea	Pos	G	AB	R	H	2B	3B	HR	RBI	SB	Avg
1992 South Oregon....	Northwest		3B	13	41	9	13	3	0	3	13	1	.317
1993 Modesto........	California		3B	89	313	72	91	16	2	12	60	2	.291
1994 Huntsville.......	Southern		3B-1B	56	193	31	43	9	0	6	30	0	.223
1994 Tacoma	P.C.		3B-1B-SS	52	176	28	56	20	0	4	38	1	.318
1995 Edmonton	P.C.		3B-1B	55	190	34	65	26	1	3	41	0	.342
1995 Oakland	A.L.		3B-1B	54	176	27	45	7	0	6	25	2	.256
1996 Oakland	A.L.		1B-OF-3B	140	536	84	156	40	1	20	79	0	.291
1997 Oakland	A.L.		OF-1B	142	519	66	152	41	2	20	81	0	.293
1998 Oakland	A.L.		1B	153	562	92	166	28	0	27	110	2	.295
1999 Oakland	A.L.		1B-3B	158	575	115	181	36	1	33	123	1	.315
2000 Oakland a...........	A.L.		1B	152	510	108	170	29	1	43	137	2	.333
2001 Oakland b...........	A.L.		1B	154	520	109	178	*47	2	38	120	2	.342
2002 New York	A.L.		1B	155	560	120	176	34	1	41	122	2	.314
2003 New York	A.L.		1B	156	535	97	134	25	0	41	107	2	.250
2004 Tampa	Fla.St.		1B	2	6	0	1	0	0	0	0	0	.167
2004 New York c...........	A.L.		1B	80	264	33	55	9	0	12	40	0	.208
2005 New York	A.L.		1B	139	417	74	113	14	0	32	87	0	.271
2006 New York	A.L.		DH-1B	139	446	92	113	25	0	37	113	2	.253
2007 Tampa	Fla.St.		DH	5	13	0	4	1	0	0	1	0	.308
2007 Scranton-WB	Int.		1B	4	9	1	1	0	0	1	1	0	.111
2007 New York d...........	A.L.		DH-1B	83	254	31	60	8	0	14	39	1	.236
2008 New York e...........	A.L.		1B	145	458	68	113	19	1	32	96	2	.247
2009 Colorado Springs.......	P.C.		1B	6	18	4	8	1	0	2	4	0	.444
2009 Oakland	A.L.		1B	83	269	39	52	13	0	11	40	0	.193
2009 Colorado f-g-h	N.L.		1B	19	24	4	7	1	0	2	11	0	.292
2010 Colorado i	N.L.		1B	87	176	17	43	9	0	6	35	2	.244
2011 Colorado Springs.......	P.C.		1B	3	7	2	3	0	0	0	3	0	.429
2011 Colorado j	N.L.		1B	64	131	20	34	6	0	13	32	0	.260
2012 Tulsa	Texas		1B	3	7	1	3	0	0	0	1	0	.429
2012 Colorado Springs.....	P.C.		1B	2	6	0	2	1	0	0	0	0	.333
2012 Colorado k-l..........	N.L.		1B	60	89	7	20	4	0	1	8	0	.225
Major League Totals			18 Yrs.	2163	7021	1203	1968	395	9	429	1405	20	.280
Division Series													
2000 Oakland	A.L.		1B	5	14	2	4	0	0	0	1	1	.286
2001 Oakland	A.L.		1B	5	17	2	6	0	0	1	4	0	.353
2002 New York	A.L.		1B-DH	4	14	5	5	0	0	1	3	0	.357
2003 New York	A.L.		DH	4	16	1	4	2	0	0	2	0	.250
2005 New York	A.L.		1B-DH	5	19	1	8	3	0	0	2	0	.421
2006 New York	A.L.		DH-1B	3	8	1	1	0	0	1	2	1	.125
2007 New York	A.L.		1B	3	4	0	1	0	0	0	0	0	.250
2009 Colorado	N.L.		PH	3	3	1	1	0	0	0	1	0	.333
Division Series Totals				32	95	13	30	5	0	3	15	2	.316
Championship Series													
2003 New York	A.L.		DH	7	26	4	6	0	0	3	3	0	.231
World Series Record													
2003 New York	A.L.		1B	6	17	2	4	1	0	1	1	0	.235

a Selected Most Valuable Player in American League for 2000.
b Filed for free agency, November 5, 2001. Signed with New York Yankees, December 13, 2001.
c On disabled list from May 22 to June 6 and from July 26 to September 14, 2004.
d On disabled list from May 31 to August 7, 2007.
e Not offered contract, November 4, 2008. Signed with Oakland A's, January 7, 2009.
f On disabled list from July 20 to August 7, 2009.
g Released by Oakland Athletics, August 7, 2009. Signed with Colorado Rockies organization, August 24, 2009.
h Filed for free agency, November 5, 2009, re-signed with Colorado Rockies, January 28, 2010.
i Filed for free agency, November 1, 2010, re-signed with Colorado Rockies organization, January 17, 2011.
j On disabled list from July 26 to August 12, 2011.
k On disabled list from July 21 to September 1, 2012.
l Filed for free agency, November 3, 2012.

GIAVOTELLA, JOHNNY ARTHUR

Born, Metairie, Louisiana, July 10, 1987.
Bats Right. Throws Right. Height, 5 feet, 8 inches. Weight, 185 pounds.

Year Club	Lea	Pos	G	AB	R	H	2B	3B	HR	RBI	SB	Avg
2008 Burlington	Midwest	2B	68	278	50	83	18	2	4	26	10	.299
2009 Wilmington	Carolina	2B	133	476	84	123	24	8	6	52	26	.258
2010 NW Arkansas	Texas	2B	134	522	92	168	35	5	9	65	13	.322
2011 Omaha	P.C.	2B-OF-3B	110	453	67	153	34	2	9	72	9	.338
2011 Kansas City	A.L.	2B	46	178	20	44	9	4	2	21	5	.247
2012 Omaha	P.C.	2B-3B	89	362	67	117	20	2	10	71	7	.323
2012 Kansas City	A.L.	2B	53	181	21	43	7	1	1	15	3	.238
Major League Totals		2 Yrs.	99	359	41	87	16	5	3	36	8	.242

GOLDSCHMIDT, PAUL EDWARD

Born, Wilmington, Delaware, September 10, 1987.
Bats Right. Throws Right. Height, 6 feet, 3 inches. Weight, 245 pounds.

Year Club	Lea	Pos	G	AB	R	H	2B	3B	HR	RBI	SB	Avg
2009 Missoula	Pioneer	1B-OF	72	278	48	91	26	2	17	61	4	.327
2010 Visalia	Calif.	1B	138	525	102	165	42	3	35	108	5	.314
2011 Mobile	Southern	1B	103	366	84	112	21	3	30	94	9	.306
2011 Arizona	N.L.	1B	48	156	28	39	9	1	8	26	4	.250
2012 Arizona	N.L.	1B	145	514	82	147	43	1	20	82	18	.286
Major League Totals		2 Yrs.	193	670	110	186	52	2	28	108	22	.278
Division Series												
2011 Arizona	N.L.	1B	4	16	4	7	0	0	2	6	1	.438

GOMES, JONNY JOHNSON

Born, Petaluma, California, November 22, 1980.
Bats Right. Throws Right. Height, 6 feet, 1 inch. Weight, 225 pounds.

Year Club	Lea	Pos	G	AB	R	H	2B	3B	HR	RBI	SB	Avg
2001 Princeton	Appal.	OF	62	206	58	60	11	2	16	44	15	.291
2002 Bakersfield	California	OF	133	446	102	123	24	9	30	72	15	.276
2003 Orlando	Southern	OF	120	442	68	110	28	3	17	56	23	.249
2003 Durham	Int.	OF	5	19	2	6	2	1	0	1	0	.316
2003 Tampa Bay	A.L.	DH	8	15	1	2	1	0	0	0	0	.133
2004 Durham	Int.	OF	114	389	73	100	27	1	26	78	8	.257
2004 Tampa Bay	A.L.	DH	5	14	0	1	0	0	0	1	0	.071
2005 Durham	Int.	OF	45	162	34	52	13	0	14	46	7	.321
2005 Tampa Bay	A.L.	OF	101	348	61	98	13	6	21	54	9	.282
2006 Tampa Bay a	A.L.	DH-OF	117	385	53	83	21	1	20	59	1	.216
2007 Durham	Int.	OF	13	43	6	13	2	0	1	7	4	.302
2007 Tampa Bay	A.L.	OF	107	348	48	85	20	2	17	49	12	.244
2008 Durham	Int.	OF	26	107	19	27	11	0	2	14	0	.252
2008 Tampa Bay b	A.L.	DH-OF	77	154	23	28	5	1	8	21	8	.182
2009 Louisville	Int.	OF	37	131	18	37	10	1	9	27	4	.282
2009 Cincinnati c	N.L.	OF	98	281	39	75	17	0	20	51	3	.267
2010 Cincinnati	N.L.	OF	148	511	77	136	24	3	18	86	5	.266
2011 Cincinnati-Washington d-e	N.L.	OF	120	311	41	65	12	1	14	43	7	.209
2012 Oakland f	A.L.	DH-OF	99	279	46	73	10	0	18	47	3	.262
Major League Totals		10 Yrs.	880	2646	389	646	123	14	136	411	48	.244
Division Series												
2010 Cincinnati	N.L.	OF	2	6	0	0	0	0	0	0	0	.000
2012 Oakland	A.L.	PH	1	1	0	0	0	0	0	0	0	.000
Division Series Totals			3	7	0	0	0	0	0	0	0	.000

a On disabled list from August 22 to October 2, 2006.
b Not offered contract, December 12, 2008. Signed with Cincinnati Reds organization, January 19, 2009.
c Not offered contract, December 12, 2009, re-signed with Cincinnati Reds, February 22, 2010.
d Traded to Washington Nationals with cash for pitcher Chris Manno and outfielder Bill Rhinehart, July 26, 2011.
e Filed for free agency, October 30, 2011. Signed with Oakland Athletics, January 26, 2012.
f Filed for free agency, November 3, 2012. Signed with Boston Red Sox, November 22, 2012.

GOMEZ (PENA), CARLOS ARGELIS

Born, Santiago, Dominican Republic, December 4, 1985.
Bats Right. Throws Right. Height, 6 feet, 4 inches. Weight, 195 pounds.

Year	Club	Lea	Pos	G	AB	R	H	2B	3B	HR	RBI	SB	Avg
2004 Kingsport	Appal.	OF	38	150	24	43	10	4	1	20	8	.287
2004 Mets	Gulf Coast	OF	19	71	10	19	7	0	0	11	9	.268
2005 Hagerstown	So.Atl.	OF	120	487	75	134	13	6	8	48	64	.275
2006 Binghamton	Eastern	OF	120	430	53	121	24	8	7	48	41	.281
2007 New Orleans	P.C.	OF	36	140	24	40	8	2	2	13	17	.286
2007 St. Lucie	Fla.St.	OF	5	13	1	2	0	0	0	0	2	.154
2007 New York a	N.L.	OF	58	125	14	29	3	0	2	12	12	.232
2008 Minnesota b	A.L.	OF	153	577	79	149	24	7	7	59	33	.258
2009 Minnesota c	A.L.	OF	137	315	51	72	15	5	3	28	14	.229
2010 Wisconsin	Midwest	OF	2	7	0	2	0	0	0	0	2	.286
2010 Nashville	P.C.	OF	8	28	7	8	0	0	0	2	2	.286
2010 Milwaukee	N.L.	OF	97	291	38	72	11	3	5	24	18	.247
2011 Wisconsin	Midwest	OF	4	12	3	4	0	0	0	0	3	.333
2011 Milwaukee e	N.L.	OF	94	231	37	52	11	3	8	24	16	.225
2012 Wisconsin	Midwest	OF	4	13	2	2	0	0	1	3	0	.154
2012 Milwaukee f	N.L.	OF	137	415	72	108	19	4	19	51	37	.260
Major League Totals		6 Yrs.	676	1954	291	482	83	22	44	198	130	.247
Division Series												
2009 Minnesota	A.L.	OF	1	4	1	0	0	0	0	0	0	.000
2011 Milwaukee	N.L.	OF	3	4	2	3	0	0	1	2	2	.750
Division Series Totals			4	8	3	3	0	0	1	2	2	.375
Championship Series												
2011 Milwaukee	N.L.	OF	5	10	1	2	0	0	0	0	0	.200

a On disabled list from July 5 to September 7, 2007.
b Traded to Minnesota Twins with pitcher Philip Humber, pitcher Kevin Mulvey and pitcher Deolis Garcia for pitcher Johan Santana, February 2, 2008.
c Traded to Milwaukee Brewers for infielder J.J. Hardy, November 6, 2009.
d On disabled list from May 6 to May 21 and August 3 to August 24, 2010.
e On disabled list from July 21 to September 1, 2011.
f On disabled list from May 5 to May 20, 2012.

GONZALEZ, ADRIAN

Born, San Diego, California, May 8, 1982.
Bats Left. Throws Left. Height, 6 feet, 2 inches. Weight, 220 pounds.

Year	Club	Lea	Pos	G	AB	R	H	2B	3B	HR	RBI	SB	Avg
2000 Marlins	Gulf Coast	1B	53	193	24	57	10	1	0	30	0	.295
2000 Utica	N.Y.-Penn.	1B	8	29	7	9	3	0	0	3	0	.310
2001 Kane County	Midwest	1B	127	516	86	161	37	1	17	103	5	.312
2002 Portland	Eastern	1B	138	508	70	135	34	1	17	96	6	.266
2003 Albuquerque	P.C.	1B	39	139	17	30	5	1	1	18	1	.216
2003 Carolina	Southern	1B	36	137	15	42	9	1	1	16	1	.307
2003 Frisco a	Texas	1B	45	173	16	49	6	2	3	17	0	.283
2004 Oklahoma	P.C.	1B	123	457	61	139	28	3	12	88	1	.304
2004 Texas	A.L.	1B	16	42	7	10	3	0	1	7	0	.238
2005 Oklahoma	P.C.	1B	84	328	61	111	17	1	18	65	0	.338
2005 Texas	A.L.	DH-1B-OF	43	150	17	34	7	1	6	17	0	.227
2006 San Diego b	N.L.	1B	156	570	83	173	38	1	24	82	0	.304
2007 San Diego	N.L.	1B	161	646	101	182	46	3	30	100	0	.282
2008 San Diego	N.L.	1B	*162	616	103	172	32	1	36	119	0	.279
2009 San Diego	N.L.	1B	160	552	90	153	27	2	40	99	1	.277
2010 San Diego c	N.L.	1B	160	591	87	176	33	0	31	101	0	.298
2011 Boston	A.L.	1B-OF	159	630	108	*213	45	3	27	117	1	.338
2012 Boston	A.L.	1B-OF	123	484	63	145	37	0	15	86	0	.300
2012 Los Angeles d	N.L.	1B	36	145	12	43	10	1	3	22	2	.297
Major League Totals		9 Yrs.	1176	4426	671	1301	278	12	213	750	4	.294
Division Series												
2006 San Diego	N.L.	1B	4	14	2	5	0	0	0	0	0	.357

a Traded to Texas Rangers with pitcher Ryan Snare and outfielder Will Smith for pitcher Ugueth Urbina, July 11, 2003.
b Traded to San Diego Padres with pitcher Chris Young and outfielder Terrmel Sledge for pitcher Adam Eaton, pitcher Akinori Otsuka and catcher Billy Killian, January 4, 2006.
c Traded to Boston Red Sox for pitcher Casey Kelly, outfielder Reymond Fuentes, infielder Anthony Rizzo and player to be named later, December 5, 2010. San Diego Padres received outfielder Eric Patterson to complete trade, December 16, 2010.
d Traded to Los Angeles Dodgers with outfielder Carl Crawford, pitcher Josh Beckett, infielder Nick Punto and cash for infielder James Loney, infielder Ivan DeJesus, pitcher Allen Webster and player to be named later, August 25, 2012. Boston Red Sox received pitcher Rubby De La Rosa to complete trade, October 4, 2012.

GONZALEZ, CARLOS EDUARDO

Born, Maracaibo, Venezuela, October 17, 1985.
Bats Left. Throws Left. Height, 6 feet, 1 inch. Weight, 200 pounds.

Year	Club	Lea	Pos	G	AB	R	H	2B	3B	HR	RBI	SB	Avg
2003	Missoula	Pioneer	OF	72	275	45	71	14	4	6	25	12	.258
2004	South Bend	Midwest	OF	12	42	3	11	4	0	1	6	0	.262
2004	Yakima	Northwest	OF	73	300	44	83	15	2	9	44	2	.277
2005	South Bend	Midwest	OF	129	515	91	158	28	6	18	92	7	.307
2006	Lancaster	Calif.	OF	104	403	82	121	35	4	21	94	15	.300
2006	Tennessee	Southern	OF	18	61	11	13	6	0	2	5	1	.213
2007	Tucson	P.C.	OF	10	42	9	13	5	0	1	11	1	.310
2007	Mobile a	Southern	OF	120	458	63	131	33	3	16	75	9	.286
2008	Sacramento	P.C.	OF	46	173	23	49	9	1	4	28	1	.283
2008	Oakland b	A.L.	OF	85	302	31	73	22	1	4	26	4	.242
2009	Colorado Springs	P.C.	OF	48	192	43	65	12	7	10	59	6	.339
2009	Colorado	N.L.	OF	89	278	53	79	14	7	13	29	16	.284
2010	Colorado	N.L.	OF	145	587	111	*197	34	9	34	117	26	*.336
2011	Colorado Springs	P.C.	OF	3	10	1	3	0	0	0	0	0	.300
2011	Colorado c	N.L.	OF	127	481	92	142	27	3	26	92	20	.295
2012	Colorado	N.L.	OF	135	518	89	157	31	5	22	85	20	.303
Major League Totals			5 Yrs.	581	2166	376	648	128	25	99	349	86	.299
Division Series													
2009	Colorado	N.L.	OF	4	17	5	10	2	0	1	1	2	.588

a Traded by Arizona Diamondbacks to Oakland Athletics with pitcher Brett Anderson, pitcher Dana Eveland, pitcher Greg Smith, infielder Chris Carter and outfielder Aaron Cunningham for pitcher Danny Haren and pitcher Connor Robertson, December 14, 2007.
b Traded to Colorado Rockies with pitcher Greg Smith and pitcher Huston Street for outfielder Matt Holliday, November 12, 2008.
c On disabled list from July 22 to August 6, 2011.

GORDON, ALEX JONATHAN

Born, Lincoln, Nebraska, February 10, 1984.
Bats Left. Throws Right. Height, 6 feet, 1 inch. Weight, 220 pounds.

Year	Club	Lea	Pos	G	AB	R	H	2B	3B	HR	RBI	SB	Avg
2006	Wichita	Texas	3B-1B	130	486	111	158	39	1	29	101	22	.325
2007	Kansas City	A.L.	3B-1B-SS	151	543	60	134	36	4	15	60	14	.247
2008	Kansas City a	A.L.	3B	134	493	72	128	35	1	16	59	9	.260
2009	Azl Royals	Arizona	3B	4	7	1	2	0	0	1	3	0	.286
2009	NW Arkansas	Texas	3B	8	30	4	11	3	0	2	10	0	.367
2009	Omaha	P.C.	3B	18	67	17	21	4	1	2	10	0	.313
2009	Kansas City b	A.L.	3B	49	164	28	38	6	0	6	22	5	.232
2010	Wilmington	Carolina	3B	7	17	7	4	3	0	0	2	1	.235
2010	Omaha	P.C.	OF	68	260	59	82	20	3	14	44	7	.315
2010	Kansas City c	A.L.	OF-3B-1B	74	242	34	52	10	0	8	20	1	.215
2011	Kansas City	A.L.	OF-1B	151	611	101	185	45	4	23	87	17	.303
2012	Kansas City	A.L.	OF	161	642	93	189	*51	5	14	72	10	.294
Major League Totals			6 Yrs.	720	2695	388	726	183	14	82	320	56	.269

a On disabled list from August 22 to September 12, 2008.
b On disabled list from April 16 to July 16, 2009.
c On disabled list from March 26 to April 17, 2010.

GORDON, DEVARIS (DEE)

Born, Windermere, Florida, April 22, 1988.
Bats Left. Throws Right. Height, 5 feet, 11 inches. Weight, 150 pounds.

Year	Club	Lea	Pos	G	AB	R	H	2B	3B	HR	RBI	SB	Avg
2008	Ogden	Pioneer	SS	60	251	45	83	13	3	2	27	18	.331
2009	Great Lakes	Midwest	SS	131	538	96	162	17	12	3	35	73	.301
2010	Chattanooga	Southern	SS	133	555	86	154	17	10	2	39	53	.277
2011	Rancho Cucamonga	Calif.	SS	3	11	4	3	0	0	0	0	2	.273
2011	Albuquerque	P.C.	SS	70	288	51	96	10	6	0	24	30	.333
2011	Los Angeles a	N.L.	SS	56	224	34	68	9	2	0	11	24	.304
2012	Albuquerque	P.C.	SS	8	30	3	8	0	1	0	1	2	.267
2012	Los Angeles b	N.L.	SS	87	303	38	69	9	2	1	17	32	.228
Major League Totals			2 Yrs.	143	527	72	137	18	4	1	28	56	.260

a On disabled list from August 10 to September 1, 2011.
b On disabled list from July 5 to September 11, 2012.

GRANDAL, YASMANI
Born, Havana, Cuba, November 8, 1988.
Bats Both. Throws Right. Height, 6 feet, 2 inches. Weight, 210 pounds.

Year Club	Lea	Pos	G	AB	R	H	2B	3B	HR	RBI	SB	Avg
2010 Reds............	Arizona	C	8	28	4	8	1	0	0	1	0	.286
2011 Bakersfield..........	Calif.	C	56	206	47	61	14	0	10	40	0	.296
2011 Louisville..........	Int.	C	4	12	2	6	2	0	0	2	0	.500
2011 Carolina a........	Southern	C	45	156	20	47	15	0	4	26	0	.301
2012 Lake Elsinore.........	Calif.	C	2	7	0	0	0	0	0	0	0	.000
2012 Tucson.............	P.C.	C	56	194	40	65	18	0	6	35	0	.335
2012 San Diego b..........	N.L.	C	60	192	28	57	7	1	8	36	0	.297

a Traded by Cincinnati Reds to San Diego Padres with pitcher Edinson Volquez, pitcher Brad Boxberger and infielder Yonder Alonso for pitcher Mat Latos, December 17, 2011.

b On disabled list from July 31 to August 17, 2012.

GRANDERSON, CURTIS
Born, Blue Island, Illinois, March 16, 1981.
Bats Left. Throws Right. Height, 6 feet, 1 inch. Weight, 185 pounds.

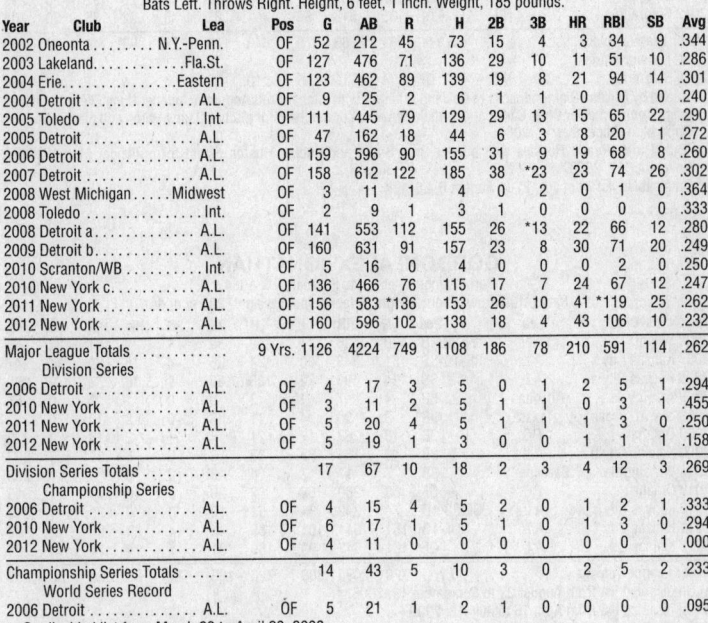

Year Club	Lea	Pos	G	AB	R	H	2B	3B	HR	RBI	SB	Avg
2002 Oneonta........	N.Y.-Penn.	OF	52	212	45	73	15	4	3	34	9	.344
2003 Lakeland...........	Fla.St.	OF	127	476	71	136	29	10	11	51	10	.286
2004 Erie...........	Eastern	OF	123	462	89	139	19	8	21	94	14	.301
2004 Detroit.............	A.L.	OF	9	25	2	6	1	1	0	0	0	.240
2005 Toledo.............	Int.	OF	111	445	79	129	29	13	15	65	22	.290
2005 Detroit.............	A.L.	OF	47	162	18	44	6	3	8	20	1	.272
2006 Detroit.............	A.L.	OF	159	596	90	155	31	9	19	68	8	.260
2007 Detroit.............	A.L.	OF	158	612	122	185	38	*23	23	74	26	.302
2008 West Michigan.....	Midwest	OF	3	11	1	4	0	2	0	1	0	.364
2008 Toledo.............	Int.	OF	2	9	1	3	1	0	0	0	0	.333
2008 Detroit a............	A.L.	OF	141	553	112	155	26	*13	22	66	12	.280
2009 Detroit b............	A.L.	OF	160	631	91	157	23	8	30	71	20	.249
2010 Scranton/WB..........	Int.	OF	5	16	0	4	0	0	0	2	0	.250
2010 New York c..........	A.L.	OF	136	466	76	115	17	7	24	67	12	.247
2011 New York...........	A.L.	OF	156	583	*136	153	26	10	41	*119	25	.262
2012 New York...........	A.L.	OF	160	596	102	138	18	4	43	106	10	.232
Major League Totals...........		9 Yrs.	1126	4224	749	1108	186	78	210	591	114	.262
Division Series												
2006 Detroit.............	A.L.	OF	4	17	3	5	0	1	2	5	1	.294
2010 New York...........	A.L.	OF	3	11	2	5	1	1	0	3	1	.455
2011 New York...........	A.L.	OF	5	20	4	5	1	1	1	3	0	.250
2012 New York...........	A.L.	OF	5	19	1	3	0	0	1	1	1	.158
Division Series Totals...........			17	67	10	18	2	3	4	12	3	.269
Championship Series												
2006 Detroit.............	A.L.	OF	4	15	4	5	2	0	1	2	1	.333
2010 New York...........	A.L.	OF	6	17	1	5	1	0	1	3	0	.294
2012 New York...........	A.L.	OF	4	11	0	0	0	0	0	0	1	.000
Championship Series Totals......			14	43	5	10	3	0	2	5	2	.233
World Series Record												
2006 Detroit.............	A.L.	OF	5	21	1	2	1	0	0	0	0	.095

a On disabled list from March 23 to April 23, 2008.

b Traded to New York Yankees for outfielder Austin Jackson, pitcher Phil Coke and pitcher Ian Kennedy, December 9, 2009.

c On disabled list from May 2 to May 28, 2010.

GREENE, JAMES TYLER (TYLER)
Born, Raleigh, North Carolina, August 17, 1983.
Bats Right. Throws Right. Height, 6 feet, 2 inches. Weight, 190 pounds.

Year Club	Lea	Pos	G	AB	R	H	2B	3B	HR	RBI	SB	Avg
2005 Palm Beach.....	Fla.St.	SS	20	85	17	23	4	0	2	5	6	.271
2005 New Jersey..	N.Y.-Penn.	SS	35	138	28	36	12	0	1	18	13	.261
2006 Palm Beach.....	Fla.St.	SS	71	268	38	60	10	1	5	19	22	.224
2006 Quad Cities.....	Midwest	SS	59	223	42	64	8	3	15	47	11	.287
2007 Springfield........	Texas	SS	65	221	41	54	17	2	8	25	10	.244
2008 Memphis.........	P.C.	SS	30	111	17	26	7	0	0	7	6	.234
2008 Springfield.......	Texas	SS-3B	97	374	62	97	15	4	16	41	14	.259
2009 Memphis..........	P.C.	SS-3B	89	340	70	99	10	5	15	42	31	.291
2009 St. Louis..........	N.L.	SS-3B-2B-1B	48	108	9	24	5	0	2	7	3	.222
2010 Palm Beach.....	Fla.St.	SS	2	7	0	0	0	0	0	0	0	.000

Year	Club	Lea	Pos	G	AB	R	H	2B	3B	HR	RBI	SB	Avg
2010 Memphis	P.C.		SS	82	338	67	96	21	5	9	34	12	.284
2010 St. Louis a	N.L.		SS-2B-3B	44	104	14	23	3	1	2	10	2	.221
2011 Memphis	P.C.		SS-2B	66	254	53	82	19	2	14	43	19	.323
2011 St. Louis	N.L.		2B-SS-OF	58	104	22	22	5	0	1	11	11	.212
2012 St. Louis-Houston b	N.L.		2B-SS-OF	116	305	34	70	15	2	11	30	12	.230
Major League Totals			4 Yrs.	266	621	79	139	28	3	16	58	28	.224

a On disabled list from August 1 to August 17, 2010.
b Sold to Houston Astros, August 9, 2012.

GUTIERREZ, FRANKLIN RAFAEL

Born, Caracas, Venezuela, February 21, 1983.
Bats Right. Throws Right. Height, 6 feet, 2 inches. Weight, 180 pounds.

Year	Club	Lea	Pos	G	AB	R	H	2B	3B	HR	RBI	SB	Avg
2001 Dodgers	Gulf Coast		OF	56	234	38	63	16	0	4	30	9	.269
2002 Las Vegas	P.C.		OF	2	10	2	3	2	0	0	2	0	.300
2002 South Bend	So.Atl.		OF	92	361	61	102	18	4	12	45	13	.283
2003 Vero Beach	Fla.St.		OF	110	425	65	120	28	5	20	68	17	.282
2003 Jacksonville	Southern		OF	18	67	12	21	3	2	4	12	3	.313
2004 Akron	Eastern		OF	70	262	38	79	24	2	5	35	6	.302
2004 Buffalo a	Int.		DH	7	27	4	4	1	0	1	3	0	.148
2005 Akron	Eastern		OF	95	383	70	100	25	2	11	42	14	.261
2005 Buffalo	Int.		OF	19	67	10	17	6	2	0	7	2	.254
2005 Cleveland	A.L.		OF	7	1	2	0	0	0	0	0	0	.000
2006 Buffalo	Int.		OF	90	349	63	97	27	0	9	38	13	.278
2006 Cleveland	A.L.		OF	43	136	21	37	9	0	1	8	0	.272
2007 Buffalo	Int.		OF	30	129	29	44	7	0	4	16	7	.341
2007 Cleveland b	A.L.		OF	100	271	41	72	13	2	13	36	8	.266
2008 Cleveland c	A.L.		OF	134	399	54	99	26	2	8	41	9	.248
2009 Seattle	A.L.		OF	153	565	85	160	24	1	18	70	16	.283
2010 Seattle	A.L.		OF	152	568	61	139	25	3	12	64	25	.245
2011 Tacoma	P.C.		OF	11	40	7	11	2	2	0	6	0	.275
2011 Seattle d	A.L.		OF	92	322	26	72	13	0	1	19	13	.224
2012 Tacoma	P.C.		OF	17	62	11	16	5	0	2	8	0	.258
2012 Seattle e	A.L.		OF	40	150	18	39	10	1	4	17	3	.260
Major League Totals			8 Yrs.	721	2412	308	618	120	9	57	255	74	.256
Division Series													
2007 Cleveland	A.L.		OF	4	10	2	2	0	0	0	0	0	.200
Championship Series													
2007 Cleveland	A.L.		OF	6	19	3	4	0	0	1	4	0	.211

a Traded to Cleveland Indians with player to be named later for outfielder Milton Bradley, April 4, 2004. Cleveland Indians received pitcher Andrew Brown to complete trade, May 19, 2004.
b On disabled list from March 23 to April 13, 2007.
c Traded to Seattle Mariners for infielder Luis Valbuena and pitcher Joe Smith, December 10, 2008.
d On disabled list from March 22 to May 18 and September 6 to October 31, 2011.
e On disabled list from March 24 to June 13 and June 29 to August 27, 2012.

GUZMAN, JESUS ANTONIO

Born, Cumana, Venezuela, June 14, 1984.
Bats Right. Throws Right. Height, 6 feet, 1 inch. Weight, 215 pounds.

Year	Club	Lea	Pos	G	AB	R	H	2B	3B	HR	RBI	SB	Avg
2004 Inland Empire	Calif.		3B-SS	114	442	80	137	35	3	6	71	10	.310
2005 San Antonio	Texas		3B	119	453	61	117	18	8	9	53	6	.258
2006 San Antonio	Texas		3B-2B	115	408	57	105	18	3	9	55	7	.257
2007 High Desert a	Calif.		2B-3B-OF-1B	130	518	102	156	38	5	25	112	3	.301
2008 Sacramento	P.C.		3B	15	59	5	14	2	0	2	9	0	.237
2008 Athletics	Arizona		3B-SS	5	15	2	7	3	0	1	3	1	.467
2008 Midland b	Texas		3B-2B	80	341	57	124	21	2	14	76	5	.364
2009 Fresno	P.C.		1B-3B	115	452	75	145	26	5	16	71	0	.321
2009 San Francisco	N.L.		1B	12	20	0	5	0	0	0	0	0	.250
2010 Fresno c	P.C.		3B-OF-1B	125	445	66	143	28	1	18	72	6	.321
2011 Tucson	P.C.		3B-OF-1B-2B	63	244	40	81	22	1	8	57	4	.332
2011 San Diego	N.L.		1B-OF	76	247	33	77	22	2	5	44	9	.312
2012 San Diego	N.L.		OF-1B-2B	120	287	32	71	18	2	9	48	3	.247
Major League Totals			3 Yrs.	208	554	65	153	40	4	14	92	12	.276

a Filed for free agency from Seattle Mariners, October 29, 2007. Signed with Oakland Athletics organization, November 16, 2007.
b Filed for free agency, November 3, 2008. Signed with San Francisco Giants organization, November 18, 2008.
c Filed for free agency, November 6, 2010. Signed with San Diego Padres organization, November 29, 2010.

GWYNN, ANTHONY KEITH JR. (TONY)

Born, Long Beach, California, October 4, 1982.
Bats Left. Throws Right. Height, 6 feet. Weight, 195 pounds.

Year Club	Lea	Pos	G	AB	R	H	2B	3B	HR	RBI	SB	Avg
2003 Beloit	Midwest	OF	61	236	35	66	8	0	1	33	14	.280
2004 Huntsville	Southern	OF	138	534	74	130	20	5	2	37	35	.243
2005 Huntsville	Southern	OF	133	509	83	138	21	5	1	41	34	.271
2006 Nashville	.P.C.	OF	112	447	73	134	21	5	4	42	30	.300
2006 Milwaukee	N.L.	OF	32	77	5	20	2	1	0	4	3	.260
2007 Nashville	.P.C.	OF	32	126	19	36	3	3	0	13	4	.286
2007 Milwaukee	N.L.	OF	69	123	13	32	3	2	0	10	8	.260
2008 Nashville	.P.C.	OF	93	375	47	103	9	3	2	26	20	.275
2008 Milwaukee a	N.L.	OF	29	42	5	8	1	0	0	1	3	.190
2009 Nashville	.P.C.	OF	38	152	34	47	8	1	1	9	15	.309
2009 San Diego b	N.L.	OF	119	393	59	106	11	6	2	21	11	.270
2010 San Diego c-d	N.L.	OF	117	289	30	59	9	3	3	20	17	.204
2011 Los Angeles	N.L.	OF	136	312	37	80	12	6	2	22	22	.256
2012 Albuquerque	.P.C.	OF	19	68	12	23	4	1	0	7	4	.338
2012 Los Angeles	N.L.	OF	103	259	29	60	8	4	0	17	13	.232
Major League Totals	7 Yrs.		605	1495	178	365	46	22	7	95	77	.244
Division Series												
2008 Milwaukee	N.L.	PH	3	3	0	1	0	0	0	0	0	.333

a On disabled list from April 4 to April 23, 2008.
b Traded to San Diego Padres for outfielder Jody Gerut, May 21, 2009.
c On disabled list from August 19 to September 13, 2010.
d Not offered contract, December 2, 2010. Signed with Los Angeles Dodgers, December 11, 2010.

HAFNER, TRAVIS LEE

Born, Jamestown, North Dakota, June 3, 1977.
Bats Left. Throws Right. Height, 6 feet, 3 inches. Weight, 240 pounds.

Year Club	Lea	Pos	G	AB	R	H	2B	3B	HR	RBI	SB	Avg
1997 Rangers	Gulf Coast	1B-OF	55	189	38	54	14	0	5	24	7	.286
1998 Savannah	So.Atl.	1B-3B-OF	123	405	62	96	15	4	16	84	7	.237
1999 Savannah	So.Atl.	1B	134	480	94	140	30	4	28	111	5	.292
2000 Charlotte a	Fla.St.	1B-3B	122	436	90	151	34	1	22	109	0	.346
2001 Tulsa b	Texas	1B	88	323	59	91	25	0	20	74	3	.282
2002 Oklahoma	.P.C.	1B	110	401	79	137	22	1	21	77	2	.342
2002 Texas c	A.L.	DH-1B	23	62	6	15	4	1	1	6	0	.242
2003 Buffalo	Int.	1B	29	100	15	27	4	0	2	10	2	.270
2003 Cleveland d	A.L.	DH-1B	91	291	35	74	19	3	14	40	2	.254
2004 Cleveland	A.L.	DH-1B	140	482	96	150	41	3	28	109	3	.311
2005 Akron	Eastern	DH	3	9	0	0	0	0	0	0	0	.000
2005 Cleveland e	A.L.	DH-1B	137	486	94	148	42	0	33	108	0	.305
2006 Cleveland	A.L.	DH-1B	129	454	100	140	31	1	42	117	0	.308
2007 Cleveland	A.L.	DH-1B	152	545	80	145	25	2	24	100	1	.266
2008 Buffalo	Int.	DH	7	22	4	7	3	0	0	4	0	.318
2008 Cleveland f	A.L.	DH	57	198	21	39	10	0	5	24	1	.197
2009 Columbus	Int.	DH	12	39	6	13	4	0	1	8	0	.333
2009 Cleveland g	A.L.	DH	94	338	46	92	19	0	16	49	0	.272
2010 Cleveland h	A.L.	DH	118	396	46	110	29	0	13	50	2	.278
2011 Akron	Eastern	DH	2	6	2	3	1	0	0	0	0	.500
2011 Cleveland i	A.L.	DH	94	325	41	91	16	0	13	57	0	.280
2012 Columbus	Int.	DH	3	10	0	1	0	0	0	1	0	.100
2012 Cleveland j-k	A.L.	DH	66	219	23	50	6	2	12	34	0	.228
Major League Totals	11 Yrs.		1101	3796	588	1054	242	12	201	694	9	.278
Division Series												
2007 Cleveland	A.L.	DH	4	16	4	4	0	0	1	2	0	.250
Championship Series												
2007 Cleveland	A.L.	DH	7	27	2	4	1	0	1	2	0	.148

a On disabled list from August 6 to 22, 2000.
b On disabled list from April 5 to May 11, 2001.
c Traded to Cleveland Indians with pitcher Aaron Myette for catcher Einar Diaz and pitcher Ryan Drese, December 6, 2002.
d On disabled list from May 10 to May 26, 2003.
e On disabled list from July 17 to August 4, 2005.
f On disabled list from May 26 to September 9, 2008.
g On disabled list from April 29 to June 5, 2009.
h On disabled list from July 29 to August 15, 2010.
i On disabled list from May 18 to June 17 and August 22 to September 11, 2011.
j On disabled list from May 24 to July 4 and August 6 to September 18, 2012.
k Filed for free agency, November 3, 2012.

HAIRSTON, JERRY WAYNE JR.

Born, Naperville, Illinois, May 29, 1976.
Bats Right. Throws Right. Height, 5 feet, 10 inches. Weight, 185 pounds.

Year	Club	Lea	Pos	G	AB	R	H	2B	3B	HR	RBI	SB	Avg
1997	Bluefield	Appal.	SS	59	221	44	73	13	4	2	36	13	.330
1998	Frederick	Carolina	SS-2B	80	293	56	83	22	3	5	33	13	.283
1998	Bowie	Eastern	2B-SS	55	221	42	72	12	3	5	37	6	.326
1998	Baltimore	A.L.	2B	6	7	2	0	0	0	0	0	0	.000
1999	Rochester	Int.	2B	107	413	65	120	24	5	7	48	19	.291
1999	Baltimore	A.L.	2B	50	175	26	47	12	1	4	17	9	.269
2000	Rochester	Int.	2B-SS	58	201	43	59	15	1	4	21	6	.294
2000	Orioles	Gulf Coast	2B	4	10	3	3	2	0	0	3	4	.300
2000	Frederick	Carolina	2B	2	8	1	3	2	0	0	1	0	.375
2000	Baltimore a	A.L.	2B	49	180	27	46	5	0	5	19	8	.256
2001	Baltimore	A.L.	2B	159	532	63	124	25	5	8	47	29	.233
2002	Baltimore	A.L.	2B	122	426	55	114	25	3	5	32	21	.268
2003	Aberdeen	N.Y.-Penn.	2B	2	3	2	1	0	0	0	0	1	.333
2003	Bowie	Eastern	2B	6	20	4	6	1	0	1	2	0	.300
2003	Baltimore b	A.L.	2B	58	218	25	59	12	2	2	21	14	.271
2004	Bowie	Eastern	2B	5	13	4	2	1	0	0	2	2	.154
2004	Baltimore c	A.L.	OF-2B-3B	86	287	43	87	19	1	2	24	13	.303
2005	Iowa	P.C.	2B-OF	5	22	3	7	0	1	0	2	3	.318
2005	Chicago d-e	N.L.	OF-2B-SS	114	380	51	99	25	2	4	30	8	.261
2006	Chicago	N.L.	2B-OF-1B	38	82	8	17	3	0	0	4	3	.207
2006	Texas f-g	A.L.	OF-SS-2B-3B	63	88	17	18	3	1	0	6	2	.205
2007	Frisco	Texas	DH	3	12	2	2	1	0	1	2	0	.167
2007	Oklahoma	P.C.	SS-OF	4	15	2	2	0	0	1	1	0	.133
2007	Texas h-i	A.L.	OF-2B-SS	73	159	22	30	7	0	3	16	5	.189
2008	Louisville	Int.	OF-SS-3B-2B	20	79	11	30	8	2	4	19	1	.380
2008	Cincinnati j-k	N.L.	OF-SS-2B-3B	80	261	47	85	20	2	6	36	15	.326
2009	Cincinnati	N.L.	3B-SS-OF-2B	86	307	47	78	18	1	8	27	7	.254
2009	New York l-m	A.L.	OF-3B-SS-2B	45	76	15	18	5	0	2	12	0	.237
2010	San Diego n-o	N.L.	SS-2B-OF-3B	119	430	53	105	13	2	10	50	9	.244
2011	Harrisburg	Eastern	SS	2	6	1	1	0	0	0	0	0	.167
2011	Wash.-Milwaukee p-q-r	N.L.	3B-OF-2B-SS	120	337	43	91	21	1	5	31	3	.270
2012	Albuquerque	P.C.	2B-3B-OF	2	6	0	0	0	0	0	0	0	.000
2012	Los Angeles s	N.L.	3B-2B-OF-SS	78	238	19	65	13	1	4	26	1	.273
Major League Totals			15 Yrs.	1346	4183	563	1083	226	22	68	398	147	.259
Division Series													
2009	New York	A.L.	PH	1	0	0	0	0	0	0	0	0	.000
2011	Milwaukee	N.L.	3B	5	16	2	6	2	0	0	3	0	.375
Division Series Totals				6	16	2	6	2	0	0	3	0	.375
Championship Series													
2009	New York	A.L.	OF	2	2	1	1	0	0	0	0	0	.500
2011	Milwaukee	N.L.	3B	6	23	6	9	4	0	0	1	0	.391
Championship Series Totals				8	25	7	10	4	0	0	1	0	.400
World Series Record													
2009	New York	A.L.	OF	3	6	0	1	0	0	0	0	0	.167

a On disabled list from May 16 to July 4, 2000.
b On disabled list from May 21 to September 4, 2003.
c On disabled list from March 31 to May 11 and from August 18 to November 3, 2004.
d Traded to Chicago Cubs with infielder Mike Fontenot and pitcher Dave Crouthers for outfielder Sammy Sosa, February 2, 2005.
e On disabled list from August 4 to August 19, 2005.
f Traded to Texas Rangers for infielder Phil Nevin, May 31, 2006.
g Filed for free agency, October 13, 2006, re-signed with Texas Rangers organization, January 5, 2007.
h On disabled list from May 17 to June 5 and August 8 to August 29, 2007.
i Filed for free agency, October 30, 2007. Signed with Cincinnati Reds organization, March 3, 2008.
j On disabled list from June 10 to June 26 and July 14 to August 1 and August 18 to September 8, 2008.
k Filed for free agency, October 31, 2008, re-signed with Cincinnati Reds, January 7, 2009.
l Traded to New York Yankees for catcher Chase Weems, July 31, 2009.
m Filed for free agency, November 10, 2009. Signed with the San Diego Padres, January 18, 2010.
n On disabled list from August 28 to September 12, 2010.
o Filed for free agency, November 1, 2010. Signed with Washington Nationals, January 19, 2011.
p On disabled list from June 30 to July 18, 2011.
q Traded to Milwaukee Brewers for outfielder Erik Komatsu, July 30, 2011.
r Filed for free agency, October 30, 2011. Signed with Los Angeles Dodgers, December 5, 2011.
s On disabled list from May 7 to May 25 and August 12 to October 29, 2012.

HAIRSTON, SCOTT ALEXANDER

Born, Fort Worth, Texas, May 25, 1980.
Bats Right. Throws Right. Height, 6 feet. Weight, 190 pounds.

Year Club	Lea	Pos	G	AB	R	H	2B	3B	HR	RBI	SB	Avg
2001 Missoula	Pioneer	2B	74	291	81	101	16	6	14	65	2	.347
2002 Lancaster	Calif.	2B-3B	18	79	20	32	11	1	6	26	1	.405
2002 South Bend	Midwest	2B-3B	109	394	79	131	35	4	16	72	9	.332
2003 Tucson	P.C.	DH	1	0	0	0	0	0	0	1	0	.000
2003 El Paso	Texas	2B	88	337	53	93	21	7	10	47	6	.276
2004 Tucson	P.C.	2B-OF	28	115	29	36	8	3	5	20	0	.313
2004 Arizona	N.L.	2B-OF	101	339	39	84	15	6	13	29	3	.248
2005 Arizona	N.L.	OF	15	20	0	2	1	0	0	0	0	.100
2005 Tucson a	P.C.	OF-2B	58	209	45	65	8	3	16	40	3	.311
2006 Tucson	P.C.	OF	98	381	83	123	22	1	26	81	3	.323
2006 Arizona b	N.L.	OF	9	15	2	6	2	0	0	2	0	.400
2007 Arizona-San Diego c-d	N.L.	OF	107	263	37	64	18	2	11	36	2	.243
2008 San Diego e	N.L.	OF-2B	112	326	42	81	18	3	17	31	3	.248
2009 Lake Elsinore	Calif.	OF	3	10	1	1	0	0	0	0	0	.100
2009 San Diego	N.L.	OF	56	197	26	59	14	1	10	29	8	.299
2009 Oakland f-g-h	A.L.	OF	60	233	24	55	13	1	7	35	3	.236
2010 Lake Elsinore	Calif.	OF	3	7	1	4	1	0	0	1	0	.571
2010 San Diego i-j	N.L.	OF	104	295	34	62	10	0	10	36	6	.210
2011 New York k-l	N.L.	OF-2B	79	132	20	31	8	1	7	24	1	.235
2012 New York m	N.L.	OF	134	377	52	99	25	3	20	57	8	.263
Major League Totals		9 Yrs.	777	2197	276	543	124	17	95	279	34	.247

a On disabled list from September 2 to November 14, 2005.
b On disabled list from June 20 to July 29, 2006.
c Traded to San Diego Padres for pitcher Leo Rosales, July 27, 2007.
d On disabled list from August 10 to September 8, 2007.
e On disabled list from August 28 to October 2, 2008.
f On disabled list from June 3 to June 23, 2009.
g Traded to Oakland Athletics for pitcher Ryan Webb, pitcher Craig Italiano and player to be named later, July 5, 2009. San Diego Padres received pitcher Sean Gallagher to complete trade, July 28, 2009.
h Traded to San Diego Padres with outfielder Aaron Cunningham for third baseman Kevin Kouzmanoff and infielder Eric Sogard, January 16, 2010.
i On disabled list from May 16 to June 2, 2010.
j Not offered contract, December 2, 2010. Signed with New York Mets, January 20, 2011.
k On disabled list from August 24 to September 30, 2011.
l Filed for free agency, October 30, 2011, re-signed with New York Mets, January 6, 2012.
m Filed for free agency, November 3, 2012.

HAMILTON, JOSHUA HOLT (JOSH)

Born, Raleigh, North Carolina, May 21, 1981.
Bats Left. Throws Left. Height, 6 feet, 4 inches. Weight, 235 pounds.

Year Club	Lea	Pos	G	AB	R	H	2B	3B	HR	RBI	SB	Avg
1999 Princeton	Appal.	OF	56	236	49	82	20	4	10	48	17	.347
1999 Hudson Valley	N.Y.-Penn.	OF	16	72	7	14	3	0	0	7	1	.194
2000 Charleston-SC	So.Atl.	OF	96	391	62	118	23	3	13	61	14	.302
2001 Charleston-SC	So.Atl.	OF	4	11	3	4	1	0	1	2	0	.364
2001 Orlando	Southern	OF	23	89	5	16	5	0	0	4	2	.180
2002 Bakersfield	Calif.	OF	56	211	32	64	14	1	9	44	10	.303
2003-05					Did Not Play							
2006 Hudson Valley a	N.Y.-Penn.	OF	15	50	7	13	3	1	0	5	0	.260
2007 Louisville	Int.	OF	11	40	9	14	1	0	4	8	3	.350
2007 Cincinnati b-c	N.L.	OF	90	298	52	87	17	2	19	47	3	.292
2008 Texas	A.L.	OF	156	624	98	190	35	5	32	*130	9	.304
2009 Frisco	Texas	DH	1	4	1	1	0	0	0	1	1	.250
2009 Oklahoma	P.C.	OF	7	28	3	5	2	1	0	0	1	.179
2009 Texas d	A.L.	OF	89	336	43	90	19	2	10	54	8	.268
2010 Texas e	A.L.	OF	133	518	95	186	40	3	32	100	8	*.359
2011 Frisco	Texas	DH	2	7	3	2	0	0	1	3	0	.286
2011 Round Rock	P.C.	DH	3	11	2	2	1	0	1	3	0	.182
2011 Texas f	A.L.	OF	121	487	80	145	31	5	25	94	8	.298
2012 Texas g	A.L.	OF	148	562	103	160	31	2	43	128	7	.285
Major League Totals		6 Yrs.	737	2825	471	858	173	19	161	553	43	.304
Wild Card Playoff												
2012 Texas	A.L.	OF	1	4	0	0	0	0	0	0	0	.000
Division Series												
2010 Texas	A.L.	OF	5	18	1	2	0	0	0	1	1	.111

Year	Club	Lea	Pos	G	AB	R	H	2B	3B	HR	RBI	SB	Avg
2011 Texas	A.L.	OF	4	15	1	4	1	0	0	2	0	.267
Division Series Totals			9	33	2	6	1	0	0	3	1	.182
Championship Series													
2010 Texas	A.L.	OF	6	20	6	7	1	0	4	7	3	.350
2011 Texas	A.L.	OF	6	26	4	8	4	0	0	5	0	.308
Championship Series Totals			12	46	10	15	5	0	4	12	3	.326
World Series Record													
2010 Texas	A.L.	OF	5	20	2	2	0	0	1	1	0	.100
2011 Texas	A.L.	OF	7	29	4	7	2	0	1	6	0	.241
World Series Totals............			12	49	6	9	2	0	2	7	0	.184

a Selected by Chicago Cubs from Tampa Bay Devil Rays in Rule V draft, December 7, 2006. Sold to Cincinnati Reds, December 7, 2006.
b On disabled list from May 19 to June 4 and July 8 to August 12, 2007.
c Traded to Texas Rangers for pitcher Edinson Volquez and pitcher Danny Herrera, December 21, 2007.
d On disabled list from April 27 to May 12 and June 1 to July 6, 2009.
e Selected Most Valuable Player in American League for 2010.
f On disabled list from April 13 to May 23, 2011.
g Filed for free agency, November 3, 2012. Signed with Los Angeles Angels, December 15, 2012.

HANIGAN, RYAN M.

Born, Washington, District of Columbia, August 16, 1980.
Bats Right. Throws Right. Height, 6 feet. Weight, 195 pounds.

Year	Club	Lea	Pos	G	AB	R	H	2B	3B	HR	RBI	SB	Avg
2002 Dayton	Midwest	C	6	11	1	3	1	0	0	0	0	.273
2003 Louisville	Int.	C	1	3	1	1	0	0	0	0	0	.333
2003 Dayton	Midwest	C	92	311	43	86	12	0	1	31	3	.277
2004 Potomac.........	Carolina	C	119	429	58	127	21	0	5	56	6	.296
2005 Chattanooga......	Southern	1B-C	100	333	45	107	14	1	4	29	4	.321
2006 Louisville	Int.	C-1B	8	13	2	2	0	0	0	1	0	.154
2006 Chattanooga......	Southern	C-1B-OF	56	126	17	31	2	0	0	14	0	.246
2007 Chattanooga......	Southern	C-1B	60	197	30	59	14	1	3	27	0	.299
2007 Louisville	Int.	C-1B	41	127	16	32	5	0	1	9	0	.252
2007 Cincinnati............	N.L.	C	5	10	3	3	1	0	0	2	0	.300
2008 Louisville	Int.	C-1B	75	272	37	88	14	0	4	35	1	.324
2008 Cincinnati............	N.L.	C	31	85	9	23	2	0	2	9	0	.271
2009 Louisville	Int.	C	5	18	4	7	2	0	0	2	0	.389
2009 Cincinnati a	N.L.	C	90	251	22	66	6	1	3	11	0	.263
2010 Louisville	Int.	C	13	46	6	11	3	0	0	2	0	.239
2010 Cincinnati b	N.L.	C	70	203	25	61	11	0	5	40	0	.300
2011 Cincinnati............	N.L.	C	91	266	27	71	6	0	6	31	0	.267
2012 Cincinnati............	N.L.	C	112	317	25	87	14	0	2	24	0	.274
Major League Totals		6 Yrs.	399	1132	111	311	40	1	18	117	0	.275	
Division Series													
2010 Cincinnati............	N.L.	C	2	4	0	0	0	0	0	0	0	.000
2012 Cincinnati............	N.L.	C	4	15	3	3	0	0	0	3	0	.200
Division Series Totals			6	19	3	3	0	0	0	3	0	.158

a On disabled list from August 24 to September 9, 2009.
b On disabled list from May 29 to July 9, 2010.

HANNAHAN, JOHN JOSEPH (JACK)

Born, St.Paul, Minnesota, March 4, 1980.
Bats Left. Throws Right. Height, 6 feet, 2 inches. Weight, 210 pounds.

Year	Club	Lea	Pos	G	AB	R	H	2B	3B	HR	RBI	SB	Avg
2001 Oneonta	N.Y.-Penn.	3B	14	55	11	16	4	1	0	8	2	.291
2001 West Michigan .	Midwest	3B	46	170	24	54	11	0	1	27	4	.318
2002 Lakeland.......	Fla.St.	3B	66	246	28	67	11	4	6	42	9	.272
2002 Erie...........	Eastern	3B	65	226	17	54	12	1	3	20	2	.239
2003 Erie...........	Eastern	3B	135	471	64	121	18	0	9	45	2	.257
2004 Erie...........	Eastern	3B-SS	108	374	48	102	21	1	8	39	7	.273
2005 Erie...........	Eastern	3B	7	22	1	3	0	0	0	1	0	.136
2005 Toledo	Int.	3B-1B-2B	68	238	31	64	15	0	4	28	6	.269
2006 Detroit	A.L.	1B	3	9	0	0	0	0	0	0	0	.000
2006 Toledo	Int.	2B-3B-1B	119	415	59	117	27	0	9	62	9	.282
2007 Toledo	Int.	2B-3B-1B	101	336	56	99	20	1	13	63	5	.295
2007 Oakland a	A.L.	3B	41	144	16	40	12	0	3	24	1	.278
2008 Oakland	A.L.	3B-1B	143	436	48	95	27	0	9	47	2	.218

Year Club Lea	Pos	G	AB	R	H	2B	3B	HR	RBI	SB	Avg
2009 Sacramento .... P.C.	3B-2B	21	81	8	18	7	0	2	11	0	.222
2009 Oakland-Seattle b... A.L.	3B-1B-SS-2B	103	267	27	57	14	2	4	19	1	.213
2010 Pawtucket .... Int.	3B-2B-1B	33	110	15	28	8	0	4	12	2	.255
2010 Tacoma c .... P.C.	2B-3B-SS	63	224	32	51	9	1	5	33	1	.228
2011 Cleveland .... A.L.	3B-1B	110	320	38	80	16	2	8	40	2	.250
2012 Lake County ... Midwest	3B	2	8	0	1	0	0	0	1	0	.125
2012 Columbus........ Int.	DH	1	4	0	0	0	0	0	0	0	.000
2012 Cleveland d-e ..... A.L.	3B-SS-1B	105	287	23	70	16	0	4	29	0	.244
Major League Totals .... 6 Yrs.		505	1463	152	342	85	4	28	159	6	.234

a Traded by Detroit Tigers to Oakland Athletics for outfielder Jason Perry, August 13, 2007.
b Traded to Seattle Mariners for pitcher Justin Souza, July 11, 2009.
c On disabled list from March 26 to April 30, 2010.
d On disabled list from May 27 to June 14, 2012.
e Not offered contract, November 30, 2012. Signed with Cincinnati Reds, December 13, 2012.

HARDY, JAMES JERRY (J.J.)

Born, Tucson, Arizona, August 19, 1982.
Bats Right. Throws Right. Height, 6 feet, 2 inches. Weight, 190 pounds.

Year Club Lea	Pos	G	AB	R	H	2B	3B	HR	RBI	SB	Avg
2001 Brewers .... Arizona	SS	5	20	6	5	2	1	0	1	0	.250
2001 Ogden .... Pioneer	SS	35	125	20	31	5	0	2	15	1	.248
2002 High Desert ..... California	SS	84	335	53	98	19	1	6	48	9	.293
2002 Huntsville....... Southern	SS	38	145	14	33	7	0	1	13	1	.228
2003 Huntsville....... Southern	SS	114	416	.67	116	26	0	12	62	6	.279
2004 Indianapolis .... Int.	SS	26	101	17	28	10	0	4	20	0	.277
2005 Milwaukee .... N.L.	SS	124	372	46	92	22	1	9	50	0	.247
2006 Milwaukee a .... N.L.	SS	35	128	13	31	5	0	5	14	1	.242
2007 Milwaukee .... N.L.	SS	151	592	89	164	30	1	26	80	2	.277
2008 Milwaukee .... N.L.	SS	146	569	78	161	31	4	24	74	2	.283
2009 Nashville .... P.C.	SS	18	71	7	18	2	0	4	12	0	.254
2009 Milwaukee b .... N.L.	SS	115	414	53	95	16	2	11	47	0	.229
2010 Beloit .... Midwest	SS	3	10	0	2	0	0	0	0	0	.200
2010 Minnesota c-d .... A.L.	SS	101	340	44	91	19	3	6	38	1	.268
2011 Norfolk............... Int.	SS	3	9	2	2	0	0	0	0	0	.222
2011 Baltimore e........... A.L.	SS	129	527	76	142	27	0	30	80	0	.269
2012 Baltimore .... A.L.	SS	158	663	85	158	30	2	22	68	0	.238
Major League Totals .... 8 Yrs.		959	3605	484	934	180	13	133	451	6	.259
Wild Card Playoff											
2012 Baltimore .... A.L.	SS	1	5	1	2	0	0	0	1	0	.400
Division Series											
2008 Milwaukee .... N.L.	SS	4	14	2	6	1	0	0	2	0	.429
2010 Minnesota .... A.L.	SS	3	10	0	1	1	0	0	0	0	.100
2012 Baltimore .... A.L.	SS	5	22	0	3	2	0	0	1	0	.136
Division Series Totals		12	46	2	10	4	0	0	3	0	.217

a On disabled list from May 17 to October 31, 2006.
b Traded to Minnesota Twins for outfielder Carlos Gomez, November 6, 2009.
c On disabled list from May 5 to May 25 and June 7 to July 3, 2010.
d Traded to Baltimore Orioles with infielder Brendan Harris and cash for pitcher Jim Hoey and pitcher Brett Jacobson, December 9, 2010.
e On disabled list from April 10 to May 10, 2011.

HARPER, BRYCE ARON MAX (BRYCE)

Born, Las Vegas, Nevada, October 16, 1992.
Bats Left. Throws Right. Height, 6 feet, 3 inches. Weight, 215 pounds.

Year Club Lea	Pos	G	AB	R	H	2B	3B	HR	RBI	SB	Avg
2011 Harrisburg .... Eastern	OF	37	129	14	33	7	1	3	12	7	.256
2011 Hagerstown .... So.Atl.	OF	72	258	49	82	17	1	14	46	19	.318
2012 Syracuse .... Int.	OF	21	74	8	18	4	1	1	3	1	.243
2012 Washington a......... N.L.	OF	139	533	98	144	26	9	22	59	18	.270
Division Series											
2012 Washington .... N.L.	OF	5	23	2	3	1	1	1	2	0	.130

a Selected Rookie of the Year in National League for 2012.

HARRISON, JOSH ISAIAH

Born, Cincinnati, Ohio, July 8, 1987.
Bats Right. Throws Right. Height, 5 feet, 8 inches. Weight, 185 pounds.

Year	Club	Lea	Pos	G	AB	R	H	2B	3B	HR	RBI	SB	Avg
2008 Boise	Northwest	2B-OF	33	114	27	40	11	2	1	25	12	.351
2008 Peoria	Midwest	2B-OF	31	122	15	32	4	1	1	4	6	.262
2009 Peoria	Midwest	OF-2B-3B	79	303	51	102	17	7	4	33	16	.337
2009 Daytona a	Fla.St.	OF-2B-3B	18	70	10	20	3	1	1	9	10	.286
2009 Lynchburg	Carolina	3B-2B-OF	34	141	15	38	8	1	1	13	4	.270
2010 Altoona	Eastern	3B-2B	135	520	74	156	33	3	4	75	19	.300
2011 Indianapolis	Int.	3B-2B-SS	62	226	35	70	15	2	5	23	13	.310
2011 Pittsburgh	N.L.	3B-2B	65	195	21	53	13	2	1	16	4	.272
2012 Pittsburgh	N.L.	2B-SS-3B-OF	104	249	34	58	9	5	3	16	7	.233
Major League Totals		2 Yrs.	169	444	55	111	22	7	4	32	11	.250

a Traded by Chicago Cubs to Pittsburgh Pirates with pitcher Kevin Hart and pitcher Jose Ascanio for pitcher John Grabow and pitcher Tom Gorzelanny, July 30, 2009.

HART, JON COREY (COREY)

Born, Bowling Green, Kentucky, March 24, 1982.
Bats Right. Throws Right. Height, 6 feet, 6 inches. Weight, 215 pounds.

Year	Club	Lea	Pos	G	AB	R	H	2B	3B	HR	RBI	SB	Avg
2000 Ogden	Pioneer	1B	57	216	32	62	9	1	2	30	6	.287
2001 Ogden	Pioneer	1B-OF	69	262	53	89	18	1	11	62	14	.340
2002 High Desert	Calif.	3B-1B	100	393	76	113	26	10	22	84	24	.288
2002 Huntsville	Southern	3B-1B	28	94	16	25	3	0	2	15	3	.266
2003 Huntsville	Southern	3B-OF	130	493	70	149	40	1	13	94	25	.302
2004 Indianapolis	Int.	OF-1B	121	440	68	124	29	8	15	67	17	.282
2004 Milwaukee	N.L.	DH	1	1	0	0	0	0	0	0	0	.000
2005 Milwaukee	N.L.	OF	21	57	9	11	2	1	2	7	2	.193
2005 Nashville	P.C.	OF-1B	113	429	85	132	29	9	17	69	31	.308
2006 Milwaukee	N.L.	OF-1B	87	237	32	67	13	2	9	33	5	.283
2007 Milwaukee	N.L.	OF	140	505	86	149	33	9	24	81	23	.295
2008 Milwaukee	N.L.	OF	157	612	76	164	45	6	20	91	23	.268
2009 Nashville	P.C.	OF	4	10	5	5	1	0	1	3	0	.500
2009 Milwaukee a	N.L.	OF	115	419	64	109	24	3	12	48	11	.260
2010 Milwaukee	N.L.	OF	145	558	91	158	34	4	31	102	7	.283
2011 Nashville	P.C.	OF	5	15	1	2	2	0	0	1	0	.133
2011 Milwaukee b	N.L.	OF	130	492	80	140	25	4	26	63	7	.285
2012 Milwaukee	N.L.	1B-OF	149	562	91	152	35	4	30	83	5	.270
Major League Totals		9 Yrs.	945	3443	529	950	211	33	154	508	83	.276
Division Series													
2008 Milwaukee	N.L.	OF	4	13	0	3	0	0	0	0	0	.231
2011 Milwaukee	N.L.	OF	5	21	4	5	0	0	1	3	0	.238
Division Series Totals			9	34	4	8	0	0	1	3	0	.235
Championship Series													
2011 Milwaukee	N.L.	OF	5	20	2	5	0	0	1	2	0	.250

a On disabled list from August 2 to September 8, 2009.
b On disabled list from March 22 to April 26, 2011.

HEADLEY, CHASE JORDAN

Born, Fountain, Colorado, May 9, 1984.
Bats Both. Throws Right. Height, 6 feet, 2 inches. Weight, 195 pounds.

Year	Club	Lea	Pos	G	AB	R	H	2B	3B	HR	RBI	SB	Avg
2005 Fort Wayne	Midwest	3B	4	15	2	3	0	0	0	1	0	.200
2005 Eugene	Northwest	3B	57	220	29	59	14	3	6	33	1	.268
2006 Lake Elsinore	Calif.	3B	129	484	79	141	33	0	12	73	4	.291
2007 San Antonio	Texas	3B	121	433	82	143	38	5	20	78	1	.330
2007 San Diego	N.L.	3B	18	11	4	1	1	0	0	0	0	.222
2008 Portland	P.C.	OF-3B	65	259	49	79	24	1	13	40	0	.305
2008 San Diego	N.L.	OF-3B	91	331	34	89	19	2	9	38	4	.269
2009 San Diego	N.L.	OF-3B-1B	156	543	62	142	31	2	12	64	10	.262
2010 San Diego	N.L.	3B	161	610	77	161	29	3	11	58	17	.264
2011 San Diego a	N.L.	3B	113	381	43	110	28	1	4	44	13	.289
2012 San Diego	N.L.	3B-1B	161	604	95	173	31	2	31	*115	17	.286
Major League Totals		6 Yrs.	690	2487	312	679	139	10	67	319	61	.273

a On disabled list from August 7 to September 19, 2011.

HECHAVARRIA (BARETTA), ADEINY
Born, Santiago de Cuba, Cuba, April 15, 1989.
Bats Right. Throws Right. Height, 5 feet, 11 inches. Weight, 180 pounds.

Year	Club	Lea	Pos	G	AB	R	H	2B	3B	HR	RBI	SB	Avg
2010 New Hampshire	Eastern		SS	61	253	36	69	11	1	3	34	6	.273
2010 Dunedin	Fla.St.		SS	41	161	21	31	7	3	1	7	7	.193
2011 New Hampshire	Eastern		SS	111	464	58	109	22	6	6	46	19	.235
2011 Las Vegas	P.C.		SS	25	108	16	42	6	2	2	11	1	.389
2012 Las Vegas	P.C.		SS-2B	102	443	78	138	20	6	6	63	8	.312
2012 Toronto a	A.L.		3B-SS-2B	41	126	10	32	8	0	2	15	0	.254

a Traded to Miami Marlins with pitcher Henderson Alvarez, infielder Yunel Escobar, catcher Jeff Mathis, pitcher Anthony De Sclafani, outfielder Jake Marisnick and pitcher Justin Nicolino for outfielder Emilio Bonifacio, catcher John Buck, pitcher Mark Buehrle, pitcher Josh Johnson and infielder Jose Reyes, November 19, 2012.

HEISEY, CHRISTOPHER J. (CHRIS)
Born, Lancaster, Pennsylvania, December 14, 1984.
Bats Right. Throws Right. Height, 6 feet. Weight, 215 pounds.

Year	Club	Lea	Pos	G	AB	R	H	2B	3B	HR	RBI	SB	Avg
2006 Billings	Pioneer		OF	70	245	46	70	10	0	6	37	11	.286
2007 Sarasota	Fla.St.		OF	12	43	6	15	1	0	1	5	3	.349
2007 Dayton	Midwest		OF	104	374	60	108	24	2	9	46	19	.289
2008 Sarasota	Fla.St.		OF	117	436	77	125	31	7	7	51	27	.287
2008 Chattanooga	Southern		OF	19	79	11	25	6	1	2	10	5	.316
2009 Louisville	Int.		OF	63	245	37	68	17	1	9	37	8	.278
2009 Carolina	Southern		OF	71	271	54	94	18	2	13	40	13	.347
2010 Louisville	Int.		OF	20	79	6	19	3	0	4	13	2	.241
2010 Cincinnati	N.L.		OF	97	201	33	51	10	1	8	21	1	.254
2011 Louisville	Int.		OF	4	12	1	1	0	0	1	2	0	.083
2011 Cincinnati a	N.L.		OF	120	279	44	71	9	1	18	50	6	.254
2012 Cincinnati	N.L.		OF	120	347	44	92	16	5	7	31	6	.265
Major League Totals		3 Yrs.		337	827	121	214	35	7	33	102	13	.259
Division Series													
2010 Cincinnati	N.L.		OF	1	2	0	0	0	0	0	0	0	.000
2012 Cincinnati	N.L.		OF	4	3	1	0	0	0	0	0	0	.000
Division Series Totals				5	5	1	0	0	0	0	0	0	.000

a On disabled list from August 6 to September 1, 2011.

HELTON, TODD LYNN
Born, Knoxville, Tennessee, August 20, 1973.
Bats Left. Throws Left. Height, 6 feet, 2 inches. Weight, 210 pounds.

Year	Club	Lea	Pos	G	AB	R	H	2B	3B	HR	RBI	SB	Avg
1995 Asheville	So. Atl.		1B	54	201	24	51	11	1	1	15	1	.254
1996 New Haven	Eastern		1B	93	319	46	106	24	2	7	51	2	.332
1996 Colo Sprngs	P.C.		1B-OF	21	71	13	25	4	1	2	13	0	.352
1997 Colo Sprngs	P.C.		1B-OF	99	392	87	138	31	2	16	88	3	.352
1997 Colorado	N.L.		OF-1B	35	93	13	26	2	1	5	11	0	.280
1998 Colorado	N.L.		1B	152	530	78	167	37	1	25	97	3	.315
1999 Colorado	N.L.		1B	159	578	114	185	39	5	35	113	7	.320
2000 Colorado	N.L.		1B	160	580	138	*216	*59	2	42	*147	5	*.372
2001 Colorado	N.L.		1B	159	587	132	197	54	2	49	146	7	.336
2002 Colorado	N.L.		1B	156	553	107	182	39	4	30	109	5	.329
2003 Colorado	N.L.		1B	160	583	135	209	49	5	33	117	0	.358
2004 Colorado	N.L.		1B	154	547	115	190	49	2	32	96	3	.347
2005 Colo Sprngs	P.C.		2B	2	5	1	3	2	0	0	1	0	.600
2005 Colorado a	N.L.		1B	144	509	92	163	45	2	20	79	3	.320
2006 Colo Sprngs	P.C.		1B	2	6	0	2	0	0	0	0	0	.333
2006 Colorado b	N.L.		1B	145	546	94	165	40	5	15	81	3	.302
2007 Colorado	N.L.		1B	154	557	86	178	42	2	17	91	0	.320
2008 Colorado c	N.L.		1B	83	299	39	79	16	0	7	29	0	.264
2009 Colorado	N.L.		1B	151	544	79	177	38	3	15	86	0	.325
2010 Casper	Pioneer		1B	3	10	1	5	1	0	0	5	0	.500
2010 Colorado d	N.L.		1B	118	398	48	102	18	1	8	37	0	.256
2011 Colorado	N.L.		1B	124	421	59	127	27	0	14	69	0	.302
2012 Grand Junction	Pioneer		1B	2	5	0	3	0	0	0	2	0	.600
2012 Colorado e	N.L.		1B	69	240	31	57	16	1	7	37	1	.237
Major League Totals		16 Yrs.		2123	7565	1360	2420	570	36	354	1345	37	.320
Division Series													
2007 Colorado	N.L.		1B	3	12	1	1	0	1	0	0	0	.083

Year	Club	Lea	Pos	G	AB	R	H	2B	3B	HR	RBI	SB	Avg
2009 Colorado	N.L.		1B	4	16	5	3	0	0	0	2	0	.188
Division Series Totals				7	28	6	4	0	1	0	2	0	.143
Championship Series													
2007 Colorado	N.L.		1B	4	14	3	3	0	0	0	1	0	.214
World Series Record													
2007 Colorado	N.L.		1B	4	15	2	5	2	0	0	1	0	.333

a On disabled list from July 26 to August 10, 2005.
b On disabled list from April 20 to May 5, 2006.
c On disabled list from July 3 to September 12, 2008.
d On disabled list from July 7 to August 3, 2010.
e On disabled list from July 9 to July 27 and August 6 to November 2, 2012.

HERNANDEZ (LUGO), GORKYS GUSTAVO
Born, Guiria, Venezuela, September 7, 1987.
Bats Right. Throws Right. Height, 6 feet. Weight, 190 pounds.

Year	Club	Lea	Pos	G	AB	R	H	2B	3B	HR	RBI	SB	Avg
2006 Tigers.........	Gulf Coast		OF	50	205	41	67	9	2	5	23	20	.327
2007 West Michigan a ...	Midwest		OF	124	481	84	141	25	5	4	50	54	.293
2008 Myrtle Beach	Carolina		OF	100	406	75	107	23	6	5	42	20	.264
2009 Altoona...........	Eastern		OF	86	344	45	90	14	2	3	31	9	.262
2009 Mississippi b	Southern		OF	52	212	33	67	11	2	0	19	10	.316
2010 Altoona...........	Eastern		OF	92	368	45	98	11	4	2	26	17	.266
2011 Indianapolis	Int.		OF	126	424	48	120	25	9	1	40	21	.283
2012 Indianapolis	Int.		OF	67	237	43	61	11	2	2	25	13	.257
2012 Pittsburgh-Miami c	N.L.		OF	70	156	18	30	2	3	3	13	7	.192
Major League Totals		1 Yrs.		70	156	18	30	2	3	3	13	7	.192

a Traded by Detroit Tigers to Atlanta Braves with pitcher Jair Jurrjens for infielder Edgar Renteria, October 29, 2007.
b Traded to Pittsburgh Pirates with pitcher Jeff Locke and pitcher Charlie Morton for outfielder Nate McLouth, June 3, 2009.
c Traded to Miami Marlins with a competitive balance draft pick for infielder Gaby Sanchez and pitcher Kyle Kaminska, July 31, 2012.

HERRERA, JONATHAN ALEJANDRO
Born, Maracaibo, Venezuela, November 3, 1984.
Bats Both. Throws Right. Height, 5 feet, 9 inches. Weight, 150 pounds.

Year	Club	Lea	Pos	G	AB	R	H	2B	3B	HR	RBI	SB	Avg
2003 Casper	Pioneer		2B	39	159	27	49	7	1	1	25	12	.308
2004 Asheville.......	So.Atl.		SS	95	380	71	106	20	2	6	35	21	.279
2005 Modesto........	Calif.		SS-2B	73	310	48	80	9	4	2	30	9	.258
2005 Asheville.......	So.Atl.		SS-2B	19	87	17	27	2	0	0	5	6	.310
2006 Modesto........	Calif.		SS-2B-3B	127	487	87	151	20	8	7	77	34	.310
2007 Tulsa	Texas		SS	131	509	65	131	24	4	3	40	18	.257
2008 Colorado	N.L.		2B-SS	28	61	5	14	1	1	0	3	1	.230
2008 Colorado Springs a .	P.C.		SS-2B	66	226	40	70	7	0	3	31	15	.310
2009 Colorado Springs...	P.C.		SS-2B	119	381	63	102	11	5	2	33	16	.268
2010 Colorado Springs...	P.C.		SS-2B-3B	58	222	30	58	6	1	2	17	3	.261
2010 Colorado	N.L.		2B-3B-SS	76	222	34	63	6	2	1	21	2	.284
2011 Colorado b.......	N.L.		2B-SS-3B	104	281	28	68	5	1	3	14	4	.242
2012 Tulsa	Texas		2B-SS	5	17	2	3	0	0	1	1	0	.176
2012 Colorado Springs ..	P.C.		2B	4	12	1	2	1	0	0	1	0	.167
2012 Colorado c........	N.L.		SS-2B-3B	86	225	29	59	9	1	3	12	4	.262
Major League Totals		4 Yrs.		294	789	96	204	21	5	7	50	11	.259

a Not offered contract, December 12, 2008, re-signed with Colorado Rockies, December 13, 2008.
b On disabled list from September 6 to October 31, 2011.
c On disabled list from May 22 to June 23 and July 16 to July 31, 2012.

HEYWARD, JASON ADENOLITH
Born, Ridgewood, New Jersey, August 9, 1989.
Bats Left. Throws Left. Height, 6 feet, 5 inches. Weight, 240 pounds.

Year	Club	Lea	Pos	G	AB	R	H	2B	3B	HR	RBI	SB	Avg
2007 Danville	Appal.		OF	4	16	3	5	1	0	0	1	0	.313
2007 Braves	Gulf Coast		OF	8	27	1	8	4	0	1	5	1	.296
2008 Myrtle Beach	Carolina		OF	7	22	3	4	2	0	0	4	0	.182
2008 Rome.............	So.Atl.		OF	120	449	88	145	27	6	11	52	15	.323
2009 Myrtle Beach	Carolina		OF	49	189	34	56	12	0	10	31	4	.296
2009 Gwinnett.	Int.		OF	3	11	3	4	0	0	0	2	1	.364

Year Club	Lea	Pos	G	AB	R	H	2B	3B	HR	RBI	SB	Avg
2009 Mississippi.......	Southern	OF	47	162	32	57	13	4	7	30	5	.352
2010 Atlanta a.............	N.L.	OF	142	520	83	144	29	5	18	72	11	.277
2011 Gwinnett.............	Int.	OF	2	6	1	1	1	0	0	0	0	.167
2011 Atlanta b.............	N.L.	OF	128	396	50	90	18	2	14	42	9	.227
2012 Atlanta	N.L.	OF	158	587	93	158	30	6	27	82	21	.269
Major League Totals	3 Yrs.		428	1503	226	392	77	13	59	196	41	.261
Wild Card Playoff												
2012 Atlanta	N.L.	OF	1	5	0	1	1	0	0	0	0	.200
Division Series												
2010 Atlanta	N.L.	OF	4	16	0	2	0	0	0	0	0	.125

a On disabled list from June 27 to July 15, 2010.
b On disabled list from May 22 to June 15, 2011.

HILL, AARON WALTER
Born, Visalia, California, March 21, 1982.
Bats Right. Throws Right. Height, 5 feet, 11 inches. Weight, 195 pounds.

Year Club	Lea	Pos	G	AB	R	H	2B	3B	HR	RBI	SB	Avg
2003 Dunedin........	Fla.St.	SS	32	119	26	34	7	0	0	11	1	.286
2003 Auburn......	N.Y.-Penn.	SS	33	122	22	44	4	0	4	34	1	.361
2004 New Hampshire .	Eastern	SS	135	479	78	134	26	2	11	80	3	.280
2005 Syracuse	Int.	SS	38	156	22	47	11	0	5	18	2	.301
2005 Toronto	A.L.	3B-2B-SS	105	361	49	99	25	3	3	40	2	.274
2006 Toronto	A.L.	2B-SS	155	546	70	159	28	3	6	50	5	.291
2007 Toronto	A.L.	2B	160	608	87	177	47	2	17	78	4	.291
2008 Toronto a........	A.L.	2B	55	205	19	54	14	0	2	20	4	.263
2009 Toronto	A.L.	2B	158	*682	103	195	37	0	36	108	6	.286
2010 Toronto b........	A.L.	2B	138	528	70	108	22	0	26	68	2	.205
2011 Dunedin........	Fla.St.	2B	2	6	2	1	0	0	0	1	0	.167
2011 Toronto	A.L.	2B	104	396	38	89	15	1	6	45	16	.225
2011 Arizona c-d-e	N.L.	2B	33	124	23	39	12	2	2	16	5	.315
2012 Arizona...........	N.L.	2B	156	609	93	184	44	6	26	85	14	.302
Major League Totals	8 Yrs.		1064	4059	552	1104	244	17	124	510	58	.272
Division Series												
2011 Arizona...........	N.L.	2B	5	18	3	5	0	0	1	1	0	.278

a On disabled list from June 5 to November 14, 2008.
b On disabled list from April 8 to April 23, 2010.
c On disabled list from April 20 to May 8, 2011.
d Traded to Arizona Diamondbacks with infielder John McDonald for infielder Kelly Johnson, August 23, 2011.
e Filed for free agency, October 31, 2011, re-signed with Arizona Diamondbacks, November 15, 2011.

HINSKE, ERIC SCOTT
Born, Menasha, Wisconsin, August 5, 1977.
Bats Left. Throws Right. Height, 6 feet, 2 inches. Weight, 235 pounds.

Year Club	Lea	Pos	G	AB	R	H	2B	3B	HR	RBI	SB	Avg
1998 Williamsprt......	N.Y.-Penn.	1B	68	248	46	74	20	0	9	57	19	.298
1998 Rockford	Midwest	1B-OF	6	20	8	9	4	0	1	4	1	.450
1999 Daytona	Fla.St.	3B	130	445	76	132	28	6	19	79	16	.297
1999 Iowa.............	P.C.	1B	4	15	3	4	0	1	1	2	0	.267
2000 West Tenn	Southern	3B-1B-OF	131	436	76	113	21	9	20	73	14	.259
2001 Sacramento a-b-c	P.C.	3B-2B	121	436	71	123	27	1	25	79	20	.282
2002 Toronto d...........	A.L.	3B	151	566	99	158	38	2	24	84	13	.279
2003 Syracuse	Int.	3B	2	8	2	4	1	0	1	2	0	.500
2003 Toronto e...........	A.L.	3B	124	449	74	109	45	3	12	63	12	.243
2004 Toronto	A.L.	3B	155	570	66	140	23	3	15	69	12	.246
2005 Toronto	A.L.	1B	147	477	79	125	31	2	15	68	8	.262
2006 Toronto-Boston f	A.L.	OF-1B-3B	109	277	43	75	17	2	13	34	2	.271
2007 Boston g...........	A.L.	1B-OF	84	186	25	38	12	3	6	21	3	.204
2008 Tampa Bay h........	A.L.	OF-1B-3B	133	381	59	94	21	1	20	60	10	.247
2009 Pittsburgh	N.L.	OF-1B-3B	54	106	18	27	9	0	1	11	0	.255
2009 New York i-j........	N.L.	OF-3B	39	84	13	19	3	0	7	14	1	.226
2010 Atlanta k...........	N.L.	OF-1B-3B	131	281	38	72	21	1	11	51	0	.256
2011 Atlanta	N.L.	OF-1B	117	236	24	55	10	0	10	28	0	.233
2012 Atlanta l.............	N.L.	1B-OF	91	132	9	26	7	1	2	13	0	.197
Major League Totals	11 Yrs.		1335	3745	547	938	237	18	136	516	61	.250
Division Series												
2007 Boston	A.L.	PH	1	1	0	0	0	0	0	0	0	.000

<table>
Year Club	Lea	Pos	G	AB	R	H	2B	3B	HR	RBI	SB	Avg
2010 Atlanta	N.L.	PH	4	3	1	1	0	0	1	2	0	.333
Division Series Totals			5	4	1	1	0	0	1	2	0	.250
Championship Series												
2007 Boston	A.L.	PH	1	0	0	0	0	0	0	0	0	.000
World Series Record												
2007 Boston	A.L.	PH	1	1	0	0	0	0	0	0	0	.000
2008 Tampa Bay	A.L.	PH	2	2	1	1	0	0	1	1	0	.500
2009 New York	A.L.	PH	1	0	1	0	0	0	0	0	0	.000
World Series Totals.............			4	3	2	1	0	0	1	1	0	.333
</table>

a Traded by Chicago Cubs with pitcher Scott Chiasson to Oakland A's for infielder Miguel Cairo, March 28, 2001.
b On disabled list from May 1 to 12, 2001.
c Traded by Oakland A's to Toronto Blue Jays with pitcher Justin Miller for pitcher Billy Koch, December 7, 2001.
d Selected Rookie of the Year in American League for 2002.
e On disabled list from May 2 to June 26, 2003.
f Sold to Boston Red Sox, August 17, 2006.
g Filed for free agency, October 30, 2007. Signed with Tampa Bay Rays organization, February 7, 2008.
h Filed for free agency, November 1, 2008. Signed with Pittsburgh Pirates, January 30, 2009.
i Traded to New York Yankees for outfielder Eric Fryer and pitcher Casey Erickson, June 30, 2009.
j Filed for free agency, November 9, 2009. Signed with Atlanta Braves, January 12, 2010.
k Filed for free agency, November 1, 2010, re-signed with Atlanta Braves, December 2, 2010.
l Filed for free agency, November 3, 2012. Signed with Arizona Diamondbacks, December 6, 2012.

HOLLIDAY, MATTHEW THOMAS (MATT)

Born, Stillwater, Oklahoma, January 15, 1980.
Bats Right. Throws Right. Height, 6 feet, 4 inches. Weight, 235 pounds.

<table>
Year Club	Lea	Pos	G	AB	R	H	2B	3B	HR	RBI	SB	Avg
1998 Rockies	Arizona	3B	32	117	20	40	4	1	5	23	2	.342
1999 Asheville...........	So.Atl.	3B	121	444	76	117	28	0	16	64	10	.264
2000 Salem...........	Carolina	3B	123	460	64	126	28	2	7	72	11	.274
2001 Salem...........	Carolina	OF	72	255	36	70	16	1	11	52	11	.275
2002 Carolina	Southern	OF	130	463	79	128	19	2	10	64	16	.276
2003 Tulsa	Texas	OF	135	522	65	132	28	5	12	72	15	.253
2004 Colorado Springs......	P.C.	OF	6	22	8	8	5	0	2	4	2	.364
2004 Colorado	N.L.	OF	121	400	65	116	31	3	14	57	3	.290
2005 Tulsa	Texas	OF	7	26	6	14	3	0	1	6	1	.538
2005 Colorado a	N.L.	OF	125	479	68	147	24	7	19	87	14	.307
2006 Colorado	N.L.	OF	155	602	119	196	45	5	34	114	10	.326
2007 Colorado	N.L.	OF	158	636	120	*216	*50	6	36	*137	11	*.340
2008 Colorado Springs......	P.C.	OF	3	10	4	6	1	0	1	3	0	.600
2008 Colorado b-c	N.L.	OF	139	539	107	173	38	2	25	88	28	.321
2009 Oakland	A.L.	OF	93	346	52	99	23	1	11	54	12	.286
2009 St. Louis d-e	N.L.	OF	63	235	42	83	16	2	13	55	2	.353
2010 St. Louis...........	N.L.	OF	158	596	95	186	45	1	28	103	9	.312
2011 St. Louis f	N.L.	OF	124	446	83	132	36	0	22	75	2	.296
2012 St. Louis..............	N.L.	OF	157	599	95	177	36	2	27	102	4	.295
Major League Totals	9 Yrs.		1293	4878	846	1525	344	29	229	872	95	.313
Wild Card Playoff												
2012 St. Louis.............	N.L.	OF	1	3	2	2	0	0	1	1	0	.667
Division Series												
2007 Colorado	N.L.	OF	3	13	2	3	0	0	2	3	0	.231
2009 St. Louis.............	N.L.	OF	3	12	1	2	0	0	1	1	0	.167
2011 St. Louis.............	N.L.	OF	4	9	2	2	0	0	0	0	0	.222
2012 St. Louis.............	N.L.	OF	5	21	2	4	1	0	0	4	0	.190
Division Series Totals			15	55	7	11	1	0	3	8	0	.200
Championship Series												
2007 Colorado	N.L.	OF	4	15	3	5	0	0	2	4	0	.333
2011 St. Louis.............	N.L.	OF	6	23	6	10	2	0	1	5	0	.435
2012 St. Louis.............	N.L.	OF	6	25	1	5	0	0	0	2	1	.200
Championship Series Totals			16	63	10	20	2	0	3	11	1	.317
World Series Record												
2007 Colorado	N.L.	OF	4	17	1	5	0	0	1	3	0	.294
2011 St. Louis.............	N.L.	OF	6	19	5	3	1	0	0	0	0	.158
World Series Totals.............			10	36	6	8	1	0	1	3	0	.222
</table>

a On disabled list from June 9 to July 19, 2005.
b On disabled list from May 25 to June 10, 2008.
c Traded to Oakland Athletics for outfielder Carlos Gonzalez, pitcher Greg Smith and pitcher Huston Street, November 12, 2008.

d Traded to St. Louis Cardinals for pitcher Clayton Mortensen, infielder Brett Wallace and outfielder Shane Peterson, July 24, 2009.
e Filed for free agency, November 5, 2009, re-signed with St. Louis Cardinals, January 5, 2010.
f On disabled list from June 1 to June 16, 2011.

HOSMER, ERIC JOHN

Born, South Miami, Florida, October 24, 1989.
Bats Left. Throws Left. Height, 6 feet, 4 inches. Weight, 230 pounds.

Year	Club	Lea	Pos	G	AB	R	H	2B	3B	HR	RBI	SB	Avg
2008 Idaho Falls	Pioneer	1B	3	11	2	4	2	0	0	2	0	.364
2009 Burlington	Midwest	1B	79	280	31	71	17	2	5	49	3	.254
2009 Wilmington	Carolina	1B	27	97	9	20	2	2	1	10	0	.206
2010 Wilmington	Carolina	1B	87	325	48	115	29	6	7	51	11	.354
2010 NW Arkansas	Texas	1B	50	195	39	61	14	3	13	35	3	.313
2011 Omaha	P.C.	1B	26	98	21	43	5	0	3	15	3	.439
2011 Kansas City	A.L.	1B	128	523	66	153	27	3	19	78	11	.293
2012 Kansas City	A.L.	1B-OF	152	535	65	124	22	2	14	60	16	.232
Major League Totals		2 Yrs.	280	1058	131	277	49	5	33	138	27	.262

HOWARD, RYAN JAMES

Born, St. Louis, Missouri, November 19, 1979.
Bats Left. Throws Left. Height, 6 feet, 4 inches. Weight, 250 pounds.

Year	Club	Lea	Pos	G	AB	R	H	2B	3B	HR	RBI	SB	Avg
2001 Batavia	N.Y.-Penn.	1B	48	169	26	46	7	3	6	35	0	.272
2002 Lakewood	So.Atl.	1B	135	493	56	138	20	6	19	87	5	.280
2003 Clearwater	Fla.St.	1B	130	490	67	149	32	1	23	82	0	.304
2004 Reading	Eastern	1B	102	374	73	111	18	1	37	102	1	.297
2004 Scranton/WB	Int.	1B	29	111	21	30	10	0	9	29	0	.270
2004 Philadelphia	N.L.	1B	19	39	5	11	5	0	2	5	0	.282
2005 Scranton/WB	Int.	1B	61	210	38	78	19	0	16	54	0	.371
2005 Philadelphia a	N.L.	1B	88	312	52	90	17	2	22	63	0	.288
2006 Philadelphia b	N.L.	1B	159	581	104	182	25	1	*58	*149	0	.313
2007 Lakewood	So.Atl.	1B	2	6	1	2	1	0	1	4	0	.333
2007 Philadelphia c	N.L.	1B	144	529	94	142	26	0	47	136	1	.268
2008 Philadelphia	N.L.	1B	*162	610	105	153	26	4	*48	*146	1	.251
2009 Philadelphia	N.L.	1B	160	616	105	172	37	4	45	*141	8	.279
2010 Lakewood	So.Atl.	1B	1	2	0	1	1	0	0	1	0	.500
2010 Philadelphia d	N.L.	1B	143	550	87	152	23	5	31	108	1	.276
2011 Philadelphia	N.L.	1B	152	557	81	141	30	1	33	116	1	.253
2012 Lakewood	So.Atl.	1B	3	8	2	5	1	0	0	4	0	.625
2012 Lehigh Valley	Int.	1B	4	12	1	5	1	0	1	6	0	.417
2012 Philadelphia e	N.L.	1B	71	260	28	57	11	0	14	56	0	.219
Major League Totals		9 Yrs.	1098	4054	661	1100	200	17	300	920	12	.271
Division Series													
2007 Philadelphia	N.L.	1B	3	12	1	3	0	0	1	1	0	.250
2008 Philadelphia	N.L.	1B	4	11	1	2	1	0	0	1	0	.182
2009 Philadelphia	N.L.	1B	4	16	3	6	3	0	0	6	0	.375
2010 Philadelphia	N.L.	1B	3	11	0	3	0	0	0	0	0	.273
2011 Philadelphia	N.L.	1B	5	19	1	2	0	0	1	6	0	.105
Division Series Totals			19	69	6	16	4	0	2	14	0	.232
Championship Series													
2008 Philadelphia	N.L.	1B	5	20	4	6	1	0	0	2	0	.300
2009 Philadelphia	N.L.	1B	5	15	5	5	1	1	2	8	0	.333
2010 Philadelphia	N.L.	1B	6	22	1	7	4	0	0	0	0	.318
Championship Series Totals			16	57	10	18	6	1	2	10	0	.316
World Series Record													
2008 Philadelphia	N.L.	1B	5	21	3	6	1	0	3	6	0	.286
2009 Philadelphia	N.L.	1B	6	23	3	4	2	0	1	3	1	.174
World Series Totals			11	44	6	10	3	0	4	9	1	.227

a Selected Rookie of the Year in National League for 2005.
b Selected Most Valuable Player in National League for 2006.
c On disabled list from May 10 to May 25, 2007.
d On disabled list from August 2 to August 21, 2010.
e On disabled list from March 26 to July 6, 2012.

HUDSON, ORLANDO THILL

Born, Darlington, South Carolina, December 12, 1977.
Bats Both. Throws Right. Height, 6 feet. Weight, 185 pounds.

Year	Club	Lea	Pos	G	AB	R	H	2B	3B	HR	RBI	SB	Avg
1998 Medicine Hat	Pioneer		2B	65	242	50	71	18	1	8	42	6	.293
1999 Hagerstown	So.Atl.		3B	132	513	66	137	36	6	7	74	8	.267
2000 Dunedin	Fla.St.		3B-2B-SS	96	358	54	102	16	2	7	48	9	.285
2000 Tennessee	Southern		3B	39	134	17	32	4	3	2	15	3	.239
2001 Syracuse	Int.		2B-3B	55	194	31	59	14	3	4	27	11	.304
2001 Tennessee	Southern		2B-3B	84	306	51	94	22	8	4	52	8	.307
2002 Syracuse	Int.		2B	100	417	63	127	27	3	10	37	8	.305
2002 Toronto	A.L.		2B	54	192	20	53	10	5	4	23	0	.276
2003 Toronto	A.L.		2B	142	474	54	127	21	6	9	57	5	.268
2004 Toronto a	A.L.		2B	135	489	73	132	32	7	12	58	7	.270
2005 Toronto b	A.L.		2B	131	461	62	125	25	5	10	63	7	.271
2006 Arizona	N.L.		2B	157	579	87	166	34	9	15	67	9	.287
2007 Arizona	N.L.		2B	139	517	69	152	28	9	10	63	10	.294
2008 Arizona c-d	N.L.		2B	107	407	54	124	29	3	8	41	4	.305
2009 Los Angeles e	N.L.		2B	149	551	74	156	35	6	9	62	8	.283
2010 Minnesota f-g	A.L.		2B	126	497	80	133	24	5	6	37	10	.268
2011 Lake Elsinore	Calif.		2B	4	7	6	4	0	0	1	3	2	.571
2011 Tucson	P.C.		2B	2	4	4	3	2	0	0	1	0	.750
2011 San Diego h	N.L.		2B	119	398	54	98	15	3	7	43	19	.246
2012 Charlotte	Int.		2B	5	16	1	5	1	0	0	1	2	.313
2012 San Diego	N.L.		2B	35	123	11	26	0	5	1	11	3	.211
2012 Chicago i-j-k	A.L.		3B-2B	51	137	10	27	3	3	2	17	3	.197
Major League Totals		11 Yrs.		1345	4825	648	1319	256	66	93	542	85	.273
Division Series													
2009 Los Angeles	N.L.		2B	3	0	0	0	0	0	0	0	0	.000
2010 Minnesota	A.L.		2B	3	12	2	4	0	0	1	2	0	.333
Division Series Totals				6	12	2	4	0	0	1	2	0	.333
Championship Series													
2009 Los Angeles	N.L.		2B	5	4	1	1	0	0	1	1	0	.250

a On disabled list from May 24 to June 16, 2004.
b Traded to Arizona Diamondbacks with pitcher Miguel Batista for infielder Troy Glaus and infielder Sergio Santos, December 27, 2005.
c On disabled list from August 10 to November 1, 2008.
d Filed for free agency, November 1, 2008. Signed with Los Angeles Dodgers, February 21, 2009.
e Filed for free agency, November 5, 2009. Signed with Minnesota Twins, February 4, 2010.
f On disabled list from May 31 to June 18 and July 24 to August 8, 2010.
g Filed for free agency, November 1, 2010. Signed with San Diego Padres, December 20, 2010.
h On disabled list from May 4 to May 19 and May 26 to June 19, 2011.
i Released by San Diego Padres, May 17, 2012. Signed with Chicago White Sox, May 22, 2012.
j On disabled list from August 16 to September 1, 2012.
k Filed for free agency, November 3, 2012.

HUNDLEY, NICHOLAS JOHN (NICK)

Born, Corvallis, Oregon, September 8, 1983.
Bats Right. Throws Right. Height, 6 feet, 1 inch. Weight, 210 pounds.

Year	Club	Lea	Pos	G	AB	R	H	2B	3B	HR	RBI	SB	Avg
2005 Fort Wayne	Midwest		C	10	36	2	8	2	0	0	5	0	.222
2005 Eugene	Northwest		C	43	148	30	37	7	1	7	22	1	.250
2006 Lake Elsinore	Calif.		C	47	176	18	49	13	0	3	23	1	.278
2006 Fort Wayne	Midwest		C	57	215	29	59	19	0	8	44	1	.274
2007 San Antonio	Texas		C	101	373	55	92	23	1	20	72	0	.247
2008 Portland	P.C.		C	58	224	33	52	13	0	12	39	0	.232
2008 San Diego	N.L.		C	60	198	21	47	7	1	5	24	0	.237
2009 Portland	P.C.		C	5	16	2	4	1	0	1	2	0	.250
2009 San Diego a	N.L.		C-OF	78	256	23	61	15	2	8	30	5	.238
2010 San Diego	N.L.		C	85	273	33	68	18	2	8	43	0	.249
2011 San Antonio	Texas		C	7	23	1	4	0	0	0	1	0	.174
2011 Tucson	P.C.		C	4	11	3	3	2	0	1	5	0	.273
2011 San Diego b	N.L.		C	82	281	34	81	16	5	9	29	1	.288
2012 Tucson	P.C.		C	13	42	4	8	1	1	0	7	0	.190
2012 San Diego c	N.L.		C	58	204	14	32	7	1	3	22	0	.157
Major League Totals		5 Yrs.		363	1212	125	289	63	11	33	148	6	.238

a On disabled list from June 18 to August 12, 2009.
b On disabled list from May 5 to June 8 and July 6 to August 12, 2011.
c On disabled list from August 16 to November 2, 2012.

HUNTER, TORII KEDAR

Born, Pine Bluff, Arkansas, July 18, 1975.
Bats Right. Throws Right. Height, 6 feet, 2 inches. Weight, 215 pounds.

Year Club	Lea	Pos	G	AB	R	H	2B	3B	HR	RBI	SB	Avg
1993 Twins .... Gulf Coast		OF	28	100	6	19	3	0	0	8	4	.190
1994 Fort Wayne........ Midwest		OF	91	335	57	98	17	1	10	50	8	.293
1995 Fort Myers .... Fla.St.		OF	113	391	64	96	15	2	7	36	7	.246
1996 Fort Myers .... Fla.St.		OF	4	16	1	3	0	0	0	1	1	.188
1996 New Britain .... Eastern		OF	99	342	49	90	20	3	7	33	7	.263
1997 New Britain .... Eastern		OF	127	471	57	109	22	2	8	56	8	.231
1997 Minnesota .... A.L.		OF	1	0	0	0	0	0	0	0	0	.000
1998 New Britain .... Eastern		OF	82	308	42	87	24	3	6	32	11	.282
1998 Salt Lake .... P.C.		OF	26	92	15	31	7	0	4	20	2	.337
1998 Minnesota .... A.L.		OF	6	17	0	4	1	0	0	2	0	.235
1999 Minnesota .... A.L.		OF	135	384	52	98	17	2	9	35	10	.255
2000 Salt Lake .... P.C.		OF	55	209	58	77	17	2	18	61	11	.368
2000 Minnesota .... A.L.		OF	99	336	44	94	14	7	5	44	4	.280
2001 Minnesota a .... A.L.		OF	148	564	82	147	32	5	27	92	9	.261
2002 Minnesota .... A.L.		OF	148	561	89	162	37	4	29	94	23	.289
2003 Minnesota .... A.L.		OF	154	581	83	145	31	4	26	102	6	.250
2004 Minnesota b .... A.L.		OF	138	520	79	141	37	0	23	81	21	.271
2005 Minnesota c .... A.L.		OF	98	372	63	100	24	1	14	56	23	.269
2006 Minnesota d .... A.L.		OF	147	557	86	155	21	2	31	98	12	.278
2007 Minnesota e .... A.L.		OF	160	600	94	172	45	1	28	107	18	.287
2008 Los Angeles .... A.L.		OF	146	551	85	153	37	2	21	78	19	.278
2009 Rancho Cucamonga.... Calif.		OF	3	9	3	3	0	0	1	3	1	.333
2009 Los Angeles f .... A.L.		OF	119	451	74	135	26	1	22	90	18	.299
2010 Los Angeles .... A.L.		OF	152	573	76	161	36	0	23	90	9	.281
2011 Los Angeles .... A.L.		OF	156	580	80	152	24	2	23	82	5	.262
2012 Los Angeles g .... A.L.		OF	140	534	81	167	24	1	16	92	9	.313
Major League Totals	16 Yrs.		1947	7181	1068	1986	406	32	297	1143	186	.277
Division Series												
2002 Minnesota .... A.L.		OF	5	20	4	6	4	0	0	2	0	.300
2003 Minnesota .... A.L.		OF	4	14	3	6	0	1	1	2	0	.429
2004 Minnesota .... A.L.		OF	4	17	5	6	1	0	1	2	2	.353
2006 Minnesota .... A.L.		OF	3	11	1	3	1	0	1	2	0	.273
2008 Los Angeles .... A.L.		OF	4	18	0	7	0	0	0	5	0	.389
2009 Los Angeles .... A.L.		OF	3	10	2	2	1	0	1	3	0	.200
Division Series Totals			23	90	15	30	7	1	4	16	2	.333
Championship Series												
2002 Minnesota .... A.L.		OF	5	18	2	3	2	0	0	0	0	.167
2009 Los Angeles .... A.L.		OF	6	23	2	7	1	0	0	2	1	.304
Championship Series Totals			11	41	4	10	3	0	0	2	1	.244

a On disabled list from April 6 to April 21, 2001.
b On disabled list from April 7 to April 25, 2004.
c On disabled list from July 30 to October 6, 2005.
d On disabled list from July 16 to July 31, 2006.
e Filed for free agency, October 29, 2007. Signed with Los Angeles Angels, November 21, 2007.
f On disabled list from July 8 to August 16, 2009.
g Filed for free agency, November 3, 2012. Signed with Detroit Tigers, November 16, 2012.

IANNETTA, CHRISTOPHER DOMENIC (CHRIS)

Born, Providence, Rhode Island, April 8, 1983.
Bats Right. Throws Right. Height, 5 feet, 11 inches. Weight, 225 pounds.

Year Club	Lea	Pos	G	AB	R	H	2B	3B	HR	RBI	SB	Avg
2004 Asheville .... So.Atl.		C	36	121	23	38	5	1	5	17	0	.314
2005 Tulsa .... Texas		C	19	60	7	14	3	1	2	11	0	.233
2006 Tulsa .... Texas		C	44	156	38	50	10	2	11	26	1	.321
2006 Colorado Springs....... P.C.		C	47	151	23	53	11	2	3	22	0	.351
2006 Colorado .... N.L.		C	21	77	12	20	4	0	2	10	0	.260
2007 Colorado Springs....... P.C.		C	16	54	8	16	3	0	1	7	0	.296
2007 Colorado .... N.L.		C	67	197	22	43	8	3	4	27	0	.218
2008 Colorado .... N.L.		C-3B	104	333	50	88	22	2	18	65	0	.264
2009 Colorado Springs....... P.C.		C	4	15	3	5	2	0	1	3	0	.333
2009 Colorado a .... N.L.		C	93	289	41	66	15	2	16	52	0	.228
2010 Colorado Springs....... P.C.		C-1B	17	63	17	22	7	0	5	21	0	.349
2010 Colorado .... N.L.		C-1B-3B	61	188	20	37	6	1	9	27	1	.197
2011 Colorado b .... N.L.		C-1B-3B	112	345	51	82	17	1	14	55	6	.238
2012 Salt Lake .... P.C.		C	6	22	3	6	2	0	0	2	0	.273

Year	Club	Lea	Pos	G	AB	R	H	2B	3B	HR	RBI	SB	Avg
2012 Los Angeles c		A.L.	C	79	221	27	53	6	1	9	26	1	.240
Major League Totals			7 Yrs.	537	1650	223	389	78	10	72	262	8	.236

a On disabled list from May 24 to June 9, 2009.
b Traded to Los Angeles Angels for pitcher Tyler Chatwood, November 30, 2011.
c On disabled list from May 10 to July 28, 2012.

IBANEZ, RAUL JAVIER

Born, New York, New York, June 2, 1972.
Bats Left. Throws Right. Height, 6 feet, 2 inches. Weight, 220 pounds.

Year	Club	Lea	Pos	G	AB	R	H	2B	3B	HR	RBI	SB	Avg
1992 Mariners		Arizona	DH-1B-C-OF	33	120	25	37	8	2	1	16	1	.308
1993 Appleton		Midwest	DH-1B-OF-C	52	157	26	43	9	0	5	21	0	.274
1993 Bellingham		Northwest	C	43	134	16	38	5	2	0	15	0	.284
1994 Appleton		Midwest	DH-C-1B-OF	91	327	55	102	30	3	7	59	10	.312
1995 Riverside		California	C-1B	95	361	59	120	23	9	20	108	4	.332
1996 Port City		Southern	OF-1B-C	19	76	12	28	8	1	1	13	3	.368
1996 Seattle		A.L.	DH	4	5	0	0	0	0	0	0	0	.000
1996 Tacoma		P.C.	OF-1B	111	405	59	115	20	3	11	47	7	.284
1997 Tacoma		P.C.	OF	111	438	84	133	30	5	15	84	7	.304
1997 Seattle		A.L.	OF	11	26	3	4	0	1	1	4	0	.154
1998 Tacoma		P.C.	OF	52	190	24	41	8	1	6	25	1	.216
1998 Seattle		A.L.	OF-1B	37	98	12	25	7	1	2	12	0	.255
1999 Tacoma		P.C.	OF	8	31	6	11	1	0	3	5	1	.355
1999 Seattle a		A.L.	OF-1B-C	87	209	23	54	7	0	9	27	5	.258
2000 Tacoma		P.C.	OF	10	40	3	10	4	0	0	6	0	.250
2000 Seattle b-c		A.L.	OF-1B	92	140	21	32	8	0	2	15	2	.229
2001 Omaha		P.C.	OF-SS	8	27	3	4	1	0	2	5	0	.148
2001 Kansas City		A.L.	OF-1B-3B	104	279	44	78	11	5	13	54	0	.280
2002 Kansas City		A.L.	OF-1B	137	497	70	146	37	6	24	103	5	.294
2003 Kansas City d		A.L.	OF-1B	157	608	95	179	33	5	18	90	8	.294
2004 Tacoma		P.C.	OF	4	17	2	4	1	0	0	1	0	.235
2004 Seattle e		A.L.	OF-1B	123	481	67	146	31	1	16	62	1	.304
2005 Seattle		A.L.	DH-OF-1B	*162	614	92	172	32	2	20	89	9	.280
2006 Seattle		A.L.	OF	159	626	103	181	33	5	33	123	2	.289
2007 Seattle		A.L.	OF	149	573	80	167	35	5	21	105	0	.291
2008 Seattle f		A.L.	OF	162	635	85	186	43	3	23	110	2	.293
2009 Reading		Eastern	OF	1	2	1	0	0	0	0	0	0	.000
2009 Lehigh Valley		Int.	OF	2	5	1	2	1	0	0	2	0	.400
2009 Philadelphia g		N.L.	OF	134	500	93	136	32	3	34	93	4	.272
2010 Philadelphia		N.L.	OF-1B	155	561	75	154	37	5	16	83	4	.275
2011 Philadelphia h		N.L.	OF	144	535	65	131	31	1	20	84	2	.245
2012 New York i		A.L.	OF	130	384	50	92	19	3	19	62	3	.240
Major League Totals			17 Yrs.	1947	6771	978	1883	396	46	271	1116	47	.278
Division Series													
2000 Seattle		A.L.	OF	3	8	2	3	0	0	0	0	0	.375
2009 Philadelphia		N.L.	OF	4	13	2	4	1	0	0	5	0	.308
2010 Philadelphia		N.L.	OF	3	12	0	3	1	0	0	0	0	.250
2011 Philadelphia		N.L.	OF	4	15	1	3	0	0	1	4	0	.200
2012 New York		A.L.	DH	4	9	2	4	0	0	2	3	0	.444
Division Series Totals				18	57	7	17	2	0	3	12	0	.298
Championship Series													
2000 Seattle		A.L.	OF	6	9	0	0	0	0	0	0	0	.000
2009 Philadelphia		N.L.	OF	5	18	4	3	1	0	1	4	0	.167
2010 Philadelphia		N.L.	OF	5	19	1	4	1	0	0	0	0	.211
2012 New York		A.L.	DH	4	13	1	3	1	0	1	2	0	.231
Championship Series Totals				20	59	6	10	3	0	2	6	0	.169
World Series Record													
2009 Philadelphia		N.L.	OF-DH	6	23	2	7	4	0	1	4	0	.304

a On disabled list from May 18 to June 3, 1999.
b On disabled list from August 7 to August 21, 2000.
c Not offered contract, December 21, 2000. Signed with Kansas City Royals organization, January 13, 2001.
d Filed for free agency, October 27, 2003. Signed with Seattle Mariners, November 19, 2003.
e On disabled list from June 3 to July 10, 2004.
f Filed for free agency, October 30, 2008. Signed with Philadelphia Phillies, December 16, 2008.
g On disabled list from June 18 to July 10, 2009.
h Filed for free agency, October 30, 2011. Signed with New York Yankees, February 21, 2012.
i Filed for free agency, November 3, 2012. Signed with Seattle Mariners, December 26, 2012.

IGLESIAS (ALEMAN), JOSE ANTONIO
Born, Havana, Cuba, January 5, 1990.
Bats Right. Throws Right. Height, 5 feet, 11 inches. Weight, 175 pounds.

Year	Club	Lea	Pos	G	AB	R	H	2B	3B	HR	RBI	SB	Avg
2010 Portland	....	Eastern	SS	57	221	29	63	10	3	0	13	5	.285
2010 Lowell	....	N.Y.-Penn.	SS	13	40	8	14	2	2	0	7	2	.350
2011 Pawtucket	....	Int.	SS	101	357	35	84	9	0	1	31	12	.235
2011 Boston	....	A.L.	SS	10	6	3	2	0	0	0	0	0	.333
2012 Lowell	....	N.Y.-Penn.	SS	2	8	1	3	1	0	0	0	1	.375
2012 Pawtucket	....	Int.	SS	88	353	46	94	9	1	1	23	12	.266
2012 Boston	....	A.L.	SS	25	68	5	8	2	0	1	2	1	.118
Major League Totals	....		2 Yrs.	35	74	8	10	2	0	1	2	1	.135

INFANTE, OMAR RAFAEL
Born, Puerto La Cruz, Venezuela, December 26, 1981.
Bats Right. Throws Right. Height, 6 feet. Weight, 180 pounds.

Year	Club	Lea	Pos	G	AB	R	H	2B	3B	HR	RBI	SB	Avg
1999 Tigers	....	Gulf Coast	SS	21	75	9	20	0	0	0	4	4	.267
2000 Lakeland	....	Fla.St.	SS	79	259	35	71	11	0	2	24	11	.274
2000 West Michigan	.	Midwest	SS-2B	12	48	7	11	0	0	0	5	1	.229
2001 Erie	....	Eastern	SS	132	540	86	163	21	4	2	62	27	.302
2002 Toledo	....	Int.	SS	120	436	49	117	16	8	4	51	19	.268
2002 Detroit	....	A.L.	SS-2B	18	72	4	24	3	0	1	6	0	.333
2003 Toledo	....	Int.	SS	64	224	28	50	10	0	2	18	22	.223
2003 Detroit	....	A.L.	SS-3B-2B	69	221	24	49	6	1	0	8	6	.222
2004 Detroit	....	A.L.	2B-SS-3B-OF	142	503	69	133	27	9	16	55	13	.264
2005 Detroit	....	A.L.	2B-SS	121	406	36	90	28	2	9	43	8	.222
2006 Detroit	....	A.L.	2B-SS-3B	78	224	35	62	11	4	4	25	3	.277
2007 Toledo	....	Int.	SS-2B	10	38	3	14	2	0	0	4	1	.368
2007 Detroit a-b	....	A.L.	2B-OF-SS-3B	66	166	24	45	6	1	2	17	4	.271
2008 Richmond	....	Int.	OF	3	11	3	4	1	0	0	3	0	.364
2008 Atlanta c	....	N.L.	OF-3B-SS-2B	96	317	45	93	24	3	3	40	0	.293
2009 Rome	....	So.Atl.	2B-3B-SS-OF	5	17	1	5	0	0	0	1	1	.294
2009 Gwinnett	....	Int.	SS	1	3	1	1	0	0	1	2	0	.333
2009 Atlanta d	....	N.L.	2B-OF-3B-SS	70	203	24	62	9	1	2	27	2	.305
2010 Atlanta e	....	N.L.	2B-3B-OF-SS	134	471	65	151	15	3	8	47	7	.321
2011 Jupiter	....	Fla.St.	2B	1	5	0	3	0	0	0	0	0	.600
2011 Florida f	....	N.L.	2B	148	579	55	160	24	8	7	49	4	.276
2012 Miami	....	N.L.	2B	85	328	42	94	23	2	8	33	10	.287
2012 Detroit g	....	A.L.	2B-3B	64	226	27	58	7	5	4	20	7	.257
Major League Totals	....		11 Yrs.	1091	3716	450	1021	183	39	64	370	64	.275
Division Series													
2010 Atlanta	....	N.L.	3B-2B	4	18	1	4	1	0	0	0	0	.222
2012 Detroit	....	A.L.	2B	5	17	6	6	1	0	0	0	1	.353
Division Series Totals	....			9	35	7	10	2	0	0	0	1	.286
Championship Series													
2006 Detroit	....	A.L.	DH	1	2	0	1	0	0	0	0	1	.500
2012 Detroit	....	A.L.	2B	4	18	3	4	0	0	0	0	1	.222
Championship Series Totals	......			5	20	3	5	0	0	0	0	2	.250
World Series Record													
2006 Detroit	....	A.L.	PH	1	1	0	0	0	0	0	0	0	.000
2012 Detroit	....	A.L.	2B	4	15	0	5	0	0	0	0	0	.333
World Series Totals	....			5	16	0	5	0	0	0	0	0	.313

a Traded to Chicago Cubs for outfielder Jacque Jones, November 12, 2007.
b Traded to Atlanta Braves with pitcher Will Ohman for pitcher Jose Ascanio, December 4, 2007.
c On disabled list from March 21 to May 8 and July 7 to July 22, 2008.
d On disabled list from May 21 to August 11, 2009.
e Traded to Florida Marlins with pitcher Michael Dunn for infielder Dan Uggla, November 16, 2010.
f On disabled list from August 5 to August 20, 2011.
g Traded to Detroit Tigers with pitcher Anibal Sanchez for pitcher Jacob Turner, catcher Rob Brantley and pitcher Brian Flynn, July 23, 2012.

INGE, CHARLES BRANDON (BRANDON)

Born, Lynchburg, Virginia, May 19, 1977.
Bats Both. Throws Right. Height, 5 feet, 11 inches. Weight, 190 pounds.

Year	Club	Lea	Pos	G	AB	R	H	2B	3B	HR	RBI	SB	Avg
1998 Jamestown	N.Y.-Penn.	C	51	191	24	44	10	1	8	29	8	.230
1999 West Michigan	Midwest	C	100	352	54	86	25	2	9	46	15	.244
2000 Toledo	Int.	C	55	190	24	42	9	3	5	20	2	.221
2000 Jacksonville	Southern	C-OF	78	298	39	77	25	1	6	53	10	.258
2001 Tigers	Gulf Coast	C	3	10	1	1	0	0	1	2	0	.100
2001 West Michigan	Midwest	C	4	16	3	3	1	0	0	2	0	.188
2001 Toledo	Int.	C	27	90	11	26	11	1	2	15	1	.289
2001 Detroit a	A.L.	C	79	189	13	34	11	0	0	15	1	.180
2002 Toledo	Int.	C	21	65	10	17	2	4	3	13	1	.262
2002 Detroit b	A.L.	C	95	321	27	65	15	3	7	24	1	.202
2003 Toledo	Int.	C	39	142	15	39	9	0	5	15	3	.275
2003 Detroit	A.L.	C	104	330	32	67	15	3	8	30	4	.203
2004 Detroit c	A.L.	3B-C-OF	131	408	43	117	15	7	13	64	5	.287
2005 Detroit	A.L.	3B-OF	160	616	75	161	31	9	16	72	7	.261
2006 Detroit	A.L.	3B	159	542	83	137	29	2	27	83	7	.253
2007 Detroit	A.L.	3B	151	508	64	120	25	2	14	71	9	.236
2008 Toledo	Int.	C-3B	3	10	2	3	0	0	1	4	0	.300
2008 Detroit d	A.L.	C-3B-OF	113	347	41	71	16	4	11	51	4	.205
2009 Detroit	A.L.	3B	*161	562	71	129	16	1	27	84	2	.230
2010 West Michigan	Midwest	3B	1	5	0	2	2	0	0	1	0	.400
2010 Detroit e	A.L.	3B	144	514	47	127	28	5	13	70	4	.247
2011 Toledo	Int.	3B	29	108	18	31	4	0	7	19	0	.287
2011 Detroit f	A.L.	3B	102	269	29	53	10	2	3	23	1	.197
2012 Sacramento	P.C.	3B	8	27	6	10	4	0	2	9	0	.370
2012 Toledo	Int.	2B	3	9	1	1	0	0	0	0	0	.111
2012 Detroit-Oakland g-h-i	A.L.	3B-2B	83	303	33	66	14	0	12	54	0	.218
Major League Totals			12 Yrs.	1482	4909	558	1147	225	38	151	641	45	.234
Division Series													
2006 Detroit	A.L.	3B	4	15	1	2	0	0	0	0	0	.133
2011 Detroit	A.L.	3B	4	7	3	3	1	0	0	0	0	.429
Division Series Totals			8	22	4	5	1	0	0	0	0	.227
Championship Series													
2006 Detroit	A.L.	3B	4	12	3	4	1	0	1	3	0	.333
2011 Detroit	A.L.	3B	6	15	3	4	0	0	1	1	0	.267
Championship Series Totals			10	27	6	8	1	0	2	4	0	.296
World Series Record													
2006 Detroit	A.L.	3B	5	17	0	6	2	0	0	1	0	.353

a On disabled list from June 25 to August 6, 2001.
b On disabled list from May 12 to May 27, 2002.
c On disabled list from June 26 to July 15, 2004.
d On disabled list from June 23 to July 10, 2008.
e On disabled list from July 20 to August 4, 2010.
f On disabled list from June 2 to June 23, 2011.
g Released by Detroit Tigers, April 26, 2012. Signed with Oakland Athletics, April 30, 2012.
h On disabled list from March 30 to April 14 and May 13 to May 28 and August 12 to September 1 and September 6 to October 29, 2012.
i Filed for free agency, November 3, 2012.

ISHIKAWA, TRAVIS TAKASHI

Born, Seattle, Washington, September 24, 1983.
Bats Left. Throws Left. Height, 6 feet, 3 inches. Weight, 225 pounds.

Year	Club	Lea	Pos	G	AB	R	H	2B	3B	HR	RBI	SB	Avg
2002 Giants	Arizona	1B-OF	19	68	10	19	4	2	1	10	7	.279
2002 Salem-Keizer	Northwest	1B	23	88	14	27	2	1	1	17	1	.307
2003 Salem-Keizer	Northwest	1B	66	248	53	63	17	4	3	31	0	.254
2003 Hagerstown	So.Atl.	1B	57	194	20	40	5	0	3	22	3	.206
2004 San Jose	Calif.	1B	16	56	10	13	7	0	1	10	0	.232
2004 Hagerstown	So.Atl.	1B	98	358	59	92	19	2	15	54	10	.257
2005 San Jose	Calif.	1B	127	432	87	122	28	7	22	79	1	.282
2006 San Francisco	N.L.	1B	12	24	1	7	3	1	0	4	0	.292
2006 Connecticut	Eastern	1B	86	298	33	69	13	4	10	42	0	.232
2007 San Jose	Calif.	1B	56	198	35	53	15	1	13	34	0	.268
2007 Connecticut	Eastern	1B	48	173	17	37	3	1	3	17	0	.214
2008 Connecticut	Eastern	1B	64	234	34	68	16	0	8	48	10	.291
2008 Fresno	P.C.	1B	48	171	35	53	19	3	16	46	0	.310

Year	Club	Lea	Pos	G	AB	R	H	2B	3B	HR	RBI	SB	Avg
2008 San Francisco		N.L.	1B	33	95	12	26	6	0	3	15	1	.274
2009 San Francisco		N.L.	1B	120	326	49	85	10	2	9	39	2	.261
2010 San Francisco		N.L.	1B	116	158	18	42	11	0	3	22	0	.266
2011 Fresno a		P.C.	OF-1B	56	175	21	44	14	0	3	18	3	.251
2012 Nashville		P.C.	1B	6	18	1	4	3	0	0	5	0	.222
2012 Milwaukee b-c		N.L.	1B-OF	94	152	19	39	12	1	4	30	0	.257
Major League Totals			5 Yrs.	375	755	99	199	42	4	19	110	3	.264
Division Series													
2010 San Francisco		N.L.	1B	3	2	1	0	0	0	0	0	0	.000
Championship Series													
2010 San Francisco		N.L.	1B	5	4	0	1	0	0	0	0	0	.250
World Series Record													
2010 San Francisco		N.L.	1B	2	4	1	1	1	0	0	1	0	.250

a Filed for free agency, November 2, 2011. Signed with Milwaukee Brewers organization, December 12, 2011.
b On disabled list from May 26 to June 23, 2012.
c Filed for free agency, November 3, 2012. Signed with Baltimore Orioles organization, December 19, 2012.

IZTURIS, MAICER

Born, Barquisimeto, Venezuela, September 12, 1980.
Bats Both. Throws Right. Height, 5 feet, 8 inches. Weight, 160 pounds.

Year	Club	Lea	Pos	G	AB	R	H	2B	3B	HR	RBI	SB	Avg
1998 Burlington		Appal.	SS	55	217	33	63	8	2	2	33	16	.290
1999 Columbus		So.Atl.	SS	57	220	46	66	5	3	4	23	14	.300
2000 Columbus		So.Atl.	SS	10	29	4.	8	1	0	0	1	0	.276
2001 Kinston		Carolina	2B	114	433	47	104	16	6	1	39	32	.240
2002 Kinston		Carolina	2B	58	233	28	61	13	1	1	30	24	.262
2002 Akron		Eastern	2B	67	253	34	70	12	7	0	32	8	.277
2003 Akron		Eastern	2B-SS-OF	54	218	31	61	11	5	1	20	14	.280
2003 Buffalo		Int.	SS-2B	85	301	43	79	16	4	2	29	14	.262
2004 Edmonton		P.C.	SS-2B	99	376	65	127	19	2	3	36	14	.338
2004 Montreal a-b		N.L.	SS-2B	32	107	10	22	5	2	1	4	4	.206
2005 Salt Lake		P.C.	SS-3B-2B	10	31	10	14	4	0	0	2	4	.452
2005 Los Angeles c		A.L.	3B-SS-2B-OF	77	191	18	47	8	4	1	15	9	.246
2006 Salt Lake		P.C.	SS-3B-2B	9	36	5	11	5	1	0	5	1	.306
2006 Los Angeles d		A.L.	3B-SS-2B	104	352	64	103	21	3	5	44	14	.293
2007 Rancho Cucamonga		Calif.	3B	7	22	5	7	1	0	0	3	0	.318
2007 Salt Lake		P.C.	2B-SS	5	17	3	6	1	0	0	0	0	.353
2007 Los Angeles e		A.L.	3B-2B-SS	102	336	47	97	17	2	6	51	7	.289
2008 Rancho Cucamonga		Calif.	2B	1	2	0	1	0	0	0	0	0	.500
2008 Los Angeles f		A.L.	SS-2B-3B	79	290	44	78	14	2	.3	37	11	.269
2009 Los Angeles		A.L.	2B-SS-3B-OF	114	387	74	116	22	3	8	65	13	.300
2010 Salt Lake		P.C.	3B-SS	2	7	1	2	0	0	0	1	0	.286
2010 Los Angeles g		A.L.	3B-2B-SS	61	212	27	53	13	1	3	27	7	.250
2011 Los Angeles		A.L.	2B-3B-SS	122	449	51	124	35	0	5	38	9	.276
2012 Los Angeles h		A.L.	3B-2B-SS	100	289	35	74	11	0	2	20	17	.256
Major League Totals			9 Yrs.	791	2613	370	714	146	17	34	301	91	.273
Division Series													
2007 Los Angeles		A.L.	3B	3	12	1	4	2	0	0	0	2	.333
2009 Los Angeles		A.L.	2B	2	7	1	1	0	0	0	1	1	.143
Division Series Totals				5	19	2	5	2	0	0	1	3	.263
Championship Series													
2005 Los Angeles		A.L.	SS	1	0	0	0	0	0	0	0	0	.000
2009 Los Angeles		A.L.	2B	4	10	1	1	1	0	0	1	0	.100
Championship Series Totals				5	10	1	1	1	0	0	1	0	.100

a Traded by Cleveland Indians to Montreal Expos with outfielder Ryan Church for pitcher Scott Stewart, January 5, 2004.
b Traded to Anaheim Angels with outfielder Juan Rivera for outfielder Jose Guillen, November 19, 2004.
c On disabled list from April 26 to June 18, 2005.
d On disabled list from April 24 to June 9, 2006.
e On disabled list from April 30 to May 15 and May 21 to July 3, 2007.
f On disabled list from April 28 to May 13 and August 14 to October 9, 2008.
g On disabled list from May 6 to May 25 and June 16 to July 18 and August 20 to September 27, 2010.
h Filed for free agency, November 3, 2012. Signed with Toronto Blue Jays, November 8, 2012.

JACKSON, AUSTIN JARRIEL

Born, Denton, Texas, February 1, 1987.
Bats Right. Throws Right. Height, 6 feet, 1 inch. Weight, 185 pounds.

Year Club	Lea	Pos	G	AB	R	H	2B	3B	HR	RBI	SB	Avg
2005 Yankees	Gulf Coast	OF	40	148	32	45	11	2	0	14	11	.304
2006 Charleston	So.Atl.	OF	134	535	90	139	24	5	4	47	37	.260
2007 Tampa	Fla.St.	OF	67	258	53	89	15	6	10	34	13	.345
2007 Scranton/WB	Int.	OF	1	3	2	1	1	0	0	0	1	.333
2007 Charleston	So.Atl.	OF	60	235	33	61	16	1	3	25	19	.260
2008 Trenton...........	Eastern	OF	131	520	75	148	33	5	9	69	19	.285
2009 Scranton/WB a	Int.	OF	132	504	67	151	23	9	4	65	24	.300
2010 Detroit	A.L.	OF	151	618	103	181	34	10	4	41	27	.293
2011 Detroit	A.L.	OF	153	591	90	147	22	11	10	45	22	.249
2012 Toledo	Int.	OF	2	8	0	1	0	0	0	0	0	.125
2012 Detroit b	A.L.	OF	137	543	103	163	29	*10	16	66	12	.300
Major League Totals		3 Yrs.	441	1752	296	491	85	31	30	152	61	.280
Division Series												
2011 Detroit	A.L.	OF	5	16	3	2	1	0	0	0	1	.125
2012 Detroit	A.L.	OF	5	20	4	5	2	0	0	3	0	.250
Division Series Totals			10	36	7	7	3	0	0	3	1	.194
Championship Series												
2011 Detroit	A.L.	OF	6	25	3	6	1	0	1	4	0	.240
2012 Detroit	A.L.	OF	4	17	3	6	1	1	1	1	0	.353
Championship Series Totals			10	42	6	12	2	1	2	5	0	.286
World Series Record												
2012 Detroit	A.L.	OF	4	13	2	3	1	0	0	0	0	.231

a Traded by New York Yankees to Detroit Tigers with pitcher Phil Coke and pitcher Ian Kennedy for outfielder Curtis Granderson, December 9, 2009.
b On disabled list from May 17 to June 9, 2012.

JASO, JOHN EDWARD

Born, Chula Vista, California, September 19, 1983.
Bats Left. Throws Right. Height, 6 feet, 2 inches. Weight, 205 pounds.

Year Club	Lea	Pos	G	AB	R	H	2B	3B	HR	RBI	SB	Avg
2003 Hudson Valley ...	N.Y.-Penn.	C	47	154	20	34	7	0	2	20	2	.221
2004 Hudson Valley ...	N.Y.-Penn.	C-1B-SS	57	199	34	60	17	2	2	35	1	.302
2005 SW Michigan	Midwest	C-1B	92	332	61	102	25	1	14	50	3	.307
2006 Visalia	Calif.	C	95	366	58	113	22	0	10	55	1	.309
2007 Montgomery	Southern	C	109	380	62	120	24	2	12	71	2	.316
2008 Montgomery	Southern	C	85	284	51	77	13	2	7	43	1	.271
2008 Durham	Int.	C	31	108	14	30	7	0	5	24	1	.278
2008 Tampa Bay	A.L.	C	5	10	2	2	0	0	0	0	0	.200
2009 Durham	Int.	C	104	331	42	88	14	2	5	30	1	.266
2010 Durham	Int.	C	3	11	1	4	1	0	0	2	0	.364
2010 Tampa Bay	A.L.	C-1B	109	339	57	89	18	3	5	44	4	.263
2011 Durham	Int.	C	6	20	2	6	2	0	0	4	0	.300
2011 Tampa Bay a-b	A.L.	C	89	246	26	55	15	1	5	27	1	.224
2012 Seattle	A.L.	DH-C	108	294	41	81	19	2	10	50	5	.276
Major League Totals		4 Yrs.	311	889	126	227	52	6	20	121	10	.255
Division Series												
2010 Tampa Bay	A.L.	C	3	10	0	3	0	0	0	0	0	.300
2011 Tampa Bay	A.L.	C	2	4	0	0	0	0	0	0	0	.000
Division Series Totals			5	14	0	3	0	0	0	1	0	.214

a On disabled list from July 15 to August 19, 2011.
b Traded to Seattle Mariners for pitcher Josh Lueke, November 27, 2011.

JAY, JONATHAN HENRY (JON)

Born, Miami, Florida, March 15, 1985.
Bats Left. Throws Left. Height, 5 feet, 11 inches. Weight, 200 pounds.

Year Club	Lea	Pos	G	AB	R	H	2B	3B	HR	RBI	SB	Avg
2006 Quad Cities........	Midwest	OF	60	234	42	80	13	3	3	45	9	.342
2007 Palm Beach	Fla.St.	OF	32	126	19	36	8	0	2	10	5	.286
2007 Cardinals	Gulf Coast	DH	1	2	0	1	0	0	0	0	0	.500
2007 Springfield	Texas	OF	26	102	17	24	4	2	2	11	4	.235
2008 Memphis	P.C.	OF	16	58	8	20	4	1	1	10	0	.345
2008 Springfield	Texas	OF	96	372	57	114	17	3	11	47	10	.306
2009 Memphis	P.C.	OF-1B	136	505	72	142	23	2	10	54	20	.281

Year Club	Lea	Pos	G	AB	R	H	2B	3B	HR	RBI	SB	Avg
2010 Memphis . . . . .P.C.		OF-1B	42	165	31	53	16	0	4	32	13	.321
2010 St. Louis. . . . . N.L.		OF	105	287	47	86	19	2	4	27	2	.300
2011 St. Louis. . . . . N.L.		OF	159	455	56	135	24	2	10	37	6	.297
2012 Memphis . . . . .P.C.		OF	2	7	3	3	0	1	1	3	0	.429
2012 St. Louis a . . . . N.L.		OF	117	443	70	135	22	4	4	40	19	.305
Major League Totals		3 Yrs.	381	1185	173	356	65	8	18	104	27	.300
Wild Card Playoff												
2012 St. Louis. . . . . N.L.		OF	1	4	0	0	0	0	0	0	0	.000
Division Series												
2011 St. Louis. . . . . N.L.		OF	5	12	0	2	0	0	0	2	0	.167
2012 St. Louis. . . . . N.L.		OF	5	20	4	4	0	1	0	4	2	.200
Division Series Totals			10	32	4	6	0	1	0	6	2	.188
Championship Series												
2011 St. Louis. . . . . N.L.		OF	6	25	7	6	2	0	0	1	1	.240
2012 St. Louis. . . . . N.L.		OF	7	29	3	6	1	0	0	3	0	.207
Championship Series Totals			13	54	10	12	3	0	0	4	1	.222
World Series Record												
2011 St. Louis. . . . . N.L.		OF	7	18	1	2	0	0	0	0	0	.111

a On disabled list from May 15 to June 22, 2012.

JENNINGS, DESMOND DELANE

Born, Birmingham, Alabama, October 30, 1986.
Bats Right. Throws Right. Height, 6 feet, 2 inches. Weight, 200 pounds.

Year Club	Lea	Pos	G	AB	R	H	2B	3B	HR	RBI	SB	Avg
2006 Princeton . . . . .Appal.		OF	56	213	48	59	10	1	4	20	32	.277
2007 Columbus. . . . . So.Atl.		OF	99	387	75	122	21	5	9	37	45	.315
2008 Vero Beach. . . . . .Fla.St.		OF	24	85	17	22	5	1	2	6	5	.259
2009 Montgomery . . . . . Southern		OF	100	383	69	121	25	8	8	45	37	.316
2009 Durham . . . . .Int.		OF	32	114	23	37	6	2	3	17	15	.325
2010 Durham . . . . .Int.		OF	109	399	82	111	25	6	3	36	37	.278
2010 Tampa Bay . . . . A.L.		OF	17	21	5	4	1	1	0	2	2	.190
2011 Durham . . . . .Int.		OF	89	338	68	93	19	3	12	39	17	.275
2011 Tampa Bay . . . . A.L.		OF	63	247	44	64	9	4	10	25	20	.259
2012 Charlotte . . . . .Fla.St.		OF	1	3	1	1	1	0	0	0	0	.333
2012 Durham . . . . .Int.		OF	3	12	1	2	0	0	0	0	0	.167
2012 Tampa Bay a . . . . A.L.		OF	132	505	85	124	19	7	13	47	31	.246
Major League Totals		3 Yrs.	212	773	134	192	29	12	23	74	53	.248
Division Series												
2010 Tampa Bay . . . . A.L.		OF	2	2	1	0	0	0	0	0	0	.000
2011 Tampa Bay . . . . A.L.		OF	4	15	3	5	1	0	2	2	0	.333
Division Series Totals			6	17	4	5	1	0	2	2	0	.294

a On disabled list from May 12 to June 5, 2012.

JETER, DEREK SANDERSON

Born, Pequannock, New Jersey, June 26, 1974.
Bats Right. Throws Right. Height, 6 feet, 3 inches. Weight, 195 pounds.

Year Club	Lea	Pos	G	AB	R	H	2B	3B	HR	RBI	SB	Avg
1992 Tampa Yankees . . . . . Gulf C.		SS	47	173	19	35	10	0	3	25	2	.202
1992 Greensboro . . . . .So. Atl.		SS	11	37	4	9	0	0	1	4	0	.243
1993 Greensboro . . . . .So. Atl.		SS	128	515	85	152	14	11	5	71	18	.295
1994 Tampa . . . . Fla. St.		SS	69	292	61	96	13	8	0	39	28	.329
1994 Albany . . . . .Eastern		SS	34	122	17	46	7	2	2	13	12	.377
1994 Columbus. . . . . .Int.		SS	35	126	25	44	7	1	3	16	10	.349
1995 Columbus. . . . . .Int.		SS	123	486	96	154	27	9	2	45	20	.317
1995 New York . . . . A.L.		SS	15	48	5	12	4	1	0	7	0	.250
1996 New York a . . . . A.L.		SS	157	582	104	183	25	6	10	78	14	.314
1997 New York . . . . A.L.		SS	159	654	116	190	31	7	10	70	23	.291
1998 Columbus. . . . . .Int.		SS	1	5	2	2	2	0	0	0	0	.400
1998 New York b . . . . A.L.		SS	149	626	*127	203	25	8	19	84	30	.324
1999 New York . . . . A.L.		SS	158	627	134	219	37	9	24	102	19	.349
2000 Tampa . . . . .Fla.St.		SS	1	3	2	2	1	0	0	0	0	.667
2000 New York c . . . . A.L.		SS	148	593	119	201	31	4	15	73	22	.339
2001 New York d . . . . A.L.		SS	150	614	110	191	35	3	21	74	27	.311
2002 New York . . . . A.L.		SS	157	644	124	191	26	0	18	75	32	.297
2003 Trenton . . . . .Eastern		SS	5	18	2	8	1	0	0	5	0	.444
2003 New York e . . . . A.L.		SS	119	482	87	156	25	3	10	52	11	.324

Year	Club	Lea	Pos	G	AB	R	H	2B	3B	HR	RBI	SB	Avg
2004	New York	A.L.	SS	154	643	111	188	44	1	23	78	23	.292
2005	New York	A.L.	SS	159	654	122	202	25	5	19	70	14	.309
2006	New York	A.L.	SS	154	623	118	214	39	3	14	97	34	.343
2007	New York	A.L.	SS	156	639	102	206	39	4	12	73	15	.322
2008	New York	A.L.	SS	150	596	88	179	25	3	11	69	11	.300
2009	New York	A.L.	SS	153	634	107	212	27	1	18	66	30	.334
2010	New York f	A.L.	SS	157	663	111	179	30	3	10	67	18	.270
2011	Trenton	Eastern	SS	2	4	1	2	0	0	0	0	0	.500
2011	New York g	A.L.	SS	131	546	84	162	24	4	6	61	16	.297
2012	New York	A.L.	SS	159	*683	99	*216	32	0	15	58	9	.316
Major League Totals		18 Yrs.		2585	10551	1868	3304	524	65	255	1254	348	.313

Division Series

Year	Club	Lea	Pos	G	AB	R	H	2B	3B	HR	RBI	SB	Avg
1996	New York	A.L.	SS	4	17	2	7	1	0	0	1	0	.412
1997	New York	A.L.	SS	5	21	6	7	1	0	2	2	1	.333
1998	New York	A.L.	SS	3	9	0	1	0	0	0	0	0	.111
1999	New York	A.L.	SS	3	11	3	5	1	1	0	0	0	.455
2000	New York	A.L.	SS	5	19	1	4	0	0	0	2	0	.211
2001	New York	A.L.	SS	5	18	2	8	1	0	0	1	0	.444
2002	New York	A.L.	SS	4	16	6	8	0	0	2	3	0	.500
2003	New York	A.L.	SS	4	14	2	6	0	0	1	1	1	.429
2004	New York	A.L.	SS	4	19	3	6	1	0	1	4	1	.316
2005	New York	A.L.	SS	5	21	4	7	0	0	2	5	1	.333
2006	New York	A.L.	SS	4	16	4	8	4	0	1	1	0	.500
2007	New York	A.L.	SS	4	17	0	3	0	0	0	1	0	.176
2009	New York	A.L.	SS	3	10	4	4	2	0	1	2	0	.400
2010	New York	A.L.	SS	3	14	0	4	0	0	0	1	1	.286
2011	New York	A.L.	SS	5	24	6	6	1	0	0	2	1	.250
2012	New York	A.L.	SS-DH	5	22	4	8	1	1	0	2	0	.364
Division Series Totals				66	268	47	92	13	2	10	28	6	.343

Championship Series

Year	Club	Lea	Pos	G	AB	R	H	2B	3B	HR	RBI	SB	Avg
1996	New York	A.L.	SS	5	24	5	10	2	0	1	1	2	.417
1998	New York	A.L.	SS	6	25	3	5	1	1	0	2	3	.200
1999	New York	A.L.	SS	5	20	3	7	1	0	1	3	0	.350
2000	New York	A.L.	SS	6	22	6	7	0	0	2	5	1	.318
2001	New York	A.L.	SS	5	17	0	2	0	0	0	2	0	.118
2003	New York	A.L.	SS	7	30	3	7	2	0	1	2	1	.233
2004	New York	A.L.	SS	7	30	5	6	1	0	0	5	1	.200
2009	New York	A.L.	SS	6	27	5	7	0	0	2	3	0	.259
2010	New York	A.L.	SS	6	26	2	6	3	1	0	1	0	.231
2012	New York	A.L.	SS	1	5	0	1	0	0	0	0	0	.200
Championship Series Totals				54	226	32	58	10	2	7	24	8	.257

World Series

Year	Club	Lea	Pos	G	AB	R	H	2B	3B	HR	RBI	SB	Avg
1996	New York	A.L.	SS	6	20	5	5	0	0	0	1	1	.250
1998	New York	A.L.	SS	4	17	4	6	0	0	0	1	0	.353
1999	New York	A.L.	SS	4	17	4	6	1	0	0	1	3	.353
2000	New York	A.L.	SS	5	22	6	9	2	1	2	2	0	.409
2001	New York	A.L.	SS	7	27	3	4	0	0	1	1	0	.148
2003	New York	A.L.	SS	6	26	5	9	3	0	0	2	0	.346
2009	New York	A.L.	SS	6	27	5	11	3	0	0	1	0	.407
World Series Totals				38	156	32	50	9	1	3	9	4	.321

a Selected Rookie of the Year in American League for 1996.
b On disabled list from June 4 to June 19, 1998.
c On disabled list from May 12 to May 26, 2000.
d On disabled list from March 23 to April 7, 2001.
e On disabled list from April 1 to May 13, 2003.
f Filed for free agency, November 1, 2010, re-signed with New York Yankees, December 7, 2010.
g On disabled list from June 14 to July 4, 2011.

JOHNSON, CHRISTOPHER DALTON (CHRIS)

Born, Naples, Florida, October 1, 1984.
Bats Right. Throws Right. Height, 6 feet, 3 inches. Weight, 220 pounds.

Year	Club	Lea	Pos	G	AB	R	H	2B	3B	HR	RBI	SB	Avg
2006	Tri-City	N.Y.-Penn.	3B-1B	60	222	18	47	7	1	1	29	7	.212
2007	Salem	Carolina	3B-1B	60	224	24	59	11	0	6	38	1	.263
2007	Lexington	So.Atl.	3B-SS-1B	64	255	37	66	14	0	8	44	3	.259
2008	Round Rock	P.C.	3B	30	101	10	22	2	1	1	9	0	.218
2008	Corpus Christi	Texas	3B	84	330	43	107	24	0	12	58	5	.324
2009	Lancaster	Calif.	3B	4	16	5	7	5	0	0	6	0	.438

Year	Club	Lea	Pos	G	AB	R	H	2B	3B	HR	RBI	SB	Avg
2009 Round Rock..........P.C.			3B	104	384	48	108	20	5	13	42	2	.281
2009 Houston.............N.L.			3B	11	22	1	2	0	0	0	1	0	.091
2010 Round Rock..........P.C.			3B	38	149	26	49	10	1	8	33	0	.329
2010 Houston a ..........N.L.			3B	94	341	40	105	22	2	11	52	3	.308
2011 Oklahoma.............P.C.			3B	21	81	18	22	7	0	4	15	1	.272
2011 Houston.............N.L.			3B	107	378	32	95	21	3	7	42	2	.251
2012 Houston-Arizona b.....N.L.		3B-1B-OF	136	488	48	137	28	5	15	76	5	.281
Major League Totals			4 Yrs.	348	1229	121	339	71	10	33	171	10	.276

a On disabled list from April 18 to May 8, 2010.

b Traded to Arizona Diamondbacks for outfielder Marc Krauss and outfielder Bobby Borchering, July 29, 2012.

JOHNSON, ELLIOT TYLER
Born, Safford, Arizona, March 9, 1984.
Bats Both. Throws Right. Height, 6 feet. Weight, 190 pounds.

Year	Club	Lea	Pos	G	AB	R	H	2B	3B	HR	RBI	SB	Avg
2002 Princeton.......Appal.			2B-SS	42	152	21	40	10	1	1	13	14	.263
2003 Charleston......So.Atl.		2B-SS-OF	54	151	22	32	4	0	0	15	8	.212
2004 Charleston......So.Atl.			2B	126	503	92	132	22	7	6	41	43	.262
2005 Visalia ....Calif.			2B	56	227	42	62	10	3	8	33	28	.273
2005 Montgomery ..Southern		2B-SS	63	264	31	69	9	6	3	21	15	.261
2006 Montgomery ..Southern			2B	122	494	69	139	21	10	15	50	20	.281
2007 Durham ....Int.			2B	129	463	56	96	17	6	11	45	16	.207
2008 Tampa Bay .........A.L.		SS-OF-2B	7	19	0	3	0	0	0	0	0	.158
2008 Durham ....Int.		2B-SS-OF	107	387	49	101	26	5	9	50	15	.261
2009 Rays.......Gulf Coast			2B	5	16	2	5	2	0	0	2	0	.313
2009 Durham ....Int.		2B-3B-SS-OF	63	233	31	61	9	1	11	35	7	.262
2010 Durham ....Int.		SS-OF-2B	109	427	72	136	24	5	11	56	30	.319
2011 Durham ....Int.			SS	2	9	1	2	0	0	0	0	0	.222
2011 Tampa Bay a.......A.L.		SS-2B-1B-OF	70	160	20	31	7	2	4	17	6	.194
2012 Tampa Bay .......A.L.		SS-2B-3B-OF	123	297	32	72	10	2	6	33	18	.242
Major League Totals			3 Yrs.	200	476	52	106	17	4	10	50	24	.223
Division Series													
2011 Tampa Bay ........A.L.			PH	1	0	0	0	0	0	0	0	0	.000

a On disabled list from May 22 to June 12, 2011.

JOHNSON, KELLY ANDREW
Born, Austin, Texas, February 22, 1982.
Bats Left. Throws Right. Height, 6 feet, 1 inch. Weight, 205 pounds.

Year	Club	Lea	Pos	G	AB	R	H	2B	3B	HR	RBI	SB	Avg
2000 Braves .... Gulf Coast		SS-3B	53	193	27	52	12	3	4	29	6	.269
2001 Macon ....So.Atl.			SS	124	415	75	120	22	1	23	66	25	.289
2002 Myrtle Beach ...... Carolina		SS-3B	126	482	62	123	21	5	12	49	12	.255
2003 Braves .... Gulf Coast			SS	6	26	10	10	1	1	1	3	1	.385
2003 Greenville.........Southern			SS	98	334	46	92	22	5	6	45	10	.275
2004 Greenville........Southern		OF-3B-2B	135	479	70	135	35	3	16	50	9	.282
2005 Richmond ....Int.		OF-3B-SS	44	155	35	48	12	3	8	22	7	.310
2005 Atlanta .............N.L.			OF	87	290	46	70	12	3	9	40	2	.241
2006 Richmond ....Int.			OF	10	39	3	13	4	0	1	7	1	.333
2006 Rome a ....So.Atl.			OF	5	19	5	9	2	1	1	3	2	.474
2007 Atlanta .............N.L.			2B	147	521	91	144	26	10	16	68	9	.276
2008 Atlanta .............N.L.			2B	150	547	86	157	39	6	12	69	11	.287
2009 Gwinnett ....Int.			2B	13	52	9	16	2	2	3	16	1	.308
2009 Atlanta b-c .........N.L.			2B	106	303	47	68	20	3	8	29	7	.224
2010 Arizona.............N.L.			2B	154	585	93	166	36	5	26	71	13	.284
2011 Arizona.............N.L.			2B	114	430	59	90	23	5	18	49	13	.209
2011 Toronto d-e ........A.L.			2B	33	115	16	31	4	2	3	9	3	.270
2012 Toronto f ..........A.L.			2B	142	507	61	114	19	2	16	55	14	.225
Major League Totals			7 Yrs.	933	3298	499	840	179	36	108	390	72	.255
Division Series													
2005 Atlanta .............N.L.			PH	4	2	0	0	0	0	0	0	0	.000

a On disabled list from March 24 to November 1, 2006.

b On disabled list from July 3 to July 23, 2009.

c Not offered contract, December 12, 2009. Signed with Arizona Diamondbacks, December 30, 2009.

d Traded to Toronto Blue Jays for infielder Aaron Hill and infielder John McDonald, August 23, 2011.

e Filed for free agency, October 30, 2011. Accepted arbitration, December 7, 2011.

f Filed for free agency, November 3, 2012.

JOHNSON, REED CAMERON

Born, Riverside, California, December 8, 1976.
Bats Right. Throws Right. Height, 5 feet, 10 inches. Weight, 180 pounds.

Year	Club	Lea	Pos	G	AB	R	H	2B	3B	HR	RBI	SB	Avg
1999 St. Catharines....	N.Y.-Penn.	OF	60	189	24	44	8	2	2	23	5	.233
2000 Dunedin...........	Fla.St.	OF	36	133	26	42	9	2	4	28	3	.316
2000 Hagerstown........	So.Atl.	OF	95	324	66	94	24	5	8	70	14	.290
2001 Tennessee........	Southern	OF	136	554	104	174	29	4	13	74	42	.314
2002 Dunedin...........	Fla.St.	OF	8	33	7	9	3	0	0	6	0	.273
2002 Syracuse.........	Int.	OF	44	159	27	37	8	3	2	10	1	.233
2003 Syracuse.........	Int.	OF	26	101	14	33	4	1	2	16	3	.327
2003 Toronto..........	A.L.	OF	114	412	79	121	21	2	10	52	5	.294
2004 Toronto..........	A.L.	OF	141	537	68	145	25	2	10	61	6	.270
2005 Toronto..........	A.L.	OF	142	398	55	107	21	6	8	58	5	.269
2006 Toronto..........	A.L.	OF	134	461	86	147	34	2	12	49	8	.319
2007 Dunedin..........	Fla.St.	OF	4	12	1	4	1	0	1	1	0	.333
2007 Syracuse.........	Int.	OF	2	8	1	3	0	0	0	1	0	.375
2007 Toronto a........	A.L.	OF	79	275	31	65	13	2	2	14	4	.236
2008 Chicago b-c......	N.L.	OF	109	333	52	101	21	0	6	50	5	.303
2009 Peoria..........	Midwest	OF	3	6	2	2	0	0	0	0	0	.333
2009 Chicago d-e......	N.L.	OF	65	165	23	42	10	2	4	22	2	.255
2010 Inland Empire.....	Calif.	OF	2	6	2	3	1	0	0	0	0	.500
2010 Los Angeles f-g...	N.L.	OF	102	202	24	53	11	2	2	15	2	.262
2011 Iowa.............	P.C.	OF	3	6	0	0	0	0	0	0	0	.000
2011 Chicago h-i......	N.L.	OF	111	246	33	76	22	1	5	28	2	.309
2012 Chicago-Atlanta j-k.	N.L.	OF	119	269	30	78	14	3	3	20	2	.290
Major League Totals...........	10 Yrs.	1116	3298	481	935	192	22	62	369	41	.284

a On disabled list from April 12 to July 6, 2007.
b Released by Toronto Blue Jays, March 23, 2008. Signed with Chicago Cubs, March 25, 2008.
c On disabled list from June 18 to July 3, 2008.
d On disabled list from June 21 to July 6 and July 30 to September 21, 2009.
e Filed for free agency, November 5, 2009. Signed with Los Angeles Dodgers, February 1, 2010.
f On disabled list from July 9 to August 4, 2010.
g Filed for free agency, November 1, 2010. Signed with Chicago Cubs organization, January 12, 2011.
h On disabled list from May 29 to June 14, 2011.
i Filed for free agency, October 30, 2011, re-signed with Chicago Cubs, January 3, 2012.
j Traded to Atlanta Braves with pitcher Paul Maholm and cash for pitcher Jaye Chapman and pitcher Arodys Vizcaino, July 31, 2012.
k Filed for free agency, November 3, 2012, re-signed with Atlanta Braves, December 6, 2012.

JONES, ADAM LA MARQUE

Born, San Diego, California, August 1, 1985.
Bats Right. Throws Right. Height, 6 feet, 2 inches. Weight, 200 pounds.

Year	Club	Lea	Pos	G	AB	R	H	2B	3B	HR	RBI	SB	Avg
2003 Mariners..........	Arizona	SS	28	109	18	31	5	1	0	8	5	.284
2003 Everett........	Northwest	SS	3	13	2	6	1	0	0	4	0	.462
2004 Wisconsin........	Midwest	SS-3B	130	510	76	136	23	7	11	72	8	.267
2005 Inland Empire........	Calif.	SS	68	271	43	80	20	5	8	46	4	.295
2005 San Antonio........	Texas	SS-OF	63	228	33	68	10	3	7	20	9	.298
2006 Tacoma..............	P.C.	OF	96	380	69	109	19	4	16	62	13	.287
2006 Seattle..............	A.L.	OF	32	74	6	16	4	0	1	8	3	.216
2007 Tacoma..............	P.C.	OF	101	420	75	132	27	6	25	84	8	.314
2007 Seattle..............	A.L.	OF	41	65	16	16	2	1	2	4	2	.246
2008 Baltimore a-b........	A.L.	OF	132	477	61	129	21	7	9	57	10	.270
2009 Baltimore c........	A.L.	OF	119	473	83	131	22	3	19	70	10	.277
2010 Baltimore..........	A.L.	OF	149	581	76	165	25	5	19	69	7	.284
2011 Baltimore..........	A.L.	OF	151	567	68	159	26	2	25	83	12	.280
2012 Baltimore..........	A.L.	OF	*162	648	103	186	39	3	32	82	16	.287
Major League Totals............	7 Yrs.	786	2885	413	802	139	21	107	373	60	.278
Wild Card Playoff												
2012 Baltimore..........	A.L.	OF	1	3	0	0	0	0	0	1	0	.000
Division Series												
2012 Baltimore..........	A.L.	OF	5	23	0	2	0	0	0	0	0	.087

a Traded to Baltimore Orioles with pitcher Tony Butler, pitcher Kam Mickolio, pitcher George Sherrill and pitcher Chris Tillman for pitcher Erik Bedard, February 8, 2008.
b On disabled list from August 3 to September 1, 2008.
c On disabled list from September 2 to November 6, 2009.

JONES, ANDRUW RUDOLF

Born, Willemstad, Curacao, Netherlands Antilles, April 23, 1977.
Bats Right. Throws Right. Height, 6 feet, 1 inch. Weight, 240 pounds.

Year	Club	Lea	Pos	G	AB	R	H	2B	3B	HR	RBI	SB	Avg
1994 Braves	Gulf Coast	OF	27	95	22	21	5	1	2	10	5	.221
1994 Danville	Appal.	OF	36	143	20	48	9	2	1	16	16	.336
1995 Macon	So.Atl.	OF	139	537	104	149	41	5	25	100	56	.277
1996 Durham	Carolina	OF	66	243	65	76	14	3	17	43	16	.313
1996 Greenville	Southern	OF	38	157	39	58	10	1	12	37	12	.369
1996 Richmond	Int.	OF	12	45	11	17	3	1	5	12	2	.378
1996 Atlanta	N.L.	OF	31	106	11	23	7	1	5	13	3	.217
1997 Atlanta	N.L.	OF	153	399	60	92	18	1	18	70	20	.231
1998 Atlanta	N.L.	OF	159	582	89	158	33	8	31	90	27	.271
1999 Atlanta	N.L.	OF	162	592	97	163	35	5	26	84	24	.275
2000 Atlanta	N.L.	OF	161	*656	122	199	36	6	36	104	21	.303
2001 Atlanta	N.L.	OF	161	625	104	157	25	2	34	104	11	.251
2002 Atlanta	N.L.	OF	154	560	91	148	34	0	35	94	8	.264
2003 Atlanta	N.L.	OF	156	595	101	165	28	2	36	116	4	.277
2004 Atlanta	N.L.	OF	154	570	85	149	34	4	29	91	6	.261
2005 Atlanta	N.L.	OF	160	586	95	154	24	3	*51	*128	5	.263
2006 Atlanta	N.L.	OF	156	565	107	148	29	0	41	129	4	.262
2007 Atlanta a	N.L.	OF	154	572	83	127	27	2	26	94	5	.222
2008 Las Vegas	P.C.	1B-OF	11	31	7	10	0	0	4	11	2	.323
2008 Los Angeles b-c	N.L.	OF	75	209	21	33	8	1	3	14	0	.158
2009 Frisco	Texas	1B	3	9	0	2	0	0	0	0	1	.222
2009 Texas d-e	A.L.	DH-OF-1B	82	281	43	60	18	0	17	43	5	.214
2010 Chicago f	A.L.	OF	107	278	41	64	12	1	19	48	9	.230
2011 New York g	A.L.	OF	77	190	27	47	8	0	13	33	0	.247
2012 New York h	A.L.	OF	94	233	27	46	7	0	14	34	0	.197
Major League Totals	17 Yrs.			2196	7599	1204	1933	383	36	434	1289	152	.254
Division Series													
1996 Atlanta	N.L.	OF	3	0	0	0	0	0	0	0	0	.000
1997 Atlanta	N.L.	OF	3	5	1	0	0	0	0	1	0	.000
1998 Atlanta	N.L.	OF	3	9	2	0	0	0	0	1	2	.000
1999 Atlanta	N.L.	OF	4	18	1	4	1	0	0	2	0	.222
2000 Atlanta	N.L.	OF	3	9	3	1	0	0	1	1	0	.111
2001 Atlanta	N.L.	OF	3	12	2	6	0	0	1	1	0	.500
2002 Atlanta	N.L.	OF	5	19	4	6	1	0	0	2	0	.316
2003 Atlanta	N.L.	OF	5	17	1	1	0	0	0	1	0	.059
2004 Atlanta	N.L.	OF	5	19	4	10	2	0	2	5	1	.526
2005 Atlanta	N.L.	OF	4	17	5	8	3	0	1	5	0	.471
2011 New York	A.L.	OF	1	0	0	0	0	0	0	1	0	.000
Division Series Totals			39	125	23	36	7	0	5	20	3	.288
Championship Series													
1996 Atlanta	N.L.	OF	5	9	3	2	0	0	1	3	0	.222
1997 Atlanta	N.L.	OF	5	9	0	4	0	0	0	1	0	.444
1998 Atlanta	N.L.	OF	6	22	3	6	0	0	1	2	1	.273
1999 Atlanta	N.L.	OF	6	23	5	5	0	0	0	1	0	.217
2001 Atlanta	N.L.	OF	5	17	4	3	0	0	1	1	0	.176
Championship Series Totals			27	80	15	20	0	0	3	8	1	.250
World Series													
1996 Atlanta	N.L.	OF	6	20	4	8	1	0	2	6	1	.400
1999 Atlanta	N.L.	OF	4	13	1	1	0	0	0	0	0	.077
World Series Totals			10	33	5	9	1	0	2	6	1	.273

a Filed for free agency, October 31, 2007. Signed with Los Angeles Dodgers, December 12, 2007.
b On disabled list from May 24 to July 4 and August 10 to September 1 and September 13 to November 4, 2008.
c Released, January 15, 2009. Signed with Texas Rangers organization, February 8, 2009.
d On disabled list from August 24 to September 8, 2009.
e Filed for free agency, November 6, 2009. Signed with Chicago White Sox, November 25, 2009.
f Filed for free agency, November 1, 2010. Signed with New York Yankees, February 14, 2011.
g Filed for free agency, October 30, 2011, re-signed with New York Yankees January 25, 2012.
h Filed for free agency, November 3, 2012. Signed with Rakuten Golden Eagles (Japan), December 16, 2012.

JONES, GARRETT THOMAS

Born, Harvey, Illinois, June 21, 1981.
Bats Left. Throws Left. Height, 6 feet, 4 inches. Weight, 245 pounds.

Year	Club	Lea	Pos	G	AB	R	H	2B	3B	HR	RBI	SB	Avg
1999 Braves	Gulf Coast	1B	46	170	17	41	3	0	3	18	1	.241
2000 Danville	Appal.	1B	40	138	12	24	7	2	0	16	0	.174

Year	Club	Lea	Pos	G	AB	R	H	2B	3B	HR	RBI	SB	Avg
2001	Danville	Appal.	1B	40	149	13	43	11	0	3	23	0	.289
2002	Quad Cities a	Midwest	1B-OF	63	223	21	45	8	0	10	32	3	.202
2003	Fort Myers	Fla.St.	1B-OF	117	404	52	89	12	5	18	67	5	.220
2004	New Britain	Eastern	1B	122	450	68	140	33	2	30	92	11	.311
2004	Fort Myers	Fla.St.	1B	19	66	6	16	5	0	1	6	2	.242
2005	Rochester	Int.	1B-OF	134	488	71	119	22	2	24	72	5	.244
2006	Rochester	Int.	1B-OF	140	525	72	125	32	3	21	92	3	.238
2007	Rochester	Int.	OF-1B	107	400	57	112	32	3	13	70	2	.280
2007	Minnesota	A.L.	DH-1B-OF	31	77	7	16	2	1	2	5	1	.208
2008	Rochester b	Int.	1B-OF	138	527	82	147	33	3	23	92	9	.279
2009	Indianapolis	Int.	OF-1B	72	277	44	85	18	0	12	49	14	.307
2009	Pittsburgh	N.L.	OF-1B	82	314	45	92	21	1	21	44	10	.293
2010	Pittsburgh	N.L.	1B-OF	158	592	64	146	34	1	21	86	7	.247
2011	Pittsburgh	N.L.	OF-1B	148	423	51	103	30	1	16	58	6	.243
2012	Pittsburgh	N.L.	1B-OF	145	475	68	130	28	3	27	86	2	.274
Major League Totals		5 Yrs.		564	1881	235	487	115	7	87	279	26	.259

a Released by Atlanta Braves, May 21, 2002. Signed with Minnesota Twins organization, May 24, 2002.
b Filed for free agency, November 3, 2008. Signed with Pittsburgh Pirates organization, December 16, 2008.

JONES, LARRY WAYNE (CHIPPER)

Born, Deland, Florida, April 24, 1972.
Bats Both. Throws Right. Height, 6 feet, 4 inches. Weight, 210 pounds.

Year	Club	Lea	Pos	G	AB	R	H	2B	3B	HR	RBI	SB	Avg
1990	Bradenton Braves....	Gulf C.	SS	44	140	20	32	1	1	1	18	5	.229
1991	Macon	So. Atl.	SS	136	473	*104	154	24	11	15	98	40	.326
1992	Durham	Carolina	SS	70	264	43	73	22	1	4	31	10	.277
1992	Greenville	Southern	SS	67	266	43	92	17	11	9	42	14	.346
1993	Richmond	Int.	SS	139	536	97	174	31	12	13	89	23	.325
1993	Atlanta	N.L.	SS	8	3	2	2	1	0	0	0	0	.667
1994	Atlanta a	N.L.	INJURED—Did Not Play										
1995	Atlanta	N.L.	3B-OF	140	524	87	139	22	3	23	86	8	.265
1996	Atlanta b	N.L.	3B-SS-OF	157	598	114	185	32	5	30	110	14	.309
1997	Atlanta	N.L.	3B-OF	157	597	100	176	41	3	21	111	20	.295
1998	Atlanta	N.L.	3B	160	601	123	188	29	5	34	107	16	.313
1999	Atlanta c	N.L.	3B-SS	157	567	116	181	41	1	45	110	25	.319
2000	Atlanta	N.L.	3B-SS	156	579	118	180	38	1	36	111	14	.311
2001	Atlanta	N.L.	3B-OF	159	572	113	189	33	5	38	102	9	.330
2002	Atlanta	N.L.	OF	158	548	90	179	35	1	26	100	8	.327
2003	Atlanta	N.L.	OF	153	555	103	169	33	2	27	106	2	.305
2004	Rome	So.Atl.	OF	1	4	0	0	0	0	0	0	0	.000
2004	Atlanta d	N.L.	3B-OF	137	472	69	117	20	1	30	96	2	.248
2005	Rome	So.Atl.	3B	3	6	1	3	0	0	0	2	0	.500
2005	Atlanta e	N.L.	3B	109	358	66	106	30	0	21	72	5	.296
2006	Mississippi	Southern	3B	2	6	1	1	0	0	0	0	0	.167
2006	Atlanta f	N.L.	3B	110	411	87	133	28	3	26	86	6	.324
2007	Atlanta g	N.L.	3B-SS	134	513	108	173	42	4	29	102	5	.337
2008	Atlanta h	N.L.	3B	128	439	82	160	24	1	22	75	4	*.364
2009	Atlanta	N.L.	3B	143	488	80	129	23	2	18	71	4	.264
2010	Atlanta i	N.L.	3B	95	317	47	84	21	0	10	46	5	.265
2011	Rome	So.Atl.	3B	2	3	0	1	0	0	0	1	0	.333
2011	Atlanta j	N.L.	3B	126	455	56	125	33	1	18	70	2	.275
2012	Rome	So.Atl.	3B	2	4	0	1	0	0	0	1	0	.250
2012	Atlanta k-l.	N.L.	3B	112	387	58	111	23	0	14	62	1	.287
Major League Totals		19 Yrs.		2499	8984	1619	2726	549	38	468	1623	150	.303
Wild Card Playoff													
2012	Atlanta	N.L.	3B	1	5	0	1	0	0	0	0	0	.200
Division Series													
1995	Atlanta	N.L.	3B	4	18	4	7	2	0	2	4	0	.389
1996	Atlanta	N.L.	3B	3	9	2	2	0	0	1	2	1	.222
1997	Atlanta	N.L.	3B	3	8	3	4	0	0	1	2	1	.500
1998	Atlanta	N.L.	3B	3	10	2	2	0	0	0	1	0	.200
1999	Atlanta	N.L.	3B	4	13	2	3	0	0	0	1	0	.231
2000	Atlanta	N.L.	3B	3	12	2	4	1	0	0	1	0	.333
2001	Atlanta	N.L.	3B	3	9	2	4	0	0	2	5	0	.444
2002	Atlanta	N.L.	OF	5	17	3	5	0	0	0	2	0	.294
2003	Atlanta	N.L.	OF	5	18	3	3	0	0	2	6	0	.167
2004	Atlanta	N.L.	3B	5	20	4	4	0	0	0	0	0	.200
2005	Atlanta	N.L.	3B	4	17	3	3	2	0	1	2	0	.176
Division Series Totals				42	151	30	41	5	0	9	26	2	.272

Year	Club	Lea	Pos	G	AB	R	H	2B	3B	HR	RBI	SB	Avg
Championship Series													
1995 Atlanta	N.L.	3B	4	16	3	7	0	0	1	3	1	.438
1996 Atlanta	N.L.	3B	7	25	6	11	2	0	0	4	1	.440
1997 Atlanta	N.L.	3B	6	24	5	7	1	0	2	4	0	.292
1998 Atlanta	N.L.	3B	6	24	2	5	1	0	0	1	0	.208
1999 Atlanta	N.L.	3B	6	19	3	5	2	0	0	1	3	.263
2001 Atlanta	N.L.	3B	5	19	1	5	1	0	0	2	0	.263
Championship Series Totals			34	127	20	40	7	0	3	15	5	.315
World Series Record													
1995 Atlanta	N.L.	3B	6	21	3	6	3	0	0	1	0	.286
1996 Atlanta	N.L.	3B-SS	6	21	3	6	3	0	0	3	1	.286
1999 Atlanta	N.L.	3B	4	13	2	3	0	0	1	2	0	.231
World Series Totals............			16	55	8	15	6	0	1	6	1	.273

a On disabled list from March 20 to end of 1994 season.
b On disabled list from April 1 to April 6, 1996.
c Selected Most Valuable Player in National League for 1999.
d On disabled list from April 19 to May 8, 2004.
e On disabled list from June 6 to July 18, 2005.
f On disabled list from April 10 to April 25 and July 30 to August 13 and September 4 to September 19, 2006.
g On disabled list from May 24 to June 13, 2007.
h On disabled list from July 24 to August 8, 2008.
i On disabled list from August 11 to October 19, 2010.
j On disabled list from July 9 to July 25, 2011.
k On disabled list from March 26 to April 10 and May 24 to June 10, 2012.
l Announced retirement, October 29, 2012.

JOYCE, MATTHEW R. (MATT)
Born, Tampa, Florida, August 3, 1984.
Bats Left. Throws Right. Height, 6 feet, 2 inches. Weight, 205 pounds.

Year	Club	Lea	Pos	G	AB	R	H	2B	3B	HR	RBI	SB	Avg
2005 Oneonta	N.Y.-Penn.	OF	65	245	51	81	10	4	4	45	9	.331
2006 West Michigan.....	Midwest	OF	122	465	75	120	30	5	11	86	5	.258
2007 Erie..............	Eastern	OF	130	456	61	117	33	3	17	70	4	.257
2008 Toledo	Int.	OF	56	200	36	54	13	2	13	41	2	.270
2008 Detroit a	A.L.	OF	92	242	40	61	16	3	12	33	0	.252
2009 Tampa Bay	A.L.	OF	11	32	3	6	1	0	3	7	1	.188
2009 Durham	Int.	OF	111	417	73	114	35	2	16	66	14	.273
2010 Charlotte	Fla.St.	OF	10	29	6	11	5	0	2	8	1	.379
2010 Durham	Int.	OF	25	92	18	27	8	0	3	12	1	.293
2010 Tampa Bay b	A.L.	OF	77	216	30	52	15	3	10	40	2	.241
2011 Tampa Bay	A.L.	OF	141	462	69	128	32	2	19	75	13	.277
2012 Charlotte	Fla.St.	OF	2	8	2	2	1	0	0	2	0	.250
2012 Durham	Int.	OF	1	2	0	0	0	0	0	0	0	.000
2012 Tampa Bay c	A.L.	OF	124	399	55	96	18	3	17	59	4	.241
Major League Totals	5 Yrs.		445	1351	197	343	82	11	61	214	20	.254
Division Series													
2010 Tampa Bay	A.L.	OF	4	9	0	2	0	0	0	0	1	.222
2011 Tampa Bay	A.L.	OF	4	15	1	3	1	0	1	4	0	.200
Division Series Totals			8	24	1	5	1	0	1	4	1	.208

a Traded to Tampa Bay Rays for pitcher Edwin Jackson, December 10, 2008.
b On disabled list from March 26 to May 31, 2010.
c On disabled list from June 20 to July 17, 2012.

KEARNS, AUSTIN RYAN
Born, Lexington, Kentucky, May 20, 1980.
Bats Right. Throws Right. Height, 6 feet, 3 inches. Weight, 240 pounds.

Year	Club	Lea	Pos	G	AB	R	H	2B	3B	HR	RBI	SB	Avg
1998 Billings...........	Pioneer	OF-3B	30	108	17	34	9	0	1	14	1	.315
1999 Rockford	Midwest	OF	124	426	72	110	36	5	13	48	21	.258
2000 Dayton	Midwest	OF	136	484	110	148	37	2	27	104	18	.306
2001 Reds..........	Gulf Coast	OF	6	17	2	3	2	0	0	4	0	.176
2001 Chattanooga a	Southern	OF	59	205	30	55	11	2	6	36	7	.268
2002 Chattanooga......	Southern	OF	12	41	10	11	2	0	5	13	1	.268
2002 Cincinnati...........	N.L.	OF	107	372	66	117	24	3	13	56	6	.315
2002 Louisville b.........	Int.	OF	1	4	3	3	2	0	0	2	0	.750
2003 Chattanooga......	Southern	OF	3	5	2	1	0	0	0	1	0	.200
2003 Cincinnati c	N.L.	OF	82	292	39	77	11	0	15	58	5	.264

Year Club	Lea	Pos	G	AB	R	H	2B	3B	HR	RBI	SB	Avg
2004 Louisville	Int.	OF	25	83	19	28	7	1	2	15	3	.337
2004 Cincinnati d	N.L.	OF	64	217	28	50	10	2	9	32	2	.230
2005 Louisville	Int.	OF	28	111	24	38	15	1	7	21	0	.342
2005 Cincinnati	N.L.	OF	112	387	62	93	26	1	18	67	0	.240
2006 Cincinnati-Washington e	N.L.	OF	150	537	86	142	33	2	24	86	9	.264
2007 Washington	N.L.	OF	161	587	84	156	35	1	16	74	2	.266
2008 Hagerstown	So.Atl.	DH	2	3	2	1	0	0	0	1	0	.333
2008 Columbus.	Int.	OF	5	14	2	6	1	1	1	6	0	.429
2008 Washington f	N.L.	OF	86	313	40	68	10	0	7	32	2	.217
2009 Washington g	N.L.	OF	80	174	20	34	6	2	3	17	1	.195
2010 Cleveland-New York h-i-j	A.L.	OF	120	403	55	106	21	1	10	49	4	.263
2011 Cleveland k.	A.L.	OF	57	150	18	30	5	1	2	7	0	.200
2012 Jupiter	Fla.St.	OF	3	6	1	1	0	0	0	1	0	.167
2012 Miami l-m	N.L.	OF-1B	87	147	21	36	6	0	4	16	2	.245
Major League Totals	11 Yrs.		1106	3579	519	909	187	13	121	494	33	.254

a On disabled list from May 27 to August 13, 2001.
b On disabled list from August 27 to September 30, 2002.
c On disabled list from July 9 to November 5, 2003.
d On disabled list from April 27 to May 19 and from June 2 to August 24, 2004.
e Traded to Washington Nationals with infielder Felipe Lopez and pitcher Ryan Wagner for pitcher Gary Majewski, pitcher Bill Bray, infielder Royce Clayton, infielder Brendan Harris and pitcher Daryl Thompson, July 13, 2006.
f On disabled list from May 22 to July 3 and from August 25 to October 3, 2008.
g On disabled list from August 4 to October 13, 2009.
h Filed for free agency, November 6, 2009. Signed with Cleveland Indians organization, January 5, 2010.
i Traded to New York Yankees for player to be named later, July 31, 2010. Cleveland Indians received pitcher Zach McAllister to complete trade, August 20, 2010.
j Filed for free agency, November 1, 2010. Signed with Cleveland Indians, December 20, 2010.
k Released by Cleveland Indians, August 17, 2011. Signed with Florida Marlins organization, January 25, 2012.
l On disabled list from May 23 to June 8, 2012.
m Filed for free agency, November 3, 2012, re-signed with Miami Marlins, January 15, 2013.

KEMP, MATTHEW RYAN (MATT)

Born, Midwest City, Oklahoma, September 23, 1984.
Bats Right. Throws Right. Height, 6 feet, 2 inches. Weight, 230 pounds.

Year Club	Lea	Pos	G	AB	R	H	2B	3B	HR	RBI	SB	Avg
2003 Dodgers	Gulf Coast	OF	42	159	11	43	5	2	1	17	2	.270
2004 Vero Beach.	Fla.St.	OF	11	37	5	13	5	0	1	9	2	.351
2004 Columbus.	So.Atl.	OF	112	423	67	122	22	8	17	66	8	.288
2005 Vero Beach.	Fla.St.	OF	109	418	76	128	21	4	27	90	23	.306
2006 Jacksonville	Southern	OF	48	199	38	65	15	2	7	34	11	.327
2006 Las Vegas	P.C.	OF	44	182	37	67	14	6	3	36	14	.368
2006 Los Angeles	N.L.	OF	52	154	30	39	7	1	7	23	6	.253
2007 Las Vegas	P.C.	OF	39	161	32	53	16	3	4	20	9	.329
2007 Los Angeles a	N.L.	OF	98	292	47	100	12	5	10	42	10	.342
2008 Los Angeles	N.L.	OF	155	606	93	176	38	5	18	76	35	.290
2009 Los Angeles	N.L.	OF	159	606	97	180	25	7	26	101	34	.297
2010 Los Angeles	N.L.	OF	*162	602	82	150	25	6	28	89	19	.249
2011 Los Angeles	N.L.	OF	161	602	*115	195	33	4	*39	*126	40	.324
2012 Rancho Cucamonga. . . .	Calif.	OF	4	14	2	6	1	0	0	4	0	.429
2012 Albuquerque.	P.C.	OF	4	16	6	8	2	0	2	6	0	.500
2012 Los Angeles b	N.L.	OF	106	403	74	122	22	2	23	69	9	.303
Major League Totals	7 Yrs.		893	3265	538	962	162	30	151	526	153	.295
Division Series												
2008 Los Angeles	N.L.	OF	3	13	0	2	2	0	0	1	0	.154
2009 Los Angeles	N.L.	OF	3	14	2	2	0	0	1	2	0	.143
Division Series Totals			6	27	2	4	2	0	1	3	0	.148
Championship Series												
2008 Los Angeles	N.L.	OF	5	15	1	5	1	0	0	0	0	.333
2009 Los Angeles	N.L.	OF	5	20	2	5	0	0	1	2	0	.250
Championship Series Totals			10	35	3	10	1	0	1	2	0	.286

a On disabled list from April 10 to April 27, 2007.
b On disabled list from May 31 to July 13 and May 14 to May 29, 2012.

KENDRICK, HOWARD JOSEPH
Born, Jacksonville, Florida, July 12, 1983.
Bats Right. Throws Right. Height, 5 feet, 10 inches. Weight, 195 pounds.

Year Club	Lea	Pos	G	AB	R	H	2B	3B	HR	RBI	SB	Avg
2002 Angels	Arizona	2B	42	157	24	50	6	4	0	13	12	.318
2003 Provo	Pioneer	2B	63	234	65	86	20	3	3	36	8	.368
2004 Angels	Arizona	2B	3	12	1	3	1	0	0	0	2	.250
2004 Cedar Rapids	Midwest	2B	75	313	66	115	24	6	10	49	15	.367
2005 Rancho Cucamonga	Calif.	2B	63	279	69	107	23	6	12	47	13	.384
2005 Arkansas	Texas	2B	46	190	35	65	20	2	7	42	12	.342
2006 Salt Lake	P.C.	2B-3B	69	290	57	107	25	6	13	62	11	.369
2006 Los Angeles	A.L.	1B-2B-3B	72	267	25	76	21	1	4	30	6	.285
2007 Rancho Cucamonga	Calif.	DH	1	4	0	1	0	0	0	0	0	.250
2007 Salt Lake	P.C.	2B	13	50	9	15	1	0	3	11	1	.300
2007 Los Angeles a	A.L.	2B	88	338	55	109	24	2	5	39	5	.322
2008 Rancho Cucamonga	Calif.	2B	2	6	3	5	0	0	2	2	1	.833
2008 Salt Lake	P.C.	2B	2	5	0	1	0	0	0	1	0	.200
2008 Los Angeles b	A.L.	2B	92	340	43	104	26	2	3	37	11	.306
2009 Salt Lake	P.C.	2B	20	78	11	27	6	1	2	11	4	.346
2009 Los Angeles	A.L.	2B	105	374	61	109	21	3	10	61	11	.291
2010 Los Angeles	A.L.	2B-1B-OF	158	616	67	172	41	4	10	75	14	.279
2011 Los Angeles c	A.L.	2B-OF-1B	140	537	86	153	30	6	18	63	14	.285
2012 Los Angeles	A.L.	2B-1B-OF	147	550	57	158	32	3	8	67	14	.287
Major League Totals		7 Yrs.	802	3022	394	881	195	21	58	372	75	.292
Division Series												
2007 Los Angeles	A.L.	2B	3	10	0	2	0	0	0	1	2	.200
2008 Los Angeles	A.L.	2B	4	17	0	2	0	0	0	0	0	.118
2009 Los Angeles	A.L.	2B	2	5	1	1	0	0	0	0	1	.200
Division Series Totals			9	32	1	5	0	0	0	1	3	.156
Championship Series												
2009 Los Angeles	A.L.	2B	4	14	3	4	0	1	1	1	0	.286

a On disabled list from April 18 to May 23 and July 8 to August 20, 2007.
b On disabled list from April 14 to May 30 and August 28 to September 22, 2008.
c On disabled list from May 20 to June 4, 2011.

KENNEDY, ADAM THOMAS
Born, Riverside, California, January 10, 1976.
Bats Left. Throws Right. Height, 6 feet. Weight, 185 pounds.

Year Club	Lea	Pos	G	AB	R	H	2B	3B	HR	RBI	SB	Avg
1997 New Jersey	N.Y.-Penn.	SS	29	114	20	39	6	3	0	19	9	.342
1997 Pr William	Carolina	SS	35	154	24	48	9	3	1	27	4	.312
1998 Pr William	Carolina	2B-SS	17	69	9	18	6	0	0	7	5	.261
1998 Arkansas	Texas	SS-2B	52	205	35	57	11	2	6	24	6	.278
1998 Memphis	P.C.	SS-2B	74	305	36	93	22	7	4	41	15	.305
1999 Memphis	P.C.	2B	91	367	69	120	22	4	10	63	20	.327
1999 St. Louis	N.L.	2B	33	102	12	26	10	1	1	16	0	.255
2000 Anaheim a	A.L.	2B	156	598	82	159	33	11	9	72	22	.266
2001 Rancho Cucamonga	Calif.	2B	3	8	3	3	2	0	0	1	3	.375
2001 Anaheim b	A.L.	2B	137	478	48	129	25	3	6	40	12	.270
2002 Anaheim	A.L.	2B-OF	144	474	65	148	32	6	7	52	17	.312
2003 Rancho Cucamonga	Calif.	2B	3	11	3	3	1	0	1	1	0	.273
2003 Anaheim c	A.L.	2B	143	449	71	121	17	1	13	49	22	.269
2004 Anaheim	A.L.	2B	144	468	70	130	20	5	10	48	15	.278
2005 Rancho Cucamonga	Calif.	2B	2	5	1	2	0	0	0	1	1	.400
2005 Salt Lake	P.C.	2B	4	17	4	7	1	0	0	4	2	.412
2005 Los Angeles d	A.L.	2B	129	416	49	125	23	0	2	37	19	.300
2006 Los Angeles e	A.L.	2B	139	451	50	123	26	6	4	55	16	.273
2007 St. Louis f	N.L.	2B-SS-OF	87	279	27	61	9	1	3	18	6	.219
2008 St. Louis	N.L.	2B-OF-1B	115	339	42	95	17	4	2	36	7	.280
2009 Durham	Int.	2B	23	82	11	23	4	0	3	9	2	.280
2009 Oakland g-h-i	A.L.	3B-2B-1B-OF	129	529	65	153	29	1	11	63	20	.289
2010 Washington j	N.L.	2B-1B-3B	135	342	43	85	16	1	3	31	14	.249
2011 Seattle k	A.L.	1B-2B-3B	114	380	36	89	23	1	7	38	8	.234
2012 Rancho Cucamonga	Calif.	2B-3B	5	16	4	4	0	1	0	1	0	.250
2012 Albuquerque	P.C.	3B	1	4	0	2	0	0	0	0	0	.500
2012 Los Angeles l-m	N.L.	3B-2B-1B-OF	86	168	22	44	8	1	2	16	1	.262
Major League Totals		14 Yrs.	1691	5473	682	1488	288	42	80	571	179	.272
Division Series												
2002 Anaheim	A.L.	2B	4	8	4	4	1	0	1	3	1	.500

90

Year	Club	Lea	Pos	G	AB	R	H	2B	3B	HR	RBI	SB	Avg
2005 Los Angeles . . . . . . .A.L.			2B	5	17	0	4	0	1	0	2	0	.235
Division Series Totals				9	25	4	8	1	1	1	5	1	.320
Championship Series													
2002 Anaheim . . . . .A.L.			2B	4	14	5	5	0	0	3	5	0	.357
2005 Los Angeles . . . . . . .A.L.			2B	5	14	3	4	0	0	0	1	0	.286
Championship Series Totals				9	28	8	9	0	0	3	6	0	.321
World Series Record													
2002 Anaheim . . . . .A.L.			2B	7	25	1	7	2	0	0	2	0	.280

a Traded to Anaheim Angels with pitcher Kent Bottenfield for outfielder Jim Edmonds, March 23, 2000.
b On disabled list from March 23 to April 13, 2001.
c On disabled list from April 7 to April 22, 2003.
d On disabled list from March 25 to May 2, 2005.
e Filed for free agency, October 29, 2006. Signed with St. Louis Cardinals, November 28, 2006.
f On disabled list from August 12 to November 2, 2007.
g Released by St. Louis Cardinals, February 9, 2009. Signed with Tampa Bay Rays organization, February 17, 2009.
h Traded to Oakland Athletics for player to be named later, May 8, 2009. Tampa Bay Rays received infielder Joe Dillon to complete trade, May 9, 2009.
i Filed for free agency, November 5, 2009. Signed with Washington Nationals, February 12, 2010.
j Filed for free agency, November 3, 2010. Signed with Seattle Mariners organization, January 10, 2011.
k Filed for free agency, October 30, 2011. Signed with Los Angeles Dodgers, November 30, 2011.
l On disabled list from July 25 to August 10 and September 8 to October 29, 2012.
m Filed for free agency, November 3, 2012.

KEPPINGER, JEFFREY SCOTT (JEFF)

Born, Miami, Florida, April 21, 1980.
Bats Right. Throws Right. Height, 6 feet. Weight, 180 pounds.

Year	Club	Lea	Pos	G	AB	R	H	2B	3B	HR	RBI	SB	Avg
2002 Hickory . . . . .So.Atl.			2B	126	478	75	132	23	4	10	73	6	.276
2003 Lynchburg . . . . Carolina			2B-3B-1B	92	342	55	111	21	2	3	51	3	.325
2004 Altoona . . . . Eastern			2B	82	323	45	108	17	2	1	33	10	.334
2004 Binghamton . . . . Eastern			2B-3B	14	47	14	17	3	1	0	5	2	.362
2004 Norfolk . . . . Int.			2B	6	19	1	6	1	0	0	2	0	.316
2004 New York a . . . . . . .N.L.			2B	33	116	9	33	2	0	3	9	2	.284
2005 Norfolk b . . . . Int.			2B-3B-SS	64	255	40	86	15	3	3	29	5	.337
2006 Norfolk . . . . Int.			2B-OF-3B	87	323	36	97	13	0	2	26	0	.300
2006 Omaha . . . . .P.C.			2B-3B-1B-SS	32	127	21	45	6	1	2	17	0	.354
2006 Kansas City c . . . . . . .A.L.			3B-1B-2B-OF	22	60	11	16	2	0	2	8	0	.267
2007 Sarasota . . . . . . .Fla.St.			3B-2B	3	12	1	4	2	0	0	1	0	.333
2007 Louisville . . . . Int.			3B-2B-OF-1B	57	228	31	84	15	1	2	18	1	.368
2007 Cincinnati d-e . . . .N.L.			SS-3B-2B-OF	67	241	39	80	16	2	5	32	2	.332
2008 Sarasota . . . . .Fla.St.			3B	2	7	1	2	0	0	0	1	0	.286
2008 Louisville . . . . Int.			3B-SS	6	22	3	11	2	0	1	2	0	.500
2008 Cincinnati f . . . . . . .N.L.			SS-3B-1B-2B	121	459	45	122	24	2	3	43	3	.266
2009 Houston g . . . . .N.L.			3B-2B-SS-OF	107	305	35	78	13	3	7	29	0	.256
2010 Corpus Christi . . . Texas			2B	2	5	0	2	0	0	0	1	0	.400
2010 Houston h . . . . . . .N.L.			2B-SS	137	514	62	148	34	1	6	59	4	.288
2011 Corpus Christi . . . Texas			2B	4	16	4	7	1	0	1	2	0	.438
2011 Oklahoma . . . . .P.C.			2B	7	28	2	7	0	0	0	1	0	.250
2011 Houston-San Fran. i-j-k N.L.			2B	99	379	39	105	20	0	6	35	0	.277
2012 Durham . . . . Int.			3B-1B	6	21	4	6	1	0	0	1	0	.286
2012 Tampa Bay l-m . . . . .A.L.			3B-1B-2B	115	385	46	125	15	1	9	40	1	.325
Major League Totals	8 Yrs.			701	2459	286	707	126	9	41	255	12	.288

a Traded by Pittsburgh Pirates to New York Mets with pitcher Kris Benson for infielder Ty Wigginton, pitcher Matt Peterson and infielder Jose Bautista, July 30, 2004.
b On disabled list from September 9 to October 31, 2005.
c Traded to Kansas City Royals for infielder Ruben Gotay, July 19, 2006.
d Traded to Cincinnati Reds for pitcher Russ Haltiwanger, January 11, 2007.
e On disabled list from March 23 to April 22, 2007.
f On disabled list from May 14 to June 22, 2008.
g Traded to Houston Astros for player to be named later, March 31, 2009. Cincinnati Reds received infielder Drew Sutton to complete trade, April 16, 2009.
h On disabled list from August 17 to September 1, 2010.
i On disabled list from March 22 to May 27, 2011.
j Traded to San Francisco Giants for pitcher Henry Sosa and pitcher Jason Stoffel, July 19, 2011.
k Not offered contract, December 12, 2011. Signed with Tampa Bay Rays, January 27, 2012.
l On disabled list from May 19 to June 22, 2012.
m Filed for free agency, November 3, 2012. Signed with Chicago White Sox, December 10, 2012.

KINSLER, IAN MICHAEL
Born, Tucson, Arizona, June 22, 1982.
Bats Right. Throws Right. Height, 6 feet. Weight, 200 pounds.

Year Club	Lea	Pos	G	AB	R	H	2B	3B	HR	RBI	SB	Avg
2003 Spokane.....	Northwest	SS	51	188	32	52	10	6	1	15	11	.277
2004 Clinton......	Midwest	SS	60	227	52	91	30	1	11	53	16	.401
2004 Frisco.........	Texas	SS	71	277	51	83	21	1	9	46	7	.300
2005 Oklahoma.........	P.C.	2B-SS-3B	131	530	102	145	28	2	23	94	19	.274
2006 Oklahoma........	P.C.	2B	10	39	7	10	3	0	2	6	1	.256
2006 Texas a..........	A.L.	2B	120	423	65	121	27	1	14	55	11	.286
2007 Oklahoma........	P.C.	2B	3	13	1	5	0	0	0	3	2	.385
2007 Texas b..........	A.L.	2B	130	483	96	127	22	2	20	61	23	.263
2008 Texas c..........	A.L.	2B	121	518	102	165	41	4	18	71	26	.319
2009 Frisco.........	Texas	2B	2	7	1	0	0	0	0	0	0	.000
2009 Texas d..........	A.L.	2B	144	566	101	143	32	4	31	86	31	.253
2010 Frisco.........	Texas	2B	6	19	3	5	0	1	0	6	2	.263
2010 Texas e..........	A.L.	2B	103	391	73	112	20	1	9	45	15	.286
2011 Texas...........	A.L.	2B	155	620	121	158	34	4	32	77	30	.255
2012 Texas...........	A.L.	2B-3B	157	655	105	168	42	5	19	72	21	.256
Major League Totals.........		7 Yrs.	930	3656	663	994	218	21	143	467	157	.272
Wild Card Playoff												
2012 Texas...........	A.L.	2B	1	3	1	2	0	0	0	0	0	.667
Division Series												
2010 Texas...........	A.L.	2B	5	18	5	8	0	0	3	6	0	.444
2011 Texas...........	A.L.	2B	4	16	2	4	2	0	1	3	1	.250
Division Series Totals..........			9	34	7	12	2	0	4	9	1	.353
Championship Series												
2010 Texas...........	A.L.	2B	6	20	1	5	1	1	0	3	2	.250
2011 Texas...........	A.L.	2B	6	24	6	7	2	0	0	6	1	.292
Championship Series Totals......			12	44	7	12	3	1	0	9	3	.273
World Series Record												
2010 Texas...........	A.L.	2B	5	16	1	3	1	0	0	0	1	.188
2011 Texas...........	A.L.	2B	7	25	2	9	1	0	0	2	1	.360
World Series Totals...........			12	41	3	12	2	0	0	2	2	.293

a On disabled list from April 12 to May 25, 2006.
b On disabled list from July 2 to July 31, 2007.
c On disabled list from August 18 to November 14, 2008.
d On disabled list from July 29 to August 14, 2009.
e On disabled list from March 26 to April 30 and July 28 to September 1, 2010.

KIPNIS, JASON MICHAEL
Born, Northbrook, Illinois, April 3, 1987.
Bats Left. Throws Right. Height, 5 feet, 11 inches. Weight, 185 pounds.

Year Club	Lea	Pos	G	AB	R	H	2B	3B	HR	RBI	SB	Avg
2009 Mahoning Valley..	N.Y.-Penn.	OF	29	111	19	34	8	3	1	19	3	.306
2010 Kinston..........	Carolina	2B	54	203	33	61	12	3	6	31	2	.300
2010 Akron............	Eastern	2B	79	315	63	98	20	5	10	43	7	.311
2011 Columbus...........	Int.	2B	92	343	65	96	16	9	12	55	12	.280
2011 Cleveland a..........	A.L.	2B	36	136	24	37	9	1	7	19	5	.272
2012 Cleveland............	A.L.	2B	152	591	86	152	22	4	14	76	31	.257
Major League Totals..........		2 Yrs.	188	727	110	189	31	5	21	95	36	.260

a On disabled list from August 14 to September 6, 2011.

KONERKO, PAUL HENRY
Born, Providence, Rhode Island, March 5, 1976.
Bats Right. Throws Right. Height, 6 feet, 2 inches. Weight, 220 pounds.

Year Club	Lea	Pos	G	AB	R	H	2B	3B	HR	RBI	SB	Avg
1994 Yakima........	Northwest	C	67	257	25	74	15	2	6	58	1	.288
1995 San Berndno.....	California	C	118	448	77	124	21	1	19	77	3	.277
1996 San Antonio.........	Texas	1B	133	470	78	141	23	2	29	86	1	.300
1996 Albuquerque..........	P.C.	1B	4	14	2	6	0	0	1	2	0	.429
1997 Albuquerque..........	P.C.	3B-1B-2B	130	483	97	156	31	1	37	127	2	.323
1997 Los Angeles.........	N.L.	1B-3B	6	7	0	1	0	0	0	0	0	.143
1998 Albuquerque..........	P.C.	OF-1B-3B	24	87	16	33	10	0	6	26	0	.379
1998 Indianapolis.........	Int.	3B	39	150	25	49	8	0	8	39	1	.327
1998 Los Angeles-Cinc. a-b..	N.L.	1B-3B-OF	75	217	21	47	4	0	7	29	0	.217
1999 Chicago...........	A.L.	1B-3B	142	513	71	151	31	4	24	81	1	.294

Year	Club	Lea	Pos	G	AB	R	H	2B	3B	HR	RBI	SB	Avg
2000 Chicago	A.L.	1B-3B	143	524	84	156	31	1	21	97	1	.298
2001 Chicago	A.L.	1B	156	582	92	164	35	0	32	99	1	.282
2002 Chicago	A.L.	1B	151	570	81	173	30	0	27	104	0	.304
2003 Chicago	A.L.	1B	137	444	49	104	19	0	18	65	0	.234
2004 Chicago	A.L.	1B	155	563	84	156	22	0	41	117	1	.277
2005 Chicago c............	A.L.	1B	158	575	98	163	24	0	40	100	0	.283
2006 Chicago	A.L.	1B	152	566	97	177	30	0	35	113	1	.313
2007 Chicago	A.L.	1B	151	549	71	142	34	0	31	90	0	.259
2008 Charlotte	Int.	1B	4	11	3	5	2	0	0	3	0	.455
2008 Chicago d............	A.L.	1B	122	438	59	105	19	1	22	62	2	.240
2009 Chicago	A.L.	1B	152	546	75	151	30	1	28	88	1	.277
2010 Chicago e............	A.L.	1B	149	548	89	171	30	1	39	111	0	.312
2011 Chicago	A.L.	1B	149	543	69	163	25	0	31	105	1	.300
2012 Chicago f............	A.L.	1B	144	533	66	159	22	0	26	75	0	.298
Major League Totals		16 Yrs.	2142	7718	1106	2183	386	8	422	1336	9	.283
Division Series												
2000 Chicago	A.L.	1B	3	9	1	0	0	0	0	0	0	.000
2005 Chicago	A.L.	1B	3	12	3	3	0	0	2	4	0	.250
2008 Chicago	A.L.	1B	4	16	3	5	0	0	2	2	0	.313
Division Series Totals			10	37	7	8	0	0	4	6	0	.216
Championship Series												
2005 Chicago	A.L.	1B	5	21	2	6	1	0	2	7	0	.286
World Series Record												
2005 Chicago	A.L.	1B	4	16	1	4	1	0	1	4	0	.250

a Traded to Cincinnati Reds with pitcher Dennis Reyes for pitcher Jeff Shaw, July 4, 1998.
b Traded to Chicago White Sox for outfielder Mike Cameron, November 11, 1998.
c Filed for free agency, October 27, 2005, re-signed with Chicago White Sox, November 30, 2005.
d On disabled list from June 15 to July 8, 2008.
e Filed for free agency, November 1, 2010, re-signed with Chicago White Sox, December 8, 2010.
f On disabled list from August 10 to August 17, 2012.

KOTCHMAN, CASEY JOHN
Born, St. Petersburg, Florida, February 22, 1983.
Bats Left. Throws Left. Height, 6 feet, 3 inches. Weight, 215 pounds.

Year	Club	Lea	Pos	G	AB	R	H	2B	3B	HR	RBI	SB	Avg
2001 Angels	Arizona	1B	4	15	5	9	1	0	1	5	0	.600
2001 Provo	Pioneer	1B	7	22	6	11	3	0	0	7	0	.500
2002 Cedar Rapids	Midwest	1B	81	288	42	81	30	1	5	50	2	.281
2003 Angels	Arizona	1B	7	27	5	9	1	0	2	6	0	.333
2003 Rancho Cucamonga...	Calif.	1B	57	206	42	72	12	0	8	28	2	.350
2004 Arkansas	Texas	1B	28	114	19	42	11	0	3	18	0	.368
2004 Anaheim............	A.L.	1B	38	116	7	26	6	0	0	15	3	.224
2004 Salt Lake	P.C.	1B	49	199	32	74	22	0	5	38	0	.372
2005 Salt Lake	P.C.	1B	94	363	62	105	23	1	10	58	0	.289
2005 Los Angeles	A.L.	1B	47	126	16	35	5	0	7	22	1	.278
2006 Salt Lake	P.C.	1B	3	7	0	0	0	0	0	1	0	.000
2006 Los Angeles a........	A.L.	1B	29	79	6	12	2	0	1	6	0	.152
2007 Los Angeles	A.L.	1B	137	443	64	131	37	3	11	68	2	.296
2008 Los Angeles	A.L.	1B	100	373	47	107	24	0	12	54	2	.287
2008 Atlanta b...........	N.L.	1B	43	152	18	36	4	1	2	20	0	.237
2009 Gwinnett...........	Int.	1B	2	3	2	0	0	0	0	3	0	.000
2009 Atlanta	N.L.	1B	87	298	28	84	20	0	6	41	0	.282
2009 Boston c-d-e	A.L.	1B	39	87	9	19	3	0	1	7	1	.218
2010 Seattle f	A.L.	1B	125	414	37	90	20	1	9	51	0	.217
2011 Durham	Int.	1B	1	4	0	1	0	0	0	0	0	.250
2011 Tampa Bay g	A.L.	1B	146	500	44	153	24	2	10	48	2	.306
2012 Cleveland h	A.L.	1B	142	463	46	106	12	0	12	55	3	.229
Major League Totals		9 Yrs.	933	3051	322	799	157	7	71	387	14	.262
Division Series												
2004 Anaheim............	A.L.	PH	2	1	0	0	0	0	0	0	0	.000
2005 Los Angeles	A.L.	PH	2	2	0	0	0	0	0	0	0	.000
2007 Los Angeles	A.L.	1B	2	5	1	0	0	0	0	0	0	.000
2009 Boston	A.L.	1B	3	1	0	0	0	0	0	0	0	.000
2011 Tampa Bay	A.L.	1B	4	16	1	4	1	0	0	2	0	.250
Division Series Totals			13	25	2	4	1	0	0	2	0	.160
Championship Series												
2005 Los Angeles	A.L.	DH	2	7	0	2	1	0	0	1	0	.286

a On disabled list from May 9 to October 2, 2006.

b Traded to Atlanta Braves with pitcher Steve Marek for infielder Mark Teixeira, July 29, 2008.
c On disabled list from June 1 to June 16, 2009.
d Traded to Boston Red Sox for infielder Adam LaRoche, July 31, 2009. Boston Red Sox received pitcher Miguel Celestino to complete trade, March 18, 2010.
e Traded to Seattle Mariners for infielder Bill Hall and cash, January 7, 2010.
f Filed for free agency, November 4, 2010. Signed with Tampa Bay Rays organization, January 28, 2011.
g Filed for free agency, October 30, 2011. Signed with Cleveland Indians, February 3, 2012.
h Filed for free agency, November 3, 2012.

KOTSAY, MARK STEVEN
Born, Whittier, California, December 2, 1975.
Bats Left. Throws Left. Height, 6 feet. Weight, 205 pounds.

Year	Club	Lea	Pos	G	AB	R	H	2B	3B	HR	RBI	SB	Avg
1996 Kane County	Midwest		OF	17	60	16	17	5	0	2	8	3	.283
1997 Florida	N.L.		OF	14	52	5	10	1	1	0	4	3	.192
1997 Portland	Eastern		OF	114	438	103	134	27	2	20	77	17	.306
1998 Florida	N.L.		OF-1B	154	578	72	161	25	7	11	68	10	.279
1999 Florida	N.L.		OF-1B	148	495	57	134	23	9	8	50	7	.271
2000 Florida	N.L.		OF-1B	152	530	87	158	31	5	12	57	19	.298
2001 San Diego a-b	N.L.		OF	119	406	67	118	29	1	10	58	13	.291
2002 San Diego	N.L.		OF	153	578	82	169	27	7	17	61	11	.292
2003 San Diego c-d	N.L.		OF	128	482	64	128	28	4	7	38	6	.266
2004 Oakland	A.L.		OF	148	606	78	190	37	3	15	63	8	.314
2005 Oakland	A.L.		OF	139	582	75	163	35	1	15	82	5	.280
2006 Oakland	A.L.		OF-1B	129	502	57	138	29	3	7	59	6	.275
2007 Sacramento	P.C.		OF	10	37	2	10	1	0	0	2	2	.270
2007 Oakland e-f	A.L.		OF	56	206	20	44	14	0	1	20	1	.214
2008 Mississippi	Southern		OF	5	18	4	6	1	0	0	1	0	.333
2008 Atlanta	N.L.		OF	88	318	39	92	17	3	6	37	2	.289
2008 Boston g-h-i	A.L.		OF-1B	22	84	6	19	8	1	0	12	0	.226
2009 Pawtucket	Int.		OF-1B	10	33	2	10	1	0	0	5	1	.303
2009 Boston-Chicago j-k	A.L.		1B-OF	67	187	16	52	9	0	4	23	3	.278
2010 Chicago l	A.L.		DH-1B-OF	107	327	30	78	17	2	8	31	1	.239
2011 Milwaukee m	N.L.		OF-1B	104	233	18	63	13	1	3	31	3	.270
2012 Lake Elsinore	Calif.		DH	1	4	0	0	0	0	0	0	0	.000
2012 San Diego n	N.L.		OF-1B	82	143	9	37	8	0	2	14	0	.259
Major League Totals		16 Yrs.		1810	6309	782	1754	351	48	126	708	98	.278
Division Series													
2006 Oakland	A.L.		OF	3	14	2	2	0	0	1	2	0	.143
2008 Boston	A.L.		1B	3	10	1	3	0	0	0	0	0	.300
2011 Milwaukee	N.L.		PH	4	3	1	0	0	0	0	0	0	.000
Division Series Totals				10	27	4	5	0	0	1	2	0	.185
Championship Series													
2006 Oakland	A.L.		OF	4	16	3	4	2	0	0	0	0	.250
2008 Boston	A.L.		1B	7	30	1	7	3	0	0	0	0	.233
2011 Milwaukee	N.L.		OF	5	9	1	1	0	0	1	1	0	.111
Championship Series Totals				16	55	5	12	5	0	1	1	0	.218

a Traded to San Diego Padres with outfielder Cesar Crespo for pitcher Matt Clement, pitcher Omar Ortiz and outfielder Eric Owens, March 28, 2001.
b On disabled list from April 16 to May 1, 2001.
c On disabled list from May 19 to June 5, 2003.
d Traded to Oakland Athletics for catcher Ramon Hernandez and outfielder Terrence Long, November 26, 2003.
e On disabled list from March 23 to June 1 and August 15 to October 8, 2007.
f Traded to Atlanta Braves for pitcher Joey Devine, pitcher Jamie Richmond and cash, January 14, 2008.
g On disabled list from May 26 to July 1, 2008.
h Traded to Boston Red Sox for outfielder Luis Sumoza, August 29, 2008.
i Filed for free agency, November 1, 2008, re-signed with Boston Red Sox, January 15, 2009.
j On disabled list from March 27 to June 2, 2009.
k Traded to Chicago White Sox for outfielder Brian Anderson, July 28, 2009.
l Filed for free agency, November 1, 2010. Signed with Milwaukee Brewers, February 4, 2011.
m Filed for free agency, October 30, 2011. Signed with San Diego Padres, November 16, 2011.
n On disabled list from April 1 to April 16 and May 13 to June 3, 2012.

KOTTARAS, GEORGE

Born, Scarborough, Ontario, Canada, May 16, 1983.
Bats Left. Throws Right. Height, 6 feet. Weight, 185 pounds.

Year	Club	Lea	Pos	G	AB	R	H	2B	3B	HR	RBI	SB	Avg
2003 Idaho Falls	Pioneer		C-1B	42	143	27	37	8	1	7	24	1	.259
2004 Fort Wayne	Midwest		C	78	271	40	84	18	1	7	46	0	.310
2005 Lake Elsinore	Calif.		C	91	337	54	102	29	0	9	50	2	.303
2005 Mobile	Southern		C	29	101	16	29	7	0	2	15	0	.287
2006 Portland	P.C.		C	33	119	14	25	10	1	2	17	0	.210
2006 Mobile a	Southern		C	78	257	40	71	19	1	8	33	0	.276
2007 Pawtucket	Int.		C	87	294	32	71	22	0	9	39	1	.241
2008 Pawtucket	Int.		C	107	395	63	96	18	0	22	65	0	.243
2008 Boston	A.L.		C	3	5	1	1	1	0	0	0	0	.200
2009 Pawtucket	Int.		C	10	24	1	7	3	0	0	0	0	.292
2009 Boston b-c	A.L.		C-3B	45	93	15	22	11	0	1	10	0	.237
2010 Milwaukee	N.L.		C-1B-OF	67	212	24	43	12	1	9	26	2	.203
2011 Nashville	P.C.		C	29	102	19	35	8	1	4	21	0	.343
2011 Milwaukee	N.L.		C	49	111	15	28	6	1	5	17	0	.252
2012 Milwaukee	N.L.		C-1B	58	86	10	18	4	0	3	12	0	.209
2012 Oakland d	A.L.		C	27	85	10	18	2	1	6	19	0	.212
Major League Totals		5 Yrs.		249	592	75	130	36	3	24	84	2	.220
Division Series													
2011 Milwaukee	N.L.		C	1	3	0	0	0	0	0	1	0	.000
2012 Oakland	A.L.		C	4	4	0	0	0	0	0	0	0	.000
Division Series Totals				5	7	0	0	0	0	0	1	0	.000
Championship Series													
2011 Milwaukee	N.L.		C	2	5	0	0	0	0	0	1	0	.000

a Sent by San Diego Padres to Boston Red Sox as player to be named later for pitcher David Wells, September 5, 2006.
b On disabled list from July 30 to September 1, 2009.
c Claimed on waivers by Milwaukee Brewers, November 18, 2009.
d Traded to Oakland Athletics for pitcher Faustino De Los Santos, July 29, 2012.

KUBEL, JASON JAMES

Born, Belle Fourche, South Dakota, May 25, 1982.
Bats Left. Throws Right. Height, 5 feet, 11 inches. Weight, 200 pounds.

Year	Club	Lea	Pos	G	AB	R	H	2B	3B	HR	RBI	SB	Avg
2000 Twins	Gulf Coast		OF	23	78	17	22	3	2	0	13	0	.282
2001 Twins	Gulf Coast		OF	37	124	14	41	10	4	1	30	3	.331
2002 Quad Cities	Midwest		OF	115	424	60	136	26	4	17	69	3	.321
2003 Fort Myers	Fla.St.		OF	116	420	56	125	20	4	5	82	4	.298
2004 New Britain	Eastern		OF	37	138	25	52	14	4	6	29	0	.377
2004 Rochester	Int.		OF	90	350	71	120	28	0	16	71	16	.343
2004 Minnesota a	A.L.		OF	23	60	10	18	2	0	2	7	1	.300
2005 Minnesota					INJURED—Did Not Play								
2006 Rochester	Int.		OF	30	120	18	34	7	2	4	22	2	.283
2006 Minnesota	A.L.		OF	73	220	23	53	8	0	8	26	2	.241
2007 Minnesota	A.L.		OF	128	418	49	114	31	2	13	65	5	.273
2008 Minnesota	A.L.		DH-OF	141	463	74	126	22	5	20	78	0	.272
2009 Minnesota	A.L.		DH-OF	146	514	73	154	35	2	28	103	1	.300
2010 Minnesota	A.L.		OF	143	518	68	129	23	3	21	92	0	.249
2011 Fort Myers	Fla.St.		OF	2	3	0	0	0	0	0	1	0	.000
2011 Rochester	Int.		OF	5	18	3	6	1	0	1	2	0	.333
2011 Minnesota b-c	A.L.		OF	99	366	37	100	21	1	12	58	1	.273
2012 Arizona	N.L.		OF	141	506	75	128	30	4	30	90	1	.253
Major League Totals		8 Yrs.		894	3065	409	822	172	17	134	519	11	.268
Division Series													
2004 Minnesota	A.L.		DH	2	7	0	1	1	0	0	0	0	.143
2009 Minnesota	A.L.		OF-DH	3	14	0	1	0	0	0	0	0	.071
2010 Minnesota	A.L.		OF	3	8	0	0	0	0	0	0	0	.000
Division Series Totals				8	29	0	2	1	0	0	0	0	.069

a On disabled list from March 15 to October 14, 2005.
b On disabled list from May 31 to July 22, 2011.
c Filed for free agency, October 30, 2011. Signed with Arizona Diamondbacks, December 20, 2011.

LAIRD, GERALD LEE

Born, Westminster, California, November 13, 1979.
Bats Right. Throws Right. Height, 6 feet, 2 inches. Weight, 225 pounds.

Year	Club	Lea	Pos	G	AB	R	H	2B	3B	HR	RBI	SB	Avg
1999 Southern Oregon	Northwest		C	60	228	45	65	7	2	2	39	10	.285
2000 Athletics	Arizona		C	14	50	10	15	2	1	0	9	2	.300
2000 Visalia	Calif.		C	33	103	14	25	3	0	0	13	7	.243
2001 Modesto	Calif.		C-OF-1B-2B	119	443	71	113	13	5	5	46	10	.255
2002 Tulsa a	Texas		C-OF	123	442	70	122	21	4	11	67	8	.276
2003 Oklahoma	P.C.		C	99	338	50	88	20	5	9	42	9	.260
2003 Texas	A.L.		C	19	44	9	12	2	1	1	4	0	.273
2004 Texas	A.L.		C	49	147	20	33	6	0	1	16	0	.224
2004 Oklahoma b	P.C.		C	6	22	2	4	2	0	0	2	1	.182
2005 Rangers	Arizona		C	8	26	4	5	2	2	0	3	1	.192
2005 Oklahoma	P.C.		C	75	281	51	87	12	4	17	55	12	.310
2005 Texas	A.L.		C-OF	13	40	7	9	2	0	1	4	0	.225
2006 Texas	A.L.		C-OF	78	243	46	72	20	1	7	22	3	.296
2007 Texas	A.L.		C-OF	120	407	48	91	18	3	9	47	6	.224
2008 Oklahoma	P.C.		C	4	12	1	0	0	0	0	2	0	.000
2008 Texas c-d	A.L.		C-3B	95	344	54	95	24	0	6	41	2	.276
2009 Detroit	A.L.		C-1B	135	413	49	93	23	2	4	33	5	.225
2010 Detroit e	A.L.		C	89	270	22	56	11	0	5	25	3	.207
2011 Memphis	P.C.		1B-C	2	7	2	3	1	0	0	1	0	.429
2011 St. Louis f-g	N.L.		C-1B	37	95	11	22	7	1	1	12	1	.232
2012 Detroit h	A.L.		C	63	174	24	49	8	1	2	11	0	.282
Major League Totals			10 Yrs.	698	2177	290	532	121	9	37	215	20	.244
Division Series													
2011 St. Louis	N.L.		PH	1	0	0	0	0	0	0	0	0	.000
2012 Detroit	A.L.		C	2	5	0	0	0	0	0	0	0	.000
Division Series Totals				3	5	0	0	0	0	0	0	0	.000
Championship Series													
2011 St. Louis	N.L.		C	1	1	0	0	0	0	0	0	0	.000
2012 Detroit	A.L.		C	2	8	0	1	0	0	0	0	0	.125
Championship Series Totals				3	9	0	1	0	0	0	0	0	.111
World Series Record													
2011 St. Louis	N.L.		PH	2	0	0	0	0	0	0	0	0	.000
2012 Detroit	A.L.		C	2	7	0	0	0	0	0	0	0	.000
World Series Totals				4	7	0	0	0	0	0	0	0	.000

a Traded by Oakland Athletics to Texas Rangers with pitcher Mario Ramos, outfielder Ryan Ludwick and infielder Jason Hart for pitcher Mike Venafro and outfielder Carlos Pena, January 14, 2002.
b On disabled list from May 21 to July 23, 2004.
c On disabled list from June 21 to July 26, 2008.
d Traded to Detroit Tigers for pitcher Guillermo Moscoso and pitcher Carlos Melo, December 9, 2008.
e Filed for free agency, November 1, 2010. Signed with St. Louis Cardinals, December 14, 2010.
f On disabled list from May 23 to July 7, 2011.
g Filed for free agency, October 30, 2011. Signed with Detroit Tigers, November 18, 2011.
h Filed for free agency, November 3, 2012. Signed with Atlanta Braves, November 16, 2012.

LA ROCHE, DAVID ADAM (ADAM)

Born, Orange Co., California, November 6, 1979.
Bats Left. Throws Left. Height, 6 feet, 3 inches. Weight, 200 pounds.

Year	Club	Lea	Pos	G	AB	R	H	2B	3B	HR	RBI	SB	Avg
2000 Danville	Appal.		1B	56	201	38	62	13	3	7	45	4	.308
2001 Myrtle Beach	Carolina		1B-OF	126	471	49	118	31	0	7	47	10	.251
2002 Myrtle Beach	Carolina		1B	69	250	30	84	17	0	9	53	0	.336
2002 Greenville	Southern		1B	45	173	17	50	9	0	4	19	1	.289
2003 Greenville	Southern		1B	61	219	42	62	12	1	12	37	1	.283
2003 Richmond	Int.		1B	72	264	33	78	21	0	8	35	1	.295
2004 Richmond	Int.		1B	4	11	1	2	0	0	1	2	0	.182
2004 Atlanta a	N.L.		1B	110	324	45	90	27	1	13	45	0	.278
2005 Atlanta	N.L.		1B	141	451	53	117	28	0	20	78	0	.259
2006 Atlanta b	N.L.		1B	149	492	89	140	38	1	32	90	0	.285
2007 Pittsburgh	N.L.		1B	152	563	71	153	42	0	21	88	1	.272
2008 Hickory	So.Atl.		1B	3	10	2	6	1	0	0	4	0	.600
2008 Pittsburgh c	N.L.		1B	136	492	66	133	32	3	25	85	1	.270
2009 Boston	A.L.		1B	6	19	2	5	2	0	1	3	0	.263
2009 Pittsburgh-Atlanta d-e-f	N.L.		1B	144	536	76	149	36	2	24	80	2	.278
2010 Arizona g	N.L.		1B	151	560	75	146	37	2	25	100	0	.261
2011 Washington h	N.L.		1B	43	151	15	26	4	0	3	15	1	.172

Year	Club	Lea	Pos	G	AB	R	H	2B	3B	HR	RBI	SB	Avg
2012 Washington i	N.L.	1B	154	571	76	155	35	1	33	100	1	.271
Major League Totals	9 Yrs.	1186	4159	568	1114	281	10	197	684	6	.268
Division Series												
2004 Atlanta ...	N.L.	1B	5	17	1	4	1	0	1	4	0	.235
2005 Atlanta ...	N.L.	1B	3	8	2	4	1	0	1	6	0	.500
2012 Washington ...	N.L.	1B	5	17	4	3	0	0	2	2	0	.176
Division Series Totals			13	42	7	11	2	0	4	12	0	.262

a On disabled list from May 29 to July 2, 2004.
b Traded to Pittsburgh Pirates with outfielder Jamie Romak for pitcher Mike Gonzalez and infielder Brent Lillibridge, January 17, 2007.
c On disabled list from July 28 to August 14, 2008.
d Traded to Boston Red Sox for infielder Argenis Diaz and pitcher Hunter Strickland, July 22, 2009.
e Traded to Atlanta Braves for infielder Casey Kotchman, July 31, 2009.
f Filed for free agency, November 5, 2009. Signed with Arizona Diamondbacks, January 15, 2010.
g Filed for free agency, November 2, 2010. Signed with Washington Nationals, January 7, 2011.
h On disabled list from May 22 to October 31, 2011.
i Filed for free agency, November 3, 2012, re-signed with Washington Nationals, January 8, 2013.

LAWRIE, BRETT R.

Born, Langley, British Columbia, Canada, January 18, 1990.
Bats Right. Throws Right. Height, 6 feet. Weight, 215 pounds.

Year	Club	Lea	Pos	G	AB	R	H	2B	3B	HR	RBI	SB	Avg
2009 Wisconsin	Midwest	2B	105	372	48	102	18	5	13	65	19	.274
2009 Huntsville	Southern	2B	13	52	6	14	0	1	0	0	0	.269
2010 Huntsville a	Southern	2B	135	554	90	158	36	16	8	63	30	.285
2011 Dunedin	Fla.St.	3B	4	8	0	1	0	0	0	1	0	.125
2011 Las Vegas...........	P.C.	3B	69	292	64	103	24	6	18	61	13	.353
2011 Toronto b	A.L.	3B	43	150	26	44	8	4	9	25	7	.293
2012 Blue Jays	Gulf Coast	3B	1	1	0	0	0	0	0	0	0	.000
2012 Dunedin	Fla.St.	3B	1	3	0	0	0	0	0	0	0	.000
2012 Toronto c	A.L.	3B-SS	125	494	73	135	26	3	11	48	13	.273
Major League Totals	2 Yrs.	168	644	99	179	34	7	20	73	20	.278

a Traded by Milwaukee Brewers to Toronto Blue Jays for pitcher Shaun Marcum, December 6, 2010.
b On disabled list from September 22 to September 29, 2011.
c On disabled list from August 4 to September 7, 2012.

LEE, CARLOS

Born, Aguadulce, Panama, June 20, 1976.
Bats Right. Throws Right. Height, 6 feet, 2 inches. Weight, 240 pounds.

Year	Club	Lea	Pos	G	AB	R	H	2B	3B	HR	RBI	SB	Avg
1994 White Sox	Gulf Coast	3B	29	56	6	7	1	0	0	1	0	.125
1995 Hickory...........	So.Atl.	3B-SS	63	218	18	54	9	1	4	30	1	.248
1995 Bristol	Appal.	3B-1B	67	269	43	93	17	1	7	45	17	.346
1996 Hickory...........	So.Atl.	3B-1B	119	480	65	150	23	6	8	70	18	.313
1997 Winston-Sal	Carolina	3B	139	546	81	173	50	4	17	82	11	.317
1998 Birmingham	Southern	3B	138	549	77	166	33	2	21	106	11	.302
1999 Charlotte	Int.	3B	25	94	16	33	5	0	4	20	2	.351
1999 Chicago	A.L.	OF-1B	127	492	66	144	32	2	16	84	4	.293
2000 Chicago	A.L.	OF	152	572	107	172	29	2	24	92	13	.301
2001 Chicago	A.L.	OF	150	558	75	150	33	3	24	84	17	.269
2002 Chicago	A.L.	OF	140	492	82	130	26	2	26	80	1	.264
2003 Chicago	A.L.	OF	158	623	100	181	35	4	31	113	18	.291
2004 Chicago a	A.L.	OF	153	591	103	180	37	0	31	99	11	.305
2005 Milwaukee	N.L.	OF *162	618	85	164	41	0	32	114	13	.265
2006 Milwaukee	N.L.	OF	102	388	60	111	18	0	28	81	12	.286
2006 Texas b-c	A.L.	OF	59	236	42	76	19	1	9	35	7	.322
2007 Houston	N.L.	OF *162	627	93	190	43	1	32	119	10	.303
2008 Houston d	N.L.	OF	115	436	61	137	27	0	28	100	4	.314
2009 Houston	N.L.	OF-1B	160	610	65	183	35	1	26	102	5	.300
2010 Houston	N.L.	OF-1B	157	605	67	149	29	1	24	89	3	.246
2011 Houston	N.L.	OF-1B	155	585	66	161	38	4	18	94	4	.275
2012 Corpus Christi	Texas	1B	3	10	1	5	0	0	1	2	0	.500
2012 Houston-Miami e-f-g ...	N.L.	1B	147	550	53	145	27	1	9	77	3	.264
Major League Totals	14 Yrs.	2099	7983	1125	2273	469	19	358	1363	125	.285
Division Series												
2000 Chicago	A.L.	OF	3	11	0	1	1	0	0	1	0	.091

97

a Traded to Milwaukee Brewers for outfielder Scott Podsednik, pitcher Luis Vizcaino and player to be named later, December 13, 2004. Chicago White Sox received infielder Travis Hinton to complete trade, January 10, 2005.
b Traded to Texas Rangers with outfielder Nelson Cruz for pitcher Francisco Cordero, outfielder Kevin Mench, outfielder Laynce Nix and pitcher Julian Cordero, July 28, 2006.
c Filed for free agency, October 30, 2006. Signed with Houston Astros, November 24, 2006.
d On disabled list from August 10 to September 30, 2008.
e On disabled list from June 2 to June 17, 2012.
f Traded to Miami Marlins with cash for infielder Matt Dominguez and pitcher Rob Rasmussen, July 5, 2012.
g Filed for free agency, November 3, 2012.

LILLIBRIDGE, BRENT STUART
Born, Everett, Washington, September 18, 1983.
Bats Right. Throws Right. Height, 5 feet, 11 inches. Weight, 190 pounds.

Year Club	Lea	Pos	G	AB	R	H	2B	3B	HR	RBI	SB	Avg
2005 Williamsport. .N.Y.-Penn.		SS	42	169	19	41	12	4	4	18	10	.243
2006 Lynchburg .... Carolina		SS	54	201	47	63	10	3	2	28	24	.313
2006 Hickory.........So.Atl.		SS-2B	74	274	59	82	18	5	11	43	29	.299
2007 Richmond .... Int.		SS	87	321	47	92	14	2	10	41	28	.287
2007 Mississippi a ..Southern		SS	52	204	31	56	8	3	3	17	14	.275
2008 Richmond .... Int.		SS	90	355	46	78	18	7	4	39	23	.220
2008 Atlanta b.........N.L.		SS-3B	29	80	9	16	6	1	1	8	2	.200
2009 Charlotte .... Int.		SS-OF-2B	67	246	34	62	9	4	3	24	17	.252
2009 Chicago .........A.L.		2B-OF-SS-3B	46	95	9	15.	2	0	0	3	6	.158
2010 Charlotte .... Int.		SS-2B-OF	48	185	26	50	8	0	4	16	19	.270
2010 Chicago ..........A.L.		2B-OF-SS	64	98	19	22	5	2	2	16	5	.224
2011 Chicago c ........A.L.		OF-1B-2B	97	186	38	48	5	1	13	29	10	.258
2012 Chi.-Boston-Clev. d-e-f A.L.		OF-1B-SS-3B	102	190	25	37	6	0	3	10	13	.195

Major League Totals .... 5 Yrs. 338 649 100 138 24 4 19 66 36 .213

a Traded by Pittsburgh Pirates to Atlanta Braves with pitcher Mike Gonzalez for infielder Adam LaRoche and outfielder Jamie Romak, January 18, 2007.
b Traded to Chicago White Sox with catcher Tyler Flowers, infielder Jonathan Gilmore and pitcher Santos Rodriguez for pitcher Javier Vazquez and pitcher Boone Logan, December 4, 2008.
c On disabled list from September 9 to September 30, 2011.
d Traded to Boston Red Sox with pitcher Zach Stewart for infielder Kevin Youkilis and cash, June 25, 2012.
e Traded to Cleveland Indians for pitcher Jose De La Torre, July 24, 2012.
f Filed for free agency, November 26, 2012. Signed with the Chicago Cubs, January 10, 2013.

LIND, ADAM ALAN
Born, Anderson, Indiana, July 17, 1983.
Bats Left. Throws Left. Height, 6 feet, 2 inches. Weight, 195 pounds.

Year Club	Lea	Pos	G	AB	R	H	2B	3B	HR	RBI	SB	Avg
2004 Auburn.........N.Y.-Penn.		OF	70	266	43	82	23	0	7	50	1	.308
2005 Dunedin ....Fla.St.		OF	126	495	80	155	42	4	12	84	2	.313
2006 New Hampshire .....Eastern		OF	91	348	43	108	24	0	19	71	2	.310
2006 Syracuse ....Int.		OF	34	109	20	43	7	0	5	18	1	.394
2006 Toronto ............A.L.		DH-OF	18	60	8	22	8	0	2	8	0	.367
2007 Syracuse ....Int.		OF	46	174	20	52	8	2	6	28	0	.299
2007 Toronto ............A.L.		OF	89	290	34	69	14	0	11	46	1	.238
2008 Syracuse ....Int.		OF-1B	51	189	24	62	17	2	6	50	1	.328
2008 Toronto ............A.L.		OF	88	326	48	92	16	4	9	40	2	.282
2009 Toronto ............A.L.		DH-OF	151	587	93	179	46	0	35	114	1	.305
2010 Toronto ............A.L.		DH-OF-1B	150	569	57	135	32	3	23	72	0	.237
2011 Dunedin ....Fla.St.		1B	3	10	2	6	3	0	0	4	2	.600
2011 Toronto a ...........A.L.		1B	125	499	56	125	16	0	26	87	1	.251
2012 New Hampshire .....Eastern		1B	3	11	2	6	0	0	1	1	0	.545
2012 Las Vegas...........P.C.		1B	32	125	24	49	10	0	8	29	1	.392
2012 Toronto b ............A.L.		1B	93	321	28	82	14	2	11	45	0	.255

Major League Totals .... 7 Yrs. 714 2652 324 704 146 9 117 412 5 .265

a On disabled list from May 8 to June 4, 2011.
b On disabled list from July 26 to August 26, 2012.

LOBATON, JOSE MANUEL
Born, Acarigua, Venezuela, October 21, 1984.
Bats Both. Throws Right. Height, 6 feet. Weight, 210 pounds.

Year Club	Lea	Pos	G	AB	R	H	2B	3B	HR	RBI	SB	Avg
2003 Idaho Falls ....Pioneer		C	56	191	22	52	15	0	1	32	0	.272
2004 Eugene.........Northwest		C	44	151	13	33	12	0	7	23	0	.219
2005 Padres ....Arizona		C	5	14	2	5	2	0	0	2	1	.357

Year	Club	Lea	Pos	G	AB	R	H	2B	3B	HR	RBI	SB	Avg
2005 Fort Wayne	Midwest		C	9	34	2	6	1	0	0	1	0	.176
2005 Eugene	Northwest		C	11	32	4	9	2	0	0	3	0	.281
2006 Lake Elsinore	Calif.		C	42	122	12	26	7	0	4	15	0	.213
2006 Fort Wayne	Midwest		C	20	61	15	17	3	1	1	11	0	.279
2007 Lake Elsinore	Calif.		C	90	304	50	79	15	3	10	47	0	.260
2008 San Antonio	Texas		C	92	294	35	76	21	0	9	45	1	.259
2009 Portland	P.C.		C	39	133	14	32	6	0	3	8	0	.241
2009 San Diego	N.L.		C-2B	7	17	0	3	0	0	0	0	0	.176
2009 Montgomery a	Southern		C	26	84	13	22	7	0	3	11	0	.262
2010 Durham	Int.		C	72	241	26	63	11	0	7	33	1	.261
2010 Montgomery b	Southern		C	7	24	3	6	1	0	0	2	0	.250
2011 Charlotte	Fla.St.		C	6	18	0	8	4	0	0	2	0	.444
2011 Durham	Int.		C	54	184	24	54	10	1	8	31	0	.293
2011 Tampa Bay c	A.L.		C	15	34	2	4	1	0	0	0	0	.118
2012 Charlotte	Fla.St.		C	2	5	0	0	0	0	0	0	0	.000
2012 Montgomery	Southern		C	4	13	1	2	1	0	0	1	0	.154
2012 Durham	Int.		C	4	15	0	1	1	0	0	0	0	.067
2012 Tampa Bay d	A.L.		C	69	167	16	37	10	0	2	20	0	.222
Major League Totals		3 Yrs.		91	218	18	44	11	0	2	20	0	.202

a Claimed on waivers by Tampa Bay Rays, July 30, 2009.
b On disabled list from August 31 to October 19, 2010.
c On disabled list from July 18 to September 2, 2011.
d On disabled list from April 13 to May 28, 2012.

LOMBARDOZZI, STEPHEN PAUL JR. (STEVE)
Born, Fulton, Maryland, September 20, 1988.
Bats Both. Throws Right. Height, 6 feet. Weight, 195 pounds.

Year	Club	Lea	Pos	G	AB	R	H	2B	3B	HR	RBI	SB	Avg
2008 Nationals	Gulf Coast		2B-SS	48	152	23	43	4	1	0	24	4	.283
2009 Hagerstown	So.Atl.		2B-SS	128	496	90	147	26	7	3	58	16	.296
2010 Potomac	Carolina		2B	110	440	71	129	30	9	1	38	20	.293
2010 Harrisburg	Eastern		2B	27	105	19	31	5	2	5	11	4	.295
2011 Harrisburg	Eastern		2B-SS	65	262	40	81	12	7	4	23	16	.309
2011 Syracuse	Int.		2B-SS-3B	69	294	46	91	13	2	4	29	14	.310
2011 Washington	N.L.		2B-3B-SS	13	31	3	6	1	0	0	1	0	.194
2012 Washington	N.L.		2B-OF-3B-SS	126	384	40	105	16	3	3	27	5	.273
Major League Totals		2 Yrs.		139	415	43	111	17	3	3	28	5	.267
Division Series													
2012 Washington	N.L.		PH	3	3	0	1	0	0	0	0	0	.333

LONEY, JAMES ANTHONY
Born, Houston, Texas, May 7, 1984.
Bats Left. Throws Left. Height, 6 feet, 3 inches. Weight, 220 pounds.

Year	Club	Lea	Pos	G	AB	R	H	2B	3B	HR	RBI	SB	Avg
2002 Vero Beach	Fla.St.		1B	17	67	6	20	6	0	0	5	0	.299
2002 Great Falls	Pioneer		1B	47	170	33	63	22	3	5	30	5	.371
2003 Vero Beach	Fla.St.		1B-OF	125	468	64	129	31	3	7	46	9	.276
2004 Jacksonville	Southern		1B	104	395	39	94	19	2	4	35	6	.238
2005 Jacksonville	Southern		1B-OF	138	504	74	143	31	2	11	65	1	.284
2006 Las Vegas	P.C.		1B-OF	98	366	64	139	33	2	8	67	9	.380
2006 Los Angeles	N.L.		1B-OF	48	102	20	29	6	5	4	18	1	.284
2007 Las Vegas	P.C.		1B	58	233	28	65	19	1	1	32	2	.279
2007 Los Angeles	N.L.		1B-OF	96	344	41	114	18	4	15	67	0	.331
2008 Los Angeles	N.L.		1B	161	595	66	172	35	6	13	90	7	.289
2009 Los Angeles	N.L.		1B	158	576	73	162	25	2	13	90	7	.281
2010 Los Angeles	N.L.		1B	161	588	67	157	41	2	10	88	10	.267
2011 Los Angeles	N.L.		1B	158	531	56	153	30	1	12	65	4	.288
2012 Los Angeles	N.L.		1B	114	334	32	85	18	0	4	33	0	.254
2012 Boston a-b	A.L.		1B	30	100	5	23	2	0	2	8	0	.230
Major League Totals		7 Yrs.		926	3170	360	895	175	20	73	459	29	.282
Division Series													
2006 Los Angeles	N.L.		1B	1	4	0	3	0	0	0	3	0	.750
2008 Los Angeles	N.L.		1B	3	14	2	3	1	0	1	6	0	.214
2009 Los Angeles	N.L.		1B	3	12	0	3	0	0	0	0	0	.250
Division Series Totals				7	30	2	9	1	0	1	9	0	.300
Championship Series													
2008 Los Angeles	N.L.		1B	5	16	0	7	2	0	0	2	0	.438

Year	Club	Lea	Pos	G	AB	R	H	2B	3B	HR	RBI	SB	Avg
2009 Los Angeles	N.L.	1B	5	17	3	6	0	0	2	3	0	.353
Championship Series Totals			10	33	3	13	2	0	2	5	0	.394

a Traded to Boston Red Sox with infielder Ivan DeJesus, pitcher Allen Webster and player to be named later for outfielder Carl Crawford, infielder Adrian Gonzalez, pitcher Josh Beckett, infielder Nick Punto and cash, August 25, 2012. Boston Red Sox received pitcher Rubby De La Rosa to complete trade, October 4, 2012.

b Filed for free agency, November 3, 2012. Signed with Tampa Bay Rays, December 6, 2012.

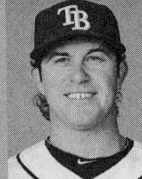

LONGORIA, EVAN MICHAEL
Born, Downey, California, October 7, 1985.
Bats Right. Throws Right. Height, 6 feet, 2 inches. Weight, 210 pounds.

Year	Club	Lea	Pos	G	AB	R	H	2B	3B	HR	RBI	SB	Avg
2006 Visalia	Calif.	3B	28	110	22	36	8	0	8	28	1	.327
2006 Hudson Valley	N.Y.-Penn.	3B	8	33	5	14	1	1	4	11	1	.424
2006 Montgomery	Southern	3B	26	105	14	28	5	0	6	19	2	.267
2007 Durham	Int.	3B	31	104	19	28	8	0	5	19	0	.269
2007 Montgomery	Southern	3B	105	381	78	117	21	0	21	76	4	.307
2008 Durham	Int.	3B	7	25	2	5	0	0	0	1	0	.200
2008 Tampa Bay a-b	A.L.	3B-SS	122	448	67	122	31	2	27	85	7	.272
2009 Tampa Bay	A.L.	3B	157	584	100	164	44	0	33	113	9	.281
2010 Tampa Bay	A.L.	3B	151	574	96	169	46	5	22	104	15	.294
2011 Montgomery	Southern	3B	4	15	5	4	0	0	3	3	0	.267
2011 Tampa Bay c	A.L.	3B	133	483	78	118	26	1	31	99	3	.244
2012 Durham	Int.	DH	10	30	0	6	0	0	0	3	0	.200
2012 Tampa Bay d	A.L.	3B	74	273	39	79	14	0	17	55	2	.289
Major League Totals	5 Yrs.		637	2362	380	652	161	8	130	456	36	.276
Division Series													
2008 Tampa Bay	A.L.	3B	4	15	2	4	0	0	2	3	1	.267
2010 Tampa Bay	A.L.	3B	5	20	2	4	2	0	1	2	0	.200
2011 Tampa Bay	A.L.	3B	4	16	2	3	0	0	1	3	0	.188
Division Series Totals			13	51	6	11	2	0	4	8	1	.216
Championship Series													
2008 Tampa Bay	A.L.	3B	7	27	8	7	3	0	4	8	0	.259
World Series Record													
2008 Tampa Bay	A.L.	3B	5	20	0	1	0	0	0	2	0	.050

a On disabled list from August 8 to September 6, 2008.

b Selected Rookie of the Year in American League for 2008.

c On disabled list from April 3 to May 3, 2011.

d On disabled list from May 1 to August 7, 2012.

LOPEZ, JOSE CELESTINO
Born, Barcelona, Venezuela, November 24, 1983.
Bats Right. Throws Right. Height, 6 feet. Weight, 200 pounds.

Year	Club	Lea	Pos	G	AB	R	H	2B	3B	HR	RBI	SB	Avg
2001 Everett	Northwest	SS-2B	70	289	42	74	15	0	2	20	13	.256
2002 San Bernardino	Calif.	SS-2B	123	522	82	169	39	5	8	60	31	.324
2003 San Antonio	Texas	SS-2B-3B	132	538	82	139	35	2	13	69	18	.258
2004 Tacoma	P.C.	SS-3B-2B	74	275	40	81	19	0	13	39	5	.295
2004 Mariners	Arizona	3B-SS-2B	4	12	3	2	1	0	0	1	1	.167
2004 Seattle	A.L.	SS-3B	57	207	28	48	13	0	5	22	0	.232
2005 Tacoma	P.C.	2B	44	182	29	58	19	0	5	31	2	.319
2005 Seattle	A.L.	2B-3B	54	190	18	47	19	0	2	25	4	.247
2006 Seattle	A.L.	2B	151	603	78	170	28	8	10	79	5	.282
2007 Seattle	A.L.	2B-3B	149	524	58	132	17	2	11	62	2	.252
2008 Seattle	A.L.	2B-1B	159	644	80	191	41	1	17	89	6	.297
2009 Seattle	A.L.	2B-1B	153	613	69	167	42	0	25	96	3	.272
2010 Seattle a	A.L.	3B	150	593	49	142	29	0	10	58	3	.239
2011 New Orleans	P.C.	2B-1B-3B	32	125	24	50	9	0	9	30	2	.400
2011 Colorado-Florida b-c	N.L.	3B-2B-1B	82	231	23	50	12	0	8	21	2	.216
2012 Charlotte	Int.	3B-2B	13	49	7	15	5	0	1	10	0	.306
2012 Columbus	Int.	3B	6	23	1	12	4	0	0	4	0	.522
2012 Cleveland-Chicago d-e	A.L.	3B-1B-2B-OF	81	236	18	58	14	0	4	28	0	.246
Major League Totals	9 Yrs.		1036	3841	421	1005	215	11	92	480	25	.262

a Traded to Colorado Rockies for pitcher Chaz Roe, December 2, 2010.

b Released by Colorado Rockies, June 7, 2011. Signed with Florida Marlins organization, June 9, 2011.

c Filed for free agency, October 30, 2011. Signed with Cleveland Indians organization, December 16, 2011.

d Released by Cleveland Indians, August 12, 2012. Signed with Chicago White Sox organization, August 14, 2012.

e Filed for free agency, November 3, 2012. Signed with Yomiuri Giants (Japan), January 7, 2013.

LOWRIE, JED CARLSON

Born, Salem, Oregon, April 17, 1984.
Bats Both. Throws Right. Height, 6 feet. Weight, 180 pounds.

Year Club	Lea	Pos	G	AB	R	H	2B	3B	HR	RBI	SB	Avg
2005 Lowell	N.Y.-Penn.	SS-2B	53	201	36	66	12	0	4	32	7	.328
2006 Wilmington	Carolina	SS	97	374	43	98	21	6	3	50	2	.262
2007 Portland	Eastern	SS-2B	93	337	61	100	31	7	8	49	5	.297
2007 Pawtucket	Int.	SS-2B-3B	40	160	21	48	16	1	5	21	0	.300
2008 Pawtucket	Int.	SS-2B-3B	53	198	35	53	14	2	5	32	1	.268
2008 Boston	A.L.	SS-3B-2B	81	260	34	67	25	3	2	46	1	.258
2009 Portland	Eastern	SS	5	5	1	3	1	0	0	2	0	.600
2009 Lowell	N.Y.-Penn.	SS	3	11	2	2	2	0	0	1	0	.182
2009 Pawtucket	Int.	SS	22	68	9	12	3	0	3	8	0	.176
2009 Boston	A.L.	SS-3B-2B	32	68	5	10	2	0	2	11	0	.147
2010 Lowell	N.Y.-Penn.	SS	6	15	2	6	1	0	0	5	0	.400
2010 Pawtucket	Int.	2B-3B-SS	4	15	3	5	3	0	1	4	1	.333
2010 Boston a	A.L.	2B-SS-1B-3B	55	171	31	49	14	0	9	24	1	.287
2011 Pawtucket	Int.	SS	5	17	2	7	4	0	0	5	0	.412
2011 Boston b-c	A.L.	SS-3B-1B-2B	88	309	40	78	14	4	6	36	1	.252
2012 Oklahoma	P.C.	SS	2	6	1	3	0	0	0	3	0	.500
2012 Houston d	N.L.	SS	97	340	43	83	18	0	16	42	2	.244
Major League Totals	5 Yrs.		353	1148	153	287	73	7	35	159	5	.250
Division Series												
2008 Boston	A.L.	SS-3B	3	11	2	4	0	0	0	1	0	.364
2009 Boston	A.L.	SS	3	2	0	0	0	0	0	0	0	.000
Division Series Totals			6	13	2	4	0	0	0	1	0	.308
Championship Series												
2008 Boston	A.L.	SS	6	18	2	2	1	0	0	1	0	.111

a On disabled list from March 26 to July 21, 2010.
b On disabled list from June 17 to August 8, 2011.
c Traded to Houston Astros with pitcher Kyle Weiland for pitcher Mark Melancon, December 14, 2011.
d On disabled list from March 29 to April 12 and July 15 to September 11, 2012.

LUCROY, JONATHAN CHARLES

Born, Eustis, Pennsylvania, June 13, 1986.
Bats Right. Throws Right. Height, 6 feet. Weight, 195 pounds.

Year Club	Lea	Pos	G	AB	R	H	2B	3B	HR	RBI	SB	Avg
2007 Helena	Pioneer	C	61	234	35	80	18	2	4	39	0	.342
2008 Brevard County	Fla.St.	C	64	236	31	69	12	1	10	44	1	.292
2008 West Tenn	So.Atl.	C	65	239	45	74	16	1	10	33	8	.310
2009 Huntsville	Southern	C	125	419	61	112	32	2	9	66	1	.267
2010 Huntsville	Southern	C	10	42	8	19	3	0	0	5	0	.452
2010 Nashville	P.C.	C	21	80	8	19	4	0	2	11	0	.237
2010 Milwaukee	N.L.	C	75	277	24	70	9	0	4	26	4	.253
2011 Huntsville a	Southern	C	4	11	3	3	1	0	0	4	1	.273
2011 Milwaukee	N.L.	C	136	430	45	114	16	1	12	59	2	.265
2012 Wisconsin	Midwest	C	4	12	0	4	1	0	0	2	1	.333
2012 Nashville	P.C.	C	2	7	4	3	0	0	0	1	1	.429
2012 Milwaukee b	N.L.	C	96	316	46	101	17	4	12	58	4	.320
Major League Totals	3 Yrs.		307	1023	115	285	42	5	28	143	10	.279
Division Series												
2011 Milwaukee	N.L.	C	4	15	1	3	0	0	0	2	0	.200
Championship Series												
2011 Milwaukee	N.L.	C	6	17	2	5	1	0	1	3	0	.294

a On disabled list from March 22 to April 11, 2011.
b On disabled list from May 28 to July 26, 2012.

LUDWICK, RYAN ANDREW

Born, Satellite Beach, Florida, July 13, 1978.
Bats Right. Throws Left. Height, 6 feet, 3 inches. Weight, 220 pounds.

Year Club	Lea	Pos	G	AB	R	H	2B	3B	HR	RBI	SB	Avg
1999 Modesto	Calif.	OF	43	171	28	47	11	3	4	34	2	.275
2000 Modesto	Calif.	OF	129	493	86	130	26	3	29	102	10	.264
2001 Sacramento	P.C.	OF	17	57	10	13	3	0	1	7	2	.228
2001 Midland	Texas	OF	119	443	82	119	23	3	25	96	9	.269
2002 Oklahoma	P.C.	OF	78	305	62	87	27	4	15	52	2	.285
2002 Texas a	A.L.	OF	23	81	10	19	6	0	1	9	2	.235

Year Club	Lea	Pos	G	AB	R	H	2B	3B	HR	RBI	SB	Avg
2003 Oklahoma............	P.C.	OF	81	317	51	96	24	3	17	63	1	.303
2003 Texas-Cleveland b-c....	A.L.	OF	47	162	17	40	8	1	7	26	2	.247
2004 Akron.............	Eastern	OF	8	26	4	7	2	0	1	5	0	.269
2004 Buffalo...............	Int.	OF	44	166	25	45	15	0	8	30	0	.271
2004 Cleveland d..........	A.L.	OF	15	50	3	11	2	0	2	4	0	.220
2005 Cleveland............	A.L.	OF	19	41	8	9	0	0	4	5	0	.220
2005 Buffalo..............	Int.	OF	54	188	27	36	10	2	4	16	0	.191
2006 Toledo e-f..........	Int.	OF	134	508	81	135	34	2	28	80	2	.266
2007 Memphis............	P.C.	OF	29	106	27	36	8	0	8	36	1	.340
2007 St. Louis............	N.L.	OF	120	303	42	81	22	0	14	52	4	.267
2008 St. Louis............	N.L.	OF	152	538	104	161	40	3	37	113	4	.299
2009 St. Louis g...........	N.L.	OF	139	486	63	129	20	1	22	97	4	.265
2010 Memphis............	P.C.	OF	3	9	2	3	1	0	2	5	0	.333
2010 St. Louis-San Diego h-i.	N.L.	OF	136	490	63	123	27	2	17	69	0	.251
2011 Indianapolis..........	Int.	OF	4	13	3	5	1	0	1	5	0	.385
2011 San Diego-Pittsburgh j-k-l.	N.L.	OF	139	490	56	116	23	0	13	75	1	.237
2012 Cincinnati m...........	N.L.	OF	125	422	53	116	28	1	26	80	0	.275
Major League Totals...........	10 Yrs.		915	3063	419	805	176	8	143	530	17	.263
Division Series												
2009 St. Louis............	N.L.	OF	3	12	1	4	0	0	0	1	0	.333
2012 Cincinnati............	N.L.	OF	5	18	4	6	0	0	3	4	0	.333
Division Series Totals...........			8	30	5	10	0	0	3	5	0	.333

a Traded to Texas Rangers by Oakland Athletics with pitcher Mario Ramos, infielder Jason Hart and catcher Gerald Laird for pitcher Mike Venafro and infielder Carlos Pena, January 14, 2002.
b Traded to Cleveland Indians for outfielder Shane Spencer and pitcher Ricardo Rodriguez, July 18, 2003.
c On disabled list from September 9 to October 28, 2003.
d On disabled list from April 2 to July 5, 2004.
e Filed for free agency, October 28, 2005. Signed with Detroit Tigers organization, January 4, 2006.
f Filed for free agency, October 15, 2006. Signed with St. Louis Cardinals organization, December 1, 2006.
g On disabled list from May 13 to May 29, 2009.
h On disabled list from June 26 to July 24, 2010.
i Traded to San Diego Padres for pitcher Nick Greenwood and pitcher Corey Kluber, July 31, 2010.
j Sold to Pittsburgh Pirates, July 31, 2011.
k On disabled list from August 23 to September 7, 2011.
l Filed for free agency, October 30, 2011. Signed with Cincinnati Reds, February 8, 2012.
n Filed for free agency, November 3, 2012, re-signed with Cincinnati Reds, December 10, 2012.

MACHADO, MANUEL AUTURO (MANNY)
Born, Hialeah, Florida, July 6, 1992.
Bats Right. Throws Right. Height, 6 feet, 3 inches. Weight, 185 pounds.

Year Club	Lea	Pos	G	AB	R	H	2B	3B	HR	RBI	SB	Avg
2010 Orioles.........	Gulf Coast	DH	2	7	1	1	0	0	1	2	0	.143
2010 Aberdeen.......	N.Y.-Penn.	SS	7	29	2	10	1	1	0	3	0	.345
2011 Frederick.........	Carolina	SS	63	237	24	58	12	3	5	26	8	.245
2011 Delmarva..........	So.Atl.	SS	38	145	24	40	8	2	6	24	3	.276
2012 Bowie............	Eastern	SS-3B	109	402	60	107	26	5	11	59	13	.266
2012 Baltimore............	A.L.	3B	51	191	24	50	8	3	7	26	2	.262
Wild Card Playoff												
2012 Baltimore............	A.L.	3B	1	3	0	1	0	0	0	1	0	.333
Division Series												
2012 Baltimore............	A.L.	3B	5	16	2	2	1	0	1	1	0	.125

MALDONADO (VALDES), MARTIN
Born, Naguabo, Puerto Rico, August 16, 1986.
Bats Right. Throws Right. Height, 6 feet, 1 inch. Weight, 225 pounds.

Year Club	Lea	Pos	G	AB	R	H	2B	3B	HR	RBI	SB	Avg
2004 Angels............	Arizona	C	25	60	5	13	1	0	0	4	2	.217
2005 Angels............	Arizona	C	27	86	6	22	2	0	0	10	0	.256
2005 Orem.............	Pioneer	C	9	32	4	8	0	0	1	2	0	.250
2006 Angels............	Arizona	C	21	63	9	14	1	1	0	6	0	.222
2007 West Virginia a.........	So.Atl.	C-1B-3B	66	208	20	46	8	0	2	22	2	.221
2008 Brevard County.....	Fla.St.	C-1B	34	94	8	25	8	0	0	9	3	.266
2008 Huntsville........	Southern	C	31	98	4	19	2	0	2	8	0	.194
2009 Brevard County.....	Fla.St.	C	81	251	25	50	9	0	2	21	2	.199
2009 Wisconsin........	Midwest	C	7	19	1	2	0	0	0	2	1	.105
2009 Nashville........	P.C.	C	7	18	1	6	1	0	0	3	0	.333
2010 Brevard County.....	Fla.St.	C	10	33	1	4	0	0	0	3	1	.121

Year Club	Lea	Pos	G	AB	R	H	2B	3B	HR	RBI	SB	Avg
2010 Nashville ............P.C.		C	52	174	19	44	9	0	7	26	0	.253
2010 Huntsville........ Southern		C	34	103	9	26	6	0	2	12	0	.252
2011 Huntsville........ Southern		C	64	208	24	55	13	0	3	34	2	.264
2011 Nashville ............P.C.		C	39	134	23	43	5	0	8	25	0	.321
2011 Milwaukee ...........N.L.		C	3	1	0	0	0	0	0	0	0	.000
2012 Nashville ............P.C.		C	35	121	10	24	6	0	4	13	0	.198
2012 Milwaukee ...........N.L.		C-1B	78	233	22	62	9	0	8	30	1	.266
Major League Totals	2 Yrs.		81	234	22	62	9	0	8	30	1	.265

a Released by Los Angeles Angels January 10, 2007. Signed with Milwaukee Brewers organization, January 24, 2007.

MARKAKIS, NICHOLAS WILLIAM (NICK)
Born, Woodstock, Georgia, November 17, 1983.
Bats Left. Throws Left. Height, 6 feet, 2 inches. Weight, 195 pounds.

Year Club	Lea	Pos	G	AB	R	H	2B	3B	HR	RBI	SB	Avg
2003 Aberdeen .... N.Y.-Penn.		OF	59	205	22	58	14	3	1	28	13	.283
2004 Delmarva .... So.Atl.		OF	96	355	57	106	22	3	11	64	12	.299
2005 Frederick .... Carolina		OF	91	350	59	105	25	1	12	62	2	.300
2005 Bowie............Eastern		OF	33	124	19	42	16	2	3	30	0	.339
2006 Baltimore .... A.L.		OF	147	491	72	143	25	2	16	62	2	.291
2007 Baltimore .... A.L.		OF	161	637	97	191	43	3	23	112	18	.300
2008 Baltimore .... A.L.		OF	157	595	106	182	48	1	20	87	10	.306
2009 Baltimore .... A.L.		OF	*161	642	94	188	45	2	18	101	6	.293
2010 Baltimore .... A.L.		OF	160	629	79	187	45	3	12	60	7	.297
2011 Baltimore .... A.L.		OF-1B	160	641	72	182	31	1	15	73	12	.284
2012 Bowie.............Eastern		OF	3	10	4	3	1	0	2	4	0	.300
2012 Baltimore a........... A.L.		OF	104	420	59	125	28	3	13	54	1	.298
Major League Totals	7 Yrs.		1050	4055	579	1198	265	15	117	549	56	.295

a On disabled list from June 1 to July 9, 2012.

MARSON, LOUIS GLENN (LOU)
Born, Scottsdale, Arizona, June 26, 1986.
Bats Right. Throws Right. Height, 6 feet, 1 inch. Weight, 200 pounds.

Year Club	Lea	Pos	G	AB	R	H	2B	3B	HR	RBI	SB	Avg
2004 Phillies......... Gulf Coast		C	38	113	18	29	3	0	4	8	4	.257
2005 Batavia .... N.Y.-Penn.		C	60	220	25	54	11	3	5	25	0	.245
2006 Lakewood........ So.Atl.		C	104	350	44	85	16	5	4	39	4	.243
2007 Clearwater .... Fla.St.		C	111	393	68	113	24	1	7	63	3	.288
2008 Reading ....Eastern		C	94	322	55	101	18	0	5	46	3	.314
2008 Philadelphia ..........N.L.		C	1	4	2	2	0	0	1	2	0	.500
2009 Philadelphia ..........N.L.		C	7	17	3	4	1	0	0	0	0	.235
2009 Lehigh Valley .... Int.		C	63	211	32	62	13	0	1	24	3	.294
2009 Columbus............. Int.		C	28	103	10	25	5	1	1	9	1	.243
2009 Cleveland a........... A.L.		C	14	44	6	11	6	0	0	4	0	.250
2010 Columbus............. Int.		C	37	124	19	25	7	1	4	14	5	.202
2010 Cleveland .... A.L.		C	87	262	29	51	15	0	3	22	8	.195
2011 Cleveland .... A.L.		C	79	243	26	56	9	2	1	19	4	.230
2012 Cleveland .... A.L.		C	70	195	27	44	8	2	0	13	4	.226
Major League Totals	5 Yrs.		258	765	93	168	39	4	5	60	16	.220

a Traded to Cleveland Indians with pitcher Jason Knapp, infielder Jason Donald and pitcher Carlos Carrasco for
pitcher Cliff Lee and outfielder Ben Francisco, July 29, 2009.

MARTE, STARLING JAVIER
Born, Santo Domingo, Dominican Republic, October 9, 1988.
Bats Right. Throws Right. Height, 6 feet, 2 inches. Weight, 180 pounds.

Year Club	Lea	Pos	G	AB	R	H	2B	3B	HR	RBI	SB	Avg
2009 Lynchburg .... Carolina		SS	1	2	0	2	0	0	0	1	0	1.000
2009 Pirates .... Gulf Coast		OF	2	7	1	0	0	0	0	0	0	.000
2009 West Virginia .... So.Atl.		OF	54	221	41	69	9	5	3	34	24	.312
2010 Bradenton ....Fla.St.		OF	60	222	41	70	16	5	0	33	22	.315
2010 Pirates .... Gulf Coast		OF	8	26	6	9	3	0	2	5	4	.346
2011 Altoona ....Eastern		OF	129	536	91	178	38	8	12	50	24	.332
2012 State College .... N.Y.-Penn.		DH	1	5	0	0	0	0	0	0	0	.000
2012 Indianapolis...........Int.		OF	99	388	64	111	21	13	12	62	21	.286
2012 Pittsburgh a.......... N.L.		OF	47	167	18	43	3	6	5	17	12	.257

a On disabled list from August 19 to September 7, 2012.

MARTIN (TAPANES), LEONYS

Born, Corralillo, Villa Clara, Cuba, March 6, 1988.
Bats Left. Throws Right. Height, 6 feet, 1 inch. Weight, 190 pounds.

Year Club	Lea	Pos	G	AB	R	H	2B	3B	HR	RBI	SB	Avg
2011 Rangers	Arizona	OF	4	15	2	4	0	2	0	1	0	.267
2011 Frisco	Texas	OF	29	112	24	39	9	2	4	24	10	.348
2011 Round Rock	P.C.	OF	40	175	27	46	7	1	0	17	9	.263
2011 Texas	A.L.	OF	8	8	2	3	1	0	0	0	0	.375
2012 Round Rock	P.C.	OF	55	231	48	83	18	2	12	42	10	.359
2012 Texas	A.L.	OF	24	46	6	8	5	2	0	6	3	.174
Major League Totals	2 Yrs.		32	54	8	11	6	2	0	6	3	.204

MARTIN, RUSSELL NATHAN

Born, East York, Ontario, Canada, February 15, 1983.
Bats Right. Throws Right. Height, 5 feet, 10 inches. Weight, 210 pounds.

Year Club	Lea	Pos	G	AB	R	H	2B	3B	HR	RBI	SB	Avg
2002 Dodgers	Gulf Coast	3B-SS	41	126	22	36	3	3	0	10	7	.286
2003 Ogden	Pioneer	C	52	188	25	51	13	0	6	36	3	.271
2003 South Georgia	So.Atl.	C-OF-3B	25	98	15	28	4	1	3	14	5	.286
2004 Vero Beach	Fla.St.	C	122	416	74	104	24	1	15	64	9	.250
2005 Jacksonville	Southern	C-OF	129	409	83	127	17	1	9	61	15	.311
2006 Las Vegas	P.C.	C	23	74	14	22	9	0	0	9	0	.297
2006 Los Angeles	N.L.	C	121	415	65	117	26	4	10	65	10	.282
2007 Los Angeles	N.L.	C	151	540	87	158	32	3	19	87	21	.293
2008 Los Angeles	N.L.	C-3B	155	553	87	155	25	0	13	69	18	.280
2009 Los Angeles	N.L.	C-3B	143	505	63	126	19	0	7	53	11	.250
2010 Los Angeles a-b	N.L.	C	97	331	45	82	13	0	5	26	6	.248
2011 New York	A.L.	C-3B-2B	125	417	57	99	17	0	18	65	8	.237
2012 New York c	A.L.	C	133	422	50	89	18	0	21	53	6	.211
Major League Totals	7 Yrs.		925	3183	454	826	150	7	93	418	80	.260
Division Series												
2006 Los Angeles	N.L.	C	3	12	2	4	0	0	0	0	0	.333
2008 Los Angeles	N.L.	C	3	13	2	4	3	0	1	5	0	.308
2009 Los Angeles	N.L.	C	3	9	0	1	0	0	0	1	0	.111
2011 New York	A.L.	C	5	17	3	3	1	0	0	0	0	.176
2012 New York	A.L.	C	5	17	2	3	1	0	1	1	0	.176
Division Series Totals			19	68	9	15	5	0	2	7	0	.221
Championship Series												
2008 Los Angeles	N.L.	C	5	17	3	2	0	0	0	1	1	.118
2009 Los Angeles	N.L.	C	5	16	2	4	1	0	0	2	0	.250
2012 New York	A.L.	C	4	14	1	2	0	0	0	0	0	.143
Championship Series Totals			14	47	6	8	1	0	0	3	1	.170

a On disabled list from August 4 to November 2, 2010.
b Not offered contract, December 2, 2010. Signed with New York Yankees, December 16, 2010.
c Filed for free agency, November 3, 2012. Signed with Pittsburgh Pirates, November 30, 2012.

MARTINEZ, JESUS FERNANDO (FERNANDO)

Born, Rio San Juan, Dominican Republic, October 10, 1988.
Bats Left. Throws Right. Height, 6 feet, 1 inch. Weight, 205 pounds.

Year Club	Lea	Pos	G	AB	R	H	2B	3B	HR	RBI	SB	Avg
2006 St. Lucie	Fla.St.	OF	30	119	18	23	4	2	5	11	1	.193
2006 Mets	Gulf Coast	OF	1	4	1	1	0	0	0	0	0	.250
2006 Hagerstown	So.Atl.	OF	45	192	24	64	14	2	5	28	7	.333
2007 Binghamton	Eastern	OF	60	236	32	64	11	1	4	21	3	.271
2007 Mets	Gulf Coast	OF-C	3	9	1	1	0	1	0	1	0	.111
2008 Binghamton	Eastern	OF	86	352	48	101	19	4	8	43	6	.287
2008 Mets	Gulf Coast	OF	4	14	2	6	1	1	0	0	0	.429
2009 Buffalo	Int.	OF	45	176	24	51	16	2	8	28	2	.290
2009 New York a	N.L.	OF	29	91	11	16	6	0	1	8	2	.176
2010 St. Lucie	Fla.St.	OF	4	15	1	4	1	0	0	0	0	.267
2010 New York	N.L.	OF	7	18	1	3	0	0	0	2	0	.167
2010 Buffalo	Int.	OF	71	257	39	65	16	0	12	33	1	.253
2011 New York	N.L.	OF	11	22	3	5	2	0	1	2	0	.227
2011 Buffalo	Int.	OF	63	223	29	58	11	0	8	30	0	.260
2012 Oklahoma	P.C.	OF	90	341	55	107	23	2	13	62	1	.314
2012 Houston b-c	N.L.	OF	41	118	12	28	7	1	6	14	0	.237
Major League Totals	4 Yrs.		88	249	27	52	15	1	8	26	2	.209

104

a On disabled list from July 9 to November 12, 2009.
b Claimed on waivers by Houston Astros, January 11, 2012.
c On disabled list from June 9 to June 26, 2012.

MARTINEZ, JULIO DANIEL (J.D.)

Born, Miami, Florida, August 21, 1987.
Bats Right. Throws Right. Height, 6 feet, 3 inches. Weight, 200 pounds.

Year	Club	Lea	Pos	G	AB	R	H	2B	3B	HR	RBI	SB	Avg
2009 Greeneville	Appal.		OF-1B	19	77	17	31	9	1	5	23	0	.403
2009 Tri-City	N.Y.-Penn.		OF-1B	53	187	25	61	15	2	7	33	1	.326
2010 Lexington	So.Atl.		OF	88	348	83	126	31	3	15	64	3	.362
2010 Corpus Christi	Texas		OF	50	189	24	57	9	1	3	25	2	.302
2011 Corpus Christi	Texas		OF	88	317	50	107	25	1	13	72	1	.338
2011 Houston	N.L.		OF	53	208	29	57	13	0	6	35	0	.274
2012 Oklahoma	P.C.		OF	23	90	6	21	6	0	0	4	0	.233
2012 Houston	N.L.		OF	113	395	34	95	14	3	11	55	0	.241
Major League Totals			2 Yrs.	166	603	63	152	27	3	17	90	0	.252

MARTINEZ, VICTOR JESUS

Born, Ciudad Bolivar, Venezuela, December 23, 1978.
Bats Both. Throws Right. Height, 6 feet, 2 inches. Weight, 210 pounds.

Year	Club	Lea	Pos	G	AB	R	H	2B	3B	HR	RBI	SB	Avg
1997 Maracay-1	Venzuelan		C	53	122	21	42	12	0	0	26	6	.344
1998 Guacara-2	Venzuelan		C	55	160	28	43	13	0	1	27	8	.269
1999 Mahoning Valley	N.Y.-Penn.		C	64	235	37	65	9	0	4	36	0	.277
2000 Kinston	Carolina		C	26	83	9	18	7	0	0	8	1	.217
2000 Columbus a	So.Atl.		C	21	70	11	26	9	1	2	12	0	.371
2001 Kinston	Carolina		C	114	420	59	138	33	2	10	57	3	.329
2002 Akron	Eastern		C	121	443	84	149	40	0	22	85	3	.336
2002 Cleveland	A.L.		C	12	32	2	9	1	0	1	5	0	.281
2003 Buffalo	Int.		C-1B	73	274	42	90	19	0	7	45	3	.328
2003 Akron	Eastern		C	3	12	1	4	2	0	0	2	0	.333
2003 Cleveland b	A.L.		C	49	159	15	46	4	0	1	16	1	.289
2004 Cleveland	A.L.		C	141	520	77	147	38	1	23	108	0	.283
2005 Cleveland	A.L.		C	147	547	73	167	33	0	20	80	0	.305
2006 Cleveland	A.L.		C-1B	153	572	82	181	37	0	16	93	0	.316
2007 Cleveland	A.L.		C-1B	147	562	78	169	40	0	25	114	0	.301
2008 Akron	Eastern		DH	2	6	1	2	0	0	1	1	0	.333
2008 Buffalo	Int.		C	6	20	2	6	2	0	0	2	0	.300
2008 Cleveland	A.L.		C-1B	73	266	30	74	17	0	2	35	0	.278
2009 Cleveland-Boston d	A.L.		C-1B	155	588	88	178	33	1	23	108	1	.303
2010 Boston e-f	A.L.		C-1B	127	493	64	149	32	1	20	79	1	.302
2011 Toledo	Int.		DH	2	6	1	3	1	0	0	2	0	.500
2011 Detroit g	A.L.		DH-C-1B	145	540	76	178	40	0	12	103	1	.330
2012 Detroit h	A.L.						INJURED—Did Not Play						
Major League Totals			10 Yrs.	1149	4279	585	1298	275	3	143	741	4	.303
Division Series													
2007 Cleveland	A.L.		C-1B	4	17	2	6	1	0	1	4	0	.353
2009 Boston	A.L.		C	3	11	0	2	0	0	0	2	0	.182
2011 Detroit	A.L.		DH	5	18	1	4	0	0	1	3	0	.222
Division Series Totals				12	46	3	12	1	0	2	9	0	.261
Championship Series													
2007 Cleveland	A.L.		C-1B	7	27	4	8	1	0	1	3	0	.296
2011 Detroit	A.L.		DH	6	22	3	6	0	1	1	2	0	.273
Championship Series Totals				13	49	7	14	1	1	2	5	0	.286

a On minor league disabled list from May 25 to July 19, 2000.
b On disabled list from August 9 to September 2, 2003.
c On disabled list from June 12 to August 29, 2008.
d Traded to Boston Red Sox for pitcher Justin Masterson, pitcher Nick Hagadone and pitcher Bryan Price, July 31, 2009.
e On disabled list from June 28 to July 26, 2010.
f Filed for free agency, November 1, 2010. Signed with Detroit Tigers, November 26, 2010.
g On disabled list from April 19 to May 4, 2011.
h On disabled list from March 12 to October 29, 2012.

MASTROIANNI, DARIN PAUL

Born, Mount Kisco, New York, August 26, 1985.
Bats Right. Throws Right. Height, 5 feet, 11 inches. Weight, 190 pounds.

Year	Club	Lea	Pos	G	AB	R	H	2B	3B	HR	RBI	SB	Avg
2007 Auburn	N.Y.-Penn.	2B-OF	68	230	50	66	11	4	3	26	20	.287
2008 Lansing	Midwest	OF-2B	95	325	51	74	10	4	3	25	30	.228
2009 New Hampshire	Eastern	OF	70	247	39	67	10	2	1	25	38	.271
2009 Dunedin	Fla.St.	OF	61	231	55	75	11	2	0	26	32	.325
2010 New Hampshire	Eastern	OF	132	525	101	158	25	7	4	46	46	.301
2011 New Hampshire	Eastern	OF	44	169	29	43	8	3	1	13	14	.254
2011 Toronto	A.L.	OF	1	2	0	0	0	0	0	0	0	.000
2011 Las Vegas	P.C.	OF	79	319	63	88	18	6	2	23	20	.276
2012 New Britain	Eastern	OF	9	35	6	5	1	0	0	0	4	.143
2012 Rochester	Int.	OF-2B	20	78	10	27	2	2	0	11	10	.346
2012 Minnesota a	A.L.	OF-2B	77	163	22	41	3	2	3	17	21	.252
Major League Totals		2 Yrs.	78	165	22	41	3	2	3	17	21	.248

a Claimed on waivers by Minnesota Twins, February 9, 2012.

MATHER, JOSEPH PAUL (JOE)

Born, Sandpoint, Idaho, July 23, 1982.
Bats Right. Throws Right. Height, 6 feet, 4 inches. Weight, 215 pounds.

Year	Club	Lea	Pos	G	AB	R	H	2B	3B	HR	RBI	SB	Avg
2001 Johnson City	Appal.	3B-SS	45	165	25	41	3	0	5	21	2	.248
2002 Johnson City	Appal.	3B-1B	62	224	29	52	15	2	8	39	9	.232
2003 New Jersey	N.Y.-Penn.	1B-3B	65	196	23	45	12	1	2	22	4	.230
2004 Peoria	Midwest	OF-3B-1B-2B	65	241	34	61	18	2	7	31	3	.253
2004 New Jersey	N.Y.-Penn.	3B	3	8	0	1	0	0	0	0	2	.125
2005 Palm Beach	Fla.St.	OF-3B	57	200	37	55	12	2	8	27	4	.275
2005 Quad Cities	Midwest	OF-1B	54	209	30	46	15	2	9	33	0	.220
2006 Palm Beach	Fla.St.	OF-1B	124	443	64	119	33	1	16	74	9	.269
2007 Memphis	P.C.	OF-1B	70	253	32	61	10	1	13	31	6	.241
2007 Springfield	Texas	1B-OF	64	234	48	71	17	0	18	46	4	.303
2008 Memphis	P.C.	OF	59	211	45	64	14	2	17	41	7	.303
2008 St. Louis a	N.L.	OF-1B-3B	54	133	20	32	7	0	8	18	1	.241
2009 Cardinals	Gulf Coast	OF	3	8	1	2	1	0	0	3	0	.250
2009 Memphis	P.C.	OF-1B	39	136	12	24	6	2	1	14	7	.176
2009 Springfield	Texas	OF-3B-1B	17	58	8	12	3	0	3	11	0	.207
2010 Memphis	P.C.	OF-1B	91	335	55	92	18	4	10	46	6	.275
2010 St. Louis b	N.L.	OF-1B-P-3B	36	60	7	13	4	0	0	3	1	.217
2011 Gwinnett	Int.	1B-OF-3B	18	62	13	16	5	0	1	4	2	.258
2011 Colorado Springs	P.C.	OF-1B	55	209	36	67	14	1	6	31	3	.321
2011 Atlanta c	N.L.	OF-1B-3B	36	75	4	16	4	0	1	9	0	.213
2012 Chicago d-e	N.L.	OF-3B-1B-P	103	225	18	47	11	0	5	19	5	.209
Major League Totals		4 Yrs.	229	493	49	108	26	0	14	49	7	.219

a On disabled list from September 2 to October 8, 2008.
b Claimed on waivers by Atlanta Braves, November 3, 2010.
c Filed for free agency, June 24, 2011. Signed with Colorado Rockies organization, July 4, 2011.
d Filed for free agency, November 2, 2011. Signed with Chicago Cubs organization, January 4, 2012.
e Filed for free agency, October 30, 2012.

MATHIS, JEFFERY STEPHEN (JEFF)

Born, Marianna, Florida, March 31, 1983.
Bats Right. Throws Right. Height, 6 feet. Weight, 180 pounds.

Year	Club	Lea	Pos	G	AB	R	H	2B	3B	HR	RBI	SB	Avg
2001 Angels	Arizona	C-OF	7	23	1	7	1	0	0	3	0	.304
2001 Provo	Pioneer	C	22	77	14	23	6	3	0	18	1	.299
2002 Cedar Rapids	Midwest	C	128	491	75	141	41	3	10	73	7	.287
2003 Rancho Cucamonga	Calif.	C	98	378	74	122	28	3	11	54	5	.323
2003 Arkansas	Texas	C	24	95	19	27	11	0	2	14	1	.284
2004 Arkansas	Texas	C	117	432	57	98	24	3	14	55	2	.227
2005 Salt Lake	P.C.	C	112	427	78	118	26	3	21	73	4	.276
2005 Los Angeles	A.L.	C	5	3	1	1	0	0	0	0	0	.333
2006 Salt Lake	P.C.	C	99	384	62	111	33	3	5	45	3	.289
2006 Los Angeles	A.L.	C	23	55	9	8	2	0	2	6	0	.145
2007 Salt Lake	P.C.	C	66	250	39	61	14	2	5	26	3	.244
2007 Los Angeles	A.L.	C	59	171	24	36	12	0	4	23	0	.211
2008 Los Angeles	A.L.	C	94	283	35	55	8	0	9	42	2	.194
2009 Los Angeles	A.L.	C	84	237	26	50	8	0	5	28	2	.211

Year	Club	Lea	Pos	G	AB	R	H	2B	3B	HR	RBI	SB	Avg
2010 Salt Lake	P.C.	C	9	33	6	8	1	1	1	5	0	.242
2010 Los Angeles a	A.L.	C	68	205	19	40	6	1	3	18	3	.195
2011 Los Angeles b	A.L.	C	93	247	18	43	12	0	3	22	1	.174
2012 Toronto c	A.L.	C-P	71	211	25	46	13	0	8	27	1	.218
Major League Totals	8 Yrs.		497	1412	157	279	61	1	34	166	9	.198
Division Series												
2007 Los Angeles	A.L.	C	2	3	0	0	0	0	0	1	0	.000
2008 Los Angeles	A.L.	C	1	2	0	1	0	0	0	0	0	.500
2009 Los Angeles	A.L.	C	2	3	0	1	0	0	0	0	0	.333
Division Series Totals			5	8	0	2	0	0	0	1	0	.250
Championship Series												
2009 Los Angeles	A.L.	C	5	12	2	7	5	0	0	1	0	.583

a On disabled list from April 20 to June 17, 2010.
b Traded to Toronto Blue Jays for pitcher Brad Mills, December 3, 2011.
c Traded to Miami Marlins with pitcher Henderson Alvarez, infielder Yunel Escobar, infielder Adeiny Hechavarria, pitcher Anthony De Sclafani, outfielder Jake Marisnick and pitcher Justin Nicolino for outfielder Emilio Bonifacio, catcher John Buck, pitcher Mark Buehrle, pitcher Josh Johnson and infielder Jose Reyes, November 19, 2012.

MAUER, JOSEPH PATRICK (JOE)
Born, St. Paul, Minnesota, April 19, 1983.
Bats Left. Throws Right. Height, 6 feet, 4 inches. Weight, 220 pounds.

Year	Club	Lea	Pos	G	AB	R	H	2B	3B	HR	RBI	SB	Avg
2001 Elizabethton	Appal.	C	32	110	14	44	6	2	0	14	4	.400
2002 Quad Cities	Midwest	C-1B	110	411	58	124	23	1	4	62	0	.302
2003 Fort Myers	Fla.St.	C-1B	62	233	25	78	13	1	1	44	3	.335
2003 New Britain	Eastern	C	73	276	48	94	17	1	4	41	0	.341
2004 Fort Myers	Fla.St.	C	2	6	0	4	0	0	0	2	0	.667
2004 Rochester	Int.	C	5	19	1	6	3	0	0	2	0	.316
2004 Minnesota a	A.L.	C	35	107	18	33	8	1	6	17	1	.308
2005 Minnesota	A.L.	C	131	489	61	144	26	2	9	55	13	.294
2006 Minnesota	A.L.	C	140	521	86	181	36	4	13	84	8	*.347
2007 Fort Myers	Fla.St.	C	1	3	0	0	0	0	0	0	0	.000
2007 Minnesota b	A.L.	C	109	406	62	119	27	3	7	60	7	.293
2008 Minnesota	A.L.	C	146	536	98	176	31	4	9	85	1	*.328
2009 Fort Myers	Fla.St.	C	5	15	2	6	2	0	0	4	0	.400
2009 Minnesota c-d	A.L.	C	138	523	94	191	30	1	28	96	4	*.365
2010 Minnesota	A.L.	C	137	510	88	167	43	1	9	75	1	.327
2011 Fort Myers	Fla.St.	C	7	23	3	6	2	0	1	6	0	.261
2011 Minnesota e	A.L.	C-1B-OF	82	296	38	85	15	0	3	30	0	.287
2012 Minnesota	A.L.	C-1B	147	545	81	174	31	4	10	85	8	.319
Major League Totals	9 Yrs.		1065	3933	626	1270	247	20	94	587	43	.323
Division Series												
2006 Minnesota	A.L.	C	3	11	0	2	0	0	0	0	0	.182
2009 Minnesota	A.L.	C	3	12	1	5	1	0	0	1	0	.417
2010 Minnesota	A.L.	C	3	12	0	3	0	0	0	0	0	.250
Division Series Totals			9	35	1	10	1	0	0	1	0	.286

a On disabled list from April 7 to June 2 and from July 16 to October 11, 2004.
b On disabled list from May 5 to June 8, 2007.
c On disabled list from March 27 to May 1, 2009.
d Selected Most Valuable Player in American League for 2009.
e On disabled list from April 13 to June 17 and September 15 to October 3, 2011.

MAXWELL, JUSTIN ADAM
Born, Olney, Maryland, November 6, 1983.
Bats Right. Throws Right. Height, 6 feet, 5 inches. Weight, 235 pounds.

Year	Club	Lea	Pos	G	AB	R	H	2B	3B	HR	RBI	SB	Avg
2006 Vermont	N.Y.-Penn.	OF	74	271	36	73	11	3	4	33	20	.269
2006 Savannah	So.Atl.	OF	17	58	8	10	2	2	1	7	1	.172
2007 Hagerstown	So.Atl.	OF	56	209	51	63	12	2	14	40	14	.301
2007 Potomac...........	Carolina	OF	58	228	35	60	13	0	13	43	21	.263
2007 Washington	N.L.	OF	15	26	5	7	0	0	2	5	0	.269
2008 Harrisburg a	Eastern	OF	43	146	35	34	6	3	7	28	13	.233
2009 Syracuse	Int.	OF	111	384	68	93	10	5	13	42	35	.242
2009 Washington	N.L.	OF	40	89	13	22	4	1	4	9	6	.247
2010 Syracuse	Int.	OF	66	230	34	66	17	0	6	21	16	.287
2010 Washington	N.L.	OF	67	104	16	15	6	0	3	12	5	.144

Year	Club	Lea	Pos	G	AB	R	H	2B	3B	HR	RBI	SB	Avg
2011 Scranton-WB b-c	Int.	OF	48	177	36	46	8	1	16	35	11	.260
2012 Corpus Christi	Texas	OF	2	8	2	2	1	0	0	1	0	.250
2012 Oklahoma	P.C.	OF	3	10	1	2	1	0	0	0	0	.200
2012 Houston d-e	N.L.	OF	124	315	46	72	13	3	18	53	9	.229
Major League Totals	4 Yrs.	246	534	80	116	23	4	27	79	20	.217	

a On disabled list from September 2 to September 29, 2008.
b Traded to New York Yankees for pitcher Adam Olbrychowski, February 2, 2011.
c On disabled list from September 1 to October 12, 2011.
d Claimed on waivers by Houston Astros, April 8, 2012.
e On disabled list from June 26 to July 13, 2012.

MAYBERRY, JOHN CLAIBORN JR.

Born, Kansas City, Missouri, December 21, 1983.
Bats Right. Throws Right. Height, 6 feet, 6 inches. Weight, 230 pounds.

Year	Club	Lea	Pos	G	AB	R	H	2B	3B	HR	RBI	SB	Avg
2005 Spokane	Northwest	OF	71	265	51	67	16	0	11	26	7	.253
2006 Clinton	Midwest	OF	126	459	77	123	26	4	21	77	9	.268
2007 Bakersfield	Calif.	OF	63	244	47	56	15	1	16	45	9	.230
2007 Frisco	Texas	OF	69	245	35	59	10	0	14	38	7	.241
2008 Frisco a	Texas	OF	21	82	16	22	8	0	4	13	4	.268
2008 Oklahoma	P.C.	OF-1B	114	437	49	115	30	7	16	58	6	.263
2009 Lehigh Valley	Int.	OF	89	316	44	81	20	2	13	43	6	.256
2009 Philadelphia	N.L.	OF	39	57	8	12	3	0	4	8	0	.211
2010 Lehigh Valley	Int.	OF	128	495	75	132	25	1	15	65	20	.267
2010 Philadelphia	N.L.	OF	11	12	4	4	0	0	2	6	0	.333
2011 Lehigh Valley	Int.	OF-1B	28	113	16	30	8	0	4	15	2	.265
2011 Philadelphia	N.L.	OF-1B	104	267	37	73	17	1	15	49	8	.273
2012 Philadelphia	N.L.	OF-1B	149	441	53	108	24	0	14	46	1	.245
Major League Totals	4 Yrs.	303	777	102	197	44	1	35	109	9	.254	
Division Series													
2011 Philadelphia	N.L.	OF	2	4	0	0	0	0	0	0	0	.000

a Traded by Texas Rangers to Philadelphia Phillies for outfielder Greg Golson, November 20, 2008.

MAYBIN, CAMERON KEITH

Born, Asheville, North Carolina, April 4, 1987.
Bats Right. Throws Right. Height, 6 feet, 4 inches. Weight, 205 pounds.

Year	Club	Lea	Pos	G	AB	R	H	2B	3B	HR	RBI	SB	Avg
2006 West Michigan	Midwest	OF	101	385	59	117	20	6	9	69	27	.304
2007 Tigers	Gulf Coast	OF	2	7	1	4	0	0	0	1	0	.571
2007 Lakeland	Fla.St.	OF	83	296	58	90	14	5	10	44	25	.304
2007 Erie	Eastern	OF	6	20	9	8	1	0	4	8	0	.400
2007 Detroit a	A.L.	OF	24	49	8	7	3	0	1	2	5	.143
2008 Carolina	Southern	OF	108	390	73	108	15	8	13	49	21	.277
2008 Florida	N.L.	OF	8	32	9	16	2	0	0	2	4	.500
2009 New Orleans	P.C.	OF	82	298	44	95	18	8	3	39	8	.319
2009 Florida	N.L.	OF	54	176	30	44	12	2	4	13	1	.250
2010 Marlins	Gulf Coast	OF	3	11	4	4	1	0	1	5	0	.364
2010 New Orleans	P.C.	OF	33	130	21	44	6	2	4	23	5	.338
2010 Florida b	N.L.	OF	82	291	46	68	7	3	8	28	9	.234
2011 Tucson	P.C.	OF	3	10	1	2	1	0	0	1	1	.200
2011 San Diego c	N.L.	OF	137	516	82	136	24	8	9	40	40	.264
2012 San Diego	N.L.	OF	147	507	67	123	20	5	8	45	26	.243
Major League Totals	6 Yrs.	452	1571	242	394	68	18	30	130	85	.251	

a Traded to Florida Marlins with pitcher Burke Badenhop, pitcher Eulogio De La Cruz, pitcher Andrew Miller and catcher Mike Rabelo for pitcher Dontrelle Willis and infielder Miguel Cabrera, December 5, 2007.
b Traded to San Diego Padres for pitcher Edward Mujica and pitcher Ryan Webb, November 13, 2010.
c On disabled list from May 28 to June 13, 2011.

MC CANN, BRIAN MICHAEL

Born, Athens, Georgia, February 20, 1984.
Bats Left. Throws Right. Height, 6 feet, 3 inches. Weight, 230 pounds.

Year	Club	Lea	Pos	G	AB	R	H	2B	3B	HR	RBI	SB	Avg
2002 Braves	Gulf Coast	C	29	100	9	22	5	0	2	11	0	.220
2003 Rome	So.Atl.	C	115	424	40	123	31	3	12	71	7	.290
2004 Myrtle Beach	Carolina	C	111	385	45	107	35	0	16	66	2	.278

Year	Club	Lea	Pos	G	AB	R	H	2B	3B	HR	RBI	SB	Avg
2005 Mississippi	Southern	C	48	166	27	44	13	2	6	26	2	.265
2005 Atlanta	N.L.	C	59	180	20	50	7	0	5	23	1	.278
2006 Rome	So.Atl.	DH	2	7	0	2	0	0	0	0	0	.286
2006 Atlanta a	N.L.	C	130	442	61	147	34	0	24	93	2	.333
2007 Atlanta	N.L.	C	139	504	51	136	38	0	18	92	0	.270
2008 Atlanta	N.L.	C	145	509	68	153	42	1	23	87	5	.301
2009 Myrtle Beach	Carolina	DH	2	6	1	2	2	0	0	1	0	.333
2009 Gwinnett	Int.	C	1	3	0	1	1	0	0	1	0	.333
2009 Atlanta b	N.L.	C	138	488	63	137	35	1	21	94	4	.281
2010 Atlanta	N.L.	C	143	479	63	129	25	0	21	77	5	.269
2011 Gwinnett	Int.	C	2	6	1	2	0	0	1	2	0	.333
2011 Atlanta c	N.L.	C	128	466	51	126	19	0	24	71	3	.270
2012 Atlanta	N.L.	C	121	439	44	101	14	0	20	67	3	.230
Major League Totals		8 Yrs.	1003	3507	421	979	214	2	156	604	23	.279
Wild Card Playoff													
2012 Atlanta	N.L.	PH	1	0	0	0	0	0	0	0	0	.000
Division Series													
2005 Atlanta	N.L.	C	3	16	2	3	0	0	2	5	0	.188
2010 Atlanta	N.L.	C	4	14	2	6	1	0	1	3	0	.429
Division Series Totals			7	30	4	9	1	0	3	8	0	.300

a On disabled list from May 24 to June 9, 2006.
b On disabled list from April 23 to May 8, 2009.
c On disabled list from July 27 to August 14, 2011.

MC CUTCHEN, ANDREW STEFAN
Born, Fort Meade, Florida, October 10, 1986.
Bats Right. Throws Right. Height, 5 feet, 11 inches. Weight, 175 pounds.

Year	Club	Lea	Pos	G	AB	R	H	2B	3B	HR	RBI	SB	Avg
2005 Pirates	Gulf Coast	OF	45	158	36	47	9	3	2	30	13	.297
2005 Williamsport	N.Y.-Penn.	OF	13	52	12	18	3	1	0	5	4	.346
2006 Altoona	Eastern	OF	20	78	12	24	4	0	3	12	1	.308
2006 Hickory	So.Atl.	OF	114	453	77	132	20	4	14	62	22	.291
2007 Altoona	Eastern	OF	118	446	70	115	20	3	10	48	17	.258
2007 Indianapolis	Int.	OF	17	67	7	21	4	0	1	5	4	.313
2008 Indianapolis	Int.	OF	135	512	75	145	26	3	9	50	34	.283
2009 Indianapolis	Int.	OF	49	201	41	61	10	8	4	20	10	.303
2009 Pittsburgh	N.L.	OF	108	433	74	124	26	9	12	54	22	.286
2010 Pittsburgh	N.L.	OF	154	570	94	163	35	5	16	56	33	.286
2011 Pittsburgh	N.L.	OF	158	572	87	148	34	5	23	89	23	.259
2012 Pittsburgh	N.L.	OF	157	593	107	*194	29	6	31	96	20	.327
Major League Totals		4 Yrs.	577	2168	362	629	124	25	82	295	98	.290

MC DONALD, JOHN JOSEPH
Born, New London, Connecticut, September 24, 1974.
Bats Right. Throws Right. Height, 5 feet, 11 inches. Weight, 175 pounds.

Year	Club	Lea	Pos	G	AB	R	H	2B	3B	HR	RBI	SB	Avg
1996 Watertown	N.Y.-Penn.	SS	75	278	48	75	11	0	2	26	11	.270
1997 Kinston	Carolina	SS	130	541	77	140	27	3	5	53	6	.259
1998 Akron	Eastern	SS	132	514	68	118	18	2	2	43	17	.230
1999 Akron	Eastern	SS	55	226	31	67	12	0	1	26	7	.296
1999 Buffalo	Int.	SS	66	237	30	75	12	1	0	25	6	.316
1999 Cleveland	A.L.	2B-SS	18	21	2	7	0	0	0	0	0	.333
2000 Buffalo	Int.	SS-2B	75	286	37	77	17	2	1	36	4	.269
2000 Mahoning Valley	N.Y.-Penn.	SS	5	17	0	2	1	0	0	1	0	.118
2000 Cleveland	A.L.	2B-SS	9	9	0	4	0	0	0	0	0	.444
2000 Kinston a	Carolina	SS	1	3	0	1	0	0	0	0	0	.333
2001 Buffalo	Int.	SS-2B-3B	116	410	52	100	17	1	2	33	17	.244
2001 Cleveland b	A.L.	SS-2B-3B	17	22	1	2	1	0	0	0	0	.091
2002 Cleveland	A.L.	2B-SS-3B	93	264	35	66	11	3	1	12	3	.250
2003 Lake County	So.Atl.	SS	1	3	0	0	0	0	0	0	0	.000
2003 Mahoning Valley	N.Y.-Penn.	SS	1	2	1	0	0	0	0	0	0	.000
2003 Cleveland c	A.L.	2B-SS-3B	82	214	21	46	9	1	1	14	3	.215
2004 Cleveland d	A.L.	SS-2B-3B	66	93	17	19	5	1	2	7	0	.204
2005 Toronto-Detroit e-f	A.L.	SS-2B-3B	68	166	18	46	6	1	0	16	6	.277
2006 Toronto g	A.L.	SS-2B-3B	104	260	35	58	7	3	3	23	7	.223
2007 Toronto	A.L.	SS-3B	123	327	32	82	20	2	1	31	7	.251

109

Year	Club	Lea	Pos	G	AB	R	H	2B	3B	HR	RBI	SB	Avg
2008 Dunedin	Fla.St.		SS	3	11	2	4	0	0	0	1	0	.364
2008 Toronto h	A.L.		SS-3B-2B	84	186	21	39	8	0	1	18	3	.210
2009 Toronto i	A.L.		SS-3B-2B-OF	73	151	18	39	7	0	4	13	0	.258
2010 Toronto	A.L.		2B-3B-SS-OF	63	152	27	38	9	2	6	23	2	.250
2011 Dunedin	Fla.St.		SS	1	4	0	1	0	0	0	0	0	.250
2011 Toronto	A.L.		3B-2B-SS	65	168	19	42	8	1	2	20	2	.250
2011 Arizona j-k-l	N.L.		SS	19	59	2	10	2	0	0	2	0	.169
2012 D-Backs	Arizona		SS	3	8	1	0	0	0	0	1	0	.000
2012 Arizona m	N.L.		SS-3B-2B	70	197	16	49	9	0	6	22	0	.249
Major League Totals			14 Yrs.	954	2289	264	547	102	14	27	201	33	.239
Division Series													
2011 Arizona	N.L.		SS	2	2	0	0	0	0	0	0	0	.000

a On disabled list from April 27 to May 9 and May 10 to June 22, 2000.
b On disabled list from May 10 to 17, 2001.
c On disabled list from June 30 to July 17 and August 27 to October 3, 2003.
d Traded to Toronto Blue Jays for player to be named later, December 2, 2004. Cleveland received pitcher Tom Mastny to complete deal, December 13, 2004.
e Sold to Detroit Tigers, July 22, 2005.
f Sold to Toronto Blue Jays, November 10, 2005.
g On disabled list from May 28 to June 12, 2006.
h On disabled list from May 7 to June 7, 2008.
i Filed for free agency, November 6, 2009, re-signed with Toronto Blue Jays, November 25, 2009.
j On disabled list from May 27 to June 17, 2011.
k Traded to Arizona Diamondbacks with infielder Aaron Hill for infielder Kelly Johnson, August 23, 2011.
l Filed for free agency, October 31, 2011, re-signed with Arizona Diamondbacks, November 2, 2011.
m On disabled list from June 25 to July 24, 2012.

MC GEHEE, CASEY MICHAEL

Born, Santa Cruz, California, October 12, 1982.
Bats Right. Throws Right. Height, 6 feet, 1 inch. Weight, 195 pounds.

Year	Club	Lea	Pos	G	AB	R	H	2B	3B	HR	RBI	SB	Avg
2003 Lansing	Midwest		3B	64	243	24	66	18	1	3	23	2	.272
2004 Daytona	Fla.St.		3B-C	119	449	56	117	30	0	10	66	2	.261
2005 West Tenn	Southern		3B-1B-2B	124	455	67	135	31	1	8	72	2	.297
2006 Iowa	P.C.		3B-1B-2B-SS	135	497	56	139	28	1	11	68	0	.280
2007 Iowa	P.C.		3B-1B	18	52	3	9	2	0	1	5	0	.173
2007 Tennessee	Southern		3B-C-1B	105	384	53	105	26	2	9	54	1	.273
2008 Iowa	P.C.		3B-C-1B-2B	133	497	68	147	30	0	12	92	0	.296
2008 Chicago a	N.L.		3B	9	24	1	4	1	0	0	5	0	.167
2009 Milwaukee	N.L.		3B-2B-1B-OF	116	355	58	107	20	1	16	66	0	.301
2010 Milwaukee	N.L.		3B-1B	157	610	70	174	38	1	23	104	1	.285
2011 Milwaukee b	N.L.		3B-1B	155	546	46	122	24	2	13	67	0	.223
2012 Charleston	So.Atl.		3B-1B	7	25	4	9	3	0	0	8	0	.360
2012 Pittsburgh	N.L.		1B-3B	92	265	27	61	13	1	8	35	1	.230
2012 New York c-d	A.L.		3B-1B-2B	22	53	9	8	3	0	1	6	0	.151
Major League Totals			5 Yrs.	551	1853	211	476	99	5	61	283	2	.257
Division Series													
2011 Milwaukee	N.L.		PH	3	3	0	1	0	0	0	0	0	.333
Championship Series													
2011 Milwaukee	N.L.		PH	3	2	0	0	0	0	0	0	0	.000

a Claimed on waivers by Milwaukee Brewers, October 29, 2008.
b Traded to Pittsburgh Pirates for pitcher Jose Veras, December 13, 2011.
c Traded to New York Yankees with cash for pitcher Chad Qualls, July 31, 2012.
d Filed for free agency, October 30, 2012. Signed with Rakuten Golden Eagles (Japan), December 19, 2012.

MC KENRY, MICHAEL CHARLES

Born, Knoxville, Tennessee, March 4, 1985.
Bats Right. Throws Right. Height, 5 feet, 10 inches. Weight, 215 pounds.

Year	Club	Lea	Pos	G	AB	R	H	2B	3B	HR	RBI	SB	Avg
2006 Tri-City	Northwest		C	66	245	28	53	16	1	4	23	3	.216
2007 Asheville	So.Atl.		C	113	408	79	117	35	1	22	90	8	.287
2008 Modesto	Calif.		C	111	400	59	103	28	1	18	75	2	.257
2009 Tulsa	Texas		C	102	358	52	100	25	1	12	50	2	.279
2010 Colorado Springs	P.C.		C	99	347	44	92	23	1	10	49	1	.265
2010 Colorado	N.L.		C	6	8	0	0	0	0	0	0	0	.000
2011 Pawtucket	Int.		C	29	95	10	26	5	0	3	12	1	.274
2011 Pittsburgh a-b	N.L.		C-3B	58	180	17	40	12	0	2	11	0	.222

Year Club	Lea	Pos	G	AB	R	H	2B	3B	HR	RBI	SB	Avg
2012 Pittsburgh	N.L.	C	88	240	25	56	14	0	12	39	0	.233
Major League Totals		3 Yrs.	152	428	42	96	26	0	14	50	0	.224

a Traded to Boston Red Sox for pitcher Daniel Turpen, March 29, 2011.
b Sold to Pittsburgh Pirates, June 13, 2011.

MC LOUTH, NATHAN RICHARD (NATE)

Born, Muskegon, Michigan, October 28, 1981.
Bats Left. Throws Right. Height, 5 feet, 11 inches. Weight, 185 pounds.

Year Club	Lea	Pos	G	AB	R	H	2B	3B	HR	RBI	SB	Avg
2001 Hickory............	So.Atl.	OF-2B	96	351	59	100	17	5	12	54	21	.285
2002 Lynchburg	Carolina	OF	114	393	58	96	23	4	9	46	20	.244
2003 Lynchburg	Carolina	OF	117	440	85	132	27	2	6	33	40	.300
2004 Altoona...........	Eastern	OF	133	515	93	166	40	4	8	73	31	.322
2005 Indianapolis	Int.	OF	110	397	64	118	20	3	5	39	34	.297
2005 Pittsburgh	N.L.	OF	41	109	20	28	6	0	5	12	2	.257
2006 Pittsburgh a	N.L.	OF	106	270	50	63	16	2	7	16	10	.233
2007 Pittsburgh	N.L.	OF	137	329	62	85	21	3	13	38	22	.258
2008 Pittsburgh	N.L.	OF	152	597	113	165	*46	4	26	94	23	.276
2009 Rome.............	So.Atl.	OF	1	2	0	0	0	0	0	0	0	.000
2009 Mississippi	Southern	OF	2	3	1	0	0	0	0	0	0	.000
2009 Pittsburgh-Atlanta b-c ..	N.L.	OF	129	507	86	130	27	2	20	70	19	.256
2010 Gwinnett............	Int.	OF	34	128	18	30	1	0	6	18	7	.234
2010 Atlanta d..........	N.L.	OF	85	242	30	46	12	1	6	24	7	.190
2011 Gwinnett............	Int.	OF	3	6	2	3	0	0	0	1	0	.500
2011 Atlanta e-f	N.L.	OF	81	267	35	61	12	2	4	16	4	.228
2012 Norfolk.............	Int.	OF	47	180	29	44	5	2	10	33	5	.244
2012 Pittsburgh	N.L.	OF	34	57	4	8	2	0	0	2	0	.140
2012 Baltimore g-h........	A.L.	OF	55	209	35	56	12	1	7	18	12	.268
Major League Totals		8 Yrs.	820	2587	435	642	154	15	88	290	99	.248
Wild Card Playoff												
2012 Baltimore	A.L.	OF	1	4	1	1	0	0	0	2	1	.250
Division Series												
2010 Atlanta	N.L.	OF	3	2	0	1	0	0	0	0	0	.500
2012 Baltimore	A.L.	OF	5	22	2	7	1	0	1	3	2	.318
Division Series Totals			8	24	2	8	1	0	1	3	2	.333

a On disabled list from August 12 to October 3, 2006.
b Traded to Atlanta Braves for outfielder Gorkys Hernandez, pitcher Jeff Locke and pitcher Charlie Morton, June 3, 2009.
c On disabled list from August 16 to September 4, 2009.
d On disabled list from June 10 to July 21, 2010.
e On disabled list from May 23 to June 19 and July 29 to October 30, 2011.
f Filed for free agency, October 31, 2011. Signed with Pittsburgh Pirates, December 7, 2011.
g Released by Pittsburgh Pirates, May 31, 2012. Signed with Baltimore Orioles organization, June 5, 2012.
h Filed for free agency, November 3, 2012, re-signed with Baltimore Orioles, December 13, 2012.

MIDDLEBROOKS, WILLIAM SCOTT (WILL)

Born, Greenville, Texas, September 9, 1988.
Bats Right. Throws Right. Height, 6 feet, 4 inches. Weight, 225 pounds.

Year Club	Lea	Pos	G	AB	R	H	2B	3B	HR	RBI	SB	Avg
2008 Lowell	N.Y.-Penn.	3B	59	209	21	53	17	2	1	21	10	.254
2009 Greenville..........	So.Atl.	3B	103	374	53	99	25	3	7	57	7	.265
2010 Salem	Carolina	3B	114	435	69	120	31	2	12	70	5	.276
2011 Portland	Eastern	3B	96	371	54	112	25	1	18	80	6	.302
2011 Pawtucket	Int.	3B	16	56	4	9	0	0	2	8	3	.161
2011 Lowell	N.Y.-Penn.	DH	4	12	4	4	1	0	3	6	1	.333
2012 Pawtucket	Int.	3B	24	93	18	31	3	1	9	27	3	.333
2012 Boston a............	A.L.	3B	75	267	34	77	14	0	15	54	4	.288

a On disabled list from August 11 to November 2, 2012.

MOLINA (MATTA), JOSE BENJAMIN

Born, Bayamon, Puerto Rico, June 3, 1975.
Bats Right. Throws Right. Height, 6 feet, 1 inch. Weight, 250 pounds.

Year Club	Lea	Pos	G	AB	R	H	2B	3B	HR	RBI	SB	Avg
1993 Cubs..........	Gulf Coast	C-1B	33	78	5	17	2	0	0	4	3	.218
1993 Daytona...........	Fla.St.	C	3	7	0	1	0	0	0	1	0	.143

Year	Club	Lea	Pos	G	AB	R	H	2B	3B	HR	RBI	SB	Avg
1994 Peoria............	Midwest	C	78	253	31	58	13	1	1	33	4	.229
1995 Daytona............	Fla.St.	C	82	233	27	55	9	1	1	19	1	.236
1996 Rockford.........	Midwest	C	96	305	35	69	10	1	2	27	2	.226
1997 Iowa................	A.A.	C	1	3	0	1	0	0	0	0	0	.333
1997 Daytona............	Fla.St.	C	55	179	17	45	9	1	0	23	4	.251
1997 Orlando.........	Southern	C	37	99	10	17	3	0	1	15	0	.172
1998 West Tenn.......	Southern	C-1B	109	320	33	71	10	1	2	28	1	.222
1999 West Tenn.......	Southern	C	14	35	2	6	3	0	0	5	0	.171
1999 Iowa................	P.C.	C	74	240	24	63	11	1	4	26	0	.262
1999 Chicago.............	N.L.	C	10	19	3	5	1	0	0	1	0	.263
2000 Iowa................	P.C.	C-1B	76	248	22	58	9	0	1	17	1	.234
2001 Salt Lake..........	P.C.	C	61	213	29	64	11	1	5	31	1	.300
2001 Anaheim a-b..........	A.L.	C	15	37	8	10	3	0	2	4	0	.270
2002 Salt Lake.............	P.C.	C	79	290	30	89	14	2	4	43	0	.307
2002 Anaheim.............	A.L.	C	29	70	5	19	3	0	0	5	0	.271
2003 Anaheim.............	A.L.	C	53	114	12	21	4	0	0	6	0	.184
2004 Anaheim.............	A.L.	C-1B	73	203	26	53	10	2	3	25	4	.261
2005 Los Angeles...........	A.L.	C-1B	75	184	14	42	4	0	6	25	2	.228
2006 Los Angeles...........	A.L.	C-1B	78	225	18	54	17	0	4	22	1	.240
2007 Los Angeles-New York c-d	A.L.	C	69	191	18	49	13	0	1	19	2	.257
2008 New York.............	A.L.	C-1B	100	268	32	58	17	0	3	18	0	.216
2009 Scranton-WB...........	Int.	C	2	4	0	1	1	0	0	1	0	.250
2009 Trenton............	Eastern	C	3	7	0	0	0	0	0	0	0	.000
2009 New York e...........	A.L.	C-1B-3B	52	138	15	30	4	0	1	11	0	.217
2010 Toronto f.............	A.L.	C	57	167	13	41	4	0	6	12	1	.246
2011 Toronto g.............	A.L.	C	55	171	19	48	12	1	3	15	2	.281
2012 Tampa Bay.............	A.L.	C	102	251	27	56	9	0	8	32	3	.223
Major League Totals		13 Yrs.	768	2038	210	486	101	3	37	195	15	.238
Division Series												
2004 Anaheim.............	A.L.	C	2	3	2	1	0	0	0	0	0	.333
2005 Los Angeles...........	A.L.	C	1	1	1	1	0	0	0	1	0	1.000
2009 New York.............	A.L.	C	1	1	0	0	0	0	0	0	0	.000
Division Series Totals			4	5	3	2	0	0	0	1	0	.400
Championship Series												
2002 Anaheim.............	A.L.	C	3	1	0	0	0	0	0	0	0	.000
2005 Los Angeles...........	A.L.	C	1	3	0	1	0	0	0	0	0	.333
2009 New York.............	A.L.	C	2	3	0	1	0	0	0	0	0	.333
Championship Series Totals			6	7	0	2	0	0	0	0	0	.286
World Series Record												
2002 Anaheim.............	A.L.	C	3	0	0	0	0	0	0	0	0	.000
2009 New York.............	A.L.	C	2	2	0	0	0	0	0	0	0	.000
World Series Totals			5	2	0	0	0	0	0	0	0	.000

a Released by Chicago Cubs November 27, 2000. Signed with Anaheim Angels organization, January 15, 2001.
b On disabled list from May 21 to July 2, 2001.
c Traded to New York Yankees for pitcher Jeff Kennard, July 21, 2007.
d Filed for free agency, October 30, 2007, re-signed with New York Yankees, December 3, 2007.
e On disabled list from May 8 to July 8, 2009.
f Filed for free agency, November 9, 2009. Signed with Toronto Blue Jays, February 19, 2010.
g Filed for free agency, October 30, 2011. Signed with Tampa Bay Rays, November 28, 2011.

MOLINA, YADIER BENJAMIN

Born, Bayamon, Puerto Rico, July 13, 1982.
Bats Right. Throws Right. Height, 5 feet, 11 inches. Weight, 225 pounds.

Year	Club	Lea	Pos	G	AB	R	H	2B	3B	HR	RBI	SB	Avg
2001 Johnson City	Appal.	C	44	158	18	41	11	0	4	18	1	.259
2002 Peoria............	Midwest	C	112	393	39	110	20	0	7	50	2	.280
2003 Tennessee	Southern	C	104	364	32	100	13	1	2	51	0	.275
2004 Memphis	P.C.	C	37	129	19	39	6	0	1	14	0	.302
2004 St. Louis	N.L.	C	51	135	12	36	6	0	2	15	0	.267
2005 St. Louis a	N.L.	C-1B	114	385	36	97	15	1	8	49	2	.252
2006 St. Louis	N.L.	C-1B	129	417	29	90	26	0	6	49	1	.216
2007 St. Louis b	N.L.	C-1B	111	353	30	97	15	0	6	40	1	.275
2008 St. Louis	N.L.	C-1B	124	444	37	135	18	0	7	56	0	.304
2009 St. Louis	N.L.	C-1B	140	481	45	141	23	1	6	54	9	.293
2010 St. Louis	N.L.	C-1B	136	465	34	122	19	0	6	62	8	.262
2011 St. Louis	N.L.	C-1B	139	475	55	145	32	1	14	65	4	.305
2012 St. Louis	N.L.	C-1B	138	505	65	159	28	0	22	76	12	.315
Major League Totals		9 Yrs.	1082	3660	343	1022	182	3	77	466	37	.279

Year	Club	Lea	Pos	G	AB	R	H	2B	3B	HR	RBI	SB	Avg
Wild Card Playoff													
2012 St. Louis............	N.L.		C	1	4	0	0	0	0	0	0	1	0	.000
Division Series													
2005 St. Louis............	N.L.		C	3	13	1	3	0	0	0	3	0	.231
2006 St. Louis............	N.L.		C	4	13	0	4	1	0	0	1	0	.308
2009 St. Louis............	N.L.		C	3	13	0	4	1	0	0	0	0	.308
2011 St. Louis............	N.L.		C	5	19	1	4	0	0	0	1	1	.211
2012 St. Louis............	N.L.		C	5	17	3	2	0	0	0	1	0	.118
Division Series Totals				20	75	5	17	2	0	0	6	1	.227
Championship Series													
2004 St. Louis............	N.L.		C	1	4	0	1	0	0	0	0	0	.250
2005 St. Louis............	N.L.		C	6	22	1	7	3	0	0	0	0	.318
2006 St. Louis............	N.L.		C	7	23	2	8	1	0	2	6	0	.348
2011 St. Louis............	N.L.		C-1B	6	24	5	8	3	0	0	2	0	.333
2012 St. Louis............	N.L.		C	7	28	2	11	1	0	0	2	0	.393
Championship Series Totals				27	101	10	35	8	0	2	10	0	.347
World Series Record													
2004 St. Louis............	N.L.		C	3	3	0	0	0	0	0	0	0	.000
2006 St. Louis............	N.L.		C	5	17	3	7	2	0	0	1	0	.412
2011 St. Louis............	N.L.		C	7	24	1	8	2	0	0	9	0	.333
World Series Totals............				15	44	4	15	4	0	0	10	0	.341

a On disabled list from July 9 to August 18, 2005.
b On disabled list from May 30 to June 28, 2007.

MONTERO (LOPEZ), JESUS ALEJANDRO

Born, Guacara, Venezuela, November 28, 1989.
Bats Right. Throws Right. Height, 6 feet, 3 inches. Weight, 235 pounds.

Year	Club	Lea	Pos	G	AB	R	H	2B	3B	HR	RBI	SB	Avg
2007 Yankees	Gulf Coast	C	33	107	13	30	6	0	3	19	0	.280
2008 Charleston	So.Atl.	C	132	525	86	171	34	1	17	87	2	.326
2009 Tampa	Fla.St.	C	48	180	26	64	15	1	8	37	0	.356
2009 Trenton.............	Eastern	C	44	167	19	53	10	0	9	33	0	.317
2010 Scranton-WB	Int.	C	123	453	66	131	34	3	21	75	0	.289
2011 Scranton-WB	Int.	C	109	420	52	121	19	1	18	67	0	.288
2011 New York a...........	A.L.	DH-C	18	61	9	20	4	0	4	12	0	.328
2012 Seattle	A.L.	DH-C	135	515	46	134	20	0	15	62	0	.260
Major League Totals		2 Yrs.	153	576	55	154	24	0	19	74	0	.267
Division Series												
2011 New York	A.L.	PH	1	2	1	2	0	0	0	1	0	1.000

a Traded to Seattle Mariners with pitcher Hector Noesi for pitcher Michael Pineda and pitcher Jose Campos, January 22, 2012.

MONTERO, MIGUEL ANGEL

Born, Caracas, Venezuela, July 9, 1983.
Bats Left. Throws Right. Height, 5 feet, 11 inches. Weight, 195 pounds.

Year	Club	Lea	Pos	G	AB	R	H	2B	3B	HR	RBI	SB	Avg
2002 Missoula ....Pioneer		C-3B-1B	50	152	21	40	10	1	3	14	2	.263
2003 Missoula ....Pioneer		C	59	196	24	59	10	2	4	32	2	.301
2004 South Bend ....Midwest		C-1B-SS	115	403	47	106	22	2	11	59	8	.263
2005 Lancaster ....Calif.		C-1B	85	355	73	124	24	1	24	82	1	.349
2005 Tennessee .... Southern		C-1B	30	108	13	27	1	2	2	13	1	.250
2006 Tennessee .... Southern		C	81	289	24	78	18	0	10	46	0	.270
2006 Tucson..............P.C.		C	36	134	21	43	5	0	7	29	1	.321
2006 Arizona.............	N.L.	C	6	16	0	4	1	0	0	3	0	.250
2007 Arizona.............	N.L.	C	84	214	30	48	7	0	10	37	0	.224
2008 Tucson .............P.C.		C	11	32	3	9	2	0	1	5	0	.281
2008 Arizona a	N.L.	C	70	184	24	47	16	1	5	18	0	.255
2009 Arizona.............	N.L.	C	128	425	61	125	30	0	16	59	1	.294
2010 Reno ...............P.C.		C	4	15	1	5	0	0	0	2	0	.333
2010 Arizona b	N.L.	C	85	297	36	79	20	2	9	43	0	.266
2011 Arizona.............	N.L.	C	140	493	65	139	36	1	18	86	1	.282
2012 Arizona.............	N.L.	C	141	486	65	139	25	2	15	88	0	.286
Major League Totals		7 Yrs.	654	2115	281	581	135	6	73	334	2	.275
Division Series												
2007 Arizona.............	N.L.	C	1	2	1	0	0	0	0	0	0	.000
2011 Arizona.............	N.L.	C	5	20	3	6	2	0	0	2	0	.300
Division Series Totals				6	22	4	6	2	0	0	2	0	.273

Year	Club	Lea	Pos	G	AB	R	H	2B	3B	HR	RBI	SB	Avg
Championship Series													
2007 Arizona.............	N.L.	C	3	5	0	2	0	0	0	0	0	.400

a On disabled list from March 23 to April 23, 2008.
b On disabled list from April 11 to June 12, 2010.

MOORE, SCOTT ALAN
Born, Long Beach, California, November 17, 1983.
Bats Left. Throws Right. Height, 6 feet, 2 inches. Weight, 195 pounds.

Year	Club	Lea	Pos	G	AB	R	H	2B	3B	HR	RBI	SB	Avg
2002 Tigers......Gulf Coast		SS	40	133	18	39	6	2	4	25	1	.293
2003 West Michigan . Midwest		3B	107	372	40	89	16	6	6	45	2	.239
2004 Lakeland........ Fla.St.		3B	118	391	52	87	13	4	14	56	2	.223
2005 Daytona a....... Fla.St.		3B	128	466	77	131	31	2	20	82	22	.281
2006 Iowa.............P.C.		SS	1	4	1	1	1	0	0	0	0	.250
2006 West Tenn ....Southern		3B-1B-SS-OF	132	463	52	128	28	0	22	75	12	.276
2006 Chicago..........N.L.		1B-3B	16	38	6	10	2	0	2	5	0	.263
2007 Chicago..........N.L.		1B	2	5	0	0	0	0	0	0	0	.000
2007 Iowa.............P.C.		3B-OF-1B-SS	103	321	61	85	19	4	19	69	4	.265
2007 Baltimore b ......A.L.		3B-1B-OF	17	47	2	12	2	0	1	11	0	.255
2008 Baltimore........A.L.		2B-3B	4	8	1	1	0	0	1	1	0	.125
2008 Norfolk...........Int.		3B-1B-2B-SS	78	287	41	71	21	2	7	44	3	.247
2009 Norfolk...........Int.		3B-1B	32	123	19	31	7	0	7	21	1	.252
2010 Baltimore........A.L.		2B-1B-3B	41	86	8	18	2	0	3	10	3	.209
2010 Norfolk c ....Int.		3B-2B-SS	61	225	34	63	9	1	11	45	2	.280
2011 Iowa d ..........P.C.		3B-1B-2B-OF	123	363	60	107	19	4	9	53	3	.295
2012 Oklahoma........P.C.		3B-OF-1B-2B	73	245	47	78	26	1	10	54	3	.318
2012 Houston e .......N.L.		3B-1B-OF-2B	72	201	23	52	11	0	9	26	0	.259
Major League Totals	5 Yrs.		152	385	40	93	17	0	16	53	3	.242

a Traded by Detroit Tigers to Chicago Cubs with pitcher Roberto Novoa and outfielder Clarence Flowers for pitcher Kyle Farnsworth, February 9, 2005.
b Traded to Baltimore Orioles with pitcher Rocky Cherry for pitcher Steve Trachsel, August 31, 2007.
c Filed for free agency, October 4, 2010. Signed wih Chicago Cubs organization, November 16, 2010.
d Filed for free agency, November 2, 2011. Signed with Houston Astros organization, November 15, 2011.
e Filed for free agency, November 21, 2012. Signed with Oakland Athletics organization, November 29, 2012.

MOORE, TYLER MICHAEL
Born, Brandon, Mississippi, January 30, 1987.
Bats Right. Throws Right. Height, 6 feet, 2 inches. Weight, 215 pounds.

Year	Club	Lea	Pos	G	AB	R	H	2B	3B	HR	RBI	SB	Avg
2008 Vermont........ N.Y.-Penn.		1B	71	265	17	53	10	0	6	28	1	.200
2009 Hagerstown .... So.Atl.		1B	111	421	38	125	30	3	9	87	2	.297
2010 Potomac......... Carolina		1B	129	502	78	135	43	3	31	111	0	.269
2011 Harrisburg .... Eastern		1B	137	519	70	140	35	4	31	90	2	.270
2012 Syracuse ....Int.		1B-OF	29	101	15	31	6	1	9	26	1	.307
2012 Washington .... N.L.		OF-1B	75	156	20	41	9	0	10	29	3	.263
Division Series													
2012 Washington .... N.L.		PH	1	1	0	1	0	0	0	2	0	1.000

MORALES, KENDRYS
Born, Fomento, Cuba, June 20, 1983.
Bats Both. Throws Right. Height, 6 feet, 1 inch. Weight, 225 pounds.

Year	Club	Lea	Pos	G	AB	R	H	2B	3B	HR	RBI	SB	Avg
2005 Rancho Cucamonga Calif.		1B-3B-OF	22	90	18	31	3	0	5	17	0	.344
2005 Arkansas .... Texas		1B-OF	74	281	47	86	12	0	17	54	2	.306
2006 Salt Lake .... P.C.		1B	66	256	41	82	13	1	12	52	0	.320
2006 Los Angeles .... A.L.		1B	57	197	21	46	10	1	5	22	1	.234
2007 Salt Lake .... P.C.		1B	74	255	42	87	20	1	5	37	0	.341
2007 Los Angeles .... A.L.		1B-OF	43	119	12	35	10	0	4	15	0	.294
2008 Angels .... Arizona		OF	5	21	4	11	3	0	1	10	0	.524
2008 Salt Lake .... P.C.		1B-OF	78	317	46	108	19	0	15	64	1	.341
2008 Los Angeles .... A.L.		OF-1B	27	61	7	13	2	0	3	8	0	.213
2009 Los Angeles .... A.L.		1B	152	566	86	173	43	2	34	108	3	.306
2010 Los Angeles a......A.L.		1B	51	193	29	56	5	0	11	39	0	.290
2011 Los Angeles b ...... A.L.		INJURED—Did Not Play										
2012 Los Angeles c....... A.L.		DH-1B	134	484	61	132	26	1	22	73	0	.273
Major League Totals	6 Yrs.		464	1620	216	455	96	4	79	265	4	.281

Year	Club	Lea	Pos	G	AB	R	H	2B	3B	HR	RBI	SB	Avg
	Division Series												
2007 Los Angeles	....	A.L.	1B-DH	3	9	1	1	0	0	0	0	0	.111
2008 Los Angeles	....	A.L.	PH	4	4	0	2	1	0	0	0	0	.500
2009 Los Angeles	....	A.L.	1B	3	10	1	2	0	0	1	3	0	.200
Division Series Totals	....			10	23	2	5	1	0	1	3	0	.217
	Championship Series												
2009 Los Angeles	....	A.L.	1B	6	24	1	4	0	0	1	4	0	.167

a On disabled list from May 30 to November 2, 2010.
b On disabled list from March 22 to October 30, 2011.
c Traded to Seattle Mariners for pitcher Jason Vargas, December 19, 2012.

MORELAND, MITCHELL AUSTIN (MITCH)

Born, Amory, Mississippi, September 6, 1985.
Bats Left. Throws Left. Height, 6 feet, 2 inches. Weight, 230 pounds.

Year	Club	Lea	Pos	G	AB	R	H	2B	3B	HR	RBI	SB	Avg
2007 Spokane	....	Northwest	1B-OF	27	108	10	28	7	1	2	15	1	.259
2008 Clinton	....	Midwest	1B-OF	123	466	64	151	37	4	18	99	2	.324
2009 Bakersfield	....	Calif.	1B-OF	43	170	34	58	19	0	8	26	1	.341
2009 Frisco	....	Texas	OF-1B	73	301	51	98	19	3	8	59	1	.326
2010 Oklahoma	....	P.C.	OF-1B	95	353	52	102	29	2	12	65	2	.289
2010 Texas	....	A.L.	1B-OF	47	145	20	37	4	0	9	25	3	.255
2011 Texas	....	A.L.	1B-OF	134	464	60	120	22	1	16	51	2	.259
2012 Frisco	....	Texas	1B	3	13	4	4	2	0	0	1	0	.308
2012 Round Rock	....	P.C.	1B	2	6	0	1	0	0	0	0	0	.167
2012 Texas a	....	A.L.	1B-OF	114	327	41	90	18	0	15	50	1	.275
Major League Totals	....	3 Yrs.		295	936	121	247	44	1	40	126	6	.264
	Wild Card Playoff												
2012 Texas	....	A.L.	PH	1	1	0	0	0	0	0	0	0	.000
	Division Series												
2010 Texas	....	A.L.	1B	4	15	1	3	3	0	0	1	0	.200
2011 Texas	....	A.L.	1B	3	10	1	1	0	0	1	2	0	.100
Division Series Totals	....			7	25	2	4	3	0	1	3	0	.160
	Championship Series												
2010 Texas	....	A.L.	1B	6	18	3	7	0	0	0	3	0	.389
2011 Texas	....	A.L.	1B	3	9	0	1	0	0	0	0	0	.111
Championship Series Totals	......			9	27	3	8	0	0	0	3	0	.296
	World Series Record												
2010 Texas	....	A.L.	1B	5	13	1	6	1	0	1	3	0	.462
2011 Texas	....	A.L.	1B	3	10	1	1	0	0	1	1	0	.100
World Series Totals	....			8	23	2	7	1	0	2	4	0	.304

a On disabled list from June 20 to July 30, 2012.

MORGAN, NYJER JAMID

Born, San Francisco, California, July 2, 1980.
Bats Left. Throws Left. Height, 6 feet. Weight, 170 pounds.

Year	Club	Lea	Pos	G	AB	R	H	2B	3B	HR	RBI	SB	Avg
2003 Williamsport	.....	N.Y.-Penn.	OF	72	268	49	92	7	4	0	23	26	.343
2004 Hickory	....	So.Atl.	OF	134	514	83	131	16	7	4	41	55	.255
2005 Lynchburg	....	Carolina	OF	60	252	36	72	12	3	0	24	24	.286
2006 Lynchburg	....	Carolina	OF	61	228	43	69	7	3	0	22	38	.303
2006 Altoona	....	Eastern	OF	56	219	39	67	6	5	1	10	21	.306
2007 Pirates	....	Gulf Coast	OF	4	13	3	4	0	0	1	1	0	.308
2007 Indianapolis	....	Int.	OF	44	164	30	50	4	2	0	10	26	.305
2007 Pittsburgh a	....	N.L.	OF	28	107	15	32	3	4	1	7	7	.299
2008 Indianapolis	....	Int.	OF	82	322	54	96	13	4	1	33	44	.298
2008 Pittsburgh	....	N.L.	OF	58	160	26	47	13	0	0	7	9	.294
2009 Pittsburgh-Washington b-c		N.L.	OF	120	469	74	144	15	7	3	39	42	.307
2010 Hagerstown	....	So.Atl.	OF	1	3	0	0	0	0	0	0	0	.000
2010 Potomac	....	Carolina	DH	1	3	0	0	0	0	0	0	0	.000
2010 Washington d	....	N.L.	OF	136	509	60	129	17	7	0	24	34	.253
2011 Nashville	....	P.C.	OF	2	4	1	2	0	0	0	0	1	.500
2011 Milwaukee e-f	....	N.L.	OF	119	316	61	115	20	6	4	37	13	.304
2012 Milwaukee g	....	N.L.	OF	122	289	44	69	5	3	3	16	12	.239
Major League Totals	....	6 Yrs.		583	1912	280	536	73	27	11	130	117	.280
	Division Series												
2011 Milwaukee	....	N.L.	OF	4	16	1	3	1	0	0	3	0	.188

Year	Club	Lea	Pos	G	AB	R	H	2B	3B	HR	RBI	SB	Avg
Championship Series													
2011 Milwaukee ..........N.L.			OF	6	12	1	2	1	0	0	0	0	.167

a On minor league disabled list from May 14 through August 23, 2007.
b Traded to Washington Nationals with pitcher Sean Burnett for outfielder Lastings Milledge and pitcher Joel Hanrahan, June 30, 2009.
c On disabled list from August 28 to October 13, 2009.
d On disabled list from August 4 to August 19, 2010.
e Traded to Milwaukee Brewers for infielder Cutter Dykstra, March 27, 2011.
f On disabled list from April 18 to May 3 and May 6 to May 27, 2011.
g Filed for free agency, November 1, 2012.

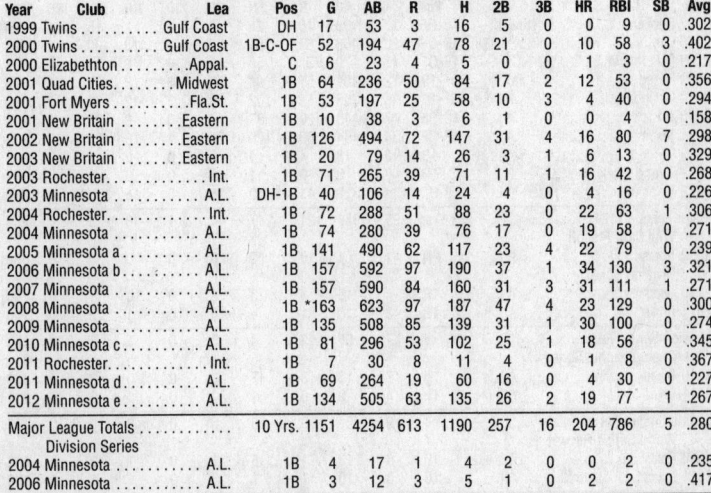

MORNEAU, JUSTIN ERNEST GEORGE
Born, New Westminster, British Columbia, Canada, May 15, 1981.
Bats Left. Throws Right. Height, 6 feet, 4 inches. Weight, 225 pounds.

Year	Club	Lea	Pos	G	AB	R	H	2B	3B	HR	RBI	SB	Avg
1999 Twins	Gulf Coast		DH	17	53	3	16	5	0	0	9	0	.302
2000 Twins	Gulf Coast		1B-C-OF	52	194	47	78	21	0	10	58	3	.402
2000 Elizabethton	.Appal.		C	6	23	4	5	0	0	1	3	0	.217
2001 Quad Cities.......	Midwest		1B	64	236	50	84	17	2	12	53	0	.356
2001 Fort Myers	.Fla.St.		1B	53	197	25	58	10	3	4	40	0	.294
2001 New Britain	Eastern		1B	10	38	3	6	1	0	0	4	0	.158
2002 New Britain	Eastern		1B	126	494	72	147	31	4	16	80	7	.298
2003 New Britain	Eastern		1B	20	79	14	26	3	1	6	13	0	.329
2003 Rochester...........	Int.		1B	71	265	39	71	11	1	16	42	0	.268
2003 Minnesota	A.L.		DH-1B	40	106	14	24	4	0	4	16	0	.226
2004 Rochester...........	Int.		1B	72	288	51	88	23	0	22	63	1	.306
2004 Minnesota	A.L.		1B	74	280	39	76	17	0	19	58	0	.271
2005 Minnesota a	A.L.		1B	141	490	62	117	23	4	22	79	0	.239
2006 Minnesota b	A.L.		1B	157	592	97	190	37	1	34	130	3	.321
2007 Minnesota	A.L.		1B	157	590	84	160	31	3	31	111	0	.271
2008 Minnesota	A.L.		1B	*163	623	97	187	47	4	23	129	0	.300
2009 Minnesota	A.L.		1B	135	508	85	139	31	1	30	100	0	.274
2010 Minnesota c	A.L.		1B	81	296	53	102	25	1	18	56	0	.345
2011 Rochester............	Int.		1B	7	30	8	11	4	0	1	8	0	.367
2011 Minnesota d	A.L.		1B	69	264	19	60	16	0	4	30	0	.227
2012 Minnesota e	A.L.		1B	134	505	63	135	26	2	19	77	1	.267
Major League Totals		10 Yrs.		1151	4254	613	1190	257	16	204	786	5	.280
Division Series													
2004 Minnesota	A.L.		1B	4	17	1	4	2	0	0	2	0	.235
2006 Minnesota	A.L.		1B	3	12	3	5	1	0	2	2	0	.417
Division Series Totals				7	29	4	9	3	0	2	4	0	.310

a On disabled list from April 7 to April 22, 2005.
b Selected Most Valuable Player in American League for 2006.
c On disabled list from July 8 to November 2, 2010.
d On disabled list from June 10 to August 12 and September 12 to October 3, 2011.
e On disabled list from May 1 to May 16, 2012.

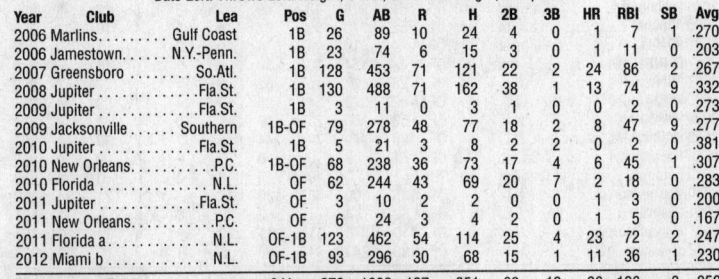

MORRISON, JUSTIS LOGAN (LOGAN)
Born, Kansas City, Missouri, August 25, 1987.
Bats Left. Throws Left. Height, 6 feet, 3 inches. Weight, 235 pounds.

Year	Club	Lea	Pos	G	AB	R	H	2B	3B	HR	RBI	SB	Avg
2006 Marlins.........	Gulf Coast		1B	26	89	10	24	4	0	1	7	0	.270
2006 Jamestown......	N.Y.-Penn.		1B	23	74	6	15	3	0	1	11	0	.203
2007 Greensboro	So.Atl.		1B	128	453	71	121	22	2	24	86	2	.267
2008 Jupiter	.Fla.St.		1B	130	488	71	162	38	1	13	74	9	.332
2009 Jupiter	.Fla.St.		1B	3	11	0	3	1	0	0	2	0	.273
2009 Jacksonville	Southern		1B-OF	79	278	48	77	18	2	8	47	9	.277
2010 Jupiter	.Fla.St.		1B	5	21	3	8	2	2	0	2	0	.381
2010 New Orleans..........	.P.C.		1B-OF	68	238	36	73	17	4	6	45	1	.307
2010 Florida	N.L.		OF	62	244	43	69	20	7	2	18	0	.283
2011 Jupiter	.Fla.St.		OF	3	10	2	2	0	0	1	3	0	.200
2011 New Orleans..........	.P.C.		OF	6	24	3	4	2	0	1	5	0	.167
2011 Florida a	N.L.		OF-1B	123	462	54	114	25	4	23	72	2	.247
2012 Miami b	N.L.		OF-1B	93	296	30	68	15	1	11	36	1	.230
Major League Totals		3 Yrs.		278	1002	127	251	60	12	36	126	3	.250

a On disabled list from April 20 to May 13, 2011.
b On disabled list from July 29 to October 31, 2012.

MORSE, MICHAEL JOHN (MIKE)

Born, Fort Lauderdale, Florida, March 22, 1982.
Bats Right. Throws Right. Height, 6 feet, 4 inches. Weight, 230 pounds.

Year	Club	Lea	Pos	G	AB	R	H	2B	3B	HR	RBI	SB	Avg
2000 White Sox	.....	Arizona	SS	45	180	32	46	6	1	2	24	5	.256
2001 Bristol	....	Appal.	SS	57	181	23	41	7	3	4	27	6	.227
2002 Kannapolis	.....	So.Atl.	SS-3B	113	417	43	107	30	4	2	56	7	.257
2003 Winston-Salem		Carolina	SS	122	432	45	106	30	2	10	55	4	.245
2004 Birmingham	..	.Southern	SS	54	209	30	60	9	5	11	38	0	.287
2004 San Antonio a.	....	Texas	SS	41	157	18	43	10	1	6	33	0	.274
2005 Tacoma	....	P.C.	SS	49	182	20	46	12	2	4	23	1	.253
2005 Seattle	....	A.L.	SS-OF	72	230	27	64	10	1	3	23	3	.278
2006 Tacoma	.....	P.C.	1B-3B-SS-OF	57	206	23	51	15	1	5	34	0	.248
2006 Seattle	....	A.L.	OF-3B-1B-SS	21	43	5	16	5	0	0	11	1	.372
2007 Mariners.	......	Arizona	3B-SS	5	15	2	3	1	0	0	2	0	.200
2007 Tacoma	.....	P.C.	3B-SS-OF	76	291	48	90	26	0	6	39	5	.309
2007 Seattle	....	A.L.	1B-3B-SS-OF	9	18	1	8	2	0	0	3	0	.444
2008 Seattle b	....	A.L.	OF	5	9	0	2	1	0	0	0	0	.222
2009 Tacoma	.....	P.C.	SS-2B-3B-OF	66	260	38	81	14	0	10	52	0	.312
2009 Syracuse	....	Int.	1B-3B-OF-SS	44	165	21	56	12	3	6	34	2	.339
2009 Washington c	.....	.N.L.	1B-OF-3B	32	52	4	13	3	0	3	10	0	.250
2010 Syracuse	.....	Int.	1B-OF-3B	15	51	12	13	2	0	3	8	0	.255
2010 Washington d.	..	...N.L.	OF-1B	98	266	36	77	12	2	15	41	0	.289
2011 Washington	.....	.N.L.	1B-OF	146	522	73	158	36	0	31	95	2	.303
2012 Hagerstown	.....	So.Atl.	OF	1	4	1	2	0	0	0	0	0	.500
2012 Potomac.	......	Carolina	OF	3	9	0	3	1	0	0	1	0	.333
2012 Harrisburg	.....	Eastern	OF	3	8	1	3	2	0	1	4	0	.375
2012 Washington e.	..	...N.L.	OF-1B	102	406	53	118	17	1	18	62	0	.291
Major League Totals	....		8 Yrs.	485	1546	199	456	86	4	70	245	6	.295
Division Series													
2012 Washington	....	.N.L.	OF	5	19	2	5	0	0	1	2	0	.263

a Traded by Chicago White Sox to Seattle Mariners with catcher Miguel Olivo and outfielder Jeremy Reed for pitcher Freddy Garcia, catcher Ben Davis and cash, June 27, 2004.
b On disabled list from April 14 to September 29, 2008.
c Traded to Washington Nationals for outfielder Ryan Langerhans, June 28, 2009.
d On disabled list from April 11 to May 16, 2010.
e On disabled list from March 26 to June 1, 2012.

MOSS, BRANDON DOUGLAS

Born, Monroe, Georgia, September 16, 1983.
Bats Left. Throws Right. Height, 6 feet. Weight, 210 pounds.

Year	Club	Lea	Pos	G	AB	R	H	2B	3B	HR	RBI	SB	Avg
2002 Red Sox	....	Gulf Coast	2B-3B	42	113	10	23	6	2	0	6	1	.204
2003 Lowell	....	N.Y.-Penn.	OF	65	228	29	54	15	4	7	34	7	.237
2004 Sarasota.	....	.Fla.St.	OF	23	83	16	35	2	1	2	10	2	.422
2004 Augusta	....	So.Atl.	OF	109	433	66	147	25	6	13	104	19	.339
2005 Portland	....	Eastern	OF	135	503	87	135	31	4	16	61	6	.268
2006 Portland	....	Eastern	OF	133	508	76	145	36	3	12	83	8	.285
2007 Pawtucket	....	Int.	OF-1B	133	493	66	139	41	2	16	78	3	.282
2007 Boston	....	A.L.	OF	15	25	6	7	2	1	0	1	0	.280
2008 Boston	....	A.L.	OF-1B	34	78	7	23	5	1	2	11	1	.295
2008 Pawtucket	....	Int.	1B-OF	43	163	29	46	8	4	8	30	2	.282
2008 Pittsburgh a-b	....	N.L.	OF	45	158	12	35	10	2	6	23	0	.222
2009 Pittsburgh	....	N.L.	OF	133	385	47	91	20	4	7	41	1	.236
2010 Indianapolis	....	Int.	OF	136	500	73	133	32	2	22	96	12	.266
2010 Pittsburgh c	....	N.L.	OF	17	26	2	4	1	0	0	2	0	.154
2011 Lehigh Valley	....	Int.	OF	124	436	66	120	31	1	23	80	4	.275
2011 Philadelphia d	....	N.L.	OF	5	6	0	0	0	0	0	0	0	.000
2012 Sacramento	....	.P.C.	OF-1B	51	196	32	56	11	1	15	33	4	.286
2012 Oakland	....	A.L.	1B-OF	84	265	48	77	18	0	21	52	1	.291
Major League Totals	....		6 Yrs.	333	943	122	237	56	8	36	130	3	.251
Division Series													
2012 Oakland	....	A.L.	1B	5	15	0	2	0	0	0	0	0	.133

a On disabled list from May 3 to May 23, 2008.
b Traded to Pittsburgh Pirates with outfielder Manny Ramirez and pitcher Craig Hansen for outfielder Jason Bay, July 31, 2008.
c Filed for free agency, November 6, 2010. Signed with Philadelphia Phillies organization, November 19, 2010.
d Filed for free agency, October 18, 2011. Signed with Oakland Athletics organization, November 19, 2011.

MOUSTAKAS, MICHAEL CHRISTOPHER (MIKE)
Born, Los Angeles, California, September 11, 1988.
Bats Left. Throws Right. Height, 5 feet, 11 inches. Weight, 230 pounds.

Year	Club	Lea	Pos	G	AB	R	H	2B	3B	HR	RBI	SB	Avg
2007 Idaho Falls	Pioneer		SS	11	41	6	12	4	1	0	10	0	.293
2008 Burlington	Midwest		3B-SS	126	496	77	135	25	3	22	71	8	.272
2009 Wilmington	Carolina		3B	129	492	66	123	32	2	16	86	10	.250
2010 Omaha	P.C.		3B	52	225	36	66	16	0	15	48	2	.293
2010 NW Arkansas	Texas		3B	66	259	58	90	25	0	21	76	0	.347
2011 Omaha	P.C.		3B	55	223	38	64	15	1	10	44	1	.287
2011 Kansas City	A.L.		3B	89	338	26	89	18	1	5	30	2	.263
2012 Kansas City	A.L.		3B	149	563	69	136	34	1	20	73	5	.242
Major League Totals		2 Yrs.		238	901	95	225	52	2	25	103	7	.250

MURPHY, DANIEL THOMAS
Born, Jacksonville, Florida, April 1, 1985.
Bats Left. Throws Right. Height, 6 feet, 3 inches. Weight, 205 pounds.

Year	Club	Lea	Pos	G	AB	R	H	2B	3B	HR	RBI	SB	Avg
2006 Mets	Gulf Coast		DH	8	18	2	1	0	0	0	0	0	.056
2006 Kingsport	Appal.		DH	9	33	2	9	0	0	2	7	0	.273
2006 Brooklyn	N.Y.-Penn.		DH	8	29	2	7	1	0	0	3	0	.241
2007 St. Lucie	Fla.St.		3B	135	502	68	143	34	3	11	78	6	.285
2008 Brooklyn	N.Y.-Penn.		DH	3	14	1	7	0	0	0	2	0	.500
2008 Binghamton	Eastern		3B-2B-1B-OF	95	357	56	110	26	1	13	67	14	.308
2008 New Orleans	P.C.		3B	1	4	2	1	0	0	0	0	0	.250
2008 New York	N.L.		OF	49	131	24	41	9	3	2	17	0	.313
2009 New York	N.L.		1B-OF	155	508	60	135	38	4	12	63	4	.266
2010 St. Lucie	Fla.St.		1B	3	11	2	8	1	0	1	6	0	.727
2010 Buffalo a	Int.		1B-2B	8	34	4	10	3	0	1	8	1	.294
2011 New York b	N.L.		1B-3B-2B-OF	109	391	49	125	28	2	6	49	5	.320
2012 New York	N.L.		2B-1B	156	571	62	166	40	3	6	65	10	.291
Major League Totals		4 Yrs.		469	1601	195	467	115	12	26	194	19	.292

a On disabled list from March 31 to May 24, 2010.
b On disabled list from August 8 to October 24, 2011.

MURPHY, DAVID MATTHEW
Born, Houston, Texas, October 18, 1981.
Bats Left. Throws Left. Height, 6 feet, 4 inches. Weight, 205 pounds.

Year	Club	Lea	Pos	G	AB	R	H	2B	3B	HR	RBI	SB	Avg
2003 Sarasota	Fla.St.		OF	45	153	18	37	5	1	1	18	6	.242
2003 Lowell	N.Y.-Penn.		OF	21	78	13	27	4	0	0	13	4	.346
2004 Sarasota	Fla.St.		OF	73	272	35	71	11	0	4	38	3	.261
2004 Red Sox	Gulf Coast		OF	5	18	3	5	1	0	0	1	1	.278
2005 Portland	Eastern		OF	135	484	71	133	25	4	14	75	13	.275
2006 Portland	Eastern		OF	42	172	22	47	17	1	3	25	4	.273
2006 Pawtucket	Int.		OF	84	318	45	85	23	5	8	44	3	.267
2006 Boston	A.L.		OF	20	22	4	5	1	0	1	2	0	.227
2007 Oklahoma	P.C.		OF	2	7	0	2	0	0	0	0	0	.286
2007 Pawtucket	Int.		OF	100	400	50	112	20	5	9	47	8	.280
2007 Boston-Texas a	A.L.		OF	46	105	17	36	12	2	2	14	0	.343
2008 Texas b	A.L.		OF	108	415	64	114	28	3	15	74	7	.275
2009 Texas	A.L.		OF	128	432	61	116	24	1	17	57	9	.269
2010 Texas	A.L.		OF	138	419	54	122	26	2	12	65	14	.291
2011 Texas	A.L.		OF	120	404	46	111	14	2	11	46	11	.275
2012 Texas	A.L.		OF	147	457	65	139	29	3	15	61	10	.304
Major League Totals		7 Yrs.		707	2254	311	643	134	13	73	319	51	.285
Wild Card Playoff													
2012 Texas	A.L.		OF	1	2	0	0	0	0	0	0	0	.000
Division Series													
2010 Texas	A.L.		OF	2	7	0	1	0	0	0	0	0	.143
2011 Texas	A.L.		OF	3	6	0	2	0	0	0	0	0	.333
Division Series Totals				5	13	0	3	0	0	0	0	0	.231
Championship Series													
2010 Texas	A.L.		OF	6	13	6	3	1	0	1	2	0	.231
2011 Texas	A.L.		OF-DH	5	17	4	7	2	1	0	3	1	.412
Championship Series Totals				11	30	10	10	3	1	1	5	1	.333

Year	Club	Lea	Pos	G	AB	R	H	2B	3B	HR	RBI	SB	Avg
	World Series Record												
2010 Texas		A.L.	OF	3	7	0	1	0	0	0	1	0	.143
2011 Texas		A.L.	OF	7	18	1	4	1	0	0	0	0	.222
World Series Totals				10	25	1	5	1	0	0	1	0	.200

a Traded to Texas Rangers with pitcher Kason Gabbard and outfielder Engle Beltre for pitcher Eric Gagne, July 31, 2007.

b On disabled list from August 7 to October 2, 2008.

MYERS, WILLIAM BRADFORD (WIL)
Born, High Point, North Carolina, December 10, 1990.
Bats Right. Throws Right. Height, 6 feet, 1 inches. Weight, 205 pounds.

Year	Club	Lea	Pos	G	AB	R	H	2B	3B	HR	RBI	SB	Avg
2009 Burlington	Appal.		C	4	16	1	2	0	1	1	4	0	.125
2009 Idaho Falls	Pioneer		C	18	68	18	29	7	1	4	14	2	.426
2010 Burlington	Midwest		C	68	242	42	70	19	1	10	45	10	.289
2010 Wilmington	Carolina		C	58	205	28	71	18	2	4	38	2	.346
2011 NW Arkansas	Texas		OF	99	354	50	90	23	1	8	49	9	.254
2012 NW Arkansas	Texas		OF-3B	35	134	32	46	11	1	13	30	4	.343
2012 Omaha a.	Pacific		OF-3B	99	388	66	118	15	5	24	79	2	.304

a Traded by Kansas City Royals to Tampa Bay Rays with pitcher Mike Montgomery, pitcher Jake Odorizzi and infielder Patrick Leonard for pitcher James Shields, pitcher Wade Davis and player to be named later, December 9, 2012.

NAPOLI, MICHAEL ANTHONY (MIKE)
Born, Hollywood, Florida, October 31, 1981.
Bats Right. Throws Right. Height, 6 feet. Weight, 205 pounds.

Year	Club	Lea	Pos	G	AB	R	H	2B	3B	HR	RBI	SB	Avg
2000 Butte	Pioneer		1B-C	10	26	3	6	2	0	0	3	1	.231
2001 Rancho Cucamonga	Calif.		C	7	20	3	4	0	0	1	4	0	.200
2001 Cedar Rapids	Midwest		C-1B	43	155	23	36	10	1	5	18	3	.232
2002 Cedar Rapids	Midwest		C-1B-3B	106	362	57	91	19	1	10	50	6	.251
2003 Rancho Cucamonga	Calif.		C-1B	47	165	28	44	10	1	4	26	5	.267
2004 Rancho Cucamonga	Calif.		C-1B-3B	132	482	94	136	29	4	29	118	9	.282
2005 Arkansas	Texas		C-1B	131	439	96	104	22	2	31	99	12	.237
2006 Salt Lake	P.C.		C-1B	21	78	12	19	6	0	3	10	1	.244
2006 Los Angeles a.	A.L.		C	99	268	47	61	13	0	16	42	2	.228
2007 Los Angeles	A.L.		C	75	219	40	54	11	1	10	34	5	.247
2008 Rancho Cucamonga	Calif.		C	5	14	3	8	3	0	1	4	0	.571
2008 Los Angeles b	A.L.		C	78	227	39	62	9	1	20	49	7	.273
2009 Los Angeles	A.L.		C	114	382	60	104	22	1	20	56	3	.272
2010 Los Angeles	A.L.		1B-C	140	453	60	108	24	1	26	68	4	.238
2011 Round Rock	P.C.		C-1B	4	15	3	4	1	0	3	9	0	.267
2011 Texas c-d-e.	A.L.		C-1B	113	369	72	118	25	0	30	75	4	.320
2012 Texas f	A.L.		C-1B	108	352	53	80	9	2	24	56	1	.227
Major League Totals	7 Yrs.			727	2270	371	587	113	6	146	380	26	.259
	Wild Card Playoff												
2012 Texas		A.L.	C-DH	1	3	0	0	0	0	0	0	0	.000
	Division Series												
2007 Los Angeles		A.L.	C	3	6	0	1	0	0	0	0	0	.167
2008 Los Angeles		A.L.	C	4	12	3	3	0	0	2	4	0	.250
2009 Los Angeles		A.L.	C	2	4	1	1	1	0	0	0	0	.250
2011 Texas		A.L.	C	4	14	3	5	0	0	1	4	1	.357
Division Series Totals				13	36	7	10	1	0	3	8	1	.278
	Championship Series												
2009 Los Angeles		A.L.	C	5	9	0	1	0	0	0	0	0	.111
2011 Texas		A.L.	C-1B-DH	6	24	6	7	0	0	0	1	0	.292
Championship Series Totals				11	33	6	8	0	0	0	1	0	.242
	World Series Record												
2011 Texas		A.L.	C-1B	7	20	2	7	1	0	2	10	0	.350

a On disabled list from July 2 to July 18 and July 28 to September 1, 2007.

b On disabled list from July 6 to August 8, 2008.

c Traded to Toronto Blue Jays with outfielder Juan Rivera for outfielder Vernon Wells, January 21, 2011.

d Traded to Texas Rangers for pitcher Frank Francisco, January 25, 2011.

e On disabled list from June 12 to July 4, 2011.

f On disabled list from August 11 to September 15, 2012.

NAVA, DANIEL JAMES
Born, Redwood City, California, February 22, 1983.
Bats Both. Throws Left. Height, 5 feet, 10 inches. Weight, 200 pounds.

Year Club	Lea	Pos	G	AB	R	H	2B	3B	HR	RBI	SB	Avg
2007 Chico a	Golden	OF	72	256	70	95	23	3	12	59	18	.371
2008 Lancaster b	Calif.	OF	85	323	54	110	27	1	10	59	4	.341
2009 Salem	Carolina	OF	29	109	18	37	12	1	1	13	0	.339
2009 Portland	Eastern	OF	32	118	25	43	10	1	4	23	0	.364
2010 Pawtucket	Int.	OF	77	284	41	82	16	1	10	48	4	.289
2010 Boston	A.L.	OF	60	161	23	39	14	1	1	26	1	.242
2011 Pawtucket	Int.	OF	121	441	69	118	·27	2	10	48	10	.268
2012 Pawtucket	Int.	OF	29	99	20	31	7	1	4	18	1	.313
2012 Boston c	A.L.	OF	88	267	38	65	21	0	6	33	3	.243
Major League Totals		2 Yrs.	148	428	61	104	35	1	7	59	4	.243

a Signed by independent Chico, 2007.
b Signed by Boston Red Sox organization, January 17, 2008.
c On disabled list from July 29 to August 21 and August 25 to September 9, 2012.

NELSON, CHRISTOPHER L. (CHRIS)
Born, Escondido, California, September 3, 1985.
Bats Right. Throws Right. Height, 5 feet, 11 inches. Weight, 175 pounds.

Year Club	Lea	Pos	G	AB	R	H	2B	3B	HR	RBI	SB	Avg
2004 Casper	Pioneer	SS	38	147	36	51	6	3	4	20	6	.347
2005 Asheville	So.Atl.	SS	79	315	51	76	13	3	3	38	7	.241
2006 Asheville	So.Atl.	SS	118	466	69	121	38	1	11	76	14	.260
2007 Modesto	Calif.	SS	133	529	97	153	42	7	19	99	27	.289
2008 Modesto	Calif.	SS	8	30	2	5	1	0	1	5	0	.167
2008 Tulsa	Texas	SS	73	283	38	67	18	2	3	42	6	.237
2009 Tulsa	Texas	SS-2B	29	107	21	30	5	2	4	17	5	.280
2010 Colorado Springs	P.C.	SS-2B-3B-OF	85	319	60	100	15	3	12	55	7	.313
2010 Colorado	N.L.	2B-3B	17	25	7	7	1	0	0	0	1	.280
2011 Colorado Springs	P.C.	SS-2B-3B	73	289	52	95	20	5	11	65	3	.329
2011 Colorado	N.L.	2B-3B-SS	63	180	20	45	10	1	4	16	3	.250
2012 Colorado Springs	P.C.	3B-2B	13	51	12	15	4	1	0	8	1	.294
2012 Colorado a	N.L.	3B-2B-SS	111	345	45	104	21	3	9	53	2	.301
Major League Totals		3 Yrs.	191	550	72	156	32	4	13	69	6	.284

a On disabled list from May 15 to May 31 and July 16 to August 6, 2012.

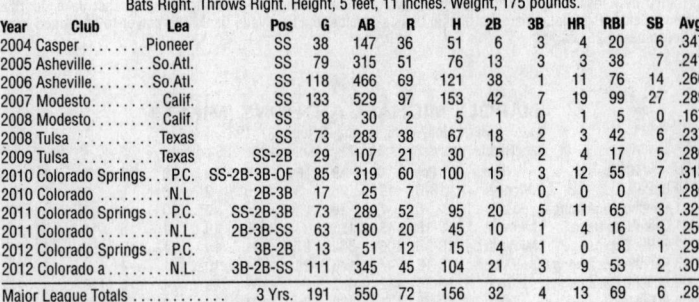

NIEUWENHUIS, KIRK ROBERT
Born, Santa Monica, California, August 7, 1987.
Bats Left. Throws Right. Height, 6 feet, 3 inches. Weight, 215 pounds.

Year Club	Lea	Pos	G	AB	R	H	2B	3B	HR	RBI	SB	Avg
2008 Brooklyn	N.Y.-Penn.	OF	74	285	34	79	15	5	3	29	11	.277
2009 Binghamton	Eastern	OF	8	32	8	13	3	1	1	2	1	.406
2009 St. Lucie	Fla.St.	OF-1B	123	482	91	132	35	5	16	71	16	.274
2010 Binghamton	Eastern	OF	94	394	81	114	35	2	16	60	13	.289
2010 Buffalo	Int.	OF	30	120	10	27	8	1	2	17	0	.225
2011 Buffalo	Int.	OF	53	188	33	56	17	2	6	14	5	.298
2012 Buffalo	Int.	OF	5	11	0	2	1	0	0	1	1	.182
2012 New York	N.L.	OF	91	282	40	71	12	1	7	28	4	.252

NIX, JAYSON TRUITT EDWARD
Born, Dallas, Texas, August 26, 1982.
Bats Right. Throws Right. Height, 5 feet, 11 inches. Weight, 195 pounds.

Year Club	Lea	Pos	G	AB	R	H	2B	3B	HR	RBI	SB	Avg
2001 Casper	Pioneer	SS	42	153	28	45	10	1	5	24	1	.294
2002 Asheville	So.Atl.	2B	132	487	73	120	29	2	14	79	14	.246
2003 Visalia	Calif.	2B	137	562	107	158	46	0	21	86	24	.281
2004 Tulsa	Texas	2B	123	456	58	97	17	1	14	58	14	.213
2005 Tulsa	Texas	2B	131	501	68	118	27	0	11	47	10	.236
2006 Colorado Springs	P.C.	2B-3B	103	358	39	90	14	1	2	26	15	.251
2007 Colorado Springs	P.C.	2B-3B	124	439	80	128	33	2	11	58	24	.292
2008 Colorado	N.L.	2B	22	56	2	7	2	0	0	2	1	.125
2008 Colorado Springs a	P.C.	2B-3B	67	264	63	80	21	2	17	51	11	.303
2009 Birmingham	Southern	SS	3	10	1	3	0	0	0	3	0	.300
2009 Charlotte	Int.	SS-2B	5	20	4	9	1	0	0	5	1	.450

Year Club	Lea	Pos	G	AB	R	H	2B	3B	HR	RBI	SB	Avg
2009 Chicago b . . . . .A.L.		2B-SS-3B-OF	94	255	36	57	11	0	12	32	10	.224
2010 Chicago-Cleveland c	A.L.	3B-2B-OF-SS	102	331	32	74	15	0	14	34	1	.224
2011 Dunedin . . . . .Fla.St.		3B	3	12	0	1	0	0	0	2	0	.083
2011 Toronto . . . . .A.L.		3B-2B-OF	46	136	15	23	5	1	4	16	4	.169
2011 Las Vegas d-e-f . . . .P.C.		3B-SS-OF-2B	41	163	30	44	12	2	8	29	3	.270
2012 Scranton-WB . . . . . . Int.		2B-3B-OF	8	30	5	7	4	0	0	4	0	.233
2012 New York . . . . .A.L.		3B-SS-2B-OF	74	177	24	43	13	0	4	18	6	.243
Major League Totals		5 Yrs.	338	955	109	204	46	1	34	102	22	.214
Division Series												
2012 New York . . . . .A.L.		SS	2	4	0	2	1	0	0	0	0	.500
Championship Series												
2012 New York . . . . .A.L.		SS-3B	4	4	0	0	0	0	0	0	0	.000

a Filed for free agency, October 15, 2008. Signed with Chicago White Sox, October 24, 2008.
b On disabled list from March 27 to May 1, 2009.
c Claimed on waivers by Cleveland Indians, June 25, 2010.
d Sold to Toronto Blue Jays, March 29, 2011.
e On disabled list from April 23 to May 16, 2011.
f Filed for free agency, November 2, 2011. Signed with New York Yankees organization, November 22, 2011.

NIX, LAYNCE MICHAEL
Born, Houston, Texas, October 30, 1980.
Bats Left. Throws Left. Height, 6 feet. Weight, 220 pounds.

Year Club	Lea	Pos	G	AB	R	H	2B	3B	HR	RBI	SB	Avg
2000 Rangers	Gulf Coast	OF	51	199	34	45	7	1	2	25	4	.226
2001 Charlotte . . . . .Fla.St.		OF	9	37	4	11	3	1	0	2	0	.297
2001 Savannah . . . . So.Atl.		OF	104	407	50	113	26	8	8	59	9	.278
2002 Charlotte . . . . .Fla.St.		OF	137	512	86	146	27	3	21	110	17	.285
2003 Frisco. . . . . Texas		OF	87	335	52	95	23	0	15	63	9	.284
2003 Texas . . . . A.L.		OF	53	184	25	47	10	0	8	30	3	.255
2004 Frisco. . . . . Texas		OF	7	26	2	7	1	0	0	2	0	.269
2004 Texas a. . . . . A.L.		OF	115	371	58	92	20	4	14	46	1	.248
2005 Oklahoma. . . . . .P.C.		OF	10	36	8	12	1	1	3	6	0	.333
2005 Texas b. . . . . A.L.		OF	63	229	28	55	12	3	6	32	2	.240
2006 Texas . . . . A.L.		OF	9	32	1	3	1	0	0	4	0	.094
2006 Oklahoma. . . . . .P.C.		OF	77	286	39	77	14	1	10	55	4	.269
2006 Nashville . . . . .P.C.		OF	18	68	16	28	5	1	7	13	0	.412
2006 Milwaukee c-d . . . . N.L.		OF	10	35	2	8	1	0	1	6	0	.229
2007 Huntsville . . . . Southern		OF	4	11	2	4	1	0	1	6	0	.364
2007 Nashville . . . . .P.C.		OF	95	347	60	93	20	1	24	74	5	.268
2007 Milwaukee e. . . . . N.L.		OF	10	12	0	0	0	0	0	0	0	.000
2008 Nashville . . . . .P.C.		OF	103	380	63	108	22	3	23	60	5	.284
2008 Milwaukee f . . . . N.L.		OF	10	12	1	1	0	0	0	0	0	.083
2009 Cincinnati g-h. . . . . . . N.L.		OF	116	309	42	74	26	1	15	46	0	.239
2010 Cincinnati i-j. . . . . N.L.		OF	97	165	16	48	11	2	4	18	0	.291
2011 Washington k. . . . . N.L.		OF-1B	124	324	38	81	15	1	16	44	2	.250
2012 Clearwater . . . . .Fla.St.		1B	6	16	1	4	2	0	1	4	0	.250
2012 Lehigh Valley . . . . Int.		1B-OF	2	8	1	2	0	0	0	0	0	.250
2012 Philadelphia l . . . . N.L.		OF-1B	70	114	13	28	10	0	3	16	0	.246
Major League Totals		10 Yrs.	677	1787	224	437	106	11	67	242	8	.245
Division Series												
2010 Cincinnati. . . . . N.L.		OF	1	3	1	0	0	0	0	0	0	.000

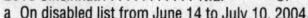

a On disabled list from June 14 to July 10, 2004.
b On disabled list from July 15 to October 12, 2005.
c Traded to Milwaukee Brewers with pitcher Francisco Cordero, outfielder Kevin Mench and pitcher Julian Cordero for outfielder Carlos Lee and outfielder Nelson Cruz, July 28, 2006.
d On disabled list from September 9 to October 2, 2006.
e On disabled list from March 23 to May 14, 2007.
f Filed for free agency, October 9, 2008. Signed with Cincinnati Reds organization, December 15, 2008.
g On disabled list from August 31 to September 15, 2009.
h Filed for free agency, November 20, 2009, re-signed with Cincinnati Reds organization, December 18, 2009.
i On disabled list from August 26 to September 18, 2010.
j Filed for free agency, November 9, 2010. Signed with Washington Nationals organization, February 3, 2011.
k Filed for free agency, October 30, 2011. Signed with Philadelphia Phillies, December 5, 2011.
l On disabled list from May 10 to July 22, 2012.

NORRIS, DEREK RYAN
Born, Ryan, Kansas, February 14, 1989.
Bats Right. Throws Right. Height, 6 feet. Weight, 210 pounds.

Year	Club	Lea	Pos	G	AB	R	H	2B	3B	HR	RBI	SB	Avg
2007 Nationals	Gulf Coast	C-1B	37	123	16	25	6	2	4	15	2	.203
2008 Vermont	N.Y.-Penn.	C	70	227	42	63	12	0	10	38	11	.278
2009 Hagerstown	So.Atl.	C	126	437	78	125	30	0	23	84	6	.286
2010 Potomac.	Carolina	C	94	298	67	70	19	0	12	49	6	.235
2011 Harrisburg a	Eastern	C	104	334	75	70	17	1	20	46	13	.210
2012 Sacramento	P.C.	C	58	218	39	59	14	2	9	38	5	.271
2012 Oakland	A.L.	C	60	209	19	42	8	1	7	34	5	.201
Division Series													
2012 Oakland	A.L.	C	5	12	0	1	0	0	0	0	0	.083

a Traded by Washington Nationals to Oakland Athletics with pitcher A.J. Cole, pitcher Brad Peacock and pitcher Tom Milone for pitcher Gio Gonzalez and pitcher Robert Gilliam, December 23, 2011.

NUNEZ (MENDEZ), EDUARDO MICHELLE
Born, Santo Domingo, Dominican Republic, June 15, 1987.
Bats Right. Throws Right. Height, 6 feet. Weight, 155 pounds.

Year	Club	Lea	Pos	G	AB	R	H	2B	3B	HR	RBI	SB	Avg
2005 Staten Island	N.Y.-Penn.	SS	73	281	37	88	11	6	3	46	6	.313
2006 Tampa	Fla.St.	SS	37	147	17	27	5	3	4	26	6	.184
2006 Charleston	So.Atl.	SS-2B-3B	90	344	36	78	11	3	2	40	16	.227
2007 Charleston	So.Atl.	SS	91	328	36	78	10	2	1	28	20	.238
2007 Tampa	Fla.St.	SS	30	123	16	35	5	0	1	13	9	.285
2008 Tampa	Fla.St.	SS	94	373	45	101	18	3	6	42	14	.271
2009 Trenton	Eastern	SS	123	497	70	160	26	1	9	55	19	.322
2010 Scranton-WB	Int.	SS-3B-2B	118	464	55	134	25	3	4	50	23	.289
2010 New York	A.L.	3B-SS-2B	30	50	12	14	1	0	1	7	5	.280
2011 New York	A.L.	SS-3B-2B-OF	112	309	38	82	18	2	5	30	22	.265
2012 Yankees	Gulf Coast	SS	4	10	1	2	0	0	1	1	0	.200
2012 Tampa	Fla.St.	SS	2	7	2	2	0	0	0	0	1	.286
2012 Scranton-WB	Int.	SS	38	163	18	37	4	0	2	16	16	.227
2012 New York	A.L.	SS-3B-OF-2B	38	89	14	26	4	1	1	11	11	.292
Major League Totals		3 Yrs.	180	448	64	122	23	3	7	48	38	.272
Division Series													
2011 New York	A.L.	PH	1	0	0	0	0	0	0	0	1	.000
2012 New York	A.L.	SS-DH	3	5	2	1	1	0	0	0	0	.200
Division Series Totals			4	5	2	1	1	0	0	0	1	.200
Championship Series													
2012 New York	A.L.	SS	2	6	2	2	0	1	1	1	1	.333

OLIVO (PENA), MIGUEL EDUARDO
Born, Villa Vasquez, Dominican Republic, July 15, 1978.
Bats Right. Throws Right. Height, 6 feet. Weight, 220 pounds.

Year	Club	Lea	Pos	G	AB	R	H	2B	3B	HR	RBI	SB	Avg
1997 Oakland-East	Dominican	C	63	221	37	60	11	4	6	57	6	.271
1998 Athletics	Arizona	C-OF	46	164	30	51	11	3	2	23	2	.311
1999 Modesto.	California	C	73	243	46	74	13	6	9	42	4	.305
2000 Modesto.	California	C	58	227	40	64	11	5	5	35	5	.282
2000 Midland a-b-c.	Texas	C	19	59	8	14	2	0	1	9	0	.237
2001 Birmingham d	Southern	C	93	316	45	82	23	1	14	55	6	.259
2002 Birmingham	Southern	C	106	359	51	110	24	10	6	49	29	.306
2002 Chicago e	A.L.	C	6	19	2	4	1	0	1	5	0	.211
2003 Chicago	A.L.	C	114	317	37	75	19	1	6	27	6	.237
2004 Everett	Northwest	C	2	6	0	0	0	0	0	0	0	.000
2004 Chicago-Seattle f-g	A.L.	C	96	301	46	70	15	4	13	40	7	.233
2005 Tacoma	P.C.	C	24	90	13	21	4	1	3	21	8	.233
2005 Seattle	A.L.	C	54	152	14	23	4	0	5	18	1	.151
2005 San Diego h	N.L.	C	37	115	16	35	7	1	4	16	6	.304
2006 Florida i	N.L.	C-1B	127	430	52	113	22	3	16	58	2	.263
2007 Florida j	N.L.	C	122	452	43	107	20	4	16	60	3	.237
2008 Kansas City	A.L.	C	84	306	29	78	22	0	12	41	7	.255
2009 Kansas City k	A.L.	C	114	390	51	97	15	5	23	65	5	.249
2010 Colorado l-m	N.L.	C	112	394	55	106	17	6	14	58	7	.269
2011 Seattle	A.L.	C	130	477	54	107	19	1	19	62	6	.224
2012 Tacoma	P.C.	C	3	13	3	3	0	0	1	1	0	.231

Year	Club	Lea	Pos	G	AB	R	H	2B	3B	HR	RBI	SB	Avg
2012 Seattle n-o	A.L.	C	87	315	27	70	14	0	12	29	3	.222
Major League Totals	11 Yrs.		1083	3668	426	885	175	25	141	479	53	.241
Division Series												
2005 San Diego	N.L.	PH	1	1	0	0	0	0	0	0	0	.000

a On disabled list from August 8 to September 29, 2000.
b Chicago White Sox traded pitcher Chad Bradford to Oakland Athletics for player to be named later, December 7, 2000.
c Sent by Oakland Athletics to Chicago White Sox to complete trade, December 12, 2000.
d On disabled list from April 22 to May 2, 2001.
e On disabled list from June 4 to 11, 2002.
f Traded to Seattle Mariners with outfielder Jeremy Reed and infielder Michael Morse for pitcher Freddy Garcia, catcher Ben Davis and cash, June 27, 2004.
g On disabled list from June 30 to July 15, 2004.
h Traded to San Diego Padres for catcher Miguel Ojeda and pitcher Nathaniel Mateo, July 31, 2005.
i Filed for free agency, December 21, 2005. Signed with Florida Marlins, January 3, 2006.
j Not offered contract, December 12, 2007. Signed with Kansas City Royals, December 27, 2007.
k Filed for free agency, November 6, 2009. Signed with Colorado Rockies, January 4, 2010.
l Sold to Toronto Blue Jays, November 4, 2010.
m Filed for free agency, November 4, 2010. Signed with Seattle Mariners, December 10, 2010.
n On disabled list from May 1 to May 24, 2012.
o Filed for free agency, November 3, 2012.

OLT, MICHAEL GEORGE (MIKE)

Born, New Haven, Connecticut, August 27, 1988.
Bats Right. Throws Right. Height, 6 feet, 2 inches. Weight, 210 pounds.

Year	Club	Lea	Pos	G	AB	R	H	2B	3B	HR	RBI	SB	Avg
2010 Spokane	Northwest	3B	69	263	57	77	16	1	9	43	6	.293
2011 Rangers	Arizona	3B	4	14	2	3	0	0	1	4	0	.214
2011 Myrtle Beach	Carolina	3B	69	240	39	64	15	0	14	42	0	.267
2012 Frisco	Texas	3B-1B-OF	95	354	65	102	17	1	28	82	4	.288
2012 Texas	A.L.	1B-3B-OF	16	33	2	5	1	0	0	5	1	.152

ORTIZ (ARIAS), DAVID AMERICO

Born, Santo Domingo, Dominican Republic, November 18, 1975.
Bats Left. Throws Left. Height, 6 feet, 4 inches. Weight, 230 pounds.

Year	Club	Lea	Pos	G	AB	R	H	2B	3B	HR	RBI	SB	Avg
1993 Seattle	Dominican	1B	61	201	37	53	17	1	7	31	1	.264
1994 Mariners	Arizona	1B	53	167	14	41	10	1	2	20	1	.246
1995 Mariners	Arizona	1B	48	184	30	61	18	4	4	37	2	.332
1996 Wisconsin a	Midwest	1B	129	485	89	156	34	2	18	93	3	.322
1997 Salt Lake	P.C.	1B	10	42	5	9	1	0	4	10	0	.214
1997 New Britain	Eastern	DH-1B	69	258	40	83	22	2	14	56	2	.322
1997 Fort Myers	Fla.St.	1B	61	239	45	79	15	0	13	58	2	.331
1997 Fort Myers	A.L.	1B	15	49	10	16	3	0	1	6	0	.327
1998 Salt Lake	P.C.	1B	11	37	5	9	3	0	2	6	0	.243
1998 Minnesota b	A.L.	1B	86	278	47	77	20	0	9	46	1	.277
1999 Salt Lake	P.C.	1B	130	476	85	150	35	3	30	110	2	.315
1999 Minnesota	A.L.	1B	10	20	1	0	0	0	0	0	0	.000
2000 Minnesota	A.L.	DH-1B	130	415	59	117	36	1	10	63	1	.282
2001 Twins	Gulf Coast	DH	4	10	3	4	0	0	0	1	1	.400
2001 Fort Myers	Fla.St.	1B	1	3	0	0	0	0	0	0	0	.000
2001 New Britain	Eastern	1B	9	37	3	9	4	0	1	6	0	.243
2001 Minnesota c	A.L.	DH-1B	89	303	46	71	17	1	18	48	1	.234
2002 Minnesota d-e	A.L.	DH-1B	125	412	52	112	32	1	20	75	1	.272
2003 Boston	A.L.	DH-1B	128	448	79	129	39	2	31	101	0	.288
2004 Boston	A.L.	DH-1B	150	582	94	175	47	3	41	139	0	.301
2005 Boston	A.L.	DH-1B	159	601	119	180	40	1	47	*148	1	.300
2006 Boston	A.L.	DH-1B	151	558	115	160	29	2	*54	*137	1	.287
2007 Boston	A.L.	DH-1B	149	549	116	182	52	1	35	117	3	.332
2008 Portland	Eastern	DH	3	8	2	2	0	0	0	1	0	.250
2008 Pawtucket	Int.	DH	3	9	4	3	0	0	3	5	0	.333
2008 Boston f	A.L.	DH	109	416	74	110	30	1	23	89	1	.264
2009 Boston	A.L.	DH-1B	150	541	77	129	35	1	28	99	0	.238
2010 Boston	A.L.	DH-1B	145	518	86	140	36	1	32	102	0	.270
2011 Boston g	A.L.	DH-1B	146	525	84	162	40	1	29	96	1	.309
2012 Boston h-i	A.L.	DH-1B	90	324	65	103	26	0	23	60	0	.318
Major League Totals	16 Yrs.		1832	6539	1124	1863	482	16	401	1326	11	.285

Year Club	Lea	Pos	G	AB	R	H	2B	3B	HR	RBI	SB	Avg
Division Series												
2002 Minnesota	A.L.	DH	4	13	0	3	2	0	0	2	0	.231
2003 Boston	A.L.	DH	5	21	0	2	1	0	0	2	0	.095
2004 Boston	A.L.	DH	3	11	4	6	2	0	1	4	0	.545
2005 Boston	A.L.	DH	3	12	2	4	2	0	1	1	0	.333
2007 Boston	A.L.	DH	3	7	5	5	0	0	2	3	0	.714
2008 Boston	A.L.	DH	4	17	1	4	1	0	0	1	0	.235
2009 Boston	A.L.	DH	3	12	0	1	0	0	0	0	0	.083
Division Series Totals			25	93	12	25	8	0	4	13	0	.269
Championship Series												
2002 Minnesota	A.L.	DH	5	16	0	5	1	0	0	2	0	.313
2003 Boston	A.L.	DH	7	26	4	7	1	0	2	6	0	.269
2004 Boston	A.L.	DH	7	31	6	12	0	1	3	11	0	.387
2007 Boston	A.L.	DH	7	24	7	7	3	0	1	3	0	.292
2008 Boston	A.L.	DH	7	26	3	4	1	1	1	4	0	.154
Championship Series Totals			33	123	20	35	6	2	7	26	0	.285
World Series Record												
2004 Boston	A.L.	1B-DH	4	13	3	4	1	0	1	4	0	.308
2007 Boston	A.L.	1B-DH	4	15	4	5	3	0	0	4	0	.333
World Series Totals			8	28	7	9	4	0	1	8	0	.321

a Sent to Minnesota Twins by Seattle Mariners to complete trade for infielder Dave Hollins, September 13, 1996.
b On disabled list from May 10 to July 9, 1998.
c On disabled list from May 5 to July 21, 2001.
d On disabled list from April 20 to May 13, 2002.
e Released by Minnesota Twins, December 16, 2002. Signed with Boston Red Sox, January 22, 2003.
f On disabled list from June 1 to July 25, 2008.
g Filed for free agency, October 30, 2011. Accepted arbitration, December 7, 2011.
h On disabled list from July 17 to August 24 and August 25 to October 5, 2012.
i Filed for free agency, November 3, 2012, re-signed with Boston Red Sox, November 5, 2012.

OVERBAY, LYLE STEFAN
Born, Centralia, Washington, January 28, 1977.
Bats Left. Throws Left. Height, 6 feet, 2 inches. Weight, 235 pounds.

Year Club	Lea	Pos	G	AB	R	H	2B	3B	HR	RBI	SB	Avg
1999 Missoula	Pioneer	1B	75	306	66	105	25	7	12	101	10	.343
2000 South Bend	Midwest	1B	71	259	47	86	19	3	6	47	9	.332
2000 El Paso............	Texas	1B	62	244	43	86	16	2	8	49	3	.352
2001 El Paso............	Texas	1B-OF	138	532	82	187	49	3	13	100	5	.352
2001 Arizona............	N.L.	PH	2	2	0	1	0	0	0	0	0	.500
2002 Tucson	P.C.	1B	134	525	83	180	40	0	19	109	0	.343
2002 Arizona............	N.L.	PH	10	10	0	1	0	0	0	1	0	.100
2003 Tucson	P.C.	1B	35	119	24	34	11	0	4	16	0	.286
2003 Arizona a	N.L.	1B	86	254	23	70	20	0	4	28	1	.276
2004 Milwaukee	N.L.	1B	159	579	83	174	*53	1	16	87	2	.301
2005 Milwaukee b.......	N.L.	1B	158	537	80	148	34	1	19	72	1	.276
2006 Toronto	A.L.	1B	157	581	82	181	46	1	22	92	5	.312
2007 New Hampshire	Eastern	1B	4	15	2	4	1	0	1	5	0	.267
2007 Toronto c..........	A.L.	1B	122	425	49	102	30	2	10	44	2	.240
2008 Toronto	A.L.	1B	158	544	74	147	32	2	15	69	1	.270
2009 Toronto	A.L.	1B	132	423	57	112	35	1	16	64	0	.265
2010 Toronto d..........	A.L.	1B	154	534	75	130	37	2	20	67	1	.243
2011 Pittsburgh-Arizona e-f ..	N.L.	1B	121	394	43	92	21	1	9	47	2	.234
2012 Gwinnett	Int.	1B	7	22	3	6	3	0	0	3	0	.273
2012 Arizona-Atlanta g-h ..	N.L.	1B	65	116	12	30	10	0	2	10	0	.259
Major League Totals			12 Yrs. 1324	4399	578	1188	318	11	133	581	15	.270
Division Series												
2011 Arizona............	N.L.	1B	2	4	0	0	0	0	0	0	0	.000

a Traded to Milwaukee Brewers with infielder Junior Spivey, infielder Craig Counsell, catcher Chad Moeller, pitcher Chris Capuano and pitcher Jorge De La Rosa for infielder Richie Sexson, pitcher Shane Nance and player to be named later, December 1, 2003. Arizona Diamondbacks received outfielder Gary Varner to complete trade, December 15, 2003.
b Traded to Toronto Blue Jays with pitcher Ty Taubenheim for pitcher Dave Bush, outfielder Gabe Gross and pitcher Zach Jackson, December 7, 2005.
c On disabled list from June 4 to July 12, 2007.
d Filed for free agency, November 1, 2010. Signed with Pittsburgh Pirates, December 14, 2010.
e Released by Pittsburgh Pirates, August 5, 2011. Signed with Arizona Diamondbacks, August 13, 2011.
f Filed for free agency, October 31, 2011, re-signed with Arizona Diamondbacks, December 9, 2011.
g Released by Arizona Diamondbacks, August 3, 2012. Signed with Atlanta Braves organization, August 20, 2012.
h Filed for free agency, November 3, 2012.

PACHECO, JORDAN PATRICK

Born, Albuquerque, New Mexico, January 30, 1986.
Bats Right. Throws Right. Height, 6 feet, 1 inch. Weight, 200 pounds.

Year	Club	Lea	Pos	G	AB	R	H	2B	3B	HR	RBI	SB	Avg
2007	Tri-City	Northwest	2B-SS	8	31	5	8	2	0	0	3	0	.258
2007	Casper	Pioneer	3B-SS-2B	55	192	27	56	10	2	3	29	3	.292
2008	Tri-City	Northwest	C	54	214	25	60	8	3	1	35	3	.280
2009	Asheville	So.Atl.	C	117	451	67	145	30	4	13	79	12	.322
2010	Modesto	Calif.	C	104	390	59	125	27	3	5	70	5	.321
2010	Tulsa	Texas	C	21	78	11	26	5	0	1	19	1	.333
2011	Colorado Springs	P.C.	C-3B	97	363	57	101	21	3	3	50	2	.278
2011	Colorado	N.L.	1B-3B-C-2B	21	84	5	24	1	0	2	14	0	.286
2012	Colorado Springs	P.C.	3B-C	17	67	10	29	4	0	3	10	1	.433
2012	Colorado	N.L.	3B-1B-C	132	475	51	147	32	3	5	54	7	.309
Major League Totals			2 Yrs.	153	559	56	171	33	3	7	68	7	.306

PAGAN, ANGEL ANTHONY

Born, Rio Piedras, Puerto Rico, July 2, 1981.
Bats Both. Throws Right. Height, 6 feet, 1 inch. Weight, 195 pounds.

Year	Club	Lea	Pos	G	AB	R	H	2B	3B	HR	RBI	SB	Avg
2000	Kingsport	Appal.	OF	19	72	13	26	5	1	0	8	6	.361
2001	Brooklyn	N.Y.-Penn.	OF	62	238	46	75	10	2	0	15	30	.315
2001	Columbia	So.Atl.	OF	15	57	4	17	1	1	0	5	3	.298
2002	St. Lucie	Fla.St.	OF	16	67	12	23	2	1	1	7	10	.343
2002	Columbia	So.Atl.	OF	108	458	79	128	14	5	1	36	52	.279
2003	St. Lucie	Fla.St.	OF	113	441	64	110	15	5	1	33	35	.249
2004	Binghamton	Eastern	OF	112	448	71	129	25	8	4	63	29	.288
2004	Norfolk	Int.	OF	12	45	13	13	3	3	0	1	4	.289
2005	Norfolk	Int.	OF	129	516	69	140	20	10	8	40	27	.271
2006	Cubs	Arizona	OF	3	9	1	1	0	0	0	0	1	.111
2006	Iowa	P.C.	OF	4	15	2	4	1	0	0	0	1	.267
2006	Chicago a-b	N.L.	OF	77	170	28	42	6	2	5	18	4	.247
2007	Iowa	P.C.	OF	33	116	18	29	4	3	3	9	6	.250
2007	Chicago c-d	N.L.	OF	71	148	21	39	10	2	4	21	4	.264
2008	Mets	Gulf Coast	OF	2	5	1	3	1	0	0	2	2	.600
2008	Brooklyn	N.Y.-Penn.	OF	4	13	0	4	0	0	0	1	3	.308
2008	St. Lucie	Fla.St.	OF	1	4	1	0	0	0	0	0	0	.000
2008	New York e	N.L.	OF	31	91	12	25	7	1	0	13	4	.275
2009	St. Lucie	Fla.St.	OF	4	12	4	5	2	0	0	3	2	.417
2009	Buffalo	Int.	OF	3	14	2	4	0	2	0	2	0	.286
2009	New York f	N.L.	OF	88	343	54	105	22	11	6	32	14	.306
2010	New York	N.L.	OF	151	579	80	168	31	7	11	69	37	.290
2011	St. Lucie	Fla.St.	OF	8	31	6	7	1	1	1	2	0	.226
2011	New York g-h	N.L.	OF	123	478	68	125	24	4	7	56	32	.262
2012	San Francisco i	N.L.	OF	154	605	95	174	38	*15	8	56	29	.288
Major League Totals			7 Yrs.	695	2414	358	678	138	42	41	265	124	.281
Division Series													
2012	San Francisco	N.L.	OF	5	20	3	3	1	0	1	4	0	.150
Championship Series													
2012	San Francisco	N.L.	OF	7	33	4	8	0	1	1	2	0	.242
World Series Record													
2012	San Francisco	N.L.	OF	4	16	3	2	2	0	0	0	1	.125

a Sold to Chicago by New York Mets, January 25, 2006.
b On disabled list from April 16 to June 30, 2006.
c On disabled list from August 8 to November 1, 2007.
d Traded to New York Mets for pitcher Ryan Meyers and outfielder Corey Coles, January 5, 2008.
e On disabled list from May 13 to November 3, 2008.
f On disabled list from March 27 to May 16 and June 1 to July 10, 2009.
g On disabled list from April 22 to May 27, 2011.
h Traded to San Francisco Giants for pitcher Ramon Ramirez and outfielder Andres Torres, December 7, 2011.
i Filed for free agency, November 3, 2012, re-signed with San Francisco Giants, December 4, 2012.

PAREDES, JIMMY SANTIAGO

Born, Haina, Dominican Republic, November 25, 1988.
Bats Both. Throws Right. Height, 6 feet, 1 inch. Weight, 200 pounds.

Year	Club	Lea	Pos	G	AB	R	H	2B	3B	HR	RBI	SB	Avg
2008	Yankees	Gulf Coast	3B-SS	47	161	23	45	9	2	1	15	6	.280
2009	Staten Island	N.Y.-Penn.	2B-3B	54	205	36	62	8	4	2	17	23	.302

Year Club	Lea	Pos	G	AB	R	H	2B	3B	HR	RBI	SB	Avg
2010 Charleston	So.Atl.	2B-SS-3B	99	404	59	114	24	6	5	48	36	.282
2010 Lexington a	So.Atl.	2B	34	147	24	44	10	1	3	17	14	.299
2011 Corpus Christi	Texas	2B-3B	93	385	69	104	22	4	10	41	29	.270
2011 Houston	N.L.	3B	46	168	16	48	8	2	2	18	5	.286
2012 Oklahoma............	P.C.	2B-OF	124	507	92	161	28	7	13	59	37	.318
2012 Houston	N.L.	OF-2B	24	74	7	14	1	1	0	3	2	.189
Major League Totals		2 Yrs.	70	242	23	62	9	3	2	21	7	.256

a Traded by New York Yankees to Houston Astros with pitcher Mark Melancon for infielder Lance Berkman and cash, July 31, 2010.

PARMELEE, CHRISTOPHER MATTHEW (CHRIS)
Born, Long Beach, California, February 24, 1988.
Bats Left. Throws Left. Height, 6 feet, 1 inch. Weight, 230 pounds.

Year Club	Lea	Pos	G	AB	R	H	2B	3B	HR	RBI	SB	Avg
2006 Twins	Gulf Coast	OF-1B	45	154	29	43	7	4	8	32	3	.279
2006 Beloit	Midwest	1B	11	22	2	5	1	0	0	2	0	.227
2007 Beloit	Midwest	OF-1B	128	447	56	107	23	5	15	70	8	.239
2008 Beloit	Midwest	1B-OF	69	226	41	54	10	3	14	49	3	.239
2009 Fort Myers	Fla.St.	1B-OF	123	422	61	109	27	1	16	73	2	.258
2010 New Britain	Eastern	1B-OF	111	411	51	113	25	2	6	44	3	.275
2010 Fort Myers	Fla.St.	1B-OF	22	80	9	27	2	1	2	17	0	.338
2011 New Britain	Eastern	1B-OF	142	530	76	152	30	5	13	83	0	.287
2011 Minnesota	A.L.	1B	21	76	8	27	6	0	4	14	0	.355
2012 Rochester............	Int.	1B	64	228	45	77	17	1	17	49	1	.338
2012 Minnesota	A.L.	1B-OF	64	192	18	44	10	2	5	20	0	.229
Major League Totals		2 Yrs.	85	268	26	71	16	2	9	34	0	.265

PARRA, GERARDO ENRIQUE
Born, Santa Barbara Del Zulia, Venezuela, May 6, 1987.
Bats Left. Throws Left. Height, 5 feet, 11 inches. Weight, 195 pounds.

Year Club	Lea	Pos	G	AB	R	H	2B	3B	HR	RBI	SB	Avg
2006 Missoula	Pioneer	OF	69	271	46	89	18	4	4	43	23	.328
2007 Visalia	Calif.	OF	24	102	11	29	2	1	2	14	2	.284
2007 South Bend	Midwest	OF	110	444	64	142	25	4	6	57	24	.320
2008 Visalia	Calif.	OF	50	196	26	59	8	4	2	19	12	.301
2008 Mobile	Southern	OF	73	265	35	73	14	6	4	33	16	.275
2009 Mobile	Southern	OF	29	108	23	39	3	1	3	12	7	.361
2009 Arizona.............	N.L.	OF	120	455	59	132	21	8	5	60	5	.290
2010 Reno	P.C.	OF	9	36	8	15	4	0	1	7	3	.417
2010 Arizona.............	N.L.	OF	133	364	31	95	19	6	3	30	1	.261
2011 Arizona.............	N.L.	OF	141	445	55	130	20	8	8	46	15	.292
2012 Arizona.............	N.L.	OF	133	385	58	105	21	2	7	36	15	.273
Major League Totals		4 Yrs.	527	1649	203	462	81	24	23	172	36	.280
Division Series												
2011 Arizona.............	N.L.	OF	5	18	1	1	1	0	0	0	0	.056

PASTORNICKY, TYLER BROCK
Born, Bradenton, Florida, December 13, 1989.
Bats Right. Throws Right. Height, 5 feet, 11 inches. Weight, 190 pounds.

Year Club	Lea	Pos	G	AB	R	H	2B	3B	HR	RBI	SB	Avg
2008 Blue Jays	Gulf Coast	SS	50	160	32	42	6	3	1	17	27	.262
2009 Dunedin	Fla.St.	SS	15	63	9	17	3	0	0	3	6	.270
2009 Lansing	Midwest	SS	109	413	63	111	11	9	1	31	51	.269
2010 Dunedin	Fla.St.	SS-2B	77	287	50	74	16	0	6	35	24	.258
2010 Mississippi a	Southern	SS	38	134	22	34	5	2	2	15	11	.254
2011 Gwinnett...........	Int.	SS	27	104	15	38	2	0	1	9	7	.365
2011 Mississippi.......	Southern	SS	90	355	50	106	13	5	6	36	20	.299
2012 Gwinnett............	Int.	SS-2B	38	153	15	41	15	1	1	20	3	.268
2012 Atlanta	N.L.	SS-2B	76	169	21	41	6	1	2	13	2	.243
Wild Card Playoff												
2012 Atlanta	N.L.	PH	1	0	0	0	0	0	0	0	0	.000

a Traded by Toronto Blue Jays to Atlanta Braves with infielder Alex Gonzalez and pitcher Tim Collins for infielder Yunel Escobar and pitcher Jo-Jo Reyes, July 14, 2010.

PAUL, XAVIER BROOKS

Born, Slidell, Louisiana, February 25, 1985.
Bats Left. Throws Right. Height, 6 feet. Weight, 205 pounds.

Year	Club	Lea	Pos	G	AB	R	H	2B	3B	HR	RBI	SB	Avg
2003 Ogden		Pioneer	OF	69	264	60	81	15	6	7	47	11	.307
2004 Columbus		So.Atl.	OF	126	460	69	122	26	6	9	72	10	.265
2005 Vero Beach		Fla.St.	OF	85	288	42	71	15	3	7	41	1	.247
2006 Vero Beach		Fla.St.	OF	120	470	62	134	23	3	13	49	22	.285
2007 Jacksonville		Southern	OF	118	422	64	123	21	2	11	50	17	.291
2008 Las Vegas		P.C.	OF	115	443	82	140	28	5	9	68	17	.316
2009 Los Angeles		N.L.	OF	11	14	3	3	1	0	1	1	0	.214
2009 Albuquerque a		P.C.	OF	31	116	13	38	10	2	2	16	8	.328
2010 Los Angeles		N.L.	OF	44	121	16	28	8	1	0	11	3	.231
2010 Albuquerque		P.C.	OF	57	228	46	74	20	1	12	38	7	.325
2011 Los Angeles-Pittsburgh b-c		N.L.	OF	128	243	30	62	6	5	2	20	16	.255
2012 Louisville		Int.	OF	6	25	4	12	2	0	1	4	3	.480
2012 Syracuse		Int.	OF	60	213	30	.67	16	1	8	44	6	.315
2012 Cincinnati d		N.L.	OF	55	86	8	27	5	1	2	7	4	.314
Major League Totals			4 Yrs.	238	464	57	120	20	7	5	39	23	.259
Division Series													
2012 Cincinnati		N.L.	PH	3	3	1	1	0	0	0	0	0	.333

a On disabled list from May 21 to November 9, 2009.
b Claimed on waivers by Pittsburgh Pirates, April 26, 2011.
c Filed for free agency, November 30, 2011. Signed with Washington Nationals organization, December 20, 2011.
d Released by Washington Nationals, July 3, 2012. Signed with Cincinnati Reds organization, July 7, 2012.

PEARCE, STEVEN WAYNE (STEVE)

Born, Lakeland, Florida, April 13, 1983.
Bats Right. Throws Right. Height, 5 feet, 11 inches. Weight, 210 pounds.

Year	Club	Lea	Pos	G	AB	R	H	2B	3B	HR	RBI	SB	Avg
2005 Williamsport		N.Y.-Penn.	1B	72	272	48	82	26	0	7	52	2	.301
2006 Lynchburg		Carolina	1B	90	328	48	87	27	1	14	60	7	.265
2006 Hickory		So.Atl.	1B	41	160	35	46	13	1	12	38	1	.287
2007 Lynchburg		Carolina	1B	19	75	19	26	4	1	11	24	2	.347
2007 Altoona		Eastern	1B	81	290	57	97	27	2	14	72	7	.334
2007 Indianapolis		Int.	1B-OF	34	122	18	39	9	1	6	17	5	.320
2007 Pittsburgh		N.L.	OF-1B	23	68	13	20	5	1	0	6	2	.294
2008 Indianapolis		Int.	OF-1B	103	386	47	97	26	1	12	60	10	.251
2008 Pittsburgh		N.L.	OF	37	109	6	27	7	0	4	15	2	.248
2009 Indianapolis		Int.	1B-OF	77	273	37	78	18	1	13	54	3	.286
2009 Pittsburgh		N.L.	1B-OF	60	165	19	34	13	1	4	16	1	.206
2010 Pittsburgh		N.L.	1B	15	29	4	8	2	1	0	5	0	.276
2010 Bradenton		Fla.St.	1B	2	7	2	3	2	0	0	2	0	.429
2010 Indianapolis a		Int.	1B-3B-OF	35	129	25	42	14	2	3	15	7	.326
2011 Pirates		Gulf Coast	3B	1	3	0	2	0	0	0	2	0	.667
2011 Bradenton		Fla.St.	3B	3	6	2	0	0	0	0	0	0	.000
2011 Indianapolis		Int.	1B-3B-OF-SS	7	30	5	8	2	0	3	6	0	.267
2011 Pittsburgh b-c		N.L.	1B-3B-OF	50	94	8	19	2	0	1	10	0	.202
2012 Scranton-WB		Int.	1B-3B-OF	53	192	37	61	15	0	11	30	3	.318
2012 Houston		N.L.	OF-1B	21	63	2	16	4	1	0	8	1	.254
2012 Baltimore-N.Y. d-e-f-g		A.L.	OF-1B	40	96	14	22	4	0	4	18	0	.229
Major League Totals			6 Yrs.	246	624	66	146	37	4	13	78	6	.234

a On disabled list from May 25 to November 3, 2010.
b On disabled list from May 29 to July 22 and August 23 to October 31, 2011.
c Filed for free agency, November 2, 2011. Signed with Minnesota Twins organization, December 15, 2011.
d Released by Minnesota Twins, March 27, 2012. Signed with New York Yankees organization, March 28, 2012.
e Sold to Baltimore Orioles, June 2, 2012.
f Claimed on waivers by Houston Astros, July 28, 2012.
g Sold to New York Yankees, August 27, 2012. Claimed on waivers by Baltimore Orioles, September 29, 2012.

PEDROIA, DUSTIN LUIS

Born, Woodland, California, August 17, 1983.
Bats Right. Throws Right. Height, 5 feet, 9 inches. Weight, 180 pounds.

Year	Club	Lea	Pos	G	AB	R	H	2B	3B	HR	RBI	SB	Avg
2004 Sarasota		Fla.St.	SS	30	107	23	36	8	3	2	14	0	.336
2004 Augusta		So.Atl.	SS	12	50	11	20	5	0	1	5	2	.400
2005 Portland		Eastern	2B-SS	66	256	39	83	19	2	8	40	7	.324
2005 Pawtucket		Int.	2B-SS	51	204	39	52	9	1	5	24	1	.255

Year Club	Lea	Pos	G	AB	R	H	2B	3B	HR	RBI	SB	Avg
2006 Pawtucket	Int.	SS-2B-3B	111	423	55	129	30	3	5	50	1	.305
2006 Boston	A.L.	2B-SS	31	89	5	17	4	0	2	7	0	.191
2007 Boston a	A.L.	2B	139	520	86	165	39	1	8	50	7	.317
2008 Boston b	A.L.	2B	157	653	*118	*213	*54	2	17	83	20	.326
2009 Boston	A.L.	2B	154	626	*115	185	48	1	15	72	20	.296
2010 Pawtucket	Int.	2B	2	6	1	1	0	0	0	0	0	.167
2010 Boston c	A.L.	2B	75	302	53	87	24	1	12	41	9	.288
2011 Boston	A.L.	2B	159	635	102	195	37	3	21	91	26	.307
2012 Boston d	A.L.	2B	141	563	81	163	39	3	15	65	20	.290
Major League Totals		7 Yrs.	856	3388	560	1025	245	11	90	409	102	.303
Division Series												
2007 Boston	A.L.	2B	3	13	2	2	2	0	0	1	0	.154
2008 Boston	A.L.	2B	4	17	0	1	1	0	0	1	0	.059
2009 Boston	A.L.	2B	3	12	1	2	1	0	0	2	0	.167
Division Series Totals			10	42	3	5	4	0	0	4	0	.119
Championship Series												
2007 Boston	A.L.	2B	7	29	8	10	3	0	1	5	0	.345
2008 Boston	A.L.	2B	7	26	9	9	1	0	3	5	2	.346
Championship Series Totals			14	55	17	19	4	0	4	10	2	.345
World Series Record												
2007 Boston	A.L.	2B	4	18	2	5	1	0	1	4	0	.278

a Selected Rookie of the Year in American League for 2007.
b Selected Most Valuable Player in American League for 2008.
c On disabled list from June 26 to August 17 and August 19 to October 13, 2010.
d On disabled list from July 4 to July 19, 2012.

PENA, BRAYAN EDUARDO

Born, Havana, Cuba, January 7, 1982.
Bats Both. Throws Right. Height, 5 feet, 11 inches. Weight, 245 pounds.

Year Club	Lea	Pos	G	AB	R	H	2B	3B	HR	RBI	SB	Avg
2001 Danville	Appal.	C	64	235	39	87	16	2	1	33	3	.370
2002 Myrtle Beach ..	Carolina	C	6	19	3	4	1	0	0	1	0	.211
2002 Macon	So.Atl.	C	81	271	26	62	10	0	3	25	0	.229
2003 Myrtle Beach ..	Carolina	C	82	286	24	84	14	1	2	27	2	.294
2004 Greenville.....	Southern	C	77	277	30	87	10	4	2	30	3	.314
2005 Richmond	Int.	C-1B	81	282	27	92	21	2	0	25	3	.326
2005 Atlanta	N.L.	C	18	39	2	7	2	0	0	4	0	.179
2006 Richmond	Int.	C	87	325	32	98	18	1	1	33	6	.302
2006 Atlanta	N.L.	C-3B	23	41	9	11	2	0	1	5	0	.268
2007 Richmond	Int.	C-1B-OF-3B	94	345	42	104	20	2	6	48	5	.301
2007 Atlanta a	N.L.	C	16	33	2	7	0	0	1	3	0	.212
2008 Atlanta	N.L.	PH	14	14	3	4	1	0	0	0	0	.286
2008 Omaha b-c	P.C.	C-OF-3B	60	234	33	71	17	1	6	31	7	.303
2009 Omaha	P.C.	OF-C	22	88	11	27	6	1	4	18	2	.307
2009 Kansas City	A.L.	C	64	165	17	45	10	0	6	18	0	.273
2010 Kansas City	A.L.	C	60	158	11	40	10	0	1	19	2	.253
2011 Kansas City	A.L.	C	72	222	17	55	11	0	3	24	0	.248
2012 Kansas City d	A.L.	C-1B	68	212	16	50	10	1	2	25	0	.236
Major League Totals		8 Yrs.	335	884	77	219	46	1	14	98	2	.248

a On disabled list from May 2 to May 17, 2007.
b On disabled list from May 5 to May 23, 2008.
c Claimed on waivers by Kansas City Royals, May 30, 2008.
d Filed for free agency, November 28, 2012. Signed with Detroit Tigers, December 10, 2012.

PENA, CARLOS FELIPE

Born, Santo Domingo, Dominican Republic, May 17, 1978.
Bats Left. Throws Left. Height, 6 feet, 2 inches. Weight, 210 pounds.

Year Club	Lea	Pos	G	AB	R	H	2B	3B	HR	RBI	SB	Avg
1998 Rangers	Gulf Coast	1B	2	5	1	2	0	0	0	0	1	.400
1998 Savannah..........	So.Atl.	1B-OF	30	117	22	38	14	0	6	20	3	.325
1998 Charlotte	Fla.St.	1B	7	22	1	6	1	0	0	3	0	.273
1999 Charlotte	Fla.St.	1B	136	501	85	128	31	8	18	103	2	.255
2000 Tulsa	Texas	1B	138	529	117	158	36	2	28	105	12	.299
2001 Oklahoma............	P.C.	1B	119	431	71	124	38	3	23	74	11	.288
2001 Texas	A.L.	1B	22	62	6	16	4	1	3	12	0	.258
2002 Sacramento	P.C.	1B	44	175	30	42	10	1	10	33	3	.240
2002 Oakland-Detroit a-b ..	A.L.	1B	115	397	43	96	17	4	19	52	2	.242
2003 Toledo	Int.	1B	8	30	4	10	4	1	0	5	0	.333

Year	Club	Lea	Pos	G	AB	R	H	2B	3B	HR	RBI	SB	Avg
2003 Detroit c	A.L.	1B	131	452	51	112	21	6	18	50	4	.248
2004 Detroit	A.L.	1B	142	481	89	116	22	4	27	82	7	.241
2005 Toledo	Int.	1B	71	257	43	80	17	1	12	45	3	.311
2005 Detroit	A.L.	1B	79	260	37	61	9	0	18	44	0	.235
2006 Columbus	Int.	1B	105	381	65	99	17	0	19	66	4	.260
2006 Pawtucket	Int.	1B	11	37	7	17	3	0	4	8	0	.459
2006 Boston d-e-f	A.L.	1B-OF	18	33	3	9	2	0	1	3	0	.273
2007 Tampa Bay	A.L.	1B	148	490	99	138	29	1	46	121	1	.282
2008 Vero Beach	Fla.St.	DH	1	4	0	0	0	0	0	0	1	.000
2008 Tampa Bay g	A.L.	1B	139	490	76	121	24	2	31	102	1	.247
2009 Tampa Bay h	A.L.	1B	135	471	91	107	25	2	*39	100	3	.227
2010 Charlotte	Fla.St.	DH	1	3	1	2	0	0	0	1	0	.667
2010 Tampa Bay i-j	A.L.	1B	144	484	64	95	18	0	28	84	5	.196
2011 Chicago k	N.L.	1B	153	493	72	111	27	3	28	80	2	.225
2012 Tampa Bay l	A.L.	1B	160	497	72	98	17	2	19	61	2	.197
Major League Totals	12 Yrs.		1386	4610	703	1080	215	25	277	791	27	.234
Division Series												
2008 Tampa Bay	A.L.	1B	3	10	0	5	0	0	0	2	2	.500
2010 Tampa Bay	A.L.	1B	4	14	4	4	1	1	1	4	0	.286
Division Series Totals			7	24	4	9	1	1	1	6	2	.375
Championship Series												
2008 Tampa Bay	A.L.	1B	7	26	8	7	1	0	3	6	1	.269
World Series Record												
2008 Tampa Bay	A.L.	1B	5	17	1	2	1	0	0	2	0	.118

a Traded to Oakland Athletics with pitcher Mike Venafro for pitcher Mario Ramos, outfielder Ryan Ludwick, infielder Jason Hart and catcher Gerald Laird, January 14, 2002.
b Traded to Detroit Tigers with pitcher Franklyn German and player to be named later for pitcher Jeff Weaver, July 5, 2002. Detroit Tigers received pitcher Jeremy Bonderman to complete trade, August 22, 2002.
c On disabled list from June 2 to June 27, 2003.
d Released by Detroit Tigers, March 26, 2006. Signed with New York Yankees organization, April 15, 2006.
e Filed for free agency, August 16, 2006. Signed with Boston Red Sox organization, August 17, 2006.
f Filed for free agency, October 13, 2006. Signed with Tampa Bay Devil Rays organization, February 1, 2007.
g On disabled list from June 4 to June 27, 2008.
h On disabled list from September 7 to November 19, 2009.
i On disabled list from August 1 to August 16, 2010.
j Filed for free agency, November 1, 2010. Signed with Chicago Cubs, December 8, 2010.
k Filed for free agency, October 30, 2011. Signed with Tampa Bay Rays, January 24, 2012.
l Filed for free agency, November 3, 2012. Signed with Houston Astros, December 17, 2012.

PENCE, HUNTER ANDREW

Born, Arlington, Texas, April 13, 1983.
Bats Right. Throws Right. Height, 6 feet, 4 inches. Weight, 210 pounds.

Year	Club	Lea	Pos	G	AB	R	H	2B	3B	HR	RBI	SB	Avg
2004 Tri-City	N.Y.-Penn.	OF	51	199	36	59	18	1	8	37	3	.296
2005 Lexington	So.Atl.	OF	80	302	59	102	14	3	25	60	8	.338
2005 Salem	Carolina	OF	41	151	24	46	8	1	6	30	1	.305
2006 Corpus Christi	Texas	OF	136	523	97	148	31	8	28	95	17	.283
2007 Round Rock	P.C.	OF	25	95	17	31	11	1	3	21	2	.326
2007 Houston a	N.L.	OF	108	456	57	147	30	9	17	69	11	.322
2008 Houston	N.L.	OF	157	595	78	160	34	4	25	83	11	.269
2009 Houston	N.L.	OF	159	585	76	165	26	5	25	72	14	.282
2010 Houston	N.L.	OF	156	614	93	173	29	3	25	91	18	.282
2011 Houston-Philadelphia b	N.L.	OF	154	606	84	190	38	5	22	97	8	.314
2012 Philadelphia-San Fran. c	N.L.	OF	160	617	87	156	26	4	24	104	5	.253
Major League Totals	6 Yrs.		894	3473	475	991	183	30	138	516	67	.285
Division Series												
2011 Philadelphia	N.L.	OF	5	19	3	4	0	0	0	4	0	.211
2012 San Francisco	N.L.	OF	5	20	0	4	0	0	0	0	1	.200
Division Series Totals			10	39	3	8	0	0	0	4	1	.205
Championship Series												
2012 San Francisco	N.L.	OF	7	28	4	5	1	0	1	3	0	.179
World Series Record												
2012 San Francisco	N.L.	OF	4	14	3	4	1	0	0	1	1	.286

a On disabled list from July 23 to August 21, 2007.
b Traded to Philadelphia Phillies with cash for infielder Jonathan Singleton, pitcher Jarred Cosart, pitcher Josh Zeid and player to be named later, July 30, 2011. Houston Astros received pitcher Domingo Santana to complete trade, August 15, 2011.
c Traded to San Francisco Giants with cash for outfielder Nate Schierholtz, catcher Tommy Joseph and pitcher Seth Rosin, July 31, 2012.

PENNINGTON, CLIFTON RANDOLPH (CLIFF)

Born, Corpus Christi, Texas, June 15, 1984.
Bats Both. Throws Right. Height, 5 feet, 11 inches. Weight, 190 pounds.

Year	Club	Lea	Pos	G	AB	R	H	2B	3B	HR	RBI	SB	Avg
2005 Kane County...	Midwest		SS	69	290	49	80	15	0	3	29	25	.276
2006 Athletics......	Arizona		SS	9	28	3	13	3	1	0	6	0	.464
2006 Stockton........	Calif.		SS	46	177	36	36	7	0	2	21	7	.203
2007 Stockton........	Calif.		SS-2B	68	286	50	73	17	3	6	36	9	.255
2007 Midland.......	Texas		SS-2B	70	271	41	68	13	2	2	21	8	.251
2008 Midland.......	Texas		SS-2B	50	204	42	53	7	2	0	18	20	.260
2008 Sacramento......	P.C.		SS-2B-3B	65	236	47	70	9	3	2	16	11	.297
2008 Oakland.........	A.L.		2B-SS-3B	36	99	14	24	5	0	0	9	4	.242
2009 Sacramento......	P.C.		SS-2B-3B-OF	99	360	48	95	22	3	3	40	27	.264
2009 Oakland.........	A.L.		SS	60	208	27	58	11	3	4	21	7	.279
2010 Oakland.........	A.L.		SS	156	508	64	127	26	8	6	46	29	.250
2011 Oakland.........	A.L.		SS	148	515	57	136	26	2	8	58	14	.264
2012 Sacramento......	P.C.		SS	3	11	2	5	1	0	0	1	1	.455
2012 Oakland a-b......	A.L.		SS-2B	125	418	50	90	18	2	6	28	15	.215
Major League Totals...........			5 Yrs.	525	1748	212	435	86	15	24	162	69	.249
Division Series													
2012 Oakland.........	A.L.		2B	5	14	1	4	0	0	0	1	0	.286

a On disabled list from July 20 to August 7, 2012.

b Traded to Arizona Diamondbacks with infielder Yordy Cabrera for outfielder Chris Young and cash, October 20, 2012.

PERALTA, JHONNY ANTONIO

Born, Santiago, Dominican Republic, May 28, 1982.
Bats Right. Throws Right. Height, 6 feet, 1 inch. Weight, 210 pounds.

Year	Club	Lea	Pos	G	AB	R	H	2B	3B	HR	RBI	SB	Avg
2001 Kinston..........	Carolina		SS	125	441	57	106	24	2	7	47	4	.240
2002 Akron..........	Eastern		SS	130	470	62	132	28	5	15	62	4	.281
2003 Buffalo.............	Int.		SS-3B	63	237	25	61	12	1	1	21	1	.257
2003 Cleveland...........	A.L.		SS-3B	77	242	24	55	10	1	4	21	1	.227
2004 Buffalo.............	Int.		SS-3B	138	556	109	181	44	2	15	86	8	.326
2004 Cleveland...........	A.L.		SS-3B	8	25	2	6	1	0	0	2	0	.240
2005 Cleveland...........	A.L.		SS	141	504	82	147	35	4	24	78	0	.292
2006 Cleveland...........	A.L.		SS	149	569	84	146	28	3	13	68	0	.257
2007 Cleveland...........	A.L.		SS	152	574	87	155	27	1	21	72	4	.270
2008 Cleveland...........	A.L.		SS-3B	154	605	104	167	42	4	23	89	3	.276
2009 Cleveland...........	A.L.		3B-SS	151	582	57	148	35	1	11	83	0	.254
2010 Cleveland-Detroit a-b...	A.L.		3B-SS-1B	148	551	60	137	30	2	15	81	1	.249
2011 Detroit.............	A.L.		SS-1B	146	525	68	157	25	3	21	86	0	.299
2012 Detroit.............	A.L.		SS	150	531	58	127	32	3	13	63	1	.239
Major League Totals...........			10 Yrs.	1276	4708	626	1245	265	22	145	643	10	.264
Division Series													
2007 Cleveland.............	A.L.		SS	4	15	2	7	3	0	0	2	1	.467
2011 Detroit.............	A.L.		SS	5	18	0	4	2	0	0	1	0	.222
2012 Detroit.............	A.L.		SS	5	17	1	5	0	0	0	0	1	.294
Division Series Totals...........				14	50	3	16	5	0	0	3	2	.320
Championship Series													
2007 Cleveland.............	A.L.		SS	7	27	4	7	4	0	2	8	0	.259
2011 Detroit.............	A.L.		SS	6	23	2	5	1	0	2	2	0	.217
2012 Detroit.............	A.L.		SS	4	18	3	7	1	0	2	3	0	.389
Championship Series Totals......				17	68	9	19	4	0	6	13	0	.279
World Series Record													
2012 Detroit.............	A.L.		SS	4	15	1	1	0	0	1	2	0	.067

a Traded to Detroit Tigers for pitcher Giovanni Soto, July 28, 2010.

b Filed for free agency, November 2, 2010, re-signed with Detroit Tigers, November 8, 2010.

PEREZ (DIAZ), SALVADOR

Born, Valencia, Venezuela, May 10, 1990.
Bats Right. Throws Right. Height, 6 feet, 3 inches. Weight, 230 pounds.

Year	Club	Lea	Pos	G	AB	R	H	2B	3B	HR	RBI	SB	Avg
2007 Royals...........	Arizona		C	30	86	10	21	3	0	0	10	1	.244
2008 Burlington.........	Appal.		C-2B	13	40	4	13	0	1	0	10	0	.325
2008 Idaho Falls........	Pioneer		C	12	43	7	17	3	1	1	6	0	.395
2009 Burlington........	Midwest		C	36	127	10	24	6	0	0	7	0	.189
2009 Idaho Falls........	Pioneer		C	57	226	33	71	14	3	2	37	0	.314

Year Club	Lea	Pos	G	AB	R	H	2B	3B	HR	RBI	SB	Avg
2010 Wilmington	Carolina	C	99	365	35	106	21	1	7	53	1	.290
2011 NW Arkansas	Texas	C	79	286	35	81	14	0	9	43	0	.283
2011 Omaha..............	P.C.	C	12	48	5	16	5	0	1	10	0	.333
2011 Kansas City	A.L.	C	39	148	20	49	8	2	3	21	0	.331
2012 Omaha..............	P.C.	C	12	50	11	17	2	0	0	7	0	.340
2012 Kansas City a	A.L.	C	76	289	38	87	16	0	11	39	0	.301
Major League Totals	2 Yrs.		115	437	58	136	24	2	14	60	0	.311

a On disabled list from March 20 to June 22, 2012.

PETERSEN, BRYAN E.
Born, Agoura, California, April 9, 1986.
Bats Left. Throws Right. Height, 6 feet. Weight, 205 pounds.

Year Club	Lea	Pos	G	AB	R	H	2B	3B	HR	RBI	SB	Avg
2007 Jamestown......	N.Y.-Penn.	OF	57	216	27	54	13	1	5	24	11	.250
2008 Greensboro	So.Atl.	OF	79	296	60	89	10	2	19	58	15	.301
2008 Carolina	Southern	OF	12	37	5	13	2	0	1	10	1	.351
2008 Jupiter	Fla.St.	OF	40	155	23	41	5	0	3	12	7	.265
2009 Jacksonville	Southern	OF	121	431	64	128	15	7	7	49	13	.297
2010 Florida	N.L.	OF	23	24	1	2	0	0	0	2	0	.083
2010 New Orleans.........	P.C.	OF	91	322	47	82	13	2	5	27	5	.255
2011 New Orleans.........	P.C.	OF	67	248	47	87	21	0	11	26	6	.351
2011 Florida	N.L.	OF-P	74	204	18	54	13	3	2	10	7	.265
2012 New Orleans.........	P.C.	OF	64	243	45	78	8	2	3	28	8	.321
2012 Miami...............	N.L.	OF	84	241	29	47	9	3	0	17	8	.195
Major League Totals	3 Yrs.		181	469	48	103	22	6	2	29	15	.220

PHILLIPS, BRANDON EMIL
Born, Raleigh, North Carolina, June 28, 1981.
Bats Right. Throws Right. Height, 6 feet. Weight, 195 pounds.

Year Club	Lea	Pos	G	AB	R	H	2B	3B	HR	RBI	SB	Avg
1999 Expos..........	Gulf Coast	SS	47	169	23	49	11	3	1	21	12	.290
2000 Cape Fear..........	So.Atl.	SS-2B	126	484	74	117	17	8	11	72	23	.242
2001 Harrisburg	Eastern	SS-2B-3B	67	265	35	79	19	0	7	36	13	.298
2001 Jupiter	Fla.St.	SS	55	194	36	55	12	2	4	23	17	.284
2002 Harrisburg	Eastern	SS	60	245	40	80	13	2	9	35	6	.327
2002 Ottawa	Int.	SS	10	35	1	9	4	0	1	5	0	.257
2002 Buffalo	Int.	SS-2B	55	223	30	63	14	0	8	27	8	.283
2002 Cleveland a..........	A.L.	2B	11	31	5	8	3	1	0	4	0	.258
2003 Cleveland	A.L.	2B	112	370	36	77	18	1	6	33	4	.208
2003 Buffalo	Int.	2B	43	154	14	27	7	0	3	13	7	.175
2004 Buffalo	Int.	2B-SS	135	521	83	158	34	4	8	50	14	.303
2004 Cleveland	A.L.	2B	6	22	1	4	2	0	0	1	0	.182
2005 Cleveland	A.L.	2B-SS	6	9	1	0	0	0	0	0	0	.000
2005 Buffalo	Int.	SS	112	465	79	119	24	1	15	46	7	.256
2006 Cincinnati b	N.L.	2B-SS	149	536	65	148	28	1	17	75	25	.276
2007 Cincinnati...........	N.L.	2B-SS	158	650	107	187	26	6	30	94	32	.288
2008 Cincinnati c	N.L.	2B	141	559	80	146	24	7	21	78	23	.261
2009 Cincinnati...........	N.L.	2B	153	584	78	161	30	5	20	98	25	.276
2010 Cincinnati...........	N.L.	2B	155	626	100	172	33	5	18	59	16	.275
2011 Cincinnati...........	N.L.	2B	150	610	94	183	38	2	18	82	14	.300
2012 Cincinnati...........	N.L.	2B	147	580	86	163	30	1	18	77	15	.281
Major League Totals	11 Yrs.		1188	4577	653	1249	232	29	148	601	154	.273
Division Series												
2010 Cincinnati...........	N.L.	2B	3	12	2	4	1	0	1	1	0	.333
2012 Cincinnati...........	N.L.	2B	5	24	1	9	3	0	1	7	1	.375
Division Series Totals			8	36	3	13	4	0	2	8	1	.361

a Traded to Cleveland Indians with infielder Lee Stevens, outfielder Grady Sizemore and pitcher Cliff Lee for pitcher Bartolo Colon and player to be named later, June 27, 2002. Montreal Expos received pitcher Tim Drew to complete trade, June 28, 2002.

b Traded to Cincinnati Reds for player to be named later, April 7, 2006. Cleveland Indians received pitcher Jeff Stevens to complete trade, June 13, 2006.

c On disabled list from September 12 to November 6, 2008.

PIERRE, JUAN D'VAUGHN
Born, Mobile, Alabama, August 14, 1977.
Bats Left. Throws Left. Height, 6 feet. Weight, 180 pounds.

Year Club	Lea	Pos	G	AB	R	H	2B	3B	HR	RBI	SB	Avg
1998 Portland........	Northwest	OF	64	264	55	93	9	2	0	30	38	.352
1999 Asheville..........	So.Atl.	OF	140	585	93	187	28	5	1	55	66	.320
2000 Carolina.........	Southern	OF	107	439	63	143	16	4	0	32	46	.326
2000 Colorado Spgs........	.P.C.	OF	4	17	3	8	0	1	0	1	1	.471
2000 Colorado	N.L.	OF	51	200	26	62	2	0	0	20	7	.310
2001 Colorado	N.L.	OF	156	617	108	202	26	11	2	55	*46	.327
2002 Colorado a...........	N.L.	OF	152	592	90	170	20	5	1	35	47	.287
2003 Florida	N.L.	OF	*162	*668	100	204	28	7	1	41	*65	.305
2004 Florida	N.L.	OF	*162	*678	100	*221	22	*12	3	49	45	.326
2005 Florida b...........	N.L.	OF	*162	656	96	181	19	13	2	47	57	.276
2006 Chicago c...........	N.L.	OF	*162	*699	87	*204	32	13	3	40	58	.292
2007 Los Angeles	N.L.	OF	*162	668	96	196	24	8	0	41	64	.293
2008 Las Vegas...........	.P.C.	OF	2	6	2	3	1	0	0	0	0	.500
2008 Los Angeles d........	N.L.	OF	119	375	44	106	10	2	1	28	40	.283
2009 Los Angeles e........	N.L.	OF	145	380	57	117	16	8	0	31	30	.308
2010 Chicago	A.L.	OF	160	651	96	179	18	3	1	47	*68	.275
2011 Chicago f...........	A.L.	OF	158	639	80	178	17	4	2	50	27	.279
2012 Philadelphia g........	N.L.	OF	130	394	59	121	10	6	1	25	37	.307
Major League Totals	13 Yrs.		1881	7217	1039	2141	244	92	17	509	591	.297
Division Series												
2003 Florida	N.L.	OF	4	19	5	5	1	0	0	3	1	.263
2008 Los Angeles	N.L.	OF	1	1	1	0	0	0	0	0	0	.000
2009 Los Angeles	N.L.	OF	3	0	1	0	0	0	0	0	0	.000
Division Series Totals			8	20	7	5	1	0	0	3	1	.250
Championship Series												
2003 Florida	N.L.	OF	7	33	5	10	1	2	0	1	1	.303
2008 Los Angeles	N.L.	OF	1	3	1	2	1	0	0	0	0	.667
2009 Los Angeles	N.L.	OF	4	2	1	0	0	0	0	0	0	.000
Championship Series Totals			12	38	7	12	2	2	0	1	1	.316
World Series Record												
2003 Florida	N.L.	OF	6	21	2	7	2	0	0	3	1	.333

a Traded to Florida Marlins with pitcher Mike Hampton for outfielder Preston Wilson, catcher Charles Johnson, pitcher Vic Darensbourg and infielder Pablo Ozuna, November 16, 2002.
b Traded to Chicago Cubs for pitcher Sergio Mitre, pitcher Ricky Nolasco and pitcher Renyel Pinto, December 7, 2005.
c Filed for free agency, October 29, 2006. Signed with Los Angeles Dodgers, November 22, 2006.
d On disabled list from June 30 to July 25, 2008.
e Traded with cash to Chicago White Sox for pitcher John Ely and pitcher Jon Link, December 15, 2009.
f Filed for free agency, October 30, 2011. Signed with Philadelphia Phillies organization, January 27, 2012.
g Filed for free agency, November 3, 2012. Signed with Miami Marlins, November 19, 2012.

PIERZYNSKI, ANTHONY JOHN (A.J.)
Born, Bridgehampton, New York, December 30, 1976.
Bats Left. Throws Right. Height, 6 feet, 3 inches. Weight, 235 pounds.

Year Club	Lea	Pos	G	AB	R	H	2B	3B	HR	RBI	SB	Avg
1994 Twins..........	Gulf Coast	C	43	152	21	44	8	1	1	19	0	.289
1995 Ft. Wayne.........	Midwest	C	22	84	10	26	5	1	2	14	0	.310
1995 Elizabethtn..........	Appal.	C-1B	56	205	29	68	13	1	7	45	0	.332
1996 Ft. Wayne..........	Midwest	C-OF	114	431	48	118	30	3	7	70	0	.274
1997 Ft. Myers...........	Fla.St.	C-1B	118	412	49	115	23	1	9	64	2	.279
1998 New Britain	Eastern	C	59	212	30	63	11	0	3	17	0	.297
1998 Salt Lake	.P.C.	C	59	208	29	53	7	2	7	30	3	.255
1998 Minnesota	A.L.	C	7	10	1	3	0	0	0	1	0	.300
1999 Salt Lake	.P.C.	C	67	228	29	59	10	0	1	25	0	.259
1999 Minnesota a...........	A.L.	C	9	22	3	6	2	0	0	3	0	.273
2000 New Britain	Eastern	C	62	228	36	68	17	2	4	34	0	.298
2000 Salt Lake	.P.C.	C	41	155	22	52	14	1	4	25	1	.335
2000 Minnesota	A.L.	C	33	88	12	27	5	1	2	11	1	.307
2001 Minnesota	A.L.	C	114	381	51	110	33	2	7	55	1	.289
2002 Minnesota	A.L.	C	130	440	54	132	31	6	6	49	1	.300
2003 Minnesota b...........	A.L.	C	137	487	63	152	35	3	11	74	3	.312
2004 San Francisco c.......	N.L.	C	131	471	45	128	28	2	11	77	0	.272
2005 Chicago	A.L.	C	128	460	61	118	21	0	18	56	0	.257
2006 Chicago	A.L.	C	140	509	65	150	24	0	16	64	1	.295
2007 Chicago	A.L.	C	136	472	54	124	24	0	14	50	1	.263

132

Year	Club	Lea	Pos	G	AB	R	H	2B	3B	HR	RBI	SB	Avg
2008 Chicago		A.L.	C	134	534	66	150	31	1	13	60	1	.281
2009 Chicago		A.L.	C	138	504	57	151	22	1	13	49	1	.300
2010 Chicago d		A.L.	C	128	474	43	128	29	0	9	56	3	.270
2011 Charlotte		Int.	C	3	10	2	2	0	0	0	1	0	.200
2011 Chicago e		A.L.	C	129	464	38	133	29	1	8	48	0	.287
2012 Chicago f		A.L.	C	135	479	68	133	18	4	27	77	0	.278
Major League Totals		15 Yrs.	1629	5795	681	1645	332	21	155	730	13	.284
Division Series													
2002 Minnesota		A.L.	C	5	16	4	7	0	1	1	4	0	.438
2003 Minnesota		A.L.	C	4	13	1	3	0	0	1	1	0	.231
2005 Chicago		A.L.	C	3	9	5	4	2	0	2	4	1	.444
2008 Chicago		A.L.	C	4	13	1	5	1	0	0	1	0	.385
Division Series Totals			16	51	11	19	3	1	4	10	1	.373
Championship Series													
2002 Minnesota		A.L.	C	5	16	1	4	0	0	0	2	0	.250
2005 Chicago		A.L.	C	5	18	1	3	0	0	1	2	0	.167
Championship Series Totals			10	34	2	7	0	0	1	4	0	.206
World Series Record													
2005 Chicago		A.L.	C	4	15	3	4	2	0	0	3	1	.267

a On disabled list from August 24 to September 30, 1999.
b Traded to San Francisco Giants with cash for pitcher Joe Nathan, pitcher Boof Bonser and pitcher Francisco Liriano, November 14, 2003.
c Released by San Francisco Giants, December 16, 2004. Signed with Chicago White Sox, January 5, 2005.
d Filed for free agency, November 1, 2010, re-signed with Chicago White Sox, December 3, 2010.
e On disabled list from August 13 to September 2, 2011.
f Filed for free agency, November 3, 2012. Signed with Texas Rangers, December 26, 2012.

PLOUFFE, TREVOR PATRICK

Born, West Hills, California, June 15, 1986.
Bats Right. Throws Right. Height, 6 feet, 2 inches. Weight, 200 pounds.

Year	Club	Lea	Pos	G	AB	R	H	2B	3B	HR	RBI	SB	Avg
2004 Elizabethton		Appal.	SS	60	237	29	67	7	2	4	28	3	.283
2005 Beloit		Midwest	SS	127	466	58	104	18	0	13	60	8	.223
2006 Fort Myers		Fla.St.	SS-3B	125	455	60	112	26	4	4	45	8	.246
2007 New Britain		Eastern	SS-3B	126	497	75	136	37	2	9	50	12	.274
2008 New Britain		Eastern	SS-3B	58	227	32	61	17	3	3	21	4	.269
2008 Rochester		Int.	3B-2B-SS	66	250	34	64	17	3	6	39	1	.256
2009 Rochester		Int.	SS	118	430	53	112	23	5	10	60	3	.260
2010 Rochester		Int.	SS-3B-2B	102	402	53	98	22	4	15	49	5	.244
2010 Minnesota		A.L.	SS-2B	22	41	7	6	1	0	2	6	0	.146
2011 Rochester		Int.	SS-2B-1B-OF	51	192	33	60	11	3	15	33	3	.313
2011 Minnesota		A.L.	SS-2B-OF-1B	81	286	47	68	18	1	8	31	3	.238
2012 Rochester		Int.	3B	2	8	0	0	0	0	0	0	0	.000
2012 Minnesota a		A.L.	3B-OF-2B-1B	119	422	56	99	19	1	24	55	1	.235
Major League Totals		3 Yrs.	222	749	110	173	38	2	34	92	4	.231

a On disabled list from July 21 to August 13, 2012.

PODSEDNIK, SCOTT ERIC

Born, West, Texas, March 18, 1976.
Bats Left. Throws Left. Height, 6 feet. Weight, 185 pounds.

Year	Club	Lea	Pos	G	AB	R	H	2B	3B	HR	RBI	SB	Avg
1994 Rangers		Gulf Coast	OF	60	211	34	48	7	1	1	17	18	.227
1995 Hudson Val a		N.Y.-Penn.	OF	65	252	42	67	3	0	0	20	20	.266
1996 Brevard Cty		Fla.St.	OF	108	383	39	100	9	2	0	20	20	.261
1997 Kane County b		Midwest	OF	135	531	80	147	23	4	3	49	28	.277
1998 Tulsa		Texas	OF	17	75	9	18	4	1	0	4	5	.240
1998 Charlotte		Fla.St.	OF	81	302	55	86	12	4	4	39	26	.285
1999 Rangers		Gulf Coast	OF	5	17	6	7	2	0	0	5	1	.412
1999 Tulsa		Texas	OF	37	116	10	18	4	0	0	1	6	.155
2000 Tulsa c-d		Texas	OF	49	169	20	42	7	2	2	13	19	.249
2001 Tacoma		P.C.	OF	66	269	46	78	15	4	3	30	12	.290
2001 Seattle e		A.L.	OF	5	6	1	1	0	1	0	3	0	.167
2002 Tacoma		P.C.	OF	125	438	63	122	25	6	9	61	35	.279
2002 Seattle f		A.L.	OF	14	20	2	4	0	0	1	5	0	.200
2003 Milwaukee		N.L.	OF	154	558	100	175	29	8	9	58	43	.314
2004 Milwaukee		N.L.	OF	154	640	85	156	27	7	12	39	70	.244
2005 Charlotte		Int.	OF	2	9	2	2	2	0	0	1	0	.222

Year	Club	Lea	Pos	G	AB	R	H	2B	3B	HR	RBI	SB	Avg
2005 Chicago g-h	A.L.	OF	129	507	80	147	28	1	0	25	59	.290
2006 Chicago	A.L.	OF	139	524	86	137	27	6	3	45	40	.261
2007 Charlotte	Int.	OF	20	73	12	21	5	0	1	6	2	.288
2007 Chicago i	A.L.	OF	62	214	30	52	13	4	2	11	12	.243
2008 Colorado Springs	P.C.	OF	4	16	2	7	0	0	0	3	3	.438
2008 Colorado j-k	N.L.	OF	93	162	22	41	8	1	1	15	12	.253
2009 Charlotte	Int.	OF	10	42	6	11	4	0	0	2	1	.262
2009 Chicago l-m	A.L.	OF	132	537	75	163	25	6	7	48	30	.304
2010 Kansas City	A.L.	OF	95	390	46	121	8	6	5	44	30	.310
2010 Los Angeles n-o	N.L.	OF	39	149	17	39	6	1	1	7	5	.262
2011 Dunedin	Fla.St.	OF	3	12	1	3	1	0	0	1	0	.250
2011 Phillies	Gulf Coast	OF	3	10	2	3	2	1	0	1	1	.300
2011 Lehigh Valley	Int.	OF	14	53	4	13	6	1	0	0	2	.245
2011 Las Vegas p-q-r	P.C.	OF	14	59	12	15	2	2	0	6	3	.254
2012 Lehigh Valley	Int.	OF	23	76	13	15	1	0	0	4	6	.197
2012 Pawtucket	Int.	OF	25	89	10	25	2	1	1	11	4	.281
2012 Boston s-t-u-v-w	A.L.	OF	63	199	19	60	7	0	1	12	8	.302
Major League Totals		11 Yrs.	1079	3906	563	1096	178	41	42	312	309	.281
Division Series													
2005 Chicago	A.L.	OF	3	11	3	3	1	0	1	4	1	.273
Championship Series													
2005 Chicago	A.L.	OF	5	17	4	5	0	1	0	0	3	.294
World Series Record													
2005 Chicago	A.L.	OF	4	21	2	6	0	2	1	2	2	.286

a Sent to Florida Marlins for Texas Rangers to complete trade for pitcher Bobby Witt, August 8, 1995.
b Selected by Texas Rangers organization in Rule V draft, December 15, 1997.
c On disabled list from April 6 to May 22, 2000.
d Filed for free agency, October 15, 2000. Signed with Seattle Mariners organization, November 7, 2000.
e On disabled list from May 4 to June 12 and August 14 to 26, 2001.
f Claimed on waivers by Milwaukee Brewers, October 11, 2002.
g Traded to Chicago White Sox with pitcher Luis Vizcaino and player to be named later for outfielder Carlos Lee, December 13, 2004. Chicago White Sox received infielder Travis Hinton to complete trade, January 10, 2005.
h On disabled list from August 13 to August 29, 2005.
i On disabled list from April 16 to June 23 and from July 2 to July 24, 2007.
j Released by Chicago White Sox, November 28, 2007. Signed with Colorado Rockies organization, February 5, 2008.
k On disabled list from July 28 to August 22, 2008.
l Filed for free agency, November 1, 2008, re-signed with Colorado Rockies organization, January 14, 2009.
m Released by Colorado Rockies, April 1, 2009. Signed with Chicago White Sox organization, April 14, 2009.
n Filed for free agency, November 5, 2009. Signed with Kansas City Royals, January 8, 2010.
o Traded to Los Angeles Dodgers for catcher Lucas May and pitcher Elisaul Pimentel, July 29, 2010.
p Filed for free agency, November 4, 2010. Signed with Toronto Blue Jays organization, February 16, 2011.
q Released by Toronto Blue Jays, May 11, 2011. Signed with Philadelphia Phillies organization , May 26, 2011.
r Filed for free agency, November 2, 2011, re-signed with Philadelphia Phillies organization, November 30, 2011.
s Sold to Boston Red Sox, May 11, 2012.
t On disabled list from June 18 to July 6, 2012.
u Traded to Arizona Diamondbacks with pitcher Matt Albers for pitcher Craig Breslow, July 31, 2012.
v Released by Arizona Diamondbacks, August 2, 2012. Signed with Boston Red Sox, August 10, 2012.
w Filed for free agency, November 3, 2012.

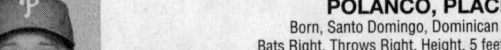

POLANCO, PLACIDO ENRIQUE

Born, Santo Domingo, Dominican Republic, October 10, 1975.
Bats Right. Throws Right. Height, 5 feet, 10 inches. Weight, 195 pounds.

Year	Club	Lea	Pos	G	AB	R	H	2B	3B	HR	RBI	SB	Avg
1994 Cardinals	Arizona	SS-2B	32	127	17	27	4	0	1	10	4	.213
1995 Peoria	Midwest	SS-2B	103	361	43	96	7	4	2	41	7	.266
1996 St. Pete	Fla.St.	2B	137	540	65	157	29	5	0	51	4	.291
1997 Arkansas	Texas	2B	129	508	71	148	16	3	2	51	19	.291
1998 Memphis	P.C.	2B-SS	70	246	36	69	19	1	1	21	6	.280
1998 St. Louis	N.L.	SS-2B	45	114	10	29	3	2	1	11	2	.254
1999 Memphis	P.C.	2B	29	120	18	33	4	1	0	10	2	.275
1999 St. Louis	N.L.	2B-3B-SS	88	220	24	61	9	3	1	19	1	.277
2000 St. Louis a	N.L.	2B-3B-SS-1B	118	323	50	102	12	3	5	39	4	.316
2001 St. Louis	N.L.	3B-SS-2B	144	564	87	173	26	4	3	38	12	.307
2002 St. Louis-Phil. b	N.L.	3B-SS-2B	147	548	75	158	32	2	9	49	5	.288
2003 Philadelphia c	N.L.	2B-3B	122	492	87	142	30	3	14	63	14	.289
2004 Reading	Eastern	2B	1	3	0	2	0	0	0	0	0	.667
2004 Scranton/WB	Int.	2B	1	3	1	0	0	0	0	0	0	.000
2004 Philadelphia d-e	N.L.	2B-3B	126	503	74	150	21	0	17	55	7	.298

Year	Club	Lea	Pos	G	AB	R	H	2B	3B	HR	RBI	SB	Avg
2005 Philadelphia	. . . .	N.L.	2B-3B-OF-SS	43	158	26	50	7	0	3	20	0	.316
2005 Detroit f-g	. . . .	A.L.	2B-3B	86	343	58	116	20	2	6	36	4	.338
2006 Detroit h	. . . .	A.L.	2B	110	461	58	136	18	1	4	52	1	.295
2007 Detroit	. . . .	A.L.	2B	142	587	105	200	36	3	9	67	7	.341
2008 Detroit	. . . .	A.L.	2B	141	580	90	178	34	3	8	58	7	.307
2009 Detroit i	. . . .	A.L.	2B	153	618	82	176	31	4	10	72	7	.285
2010 Phillies	. . . . . .	Gulf Coast	2B	1	3	1	3	1	0	0	2	0	1.000
2010 Clearwater	. . . . . .	Fla.St.	3B	1	4	1	1	0	0	0	0	0	.250
2010 Philadelphia j	. . . . . .	N.L.	3B-2B	132	554	76	165	27	2	6	52	5	.298
2011 Lehigh Valley	. . . . . .	Int.	3B	2	6	0	0	0	0	0	0	0	.000
2011 Philadelphia k	. . . . .	N.L.	3B-2B	122	469	46	130	14	0	5	50	3	.277
2012 Clearwater	. . . . . .	Fla.St.	3B	3	12	3	5	0	0	0	2	0	.417
2012 Philadelphia l-m	. . . .	N.L.	3B	90	303	28	78	15	0	2	19	0	.257
Major League Totals	. . . .		15 Yrs.	1809	6837	976	2044	335	32	103	700	79	.299
Division Series													
2000 St. Louis	. . . .	N.L.	3B	3	10	1	3	0	0	0	3	1	.300
2001 St. Louis	. . . .	N.L.	3B	5	15	1	4	0	0	0	1	1	.267
2006 Detroit	. . . .	A.L.	2B	4	17	3	7	1	0	0	2	0	.412
2010 Philadelphia	. . . .	N.L.	3B	2	9	1	1	0	0	0	0	0	.111
2011 Philadelphia	. . . .	N.L.	3B	5	19	0	2	0	0	0	0	0	.105
Division Series Totals	. . . .			19	70	6	17	1	0	0	6	2	.243
Championship Series													
2000 St. Louis	. . . .	N.L.	3B	4	5	0	1	0	0	0	0	0	.200
2006 Detroit	. . . .	A.L.	2B	4	17	2	9	1	0	0	2	0	.529
2010 Philadelphia	. . . .	N.L.	3B	6	20	3	5	2	0	0	5	1	.250
Championship Series Totals	. . . . . .			14	42	5	15	3	0	0	7	1	.357
World Series Record													
2006 Detroit	. . . .	A.L.	2B	5	17	0	0	0	0	0	0	0	.000

a On disabled list from July 1 to July 15, 2000.
b Traded to Philadelphia Phillies with pitcher Bud Smith and pitcher Mike Timlin for infielder Scott Rolen and pitcher Doug Nickle, July 29, 2002.
c On disabled list from April 16 to May 1, 2003.
d On disabled list from May 8 to June 7, 2004.
e Filed for free agency, October 29, 2004, re-signed with Philadelphia Phillies, December 19, 2004.
f Traded to Detroit Tigers for pitcher Ugueth Urbina and infielder Ramon Martinez, June 8, 2005.
g On disabled list from July 12 to July 27, 2005.
h On disabled list from August 16 to September 22, 2006.
i Filed for free agency, November 5, 2009. Signed with Philadelphia Phillies, December 3, 2009.
j On disabled list from June 26 to July 17, 2010.
k On disabled list from July 5 to July 30 and August 7 to August 22, 2011.
l On disabled list from July 23 to August 20 and September 5 to October 5, 2012.
m Filed for free agency, November 3, 2012. Signed with Miami Marlins, December 20, 2012.

POSEY, GERALD DEMP (BUSTER)

Born, Leesburg, Georgia, March 27, 1987.
Bats Right. Throws Right. Height, 6 feet, 1 inch. Weight, 205 pounds.

Year	Club	Lea	Pos	G	AB	R	H	2B	3B	HR	RBI	SB	Avg
2008 Giants	. . . .	Arizona	C	7	26	8	10	3	1	1	4	0	.385
2008 Salem-Keizer	. . . .	Northwest	C	3	11	2	3	2	0	0	2	0	.273
2009 San Jose	. . . .	Calif.	C	80	291	63	95	23	0	13	58	6	.326
2009 Fresno	. . . .	P.C.	C	35	131	21	42	8	1	5	22	0	.321
2009 San Francisco	. . . .	N.L.	C	7	17	1	2	0	0	0	0	0	.118
2010 Fresno	. . . .	P.C.	C-1B	47	172	31	60	13	2	6	32	1	.349
2010 San Francisco a	. . . .	N.L.	C-1B	108	406	58	124	23	2	18	67	0	.305
2011 San Francisco b	. . . .	N.L.	C-1B	45	162	17	46	5	0	4	21	3	.284
2012 San Francisco c	. . . .	N.L.	C-1B	148	530	78	178	39	1	24	103	1	*.336
Major League Totals	. . . .		4 Yrs.	308	1115	154	350	67	3	46	191	4	.314
Division Series													
2010 San Francisco	. . . .	N.L.	C	4	16	3	6	1	0	0	0	1	.375
2012 San Francisco	. . . .	N.L.	C-1B	5	19	3	4	0	0	2	5	0	.211
Division Series Totals	. . . .			9	35	6	10	1	0	2	5	1	.286
Championship Series													
2010 San Francisco	. . . .	N.L.	C	6	23	1	5	2	0	0	3	0	.217
2012 San Francisco	. . . .	N.L.	C-1B	7	26	1	4	0	0	0	1	0	.154
Championship Series Totals	. . . . . .			13	49	2	9	2	0	0	4	0	.184
World Series Record													
2010 San Francisco	. . . .	N.L.	C	5	20	2	6	0	0	1	2	0	.300

Year	Club	Lea	Pos	G	AB	R	H	2B	3B	HR	RBI	SB	Avg
2012 San Francisco	N.L.		C	4	15	1	4	0	0	1	3	0	.267
World Series Totals.............				9	35	3	10	0	0	2	5	0	.286

a Selected Rookie of the Year in National League for 2010.
b On disabled list from May 26 to October 31, 2011.
c Selected Most Valuable Player in National League for 2012.

PRADO, MARTIN MANUEL
Born, Maracay, Venezuela, October 27, 1983.
Bats Right. Throws Right. Height, 6 feet, 1 inch. Weight, 170 pounds.

Year	Club	Lea	Pos	G	AB	R	H	2B	3B	HR	RBI	SB	Avg
2003 Braves ......Gulf Coast			2B-3B	59	220	28	63	2	6	0	23	9	.286
2004 Rome..........	So.Atl.		2B	107	429	68	135	25	6	3	38	14	.315
2005 Myrtle Beach ..	Carolina		2B	75	297	44	91	13	3	4	34	9	.306
2005 Mississippi....	Southern		2B	39	143	17	40	7	1	1	11	3	.280
2006 Richmond	Int.		2B-3B	60	241	30	68	12	1	2	23	2	.282
2006 Mississippi....	Southern		2B-3B	43	176	17	49	6	2	1	15	2	.278
2006 Atlanta	N.L.		2B-3B	24	42	3	11	1	1	1	9	0	.262
2007 Richmond	Int.		2B-3B-SS	103	395	61	125	23	3	4	41	5	.316
2007 Atlanta	N.L.		2B-3B	28	59	5	17	3	0	0	2	0	.288
2008 Mississippi....	Southern		2B-3B-SS-OF	5	19	2	5	2	0	0	3	0	.263
2008 Atlanta a..........	N.L.		3B-1B-2B-OF	78	228	36	73	18	4	2	33	3	.320
2009 Atlanta	N.L.		2B-3B-1B-OF	128	450	64	138	38	0	11	49	1	.307
2010 Gwinnett.	Int.		2B-3B	1	4	0	1	0	0	0	0	0	.250
2010 Atlanta b..........	N.L.		2B-3B-1B	140	599	100	184	40	3	15	66	5	.307
2011 Mississippi.......	Southern		3B	2	9	2	2	0	0	0	2	0	.222
2011 Gwinnett.	Int.		3B-OF	6	17	2	3	0	0	0	1	0	.176
2011 Atlanta c..........	N.L.		OF-3B-1B	129	551	66	143	26	2	13	57	4	.260
2012 Atlanta	N.L.		OF-3B-SS-2B	156	617	81	186	42	6	10	70	17	.301
Major League Totals		7 Yrs.		683	2546	355	752	168	16	52	286	30	.295
Wild Card Playoff													
2012 Atlanta	N.L.		OF	1	5	0	1	0	0	0	0	0	.200

a On disabled list from May 5 to July 3, 2008.
b On disabled list from July 31 to August 17, 2010.
c On disabled list from June 8 to July 15, 2011.

PRESLEY, ALEXANDER CRAWFORD (ALEX)
Born, Monroe, Louisiana, July 25, 1985.
Bats Left. Throws Left. Height, 5 feet, 9 inches. Weight, 190 pounds.

Year	Club	Lea	Pos	G	AB	R	H	2B	3B	HR	RBI	SB	Avg
2006 Williamsport.....	N.Y.-Penn.		OF	61	223	26	58	7	8	3	23	3	.260
2007 Hickory............	So.Atl.		OF	121	495	79	145	22	8	11	63	18	.293
2008 Lynchburg	Carolina		OF	82	287	39	74	15	1	6	35	13	.258
2009 Lynchburg	Carolina		OF	115	417	51	107	17	11	4	37	9	.257
2010 Altoona...........	Eastern		OF	67	246	42	86	13	7	6	47	5	.350
2010 Indianapolis	Int.		OF	69	272	44	80	15	6	6	38	8	.294
2010 Pittsburgh	N.L.		OF	19	23	2	6	1	0	0	0	1	.261
2011 Bradenton	Fla.St.		OF	2	6	2	1	0	0	0	0	0	.167
2011 Indianapolis	Int.		OF	87	342	58	114	18	5	8	41	22	.333
2011 Pittsburgh a	N.L.		OF	52	215	24	64	12	6	4	20	9	.298
2012 Indianapolis	Int.		OF	40	153	24	47	3	4	5	22	7	.307
2012 Pittsburgh b	N.L.		OF	104	346	46	82	14	7	10	25	9	.237
Major League Totals		3 Yrs.		175	584	75	152	27	13	14	45	19	.260

a On disabled list from July 23 to August 25, 2011.
b On disabled list from July 5 to July 16, 2012.

PUJOLS, JOSE ALBERTO (ALBERT)
Born, Santo Domingo, Dominican Republic, January 16, 1980.
Bats Right. Throws Right. Height, 6 feet, 3 inches. Weight, 225 pounds.

Year	Club	Lea	Pos	G	AB	R	H	2B	3B	HR	RBI	SB	Avg
2000 Potomac......	Carolina		3B	21	81	11	23	8	1	2	10	1	.284
2000 Peoria........	Midwest		3B	109	395	62	128	32	6	17	84	2	.324
2000 Memphis	P.C.		3B-OF	3	14	1	3	1	0	0	2	1	.214
2001 St. Louis a	N.L.		OF-3B-1B	161	590	112	194	47	4	37	130	1	.329
2002 St. Louis.........	N.L.		OF-3B-1B-SS	157	590	118	185	40	2	34	127	2	.314
2003 St. Louis.........	N.L.		OF-1B	157	591	*137	*212	*51	1	43	124	5	*.359

136

Year	Club	Lea	Pos	G	AB	R	H	2B	3B	HR	RBI	SB	Avg
2004 St. Louis.........N.L.			1B	154	592	*133	196	51	2	46	123	5	.331
2005 St. Louis b.......N.L.			1B	161	591	*129	195	38	2	41	117	16	.330
2006 St. Louis c.......N.L.			1B	143	535	119	177	33	1	49	137	7	.331
2007 St. Louis.........N.L.			1B	158	565	99	185	38	1	32	103	2	.327
2008 St. Louis d-e.....N.L.			1B-2B	148	524	100	187	44	0	37	116	7	.357
2009 St. Louis f.......N.L.			1B	160	568	*124	186	45	1	*47	135	16	.327
2010 St. Louis.........N.L.			1B	159	587	*115	183	39	1	*42	*118	14	.312
2011 St. Louis g-h.....N.L.			1B-3B	147	579	105	173	29	0	37	99	9	.299
2012 Los Angeles......A.L.			1B-3B	154	607	85	173	50	0	30	105	8	.285
Major League Totals...........		12 Yrs.		1859	6919	1376	2246	505	15	475	1434	92	.325
Division Series													
2001 St. Louis.........N.L.			1B-OF	5	18	1	2	0	0	1	2	0	.111
2002 St. Louis.........N.L.			OF-1B-3B	3	10	3	3	0	0	1	3	0	.300
2004 St. Louis.........N.L.			1B	4	15	4	5	0	0	2	5	0	.333
2005 St. Louis.........N.L.			1B	3	9	4	5	2	0	0	2	0	.556
2006 St. Louis.........N.L.			1B	4	15	3	5	1	0	1	3	0	.333
2009 St. Louis.........N.L.			1B	3	10	0	3	0	0	0	1	0	.300
2011 St. Louis.........N.L.			1B	5	20	2	7	3	0	0	1	1	.350
Division Series Totals..........				27	97	17	30	6	1	4	17	1	.309
Championship Series													
2002 St. Louis.........N.L.			OF-3B-1B	5	19	2	5	1	0	1	2	0	.263
2004 St. Louis.........N.L.			1B	7	28	10	14	2	0	4	9	0	.500
2005 St. Louis.........N.L.			1B	6	23	3	7	0	0	2	6	0	.304
2006 St. Louis.........N.L.			1B	7	22	5	7	1	0	1	1	0	.318
2011 St. Louis.........N.L.			1B	6	23	5	11	4	0	2	9	0	.478
Championship Series Totals......				31	115	25	44	8	0	10	27	0	.383
World Series Record													
2004 St. Louis.........N.L.			1B	4	15	1	5	2	0	0	0	0	.333
2006 St. Louis.........N.L.			1B	5	15	3	3	1	0	1	2	0	.200
2011 St. Louis.........N.L.			1B	7	25	8	6	1	0	3	6	0	.240
World Series Totals............				16	55	12	14	4	0	4	8	0	.255

a Selected Rookie of the Year in National League for 2001.
b Selected Most Valuable Player in National League for 2005.
c On disabled list from June 4 to June 22, 2006.
d On disabled list from June 11 to June 26, 2008.
e Selected Most Valuable Player in National League for 2008.
f Selected Most Valuable Player in National League for 2009.
g On disabled list from June 20 to July 5, 2011.
h Filed for free agency, October 30, 2011. Signed with Los Angeles Angels, December 10, 2011.

PUNTO, NICHOLAS PAUL (NICK)

Born, San Diego, California, November 8, 1977.
Bats Both. Throws Right. Height, 5 feet, 9 inches. Weight, 185 pounds.

Year	Club	Lea	Pos	G	AB	R	H	2B	3B	HR	RBI	SB	Avg
1998 Batavia......N.Y.-Penn.			SS-2B	72	279	51	69	9	4	1	20	19	.247
1999 Clearwater......Fla.St.			SS	106	400	65	122	18	6	1	48	16	.305
2000 Reading......Eastern			SS	121	456	77	116	15	4	5	47	33	.254
2001 Scranton-WB......Int.			SS	123	463	57	106	19	5	1	39	33	.229
2001 Philadelphia.......N.L.			SS	4	5	0	2	0	0	0	0	0	.400
2002 Philadelphia.......N.L.			2B-SS	9	6	0	1	0	0	0	0	0	.167
2002 Scranton-WB......Int.			SS	115	443	74	120	12	5	1	29	42	.271
2003 Philadelphia.......N.L.			2B-3B-SS	64	92	14	20	2	0	1	4	2	.217
2003 Scranton/WB a...... Int.			SS	25	111	19	35	7	1	0	9	7	.315
2004 Minnesota.......A.L.			2B-SS-3B-OF	38	91	17	23	0	0	2	12	6	.253
2004 Quad Cities b.. Midwest			SS-2B-3B	4	16	4	7	1	0	1	6	1	.438
2005 Rochester.........Int.			2B	4	15	2	3	1	0	0	1	0	.200
2005 Minnesota c.......A.L.			2B-SS-3B-OF	112	394	45	94	18	4	4	26	13	.239
2006 Minnesota.......A.L.			3B-SS-2B-OF	135	459	73	133	21	7	1	45	17	.290
2007 Minnesota.......A.L.			3B-SS-2B	150	472	53	99	18	4	1	25	16	.210
2008 Fort Myers......Fla.St.			SS	3	12	0	3	0	0	0	1	1	.250
2008 Minnesota d-e.....A.L.			SS-2B-3B-OF	99	338	43	96	19	4	2	28	15	.284
2009 Minnesota f.......A.L.			2B-SS-3B	125	359	56	82	15	1	1	38	16	.228
2010 Minnesota g-h.....A.L.			3B-SS-2B	88	252	24	60	11	1	1	20	6	.238
2011 Springfield......Texas			2B	7	24	3	8	1	0	0	2	1	.333
2011 Memphis.........P.C.			2B-3B	5	15	2	3	0	0	0	0	0	.200
2011 St. Louis i-j.......A.L.			2B-SS-3B	63	133	21	37	8	4	1	20	1	.278
2012 Boston..........A.L.			3B-2B-SS-1B	65	125	14	25	6	0	1	10	5	.200
2012 Los Angeles k.....N.L.			2B-3B	22	35	6	10	1	0	0	0	1	.286

Year	Club	Lea	Pos	G	AB	R	H	2B	3B	HR	RBI	SB	Avg
Major League Totals			12 Yrs.	974	2761	366	682	119	25	15	228	98	.247
Division Series													
2006 Minnesota	A.L.		3B	3	12	0	2	0	0	0	0	0	.167
2009 Minnesota	A.L.		2B	3	9	0	4	1	0	0	1	0	.444
2011 St. Louis	N.L.		2B	3	6	0	1	0	0	0	0	0	.167
Division Series Totals				9	27	0	7	1	0	0	1	0	.259
Championship Series													
2011 St. Louis	N.L.		2B	6	15	0	2	0	0	0	3	0	.133
World Series Record													
2011 St. Louis	N.L.		2B	6	14	0	3	0	0	0	0	0	.214

a Traded to Minnesota Twins with pitcher Carlos Silva and cash for pitcher Eric Milton, December 3, 2003.
b On disabled list from May 9 to June 30 and July 27 to October 28, 2004.
c On disabled list from June 3 to July 3, 2005.
d On disabled list from May 8 to May 31 and June 6 to June 24, 2008.
e Filed for free agency, October 30, 2008, re-signed with Minnesota Twins, December 11, 2008.
f On disabled list from May 28 to June 12, 2009.
g On disabled list from April 16 to May 1 and July 29 to August 17 and August 20 to September 10, 2010.
h Filed for free agency, November 1, 2010. Signed with St. Louis Cardinals, January 21, 2011.
i On disabled list from March 22 to April 19 and May 18 to June 27 and July 29 to September 6, 2011.
j Filed for free agency, October 30, 2011. Signed with Boston Red Sox, December 14, 2011.
k Traded to Los Angeles Dodgers with outfielder Carl Crawford, infielder Adrian Gonzalez, pitcher Josh Beckett and cash for infielder James Loney, infielder Ivan DeJesus, pitcher Allen Webster and player to be named later, August 25, 2012. Boston Red Sox received pitcher Rubby De La Rosa to complete trade, October 4, 2012.

QUENTIN, CARLOS JOSE
Born, Bellflower, California, August 28, 1982.
Bats Right. Throws Right. Height, 6 feet, 1 inch. Weight, 225 pounds.

Year	Club	Lea	Pos	G	AB	R	H	2B	3B	HR	RBI	SB	Avg
2004 Lancaster	Calif.		OF	65	242	64	75	14	1	15	51	5	.310
2004 El Paso	Texas		OF	60	210	39	75	19	0	6	38	0	.357
2005 Tucson	P.C.		OF	136	452	98	136	28	4	21	89	9	.301
2006 Tucson	P.C.		OF	85	318	66	92	30	3	9	52	5	.289
2006 Arizona	N.L.		OF	57	166	23	42	13	3	9	32	1	.253
2007 Tucson	P.C.		OF	33	115	30	40	12	1	4	27	0	.348
2007 Arizona a-b	N.L.		OF	81	229	29	49	16	0	5	31	2	.214
2008 Chicago	A.L.		OF	130	480	96	138	26	1	36	100	7	.287
2009 Kannapolis	So.Atl.		OF	2	3	0	1	1	0	0	1	0	.333
2009 Charlotte	Int.		OF	12	37	10	14	3	0	1	9	0	.378
2009 Chicago c	A.L.		OF	99	351	47	83	14	0	21	56	3	.236
2010 Chicago	A.L.		OF	131	453	73	110	25	2	26	87	2	.243
2011 Chicago d-e	A.L.		OF	118	421	53	107	31	0	24	77	1	.254
2012 Lake Elsinore	Calif.		OF	4	14	3	6	1	0	1	5	0	.429
2012 Tucson	P.C.		OF	5	14	5	4	0	0	1	4	0	.286
2012 San Diego f	N.L.		OF	86	284	44	74	21	0	16	46	0	.261
Major League Totals			7 Yrs.	702	2384	365	603	146	6	137	429	16	.253

a On disabled list from March 23 to April 16 and August 2 to September 1, 2007.
b Traded to Chicago White Sox for infielder Chris Carter, December 3, 2007.
c On disabled list from May 26 to July 20, 2009.
d On disabled list from August 21 to September 12, 2011.
e Traded to San Diego Padres for pitcher Simon Castro and pitcher Pedro Hernandez, December 31, 2011.
f On disabled list from April 3 to May 28, 2012.

RAMIREZ, ALEXEI FERNANDO
Born, Pinar Del Rio, Cuba, September 22, 1981.
Bats Right. Throws Right. Height, 6 feet, 3 inches. Weight, 185 pounds.

Year	Club	Lea	Pos	G	AB	R	H	2B	3B	HR	RBI	SB	Avg
2008 Chicago a-b	A.L.		2B-SS-OF-3B	136	480	65	139	22	2	21	77	13	.290
2009 Chicago	A.L.		SS	148	542	71	150	14	1	15	68	14	.277
2010 Chicago	A.L.		SS	156	585	83	165	29	2	18	70	13	.282
2011 Chicago	A.L.		SS	158	614	81	165	31	2	15	70	7	.269
2012 Chicago	A.L.		SS	158	593	59	157	24	4	9	73	20	.265
Major League Totals			5 Yrs.	756	2814	359	776	120	11	78	358	67	.276
Division Series													
2008 Chicago	A.L.		2B	4	12	1	3	0	0	0	2	0	.250

a Played in Cuba 2001-2007.
b Signed with Chicago White Sox, January 1, 2008.

RAMIREZ (NIN), ARAMIS

Born, Santo Domingo, Dominican Republic, June 25, 1978.
Bats Right. Throws Right. Height, 6 feet, 1 inch. Weight, 215 pounds.

Year Club	Lea	Pos	G	AB	R	H	2B	3B	HR	RBI	SB	Avg
1995 Pittsburgh . . . . . . .Dominican		3B	64	214	41	63	13	0	11	54	2	.294
1996 Erie.	N.Y.-Penn.	3B	61	223	37	68	14	4	9	42	0	.305
1996 Augusta	So.Atl.	3B	6	20	3	4	1	0	1	2	0	.200
1997 Lynchburg	Carolina	3B	137	482	85	134	24	2	29	114	5	.278
1998 Nashville . .	P.C.	3B-SS	47	168	19	46	10	0	5	18	0	.274
1998 Pittsburgh a	N.L.	3B	72	251	23	59	9	1	6	24	0	.235
1999 Nashville	P.C.	3B	131	460	92	151	35	1	21	74	5	.328
1999 Pittsburgh	N.L.	3B	18	56	2	10	2	1	0	7	0	.179
2000 Nashville	P.C.	3B	44	167	28	59	12	2	4	26	2	.353
2000 Pittsburgh b	N.L.	3B	73	254	19	65	15	2	6	35	0	.256
2001 Pittsburgh	N.L.	3B	158	603	83	181	40	0	34	112	5	.300
2002 Pittsburgh	N.L.	3B	142	522	51	122	26	0	18	71	2	.234
2003 Pittsburgh-Chicago c-d .	N.L.	3B	159	607	75	165	32	2	27	106	2	.272
2004 Chicago	N.L.	3B	145	547	99	174	32	1	36	103	0	.318
2005 Chicago e	N.L.	3B	123	463	72	140	30	0	31	92	0	.302
2006 Chicago f	N.L.	3B	157	594	93	173	38	4	38	119	2	.291
2007 Chicago g	N.L.	3B	132	506	72	157	35	4	26	101	0	.310
2008 Chicago	N.L.	3B	149	554	97	160	44	1	27	111	2	.289
2009 Peoria.	Midwest	3B	3	6	2	3	1	0	0	1	0	.500
2009 Chicago h	N.L.	3B	82	306	46	97	14	1	15	65	2	.317
2010 Peoria.	Midwest	3B	2	6	1	1	0	0	0	1	0	.167
2010 Chicago i	N.L.	3B	124	465	61	112	21	1	25	83	0	.241
2011 Chicago j	N.L.	3B	149	565	80	173	35	1	26	93	1	.306
2012 Milwaukee	N.L.	3B	149	570	92	171	*50	3	27	105	9	.300
Major League Totals		15 Yrs.	1832	6863	965	1959	423	22	342	1227	25	.285
Division Series												
2003 Chicago	N.L.	3B	5	18	2	5	1	0	1	3	0	.278
2007 Chicago	N.L.	3B	3	12	0	0	0	0	0	0	0	.000
2008 Chicago	N.L.	3B	3	11	1	2	1	0	0	0	0	.182
Division Series Totals.			11	41	3	7	2	0	1	3	0	.171
Championship Series												
2003 Chicago	N.L.	3B	7	26	4	6	0	1	3	7	0	.231

a On disabled list from August 10 to September 4, 1998.
b On disabled list from August 29 to October 1, 2000.
c Traded to Chicago Cubs with outfielder Kenny Lofton for infielder Jose Hernandez, pitcher Matt Bruback and player to be named later, July 22, 2003.
d Pittsburgh Pirates received infielder Bobby Hill to complete trade, August 15, 2003.
e On disabled list from August 25 to October 3, 2005.
f Filed for free agency, October 30, 2006, re-signed with Chicago Cubs, November 12, 2006.
g On disabled list from June 7 to June 22, 2007.
h On disabled list from May 9 to July 6, 2009.
i On disabled list from June 8 to June 25, 2010.
j Filed for free agency, November 1, 2011. Signed with Milwaukee Brewers, December 12, 2011.

RAMIREZ, HANLEY

Born, Samana, Dominican Republic, December 23, 1983.
Bats Right. Throws Right. Height, 6 feet, 3 inches. Weight, 195 pounds.

Year Club	Lea	Pos	G	AB	R	H	2B	3B	HR	RBI	SB	Avg
2002 Red Sox	Gulf Coast	SS-2B-3B	45	164	29	56	11	3	6	26	8	.341
2002 Lowell	N.Y.-Penn.	SS	22	97	17	36	9	2	1	19	4	.371
2003 Augusta	So.Atl.	SS	111	422	69	116	24	3	8	50	36	.275
2004 Portland	Eastern	SS	32	129	26	40	7	2	5	15	12	.310
2004 Sarasota	Fla.St.	SS	62	239	33	74	8	4	1	24	12	.310
2004 Red Sox	Gulf Coast	SS-2B	6	20	5	8	0	1	0	7	1	.400
2005 Portland	Eastern	SS-2B-3B	122	465	66	126	21	7	6	52	26	.271
2005 Boston a	A.L.	SS	2	2	0	0	0	0	0	0	0	.000
2006 Florida b	N.L.	SS	158	633	119	185	46	11	17	59	51	.292
2007 Florida	N.L.	SS	154	639	125	212	48	6	29	81	51	.332
2008 Florida	N.L.	SS	153	589	*125	177	34	4	33	67	35	.301
2009 Florida	N.L.	SS	151	576	101	197	42	1	24	106	27	*.342
2010 Florida	N.L.	SS	142	543	92	163	28	2	21	76	32	.300
2011 Jupiter	Fla.St.	SS	6	21	6	10	1	1	0	4	1	.476
2011 Florida c	N.L.	SS	92	338	55	82	16	0	10	45	20	.243
2012 Miami-Los Angeles d	N.L.	3B-SS	157	604	79	155	29	4	24	92	21	.257
Major League Totals		8 Yrs.	1009	3924	696	1171	243	28	158	526	237	.298

a Traded to Florida Marlins with pitcher Anibal Sanchez and pitcher Jesus Delgado for pitcher Josh Beckett, infielder Mike Lowell and pitcher Guillermo Mota, November 24, 2005.

b Selected Rookie of the Year in National League for 2006.

c On disabled list from May 30 to June 14 and August 3 to October 31, 2011.

d Traded to Los Angeles Dodgers with pitcher Randy Choate for pitcher Nathan Eovaldi and pitcher Scott McGough, July 25, 2012.

RAMOS (CAMPOS), WILSON ABRAHAM

Born, Valencia, Venezuela, August 10, 1987.
Bats Right. Throws Right. Height, 6 feet. Weight, 220 pounds.

Year	Club	Lea	Pos	G	AB	R	H	2B	3B	HR	RBI	SB	Avg
2006	Twins	Gulf Coast	C-1B	46	154	18	44	12	1	3	26	4	.286
2007	Beloit	Midwest	C	73	292	40	85	17	1	8	42	1	.291
2008	Fort Myers	Fla.St.	C	126	452	50	130	23	2	13	78	0	.288
2009	Twins	Gulf Coast	C	5	19	4	6	1	1	3	6	0	.316
2009	New Britain	Eastern	C	54	205	31	65	16	0	4	29	0	.317
2010	Minnesota	A.L.	C	7	27	2	8	3	0	0	1	0	.296
2010	Rochester	Int.	C	71	278	25	67	14	0	5	30	1	.241
2010	Syracuse	Int.	C	20	79	14	25	3	1	3	8	0	.316
2010	Washington a	N.L.	C	15	52	3	14	4	0	1	4	0	.269
2011	Washington	N.L.	C	113	389	48	104	22	1	15	52	0	.267
2012	Washington b	N.L.	C	25	83	11	22	2	0	3	10	0	.265

Major League Totals			3 Yrs.	160	551	64	148	31	1	19	67	0	.269

a Traded to Washington Nationals with pitcher Joe Testa and cash for pitcher Matt Capps, July 30, 2010.

b On disabled list from May 13 to November 2, 2012.

RANSOM, BRYAN CODY (CODY)

Born, Mesa, Arizona, February 17, 1976.
Bats Right. Throws Right. Height, 6 feet, 2 inches. Weight, 205 pounds.

Year	Club	Lea	Pos	G	AB	R	H	2B	3B	HR	RBI	SB	Avg
1998	Salem-Keizr	Northwest	SS	71	236	52	55	12	7	6	27	19	.233
1999	Bakersfield	Calif.	SS	99	356	69	98	12	6	11	47	15	.275
1999	Shreveport	Texas	SS	14	41	6	5	0	0	2	4	0	.122
2000	Shreveport	Texas	SS	130	459	58	92	21	2	7	47	9	.200
2001	Fresno	P.C.	SS	134	469	77	113	21	6	23	78	17	.241
2001	San Francisco	N.L.	SS	9	7	1	0	0	0	0	0	0	.000
2002	Fresno	P.C.	SS	135	449	53	93	18	4	13	46	6	.207
2002	San Francisco	N.L.	SS	7	3	2	2	0	0	0	1	0	.667
2003	Fresno	P.C.	SS	112	396	56	100	16	4	12	50	14	.253
2003	San Francisco	N.L.	SS	20	27	7	6	1	0	1	1	0	.222
2004	San Francisco	N.L.	SS-2B-3B-OF	78	68	13	17	6	0	1	11	2	.250
2004	Fresno	P.C.	2B-SS-3B	36	136	29	42	6	2	10	21	8	.309
2005	Iowa	P.C.	SS-3B-2B-1B	65	171	22	40	5	1	2	16	6	.234
2005	Oklahoma a-b-c	P.C.	SS-3B-2B	24	92	13	24	5	0	5	17	0	.261
2006	Round Rock d-e	P.C.	SS-3B-2B	122	380	64	94	23	1	21	62	2	.247
2007	Round Rock	P.C.	3B-SS-1B-OF	135	503	75	131	35	0	28	90	21	.260
2007	Houston f	N.L.	SS-2B-3B	19	35	9	8	2	0	1	3	0	.229
2008	Scranton-WB	Int.	3B-SS-2B-1B	116	423	69	108	24	3	22	71	9	.255
2008	New York	A.L.	1B-SS-3B-2B	33	43	9	13	3	0	4	8	0	.302
2009	New York	N.L.	3B-SS-1B-2B	31	79	11	15	9	1	0	10	2	.190
2009	Scranton-WB g-h-i	Int.	3B-SS-2B-1B	31	96	24	23	7	1	3	16	0	.240
2010	Philadelphia	N.L.	3B-2B-1B	22	42	6	8	0	0	2	5	1	.190
2010	Lehigh Valley	Int.	3B-SS-OF-2B	110	394	58	103	25	1	18	63	5	.261
2011	Arizona	N.L.	SS-3B	12	33	3	5	2	0	1	4	1	.152
2011	Reno j-k	P.C.	SS-3B-2B	101	372	86	118	29	3	27	92	10	.317
2012	Reno	P.C.	SS-3B	10	34	5	10	2	0	2	9	0	.294
2012	Milwaukee-Arizona l-m-n	N.L.	SS-3B-2B-1B	90	246	29	54	14	0	11	42	0	.220

Major League Totals			10 Yrs.	321	583	90	128	37	1	21	85	6	.220

a Not offered contract, December 20, 2004. Signed with Chicago Cubs organization, January 20, 2005.

b Sold to Texas Rangers, March 30, 2005.

c Released by Texas Rangers, may 25, 2005. Signed with Chicago Cubs organization, May 27, 2005.

d Filed for free agency, October 15, 2005. Signed with Seattle Mariners organization, January 8, 2006.

e Sold to Houston Astros, March 30, 2006.

f Filed for free agency, October 21, 2007. Signed with New York Yankees organization, November 27, 2007.

g On disabled list from April 26 to June 24, 2009.

h Filed for free agency, August 8, 2009, re-signed with New York Yankees organization, August 10, 2009.

i Filed for free agency, November 9, 2009. Signed with Philadelphia Phillies organization, December 11, 2009.

j Filed for free agency, November 6, 2010. Signed with Arizona Diamondbacks organization, January 19, 2011.

k Filed for free agency, November 2, 2011, re-signed with Arizona Diamondbacks organization, December 11, 2011.
l Claimed on waivers by Milwaukee Brewers, May 23, 2012.
m Claimed on waivers by Arizona Diamondbacks, August 31, 2012.
n Filed for free agency, October 25, 2012. Signed with San Diego Padres organization, December 21, 2012.

RASMUS, COLBY RYAN

Born, Columbus, Georgia, August 11, 1986.
Bats Left. Throws Left. Height, 6 feet, 2 inches. Weight, 200 pounds.

Year	Club	Lea	Pos	G	AB	R	H	2B	3B	HR	RBI	SB	Avg
2005	Johnson City	Appal.	OF	62	216	47	64	16	5	7	27	13	.296
2006	Palm Beach	Fla.St.	OF	53	193	22	49	4	5	5	35	11	.254
2006	Quad Cities	Midwest	OF	78	303	49	94	22	3	11	50	17	.310
2007	Springfield	Texas	OF	128	472	93	130	37	3	29	72	18	.275
2008	Palm Beach	Fla.St.	OF	3	9	1	0	0	0	0	0	0	.000
2008	Cardinals	Gulf Coast	OF	3	9	1	5	1	0	1	2	0	.556
2008	Memphis	P.C.	OF	90	331	56	83	15	0	11	36	15	.251
2009	St. Louis	N.L.	OF	147	474	72	119	22	2	16	52	3	.251
2010	St. Louis	N.L.	OF	144	464	85	128	28	3	23	66	12	.276
2011	St. Louis	N.L.	OF	94	338	61	83	14	6	11	40	5	.246
2011	Toronto a-b	A.L.	OF	35	133	14	23	10	0	3	13	0	.173
2012	Toronto	A.L.	OF	151	565	75	126	21	5	23	75	4	.223
Major League Totals			4 Yrs.	571	1974	307	479	95	16	76	246	24	.243
Division Series													
2009	St. Louis	N.L.	OF	3	9	1	4	3	0	1	0	0	.444

a Traded to Toronto Blue Jays with pitcher Trever Miller, pitcher Brian Tallet and pitcher P.J. Walters for pitcher Edwin Jackson, pitcher Octavio Dotel, pitcher Marc Rzepczynski, outfielder Corey Patterson and cash, July 27, 2011.
b On disabled list from August 24 to September 16, 2011.

REDDICK, WILLIAM JOSHUA (JOSH)

Born, Savannah, Georgia, February 19, 1987.
Bats Left. Throws Right. Height, 6 feet, 2 inches. Weight, 180 pounds.

Year	Club	Lea	Pos	G	AB	R	H	2B	3B	HR	RBI	SB	Avg
2007	Greenville	So.Atl.	OF	94	369	60	113	17	6	18	72	8	.306
2007	Portland	Eastern	PH	1	1	0	0	0	0	0	0	0	.000
2008	Greenville	So.Atl.	OF	14	53	7	18	4	2	0	9	2	.340
2008	Lancaster	Calif.	OF	76	312	60	107	11	8	17	57	9	.343
2008	Portland	Eastern	OF	34	117	22	25	4	2	6	25	3	.214
2009	Portland	Eastern	OF	63	256	47	71	17	3	13	29	5	.277
2009	Pawtucket	Int.	OF	18	71	1	9	0	2	0	6	0	.127
2009	Boston	A.L.	OF	27	59	5	10	4	0	2	4	0	.169
2010	Pawtucket	Int.	OF	114	451	59	120	28	4	18	65	4	.266
2010	Boston	A.L.	OF	29	62	5	12	3	1	1	5	1	.194
2011	Pawtucket	Int.	OF	52	191	37	44	9	1	14	36	4	.230
2011	Boston a	A.L.	OF	87	254	41	71	18	3	7	28	1	.280
2012	Oakland	A.L.	OF	156	611	85	148	29	5	32	85	11	.242
Major League Totals			4 Yrs.	299	986	136	241	54	9	42	122	13	.244
Division Series													
2012	Oakland	A.L.	OF	5	17	2	2	0	0	1	1	0	.118

a Traded to Oakland Athletics with infielder Miles Head and pitcher Raul Alcantara for pitcher Andrew Bailey and outfielder Ryan Sweeney, December 28, 2011.

REIMOLD, NOLAN GALLAGHER

Born, Greenville, Pennsylvania, October 12, 1983.
Bats Right. Throws Right. Height, 6 feet, 4 inches. Weight, 215 pounds.

Year	Club	Lea	Pos	G	AB	R	H	2B	3B	HR	RBI	SB	Avg
2005	Aberdeen	N.Y.-Penn.	OF-1B	50	180	33	53	15	2	9	30	2	.294
2005	Frederick	Carolina	OF	23	83	17	22	6	0	6	11	3	.265
2006	Frederick	Carolina	OF	119	415	73	106	26	0	19	75	14	.255
2007	Orioles	Gulf Coast	OF	9	30	4	7	4	1	0	8	0	.233
2007	Bowie	Eastern	OF	50	186	30	57	15	0	11	34	2	.306
2008	Bowie	Eastern	OF	139	507	87	144	29	3	25	84	7	.284
2009	Norfolk	Int.	OF	31	109	21	43	11	0	9	27	6	.394
2009	Baltimore a	A.L.	OF	104	358	49	100	18	2	15	45	8	.279
2010	Norfolk	Int.	OF-1B	94	337	52	84	12	0	10	37	9	.249
2010	Baltimore	A.L.	OF	39	116	9	24	5	0	3	14	0	.207
2011	Norfolk	Int.	OF	39	139	16	33	6	0	6	22	2	.237
2011	Baltimore	A.L.	OF	87	267	40	66	10	3	13	45	7	.247

Year	Club	Lea	Pos	G	AB	R	H	2B	3B	HR	RBI	SB	Avg
2012 Baltimore b	A.L.	OF	16	67	10	21	6	0	5	10	1	.313
Major League Totals	4 Yrs.	246	808	108	211	39	5	36	114	16	.261

a On disabled list from September 18 to October 13, 2009.
b On disabled list from May 1 to November 2, 2012.

REVERE, BEN DANIEL
Born, Atlanta, Georgia, May 3, 1988.
Bats Left. Throws Right. Height, 5 feet, 9 inches. Weight, 170 pounds.

Year	Club	Lea	Pos	G	AB	R	H	2B	3B	HR	RBI	SB	Avg
2007 Twins	Gulf Coast	OF	50	191	46	62	6	10	0	29	21	.325
2008 Beloit	Midwest	OF	83	340	51	129	17	10	1	43	44	.379
2009 Fort Myers	Fla.St.	OF	121	466	75	145	13	4	2	48	45	.311
2010 New Britain	Eastern	OF	94	361	44	110	10	4	1	23	36	.305
2010 Minnesota	A.L.	OF	13	28	1	5	0	0	0	2	0	.179
2011 Rochester	Int.	OF	32	132	15	40	3	1	1	9	8	.303
2011 Minnesota	A.L.	OF	117	450	56	120	9	5	0	30	34	.267
2012 Rochester	Int.	OF	23	94	9	31	1	0	0	6	6	.330
2012 Minnesota a	A.L.	OF	124	511	70	150	13	6	0	32	40	.294
Major League Totals	3 Yrs.	254	989	127	275	22	11	0	64	74	.278

a Traded to Philadelphia Phillies for pitcher Trevor May and pitcher Vance Worley, December 6, 2012.

REYES, JOSE BERNABE
Born, Villa Gonzalez, Dominican Republic, June 11, 1983.
Bats Both. Throws Right. Height, 6 feet. Weight, 200 pounds.

Year	Club	Lea	Pos	G	AB	R	H	2B	3B	HR	RBI	SB	Avg
2000 Kingsport	Appal.	SS-3B-2B-OF	49	132	22	33	3	3	0	8	10	.250
2001 Columbia	So.Atl.	SS	108	407	71	125	22	15	5	48	30	.307
2002 Binghamton	Eastern	SS	65	275	46	79	16	8	2	24	27	.287
2002 St. Lucie	Fla.St.	SS	69	288	58	83	10	11	6	38	31	.288
2003 Norfolk	Int.	SS	42	160	28	43	6	4	0	13	26	.269
2003 New York a	N.L.	SS	69	274	47	84	12	4	5	32	13	.307
2004 St. Lucie	Fla.St.	2B	6	23	3	6	2	0	0	1	2	.261
2004 Binghamton	Eastern	2B	4	18	2	2	0	0	0	3	3	.111
2004 New York b	N.L.	2B-SS	53	220	33	56	16	2	2	14	19	.255
2005 New York	N.L.	SS	161	*696	99	190	24	*17	7	58	*60	.273
2006 New York	N.L.	SS	153	647	*122	194	30	17	19	81	*64	.300
2007 New York	N.L.	SS	160	681	119	191	36	12	12	57	*78	.280
2008 New York	N.L.	SS	159	*688	113	*204	37	*19	16	68	56	.297
2009 New York c	N.L.	SS	36	147	18	41	7	2	2	15	11	.279
2010 St. Lucie	Fla.St.	SS	1	4	0	0	0	0	0	1	0	.000
2010 New York d	N.L.	SS	133	563	83	159	29	10	11	54	30	.282
2011 Brooklyn	N.Y.-Penn.	SS	1	3	1	1	1	0	0	0	0	.333
2011 Binghamton	Eastern	SS	3	9	3	3	0	1	0	1	0	.333
2011 New York e-f	N.L.	SS	126	537	101	181	31	*16	7	44	39	*.337
2012 Miami g	N.L.	SS	160	642	86	184	37	12	11	57	40	.287
Major League Totals	10 Yrs.	1210	5095	821	1484	259	111	92	480	410	.291
Division Series												
2006 New York	N.L.	SS	3	12	2	2	0	0	0	3	1	.167
Championship Series												
2006 New York	N.L.	SS	7	32	5	9	1	1	1	2	2	.281

a On disabled list from September 1 to November 6, 2003.
b On disabled list from March 26 to June 19 and August 12 to September 24, 2004.
c On disabled list from May 21 to October 14, 2009.
d On disabled list from March 26 to April 8, 2010.
e On disabled list from July 3 to July 19 and August 8 to August 29, 2011.
f Filed for free agency, October 30, 2011. Signed with Florida Marlins, December 7, 2011.
g Traded to Toronto Blue Jays with outfielder Emilio Bonifacio, catcher John Buck, pitcher Mark Buehrle and pitcher Josh Johnson for pitcher Henderson Alvarez, infielder Yunel Escobar, infielder Adeiny Hechavarria, catcher Jeff Mathis, pitcher Anthony De Sclafani, outfielder Jake Marisnick and pitcher Justin Nicolino, November 19, 2012.

REYNOLDS, MARK ANDREW
Born, Pikeville, Kentucky, August 3, 1983.
Bats Right. Throws Right. Height, 6 feet, 1 inch. Weight, 220 pounds.

Year	Club	Lea	Pos	G	AB	R	H	2B	3B	HR	RBI	SB	Avg
2004 Lancaster	Calif.	3B-SS	4	12	1	1	0	0	0	1	0	.083
2004 South Bend ...	Midwest	3B	4	15	0	1	1	0	0	0	0	.067

Year	Club	Lea	Pos	G	AB	R	H	2B	3B	HR	RBI	SB	Avg
2004 Yakima . . . . . . Northwest			SS-3B-2B	64	234	58	64	19	1	12	41	5	.274
2005 South Bend . . . Midwest			SS-3B	118	434	65	110	26	2	19	76	4	.253
2006 Lancaster . . . . Calif.			SS-3B-2B-1B	76	273	64	92	18	2	23	77	1	.337
2006 Tennessee . . . . Southern			OF-3B-2B	30	114	23	31	7	0	8	21	0	.272
2007 Mobile . . . . Southern			3B-2B	37	134	28	41	9	2	6	22	2	.306
2007 Arizona . . . . N.L.			3B-2B-OF	111	366	62	102	20	4	17	62	0	.279
2008 Arizona . . . . N.L.			3B-1B	152	539	87	129	28	3	28	97	11	.239
2009 Arizona . . . . N.L.			3B-1B	155	578	98	150	30	1	44	102	24	.260
2010 Arizona a . . . . N.L.			3B-1B	145	499	79	99	17	2	32	85	7	.198
2011 Baltimore . . . . A.L.			3B-1B	155	534	84	118	27	1	37	86	6	.221
2012 Bowie . . . . Eastern			3B	2	7	0	1	0	0	0	0	0	.143
2012 Baltimore b-c . . . . . . A.L.			1B-3B	135	457	65	101	26	0	23	69	1	.221
Major League Totals	6 Yrs.			853	2973	475	699	148	11	181	501	49	.235
Wild Card Playoff													
2012 Baltimore . . . . A.L.			1B	1	3	0	0	0	0	0	0	1	.000
Division Series													
2007 Arizona . . . . N.L.			3B	3	10	2	2	0	0	1	1	0	.200
2012 Baltimore . . . . A.L.			1B	5	19	0	3	0	0	0	1	0	.158
Division Series Totals				8	29	2	5	0	0	1	2	0	.172
Championship Series													
2007 Arizona . . . . N.L.			3B	4	16	1	2	0	0	1	1	0	.125

a Traded to Baltimore Orioles with player to be named later for pitcher Kam Mickolio and pitcher David Hernandez, December 6, 2010. Baltimore Orioles received catcher John Hester to complete trade, April 30, 2011.

b On disabled list from May 12 to May 28, 2012.

c Not offered contract, November 30, 2012. Signed with Cleveland Indians, December 18 , 2012.

RIOS, ALEXIS ISRAEL

Born, Coffee County, Alabama, February 18, 1981.
Bats Right. Throws Right. Height, 6 feet, 5 inches. Weight, 195 pounds.

Year	Club	Lea	Pos	G	AB	R	H	2B	3B	HR	RBI	SB	Avg
1999 Medicine Hat . . . . Pioneer			OF	67	234	35	63	7	3	0	13	8	.269
2000 Hagerstown . . . . So.Atl.			DH	22	74	5	17	3	1	0	5	2	.230
2000 Queens . . . . N.Y.-Penn.			OF	50	206	22	55	9	2	1	25	5	.267
2001 Charleston-WV . . . . . . So.Atl.			OF	130	480	40	126	20	9	2	58	22	.262
2002 Dunedin . . . . Fla.St.			OF	111	456	60	139	22	8	3	61	14	.305
2003 New Haven . . . . Eastern			OF	127	514	86	181	32	11	11	82	11	.352
2004 Syracuse . . . . Int.			OF	46	185	14	48	10	1	3	23	2	.259
2004 Toronto . . . . A.L.			OF	111	426	55	122	24	7	1	28	15	.286
2005 Toronto . . . . A.L.			OF	146	481	71	126	23	6	10	59	14	.262
2006 Syracuse . . . . Int.			OF	3	10	0	3	1	0	0	1	0	.300
2006 Toronto a . . . . A.L.			OF	128	450	68	136	33	6	17	82	15	.302
2007 Toronto . . . . A.L.			OF	161	643	114	191	43	7	24	85	17	.297
2008 Toronto . . . . A.L.			OF	155	635	91	185	47	8	15	79	32	.291
2009 Toronto-Chicago b . . . . . . A.L.			OF	149	582	63	144	31	2	17	71	24	.247
2010 Chicago . . . . A.L.			OF	147	567	89	161	29	3	21	88	34	.284
2011 Chicago . . . . A.L.			OF	145	537	64	122	22	2	13	44	11	.227
2012 Chicago . . . . A.L.			OF	157	605	93	184	37	8	25	91	23	.304
Major League Totals	9 Yrs.			1299	4926	708	1371	289	49	143	627	185	.278

a On disabled list from June 28 to July 28, 2006.

b Claimed on waivers by Chicago White Sox, August 10, 2009.

RIVERA, JUAN LUIS

Born, Guarenas, Venezuela, July 3, 1978.
Bats Right. Throws Right. Height, 6 feet, 2 inches. Weight, 225 pounds.

Year	Club	Lea	Pos	G	AB	R	H	2B	3B	HR	RBI	SB	Avg
1996 NY Yankees . . . . . Dominican			OF	10	18	0	3	0	0	0	2	0	.167
1997 Maracay-2 . . . . Venzuelan			OF	52	142	25	40	9	0	0	14	12	.282
1998 Yankees . . . . . . Gulf Coast			OF	57	210	43	70	9	1	12	45	8	.333
1998 Oneonta . . . . N.Y.-Penn.			OF	6	18	2	5	0	0	1	3	1	.278
1999 Tampa . . . . Fla.St.			OF	109	427	50	112	20	2	14	77	5	.262
1999 Yankees . . . . . . Gulf Coast			OF	5	18	7	6	0	0	1	4	0	.333
2000 Norwich . . . . Eastern			OF	17	62	9	14	5	0	2	12	0	.226
2000 Tampa . . . . Fla.St.			OF-1B	115	409	62	113	26	1	14	69	11	.276
2001 Norwich . . . . Eastern			OF	77	316	50	101	18	3	14	58	5	.320
2001 Columbus . . . . Int.			OF	55	199	39	65	11	1	14	40	4	.327
2001 New York . . . . A.L.			OF	3	4	0	0	0	0	0	0	0	.000
2002 Columbus . . . . Int.			OF	65	265	40	86	21	1	8	47	5	.325

Year	Club	Lea	Pos	G	AB	R	H	2B	3B	HR	RBI	SB	Avg
2002 New York a...........	A.L.	OF	28	83	9	22	5	0	1	6	1	.265
2003 Columbus.............	Int.	OF	79	308	47	100	21	0	7	37	1	.325
2003 New York b..........	A.L.	OF	57	173	22	46	14	0	7	26	0	.266
2004 Montreal c	N.L.	OF	134	391	48	120	24	1	12	49	6	.307
2005 Los Angeles	A.L.	OF	106	350	46	95	17	1	15	59	1	.271
2006 Salt Lake	P.C.	OF	2	9	3	5	3	0	1	6	0	.556
2006 Los Angeles d	A.L.	OF	124	448	65	139	27	0	23	85	0	.310
2007 Rancho Cucamonga....	Calif.	OF	3	10	3	4	1	0	0	2	0	.400
2007 Salt Lake	P.C.	OF	15	61	4	16	8	0	0	17	0	.262
2007 Los Angeles e........	A.L.	OF	14	43	3	12	1	0	2	8	0	.279
2008 Los Angeles f........	A.L.	OF-1B-2B	89	256	31	63	13	0	12	45	1	.246
2009 Los Angeles	A.L.	OF	138	529	72	152	24	1	25	88	0	.287
2010 Los Angeles	A.L.	OF-1B	124	416	53	105	20	0	15	52	2	.252
2011 Toronto	A.L.	OF-1B	70	247	22	60	11	0	6	28	3	.243
2011 Los Angeles g-h-i......	N.L.	OF-1B	62	219	24	60	12	1	5	46	2	.274
2012 Rancho Cucamonga....	Calif.	1B-OF	2	7	1	1	0	0	1	2	0	.143
2012 Albuquerque..........	P.C.	OF-1B	2	5	2	2	0	0	1	3	0	.400
2012 Los Angeles j-k	N.L.	1B-OF	109	312	30	76	14	0	9	47	1	.244
Major League Totals		12 Yrs.	1058	3471	425	950	182	4	132	539	17	.274
Division Series												
2002 New York	A.L.	OF	4	12	2	3	0	0	0	3	0	.250
2003 New York	A.L.	OF	4	12	2	4	0	0	0	0	0	.333
2005 Los Angeles	A.L.	DH	5	17	3	6	1	0	1	1	0	.353
2007 Los Angeles	A.L.	DH	2	3	0	1	0	0	0	0	0	.333
2008 Los Angeles	A.L.	OF	3	8	1	1	0	0	0	1	0	.125
2009 Los Angeles	A.L.	OF	3	11	1	3	1	0	0	2	1	.273
Division Series Totals			21	63	9	18	2	0	1	7	1	.286
Championship Series												
2003 New York	A.L.	OF	2	2	0	0	0	0	0	0	0	.000
2005 Los Angeles	A.L.	OF-DH	3	9	1	1	1	0	0	0	0	.111
2009 Los Angeles	A.L.	OF	6	25	0	5	1	0	0	0	0	.200
Championship Series Totals			11	36	1	6	2	0	0	0	0	.167
World Series Record												
2003 New York	A.L.	OF	4	6	0	1	1	0	0	1	0	.167

a On disabled list from June 8 to August 19, 2002.
b Traded to Montreal Expos with infielder Nick Johnson and pitcher Randy Choate for pitcher Javier Vazquez, December 4, 2003.
c Traded to Anaheim Angels with infielder Maicer Izturis for outfielder Jose Guillen, November 19, 2004.
d On disabled list from April 17 to May 8, 2006.
e On disabled list from March 23 to September 2, 2007.
f Filed for free agency, October 31, 2008, re-signed with Los Angeles Angels, December 19, 2008.
g Traded to Toronto Blue Jays with catcher Mike Napoli for outfielder Vernon Wells, January 21, 2011.
h Sold to Los Angeles Dodgers, July 12, 2011.
i Filed for free agency, October 30, 2011, re-signed with Los Angeles Dodgers, November 3, 2011.
j On disabled list from May 9 to June 4, 2012.
k Filed for free agency, November 3, 2012.

RIZZO, ANTHONY VINCENT

Born, Ft. Lauderdale, Florida, August 8, 1989.
Bats Left. Throws Left. Height, 6 feet, 3 inches. Weight, 220 pounds.

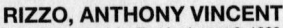

Year	Club	Lea	Pos	G	AB	R	H	2B	3B	HR	RBI	SB	Avg
2007 Red Sox	Gulf Coast	1B	6	21	6	6	0	0	1	3	0	.286
2008 Greenville..........	So.Atl.	1B	21	83	9	31	6	0	0	11	0	.373
2009 Salem............	Carolina	1B	55	200	23	59	16	0	3	24	2	.295
2009 Greenville..........	So.Atl.	1B	64	245	40	73	21	0	9	42	2	.298
2010 Salem............	Carolina	1B	29	117	26	29	12	0	5	20	3	.248
2010 Portland a	Eastern	1B	107	414	66	109	30	0	20	80	7	.263
2011 Tucson.............	P.C.	1B	93	356	64	118	34	1	26	101	7	.331
2011 San Diego	N.L.	1B	49	128	9	18	8	1	1	9	2	.141
2012 Iowa..............	P.C.	1B	70	257	48	88	18	2	23	62	2	.342
2012 Chicago b...........	N.L.	1B	87	337	44	96	15	0	15	48	3	.285
Major League Totals		2 Yrs.	136	465	53	114	23	1	16	57	5	.245

a Traded by Boston Red Sox to San Diego Padres with pitcher Casey Kelly, outfielder Reymond Fuentes and player to be named later for infielder Adrian Gonzalez, December 5, 2010.
b Traded to Chicago Cubs with pitcher Zach Cates for pitcher Andrew Cashner and outfielder Kyung-Min Na, January 6, 2012. San Diego Padres received outfielder Eric Patterson to complete trade, December 16, 2010.

ROBERTS, BRIAN MICHAEL

Born, Durham, North Carolina, October 9, 1977.
Bats Both. Throws Right. Height, 5 feet, 9 inches. Weight, 175 pounds.

Year Club	Lea	Pos	G	AB	R	H	2B	3B	HR	RBI	SB	Avg
1999 Delmarva a	So.Atl.	SS	47	167	22	40	12	1	0	21	17	.240
2000 Frederick	Carolina	SS	48	163	27	49	6	3	0	16	13	.301
2000 Orioles b	Gulf Coast	SS	9	29	8	9	1	2	1	3	7	.310
2001 Bowie	Eastern	2B-SS	22	81	12	24	7	0	1	7	10	.296
2001 Rochester	Int.	SS	44	161	16	43	4	1	1	12	23	.267
2001 Baltimore	A.L.	SS-2B	75	273	42	69	12	3	2	17	12	.253
2002 Rochester	Int.	2B	78	313	49	86	9	7	3	30	22	.275
2002 Baltimore	A.L.	2B	38	128	18	29	6	0	1	11	9	.227
2003 Ottawa	Int.	2B-SS	44	178	36	56	13	1	0	15	19	.315
2003 Baltimore	A.L.	2B-SS	112	460	65	124	22	4	5	41	23	.270
2004 Baltimore	A.L.	2B	159	641	107	175	*50	2	4	53	29	.273
2005 Baltimore	A.L.	2B	143	561	92	176	45	7	18	73	27	.314
2006 Bowie	Eastern	2B	2	5	0	1	0	0	0	0	0	.200
2006 Baltimore c	A.L.	2B	138	563	85	161	34	3	10	55	36	.286
2007 Baltimore	A.L.	2B	156	621	103	180	42	5	12	57	*50	.290
2008 Baltimore	A.L.	2B	155	611	107	181	51	8	9	57	40	.296
2009 Baltimore	A.L.	2B	159	632	110	179	*56	1	16	79	30	.283
2010 Orioles	Gulf Coast	2B	5	15	1	8	1	0	0	0	0	.533
2010 Bowie	Eastern	2B	3	14	3	6	2	0	0	3	0	.429
2010 Baltimore d	A.L.	2B	59	230	28	64	14	0	4	15	12	.278
2011 Baltimore e	A.L.	2B	39	163	18	36	7	1	3	19	6	.221
2012 Aberdeen	N.Y.-Penn.	2B	1	4	1	0	0	0	0	0	0	.000
2012 Delmarva	So.Atl.	2B	2	5	0	1	0	0	0	0	0	.200
2012 Bowie	Eastern	2B	7	16	4	4	3	0	1	3	0	.250
2012 Norfolk	Int.	2B	5	21	2	5	2	0	0	1	0	.238
2012 Baltimore f	A.L.	2B	17	66	2	12	0	0	0	5	1	.182
Major League Totals		12 Yrs.	1250	4949	777	1386	339	34	84	482	275	.280

a Drafted by Baltimore Orioles with choice received for Texas Rangers signing infielder Rafael Palmeiro, June 2, 1999.
b On disabled list from April 19 to July 13, 2000.
c On disabled list from April 30 to May 24, 2006.
d On disabled list from April 10 to July 23, 2010.
e On disabled list from May 17 to May 31 and May 31 to November 2, 2011.
f On disabled list from March 26 to June 12 and July 3 to November 2, 2012.

ROBERTS, RYAN ALAN

Born, Fort Worth, Texas, September 19, 1980.
Bats Right. Throws Right. Height, 5 feet, 11 inches. Weight, 185 pounds.

Year Club	Lea	Pos	G	AB	R	H	2B	3B	HR	RBI	SB	Avg
2003 Auburn	N.Y.-Penn.	3B-SS	66	248	52	69	10	3	8	36	7	.278
2004 Charleston	So.Atl.	2B	64	225	38	64	9	0	13	39	0	.284
2004 Dunedin	Fla.St.	2B	59	205	29	49	1	1	7	25	0	.239
2005 Dunedin	Fla.St.	2B	42	164	33	47	9	0	9	35	6	.287
2005 New Hampshire	Eastern	2B	92	338	54	92	19	3	15	44	5	.272
2006 Toronto	A.L.	2B	9	13	1	1	0	0	1	1	0	.077
2006 Syracuse	Int.	2B-3B	98	362	44	99	28	1	10	49	5	.273
2007 Toronto	A.L.	3B-2B-OF	8	13	2	1	0	0	0	0	0	.077
2007 Syracuse a	Int.	3B-2B-SS-1B	100	337	46	84	16	1	12	47	1	.249
2008 Texas	A.L.	DH	1	1	0	0	0	0	0	0	0	.000
2008 Oklahoma b	P.C.	2B-3B-SS-OF	130	453	71	136	28	8	10	66	15	.300
2009 Reno	P.C.	2B-SS	10	42	10	13	1	1	1	10	7	.310
2009 Arizona	N.L.	2B-3B-OF	110	305	41	85	17	2	7	25	7	.279
2010 Reno	P.C.	2B-OF-3B-SS	94	347	62	92	25	2	11	55	16	.265
2010 Arizona	N.L.	OF-2B-3B	36	66	8	13	4	0	2	9	0	.197
2011 Arizona	N.L.	3B-2B-OF-SS	143	482	86	120	25	2	19	65	18	.249
2012 Arizona	N.L.	3B-2B-OF	83	252	28	63	9	0	6	34	6	.250
2012 Tampa Bay c	A.L.	2B-3B	60	187	23	40	10	0	6	18	4	.214
Major League Totals		7 Yrs.	450	1319	189	323	65	4	41	152	35	.245
Division Series												
2011 Arizona	N.L.	3B	5	20	2	7	1	0	2	6	0	.350

a Filed for free agency, October 10, 2007. Signed with Texas Rangers organization, November 21, 2007.
b Filed for free agency, September 29, 2008. Signed with Arizona Diamondbacks organization, November 6, 2008.
c Traded to Tampa Bay Rays for infielder Tyler Bortnick, July 24, 2012.

ROBINSON, SHANE M.
Born, Tampa, Florida, October 30, 1984.
Bats Right. Throws Right. Height, 5 feet, 9 inches. Weight, 160 pounds.

Year Club	Lea	Pos	G	AB	R	H	2B	3B	HR	RBI	SB	Avg
2006 Quad Cities........ Midwest		OF	63	252	41	71	9	2	0	21	13	.282
2007 Palm Beach ....Fla.St.		OF	43	166	22	42	6	1	3	13	14	.253
2007 Cardinals ...... Gulf Coast		OF	4	11	1	2	0	0	0	1	0	.182
2008 Memphis .............P.C.		OF	42	141	10	31	4	1	1	10	2	.220
2008 Springfield .... Texas		OF	63	244	46	86	17	3	4	32	13	.352
2009 St. Louis............. N.L.		OF	11	25	1	6	1	0	0	1	1	.240
2009 Memphis .............P.C.		OF	100	345	46	82	18	3	5	40	16	.238
2010 Memphis .............P.C.		OF	26	86	9	24	5	0	2	13	3	.279
2011 Cardinals ...... Gulf Coast		OF	6	22	4	3	2	1	0	0	0	.136
2011 Springfield .... Texas		OF	7	31	8	15	2	0	3	8	0	.484
2011 Memphis .............P.C.		OF	43	167	35	50	8	3	4	23	9	.299
2011 St. Louis............. N.L.		OF	9	7	0	0	0	0	0	0	0	.000
2012 Memphis .............P.C.		OF	18	70	15	21	4	2	0	3	5	.300
2012 St. Louis............. N.L.		OF	102	166	20	42	8	0	3	16	1	.253
Major League Totals		3 Yrs.	122	198	21	48	9	0	3	17	2	.242
Wild Card Playoff												
2012 St. Louis............. N.L.		OF	1	1	0	0	0	0	0	0	0	.000
Division Series												
2012 St. Louis............. N.L.		OF	3	1	1	0	0	0	0	0	0	.000
Championship Series												
2012 St. Louis............. N.L.		OF	6	6	0	0	0	0	0	1	0	.000

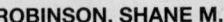

RODRIGUEZ, ALEXANDER EMMANUEL (ALEX)
Born, New York, New York, July 27, 1975.
Bats Right. Throws Right. Height, 6 feet, 3 inches. Weight, 225 pounds.

Year Club	Lea	Pos	G	AB	R	H	2B	3B	HR	RBI	SB	Avg
1994 Appleton.......... Midwest		SS	65	248	49	79	17	6	14	55	16	.319
1994 Jacksonville ...... Southern		SS	17	59	7	17	4	1	1	8	2	.288
1994 Seattle.............. A.L.		SS	17	54	4	11	0	0	0	2	3	.204
1994 Calgary..............P.C.		SS	32	119	22	37	7	4	6	21	2	.311
1995 Tacoma ..............P.C.		SS	54	214	37	77	12	3	15	45	2	.360
1995 Seattle.............. A.L.		SS	48	142	15	33	6	2	5	19	4	.232
1996 Tacoma a ............P.C.		SS	2	5	0	1	0	0	0	0	0	.200
1996 Seattle .... A.L.		SS	146	601	*141	215	*54	1	36	123	15	*.358
1997 Seattle b............. A.L.		SS	141	587	100	176	40	3	23	84	29	.300
1998 Seattle .... A.L.		SS	161	*686	123	*213	35	5	42	124	46	.310
1999 Seattle c............. A.L.		SS	129	502	110	143	25	0	42	111	21	.285
2000 Seattle d-e .... A.L.		SS	148	554	134	175	34	2	41	132	15	.316
2001 Texas .... A.L.		SS	*162	632	*133	201	34	1	*52	135	18	.318
2002 Texas .... A.L.		SS	*162	624	125	187	27	2	*57	*142	9	.300
2003 Texas .... A.L.		SS	161	607	*124	181	30	6	*47	118	17	.298
2004 New York f-g .... A.L.		3B-SS	155	601	112	172	24	2	36	106	28	.286
2005 New York h........... A.L.		3B-SS	*162	605	*124	194	29	1	*48	130	21	.321
2006 New York .... A.L.		3B	154	572	113	166	26	1	35	121	15	.290
2007 New York i-j.......... A.L.		3B	158	583	*143	183	31	0	*54	*156	24	.314
2008 New York k........... A.L.		3B	138	510	104	154	33	0	35	103	18	.302
2009 New York l .... A.L.		3B	124	444	78	127	17	1	30	100	14	.286
2010 New York m.......... A.L.		3B	137	522	74	141	29	2	30	125	4	.270
2011 Tampa ....Fla.St.		DH	2	6	2	2	1	0	1	2	0	.333
2011 Scranton-WB .... Int.		3B	2	5	0	2	0	0	0	1	0	.400
2011 New York n........... A.L.		3B	99	373	67	103	21	0	16	62	4	.276
2012 Tampa ....Fla.St.		3B	2	7	1	0	0	0	0	0	0	.000
2012 New York o........... A.L.		3B	122	463	74	126	17	1	18	57	13	.272
Major League Totals		19 Yrs.	2524	9662	1898	2901	512	30	647	1950	318	.300
Division Series												
1995 Seattle .... A.L.		SS	1	1	1	0	0	0	0	0	0	.000
1997 Seattle .... A.L.		SS	4	16	1	5	1	0	1	1	0	.313
2000 Seattle .... A.L.		SS	3	13	0	4	0	0	0	2	0	.308
2004 New York .... A.L.		3B	4	19	3	8	3	0	1	3	2	.421
2005 New York .... A.L.		3B	5	15	2	2	1	0	0	0	0	.133
2006 New York .... A.L.		3B	4	14	0	1	0	0	0	0	0	.071
2007 New York .... A.L.		3B	4	15	2	4	0	0	1	1	0	.267
2009 New York .... A.L.		3B	3	11	4	5	0	0	2	6	0	.455
2010 New York .... A.L.		3B	3	11	1	3	0	0	0	1	1	.273
2011 New York .... A.L.		3B	5	18	1	2	0	0	0	3	0	.111

Year Club	Lea	Pos	G	AB	R	H	2B	3B	HR	RBI	SB	Avg
2012 New York............	A.L.	3B-DH	4	16	1	2	0	0	0	0	0	.125
Division Series Totals...........			40	149	16	36	5	0	5	17	4	.242
Championship Series												
1995 Seattle..............	A.L.	PH	1	1	0	0	0	0	0	0	0	.000
2000 Seattle..............	A.L.	SS	6	22	4	9	2	0	2	5	1	.409
2004 New York............	A.L.	3B	7	31	8	8	2	0	2	5	0	.258
2009 New York............	A.L.	3B	6	21	6	9	2	0	3	6	1	.429
2010 New York............	A.L.	3B	6	21	4	4	2	0	0	2	1	.190
2012 New York............	A.L.	3B	3	9	0	1	0	0	0	0	0	.111
Championship Series Totals......			29	105	22	31	8	0	7	18	3	.295
World Series Record												
2009 New York............	A.L.	3B	6	20	5	5	3	0	1	6	1	.250

a On disabled list from April 22 to May 7, 1996.
b On disabled list from June 12 to June 27, 1997.
c On disabled list from April 7 to May 14, 1999.
d On disabled list from July 8 to July 23, 2000.
e Filed for free agency, October 30, 2000. Signed with Texas Rangers, December 11, 2000.
f Traded to New York Yankees for infielder Alfonso Soriano and player to be named later, February 16, 2004.
g Texas Rangers received infielder Joaquin Arias to complete trade, March 23, 2004.
h Selected Most Valuable Player in American League for 2005.
i Filed for free agency, October 29, 2007, re-signed with New York Yankees, December 13, 2007.
j Selected Most Valuable Player in American League for 2007.
k On disabled list from April 30 to May 20, 2008.
l On disabled list from March 27 to May 8, 2009.
m On disabled list from August 21 to September 5, 2010.
n On disabled list from July 14 to August 21, 2011.
o On disabled list from July 25 to September 3, 2012.

RODRIGUEZ, SEAN JOHN

Born, Miami, Florida, April 26, 1985.
Bats Right. Throws Right. Height, 6 feet, 1 inch. Weight, 215 pounds.

Year Club	Lea	Pos	G	AB	R	H	2B	3B	HR	RBI	SB	Avg
2003 Angels........	Arizona	SS-3B-2B-OF	54	216	30	58	8	5	2	25	11	.269
2004 Cedar Rapids..	Midwest	2B-OF-3B-SS	57	196	35	49	8	4	4	17	14	.250
2004 Provo........	Pioneer	SS-OF	64	225	64	76	14	4	10	55	9	.338
2005 Cedar Rapids..	Midwest	SS-3B-OF-2B	124	448	86	112	29	3	14	45	27	.250
2006 Rancho Cucamonga ..	Calif.	SS-OF	116	455	78	137	29	5	24	77	15	.301
2006 Salt Lake........	P.C.	SS	1	2	0	0	0	0	0	0	0	.000
2006 Arkansas.......	Texas	SS	18	65	16	23	5	0	5	9	0	.354
2007 Arkansas.......	Texas	SS-OF	136	508	84	129	31	2	17	73	15	.254
2008 Salt Lake........	P.C.	2B-SS-OF	66	248	68	76	19	1	21	52	4	.306
2008 Los Angeles......	A.L.	2B-SS-3B	59	167	18	34	8	1	3	10	3	.204
2009 Los Angeles......	A.L.	OF-2B	12	25	4	5	0	0	2	4	0	.200
2009 Salt Lake........	P.C.	2B-SS-OF	103	365	81	109	17	6	29	93	9	.299
2009 Durham a.......	Int.	2B-3B	5	20	6	4	2	0	1	5	0	.200
2010 Tampa Bay........	A.L.	2B-OF-3B-SS	118	343	53	86	19	2	9	40	13	.251
2011 Tampa Bay........	A.L.	SS-2B-3B-1B	131	373	45	83	20	3	8	36	11	.223
2012 Durham.......	Int.	2B-SS	2	6	2	3	2	0	1	4	0	.500
2012 Tampa Bay b.....	A.L.	3B-SS-2B	112	301	36	64	14	1	6	32	5	.213
Major League Totals............		5 Yrs.	432	1209	156	272	61	7	28	122	32	.225
Division Series												
2010 Tampa Bay........	A.L.	2B	4	10	2	2	0	0	0	0	0	.200
2011 Tampa Bay........	A.L.	SS-2B	4	12	3	2	1	0	0	1	0	.167
Division Series Totals...........			8	22	5	4	1	0	0	1	0	.182

a Sent to Tampa Bay Rays as player to be named later for pitcher Scott Kazmir, September 1, 2009.
b On disabled list from August 31 to September 15, 2012.

ROLEN, SCOTT BRUCE

Born, Evansville, Indiana, April 4, 1975.
Bats Right. Throws Right. Height, 6 feet, 4 inches. Weight, 240 pounds.

Year Club	Lea	Pos	G	AB	R	H	2B	3B	HR	RBI	SB	Avg
1993 Martinsville........	Appal.	3B	25	80	8	25	5	0	0	12	3	.313
1994 Spartanburg........	So.Atl.	3B	138	513	83	151	34	5	14	72	6	.294
1995 Clearwater.........	Fla.St.	3B	66	238	45	69	13	2	10	39	4	.290
1995 Reading..........	Eastern	3B	20	76	16	22	3	0	3	15	1	.289
1996 Reading..........	Eastern	3B	61	230	44	83	22	2	9	42	8	.361
1996 Scranton-WB..........	Int.	3B	45	168	23	46	17	0	2	19	4	.274

Year Club	Lea	Pos	G	AB	R	H	2B	3B	HR	RBI	SB	Avg
1996 Philadelphia	N.L.	3B	37	130	10	33	7	0	4	18	0	.254
1997 Philadelphia a	N.L.	3B	156	561	93	159	35	3	21	92	16	.283
1998 Philadelphia	N.L.	3B	160	601	120	174	45	4	31	110	14	.290
1999 Philadelphia	N.L.	3B	112	421	74	113	28	1	26	77	12	.268
2000 Philadelphia b	N.L.	3B	128	483	88	144	32	6	26	89	8	.298
2001 Philadelphia	N.L.	3B	151	554	96	160	39	1	25	107	16	.289
2002 Philadelphia-St. Louis c	N.L.	3B	155	580	89	154	29	8	31	110	8	.266
2003 St. Louis	N.L.	3B	154	559	98	160	49	1	28	104	13	.286
2004 St. Louis	N.L.	3B	142	500	109	157	32	4	34	124	4	.314
2005 St. Louis d	N.L.	3B	56	196	28	46	12	1	5	28	1	.235
2006 St. Louis	N.L.	3B	142	521	94	154	48	1	22	95	7	.296
2007 St. Louis e-f	N.L.	3B	112	392	55	104	24	2	8	58	5	.265
2008 Dunedin	Fla.St.	3B	3	9	0	0	0	0	0	0	0	.000
2008 Toronto g	A.L.	3B	115	408	58	107	30	3	11	50	5	.262
2009 Louisville	Int.	3B	2	6	1	2	0	0	0	1	0	.333
2009 Toronto	A.L.	3B	88	338	52	108	29	0	8	43	4	.320
2009 Cincinnati h-i	N.L.	3B	40	137	24	37	7	1	3	24	1	.270
2010 Cincinnati	N.L.	3B	133	471	66	134	34	3	20	83	1	.285
2011 Cincinnati j	N.L.	3B	65	252	31	61	20	2	5	36	1	.242
2012 Louisville	Int.	3B	2	6	1	2	0	0	1	3	0	.333
2012 Cincinnati k-l	N.L.	3B	92	294	26	72	17	2	8	39	2	.245
Major League Totals		17 Yrs.	2038	7398	1211	2077	517	43	316	1287	118	.281
Division Series												
2002 St. Louis	N.L.	3B	2	7	1	3	0	0	1	2	0	.429
2004 St. Louis	N.L.	3B	4	12	1	0	0	0	0	0	0	.000
2006 St. Louis	N.L.	3B	3	11	0	1	1	0	0	0	0	.091
2010 Cincinnati	N.L.	3B	3	11	0	1	0	0	0	0	0	.091
2012 Cincinnati	N.L.	3B	4	16	1	4	0	0	0	1	0	.250
Division Series Totals			16	57	3	9	1	0	1	3	0	.158
Championship Series												
2004 St. Louis	N.L.	3B	7	29	6	9	2	0	3	6	0	.310
2006 St. Louis	N.L.	3B	7	21	4	5	1	0	0	0	0	.238
Championship Series Totals			14	50	10	14	3	0	3	6	0	.280
World Series Record												
2004 St. Louis	N.L.	3B	4	15	0	0	0	0	0	1	0	.000
2006 St. Louis	N.L.	3B	5	19	5	8	3	0	1	2	0	.421
World Series Totals			9	34	5	8	3	0	1	3	0	.235

a Selected Rookie of the Year in National League for 1997.
b On disabled list from May 24 to June 8, 2000.
c Traded to St. Louis Cardinals with pitcher Doug Nickle for infielder Placido Polanco, pitcher Bud Smith and pitcher Mike Timlin, July 29, 2002.
d On disabled list from May 11 to June 18 and July 22 to October 31, 2005.
e On disabled list from August 29 to November 2, 2007.
f Traded to Toronto Blue Jays for infielder Troy Glaus, January 14, 2008.
g On disabled list from March 21 to April 25 and from August 11 to August 26, 2008.
h Traded to Cincinnati Reds for infielder Edwin Encarnacion, pitcher Josh Roenicke and pitcher Zach Stewart, July 31, 2009.
i On disabled list from August 8 to August 23, 2009.
j On disabled list from April 21 to May 13 and July 22 to October 3, 2011.
k On disabled list from May 12 to June 18, 2012.
l Filed for free agency, November 3, 2012.

ROLLINS, JAMES CALVIN (JIMMY)
Born, Oakland, California, November 27, 1978.
Bats Both. Throws Right. Height, 5 feet, 8 inches. Weight, 170 pounds.

Year Club	Lea	Pos	G	AB	R	H	2B	3B	HR	RBI	SB	Avg
1996 Martinsvlle	Appal.	SS	49	172	22	41	3	1	1	16	11	.238
1997 Piedmont	So.Atl.	SS	139	560	94	151	22	8	6	59	46	.270
1998 Clearwater	Fla.St.	SS	119	495	72	121	18	9	6	35	23	.244
1999 Reading	Eastern	SS	133	532	81	145	21	8	11	56	24	.273
1999 Scranton-WB	Int.	SS	4	13	0	1	1	0	0	0	1	.077
2000 Scranton-WB	Int.	SS	133	470	67	129	28	11	12	69	24	.274
2000 Philadelphia	N.L.	SS	14	53	5	17	1	1	0	5	3	.321
2001 Philadelphia	N.L.	SS	158	*656	97	180	29	*12	14	54	*46	.274
2002 Philadelphia	N.L.	SS-2B	154	*637	82	156	33	*10	11	60	31	.245
2003 Philadelphia	N.L.	SS	156	628	85	165	42	6	8	62	20	.263
2004 Philadelphia	N.L.	SS	154	657	119	190	43	*12	14	73	30	.289
2005 Philadelphia	N.L.	SS	158	677	115	196	38	11	12	54	41	.290

Year Club	Lea	Pos	G	AB	R	H	2B	3B	HR	RBI	SB	Avg
2006 Philadelphia	N.L.	SS	158	689	127	191	45	9	25	83	36	.277
2007 Philadelphia a.........	N.L.	SS	*162	*716	*139	212	38	*20	30	94	41	.296
2008 Clearwater	Fla.St.	SS	1	3	2	0	0	0	0	0	0	.000
2008 Philadelphia b	N.L.	SS	137	556	76	154	38	9	11	59	47	.277
2009 Philadelphia	N.L.	SS	155	*672	100	168	43	5	21	77	31	.250
2010 Clearwater	Fla.St.	SS	5	14	2	2	0	0	0	2	0	.143
2010 Philadelphia c.........	N.L.	SS	88	350	48	85	16	3	8	41	17	.243
2011 Philadelphia d-e.......	N.L.	SS	142	567	87	152	22	2	16	63	30	.268
2012 Philadelphia	N.L.	SS	156	632	102	158	33	5	23	68	30	.250
Major League Totals	13 Yrs.	1792	7490	1182	2024	421	105	193	793	403	.270	
Division Series												
2007 Philadelphia	N.L.	SS	3	11	1	2	0	1	1	4	1	.182
2008 Philadelphia	N.L.	SS	4	16	2	6	2	0	1	1	1	.375
2009 Philadelphia	N.L.	SS	4	19	1	5	1	0	0	0	0	.263
2010 Philadelphia	N.L.	SS	3	11	1	1	0	0	0	0	0	.091
2011 Philadelphia	N.L.	SS	5	20	6	9	4	0	0	0	2	.450
Division Series Totals			19	77	11	23	7	1	2	5	4	.299
Championship Series												
2008 Philadelphia	N.L.	SS	5	21	4	3	0	0	1	1	2	.143
2009 Philadelphia	N.L.	SS	5	22	5	5	2	0	0	3	0	.227
2010 Philadelphia	N.L.	SS	6	23	0	6	1	0	0	4	2	.261
Championship Series Totals			16	66	9	14	3	0	1	8	4	.212
World Series Record												
2008 Philadelphia	N.L.	SS	5	22	4	5	2	0	0	0	0	.227
2009 Philadelphia	N.L.	SS	6	23	3	5	0	0	0	2	3	.217
World Series Totals			11	45	7	10	2	0	0	2	3	.222

a Selected Most Valuable Player in National League for 2007.
b On disabled list from April 20 to May 9, 2008.
c On disabled list from April 13 to May 17 and May 22 to June 22, 2010.
d On disabled list from August 22 to September 8, 2011.
e Filed for free agency, October 30, 2011, re-signed with Philadelphia Phillies, December 19, 2011.

ROSALES, ADAM M.
Born, Chicago, Illinois, May 20, 1983.
Bats Right. Throws Right. Height, 6 feet, 1 inch. Weight, 195 pounds.

Year Club	Lea	Pos	G	AB	R	H	2B	3B	HR	RBI	SB	Avg
2005 Dayton	Midwest	SS	32	134	24	44	8	0	9	21	3	.328
2005 Billings........	Pioneer	SS	34	140	29	45	14	0	5	25	2	.321
2006 Sarasota	Fla.St.	SS	34	122	15	26	8	2	2	14	3	.213
2006 Dayton	Midwest	SS	55	222	36	60	9	3	6	29	5	.270
2007 Sarasota	Fla.St.	1B-SS	69	248	47	73	23	5	5	48	9	.294
2007 Chattanooga...	Southern	1B-3B-SS-OF	67	255	51	71	18	6	13	31	4	.278
2008 Louisville	Int.	3B-SS-1B-2B	117	432	70	124	29	7	11	58	7	.287
2008 Cincinnati.........	N.L.	3B-2B	18	29	0	6	1	0	0	2	1	.207
2009 Louisville	Int.	3B-SS-2B-1B	30	109	27	38	8	2	5	20	4	.349
2009 Cincinnati.........	N.L.	3B-1B-SS-2B	87	230	23	49	10	1	4	19	1	.213
2010 Oakland a.........	A.L.	2B-SS-1B-3B	80	255	31	69	8	2	7	31	2	.271
2011 Sacramento	P.C.	SS-2B-3B	40	147	23	39	5	1	3	22	1	.265
2011 Oakland	A.L.	SS-3B-1B-2B	24	61	5	6	0	0	2	8	0	.098
2012 Sacramento	P.C.	SS-2B-3B-OF	76	275	46	77	21	1	8	47	4	.280
2012 Oakland	A.L.	2B-1B-3B	42	99	12	22	5	0	2	8	0	.222
Major League Totals	5 Yrs.	251	674	71	152	24	3	15	68	4	.226	

a Traded to Oakland Athletics with outfielder Willy Taveras for infielder Aaron Miles, February 1, 2010.

ROSARIO, WILIN ARISMENDY
Born, Bonao, Dominican Republic, February 23, 1989.
Bats Right. Throws Right. Height, 5 feet, 11 inches. Weight, 215 pounds.

Year Club	Lea	Pos	G	AB	R	H	2B	3B	HR	RBI	SB	Avg
2007 Casper	Pioneer	C	34	115	11	24	4	0	2	9	2	.209
2008 Casper	Pioneer	C	66	263	48	83	15	3	12	49	4	.316
2009 Modesto...........	Calif.	C	58	203	17	54	12	2	4	33	2	.266
2010 Tulsa	Texas	C	73	270	42	77	13	1	19	52	1	.285
2011 Tulsa	Texas	C-1B	102	405	52	101	15	3	21	48	1	.249
2011 Colorado	N.L.	C	16	54	6	11	3	1	3	8	0	.204
2012 Colorado	N.L.	C-3B-1B	117	396	67	107	19	0	28	71	4	.270
Major League Totals	2 Yrs.	133	450	73	118	22	1	31	79	4	.262	

ROSS, CODY JOSEPH

Born, Portales, New Mexico, December 23, 1980.
Bats Right. Throws Left. Height, 5 feet, 9 inches. Weight, 205 pounds.

Year	Club	Lea	Pos	G	AB	R	H	2B	3B	HR	RBI	SB	Avg
1999	Tigers	Gulf Coast	OF	42	142	19	31	8	3	4	18	3	.218
2000	West Michigan	Midwest	OF	122	434	71	116	17	9	7	68	11	.267
2001	Lakeland	Fla.St.	OF	127	482	84	133	34	5	15	80	28	.276
2002	Erie	Eastern	OF	105	400	73	112	28	3	19	72	16	.280
2003	Toledo	Int.	OF	124	470	74	135	35	6	20	61	15	.287
2003	Detroit	A.L.	OF	6	19	1	4	1	0	1	5	0	.211
2004	Las Vegas a	P.C.	OF	60	238	44	65	17	2	14	49	2	.273
2005	Los Angeles	N.L.	OF	14	25	1	4	1	0	0	1	0	.160
2005	Las Vegas	P.C.	OF	115	393	79	105	21	4	22	63	4	.267
2006	L.A.-Cin.-Florida b-c-d-e	N.L.	OF	101	269	34	61	12	2	13	46	1	.227
2007	Jupiter	Fla.St.	OF	7	23	2	6	1	0	2	3	0	.261
2007	Florida f	N.L.	OF	66	173	35	58	19	0	12	39	2	.335
2008	Florida	N.L.	OF	145	461	59	120	29	5	22	73	6	.260
2009	Florida	N.L.	OF-P	151	559	73	151	37	1	24	90	5	.270
2010	Florida-San Francisco g	N.L.	OF	153	525	71	141	28	3	14	65	9	.269
2011	Fresno	P.C.	OF	2	6	1	3	1	0	0	2	0	.500
2011	San Francisco h-i	N.L.	OF	121	405	54	97	25	0	14	52	5	.240
2012	Pawtucket	Int.	OF	2	7	1	1	0	0	0	0	0	.143
2012	Boston j-k	A.L.	OF	130	476	70	127	34	1	22	81	2	.267
Major League Totals		9 Yrs.		887	2912	398	763	186	12	122	452	30	.262
Division Series													
2010	San Francisco	N.L.	OF	4	14	2	4	1	0	1	3	0	.286
Championship Series													
2010	San Francisco	N.L.	OF	6	20	4	7	3	0	3	5	0	.350
World Series Record													
2010	San Francisco	N.L.	OF	5	17	5	4	1	0	1	2	0	.235

a Traded to Los Angeles Dodgers for pitcher Steve Colyer and cash, April 1, 2004.
b Traded to Cincinnati Reds for player to be named later, April 24, 2006.
c Los Angeles Dodgers received pitcher Ben Kozlowski to complete trade, June 1, 2006.
d On disabled list from April 29 to May 23, 2006.
e Sold to Florida Marlins, May 27, 2006.
f On disabled list from May 6 to July 19, 2007.
g Claimed on waivers by San Francisco Giants, August 22, 2010.
h On disabled list from March 22 to April 20, 2011.
i Filed for free agency, October 30, 2011. Signed with Boston Red Sox, January 26, 2012.
j On disabled list from May 19 to June 19, 2012.
k Filed for free agency, November 3, 2012. Signed with Arizona Diamondbacks, December 22, 2012.

ROSS, DAVID WADE

Born, Bainbridge, Georgia, March 19, 1977.
Bats Right. Throws Right. Height, 6 feet, 2 inches. Weight, 240 pounds.

Year	Club	Lea	Pos	G	AB	R	H	2B	3B	HR	RBI	SB	Avg
1998	Yakima	Northwest	C	59	191	31	59	14	1	6	25	2	.309
1999	Vero Beach	Fla.St.	C-1B-OF	114	375	47	85	19	1	7	39	5	.227
2000	San Bernardino	Calif.	C	51	191	27	49	11	1	7	21	3	.257
2000	San Antonio	Texas	C	24	67	11	14	2	1	3	12	1	.209
2001	Jacksonville	Southern	C	74	246	35	65	13	1	11	45	1	.264
2002	Las Vegas	P.C.	C	92	293	48	87	16	2	15	68	1	.297
2002	Los Angeles	N.L.	C	8	10	2	2	1	0	1	2	0	.200
2003	Las Vegas	P.C.	C	24	86	12	19	4	0	5	16	0	.221
2003	Los Angeles	N.L.	C	40	124	19	32	7	0	10	18	0	.258
2004	Los Angeles	N.L.	C	70	165	13	28	3	1	5	15	0	.170
2005	Indianapolis	Int.	C	6	19	1	4	1	0	0	1	0	.211
2005	Portland	P.C.	C	6	21	3	3	1	0	0	1	0	.143
2005	Pittsburgh-San Diego a-b	N.L.	C	51	125	11	30	8	1	3	15	0	.240
2006	Chattanooga	Southern	C	2	6	0	2	0	0	0	2	0	.333
2006	Cincinnati c-d	N.L.	C	90	247	34	63	15	1	21	52	0	.255
2007	Louisville	Int.	C	3	9	0	2	1	0	0	0	0	.222
2007	Cincinnati e	N.L.	C	112	311	32	63	10	0	17	39	0	.203
2008	Sarasota	Fla.St.	C	4	11	2	2	0	0	0	1	0	.182
2008	Louisville	Int.	C	9	30	4	5	1	1	1	2	0	.167
2008	Cincinnati	N.L.	C	52	134	17	31	9	0	3	13	0	.231
2008	Pawtucket	Int.	C	6	28	4	7	1	0	1	3	0	.250
2008	Boston f-g-h	A.L.	C	8	8	1	1	0	0	0	0	0	.125
2009	Rome	So.Atl.	C	2	6	1	3	0	0	1	4	0	.500
2009	Atlanta i	N.L.	C	54	128	18	35	9	0	7	20	0	.273

150

Year	Club	Lea	Pos	G	AB	R	H	2B	3B	HR	RBI	SB	Avg
2010 Atlanta	N.L.	C	59	121	15	35	13	2	2	28	0	.289
2011 Atlanta	N.L.	C	52	152	14	40	7	0	6	23	0	.263
2012 Atlanta j	N.L.	C	62	176	18	45	7	0	9	23	1	.256
Major League Totals	11 Yrs.	658	1701	197	405	89	5	84	248	1	.238

Wild Card Playoff

| 2012 Atlanta .... | N.L. | C | 1 | 4 | 1 | 3 | 0 | 0 | 1 | 2 | 0 | .750 |

Division Series

2004 Los Angeles	N.L.	C	2	3	0	0	0	0	0	0	0	.000
2008 Boston	A.L.	C	1	0	0	0	0	0	0	0	0	.000
2010 Atlanta	N.L.	C	2	0	0	0	0	0	0	0	0	.000
Division Series Totals	5	3	0	0	0	0	0	0	0	.000

a Sold to Pittsburgh Pirates, March 30, 2005.
b Traded to San Diego Padres for infielder J.J. Furmaniak, July 28, 2005.
c Traded to Cincinnati Reds for pitcher Bobby Basham, March 21, 2006.
d On disabled list from July 8 to July 26, 2006.
e On disabled list from August 13 to August 28, 2007.
f On disabled list from March 30 to April 23, 2008.
g Released by Cincinnati Reds, August 19, 2008. Signed with Boston Red Sox organization, August 22, 2008.
h Filed for free agency, October 30, 2008. Signed with Atlanta Braves, December 5, 2008.
i On disabled list from April 1 to April 16, 2009.
j Filed for free agency, November 3, 2012. Signed with Boston Red Sox, November 14, 2012.

RUGGIANO, JUSTIN MARSHALL
Born, Austin, Texas, April 12, 1982.
Bats Right. Throws Right. Height, 6 feet, 2 inches. Weight, 205 pounds.

Year	Club	Lea	Pos	G	AB	R	H	2B	3B	HR	RBI	SB	Avg
2004 Ogden	Pioneer	OF	46	155	26	51	12	0	7	36	6	.329
2005 Vero Beach.........	Fla.St.	OF	71	242	47	75	15	4	9	37	16	.310
2005 Jacksonville	Southern	OF	53	161	23	55	10	1	6	29	8	.342
2006 Jacksonville	Southern	OF	89	292	51	76	19	3	9	45	10	.260
2006 Montgomery	Southern	OF	31	108	25	36	14	3	4	27	4	.333
2007 Durham	Int.	OF	127	482	78	149	29	2	20	73	26	.309
2007 Tampa Bay	A.L.	OF	7	14	2	3	0	0	0	3	0	.214
2008 Durham	Int.	OF	66	257	49	81	18	3	11	51	20	.315
2008 Tampa Bay	A.L.	OF	45	76	9	15	4	0	2	7	2	.197
2009 Durham	Int.	OF	123	471	71	119	28	1	15	72	23	.253
2010 Durham	Int.	OF-3B	117	457	77	131	31	0	15	70	24	.287
2011 Durham	Int.	OF	43	168	29	51	13	1	7	34	12	.304
2011 Tampa Bay b	A.L.	OF	46	105	11	26	4	0	4	13	1	.248
2012 Oklahoma	P.C.	OF-1B	39	117	21	38	13	1	5	29	5	.325
2012 Miami c-d...........	N.L.	OF	91	288	38	90	23	1	13	36	14	.313
Major League Totals	4 Yrs.	189	483	60	134	31	1	19	59	17	.277

a Traded by Los Angeles Dodgers to Tampa Bay Devil Rays with catcher Dioner Navarro and pitcher Jae Seo for pitcher Mark Hendrickson, catcher Toby Hall and cash, June 27, 2006.
b On disabled list from August 7 to September 1, 2011.
c Filed for free agency, January 30, 2012. Signed with Houston Astros organization, February 6, 2012.
d Traded to Miami Marlins for catcher Jobduan Morales, May 26, 2012.

RUIZ, CARLOS JOAQUIN
Born, David, Panama, January 22, 1979.
Bats Right. Throws Right. Height, 5 feet, 10 inches. Weight, 200 pounds.

Year	Club	Lea	Pos	G	AB	R	H	2B	3B	HR	RBI	SB	Avg
2000 Phillies	Gulf Coast	C	38	130	11	36	7	1	1	22	3	.277
2001 Lakewood..........	So.Atl.	C-OF	73	249	21	65	14	3	4	32	5	.261
2002 Clearwater	Fla.St.	C	92	342	35	73	18	3	5	32	3	.213
2003 Reading	Eastern	C-OF	52	169	22	45	6	0	2	16	1	.266
2003 Clearwater	Fla.St.	C	15	54	5	17	0	0	2	9	2	.315
2004 Reading	Eastern	C	101	349	45	99	15	2	17	50	8	.284
2005 Scranton-WB	Int.	C-1B	100	347	50	104	25	9	4	40	4	.300
2006 Scranton-WB	Int.	C	100	368	56	113	25	0	16	69	4	.307
2006 Philadelphia	N.L.	C	27	69	5	18	1	1	3	10	0	.261
2007 Philadelphia	N.L.	C	115	374	42	97	29	2	6	54	6	.259
2008 Philadelphia	N.L.	C-3B	117	320	47	70	14	0	4	31	1	.219
2009 Lehigh Valley	Int.	C	4	13	1	3	1	0	0	2	0	.231
2009 Philadelphia a.........	N.L.	C	107	322	32	82	26	1	9	43	3	.255
2010 Lakewood..........	So.Atl.	C	2	8	1	4	2	0	0	1	0	.500
2010 Lehigh Valley	Int.	C	1	2	0	0	0	0	0	0	0	.000

Year Club	Lea	Pos	G	AB	R	H	2B	3B	HR	RBI	SB	Avg
2010 Philadelphia b	N.L.	C	121	371	43	112	28	1	8	53	0	.302
2011 Clearwater	Fla.St.	C	1	3	1	1	0	0	0	0	0	.333
2011 Philadelphia c.........	N.L.	C-3B	132	410	49	116	23	0	6	40	1	.283
2012 Philadelphia d	N.L.	C	114	372	56	121	32	0	16	68	4	.325
Major League Totals		7 Yrs.	733	2238	274	616	153	5	52	299	15	.275
Division Series												
2007 Philadelphia	N.L.	C	3	9	1	3	1	0	0	0	1	.333
2008 Philadelphia	N.L.	C	4	14	1	1	0	0	0	0	0	.071
2009 Philadelphia	N.L.	C	4	13	0	4	0	0	0	3	0	.308
2010 Philadelphia	N.L.	C	3	8	1	2	1	0	0	1	0	.250
2011 Philadelphia	N.L.	C	5	17	1	1	0	0	0	0	0	.059
Division Series Totals			19	61	4	11	2	0	0	4	1	.180
Championship Series												
2008 Philadelphia	N.L.	C	5	16	3	5	1	0	0	1	0	.313
2009 Philadelphia	N.L.	C	5	13	4	5	1	0	1	4	1	.385
2010 Philadelphia	N.L.	C	6	18	2	3	0	0	1	1	0	.167
Championship Series Totals			16	47	9	13	2	0	2	6	1	.277
World Series Record												
2008 Philadelphia	N.L.	C	5	16	2	6	2	0	1	3	1	.375
2009 Philadelphia	N.L.	C	6	18	4	6	2	1	1	2	0	.333
World Series Totals.............			11	34	6	12	4	1	2	5	1	.353

a On disabled list from April 11 to May 2, 2009.
b On disabled list from June 19 to July 10, 2010.
c On disabled list from April 28 to May 13, 2011.
d On disabled list from August 3 to September 7, 2012.

RUTLEDGE, JOSHUA ALAN (JOSH)

Born, Cullman, Alabama, April 21, 1989.
Bats Right. Throws Right. Height, 6 feet, 1 inch. Weight, 190 pounds.

Year Club	Lea	Pos	G	AB	R	H	2B	3B	HR	RBI	SB	Avg
2010 Tri-City	Northwest	SS	11	39	6	5	0	0	0	4	1	.128
2011 Modesto............	Calif.	SS	113	460	91	160	33	9	9	71	16	.348
2012 Tulsa	Texas	SS-2B	87	356	57	109	27	3	13	35	14	.306
2012 Colorado	N.L.	SS-2B	73	277	37	76	20	5	8	37	7	.274

RYAN, BRENDAN WOOD

Born, Los Angeles, California, March 26, 1982.
Bats Right. Throws Right. Height, 6 feet, 2 inches. Weight, 195 pounds.

Year Club	Lea	Pos	G	AB	R	H	2B	3B	HR	RBI	SB	Avg
2003 New Jersey ..	N.Y.-Penn.	SS-3B	53	193	20	60	14	4	0	13	11	.311
2004 Peoria........	Midwest	SS	105	426	72	137	21	4	2	59	30	.322
2005 Palm Beach	Fla.St.	SS	49	188	29	57	17	0	1	16	8	.303
2005 Springfield	Texas	SS	43	154	28	42	8	1	2	9	6	.273
2006 Palm Beach	Fla.St.	SS	3	14	2	6	1	0	0	1	1	.429
2006 State College ..	N.Y.-Penn.	SS	8	34	5	8	0	0	0	3	1	.235
2006 Memphis	P.C.	SS	7	26	4	4	0	0	1	6	1	.154
2006 Springfield	Texas	SS	10	43	6	13	1	0	0	3	1	.302
2007 Memphis	P.C.	SS	81	323	55	88	9	5	1	15	17	.272
2007 St. Louis.........	N.L.	SS-3B-2B	67	180	30	52	9	0	4	12	7	.289
2008 Palm Beach	Fla.St.	SS	3	12	1	3	1	0	0	1	0	.250
2008 Springfield	Texas	3B-2B-SS	4	19	5	7	3	0	1	3	1	.368
2008 Memphis	P.C.	OF-2B-SS	21	80	13	19	5	0	3	10	1	.237
2008 St. Louis a	N.L.	SS-2B-3B-OF	80	197	30	48	9	0	0	10	7	.244
2009 Memphis	P.C.	SS	3	11	0	0	0	0	0	0	0	.000
2009 St. Louis b	N.L.	SS-2B	129	390	55	114	19	7	3	37	14	.292
2010 St. Louis c	N.L.	SS	139	439	50	98	19	3	2	36	11	.223
2011 Seattle d	A.L.	SS	123	436	51	108	19	3	3	39	13	.248
2012 Seattle	A.L.	SS	141	407	42	79	19	3	3	31	11	.194
Major League Totals		6 Yrs.	679	2049	258	499	94	16	15	165	63	.244
Division Series												
2009 St. Louis.............	N.L.	SS	3	12	0	1	1	0	0	0	0	.083

a On disabled list from March 21 to April 23, 2008.
b On disabled list from April 30 to May 15, 2009.
c Traded to Seattle Mariners for pitcher Maikel Cleto, December 12, 2010.
d On disabled list from August 4 to August 19, 2011.

SALTALAMACCHIA, JARROD SCOTT

Born, West Palm Beach, Florida, May 2, 1985.
Bats Both. Throws Right. Height, 6 feet, 4 inches. Weight, 235 pounds.

Year	Club	Lea	Pos	G	AB	R	H	2B	3B	HR	RBI	SB	Avg
2003 Braves	Gulf Coast	C-3B	46	134	23	32	11	2	2	14	0	.239
2004 Rome	So.Atl.	C	91	323	42	88	19	2	10	51	1	.272
2005 Myrtle Beach	Carolina	C	129	459	70	144	35	1	19	81	4	.314
2006 Mississippi	Southern	C	92	313	30	72	18	1	9	39	0	.230
2007 Mississippi	Southern	C	22	81	18	25	7	0	6	13	2	.309
2007 Atlanta	N.L.	C-1B	47	141	11	40	6	0	4	12	0	.284
2007 Texas a	A.L.	1B-C	46	167	28	42	7	1	7	21	0	.251
2008 Oklahoma	P.C.	C	15	55	10	16	3	1	2	13	0	.291
2008 Texas	A.L.	C	61	198	27	50	13	0	3	26	0	.253
2009 Frisco	Texas	C	2	4	1	0	0	0	0	0	0	.000
2009 Texas b	A.L.	C	84	283	34	66	12	0	9	34	0	.233
2010 Oklahoma	P.C.	C	63	238	37	58	11	2	11	33	1	.244
2010 Pawtucket	Int.	C-1B	9	36	5	10	5	0	1	6	0	.278
2010 Texas-Boston c-d	A.L.	C-1B	12	24	2	4	3	0	0	2	0	.167
2011 Boston	A.L.	C	103	358	52	84	23	3	16	56	1	.235
2012 Boston	A.L.	C-1B	121	405	55	90	17	1	25	59	0	.222
Major League Totals			6 Yrs.	474	1576	209	376	81	5	64	210	1	.239

a Traded to Texas Rangers with infielder Elvis Andrews, pitcher Neftali Feliz, pitcher Matt Harrison and pitcher Beau James for infielder Mark Teixeira and pitcher Ron Mahay, July 31, 2007.
b On disabled list from August 16 to September 2, 2009.
c On disabled list from April 8 to April 27 and August 16 to September 1, 2010.
d Traded to Boston Red Sox for pitcher Roman Mendez, infielder Chris McGuiness, player to be named later and cash, July 31, 2010. Texas Rangers received catcher Michael Thomas to complete trade, August 14, 2010.

SANCHEZ, GABRIEL (GABY)

Born, Miami, Florida, September 2, 1983.
Bats Right. Throws Right. Height, 6 feet, 2 inches. Weight, 225 pounds.

Year	Club	Lea	Pos	G	AB	R	H	2B	3B	HR	RBI	SB	Avg
2005 Jamestown	N.Y.-Penn.	3B-1B-C	62	234	34	83	16	0	5	42	11	.355
2006 Jupiter	Fla.St.	1B-3B-C	16	55	13	10	3	1	1	7	1	.182
2006 Marlins	Gulf Coast	1B	3	6	1	2	1	0	0	3	0	.333
2006 Greensboro	So.Atl.	1B-C	55	189	43	60	12	0	14	40	6	.317
2007 Jupiter	Fla.St.	1B-3B-C	133	473	89	132	40	3	9	70	6	.279
2008 Carolina	Southern	1B-3B	133	478	70	150	42	1	17	92	17	.314
2008 Florida	N.L.	1B	5	8	0	3	2	0	0	1	0	.375
2009 New Orleans	P.C.	1B-3B	85	318	55	92	11	0	16	56	5	.289
2009 Florida	N.L.	1B	21	21	2	5	0	0	2	3	0	.238
2010 Florida	N.L.	1B	151	572	72	156	37	3	19	85	5	.273
2011 Florida	N.L.	1B	159	572	72	152	35	0	19	78	3	.266
2012 New Orleans	P.C.	1B	34	116	20	35	7	0	5	18	2	.302
2012 Miami-Pittsburgh a	N.L.	1B	105	299	30	65	16	0	7	30	1	.217
Major League Totals			5 Yrs.	441	1472	176	381	90	3	47	197	9	.259

a Traded to Pittsburgh Pirates with pitcher Kyle Kaminska for outfielder Gorkys Hernandez and a competitive balance draft pick, July 31, 2012.

SANCHEZ, HECTOR ENRIQUE

Born, Maracay, Venezuela, November 17, 1989.
Bats Both. Throws Right. Height, 5 feet, 11 inches. Weight, 225 pounds.

Year	Club	Lea	Pos	G	AB	R	H	2B	3B	HR	RBI	SB	Avg
2009 Giants	Arizona	C	33	117	13	35	8	1	1	22	0	.299
2010 Augusta	So.Atl.	C	89	310	29	85	20	1	5	31	0	.274
2011 Fresno	P.C.	C	46	153	15	40	9	0	1	26	0	.261
2011 San Jose	Calif.	C-1B	52	212	31	64	14	1	11	58	0	.302
2011 San Francisco	N.L.	C	13	31	0	8	2	0	0	1	0	.258
2012 Fresno	P.C.	C	4	15	0	1	0	0	0	1	0	.067
2012 San Francisco a	N.L.	C	74	218	22	61	15	0	3	34	0	.280
Major League Totals			2 Yrs.	87	249	22	69	17	0	3	35	0	.277
Division Series													
2012 San Francisco	N.L.	C	1	2	1	1	0	0	0	0	0	.500
Championship Series													
2012 San Francisco	N.L.	C	2	5	0	0	0	0	0	0	0	.000
World Series Record													
2012 San Francisco	N.L.	DH	1	4	0	0	0	0	0	0	0	.000

a On disabled list from July 18 to August 2, 2012.

SANDOVAL, PABLO E.
Born, Puerto Cabello, Venezuela, August 11, 1986.
Bats Both. Throws Right. Height, 5 feet, 11 inches. Weight, 245 pounds.

Year	Club	Lea	Pos	G	AB	R	H	2B	3B	HR	RBI	SB	Avg
2004 Giants	Arizona		C	46	177	21	47	9	5	0	26	4	.266
2005 Salem-Keizer	Northwest	3B-1B-C	75	294	46	97	15	2	3	50	2	.330
2006 Augusta	So.Atl.	1B-3B	117	438	43	116	20	1	1	49	3	.265
2007 San Jose	Calif.	C-1B	102	401	56	115	33	5	11	52	3	.287
2008 San Jose	Calif.	C-1B	68	273	61	98	25	2	12	59	2	.359
2008 Connecticut	Eastern	C-1B	44	175	29	59	13	0	8	37	0	.337
2008 San Francisco	N.L.	1B-3B-C	41	145	24	50	10	1	3	24	0	.345
2009 San Francisco	N.L.	3B-1B-C	153	572	79	189	44	5	25	90	5	.330
2010 San Francisco	N.L.	3B-1B	152	563	61	151	34	3	13	63	3	.268
2011 San Jose	Calif.	3B	1	3	1	0	0	0	0	0	0	.000
2011 Fresno	P.C.	3B-1B	5	18	4	5	0	0	2	7	0	.278
2011 San Francisco a	N.L.	3B-1B	117	426	55	134	26	3	23	70	2	.315
2012 San Jose	Calif.	3B	6	22	1	6	2	0	1	1	0	.273
2012 Fresno	P.C.	3B	3	11	3	3	1	0	2	2	0	.273
2012 San Francisco b	N.L.	3B-1B	108	396	59	112	25	2	12	63	1	.283
Major League Totals			5 Yrs.	571	2102	278	636	139	14	76	310	11	.303
Division Series													
2010 San Francisco	N.L.	3B	2	6	0	1	0	0	0	0	0	.167
2012 San Francisco	N.L.	3B	5	21	2	7	2	0	1	3	0	.333
Division Series Totals				7	27	2	8	2	0	1	3	0	.296
Championship Series													
2010 San Francisco	N.L.	3B	3	8	0	2	1	0	0	2	0	.250
2012 San Francisco	N.L.	3B	7	29	4	9	2	0	2	6	0	.310
Championship Series Totals				10	37	4	11	3	0	2	8	0	.297
World Series Record													
2010 San Francisco	N.L.	DH	1	3	0	0	0	0	0	0	0	.000
2012 San Francisco	N.L.	3B	4	16	3	8	1	0	3	4	0	.500
World Series Totals				5	19	3	8	1	0	3	4	0	.421

a On disabled list from April 30 to June 14, 2011.
b On disabled list from May 3 to June 9 and July 25 to August 13, 2012.

SANTANA, CARLOS
Born, Santo Domingo, Dominican Republic, April 8, 1986.
Bats Both. Throws Right. Height, 5 feet, 11 inches. Weight, 190 pounds.

Year	Club	Lea	Pos	G	AB	R	H	2B	3B	HR	RBI	SB	Avg
2005 Dodgers	Gulf Coast	3B-OF-C-2B	32	78	14	23	4	1	1	14	0	.295
2006 Vero Beach	Fla.St.	3B-OF	54	198	16	53	10	2	3	18	0	.268
2006 Ogden	Pioneer	OF-3B	37	132	31	40	5	1	7	27	4	.303
2007 Great Lakes	Midwest	C-3B-OF	86	292	32	65	20	1	7	36	5	.223
2008 Inland Empire	Calif.	C-OF-1B-2B	99	350	88	113	34	4	14	96	7	.323
2008 Kinston	Carolina	C	29	105	34	37	5	1	6	19	3	.352
2008 Akron a	Eastern	C	2	8	3	1	0	0	1	2	0	.125
2009 Akron	Eastern	C	130	428	91	124	30	2	23	97	2	.290
2010 Columbus	Int.	C	57	196	39	62	14	1	13	51	6	.316
2010 Cleveland b	A.L.	C	46	150	23	39	13	0	6	22	3	.260
2011 Cleveland	A.L.	C-1B	155	552	84	132	35	2	27	79	5	.239
2012 Lake County	Midwest	DH	1	4	1	1	0	0	1	2	0	.250
2012 Cleveland c	A.L.	C-1B-OF	143	507	72	128	27	2	18	76	3	.252
Major League Totals			3 Yrs.	344	1209	179	299	75	4	51	177	11	.247

a Traded by Los Angeles Dodgers to Cleveland Indians with pitcher Jonathan Meloan for infielder Casey Blake, July 26, 2008.
b On disabled list from August 3 to November 9, 2010.
c On disabled list from May 26 to June 5, 2012.

SANTIAGO, RAMON D.
Born, Las Matas de Farfan, Dominican Republic, August 31, 1979.
Bats Both. Throws Right. Height, 5 feet, 11 inches. Weight, 150 pounds.

Year	Club	Lea	Pos	G	AB	R	H	2B	3B	HR	RBI	SB	Avg
1999 Tigers	Gulf Coast	SS	35	134	25	43	9	2	0	11	20	.321
1999 Oneonta	N.Y.-Penn.	SS	12	50	9	17	1	2	1	8	5	.340
2000 West Michigan	Midwest	SS	98	379	69	103	15	1	1	42	39	.272
2001 Lakeland	Fla.St.	DH	120	429	64	115	15	3	2	46	34	.268
2002 Erie	Eastern	SS	22	75	9	21	0	2	1	7	6	.280

154

Year	Club	Lea	Pos	G	AB	R	H	2B	3B	HR	RBI	SB	Avg
2002 Toledo	....	Int.	SS	9	28	8	12	1	0	2	6	0	.429
2002 Detroit	....	A.L.	SS	65	222	33	54	5	5	4	20	8	.243
2003 Detroit	....	A.L.	SS-2B	141	444	41	100	18	1	2	29	10	.225
2004 Tacoma	....	P.C.	SS-2B	71	243	35	47	7	2	1	24	9	.193
2004 Seattle a	....	A.L.	SS	19	39	8	7	1	0	0	2	0	.179
2005 Tacoma	....	P.C.	2B-SS-3B-C	129	441	68	111	22	3	10	50	18	.252
2005 Seattle	....	A.L.	2B-SS	8	8	2	1	0	0	0	0	0	.125
2006 Toledo	....	Int.	2B-SS	25	83	13	21	6	0	2	12	2	.253
2006 Detroit b	....	A.L.	SS-2B-3B	43	80	9	18	1	1	0	3	2	.225
2007 Toledo	....	Int.	SS-2B	91	365	40	96	19	4	3	30	8	.263
2007 Detroit	....	A.L.	SS	32	67	10	19	5	1	0	7	3	.284
2008 Toledo	....	Int.	SS	8	28	3	6	2	0	0	3	0	.214
2008 Detroit c	....	A.L.	SS-2B-3B	58	124	30	35	6	2	4	18	1	.282
2009 Detroit	....	A.L.	SS-2B-3B	93	262	29	70	6	2	7	35	1	.267
2010 Detroit	....	A.L.	SS-2B	112	320	38	84	9	1	3	22	2	.262
2011 Detroit d	....	A.L.	2B-SS-3B	101	258	29	67	11	3	5	30	0	.260
2012 Detroit	....	A.L.	2B-SS-3B	93	228	19	47	7	1	2	17	1	.206
Major League Totals	....		11 Yrs.	765	2052	248	502	69	17	27	183	28	.245
Division Series													
2011 Detroit	....	A.L.	2B	4	14	0	2	1	0	0	2	0	.143
Championship Series													
2006 Detroit	....	A.L.	SS	3	7	0	0	0	0	0	0	0	.000
2011 Detroit	....	A.L.	2B	6	24	1	9	1	0	0	0	0	.375
Championship Series Totals	......			9	31	1	9	1	0	0	0	0	.290
World Series Record													
2006 Detroit	....	A.L.	SS	3	5	0	1	0	0	0	0	0	.200
2012 Detroit	....	A.L.	PH	1	1	0	0	0	0	0	0	0	.000
World Series Totals	....			4	6	0	1	0	0	0	0	0	.167

a Traded to Seattle Mariners with infielder Juan Gonzalez for infielder Carlos Guillen, January 8, 2004.
b Released by Seattle Mariners, November 18, 2005. Signed with Detroit Tigers organization, January 4, 2006.
c On disabled list from June 5, to July 8, 2008.
d Filed for free agency, October 30, 2011, re-signed with Detroit Tigers November 30, 2011.

SAUNDERS, MICHAEL EDWARD BRETT

Born, Victoria, British Columbia, Canada, November 19, 1986.
Bats Left. Throws Right. Height, 6 feet, 4 inches. Weight, 210 pounds.

Year	Club	Lea	Pos	G	AB	R	H	2B	3B	HR	RBI	SB	Avg
2005 Everett	....	Northwest	OF	56	196	24	53	13	3	7	39	2	.270
2006 Wisconsin	....	Midwest	OF	104	359	48	86	10	8	4	39	22	.240
2007 High Desert	....	Calif.	OF	108	431	91	129	25	4	14	77	27	.299
2007 West Tenn	....	Southern	OF	15	52	8	15	1	2	1	7	2	.288
2008 Tacoma	....	P.C.	OF	24	95	12	23	4	1	3	16	1	.242
2008 West Tenn	....	Southern	OF	67	248	46	72	18	3	8	30	11	.290
2009 Tacoma	....	P.C.	OF	64	248	58	77	15	2	13	32	6	.310
2009 Seattle	....	A.L.	OF	46	122	13	27	1	3	0	4	4	.221
2010 Tacoma	....	P.C.	OF	21	80	6	16	1	0	0	5	4	.200
2010 Seattle	....	A.L.	OF	100	289	29	61	11	2	10	33	6	.211
2011 Tacoma	....	P.C.	OF	64	236	51	68	11	3	7	38	10	.288
2011 Seattle	....	A.L.	OF	58	161	16	24	5	0	2	8	6	.149
2012 Seattle	....	A.L.	OF	139	507	71	125	31	3	19	57	21	.247
Major League Totals	....		4 Yrs.	343	1079	129	237	48	8	31	102	37	.220

SCHAFER, JORDAN JAMES

Born, Hammond, Indiana, September 4, 1986.
Bats Left. Throws Left. Height, 6 feet, 1 inch. Weight, 200 pounds.

Year	Club	Lea	Pos	G	AB	R	H	2B	3B	HR	RBI	SB	Avg
2005 Braves	....	Gulf Coast	OF	49	182	18	37	12	3	3	19	13	.203
2006 Rome	....	So.Atl.	OF	114	388	49	93	15	7	8	60	15	.240
2007 Rome	....	So.Atl.	OF	30	129	16	48	15	2	5	20	4	.372
2007 Myrtle Beach	......	Carolina	OF	106	436	70	128	34	8	10	43	19	.294
2008 Mississippi	....	Southern	OF	84	297	46	80	18	6	10	51	12	.269
2009 Atlanta	....	N.L.	OF	50	167	18	34	8	0	2	8	2	.204
2009 Gwinnett a	....	Int.	OF	9	35	6	8	0	0	2	3	3	.229
2010 Gwinnett	....	Int.	OF	52	189	16	38	5	1	1	8	9	.201
2010 Rome	....	So.Atl.	OF	6	22	4	6	2	0	0	1	2	.273
2010 Mississippi b	.....	Southern	OF	18	63	7	11	3	0	0	5	1	.175
2011 Oklahoma	....	P.C.	OF	5	20	4	10	2	0	0	3	3	.500

155

Year	Club	Lea	Pos	G	AB	R	H	2B	3B	HR	RBI	SB	Avg
2011 Gwinnett.............	Int.		OF	42	164	21	42	8	0	1	21	6	.256
2011 Atlanta-Houston c-d....	N.L.		OF	82	302	46	73	10	3	2	13	22	.242
2012 Astros	Gulf Coast		OF	1	2	0	1	0	0	0	0	0	.500
2012 Oklahoma.............	P.C.		OF	4	13	2	2	0	0	0	0	2	.154
2012 Houston e-f.........	N.L.		OF	106	313	40	66	10	2	4	23	27	.211
Major League Totals			3 Yrs.	238	782	104	173	28	5	8	44	51	.221

a On disabled list from September 4 to October 9, 2009.
b On disabled list from March 26 to May 17, 2010.
c Traded to Houston Astros with pitcher Juan Abreu, pitcher Paul Clemens and pitcher Brett Oberholtzer for outfielder Michael Bourn and cash, July 31, 2011.
d On disabled list from July 27 to August 22, 2011.
e On disabled list from August 7 to September 1, 2012.
f Claimed on waivers by Atlanta Braves, November 1, 2012.

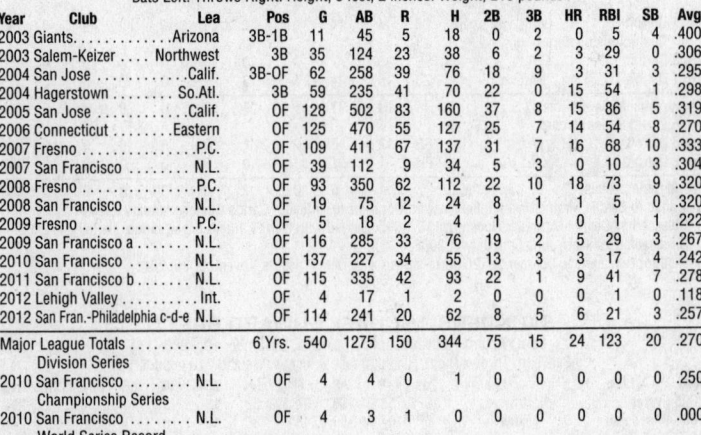

SCHIERHOLTZ, NATHAN JOHN (NATE)
Born, Reno, Nevada, February 15, 1984.
Bats Left. Throws Right. Height, 6 feet, 2 inches. Weight, 215 pounds.

Year	Club	Lea	Pos	G	AB	R	H	2B	3B	HR	RBI	SB	Avg
2003 Giants............	Arizona		3B-1B	11	45	5	18	0	2	0	5	4	.400
2003 Salem-Keizer	Northwest		3B	35	124	23	38	6	2	3	29	0	.306
2004 San Jose	Calif.		3B-OF	62	258	39	76	18	9	3	31	3	.295
2004 Hagerstown	So.Atl.		3B	59	235	41	70	22	0	15	54	1	.298
2005 San Jose	Calif.		OF	128	502	83	160	37	8	15	86	5	.319
2006 Connecticut	Eastern		OF	125	470	55	127	25	7	14	54	8	.270
2007 Fresno	P.C.		OF	109	411	67	137	31	7	16	68	10	.333
2007 San Francisco	N.L.		OF	39	112	9	34	5	3	0	10	3	.304
2008 Fresno	P.C.		OF	93	350	62	112	22	10	18	73	9	.320
2008 San Francisco	N.L.		OF	19	75	12	24	8	1	1	5	0	.320
2009 Fresno	P.C.		OF	5	18	2	4	1	0	0	1	1	.222
2009 San Francisco a	N.L.		OF	116	285	33	76	19	2	5	29	3	.267
2010 San Francisco	N.L.		OF	137	227	34	55	13	3	3	17	4	.242
2011 San Francisco b	N.L.		OF	115	335	42	93	22	1	9	41	7	.278
2012 Lehigh Valley	Int.		OF	4	17	1	2	0	0	0	1	0	.118
2012 San Fran.-Philadelphia c-d-e	N.L.		OF	114	241	20	62	8	5	6	21	3	.257
Major League Totals			6 Yrs.	540	1275	150	344	75	15	24	123	20	.270
Division Series													
2010 San Francisco	N.L.		OF	4	4	0	1	0	0	0	0	0	.250
Championship Series													
2010 San Francisco	N.L.		OF	4	3	1	0	0	0	0	0	0	.000
World Series Record													
2010 San Francisco	N.L.		OF	3	5	1	1	0	0	0	1	0	.200

a On disabled list from July 27 to August 12, 2009.
b On disabled list from August 22 to September 29, 2011.
c Traded to Philadelphia Phillies with catcher Tommy Joseph and pitcher Seth Rosin for outfielder Hunter Pence and cash, July 31, 2012.
d On disabled list from August 13 to September 1, 2012.
e Not offered contract, November 30, 2012. Signed with Chicago Cubs, December 21, 2012.

SCHUMAKER, JARED MICHAEL (SKIP)
Born, Torrance, California, February 3, 1980.
Bats Left. Throws Right. Height, 5 feet, 10 inches. Weight, 195 pounds.

Year	Club	Lea	Pos	G	AB	R	H	2B	3B	HR	RBI	SB	Avg
2001 New Jersey	N.Y.-Penn.		OF	49	162	22	41	10	1	0	14	11	.253
2002 Potomac	Carolina		OF	136	551	71	158	22	4	2	44	26	.287
2003 Tennessee	Southern		OF	91	342	43	86	20	3	2	22	6	.251
2004 Tennessee	Southern		OF-3B	138	516	78	163	29	6	4	43	19	.316
2005 Memphis	P.C.		OF	115	443	66	127	24	3	7	34	14	.287
2005 St. Louis.............	N.L.		OF	27	24	9	6	1	0	0	1	1	.250
2006 Memphis	P.C.		OF	95	369	47	113	13	3	3	27	11	.306
2006 St. Louis.............	N.L.		OF	28	54	3	10	1	0	1	2	2	.185
2007 Memphis	P.C.		OF	59	232	34	71	16	0	7	31	2	.306
2007 St. Louis.............	N.L.		OF	88	177	19	59	12	2	2	19	1	.333
2008 St. Louis.............	N.L.		OF	153	540	87	163	22	5	8	46	8	.302
2009 St. Louis.............	N.L.		2B-OF	153	532	85	161	34	1	4	35	2	.303
2010 St. Louis.............	N.L.		2B-OF	137	476	66	126	18	1	5	42	5	.265
2011 St. Louis a-b	N.L.		2B-OF-P	117	367	34	104	19	0	2	38	0	.283
2012 Memphis	P.C.		2B-OF	7	21	5	6	2	0	0	0	1	.286

Year	Club	Lea	Pos	G	AB	R	H	2B	3B	HR	RBI	SB	Avg
2012 St. Louis c-d	N.L.	2B-OF	107	272	37	75	14	4	1	28	1	.276	
Major League Totals		8 Yrs.	810	2442	340	704	121	13	23	211	20	.288	
Division Series													
2009 St. Louis.............	N.L.	2B-OF	2	6	1	2	1	0	0	1	0	.333	
2011 St. Louis.............	N.L.	OF-2B	5	10	1	6	2	0	0	3	0	.600	
2012 St. Louis.............	N.L.	PH	4	4	0	0	0	0	0	1	0	.000	
Division Series Totals			11	20	2	8	3	0	0	5	0	.400	
Championship Series													
2012 St. Louis.............	N.L.	2B	5	5	0	0	0	0	0	0	0	.000	
World Series Record													
2011 St. Louis.............	N.L.	OF	6	11	1	2	0	0	0	1	0	.182	

a On disabled list from April 16 to May 23, 2011.
b Not offered contract, December 12, 2011, re-signed with St. Louis Cardinals, December 12, 2011.
c On disabled list from April 1 to April 20 and May 31 to June 19, 2012.
d Traded to Los Angeles Dodgers for infielder Jake Lemmerman, December 12, 2012.

SCOTT, LUKE BRANDON

Born, DeLeon Springs, Florida, June 25, 1978.
Bats Left. Throws Right. Height, 6 feet. Weight, 210 pounds.

Year	Club	Lea	Pos	G	AB	R	H	2B	3B	HR	RBI	SB	Avg
2001 Kinston a	Carolina			INJURED — Did Not Play									
2002 Kinston..........	Carolina	OF-1B	48	163	22	39	7	1	8	30	2	.239	
2002 Columbus.......	So.Atl.	OF	49	171	28	44	15	4	7	32	9	.257	
2003 Kinston..........	Carolina	OF	67	241	37	67	12	1	13	44	6	.278	
2003 Akron...........	Eastern	OF	50	183	21	50	13	1	7	37	0	.273	
2004 Salem..........	Carolina	OF	66	241	45	67	20	1	8	35	6	.278	
2004 Round Rock b	Texas	OF	63	208	45	62	17	0	19	62	0	.298	
2005 Round Rock...........	P.C.	OF	103	398	69	114	25	4	31	87	2	.286	
2005 Houston.............	N.L.	OF	34	80	6	15	4	2	0	4	1	.188	
2006 Round Rock...........	P.C.	OF	87	318	63	95	15	1	20	63	6	.299	
2006 Houston.............	N.L.	OF	65	214	31	72	19	6	10	37	2	.336	
2007 Houston c	N.L.	OF	132	369	49	94	28	5	18	64	3	.255	
2008 Baltimore	A.L.	OF	148	475	67	122	29	2	23	65	2	.257	
2009 Delmarva	So.Atl.	OF	2	4	1	3	0	0	1	1	0	.750	
2009 Baltimore d	A.L.	DH-OF-1B	128	449	61	116	26	1	25	77	0	.258	
2010 Orioles	Gulf Coast	OF	3	9	1	2	0	0	0	2	0	.222	
2010 Baltimore e........	A.L.	DH-1B-OF	131	447	70	127	29	1	27	72	2	.284	
2011 Bowie	Eastern	DH	3	10	5	5	1	0	3	7	0	.500	
2011 Baltimore f-g	A.L.	OF-1B	64	209	24	46	11	0	9	22	1	.220	
2012 Charlotte	Fla.St.	1B	8	26	6	8	1	0	2	6	0	.308	
2012 Durham	Int.	DH	2	8	3	3	0	0	2	4	0	.375	
2012 Tampa Bay h-i	A.L.	DH-1B	96	314	35	72	22	1	14	55	5	.229	
Major League Totals		8 Yrs.	798	2557	343	664	168	18	126	396	16	.260	
Division Series													
2005 Houston.............	N.L.	OF	2	2	1	0	0	0	0	0	0	.000	
World Series Record													
2005 Houston.............	N.L.	PH	0	0	0	0	0	0	0	0	0	.000	

a On disabled list from June 21 to September 14, 2001.
b Traded by Cleveland Indians to Houston Astros with outfielder Willy Taveras for pitcher Jeriome Robertston, March 31, 2004.
c Traded to Baltimore Orioles with pitcher Troy Patton, pitcher Matt Albers, pitcher Dennis Sarfate and infielder Michael Costanzo for infielder Miguel Tejada, December 12, 2007.
d On disabled list from May 11 to May 27, 2009.
e On disabled list from July 1 to July 19, 2010.
f On disabled list from July 3 to July 22 and July 23 to November 2, 2011.
g Not offered contract, December 12, 2011. Signed with Tampa Bay Rays, January 12, 2012.
h On disabled list from June 9 to June 28 and July 21 to August 21, 2012.
i Filed for free agency, November 3, 2012.

SCUTARO, MARCOS (MARCO)

Born, San Felipe, Venezuela, October 30, 1975.
Bats Right. Throws Right. Height, 5 feet, 10 inches. Weight, 190 pounds.

Year	Club	Lea	Pos	G	AB	R	H	2B	3B	HR	RBI	SB	Avg
1995 Cleveland ...	Dominican	3B	66	262	71	103	18	6	0	38	32	.393	
1996 Columbus......	So.Atl.	2B-SS-3B	85	315	66	79	12	3	10	45	6	.251	
1997 Buffalo...........	A.A.	2B-3B-SS	21	57	8	15	3	0	1	6	0	.263	
1997 Kinston.......	Carolina	2B-3B	97	378	58	103	17	6	10	59	23	.272	

Year	Club	Lea	Pos	G	AB	R	H	2B	3B	HR	RBI	SB	Avg
1998 Buffalo	Int.		2B-3B	8	26	3	6	3	0	0	4	0	.231
1998 Akron	Eastern		2B-SS	124	462	68	146	27	6	11	62	33	.316
1999 Buffalo	Int.		2B-SS	129	462	76	126	24	2	8	51	21	.273
2000 Buffalo	Int.		2B-SS	124	425	67	117	20	5	5	54	9	.275
2000 Indianapolis a	Int.		2B-SS	4	13	5	7	1	1	1	3	1	.538
2001 Indianapolis	Int.		2B-3B-SS	132	495	87	146	29	3	11	50	11	.295
2002 Norfolk	Int.		2B-SS-OF-3B	97	354	48	113	22	6	7	28	7	.319
2002 New York b	N.L.		2B-SS-3B-OF	27	36	2	8	0	1	1	6	0	.222
2003 Norfolk	Int.		3B-2B-SS-OF	70	244	42	76	18	3	9	32	11	.311
2003 New York c	N.L.		2B-SS	48	75	10	16	4	0	2	6	2	.213
2004 Oakland	A.L.		2B-SS-3B	137	455	50	124	32	1	7	43	0	.273
2005 Oakland	A.L.		SS-2B-3B-OF	118	381	48	94	22	3	9	37	5	.247
2006 Oakland	A.L.		2B-SS-3B-OF	117	365	52	97	21	6	5	41	5	.266
2007 Oakland d	A.L.		SS-3B-2B-OF	104	338	49	88	13	0	7	41	2	.260
2008 Toronto	A.L.		SS-2B-3B-1B	145	517	76	138	23	1	7	60	7	.267
2009 Toronto e	A.L.		SS-2B	144	574	100	162	35	1	12	60	14	.282
2010 Boston	A.L.		SS-2B	150	632	92	174	38	0	11	56	5	.275
2011 Pawtucket	Int.		2B-SS	3	11	4	5	1	0	0	0	0	.455
2011 Boston f	A.L.		SS-2B	113	395	59	118	26	1	7	54	4	.299
2012 Colorado-San Fran. g-h-i	N.L.		2B-SS-3B	156	620	87	190	32	4	7	74	9	.306
Major League Totals	11 Yrs.			1259	4388	625	1209	246	18	75	478	53	.276
Division Series													
2006 Oakland	A.L.		SS	3	12	1	4	4	0	0	6	0	.333
2012 San Francisco	N.L.		2B	5	20	2	3	1	0	0	1	0	.150
Division Series Totals				8	32	3	7	5	0	0	7	0	.219
Championship Series													
2006 Oakland	A.L.		SS	4	15	0	1	0	0	0	0	0	.067
2012 San Francisco	N.L.		2B	7	28	6	14	3	0	0	4	0	.500
Championship Series Totals				11	43	6	15	3	0	0	4	0	.349
World Series Record													
2012 San Francisco	N.L.		2B	4	16	3	4	0	0	0	3	0	.250

a Sent by Cleveland Indians to Milwaukee Brewers as player to be named later in Richie Sexson trade, August 30, 2000.
b Claimed on waivers by New York Mets, April 3, 2002.
c Claimed on waivers by Oakland Athletics, October 9, 2003.
d Traded to Toronto Blue Jays for pitcher Kristian Bell and pitcher Graham Godfrey, November 18, 2007.
e Filed for free agency, November 6, 2009. Signed with Boston Red Sox, December 4, 2009.
f On disabled list from May 8 to June 7, 2011.
g Traded to Colorado Rockies for pitcher Clayton Mortensen, January 21, 2012.
h Traded to San Francisco Giants with cash for infielder Charlie Culberson, July 28, 2012.
i Filed for free agency, November 3, 2012, re-signed with San Francisco Giants, December 4, 2012.

SEAGER, KYLE DUERR
Born, Charlotte, North Carolina, November 3, 1987.
Bats Left. Throws Right. Height, 5 feet, 10 inches. Weight, 175 pounds.

Year	Club	Lea	Pos	G	AB	R	H	2B	3B	HR	RBI	SB	Avg
2009 Mariners	Arizona		2B	1	3	0	0	0	0	0	0	0	.000
2009 Clinton	Midwest		2B-3B-SS	41	153	17	42	8	0	1	22	4	.275
2009 High Desert	Calif.		2B	2	5	1	0	0	0	0	0	0	.000
2010 High Desert	Calif.		2B-3B-SS	135	557	126	192	40	3	14	74	13	.345
2011 Jackson	Southern		2B-SS-3B	66	266	33	83	25	1	4	37	8	.312
2011 Tacoma	P.C.		3B-2B-SS	24	106	24	41	8	2	3	17	3	.387
2011 Seattle	A.L.		3B-SS-2B	53	182	22	47	13	0	3	13	3	.258
2012 Seattle	A.L.		3B-2B	155	594	62	154	35	1	20	86	13	.259
Major League Totals	2 Yrs.			208	776	84	201	48	1	23	99	16	.259

SEGURA, JEAN CARLOS ENRIQUE
Born, San Juan, Dominican Republic, March 17, 1990.
Bats Right. Throws Right. Height, 5 feet, 10 inches. Weight, 165 pounds.

Year	Club	Lea	Pos	G	AB	R	H	2B	3B	HR	RBI	SB	Avg
2008 Angels	Arizona		2B-OF	11	36	13	9	0	0	0	4	1	.250
2009 Salt Lake	P.C.		2B	7	19	2	8	2	0	0	2	0	.421
2009 Orem	Pioneer		2B	36	162	33	56	10	4	3	21	11	.346
2010 Cedar Rapids	Midwest		2B	130	515	89	161	24	12	10	79	50	.313
2011 Angels	Arizona		SS	8	30	5	11	4	0	1	5	0	.367
2011 Inland Empire	Calif.		SS	44	185	26	52	9	4	3	21	18	.281

Year Club	Lea	Pos	G	AB	R	H	2B	3B	HR	RBI	SB	Avg
2012 Arkansas	Texas	SS-2B	94	374	50	110	10	5	7	40	33	.294
2012 Huntsville	Southern	SS	8	30	7	13	3	0	0	4	4	.433
2012 Los Angeles	A.L.	SS	1	3	0	0	0	0	0	0	0	.000
2012 Milwaukee a	N.L.	SS	44	148	19	39	4	3	0	14	7	.264
Major League Totals		1 Yrs.	45	151	19	39	4	3	0	14	7	.258

a Traded to Milwaukee Brewers with pitcher Ariel Pena and pitcher Johnny Hellweg for pitcher Zack Greinke, July 27, 2012.

SIMMONS, ANDRELTON A.
Born, Mundo-Novo, Curacao, September 4, 1989.
Bats Right. Throws Right. Height, 6 feet, 2 inches. Weight, 170 pounds.

Year Club	Lea	Pos	G	AB	R	H	2B	3B	HR	RBI	SB	Avg
2010 Danville	.Appal.	SS	62	239	36	66	11	1	2	26	18	.276
2011 Lynchburg	Carolina	SS	131	517	69	161	35	6	1	52	26	.311
2012 Mississippi.	Southern	SS	44	174	29	51	9	2	3	21	10	.293
2012 Atlanta a	N.L.	SS	49	166	17	48	8	2	3	19	1	.289
Wild Card Playoff												
2012 Atlanta	N.L.	SS	1	4	0	1	0	0	0	0	0	.250

a On disabled list from July 13 to September 10, 2012.

SIZEMORE, SCOTT DANIEL
Born, Virginia Beach, Virginia, January 4, 1985.
Bats Right. Throws Right. Height, 6 feet, 1 inch. Weight, 185 pounds.

Year Club	Lea	Pos	G	AB	R	H	2B	3B	HR	RBI	SB	Avg
2006 Oneonta	.N.Y.-Penn.	SS-2B	70	294	49	96	15	4	3	37	7	.327
2007 West Michigan .	Midwest	2B	125	438	78	116	33	5	4	48	16	.265
2008 Lakeland	Fla.St.	2B	53	203	32	58	11	4	4	20	14	.286
2009 Erie.	Eastern	2B	59	228	39	70	17	4	9	33	7	.307
2009 Toledo	Int.	2B-3B-SS	71	292	49	90	22	1	8	33	14	.308
2010 Toledo	Int.	2B-3B-SS	76	299	49	89	23	1	9	37	2	.298
2010 Detroit	.A.L.	2B-3B	48	143	19	32	7	0	3	14	0	.224
2011 Sacramento	.P.C.	3B-2B	9	30	11	8	2	0	1	3	2	.267
2011 Toledo	Int.	2B	23	76	17	31	7	1	2	15	3	.408
2011 Detroit-Oakland a . .	.A.L.	3B-2B	110	368	50	90	22	1	11	56	5	.245
2012 Oakland b	.A.L.				INJURED—Did Not Play							
Major League Totals		2 Yrs.	158	511	69	122	29	1	14	70	5	.239

a Traded to Oakland Athletics for pitcher David Purcey, May 27, 2011.
b On disabled list from March 3 to October 29, 2012.

SMITH, GARRY SETH (SETH)
Born, Jackson, Mississippi, September 30, 1982.
Bats Left. Throws Left. Height, 6 feet, 3 inches. Weight, 215 pounds.

Year Club	Lea	Pos	G	AB	R	H	2B	3B	HR	RBI	SB	Avg
2004 Tri-Cities	Northwest	OF	9	27	6	7	1	1	2	5	0	.259
2004 Casper	.Pioneer	OF	56	233	46	86	21	3	9	61	9	.369
2005 Modesto	.Calif.	OF	129	533	87	160	45	6	9	72	5	.300
2006 Tulsa	Texas	OF	130	524	79	154	46	4	15	71	4	.294
2007 Colorado Springs	.P.C.	OF	129	451	68	143	32	6	17	82	7	.317
2007 Colorado	N.L.	OF	7	8	4	5	0	1	0	0	0	.625
2008 Colorado Springs	.P.C.	OF	68	248	55	80	16	2	10	53	11	.323
2008 Colorado	N.L.	OF	67	108	13	28	7	0	4	15	1	.259
2009 Colorado	N.L.	OF	133	335	61	98	20	4	15	55	4	.293
2010 Colorado	N.L.	OF	133	358	55	88	19	5	17	52	2	.246
2011 Colorado a	N.L.	OF	147	476	67	135	32	9	15	59	10	.284
2012 Sacramento	.P.C.	DH	1	3	0	2	0	0	0	0	0	.667
2012 Oakland b	.A.L.	OF	125	383	55	92	23	2	14	52	2	.240
Major League Totals		6 Yrs.	612	1668	255	446	101	21	65	233	19	.267
Division Series												
2007 Colorado	N.L.	PH	2	2	1	1	0	0	0	0	0	.500
2009 Colorado	N.L.	OF	3	5	0	1	0	0	0	0	0	.200
2012 Oakland	A.L.	DH	5	15	3	2	1	0	1	3	0	.133
Division Series Totals			10	22	4	4	1	0	1	3	0	.182
Championship Series												
2007 Colorado	N.L.	PH	2	2	1	1	1	0	0	2	0	.500

Year	Club	Lea	Pos	G	AB	R	H	2B	3B	HR	RBI	SB	Avg
2007 Colorado	N.L.	PH	2	2	0	1	0	0	0	0	0	.500

a Traded to Oakland Athletics for pitcher Guillermo Moscoso and pitcher Josh Outman, January 16, 2012.
b On disabled list from August 3 to August 21, 2012.

SMOAK, JUSTIN KYLE
Born, Goose Creek, South Carolina, December 5, 1986.
Bats Both. Throws Left. Height, 6 feet, 4 inches. Weight, 220 pounds.

Year	Club	Lea	Pos	G	AB	R	H	2B	3B	HR	RBI	SB	Avg
2008 Clinton	Midwest	1B	14	56	9	17	3	0	3	6	0	.304
2009 Rangers	Arizona	1B	2	6	3	4	0	1	2	5	0	.667
2009 Oklahoma...........	P.C.	1B	54	197	25	48	11	0	4	23	0	.244
2009 Frisco.............	Texas	1B	50	183	30	60	10	0	6	29	0	.328
2010 Oklahoma............	P.C.	1B	15	50	10	15	6	0	2	5	0	.300
2010 Tacoma	P.C.	1B	35	133	23	36	7	0	7	25	0	.271
2010 Texas-Seattle a	A.L.	1B	100	348	40	76	14	0	13	48	1	.218
2011 Tacoma	P.C.	1B	4	11	1	0	0	0	0	0	0	.000
2011 Seattle b............	A.L.	1B	123	427	38	100	24	0	15	55	0	.234
2012 Tacoma	P.C.	1B	20	66	10	16	6	1	0	4	1	.242
2012 Seattle	A.L.	1B	132	483	49	105	14	0	19	51	1	.217
Major League Totals			3 Yrs.	355	1258	127	281	52	0	47	154	2	.223

a Traded to Seattle Mariners with pitcher Blake Beavan, pitcher Josh Lueke and infielder Matt Lawson for pitcher Cliff Lee, pitcher Mark Lowe and cash, July 9, 2010.
b On disabled list from August 13 to September 1, 2011.

SNIDER, TRAVIS JAMES
Born, Kirkland, Washington, February 2, 1988.
Bats Left. Throws Left. Height, 5 feet, 11 inches. Weight, 245 pounds.

Year	Club	Lea	Pos	G	AB	R	H	2B	3B	HR	RBI	SB	Avg
2006 Pulaski	Appal.	OF	54	194	36	63	12	1	11	41	6	.325
2007 Lansing	Midwest	OF	118	457	72	143	35	7	16	93	3	.313
2008 Dunedin	Fla.St.	DH	17	61	15	17	5	0	4	7	1	.279
2008 New Hampshire	Eastern	OF	98	362	65	95	21	0	17	67	1	.262
2008 Syracuse	Int.	OF	18	64	9	22	5	0	2	11	1	.344
2008 Toronto	A.L.	OF	24	73	9	22	6	0	2	13	0	.301
2009 Las Vegas............	P.C.	OF	48	175	32	59	13	1	14	40	2	.337
2009 Toronto	A.L.	OF	77	241	34	58	14	1	9	29	1	.241
2010 Blue Jays	Gulf Coast	OF	4	14	2	4	0	0	0	1	1	.286
2010 Dunedin	Fla.St.	DH	1	4	0	0	0	0	0	0	0	.000
2010 New Hampshire	Eastern	OF	20	81	14	24	5	0	5	17	3	.296
2010 Toronto a	A.L.	OF	82	298	36	76	20	0	14	32	6	.255
2011 Las Vegas............	P.C.	OF	61	248	47	81	22	2	4	42	12	.327
2011 Toronto	A.L.	OF	49	187	23	42	14	0	3	30	9	.225
2012 Dunedin	Fla.St.	OF	5	22	3	5	1	0	0	1	2	.227
2012 Las Vegas............	P.C.	OF	56	209	49	70	16	0	13	56	2	.335
2012 Toronto	A.L.	OF	10	36	6	9	2	0	3	8	0	.250
2012 Pittsburgh b..........	N.L.	OF	50	128	17	32	5	1	1	9	2	.250
Major League Totals			5 Yrs.	292	963	125	239	61	2	32	121	18	.248

a On disabled list from May 15 to July 17, 2010.
b Traded to Pittsburgh Pirates for pitcher Brad Lincoln, July 31, 2012.

SNYDER, CHRISTOPHER RYAN (CHRIS)
Born, Houston, Texas, February 12, 1981.
Bats Right. Throws Right. Height, 6 feet, 3 inches. Weight, 245 pounds.

Year	Club	Lea	Pos	G	AB	R	H	2B	3B	HR	RBI	SB	Avg
2002 Lancaster	Calif.	C	60	217	32	56	16	0	9	44	0	.258
2003 Lancaster	Calif.	C	69	245	53	77	16	2	10	53	0	.314
2003 El Paso............	Texas	C	53	188	21	38	14	0	4	26	0	.202
2004 El Paso............	Texas	C-1B	99	346	66	104	31	0	15	57	3	.301
2004 Arizona............	N.L.	C	29	96	10	23	6	0	5	15	0	.240
2005 Arizona.............	N.L.	C	115	326	24	66	14	0	6	28	0	.202
2006 Arizona.............	N.L.	C	61	184	19	51	9	0	6	32	0	.277
2007 Arizona.............	N.L.	C-1B-OF	110	326	37	82	20	0	13	47	0	.252
2008 Visalia	Calif.	C	1	5	1	2	0	0	1	4	0	.400
2008 Arizona a	N.L.	C	115	334	47	79	22	1	16	64	0	.237
2009 Visalia	Calif.	C	3	7	1	1	0	0	0	0	0	.143
2009 Reno	P.C.	C	3	13	2	4	1	0	1	4	0	.308

<table>
<tr><th>Year</th><th>Club</th><th>Lea</th><th>Pos</th><th>G</th><th>AB</th><th>R</th><th>H</th><th>2B</th><th>3B</th><th>HR</th><th>RBI</th><th>SB</th><th>Avg</th></tr>
<tr><td>2010 Arizona-Pittsburgh c ...</td><td></td><td>N.L.</td><td>C</td><td>105</td><td>319</td><td>34</td><td>66</td><td>9</td><td>0</td><td>15</td><td>48</td><td>0</td><td>.207</td></tr>
<tr><td>2011 Bradenton ....</td><td></td><td>Fla.St.</td><td>C</td><td>6</td><td>20</td><td>6</td><td>8</td><td>2</td><td>0</td><td>1</td><td>8</td><td>0</td><td>.400</td></tr>
<tr><td>2011 Pittsburgh d-e ....</td><td></td><td>N.L.</td><td>C</td><td>34</td><td>96</td><td>13</td><td>26</td><td>3</td><td>0</td><td>3</td><td>17</td><td>0</td><td>.271</td></tr>
<tr><td>2012 Houston f...........</td><td></td><td>N.L.</td><td>C-1B</td><td>76</td><td>221</td><td>23</td><td>39</td><td>8</td><td>0</td><td>7</td><td>24</td><td>0</td><td>.176</td></tr>
<tr><td>Major League Totals ....</td><td></td><td>9 Yrs.</td><td></td><td>706</td><td>2067</td><td>227</td><td>465</td><td>98</td><td>1</td><td>77</td><td>297</td><td>0</td><td>.225</td></tr>
<tr><td>Division Series</td><td></td><td></td><td></td><td></td><td></td><td></td><td></td><td></td><td></td><td></td><td></td><td></td><td></td></tr>
<tr><td>2007 Arizona..............</td><td></td><td>N.L.</td><td>C</td><td>3</td><td>7</td><td>2</td><td>1</td><td>0</td><td>0</td><td>0</td><td>0</td><td>0</td><td>.143</td></tr>
<tr><td>Championship Series</td><td></td><td></td><td></td><td></td><td></td><td></td><td></td><td></td><td></td><td></td><td></td><td></td><td></td></tr>
<tr><td>2007 Arizona..............</td><td></td><td>N.L.</td><td>C</td><td>3</td><td>12</td><td>1</td><td>4</td><td>2</td><td>0</td><td>1</td><td>3</td><td>0</td><td>.333</td></tr>
</table>

a On disabled list from July 1 to July 20, 2008.
b On disabled list from June 21 to July 28 and August 27 to October 15, 2009.
c Traded to Pittsburgh Pirates with infielder Pedro Ciriaco and cash for infielder Bobby Crosby, outfielder Ryan Church and pitcher D.J. Carrasco, July 31, 2010.
d On disabled list from March 25 to April 14 and June 9 to October 31, 2011.
e Filed for free agency, October 31, 2011. Signed with Houston Astros, January 20, 2012.
f Filed for free agency, November 3, 2012.

SOLANO (PRECIADO), DONOVAN
Born, Barranquilla, Colombia, December 17, 1987.
Bats Right. Throws Right. Height, 5 feet, 9 inches. Weight, 190 pounds.

<table>
<tr><th>Year</th><th>Club</th><th>Lea</th><th>Pos</th><th>G</th><th>AB</th><th>R</th><th>H</th><th>2B</th><th>3B</th><th>HR</th><th>RBI</th><th>SB</th><th>Avg</th></tr>
<tr><td>2005 Johnson City ....</td><td>Appal.</td><td></td><td>SS-2B</td><td>45</td><td>145</td><td>27</td><td>38</td><td>4</td><td>0</td><td>0</td><td>11</td><td>3</td><td>.262</td></tr>
<tr><td>2005 New Jersey ....</td><td>N.Y.-Penn.</td><td></td><td>SS-3B-2B</td><td>22</td><td>77</td><td>7</td><td>19</td><td>5</td><td>0</td><td>0</td><td>11</td><td>1</td><td>.247</td></tr>
<tr><td>2006 State College .</td><td>N.Y.-Penn.</td><td></td><td>3B-2B-SS</td><td>44</td><td>149</td><td>22</td><td>42</td><td>2</td><td>0</td><td>0</td><td>13</td><td>2</td><td>.282</td></tr>
<tr><td>2007 Palm Beach .....</td><td>Fla.St.</td><td></td><td>SS-3B-2B</td><td>50</td><td>163</td><td>17</td><td>34</td><td>2</td><td>1</td><td>0</td><td>11</td><td>0</td><td>.209</td></tr>
<tr><td>2007 Quad Cities....</td><td>Midwest</td><td></td><td>3B-SS</td><td>82</td><td>292</td><td>31</td><td>75</td><td>8</td><td>0</td><td>0</td><td>30</td><td>5</td><td>.257</td></tr>
<tr><td>2008 Palm Beach .....</td><td>Fla.St.</td><td></td><td>SS-3B-2B-OF</td><td>107</td><td>402</td><td>56</td><td>115</td><td>15</td><td>4</td><td>1</td><td>31</td><td>1</td><td>.286</td></tr>
<tr><td>2008 Springfield ......</td><td>Texas</td><td></td><td>SS-2B</td><td>26</td><td>106</td><td>11</td><td>28</td><td>5</td><td>0</td><td>1</td><td>11</td><td>2</td><td>.264</td></tr>
<tr><td>2009 Memphis ....</td><td>P.C.</td><td></td><td>SS-3B-2B</td><td>52</td><td>164</td><td>22</td><td>52</td><td>7</td><td>0</td><td>0</td><td>14</td><td>3</td><td>.317</td></tr>
<tr><td>2009 Springfield ......</td><td>Texas</td><td></td><td>3B-2B-SS</td><td>64</td><td>251</td><td>27</td><td>52</td><td>7</td><td>1</td><td>1</td><td>16</td><td>1</td><td>.207</td></tr>
<tr><td>2010 Memphis ....</td><td>P.C.</td><td></td><td>SS-2B-3B</td><td>102</td><td>330</td><td>41</td><td>84</td><td>12</td><td>1</td><td>4</td><td>27</td><td>2</td><td>.255</td></tr>
<tr><td>2011 Memphis ....</td><td>P.C.</td><td></td><td>2B-SS-3B</td><td>81</td><td>229</td><td>22</td><td>65</td><td>21</td><td>1</td><td>1</td><td>23</td><td>2</td><td>.284</td></tr>
<tr><td>2011 Springfield a....</td><td>Texas</td><td></td><td>2B-3B-SS</td><td>27</td><td>101</td><td>5</td><td>23</td><td>7</td><td>0</td><td>2</td><td>10</td><td>0</td><td>.228</td></tr>
<tr><td>2012 New Orleans......</td><td>P.C.</td><td></td><td>2B-SS</td><td>36</td><td>141</td><td>14</td><td>37</td><td>7</td><td>1</td><td>0</td><td>14</td><td>4</td><td>.262</td></tr>
<tr><td>2012 Miami...........</td><td>N.L.</td><td></td><td>2B-3B-OF-SS</td><td>93</td><td>285</td><td>29</td><td>84</td><td>11</td><td>3</td><td>2</td><td>28</td><td>7</td><td>.295</td></tr>
</table>

a Filed for free agency from St. Louis Cardinals, November 2, 2011. Signed with Miami Marlins organization, November 22, 2011.

SORIANO, ALFONSO GUILLEARD
Born, San Pedro de Macoris, Dominican Republic, January 7, 1976.
Bats Right. Throws Right. Height, 6 feet, 1 inch. Weight, 180 pounds.

<table>
<tr><th>Year</th><th>Club</th><th>Lea</th><th>Pos</th><th>G</th><th>AB</th><th>R</th><th>H</th><th>2B</th><th>3B</th><th>HR</th><th>RBI</th><th>SB</th><th>Avg</th></tr>
<tr><td>1995 Hiroshima ......</td><td>Dominican</td><td></td><td>SS</td><td>63</td><td>227</td><td>52</td><td>83</td><td>12</td><td>3</td><td>4</td><td>55</td><td>8</td><td>.366</td></tr>
<tr><td>1996 Hiroshima ......</td><td>Japan East.</td><td></td><td>SS</td><td>57</td><td>131</td><td>11</td><td>28</td><td>0</td><td>0</td><td>0</td><td>13</td><td>0</td><td>.214</td></tr>
<tr><td>1997 Hiroshima ......</td><td>Japan Cent.</td><td></td><td>SS</td><td>9</td><td>17</td><td>2</td><td>2</td><td>0</td><td>0</td><td>0</td><td>2</td><td>0</td><td>.118</td></tr>
<tr><td>1998 a ....</td><td></td><td></td><td colspan="10">Did Not Play</td></tr>
<tr><td>1999 Norwich...........</td><td>Eastern</td><td></td><td>SS</td><td>89</td><td>361</td><td>57</td><td>110</td><td>20</td><td>3</td><td>15</td><td>68</td><td>24</td><td>.305</td></tr>
<tr><td>1999 Yankees ....</td><td>Gulf Coast</td><td></td><td>SS</td><td>5</td><td>19</td><td>7</td><td>5</td><td>2</td><td>0</td><td>1</td><td>5</td><td>0</td><td>.263</td></tr>
<tr><td>1999 Columbus............</td><td>Int.</td><td></td><td>SS</td><td>20</td><td>82</td><td>8</td><td>15</td><td>5</td><td>1</td><td>2</td><td>11</td><td>1</td><td>.183</td></tr>
<tr><td>1999 New York b........</td><td>A.L.</td><td></td><td>SS</td><td>9</td><td>8</td><td>2</td><td>1</td><td>0</td><td>0</td><td>1</td><td>1</td><td>0</td><td>.125</td></tr>
<tr><td>2000 Columbus............</td><td>Int.</td><td></td><td>SS-2B</td><td>111</td><td>459</td><td>90</td><td>133</td><td>32</td><td>6</td><td>12</td><td>66</td><td>14</td><td>.290</td></tr>
<tr><td>2000 New York ....</td><td>A.L.</td><td></td><td>3B-SS-2B</td><td>22</td><td>50</td><td>5</td><td>9</td><td>3</td><td>0</td><td>2</td><td>3</td><td>2</td><td>.180</td></tr>
<tr><td>2001 New York ....</td><td>A.L.</td><td></td><td>2B</td><td>158</td><td>574</td><td>77</td><td>154</td><td>34</td><td>3</td><td>18</td><td>73</td><td>43</td><td>.268</td></tr>
<tr><td>2002 New York ....</td><td>A.L.</td><td></td><td>2B</td><td>156</td><td>*696</td><td>*128</td><td>*209</td><td>51</td><td>2</td><td>39</td><td>102</td><td>41</td><td>.300</td></tr>
<tr><td>2003 New York ....</td><td>A.L.</td><td></td><td>2B</td><td>156</td><td>*682</td><td>114</td><td>198</td><td>36</td><td>5</td><td>38</td><td>91</td><td>35</td><td>.290</td></tr>
<tr><td>2004 Texas c-d ....</td><td>A.L.</td><td></td><td>2B</td><td>145</td><td>608</td><td>77</td><td>170</td><td>32</td><td>4</td><td>28</td><td>91</td><td>18</td><td>.280</td></tr>
<tr><td>2005 Texas e.............</td><td>A.L.</td><td></td><td>2B</td><td>156</td><td>637</td><td>102</td><td>171</td><td>43</td><td>2</td><td>36</td><td>104</td><td>30</td><td>.268</td></tr>
<tr><td>2006 Washington f.........</td><td>N.L.</td><td></td><td>OF</td><td>159</td><td>647</td><td>119</td><td>179</td><td>41</td><td>2</td><td>46</td><td>95</td><td>41</td><td>.277</td></tr>
<tr><td>2007 Chicago g...........</td><td>N.L.</td><td></td><td>OF-2B</td><td>135</td><td>579</td><td>97</td><td>173</td><td>42</td><td>5</td><td>33</td><td>70</td><td>19</td><td>.299</td></tr>
<tr><td>2008 Azl Cubs..........</td><td>Arizona</td><td></td><td>DH</td><td>1</td><td>2</td><td>1</td><td>0</td><td>0</td><td>0</td><td>0</td><td>0</td><td>0</td><td>.000</td></tr>
<tr><td>2008 Iowa....................</td><td>P.C.</td><td></td><td>OF</td><td>1</td><td>3</td><td>0</td><td>1</td><td>0</td><td>0</td><td>0</td><td>0</td><td>0</td><td>.333</td></tr>
<tr><td>2008 Chicago h..........</td><td>N.L.</td><td></td><td>OF-2B</td><td>109</td><td>453</td><td>76</td><td>127</td><td>27</td><td>0</td><td>29</td><td>75</td><td>19</td><td>.280</td></tr>
<tr><td>2009 Chicago i ....</td><td>N.L.</td><td></td><td>OF-2B-3B</td><td>117</td><td>477</td><td>64</td><td>115</td><td>25</td><td>1</td><td>20</td><td>55</td><td>9</td><td>.241</td></tr>
<tr><td>2010 Chicago ....</td><td>N.L.</td><td></td><td>OF</td><td>147</td><td>496</td><td>67</td><td>128</td><td>40</td><td>3</td><td>24</td><td>79</td><td>5</td><td>.258</td></tr>
<tr><td>2011 Iowa.................</td><td>P.C.</td><td></td><td>OF</td><td>3</td><td>13</td><td>3</td><td>1</td><td>0</td><td>0</td><td>0</td><td>0</td><td>0</td><td>.077</td></tr>
<tr><td>2011 Chicago j ....</td><td>N.L.</td><td></td><td>OF</td><td>137</td><td>475</td><td>50</td><td>116</td><td>27</td><td>1</td><td>26</td><td>88</td><td>2</td><td>.244</td></tr>
<tr><td>2012 Chicago ....</td><td>N.L.</td><td></td><td>OF</td><td>151</td><td>561</td><td>68</td><td>147</td><td>33</td><td>2</td><td>32</td><td>108</td><td>6</td><td>.262</td></tr>
<tr><td>Major League Totals ....</td><td></td><td>14 Yrs.</td><td></td><td>1757</td><td>6943</td><td>1046</td><td>1897</td><td>434</td><td>30</td><td>372</td><td>1035</td><td>270</td><td>.273</td></tr>
</table>

Year	Club	Lea	Pos	G	AB	R	H	2B	3B	HR	RBI	SB	Avg
Division Series													
2001 New York	A.L.		2B	5	18	2	4	0	0	0	3	2	.222
2002 New York	A.L.		2B	4	17	2	2	1	0	1	2	1	.118
2003 New York	A.L.		2B	4	19	2	7	1	0	0	4	2	.368
2007 Chicago	N.L.		OF	3	14	0	2	0	0	0	0	0	.143
2008 Chicago	N.L.		OF	3	14	0	1	0	0	0	0	0	.071
Division Series Totals				19	82	6	16	2	0	1	9	5	.195
Championship Series													
2001 New York	A.L.		2B	5	15	5	6	0	0	1	2	2	.500
2003 New York	A.L.		2B	7	30	0	4	1	0	0	3	2	.133
Championship Series Totals				12	45	5	10	1	0	1	5	4	.222
World Series Record													
2001 New York	A.L.		2B	7	25	1	6	0	0	1	2	0	.240
2003 New York	A.L.		2B-OF	6	22	2	5	0	0	1	2	1	.227
World Series Totals				13	47	3	11	0	0	2	4	1	.234

a Signed by New York Yankees as free agent, September 29, 1998.
b On disabled list from July 15 to August 15, 1999.
c Traded to Texas Rangers with player to be named later for infielder Alex Rodriguez, February 16, 2004.
d Texas Rangers received infielder Joaquin Arias to complete trade, March 23, 2004.
e Traded to Washington Nationals for outfielder Brad Wilkerson, outfielder Terrmel Sledge and pitcher Armando Galarraga, December 13, 2005.
f Filed for free agency, October 29, 2006. Signed with Chicago Cubs, November 20, 2006.
g On disabled list from August 6 to August 28, 2007.
h On disabled list from April 16 to May 1 and June 12 to July 23, 2008.
i On disabled list from September 4 to October 14, 2009.
j On disabled list from May 31 to June 15, 2011.

SOTO, GEOVANY

Born, San Juan, Puerto Rico, January 20, 1983.
Bats Right. Throws Right. Height, 6 feet, 1 inch. Weight, 230 pounds.

Year	Club	Lea	Pos	G	AB	R	H	2B	3B	HR	RBI	SB	Avg
2001 Cubs	Arizona	C-1B-3B-OF	41	150	18	39	16	0	1	20	1	.260	
2002 Cubs	Arizona		C-1B	44	156	24	42	10	2	3	24	0	.269
2002 Boise	Northwest		C	1	5	1	2	0	0	0	0	0	.400
2003 Daytona	Fla.St.		C-3B	89	297	26	72	12	2	2	38	0	.242
2004 West Tenn	Southern		C-1B	104	332	47	90	16	0	9	48	1	.271
2005 Iowa	P.C.		C	91	292	30	74	14	0	4	39	0	.253
2005 Chicago	N.L.		PH	1	1	0	0	0	0	0	0	0	.000
2006 Iowa	P.C.		C	108	342	34	93	21	0	6	38	0	.272
2006 Chicago	N.L.		C	11	25	1	5	1	0	0	2	0	.200
2007 Iowa	P.C.		C-1B	110	385	75	136	31	3	26	109	0	.353
2007 Chicago	N.L.		C	18	54	12	21	6	0	3	8	0	.389
2008 Chicago a	N.L.		C	141	494	66	141	35	2	23	86	0	.285
2009 Azl Cubs	Arizona		DH	1	3	0	1	1	0	0	2	0	.333
2009 Tennessee	Southern		C	3	9	2	3	0	0	2	4	0	.333
2009 Chicago b	N.L.		C	102	331	27	72	19	1	11	47	1	.218
2010 Chicago c	N.L.		C	105	322	47	90	19	0	17	53	0	.280
2011 Tennessee	Southern		C	2	7	0	0	0	0	0	0	0	.000
2011 Chicago d	N.L.		C	125	421	46	96	26	0	17	54	0	.228
2012 Iowa	P.C.		C	5	16	1	3	2	0	0	0	0	.188
2012 Chicago	N.L.		C	52	176	26	35	6	1	6	14	0	.199
2012 Texas e-f-g	A.L.		C	47	148	19	29	6	0	5	25	1	.196
Major League Totals		8 Yrs.	602	1972	244	489	118	4	82	289	2	.248	
Wild Card Playoff													
2012 Texas	A.L.		C	1	2	0	0	0	0	0	0	0	.000
Division Series													
2007 Chicago	N.L.		C	2	6	1	1	0	0	1	2	0	.167
2008 Chicago	N.L.		C	3	11	0	2	1	0	0	0	0	.182
Division Series Totals				5	17	1	3	1	0	1	2	0	.176

a Selected Rookie of the Year in National League for 2008.
b On disabled list from July 7 to August 7, 2009.
c On disabled list from August 7 to August 23 and September 19 to October 6, 2010.
d On disabled list from May 11 to May 29, 2011.
e On disabled list from May 17 to June 18, 2012.
f Traded to Texas Rangers with cash for pitcher Jacon Brigham and cash, July 31, 2012.
g Not offered contract, November 30, 2012, re-signed with Texas Rangers, December 2, 2012.

SPAN, KEIUNTA DENARD (DENARD)

Born, Tampa, Florida, February 17, 1984.
Bats Left. Throws Left. Height, 6 feet. Weight, 205 pounds.

Year	Club	Lea	Pos	G	AB	R	H	2B	3B	HR	RBI	SB	Avg
2003 Elizabethton	Appal.	OF	50	207	34	56	5	1	1	18	14	.271
2004 Twins	Gulf Coast	OF	5	16	1	6	2	0	0	1	0	.375
2004 Quad Cities	Midwest	OF	64	240	29	64	4	3	0	14	15	.267
2005 New Britain	Eastern	OF	68	267	47	76	6	5	0	26	10	.285
2005 Fort Myers	Fla.St.	OF	49	186	38	63	3	3	1	19	13	.339
2006 New Britain	Eastern	OF	134	536	80	153	16	6	2	45	24	.285
2007 Rochester	Int.	OF	139	487	59	130	20	7	3	55	25	.267
2008 Rochester	Int.	OF	40	156	32	53	11	1	3	14	15	.340
2008 Minnesota	A.L.	OF	93	347	70	102	16	7	6	47	18	.294
2009 Rochester	Int.	OF	2	6	1	2	1	0	0	1	1	.333
2009 Minnesota a	A.L.	OF	145	578	97	180	16	*10	8	68	23	.311
2010 Minnesota	A.L.	OF	153	629	85	166	24	10	3	58	26	.264
2011 Rochester	Int.	OF	10	39	4	8	1	0	0	2	3	.205
2011 Minnesota b	A.L.	OF	70	284	37	75	11	5	2	16	6	.264
2012 Minnesota c-d	A.L.	OF	128	516	71	146	38	4	4	41	17	.283
Major League Totals		5 Yrs.	589	2354	360	669	105	36	23	230	90	.284
Division Series													
2009 Minnesota	A.L.	OF	3	15	1	6	1	0	0	1	1	.400
2010 Minnesota	A.L.	OF	3	13	0	4	0	0	0	0	0	.308
Division Series Totals			6	28	1	10	1	0	0	1	1	.357

a On disabled list from June 10 to June 25, 2009.
b On disabled list from June 10 to June 23 and June 23 to August 2 and August 14 to September 21, 2011.
c On disabled list from August 28 to September 12, 2012.
d Traded to Washington Nationals for pitcher Alex Meyer, November 29, 2012.

STANTON, GIANCARLO CRUZ-MICHAEL

Born, Panorama, California, November 8, 1989.
Bats Right. Throws Right. Height, 6 feet, 5 inches. Weight, 235 pounds.

Year	Club	Lea	Pos	G	AB	R	H	2B	3B	HR	RBI	SB	Avg
2007 Marlins	Gulf Coast	OF	8	26	6	7	2	0	0	1	0	.269
2007 Jamestown	N.Y.-Penn.	OF	9	30	2	2	1	0	1	2	0	.067
2008 Greensboro	So.Atl.	OF	125	468	89	137	26	3	39	97	4	.293
2009 Jupiter	Fla.St.	OF	50	180	27	53	9	3	12	39	2	.294
2009 Jacksonville	Southern	OF	79	299	49	69	15	2	16	53	1	.231
2010 Jacksonville	Southern	OF	53	192	42	60	13	2	21	52	1	.313
2010 Florida	N.L.	OF	100	359	45	93	21	1	22	59	5	.259
2011 Florida	N.L.	OF	150	516	79	135	30	5	34	87	5	.262
2012 Jupiter	Fla.St.	OF	4	16	2	5	1	0	2	5	0	.313
2012 Miami a	N.L.	OF	123	449	75	130	30	1	37	86	6	.290
Major League Totals		3 Yrs.	373	1324	199	358	81	7	93	232	16	.270

a On disabled list from July 8 to August 7, 2012.

STEWART, IAN KENNETH

Born, Long Beach, California, April 5, 1985.
Bats Left. Throws Right. Height, 6 feet, 3 inches. Weight, 215 pounds.

Year	Club	Lea	Pos	G	AB	R	H	2B	3B	HR	RBI	SB	Avg
2003 Casper	Pioneer	3B	57	224	40	71	14	5	10	43	4	.317
2004 Asheville	So.Atl.	3B	131	505	92	161	31	9	30	101	19	.319
2005 Modesto	Calif.	3B	112	435	83	119	32	7	17	86	2	.274
2006 Tulsa	Texas	3B	120	462	75	124	41	7	10	71	3	.268
2007 Colorado Springs	P.C.	3B	112	414	72	126	23	2	15	65	11	.304
2007 Colorado	N.L.	3B	35	43	3	9	4	0	1	9	0	.209
2008 Colorado Springs	P.C.	3B-2B	69	257	65	72	15	6	19	57	7	.280
2008 Colorado	N.L.	3B-2B	81	266	33	69	18	2	10	41	1	.259
2009 Colorado	N.L.	3B-2B-OF	147	425	74	97	19	3	25	70	7	.228
2010 Colorado a	N.L.	3B	121	386	54	99	14	2	18	61	5	.256
2011 Colorado	N.L.	3B	48	122	14	19	6	1	0	6	3	.156
2011 Colorado Springs b	P.C.	3B	45	171	29	47	10	1	14	42	1	.275
2012 Chicago c-d	N.L.	3B	55	179	16	36	5	2	5	17	0	.201
Major League Totals		6 Yrs.	487	1421	194	329	66	10	59	204	16	.232
Division Series													
2009 Colorado	N.L.	3B	2	1	0	0	0	0	0	0	0	.000

a On disabled list from August 26 to September 17, 2010.

b Traded to Chicago Cubs with pitcher Casey Weathers for infielder D.J. Le Mahieu and outfielder Tyler Colvin, December 8, 2011.
c On disabled list from June 13 to November 2, 2012.
d Not offered contract, November 30, 2012, re-signed with Chicago Cubs, December 8, 2012.

STUBBS, ANDREW ROBERT (DREW)
Born, Texarkana, Texas, October 4, 1984.
Bats Right. Throws Right. Height, 6 feet, 4 inches. Weight, 205 pounds.

Year Club	Lea	Pos	G	AB	R	H	2B	3B	HR	RBI	SB	Avg
2006 Billings	Pioneer	OF	56	210	39	53	7	3	6	24	19	.252
2007 Dayton	Midwest	OF	129	497	93	134	29	5	12	43	23	.270
2008 Sarasota	Fla.St.	OF	86	303	49	79	21	4	5	38	27	.261
2008 Louisville	Int.	OF	19	75	14	22	4	2	2	10	3	.293
2008 Chattanooga	Southern	OF	26	92	12	29	8	0	0	9	3	.315
2009 Louisville	Int.	OF	107	411	57	110	25	2	3	39	46	.268
2009 Cincinnati	N.L.	OF	42	180	27	48	5	1	8	17	10	.267
2010 Cincinnati	N.L.	OF	150	514	91	131	19	6	22	77	30	.255
2011 Cincinnati	N.L.	OF	158	604	92	147	22	3	15	44	40	.243
2012 Dayton	Midwest	OF	3	10	0	1	0	0	0	1	0	.100
2012 Cincinnati a-b	N.L.	OF	136	493	75	105	13	2	14	40	30	.213
Major League Totals		4 Yrs.	486	1791	285	431	59	12	59	178	110	.241
Division Series												
2010 Cincinnati	N.L.	OF	3	9	0	1	0	0	0	0	0	.111
2012 Cincinnati	N.L.	OF	5	19	4	4	1	1	0	1	0	.211
Division Series Totals			8	28	4	5	1	1	0	1	0	.179

a On disabled list from June 15 to June 25, 2012.
b Traded to Cleveland Indians with infielder Didi Gregorius for outfielder Shin-Soo Choo and infielder Jason Donald, December 11, 2012.

SUZUKI, ICHIRO
Born, Kasugai, Japan, October 22, 1973.
Bats Left. Throws Right. Height, 5 feet, 9 inches. Weight, 170 pounds.

Year Club	Lea	Pos	G	AB	R	H	2B	3B	HR	RBI	SB	Avg
1992 Orix	Japan Pac.	OF	40	95	9	24	5	0	0	5	3	.253
1993 Orix	Japan Pac.	OF	43	64	4	12	2	0	1	2	0	.188
1994 Orix	Japan Pac.	OF	130	546	111	210	41	5	13	54	29	.385
1995 Orix	Japan Pac.	OF	130	524	104	179	23	4	25	80	49	.342
1996 Orix	Japan Pac.	OF	130	542	104	193	24	4	16	84	35	.356
1997 Orix	Japan Pac.	OF	135	536	94	185	31	4	17	91	39	.345
1998 Orix	Japan Pac.	OF	135	506	79	181	36	3	13	71	11	.358
1999 Orix	Japan Pac.	OF	103	411	80	141	27	2	21	68	12	.343
2000 Orix a	Japan Pac.	OF	105	395	73	153	22	1	12	73	21	.387
2001 Seattle b-c	A.L.	OF	157	*692	127	*242	34	8	8	69	*56	*.350
2002 Seattle	A.L.	OF	157	647	111	208	27	8	8	51	31	.321
2003 Seattle	A.L.	OF	159	679	111	212	29	8	13	62	34	.312
2004 Seattle	A.L.	OF	161	*704	101	*262	24	5	8	60	36	*.372
2005 Seattle	A.L.	OF	*162	679	111	206	21	12	15	68	33	.303
2006 Seattle	A.L.	OF	161	*695	110	*224	20	9	9	49	45	.322
2007 Seattle	A.L.	OF	161	*678	111	*238	22	7	6	68	37	.351
2008 Seattle	A.L.	OF	162	*686	103	*213	20	7	6	42	43	.310
2009 Seattle d	A.L.	OF	146	639	88	*225	31	4	11	46	26	.352
2010 Seattle	A.L.	OF	*162	*680	74	*214	30	3	6	43	42	.315
2011 Seattle	A.L.	OF	*161	*677	80	184	22	3	5	47	40	.272
2012 Seattle-New York e-f	A.L.	OF	*162	629	77	178	28	6	9	55	29	.283
Major League Totals		12 Yrs.	1911	8085	1204	2606	308	80	104	660	452	.322
Division Series												
2001 Seattle	A.L.	OF	5	20	4	12	1	0	0	2	1	.600
2012 New York	A.L.	OF	5	23	2	5	2	0	0	3	1	.217
Division Series Totals			10	43	6	17	3	0	0	5	2	.395
Championship Series												
2001 Seattle	A.L.	OF	5	18	3	4	1	0	0	1	2	.222
2012 New York	A.L.	OF	4	17	1	6	0	0	1	2	0	.353
Championship Series Totals			9	35	4	10	1	0	1	3	2	.286

a Signed by Seattle Mariners as free agent, November 18, 2000.
b Selected Rookie of the Year in American League for 2001.
c Selected Most Valuable Player in American League for 2001.
d On disabled list from March 31 to April 15, 2009.
e Traded to New York Yankees with cash for pitcher D.J. Mitchell and pitcher Danny Farquar, July 23, 2012.
f Filed for free agency, November 3, 2012, re-signed with New York Yankees, December 19, 2012.

SUZUKI, KURT KIYOSHI

Born, Wailuku, Hawaii, October 4, 1983.
Bats Right. Throws Right. Height, 6 feet. Weight, 205 pounds.

Year Club	Lea	Pos	G	AB	R	H	2B	3B	HR	RBI	SB	Avg
2004 Vancouver ...... Northwest		C	46	175	27	52	10	3	3	31	0	.297
2005 Stockton............Calif.		C	114	441	85	122	26	5	12	65	5	.277
2006 Midland .... Texas		C-1B	99	376	64	107	26	1	7	55	5	.285
2007 Sacramento ..........P.C.		C	55	211	32	59	9	0	3	27	0	.280
2007 Oakland .............A.L.		C	68	213	27	53	13	0	7	39	0	.249
2008 Oakland .............A.L.		C	148	530	54	148	25	1	7	42	2	.279
2009 Oakland .............A.L.		C	147	570	74	156	37	1	15	88	8	.274
2010 Sacramento ..........P.C.		C	3	8	4	3	2	0	1	5	0	.375
2010 Oakland a............A.L.		C	131	495	55	120	18	2	13	71	3	.242
2011 Oakland .............A.L.		C	134	460	54	109	26	0	14	44	2	.237
2012 Oakland .............A.L.		C	75	262	19	57	15	0	1	18	1	.218
2012 Washington b........N.L.		C	43	146	17	39	5	0	5	25	1	.267
Major League Totals		6 Yrs.	746	2676	300	682	139	4	62	327	17	.255
Division Series												
2012 Washington ..........N.L.		C	5	17	0	4	0	0	0	2	0	.235

a On disabled list from April 24 to May 16, 2010.
b Traded to Washington Nationals with cash for pitcher David Freitas, August 3, 2012.

SWISHER, NICHOLAS THOMPSON (NICK)

Born, Columbus, Ohio, January 25, 1980.
Bats Both. Throws Left. Height, 6 feet. Weight, 215 pounds.

Year Club	Lea	Pos	G	AB	R	H	2B	3B	HR	RBI	SB	Avg
2002 Visalia .... California		OF	49	183	22	44	13	2	4	23	3	.240
2002 Vancouver ...... Northwest		OF	13	44	10	11	3	0	2	12	3	.250
2003 Modesto......... California		OF-1B	51	189	38	56	14	2	10	43	0	.296
2003 Midland .... Texas		OF-1B	76	287	36	66	24	2	5	43	0	.230
2004 Sacramento ..........P.C.		OF-1B	125	443	109	119	28	2	29	92	3	.269
2004 Oakland .............A.L.		OF-1B	20	60	11	15	4	0	2	8	0	.250
2005 Sacramento ..........P.C.		OF-1B	6	23	4	9	3	0	1	0	0	.391
2005 Oakland a............A.L.		OF-1B	131	462	66	109	32	1	21	74	0	.236
2006 Oakland b............A.L.		1B-OF	157	556	106	141	24	2	35	95	1	.254
2007 Oakland .............A.L.		OF-1B	150	539	84	141	36	1	22	78	3	.262
2008 Chicago c............A.L.		OF-1B	153	497	86	109	21	1	24	69	3	.219
2009 New York ...........A.L.		OF-1B-P	150	498	84	124	35	1	29	82	0	.249
2010 New York ...........A.L.		OF-1B	150	566	91	163	33	3	29	89	1	.288
2011 New York ...........A.L.		OF-1B	150	526	81	137	30	0	23	85	2	.260
2012 New York d...........A.L.		OF-1B	148	537	75	146	36	0	24	93	2	.272
Major League Totals		9 Yrs.	1209	4241	684	1085	251	9	209	673	12	.256
Division Series												
2006 Oakland .............A.L.		1B	3	10	3	3	2	0	0	1	0	.300
2008 Chicago .............A.L.		OF-1B	3	4	1	1	0	0	0	0	0	.250
2009 New York ...........A.L.		OF	3	12	0	1	1	0	0	1	0	.083
2010 New York ...........A.L.		OF	3	12	3	4	2	0	1	1	0	.333
2011 New York ...........A.L.		OF	5	19	1	4	0	0	1	1	0	.211
2012 New York ...........A.L.		OF	5	18	0	2	0	0	0	1	0	.111
Division Series Totals			22	75	8	15	5	0	2	5	0	.200
Championship Series												
2006 Oakland .............A.L.		1B	4	10	0	1	0	0	0	0	0	.100
2009 New York ...........A.L.		OF	6	20	2	3	0	0	0	0	0	.150
2010 New York ...........A.L.		OF-1B	6	22	3	2	1	0	1	1	0	.091
2012 New York ...........A.L.		OF	3	12	0	3	2	0	0	1	0	.250
Championship Series Totals			19	64	5	9	3	0	1	2	0	.141
World Series Record												
2009 New York ...........A.L.		OF	5	15	3	2	1	0	1	1	0	.133

a On disabled list from May 2 to May 25, 2005.
b Traded to Chicago White Sox for pitcher Gio Gonzalez, pitcher Fautino de los Santos and outfielder Ryan Sweeney, January 3, 2008.
c Traded to New York Yankees with pitcher Kaneoka Texeira for infielder Wilson Betemit, pitcher Jeff Marquez and pitcher Jhonny Nunez, November 13, 2008.
d Filed for free agency, November 3, 2012. Signed with Cleveland Indians, January 3, 2013.

TABATA, JOSE NICOLAS
Born, El Tigre, Venezuela, August 12, 1988.
Bats Right. Throws Right. Height, 5 feet, 11 inches. Weight, 210 pounds.

Year	Club	Lea	Pos	G	AB	R	H	2B	3B	HR	RBI	SB	Avg
2005 Yankees	Gulf Coast	OF	44	156	30	49	5	1	3	25	22	.314
2006 Charleston	So.Atl.	OF	86	319	50	95	22	1	5	51	15	.298
2007 Tampa	Fla.St.	OF	103	411	56	126	16	2	5	54	15	.307
2008 Altoona	Eastern	OF	22	89	16	31	6	2	3	13	8	.348
2008 Trenton	Eastern	OF	79	294	40	73	9	0	3	36	10	.248
2008 Pirates a	Gulf Coast	OF	4	11	4	5	1	0	2	7	0	.455
2009 Altoona	Eastern	OF	61	228	31	69	15	1	2	25	7	.303
2009 Indianapolis	Int.	OF	32	134	21	37	7	1	3	10	4	.276
2010 Indianapolis	Int.	OF	53	224	42	69	13	2	3	19	25	.308
2010 Pittsburgh	N.L.	OF	102	405	61	121	21	4	4	35	19	.299
2011 Bradenton	Fla.St.	OF	4	8	1	1	1	0	0	1	0	.125
2011 Indianapolis	Int.	OF	9	33	6	11	6	0	0	2	0	.333
2011 Pittsburgh b	N.L.	OF	91	334	53	89	18	1	4	21	16	.266
2012 Indianapolis	Int.	OF	41	158	21	47	9	0	0	15	5	.297
2012 Pittsburgh	N.L.	OF	103	333	43	81	20	3	3	16	8	.243
Major League Totals			3 Yrs.	296	1072	157	291	59	8	11	72	43	.271

a Traded by New York Yankees to Pittsburgh Pirates with pitcher Ross Ohlendorf, pitcher Jeff Karstens and pitcher Dan McCutchen for outfielder Xavier Nady and pitcher Damaso Marte, July 26, 2008.

b On disabled list from June 27 to August 16, 2011.

TEIXEIRA, MARK CHARLES
Born, Annapolis, Maryland, April 11, 1980.
Bats Both. Throws Right. Height, 6 feet, 3 inches. Weight, 220 pounds.

Year	Club	Lea	Pos	G	AB	R	H	2B	3B	HR	RBI	SB	Avg
2002 Charlotte	Fla.St.	3B	38	150	32	48	10	2	9	41	2	.320
2002 Tulsa	Texas	3B	48	171	31	54	11	3	10	28	3	.316
2003 Texas	A.L.	1B-OF-3B	146	529	66	137	29	5	26	84	1	.259
2004 Frisco	Texas	1B	1	3	0	0	0	0	0	0	0	.000
2004 Texas a	A.L.	1B-OF	145	545	101	153	34	2	38	112	4	.281
2005 Texas	A.L.	1B	*162	644	112	194	41	3	43	144	4	.301
2006 Texas	A.L.	1B	*162	628	99	177	45	1	33	110	2	.282
2007 Frisco	Texas	1B	1	2	0	0	0	0	0	0	0	.000
2007 Texas	A.L.	1B	78	286	48	85	24	1	13	49	0	.297
2007 Atlanta b-c	N.L.	1B	54	208	38	66	9	1	17	56	0	.317
2008 Atlanta	N.L.	1B	103	381	63	108	27	0	20	78	0	.283
2008 Los Angeles d-e	A.L.	1B	54	193	39	69	14	0	13	43	2	.358
2009 New York	A.L.	1B	156	609	103	178	43	3	*39	*122	2	.292
2010 New York	A.L.	1B	158	601	*113	154	36	0	33	108	0	.256
2011 New York	A.L.	1B	156	589	90	146	26	1	39	111	4	.248
2012 New York	A.L.	1B	123	451	66	113	27	1	24	84	2	.251
Major League Totals			10 Yrs.	1497	5664	938	1580	355	18	338	1101	21	.279
Division Series													
2008 Los Angeles	A.L.	1B	4	15	4	7	0	0	0	1	0	.467
2009 New York	A.L.	1B	3	12	3	2	0	0	1	1	0	.167
2010 New York	A.L.	1B	3	13	2	4	1	0	1	3	0	.308
2011 New York	A.L.	1B	5	18	2	3	2	0	0	1	0	.167
2012 New York	A.L.	1B	5	17	1	6	0	0	0	1	1	.353
Division Series Totals				20	75	12	22	3	0	2	7	1	.293
Championship Series													
2009 New York	A.L.	1B	6	27	2	6	1	0	0	4	0	.222
2010 New York	A.L.	1B	4	14	1	0	0	0	0	0	0	.000
2012 New York	A.L.	1B	4	15	1	3	1	0	0	0	0	.200
Championship Series Totals				14	56	4	9	2	0	0	4	0	.161
World Series Record													
2009 New York	A.L.	1B	6	22	5	3	1	0	1	3	0	.136

a On disabled list from April 13 to April 29, 2004.

b On disabled list from June 9 to July 13, 2007.

c Traded to Atlanta Braves with pitcher Ron Mahay for catcher Jarrod Saltalamacchia, infielder Elvis Andrus, pitcher Neftali Feliz, pitcher Matt Harrison and pitcher Beau James, July 31, 2007.

d Traded to Los Angeles Angels for infielder Casey Kotchman and pitcher Steve Marek, July 29, 2008.

e Filed for free agency, October 30, 2008. Signed with New York Yankees, January 6, 2009.

TEJADA, RUBEN DARIO

Born, Veraguas, Panama, September 1, 1989.
Bats Right. Throws Right. Height, 5 feet, 11 inches. Weight, 160 pounds.

Year	Club	Lea	Pos	G	AB	R	H	2B	3B	HR	RBI	SB	Avg
2007 Mets	Gulf Coast		SS-2B	35	120	13	34	4	3	0	16	2	.283
2008 St. Lucie	Fla.St.		SS	131	497	55	114	19	4	2	37	8	.229
2009 Binghamton	Eastern		SS-2B	134	488	59	141	24	3	5	46	19	.289
2010 Buffalo	Int.		SS-2B	65	218	25	61	11	0	1	16	1	.280
2010 New York	N.L.		2B-SS	78	216	28	46	12	0	1	15	2	.213
2011 Buffalo	Int.		SS-2B	54	207	26	51	7	3	3	21	4	.246
2011 New York	N.L.		2B-SS	96	328	31	93	15	1	0	36	5	.284
2012 St. Lucie	Fla.St.		SS	2	9	1	1	1	0	0	0	0	.111
2012 Buffalo	Int.		SS	6	20	3	4	1	0	0	2	0	.200
2012 New York a	N.L.		SS	114	464	53	134	26	0	1	25	4	.289
Major League Totals			3 Yrs.	288	1008	112	273	53	1	2	76	11	.271

a On disabled list from May 7 to June 24, 2012.

THAMES, ERIC ALLYN

Born, Santa Clara, California, November 10, 1986.
Bats Left. Throws Right. Height, 6 feet, 1 inch. Weight, 205 pounds.

Year	Club	Lea	Pos	G	AB	R	H	2B	3B	HR	RBI	SB	Avg
2008 a					INJURED—Did Not Play								
2009 Blue Jays	Gulf Coast		OF	7	21	4	6	3	0	0	1	0	.286
2009 Dunedin	Fla.St.		OF	52	195	33	61	15	5	3	38	1	.313
2010 New Hampshire	Eastern		OF	130	496	95	143	25	6	27	104	8	.288
2011 Las Vegas	P.C.		OF	53	210	38	74	25	4	7	45	5	.352
2011 Toronto	A.L.		OF	95	362	58	95	24	5	12	37	2	.262
2012 Las Vegas	P.C.		OF	54	197	31	65	15	3	6	32	1	.330
2012 Toronto-Seattle b	A.L.		OF	86	271	27	63	12	3	9	25	1	.232
Major League Totals			2 Yrs.	181	633	85	158	36	8	21	62	3	.250

a On minor league disabled list from June 19 to September 17, 2008.
b Traded to Seattle Mariners for pitcher Steve Delabar, July 31, 2012.

THERIOT, RYAN STEWART

Born, Baton Rouge, Louisiana, December 7, 1979.
Bats Right. Throws Right. Height, 5 feet, 11 inches. Weight, 175 pounds.

Year	Club	Lea	Pos	G	AB	R	H	2B	3B	HR	RBI	SB	Avg
2001 Daytona	Fla.St.		SS	30	103	20	21	5	0	0	9	2	.204
2002 Lansing	Midwest		2B-SS	130	489	75	123	19	4	1	37	32	.252
2003 Lansing	Midwest		2B-SS	58	220	29	57	8	1	1	17	21	.259
2003 West Tenn	Southern		SS	53	178	20	42	3	0	1	9	9	.236
2004 Daytona	Fla.St.		2B-SS-3B	103	330	47	90	14	3	1	34	13	.273
2005 West Tenn	Southern		2B-SS-3B	120	448	52	136	28	4	1	53	24	.304
2005 Chicago	N.L.		2B	9	13	3	2	1	0	0	0	0	.154
2006 Iowa	P.C.		SS-2B-OF-3B	73	280	41	85	11	5	0	22	14	.304
2006 Chicago	N.L.		2B-SS-3B	53	134	34	44	11	3	3	16	13	.328
2007 Chicago	N.L.		SS-2B-3B-OF	148	537	80	143	30	2	3	45	28	.266
2008 Chicago	N.L.		SS	149	580	85	178	19	4	1	38	22	.307
2009 Chicago	N.L.		SS	154	602	81	171	20	5	7	54	21	.284
2010 Chicago-Los Angeles a-b	N.L.		2B-SS	150	586	72	158	15	2	2	29	20	.270
2011 St. Louis c	N.L.		SS-2B	132	442	46	120	26	1	1	47	4	.271
2012 San Francisco d-e	N.L.		2B-OF	104	352	45	95	16	1	0	28	13	.270
Major League Totals			8 Yrs.	899	3246	446	911	138	18	17	257	121	.281
Division Series													
2007 Chicago	N.L.		SS	3	12	0	3	0	0	0	1	1	.250
2008 Chicago	N.L.		SS	3	11	0	3	0	0	0	0	0	.273
2011 St. Louis	N.L.		2B	3	10	2	6	2	0	0	1	1	.600
2012 San Francisco	N.L.		PH	2	2	0	0	0	0	0	0	0	.000
Division Series Totals				11	35	2	12	2	0	0	2	2	.343
Championship Series													
2011 St. Louis	N.L.		2B	4	10	0	1	0	0	0	0	0	.100
2012 San Francisco	N.L.		2B	3	3	0	2	0	0	0	3	0	.667
Championship Series Totals				7	13	0	3	0	0	0	3	0	.231
World Series Record													
2011 St. Louis	N.L.		2B	5	13	1	1	0	0	0	2	0	.077
2012 San Francisco	N.L.		DH	2	5	1	1	0	0	0	0	0	.200
World Series Totals				7	18	2	2	0	0	0	2	0	.111

a Traded to Los Angeles Dodgers with pitcher Ted Lilly and cash for infielder Blake Dewitt, pitcher Kyle Smit and pitcher Brett Wallach, July 31, 2010.
b Traded to St. Louis Cardinals for pitcher Blake Hawksworth, November 30, 2010.
c Not offered contract, December 12, 2011. Signed with San Francisco Giants, February 8, 2012.
d On disabled list from May 9 to May 24, 2012.
e Filed for free agency, November 3, 2012.

THOLE, JOSHUA MICHAEL (JOSH)

Born, Breese, Illinois, October 28, 1986.
Bats Left. Throws Right. Height, 6 feet, 1 inch. Weight, 205 pounds.

Year Club	Lea	Pos	G	AB	R	H	2B	3B	HR	RBI	SB	Avg
2005 Mets	Gulf Coast	1B-C	35	104	14	28	2	1	1	12	1	.269
2006 Kingsport	Appal.	1B-C	36	98	13	23	4	0	1	12	1	.235
2007 Savannah	So.Atl.	1B-C	117	389	46	104	17	0	0	36	4	.267
2008 St. Lucie	Fla.St.	C-1B	111	347	49	104	25	2	5	56	2	.300
2009 Binghamton	Eastern	C-1B	103	384	48	126	29	2	1	46	8	.328
2009 New York	N.L.	C	17	53	2	17	2	1	0	9	1	.321
2010 Buffalo	Int.	C	48	165	20	44	19	1	2	17	0	.267
2010 New York	N.L.	C	73	202	17	56	7	1	3	17	1	.277
2011 New York	N.L.	C	114	340	22	91	17	0	3	40	0	.268
2012 Buffalo	Int.	C	2	5	0	1	0	0	0	0	0	.200
2012 New York a-b	N.L.	C	104	321	24	75	15	0	1	21	0	.234
Major League Totals		4 Yrs.	308	916	65	239	41	2	7	87	2	.261

a On disabled list from May 8 to June 1, 2012.
b Traded to Toronto Blue Jays with catcher Mike Nickeas and pitcher R.A. Dickey for catcher John Buck, pitcher Noah Syndergaard, catcher Travis D'Arnaud and outfielder Wuilmer Becerra, December 17, 2012.

THOME, JAMES HOWARD (JIM)

Born, Peoria, Illinois, August 27, 1970.
Bats Left. Throws Right. Height, 6 feet, 4 inches. Weight, 245 pounds.

Year Club	Lea	Pos	G	AB	R	H	2B	3B	HR	RBI	SB	Avg
1989 Indians	Gulf Coast	SS-3B	55	186	22	44	5	3	0	22	6	.237
1990 Burlington	Appal.	3B	34	118	31	44	7	1	12	34	6	.373
1990 Kinston	Carolina	3B	33	117	19	36	4	1	4	16	4	.308
1991 Canton	Eastern	3B	84	294	47	99	20	2	5	45	8	.337
1991 Colorado Springs	P.C.	3B	41	151	20	43	7	3	2	28	0	.285
1991 Cleveland	A.L.	3B	27	98	7	25	4	2	1	9	1	.255
1992 Colorado Springs	P.C.	3B	12	48	11	15	4	1	2	14	0	.313
1992 Cleveland a	A.L.	3B	40	117	8	24	3	1	2	12	2	.205
1993 Charlotte	Int.	3B	115	410	85	136	21	4	25	*102	1	*.332
1993 Cleveland	A.L.	3B	47	154	28	41	11	0	7	22	2	.266
1994 Cleveland	A.L.	3B	98	321	58	86	20	1	20	52	3	.268
1995 Cleveland	A.L.	3B	137	452	92	142	29	3	25	73	4	.314
1996 Cleveland	A.L.	3B	151	505	122	157	28	5	38	116	2	.311
1997 Cleveland	A.L.	1B	147	496	104	142	25	0	40	102	1	.286
1998 Cleveland b	A.L.	1B	123	440	89	129	34	2	30	85	1	.293
1999 Cleveland	A.L.	1B	146	494	101	137	27	2	33	108	0	.277
2000 Cleveland	A.L.	1B	158	557	106	150	33	1	37	106	1	.269
2001 Cleveland	A.L.	1B	156	526	101	153	26	1	49	124	0	.291
2002 Cleveland c	A.L.	1B	147	480	101	146	19	2	52	118	1	.304
2003 Philadelphia	N.L.	1B	159	578	111	154	30	3	*47	131	0	.266
2004 Philadelphia	N.L.	1B	143	508	97	139	28	1	42	105	0	.274
2005 Clearwater	Fla.St.	DH	5	12	2	4	0	0	1	3	0	.333
2005 Philadelphia d-e	A.L.	1B	59	193	26	40	7	0	7	30	0	.207
2006 Chicago	A.L.	DH-1B	143	490	108	141	26	0	42	109	0	.288
2007 Charlotte	Int.	DH	5	14	2	3	1	0	0	5	0	.214
2007 Chicago f	A.L.	DH-1B	130	432	79	119	19	0	35	96	0	.275
2008 Chicago	A.L.	DH	149	503	93	123	28	0	34	90	1	.245
2009 Chicago	A.L.	DH	107	345	55	86	15	0	23	74	0	.249
2009 Los Angeles g-h	N.L.	PH	17	17	0	4	0	0	0	3	0	.235
2010 Minnesota i	A.L.	DH	108	276	48	78	16	2	25	59	0	.283
2011 Minnesota-Cleveland j-k-l	A.L.	DH-3B	93	277	32	71	16	0	15	50	0	.256
2012 Clearwater	Fla.St.	DH	3	10	3	5	2	0	0	4	0	.500
2012 Philadelphia	N.L.	1B	30	62	9	15	2	0	5	15	0	.242
2012 Baltimore m-n-o	A.L.	DH	28	101	8	26	5	0	3	10	0	.257
Major League Totals		22 Yrs.	2543	8422	1583	2328	451	26	612	1699	19	.276
Wild Card Playoff												
2012 Baltimore	A.L.	DH	1	3	0	1	0	0	0	0	0	.333
Division Series												
1995 Cleveland	A.L.	3B	3	13	1	2	0	0	1	3	0	.154

Year Club	Lea	Pos	G	AB	R	H	2B	3B	HR	RBI	SB	Avg
1996 Cleveland	A.L.	3B	4	10	1	3	0	0	0	0	0	.300
1997 Cleveland	A.L.	1B	4	15	1	3	0	0	0	1	0	.200
1998 Cleveland	A.L.	1B-DH	4	15	2	2	0	0	2	2	0	.133
1999 Cleveland	A.L.	1B	5	17	7	6	0	0	4	10	0	.353
2001 Cleveland	A.L.	1B	5	19	2	3	0	0	1	1	0	.158
2008 Chicago	A.L.	DH	4	16	1	2	1	0	0	1	0	.125
2009 Los Angeles	N.L.	PH	3	2	0	0	0	0	0	0	0	.000
2010 Minnesota ....\.	A.L.	DH	3	10	2	1	0	0	0	0	0	.100
2012 Baltimore	A.L.	DH	3	12	0	1	0	0	0	0	0	.083
Division Series Totals			38	129	17	23	1	0	8	18	0	.178
Championship Series												
1995 Cleveland	A.L.	3B	5	15	2	4	0	0	2	5	0	.267
1997 Cleveland	A.L.	1B	6	14	3	1	0	0	.0	0	0	.071
1998 Cleveland	A.L.	1B-DH	6	23	4	7	0	0	4	8	0	.304
2009 Los Angeles	N.L.	PH	2	1	0	1	0	0	0	0	0	1.000
Championship Series Totals			19	53	9	13	0	0	6	13	0	.245
World Series Record												
1995 Cleveland	A.L.	3B	6	19	1	4	1	0	1	2	0	.211
1997 Cleveland	A.L.	1B	7	28	8	8	0	1	2	4	0	.286
World Series Totals			13	47	9	12	1	1	3	6	0	.255

a On disabled list from March 28 to May 18 and May 29 to June 15, 1992.
b On disabled list from August 8 to September 16, 1998.
c Filed for free agency, October 28, 2002. Signed with Philadelphia Phillies, December 3, 2002.
d On disabled list from May 1 to May 21 and July 1 to November 1, 2005.
e Traded to Chicago White Sox for outfielder Aaron Rowand, pitcher Dan Haigwood and player to be named later, November 25, 2005. Philadelphia Phillies received pitcher Giovany Gonzalez to complete trade, December 8, 2005.
f On disabled list from April 28 to May 20, 2007.
g Traded to Los Angeles Dodgers with cash for infielder Justin Fuller, August 31, 2009.
h Filed for free agency, November 6, 2009. Signed with Minnesota Twins, February 5, 2010.
i Filed for free agency, November 1, 2010, re-signed with Minnesota Twins, January 14, 2011.
j On disabled list from May 1 to May 23 and June 2 to June 25, 2011.
k Sold to Cleveland Indians, August 26, 2011.
l Filed for free agency, October 30, 2011. Signed with Philadelphia Phillies, November 12, 2011.
m On disabled list from July 28 to September 21 and April 29 to June 6, 2012.
n Traded to Baltimore Orioles for catcher Gabriel Lino and outfielder Kyle Simon, July 1, 2012.
o Filed for free agency, November 3, 2012.

TORRES, ANDRES VUNGO

Born, Aguadilla, Puerto Rico, January 26, 1978.
Bats Both. Throws Right. Height, 5 feet, 10 inches. Weight, 190 pounds.

Year Club	Lea	Pos	G	AB	R	H	2B	3B	HR	RBI	SB	Avg
1998 Jamestown......	N.Y.-Penn.	OF	48	192	28	45	2	6	1	21	13	.234
1999 West Michigan.....	Midwest	OF	117	407	72	96	20	5	2	34	39	.236
2000 Lakeland...........	Fla.St.	OF	108	398	82	118	11	11	3	33	65	.296
2000 Jacksonville	Southern	OF	14	54	3	8	0	0	0	0	2	.148
2001 Erie...............	Eastern	OF	64	252	54	74	16	3	1	23	19	.294
2002 Toledo	Int.	OF	115	462	80	123	17	8	4	42	42	.266
2002 Detroit	A.L.	OF	19	70	7	14	1	1	0	3	2	.200
2003 Toledo	Int.	OF	70	271	36	69	13	3	2	16	27	.255
2003 Detroit	A.L.	OF	59	168	23	37	4	3	1	9	5	.220
2004 Detroit	A.L.	OF	3	3	0	1	0	0	0	0	1	.000
2004 Charlotte	Int.	OF	87	322	49	95	11	4	8	26	23	.295
2004 Bristol a-b	Appal.	OF	6	22	8	8	0	0	1	2	5	.364
2005 Oklahoma...........	P.C.	OF	15	63	12	19	3	1	0	1	6	.302
2005 Texas c.............	A.L.	OF	8	19	2	3	1	0	0	1	1	.158
2006 Rochester...........	Int.	OF	116	348	46	82	17	9	2	30	19	.236
2007 Erie...............	Eastern	OF	85	305	53	89	15	11	6	35	17	.292
2007 Toledo d-e	Int.	OF	42	168	23	49	6	9	4	17	5	.292
2008 Iowa f...............	P.C.	OF	118	409	91	125	27	10	11	51	29	.306
2009 Azl Giants	Arizona	OF	3	6	1	2	1	0	0	1	1	.333
2009 San Jose	Calif.	OF	3	10	0	1	1	0	0	0	0	.100
2009 Fresno	P.C.	OF	11	43	7	13	1	1	1	2	1	.302
2009 San Francisco g	N.L.	OF	75	152	30	41	6	8	6	23	6	.270
2010 San Francisco	N.L.	OF	139	507	84	136	43	8	16	63	26	.268
2011 Fresno	P.C.	OF	13	55	10	15	2	2	4	11	1	.273
2011 San Francisco h-i.......	N.L.	OF	112	348	50	77	24	1	4	19	19	.221
2012 St. Lucie...........	Fla.St.	OF	3	12	3	4	1	0	0	1	2	.333
2012 Buffalo	Int.	OF	2	7	1	1	0	0	0	0	1	.143

Year	Club	Lea	Pos	G	AB	R	H	2B	3B	HR	RBI	SB	Avg
2012 New York j-k..........		N.L.	OF	132	374	47	86	17	7	3	35	13	.230
Major League Totals		8 Yrs.		547	1638	244	394	96	28	30	153	73	.241
Division Series													
2010 San Francisco		N.L.	OF	4	16	0	2	0	0	0	0	1	.125
Championship Series													
2010 San Francisco		N.L.	OF	6	20	2	7	0	0	0	0	0	.350
World Series Record													
2010 San Francisco		N.L.	OF	5	22	4	7	4	0	1	3	1	.318

a Filed for free agency, April 22, 2004. Signed with Chicago White Sox organization, April 26, 2004.
b Filed for free agency, October 15, 2004. Signed with Texas Rangers organization, November 19, 2004.
c Filed for free agency, October 6, 2005. Signed with Minnesota Twins organization, December 20, 2005.
d Filed for free agency, October 15, 2006. Signed with Detroit Tigers organization, March 2, 2007.
e Filed for free agency, October 29, 2007. Signed with Chicago Cubs organization, November 20, 2007.
f Filed for free agency, November 3, 2008. Signed with San Francisco Giants organization, January 9, 2009.
g On disabled list from April 28 to May 26 July 31 to September 1, 2009.
h On disabled list from April 10 to May 10 and August 13 to August 28, 2011.
i Traded to New York Mets with pitcher Ramon Ramirez for outfielder Angel Pagan, December 7, 2011.
j On disabled list from April 6 to April 30, 2012.
k Not offered contract, November 30, 2012. Signed with San Francisco Giants, December 13, 2012.

TRACY, CHAD AUSTIN

Born, Charlotte, North Carolina, May 22, 1980.
Bats Left. Throws Right. Height, 6 feet, 2 inches. Weight, 220 pounds.

Year	Club	Lea	Pos	G	AB	R	H	2B	3B	HR	RBI	SB	Avg
2001 South Bend	Midwest		3B-1B	54	215	43	73	11	0	4	36	3	.340
2001 Yakima.........	Northwest		3B	10	36	2	10	1	0	0	5	1	.278
2002 El Paso............	Texas		3B-1B	129	514	80	177	39	5	8	74	2	.344
2003 Tucson.............	P.C.		3B	133	522	91	169	31	4	10	80	0	.324
2004 Tucson.............	P.C.		3B-OF	11	40	7	16	4	0	2	11	2	.400
2004 Arizona.............	N.L.		3B-1B-OF	143	481	45	137	29	3	8	53	2	.285
2005 Arizona.............	N.L.		1B-OF	145	503	73	155	34	4	27	72	3	.308
2006 Arizona.............	N.L.		3B-1B	154	597	91	168	41	0	20	80	5	.281
2007 Tucson.............	P.C.		3B	3	15	3	7	2	0	1	4	0	.467
2007 Arizona.............	N.L.		3B-1B	76	227	30	60	18	2	7	35	0	.264
2008 Tucson.............	P.C.		3B-1B	12	49	5	15	2	0	0	6	0	.306
2008 Arizona.............	N.L.		1B-3B	88	273	25	73	16	0	8	39	0	.267
2009 Reno...............	P.C.		1B-3B	10	35	4	10	1	1	0	4	0	.286
2009 Arizona.............	N.L.		1B-3B	98	257	29	61	15	0	8	39	1	.237
2010 Iowa...............	P.C.		3B	26	91	21	36	8	0	5	18	0	.396
2010 Scranton-WB.........	Int.		3B-1B	18	68	14	22	5	0	6	18	0	.324
2010 Chicago-Florida a-b-c...	N.L.		3B-1B	69	146	11	36	8	0	1	15	0	.247
2011 Hiroshima	Japan Cent.		3B-DH	40	149	10	35	12	0	1	19	0	.235
2012 Potomac.........	Carolina		1B-3B	6	18	3	4	0	0	0	2	0	.222
2012 Syracuse............	Int.		1B-3B	6	19	2	9	0	0	1	3	0	.474
2012 Washington d.........	N.L.		1B-3B	73	93	7	25	7	0	3	14	0	.269
Major League Totals		8 Yrs.		846	2577	311	715	168	9	82	347	11	.277
Division Series													
2012 Washington	N.L.		PH	5	4	0	0	0	0	0	0	0	.000

a Filed for free agency, November 5, 2009. Signed with Chicago Cubs organization, January 27, 2010.
b Released by Chicago Cubs, July 1, 2010. Signed with Florida Marlins, August 5, 2010.
c Filed for free agency, November 1, 2010. Signed with Hiroshima (Japan), November 16, 2010.
d Signed with Washington Nationals organization, December 20, 2011.

TROUT, MICHAEL NELSON (MIKE)

Born, Vineland, New Jersey, August 7, 1991.
Bats Right. Throws Right. Height, 6 feet, 1 inch. Weight, 200 pounds.

Year	Club	Lea	Pos	G	AB	R	H	2B	3B	HR	RBI	SB	Avg
2009 Angels	Arizona		OF	39	164	29	59	7	7	1	25	13	.360
2009 Cedar Rapids	Midwest		OF	5	15	1	4	0	0	0	0	0	.267
2010 Rancho Cucamonga....	Calif.		OF	50	196	30	60	9	2	4	19	11	.306
2010 Cedar Rapids......	Midwest		OF	81	312	76	113	19	7	6	39	45	.362
2011 Arkansas...........	Texas		OF	91	353	82	115	18	13	11	38	33	.326
2011 Los Angeles..........	A.L.		OF	40	123	20	27	6	0	5	16	4	.220
2012 Salt Lake	P.C.		OF	20	77	21	31	4	5	1	13	6	.403
2012 Los Angeles a........	A.L.		OF	139	559	*129	182	27	8	30	83	*49	.326
Major League Totals		2 Yrs.		179	682	149	209	33	8	35	99	53	.306

a Selected Rookie of the Year in American League for 2012.

TRUMBO, MARK DANIEL

Born, Anaheim, California, January 16, 1986.
Bats Right. Throws Right. Height, 6 feet, 4 inches. Weight, 220 pounds.

Year	Club	Lea	Pos	G	AB	R	H	2B	3B	HR	RBI	SB	Avg
2005 Orem	....	Pioneer	1B	71	299	45	82	23	1	10	45	2	.274
2006 Cedar Rapids	......	Midwest	1B	118	428	43	94	19	0	13	59	5	.220
2007 Cedar Rapids	......	Midwest	1B	128	471	57	128	27	2	14	76	10	.272
2008 Rancho Cucamonga	....	Calif.	1B	103	407	70	115	28	2	26	68	7	.283
2008 Arkansas	....	Texas	1B	32	123	13	34	7	1	6	25	1	.276
2009 Arkansas	....	Texas	1B-OF	137	533	54	155	35	3	15	88	6	.291
2010 Salt Lake	....	P.C.	1B-OF	139	532	103	160	29	5	36	122	3	.301
2010 Los Angeles	....	A.L.	1B-OF	8	15	2	1	0	0	0	2	0	.067
2011 Los Angeles	....	A.L.	1B-OF	149	539	65	137	31	1	29	87	9	.254
2012 Los Angeles	....	A.L.	OF-1B-3B	144	544	66	146	19	3	32	95	4	.268
Major League Totals	....		3 Yrs.	301	1098	133	284	50	4	61	184	13	.259

TULOWITZKI, TROY TREVER

Born, Santa Clara, California, October 10, 1984.
Bats Right. Throws Right. Height, 6 feet, 3 inches. Weight, 205 pounds.

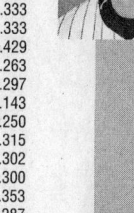

Year	Club	Lea	Pos	G	AB	R	H	2B	3B	HR	RBI	SB	Avg
2005 Modesto	....	Calif.	SS	22	94	17	25	6	0	4	14	1	.266
2006 Tulsa	....	Texas	SS	104	423	75	123	34	2	13	61	6	.291
2006 Colorado	....	N.L.	SS	25	96	15	23	2	0	1	6	3	.240
2007 Colorado	....	N.L.	SS	155	609	104	177	33	5	24	99	7	.291
2008 Modesto	....	Calif.	SS	5	12	3	4	3	0	0	1	0	.333
2008 Tulsa	....	Texas	SS	5	21	5	7	0	0	2	3	0	.333
2008 Colorado Springs	......	P.C.	SS	2	7	2	3	1	0	0	1	1	.429
2008 Colorado a	....	N.L.	SS	101	377	48	99	24	2	8	46	1	.263
2009 Colorado	....	N.L.	SS	151	543	101	161	25	9	32	92	20	.297
2010 Tulsa	....	Texas	SS	2	7	1	1	1	0	0	1	0	.143
2010 Colorado Springs	......	P.C.	SS	2	4	1	1	0	0	0	0	0	.250
2010 Colorado b	....	N.L.	SS	122	470	89	148	32	3	27	95	11	.315
2011 Colorado	....	N.L.	SS	143	537	81	162	36	2	30	105	9	.302
2012 Tulsa	....	Texas	SS	3	10	1	3	1	0	1	2	0	.300
2012 Colorado Springs	......	P.C.	SS	6	17	2	6	1	0	2	4	0	.353
2012 Colorado c	....	N.L.	SS	47	181	33	52	8	2	8	27	2	.287
Major League Totals	....		7 Yrs.	744	2813	471	822	160	23	130	470	53	.292
Division Series													
2007 Colorado	....	N.L.	SS	3	12	1	2	1	0	1	2	0	.167
2009 Colorado	....	N.L.	SS	4	16	0	4	2	0	0	3	0	.250
Division Series Totals	....			7	28	1	6	3	0	1	5	0	.214
Championship Series													
2007 Colorado	....	N.L.	SS	4	16	1	3	0	0	0	0	0	.188
World Series Record													
2007 Colorado	....	N.L.	SS	4	13	1	3	2	0	0	1	0	.231

a On disabled list from April 30 to June 20 and July 5 to July 21, 2008.
b On disabled list from June 18 to July 27, 2010.
c On disabled list from May 30 to October 5, 2012.

TURNER, JUSTIN MATTHEW

Born, Long Beach, California, November 23, 1984.
Bats Right. Throws Right. Height, 5 feet, 11 inches. Weight, 210 pounds.

Year	Club	Lea	Pos	G	AB	R	H	2B	3B	HR	RBI	SB	Avg
2006 Billings	....	Pioneer	2B-OF-3B-SS	60	231	53	78	16	3	6	41	12	.338
2007 Dayton	....	Midwest	2B-SS-3B	117	466	70	145	25	4	10	59	12	.311
2007 Sarasota	....	Fla.St.	2B	6	20	2	4	0	0	0	0	0	.200
2008 Sarasota	....	Fla.St.	2B	33	136	23	43	8	1	0	11	3	.316
2008 Chattanooga a	.Southern	2B-3B	78	280	45	81	14	1	8	42	2	.289
2009 Norfolk	....	Int.	2B-3B-SS	108	387	54	116	28	0	2	43	9	.300
2009 Baltimore	....	A.L.	3B-2B	12	18	2	3	0	0	0	3	0	.167
2010 Baltimore	....	A.L.	2B-SS	5	9	0	0	0	0	0	0	0	.000
2010 Norfolk	....	Int.	2B-SS-3B	23	84	11	21	8	0	1	8	2	.250
2010 New York	....	N.L.	2B-3B	4	8	1	1	1	0	0	0	1	.125
2010 Buffalo b	....	Int.	2B-SS-3B	78	312	58	104	22	1	11	35	5	.333
2011 Buffalo	....	Int.	2B-3B	10	40	6	12	3	2	0	2	0	.300
2011 New York	....	N.L.	2B-3B-SS	117	435	49	113	30	4	4	51	7	.260
2012 Buffalo	....	Int.	2B-SS	2	8	0	2	0	0	0	0	0	.250

Year	Club	Lea	Pos	G	AB	R	H	2B	3B	HR	RBI	SB	Avg
2012 New York c		N.L.	2B-1B-3B-SS	94	171	20	46	13	1	2	19	1	.269
Major League Totals			4 Yrs.	232	641	72	163	44	1	6	73	8	.254

a Traded by Cincinnati Reds to Baltimore Orioles with outfielder Ryan Freel and infielder Brandon Waring for catcher Ramon Hernandez and cash, December 9, 2008.
b Claimed on waivers by New York Mets, May 25, 2010.
c On disabled list from May 29 to June 16, 2012.

UGGLA, DANIEL COOLEY (DAN)
Born, Louisville, Kentucky, March 11, 1980.
Bats Right. Throws Right. Height, 5 feet, 11 inches. Weight, 200 pounds.

Year	Club	Lea	Pos	G	AB	R	H	2B	3B	HR	RBI	SB	Avg
2001 Yakima		Northwest	2B	72	278	39	77	21	0	5	40	8	.277
2002 Lancaster		Calif.	2B-3B	54	184	21	42	7	2	3	16	3	.228
2002 South Bend		Midwest	3B-2B	53	171	16	34	5	1	2	10	0	.199
2003 Lancaster		Calif.	3B-2B	134	534	104	155	31	7	23	90	24	.290
2004 Lancaster		Calif.	2B-3B-SS-1B	37	140	29	47	13	3	6	38	2	.336
2004 El Paso		Texas	3B-OF-2B	83	295	29	76	12	2	4	30	10	.258
2005 Tennessee a		Southern	2B-3B-1B-SS	135	498	88	148	33	3	21	87	15	.297
2006 Florida		N.L.	2B	154	611	105	172	26	7	27	90	6	.282
2007 Florida		N.L.	2B	159	632	113	155	49	3	31	88	2	.245
2008 Florida		N.L.	2B	146	531	97	138	37	1	32	92	5	.260
2009 Florida		N.L.	2B	158	564	84	137	27	1	31	90	2	.243
2010 Florida b		N.L.	2B	159	589	100	169	31	0	33	105	4	.287
2011 Atlanta		N.L.	2B	161	600	88	140	22	1	36	82	1	.233
2012 Atlanta		N.L.	2B	154	523	86	115	29	0	19	78	4	.220
Major League Totals			7 Yrs.	1091	4050	673	1026	221	13	209	625	24	.253
Wild Card Playoff													
2012 Atlanta		N.L.	2B	1	4	1	0	0	0	0	0	0	.000

a Selected by Florida Marlins from Arizona Diamondbacks in Rule V draft, December 8, 2005.
b Traded to Atlanta Braves for infielder Omar Infante and pitcher Michael Dunn, November 16, 2010.

UPTON, JUSTIN IRVIN
Born, Norfolk, Virginia, August 25, 1987.
Bats Right. Throws Right. Height, 6 feet, 3 inches. Weight, 205 pounds.

Year	Club	Lea	Pos	G	AB	R	H	2B	3B	HR	RBI	SB	Avg
2006 South Bend		Midwest	OF	113	438	71	115	28	1	12	66	15	.263
2007 Visalia		Calif.	OF	32	126	27	43	6	2	5	17	9	.341
2007 Mobile		Southern	OF	71	259	48	80	17	4	13	53	10	.309
2007 Arizona		N.L.	OF	43	140	17	31	8	3	2	11	2	.221
2008 Tucson		P.C.	OF	15	61	13	17	3	1	3	10	2	.279
2008 Arizona a		N.L.	OF	108	356	52	89	19	6	15	42	1	.250
2009 Visalia		Calif.	OF	2	8	1	2	0	0	1	6	1	.250
2009 Arizona b		N.L.	OF	138	526	84	158	30	7	26	86	20	.300
2010 Arizona		N.L.	OF	133	495	73	135	27	3	17	69	18	.273
2011 Arizona		N.L.	OF	159	592	105	171	39	5	31	88	21	.289
2012 Arizona		N.L.	OF	150	554	107	155	24	4	17	67	18	.280
Major League Totals			6 Yrs.	731	2663	438	739	147	28	108	363	80	.278
Division Series													
2007 Arizona		N.L.	OF	2	5	2	3	0	0	0	1	1	.600
2011 Arizona		N.L.	OF	5	20	3	4	0	0	2	3	0	.200
Division Series Totals				7	25	5	7	0	0	2	4	1	.280
Championship Series													
2007 Arizona		N.L.	OF	4	9	0	2	1	1	0	0	0	.222

a On disabled list from July 9 to August 29, 2008.
b On disabled list from August 6 to August 26, 2009.

UPTON, MELVIN EMANUEL (B.J.)
Born, Norfolk, Virginia, August 21, 1984.
Bats Right. Throws Right. Height, 6 feet, 3 inches. Weight, 180 pounds.

Year	Club	Lea	Pos	G	AB	R	H	2B	3B	HR	RBI	SB	Avg
2003 Charleston		So.Atl.	SS	101	384	70	116	22	6	7	46	38	.302
2003 Orlando		Southern	SS	29	105	14	29	8	0	1	16	2	.276
2004 Montgomery		Southern	SS	29	104	21	34	7	1	2	15	3	.327
2004 Durham		Int.	SS	69	264	65	82	17	1	12	36	17	.311
2004 Tampa Bay		A.L.	SS-3B-OF	45	159	19	41	8	2	4	12	4	.258

Year	Club	Lea	Pos	G	AB	R	H	2B	3B	HR	RBI	SB	Avg
2005 Durham	Int.		SS	139	545	98	165	36	6	18	74	44	.303
2006 Durham	Int.		SS-3B	106	398	72	107	18	4	8	41	46	.269
2006 Tampa Bay	A.L.		3B	50	175	20	43	5	0	1	10	11	.246
2007 Vero Beach.........	Fla.St.		2B-OF	7	17	4	4	0	0	1	3	0	.235
2007 Durham	Int.		2B	2	7	1	3	0	0	1	1	0	.429
2007 Tampa Bay a.........	A.L.		OF-2B	129	474	86	142	25	1	24	82	22	.300
2008 Tampa Bay	A.L.		OF	145	531	85	145	37	2	9	67	44	.273
2009 Charlotte ....Fla.St.			OF	3	9	1	4	0	0	0	2	4	.444
2009 Tampa Bay b	A.L.		OF	144	560	79	135	33	4	11	55	42	.241
2010 Tampa Bay	A.L.		OF	154	536	89	127	38	4	18	62	42	.237
2011 Tampa Bay	A.L.		OF	153	560	82	136	27	4	23	81	36	.243
2012 Charlotte ....Fla.St.			OF	4	11	1	1	0	0	0	1	2	.091
2012 Montgomery ..... Southern			OF	3	10	1	2	0	0	0	1	0	.200
2012 Tampa Bay c-d	A.L.		OF	146	573	79	141	29	3	28	78	31	.246
Major League Totals		8 Yrs.		966	3568	539	910	202	20	118	447	232	.255
Division Series													
2008 Tampa Bay	A.L.		OF	4	18	5	5	0	1	3	4	0	.278
2010 Tampa Bay	A.L.		OF	5	21	0	4	2	0	0	2	2	.190
2011 Tampa Bay	A.L.		OF	4	14	3	4	3	0	0	0	1	.286
Division Series Totals				13	53	8	13	5	1	3	6	3	.245
Championship Series													
2008 Tampa Bay	A.L.		OF	7	28	8	9	1	0	4	11	2	.321
World Series Record													
2008 Tampa Bay	A.L.		OF	5	20	3	5	0	0	0	1	4	.250

a On disabled list from June 9 to July 13, 2007.
b On disabled list from March 27 to April 13, 2009.
c On disabled list from March 26 to April 20, 2012.
d Filed for free agency, November 3, 2012. Signed with Atlanta Braves, November 29, 2012.

URIBE (TENA), JUAN C.

Born, Bani, Dominican Republic, July 22, 1979.
Bats Right. Throws Right. Height, 6 feet. Weight, 220 pounds.

Year	Club	Lea	Pos	G	AB	R	H	2B	3B	HR	RBI	SB	Avg
1997 Colorado	Dominican		SS	65	234	32	63	12	0	0	29	7	.269
1998 Rockies	Arizona		SS	40	148	25	41	5	3	0	17	8	.277
1999 Asheville......	So.Atl.		SS	125	430	57	115	28	3	9	46	11	.267
2000 Salem.......	Carolina		SS	134	485	64	124	22	7	13	65	22	.256
2001 Carolina	Southern		SS	3	13	1	3	1	0	0	1	1	.231
2001 Colo Sprngs.......	P.C.		SS	74	281	40	87	27	7	7	48	11	.310
2001 Colorado	N.L.		SS	72	273	32	82	15	11	8	53	3	.300
2002 Colorado	N.L.		SS	155	566	69	136	25	7	6	49	9	.240
2003 Visalia	California		2B-SS	2	9	4	5	1	0	0	1	0	.556
2003 Tulsa	Texas		2B-3B-SS-OF	5	20	3	5	2	0	1	4	0	.250
2003 Colorado a-b	N.L.		SS-2B-OF	87	316	45	80	19	3	10	33	7	.253
2004 Chicago	A.L.		2B-SS-3B	134	502	82	142	31	6	23	74	9	.283
2005 Chicago	A.L.		SS	146	481	58	121	23	3	16	71	4	.252
2006 Chicago	A.L.		SS	132	463	53	109	28	2	21	71	1	.235
2007 Chicago	A.L.		SS	150	513	55	120	18	2	20	68	1	.234
2008 Charlotte	Int.		2B-SS	3	11	0	2	0	0	0	2	0	.182
2008 Chicago c-d	A.L.		3B-2B-SS	110	324	38	80	22	1	7	40	1	.247
2009 San Francisco e	N.L.		3B-SS-2B	122	398	50	115	26	4	16	55	3	.289
2010 San Francisco f	N.L.		SS-3B-2B	148	521	64	129	24	2	24	85	1	.248
2011 Rancho Cucamonga .	Calif.		2B	3	8	2	4	1	0	0	0	1	.500
2011 Los Angeles g	N.L.		3B-2B-SS	77	270	21	55	12	0	4	28	2	.204
2012 Rancho Cucamonga	Calif.		3B	3	10	1	3	0	1	1	3	0	.300
2012 Los Angeles h	N.L.		3B-SS	66	162	15	31	9	0	2	17	0	.191
Major League Totals		12 Yrs.		1399	4789	582	1200	252	41	157	644	41	.251
Division Series													
2005 Chicago ..........A.L.			SS	3	10	4	4	1	0	1	4	0	.400
2008 Chicago ..........A.L.			3B	4	12	0	2	0	0	0	1	1	.167
2010 San Francisco ....N.L.			SS-3B	4	14	0	1	0	0	0	1	0	.071
Division Series Totals				11	36	4	7	1	0	1	6	1	.194
Championship Series													
2005 Chicago ..........A.L.			SS	5	16	1	4	1	0	0	0	0	.250
2010 San Francisco ....N.L.			SS-3B	5	14	1	3	0	0	1	3	0	.214
Championship Series Totals				10	30	2	7	1	0	1	3	0	.233
World Series Record													
2005 Chicago ..........A.L.			SS	4	16	2	4	3	0	0	2	1	.250

Year Club	Lea	Pos	G	AB	R	H	2B	3B	HR	RBI	SB	Avg
2010 San Francisco .....N.L.		3B	5	19	3	3	0	0	1	5	0	.158
World Series Totals............			9	35	5	7	3	0	1	7	1	.200

a On disabled list from March 18 to June 3, 2003.
b Traded to Chicago White Sox for infielder Aaron Miles, December 2, 2003.
c On disabled list from May 16 to May 31, 2008.
d Filed for free agency, October 30, 2008. Signed with San Francisco Giants organization, January 29, 2009.
e Filed for free agency, November 5, 2009, re-signed with San Francisco Giants, January 5, 2010.
f Filed for free agency, November 1, 2010. Signed with Los Angeles Dodgers, November 30, 2010.
g On disabled list from May 21 to June 6 and July 24 to September 30, 2011.
h On disabled list from May 14 to June 11, 2012.

UTLEY, CHASE CAMERON

Born, Pasadena, California, December 17, 1978.
Bats Left. Throws Right. Height, 6 feet, 1 inch. Weight, 200 pounds.

Year Club	Lea	Pos	G	AB	R	H	2B	3B	HR	RBI	SB	Avg
2000 Batavia.........	N.Y.-Penn.	2B	40	153	21	47	13	1	2	22	5	.307
2001 Clearwater	Fla.St.	2B	122	467	65	120	25	2	16	59	19	.257
2002 Scranton/W.B.	Int.	3B	125	464	73	122	39	1	17	70	8	.263
2003 Scranton/W.B.	Int.	2B	113	431	80	139	26	2	18	77	10	.323
2003 Philadelphia	N.L.	2B	43	134	13	32	10	1	2	21	2	.239
2004 Scranton/WB	Int.	2B	33	123	23	35	8	1	6	25	4	.285
2004 Philadelphia	N.L.	2B-1B	94	267	36	71	11	2	13	57	4	.266
2005 Philadelphia	N.L.	2B-1B	147	543	93	158	39	6	28	105	16	.291
2006 Philadelphia	N.L.	2B-1B	160	658	*131	203	40	4	32	102	15	.309
2007 Reading	Eastern	2B	3	10	0	1	0	0	0	0	0	.100
2007 Philadelphia a.......	N.L.	2B-1B	132	530	104	176	48	5	22	103	9	.332
2008 Philadelphia	N.L.	2B-1B	159	607	113	177	41	4	33	104	14	.292
2009 Philadelphia	N.L.	2B	156	571	112	161	28	4	31	93	23	.282
2010 Clearwater	Fla.St.	2B	4	12	1	3	0	2	0	1	0	.250
2010 Philadelphia b	N.L.	2B	115	425	75	117	20	2	16	65	13	.275
2011 Clearwater	Fla.St.	2B	9	32	4	9	2	0	1	4	1	.281
2011 Philadelphia c.......	N.L.	2B	103	398	54	103	21	6	11	44	14	.259
2012 Clearwater	Fla.St.	2B	9	32	3	5	0	0	1	5	1	.156
2012 Lehigh Valley	Int.	2B	1	5	1	2	0	0	1	1	0	.400
2012 Philadelphia d	N.L.	2B	83	301	48	77	15	2	11	45	11	.256
Major League Totals	10 Yrs.		1192	4434	779	1275	273	36	199	739	121	.288
Division Series												
2007 Philadelphia	N.L.	2B	3	11	0	2	0	0	0	0	0	.182
2008 Philadelphia	N.L.	2B	4	15	1	2	1	0	0	2	0	.133
2009 Philadelphia	N.L.	2B	4	14	5	6	0	0	1	1	2	.429
2010 Philadelphia	N.L.	2B	3	11	3	3	0	0	1	4	1	.273
2011 Philadelphia	N.L.	2B	5	16	5	7	2	1	0	1	0	.438
Division Series Totals			19	67	14	20	3	1	2	8	3	.299
Championship Series												
2008 Philadelphia	N.L.	2B	5	17	4	6	2	0	1	3	0	.353
2009 Philadelphia	N.L.	2B	5	19	3	4	0	0	1	1	0	.211
2010 Philadelphia	N.L.	2B	6	22	5	4	1	0	0	1	3	.182
Championship Series Totals			16	58	12	14	3	0	1	5	3	.241
World Series Record												
2008 Philadelphia	N.L.	2B	5	18	5	3	0	0	2	4	3	.167
2009 Philadelphia	N.L.	2B	6	21	7	6	1	0	5	8	1	.286
World Series Totals............			11	39	12	9	1	0	7	12	4	.231

a On disabled list from July 27 to August 27, 2007.
b On disabled list from June 29 to August 17, 2010.
c On disabled list from March 22 to May 23, 2011.
d On disabled list from March 26 to June 27, 2012.

VALBUENA, LUIS ADAN

Born, Caja Seca, Venezuela, November 30, 1985.
Bats Left. Throws Right. Height, 5 feet, 10 inches. Weight, 195 pounds.

Year Club	Lea	Pos	G	AB	R	H	2B	3B	HR	RBI	SB	Avg
2005 Everett	Northwest	2B	74	287	47	75	10	3	12	51	14	.261
2005 Tacoma	P.C.	2B	3	4	0	0	0	0	0	0	0	.000
2006 Inland Empire.....	Calif.	2B-SS-3B	43	163	18	41	10	1	2	10	1	.252
2006 Wisconsin	Midwest	2B	89	325	45	93	16	6	3	38	21	.286
2007 West Tenn ....Southern		2B	122	444	55	106	23	3	11	44	10	.239

Year Club Lea	Pos	G	AB	R	H	2B	3B	HR	RBI	SB	Avg
2008 West Tenn ...Southern	2B-3B	70	240	43	73	12	2	9	40	8	.304
2008 Tacoma .........P.C.	2B-3B	58	212	41	64	9	0	2	20	10	.302
2008 Seattle a.........A.L.	2B-SS	18	49	6	12	5	0	0	1	0	.245
2009 Columbus......... Int.	2B-SS-3B	22	78	15	25	4	2	3	13	3	.321
2009 Cleveland.........A.L.	2B-SS-3B	103	368	52	92	25	3	10	31	2	.250
2010 Columbus......... Int.	SS-3B-2B	25	96	23	30	8	1	6	20	2	.313
2010 Cleveland.........A.L.	2B-3B-SS-OF	91	275	22	53	12	0	2	24	1	.193
2011 Columbus......... Int.	SS-3B-OF-2B	113	420	64	127	22	0	17	75	6	.302
2011 Cleveland b ......A.L.	2B-OF-SS	17	43	4	9	0	0	1	1	1	.209
2012 Iowa.............P.C.	SS-2B-3B	58	211	38	64	17	1	8	31	1	.303
2012 Chicago c........N.L.	3B-2B	90	265	26	58	20	0	4	28	0	.219
Major League Totals	5 Yrs.	319	1000	110	224	62	3	17	85	4	.224

a Traded to Cleveland Indians with pitcher Joe Smith for outfielder Franklin Gutierrez, December 10, 2008.
b Sold to Toronto Blue Jays, November 26, 2011.
c Claimed on waivers by Chicago Cubs, April 4, 2012.

VALDESPIN (GUZMAN), JORDANY V.

Born, San Pedro de Macoris, Dominican Republic, December 23, 1987.
Bats Left. Throws Right. Height, 6 feet. Weight, 190 pounds.

Year Club Lea	Pos	G	AB	R	H	2B	3B	HR	RBI	SB	Avg
2008 Mets.......Gulf Coast	2B-SS	34	134	23	38	6	3	3	22	9	.284
2009 Mets.......Gulf Coast	2B	6	23	0	4	0	0	0	0	1	.174
2009 Brooklyn.....N.Y.-Penn.	2B-SS	18	68	10	19	3	1	1	5	4	.279
2009 Savannah.......So.Atl.	2B-SS	39	152	30	49	9	3	3	18	7	.322
2010 Binghamton .... Eastern	2B	28	112	8	26	8	0	0	8	4	.232
2010 St. Lucie........Fla.St.	2B-SS	65	270	40	78	16	3	6	33	13	.289
2011 Binghamton .... Eastern	SS-2B	107	404	62	120	24	3	15	51	33	.297
2011 Buffalo .... Int.	SS-2B	27	107	7	30	8	0	2	9	4	.280
2012 Buffalo .... Int.	2B-OF-SS	39	151	22	43	2	1	5	23	10	.285
2012 New York .........N.L.	OF-2B-SS	94	191	28	46	9	1	8	26	10	.241

VALDEZ, WILSON ANTONIO

Born, Nizao, Dominican Republic, May 20, 1978.
Bats Right. Throws Right. Height, 5 feet, 11 inches. Weight, 170 pounds.

Year Club Lea	Pos	G	AB	R	H	2B	3B	HR	RBI	SB	Avg
1997 Montreal.... Dominican	SS	62	244	39	74	13	1	2	29	19	.303
1998 Montreal.... Dominican	SS	64	247	42	74	9	0	3	30	15	.300
1999 Expos.......Gulf Coast	SS-2B	22	82	12	24	2	0	0	7	10	.293
1999 Vermont.....N.Y.-Penn.	SS-2B	36	130	19	32	7	0	1	10	4	.246
2000 Vermont.....N.Y.-Penn.	SS	65	248	32	66	8	1	1	30	16	.266
2000 Cape Fear.......So.Atl.	2B-SS-C	15	49	6	12	2	0	0	3	3	.245
2001 Jupiter ....Fla.St.	SS	64	233	34	58	13	2	2	19	7	.249
2001 Clinton ....Midwest	SS	59	214	31	54	8	1	0	11	6	.252
2002 Portland a .....Eastern	SS	114	375	51	98	19	5	1	30	18	.261
2003 Albuquerque.......P.C.	SS-2B	90	338	45	97	12	4	0	18	33	.287
2003 Carolina .....Southern	2B-SS	37	144	28	45	6	2	0	14	16	.313
2004 Albuquerque.......P.C.	SS	66	285	36	91	11	3	2	25	19	.319
2004 Charlotte .... Int.	SS	70	281	37	85	7	2	2	15	13	.302
2004 Chicago b........A.L.	SS-2B	19	43	8	10	1	0	1	4	1	.233
2005 Seattle .........A.L.	SS	42	126	9	25	5	1	0	8	2	.198
2005 Tacoma ..........P.C.	SS	1	4	0	0	0	0	0	1	0	.000
2005 San Diego .........N.L.	SS	9	13	0	3	2	0	0	1	0	.231
2005 Portland c-d-e-f ....P.C.	SS	50	155	14	38	5	3	1	15	8	.245
2006 Las Vegas g .......P.C.	SS-OF-2B	137	528	94	157	24	1	6	53	26	.297
2007 Las Vegas.........P.C.	SS-OF-2B-3B	90	361	81	124	19	1	4	29	14	.343
2007 Los Angeles......N.L.	2B-SS-3B-OF	41	74	12	16	2	1	0	7	1	.216
2008 Kia .... Korea	SS	47	156	17	34	9	1	1	16	13	.218
2008 Yakult h-i ... Japan Pac.	SS-OF	29	78	8	20	1	0	1	8	4	.256
2009 Columbus......... Int.	SS-OF-2B	41	121	17	24	1	0	0	6	5	.198
2009 Buffalo .... Int.	SS-2B-OF	36	114	13	34	4	0	0	6	1	.298
2009 New York j-k....N.L.	SS-OF-2B-3B	41	86	11	22	3	2	0	7	0	.256
2010 Lehigh Valley .... Int.	2B-SS	5	22	2	10	0	0	0	5	2	.455
2010 Philadelphia .......N.L.	SS-2B-3B	111	333	37	86	16	3	4	35	7	.258
2011 Philadelphia .......N.L.	2B-SS-3B-P	99	273	39	68	14	1	1	30	3	.249
2012 Cincinnati l-m......N.L.	SS-2B-3B-OF	77	194	15	40	4	0	0	15	3	.206
Major League Totals	7 Yrs.	439	1142	131	270	47	11	6	107	17	.236

Year	Club	Lea	Pos	G	AB	R	H	2B	3B	HR	RBI	SB	Avg
Division Series													
2010 Philadelphia	N.L.		3B	1	3	1	1	0	0	0	0	0	.333
2012 Cincinnati	N.L.		OF-SS	2	1	0	0	0	0	0	0	0	.000
Division Series Totals				3	4	1	1	0	0	0	0	0	.250
Championship Series													
2010 Philadelphia	N.L.		PH	2	0	0	0	0	0	0	0	0	.000

a Claimed on waivers from Montreal Expos by Florida Marlins, March 29, 2002.
b Traded to Chicago White Sox for pitcher Billy Koch and cash, June 17, 2004.
c Claimed on waivers by New York Mets, March 29, 2005.
d Claimed on waivers by Seattle Mariners, April 1, 2005.
e Traded to San Diego Padres for pitcher Mike Bumstead and pitcher R.D. Spiehs, June 9, 2005.
f Filed for free agency, October 3, 2005. Signed with Kansas City Royals organization, November 18, 2005.
g Traded to Los Angeles Dodgers for pitcher Jarod Plummer, March 31, 2006.
h Sold to Kia (Korea) January 8, 2008. Signed with Yakult (Japan), 2008.
i Signed with Cleveland Indians organization, December 15, 2008.
j Sold to New York Mets, May 26, 2009.
k Filed for free agency, October 27, 2009. Signed with Philadelphia Phillies organization, November 25, 2009.
l Traded to Cincinnati Reds for pitcher Jeremy Horst, January 25, 2012.
m Filed for free agency, November 7, 2012. Signed with San Francisco Giants organization, December 10, 2012.

VENABLE, WILLIAM DION (WILL)
Born, Greenbrae, California, October 29, 1982.
Bats Left. Throws Left. Height, 6 feet, 2 inches. Weight, 205 pounds.

Year	Club	Lea	Pos	G	AB	R	H	2B	3B	HR	RBI	SB	Avg
2005 Padres	Arizona	OF	15	59	13	19	4	2	1	12	4	.322
2005 Eugene	Northwest	OF	42	139	17	30	5	2	2	14	2	.216
2006 Fort Wayne	Midwest	OF	124	472	86	148	34	5	11	91	18	.314
2007 San Antonio	Texas	OF	134	515	66	143	19	3	8	68	21	.278
2008 Portland	P.C.	OF	120	442	70	129	26	4	14	58	7	.292
2008 San Diego	N.L.	OF	28	110	16	29	4	2	2	10	1	.264
2009 Portland	P.C.	OF	53	200	33	52	10	3	12	30	1	.260
2009 San Diego	N.L.	OF	95	293	38	75	14	2	12	38	6	.256
2010 Lake Elsinore	Calif.	OF	5	14	0	1	1	0	0	0	1	.071
2010 San Antonio	Texas	OF	2	6	2	2	0	0	0	1	2	.333
2010 San Diego a	N.L.	OF-1B	131	392	60	96	11	7	13	51	29	.245
2011 Tucson	P.C.	OF	14	58	14	16	3	2	3	11	3	.276
2011 San Diego	N.L.	OF	121	370	49	91	14	7	9	44	26	.246
2012 San Diego	N.L.	OF	148	417	62	110	26	8	9	45	24	.264
Major League Totals		5 Yrs.	523	1582	225	401	69	26	45	188	86	.253

a On disabled list from July 2 to July 21, 2010.

VICIEDO (PEREZ), DAYAN
Born, Remedios, Cuba, March 10, 1989.
Bats Right. Throws Right. Height, 5 feet, 11 inches. Weight, 240 pounds.

Year	Club	Lea	Pos	G	AB	R	H	2B	3B	HR	RBI	SB	Avg
2009 Birmingham a	Southern	3B-1B	130	504	72	141	20	0	12	78	5	.280
2010 Charlotte	Int.	1B-3B	86	343	42	94	15	0	20	47	1	.274
2010 Chicago	A.L.	3B-1B	38	104	17	32	7	0	5	13	1	.308
2011 Charlotte	Int.	OF-1B	119	452	60	134	28	0	20	78	2	.296
2011 Chicago b	A.L.	OF-1B	29	102	11	26	3	0	1	6	1	.255
2012 Chicago	A.L.	OF	147	505	64	129	18	1	25	78	0	.255
Major League Totals		3 Yrs.	214	711	92	187	28	1	31	97	2	.263

a Played in Cuba 2006 and 2007.
b On disabled list from March 22 to April 6, 2011.

VICTORINO, SHANE PATRICK
Born, Wailuku, Hawaii, November 30, 1980.
Bats Both. Throws Right. Height, 5 feet, 9 inches. Weight, 180 pounds.

Year	Club	Lea	Pos	G	AB	R	H	2B	3B	HR	RBI	SB	Avg
1999 Great Falls	Pioneer	OF	55	225	53	63	7	6	2	25	20	.280
2000 Yakima	Northwest	2B-SS	61	236	32	58	7	2	2	20	21	.246
2001 Vero Beach	Fla.St.	OF	2	6	2	1	0	0	0	0	2	.167
2001 Wilmington	So.Atl.	OF	112	435	71	123	21	9	4	32	47	.283
2002 Jacksonville	Southern	OF	122	481	61	124	15	1	4	34	45	.258
2003 Jacksonville	Southern	OF	66	266	37	75	9	4	2	15	16	.282

Year	Club	Lea	Pos	G	AB	R	H	2B	3B	HR	RBI	SB	Avg
2003 Las Vegas		P.C.	OF	11	41	6	16	1	2	1	9	0	.390
2003 San Diego a		N.L.	OF	36	73	8	11	2	0	0	4	7	.151
2004 Las Vegas		P.C.	OF-2B	55	200	28	47	9	1	3	20	7	.235
2004 Jacksonville b	Southern		OF	75	293	70	96	13	7	16	43	9	.328
2005 Scranton/WB		Int.	OF	126	494	93	153	25	16	18	70	17	.310
2005 Philadelphia		N.L.	OF	21	17	5	5	0	0	2	8	0	.294
2006 Philadelphia		N.L.	OF	153	415	70	119	19	8	6	46	4	.287
2007 Lakewood		So.Atl.	DH	1	5	1	1	0	0	0	0	0	.200
2007 Reading		Eastern	OF	2	6	0	2	0	0	0	1	1	.333
2007 Philadelphia c		N.L.	OF	131	456	78	128	23	3	12	46	37	.281
2008 Clearwater		Fla.St.	OF	2	5	1	2	0	0	0	1	0	.400
2008 Reading		Eastern	OF	1	3	0	1	0	0	0	0	0	.333
2008 Lehigh Valley		Int.	OF	2	8	0	3	0	0	0	0	0	.375
2008 Philadelphia d		N.L.	OF	146	570	102	167	30	8	14	58	36	.293
2009 Philadelphia		N.L.	OF	156	620	102	181	39	*13	10	62	25	.292
2010 Lehigh Valley		Int.	OF	2	6	1	4	0	1	1	3	0	.667
2010 Philadelphia e		N.L.	OF	147	587	84	152	26	10	18	69	34	.259
2011 Lakewood		So.Atl.	OF	2	6	1	1	0	0	0	2	0	.167
2011 Reading		Eastern	OF	4	15	2	5	1	0	1	3	1	.333
2011 Philadelphia f		N.L.	OF	132	519	95	145	27	*16	17	61	19	.279
2012 Philadelphia-L.A g-h		N.L.	OF	154	595	72	152	29	7	11	55	39	.255
Major League Totals			9 Yrs.	1076	3852	616	1060	195	65	90	409	201	.275
Division Series													
2007 Philadelphia		N.L.	OF	3	9	2	2	0	0	1	1	1	.222
2008 Philadelphia		N.L.	OF	4	14	2	5	3	0	1	5	3	.357
2009 Philadelphia		N.L.	OF	4	17	4	6	1	0	1	1	1	.353
2010 Philadelphia		N.L.	OF	3	13	2	3	1	0	0	3	1	.231
2011 Philadelphia		N.L.	OF	5	19	2	6	1	0	0	2	0	.316
Division Series Totals				19	72	12	22	6	0	3	12	6	.306
Championship Series													
2008 Philadelphia		N.L.	OF	5	18	2	4	0	1	1	6	0	.222
2009 Philadelphia		N.L.	OF	5	19	4	7	1	1	2	6	1	.368
2010 Philadelphia		N.L.	OF	6	24	3	5	1	0	0	2	1	.208
Championship Series Totals				16	61	9	16	2	2	3	14	2	.262
World Series Record													
2008 Philadelphia		N.L.	OF	5	20	1	5	0	0	0	2	0	.250
2009 Philadelphia		N.L.	OF	6	22	3	4	1	0	0	2	0	.182
World Series Totals				11	42	4	9	1	0	0	4	0	.214

a Selected by San Diego Padres from Los Angeles Dodgers in Rule V draft, December 16, 2002. Returned to Los Angeles Dodgers, May 28, 2003.
b Selected by Philadelphia Phillies in Rule V draft, December 13, 2004.
c On disabled list from July 31 to August 22, 2007.
d On disabled list from April 13 to April 29, 2008.
e On disabled list from July 28 to August 12, 2010.
f On disabled list from May 20 to June 3 and July 4 to July 19, 2011.
g Traded to Los Angeles Dodgers for pitcher Josh Lindblom, pitcher Ethan Martin and player to be named later, July 31, 2012. Philadelphia Phillies received infielder Stefan Jarrin to complete trade, September 28, 2012.
h Filed for free agency, November 3, 2012. Signed with Boston Red Sox, December 13, 2012.

VIZQUEL, OMAR ENRIQUE

Born, Caracas, Venezuela, April 24, 1967.
Bats Both. Throws Right. Height, 5 feet, 9 inches. Weight, 175 pounds.

Year	Club	Lea	Pos	G	AB	R	H	2B	3B	HR	RBI	SB	Avg
1984 Butte a	Pioneer		SS-2B	15	45	7	14	2	0	0	4	2	.311
1985 Bellingham	Northwest		SS-2B	50	187	24	42	9	0	5	17	4	.225
1986 Wausau	Midwest		SS-2B	105	352	60	75	13	2	4	28	19	.213
1987 Salinas	California		SS-2B	114	407	61	107	12	8	0	38	25	.263
1988 Vermont	Eastern		SS	103	375	54	95	18	2	2	35	30	.253
1988 Calgary		P.C.	SS	33	107	10	24	2	3	1	12	2	.224
1989 Seattle		A.L.	SS	143	387	45	85	7	3	1	20	1	.220
1989 Calgary		P.C.	SS	7	28	3	6	2	0	0	3	0	.214
1990 San Bernardino	California		SS	6	28	5	7	0	0	0	3	1	.250
1990 Calgary		P.C.	SS	48	150	18	35	6	2	0	8	4	.233
1990 Seattle b		A.L.	SS	81	255	19	63	3	2	2	18	4	.247
1991 Seattle		A.L.	SS-2B	142	426	42	98	16	4	1	41	7	.230
1992 Seattle c		A.L.	SS	136	483	49	142	20	4	0	21	15	.294
1992 Calgary		P.C.	SS	6	22	0	6	1	0	0	2	0	.273
1993 Seattle d		A.L.	SS	158	560	68	143	14	2	2	31	12	.255

Year	Club	Lea	Pos	G	AB	R	H	2B	3B	HR	RBI	SB	Avg
1994 Charlotte	Int.		SS	7	26	3	7	1	0	0	1	1	.269
1994 Cleveland e........	A.L.		SS	69	286	39	78	10	1	1	33	13	.273
1995 Cleveland	A.L.		SS	136	542	87	144	28	0	6	56	29	.266
1996 Cleveland	A.L.		SS	151	542	98	161	36	1	9	64	35	.297
1997 Cleveland	A.L.		SS	153	565	89	158	23	6	5	49	43	.280
1998 Cleveland	A.L.		SS	151	576	86	166	30	6	2	50	37	.288
1999 Cleveland	A.L.		SS-OF	144	574	112	191	36	4	5	66	42	.333
2000 Cleveland	A.L.		SS	156	613	101	176	27	3	7	66	22	.287
2001 Cleveland	A.L.		SS	155	611	84	156	26	8	2	50	13	.255
2002 Cleveland	A.L.		SS	151	582	85	160	31	5	14	72	18	.275
2003 Lake County	So.Atl.		SS	4	14	0	1	0	0	0	0	1	.071
2003 Cleveland f.......	A.L.		SS	64	250	43	61	13	2	2	19	8	.244
2004 Cleveland g......	A.L.		SS	148	567	82	165	28	3	7	59	19	.291
2005 San Francisco	N.L.		SS	152	568	66	154	28	4	3	45	24	.271
2006 San Francisco	N.L.		SS	153	579	88	171	22	10	4	58	24	.295
2007 San Francisco	N.L.		SS	145	513	54	126	18	3	4	51	14	.246
2008 San Jose	Calif.		SS	3	8	3	3	0	0	0	1	0	.375
2008 Fresno	P.C.		SS	2	5	0	1	0	0	0	0	0	.200
2008 San Francisco h-i ..	N.L.		SS	92	266	24	59	10	1	0	23	5	.222
2009 Texas j	A.L.		SS-3B-2B	62	177	17	47	7	2	1	14	4	.266
2010 Chicago	A.L.		3B-2B-SS	108	344	36	95	11	1	2	30	11	.276
2011 Chicago k........	A.L.		3B-2B-SS-1B	58	167	18	42	7	1	0	8	1	.251
2012 Toronto l........	A.L.		2B-3B-SS-1B	60	153	13	36	5	1	0	7	3	.235
Major League Totals			24 Yrs.	2968	10586	1445	2877	456	77	80	951	404	.272
Division Series													
1995 Cleveland	A.L.		SS	3	12	2	2	1	0	0	4	1	.167
1996 Cleveland	A.L.		SS	4	14	4	6	1	0	0	2	4	.429
1997 Cleveland	A.L.		SS	5	18	3	9	0	0	0	1	4	.500
1998 Cleveland	A.L.		SS	4	15	1	1	0	0	0	0	0	.067
1999 Cleveland	A.L.		SS	5	21	3	5	1	1	0	3	0	.238
2001 Cleveland	A.L.		SS	5	22	2	9	1	1	0	6	1	.409
Division Series Totals				26	102	15	32	4	2	0	16	10	.314
Championship Series													
1995 Cleveland	A.L.		SS	6	23	2	2	1	0	0	2	3	.087
1997 Cleveland	A.L.		SS	6	25	1	1	0	0	0	0	0	.040
1998 Cleveland	A.L.		SS	6	25	2	11	0	1	0	0	4	.440
Championship Series Totals				18	73	5	14	1	1	0	2	7	.192
World Series Record													
1995 Cleveland	A.L.		SS	6	23	3	4	0	1	0	1	1	.174
1997 Cleveland	A.L.		SS	7	30	5	7	2	0	0	1	5	.233
World Series Totals				13	53	8	11	2	1	0	2	6	.208

a Batted righthanded only from 1984 through 1988 season.
b On disabled list from April 7 to May 14, 1990.
c On disabled list from April 13 to May 11, 1992.
d Traded to Cleveland Indians for shortstop Felix Fermin and first baseman Reggie Jefferson, December 20, 1993.
e On disabled list from April 23 to June 13, 1994.
f On disabled list from June 12 to August 26 and September 6 to October 28, 2003.
g Filed for free agency, October 29, 2004. Signed with San Francisco Giants, November 14, 2004.
h On disabled list from March 21 to May 10, 2008.
i Not offered contract, November 3, 2008. Signed with Texas Rangers organization, January 21, 2009.
j Filed for free agency, November 6, 2009. Signed with Chicago White Sox, November 23, 2009.
k Filed for free agency, October 30, 2011. Signed with Toronto Blue Jays organization, January 24, 2012.
l Announced retirement, October 3, 2012.

VOTTO, JOSEPH DANIEL (JOEY)
Born, Toronto, Ontario, Canada, September 10, 1983.
Bats Left. Throws Right. Height, 6 feet, 3 inches. Weight, 220 pounds.

Year	Club	Lea	Pos	G	AB	R	H	2B	3B	HR	RBI	SB	Avg
2002 Reds..........	Gulf Coast		3B-C-OF	50	175	29	47	13	3	9	33	7	.269
2003 Dayton	Midwest		1B	60	195	19	45	8	0	1	20	2	.231
2003 Billings...........	Pioneer		1B	70	240	47	76	17	3	6	37	4	.317
2004 Potomac.........	Carolina		1B	24	84	11	25	7	0	5	20	1	.298
2004 Dayton	Midwest		1B	111	391	60	118	26	2	14	73	9	.302
2005 Sarasota...........	Fla.St.		1B	124	464	64	119	23	2	17	83	4	.256
2006 Chattanooga	Southern		1B	136	508	85	162	46	2	22	77	24	.319
2007 Louisville	Int.		1B-OF	133	496	74	146	21	2	22	92	17	.294
2007 Cincinnati............	N.L.		1B-OF	24	84	11	27	7	0	4	17	1	.321
2008 Cincinnati...........	N.L.		1B	151	526	69	156	32	3	24	84	7	.297

Year Club Lea	Pos	G	AB	R	H	2B	3B	HR	RBI	SB	Avg
2009 Dayton . . . . Midwest	1B	2	7	3	3	0	0	1	3	1	.429
2009 Sarasota . . . . Fla.St.	1B	1	2	0	0	0	0	0	0	0	.000
2009 Cincinnati a . . . . N.L.	1B	131	469	82	151	38	1	25	84	4	.322
2010 Cincinnati b . . . . N.L.	1B	150	547	106	177	36	2	37	113	16	.324
2011 Cincinnati . . . . N.L.	1B	161	599	101	185	*40	3	29	103	8	.309
2012 Dayton . . . . Midwest	1B	3	5	1	1	0	0	0	1	0	.200
2012 Louisville . . . . Int.	1B	2	6	1	1	0	0	1	1	0	.167
2012 Cincinnati c . . . . N.L.	1B	111	374	59	126	44	0	14	56	5	.337
Major League Totals	6 Yrs.	728	2599	428	822	197	9	133	457	41	.316
Division Series											
2010 Cincinnati . . . . N.L.	1B	3	10	0	1	0	0	0	1	0	.100
2012 Cincinnati . . . . N.L.	1B	5	18	3	7	0	0	0	0	0	.389
Division Series Totals		8	28	3	8	0	0	0	1	0	.286

a On disabled list from May 30 to June 23, 2009.
b Selected Most Valuable Player in National League for 2010.
c On disabled list from July 17 to September 4, 2012.

WALKER, NEIL MARTIN
Born, Pittsburgh, Pennsylvania, September 10, 1985.
Bats Both. Throws Right. Height, 6 feet, 3 inches. Weight, 210 pounds.

Year Club Lea	Pos	G	AB	R	H	2B	3B	HR	RBI	SB	Avg
2004 Pirates . . . . . . Gulf Coast	C	52	192	28	52	12	3	4	20	3	.271
2004 Williamsport . . N.Y.-Penn.	C	8	33	2	10	3	0	0	7	1	.303
2005 Lynchburg . . . . Carolina	C	9	42	4	11	2	1	0	12	0	.262
2005 Hickory . . . . So.Atl.	C	120	485	78	146	33	2	12	68	7	.301
2006 Lynchburg . . . . Carolina	C	72	264	32	75	22	1	3	35	3	.284
2006 Altoona . . . . Eastern	C	10	31	5	5	0	0	2	3	0	.161
2007 Altoona . . . . Eastern	3B	117	431	77	124	30	3	13	66	9	.288
2007 Indianapolis . . . . Int.	3B	19	64	7	13	3	0	0	1	0	.203
2008 Indianapolis . . . . Int.	3B	133	505	69	122	25	7	16	80	10	.242
2009 Pirates . . . . . . Gulf Coast	3B	8	30	2	5	2	0	1	1	0	.167
2009 Indianapolis . . . . Int.	3B	95	356	38	94	31	2	14	69	5	.264
2009 Pittsburgh . . . . N.L.	3B	17	36	5	7	1	0	0	0	1	.194
2010 Indianapolis . . . . Int.	2B-OF-1B-3B	43	168	25	54	18	2	6	26	10	.321
2010 Pittsburgh . . . . N.L.	2B-3B	110	426	57	126	29	3	12	66	2	.296
2011 Pittsburgh . . . . N.L.	2B	159	596	76	163	36	4	12	83	9	.273
2012 Pittsburgh . . . . N.L.	2B	129	472	62	132	27	0	14	69	7	.280
Major League Totals	4 Yrs.	415	1530	200	428	93	7	38	218	19	.280

WALLACE, BRETT ALEXANDER
Born, Marin, California, August 26, 1986.
Bats Left. Throws Right. Height, 6 feet, 2 inches. Weight, 205 pounds.

Year Club Lea	Pos	G	AB	R	H	2B	3B	HR	RBI	SB	Avg
2008 Quad Cities . . . . Midwest	3B	41	153	28	50	8	1	5	25	0	.327
2008 Springfield . . . . Texas	3B	13	49	13	18	5	0	3	11	0	.367
2009 Memphis . . . . P.C.	3B-1B	62	222	22	65	11	0	6	19	0	.293
2009 Sacramento . . . . P.C.	3B-1B	44	182	32	55	10	0	9	28	1	.302
2009 Springfield a-b . . . . Texas	3B	32	128	22	36	5	0	5	16	0	.281
2010 Las Vegas . . . . P.C.	1B	95	385	64	116	24	1	18	61	1	.301
2010 Houston c . . . . N.L.	1B	51	144	14	32	6	1	2	13	0	.222
2011 Oklahoma . . . . P.C.	1B	28	104	16	37	10	0	1	24	1	.356
2011 Houston . . . . N.L.	1B	115	336	37	87	22	0	5	29	1	.259
2012 Oklahoma . . . . P.C.	3B-1B-SS	86	310	54	93	16	0	16	57	0	.300
2012 Houston . . . . N.L.	1B-3B	66	229	24	58	10	1	9	24	0	.253
Major League Totals	3 Yrs.	232	709	75	177	38	2	16	66	1	.250

a Traded by St. Louis Cardinals to Oakland Athletics with pitcher Clayton Mortensen and outfielder Shane Peterson for outfielder Matt Holliday, July 24, 2009.
b Traded to Philadelphia Phillies for pitcher Michael Taylor, December 16, 2009.
c Traded to Houston Astros for outfielder Anthony Gose, July 29, 2010.

WEEKS, JEMILE NYKIWA
Born, Orlando, Florida, January 26, 1987.
Bats Both. Throws Right. Height, 5 feet, 9 inches. Weight, 160 pounds.

Year	Club	Lea	Pos	G	AB	R	H	2B	3B	HR	RBI	SB	Avg
2008 Kane County	Midwest	2B	19	74	11	22	3	1	1	8	6	.297
2009 Stockton	Calif.	2B	50	201	29	60	9	2	7	31	5	.299
2009 Midland	Texas	2B	30	105	10	25	5	0	2	13	4	.238
2010 Athletics	Arizona	2B	10	36	9	11	2	1	0	1	5	.306
2010 Midland	Texas	2B	67	273	43	73	14	7	3	33	11	.267
2011 Sacramento	P.C.	2B	45	184	30	59	6	4	3	22	10	.321
2011 Oakland	A.L.	2B	97	406	50	123	26	8	2	36	22	.303
2012 Sacramento	P.C.	2B	10	45	5	15	4	0	0	10	1	.333
2012 Oakland	A.L.	2B	118	444	54	98	15	8	2	20	16	.221
Major League Totals		2 Yrs.	215	850	104	221	41	16	4	56	38	.260

WEEKS, RICKIE DARNELL
Born, Altamonte Springs, Florida, September 13, 1982.
Bats Right. Throws Right. Height, 6 feet. Weight, 205 pounds.

Year	Club	Lea	Pos	G	AB	R	H	2B	3B	HR	RBI	SB	Avg
2003 Brewers	Arizona	DH	1	4	0	2	0	0	0	4	1	.500
2003 Beloit	Midwest	2B	20	63	13	22	8	1	1	16	2	.349
2003 Milwaukee	N.L.	2B	7	12	1	2	1	0	0	0	0	.167
2004 Huntsville	Southern	2B	133	479	67	124	35	6	8	42	11	.259
2005 Nashville	P.C.	2B	55	203	43	65	14	9	12	48	10	.320
2005 Milwaukee	N.L.	2B	96	360	56	86	13	2	13	42	15	.239
2006 Milwaukee a	N.L.	2B	95	359	73	100	15	3	8	34	19	.279
2007 Nashville	P.C.	2B	6	22	5	10	3	1	0	3	1	.455
2007 Milwaukee b	N.L.	2B	118	409	87	96	21	6	16	36	25	.235
2008 Milwaukee c	N.L.	2B	129	475	89	111	22	7	14	46	19	.234
2009 Milwaukee d	N.L.	2B	37	147	28	40	5	2	9	24	2	.272
2010 Milwaukee	N.L.	2B	160	*651	112	175	32	4	29	83	11	.269
2011 Milwaukee e	N.L.	2B	118	453	77	122	26	2	20	49	9	.269
2012 Milwaukee	N.L.	2B	157	588	85	135	29	4	21	63	16	.230
Major League Totals		9 Yrs.	917	3454	608	867	164	30	130	377	116	.251
Division Series												
2008 Milwaukee	N.L.	2B	3	4	0	0	0	0	0	0	0	.000
2011 Milwaukee	N.L.	2B	5	18	0	1	0	1	0	1	0	.056
Division Series Totals			8	22	0	1	0	1	0	1	0	.045
Championship Series												
2011 Milwaukee	N.L.	2B	6	23	5	5	1	0	2	3	0	.217

a On disabled list from July 29 to October 31, 2006.
b On disabled list from May 30 to June 18, 2007.
c On disabled list from June 7 to June 22, 2008.
d On disabled list from May 17 to November 6, 2009.
e On disabled list from July 28 to September 8, 2011.

WELLS, CASPER CHARLES
Born, Grand Rapids, Michigan, November 23, 1984.
Bats Right. Throws Right. Height, 6 feet, 2 inches. Weight, 210 pounds.

Year	Club	Lea	Pos	G	AB	R	H	2B	3B	HR	RBI	SB	Avg
2005 Tigers	Gulf Coast	OF	45	141	25	31	9	5	5	20	6	.220
2006 Lakeland	Fla.St.	OF	11	33	4	5	1	0	1	4	1	.152
2006 Oneonta	N.Y.-Penn.	OF	35	105	19	24	8	0	1	14	1	.229
2007 Lakeland	Fla.St.	OF	2	2	0	1	1	0	0	0	0	.500
2007 Oneonta	N.Y.-Penn.	OF	67	260	46	69	18	11	9	47	8	.265
2008 West Michigan	Midwest	OF	50	179	30	43	7	0	10	26	17	.240
2008 Erie	Eastern	OF	75	270	60	78	18	6	17	53	8	.289
2009 Erie	Eastern	OF	86	311	52	81	18	4	15	41	8	.260
2010 Toledo	Int.	OF	103	387	56	90	22	6	21	46	7	.233
2010 Detroit	A.L.	OF	36	93	14	30	6	1	4	17	0	.323
2011 Toledo	Int.	OF	7	27	4	10	2	2	2	6	0	.370
2011 Detroit-Seattle a	A.L.	OF	95	215	30	51	11	0	11	27	3	.237
2012 Tacoma	P.C.	OF	22	71	18	17	7	2	2	14	2	.239
2012 Seattle	A.L.	OF	93	285	42	65	12	3	10	36	3	.228
Major League Totals		3 Yrs.	224	593	86	146	29	4	25	80	6	.246

a Traded to Seattle Mariners with pitcher Charlie Furbush, infielder Francisco Martinez and player to be named later for pitcher Doug Fister and pitcher David Pauley, July 30, 2011. Seattle Mariners received pitcher Chance Ruffin to complete trade, August 17, 2011.

WELLS, VERNON M.

Born, Shreveport, Louisiana, December 8, 1978.
Bats Right. Throws Right. Height, 6 feet, 1 inch. Weight, 225 pounds.

Year	Club	Lea	Pos	G	AB	R	H	2B	3B	HR	RBI	SB	Avg
1997 St.Catherines	N.Y.-Penn.	OF	66	264	52	81	20	1	10	31	8	.307
1998 Hagerstown	So.Atl.	OF	134	509	86	145	35	2	11	65	13	.285
1999 Dunedin	Fla.St.	OF	70	265	43	91	16	2	11	43	13	.343
1999 Knoxville	Southern	OF	26	106	18	36	6	2	3	17	6	.340
1999 Syracuse	Int.	OF	33	129	20	40	8	1	4	21	5	.310
1999 Toronto	A.L.	OF	24	88	8	23	5	0	1	8	1	.261
2000 Syracuse	Int.	OF	127	493	76	120	31	7	16	66	23	.243
2000 Toronto	A.L.	OF	3	2	0	0	0	0	0	0	0	.000
2001 Syracuse	Int.	OF	107	413	57	116	27	4	12	52	15	.281
2001 Toronto a	A.L.	OF	30	96	14	30	8	0	1	6	5	.313
2002 Toronto	A.L.	OF	159	608	87	167	34	4	23	100	9	.275
2003 Toronto	A.L.	OF	161	678	118	*215	*49	5	33	117	4	.317
2004 Toronto b	A.L.	OF	134	536	82	146	34	2	23	67	9	.272
2005 Toronto	A.L.	OF	156	620	78	167	30	3	28	97	8	.269
2006 Toronto	A.L.	OF	154	611	91	185	40	5	32	106	17	.303
2007 Toronto c	A.L.	OF	149	584	85	143	36	4	16	80	10	.245
2008 Dunedin	Fla.St.	OF	2	8	3	4	0	0	0	4	0	.500
2008 Syracuse	Int.	OF	2	6	0	0	0	0	0	0	0	.000
2008 Toronto d	A.L.	OF	108	427	63	128	22	1	20	78	4	.300
2009 Toronto	A.L.	OF	158	630	84	164	37	3	15	66	17	.260
2010 Toronto	A.L.	OF	157	590	79	161	44	3	31	88	6	.273
2011 Inland Empire	Calif.	OF	2	5	3	1	1	0	0	3	0	.200
2011 Los Angeles e-f	A.L.	OF	131	505	60	110	15	4	25	66	9	.218
2012 Salt Lake	P.C.	OF	7	26	2	8	1	0	2	3	3	.308
2012 Los Angeles g	A.L.	OF	77	243	36	56	9	0	11	29	3	.230
Major League Totals		14 Yrs.	1601	6218	885	1695	363	34	259	908	102	.273

a On disabled list from April 14 to 24, 2001.
b On disabled list from June 16 to July 16, 2004.
c On disabled list from September 22 to November 13, 2007.
d On disabled list from May 10 to June 7 and July 10 to August 10, 2008.
e Traded to Los Angeles Angels for catcher Mike Napoli and outfielder Juan Rivera, January 21, 2011.
f On disabled list from May 10 to June 7, 2011.
g On disabled list from May 21 to July 27, 2012.

WERTH, JAYSON RICHARD GOWAN

Born, Springfield, Illinois, May 20, 1979.
Bats Right. Throws Right. Height, 6 feet, 5 inches. Weight, 220 pounds.

Year	Club	Lea	Pos	G	AB	R	H	2B	3B	HR	RBI	SB	Avg
1997 Orioles	Gulf Coast	C-1B-OF	32	88	16	26	6	0	1	8	7	.295
1998 Delmarva	So.Atl.	C	120	408	71	108	20	3	8	53	21	.265
1998 Bowie	Eastern	C	5	19	2	3	2	0	0	1	1	.158
1999 Frederick	Carolina	C	66	236	41	72	10	1	3	30	16	.305
1999 Bowie	Eastern	C-OF	35	121	18	33	5	1	1	11	7	.273
2000 Frederick	Carolina	C	24	83	16	23	3	0	2	18	5	.277
2000 Bowie a	Eastern	C-OF	85	276	47	63	16	2	5	26	9	.228
2001 Dunedin	Fla.St.	C	21	70	9	14	3	0	2	14	1	.200
2001 Tennessee	Southern	C-1B	104	369	51	105	23	1	18	69	12	.285
2002 Syracuse	Int.	OF-C	127	443	65	114	25	2	18	82	24	.257
2002 Toronto	A.L.	OF	15	46	4	12	2	1	0	6	1	.261
2003 Dunedin	Fla.St.	OF	18	62	10	23	5	0	4	18	1	.371
2003 Toronto	A.L.	OF	26	48	7	10	4	0	2	10	1	.208
2003 Syracuse b	Int.	OF	64	236	37	56	19	1	9	34	11	.237
2004 Los Angeles	N.L.	OF	89	290	56	76	11	3	16	47	4	.262
2004 Las Vegas c-d	P.C.	OF	14	51	13	21	2	1	5	20	2	.412
2005 Las Vegas	P.C.	OF	15	49	9	18	0	0	3	10	6	.367
2005 Los Angeles e	N.L.	OF	102	337	46	79	22	2	7	43	11	.234
2006 Los Angeles f-g	N.L.		INJURED—Did Not Play									
2007 Clearwater	Fla.St.	OF	4	13	3	1	0	0	0	0	0	.077
2007 Philadelphia h	N.L.	OF-1B	94	255	43	76	11	3	8	49	7	.298
2008 Clearwater	Fla.St.	OF	2	6	0	1	0	0	0	0	0	.167
2008 Philadelphia i	N.L.	OF	134	418	73	114	16	3	24	67	20	.273
2009 Philadelphia	N.L.	OF	159	571	98	153	26	1	36	99	20	.268
2010 Philadelphia j	N.L.	OF	156	554	106	164	*46	2	27	85	13	.296
2011 Washington	N.L.	OF	150	561	69	130	26	1	20	58	19	.232
2012 Potomac	Carolina	OF	2	6	2	3	1	0	0	1	0	.500
2012 Syracuse	Int.	OF	7	21	4	5	2	0	0	4	0	.238

Year	Club	Lea	Pos	G	AB	R	H	2B	3B	HR	RBI	SB	Avg
2012 Washington k	N.L.	OF	81	300	42	90	21	3	5	31	8	.300
Major League Totals	10 Yrs.		1006	3380	544	904	185	19	145	495	104	.267
Division Series												
2004 Los Angeles	N.L.	OF	4	14	3	4	1	0	2	3	0	.286
2007 Philadelphia	N.L.	OF	2	3	0	0	0	0	0	0	0	.000
2008 Philadelphia	N.L.	OF	4	16	3	5	3	1	1	1	1	.313
2009 Philadelphia	N.L.	OF	4	14	5	5	0	1	2	4	0	.357
2010 Philadelphia	N.L.	OF	3	12	2	2	0	0	0	1	1	.167
2012 Washington	N.L.	OF	5	21	3	5	1	0	1	1	0	.238
Division Series Totals			22	80	16	21	5	2	6	10	2	.262
Championship Series												
2008 Philadelphia	N.L.	OF	5	21	2	4	1	0	0	0	0	.190
2009 Philadelphia	N.L.	OF	5	18	5	4	0	0	3	6	0	.222
2010 Philadelphia	N.L.	OF	6	18	3	4	1	0	2	5	0	.222
Championship Series Totals			16	57	10	12	2	0	5	11	0	.211
World Series Record												
2008 Philadelphia	N.L.	OF	5	18	4	8	3	0	1	3	3	.444
2009 Philadelphia	N.L.	OF	6	19	3	5	0	0	2	3	0	.263
World Series Totals			11	37	7	13	3	0	3	6	3	.351

a Traded to Toronto Blue Jays by Baltimore Orioles for pitcher John Bale, December 11, 2000.
b On disabled list from March 21 to April 11, 2003.
c On disabled list from April 6 to June 4, 2004.
d Traded to Los Angeles Dodgers for pitcher Jason Frasor, March 30, 2004.
e On disabled list from March 25 to May 25 and from July 27 to August 11, 2005.
f On disabled list from April 1 to November 2, 2006.
g Not offered contract, December 12, 2006. Signed with Philadelphia Phillies, December 19, 2006.
h On disabled list from June 29 to August 1, 2007.
i On disabled list from May 23 to June 7, 2008.
j Filed for free agency, November 1, 2010. Signed with Washington Nationals, December 5, 2010.
k On disabled list from May 7 to August 2, 2012.

WIETERS, MATTHEW RICHARD (MATT)
Born, Goose Creek, South Carolina, May 21, 1986.
Bats Both. Throws Right. Height, 6 feet, 5 inches. Weight, 230 pounds.

Year	Club	Lea	Pos	G	AB	R	H	2B	3B	HR	RBI	SB	Avg
2008 Frederick	Carolina	C	69	229	48	79	8	0	15	40	1	.345
2008 Bowie	Eastern	C	61	208	41	76	14	2	12	51	1	.365
2009 Norfolk	Int.	C	39	141	25	43	9	2	5	30	0	.305
2009 Baltimore	A.L.	C	96	354	35	102	15	1	9	43	0	.288
2010 Baltimore a	A.L.	C	130	446	37	111	22	1	11	55	0	.249
2011 Baltimore	A.L.	C-1B	139	500	72	131	28	0	22	68	1	.262
2012 Baltimore	A.L.	C	144	526	67	131	27	1	23	83	3	.249
Major League Totals	4 Yrs.		509	1826	211	475	92	3	65	249	4	.260
Wild Card Playoff												
2012 Baltimore	A.L.	C	1	4	0	0	0	0	0	0	0	.000
Division Series												
2012 Baltimore	A.L.	C	5	20	2	3	1	0	0	0	0	.150

a On disabled list from July 10 to July 25, 2010.

WIGGINTON, TY ALLEN (TY)
Born, San Diego, California, October 11, 1977.
Bats Right. Throws Right. Height, 6 feet. Weight, 225 pounds.

Year	Club	Lea	Pos	G	AB	R	H	2B	3B	HR	RBI	SB	Avg
1998 Pittsfield	N.Y.-Penn.	2B-3B-OF	70	272	39	65	14	4	8	29	11	.239
1999 St. Lucie	Fla.St.	2B	123	456	69	133	23	5	21	73	9	.292
2000 Binghamton	Eastern	2B-3B	122	453	64	129	27	3	20	77	5	.285
2001 Binghamton	Eastern	2B-3B	8	28	5	8	3	0	0	0	1	.286
2001 St. Lucie	Fla.St.	2B	3	9	1	3	1	0	0	1	0	.333
2001 Norfolk	Int.	3B-2B-1B-OF	78	260	29	65	12	0	7	24	3	.250
2002 Norfolk	Int.	2B-OF-1B	104	383	49	115	26	3	6	48	5	.300
2002 New York	N.L.	3B-1B-2B-OF	46	116	18	35	8	0	6	18	2	.302
2003 New York	N.L.	3B	156	573	73	146	36	6	11	71	12	.255
2004 St. Lucie	Fla.St.	3B	2	8	1	3	0	0	0	0	0	.375
2004 N.Y.-Pittsburgh a-b	N.L.	3B-2B-1B	144	494	63	129	30	2	17	66	7	.261
2005 Indianapolis	Int.	3B-1B-2B	72	280	53	82	18	0	14	52	8	.293
2005 Pittsburgh c	N.L.	3B-1B-2B	57	155	20	40	9	1	7	25	0	.258

Year Club	Lea	Pos	G	AB	R	H	2B	3B	HR	RBI	SB	Avg
2006 Durham	Int.	1B	2	8	2	3	2	0	1	2	0	.375
2006 Tampa Bay d	A.L.	1B-2B-3B-OF	122	444	55	122	25	1	24	79	4	.275
2007 Tampa Bay	A.L.	2B-3B-1B	98	378	47	104	21	0	16	49	1	.275
2007 Houston e	N.L.	3B-OF-1B	50	169	24	48	12	0	6	18	2	.284
2008 Round Rock......	P.C.	3B	3	9	1	1	0	1	0	1	0	.111
2008 Houston f-g	N.L.	3B-OF	111	386	50	110	22	1	23	58	4	.285
2009 Baltimore	A.L.	1B-3B-SS	122	410	44	112	19	0	11	41	1	.273
2010 Baltimore h	A.L.	1B-2B-3B	154	581	63	144	29	1	22	76	0	.248
2011 Colorado Springs...	P.C.	3B	2	7	1	2	0	0	0	1	0	.286
2011 Colorado i-j	N.L.	3B-1B-OF	130	401	52	97	21	2	15	47	8	.242
2012 Philadelphia k.....	N.L.	1B-3B-OF	125	315	40	74	11	0	11	43	1	.235
Major League Totals		11 Yrs.	1315	4422	549	1161	243	14	169	591	42	.263

a On disabled list from April 21 to May 7, 2004.
b Traded to Pittsburgh Pirates with pitcher Matt Peterson and infielder Jose Bautista for pitcher Kris Benson and infielder Jeff Keppinger, July 30, 2004.
c Released by Pittsburgh Pirates, December 8, 2005. Signed with Tampa Bay Devil Rays, January 10, 2006.
d On disabled list from July 31 to September 1, 2006.
e Traded to Houston Astros for pitcher Dan Wheeler, July 28, 2007.
f On disabled list from April 6 to May 2, 2008.
g Not offered contract, December 12, 2008. Signed with Baltimore Orioles, February 10, 2009.
h Filed for free agency, November 1, 2010. Signed with Colorado Rockies, December 7, 2010.
i On disabled list from April 27 to May 13, 2011.
j Sold to Philadelphia Phillies, November 20, 2011.
k Filed for free agency, November 3, 2012. Signed with St. Louis Cardinals, December 14, 2012.

WILLINGHAM, JOSHUA DAVID (JOSH)

Born, Florence, Alabama, February 17, 1979.
Bats Right. Throws Right. Height, 6 feet, 1 inch. Weight, 215 pounds.

Year Club	Lea	Pos	G	AB	R	H	2B	3B	HR	RBI	SB	Avg
2000 Utica.......	N.Y.-Penn.	OF-2B-3B-SS	65	205	37	54	16	0	6	29	9	.263
2001 Kane County...	Midwest	3B-OF-2B	97	320	57	83	20	2	7	36	24	.259
2002 Jupiter	Fla.St.	1B-3B-OF	107	376	72	103	21	4	17	69	18	.274
2003 Jupiter	Fla.St.	C-1B-OF-3B	59	193	46	51	17	1	12	34	9	.264
2003 Marlins......	Gulf Coast	DH	2	7	3	3	1	0	1	3	0	.429
2003 Carolina	Southern	1B-C-3B-OF	22	67	15	20	2	1	5	14	0	.299
2004 Carolina	Southern	C-1B-OF-3B	112	338	81	95	24	0	24	76	6	.281
2004 Florida	N.L.	C-OF	12	25	2	5	0	0	1	1	0	.200
2005 Jupiter	Fla.St.	C	2	9	1	2	1	0	0	1	0	.222
2005 Albuquerque.......	P.C.	C-3B	66	219	56	71	14	3	19	54	5	.324
2005 Florida a.........	N.L.	C-OF	16	23	3	7	1	0	0	4	0	.304
2006 Carolina	Southern	OF	2	8	0	2	0	0	0	0	0	.250
2006 Florida b.........	N.L.	OF-C-1B	142	502	62	139	28	2	26	74	2	.277
2007 Florida	N.L.	OF	144	521	75	138	32	4	21	89	8	.265
2008 Carolina	Southern	OF	8	26	6	6	2	0	0	5	0	.231
2008 Florida c-d	N.L.	OF	102	351	54	89	21	5	15	51	3	.254
2009 Washington	N.L.	OF-1B	133	427	70	111	29	0	24	61	4	.260
2010 Washington e-f.....	N.L.	OF	114	370	54	99	19	2	16	56	8	.268
2011 Sacramento	P.C.	DH	2	5	1	1	0	0	1	2	0	.200
2011 Oakland g-h	A.L.	OF	136	488	69	120	26	0	29	98	4	.246
2012 Minnesota	A.L.	OF	145	519	85	135	30	1	35	110	3	.260
Major League Totals		9 Yrs.	944	3226	474	843	186	14	167	544	32	.261

a On disabled list from June 30 to September 2, 2005.
b On disabled list from June 7 to June 22, 2006.
c On disabled list from April 28 to June 23, 2008.
d Traded to Washington Nationals with pitcher Scott Olsen for infielder Emilio Bonifacio, pitcher P.J. Dean and infielder Jake Smolinkski, November 11, 2008.
e On disabled list from August 18 to November 10, 2010.
f Traded to Oakland Athletics for pitcher Henry Rodriguez and outfielder Corey Brown, December 16, 2010.
g On disabled list from June 18 to July 7, 2011.
h Filed for free agency, October 30, 2011. Signed with Minnesota Twins, December 15, 2011.

WISE, LARRY DEWAYNE (DEWAYNE)

Born, Columbia, South Carolina, February 24, 1978.
Bats Left. Throws Left. Height, 6 feet, 1 inch. Weight, 200 pounds.

Year Club	Lea	Pos	G	AB	R	H	2B	3B	HR	RBI	SB	Avg
1997 Billings............	Pioneer	OF	62	268	53	84	13	9	7	41	18	.313
1998 Burlington	Midwest	OF	127	496	61	111	15	9	2	44	27	.224
1999 Rockford a........	Midwest	OF	131	502	70	127	20	13	11	81	35	.253

Year	Club	Lea	Pos	G	AB	R	H	2B	3B	HR	RBI	SB	Avg
2000 Toronto	A.L.	OF	28	22	3	3	0	0	0	0	1	.136
2000 Tennessee b	Southern	OF	15	56	10	14	5	2	2	8	3	.250
2001 Dunedin	Fla.St.	OF	25	103	9	23	3	1	2	16	5	.223
2001 Syracuse	Int.	OF	3	13	1	3	0	0	0	0	0	.231
2001 Tennessee	Southern	OF	87	351	44	84	13	6	8	44	13	.239
2002 Tennessee	Southern	OF	86	340	59	101	21	4	10	49	15	.297
2002 Toronto	A.L.	OF	42	112	14	20	4	1	3	13	5	.179
2003 Syracuse c	Int.	OF	80	285	37	62	11	4	10	37	11	.218
2004 Atlanta	N.L.	OF	77	162	24	37	9	4	6	17	6	.228
2004 Rome	So.Atl.	OF	5	15	4	5	0	0	2	4	1	.333
2004 Myrtle Beach	Carolina	OF	4	16	1	4	0	1	0	0	0	.250
2004 Richmond d-e	Int.	OF	34	118	18	37	4	6	5	16	5	.314
2005 Toledo f	Int.	OF	108	384	42	90	12	5	8	45	22	.234
2006 Louisville	Int.	OF	44	154	27	41	10	4	4	21	6	.266
2006 Chattanooga	Southern	OF	13	50	11	21	7	0	3	7	1	.420
2006 Cincinnati g	N.L.	OF	31	38	3	7	2	0	0	1	0	.184
2007 Cincinnati	N.L.	OF	5	5	1	1	0	1	0	1	0	.200
2007 Louisville	Int.	OF	54	207	34	52	11	7	7	20	8	.251
2007 Reds	Gulf Coast	OF	2	6	2	2	1	0	0	0	1	.333
2008 Charlotte	Int.	OF	55	191	39	61	14	3	9	23	15	.319
2008 Chicago h-i	A.L.	OF	57	129	20	32	4	2	6	18	9	.248
2009 Charlotte	Int.	OF	7	27	2	9	3	1	0	3	0	.333
2009 Chicago j-k	A.L.	OF	84	142	17	32	8	3	2	11	4	.225
2010 Lehigh Valley	Int.	OF	37	137	17	37	11	5	4	13	2	.270
2010 Toronto l	A.L.	OF	52	112	20	28	3	2	3	14	4	.250
2011 Dunedin	Fla.St.	OF	3	11	4	3	2	0	1	2	0	.273
2011 Las Vegas	P.C.	OF	31	133	28	45	10	3	4	19	8	.338
2011 New Orleans	P.C.	OF	2	9	0	3	1	0	0	0	0	.333
2011 Florida	N.L.	OF	49	67	6	16	2	0	0	5	4	.239
2011 Toronto m-n-o-p	A.L.	OF	20	32	4	4	0	1	2	2	2	.125
2012 Charlotte	Int.	OF	7	31	3	5	1	1	0	3	1	.161
2012 Scranton-WB	Int.	OF	21	76	17	25	7	0	4	10	2	.329
2012 New York-Chicago q-r-s	A.L.	OF-P	101	224	31	58	10	2	8	30	19	.259
Major League Totals	10 Yrs.		546	1045	143	238	42	16	30	112	54	.228
Division Series												
2004 Atlanta	N.L.	OF	5	5	1	1	1	0	0	0	0	.200
2008 Chicago	A.L.	OF	3	7	2	2	1	0	1	5	1	.286
Division Series Totals			8	12	3	3	2	0	1	5	1	.250

a Selected by Toronto Blue Jays organization from Cincinnati Reds in Rule V draft, December 13, 1999.
b On disabled list from June 6 to August 31, 2000.
c Filed for free agency, September 30, 2003. Signed with Atlanta Braves organization, October 25, 2003.
d On disabled list from June 23 to July 15, 2004.
e Claimed on waivers by Detroit Tigers, October 15, 2004.
f Filed for free agency, October 3, 2005. Signed with Cincinnati Reds organization, November 3, 2005.
g Filed for free agency, October 6, 2006, re-signed with Cincinnati Reds organization, October 27, 2006.
h Filed for free agency, October 10, 2007. Signed with Chicago White Sox organization, March 2, 2008.
i On disabled list from August 21 to September 5, 2008.
j On disabled list from April 14 to May 29 and from August 15 to September 1, 2009.
k Filed for free agency, October 8, 2009. Signed with Philadelphia Phillies organization, November 25, 2009.
l Released by Philadelphia Phillies, June 1, 2010. Signed with Toronto Blue Jays organization, June 5, 2010.
m Filed for free agency, November 12, 2010. Signed with Florida Marlins organization, January 12, 2011.
n Released by Florida Marlins, March 30, 2011. Signed with Toronto Blue Jays organization, April 16, 2011.
o Released by Toronto Blue Jays, June 9, 2011. Signed with Florida Marlins organization, June 14, 2011.
p Claimed on waivers by Toronto Blue Jays, August 26, 2011.
q Filed for free agency, October 4, 2011. Signed with New York Yankees organization, January 4, 2012.
r Released by New York Yankees, July 30, 2012. Signed with Chicago White Sox organization, August 12, 2012.
s Filed for free agency, November 3, 2012, re-signed with Chicago White Sox, November 21, 2012.

WRIGHT, DAVID ALLEN
Born, Norfolk, Virginia, December 20, 1982.
Bats Right. Throws Right. Height, 6 feet. Weight, 215 pounds.

Year	Club	Lea	Pos	G	AB	R	H	2B	3B	HR	RBI	SB	Avg
2001 Kingsport	Appal.	3B	35	116	27	35	7	0	4	16	9	.302
2002 Columbia	So.Atl.	3B	135	496	85	132	30	2	11	93	21	.266
2003 St. Lucie	Fla.St.	3B	133	466	69	126	39	2	15	75	19	.270
2004 Binghamton	Eastern	3B	60	223	44	81	27	0	10	40	20	.363
2004 Norfolk	Int.	3B	31	114	18	34	8	0	8	17	2	.298
2004 New York	N.L.	3B	69	263	41	77	17	1	14	40	6	.293
2005 New York	N.L.	3B	160	575	99	176	42	1	27	102	17	.306

Year	Club	Lea	Pos	G	AB	R	H	2B	3B	HR	RBI	SB	Avg
2006 New York	N.L.		3B	154	582	96	181	40	5	26	116	20	.311
2007 New York	N.L.		3B	160	604	113	196	42	1	30	107	34	.325
2008 New York	N.L.		3B	160	626	115	189	42	2	33	124	15	.302
2009 New York a	N.L.		3B	144	535	88	164	39	3	10	72	27	.307
2010 New York	N.L.		3B	157	587	87	166	36	3	29	103	19	.283
2011 St. Lucie	Fla.St.		3B	6	21	9	10	3	0	0	2	1	.476
2011 New York b	N.L.		3B-SS	102	389	60	99	23	1	14	61	13	.254
2012 New York	N.L.		3B-SS	156	581	91	178	41	2	21	93	15	.306
Major League Totals		9 Yrs.		1262	4742	790	1426	322	19	204	818	166	.301
Division Series													
2006 New York	N.L.		3B	3	12	1	4	2	0	0	4	0	.333
Championship Series													
2006 New York	N.L.		3B	7	25	2	4	1	0	1	2	0	.160

a On disabled list from August 16 to September 1, 2009.
b On disabled list from May 16 to July 22, 2011.

YOUKILIS, KEVIN EDMUND

Born, Cincinnati, Ohio, March 15, 1979.
Bats Right. Throws Right. Height, 6 feet, 1 inch. Weight, 220 pounds.

Year	Club	Lea	Pos	G	AB	R	H	2B	3B	HR	RBI	SB	Avg
2001 Lowell	N.Y.-Penn.		3B	59	183	52	58	14	2	3	28	4	.317
2001 Augusta	So.Atl.		3B	5	12	0	2	0	0	0	0	0	.167
2002 Augusta	So.Atl.		3B	15	53	5	15	5	0	0	6	0	.283
2002 Sarasota	Fla.St.		1B-3B	76	268	45	79	16	0	3	48	0	.295
2002 Trenton	Eastern		3B	44	160	34	55	10	0	5	26	5	.344
2003 Portland	Eastern		3B	94	312	74	102	23	1	6	37	7	.327
2003 Pawtucket	Int.		3B	32	109	9	18	3	0	2	15	0	.165
2004 Lowell	N.Y.-Penn.		3B	2	4	1	3	1	1	0	0	0	.750
2004 Boston a	A.L.		3B	72	208	38	54	11	0	7	35	0	.260
2004 Pawtucket	Int.		3B-1B	38	154	25	41	12	0	3	18	2	.266
2005 Pawtucket	Int.	3B-1B-2B	43	152	30	49	15	1	8	27	1	.322
2005 Boston	A.L.	3B-1B-2B	44	79	11	22	7	0	1	9	0	.278
2006 Boston	A.L.	1B-OF-3B	147	569	100	159	42	2	13	72	5	.279
2007 Boston	A.L.		1B-3B	145	528	85	152	35	2	16	83	4	.288
2008 Boston	A.L.	1B-3B-OF	145	538	91	168	43	4	29	115	3	.312
2009 Pawtucket	Int.		1B	2	6	0	0	0	0	0	0	0	.000
2009 Boston b	A.L.	1B-3B-OF	136	491	99	150	36	1	27	94	7	.305
2010 Boston c	A.L.		1B-3B	102	362	77	111	26	5	19	62	4	.307
2011 Pawtucket	Int.		3B	2	8	2	2	0	0	1	1	0	.250
2011 Boston d	A.L.		3B-1B	120	431	68	111	32	2	17	80	3	.258
2012 Pawtucket	Int.		3B	4	11	1	4	2	0	0	1	0	.364
2012 Boston-Chicago e-f-g	A.L.		3B-1B	122	438	72	103	15	2	19	60	0	.235
Major League Totals		9 Yrs.		1033	3644	641	1030	247	18	148	610	26	.283
Division Series													
2004 Boston	A.L.		3B	1	2	0	0	0	0	0	0	0	.000
2007 Boston	A.L.		1B	3	12	3	3	1	0	1	2	0	.250
2008 Boston	A.L.		1B-3B	4	18	2	4	1	0	0	1	0	.222
2009 Boston	A.L.		1B-3B	3	12	0	1	1	0	0	0	0	.083
Division Series Totals				11	44	5	8	3	0	1	3	0	.182
Championship Series													
2007 Boston	A.L.		1B	7	28	10	14	1	1	3	7	0	.500
2008 Boston	A.L.		3B	7	30	4	10	3	0	2	6	0	.333
Championship Series Totals				14	58	14	24	4	1	5	13	0	.414
World Series Record													
2007 Boston	A.L.		1B	4	9	3	2	2	0	0	1	0	.222

a On disabled list from August 16 to September 1, 2004.
b On disabled list from May 5 to May 21, 2009.
c On disabled list from August 3 to November 8, 2010.
d On disabled list from August 18 to September 2 and September 28 to October 31, 2011.
e On disabled list from April 29 to May 22, 2012.
f Traded to Chicago White Sox with cash for infielder Brent Lillibridge and pitcher Zach Stewart, June 25, 2012.
g Filed for free agency, November 3, 2012. Signed with New York Yankees, December 14, 2012.

YOUNG, CHRISTOPHER BRANDON (CHRIS)

Born, Houston, Texas, September 5, 1983.
Bats Right. Throws Right. Height, 6 feet, 2 inches. Weight, 200 pounds.

Year	Club	Lea	Pos	G	AB	R	H	2B	3B	HR	RBI	SB	Avg
2002	White Sox	Arizona	OF	55	184	26	40	13	1	5	17	7	.217
2003	Bristol	Appal.	OF	64	238	47	69	18	3	7	28	21	.290
2003	Great Falls	Pioneer	OF	10	34	5	6	3	0	0	0	0	.176
2004	Kannapolis	So.Atl.	OF	136	467	83	122	31	5	24	56	31	.261
2005	Birmingham a	Southern	OF	126	466	100	129	41	3	26	77	32	.277
2006	Tucson	P.C.	OF	100	402	78	111	32	4	21	77	17	.276
2006	Arizona	N.L.	OF	30	70	10	17	4	0	2	10	2	.243
2007	Arizona	N.L.	OF	148	569	85	135	29	3	32	68	27	.237
2008	Arizona	N.L.	OF	160	625	85	155	42	7	22	85	14	.248
2009	Reno	P.C.	OF	13	54	17	20	5	1	3	9	2	.370
2009	Arizona	N.L.	OF	134	433	54	92	28	4	15	42	11	.212
2010	Arizona	N.L.	OF	156	584	94	150	33	0	27	91	28	.257
2011	Arizona	N.L.	OF	156	567	89	134	38	3	20	71	22	.236
2012	Visalia	Calif.	OF	3	13	3	4	3	0	1	7	0	.308
2012	Reno	P.C.	OF	1	2	0	0	0	0	0	1	0	.000
2012	Arizona b-c.	N.L.	OF	101	325	36	75	24	0	14	41	8	.231
Major League Totals			7 Yrs.	885	3173	453	758	198	17	132	408	112	.239
Division Series													
2007	Arizona	N.L.	OF	3	11	3	3	0	0	2	4	1	.273
2011	Arizona	N.L.	OF	5	18	5	7	1	0	3	4	2	.389
Division Series Totals				8	29	8	10	1	0	5	8	3	.345
Championship Series													
2007	Arizona	N.L.	OF	4	14	1	4	1	0	0	1	0	.286

a Traded to Arizona Diamondbacks by Chicago White Sox with pitcher Orlando Hernandez and pitcher Luis Vizcaino for pitcher Javier Vazquez, December 20, 2005.
b On disabled list from April 18 to May 18, 2012.
c Traded to Oakland Athletics with cash for infielder Cliff Pennington and infielder Yordy Cabrera, October 20, 2012.

YOUNG, DELMON DAMARCUS

Born, Birmingham, Alabama, September 14, 1985.
Bats Right. Throws Right. Height, 6 feet, 3 inches. Weight, 205 pounds.

Year	Club	Lea	Pos	G	AB	R	H	2B	3B	HR	RBI	SB	Avg
2004	Charleston	So.Atl.	OF	131	513	95	165	26	5	25	116	21	.322
2005	Durham	Int.	OF	52	228	33	65	13	3	6	28	7	.285
2005	Montgomery	Southern	OF	84	330	59	111	13	4	20	71	25	.336
2006	Durham	Int.	OF	86	342	50	108	22	4	8	59	22	.316
2006	Tampa Bay	A.L.	OF	30	126	16	40	9	1	3	10	2	.317
2007	Tampa Bay a	A.L.	OF	*162	645	65	186	38	0	13	93	10	.288
2008	Minnesota	A.L.	OF	152	575	80	167	28	4	10	69	14	.290
2009	Minnesota	A.L.	OF	108	395	50	112	16	2	12	60	2	.284
2010	Minnesota	A.L.	OF	153	570	77	170	46	1	21	112	5	.298
2011	Rochester	Int.	OF	9	31	5	9	3	0	2	5	0	.290
2011	Minnesota-Detroit b-c	A.L.	OF	124	473	54	127	21	1	12	64	1	.268
2012	Detroit d	A.L.	DH-OF	151	574	54	153	27	1	18	74	0	.267
Major League Totals			7 Yrs.	880	3358	396	955	185	10	89	482	34	.284
Division Series													
2009	Minnesota	A.L.	OF	3	12	1	1	1	0	0	0	1	.083
2010	Minnesota	A.L.	OF	3	12	1	4	0	1	0	0	0	.333
2011	Detroit	A.L.	OF	5	19	4	6	0	0	3	3	0	.316
2012	Detroit	A.L.	DH	5	17	0	4	0	0	0	2	0	.235
Division Series Totals				16	60	6	15	1	1	3	5	1	.250
Championship Series													
2011	Detroit	A.L.	OF	4	15	2	2	0	0	2	3	0	.133
2012	Detroit	A.L.	DH	4	17	3	6	1	0	2	6	0	.353
Championship Series Totals				8	32	5	8	1	0	4	9	0	.250
World Series Record													
2012	Detroit	A.L.	OF-DH	4	14	2	5	1	0	1	1	0	.357

a Traded to Minnesota Twins with infielder Brendan Harris and outfielder Jason Pridie for infielder Jason Bartlett, pitcher Matt Garza and pitcher Eduardo Morlan, November 28, 2007.
b On disabled list from April 19 to May 13 and June 26 to July 11, 2011.
c Traded to Detroit Tigers for pitcher Cole Nelson and player to be named later, August 15, 2011. Minnesota Twins received pitcher Lester Oliveros to complete trade, August 16, 2011.
d Filed for free agency, November 3, 2012.

YOUNG, ERIC ORLANDO JR.

Born, New Brunswick, New Jersey, May 25, 1985.
Bats Both. Throws Right. Height, 5 feet, 10 inches. Weight, 180 pounds.

Year	Club	Lea	Pos	G	AB	R	H	2B	3B	HR	RBI	SB	Avg
2004 Casper	Pioneer		2B	23	87	20	23	5	1	0	7	14	.264
2005 Casper	Pioneer		2B	63	219	48	66	7	7	3	25	25	.301
2006 Asheville	So.Atl.		2B	128	482	92	142	28	6	5	49	87	.295
2007 Modesto	Calif.		2B	130	540	113	157	29	11	8	63	73	.291
2008 Tulsa	Texas		2B-OF	105	403	74	117	24	4	3	33	46	.290
2009 Colorado Springs	P.C.		2B-OF	119	472	118	141	21	10	7	43	58	.299
2009 Colorado	N.L.		2B-OF	30	57	7	14	1	0	1	1	4	.246
2010 Tulsa	Texas		2B	4	13	2	3	0	0	0	0	0	.231
2010 Colorado Springs	P.C.		2B-OF	33	123	20	31	5	1	1	9	10	.252
2010 Colorado a	N.L.		2B-OF	51	172	26	42	5	1	0	8	17	.244
2011 Colorado Springs	P.C.		OF-2B	58	223	61	81	18	9	2	28	17	.363
2011 Colorado	N.L.		OF-2B	77	198	34	49	4	3	0	10	27	.247
2012 Colorado b	N.L.		OF	98	174	36	55	7	2	4	15	14	.316
Major League Totals	4 Yrs.			256	601	103	160	17	6	5	34	62	.266
Division Series													
2009 Colorado	N.L.		PH	2	1	0	0	0	0	0	0	0	.000

a On disabled list from May 13 to July 31, 2010.
b On disabled list from August 20 to October 5, 2012.

YOUNG, MICHAEL BRIAN

Born, Covina, California, October 19, 1976.
Bats Right. Throws Right. Height, 6 feet, 1 Inch. Weight, 200 pounds.

Year	Club	Lea	Pos	G	AB	R	H	2B	3B	HR	RBI	SB	Avg
1997 St.Catherines	N.Y.-Penn.		SS-2B	74	276	49	85	18	3	9	48	9	.308
1998 Hagerstown	So.Atl.		2B-SS-OF	140	522	86	147	33	5	16	87	16	.282
1999 Dunedin	Fla.St.		2B	129	495	86	155	36	3	5	83	30	.313
2000 Tennessee	Southern		2B-SS	91	345	51	95	24	5	6	47	16	.275
2000 Tulsa	Texas		SS	43	188	30	60	13	5	1	32	9	.319
2000 Texas a	A.L.		2B	2	2	0	0	0	0	0	0	0	.000
2001 Oklahoma	P.C.		2B-SS	47	189	28	55	8	0	8	28	3	.291
2001 Texas	A.L.		2B	106	386	57	96	18	4	11	49	3	.249
2002 Texas	A.L.		2B-SS-3B	156	573	77	150	26	8	9	62	6	.262
2003 Texas	A.L.		2B-SS	160	666	106	204	33	9	14	72	13	.306
2004 Texas	A.L.		SS	160	690	114	216	33	9	22	99	12	.313
2005 Texas	A.L.		SS	159	668	*114	*221	40	5	24	91	5	*.331
2006 Texas	A.L.		SS	*162	691	93	217	52	3	14	103	7	.314
2007 Texas	A.L.		SS	156	639	80	201	37	1	9	94	13	.315
2008 Texas	A.L.		SS	155	645	102	183	36	2	12	82	10	.284
2009 Texas	A.L.		3B	135	541	76	174	36	2	22	68	8	.322
2010 Texas	A.L.		3B	157	656	99	186	36	3	21	91	4	.284
2011 Texas	A.L.		DH-3B-1B-2B	159	631	88	*213	41	6	11	106	6	.338
2012 Texas b	A.L.		DH-1B-3B-2B	156	611	79	169	27	3	8	67	2	.277
Major League Totals	13 Yrs.			1823	7399	1085	2230	415	55	177	984	89	.301
Wild Card Playoff													
2012 Texas	A.L.		1B	1	4	0	2	0	0	0	0	0	.500
Division Series													
2010 Texas	A.L.		3B	5	20	1	3	0	0	1	3	0	.150
2011 Texas	A.L.		DH-1B	4	15	1	2	0	0	0	0	0	.133
Division Series Totals				9	35	2	5	0	0	1	3	0	.143
Championship Series													
2010 Texas	A.L.		3B	6	27	3	9	3	0	0	4	0	.333
2011 Texas	A.L.		1B-DH	6	28	3	7	3	0	1	7	0	.250
Championship Series Totals				12	55	6	16	6	0	1	11	0	.291
World Series Record													
2010 Texas	A.L.		3B	5	20	0	5	0	0	0	0	0	.250
2011 Texas	A.L.		1B-DH	7	27	3	7	4	0	1	5	0	.259
World Series Totals				12	47	3	12	4	0	1	5	0	.255

a Traded by Toronto Blue Jays to Texas Rangers with pitcher Darwin Cubillan for pitcher Esteban Loaiza, July 19, 2000.
b Traded to Philadelphia Phillies for pitcher Josh Lindblom and pitcher Lisalverto Bonilla, December 9, 2012.

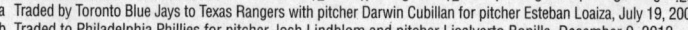

ZIMMERMAN, RYAN WALLACE

Born, Washington, North Carolina, September 28, 1984.
Bats Right. Throws Right. Height, 6 feet, 3 inches. Weight, 230 pounds.

Year Club	Lea	Pos	G	AB	R	H	2B	3B	HR	RBI	SB	Avg
2005 Savannah	So.Atl.	1B-SS	4	17	5	8	2	1	2	6	0	.471
2005 Harrisburg	Eastern	3B-SS	63	233	40	76	20	0	9	32	1	.326
2005 Washington	N.L.	3B-SS	20	58	6	23	10	0	0	6	0	.397
2006 Washington	N.L.	3B	157	614	84	176	47	3	20	110	11	.287
2007 Washington	N.L.	3B	*162	653	99	174	43	5	24	91	4	.266
2008 Potomac	Carolina	DH	2	10	1	3	2	0	0	0	0	.300
2008 Columbus	Int.	3B	4	15	4	4	1	0	1	3	0	.267
2008 Washington a	N.L.	3B	106	428	51	121	24	1	14	51	1	.283
2009 Washington	N.L.	3B	157	610	110	178	37	3	33	106	2	.292
2010 Washington	N.L.	3B	142	525	85	161	32	0	25	85	4	.307
2011 Hagerstown	So.Atl.	2B	1	2	2	2	1	1	0	1	0	1.000
2011 Potomac	Carolina	3B	3	10	0	4	2	0	0	1	0	.400
2011 Syracuse	Int.	3B	2	9	1	2	0	0	0	1	0	.222
2011 Washington b	N.L.	3B	101	395	52	114	21	2	12	49	3	.289
2012 Washington c	N.L.	3B	145	578	93	163	36	1	25	95	5	.282
Major League Totals		8 Yrs.	990	3861	580	1110	250	15	153	593	30	.287
Division Series												
2012 Washington	N.L.	3B	5	21	3	8	1	0	2	4	0	.381

a On disabled list from May 26 to July 22, 2008.
b On disabled list from April 10 to June 14, 2011.
c On disabled list from April 21 to May 8, 2012.

ZOBRIST, BENJAMIN THOMAS (BEN)

Born, Eureka, Illinois, May 26, 1981.
Bats Both. Throws Right. Height, 6 feet, 3 inches. Weight, 200 pounds.

Year Club	Lea	Pos	G	AB	R	H	2B	3B	HR	RBI	SB	Avg
2004 Tri-City	N.Y.-Penn.	SS	68	257	50	87	14	3	4	45	15	.339
2005 Salem	Carolina	SS	42	141	25	47	12	1	3	13	2	.333
2005 Lexington	So.Atl.	SS	68	247	45	75	17	2	2	32	16	.304
2006 Corpus Christi	Texas	SS-3B	83	315	57	103	25	6	3	30	9	.327
2006 Durham	Int.	SS	18	69	12	21	3	1	0	6	4	.304
2006 Tampa Bay a	A.L.	SS	52	183	10	41	6	2	2	18	2	.224
2007 Durham	Int.	SS	61	222	42	62	14	2	7	22	8	.279
2007 Tampa Bay b	A.L.	SS	31	97	8	15	2	0	1	9	2	.155
2008 Vero Beach	Fla.St.	2B-3B-SS	4	14	1	4	1	0	0	2	0	.286
2008 Durham	Int.	SS-3B-2B	20	71	15	26	3	0	4	13	4	.366
2008 Tampa Bay c	A.L.	SS-OF-2B-3B	62	198	32	50	10	2	12	30	3	.253
2009 Tampa Bay	A.L.	2B-OF-SS-1B	152	501	91	149	28	7	27	91	17	.297
2010 Tampa Bay	A.L.	OF-2B-1B-3B	151	541	77	129	28	2	10	75	24	.238
2011 Tampa Bay	A.L.	2B-OF	156	588	99	158	46	6	20	91	19	.269
2012 Tampa Bay	A.L.	OF-2B-SS	157	560	88	151	39	7	20	74	14	.270
Major League Totals		7 Yrs.	761	2668	405	693	159	26	92	388	81	.260
Division Series												
2010 Tampa Bay	A.L.	OF-2B-1B	5	20	2	6	2	0	1	2	0	.300
2011 Tampa Bay	A.L.	2B	4	17	2	4	0	0	0	0	0	.235
Division Series Totals			9	37	4	10	2	0	1	2	0	.270
Championship Series												
2008 Tampa Bay	A.L.	OF-SS	3	4	0	0	0	0	0	0	0	.000
World Series Record												
2008 Tampa Bay	A.L.	OF	4	7	0	1	0	0	0	0	0	.143

a Traded by Houston Astros to Tampa Bay Devil Rays with pitcher Mitch Talbot for infielder Aubrey Huff and cash, July 12, 2006.
b On disabled list from August 19 to November 12, 2007.
c On disabled list from March 25 to May 13, 2008.

PITCHERS

ACEVES, ALFREDO
Born, San Luis Rio Colorado, Mexico, December 8, 1982.
Bats Right. Throws Right. Height, 6 feet, 3 inches. Weight, 220 pounds.

Year	Club	Lea	G	IP	W	L	Pct	SO	BB	H	ERA	SAVES
2002	Yucatan a	Mexican	23	45	1	2	.333	25	20	42	3.00	0
2003	Yucatan	Mexican	27	43	1	1	.500	29	18	49	3.35	1
2004	Yucatan	Mexican	17	65⅓	4	2	.667	37	37	64	4.55	0
2005	Yucatan	Mexican	22	145⅔	9	8	.529	101	44	155	4.32	0
2006	Monterrey	Mexican	19	124	8	5	.615	95	26	126	4.50	0
2007	Monterrey	Mexican	18	106⅓	11	5	.688	70	33	96	3.64	0
2008	Trenton	Eastern	7	50	2	2	.500	35	6	37	1.80	0
2008	Tampa	Fla.St.	8	47	4	1	.800	37	8	32	2.11	0
2008	Scranton-WB	Int.	10	43⅔	2	3	.400	42	13	42	4.12	0
2008	New York b	A.L.	6	30	1	0	1.000	16	10	25	2.40	0
2009	Scranton-WB	Int.	4	23⅔	2	0	1.000	18	5	18	3.80	0
2009	New York	A.L.	43	84	10	1	.909	69	16	69	3.54	1
2010	New York	A.L.	10	12	3	0	1.000	2	4	10	3.00	1
2010	Trenton	Eastern	4	8	0	0	.000	7	1	10	5.63	0
2010	Scranton-WB c-d	Int.	3	3⅔	0	0	.000	4	5	4	7.36	0
2011	Pawtucket	Int.	2	8	0	1	.000	6	4	6	5.63	0
2011	Boston	A.L.	55	114	10	2	.833	80	42	84	2.61	2
2012	Boston	A.L.	69	84	2	10	.167	75	31	80	5.36	25
Major League Totals		5 Yrs.	183	324	26	13	.667	242	103	268	3.56	29

Division Series
Year	Club	Lea	G	IP	W	L	Pct	SO	BB	H	ERA	SAVES
2009	New York	A.L.	1	1	0	0	.000	1	1	1	0.00	0

Championship Series
Year	Club	Lea	G	IP	W	L	Pct	SO	BB	H	ERA	SAVES
2009	New York	A.L.	2	1⅓	0	1	.000	0	2	3	13.50	0

World Series Record
Year	Club	Lea	G	IP	W	L	Pct	SO	BB	H	ERA	SAVES
2009	New York	A.L.	1	2	0	0	.000	1	0	1	0.00	0

a Sold by Toronto Blue Jays to Yucatan (Mexican), April 24, 2002.
b Signed with New York Yankees organization, March 10, 2008.
c On disabled list from May 9 to November 3, 2010.
d Not offered contract, December 2, 2010. Signed with Boston Red Sox, February 9, 2011.

ACOSTA, MANUEL ALCIDES (MANNY)
Born, Colon, Panama, May 1, 1981.
Bats Right. Throws Right. Height, 6 feet, 4 inches. Weight, 215 pounds.

Year	Club	Lea	G	IP	W	L	Pct	SO	BB	H	ERA	SAVES
1998	NY Yankees	Dominican	9	7⅔	0	1	.000	5	10	20	16.43	1
2000	Yankees	Gulf Coast	12	62⅓	4	2	.667	46	21	64	3.47	0
2001	Tampa	Fla.St.	2	7	0	1	.000	8	6	7	7.71	0
2001	Greensboro	So.Atl.	10	65⅔	5	2	.714	67	37	37	1.51	0
2002	Staten Island	N.Y.-Penn.	3	15⅓	2	1	.667	12	8	20	4.11	0
2002	Greensboro	So.Atl.	13	52	2	5	.286	35	44	65	6.40	0
2003	Battle Creek a	Midwest	15	61	0	8	.000	45	29	80	6.64	0
2003	Myrtle Beach	Carolina	8	12⅔	2	0	1.000	10	11	19	6.39	1
2004	Myrtle Beach	Carolina	11	23⅓	4	0	1.000	21	11	20	4.24	0
2004	Braves	Gulf Coast	2	2⅔	0	0	.000	2	2	5	3.38	0
2005	Danville	Appal.	3	6	0	0	.000	8	1	3	3.00	0
2005	Myrtle Beach	Carolina	18	22⅓	2	2	.500	18	9	22	4.43	7
2006	Mississippi	Southern	13	15⅓	0	0	.000	13	15	7	2.35	4
2006	Richmond	Int.	38	44⅔	1	6	.143	44	32	38	3.63	17
2007	Richmond	Int.	40	59⅔	9	3	.750	56	35	46	2.26	12
2007	Atlanta	N.L.	21	23⅔	1	1	.500	22	14	13	2.28	0
2008	Richmond	Int.	4	3⅔	0	0	.000	4	2	4	0.00	0
2008	Atlanta b	N.L.	46	53	3	5	.375	31	26	48	3.57	3
2009	Gwinnett	Int.	18	27⅓	1	3	.250	25	13	21	2.63	2
2009	Atlanta	N.L.	36	37⅓	1	1	.500	32	19	45	4.34	0
2010	Buffalo	Int.	28	36⅓	2	3	.400	36	15	28	3.47	5
2010	New York c	N.L.	41	39⅔	3	2	.600	42	18	30	2.95	1
2011	Buffalo	Int.	20	20⅓	1	0	1.000	27	17	13	1.77	4
2011	New York	N.L.	44	47	4	1	.800	46	15	50	3.45	4
2012	Buffalo	Int.	17	28	0	0	.000	25	4	24	2.25	0

Year Club	Lea	G	IP	W	L	Pct	SO	BB	H	ERA	SAVES
2012 New York d...........	N.L.	45	47⅓	1	3	.250	46	25	48	6.46	1
Major League Totals........6 Yrs.		233	248	13	13	.500	219	117	234	3.99	9

a Released by New York Yankees, July 24, 2003. Signed with Atlanta Braves organization, July 29, 2003.
b On disabled list from July 7 to August 23, 2008.
c Claimed on waivers by New York Mets, March 30, 2010.
d Not offered contract, November 30, 2012. Signed with Yomiuri Giants (Japan), December 12, 2012.

ADAMS, JON MICHAEL (MIKE)

Born, Corpus Christi, Texas, July 29, 1978.
Bats Right. Throws Right. Height, 6 feet, 5 inches. Weight, 190 pounds.

Year Club	Lea	G	IP	W	L	Pct	SO	BB	H	ERA	SAVES
2001 Ogden	Pioneer	23	32	2	2	.500	44	6	26	2.81	12
2002 High Desert	Calif.	10	14	1	0	.667	23	7	9	2.57	5
2002 Beloit	Midwest	11	15⅓	0	0	.000	21	2	13	2.93	5
2002 Huntsville........	Southern	13	18⅔	1	0	1.000	17	12	14	3.38	1
2003 Huntsville	Southern	45	74⅓	3	7	.300	83	33	58	3.15	14
2004 Indianapolis	Int.	10	31	2	0	1.000	37	4	23	2.61	0
2004 Milwaukee	N.L.	46	53	2	3	.400	39	14	50	3.40	0
2005 Milwaukee	N.L.	13	13⅓	0	1	.000	14	10	12	2.70	1
2005 Nashville	P.C.	26	36	3	4	.429	45	12	35	5.75	2
2006 Milwaukee	N.L.	2	2⅓	0	0	.000	1	2	4	11.57	0
2006 Nashville	P.C.	15	16⅓	1	1	.500	18	8	17	3.31	2
2006 Norfolk...........	Int.	13	14⅔	0	0	.000	12	7	13	4.91	0
2006 Buffalo...........	Int.	3	4⅔	0	0	.000	3	0	4	1.93	0
2006 Portland a-b-c	P.C.	17	23⅔	0	2	.000	15	7	29	4.18	0
2007						INJURED—Did Not Play					
2008 Portland	P.C.	12	14⅔	3	1	.750	16	9	21	5.52	0
2008 San Diego d	N.L.	54	65⅓	2	3	.400	74	19	49	2.48	0
2009 San Antonio	Texas	4	4	1	0	1.000	6	2	3	2.25	0
2009 Portland	P.C.	4	5	0	0	.000	0	1	4	5.40	0
2009 San Diego e	N.L.	37	37	0	0	.000	45	8	14	0.73	0
2010 San Antonio	Texas	1	1	0	0	.000	1	0	0	0.00	0
2010 San Diego f	N.L.	70	66⅔	4	1	.800	73	23	48	1.75	0
2011 San Diego	N.L.	48	48	3	1	.750	49	9	26	1.13	1
2011 Texas g........	A.L.	27	25⅔	2	3	.400	25	5	18	2.10	1
2012 Texas h........	A.L.	61	52⅓	5	3	.625	45	17	56	3.27	1
Major League Totals........8 Yrs.		358	363⅔	18	15	.545	365	107	277	2.28	4
Division Series											
2011 Texas	A.L.	3	2	0	0	.000	1	3	1	4.50	0
Championship Series											
2011 Texas	A.L.	5	4⅓	1	0	1.000	4	1	5	2.08	0
World Series Record											
2011 Texas	A.L.	3	2	1	0	1.000	1	2	5	4.50	0

a Traded to New York Mets for pitcher Jeremi Gonzalez, May 26, 2006.
b Claimed on waivers by Cleveland Indians, July 6, 2006.
c Traded to San Diego Padres for pitcher Brian Sikorski, July 18, 2006.
d Released by San Diego Padres, March 14, 2007, re-signed with San Diego Padres organization, April 12, 2007.
e On disabled list from April 1 to June 8 and August 22 to September 17, 2009.
f On disabled list from July 12 to August 7, 2010.
g Traded to Texas Rangers for pitcher Robert Erlin and pitcher Joseph Wieland, July 31, 2011.
h Filed for free agency, November 3, 2012. Signed with Philadelphia Phillies, December 20, 2012.

AFFELDT, JEREMY DAVID

Born, Phoenix, Arizona, June 6, 1979.
Bats Left. Throws Left. Height, 6 feet, 4 inches. Weight, 225 pounds.

Year Club	Lea	G	IP	W	L	Pct	SO	BB	H	ERA	SAVES
1997 Royals	Gulf Coast	10	40	2	0	1.000	36	21	34	4.50	0
1998 Royals	Gulf Coast	12	56	4	3	.571	67	24	50	2.89	0
1998 Lansing	Midwest	6	17	0	3	.000	8	12	27	9.53	0
1999 Charleston-WV.....	So.Atl.	27	143⅓	7	7	.500	111	80	140	3.83	0
2000 Wilmington	Carolina	27	147⅓	5	15	.250	92	59	158	4.09	0
2001 Wichita...........	Texas	25	145⅓	10	6	.625	128	46	153	3.90	0
2002 Wichita...........	Texas	3	6	0	0	.000	3	3	1	1.50	0
2002 Kansas City a.........	A.L.	34	77⅔	3	4	.429	67	37	85	4.64	0
2003 Kansas City b.........	A.L.	36	126	7	6	.538	98	38	126	3.93	4
2004 Omaha	P.C.	4	4	0	0	.000	5	0	2	0.00	3
2004 Kansas City c.........	A.L.	38	76⅓	3	4	.429	49	32	91	4.95	13
2005 Omaha	P.C.	9	8⅓	0	1	.000	9	6	9	6.48	0

Year	Club	Lea	G	IP	W	L	Pct	SO	BB	H	ERA	SAVES
2005 Kansas City d	A.L.	49	49²/₃	0	2	.000	39	29	56	5.26	0
2006 Kansas City	A.L.	27	70	4	6	.400	28	42	71	5.91	0
2006 Colorado e	N.L.	27	27¹/₃	4	2	.667	20	13	30	6.91	1
2007 Colorado f	N.L.	75	59	4	3	.571	46	33	47	3.51	0
2008 Cincinnati g	N.L.	74	78¹/₃	1	1	.500	80	25	78	3.33	0
2009 San Francisco	N.L.	74	62¹/₃	2	2	.500	55	31	42	1.73	0
2010 San Jose	Calif.	2	3	0	0	.000	4	1	2	0.00	0
2010 San Francisco h	N.L.	53	50	4	3	.571	44	24	56	4.14	4
2011 San Francisco	N.L.	67	61²/₃	3	2	.600	54	24	47	2.63	3
2012 San Francisco i-j	N.L.	67	63¹/₃	1	2	.333	57	23	57	2.70	3
Major League Totals	11 Yrs.	621	801²/₃	36	37	.493	637	351	787	4.01	28
Division Series											
2007 Colorado	N.L.	1	1	0	0	.000	2	0	1	9.00	0
2012 San Francisco	N.L.	3	3²/₃	0	0	.000	2	1	3	0.00	0
Division Series Totals		4	4²/₃	0	0	.000	4	1	4	1.93	0
Championship Series											
2007 Colorado	N.L.	2	1¹/₃	0	0	.000	0	0	0	0.00	0
2010 San Francisco	N.L.	3	2²/₃	0	0	.000	4	1	0	3.38	0
2012 San Francisco	N.L.	5	4²/₃	0	0	.000	4	1	2	0.00	0
Championship Series Totals		10	8²/₃	0	0	.000	8	2	2	1.04	0
World Series Record											
2007 Colorado	N.L.	4	3	0	0	.000	2	1	2	0.00	0
2010 San Francisco	N.L.	2	1¹/₃	0	0	.000	0	1	1	6.75	0
2012 San Francisco	N.L.	2	2	0	0	.000	4	1	0	0.00	0
World Series Totals		8	6¹/₃	0	0	.000	6	3	3	1.42	0

a On disabled list from June 9 to August 1, 2002.
b On disabled list from April 20 to May 6, 2003.
c On disabled list from June 27 to August 21, 2004.
d On disabled list from April 16 to June 4 and June 19 to July 7, 2005.
e Traded to Colorado Rockies with pitcher Denny Bautista for infielder Ryan Shealy and pitcher Scott Dohmann, July 31, 2006.
f Filed for free agency, October 29, 2007. Signed with Cincinnati Reds, January 23, 2008.
g Filed for free agency, October 30, 2008. Signed with San Francisco Giants, November 17, 2008.
h On disabled list from July 21 to August 18, 2010.
i On disabled list from April 28 to May 13, 2012.
j Filed for free agency, November 3, 2012, re-signed with San Francisco Giants, November 14, 2012.

ALBERS, MATTHEW JAMES (MATT)

Born, Houston, Texas, January 20, 1983.
Bats Left. Throws Right. Height, 6 feet. Weight, 205 pounds.

Year	Club	Lea	G	IP	W	L	Pct	SO	BB	H	ERA	SAVES
2002 Martinsville	Appal.	13	59²/₃	2	3	.400	72	38	61	5.13	0
2003 Tri-City	N.Y.-Penn.	15	86¹/₃	5	4	.556	94	25	69	2.92	0
2004 Lexington	So.Atl.	22	111¹/₃	8	3	.727	140	57	95	3.31	0
2005 Salem	Carolina	28	148²/₃	8	12	.400	146	62	161	4.66	0
2006 Corpus Christi	Texas	19	116	10	2	.833	95	47	96	2.17	0
2006 Round Rock	P.C.	4	25	2	1	.667	26	10	24	3.96	0
2006 Houston	N.L.	4	15	0	2	.000	11	7	17	6.00	0
2007 Round Rock	P.C.	9	53	2	3	.400	43	22	50	3.74	0
2007 Houston a	N.L.	31	110²/₃	4	11	.267	71	50	127	5.86	0
2008 Aberdeen	N.Y.-Penn.	2	2	0	0	.000	4	1	1	0.00	0
2008 Baltimore b	A.L.	28	49	3	3	.500	26	22	43	3.49	0
2009 Norfolk	Int.	10	12²/₃	1	0	1.000	12	5	19	5.68	0
2009 Baltimore	A.L.	56	67	3	6	.333	49	36	80	5.51	0
2010 Baltimore c	A.L.	62	75²/₃	5	3	.625	49	34	78	4.52	0
2011 Pawtucket	Int.	2	3	0	0	.000	2	0	1	0.00	0
2011 Boston d	A.L.	56	64²/₃	4	4	.500	68	31	62	4.73	0
2012 Boston	A.L.	40	39¹/₃	2	0	1.000	25	15	30	2.29	0
2012 Arizona e-f	N.L.	23	21	1	1	.500	19	7	16	2.57	0
Major League Totals	7 Yrs.	300	442¹/₃	22	30	.423	318	202	453	4.68	0

a Traded to Baltimore Orioles with pitcher Troy Patton, outfielder Luke Scott, pitcher Dennis Sarfate and infielder Michael Costanzo for infielder Miguel Tejada, December 12, 2007.
b On disabled list from June 26 to October 21, 2008.
c Not offered contract, December 2, 2010. Signed with Boston Red Sox, December 16, 2010.
d On disabled list from April 8 to April 21, 2011.
e Traded to Arizona Diamondbacks with outfielder Scott Podsednik for pitcher Craig Breslow, July 31, 2012.
f Traded to Cleveland Indians with pitcher Trevor Bauer and pitcher Bryan Shaw for infielder Lars Anderson, infielder Didi Gregorius and pitcher Tony Sipp, December 11, 2012.

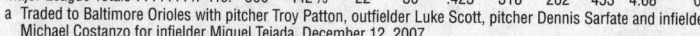

191

ALBURQUERQUE, ALBERTO JOSE (AL)
Born, San Pedro de Macoris, Dominican Republic, June 10, 1986.
Bats Right. Throws Right. Height, 6 feet. Weight, 195 pounds.

Year	Club	Lea	G	IP	W	L	Pct	SO	BB	H	ERA	SAVES
2005				INJURED—Did Not Play								
2006 Cubs	Arizona		8	12²/₃	0	2	.000	15	10	10	5.68	0
2007 Boise	Northwest		10	41	3	2	.600	49	17	42	3.73	1
2007 Peoria	Midwest		11	25¹/₃	1	4	.200	20	12	36	9.24	0
2008 a				INJURED—Did Not Play								
2009 Daytona b	Fla.St.		24	34²/₃	1	0	1.000	44	14	26	2.08	2
2009 Tulsa	Texas		23	26¹/₃	1	3	.250	31	13	23	3.76	0
2010 Tulsa c	Texas		25	34¹/₃	2	4	.333	32	19	32	4.98	3
2011 Toledo	Int.		4	4²/₃	0	0	.000	10	2	5	1.93	0
2011 Detroit d	A.L.		41	43¹/₃	6	1	.857	67	29	21	1.87	0
2012 Lakeland	Fla.St.		4	3¹/₃	0	0	.000	9	1	5	5.40	0
2012 Toledo	Int.		9	10²/₃	1	0	1.000	18	4	9	1.69	0
2012 Detroit e	A.L.		8	13¹/₃	0	0	.000	18	8	6	0.68	0
Major League Totals	2 Yrs.		49	56²/₃	6	1	.857	85	37	27	1.59	0
Division Series												
2011 Detroit	A.L.		2	0¹/₃	0	0	.000	0	1	2	81.00	0
2012 Detroit	A.L.		2	1¹/₃	1	0	1.000	1	0	0	0.00	0
Division Series Totals			4	1²/₃	1	0	1.000	1	1	2	16.20	0
Championship Series												
2011 Detroit	A.L.		2	2²/₃	0	0	.000	2	2	0	0.00	0
World Series Record												
2012 Detroit	A.L.		1	2	0	0	.000	2	0	1	4.50	0

a On minor league disabled list from June 28 to September 1, 2008.
b Traded to Colorado Rockies for outfielder Jeff Baker, July 2, 2009.
c Filed for free agency, November 6, 2010. Signed with Detroit Tigers organization, November 19, 2010.
d On disabled list from June 30 to July 16 and August 12 to September 4, 2011.
e On disabled list from April 4 to August 23, 2012.

ALVAREZ, HENDERSON JAVIER
Born, Valencia, Venezuela, April 18, 1990.
Bats Right. Throws Right. Height, 6 feet, 1 inch. Weight, 210 pounds.

Year	Club	Lea	G	IP	W	L	Pct	SO	BB	H	ERA	SAVES
2008 Blue Jays	Gulf Coast		12	46¹/₃	1	4	.200	34	6	63	5.63	0
2009 Lansing	Midwest		23	124¹/₃	9	6	.600	92	19	121	3.47	0
2010 Dunedin	Fla.St.		23	112¹/₃	8	7	.533	78	27	137	4.33	0
2011 Dunedin	Fla.St.		2	8¹/₃	0	1	.000	4	1	11	6.48	0
2011 New Hampshire	Eastern		15	88	8	4	.667	66	17	81	2.86	0
2011 Toronto	A.L.		10	63²/₃	1	3	.250	40	8	64	3.53	0
2012 Toronto a	A.L.		31	187¹/₃	9	14	.391	79	54	216	4.85	0
Major League Totals	2 Yrs.		41	251	10	17	.370	119	62	280	4.52	0

a Traded to Miami Marlins with infielder Yunel Escobar, infielder Adeiny Hechavarria, catcher Jeff Mathis, pitcher Anthony De Sclafani, outfielder Jake Marisnick and pitcher Justin Nicolino for outfielder Emilio Bonifacio, catcher John Buck, pitcher Mark Buehrle, pitcher Josh Johnson and infielder Jose Reyes, November 19, 2012.

ANDERSON, BRETT FRANKLIN
Born, Midland, Texas, February 1, 1988.
Bats Left. Throws Left. Height, 6 feet, 4 inches. Weight, 235 pounds.

Year	Club	Lea	G	IP	W	L	Pct	SO	BB	H	ERA	SAVES
2007 Visalia	Calif.		9	39	3	3	.500	40	11	50	4.85	0
2007 South Bend a	Midwest		14	81¹/₃	8	4	.667	85	10	76	2.21	0
2008 Stockton	Calif.		14	74	9	4	.692	80	18	68	4.14	0
2008 Midland	Texas		6	31	2	1	.667	38	9	27	2.61	0
2009 Oakland	A.L.		30	175¹/₃	11	11	.500	150	45	180	4.06	0
2010 Athletics	Arizona		2	6	0	0	.000	6	0	11	3.00	0
2010 Sacramento	P.C.		3	13¹/₃	1	0	1.000	12	3	19	4.05	0
2010 Oakland	A.L.		19	112¹/₃	7	6	.538	75	22	112	2.80	0
2011 Oakland	A.L.		13	83¹/₃	3	6	.333	61	25	86	4.00	0
2012 Stockton	Calif.		1	2	0	0	.000	0	0	4	9.00	0
2012 Sacramento	P.C.		5	23¹/₃	1	1	.500	18	5	27	4.24	0
2012 Oakland b	A.L.		6	35	4	2	.667	25	7	29	2.57	0
Major League Totals	4 Yrs.		68	406	25	25	.500	311	99	407	3.57	0
Division Series												
2012 Oakland	A.L.		1	6	1	0	1.000	6	2	2	0.00	0

a Traded by Arizona Diamondbacks to Oakland Athletics with outfielder Carlos Gonzalez, pitcher Dana Eveland, pitcher Greg Smith, infielder Chris Carter and outfielder Aaron Cunningham for pitcher Danny Haren and pitcher Connor Robertson, December 14, 2007.
b On disabled list from March 13 to August 20, 2012.

ARREDONDO, JOSE JUAN
Born, San Pedro de Macoris, Dominican Republic, March 30, 1984.
Bats Right. Throws Right. Height, 6 feet. Weight, 175 pounds.

Year	Club	Lea	G	IP	W	L	Pct	SO	BB	H	ERA	SAVES
2004 Angels	Arizona		8	12$\frac{1}{3}$	0	0	.000	14	4	14	2.92	1
2005 Arkansas	Texas		5	5$\frac{1}{3}$	0	0	.000	4	4	5	3.38	0
2005 Orem	Pioneer		15	68$\frac{2}{3}$	5	0	1.000	60	20	76	4.19	0
2006 Rancho Cucamonga	Calif.		15	90	5	6	.455	115	35	62	2.30	0
2006 Arkansas	Texas		11	60$\frac{2}{3}$	2	3	.400	48	22	80	6.53	0
2007 Arkansas	Texas		23	25	0	1	.000	28	12	16	2.52	10
2007 Rancho Cucamonga	Calif.		28	35	2	4	.333	34	11	46	6.43	4
2007 Salt Lake	P.C.		2	3	0	0	.000	1	2	2	3.00	0
2008 Salt Lake	P.C.		15	17	1	1	.500	15	4	12	2.12	10
2008 Los Angeles	A.L.		52	61	10	2	.833	55	22	42	1.62	0
2009 Salt Lake	P.C.		19	20$\frac{2}{3}$	1	1	.500	24	14	13	2.18	1
2009 Los Angeles	A.L.		43	45	2	3	.400	47	23	47	6.00	0
2010 Cincinnati a-b	N.L.			INJURED—Did Not Play								
2011 Carolina	Southern		6	7$\frac{2}{3}$	1	0	1.000	11	4	4	2.35	0
2011 Louisville	Int.		6	8	1	1	.500	10	2	6	2.25	0
2011 Cincinnati c	N.L.		53	53	4	4	.500	48	31	43	3.23	0
2012 Cincinnati	N.L.		66	61	6	2	.750	62	34	50	2.95	1
Major League Totals		.4 Yrs.	214	220	22	11	.667	212	110	182	3.27	1
Division Series												
2008 Los Angeles	A.L.		3	3$\frac{2}{3}$	0	0	.000	4	2	2	0.00	0
2012 Cincinnati	N.L.		2	1$\frac{1}{3}$	0	0	.000	0	2	4	20.25	0
Division Series Totals			5	5	0	0	.000	4	4	6	5.40	0

a Not offered contract, December 12, 2009. Signed with Cincinnati Reds organization, January 22, 2010.
b On disabled list from July 22 to November 2, 2010.
c On disabled list from March 25 to May 14 and July 7 to July 22, 2011.

ARRIETA, JACOB JOSEPH (JAKE)
Born, Farmington, Missouri, March 6, 1986.
Bats Right. Throws Right. Height, 6 feet, 4 inches. Weight, 225 pounds.

Year	Club	Lea	G	IP	W	L	Pct	SO	BB	H	ERA	SAVES
2008 Frederick	Carolina		20	113	6	5	.545	120	51	80	2.87	0
2009 Bowie	Eastern		11	59	6	3	.667	70	23	45	2.59	0
2009 Norfolk	Int.		17	91$\frac{2}{3}$	5	8	.385	78	33	97	3.93	0
2010 Norfolk	Int.		12	73	6	2	.750	64	34	48	1.85	0
2010 Baltimore	A.L.		18	100$\frac{1}{3}$	6	6	.500	52	48	106	4.66	0
2011 Baltimore b	A.L.		22	119$\frac{1}{3}$	10	8	.556	93	59	115	5.05	0
2012 Norfolk	Int.		10	56	5	4	.556	54	28	46	4.02	0
2012 Baltimore	A.L.		24	114$\frac{2}{3}$	3	9	.250	109	35	122	6.20	0
Major League Totals		.3 Yrs.	64	334$\frac{1}{3}$	19	23	.452	254	142	343	5.33	0

b On disabled list from August 1 to November 2, 2011.

ARROYO, BRONSON ANTHONY
Born, Key West, Florida, February 24, 1977.
Bats Right. Throws Right. Height, 6 feet, 5 inches. Weight, 190 pounds.

Year	Club	Lea	G	IP	W	L	Pct	SO	BB	H	ERA	SAVES
1995 Pirates	Gulf Coast		13	61$\frac{1}{3}$	5	4	.556	48	9	72	4.26	1
1996 Augusta	S.Atl.		26	135$\frac{2}{3}$	8	6	.571	107	36	123	3.52	0
1997 Lynchburg	Carolina		24	160$\frac{1}{3}$	12	4	.750	121	33	154	3.31	0
1998 Carolina a	Southern		23	127	9	8	.529	90	51	158	5.46	0
1999 Altoona	Eastern		25	153	15	4	.789	100	58	167	3.65	0
1999 Nashville	P.C.		3	13	0	0	.000	11	10	22	10.38	0
2000 Nashville	P.C.		13	88$\frac{2}{3}$	8	2	.800	52	25	82	3.65	0
2000 Pittsburgh	N.L.		20	71$\frac{2}{3}$	2	6	.250	50	36	88	6.40	0
2000 Lynchburg	Carolina		1	7	0	0	.000	3	2	8	3.86	0
2001 Pittsburgh	N.L.		24	88$\frac{1}{3}$	5	7	.417	39	34	99	5.09	0
2001 Nashville	P.C.		9	66$\frac{1}{3}$	6	2	.750	49	15	63	3.93	0
2002 Nashville	P.C.		22	143	8	6	.571	116	28	126	2.96	0
2002 Pittsburgh	N.L.		9	27	2	1	.667	22	15	30	4.00	0

Year	Club	Lea	G	IP	W	L	Pct	SO	BB	H	ERA	SAVES
2003 Pawtucket	Int.	24	149$^{2}/_{3}$	12	6	.667	155	23	148	3.43	0
2003 Boston b	A.L.	6	17$^{1}/_{3}$	0	0	.000	14	4	10	2.08	1
2004 Boston	A.L.	32	178$^{2}/_{3}$	10	9	.526	142	47	171	4.03	0
2005 Boston	A.L.	35	205$^{1}/_{3}$	14	10	.583	100	54	213	4.51	0
2006 Cincinnati c	N.L.	35	*240$^{2}/_{3}$	14	11	.560	184	64	222	3.29	0
2007 Cincinnati	N.L.	34	210$^{2}/_{3}$	9	15	.375	156	63	232	4.23	0
2008 Cincinnati	N.L.	34	200	15	11	.577	163	68	219	4.77	0
2009 Cincinnati	N.L.	33	220$^{1}/_{3}$	15	13	.536	127	65	214	3.84	0
2010 Cincinnati	N.L.	33	215$^{2}/_{3}$	17	10	.630	121	59	188	3.88	0
2011 Cincinnati	N.L.	32	199	9	12	.429	108	45	227	5.07	0
2012 Cincinnati	N.L.	32	202	12	10	.545	129	35	209	3.74	0
Major League Totals 13 Yrs.		359	2076$^{2}/_{3}$	124	115	.519	1355	589	2122	4.23	1
Division Series											
2004 Boston	A.L.	1	6	0	0	.000	7	2	3	3.00	0
2005 Boston	A.L.	1	1	0	0	.000	1	2	2	18.00	0
2010 Cincinnati	N.L.	1	5$^{1}/_{3}$	0	0	.000	2	3	4	1.69	0
2012 Cincinnati	N.L.	1	7	1	0	1.000	4	1	1	0.00	0
Division Series Totals		4	19$^{1}/_{3}$	1	0	1.000	14	8	10	2.33	0
Championship Series											
2003 Boston	A.L.	3	3$^{1}/_{3}$	0	0	.000	5	2	2	2.70	0
2004 Boston	A.L.	3	4	0	0	.000	3	2	8	15.75	0
Championship Series Totals		6	7$^{1}/_{3}$	0	0	.000	8	4	10	9.82	0
World Series Record											
2004 Boston	A.L.	2	2$^{2}/_{3}$	0	0	.000	4	1	4	6.75	0

a On minor league disabled list from May 18 to June 7 and June 18 to July 4, 1998.
b Claimed on waivers by Boston Red Sox, February 4, 2003.
c Traded to Cincinnati Reds for outfielder Wily Mo Pena, March 20, 2006.

ATCHISON, SCOTT BARHAM

Born, Denton, Texas, March 29, 1976.
Bats Right. Throws Right. Height, 6 feet, 2 inches. Weight, 200 pounds.

Year	Club	Lea	G	IP	W	L	Pct	SO	BB	H	ERA	SAVES
1999 Wisconsin	Midwest	15	81$^{2}/_{3}$	4	5	.444	85	25	67	3.42	0
2000 Lancaster	Calif.	19	97$^{2}/_{3}$	5	5	.500	77	21	117	3.69	0
2000 Tacoma	P.C.	5	26	1	1	.500	18	6	22	3.81	0
2001 San Antonio	Texas	24	136	9	10	.474	83	28	171	4.24	0
2002 Tacoma	P.C.	27	124$^{1}/_{3}$	5	10	.333	112	31	123	4.63	2
2003 Tacoma	P.C.	39	108$^{2}/_{3}$	6	9	.400	83	37	114	4.31	1
2004 Tacoma	P.C.	40	69$^{1}/_{3}$	5	3	.625	76	26	71	4.15	7
2004 Seattle	A.L.	25	30$^{2}/_{3}$	2	3	.400	36	14	29	3.52	0
2005 Mariners	Arizona	4	5	0	0	.000	9	1	7	5.40	0
2005 San Antonio	Texas	5	6	0	0	.000	8	2	3	0.00	0
2005 Tacoma	P.C.	10	13	0	0	.000	17	5	13	4.15	0
2005 Seattle a	A.L.	6	6$^{2}/_{3}$	0	0	.000	9	1	7	6.75	0
2006 Tacoma b	P.C.	30	50	4	0	1.000	39	15	49	2.34	1
2007 Fresno	P.C.	38	53$^{2}/_{3}$	3	2	.600	51	8	44	2.01	4
2007 San Francisco c	N.L.	22	30$^{2}/_{3}$	0	0	.000	25	10	32	4.11	0
2008 Hanshin	Japan Pac.	42	104$^{2}/_{3}$	7	6	.538	85	26	104	3.70	0
2009 Hanshin d	Japan Pac.	75	90	5	3	.625	81	20	60	1.70	0
2010 Pawtucket	Int.	11	13$^{1}/_{3}$	1	0	1.000	17	5	13	4.05	0
2010 Boston	A.L.	43	60	2	3	.400	41	19	58	4.50	0
2011 Pawtucket	Int.	36	61$^{1}/_{3}$	6	2	.750	72	9	50	2.64	5
2011 Boston	A.L.	17	30$^{1}/_{3}$	1	0	1.000	17	6	31	3.26	1
2012 Pawtucket	Int.	2	2	0	0	.000	2	0	3	13.50	0
2012 Boston e-f	A.L.	42	51$^{1}/_{3}$	2	1	.667	36	9	42	1.58	0
Major League Totals 6 Yrs.		155	209$^{2}/_{3}$	7	7	.500	164	59	199	3.48	1

a On disabled list from April 2 to September 3, 2005.
b Filed for free agency October 15, 2006. Signed with San Francisco Giants organization, November 13, 2006.
c Filed for free agency, November 28, 2007. Signed with Boston Red Sox organization, December 12, 2007.
d Sold to Hanshin (Japan), December 19, 2007. Signed with Boston Red Sox, December 5, 2009.
e On disabled list from July 14 to September 12, 2012.
f Not offered contract, November 30, 2012.

AVILAN, LUIS ARMANDO

Born, Caracas, Venezuela, July 19, 1989.
Bats Left. Throws Left. Height, 6 feet, 2 inches. Weight, 220 pounds.

Year Club	Lea	G	IP	W	L	Pct	SO	BB	H	ERA	SAVES
2008 Braves .... Gulf Coast	10	38$\frac{1}{3}$	0	3	.000	49	15	31	2.58	0
2009 Danville .... Appal.	14	38$\frac{1}{3}$	0	2	.000	34	17	25	3.05	2
2010 Myrtle Beach .... Carolina	31	48	4	3	.571	37	18	42	3.94	9
2010 Rome .... So.Atl.	10	20$\frac{2}{3}$	2	1	.667	21	9	15	2.61	0
2011 Mississippi........ Southern	36	106$\frac{1}{3}$	4	8	.333	78	36	113	4.57	1
2012 Mississippi........ Southern	16	61$\frac{1}{3}$	3	6	.333	55	31	50	3.23	1
2012 Atlanta .... N.L.	31	36	1	0	1.000	33	10	27	2.00	0

AXFORD, JOHN BERTON

Born, Simcoe, Ontario, Canada, April 1, 1983.
Bats Right. Throws Right. Height, 6 feet, 5 inches. Weight, 195 pounds.

Year Club	Lea	G	IP	W	L	Pct	SO	BB	H	ERA	SAVES
2007 Tampa .... Fla.St.	5	11$\frac{1}{3}$	0	0	.000	15	7	6	2.38	2
2007 Scranton/WB .... Int.	1	0$\frac{2}{3}$	0	0	.000	1	1	2	13.50	0
2007 Staten Island ..... N.Y.-Penn.	8	24$\frac{1}{3}$	1	1	.500	30	15	13	2.22	2
2007 Charleston .... So.Atl.	13	26$\frac{2}{3}$	0	3	.000	21	22	29	4.39	0
2008 Brevard County a ..... Fla.St.	26	95	5	10	.333	89	73	86	4.55	0
2009 Brevard County ...... Fla.St.	19	27$\frac{2}{3}$	4	1	.800	43	16	14	1.63	0
2009 Huntsville......... Southern	4	7$\frac{2}{3}$	0	0	.000	9	3	7	3.52	1
2009 Nashville .... P.C.	22	33	5	0	1.000	37	19	23	3.55	0
2009 Milwaukee .... N.L.	7	7$\frac{2}{3}$	0	0	.000	9	6	5	3.52	1
2010 Nashville .... P.C.	12	13$\frac{1}{3}$	3	2	.600	19	5	14	2.03	2
2010 Milwaukee .... N.L.	50	58	8	2	.800	76	27	42	2.48	24
2011 Milwaukee .... N.L.	74	73$\frac{2}{3}$	2	2	.500	86	25	59	1.95	*46
2012 Milwaukee .... N.L.	75	69$\frac{1}{3}$	5	8	.385	93	39	61	4.67	35
Major League Totals ....4 Yrs.	206	208$\frac{2}{3}$	15	12	.556	264	97	167	3.06	106
Division Series										
2011 Milwaukee .... N.L.	3	4	1	0	1.000	5	2	3	2.25	1
Championship Series										
2011 Milwaukee .... N.L.	3	3	0	0	.000	4	0	2	0.00	2

a Released by New York Yankees, December 14, 2007. Signed with Milwaukee Brewers organization, March 4, 2008.

AYALA, LUIS IGNACIO

Born, Los Mochis, Mexico, January 12, 1978.
Bats Right. Throws Right. Height, 6 feet, 2 inches. Weight, 190 pounds.

Year Club	Lea	G	IP	W	L	Pct	SO	BB	H	ERA	SAVES
1997 Saltillo .... Mexican	37	62	7	5	.583	30	21	76	4.62	0
1998 Saltillo .... Mexican	47	83	7	8	.467	29	45	105	5.62	7
1999 Saltillo a .... Mexican	61	79	7	3	.700	28	22	54	1.71	41
2000 Saltillo .... Mexican	55	65	5	3	.625	38	13	69	2.76	25
2001 Salem............ Carolina	13	13$\frac{1}{3}$	0	1	.000	10	5	19	4.05	7
2001 Saltillo b .... Mexican	33	40	1	2	.333	34	11	34	2.03	21
2002 Saltillo .... Mexican	49	54	3	5	.375	43	15	43	1.68	23
2002 Ottawa c-d-e .... Int.	6	7$\frac{2}{3}$	0	0	.000	6	4	7	3.52	0
2003 Expos........... Gulf Coast	2	3$\frac{2}{3}$	0	0	.000	2	2	2	0.00	0
2003 Montreal f .... N.L.	65	71	10	3	.769	46	13	65	2.92	5
2004 Montreal............. N.L.	81	90$\frac{1}{3}$	6	12	.333	63	15	92	2.69	2
2005 Washington .... N.L.	68	71	4	7	.533	40	14	75	2.66	1
2006 Washington g......... N.L.	INJURED—Did Not Play									
2007 Potomac........... Carolina	3	2$\frac{2}{3}$	0	0	.000	1	1	1	0.00	0
2007 Columbus............. Int.	5	7	0	0	.000	5	2	4	1.29	0
2007 Washington h......... N.L.	44	42$\frac{1}{3}$	2	2	.500	28	12	43	3.19	1
2008 Washington-New York i .. N.L.	81	75$\frac{2}{3}$	2	10	.167	50	24	86	5.71	9
2009 Minnesota .... A.L.	28	32$\frac{1}{3}$	1	2	.333	21	8	38	4.18	0
2009 New Orleans.......... P.C.	9	10	0	0	.000	10	3	4	0.00	4
2009 Florida j-k-l......... N.L.	10	7$\frac{2}{3}$	0	3	.000	7	6	12	11.74	0
2010 Albuquerque......... P.C.	14	14	1	3	.250	10	7	14	4.50	4
2010 Colorado Springs....... P.C.	4	7$\frac{1}{3}$	1	1	.500	4	0	8	4.91	0
2010 Reno m-n-o .... P.C.	18	26$\frac{1}{3}$	0	6	.000	17	11	38	7.86	0
2011 Scranton-WB........... Int.	3	5	0	0	.000	7	0	6	1.80	0
2011 New York p-q.......... A.L.	52	56	2	2	.500	39	20	51	2.09	0
2012 Baltimore .... A.L.	66	75	5	5	.500	51	14	81	2.64	1
Major League Totals ....8 Yrs.	495	521$\frac{1}{3}$	36	46	.439	345	126	543	3.35	19

Year	Club	Lea	G	IP	W	L	Pct	SO	BB	H	ERA	SAVES
	Division Series											
2011 New York		A.L.	2	1⅓	0	0	.000	0	0	3	6.75	0
2012 Baltimore		A.L.	1	0⅓	0	0	.000	1	0	2	0.00	0
Division Series Totals			3	1⅔	0	0	.000	1	0	5	5.40	0

a Sold to Colorado Rockies by Saltillo (Mexican), October 14, 1999.
b Sold to Saltillo (Mexican), May 15, 2001.
c Sold to Montreal Expos, August 18, 2002.
d Filed for free agency, October 15, 2002. Signed with Arizona Diamondbacks organization, October 23, 2002.
e Selected by Montreal Expos organization in Rule V draft, December 16, 2002.
f On disabled list from June 22 to July 21, 2003.
g On disabled list from March 24 to October 9, 2006.
h On disabled list from March 28 to June 20, 2007.
i Traded to New York Mets for player to be named later, August 17, 2008. Washington Nationals received infielder Anderson Hernandez to complete trade, August 20, 2008.
j Filed for free agency, October 31, 2008. Signed with Minnesota Twins, February 18, 2009.
k Released by Minnesota Twins, June 30, 2009. Signed with Florida Marlins organization, July 2, 2009.
l Filed for free agency, September 4, 2009. Signed with Los Angeles Dodgers organization, December 17, 2009.
m Released by Los Angeles Dodgers, May 17, 2010. Signed with Arizona Diamondbacks organization, May 20, 2010.
n Released by Arizona Diamondbacks, July 16, 2010. Signed with Colorado Rockies organization, August 27, 2010.
o Released by Colorado Rockies, November 22, 2010. Signed with New York Yankees organization, February 11, 2011.
p On disabled list from April 13 to May 11, 2011.
q Filed for free agency, October 30, 2011. Signed with Baltimore Orioles, February 10, 2012.

BADENHOP, BURKE HEINRICH
Born, Atlanta, Georgia, February 8, 1983.
Bats Right. Throws Right. Height, 6 feet, 5 inches. Weight, 220 pounds.

Year	Club	Lea	G	IP	W	L	Pct	SO	BB	H	ERA	SAVES
2005 Oneonta		N.Y.-Penn.	14	77	6	4	.600	55	26	69	2.92	0
2006 West Michigan		Midwest	27	171	14	3	.824	124	31	170	2.84	0
2007 Erie		Eastern	3	18⅔	2	0	1.000	12	3	8	1.45	0
2007 Lakeland a		Fla.St.	23	135⅓	10	6	.625	78	34	130	3.13	0
2008 Carolina		Southern	1	6⅓	1	0	1.000	3	0	6	0.00	0
2008 Florida		N.L.	13	47⅓	2	3	.400	35	21	55	6.08	0
2008 Marlins		Gulf Coast	1	3	0	0	.000	2	0	1	0.00	0
2009 Marlins		Gulf Coast	2	3	0	1	.000	4	0	2	0.00	0
2009 Jupiter		Fla.St.	2	8	0	0	.000	8	1	2	0.00	0
2009 New Orleans		P.C.	2	9⅓	0	1	.000	6	4	14	6.75	0
2009 Florida b		N.L.	35	72	7	4	.636	57	24	71	3.75	0
2010 New Orleans		P.C.	12	16	0	1	.000	9	7	16	2.81	0
2010 Florida		N.L.	53	67⅔	2	5	.286	47	21	62	3.99	1
2011 New Orleans		P.C.	11	14⅔	1	1	.500	10	7	20	6.75	1
2011 Florida c		N.L.	50	63⅔	2	3	.400	51	24	65	4.10	1
2012 Tampa Bay d		A.L.	66	62⅓	3	2	.600	42	12	63	3.03	0
Major League Totals		5 Yrs.	217	313	16	17	.485	232	102	316	4.08	2

a Traded by Detroit Tigers to Florida Marlins with pitcher Eulogio De La Cruz, pitcher Andrew Miller, catcher Mike Rabelo and outfielder Cameron Maybin for pitcher Dontrelle Willis and infielder Miguel Cabrera, December 5, 2007.
b On disabled list from August 2 to September 1, 2009.
c Traded to Tampa Bay Rays for catcher Jake Jefferies, December 12, 2011.
d Traded to Milwaukee Brewers for outfielder Raul Mondesi, December 1, 2012.

BAILEY, ANDREW SCOTT
Born, Voorhees, New Jersey, May 31, 1984.
Bats Right. Throws Right. Height, 6 feet, 3 inches. Weight, 235 pounds.

Year	Club	Lea	G	IP	W	L	Pct	SO	BB	H	ERA	SAVES
2006 Vancouver		Northwest	13	58	2	5	.286	53	20	39	2.02	0
2007 Stockton		Calif.	11	66	3	4	.429	72	31	56	3.82	0
2007 Kane County		Midwest	11	51	1	4	.200	74	22	42	3.35	0
2007 Sacramento		P.C.	1	8	1	0	1.000	4	1	3	1.13	0
2008 Midland		Texas	37	110⅓	5	9	.357	110	56	99	4.32	0
2009 Oakland a		A.L.	68	83⅓	6	3	.667	91	24	49	1.84	26
2010 Sacramento		P.C.	1	0⅔	0	0	.000	1	0	3	27.00	0
2010 Oakland b		A.L.	47	49	1	3	.250	42	13	34	1.47	25
2011 Sacramento		P.C.	4	4	0	0	.000	3	1	3	0.00	0
2011 Oakland c-d		A.L.	42	41⅔	0	4	.000	41	12	34	3.24	24
2012 Red Sox		Gulf Coast	2	2	0	0	.000	4	1	2	0.00	0
2012 Portland		Eastern	1	1	0	0	.000	2	0	3	9.00	0
2012 Pawtucket		Int.	3	3⅓	0	0	.000	4	0	1	0.00	0

Year Club	Lea	G	IP	W	L	Pct	SO	BB	H	ERA	SAVES
2012 Boston e............A.L.	A.L.	19	15$\frac{1}{3}$	1	1	.500	14	8	21	7.04	6
Major League Totals ....4 Yrs.		176	189$\frac{1}{3}$	8	11	.421	188	57	138	2.47	81

a Selected Rookie of the Year in American League for 2009.
b On disabled list from July 21 to August 22, 2010.
c On disabled list from March 22 to May 29, 2011.
d Traded to Boston Red Sox with outfielder Ryan Sweeney for outfielder Josh Reddick, infielder Miles Head and pitcher Raul Alcantara, December 28, 2011.
e On disabled list from April 4 to August 14, 2012.

BAILEY, DAVID DEWITT (HOMER)
Born, LaGrange, Texas, May 3, 1986.
Bats Right. Throws Right. Height, 6 feet, 4 inches. Weight, 210 pounds.

Year Club	Lea	G	IP	W	L	Pct	SO	BB	H	ERA	SAVES
2004 Reds...........Gulf Coast	Gulf Coast	6	12$\frac{1}{3}$	0	1	.000	9	3	14	4.38	0
2005 Dayton...........Midwest	Midwest	28	103$\frac{2}{3}$	8	4	.667	125	62	89	4.43	0
2006 Sarasota...........Fla.St.	Fla.St.	13	70$\frac{2}{3}$	3	5	.375	79	22	49	3.31	0
2006 Chattanooga.......Southern	Southern	13	68	7	1	.875	77	28	50	1.59	0
2007 Louisville.............Int.	Int.	12	67$\frac{1}{3}$	6	3	.667	59	32	49	3.07	0
2007 Sarasota.............Fla.St.	Fla.St.	2	8	0	1	.000	7	5	15	10.13	0
2007 Cincinnati.............N.L.	N.L.	9	45$\frac{1}{3}$	4	2	.667	28	28	43	5.76	0
2008 Cincinnati.............N.L.	N.L.	8	36$\frac{1}{3}$	0	6	.000	18	17	59	7.93	0
2008 Louisville.............Int.	Int.	19	111$\frac{1}{3}$	4	7	.364	96	46	118	4.77	0
2009 Louisville.............Int.	Int.	14	89$\frac{2}{3}$	8	5	.615	82	27	87	2.71	0
2009 Cincinnati.............N.L.	N.L.	20	113$\frac{1}{3}$	8	5	.615	86	52	115	4.53	0
2010 Dayton...........Midwest	Midwest	1	4	0	1	.000	5	1	4	6.75	0
2010 Louisville.............Int.	Int.	4	19	2	0	1.000	15	5	15	2.37	0
2010 Cincinnati a...........N.L.	N.L.	19	109	4	3	.571	100	40	109	4.46	0
2011 Louisville.............Int.	Int.	6	30	2	1	.667	22	6	34	3.00	0
2011 Cincinnati b...........N.L.	N.L.	22	132	9	7	.563	106	33	136	4.43	0
2012 Cincinnati.............N.L.	N.L.	33	208	13	10	.565	168	52	206	3.68	0
Major League Totals ....6 Yrs.		111	644	38	33	.535	506	222	668	4.50	0
Division Series											
2010 Cincinnati.............N.L.	N.L.	1	2	0	0	.000	2	0	2	0.00	0
2012 Cincinnati.............N.L.	N.L.	1	7	0	0	.000	10	1	1	1.29	0
Division Series Totals...........		2	9	0	0	.000	12	1	3	1.00	0

a On disabled list from May 24 to August 15, 2010.
b On disabled list from March 24 to May 5 and May 27 to June 26, 2011.

BALFOUR, GRANT ROBERT
Born, Sydney, New South Wales, Australia, December 30, 1977.
Bats Right. Throws Right. Height, 6 feet, 2 inches. Weight, 190 pounds.

Year Club	Lea	G	IP	W	L	Pct	SO	BB	H	ERA	SAVES
1997 Twins...........Gulf Coast	Gulf Coast	13	67	2	4	.333	43	20	73	3.76	0
1998 Elizabethtn.........Appal.	Appal.	13	77$\frac{2}{3}$	7	2	.778	75	27	70	3.36	0
1999 Quad Cities........Midwest	Midwest	19	91$\frac{2}{3}$	8	5	.615	95	37	66	3.53	1
2000 Fort Myers.........Fla.St.	Fla.St.	35	89	8	5	.615	90	34	91	4.25	6
2001 New Britain........Eastern	Eastern	35	50	2	1	.667	72	22	26	1.08	13
2001 Minnesota.............A.L.	A.L.	2	2$\frac{2}{3}$	0	0	.000	2	3	3	13.50	0
2001 Edmonton.............P.C.	P.C.	11	16$\frac{1}{3}$	2	2	.500	17	10	18	5.51	0
2002 Edmonton.............P.C.	P.C.	58	71$\frac{1}{3}$	2	4	.333	88	30	60	4.16	8
2003 Rochester.............Int.	Int.	21	71	5	2	.714	87	16	48	2.41	5
2003 Minnesota.............A.L.	A.L.	17	26	1	0	1.000	30	14	23	4.15	0
2004 Minnesota a...........A.L.	A.L.	36	39$\frac{1}{3}$	4	1	.800	42	21	35	4.35	0
2005 Minnesota b...........A.L.	A.L.	INJURED—Did Not Play									
2006 Sarasota...........Fla.St,	Fla.St,	5	5$\frac{2}{3}$	0	0	.000	7	3	8	7.94	0
2006 Reds...........Gulf Coast	Gulf Coast	2	1$\frac{1}{3}$	0	0	.000	2	3	1	13.50	0
2006 Dayton c-d........Midwest	Midwest	2	2	0	0	.000	3	0	0	0.00	0
2007 Huntsville.......Southern	Southern	8	11$\frac{1}{3}$	0	0	.000	21	4	8	2.38	2
2007 Nashville.............P.C.	P.C.	24	32	1	1	.500	47	11	17	1.69	5
2007 Milwaukee e-f.........N.L.	N.L.	3	2$\frac{2}{3}$	0	2	.000	3	4	4	20.25	0
2007 Tampa Bay.............A.L.	A.L.	22	22	1	0	1.000	27	16	26	6.14	0
2008 Durham.............Int.	Int.	15	23$\frac{2}{3}$	1	0	1.000	39	10	5	0.38	8
2008 Tampa Bay.............A.L.	A.L.	51	58$\frac{1}{3}$	6	2	.750	82	24	28	1.54	4
2009 Tampa Bay.............A.L.	A.L.	73	67$\frac{1}{3}$	5	4	.556	69	33	59	4.81	4
2010 Charlotte...........Fla.St.	Fla.St.	2	1$\frac{2}{3}$	0	1	.000	2	3	2	10.80	0
2010 Tampa Bay g-h.........A.L.	A.L.	57	55$\frac{1}{3}$	2	1	.667	56	17	43	2.28	0
2011 Sacramento...........P.C.	P.C.	1	1	0	0	.000	0	1	2	9.00	0

Year	Club	Lea	G	IP	W	L	Pct	SO	BB	H	ERA	SAVES
2011 Oakland i	A.L.	62	62	5	2	.714	59	20	44	2.47	2	
2012 Oakland	A.L.	75	74²/₃	3	2	.600	72	28	41	2.53	24	
Major League Totals ....9 Yrs.		398	410¹/₃	27	14	.659	442	180	306	3.38	34	
Division Series												
2004 Minnesota	A.L.	2	2²/₃	0	0	.000	2	0	0	0.00	0	
2008 Tampa Bay	A.L.	3	3¹/₃	0	0	.000	4	1	2	0.00	0	
2010 Tampa Bay	A.L.	3	3²/₃	0	0	.000	1	0	2	0.00	0	
2012 Oakland	A.L.	2	1²/₃	0	1	.000	2	1	3	5.40	1	
Division Series Totals		10	11¹/₃	0	1	.000	9	2	7	0.79	1	
Championship Series												
2008 Tampa Bay	A.L.	4	2¹/₃	0	0	.000	1	4	5	19.29	0	
World Series Record												
2008 Tampa Bay	A.L.	3	3	0	0	.000	2	3	4	3.00	0	

a On disabled list from April 4 to May 14 and August 2 to August 17, 2004.
b On disabled list from March 25 to October 14, 2005.
c Filed for free agency, October 15, 2005. Signed with Cincinnati Reds organization, January 12, 2006.
d On disabled list from March 31 to October 3, 2006.
e Claimed on waivers by Milwaukee Brewers, October 5, 2006.
f Traded to Tampa Bay Devil Rays for pitcher Seth McClung, July 27, 2007.
g On disabled list from July 30 to September 1, 2010.
h Filed for free agency, November 1, 2010. Signed with Oakland Athletics, January 18, 2011.
i On disabled list from June 22 to July 7, 2011.

BASS, ANTHONY E.

Born, Dearborn, Michigan, November 1, 1987.
Bats Right. Throws Right. Height, 6 feet, 2 inches. Weight, 190 pounds.

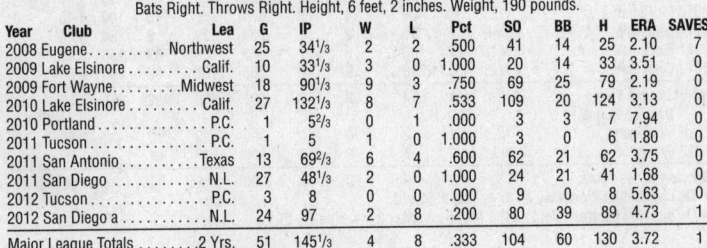

Year	Club	Lea	G	IP	W	L	Pct	SO	BB	H	ERA	SAVES
2008 Eugene..........	Northwest	25	34¹/₃	2	2	.500	41	14	25	2.10	7
2009 Lake Elsinore	Calif.	10	33¹/₃	3	0	1.000	20	14	33	3.51	0
2009 Fort Wayne........	Midwest	18	90¹/₃	9	3	.750	69	25	79	2.19	0
2010 Lake Elsinore	Calif.	27	132¹/₃	8	7	.533	109	20	124	3.13	0
2010 Portland..............	P.C.	1	5²/₃	0	1	.000	3	3	7	7.94	0
2011 Tucson..............	P.C.	1	5	1	0	1.000	3	0	6	1.80	0
2011 San Antonio..........	Texas	13	69²/₃	6	4	.600	62	21	62	3.75	0
2011 San Diego	N.L.	27	48¹/₃	2	0	1.000	24	21	41	1.68	0
2012 Tucson	P.C.	3	8	0	0	.000	9	0	8	5.63	0
2012 San Diego a	N.L.	24	97	2	8	.200	80	39	89	4.73	1
Major League Totals ....2 Yrs.		51	145¹/₃	4	8	.333	104	60	130	3.72	1

a On disabled list from June 21 to September 4, 2012.

BASTARDO, ANTONIO FRANCISCO

Born, Hato Mayor, Dominican Republic, September 21, 1985.
Bats Right. Throws Left. Height, 5 feet, 11 inches. Weight, 195 pounds.

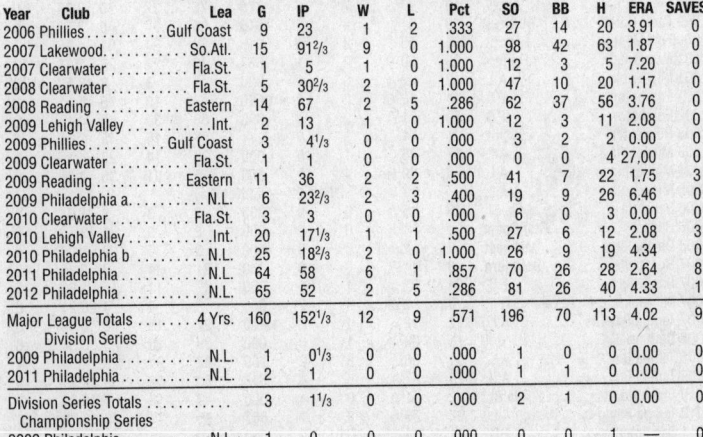

Year	Club	Lea	G	IP	W	L	Pct	SO	BB	H	ERA	SAVES
2006 Phillies..........	Gulf Coast	9	23	1	2	.333	27	14	20	3.91	0
2007 Lakewood...........	So.Atl.	15	91²/₃	9	0	1.000	98	42	63	1.87	0
2007 Clearwater	Fla.St.	1	5	1	0	1.000	12	3	5	7.20	0
2008 Clearwater	Fla.St.	5	30²/₃	2	0	1.000	47	10	20	1.17	0
2008 Reading	Eastern	14	67	2	5	.286	62	37	56	3.76	0
2009 Lehigh Valley ....Int.		2	13	1	0	1.000	12	3	11	2.08	0
2009 Phillies..........	Gulf Coast	3	4¹/₃	0	0	.000	3	2	2	0.00	0
2009 Clearwater	Fla.St.	1	1	0	0	.000	0	0	4	27.00	0
2009 Reading	Eastern	11	36	2	2	.500	41	7	22	1.75	3
2009 Philadelphia a..........	N.L.	6	23²/₃	2	3	.400	19	9	26	6.46	0
2010 Clearwater	Fla.St.	3	3	0	0	.000	6	0	3	0.00	0
2010 Lehigh Valley ....Int.		20	17¹/₃	1	1	.500	27	6	12	2.08	3
2010 Philadelphia b	N.L.	25	18²/₃	2	0	1.000	26	9	19	4.34	0
2011 Philadelphia	N.L.	64	58	6	1	.857	70	26	28	2.64	8
2012 Philadelphia	N.L.	65	52	2	5	.286	81	26	40	4.33	1
Major League Totals ....4 Yrs.		160	152¹/₃	12	9	.571	196	70	113	4.02	9
Division Series												
2009 Philadelphia	N.L.	1	0¹/₃	0	0	.000	1	0	0	0.00	0
2011 Philadelphia	N.L.	2	1	0	0	.000	1	1	0	0.00	0
Division Series Totals		3	1¹/₃	0	0	.000	2	1	0	0.00	0
Championship Series												
2009 Philadelphia	N.L.	1	0	0	0	.000	0	0	1	—	0

Year	Club	Lea	G	IP	W	L	Pct	SO	BB	H	ERA	SAVES
2010 Philadelphia	N.L.	1	$0^{1}/_{3}$	0	0	.000	0	0	1	0.00	0
Championship Series Totals		2	$0^{1}/_{3}$	0	0	.000	0	0	2	0.00	0

a On disabled list from June 26 to September 3, 2009.
b On disabled list from June 16 to July 15, 2010.

BATISTA (DECARTES), MIGUEL JEREZ

Born, Santo Domingo, Dominican Republic, February 19, 1971.
Bats Right. Throws Right. Height, 6 feet. Weight, 210 pounds.

Year	Club	Lea	G	IP	W	L	Pct	SO	BB	H	ERA	SAVES
1988 Expos...........	Dominican	0	0	0	0	.000	0	0	0	0.00	0
1989 Expos...........	Dominican	0	0	0	0	.000	0	0	0	0.00	0
1990 Expos..........	Gulf Coast	9	$39^{1}/_{3}$	4	3	.571	21	17	33	2.06	0
1990 Rockford	Midwest	3	$12^{1}/_{3}$	0	1	.000	7	5	16	8.76	0
1991 Rockford	Midwest	23	$133^{2}/_{3}$	11	5	.688	90	57	126	4.04	0
1992 Pittsburgh	N.L.	1	2	0	0	.000	1	3	4	9.00	0
1992 Wst Plm Bch a	Fla.St.	24	$135^{1}/_{3}$	7	7	.500	92	54	130	3.79	0
1993 Harrisburg	Eastern	26	141	13	5	.722	91	86	139	4.34	0
1994 Harrisburg b.......	Eastern	3	$11^{1}/_{3}$	0	1	.000	5	9	8	2.38	0
1995 Charlotte	Int.	34	$116^{1}/_{3}$	6	12	.333	58	60	118	4.80	0
1996 Charlotte	Int.	47	77	4	3	.571	56	39	93	5.38	4
1996 Florida c...........	N.L.	9	$11^{1}/_{3}$	0	0	.000	6	7	9	5.56	0
1997 Iowa...............	A.A.	31	122	9	4	.692	95	38	117	4.20	0
1997 Chicago d...........	N.L.	11	$36^{1}/_{3}$	0	5	.000	27	24	36	5.70	0
1998 Montreal............	N.L.	56	135	3	5	.375	92	65	141	3.80	0
1999 Montreal............	N.L.	39	$134^{2}/_{3}$	8	7	.533	95	58	146	4.88	1
1999 Ottawa e.............	Int.	3	8	0	1	.000	7	4	3	2.25	0
2000 Montreal............	N.L.	4	$8^{1}/_{3}$	0	1	.000	7	3	19	14.04	0
2000 Kansas City	A.L.	14	57	2	6	.250	30	34	66	7.74	0
2000 Omaha f-g	P.C.	18	$28^{1}/_{3}$	2	2	.500	27	7	35	6.04	3
2001 Arizona............	N.L.	48	$139^{1}/_{3}$	11	8	.579	90	60	113	3.36	0
2002 Arizona............	N.L.	36	$184^{2}/_{3}$	8	9	.471	112	70	172	4.29	0
2003 Arizona h...........	N.L.	36	$193^{1}/_{3}$	10	9	.526	142	60	197	3.54	0
2004 Toronto	A.L.	38	$198^{2}/_{3}$	10	13	.435	104	*96	206	4.80	5
2005 Toronto i...........	A.L.	71	$74^{2}/_{3}$	5	8	.385	54	27	80	4.10	31
2006 Arizona j...........	A.L.	34	$206^{1}/_{3}$	11	8	.579	110	84	231	4.58	0
2007 Seattle	A.L.	33	193	16	11	.593	133	85	209	4.29	0
2008 Seattle	A.L.	44	115	4	14	.222	73	79	135	6.26	1
2009 Seattle	A.L.	56	$71^{1}/_{3}$	7	4	.636	52	39	79	4.04	1
2010 Washington k.........	N.L.	58	$82^{2}/_{3}$	1	2	.333	55	39	71	3.70	2
2011 Buffalo	Int.	10	$46^{2}/_{3}$	3	0	1.000	36	25	46	4.24	0
2011 St. Louis-New York l-m-n	N.L.	35	60	5	2	.714	31	33	49	3.60	0
2012 Binghamton	Eastern	1	7	0	1	.000	3	4	4	5.14	0
2012 Gwinnett.............	Int.	6	24	1	1	.500	21	10	19	3.38	0
2012 New York-Atlanta o-p-q	N.L.	35	$52^{2}/_{3}$	1	3	.250	36	33	58	4.61	0
Major League Totals ...... 18 Yrs.		658	$1956^{1}/_{3}$	102	115	.470	1250	899	2021	4.48	41
Division Series											
2001 Arizona...............	N.L.	2	$6^{2}/_{3}$	1	0	1.000	4	1	3	2.70	0
2002 Arizona...............	N.L.	1	$3^{2}/_{3}$	0	1	.000	1	3	5	9.82	0
Division Series Totals		3	$10^{1}/_{3}$	1	1	.500	5	4	8	5.23	0
Championship Series											
2001 Arizona...............	N.L.	2	7	0	1	.000	3	4	5	5.14	0
World Series Record											
2001 Arizona...............	N.L.	2	8	0	0	.000	6	5	5	0.00	0

a Selected by Pittsburgh Pirates from Montreal Expos in Rule V draft, December 9, 1991. Returned by Pittsburgh Pirates, April 23, 1992.
b Released by Montreal Expos, November 18, 1994. Signed with Florida Marlins organization, December 9, 1994.
c Claimed on waivers by Chicago Cubs, December 17, 1996.
d Traded to Montreal Expos for outfielder Henry Rodriguez, December 12, 1997.
e On disabled list from July 16 to August 10, 1999.
f Traded to Kansas City Royals for pitcher Brad Rigby, April 25, 2000.
g Filed for free agency, October 2, 2000. Signed with Arizona Diamondbacks, November 15, 2000.
h Filed for free agency, November 7, 2003. Signed with Toronto Blue Jays, December 12, 2003.
i Traded to Arizona Diamondbacks with infielder Orlando Hudson for infielder Troy Glaus and infielder Sergio Santos, December 27, 2005.
j Filed for free agency, October 30, 2006. Signed with Seattle Mariners, December 14, 2006.
k Filed for free agency, November 6, 2009. Signed with Washington Nationals organization, January 29, 2010.
l Filed for free agency, November 1, 2010. Signed with St. Louis Cardinals organization, January 14, 2011.
m Released by St. Louis Cardinals, June 22, 2011. Signed with New York Mets organization, July 4, 2011.

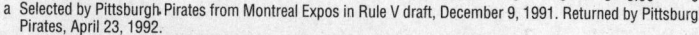

n Filed for free agency, October 30, 2011. Signed with New York Mets organization, January 10, 2012.
o On disabled list from May 20 to June 5, 2012.
p Released by New York Mets, July 24, 2012. Signed with Atlanta Braves organization, July 27, 2012.
q Filed for free agency, November 3, 2012.

BAUER, TREVOR ANDREW
Born, North Hollywood, California, January 17, 1991.
Bats Right. Throws Right. Height, 6 feet, 1 inch. Weight, 185 pounds.

Year	Club	Lea	G	IP	W	L	Pct	SO	BB	H	ERA	SAVES
2011	Visalia	Calif.	3	9	0	1	.000	17	4	7	3.00	0
2011	Mobile	Southern	4	$16^2/3$	1	1	.500	26	8	20	7.56	0
2012	Mobile	Southern	8	$48^1/3$	7	1	.875	60	26	33	1.68	0
2012	Reno	P.C.	14	82	5	1	.833	97	35	74	2.85	0
2012	Arizona a	N.L.	4	$16^1/3$	1	2	.333	17	13	14	6.06	0

a Traded to Cleveland Indians with pitcher Matt Albers and pitcher Bryan Shaw for infielder Lars Anderson, infielder Didi Gregorius and pitcher Tony Sipp, December 11, 2012.

BEACHY, BRANDON ALAN
Born, Kokomo, Indiana, September 3, 1986.
Bats Right. Throws Right. Height, 6 feet, 3 inches. Weight, 215 pounds.

Year	Club	Lea	G	IP	W	L	Pct	SO	BB	H	ERA	SAVES
2008	Danville	Appal.	6	12	2	0	1.000	16	2	12	2.25	0
2009	Rome	So.Atl.	12	$17^2/3$	0	0	.000	17	4	20	5.60	0
2009	Mississippi	Southern	1	1	0	0	.000	0	0	1	0.00	0
2009	Myrtle Beach	Carolina	22	58	4	3	.571	47	15	59	3.41	1
2010	Mississippi	Southern	27	$73^2/3$	3	1	.750	100	22	53	1.47	1
2010	Gwinnett	Int.	8	$45^2/3$	2	0	1.000	48	6	40	2.17	1
2010	Atlanta	N.L.	3	15	0	2	.000	15	7	16	3.00	0
2011	Gwinnett	Int.	1	5	1	0	1.000	8	2	4	1.80	0
2011	Atlanta a	N.L.	25	$141^2/3$	7	3	.700	169	46	125	3.68	0
2012	Atlanta b	N.L.	13	81	5	5	.500	68	29	49	2.00	0
Major League Totals		3 Yrs.	41	$237^2/3$	12	10	.545	252	82	190	3.07	

a On disabled list from May 14 to June 22, 2011.
b On disabled list from June 16 to October 10, 2012.

BEAVAN, BLAKE WILLIAM
Born, Irving, Texas, January 17, 1989.
Bats Right. Throws Right. Height, 6 feet, 7 inches. Weight, 240 pounds.

Year	Club	Lea	G	IP	W	L	Pct	SO	BB	H	ERA	SAVES
2008	Clinton	Midwest	23	$121^2/3$	10	6	.625	73	20	105	2.37	0
2009	Bakersfield	Calif.	12	$73^1/3$	5	4	.556	51	16	75	4.30	0
2009	Frisco	Texas	15	$89^2/3$	4	4	.500	34	13	113	4.01	0
2010	Tacoma	P.C.	7	$40^1/3$	2	2	.500	22	8	56	6.47	0
2010	West Tenn	Southern	3	18	2	1	.667	11	1	18	5.00	0
2010	Frisco a	Texas	17	110	10	5	.667	68	12	100	2.78	0
2011	Tacoma	P.C.	16	93	5	3	.625	64	20	118	4.45	0
2011	Seattle	A.L.	15	97	5	6	.455	42	15	106	4.27	0
2012	Tacoma a	P.C.	6	38	4	0	1.000	15	9	39	2.61	0
2012	Seattle	A.L.	26	$152^1/3$	11	11	.500	67	24	168	4.43	0
Major League Totals		2 Yrs.	41	$249^1/3$	16	17	.485	109	39	274	4.37	0

a Traded by Texas Rangers to Seattle Mariners with infielder Justin Smoak, pitcher Josh Lueke and infielder Matt Lawson for pitcher Cliff Lee, pitcher Mark Lowe and cash, July 9, 2010.

BECKETT, JOSHUA PATRICK (JOSH)
Born, Spring, Texas, May 15, 1980.
Bats Right. Throws Right. Height, 6 feet, 5 inches. Weight, 220 pounds.

Year	Club	Lea	G	IP	W	L	Pct	SO	BB	H	ERA	SAVES
2000	Kane County	Midwest	13	$59^1/3$	2	3	.400	61	15	45	2.12	0
2001	Brevard County	Fla.St.	13	$65^2/3$	6	0	1.000	101	15	32	1.23	0
2001	Portland	Eastern	13	$74^1/3$	8	1	.889	102	19	50	1.82	0
2001	Florida	N.L.	4	24	2	2	.500	24	11	14	1.50	0
2002	Marlins	Gulf Coast	1	4	0	0	.000	7	1	5	4.50	0
2002	Jupiter	Fla.St.	1	6	1	0	1.000	12	1	4	0.00	0
2002	Florida a	N.L.	23	$107^2/3$	6	7	.462	113	44	93	4.10	0
2003	Carolina	Southern	1	4	0	0	.000	7	0	4	4.50	0
2003	Jupiter	Fla.St.	1	3	0	0	.000	5	0	2	0.00	0

Year Club	Lea	G	IP	W	L	Pct	SO	BB	H	ERA	SAVES
2003 Florida b	N.L.	24	142	9	8	.529	152	56	132	3.04	0
2004 Florida c	N.L.	26	156²/₃	9	9	.500	152	54	137	3.79	0
2005 Florida d-e	N.L.	29	178²/₃	15	8	.652	166	58	153	3.38	0
2006 Boston	A.L.	33	204²/₃	16	11	.593	158	74	191	5.01	0
2007 Boston f	A.L.	30	200²/₃	*20	7	.741	194	40	189	3.27	0
2008 Boston g	A.L.	27	174¹/₃	12	10	.545	172	34	173	4.03	0
2009 Boston	A.L.	32	212¹/₃	17	6	.739	199	55	198	3.86	0
2010 Pawtucket	Int.	2	8	0	0	.000	7	1	7	4.50	0
2010 Boston h	A.L.	21	127²/₃	6	6	.500	116	45	151	5.78	0
2011 Boston	A.L.	30	193	13	7	.650	175	52	146	2.89	0
2012 Boston	A.L.	21	127¹/₃ ·	5	11	.313	94	38	131	5.23	0
2012 Los Angeles i-j	N.L.	7	43	2	3	.400	38	14	43	2.93	0
Major League Totals . . . . . . .12 Yrs.		307	1892	132	95	.581	1753	575	1751	3.91	0
Division Series											
2003 Florida	N.L.	1	7	0	1	.000	9	5	2	1.29	0
2007 Boston	A.L.	1	9	1	0	1.000	8	0	4	0.00	0
2008 Boston	A.L.	1	5	0	0	.000	6	4	9	7.20	0
2009 Boston	A.L.	1	6²/₃	0	1	.000	3	1	5	5.40	0
Division Series Totals		4	27²/₃	1	2	.333	26	10	20	2.93	0
Championship Series											
2003 Florida	N.L.	3	19¹/₃	1	0	1.000	19	2	11	3.26	0
2007 Boston	A.L.	2	14	2	0	1.000	18	1	9	1.93	0
2008 Boston	A.L.	2	9¹/₃	1	0	1.000	8	2	13	9.64	0
Championship Series Totals		7	42²/₃	4	0	1.000	45	5	33	4.22	0
World Series Record											
2003 Florida	N.L.	2	16¹/₃	1	1	.500	19	5	8	1.10	0
2007 Boston	A.L.	1	7	1	0	1.000	9	1	6	1.29	0
World Series Totals		3	23¹/₃	2	1	.667	28	6	14	1.16	0

a On disabled list from April 29 to May 14 and June 5 to July 16 and August 23 to September 11, 2002.
b On disabled list from May 8 to July 1, 2003.
c On disabled list from May 31 to June 17 and from June 18 to July 5 and July 6 to July 30, 2004.
d On disabled list from June 15 to June 30 and July 6 to July 23, 2005.
e Traded to Boston Red Sox with infielder Mike Lowell and pitcher Guillermo Mota for infielder Hanley Ramirez, pitcher Anibal Sanchez and pitcher Jesus Delgado, November 24, 2005.
f On disabled list from May 14 to May 29, 2007.
g On disabled list from March 19 to April 6 and August 18 to September 5, 2008.
h On disabled list from May 19 to July 23, 2010.
i On disabled list from June 12 to June 30, 2012.
j Traded to Los Angeles Dodgers with outfielder Carl Crawford, infielder Adrian Gonzalez, infielder Nick Punto and cash for infielder James Loney, infielder Ivan DeJesus, pitcher Allen Webster and player to be named later, August 25, 2012. Boston Red Sox received pitcher Rubby De La Rosa to complete trade, October 4, 2012.

BELISARIO, RONALD J.

Born, Maracay, Venezuela, December 31, 1982.
Bats Right. Throws Right. Height, 6 feet, 3 inches. Weight, 245 pounds.

Year Club	Lea	G	IP	W	L	Pct	SO	BB	H	ERA	SAVES
2001 Marlins	Gulf Coast	13	73	4	6	.400	54	20	62	2.34	0
2002 Kane County	Midwest	23	140¹/₃	6	5	.545	98	56	131	3.46	0
2003 Jupiter	Fla.St.	6	18¹/₃	1	2	.333	13	8	20	4.91	0
2003 Greensboro	So.Atl.	10	48	5	1	.833	45	18	41	3.00	0
2004 Jupiter	Fla.St.	6	8²/₃	1	1	.500	7	5	2	0.00	1
2004 Marlins	Gulf Coast	2	2	0	0	.000	2	0	1	0.00	0
2004 Carolina	Southern	15	73	3	5	.375	58	43	75	5.55	0
2005 a				Did Not Play							
2006 b				Did Not Play							
2007 Lynchburg	Carolina	19	34¹/₃	0	3	.000	19	13	38	4.46	4
2007 Altoona	Eastern	18	24²/₃	1	0	1.000	21	14	23	3.28	0
2008 Altoona	Eastern	38	57	4	4	.500	36	25	63	4.74	9
2009 Inland Empire	Calif.	2	2	0	0	.000	3	1	2	0.00	0
2009 Los Angeles c-d	N.L.	69	70²/₃	4	3	.571	64	29	52	2.04	0
2010 Inland Empire	Calif.	2	2	0	0	.000	1	2	1	4.50	0
2010 Los Angeles	N.L.	59	55¹/₃	3	1	.750	38	19	52	5.04	2
2011 Did not play											
2012 Rancho Cucamonga	Calif.	2	3	0	1	.000	1	0	6	12.00	0
2012 Albuquerque	P.C.	2	1²/₃	0	0	.000	0	2	2	0.00	0
2012 Los Angeles	N.L.	68	71	8	1	.889	69	29	47	2.54	1
Major League Totals . . . . .3 Yrs.		196	197	15	5	.750	171	77	151	3.06	3

Year	Club	Lea	G	IP	W	L	Pct	SO	BB	H	ERA	SAVES
Division Series												
2009 Los Angeles	N.L.		2	$1^{1}/_{3}$	0	0	.000	0	0	0	0.00	0
Championship Series												
2009 Los Angeles	N.L.		4	$3^{1}/_{3}$	0	0	.000	0	1	5	10.80	0

a On minor league disabled list April 7 to September 15, 2005.
b Filed for free agency from Florida Marlins, October 15, 2006. Signed with Pittsburgh Pirates organization, November 9, 2006.
c Filed for free agency, October 30, 2008. Signed with Los Angeles Dodgers organization, January 16, 2009.
d On disabled list from July 6 to August 8, 2009.

BELISLE, MATTHEW THOMAS (MATT)

Born, Austin, Texas, June 6, 1980.
Bats Right. Throws Right. Height, 6 feet, 3 inches. Weight, 225 pounds.

Year	Club	Lea	G	IP	W	L	Pct	SO	BB	H	ERA	SAVES
1999 Danville	Appal.		14	$71^{1}/_{3}$	2	5	.286	60	23	86	4.67	0
2000 Myrtle Beach	Carolina		12	$78^{2}/_{3}$	3	4	.429	71	11	72	3.43	0
2000 Macon	So.Atl.		15	$102^{1}/_{3}$	9	5	.643	97	18	79	2.37	0
2001 a				INJURED—Did Not Play								
2002 Greenville	Southern		26	$159^{1}/_{3}$	5	9	.357	123	39	162	4.35	0
2003 Greenville	Southern		21	$125^{1}/_{3}$	6	8	.429	94	42	128	3.52	0
2003 Richmond	Int.		3	20	1	1	.500	10	0	17	2.25	0
2003 Louisville	Int.		4	26	1	3	.250	15	5	31	3.81	0
2003 Cincinnati b	N.L.		6	$8^{2}/_{3}$	1	.	1.000	6	2	10	5.19	0
2004 Louisville	Int.		28	$162^{2}/_{3}$	9	11	.450	106	51	192	5.26	0
2005 Cincinnati	N.L.		60	$85^{2}/_{3}$	4	8	.333	59	26	101	4.41	1
2006 Dayton	Midwest		2	4	1	0	1.000	3	0	3	0.00	1
2006 Chattanooga	Southern		2	$3^{1}/_{3}$	0	0	.000	4	0	3	0.00	0
2006 Louisville	Int.		8	9	1	0	1.000	9	1	4	0.00	0
2006 Cincinnati c	N.L.		30	40	2	0	1.000	26	19	43	3.60	0
2007 Louisville	Int.		1	6	0	1	.000	7	2	7	3.00	0
2007 Cincinnati	N.L.		30	$177^{2}/_{3}$	8	9	.471	125	43	212	5.32	0
2008 Sarasota	Fla.St.		1	$8^{2}/_{3}$	1	0	1.000	3	0	2	0.00	0
2008 Chattanooga	Southern		1	9	1	0	1.000	3	0	7	2.00	0
2008 Cincinnati	N.L.		6	$29^{2}/_{3}$	1	4	.200	14	6	47	7.28	0
2008 Louisville d-e	Int.		26	38	5	1	.833	27	11	43	4.26	4
2009 Colorado Springs	P.C.		33	$58^{1}/_{3}$	1	1	.500	47	15	58	3.09	9
2009 Colorado f	N.L.		24	31	3	1	.750	22	5	35	5.52	0
2010 Colorado	N.L.		76	92	7	5	.583	91	16	84	2.93	1
2011 Colorado	N.L.		74	72	10	4	.714	58	14	77	3.25	0
2012 Colorado	N.L.		*80	80	3	8	.273	69	18	91	3.71	3
Major League Totals		9 Yrs.	386	$616^{2}/_{3}$	39	40	.494	470	149	700	4.38	5
Division Series												
2009 Colorado	N.L.		2	2	0	0	.000	2	1	0	0.00	0

a On minor league disabled list from April 6 to September 18, 2001.
b Sent by Atlanta Braves to Cincinnati Reds as player to be named later for pitcher Kent Mercker, August 14, 2003.
c On disabled list from May 28 to June 27 and July 10 to August 20, 2006.
d On disabled list from March 21 to April 21, 2008.
e On disabled list from September 9 to November 6, 2008.
f Not offered contract, December 12, 2008. Signed with Colorado Rockies organization, January 14, 2009.

BELL, HEATH JUSTIN

Born, Oceanside, California, September 29, 1977.
Bats Right. Throws Right. Height, 6 feet, 3 inches. Weight, 240 pounds.

Year	Club	Lea	G	IP	W	L	Pct	SO	BB	H	ERA	SAVES
1998 Kingsport	Appal.		22	46	1	0	1.000	61	11	40	2.54	8
1999 Columbia	So.Atl.		55	$62^{1}/_{3}$	1	7	.125	68	17	47	2.60	25
2000 St. Lucie	Fla.St.		48	60	5	1	.833	75	21	43	2.55	23
2001 Binghamton	Eastern		43	$61^{1}/_{3}$	3	1	.750	55	19	82	6.02	4
2002 Binghamton	Eastern		24	38	1	0	1.000	49	6	22	1.18	6
2002 Norfolk	Int.		22	$31^{2}/_{3}$	3	4	.429	28	9	38	4.26	1
2003 Norfolk	Int.		40	$49^{2}/_{3}$	2	3	.400	54	8	54	4.71	3
2004 Binghamton	Eastern		1	2	0	0	.000	0	0	2	0.00	0
2004 Norfolk	Int.		45	$55^{2}/_{3}$	3	1	.750	68	24	42	3.23	16
2004 New York	N.L.		17	$24^{1}/_{3}$	0	2	.000	27	6	22	3.33	0
2005 Norfolk	Int.		13	$26^{2}/_{3}$	1	0	1.000	29	5	15	1.69	6
2005 New York	N.L.		42	$46^{2}/_{3}$	1	3	.250	43	13	56	5.59	0
2006 Norfolk	Int.		30	35	3	3	.500	56	8	27	1.29	12
2006 New York a	N.L.		22	37	0	0	.000	35	11	51	5.11	0

Year	Club	Lea	G	IP	W	L	Pct	SO	BB	H	ERA	SAVES
2007 San Diego		N.L.	81	93²/₃	6	4	.600	102	30	60	2.02	2
2008 San Diego		N.L.	74	78	6	6	.500	71	28	66	3.58	0
2009 San Diego		N.L.	68	69²/₃	6	4	.600	79	24	54	2.71	*42
2010 San Diego		N.L.	67	70	6	1	.857	86	28	56	1.93	47
2011 San Diego b		N.L.	64	62²/₃	3	4	.429	51	21	51	2.44	43
2012 Miami c		N.L.	73	63²/₃	4	5	.444	59	29	70	5.09	19
Major League Totals ....9 Yrs.			508	545²/₃	32	29	.525	553	190	486	3.30	153

a Traded to San Diego Padres with pitcher Royce Ring for pitcher Jon Adkins and outfielder Ben Johnson, November 15, 2006.

b Filed for free agency, October 30, 2011. Signed with Florida Marlins, December 5, 2011.

c Traded to Arizona Diamondbacks with cash for infielder Yordy Cabrera, October 20, 2012.

BENOIT (PENA), JOAQUIN ANTONIO

Born, Santiago, Dominican Republic, July 26, 1977.
Bats Right. Throws Right. Height, 6 feet, 3 inches. Weight, 220 pounds.

Year	Club	Lea	G	IP	W	L	Pct	SO	BB	H	ERA	SAVES
1996 Texas		Dominican	14	75	6	5	.545	63	23	63	2.28	0
1997 Rangers		Gulf Coast	10	44	3	3	.500	38	11	40	2.05	0
1998 Savannah		So.Atl.	15	80	4	3	.571	68	18	79	3.83	0
1999 Charlotte		Fla.St.	22	105	7	4	.636	83	50	117	5.31	0
2000 Tulsa		Texas	16	82¹/₃	4	4	.500	72	30	73	3.83	0
2001 Tulsa		Texas	4	21²/₃	1	0	1.000	23	6	23	3.32	0
2001 Oklahoma		P.C.	24	131	9	5	.643	142	73	113	4.19	0
2001 Texas		A.L.	1	5	0	0	.000	4	3	8	10.80	0
2002 Oklahoma		P.C.	16	98²/₃	8	4	.667	103	37	74	3.56	0
2002 Texas		A.L.	17	84²/₃	4	5	.444	59	58	91	5.31	1
2002 Charlotte		Fla.St.	1	5	0	0	.000	8	3	1	0.00	0
2003 Oklahoma		P.C.	6	33	2	1	.667	31	11	28	3.82	0
2003 Texas a		A.L.	25	105	8	5	.615	87	51	99	5.49	0
2004 Texas		A.L.	28	103	3	5	.375	95	31	113	5.68	0
2004 Frisco b		Texas	1	2	0	0	.000	6	0	0	0.00	0
2005 Oklahoma		P.C.	3	5	0	1	.000	2	4	4	5.40	0
2005 Rangers		Arizona	1	2	0	0	.000	4	1	0	0.00	0
2005 Texas c		A.L.	32	87	4	4	.500	78	38	69	3.72	0
2006 Texas		A.L.	56	79²/₃	1	1	.500	85	38	48	4.86	0
2007 Texas		A.L.	70	82	7	4	.636	87	28	68	2.85	6
2008 Frisco		Texas	3	1²/₃	0	0	.000	2	4	4	16.20	0
2008 Oklahoma		P.C.	2	3	1	0	1.000	3	0	1	0.00	0
2008 Texas d		A.L.	44	45	3	2	.600	43	35	40	5.00	1
2009 Texas e-f.		A.L.					INJURED—Did Not Play					
2010 Durham		Int.	8	9²/₃	0	1	.000	17	3	8	2.79	2
2010 Tampa Bay g		A.L.	63	60¹/₃	1	2	.333	75	11	30	1.34	1
2011 Detroit		A.L.	66	61	4	3	.571	63	17	47	2.95	2
2012 Detroit		A.L.	73	71	5	3	.625	84	22	59	3.68	2
Major League Totals ....11 Yrs.			475	783²/₃	40	34	.541	760	332	692	4.28	13
Division Series												
2010 Tampa Bay		A.L.	3	3²/₃	1	0	1.000	3	0	0	0.00	0
2011 Detroit		A.L.	2	3²/₃	0	0	.000	6	1	4	2.45	0
2012 Detroit		A.L.	3	3	0	0	.000	2	1	4	6.00	0
Division Series Totals			8	10¹/₃	1	0	1.000	11	2	8	2.61	0
Championship Series												
2011 Detroit		A.L.	3	4	0	0	.000	3	2	0	0.00	0
2012 Detroit		A.L.	1	0²/₃	0	0	.000	0	0	1	0.00	0
Championship Series Totals			4	4²/₃	0	0	.000	3	2	1	0.00	0
World Series Record												
2012 Detroit		A.L.	2	1²/₃	0	0	.000	3	0	1	0.00	0

a On disabled list from June 1 to June 22, 2003.

b On disabled list from August 23 to September 7, 2004.

c On disabled list from March 25 to May 2 and June 9 to June 28, 2005.

d On disabled list from July 3 to August 6, 2008.

e On disabled list from April 5 to November 5, 2009.

f Filed for free agency, November 5, 2009. Signed with Tampa Bay Rays organization, February 15, 2010.

g Filed for free agency, November 1, 2010. Signed with Detroit Tigers, November 19, 2010.

BETANCOURT, RAFAEL JOSE
Born, Cumana, Venezuela, April 29, 1975.
Bats Right. Throws Right. Height, 6 feet, 2 inches. Weight, 200 pounds.

Year Club	Lea	G	IP	W	L	Pct	SO	BB	H	ERA	SAVES
1997 Michigan	Midwest	27	32⅓	0	3	.000	52	2	26	1.95	11
1998 Red Sox	Gulf Coast	4	5	0	2	.000	4	1	6	7.20	0
1998 Sarasota	Fla.St.	20	28	3	1	.750	33	6	22	3.54	2
1998 Trenton	Eastern	7	9⅓	0	0	.000	9	3	9	6.75	0
1999 Sarasota	Fla.St.	6	7	0	0	.000	6	1	5	0.00	4
1999 Trenton a	Eastern	39	54⅔	6	2	.750	57	10	50	3.62	13
2000 Yokohama	Japan Cen.	11	29	1	2	.333	16	11	30	4.08	0
2000 Searex b	Japan East.	20	23	1	0	1.000	29	6	17	1.17	6
2001 Trenton	Eastern	16	24	0	1	.000	27	3	28	5.63	4
2002						INJURED—Did Not Play					
2003 Akron	Eastern	31	45⅓	0	0	.000	75	13	33	1.39	16
2003 Buffalo	Int.	4	6⅔	0	0	.000	6	2	6	4.05	1
2003 Cleveland c	A.L.	33	38	2	2	.500	36	13	27	2.13	1
2004 Akron	Eastern	1	1	0	0	.000	2	1	0	0.00	0
2004 Cleveland d	A.L.	68	66⅔	5	6	.455	76	18	71	3.92	4
2005 Cleveland e	A.L.	54	67⅔	4	3	.571	73	17	57	2.79	1
2006 Akron f	Eastern	1	1	0	0	.000	2	1	0	0.00	0
2007 Cleveland	A.L.	68	79⅓	5	1	.833	80	9	51	1.47	3
2008 Cleveland	A.L.	69	71	3	4	.429	64	25	76	5.07	4
2009 Columbus	Int.	3	3⅓	1	0	1.000	4	1	0	0.00	0
2009 Cleveland g-h-i	A.L.	29	30⅔	1	2	.333	32	15	25	3.52	1
2009 Colorado	N.L.	32	25⅓	3	1	.750	29	5	17	1.78	1
2010 Colorado	N.L.	72	62⅓	5	1	.833	89	8	52	3.61	1
2011 Colorado	N.L.	68	62⅓	2	0	1.000	73	8	46	2.89	8
2012 Colorado	N.L.	60	57⅔	1	4	.200	57	12	53	2.81	31
Major League Totals	10 Yrs.	603	617⅔	34	28	.548	657	141	527	3.15	58
Division Series											
2007 Cleveland	A.L.	2	2	0	0	.000	3	0	1	0.00	0
2009 Colorado	N.L.	3	2⅓	0	0	.000	3	1	2	3.86	0
Division Series Totals		5	4⅓	0	0	.000	6	1	3	2.08	0
Championship Series											
2007 Cleveland	A.L.	5	8	0	0	.000	6	1	6	6.75	0

a Sold by Boston Red Sox to Yokohama, November 18,1999.
b Sold to Boston Red Sox, December 13, 2000.
c Filed for free agency, October 15, 2001. Signed with Cleveland Indians organization, January 20, 2003.
d On disabled list from June 26 to July 11, 2004.
e On disabled list from June 30 to July 18, 2005.
f On disabled list from April 20 to May 16, 2006.
g On disabled list from June 1 to July 9, 2009.
h Traded to Colorado Rockies for pitcher Connor Graham, July 23, 2009.
i Filed for free agency, November 14, 2009. Accepted arbitration, December 7, 2009.

BILLINGSLEY, CHAD RYAN
Born, Defiance, Ohio, July 29, 1984.
Bats Right. Throws Right. Height, 6 feet. Weight, 245 pounds.

Year Club	Lea	G	IP	W	L	Pct	SO	BB	H	ERA	SAVES
2003 Ogden	Pioneer	11	54	5	4	.556	62	15	49	2.83	0
2004 Vero Beach	Fla.St.	18	92	7	4	.636	111	49	68	2.35	0
2004 Jacksonville	Southern	8	42⅓	4	0	1.000	47	22	32	2.98	0
2005 Jacksonville	Southern	28	146	13	6	.684	162	50	116	3.51	0
2006 Las Vegas	P.C.	13	70⅔	6	3	.667	78	32	57	3.95	0
2006 Los Angeles	N.L.	18	90	7	4	.636	59	58	92	3.80	0
2007 Los Angeles	N.L.	43	147	12	5	.706	141	64	131	3.31	0
2008 Los Angeles	N.L.	35	200⅔	16	10	.615	201	80	188	3.14	0
2009 Los Angeles	N.L.	33	196⅓	12	11	.522	179	86	173	4.03	0
2010 Los Angeles a	N.L.	31	191⅔	12	11	.522	171	69	176	3.57	0
2011 Los Angeles	N.L.	32	188	11	11	.500	152	84	189	4.21	0
2012 Los Angeles b	N.L.	25	149⅔	10	9	.526	128	45	148	3.55	0
Major League Totals	7 Yrs.	217	1163⅓	80	61	.567	1031	486	1097	3.66	0
Division Series											
2006 Los Angeles	N.L.	2	2	0	0	.000	3	0	1	0.00	0
2008 Los Angeles	N.L.	1	6⅔	1	0	1.000	7	1	5	1.35	0
Division Series Totals		3	8⅔	1	0	1.000	10	1	6	1.04	0
Championship Series											
2008 Los Angeles	N.L.	2	5	0	2	.000	9	7	12	18.00	0

Year Club	Lea	G	IP	W	L	Pct	SO	BB	H	ERA	SAVES
2009 Los Angeles	N.L.	1	3⅓	0	0	.000	3	2	2	5.40	0
Championship Series Totals		3	8⅓	0	2	.000	12	9	14	12.96	0

a On disabled list from June 12 to June 28, 2010.
b On disabled list from July 8 to July 23 and August 25 to October 29, 2012.

BLACKBURN, ROBERT NICHOLAS (NICK)

Born, Ada, Oklahoma, February 24, 1982.
Bats Right. Throws Right. Height, 6 feet, 4 inches. Weight, 225 pounds.

Year Club	Lea	G	IP	W	L	Pct	SO	BB	H	ERA	SAVES
2002 Elizabethton	Appal.	13	66⅔	3	3	.500	62	21	70	4.99	0
2003 Quad Cities........	Midwest	16	76	2	9	.182	40	18	78	4.86	1
2004 Fort Myers	Fla.St.	9	37⅓	3	3	.500	21	7	51	6.27	0
2004 Quad Cities........	Midwest	20	84⅓	6	4	.600	66	23	69	2.77	1
2005 New Britain	Eastern	7	49	2	4	.333	27	10	35	1.84	0
2005 Fort Myers	Fla.St.	15	93⅔	7	5	.583	55	16	95	3.36	0
2005 Rochester............	.Int.	3	14	0	0	.000	7	3	20	5.14	0
2006 New Britain	Eastern	30	132⅓	7	8	.467	81	37	141	4.42	0
2007 New Britain	Eastern	8	38	3	1	.750	18	7	36	3.08	0
2007 Rochester............	.Int.	17	110⅔	7	3	.700	57	12	96	2.11	0
2007 Minnesota	A.L.	6	11⅔	0	2	.000	8	2	19	7.71	0
2008 Minnesota	A.L.	33	193⅓	11	11	.500	96	39	224	4.05	0
2009 Minnesota	A.L.	33	205⅔	11	11	.500	98	41	*240	4.03	0
2010 Rochester............	.Int.	4	21⅔	1	0	1.000	13	6	19	2.49	0
2010 Minnesota	A.L.	28	161	10	12	.455	68	40	194	5.42	0
2011 Minnesota a...........	A.L.	26	148⅓	7	10	.412	76	54	183	4.49	0
2012 Rochester............	.Int.	7	36⅔	3	1	.750	11	9	42	2.70	0
2012 Minnesota b...........	A.L.	19	98⅔	4	9	.308	42	26	143	7.39	0
Major League Totals ....6 Yrs.		145	818⅔	43	55	.439	388	202	1003	4.85	0
Division Series											
2009 Minnesota	A.L.	1	5⅔	0	0	.000	3	2	3	1.59	0

a On disabled list from August 22 to October 14, 2011.
b On disabled list from May 17 to June 4, 2012.

BLACKLEY, TRAVIS JARROD

Born, Melbourne, Victoria, Australia, November 4, 1982.
Bats Left. Throws Left. Height, 6 feet, 3 inches. Weight, 205 pounds.

Year Club	Lea	G	IP	W	L	Pct	SO	BB	H	ERA	SAVES
2001 Everett	Northwest	14	78⅔	6	1	.857	90	29	60	3.32	0
2002 San Bernardino	Calif.	21	121⅓	5	9	.357	152	44	102	3.49	0
2003 San Antonio	Texas	27	162⅓	17	3	.850	144	62	125	2.61	0
2004 Tacoma	P.C.	19	110⅓	8	6	.571	80	47	100	3.83	0
2004 Seattle	A.L.	6	26	1	3	.250	14	22	35	10.04	0
2005 Seattle a	A.L.			INJURED—Did Not Play							
2006 Tacoma	P.C.	2	11	1	1	.500	5	5	10	4.09	0
2006 San Antonio	Texas	25	144	8	11	.421	100	45	139	4.06	0
2007 Fresno	P.C.	28	162⅓	10	8	.556	121	68	156	4.66	0
2007 San Francisco b-c	N.L.	2	8⅔	0	0	.000	5	5	10	7.27	0
2008 Lehigh Valley d.........	.Int.	28	123	5	10	.333	87	59	132	5.41	0
2009 Reno	P.C.	38	111⅓	4	7	.364	101	38	133	4.85	3
2010 Stockton.............	Calif.	2	5	0	0	.000	2	0	5	1.80	0
2010 Buffalo	.Int.	4	6⅓	0	0	.000	4	7	6	8.53	0
2010 Sacramento e-f	P.C.	15	35⅔	2	1	.667	35	22	31	2.52	0
2011 KIA................	Korea	25	121	7	5	.583	110	60		3.48	0
2011 Melbourne g......	Australian	8	12⅔	1	0	1.000	18	7	9	3.55	1
2012 Fresno	P.C.	4	23⅓	3	0	1.000	19	3	13	0.39	1
2012 San Francisco	N.L.	4	5	0	0	.000	2	2	7	9.00	0
2012 Oakland h-i..........	A.L.	24	102⅔	6	4	.600	69	30	91	3.86	0
Major League Totals ....3 Yrs.		36	142⅓	7	7	.500	92	59	143	5.37	0

a On disabled list from March 3 to October 31, 2005.
b Traded to San Francisco Giants for outfielder Jason Ellison, April 1, 2007.
c Selected by Philadelphia Phillies in Rule V draft, December 6, 2007.
d Filed for free agency, October 14, 2008. Signed with Arizona Diamondbacks, December 29, 2008.
e Filed for free agency, October 5, 2009. Signed with New York Mets organization, February 4, 2010.
f Released by New York Mets, May 2, 2010. Signed with Oakland Athletics organization, November 5, 2010.
g Released by Oakland Athletics, December 20, 2010. Signed with KIA Tigers (Korea) for 2011.
h Signed with San Francisco Giants organization, February 16, 2012.
i Claimed on waivers by Oakland Athletics, May 15, 2012.

BLANTON, JOSEPH MATTHEW (JOE)

Born, Bowling Green, Kentucky, December 11, 1980.
Bats Right. Throws Right. Height, 6 feet, 3 inches. Weight, 255 pounds.

Year	Club	Lea	G	IP	W	L	Pct	SO	BB	H	ERA	SAVES
2002	Modesto	California	2	6	0	1	.000	6	6	8	7.50	0
2002	Vancouver	Northwest	4	14$^{1}/_{3}$	1	1	.500	15	2	11	3.14	0
2003	Kane County	Midwest	21	133	8	7	.533	144	19	110	2.57	0
2003	Midland	Texas	7	35$^{2}/_{3}$	3	1	.750	30	7	21	1.26	1
2004	Sacramento	P.C.	28	176$^{1}/_{3}$	11	8	.579	143	34	199	4.19	0
2004	Oakland	A.L.	3	8	0	0	.000	6	2	6	5.63	0
2005	Oakland	A.L.	33	201$^{1}/_{3}$	12	12	.500	116	67	178	3.53	0
2006	Oakland	A.L.	32	194$^{1}/_{3}$	16	12	.571	107	58	241	4.82	0
2007	Oakland	A.L.	34	230	14	10	.583	140	40	*240	3.95	0
2008	Oakland	A.L.	20	127	5	12	.294	62	35	145	4.96	0
2008	Philadelphia a	N.L.	13	70$^{2}/_{3}$	4	0	1.000	49	31	66	4.20	0
2009	Philadelphia	N.L.	31	195$^{1}/_{3}$	12	8	.600	163	59	198	4.05	0
2010	Lakewood	So.Atl.	1	2	0	0	.000	2	0	0	0.00	0
2010	Reading	Eastern	2	8	0	1	.000	5	2	9	5.63	0
2010	Philadelphia b	N.L.	29	175$^{2}/_{3}$	9	6	.600	134	43	206	4.82	0
2011	Lakewood	So.Atl.	1	1	0	0	.000	0	0	0	0.00	0
2011	Philadelphia c	N.L.	11	41$^{1}/_{3}$	1	2	.333	35	9	52	5.01	0
2012	Philadelphia-Los Angeles d-e	N.L.	31	191	10	13	.435	166	34	207	4.71	0
Major League Totals		9 Yrs.	237	1434$^{2}/_{3}$	83	75	.525	978	378	1539	4.37	0
Division Series												
2008	Philadelphia	N.L.	1	6	1	0	1.000	7	0	5	1.50	0
2009	Philadelphia	N.L.	2	3$^{2}/_{3}$	0	0	.000	1	0	4	4.91	0
2011	Philadelphia	N.L.	1	1	0	0	.000	0	0	0	0.00	0
Division Series Totals			4	10$^{2}/_{3}$	1	0	1.000	8	0	9	2.53	0
Championship Series												
2006	Oakland	A.L.	1	2	0	0	.000	2	2	0	0.00	0
2008	Philadelphia	N.L.	1	5	0	0	.000	4	4	7	5.40	0
2009	Philadelphia	N.L.	1	6	0	0	.000	2	2	6	4.50	0
2010	Philadelphia	N.L.	1	4$^{2}/_{3}$	0	0	.000	3	1	5	5.79	0
Championship Series Totals			4	17$^{2}/_{3}$	0	0	.000	11	9	18	4.58	0
World Series Record												
2008	Philadelphia	N.L.	1	6	1	0	1.000	7	2	4	3.00	0
2009	Philadelphia	N.L.	1	6	0	0	.000	7	2	5	6.00	0
World Series Totals			2	12	1	0	1.000	14	4	9	4.50	0

a Traded to Philadelphia Phillies for pitcher Josh Outman, infielder Adrian Cardenas and outfielder Matt Spencer, July 17, 2008.

b On disabled list from March 26 to May 3, 2010.

c On disabled list from April 24 to May 9 and May 16 to September 5, 2011.

d Traded to Los Angeles Dodgers for player to be named later, August 3, 2012. Philadelphia Phillies received pitcher Ryan O'Sullivan to complete trade, August 16, 2012.

e Filed for free agency, November 3, 2012. Signed with Los Angeles Angels, December 12, 2012.

BLEVINS, JERRY RICHARD

Born, Johnson City, Tennessee, September 6, 1983.
Bats Left. Throws Left. Height, 6 feet, 6 inches. Weight, 175 pounds.

Year	Club	Lea	G	IP	W	L	Pct	SO	BB	H	ERA	SAVES
2004	Boise	Northwest	23	33$^{1}/_{3}$	6	1	.857	42	21	17	1.62	5
2005	Peoria	Midwest	48	76$^{1}/_{3}$	3	7	.300	96	38	75	5.54	14
2006	Daytona	Fla.St.	8	11	0	1	.000	9	4	18	9.00	1
2006	Boise	Northwest	16	22$^{1}/_{3}$	1	2	.333	19	8	27	6.04	0
2006	West Tenn	Southern	5	6$^{1}/_{3}$	0	0	.000	8	1	5	1.42	1
2007	Daytona	Fla.St.	15	23$^{2}/_{3}$	1	0	1.000	32	5	13	0.38	6
2007	Tennessee	Southern	23	29$^{1}/_{3}$	2	2	.500	37	8	23	1.53	3
2007	Midland	Texas	17	21$^{2}/_{3}$	1	3	.250	29	5	18	3.32	1
2007	Sacramento	P.C.	1	2$^{2}/_{3}$	1	0	1.000	4	0	1	0.00	0
2007	Oakland a	A.L.	6	4$^{2}/_{3}$	0	1	.000	3	2	8	9.64	0
2008	Sacramento	P.C.	28	32$^{1}/_{3}$	2	2	.500	36	6	31	2.78	10
2008	Oakland	A.L.	36	37$^{2}/_{3}$	1	3	.250	35	13	32	3.11	0
2009	Sacramento	P.C.	45	63$^{1}/_{3}$	5	3	.625	62	18	65	3.84	2
2009	Oakland	A.L.	20	22$^{1}/_{3}$	0	0	.000	23	6	19	4.84	0
2010	Oakland	A.L.	63	48$^{2}/_{3}$	2	1	.667	46	18	54	3.70	1
2011	Sacramento	P.C.	27	29$^{2}/_{3}$	2	0	1.000	35	7	25	4.85	0
2011	Oakland	A.L.	26	28$^{1}/_{3}$	0	0	.000	26	14	24	2.86	0
2012	Oakland	A.L.	63	65$^{1}/_{3}$	5	1	.833	54	25	45	2.48	1
Major League Totals		6 Yrs.	214	207	8	6	.571	187	78	182	3.35	2

Division Series

Year	Club	Lea	G	IP	W	L	Pct	SO	BB	H	ERA	SAVES
2012 Oakland	A.L.	3	3²/₃	0	0	.000	0	0	1	0.00	0	

a Traded by Chicago Cubs to Oakland Athletics with catcher Rob Bowen for catcher Jason Kendall and cash, July 17, 2007.

BOGGS, MITCHELL THOMAS

Born, Dalton, Georgia, February 15, 1984.
Bats Right. Throws Right. Height, 6 feet, 4 inches. Weight, 215 pounds.

Year	Club	Lea	G	IP	W	L	Pct	SO	BB	H	ERA	SAVES
2005 New Jersey	N.Y.-Penn.	15	71²/₃	4	4	.500	61	24	77	3.89	0
2006 Palm Beach	Fla.St.	27	145	10	6	.625	126	51	153	3.41	0
2007 Springfield	Texas	26	152¹/₃	11	7	.611	117	62	167	3.84	0
2008 St. Louis	N.L.	8	34	3	2	.600	13	22	42	7.41	0
2008 Memphis	P.C.	21	125¹/₃	9	3	.750	81	46	107	3.45	0
2009 Memphis	P.C.	14	76¹/₃	6	4	.600	58	32	90	4.83	0
2009 St. Louis	N.L.	16	58	2	3	.400	46	33	71	4.19	0
2010 St. Louis	N.L.	61	67¹/₃	2	3	.400	52	27	60	3.61	0
2011 Memphis	P.C.	4	14²/₃	0	2	.000	14	5	12	2.45	0
2011 St. Louis	N.L.	51	60²/₃	2	3	.400	48	21	62	3.56	4
2012 St. Louis	N.L.	78	73¹/₃	4	1	.800	58	21	56	2.21	0
Major League Totals	5 Yrs.	214	293¹/₃	13	12	.520	217	124	291	3.80	4

Wild Card Playoff

Year	Club	Lea	G	IP	W	L	Pct	SO	BB	H	ERA	SAVES
2012 St. Louis	N.L.	1	0²/₃	0	0	.000	0	1	1	0.00	0

Division Series

Year	Club	Lea	G	IP	W	L	Pct	SO	BB	H	ERA	SAVES
2009 St. Louis	N.L.	1	1	0	0	.000	1	2	0	0.00	0
2011 St. Louis	N.L.	2	2	0	0	.000	1	1	4	9.00	0
2012 St. Louis	N.L.	4	3²/₃	0	1	.000	2	1	3	0.00	0
Division Series Totals		7	6²/₃	0	1	.000	4	4	7	2.70	0

Championship Series

Year	Club	Lea	G	IP	W	L	Pct	SO	BB	H	ERA	SAVES
2011 St. Louis	N.L.	3	3	0	0	.000	0	1	4	6.00	0
2012 St. Louis	N.L.	4	3¹/₃	0	0	.000	3	2	4	5.40	0
Championship Series Totals		7	6¹/₃	0	0	.000	3	3	8	5.68	0

World Series Record

Year	Club	Lea	G	IP	W	L	Pct	SO	BB	H	ERA	SAVES
2011 St. Louis	N.L.	2	2²/₃	0	0	.000	4	0	2	3.38	0

BRACH, BRAD

Born, Freehold, New Jersey, April 12, 1986.
Bats Right. Throws Right. Height, 6 feet, 6 inches. Weight, 210 pounds.

Year	Club	Lea	G	IP	W	L	Pct	SO	BB	H	ERA	SAVES
2008 Padres	Arizona	17	22¹/₃	1	1	.500	33	5	21	2.01	4
2009 Fort Wayne	Midwest	60	63²/₃	3	3	.500	82	11	36	1.27	33
2010 Lake Elsinore	Calif.	62	65²/₃	5	2	.714	74	11	50	2.47	41
2011 San Antonio	Texas	42	44	2	2	.500	64	5	32	2.25	23
2011 Tucson	P.C.	25	27²/₃	1	3	.250	30	7	28	3.90	11
2011 San Diego	N.L.	9	7	0	2	.000	11	7	9	5.14	0
2012 Tucson	P.C.	10	9²/₃	2	1	.667	5	1	11	2.79	3
2012 San Diego	N.L.	67	66²/₃	2	4	.333	75	33	50	3.78	0
Major League Totals	2 Yrs.	76	73²/₃	2	6	.250	86	40	59	3.91	0

BRESLOW, CRAIG ANDREW

Born, New Haven, Connecticut, August 8, 1980.
Bats Left. Throws Left. Height, 6 feet, 1 inch. Weight, 185 pounds.

Year	Club	Lea	G	IP	W	L	Pct	SO	BB	H	ERA	SAVES
2002 Ogden	Pioneer	23	54¹/₃	6	2	.750	56	24	42	1.82	2
2003 Beloit	Midwest	33	65	3	4	.429	80	27	64	5.12	2
2004 High Desert	Calif.	23	41¹/₃	1	3	.250	41	24	54	7.19	0
2004 New Jersey a	Northeast	19	26¹/₃	3	1	.750	37	13	19	4.10	0
2005 Mobile	Southern	40	52¹/₃	2	1	.667	47	17	38	2.75	0
2005 Portland	P.C.	7	9	0	1	.000	9	1	11	4.00	0
2005 San Diego b	N.L.	14	16¹/₃	0	0	.000	14	13	15	2.20	0
2006 Pawtucket	Int.	39	67	7	1	.875	77	24	49	2.69	7
2006 Boston c.	A.L.	13	12	0	2	.000	12	6	12	3.75	0
2007 Pawtucket	Int.	49	68²/₃	2	3	.400	73	25	70	4.06	1
2008 Cleveland-Minnesota d-e	A.L.	49	47	0	2	.000	39	19	34	1.91	1
2009 Minnesota-Oakland f	A.L.	77	69²/₃	8	7	.533	55	29	48	3.36	0
2010 Oakland	A.L.	75	74²/₃	4	4	.500	71	29	53	3.01	5

Year Club	Lea	G	IP	W	L	Pct	SO	BB	H	ERA	SAVES
2011 Oakland g	A.L.	67	59 1/3	0	2	.000	44	21	69	3.79	0
2012 Arizona	N.L.	40	43 1/3	2	0	1.000	42	13	38	2.70	0
2012 Boston h	A.L.	23	20	1	0	1.000	19	9	14	2.70	0
Major League Totals 7 Yrs.		358	342 1/3	15	17	.469	296	139	283	3.00	6

a Released by Milwaukee Brewers, July 6, 2004. Signed with independent New Jersey (Northeast), July 2004.
b Signed with San Diego Padres organization, March 6, 2005.
c Not offered contract, December 21, 2005. Signed with Boston Red Sox organization, February 1, 2006.
d Claimed on waivers by Cleveland Indians, March 23, 2008.
e Claimed on waivers by Minnesota Twins, May 29, 2008.
f Claimed on waivers by Oakland Athletics, May 20, 2009.
g Traded to Arizona Diamondbacks with pitcher Trevor Cahill for outfielder Collin Cowgill, pitcher Jarrod Parker and pitcher Ryan Cook, December 9, 2011.
h Traded to Boston Red Sox for pitcher Matt Albers and outfielder Scott Podsednik, July 31, 2012.

BRITTON, ZACHARY GRANT (ZACH)
Born, Panorama City, California, December 22, 1987.
Bats Left. Throws Left. Height, 6 feet, 3 inches. Weight, 195 pounds.

Year Club	Lea	G	IP	W	L	Pct	SO	BB	H	ERA	SAVES
2006 Bluefield	Appal.	11	34	0	4	.000	21	20	35	5.29	0
2007 Aberdeen	N.Y.-Penn.	15	63 2/3	6	4	.600	45	22	64	3.68	0
2008 Delmarva	So.Atl.	27	147 1/3	12	7	.632	114	49	118	3.12	0
2009 Frederick	Carolina	25	140	9	6	.600	131	55	123	2.70	0
2010 Bowie	Eastern	15	87	7	3	.700	68	28	76	2.48	0
2010 Norfolk	Int.	12	66 1/3	3	4	.429	56	23	63	2.98	0
2011 Bowie	Eastern	3	11 2/3	0	2	.000	15	2	14	5.40	0
2011 Norfolk	Int.	1	5	0	1	.000	3	1	3	1.80	0
2011 Baltimore a	A.L.	28	154 1/3	11	11	.500	97	62	162	4.61	0
2012 Bowie	Eastern	2	12	1	0	1.000	11	3	8	0.75	0
2012 Norfolk	Int.	9	51 1/3	4	2	.667	37	20	49	4.91	0
2012 Baltimore a	A.L.	12	60 1/3	5	3	.625	53	32	61	5.07	0
Major League Totals 2 Yrs.		40	214 2/3	16	14	.533	150	94	223	4.74	0

a On disabled list from August 5 to August 22, 2011.
a On disabled list from March 26 to June 6, 2012.

BROTHERS, REX COLEMAN
Born, Murfreesboro, Tennessee, December 18, 1987.
Bats Left. Throws Left. Height, 6 feet. Weight, 205 pounds.

Year Club	Lea	G	IP	W	L	Pct	SO	BB	H	ERA	SAVES
2009 Tri-City	Northwest	8	10 2/3	2	0	1.000	18	5	10	3.38	0
2009 Asheville	So.Atl.	9	10 2/3	0	0	.000	10	3	6	3.38	0
2010 Modesto	Calif.	33	37	0	2	.000	43	19	20	2.68	3
2010 Tulsa	Texas	24	23	2	1	.667	27	18	14	3.91	4
2011 Colorado Springs	P.C.	25	28	3	2	.600	45	15	29	2.89	1
2011 Colorado	N.L.	48	40 2/3	1	2	.333	59	20	33	2.88	1
2012 Colorado Springs	P.C.	4	5 1/3	0	0	.000	13	3	3	1.69	1
2012 Colorado	N.L.	75	67 2/3	8	2	.800	83	37	63	3.86	0
Major League Totals 2 Yrs.		123	108 1/3	9	4	.692	142	57	96	3.49	1

BROXTON, JONATHAN ROY
Born, Augusta, Georgia, June 16, 1984.
Bats Right. Throws Right. Height, 6 feet, 4 inches. Weight, 290 pounds.

Year Club	Lea	G	IP	W	L	Pct	SO	BB	H	ERA	SAVES
2002 Great Falls	Pioneer	11	29 1/3	2	0	1.000	33	16	22	2.76	2
2003 South Bend	So.Atl.	9	37 1/3	4	2	.667	30	22	27	3.13	0
2004 Vero Beach	Fla.St.	23	128 1/3	11	6	.647	144	43	110	3.23	0
2005 Jacksonville	Southern	33	96 2/3	5	3	.625	107	31	79	3.17	5
2005 Los Angeles	N.L.	14	13 2/3	1	0	1.000	22	12	13	5.93	0
2006 Las Vegas	P.C.	11	11 1/3	1	0	1.000	18	3	6	0.00	5
2006 Los Angeles	N.L.	68	76 1/3	4	1	.800	97	33	61	2.59	3
2007 Los Angeles	N.L.	83	82	4	4	.500	99	25	69	2.85	2
2008 Los Angeles	N.L.	70	69	3	5	.375	88	27	54	3.13	14
2009 Los Angeles	N.L.	73	76	7	2	.778	114	29	44	2.61	36
2010 Los Angeles	N.L.	64	62 1/3	5	6	.455	73	28	64	4.04	22
2011 Albuquerque	P.C.	2	2	0	0	.000	5	1	2	4.50	0
2011 Los Angeles a-b	N.L.	14	12 2/3	1	2	.333	10	9	15	5.68	7
2012 Kansas City	A.L.	35	35 2/3	1	2	.333	25	14	36	2.27	23

Year Club	Lea	G	IP	W	L	Pct	SO	BB	H	ERA	SAVES
2012 Cincinnati c-d.........N.L.	25	22$^{1}/_{3}$	3	3	.500	20	3	20	2.82	4
Major League Totals.......8 Yrs.	446	450	29	25	.537	548	180	376	3.10	111
Division Series										
2006 Los Angeles...........N.L.	2	2	0	1	.000	3	2	5	13.50	0
2008 Los Angeles...........N.L.	3	3$^{1}/_{3}$	0	0	.000	5	2	0	0.00	1
2009 Los Angeles...........N.L.	3	3$^{2}/_{3}$	0	0	.000	4	0	4	2.45	1
2012 Cincinnati............N.L.	3	3	0	1	.000	4	1	4	0.00	0
Division Series Totals...........	11	12	0	2	.000	16	5	13	3.00	2
Championship Series										
2008 Los Angeles...........N.L.	2	2$^{1}/_{3}$	0	0	.000	2	1	3	3.86	0
2009 Los Angeles...........N.L.	3	3	0	1	.000	1	1	2	6.00	1
Championship Series Totals......	5	5$^{1}/_{3}$	0	1	.000	3	2	5	5.06	1

a On disabled list from May 4 to September 30, 2011.
b Filed for free agency, October 30, 2011. Signed with Kansas City Royals, November 29, 2011.
c Traded to Cincinnati Reds for pitcher Donnie Joseph and pitcher J.C. Sulbaran, July 31, 2012.
d Filed for free agency, November 3, 2012, re-signed with Cincinnati Reds, November 28, 2012.

BUCHHOLZ, CLAY DANIEL
Born, Nederland, Texas, August 14, 1984.
Bats Left. Throws Right. Height, 6 feet, 3 inches. Weight, 190 pounds.

Year Club	Lea	G	IP	W	L	Pct	SO	BB	H	ERA	SAVES
2005 Lowell ..........N.Y.-Penn.	15	41$^{1}/_{3}$	0	1	.000	45	9	34	2.61	0
2006 Wilmington ....Carolina	3	16	2	0	1.000	23	4	10	1.13	0
2006 Greenville...........So.Atl.	21	103	9	4	.692	117	29	78	2.62	0
2007 Portland...........Eastern	16	86$^{2}/_{3}$	7	2	.778	116	22	55	1.77	0
2007 Pawtucket ....Int.	8	38$^{2}/_{3}$	1	3	.250	55	13	32	3.96	0
2007 Boston a.............A.L.	4	22$^{2}/_{3}$	3	1	.750	22	10	14	1.59	0
2008 Portland ....Eastern	2	15	1	0	1.000	18	1	7	1.80	0
2008 Pawtucket ....Int.	9	43$^{2}/_{3}$	4	2	.667	43	17	36	2.47	0
2008 Boston b .............A.L.	16	76	2	9	.182	72	41	93	6.75	0
2009 Pawtucket ....Int.	17	99	7	2	.778	89	30	67	2.36	0
2009 Boston ...............A.L.	16	92	7	4	.636	68	36	91	4.21	0
2010 Pawtucket ....Int.	1	3$^{2}/_{3}$	0	0	.000	2	1	4	4.91	0
2010 Boston c.............A.L.	28	173$^{2}/_{3}$	17	7	.708	120	67	142	2.33	0
2011 Boston d .............A.L.	14	82$^{2}/_{3}$	6	3	.667	60	31	76	3.48	0
2012 Pawtucket ....Int.	1	2$^{1}/_{3}$	0	0	.000	3	2	1	0.00	0
2012 Boston e.............A.L.	29	189$^{1}/_{3}$	11	8	.579	129	64	187	4.56	0
Major League Totals........6 Yrs.	107	636$^{1}/_{3}$	46	32	.590	471	249	603	3.92	0
Division Series										
2009 Boston ...............A.L.	1	5	0	0	.000	3	1	6	3.60	0

a Pitched no-hit, no-run game against Baltimore Orioles, September 1, 2007.
b On disabled list from May 13 to May 31, 2008.
c On disabled list from June 27 to July 21, 2010.
d On disabled list from June 17 to September 28, 2011.
e On disabled list from June 20 to July 14, 2012.

BUEHRLE, MARK ANTHONY
Born, St. Charles, Missouri, March 23, 1979.
Bats Left. Throws Left. Height, 6 feet, 2 inches. Weight, 225 pounds.

Year Club	Lea	G	IP	W	L	PCT	SO	BB	H	ERA	SAVES
1999 Burlington ....Midwest	20	98$^{2}/_{3}$	7	4	.636	91	16	105	4.10	3
2000 Birmingham.......Southern	16	118$^{2}/_{3}$	8	4	.667	68	17	95	2.28	0
2000 Chicago .............A.L.	28	51$^{1}/_{3}$	4	1	.800	37	19	55	4.21	0
2001 Chicago .............A.L.	32	221$^{1}/_{3}$	16	8	.667	126	48	188	3.29	0
2002 Chicago .............A.L.	34	239	19	12	.613	134	61	236	3.58	0
2003 Chicago .............A.L.	35	230$^{1}/_{3}$	14	14	.500	119	61	250	4.14	0
2004 Chicago .............A.L.	35	*245$^{1}/_{3}$	16	10	.615	165	51	257	3.89	0
2005 Chicago .............A.L.	33	*236$^{2}/_{3}$	16	8	.667	149	40	*240	3.12	0
2006 Chicago .............A.L.	32	204	12	13	.480	98	48	*247	4.99	0
2007 Chicago a............A.L.	30	201	10	9	.526	115	45	208	3.63	0
2008 Chicago .............A.L.	34	218$^{2}/_{3}$	15	12	.556	140	52	*240	3.79	0
2009 Chicago b............A.L.	33	213$^{1}/_{3}$	13	10	.565	105	45	222	3.84	0
2010 Chicago .............A.L.	33	210$^{1}/_{3}$	13	13	.500	99	49	*246	4.28	0
2011 Chicago c............A.L.	31	205$^{1}/_{3}$	13	9	.591	109	45	221	3.59	0
2012 Miami d .............N.L.	31	202$^{1}/_{3}$	13	13	.500	125	40	197	3.74	0
Major League Totals ....13 Yrs.	421	2679	174	132	.569	1521	604	2807	3.82	0

Year	Club	Lea	G	IP	W	L	Pct	SO	BB	H	ERA	SAVES
	Division Series											
2000 Chicago		A.L.	1	0⅓	0	0	.000	1	0	2	0.00	0
2005 Chicago		A.L.	1	7	1	0	1.000	2	1	8	5.14	0
2008 Chicago		A.L.	1	7	0	1	.000	3	0	10	6.43	0
Division Series Totals			3	14⅓	1	1	.500	6	1	20	5.65	0
	Championship Series											
2005 Chicago		A.L.	1	9	1	0	1.000	4	0	5	1.00	0
	World Series Record											
2005 Chicago		A.L.	2	7⅓	0	0	.000	6	0	7	4.91	1

a Pitched no-hit, no-run game against Texas Rangers, April 18, 2007.
b Pitched no-hit, no-run perfect game against Tampa Bay Rays, July 23, 2009.
c Filed for free agency, October 30, 2011. Signed with Florida Marlins, December 9, 2011.
d Traded to Toronto Blue Jays with outfielder Emilio Bonifacio, catcher John Buck, pitcher Josh Johnson and infielder Jose Reyes for pitcher Henderson Alvarez, infielder Yunel Escobar, infielder Adeiny Hechavarria, catcher Jeff Mathis, pitcher Anthony De Sclafani, outfielder Jake Marisnick and pitcher Justin Nicolino, November 19, 2012.

BUMGARNER, MADISON K.
Born, Hickory, North Carolina, August 1, 1989.
Bats Right. Throws Left. Height, 6 feet, 4 inches. Weight, 215 pounds.

Year	Club	Lea	G	IP	W	L	Pct	SO	BB	H	ERA	SAVES
2008 Augusta		So.Atl.	24	141⅔	15	3	.833	164	21	111	1.46	0
2009 San Jose		Calif.	5	24⅓	3	1	.750	23	4	20	1.48	0
2009 Connecticut		Eastern	20	107	9	1	.900	69	30	80	1.93	0
2009 San Francisco		N.L.	4	10	0	0	.000	10	3	8	1.80	0
2010 Fresno		P.C.	14	82⅔	7	1	.875	59	22	88	3.16	0
2010 San Francisco		N.L.	18	111	7	6	.538	86	26	119	3.00	0
2011 San Francisco		N.L.	33	204⅔	13	13	.500	191	46	202	3.21	0
2012 San Francisco		N.L.	32	208⅓	16	11	.593	191	49	183	3.37	0
Major League Totals	4 Yrs.		87	534	36	30	.545	478	124	512	3.20	0
	Division Series											
2010 San Francisco		N.L.	1	6	1	0	1.000	5	1	6	3.00	0
2012 San Francisco		N.L.	1	4⅓	0	1	.000	4	1	7	8.31	0
Division Series Totals			2	10⅓	1	1	.500	9	2	13	5.23	0
	Championship Series											
2010 San Francisco		N.L.	2	6⅔	0	0	.000	7	2	9	4.05	0
2012 San Francisco		N.L.	1	3⅔	0	1	.000	2	1	8	14.73	0
Championship Series Totals			3	10⅓	0	1	.000	9	3	17	7.84	0
	World Series Record											
2010 San Francisco		N.L.	1	8	1	0	1.000	6	2	3	0.00	0
2012 San Francisco		N.L.	1	7	1	0	1.000	8	2	2	0.00	0
World Series Totals			2	15	2	0	1.000	14	4	5	0.00	0

BURNETT, ALEX JAMES
Born, Anaheim, California, July 26, 1987.
Bats Right. Throws Right. Height, 6 feet. Weight, 210 pounds.

Year	Club	Lea	G	IP	W	L	Pct	SO	BB	H	ERA	SAVES
2005 Twins		Gulf Coast	13	48⅓	4	2	.667	33	14	50	4.10	0
2006 Elizabethton		Appal.	13	71⅓	4	3	.571	71	13	66	4.04	0
2007 Beloit		Midwest	27	155	9	8	.529	117	38	140	3.02	0
2008 Fort Myers		Fla.St.	28	143⅔	8	6	.571	84	36	151	3.76	0
2009 New Britain		Eastern	40	55⅓	1	2	.333	52	19	36	1.79	9
2009 Fort Myers		Fla.St.	18	22⅔	2	1	.667	26	7	14	1.99	4
2010 Rochester		Int.	14	19⅔	0	2	.000	18	8	26	5.49	2
2010 Minnesota		A.L.	41	47⅔	2	2	.500	37	23	52	5.29	0
2011 Rochester		Int.	4	3⅔	0	0	.000	3	1	5	7.36	1
2011 Minnesota		A.L.	66	50⅔	2	5	.286	33	21	50	5.51	0
2012 Minnesota		A.L.	67	71⅔	4	4	.500	36	26	71	3.52	0
Major League Totals	3 Yrs.		174	170	8	11	.421	106	70	173	4.61	0

BURNETT, ALLAN JAMES (A.J.)
Born, North Little Rock, Arkansas, January 3, 1977.
Bats Right. Throws Right. Height, 6 feet, 4 inches. Weight, 230 pounds.

Year	Club	Lea	G	IP	W	L	Pct	SO	BB	H	ERA	SAVES
1995 Mets		Gulf Coast	9	33⅔	2	3	.400	26	23	27	4.28	0
1996 Kingsport		Appal.	12	58	4	0	1.000	68	54	31	3.88	0

Year	Club	Lea	G	IP	W	L	Pct	SO	BB	H	ERA	SAVES
1997 Mets.	Gulf Coast		3	11⅓	0	1	.000	15	8	8	3.18	0
1997 Pittsfield.	N.Y.-Penn.		9	44	3	1	.750	48	35	28	4.70	0
1998 Kane County a	Midwest		20	119	10	4	.714	186	45	74	1.97	0
1999 Portland	Eastern		26	120⅔	6	12	.333	121	71	132	5.52	0
1999 Florida	N.L.		7	41⅓	4	2	.667	33	25	37	3.48	0
2000 Brevard County	Fla.St.		2	7⅓	0	0	.000	6	6	4	3.68	0
2000 Calgary.	P.C.		1	5	0	0	.000	6	3	0	0.00	0
2000 Florida b.	N.L.		13	82⅔	3	7	.300	57	44	80	4.79	0
2001 Brevard County	Fla.St.		2	9⅓	0	0	.000	10	4	4	1.93	0
2001 Florida c-d	N.L.		27	173⅓	11	12	.478	128	83	145	4.05	0
2002 Florida e	N.L.		31	204⅓	12	9	.571	203	90	153	3.30	0
2003 Florida f	N.L.		4	23	0	2	.000	21	18	18	4.70	0
2004 Jupiter	Fla.St.		1	4	0	0	.000	4	2	2	0.00	0
2004 Albuquerque.	P.C.		1	3⅓	0	0	.000	6	2	7	10.80	0
2004 Florida g.	N.L.		20	120	7	6	.538	113	38	102	3.68	0
2005 Florida h.	N.L.		32	209	12	12	.500	198	79	184	3.44	0
2006 Dunedin	Fla.St.		2	8	0	0	.000	6	2	9	3.38	0
2006 New Hampshire	Eastern		1	6	1	0	1.000	9	3	2	1.50	0
2006 Syracuse	Int.		1	5	1	0	1.000	7	1	0	0.00	0
2006 Toronto i.	A.L.		21	135⅔	10	8	.556	118	39	138	3.98	0
2007 Syracuse	Int.		1	5	0	0	.000	7	1	3	1.80	0
2007 Toronto j.	A.L.		25	165⅔	10	8	.556	176	66	131	3.75	0
2008 Toronto k	A.L.		35	221⅓	18	10	.643	*231	86	211	4.07	0
2009 New York	A.L.		33	207	13	9	.591	195	*97	193	4.04	0
2010 New York	A.L.		33	186⅔	10	15	.400	145	78	204	5.26	0
2011 New York	A.L.		33	190⅓	11	11	.500	173	83	190	5.15	0
2012 Bradenton	Fla.St.		2	6⅓	0	2	.000	9	2	7	8.53	0
2012 Indianapolis	Int.		1	4	0	1	.000	0	4	7	11.25	0
2012 Pittsburgh l-m	N.L.		31	202⅓	16	10	.615	180	62	189	3.51	0
Major League Totals	14 Yrs.		345	2162⅔	137	121	.531	1971	888	1975	4.05	0

Division Series

Year	Club	Lea	G	IP	W	L	Pct	SO	BB	H	ERA	SAVES
2009 New York	A.L.		1	6	0	0	.000	6	5	3	1.50	0
2011 New York	A.L.		1	5⅔	1	0	1.000	3	4	4	1.59	0
Division Series Totals			2	11⅔	1	0	1.000	9	9	7	1.54	0

Championship Series

Year	Club	Lea	G	IP	W	L	Pct	SO	BB	H	ERA	SAVES
2009 New York	A.L.		2	12⅓	0	0	.000	7	5	11	5.84	0
2010 New York	A.L.		1	6	0	1	.000	4	3	6	7.50	0
Championship Series Totals			3	18⅓	0	1	.000	11	8	17	6.38	0

World Series Record

Year	Club	Lea	G	IP	W	L	Pct	SO	BB	H	ERA	SAVES
2009 New York	A.L.		2	9	1	1	.500	11	6	8	7.00	0

a Traded to Florida Marlins by New York Mets with pitcher Jesus Sanchez and outfielder Robert Stratton for pitcher Al Leiter and infielder Ralph Milliard, February 6, 1998.
b On disabled list from March 17 to July 19, 2000.
c On disabled list from March 23 to May 7, 2001.
d Pitched no-hit, no-run game against San Diego Padres, May 12, 2001.
e On disabled list from August 19 to September 14, 2002.
f On disabled list from March 21 to April 9 and April 26 to September 29, 2003.
g On disabled list from March 26 to June 3, 2004.
h Filed for free agency, October 27, 2005. Signed with Toronto Blue Jays, December 6, 2005.
i On disabled list from March 24 to April 15 and April 22 to June 22, 2006.
j On disabled list from June 13 to June 28 and June 29 to August 12, 2007.
k Filed for free agency, November 13, 2008. Signed with New York Yankees, December 18, 2008.
l Traded to Pittsburgh Pirates with cash for outfielder Exicardo Cayones and pitcher Diego Moreno, February 20, 2012.
m On disabled list from March 26 to April 21, 2012.

BURNETT, SEAN RICHARD

Born, Dunedin, Florida, September 17, 1982.
Bats Left. Throws Left. Height, 5 feet, 11 inches. Weight, 190 pounds.

Year	Club	Lea	G	IP	W	L	Pct	SO	BB	H	ERA	SAVES
2000 Pirates	Gulf Coast		8	31	2	1	.667	24	3	31	4.06	0
2001 Hickory.	So.Atl.		26	161⅓	11	8	.579	134	33	164	2.62	0
2002 Lynchburg	Carolina		26	155⅓	13	4	.765	96	33	118	1.80	0
2003 Altoona.	Eastern		27	159⅔	14	6	.700	86	29	158	3.21	0
2004 Nashville	P.C.		10	47	1	5	.167	25	17	58	5.36	0
2004 Pittsburgh a	N.L.		13	71⅔	5	5	.500	30	28	86	5.02	0
2005 Pittsburgh b	N.L.			INJURED—Did Not Play								
2006 Indianapolis	Int.		25	120⅓	8	11	.421	46	46	136	5.16	0
2007 Indianapolis	Int.		15	70⅓	4	5	.444	31	39	83	4.48	0

Year Club	Lea	G	IP	W	L	Pct	SO	BB	H	ERA	SAVES
2008 Indianapolis	Int.	12	17⅓	1	1	.500	15	8	9	1.04	3
2008 Pittsburgh	N.L.	58	56⅔	1	1	.500	42	34	57	4.76	0
2009 Pittsburgh-Washington c	N.L.	71	57⅔	2	3	.400	43	28	36	3.12	1
2010 Washington	N.L.	73	63	1	7	.125	62	20	52	2.14	3
2011 Washington	N.L.	69	56⅔	5	5	.500	33	21	54	3.81	4
2012 Washington d	N.L.	70	56⅔	1	2	.333	57	12	58	2.38	2
Major League Totals	.6 Yrs.	354	362⅓	15	23	.395	267	143	343	3.58	10
Division Series											
2012 Washington	N.L.	2	1	0	0	.000	1	1	3	27.00	0

a On disabled list from August 22 to October 4, 2004.
b On disabled list from April 2 to October 3, 2005.
c Traded to Washington Nationals with outfielder Nyjer Morgan for outfielder Lastings Milledge and pitcher Joel Hanrahan, June 30, 2009.
d Filed for free agency, November 3, 2012. Signed with Los Angeles Angels, December 5, 2012.

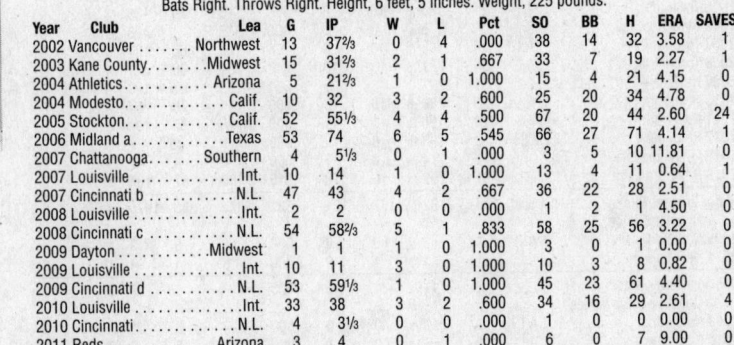

BURTON, LEVI JARED (JARED)
Born, Westminster, South Carolina, June 2, 1981.
Bats Right. Throws Right. Height, 6 feet, 5 inches. Weight, 225 pounds.

Year Club	Lea	G	IP	W	L	Pct	SO	BB	H	ERA	SAVES
2002 Vancouver	Northwest	13	37⅔	0	4	.000	38	14	32	3.58	1
2003 Kane County	Midwest	15	31⅔	2	1	.667	33	7	19	2.27	1
2004 Athletics	Arizona	5	21⅔	1	0	1.000	15	4	21	4.15	0
2004 Modesto	Calif.	10	32	3	2	.600	25	20	34	4.78	0
2005 Stockton	Calif.	52	55⅓	4	4	.500	67	20	44	2.60	24
2006 Midland a	Texas	53	74	6	5	.545	66	27	71	4.14	1
2007 Chattanooga	Southern	4	5⅓	0	1	.000	3	5	10	11.81	0
2007 Louisville	Int.	10	14	1	0	1.000	13	4	11	0.64	1
2007 Cincinnati b	N.L.	47	43	4	2	.667	36	22	28	2.51	0
2008 Louisville	Int.	2	2	0	0	.000	1	2	1	4.50	0
2008 Cincinnati c	N.L.	54	58⅔	5	1	.833	58	25	56	3.22	0
2009 Dayton	Midwest	1	1	1	0	1.000	3	0	1	0.00	0
2009 Louisville	Int.	10	11	3	0	1.000	10	3	8	0.82	0
2009 Cincinnati d	N.L.	53	59⅓	1	0	1.000	45	23	61	4.40	0
2010 Louisville	Int.	33	38	3	2	.600	34	16	29	2.61	4
2010 Cincinnati	N.L.	4	3⅓	0	0	.000	1	0	0	0.00	0
2011 Reds	Arizona	3	4	0	1	.000	6	0	7	9.00	0
2011 Louisville	Int.	11	13	2	0	1.000	11	5	12	4.15	0
2011 Cincinnati e-f	N.L.	6	4⅔	0	0	.000	3	3	6	3.86	0
2012 Minnesota	A.L.	64	62	3	2	.600	55	16	41	2.18	5
Major League Totals	.6 Yrs.	228	231	13	5	.722	198	89	192	3.08	5

a Selected by Cincinnati Reds from Oakland Athletics in Rule V draft, December 7, 2006.
b On disabled list from April 8 to May 9, 2007 and from June 11 to July 7, 2007.
c On disabled list from July 11 to September 2, 2008.
d On disabled list from July 25 to August 10, 2009.
e On disabled list from March 29 to August 22, 2011.
f Filed for free agency, November 1, 2011. Signed with Minnesota Twins organization, November 11, 2011.

BYRDAK, TIMOTHY CHRISTOPHER (TIM)
Born, Oak Lawn, Illinois, October 31, 1973.
Bats Left. Throws Left. Height, 5 feet, 11 inches. Weight, 195 pounds.

Year Club	Lea	G	IP	W	L	Pct	SO	BB	H	ERA	SAVES
1994 Eugene	Northwest	15	73⅓	4	5	.444	77	20	60	3.07	0
1995 Wilmington	Carolina	27	166⅓	11	5	.688	127	45	118	2.16	0
1996 Wichita	Texas	15	84⅔	5	7	.417	47	44	112	6.91	0
1997 Wilmington	Carolina	22	41	4	3	.571	47	12	34	3.51	3
1998 Wichita	Texas	34	52	3	5	.375	37	28	58	4.15	2
1998 Kansas City	A.L.	3	1⅔	0	0	.000	1	0	5	5.40	0
1998 Omaha	P.C.	26	36⅔	2	1	.667	32	20	31	2.45	1
1999 Omaha	P.C.	33	49⅔	3	1	.750	51	28	39	1.81	4
1999 Kansas City	A.L.	33	24⅔	0	3	.000	17	20	32	7.66	1
2000 Omaha	P.C.	34	52⅔	6	2	.750	47	29	59	4.44	4
2000 Kansas City	A.L.	12	6⅓	0	1	.000	8	4	11	11.37	0
2000 Wichita a	Texas	4	6⅔	0	0	.000	1	3	9	5.40	0
2001 Buffalo	Int.	4	17⅓	2	0	1.000	17	5	18	4.67	0
2002 Kinston	Carolina	2	4	1	0	1.000	3	4	3	4.50	0
2002 Akron	Eastern	9	13	0	0	.000	8	11	16	6.23	1
2003 Joliet	Northern	5	34	2	1	.667	18	10	31	2.67	0
2003 Gary	Northern	10	66	2	4	.333	58	25	60	4.34	0

Year	Club	Lea	G	IP	W	L	Pct	SO	BB	H	ERA	SAVES
2004 Ottawa ....Int.			33	34⅓	2	1	.667	43	12	46	4.19	2
2004 Portland b-c-d ........P.C.			20	38	3	0	1.000	25	17	47	5.45	0
2005 Ottawa ....Int.			37	38⅔	3	2	.600	44	15	23	2.09	11
2005 Baltimore ............A.L.			41	26⅔	0	1	.000	31	21	27	4.05	1
2006 Aberdeen ......N.Y.-Penn.			1	1	0	0	.000	3	0	2	9.00	0
2006 Frederick ....Carolina			1	1⅓	0	0	.000	0	1	4	13.50	0
2006 Bowie.............Eastern			3	4	0	0	.000	7	2	4	2.25	0
2006 Baltimore e-f ..........A.L.			16	7	1	0	1.000	2	8	14	12.86	0
2007 Toledo ....Int.			17	24⅓	1	0	1.000	30	8	22	2.59	0
2007 Detroit g..............A.L.			39	45	3	0	1.000	49	26	38	3.20	1
2008 Round Rock...........P.C.			7	7⅓	0	0	.000	10	0	8	3.68	0
2008 Houston h ............N.L.			59	55⅓	2	1	.667	47	29	45	3.90	0
2009 Houston..............N.L.			76	61⅓	1	2	.333	58	36	39	3.23	0
2010 Round Rock...........P.C.			2	2	0	0	.000	1	2	1	4.50	0
2010 Houston i-j............N.L.			64	38⅔	2	2	.500	29	20	40	3.49	0
2011 New York.............N.L.			72	37⅔	2	1	.667	47	19	34	3.82	1
2012 New York k-l..........N.L.			56	30⅔	2	2	.500	34	18	18	4.40	0
Major League Totals ....11 Yrs.			471	335	13	13	.500	323	201	303	4.30	4

a Not offered contract, December 1, 2000. Signed with Cleveland Indians organization, December 24, 2000.
b Released by Cleveland Indians, June 28, 2002. Signed with San Diego Padres organization, January 30, 2004.
c Sold to Baltimore Orioles, June 22, 2004.
d Filed for free agency, October 15, 2004, re-signed with Baltimore Orioles organization, November 16, 2004.
e On disabled list from April 19 to July 30, 2006.
f Filed for free agency, October 15, 2006. Signed with Detroit Tigers organization, November 18, 2006.
g On disabled list from June 27 to July 25, 2007.
h Released by Detroit Tigers, March 26, 2008. Signed with Houston Astros organization, April 3, 2008.
i On disabled list from May 4 to May 24, 2010.
j Filed for free agency, November 29, 2010. Signed with New York Mets organization, January 25, 2011.
k On disabled list from August 2 to October 29, 2012.
l Filed for free agency, November 3, 2012, re-signed with New York Mets organization, November 26, 2012.

CAHILL, TREVOR JOHN
Born, Oceanside, California, March 1, 1988.
Bats Right. Throws Right. Height, 6 feet, 3 inches. Weight, 210 pounds.

Year	Club	Lea	G	IP	W	L	Pct	SO	BB	H	ERA	SAVES
2006 Athletics...........Arizona			4	9	0	0	.000	11	7	2	3.00	0
2007 Kane County.......Midwest			20	105⅓	11	4	.733	117	40	85	2.73	0
2008 Stockton............Calif.			14	87⅓	5	4	.556	103	31	52	2.78	0
2008 Midland ....Texas			7	37	6	1	.857	33	19	24	2.19	0
2009 Oakland .............A.L.			32	178⅔	10	13	.435	90	72	185	4.63	0
2010 Sacramento ...........P.C.			2	8⅔	1	0	1.000	8	5	7	1.04	0
2010 Oakland a.............A.L.			30	196⅔	18	8	.692	118	63	155	2.97	0
2011 Oakland b.............A.L.			34	207⅔	12	14	.462	147	82	214	4.16	0
2012 Arizona................N.L.			32	200	13	12	.520	156	74	184	3.78	0
Major League Totals ....4 Yrs.			128	783	53	47	.530	511	291	738	3.87	0

a On disabled list from April 4 to April 10, 2010.
b Traded to Arizona Diamondbacks with pitcher Craig Breslow for outfielder Collin Cowgill, pitcher Jarrod Parker and pitcher Ryan Cook, December 9, 2011.

CAIN, MATTHEW THOMAS (MATT)
Born, Dothan, Alabama, October 1, 1984.
Bats Right. Throws Right. Height, 6 feet, 3 inches. Weight, 235 pounds.

Year	Club	Lea	G	IP	W	L	Pct	SO	BB	H	ERA	SAVES
2002 Giants.............Arizona			8	19⅓	0	1	.000	20	11	13	3.72	0
2003 Hagerstown ....So.Atl.			14	74	4	4	.500	90	24	57	2.55	0
2004 San Jose ....Calif.			13	72⅔	7	1	.875	89	17	58	1.86	0
2004 Norwich ....Eastern			15	86	6	4	.600	72	40	73	3.35	0
2005 Fresno ...............P.C.			26	145⅔	10	5	.667	176	73	118	4.39	0
2005 San Francisco ........N.L.			7	46⅓	2	1	.667	30	19	24	2.33	0
2006 San Francisco ........N.L.			32	190⅔	13	12	.520	179	87	157	4.15	0
2007 San Francisco ........N.L.			32	200	7	16	.304	163	79	173	3.65	0
2008 San Francisco ........N.L.			34	217⅔	8	14	.364	186	91	206	3.76	0
2009 San Francisco ........N.L.			33	217⅔	14	8	.636	171	73	184	2.89	0
2010 San Francisco ........N.L.			33	223⅓	13	11	.542	177	61	181	3.14	0
2011 San Francisco ........N.L.			33	221⅓	12	11	.522	179	63	177	2.88	0
2012 San Francisco a ........N.L.			32	219⅓	16	5	.762	193	51	177	2.79	0
Major League Totals ....8 Yrs.			236	1536⅔	85	78	.521	1278	524	1279	3.27	0

Year	Club	Lea	G	IP	W	L	Pct	SO	BB	H	ERA	SAVES
Division Series												
2010 San Francisco .... N.L.			1	6⅔	0	0	.000	6	2	7	0.00	0
2012 San Francisco .... N.L.			2	10⅔	1	1	.500	9	3	11	5.06	0
Division Series Totals			3	17⅓	1	1	.500	15	5	18	3.12	0
Championship Series												
2010 San Francisco .... N.L.			1	7	1	0	1.000	5	3	2	0.00	0
2012 San Francisco .... N.L.			2	12⅓	1	1	.500	6	2	11	2.19	0
Championship Series Totals			3	19⅓	2	1	.667	11	5	13	1.40	0
World Series Record												
2010 San Francisco .... N.L.			1	7⅔	1	0	1.000	2	2	4	0.00	0
2012 San Francisco .... N.L.			1	7	0	0	.000	5	2	5	3.86	0
World Series Totals............			2	14⅔	1	0	1.000	7	4	9	1.84	0

a Pitched no-hit, no-run perfect game against Houston Astros, June 13, 2012.

CAMP, SHAWN ANTHONY
Born, Fairfax, Virginia, November 18, 1975.
Bats Right. Throws Right. Height, 6 feet, 1 inch. Weight, 205 pounds.

Year	Club	Lea	G	IP	W	L	Pct	SO	BB	H	ERA	SAVES
1997 Idaho Falls .... Pioneer			30	32⅔	2	1	.667	41	14	41	5.51	12
1998 Clinton .... Midwest			47	55	3	5	.375	62	20	48	2.62	13
1999 Rancho Cucamonga.... Calif.			53	66	1	5	.167	78	25	68	3.95	6
2000 Rancho Cucamonga.... Calif.			14	18⅔	1	0	1.000	18	5	10	1.45	6
2000 Mobile .... Southern			45	59⅓	3	3	.500	53	30	47	2.43	1
2001 Altoona............ Eastern			8	23⅓	4	0	1.000	19	8	25	4.24	0
2001 Nashville .... P.C.			11	17	0	0	.000	15	8	11	2.12	0
2001 Portland.............. P.C.			4	7	1	0	1.000	6	1	2	0.00	0
2001 Mobile a.......... Southern			35	48⅔	6	2	.750	55	15	46	4.44	0
2002 Nashville .... P.C.			39	58⅓	4	1	.800	59	15	50	3.24	2
2003 Altoona........... Eastern			18	29	0	2	.000	35	11	26	4.34	0
2003 Nashville b........... P.C.			33	43⅓	0	1	.000	36	15	50	4.98	0
2004 Kansas City .... A.L.			42	66⅔	2	2	.500	51	16	74	3.92	2
2004 Omaha................ P.C.			15	22	1	1	.500	21	6	26	5.32	1
2005 Omaha................ P.C.			21	67⅔	3	6	.333	42	22	71	3.86	1
2005 Kansas City .... A.L.			29	49	1	4	.200	28	13	69	6.43	0
2006 Tampa Bay c.......... A.L.			75	75	7	4	.636	53	19	93	4.68	4
2007 Tampa Bay .... A.L.			50	40	0	3	.000	36	18	63	7.20	0
2007 Durham .... Int.			12	15⅓	1	0	1.000	16	2	13	1.17	4
2008 Syracuse .... Int.			7	10	1	0	1.000	13	0	4	0.00	4
2008 Toronto d .... A.L.			40	39⅓	3	1	.750	31	11	40	4.12	0
2009 Toronto .... A.L.			59	79⅔	2	6	.250	58	29	73	3.50	1
2010 Toronto .... A.L.			70	72⅓	4	3	.571	46	18	71	2.99	2
2011 Toronto e .... A.L.			67	66⅓	6	3	.667	32	22	79	4.21	1
2012 Chicago f-g-h .... N.L.			*80	77⅔	3	6	.333	54	21	79	3.59	2
Major League Totals .... 9 Yrs.			512	566	28	32	.467	389	167	641	4.29	12

a Traded by San Diego Padres to Pittsburgh Pirates for outfielder Emil Brown, July 10, 2001.
b Filed for free agency, October 15, 2003. Signed with Kansas City Royals organization, October 29, 2003.
c Not offered contract, December 21, 2005. Signed with Tampa Bay Devil Rays, January 17, 2006.
d Filed for free agency, October 31, 2007. Signed with Toronto Blue Jays organization, January 7, 2008.
e Filed for free agency, October 30, 2011.
f Signed with Seattle Mariners, February 6, 2012.
g Released by Seattle Mariners, March 21, 2012. Signed with Chicago Cubs organization, March 26, 2012.
h Filed for free agency, November 3, 2012, re-signed with Chicago Cubs, November 19, 2012.

CAPPS, CARTER LEWIS
Born, Kinston, North Carolina, August 7, 1990.
Bats Right. Throws Right. Height, 6 feet, 5 inches. Weight, 220 pounds.

Year	Club	Lea	G	IP	W	L	Pct	SO	BB	H	ERA	SAVES
2011 Clinton .... Midwest			4	18	1	1	.500	21	10	19	6.00	0
2012 Jackson .... Southern			38	50	2	3	.400	72	12	40	1.26	19
2012 Tacoma .... P.C.			1	1⅓	0	0	.000	3	0	0	0.00	0
2012 Seattle .... A.L.			18	25	0	0	.000	28	11	25	3.96	0

CAPPS, MATTHEW DICUS (MATT)

Born, Douglasville, Georgia, September 3, 1983.
Bats Right. Throws Right. Height, 6 feet, 2 inches. Weight, 240 pounds.

Year	Club	Lea	G	IP	W	L	Pct	SO	BB	H	ERA	SAVES
2002	Pirates	Gulf Coast	7	13	1	0	1.000	8	6	13	0.69	1
2003	Lynchburg	Carolina	1	5	0	0	.000	5	4	3	5.40	0
2003	Pirates	Gulf Coast	10	62²/₃	5	1	.833	54	9	40	1.87	0
2004	Williamsport	N.Y.-Penn.	11	65	3	5	.375	33	4	84	4.85	0
2004	Hickory	So.Atl.	12	42	2	3	.400	27	16	82	10.07	0
2005	Hickory	So.Atl.	35	53²/₃	3	4	.429	39	5	47	2.52	14
2005	Altoona	Eastern	17	20	0	2	.000	26	1	21	2.70	7
2005	Pittsburgh	N.L.	4	4	0	0	.000	3	0	5	4.50	0
2006	Pittsburgh	N.L.	85	80²/₃	9	1	.900	56	12	81	3.79	1
2007	Pittsburgh	N.L.	76	79	4	7	.364	64	16	64	2.28	18
2008	Pirates	Gulf Coast	2	2	0	0	.000	2	0	2	0.00	0
2008	Altoona	Eastern	3	3	0	0	.000	5	1	0	0.00	0
2008	Indianapolis	Int.	1	1²/₃	0	0	.000	1	3	0	0.00	0
2008	Pittsburgh a	N.L.	49	53²/₃	2	3	.400	39	5	47	3.02	21
2009	Pittsburgh b	N.L.	57	54¹/₃	4	8	.333	46	17	73	5.80	27
2010	Washington	N.L.	47	46	3	3	.500	38	9	51	2.74	26
2010	Minnesota c	A.L.	27	27	2	0	1.000	21	8	24	2.00	16
2011	Minnesota d	A.L.	69	65²/₃	4	7	.364	34	13	66	4.25	15
2012	Fort Myers	Fla.St.	2	2	1	0	1.000	1	0	1	0.00	0
2012	Minnesota e-f	A.L.	30	29¹/₃	1	4	.200	18	4	28	3.68	14
Major League Totals	8 Yrs.		444	439²/₃	29	33	.468	319	84	439	3.52	138
Division Series												
2010	Minnesota	A.L.	1	1	0	0	.000	0	0	2	9.00	0

a On disabled list from July 2 to August 23, 2008.
b Not offered contract, December 12, 2009. Signed with Washington Nationals, December 24, 2009.
c Traded to Minnesota Twins for catcher Wilson Ramos, pitcher Joe Testa and cash, July 30, 2010.
d Filed for free agency, October 30, 2011, re-signed with Minnesota Twins, December 7, 2011.
e On disabled list from June 24 to July 13 and July 17 to September 24, 2012.
f Filed for free agency, November 3, 2012.

CAPUANO, CHRISTOPHER FRANK (CHRIS)

Born, Springfield, Massachusetts, August 19, 1978.
Bats Left. Throws Left. Height, 6 feet, 3 inches. Weight, 225 pounds.

Year	Club	Lea	G	IP	W	L	Pct	SO	BB	H	ERA	SAVES
2000	South Bend	Midwest	18	101²/₃	10	4	.714	105	45	68	2.21	0
2001	El Paso	Texas	28	159¹/₃	10	11	.476	167	75	184	5.31	0
2002	Tucson	P.C.	6	36¹/₃	4	1	.800	29	11	30	2.72	0
2003	Tucson	P.C.	23	142²/₃	9	5	.643	108	43	133	3.34	0
2003	Arizona a	N.L.	9	33	2	4	.333	23	11	27	4.64	0
2004	Milwaukee	N.L.	17	88¹/₃	6	8	.429	80	37	91	4.99	0
2004	Beloit	Midwest	1	2²/₃	0	0	.000	4	1	3	3.38	0
2004	Indianapolis	Int.	2	8²/₃	0	1	.000	9	5	10	8.31	0
2004	High Desert b	Calif.	1	2	0	1	.000	2	3	6	27.00	0
2005	Milwaukee	N.L.	35	219	18	12	.600	176	91	212	3.99	0
2006	Milwaukee	N.L.	34	221¹/₃	11	12	.478	174	47	229	4.03	0
2007	Milwaukee c	N.L.	29	150	5	12	.294	132	54	170	5.10	0
2008	Milwaukee d-e	N.L.			INJURED—Did Not Play							
2009	Brewers	Arizona	3	3	0	0	.000	4	2	5	6.00	0
2009	Helena	Pioneer	2	4	0	0	.000	3	0	2	0.00	0
2010	Brevard County	Fla.St.	3	14²/₃	2	0	1.000	17	0	12	1.23	0
2010	Nashville	P.C.	4	25	1	1	.500	16	4	21	1.80	0
2010	Milwaukee f	N.L.	24	66	4	4	.500	54	21	65	3.95	0
2011	New York g	N.L.	33	186	11	12	.478	168	53	198	4.55	0
2012	Los Angeles	N.L.	33	198¹/₃	12	12	.500	162	54	188	3.72	0
Major League Totals	8 Yrs.		214	1162	69	76	.476	969	368	1180	4.28	0

a Traded to Milwaukee Brewers with infielder Junior Spivey, infielder Craig Counsell, infielder Lyle Overbay, catcher Chad Moeller and pitcher Jorge DeRosa for infielder Richie Sexson, pitcher Shane Nance and player to be named later, December 1, 2003. Arizona Diamondbacks received outfielder Noochie Varner to complete trade, December 15, 2003.
b On disabled list from April 19 to May 26 and May 27 to June 12 and August 25 to October 6, 2004.
c On disabled list from June 9 to July 1, 2007.
d Not offered contract, December 12, 2008, re-signed with Milwaukee Brewers organization, December 16, 2008.
e On disabled list from March 21 to September 29, 2008.
f Filed for free agency, November 1, 2010. Signed with New York Mets, January 3, 2011.
g Filed for free agency, October 30, 2011. Signed with Los Angeles Dodgers, December 2, 2011.

CARPENTER, CHRISTOPHER JOHN (CHRIS)

Born, Exeter, New Hampshire, April 27, 1975.
Bats Right. Throws Right. Height, 6 feet, 6 inches. Weight, 230 pounds.

Year	Club	Lea	G	IP	W	L	Pct	SO	BB	H	ERA	SAVES
1994	Medicne Hat	Pioneer	15	84²/₃	6	3	.667	80	39	76	2.76	0
1995	Dunedin	Fla.St.	15	99¹/₃	3	5	.375	56	50	83	2.17	0
1995	Knoxville	Southern	12	64¹/₃	3	7	.300	53	31	71	5.18	0
1996	Knoxville	Southern	28	171¹/₃	7	9	.438	150	91	161	3.94	0
1997	Syracuse	Int.	19	120	4	9	.308	97	53	113	4.50	0
1997	Toronto	A.L.	14	81¹/₃	3	7	.300	55	37	108	5.09	0
1998	Toronto	A.L.	33	175	12	7	.632	136	61	177	4.37	0
1999	Toronto	A.L.	24	150	9	8	.529	106	48	177	4.38	0
1999	St. Catharines a	N.Y.-Penn.	1	4	0	0	.000	6	1	5	4.50	0
2000	Toronto	A.L.	34	175¹/₃	10	12	.455	113	83	204	6.26	0
2001	Toronto	A.L.	34	215²/₃	11	11	.500	157	75	229	4.09	0
2002	Toronto	A.L.	13	73¹/₃	4	5	.444	45	27	89	5.28	0
2002	Tennessee	Southern	5	18²/₃	0	1	.000	9	8	26	8.20	0
2002	Syracuse b-c	Int.	1	6	0	1	.000	6	2	8	4.50	0
2003	Palm Beach	Fla.St.	4	7	0	1	.000	6	1	6	1.29	0
2003	Memphis	P.C.	3	8¹/₃	0	0	.000	4	2	11	5.40	0
2003	Tennessee d-e	Southern	1	3¹/₃	0	1	.000	2	2	7	13.50	0
2004	St. Louis	N.L.	28	182	15	5	.750	152	38	169	3.46	0
2005	St. Louis f	N.L.	33	241²/₃	21	5	*.808	213	51	204	2.83	0
2006	St. Louis g	N.L.	32	221²/₃	15	8	.652	184	43	194	3.09	0
2007	Palm Beach	Fla.St.	2	4¹/₃	0	1	.000	4	1	7	6.23	0
2007	St. Louis h	N.L.	1	6	0	1	.000	3	1	9	7.50	0
2008	Springfield	Texas	1	4	0	0	.000	4	4	1	0.00	0
2008	Memphis	P.C.	1	5²/₃	0	1	.000	5	1	4	3.18	0
2008	St. Louis i	N.L.	4	15¹/₃	0	1	.000	7	4	16	1.76	0
2009	St. Louis j	N.L.	28	192²/₃	17	4	*.810	144	38	156	*2.24	0
2010	St. Louis	N.L.	35	235	16	9	.640	179	63	214	3.22	0
2011	St. Louis	N.L.	34	*237¹/₃	11	9	.550	191	55	243	3.45	0
2012	St. Louis k	N.L.	3	17	0	2	.000	12	3	16	3.71	0
Major League Totals	15 Yrs.		350	2219¹/₃	144	94	.605	1697	627	2205	3.76	0
Division Series												
2005	St. Louis	N.L.	1	6	1	0	1.000	3	3	3	0.00	0
2006	St. Louis	N.L.	2	13¹/₃	2	0	1.000	12	4	12	2.03	0
2009	St. Louis	N.L.	1	5	0	1	.000	3	4	9	7.20	0
2011	St. Louis	N.L.	2	12	1	0	1.000	5	3	8	3.00	0
2012	St. Louis	N.L.	1	5²/₃	1	0	1.000	2	2	7	0.00	0
Division Series Totals			7	42	5	1	.833	25	16	39	2.36	0
Championship Series												
2005	St. Louis	N.L.	2	15	1	0	1.000	9	4	14	3.00	0
2006	St. Louis	N.L.	2	11	0	1	.000	5	4	13	5.73	0
2011	St. Louis	N.L.	1	5	1	0	1.000	3	3	6	5.40	0
2012	St. Louis	N.L.	2	8	0	2	.000	7	4	12	4.50	0
Championship Series Totals			7	39	2	3	.400	24	15	45	4.38	0
World Series Record												
2006	St. Louis	N.L.	1	8	1	0	1.000	6	0	3	0.00	0
2011	St. Louis	N.L.	3	19	2	0	1.000	13	5	17	2.84	0
World Series Totals			4	27	3	0	1.000	19	5	20	2.00	0

a On disabled list from June 3 to June 28, 1999.
b On disabled list from April 2 to April 20 and April 22 to June 21 and August 14 to October 7, 2002.
c Filed for free agency, October 9, 2002. Signed with St. Louis Cardinals, December 15, 2002.
d On disabled list from March 27 to September 30, 2003.
e Filed for free agency, November 3, 2003, re-signed with St. Louis Cardinals, December 1, 2003.
f Selected Cy Young Award Winner in National League for 2005.
g On disabled list from May 22 to June 6, 2006.
h On disabled list from April 2 to November 2, 2007.
i On disabled list from March 21 to July 30 and August 11 to September 1, 2008.
j On disabled list from April 15 to May 20, 2009.
k On disabled list from March 26 to September 21, 2012.

CASHNER, ANDREW BURTON

Born, Conroe, Texas, September 11, 1986.
Bats Right. Throws Right. Height, 6 feet, 6 inches. Weight, 210 pounds.

Year	Club	Lea	G	IP	W	L	Pct	SO	BB	H	ERA	SAVES
2008	Cubs	Arizona	1	1	0	0	.000	2	0	1	0.00	0
2008	Daytona	Fla.St.	1	2²/₃	0	1	.000	1	4	4	13.50	0

Year	Club	Lea	G	IP	W	L	Pct	SO	BB	H	ERA	SAVES
2008 Boise	Northwest		6	16⅓	1	1	.500	16	19	19	4.96	0
2009 Daytona	Fla.St.		12	42	0	0	.000	34	15	31	1.50	0
2009 Tennessee	Southern		12	58⅓	3	4	.429	41	27	45	3.39	0
2010 Tennessee	Southern		6	36	3	1	.750	42	13	22	2.75	0
2010 Iowa	P.C.		5	21	3	0	1.000	17	2	17	0.86	0
2010 Chicago	N.L.		53	54⅓	2	6	.250	50	30	55	4.80	0
2011 Tennessee	Southern		3	2⅔	0	1	.000	6	0	3	6.75	0
2011 Iowa	P.C.		2	2	0	0	.000	2	0	0	0.00	0
2011 Chicago a-b	N.L.		7	10⅔	0	0	.000	8	4	3	1.69	0
2012 San Antonio	Texas		3	14⅓	2	0	1.000	22	3	10	1.88	0
2012 Tucson	P.C.		3	9	0	1	.000	8	2	8	3.00	0
2012 San Diego c	N.L.		33	46⅓	3	4	.429	52	19	42	4.27	0
Major League Totals	3 Yrs.		93	111⅓	5	10	.333	110	53	100	4.28	0

a On disabled list from April 8 to September 5, 2011.
b Traded to San Diego Padres with outfielder Kyung-Min Na for infielder Anthony Rizzo and pitcher Xach Cates, January 6, 2012.
c On disabled list from July 4 to September 1, 2012.

CASILLA, SANTIAGO

Born, Don Gregorio, Dominican Republic, June 25, 1980.
Bats Right. Throws Right. Height, 6 feet. Weight, 200 pounds.

Year	Club	Lea	G	IP	W	L	Pct	SO	BB	H	ERA	SAVES
2001 Athletics	Arizona		12	47⅓	4	2	.667	50	6	37	2.85	0
2002 Athletics	Arizona		13	59	2	1	.667	66	17	56	2.44	1
2002 Vancouver	Northwest		3	12⅓	0	3	.000	16	7	15	7.30	0
2003 Kane County	Midwest		14	42⅓	0	1	.000	28	19	40	2.55	0
2004 Kane County	Midwest		25	30	1	0	1.000	49	6	16	0.30	16
2004 Midland	Texas		13	18	2	0	1.000	32	15	10	1.50	2
2004 Sacramento	P.C.		11	13⅔	1	2	.333	21	9	10	5.93	1
2004 Oakland	A.L.		4	5⅔	0	0	.000	5	9	5	12.71	0
2005 Midland	Texas		10	16⅔	0	0	.000	30	9	9	1.08	6
2005 Sacramento	P.C.		44	48⅓	3	6	.333	73	20	45	4.47	20
2005 Oakland a	A.L.		3	3	0	0	.000	1	1	2	3.00	0
2006 Oakland	A.L.		2	2⅓	0	0	.000	2	2	2	11.57	0
2006 Sacramento	P.C.		25	33	2	0	1.000	32	10	25	3.27	4
2007 Sacramento	P.C.		22	24	2	1	.667	29	14	18	4.13	3
2007 Oakland	A.L.		46	50⅔	3	1	.750	52	23	43	4.44	2
2008 Stockton	Calif.		1	1	0	0	.000	2	0	0	0.00	0
2008 Sacramento	P.C.		2	2⅔	0	0	.000	5	1	3	3.38	0
2008 Oakland b	A.L.		51	50⅓	2	1	.667	43	20	60	3.93	2
2009 Stockton	Calif.		1	1	0	0	.000	0	0	0	0.00	0
2009 Sacramento	P.C.		1	1	0	0	.000	0	0	0	0.00	0
2009 Oakland c	A.L.		46	48⅓	1	2	.333	35	25	61	5.96	0
2010 Fresno	P.C.		4	4	0	0	.000	7	2	2	0.00	2
2010 San Francisco	N.L.		52	55⅓	7	2	.778	56	26	40	1.95	2
2011 San Jose	Calif.		2	3	0	0	.000	1	2	3	0.00	0
2011 Fresno	P.C.		4	5	0	0	.000	4	1	3	1.80	0
2011 San Francisco d	N.L.		49	51⅔	2	2	.500	45	25	33	1.74	6
2012 San Francisco	N.L.		73	63⅓	7	6	.538	55	22	55	2.84	25
Major League Totals	9 Yrs.		326	330⅔	22	14	.611	294	153	301	3.62	37
Division Series												
2010 San Francisco	N.L.		1	1⅔	0	0	.000	2	0	1	0.00	0
2012 San Francisco	N.L.		5	3⅓	0	0	.000	5	1	6	2.70	0
Division Series Totals			6	5	0	0	.000	7	1	7	1.80	0
Championship Series												
2010 San Francisco	N.L.		2	1⅔	0	0	.000	2	1	2	5.40	0
2012 San Francisco	N.L.		4	2⅓	0	0	.000	3	0	2	0.00	0
Championship Series Totals			6	4	0	0	.000	5	1	4	2.25	0
World Series Record												
2010 San Francisco	N.L.		1	1⅓	0	0	.000	1	0	0	0.00	0
2012 San Francisco	N.L.		2	1⅓	1	0	1.000	0	0	0	0.00	0
World Series Totals			3	2⅔	1	0	1.000	1	0	0	0.00	0

a Played under name of Jairo Garcia 2001-2005.
b On disabled list from May 16 to June 19, 2008.
c Released by Oakland Athletics, December 10, 2009. Signed with San Francisco Giants organization, January 21, 2010.
d On disabled list from April 6 to May 28, 2011.

CECIL, BRETT AARION
Born, Dunkirk, Maryland, July 2, 1986.
Bats Right. Throws Left. Height, 6 feet, 2 inches. Weight, 225 pounds.

Year	Club	Lea	G	IP	W	L	Pct	SO	BB	H	ERA	SAVES
2007 Auburn	N.Y.-Penn.	14	49²/₃	1	0	1.000	56	11	36	1.27	0
2008 New Hampshire	Eastern	18	77²/₃	6	2	.750	87	23	66	2.55	0
2008 Dunedin	Fla.St.	4	10¹/₃	0	0	.000	11	2	6	1.74	0
2008 Syracuse	Int.	6	30²/₃	2	3	.400	31	16	28	4.11	0
2009 Las Vegas	P.C.	9	49	1	5	.167	32	19	53	5.69	0
2009 Toronto	A.L.	18	93¹/₃	7	4	.636	69	38	116	5.30	0
2010 Las Vegas	P.C.	2	11	2	0	1.000	11	2	13	2.45	0
2010 Toronto	A.L.	28	172²/₃	15	7	.682	117	54	175	4.22	0
2011 Las Vegas	P.C.	12	78²/₃	8	2	.800	63	24	89	5.26	0
2011 Toronto	A.L.	20	123²/₃	4	11	.267	87	42	122	4.73	0
2012 New Hampshire	Eastern	9	42²/₃	3	2	.600	34	14	44	3.38	0
2012 Las Vegas	P.C.	6	39²/₃	1	2	.333	33	7	36	2.50	0
2012 Toronto	A.L.	21	61¹/₃	2	4	.333	51	23	70	5.72	0
Major League Totals	4 Yrs.		87	451	28	26	.519	324	157	483	4.79	0

CHACIN (MOLINA), JHOULYS JOSE
Born, Maracaibo, Venezuela, January 7, 1988.
Bats Right. Throws Right. Height, 6 feet, 3 inches. Weight, 215 pounds.

Year	Club	Lea	G	IP	W	L	Pct	SO	BB	H	ERA	SAVES
2007 Casper	Pioneer	16	73	6	5	.545	77	26	85	3.13	0
2008 Asheville	So.Atl.	16	111¹/₃	10	1	.909	98	30	82	1.86	0
2008 Modesto	Calif.	12	66¹/₃	8	2	.800	62	12	61	2.31	0
2009 Tulsa	Texas	18	103¹/₃	8	6	.571	86	35	87	3.14	0
2009 Colorado Springs	P.C.	4	14¹/₃	1	2	.333	11	13	11	3.77	0
2009 Colorado	N.L.	9	11	0	1	.000	13	11	6	4.91	0
2010 Colorado Springs	P.C.	7	35²/₃	3	2	.600	34	17	27	1.51	0
2010 Colorado	N.L.	28	137¹/₃	9	11	.450	138	61	114	3.28	0
2011 Colorado	N.L.	31	194	11	14	.440	150	*87	168	3.62	0
2012 Modesto	Calif.	1	2¹/₃	0	1	.000	1	0	7	19.29	0
2012 Tulsa	Texas	2	9	0	1	.000	7	2	9	6.00	0
2012 Colorado Springs	P.C.	2	13²/₃	1	1	.500	5	5	10	2.63	0
2012 Colorado a	N.L.	14	69	3	5	.375	45	32	80	4.43	0
Major League Totals	4 Yrs.		82	411¹/₃	23	31	.426	346	191	368	3.68	0

a On disabled list from May 2 to August 21, 2012.

CHAMBERLAIN, JUSTIN LOUIS (JOBA)
Born, Lincoln, Nebraska, September 23, 1985.
Bats Right. Throws Right. Height, 6 feet, 2 inches. Weight, 230 pounds.

Year	Club	Lea	G	IP	W	L	Pct	SO	BB	H	ERA	SAVES
2007 Tampa	Fla.St.	7	40	4	0	1.000	51	11	25	2.03	0
2007 Trenton	Eastern	8	40¹/₃	4	2	.667	66	15	32	3.35	0
2007 Scranton-WB	Int.	3	8	1	0	1.000	18	1	5	0.00	0
2007 New York	A.L.	19	24	2	0	1.000	34	6	12	0.38	1
2008 New York a	A.L.	42	100¹/₃	4	3	.571	118	39	87	2.60	0
2009 New York	A.L.	32	157¹/₃	9	6	.600	133	76	167	4.75	0
2010 New York	A.L.	73	71¹/₃	3	4	.429	77	22	71	4.40	3
2011 New York b	A.L.	27	28²/₃	2	0	1.000	24	7	23	2.83	0
2012 Yankees	Gulf Coast	3	4	0	0	.000	6	0	0	0.00	0
2012 Tampa	Fla.St.	3	4	0	1	.000	1	1	3	2.25	0
2012 Trenton	Eastern	1	1¹/₃	1	0	1.000	3	0	1	0.00	0
2012 New York c	A.L.	22	20²/₃	1	0	1.000	22	6	26	4.35	0
Major League Totals	6 Yrs.		215	402²/₃	21	13	.618	408	156	386	3.73	4
Division Series												
2007 New York	A.L.	2	3²/₃	0	0	.000	4	3	3	4.91	0
2009 New York	A.L.	3	1²/₃	0	0	.000	1	0	2	0.00	0
2012 New York	A.L.	1	1	0	0	.000	1	0	1	0.00	0
Division Series Totals			6	6¹/₃	0	0	.000	6	3	6	2.84	0
Championship Series												
2009 New York	A.L.	4	1²/₃	0	0	.000	2	0	5	5.40	0
2010 New York	A.L.	3	3¹/₃	0	0	.000	3	2	4	2.70	0
2012 New York	A.L.	3	1¹/₃	0	0	.000	0	0	3	0.00	0
Championship Series Totals			10	6¹/₃	0	0	.000	5	2	12	2.84	0

Year	Club	Lea	G	IP	W	L	Pct	SO	BB	H	ERA	SAVES
	World Series Record											
2009 New York . . . . A.L.			3	3	1	0	1.000	4	1	2	3.00	0

a On disabled list from August 5 to September 2, 2008.
b On disabled list from June 8 to October 12, 2011.
c On disabled list from March 26 to July 31, 2012.

CHAPMAN, ALBERTIN AROLDIS (AROLDIS)
Born, Holguin, Cuba, February 28, 1988.
Bats Left. Throws Left. Height, 6 feet, 4 inches. Weight, 185 pounds.

Year	Club	Lea	G	IP	W	L	Pct	SO	BB	H	ERA	SAVES
2010 Louisville . . . . Int.			39	95²/₃	9	6	.600	125	52	77	3.57	8
2010 Cincinnati a . . . . N.L.			15	13¹/₃	2	2	.500	19	5	9	2.03	0
2011 Carolina . . . . Southern			5	7¹/₃	1	1	.500	11	6	5	6.14	0
2011 Louisville . . . . Int.			4	5²/₃	0	1	.000	9	2	9	11.12	0
2011 Cincinnati b . . . . N.L.			54	50	4	1	.800	71	41	24	3.60	1
2012 Cincinnati . . . . N.L.			68	71²/₃	5	5	.500	122	23	35	1.51	38
Major League Totals . . . . .3 Yrs.			137	135	11	8	.579	212	69	68	2.33	39
	Division Series											
2010 Cincinnati . . . . N.L.			2	1²/₃	0	1	.000	1	0	3	0.00	0
2012 Cincinnati . . . . N.L.			3	3	0	0	.000	3	2	2	3.00	0
Division Series Totals			5	4²/₃	0	1	.000	4	2	5	1.93	0

a Played in Cuba 2005 through 2009. Signed with Cincinnati Reds, January 12, 2010.
b On disabled list from May 16 to June 24, 2011.

CHATWOOD, TYLER COLE
Born, Fontana, California, December 16, 1989.
Bats Right. Throws Right. Height, 6 feet. Weight, 185 pounds.

Year	Club	Lea	G	IP	W	L	Pct	SO	BB	H	ERA	SAVES
2008 Angels . . . . Arizona			11	38	1	2	.333	48	36	25	3.08	0
2009 Cedar Rapids . . . . . . .Midwest			24	116¹/₃	8	7	.533	106	66	99	4.02	0
2010 Rancho Cucamonga. . . . Calif.			14	81¹/₃	8	3	.727	70	36	71	1.77	0
2010 Salt Lake . . . . P.C.			1	5¹/₃	1	0	1.000	3	0	9	6.35	0
2010 Arkansas . . . . .Texas			12	68¹/₃	4	6	.400	36	27	72	3.82	0
2011 Salt Lake . . . . P.C.			4	16	1	2	.333	11	11	21	5.06	0
2011 Los Angeles a . . . . A.L.			27	142	6	11	.353	74	71	166	4.75	0
2012 Tulsa . . . . .Texas			4	24	1	1	.500	22	7	17	3.00	0
2012 Colorado Springs . . . . . . .P.C.			9	37¹/₃	0	2	.000	31	19	52	5.79	0
2012 Colorado . . . . .N.L.			19	64²/₃	5	6	.455	41	33	74	5.43	1
Major League Totals . . . . .2 Yrs.			46	206²/₃	11	17	.393	115	104	240	4.96	1

a Traded to Colorado Rockies for catcher Chris Iannetta, November 30, 2011.

CHEN, BRUCE KASTULO
Born, Panama City, Panama, June 19, 1977.
Bats Left. Throws Left. Height, 6 feet, 2 inches. Weight, 215 pounds.

Year	Club	Lea	G	IP	W	L	Pct	SO	BB	H	ERA	SAVES
1994 Braves . . . . Gulf Coast			9	42²/₃	1	4	.200	26	3	42	3.80	1
1995 Danville . . . . Appal.			14	70¹/₃	4	4	.500	56	19	78	3.97	0
1996 Eugene . . . . Northwest			11	35²/₃	4	1	.800	55	14	23	2.27	0
1997 Macon . . . . .So.Atl.			28	146¹/₃	12	7	.632	182	44	120	3.51	0
1998 Greenville . . . . Southern			24	139¹/₃	13	7	.650	164	48	106	3.29	0
1998 Richmond . . . . .Int.			4	24	2	1	.667	29	19	17	1.88	0
1998 Atlanta . . . . N.L.			4	20¹/₃	2	0	1.000	17	9	23	3.98	0
1999 Richmond . . . . .Int.			14	78	6	3	.667	90	26	73	3.81	0
1999 Atlanta . . . . N.L.			16	51	2	2	.500	45	27	38	5.47	0
2000 Richmond . . . . .Int.			1	6	1	0	1.000	6	1	5	0.00	0
2000 Atlanta-Philadelphia a . . . N.L.			37	134	7	4	.636	112	46	116	3.29	0
2001 Reading . . . . Eastern			1	6	1	0	1.000	7	0	3	0.00	0
2001 Scranton-WB . . . . .Int.			3	18²/₃	1	0	1.000	14	5	14	3.86	0
2001 Philadelphia-New York b . N.L.			27	146	7	7	.500	126	59	146	4.87	0
2002 NY-Montreal-Cincinnati c-d .. N.L.			55	77²/₃	2	5	.286	80	43	85	5.56	0
2003 Houston . . . . .N.L.			11	12	0	0	.000	8	8	14	6.00	0
2003 Boston . . . . A.L.			5	12¹/₃	0	1	.000	12	2	12	5.11	0
2003 Pawtucket e-f-g . . . . .Int.			16	85	5	5	.500	73	15	80	4.24	1
2004 Syracuse . . . . .Int.			3	10¹/₃	0	1	.000	8	5	17	8.71	0
2004 Ottawa . . . . .Int.			22	95	4	3	.571	108	30	85	3.22	0
2004 Baltimore h . . . . .A.L.			8	47²/₃	2	1	.667	32	16	39	3.02	0

Year	Club	Lea	G	IP	W	L	Pct	SO	BB	H	ERA	SAVES
2005 Baltimore	A.L.	34	$197\frac{1}{3}$	13	10	.565	133	63	187	3.83	0
2006 Baltimore	A.L.	40	$98\frac{2}{3}$	0	7	.000	70	35	137	6.93	0
2007 Texas	A.L.	5	10	0	0	.000	7	6	11	7.20	0
2007 Oklahoma i	P.C.	4	16	1	1	.500	12	3	17	5.63	0
2008				Did Not Play								
2009 Omaha	P.C.	14	82	4	2	.667	69	23	57	3.40	0
2009 Kansas City j-k-l	A.L.	17	$62\frac{1}{3}$	1	6	.143	45	25	74	5.78	0
2010 Omaha	P.C.	3	$20\frac{2}{3}$	0	1	.000	20	5	13	1.31	0
2010 Kansas City m	A.L.	33	$140\frac{1}{3}$	12	7	.632	98	57	136	4.17	1
2011 NW Arkansas	Texas	1	2	0	1	.000	2	0	5	18.00	0
2011 Omaha	P.C.	2	9	0	0	.000	8	1	11	6.00	0
2011 Kansas City n-o	A.L.	25	155	12	8	.600	97	50	152	3.77	0
2012 Kansas City	A.L.	34	$191\frac{2}{3}$	11	14	.440	140	47	215	5.07	0
Major League Totals	14 Yrs.	351	$1356\frac{1}{3}$	71	72	.497	1022	493	1385	4.60	1

a Traded to Philadelphia Phillies with pitcher Jim Osting for pitcher Andy Ashby, July 12, 2000.
b Traded to New York Mets with pitcher Adam Walker for pitcher Turk Wendell and pitcher Dennis Cook, July 27, 2001.
c Traded to Montreal Expos with pitcher Dicky Gonzalez, infielder Luis Figueroa and player to be named later for pitcher Scott Strickland, pitcher Paul Seubel and outfielder Matt Watson, April 5, 2002. Montreal Expos received pitcher Saul Rivera to complete trade, July 14, 2002.
d Traded to Cincinnati Reds for pitcher Jim Brower, June 14, 2002.
e Released by Cincinnati Reds, March 12, 2003. Signed with Houston Astros organization, March 14, 2003.
f Claimed on waivers by Boston Red Sox, May 7, 2003.
g Filed for free agency, October 3, 2003. Signed with Toronto Blue Jays organization, November 26, 2003.
h Sold to Baltimore Orioles, May 1, 2004.
i Filed for free agency, October 29, 2006. Signed with Texas Rangers organization, February 6, 2007.
j Filed for free agency, October 15, 2007. Signed with Kansas City Royals organization, March 1, 2009.
k On disabled list from September 23 to November 6, 2009.
l Filed for free agency, November 6, 2009, re-signed with Kansas City Royals organization, December 11, 2009.
m Filed for free agency, November 1, 2010, re-signed with Kansas City Royals, January 15, 2011.
n On disabled list from May 6 to June 24, 2011.
o Filed for free agency, October 30, 2011, re-signed with Kansas City Royals, November 22, 2011.

CHEN, WEI-YIN

Born, Kaohsiung City, Taiwan, July 21, 1985.
Bats Left. Throws Left. Height, 6 feet. Weight, 195 pounds.

Year	Club	Lea	G	IP	W	L	Pct	SO	BB	H	ERA	SAVES
2005 Chunichi	Japan Cent.	10	$19\frac{1}{3}$	0	0	.000	20	6	29	6.16	1
2006-2007				Did Not Play								
2008 Chunichi	Japan Cent.	39	$114\frac{2}{3}$	7	6	.538	107	33	101	2.90	0
2009 Chunichi	Japan Cent.	24	164	8	4	.667	146	40	113	1.54	0
2010 Chunichi	Japan Cent.	29	188	13	10	.565	153	49	166	2.87	0
2011 Chunichi	Japan Cent.	25	$164\frac{2}{3}$	8	10	.444	94	31	138	2.67	0
2012 Baltimore a	A.L.	32	$192\frac{2}{3}$	12	11	.522	154	57	186	4.02	0
Division Series												
2012 Baltimore	A.L.	1	$6\frac{1}{3}$	1	0	1.000	3	1	8	1.42	0

a Signed with Baltimore Orioles, December 10, 2012.

CHOATE, RANDOL DOYLE (RANDY)

Born, San Antonio, Texas, September 5, 1975.
Bats Left. Throws Left. Height, 6 feet, 3 inches. Weight, 200 pounds.

Year	Club	Lea	G	IP	W	L	Pct	SO	BB	H	ERA	SAVES
1997 Oneonta	N.Y.-Penn.	10	$62\frac{1}{3}$	5	1	.833	61	12	49	1.73	0
1998 Tampa	Fla.St.	13	70	1	8	.111	55	22	83	5.27	0
1998 Greensboro	So.Atl.	8	39	1	5	.167	32	7	46	3.00	0
1999 Tampa	Fla.St.	47	50	2	2	.500	62	24	51	4.50	1
2000 Columbus	Int.	33	$35\frac{1}{3}$	2	0	1.000	37	14	34	2.04	1
2000 New York	A.L.	22	17	0	1	.000	12	8	14	4.76	0
2001 New York	A.L.	37	$48\frac{1}{3}$	3	1	.750	35	27	34	3.35	0
2001 Columbus	Int.	4	$4\frac{1}{3}$	1	1	.500	4	3	7	2.08	0
2002 New York	A.L.	18	$22\frac{1}{3}$	0	0	.000	17	15	18	6.04	0
2002 Columbus	Int.	31	$36\frac{2}{3}$	3	2	.600	32	15	25	1.72	1
2003 Columbus	Int.	54	$71\frac{1}{3}$	3	5	.375	56	24	75	3.91	1
2003 New York a	A.L.	5	$3\frac{2}{3}$	0	0	.000	0	1	7	7.36	0
2004 Arizona	N.L.	74	$50\frac{2}{3}$	2	4	.333	49	28	52	4.62	0
2004 Tucson b	P.C.	15	$12\frac{2}{3}$	0	0	.000	7	8	10	5.68	0
2005 Arizona	N.L.	8	7	0	0	.000	4	5	13	9.00	0
2005 Tucson	P.C.	47	40	1	1	.500	20	22	44	3.38	3
2006 Tucson	P.C.	43	$45\frac{2}{3}$	6	0	1.000	44	10	39	2.17	8

Year Club	Lea	G	IP	W	L	Pct	SO	BB	H	ERA	SAVES
2006 Arizona.............	N.L.	30	16	0	1	.000	12	3	21	3.94	0
2007 Arizona.............	N.L.	2	0	0	0	.000	0	0	3	0.00	0
2007 Tucson c-d-e	P.C.	55	63⅓	3	1	.750	61	16	68	2.98	3
2008 Brevard County	Fla.St.	1	1	0	0	.000	1	0	0	0.00	0
2008 Nashville f-g..........	P.C.	26	39	0	4	.000	31	20	42	5.08	2
2009 Durham..............	Int.	21	19⅓	3	0	1.000	15	9	16	3.72	0
2009 Tampa Bay...........	A.L.	61	36⅓	1	0	1.000	28	11	28	3.47	5
2010 Tampa Bay h	A.L.	*85	44⅔	4	3	.571	40	17	41	4.23	0
2011 Florida i..............	N.L.	54	24⅔	1	1	.500	31	13	13	1.82	0
2012 Miami-Los Angeles j-k..	N.L.	*80	38⅔	0	0	.000	38	18	29	3.03	1
Major League Totals ....12 Yrs.		476	309⅓	11	11	.500	266	146	268	4.02	6
Division Series											
2000 New York.............	A.L.	1	1⅓	0	0	.000	1	1	0	6.75	0
2010 Tampa Bay...........	A.L.	3	1	0	0	.000	0	0	0	0.00	0
Division Series Totals		4	2⅓	0	0	.000	1	1	0	3.86	0
Championship Series											
2000 New York.............	A.L.	1	0⅓	0	0	.000	1	0	0	0.00	0
World Series Record											
2001 New York.............	A.L.	2	3⅔	0	0	.000	2	1	7	2.45	0

a Traded to Montreal Expos with infielder Nick Johnson and outfielder Juan Rivera for pitcher Javier Vazquez, December 4, 2003.
b Traded to Arizona Diamondbacks for pitcher John Patterson, March 25, 2004.
c Filed for free agency, October 31, 2006. Signed with Minnesota Twins organization, January 29, 2007.
d Released by Minnesota Twins, March 23, 2007. Signed with Arizona Diamondbacks organization, April 17, 2007.
e Filed for free agency, October 4, 2007. Signed with Milwaukee Brewers, November 13, 2007.
f On disabled list from March 21 to July 10, 2008.
g Filed for free agency, October 1, 2008. Signed with Tampa Bay Rays organization, December 23, 2008.
h Filed for free agency, November 1, 2010. Signed with Florida Marlins organization, December 15, 2010.
i On disabled list from August 16 to October 31, 2011.
j Traded to Los Angeles Dodgers with infielder Hanley Ramirez for pitcher Nathan Eovaldi and pitcher Scott McGough, July 25, 2012.
k Filed for free agency, November 3, 2012. Signed with St. Louis Cardinals, December 7, 2012.

CISHEK, STEVEN R. (STEVE)

Born, Falmouth, Massachusetts, June 18, 1986.
Bats Right. Throws Right. Height, 6 feet, 6 inches. Weight, 215 pounds.

Year Club	Lea	G	IP	W	L	Pct	SO	BB	H	ERA	SAVES
2007 Jamestown.......	N.Y.-Penn.	25	32⅓	1	2	.333	30	19	20	1.95	9
2008 Greensboro	So.Atl.	50	75⅓	3	5	.375	75	34	69	4.66	2
2009 Jupiter	Fla.St.	37	57	3	4	.429	45	16	36	2.84	2
2010 Jupiter	Fla.St.	26	35	0	6	.000	28	19	29	2.83	4
2010 Jacksonville	Southern	22	31⅓	3	1	.750	34	10	30	4.31	2
2010 Florida	N.L.	3	4⅓	0	0	.000	3	1	1	0.00	0
2011 New Orleans..........	P.C.	15	23	1	1	.500	19	12	18	2.35	0
2011 Florida	N.L.	45	54⅔	2	1	.667	55	19	45	2.63	3
2012 Miami................	N.L.	68	63⅔	5	2	.714	68	29	54	2.69	15
Major League Totals ....3 Yrs.		116	122⅔	7	3	.700	126	49	100	2.57	18

CLIPPARD, TYLER LEE

Born, Lexington, Kentucky, February 14, 1985.
Bats Right. Throws Right. Height, 6 feet, 4 inches. Weight, 200 pounds.

Year Club	Lea	G	IP	W	L	Pct	SO	BB	H	ERA	SAVES
2003 Yankees	Gulf Coast	11	43⅔	3	3	.500	56	5	33	2.89	0
2004 Battle Creek	Midwest	26	149	10	10	.500	145	32	153	3.44	0
2005 Tampa	Fla.St.	26	147⅓	10	9	.526	169	34	118	3.18	0
2005 Columbus.............	Int.	1	1	0	0	.000	2	0	0	0.00	0
2005 Charleston	So.Atl.	1	6	0	1	.000	10	0	9	7.50	0
2006 Trenton	Eastern	28	166⅓	12	10	.545	175	55	118	3.35	0
2007 New York.............	A.L.	6	27	3	1	.750	18	17	29	6.33	0
2007 Scranton/WB	Int.	14	69⅓	4	4	.500	55	35	82	4.15	0
2007 Trenton a	Eastern	6	26⅔	2	1	.667	28	12	22	5.40	0
2008 Washington	N.L.	2	10⅓	1	1	.500	8	7	14	4.35	0
2008 Columbus.............	Int.	27	143	6	13	.316	125	66	129	4.66	0
2009 Syracuse	Int.	24	39	4	1	.800	42	15	20	0.92	1
2009 Washington	N.L.	41	60⅓	4	2	.667	67	32	36	2.69	0
2010 Washington	N.L.	78	91	11	8	.579	112	41	69	3.07	1
2011 Washington	N.L.	72	88⅓	3	0	1.000	104	26	48	1.83	0
2012 Washington	N.L.	74	72⅔	2	6	.250	84	29	55	3.72	32

Year Club	Lea	G	IP	W	L	Pct	SO	BB	H	ERA	SAVES
Major League Totals . . . . .6 Yrs.		273	349²/₃	24	18	.571	393	152	249	3.11	33
Division Series											
2012 Washington	N.L.	3	3	0	0	.000	5	1	1	3.00	0

a Traded to Washington Nationals for pitcher Jonathan Albaladejo, December 5, 2007.

CLOYD, TYLER JAMES
Born, Bellevue, Nebraska, May 16, 1987.
Bats Right. Throws Right. Height, 6 feet, 2 inches. Weight, 190 pounds.

Year Club	Lea	G	IP	W	L	Pct	SO	BB	H	ERA	SAVES
2008 Phillies	Gulf Coast	2	11	2	0	1.000	11	1	5	0.00	0
2008 Williamsport	N.Y.-Penn.	12	65	5	4	.556	58	21	76	4.57	0
2009 Clearwater	Fla.St.	13	76²/₃	5	6	.455	39	23	83	4.11	0
2009 Lakewood	So.Atl.	14	88²/₃	7	3	.700	77	19	90	3.05	0
2010 Reading	Eastern	2	9	1	1	.500	6	1	5	4.00	0
2010 Clearwater	Fla.St.	35	69¹/₃	4	3	.571	67	16	85	5.32	0
2011 Reading	Eastern	18	106²/₃	6	3	.667	99	15	101	2.78	0
2011 Clearwater	Fla.St.	13	39¹/₃	3	1	.750	39	7	31	2.75	0
2012 Reading	Eastern	4	25	3	0	1.000	20	3	22	1.80	0
2012 Lehigh Valley	Int.	22	142	12	1	.923	93	38	105	2.35	0
2012 Philadelphia	N.L.	6	33	2	2	.500	30	7	33	4.91	0

COBB, ALEXANDER MILLER (ALEX)
Born, Boston, Massachusetts, October 7, 1987.
Bats Right. Throws Right. Height, 6 feet, 2 inches. Weight, 195 pounds.

Year Club	Lea	G	IP	W	L	Pct	SO	BB	H	ERA	SAVES
2006 Princeton	Appal.	6	8²/₃	0	0	.000	8	3	9	5.19	0
2007 Hudson Valley	N.Y.-Penn.	16	81¹/₃	5	6	.455	62	31	78	3.54	0
2008 Columbus	So.Atl.	25	139²/₃	9	7	.563	97	35	113	3.29	0
2009 Charlotte	Fla.St.	24	124²/₃	8	5	.615	107	31	116	3.03	0
2010 Montgomery	Southern	23	119²/₃	7	5	.583	128	35	120	2.71	0
2011 Durham	Int.	12	67¹/₃	5	1	.833	70	16	61	1.87	0
2011 Tampa Bay a	A.L.	9	52²/₃	3	2	.600	37	21	49	3.42	0
2012 Durham	Int.	8	41¹/₃	1	4	.200	44	18	44	4.14	0
2012 Tampa Bay	A.L.	23	136¹/₃	11	9	.550	106	40	130	4.03	0
Major League Totals . . . . . . .2 Yrs.		32	189	14	11	.560	143	61	179	3.86	0

a On disabled list from August 7 to October 5, 2011.

COFFEY, JUSTIN TODD (TODD)
Born, Shelby, North Carolina, September 9, 1980.
Bats Right. Throws Right. Height, 6 feet, 5 inches. Weight, 240 pounds.

Year Club	Lea	G	IP	W	L	Pct	SO	BB	H	ERA	SAVES
1998 Billings	Pioneer	3	12	0	0	.000	8	1	13	3.00	0
1999 Reds	Gulf Coast	5	16	1	1	.500	14	14	9	3.38	0
2000 a					INJURED—Did Not Play						
2001 Reds	Gulf Coast	3	12²/₃	0	1	.000	15	5	11	4.26	0
2001 Billings	Pioneer	14	33¹/₃	2	2	.500	33	15	34	3.51	1
2002 Dayton	Midwest	38	80¹/₃	6	4	.600	62	25	78	3.59	2
2003 Potomac	Carolina	11	23	0	2	.000	21	3	16	1.96	2
2003 Dayton	Midwest	39	56	3	3	.500	53	14	61	2.25	9
2004 Louisville	Int.	15	13²/₃	1	0	1.000	11	2	15	5.27	4
2004 Chattanooga	Southern	40	45¹/₃	4	1	.800	53	4	36	2.38	20
2005 Louisville	Int.	8	8²/₃	0	0	.000	5	2	8	5.19	3
2005 Cincinnati	N.L.	57	58	4	1	.800	26	11	84	4.50	1
2006 Cincinnati	N.L.	81	78	6	7	.462	60	27	85	3.58	8
2007 Louisville	Int.	19	27	2	0	1.000	25	5	17	1.33	1
2007 Cincinnati	N.L.	58	51	2	1	.667	43	19	70	5.82	0
2008 Louisville	Int.	34	39¹/₃	3	3	.500	43	15	49	4.35	2
2008 Cincinnati-Milwaukee b	N.L.	26	26²/₃	1	0	1.000	15	8	31	4.39	0
2009 Milwaukee	N.L.	78	83²/₃	4	4	.500	65	21	76	2.90	2
2010 Nashville	P.C.	1	1	0	0	.000	1	0	0	0.00	0
2010 Milwaukee c-d	N.L.	69	62¹/₃	2	4	.333	56	23	65	4.76	0
2011 Washington e-f	N.L.	69	59²/₃	5	1	.833	46	20	55	3.62	0
2012 Rancho Cucamonga . .	Calif.	2	2	0	1	.000	1	0	3	4.50	0
2012 Los Angeles g-h	N.L.	23	19¹/₃	1	0	1.000	18	9	17	4.66	0
Major League Totals . . . . . . .8 Yrs.		461	438²/₃	25	18	.581	329	138	483	4.10	11

a On minor league disabled list, June 19 to September 27, 2000.

b Claimed on waivers by Milwaukee Brewers, September 10, 2008.
c On disabled list from May 30 to June 20, 2010.
d Not offered contract, December 2, 2010. Signed with Washington Nationals, January 24, 2011.
e On disabled list from April 9 to April 24, 2011.
f Filed for free agency, October 30, 2011. Signed with Los Angeles Dodgers, February 3, 2012.
g On disabled list from July 3 to October 29 and April 14 to April 30, 2012.
h Filed for free agency, November 3, 2012.

COKE, PHILLIP DOUGLAS (PHIL)

Born, Sonora, California, July 19, 1982.
Bats Left. Throws Left. Height, 6 feet, 1 inch. Weight, 210 pounds.

Year	Club	Lea	G	IP	W	L	Pct	SO	BB	H	ERA	SAVES
2003 Yankees	Gulf Coast		10	12	0	0	.000	5	3	13	3.75	0
2004 Yankees	Gulf Coast		7	11⅓	0	1	.000	13	3	18	3.97	0
2004 Staten Island	N.Y.-Penn.		3	8	0	0	.000	7	3	9	6.75	0
2005 Charleston	So.Atl.		24	103	8	11	.421	68	34	122	5.42	0
2006 Tampa	Fla.St.		22	110	5	7	.417	88	35	101	3.60	0
2006 Charleston	So.Atl.		5	17	0	1	.000	19	4	10	0.53	1
2007 Tampa	Fla.St.		17	99	7	3	.700	76	37	93	3.09	0
2008 Trenton	Eastern		23	118⅓	9	4	.692	115	39	105	2.51	0
2008 Scranton-WB	Int.		14	17⅓	2	2	.500	22	5	19	4.67	0
2008 New York	A.L.		12	14⅔	1	0	1.000	14	2	8	0.61	0
2009 New York a	A.L.		72	60	4	3	.571	49	20	44	4.50	2
2010 Detroit	A.L.		74	64⅔	7	5	.583	53	26	67	3.76	2
2011 Toledo	Int.		1	5⅓	0	0	.000	6	2	8	5.06	0
2011 Detroit b	A.L.		48	108⅔	3	9	.250	69	40	118	4.47	1
2012 Detroit	A.L.		66	54	2	3	.400	51	18	71	4.00	1
Major League Totals	5 Yrs.		272	302	17	20	.459	236	106	308	4.05	6
Division Series												
2009 New York	A.L.		2	0⅔	0	0	.000	1	0	0	0.00	0
2011 Detroit	A.L.		1	1	0	0	.000	1	0	3	27.00	0
2012 Detroit	A.L.		3	1⅔	0	0	.000	1	2	1	0.00	0
Division Series Totals			6	3⅓	0	0	.000	3	3	4	8.10	0
Championship Series												
2009 New York	A.L.		2	0⅔	0	0	.000	1	1	1	0.00	0
2011 Detroit	A.L.		4	3⅓	0	0	.000	2	1	3	2.70	1
2012 Detroit	A.L.		4	5⅔	0	0	.000	4	0	3	0.00	2
Championship Series Totals			10	9⅔	0	0	.000	7	2	7	0.93	3
World Series Record												
2009 New York	A.L.		2	1⅓	0	0	.000	1	0	3	13.50	0
2012 Detroit	A.L.		3	3⅓	0	1	.000	8	0	2	2.70	0
World Series Totals			5	4⅔	0	1	.000	9	0	5	5.79	0

a Traded to Detroit Tigers with outfielder Austin Jackson and pitcher Ian Kennedy for outfielder Curtis Granderson, December 9, 2009.
b On disabled list from May 24 to June 8, 2011.

COLEMAN, HAROLD LOUIS (LOUIS)

Born, Greenwood, Mississippi, April 4, 1986.
Bats Right. Throws Right. Height, 6 feet, 4 inches. Weight, 200 pounds.

Year	Club	Lea	G	IP	W	L	Pct	SO	BB	H	ERA	SAVES
2009 Burlington	Midwest		4	7⅓	1	0	1.000	6	1	2	2.45	1
2009 Wilmington	Carolina		10	14⅓	3	1	.750	16	3	8	1.26	1
2010 Omaha	P.C.		21	40⅓	5	2	.714	48	11	31	2.23	1
2010 NW Arkansas	Texas		21	51⅔	2	1	.667	55	14	31	2.09	6
2011 Omaha	P.C.		6	7	0	1	.000	16	4	4	3.86	2
2011 Kansas City	A.L.		48	59⅔	1	4	.200	64	26	44	2.87	1
2012 Omaha	P.C.		11	19⅔	0	2	.000	26	8	13	3.20	3
2012 Kansas City	A.L.		42	51	0	0	.000	65	26	41	3.71	0
Major League Totals	2 Yrs.		90	110⅔	1	4	.200	129	52	85	3.25	1

COLLINS, TIMOTHY M. (TIM)

Born, Worcester, Massachusetts, August 21, 1989.
Bats Left. Throws Left. Height, 5 feet, 7 inches. Weight, 170 pounds.

Year	Club	Lea	G	IP	W	L	Pct	SO	BB	H	ERA	SAVES
2007 Blue Jays	Gulf Coast		7	6	0	0	.000	7	2	6	4.50	0
2008 Lansing	Midwest		39	68⅓	4	2	.667	98	32	36	1.58	14

Year	Club	Lea	G	IP	W	L	Pct	SO	BB	H	ERA	SAVES
2009 Dunedin	Fla.St.	40	64²/₃	7	4	.636	99	28	47	2.37	3
2009 New Hampshire	Eastern	9	12²/₃	2	3	.400	17	7	12	5.68	0
2010 New Hampshire	Eastern	35	43	1	0	1.000	73	16	27	2.51	9
2010 Mississippi a-b.	Southern	6	8	0	0	.000	14	3	4	1.13	2
2010 Omaha	P.C.	15	20¹/₃	2	1	.667	21	8	9	1.33	4
2011 Kansas City	A.L.	68	67	4	4	.500	60	48	52	3.63	0
2012 Kansas City	A.L.	72	69²/₃	5	4	.556	93	34	55	3.36	0

| Major League Totals | 2 Yrs. | 140 | 136²/₃ | 9 | 8 | .529 | 153 | 82 | 107 | 3.49 | 0 |

a Traded to Atlanta Braves with infielder Alex Gonzalez and infielder Tyler Pastornicky for infielder Yunel Escobar and pitcher Jo-Jo Reyes, July 14, 2010.

b Traded to Kansas City Royals with outfielder Gregor Blanco and pitcher Jesse Chavez for outfielder Rick Ankiel, pitcher Kyle Farnsworth and cash, July 31, 2010.

COLLMENTER, JOSHUA MICHAEL (JOSH)

Born, Homer, Michigan, February 7, 1986.
Bats Right. Throws Right. Height, 6 feet, 2 inches. Weight, 235 pounds.

Year	Club	Lea	G	IP	W	L	Pct	SO	BB	H	ERA	SAVES
2007 Yakima	Northwest	14	66¹/₃	6	3	.667	57	21	60	2.71	0
2008 South Bend	Midwest	27	145¹/₃	12	8	.600	123	47	126	3.41	0
2009 Visalia	Calif.	27	145¹/₃	8	10	.444	152	55	127	4.15	0
2010 Visalia	Calif.	3	15	2	0	1.000	21	3	11	2.40	0
2010 Reno	P.C.	10	57²/₃	4	3	.571	39	26	64	5.77	0
2010 Mobile	Southern	12	79¹/₃	8	3	.727	73	22	61	1.82	0
2011 Reno	P.C.	1	6	1	0	1.000	7	2	2	1.50	0
2011 Arizona	N.L.	31	154¹/₃	10	10	.500	100	28	137	3.38	0
2012 D-Backs	Arizona	3	8	0	0	.000	11	0	5	0.00	0
2012 Arizona a	N.L.	28	90¹/₃	5	3	.625	80	22	92	3.69	0

Major League Totals	2 Yrs.	59	244²/₃	15	13	.536	180	50	229	3.49	0
Division Series											
2011 Arizona	N.L.	1	7	1	0	1.000	6	2	2	1.29	0

a On disabled list from August 9 to September 1, 2012.

COLON, BARTOLO

Born, Altamira, Dominican Republic, May 24, 1973.
Bats Right. Throws Right. Height, 6 feet. Weight, 265 pounds.

Year	Club	Lea	G	IP	W	L	Pct	SO	BB	H	ERA	SAVES
1993 Cleveland	Dominican	11	66	6	1	.857	43	33	44	2.59	1
1994 Burlington	Appal.	12	66	7	4	.636	84	44	46	3.14	0
1995 Kinston	Carolina	21	128²/₃	13	3	.813	152	39	91	1.96	0
1996 Canton-Akrn.	Eastern	13	62	2	2	.500	56	25	44	1.74	0
1996 Buffalo	A.A.	8	15	0	0	.000	19	8	16	6.00	0
1997 Buffalo	A.A.	10	56²/₃	7	1	.875	54	23	45	2.22	0
1997 Cleveland	A.L.	19	94	4	7	.364	66	45	107	5.65	0
1998 Cleveland	A.L.	31	204	14	9	.609	158	79	205	3.71	0
1999 Cleveland	A.L.	32	205	18	5	.783	161	76	185	3.95	0
2000 Cleveland	A.L.	30	188	15	8	.652	212	98	163	3.88	0
2000 Buffalo a	Int.	1	5	1	0	1.000	4	0	6	1.80	0
2001 Cleveland	A.L.	34	222¹/₃	14	12	.538	201	90	220	4.09	0
2002 Cleveland	A.L.	16	116¹/₃	10	4	.714	75	31	104	2.55	0
2002 Montreal b	N.L.	17	117	10	4	.714	74	39	115	3.31	0
2003 Chicago c-d	A.L.	34	242	15	13	.536	173	67	223	3.87	0
2004 Anaheim	A.L.	34	208¹/₃	18	12	.600	158	71	215	5.01	0
2005 Los Angeles	A.L.	33	222²/₃	*21	8	.724	157	43	215	3.48	0
2006 Rancho Cucamonga	Calif.	1	4	0	0	.000	3	1	2	0.00	0
2006 Salt Lake	P.C.	2	11²/₃	0	1	.000	3	2	14	6.17	0
2006 Los Angeles e	A.L.	10	56¹/₃	1	5	.167	31	11	71	5.11	0
2007 Rancho Cucamonga	Calif.	2	9²/₃	1	0	1.000	10	1	6	1.86	0
2007 Salt Lake	P.C.	3	15	2	0	1.000	8	3	12	2.40	0
2007 Los Angeles f-g	A.L.	19	99¹/₃	6	8	.429	76	29	132	6.34	0
2008 Pawtucket	Int.	9	31²/₃	3	1	.750	21	6	23	2.27	0
2008 Boston h-i	A.L.	7	39	4	2	.667	27	10	44	3.92	0
2009 Kannapolis	So.Atl.	1	7	0	1	.000	8	1	7	2.57	0
2009 Charlotte	Int.	2	12	1	1	.500	1	4	10	3.75	0
2009 Chicago j-k	A.L.	12	62¹/₃	3	6	.333	38	21	69	4.19	0
2010								Did not play				
2011 New York l-m-n	A.L.	29	164¹/₃	8	10	.444	135	40	172	4.00	0
2012 Oakland o-p	A.L.	24	152¹/₃	10	9	.526	91	23	161	3.43	0

| Major League Totals | 15 Yrs. | 381 | 2393¹/₃ | 171 | 122 | .584 | 1833 | 773 | 2401 | 4.05 | 0 |

Year	Club	Lea	G	IP	W	L	Pct	SO	BB	H	ERA	SAVES
	Division Series											
1998 Cleveland	A.L.	1	5²/₃	0	0	.000	3	3	5	1.59	0	
1999 Cleveland	A.L.	2	9	0	1	.000	12	4	11	9.00	0	
2001 Cleveland	A.L.	2	14²/₃	1	1	.500	13	6	12	1.84	0	
2004 Anaheim	A.L.	1	6	0	0	.000	3	3	7	4.50	0	
2005 Los Angeles	A.L.	2	8	0	1	.000	7	1	10	4.50	0	
Division Series Totals		8	43¹/₃	1	3	.250	38	17	45	4.15	0	
	Championship Series											
1998 Cleveland	A.L.	1	9	1	0	1.000	3	4	4	1.00	0	

a On disabled list from April 16 to May 11, 2000.
b Traded to Montreal Expos with player to be named later for infielder Lee Stevens, infielder Brandon Phillips, outfielder Grady Sizemore and pitcher Cliff Lee, June 27, 2002. Montreal Expos received pitcher Tim Drew to complete trade, June 28, 2002.
c Traded with infielder Jorge Nunez to Chicago White Sox for pitcher Rocky Biddle, pitcher Orlando Hernandez, outfielder Jeff Liefer and cash, January 15, 2003.
d Filed for free agency, October 27, 2003. Signed with Anaheim Angels, December 9, 2003.
e On disabled list from April 16 to June 18 and July 30 to October 2, 2006.
f On disabled list from March 23 to April 21, 2007.
g On disabled list from July 24 to September 9, 2007.
h Filed for free agency, October 29, 2007. Signed with Boston Red Sox organization, February 25, 2008.
i On disabled list from June 17 to September 7, 2008.
j Filed for free agency, October 31, 2008. Signed with Chicago White Sox, January 15, 2009.
k On disabled list from June 8 to July 23, 2009.
l Released by Chicago White Sox, September 16, 2009. Signed with New York Yankees organization, January 26, 2011.
m On disabled list from June 12 to July 2, 2011.
n Filed for free agency, October 30, 2011. Signed with Oakland Athletics, January 24, 2012.
o On disabled list from June 18 to July 3, 2012.
p Filed for free agency, November 3, 2012, re-signed with Oakland Athletics, November 3, 2012.

COOK, AARON LANE

Born, Fort Campbell, Kentucky, February 8, 1979.
Bats Right. Throws Right. Height, 6 feet, 3 inches. Weight, 215 pounds.

Year	Club	Lea	G	IP	W	L	Pct	SO	BB	H	ERA	SAVES
1997 Rockies	Arizona	9	46	1	3	.250	35	17	48	3.13	0	
1998 Portland	Northwest	15	79¹/₃	5	8	.385	38	39	87	4.88	0	
1999 Asheville	So.Atl.	25	121²/₃	4	12	.250	73	42	157	6.44	0	
2000 Salem	Carolina	7	43	1	6	.143	37	12	52	5.44	0	
2000 Asheville	So.Atl.	21	142²/₃	10	7	.588	118	23	130	2.96	0	
2001 Salem	Carolina	27	155	11	11	.500	122	38	157	3.08	0	
2002 Carolina	Southern	14	95	7	2	.778	58	19	73	1.42	0	
2002 Colorado Springs	P.C.	10	64¹/₃	4	4	.500	32	18	67	3.78	0	
2002 Colorado	N.L.	9	35²/₃	2	1	.667	14	13	41	4.54	0	
2003 Colorado Springs	P.C.	2	16	1	1	.500	12	4	10	2.25	0	
2003 Colorado	N.L.	43	124	4	6	.400	43	57	160	6.02	0	
2004 Colorado Springs	P.C.	7	46	3	1	.750	25	8	34	2.74	0	
2004 Colorado a	N.L.	16	96²/₃	6	4	.600	40	39	112	4.28	0	
2005 Tri-City	Northwest	2	7	0	0	.000	0	0	1	0.00	0	
2005 Modesto	California	1	5	1	0	1.000	5	0	5	1.80	0	
2005 Tulsa	Texas	1	3²/₃	1	0	1.000	1	1	10	17.18	0	
2005 Colorado Springs	P.C.	3	16¹/₃	1	0	1.000	11	7	18	5.51	0	
2005 Colorado b	N.L.	13	83¹/₃	7	2	.778	24	16	101	3.67	0	
2006 Colorado	N.L.	32	212²/₃	9	15	.375	92	55	242	4.23	0	
2007 Colorado Springs	P.C.	1	1	0	0	.000	0	1	4	27.00	0	
2007 Colorado c	N.L.	25	166	8	7	.533	61	44	178	4.12	0	
2008 Colorado	N.L.	32	211¹/₃	16	9	.640	96	48	*236	3.96	0	
2009 Colorado d	N.L.	27	158	11	6	.647	78	47	175	4.16	0	
2010 Tulsa	Texas	2	10²/₃	1	1	.500	10	3	8	2.53	0	
2010 Colorado e	N.L.	23	127²/₃	6	8	.429	62	52	147	5.08	0	
2011 Tulsa	Texas	3	14	0	1	.000	13	3	16	5.79	0	
2011 Colorado Springs	P.C.	2	14²/₃	1	0	1.000	5	2	13	5.52	0	
2011 Colorado f-g	N.L.	18	97	3	10	.231	48	37	127	6.03	0	
2012 Pawtucket	Int.	6	37¹/₃	3	0	1.000	16	12	33	2.41	0	
2012 Boston h-i	A.L.	18	94	4	11	.267	20	21	117	5.65	0	
Major League Totals	11 Yrs.	256	1406¹/₃	76	79	.490	578	429	1636	4.60	0	
	Division Series											
2009 Colorado	N.L.	1	5	1	0	1.000	4	2	7	5.40	0	
	World Series Record											
2007 Colorado	N.L.	1	6	0	1	.000	2	0	6	4.50	0	

a On disabled list from August 8 to November 3, 2004.

b On disabled list from March 25 to July 30, 2005.
c On disabled list from August 16 to October 10, 2007.
d On disabled list from August 22 to September 25, 2009.
e On disabled list from August 4 to September 3 and September 9 to October 4, 2010.
f On disabled list from March 22 to June 8, 2011.
g Filed for free agency, October 31, 2011. Signed with Boston Red Sox organization, January 9, 2012.
h On disabled list from May 6 to June 24, 2012.
i Filed for free agency, November 3, 2012. Signed with Philadelphia Phillies organization, January 16, 2013.

COOK, RYAN WILLIAM
Born, Clovis, California, June 30, 1987.
Bats Right. Throws Right. Height, 6 feet, 3 inches. Weight, 215 pounds.

Year	Club	Lea	G	IP	W	L	Pct	SO	BB	H	ERA	SAVES
2008 Yakima	Northwest	7	33	2	2	.500	23	11	37	4.64	0
2009 South Bend	Midwest	25	142²/₃	11	11	.500	103	44	140	3.66	0
2010 Visalia	Calif.	20	108¹/₃	4	7	.364	100	36	110	4.24	0
2010 Reno	P.C.	1	5	0	0	.000	5	2	7	10.80	0
2010 Mobile	Southern	3	18²/₃	1	1	.500	12	10	13	2.89	0
2011 Mobile	Southern	34	44	1	4	.200	50	14	28	2.25	13
2011 Reno	P.C.	14	17	0	1	.000	12	8	13	2.12	6
2011 Arizona a	N.L.	12	7²/₃	0	1	.000	7	8	11	7.04	0
2012 Oakland	A.L.	71	73¹/₃	6	2	.750	80	27	42	2.09	14
Major League Totals	2 Yrs.	83	81	6	3	.667	87	35	53	2.56	14

Division Series

Year	Club	Lea	G	IP	W	L	Pct	SO	BB	H	ERA	SAVES
2012 Oakland	A.L.	4	3¹/₃	1	0	1.000	4	1	4	8.10	0

a Traded to Oakland Athletics with outfielder Collin Cowgill and pitcher Jarrod Parker for pitcher Craig Breslow and pitcher Trevor Cahill, December 9, 2011.

CORBIN, PATRICK A.
Born, Clay, New York, July 19, 1989.
Bats Left. Throws Left. Height, 6 feet, 2 inches. Weight, 185 pounds.

Year	Club	Lea	G	IP	W	L	Pct	SO	BB	H	ERA	SAVES
2009 Orem	Pioneer	13	46¹/₃	4	2	.667	46	11	59	5.05	0
2010 Rancho Cucamonga	Calif.	11	60¹/₃	5	3	.625	64	18	57	3.88	0
2010 Visalia	Calif.	8	26	0	1	.000	30	9	17	1.38	0
2010 Cedar Rapids a	Midwest	9	58¹/₃	8	0	1.000	42	10	52	3.86	0
2011 Mobile	Southern	26	160¹/₃	9	8	.529	142	40	172	4.21	0
2012 Mobile	Southern	4	27	2	0	1.000	25	8	22	1.67	0
2012 Reno	P.C.	9	52¹/₃	3	2	.600	55	15	57	3.44	0
2012 Arizona	N.L.	22	107	6	8	.429	86	25	117	4.54	1

a Traded from Los Angeles Angels to Arizona Diamondbacks with pitcher Joe Saunders, pitcher Rafael Rodriguez and player to be named later for pitcher Danny Haren, July 25, 2010. Arizona Diamondbacks received pitcher Tyler Skaggs to complete trade, August 7, 2010.

CORPAS, MANUEL
Born, Panama City, Panama, December 3, 1982.
Bats Right. Throws Right. Height, 6 feet, 3 inches. Weight, 210 pounds.

Year	Club	Lea	G	IP	W	L	Pct	SO	BB	H	ERA	SAVES
2002 Casper	Pioneer	29	33	2	4	.333	42	18	37	5.73	2
2003 Tri-City	Northwest	15	84	5	6	.455	47	22	98	5.79	0
2004 Asheville	So.Atl.	43	44¹/₃	2	2	.500	52	13	48	3.05	3
2005 Modesto	Calif.	47	69	3	2	.600	52	14	83	3.78	2
2006 Tulsa	Texas	34	36²/₃	2	1	.667	35	4	22	0.98	19
2006 Colorado Springs	P.C.	8	8²/₃	0	0	.000	7	2	5	1.04	0
2006 Colorado	N.L.	35	32¹/₃	1	2	.333	27	8	36	3.62	0
2007 Colorado	N.L.	78	78	4	2	.667	58	20	63	2.08	19
2008 Colorado	N.L.	76	79²/₃	3	4	.429	50	23	93	4.52	4
2009 Colorado Springs	P.C.	3	2²/₃	0	0	.000	3	1	2	0.00	0
2009 Colorado a	N.L.	35	33²/₃	1	3	.250	24	7	44	5.88	1
2010 Colorado b	N.L.	56	62¹/₃	2	2	.375	47	22	66	4.62	10
2011 c-d-e				INJURED—Did Not Play								
2012 Iowa	P.C.	19	33²/₃	0	2	.000	19	9	30	4.01	0
2012 Chicago f	N.L.	48	46²/₃	0	2	.000	28	16	50	5.01	0
Major League Totals	6 Yrs.	328	332²/₃	12	18	.400	234	96	352	4.09	34

Division Series

Year	Club	Lea	G	IP	W	L	Pct	SO	BB	H	ERA	SAVES
2007 Colorado	N.L.	3	3¹/₃	0	0	.000	3	0	2	0.00	3

Championship Series

Year	Club	Lea	G	IP	W	L	Pct	SO	BB	H	ERA	SAVES
2007 Colorado	N.L.	4	5¹/₃	1	0	1.000	3	0	3	1.69	2

Year	Club	Lea	G	IP	W	L	Pct	SO	BB	H	ERA	SAVES
	World Series Record											
2007 Colorado	N.L.	2	1^{2}/$_{3}$	0	0	.000	1	0	1	0.00	0

a On disabled list from June 19 to July 16 and from July 21 to November 6, 2009.
b On disabled list from August 26 to November 2, 2010.
c Released by Colorado Rockies, November 16, 2010. Signed with Texas Rangers organization, April 11, 2011.
d On minor league disabled list from April 11 to September 21, 2011.
e Filed for free agency, November 2, 2011. Signed with Chicago Cubs, December 26, 2011.
f Filed for free agency, October 26, 2012.

CORREIA, KEVIN JOHN
Born, San Diego, California, August 24, 1980.
Bats Right. Throws Right. Height, 6 feet, 3 inches. Weight, 200 pounds.

Year	Club	Lea	G	IP	W	L	Pct	SO	BB	H	ERA	SAVES
2002 Salem-Keizer	Northwest	10	37^{2}/$_{3}$	2	2	.500	31	14	37	4.54	0
2003 Norwich	Eastern	16	86^{1}/$_{3}$	6	6	.500	73	30	80	3.65	0
2003 San Francisco	N.L.	10	39^{1}/$_{3}$	3	1	.750	28	18	41	3.66	0
2003 Fresno	P.C.	3	19	1	0	1.000	23	2	16	2.84	0
2004 Fresno	P.C.	29	105^{1}/$_{3}$	3	7	.300	70	35	118	4.53	0
2004 San Francisco	N.L.	12	19	0	1	.000	14	10	25	8.05	0
2005 San Jose	California	1	7	0	1	.000	7	5	5	2.57	0
2005 Fresno	P.C.	31	46	3	2	.600	35	23	50	6.07	7
2005 San Francisco	N.L.	16	58^{1}/$_{3}$	2	5	.286	44	31	61	4.63	0
2006 San Francisco	N.L.	48	69^{2}/$_{3}$	2	0	1.000	57	22	64	3.49	0
2007 San Francisco	N.L.	59	101^{2}/$_{3}$	4	7	.364	80	40	94	3.45	0
2008 San Jose	Calif.	1	3^{1}/$_{3}$	0	0	.000	1	1	1	0.00	0
2008 Fresno	P.C.	2	12	1	0	1.000	15	0	8	1.50	0
2008 San Francisco a-b	N.L.	25	110	3	8	.273	66	47	141	6.05	0
2009 San Diego	N.L.	33	198	12	11	.522	142	64	194	3.91	0
2010 San Diego c	N.L.	28	145	10	10	.500	115	64	152	5.40	0
2011 Pittsburgh d..........	N.L.	27	154	12	11	.522	77	39	175	4.79	0
2012 Pittsburgh e..........	N.L.	32	171	12	11	.522	89	46	176	4.21	0
Major League Totals	10 Yrs.	290	1066	60	65	.480	712	381	1123	4.54	0

a On disabled list from April 27 to June 15, 2008.
b Filed for free agency, October 14, 2008. Signed with San Diego Padres organization, December 24, 2008.
c Filed for free agency, November 1, 2010. Signed with Pittsburgh Pirates, December 7, 2010.
d On disabled list from August 20 to November 1, 2011.
e Filed for free agency, November 3, 2012. Signed with Minnesota Twins, December 13, 2012.

CRAIN, JESSE ALAN
Born, Toronto, Ontario, Canada, July 5, 1981.
Bats Right. Throws Right. Height, 6 feet, 1 inch. Weight, 205 pounds.

Year	Club	Lea	G	IP	W	L	Pct	SO	BB	H	ERA	SAVES
2002 Elizabethton	Appal.	9	15^{2}/$_{3}$	2	1	.667	18	7	4	0.57	2
2002 Quad Cities	Midwest	9	12	1	1	.500	11	4	6	1.50	1
2003 New Britain	Eastern	22	39	1	1	.500	56	10	13	0.69	9
2003 Fort Myers	Fla.St.	10	19	2	1	.667	25	5	10	2.84	0
2003 Rochester.............	Int.	23	26	3	1	.750	33	10	24	3.12	10
2004 Rochester.............	Int.	41	50^{2}/$_{3}$	3	2	.600	64	17	38	2.49	19
2004 Minnesota	A.L.	22	27	3	0	1.000	14	12	17	2.00	0
2005 Minnesota	A.L.	75	79^{2}/$_{3}$	12	5	.706	25	29	61	2.71	1
2006 Minnesota	A.L.	68	76^{2}/$_{3}$	4	5	.444	60	18	79	3.52	1
2007 Minnesota a	A.L.	18	16^{1}/$_{3}$	1	2	.333	10	4	19	5.51	0
2008 Minnesota	A.L.	66	62^{2}/$_{3}$	5	4	.556	50	24	62	3.59	0
2009 Rochester.............	Int.	12	17^{2}/$_{3}$	1	0	1.000	22	8	13	2.55	1
2009 Minnesota b..........	A.L.	56	51^{2}/$_{3}$	7	4	.636	43	27	48	4.70	0
2010 Minnesota c	A.L.	71	68	1	1	.500	62	27	53	3.04	1
2011 Chicago	A.L.	67	65^{1}/$_{3}$	8	3	.727	70	31	50	2.62	1
2012 Charlotte	Int.	2	2	0	0	.000	3	0	0	0.00	0
2012 Chicago d.............	A.L.	51	48	2	3	.400	60	23	29	2.44	0
Major League Totals	9 Yrs.	494	495^{1}/$_{3}$	43	27	.614	394	195	418	3.22	4
	Division Series											
2004 Minnesota	A.L.	1	0^{1}/$_{3}$	0	0	.000	0	0	1	0.00	0
2006 Minnesota	A.L.	2	1	0	0	.000	1	1	3	9.00	0
2010 Minnesota	A.L.	1	0^{1}/$_{3}$	0	1	.000	0	0	3	54.00	0
Division Series Totals..........		4	1^{2}/$_{3}$	0	1	.000	1	1	7	16.20	0

a On disabled list from May 16 to October 10, 2007.
b On disabled list from April 18 to May 4, 2009.
c Filed for free agency, November 1, 2010. Signed with Chicago White Sox, December 20, 2010.
d On disabled list from April 21 to May 15 and July 4 to July 21, 2012.

CROW, AARON J.
Born, Topeka, Kansas, November 10, 1986.
Bats Right. Throws Right. Height, 6 feet, 3 inches. Weight, 190 pounds.

Year Club	Lea	G	IP	W	L	Pct	SO	BB	H	ERA	SAVES
2008 Fort Worth . . . . . Amer. Assoc.		1	1	0	0	.000	0	0	1	0.00	0
2009 Fort Worth . . . . . Amer. Assoc.		3	17	3	0	1.000	17	5	11	1.06	0
2010 Wilmington . . . . Carolina		7	44	2	3	.400	53	6	51	5.93	0
2010 NW Arkansas . . . . Texas		22	119⅓	7	7	.500	90	59	130	5.66	0
2011 Kansas City . . . . A.L.		57	62	4	4	.500	65	31	55	2.76	0
2012 Kansas City . . . . A.L.		73	64⅔	3	1	.750	65	22	54	3.48	2
Major League Totals . . . . 2 Yrs.		130	126⅔	7	5	.583	130	53	109	3.13	2

CRUZ (MONTERO), RHINER ALLEN
Born, Santo Domingo, Dominican Republic, November 1, 1986.
Bats Right. Throws Right. Height, 6 feet, 2 inches. Weight, 205 pounds.

Year Club	Lea	G	IP	W	L	Pct	SO	BB	H	ERA	SAVES
2004 Tigers . . . . Gulf Coast		16	32	0	1	.000	26	19	37	4.78	0
2005 Tigers . . . . Gulf Coast		14	28	1	0	1.000	23	12	35	4.50	1
2006						Did Not Play					
2007 Kingsport . . . . Appal.		11	12⅔	1	1	.500	13	14	7	0.71	4
2007 Mets a . . . . Gulf Coast		4	6	2	0	1.000	4	5	1	0.00	0
2008 Brooklyn. . . . . N.Y.-Penn.		6	9⅔	0	0	.000	13	6	9	3.72	1
2008 Savannah . . . . So.Atl.		15	30⅓	2	2	.500	33	14	27	5.04	1
2009 Savannah . . . . So.Atl.		50	61	3	3	.500	55	31	42	1.92	22
2010 St. Lucie. . . . . Fla.St.		51	75⅓	0	5	.000	66	53	62	3.46	6
2011 Binghamton . . . . Eastern		36	58⅔	3	2	.600	51	39	43	4.14	7
2011 St. Lucie b . . . . Fla.St.		8	13	2	1	.667	18	6	9	2.77	0
2012 Oklahoma . . . . P.C.		2	1⅔	0	0	.000	3	1	1	5.40	0
2012 Houston c . . . . N.L.		52	55	1	1	.500	46	29	65	6.05	0

a Released by Detroit Tigers, June 16, 2006. Signed with New York Mets organization, February 15, 2007.
b Selected by Houston Astros in Rule V draft, December 8, 2011.
c On disabled list from April 24 to May 9, 2012.

CUETO (ORTIZ), JOHNNY
Born, San Pedro de Macoris, Dominican Republic, February 15, 1985.
Bats Right. Throws Right. Height, 5 feet, 10 inches. Weight, 185 pounds.

Year Club	Lea	G	IP	W	L	Pct	SO	BB	H	ERA	SAVES
2005 Sarasota . . . . Fla.St.		2	6	0	1	.000	6	2	5	3.00	0
2005 Reds . . . . Gulf Coast		13	43	2	2	.500	38	8	49	5.02	1
2006 Sarasota . . . . Fla.St.		12	61⅔	7	2	.778	61	23	48	3.50	0
2006 Dayton . . . . Midwest		14	76⅓	8	1	.889	82	15	52	2.59	0
2007 Sarasota . . . . Fla.St.		14	78⅓	4	5	.444	72	21	72	3.33	0
2007 Louisville . . . . Int.		4	22	2	1	.667	21	2	22	2.05	0
2007 Chattanooga . . . . . . Southern		10	61	6	3	.667	77	11	52	3.10	0
2008 Cincinnati . . . . N.L.		31	174	9	14	.391	158	68	178	4.81	0
2009 Cincinnati a . . . . N.L.		30	171⅓	11	11	.500	132	61	172	4.41	0
2010 Cincinnati . . . . N.L.		31	185⅔	12	7	.632	138	56	181	3.64	0
2011 Louisville . . . . Int.		4	14⅓	0	2	.000	13	6	19	6.28	0
2011 Cincinnati b . . . . N.L.		24	156	9	5	.643	104	47	123	2.31	0
2012 Cincinnati . . . . N.L.		33	217	19	9	.679	170	49	205	2.78	0
Major League Totals . . . . 5 Yrs.		149	904	60	46	.566	702	281	859	3.57	0
Division Series											
2010 Cincinnati . . . . N.L.		1	5	0	1	.000	2	1	5	1.80	0
2012 Cincinnati . . . . N.L.		1	0⅓	0	0	.000	1	0	0	0.00	0
Division Series Totals		2	5⅓	0	1	.000	3	1	5	1.69	0

a On disabled list from August 16 to August 31, 2009.
b On disabled list from March 22 to May 8, 2011.

DANKS, JOHN WILLIAM
Born, Austin, Texas, April 15, 1985.
Bats Left. Throws Left. Height, 6 feet, 1 inch. Weight, 200 pounds.

Year Club	Lea	G	IP	W	L	Pct	SO	BB	H	ERA	SAVES
2003 Rangers . . . . Arizona		5	13	1	0	1.000	22	4	6	0.69	0
2003 Spokane . . . . Northwest		5	12⅔	0	2	.000	13	7	12	8.53	0
2004 Stockton . . . . Calif.		13	55	1	4	.200	48	26	62	5.24	0
2004 Clinton . . . . Midwest		14	49⅔	3	2	.600	64	14	38	2.17	0

Year Club	Lea	G	IP	W	L	Pct	SO	BB	H	ERA	SAVES
2005 Bakersfield	Calif.	10	57²/₃	3	3	.500	53	16	50	2.50	0
2005 Frisco	Texas	18	98¹/₃	4	10	.286	85	34	117	5.49	0
2006 Oklahoma	P.C.	14	70²/₃	4	5	.444	72	34	67	4.33	0
2006 Frisco a	Texas	13	69¹/₃	5	4	.556	82	22	74	4.15	0
2007 Chicago	A.L.	26	139	6	13	.316	109	54	160	5.50	0
2008 Chicago	A.L.	33	195	12	9	.571	159	57	182	3.32	0
2009 Chicago	A.L.	32	200¹/₃	13	11	.542	149	73	184	3.77	0
2010 Chicago	A.L.	32	213	15	11	.577	162	70	189	3.72	0
2011 Charlotte	Int.	2	9	1	0	1.000	6	2	9	2.00	0
2011 Chicago b	A.L.	27	170¹/₃	8	12	.400	135	46	182	4.33	0
2012 Charlotte	Int.	1	4	0	0	.000	1	1	4	2.25	0
2012 Chicago c	A.L.	9	53²/₃	3	4	.429	30	23	57	5.70	0
Major League Totals . . . . .6 Yrs.		159	971¹/₃	57	60	.487	744	323	954	4.12	0
Division Series											
2008 Chicago	A.L.	1	6²/₃	1	0	1.000	7	3	7	4.05	0

a Traded to Chicago White Sox by Texas Rangers with pitcher Nick Masset and pitcher Jacob Rasner for pitcher Brandon McCarthy and outfielder David Paisano, December 23, 2006.
b On disabled list from June 26 to July 20, 2011.
c On disabled list from May 20 to October 29, 2012.

DARVISH, SEFAT FARID YU (YU)
Born, Osaka, Japan, August 16, 1986.
Bats Right. Throws Right. Height 6 feet, 5 inches. Weight, 187 pounds.

Year Club	Lea	G	IP	W	L	Pct	SO	BB	H	ERA	SAVES
2005 Nippon Ham . . . . . .Japan Pac.		14	94¹/₃	5	5	.500	52	48	97	3.53	0
2006 Nippon Ham . . . . . .Japan Pac.		25	149²/₃	12	5	.706	115	64	128	2.89	0
2007 Nippon Ham . . . . . .Japan Pac.		26	207²/₃	15	5	.750	210	49	123	1.82	0
2008 Nippon Ham . . . . . .Japan Pac.		25	200²/₃	16	4	.800	208	44	136	1.80	0
2009 Nippon Ham . . . . . .Japan Pac.		23	182	15	5	.750	167	45	118	1.73	0
2010 Nippon Ham . . . . . .Japan Pac.		26	202	12	8	.600	222	47	158	1.78	0
2011 Nippon Ham . . . . . .Japan Pac.		28	232	18	6	.750	276	36	156	1.44	0
2012 Texas a	A.L.	29	191¹/₃	16	9	.640	221	89	156	3.90	0
Wild Card Playoff											
2012 Texas	A.L.	1	6²/₃	0	1	.000	7	0	5	2.70	0

a Signed with Texas Rangers, January 18, 2012.

DAVIS, WADE ALLEN
Born, Lake Wales, Florida, September 7, 1985.
Bats Right. Throws Right. Height, 6 feet, 5 inches. Weight, 220 pounds.

Year Club	Lea	G	IP	W	L	Pct	SO	BB	H	ERA	SAVES
2004 Princeton	Appal.	13	57²/₃	3	5	.375	38	19	71	5.93	0
2005 Hudson Valley . . . . .N.Y.-Penn.		15	86	7	4	.636	97	23	75	2.72	0
2006 SW Michigan . . . . .Midwest		27	146	7	12	.368	165	64	124	3.02	0
2007 Vero Beach	Fla.St.	13	78¹/₃	3	0	1.000	88	21	54	1.84	0
2007 Montgomery	Southern	14	80	7	3	.700	81	30	74	3.15	0
2008 Durham	Int.	9	53	4	2	.667	55	24	39	2.72	0
2008 Montgomery	Southern	19	107²/₃	9	6	.600	81	42	104	3.85	0
2009 Durham	Int.	28	158²/₃	10	8	.556	140	60	139	3.40	0
2009 Tampa Bay	A.L.	6	36¹/₃	2	2	.500	36	13	33	3.72	0
2010 Tampa Bay a	A.L.	29	168	12	10	.545	113	62	165	4.07	0
2011 Tampa Bay b	A.L.	29	184	11	10	.524	105	63	190	4.45	0
2012 Tampa Bay c	A.L.	54	70¹/₃	3	0	1.000	87	29	48	2.43	0
Major League Totals . . . . .4 Yrs.		118	458²/₃	28	22	.560	341	167	436	3.94	0
Division Series											
2010 Tampa Bay	A.L.	1	5	1	0	1.000	7	3	7	3.60	0
2011 Tampa Bay	A.L.	2	2¹/₃	0	0	.000	1	1	1	0.00	0
Division Series Totals		3	7¹/₃	1	0	1.000	8	4	8	2.45	0

a On disabled list from August 6 to August 24, 2010.
b On disabled list from July 7 to July 22, 2011.
c Traded to Kansas City Royals with pitcher James Shields and player to be named later for pitcher Mike Montgomery, pitcher Jake Odorizzi, infielder Patrick Leonard and outfielder Wil Myers, December 9, 2012.

DELABAR, STEVEN EDWARD (STEVE)
Born, Fort Knox, Kentucky, July 17, 1983.
Bats Right. Throws Right. Height, 6 feet, 5 inches. Weight, 220 pounds.

Year	Club	Lea	G	IP	W	L	Pct	SO	BB	H	ERA	SAVES
2004	Padres	Arizona	14	45$\frac{1}{3}$	3	4	.429	39	21	51	4.37	0
2004	Eugene	Northwest	3	17	1	1	.500	11	3	13	2.65	0
2005	Eugene	Northwest	16	75$\frac{2}{3}$	4	6	.400	59	18	84	4.76	0
2006	Fort Wayne	Midwest	27	145	8	9	.471	118	65	129	3.41	0
2007	Lake Elsinore	Calif.	20	29	2	6	.250	33	16	26	5.59	0
2007	Fort Wayne	Midwest	21	68	2	5	.286	48	46	63	5.96	0
2008	Fort Wayne	Midwest	11	13$\frac{2}{3}$	2	1	.667	12	5	17	5.27	0
2008	Florence	Frontier	4	6	0	0	.000	7	2	6	2.84	0
2008	Brockton a-b	Can.-Amer.	11	69	3	3	.500	43	16	67	3.01	0
2009	Brockton	Can.-Amer.	12	26	3	3	.500	23	12	23	3.76	0
2010							Did Not Play					
2011	High Desert	Calif.	7	12$\frac{1}{3}$	1	1	.500	20	8	12	4.38	3
2011	Jackson	Southern	23	30$\frac{2}{3}$	1	3	.250	30	26	23	2.05	12
2011	Tacoma	P.C.	10	13	1	1	.500	18	6	11	0.69	0
2011	Seattle c	A.L.	6	7	1	1	.500	7	4	5	2.57	0
2012	Tacoma	P.C.	9	12	0	1	.000	12	12	11	3.75	1
2012	Seattle-Toronto d	A.L.	61	66	4	3	.571	92	26	46	3.82	0

Major League Totals ....2 Yrs. 67 73 5 4 .556 99 30 51 3.70 0

a Released by San Diego Padres, May 23, 2008. Signed with Florence, June 2008.
b Signed with Brockton, June 2008.
c Signed with Seattle Mariners organization, April 19, 2011.
d Traded to Toronto Blue Jays for outfielder Eric Thames, July 31, 2012.

DE LA ROSA, JORGE ALBERTO
Born, Monterrey, Mexico, April 5, 1981.
Bats Left. Throws Left. Height, 6 feet, 1 inch. Weight, 220 pounds.

Year	Club	Lea	G	IP	W	L	Pct	SO	BB	H	ERA	SAVES
1998	Arizona	Dominican	13	14	1	0	1.000	21	8	8	4.50	1
1999	Diamondbacks	Arizona	8	14	0	0	.000	17	3	12	3.21	2
1999	High Desert	Calif.	2	3	0	0	.000	3	2	1	0.00	0
1999	Missoula	Pioneer	13	14$\frac{2}{3}$	0	1	.000	14	9	22	7.98	2
2000	Monterrey a	Mexican	37	39	3	2	.600	50	32	38	6.28	1
2001	Trenton	Eastern	29	37	1	3	.250	27	20	56	5.84	0
2001	Sarasota b	Fla.St.	12	29$\frac{2}{3}$	0	1	.000	27	12	13	1.21	2
2002	Trenton	Eastern	4	18	1	2	.333	15	9	17	5.50	0
2002	Sarasota	Fla.St.	23	120$\frac{2}{3}$	7	7	.500	95	52	105	3.65	0
2003	Portland	Eastern	22	99$\frac{2}{3}$	6	3	.667	102	36	87	2.80	1
2003	Pawtucket c-d	Int.	5	24	1	2	.333	17	12	27	3.75	0
2004	Indianapolis	Int.	20	85$\frac{2}{3}$	5	6	.455	86	36	80	4.52	0
2004	Milwaukee	N.L.	5	22$\frac{2}{3}$	0	3	.000	5	14	29	6.35	0
2005	Milwaukee	N.L.	38	42$\frac{1}{3}$	2	2	.500	42	38	48	4.46	0
2006	Milwaukee	N.L.	18	30$\frac{1}{3}$	2	2	.500	31	22	32	8.60	0
2006	Huntsville	Southern	6	30	3	1	.750	23	3	31	2.40	0
2006	Kansas City e	A.L.	10	48$\frac{2}{3}$	3	4	.429	36	32	49	5.18	0
2007	Wichita	Texas	3	5$\frac{2}{3}$	0	1	.000	7	4	10	11.12	0
2007	Kansas City	A.L.	26	130	8	12	.400	82	53	160	5.82	0
2008	Omaha	P.C.	4	22	3	0	1.000	23	7	18	1.64	0
2008	Colorado f	N.L.	28	130	10	8	.556	128	62	128	4.92	0
2009	Colorado	N.L.	33	185	16	9	.640	193	83	172	4.38	0
2010	Colorado Springs	P.C.	3	14$\frac{2}{3}$	1	2	.333	15	4	17	5.52	0
2010	Colorado g	N.L.	20	121$\frac{2}{3}$	8	7	.533	113	55	105	4.22	0
2011	Colorado	N.L.	10	59	5	2	.714	52	22	48	3.51	0
2012	Grand Junction	Pioneer	1	3	0	0	.000	5	0	3	0.00	0
2012	Modesto	Calif.	2	5$\frac{2}{3}$	0	0	.000	7	3	7	4.76	0
2012	Tulsa	Texas	2	5	0	0	.000	5	3	8	9.00	0
2012	Colorado Springs	P.C.	2	6$\frac{2}{3}$	0	1	.000	5	3	9	9.45	0
2012	Colorado h	N.L.	3	10$\frac{2}{3}$	0	2	.000	6	2	17	9.28	0

Major League Totals ....9 Yrs. 191 780$\frac{1}{3}$ 54 51 .514 688 383 788 4.96 0

a Sold by Arizona Diamondbacks to Monterrey, April 2, 2000.
b Sold to Boston Red Sox, February 22, 2001.
c Traded by Boston Red Sox to Arizona Diamondbacks with pitcher Casey Fossum, pitcher Brandon Lyon and outfielder Michael Goss for pitcher Curt Schilling, November 28, 2003.
d Traded to Milwaukee Brewers with infielder Junior Spivey, infielder Craig Counsell, infielder Lyle Overbay, catcher Chad Moeller and pitcher Chris Capuano for infielder Richie Sexson, pitcher Shane Nance and player to be named later, December 1, 2003. Arizona Diamondbacks received outfielder Noochie Varner to complete trade, December 15, 2003.

e Traded to Kansas City Royals for infielder Tony Graffanino, July 25, 2006.
f Sent to Colorado Rockies as player to be named later for pitcher Ramon Ramirez, April 30, 2008.
g Filed for free agency, November 1, 2010, re-signed with Colorado Rockies, December 3, 2010.
h On disabled list from March 26 to September 20, 2012.

DELGADO, RANDALL ENRIQUE

Born, Las Tablas, Panama, February 9, 1990.
Bats Right. Throws Right. Height, 6 feet, 3 inches. Weight, 200 pounds.

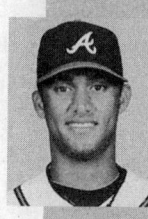

Year	Club	Lea	G	IP	W	L	Pct	SO	BB	H	ERA	SAVES
2008 Danville	....	Appal.	14	69	3	8	.273	81	30	63	3.13	0
2009 Rome	....	So.Atl.	25	124	5	10	.333	141	49	123	4.35	0
2010 Myrtle Beach	....	Carolina	20	117¹/₃	4	7	.364	120	32	89	2.76	0
2010 Mississippi	....	Southern	8	43²/₃	3	5	.375	42	20	36	4.74	0
2011 Mississippi		Southern	21	117¹/₃	5	5	.500	110	46	116	3.84	0
2011 Gwinnett	....	Int.	4	21²/₃	2	2	.500	25	11	19	4.15	0
2011 Atlanta	....	N.L.	7	35	1	1	.500	18	14	29	2.83	0
2012 Gwinnett	....	Int.	8	44¹/₃	4	3	.571	51	21	47	4.06	0
2012 Atlanta	....	N.L.	18	92²/₃	4	9	.308	76	42	89	4.37	0
Major League Totals	....	2 Yrs.	25	127²/₃	5	10	.333	94	56	118	3.95	0

DEMPSTER, RYAN SCOTT

Born, Sechelt, British Columbia, Canada, May 3, 1977.
Bats Right. Throws Right. Height, 6 feet, 2 inches. Weight, 215 pounds.

Year	Club	Lea	G	IP	W	L	Pct	SO	BB	H	ERA	SAVES
1995 Rangers	....	Gulf Coast	8	34¹/₃	3	1	.750	37	17	34	2.36	0
1995 Hudson Val.	....	N.Y.-Penn.	1	5²/₃	1	0	1.000	6	1	7	3.18	0
1996 Chston-SC	....	So.Atl.	23	144¹/₃	7	11	.389	141	58	120	3.30	0
1996 Kane County a	.....	Midwest	4	26¹/₃	2	1	.667	16	18	18	2.73	0
1997 Brevard Cty	....	Fla.St.	28	165¹/₃	10	9	.526	131	46	190	4.90	0
1998 Portland	....	Eastern	7	44²/₃	4	3	.571	33	15	34	3.22	0
1998 Florida	....	N.L.	14	54²/₃	1	5	.167	35	38	72	7.08	0
1998 Charlotte	....	Int.	5	33	3	1	.750	24	12	33	3.27	0
1999 Calgary	....	P.C.	5	30²/₃	1	1	.500	29	10	30	4.99	0
1999 Florida	....	N.L.	25	147	7	8	.467	126	93	146	4.71	0
2000 Florida	....	N.L.	33	226¹/₃	14	10	.583	209	97	210	3.66	0
2001 Florida	....	N.L.	34	211¹/₃	15	12	.556	171	112	218	4.94	0
2002 Florida-Cincinnati b	.....	N.L.	33	209	10	13	.435	153	93	228	5.38	0
2003 Cincinnati	....	N.L.	22	115²/₃	3	7	.300	84	70	134	6.54	0
2003 Louisville c	....	Int.	2	13²/₃	1	1	.500	9	3	13	3.29	0
2004 Lansing	....	Midwest	5	18¹/₃	0	0	.000	21	2	20	1.96	0
2004 Iowa	....	P.C.	6	21	1	1	.500	20	10	19	3.86	0
2004 Chicago d-e	....	N.L.	23	20²/₃	1	1	.500	18	13	16	3.92	2
2005 Chicago	....	N.L.	63	92	5	3	.625	89	49	83	3.13	33
2006 Chicago	....	N.L.	74	75	1	9	.100	67	36	77	4.80	24
2007 Iowa	....	P.C.	2	2	0	0	.000	4	1	1	0.00	0
2007 Chicago f	....	N.L.	66	66²/₃	2	7	.222	55	30	59	4.72	28
2008 Chicago g	....	N.L.	33	206²/₃	17	6	.739	187	76	174	2.96	0
2009 Chicago h	....	N.L.	31	200	11	9	.550	172	65	196	3.65	0
2010 Chicago	....	N.L.	34	215¹/₃	15	12	.556	208	86	198	3.85	0
2011 Chicago	....	N.L.	34	202¹/₃	10	14	.417	191	82	211	4.80	0
2012 Chicago	....	N.L.	16	104	5	5	.500	83	27	81	2.25	0
2012 Texas i-j-k.	....	A.L.	12	69	7	3	.700	70	25	74	5.09	0
Major League Totals	....	15 Yrs.	547	2215²/₃	124	124	.500	1918	992	2177	4.33	87
Division Series												
2007 Chicago	....	N.L.	1	1	0	0	.000	2	0	0	0.00	0
2008 Chicago	....	N.L.	1	4²/₃	0	1	.000	2	7	4	7.71	0
Division Series Totals	....		2	5²/₃	0	1	.000	4	7	4	6.35	0

a Traded by Texas Rangers to Florida Marlins with player to be named later for pitcher John Burkett, August 8, 1996. Florida Marlins received pitcher Rick Helling to complete trade, September 3, 1996.
b Traded to Cincinnati Reds for outfielder Juan Encarnacion, infielder Wilton Guerrero and pitcher Ryan Snare, July 11, 2002.
c On disabled list from May 23 to June 7 and July 29 to November 3, 2003.
d Waived by Cincinnati Reds, November 4, 2003. Signed with Chicago Cubs, January 21, 2004.
e On disabled list from March 26 to August 1, 2004.
f On disabled list from June 23 to July 20, 2007.
g Filed for free agency, October 30, 2008, re-signed with Chicago Cubs, November 18, 2008.
h On disabled list from July 7 to July 28, 2009.
i On disabled list from April 18 to May 3 and June 16 to July 8, 2012.

j Traded to Texas Rangers for pitcher Kyle Hendricks and infielder Christian Villanueva, July 31, 2012.
k Filed for free agency, November 3, 2012. Signed with Boston Red Sox, December 19, 2012.

DETWILER, ROSS EMERY
Born, St.Louis, Missouri, March 6, 1986.
Bats Right. Throws Right. Height, 6 feet, 5 inches. Weight, 185 pounds.

Year Club	Lea	G	IP	W	L	Pct	SO	BB	H	ERA	SAVES
2007 Nationals . . . . Gulf Coast		4	12	0	0	.000	15	3	11	2.25	0
2007 Potomac. . . . . .Carolina		5	21¹/₃	2	2	.500	13	9	27	4.22	0
2007 Washington . . . . .N.L.		1	1	0	0	.000	1	0	0	0.00	0
2008 Potomac. . . . . .Carolina		26	124	8	8	.500	114	57	140	4.86	0
2009 Harrisburg . . . . Eastern		6	27¹/₃	0	3	.000	28	10	28	2.96	0
2009 Syracuse . . . . .Int.		10	49¹/₃	4	2	.667	42	20	56	3.10	0
2009 Washington . . . . .N.L.		15	75²/₃	1	6	.143	43	33	87	5.00	0
2010 Potomac. . . . . .Carolina		2	6	0	0	.000	6	1	6	1.50	0
2010 Harrisburg . . . . Eastern		7	32²/₃	2	2	.500	31	7	38	2.48	0
2010 Syracuse . . . . .Int.		1	5	1	0	1.000	2	1	5	1.80	0
2010 Washington a. . . . . .N.L.		8	29²/₃	1	3	.250	17	14	34	4.25	0
2011 Syracuse . . . . .Int.		16	87¹/₃	6	6	.500	63	32	98	4.53	0
2011 Washington . . . . .N.L.		15	66	4	5	.444	41	20	63	3.00	0
2012 Washington . . . . .N.L.		33	164¹/₃	10	8	.556	105	52	149	3.40	0
Major League Totals . . . . .5 Yrs.		72	336²/₃	16	22	.421	207	119	333	3.74	
Division Series											
2012 Washington . . . . .N.L.		1	6	0	0	.000	2	3	3	0.00	0

a On disabled list from April 4 to June 21 and August 6 to September 7, 2010.

DE VRIES, COLE WILLIAM
Born, St.Louis Park, Minnesota, February 12, 1985.
Bats Right. Throws Right. Height, 6 feet, 2 inches. Weight, 180 pounds.

Year Club	Lea	G	IP	W	L	Pct	SO	BB	H	ERA	SAVES
2007 Beloit . . . . .Midwest		27	148	9	5	.643	108	36	161	3.41	0
2008 Fort Myers . . . . Fla.St.		24	135¹/₃	10	9	.526	105	38	138	2.93	0
2009 New Britain . . . . Eastern		26	137²/₃	7	14	.333	90	46	162	4.84	0
2010 New Britain . . . . Eastern		39	68¹/₃	1	5	.167	63	25	87	5.80	1
2010 Rochester. . . . . .Int.		9	23¹/₃	0	3	.000	24	14	26	5.79	0
2011 New Britain . . . . Eastern		15	27²/₃	0	0	.000	33	5	17	2.28	9
2011 Rochester. . . . . .Int.		30	62¹/₃	4	2	.667	42	18	74	3.90	0
2012 Rochester. . . . . .Int.		12	70	3	5	.375	50	10	75	4.37	0
2012 Minnesota a . . . . .A.L.		17	87²/₃	5	5	.500	58	18	88	4.11	0

a On disabled list from September 9 to October 22, 2012.

DIAMOND, SCOTT MICHAEL
Born, Guelph, Ontario, Canada, July 30, 1986.
Bats Left. Throws Left. Height, 6 feet, 3 inches. Weight, 220 pounds.

Year Club	Lea	G	IP	W	L	Pct	SO	BB	H	ERA	SAVES
2008 Myrtle Beach . . . . . . .Carolina		17	100	12	2	.857	85	28	95	2.79	0
2008 Rome . . . . .So.Atl.		9	52²/₃	3	1	.750	38	11	47	3.08	0
2009 Mississippi. . . . . Southern		23	131	5	10	.333	111	53	152	3.50	0
2010 Gwinnett. . . . . .Int.		10	56¹/₃	4	1	.800	33	15	53	3.36	0
2010 Mississippi a . . . . . . Southern		17	102¹/₃	4	6	.400	90	39	113	3.52	0
2011 Rochester. . . . . .Int.		23	123	4	14	.222	90	36	158	5.56	0
2011 Minnesota b . . . . .A.L.		7	39	1	5	.167	19	17	51	5.08	0
2012 Rochester. . . . . .Int.		6	34²/₃	4	1	.800	26	7	35	2.60	0
2012 Minnesota . . . . .A.L.		27	173	12	9	.571	90	31	184	3.54	0
Major League Totals . . . . .2 Yrs.		34	212	13	14	.481	109	48	235	3.82	0

a Selected by Minnesota Twins from Atlanta Braves in Rule V draft, December 9, 2010.
b Retained by Minnesota Twins from Atlanta Braves for pitcher Billy Bullock, March 28, 2011.

DICKEY, ROBERT ALAN (R.A.)
Born, Nashville, Tennessee, October 29, 1974.
Bats Right. Throws Right. Height, 6 feet, 3 inches. Weight, 220 pounds.

Year Club	Lea	G	IP	W	L	Pct	SO	BB	H	ERA	SAVES
1997 Charlotte . . . . Fla.St.		8	35	1	4	.200	32	12	51	6.94	0
1998 Charlotte . . . . Fla.St.		57	60	1	5	.167	53	22	58	3.30	38
1999 Oklahoma. . . . . .P.C.		6	22²/₃	2	2	.500	17	7	23	4.37	0
1999 Tulsa . . . . .Texas		35	95	6	7	.462	59	40	105	4.55	10

Year	Club	Lea	G	IP	W	L	Pct	SO	BB	H	ERA	SAVES
2000 Oklahoma	P.C.	30	158^1/$_3$	8	9	.471	85	65	167	4.49	1
2001 Oklahoma	P.C.	24	163	11	7	.611	120	45	164	3.75	0
2001 Texas	A.L.	4	12	0	1	.000	4	7	13	6.75	0
2002 Oklahoma	P.C.	37	154	8	7	.533	109	47	176	4.09	0
2003 Oklahoma	P.C.	3	15	1	1	.500	4	3	14	1.20	0
2003 Texas	A.L.	38	116^2/$_3$	9	8	.529	94	38	135	5.09	1
2004 Frisco	Texas	4	13^2/$_3$	1	1	.500	9	1	16	1.98	0
2004 Texas a	A.L.	25	104^1/$_3$	6	7	.462	57	33	136	5.61	1
2005 Oklahoma	P.C.	19	121^2/$_3$	10	6	.625	81	39	152	5.99	0
2005 Texas b	A.L.	9	29^2/$_3$	1	2	.333	15	17	29	6.67	0
2006 Texas	A.L.	1	3^1/$_3$	0	1	.000	1	1	8	18.90	0
2006 Oklahoma	P.C.	22	131^2/$_3$	9	8	.529	61	46	134	4.92	1
2007 Nashville c-d-e	P.C.	31	169^1/$_3$	13	6	.684	119	60	159	3.72	0
2008 Tacoma	P.C.	7	49^2/$_3$	2	5	.286	30	8	58	3.44	0
2008 Seattle f-g	A.L.	32	112^1/$_3$	5	8	.385	58	51	124	5.21	0
2009 Rochester	Int.	5	33^1/$_3$	2	1	.667	18	9	39	5.13	0
2009 Minnesota h	A.L.	35	64^1/$_3$	1	1	.500	42	30	74	4.62	0
2010 Buffalo	Int.	8	60^2/$_3$	4	2	.667	37	8	55	2.23	0
2010 New York	N.L.	27	174^1/$_3$	11	9	.550	104	42	165	2.84	0
2011 New York	N.L.	33	208^2/$_3$	8	13	.381	134	54	202	3.28	0
2012 New York i-j	N.L.	34	*233^2/$_3$	20	6	.769	*230	54	192	2.73	0
Major League Totals	10 Yrs.	238	1059^1/$_3$	61	56	.521	739	327	1078	3.98	2

a On disabled list from June 25 to July 19 and July 30 to August 23, 2004.
b On disabled list from April 13 to May 25, 2005.
c Filed for free agency, October 11, 2006. Signed with Milwaukee Brewers organization, January 10, 2007.
d Filed for free agency, October 29, 2007. Signed with Minnesota Twins organization, November 29, 2007.
e Selected by Seattle Mariners in Rule V draft, December 6, 2007.
f Seattle retained rights to Dickey for catcher Jair Fernandez, March 29, 2008.
g Filed for free agency, December 9, 2008. Signed with Minnesota Twins organization, December 26, 2008.
h Filed for free agency, October 6, 2009. Signed with New York Mets organization, December 23, 2009.
i Selected Cy Young Award Winner in National League for 2012.
j Traded to Toronto Blue Jays with catcher Josh Thole and catcher Mike Nickeas for catcher John Buck, pitcher Noah Syndergaard, catcher Travis D'Arnaud and outfielder Wuilmer Becerra, December 17, 2012.

DOOLITTLE, SEAN ROBERT

Born, Rapid City, South Dakota, September 26, 1986.
Bats Left. Throws Left. Height, 6 feet, 3 inches. Weight, 210 pounds.

Year	Club	Lea	G	IP	W	L	Pct	SO	BB	H	ERA	SAVES
2010 a-b							INJURED—Did Not Play					
2011 Athletics	Arizona	1	1	0	0	.000	2	1	0	9.00	0
2012 Stockton	Calif.	6	10^1/$_3$	0	0	.000	21	2	5	0.87	0
2012 Midland	Texas	8	11	0	0	.000	19	4	2	0.82	1
2012 Sacramento	P.C.	2	3^2/$_3$	0	0	.000	8	1	1	0.00	0
2012 Oakland	A.L.	44	47^1/$_3$	2	1	.667	60	11	40	3.04	1
Division Series												
2012 Oakland	A.L.	3	2^2/$_3$	0	0	.000	5	0	5	3.38	0

a Played first base in Oakland Athletics system from 2007 through 2009.
b On minor league disabled list from April 8 to September 23, 2010.

DOTEL (DIAZ), OCTAVIO EDUARDO

Born, Santo Domingo, Dominican Republic, November 25, 1973.
Bats Right. Throws Right. Height, 6 feet. Weight, 215 pounds.

Year	Club	Lea	G	IP	W	L	Pct	SO	BB	H	ERA	SAVES
1993 Mets	Dominican	15	59^1/$_3$	6	2	.750	48	38	46	4.10	0
1994 Mets	Dominican	15	81^1/$_3$	5	0	1.000	95	31	84	4.32	0
1995 Mets	Gulf Coast	13	74^1/$_3$	7	4	.636	86	17	48	2.18	0
1995 St. Lucie	Fla.St.	3	8	1	0	1.000	9	4	10	5.63	0
1996 Columbia	So.Atl.	22	115^1/$_3$	11	3	.786	142	49	89	3.59	0
1997 Mets	Gulf Coast	3	9^1/$_3$	0	0	.000	7	2	9	0.96	1
1997 St. Lucie	Fla.St.	9	50	7	2	.714	39	23	44	2.52	0
1997 Binghamton	Eastern	12	55^2/$_3$	3	4	.429	40	38	66	5.98	0
1998 Binghamton	Eastern	10	68^2/$_3$	4	2	.667	82	24	41	1.97	0
1998 Norfolk	Int.	17	99	8	6	.571	118	43	82	3.45	0
1999 Norfolk	Int.	13	70^1/$_3$	5	2	.714	90	34	52	3.84	0
1999 New York a	N.L.	19	85^1/$_3$	8	3	.727	85	49	69	5.38	0
2000 Houston	N.L.	50	125	3	7	.300	142	61	127	5.40	16
2001 Houston	N.L.	61	105	7	5	.583	145	47	79	2.66	2
2002 Houston	N.L.	83	97^1/$_3$	6	4	.600	118	27	58	1.85	6

Year	Club	Lea	G	IP	W	L	Pct	SO	BB	H	ERA	SAVES
2003 Houston	N.L.	76	87	6	4	.600	97	31	53	2.48	4
2004 Houston	N.L.	32	34²/₃	0	4	.000	50	15	27	3.12	14
2004 Oakland b-c	A.L.	45	50²/₃	6	2	.750	72	18	41	4.09	22
2005 Oakland d-e	A.L.	15	15¹/₃	1	2	.333	16	11	10	3.52	7
2006 Staten Island	N.Y.-Penn.	1	1	0	0	.000	1	0	2	0.00	0
2006 Yankees	Gulf Coast	3	3	0	0	.000	6	1	0	0.00	0
2006 Tampa	Fla.St.	2	2	0	0	.000	2	0	1	0.00	0
2006 Trenton	Eastern	2	2	0	0	.000	3	0	1	0.00	0
2006 Columbus	Int.	5	5¹/₃	0	0	.000	8	0	6	3.38	0
2006 New York f-g	A.L.	14	10	0	0	.000	7	11	18	10.80	0
2007 Wichita	Texas	3	3	0	1	.000	4	0	2	3.00	1
2007 Kansas City	A.L.	24	23	2	1	.667	29	11	24	3.91	11
2007 Atlanta h-i-j	N.L.	9	7²/₃	0	0	.000	12	1	5	4.70	0
2008 Chicago	A.L.	72	67	4	4	.500	92	29	52	3.76	1
2009 Chicago k	A.L.	62	62¹/₃	3	3	.500	75	36	54	3.32	0
2010 Pitt-LA-Col l-m-n	N.L.	68	64	3	4	.429	75	32	52	4.08	22
2011 Toronto	A.L.	36	29¹/₃	2	1	.667	30	12	20	3.68	1
2011 St. Louis o-p-q	N.L.	29	24²/₃	3	3	.500	32	5	16	3.28	2
2012 Detroit r	A.L.	57	58	5	3	.625	62	12	50	3.57	1
Major League Totals	14 Yrs.	752	946¹/₃	59	50	.541	1139	408	755	3.73	109
Division Series											
1999 New York	N.L.	1	0¹/₃	0	0	.000	0	2	1	54.00	0
2001 Houston	N.L.	2	3¹/₃	0	0	.000	5	0	5	5.40	0
2008 Chicago	A.L.	4	1¹/₃	0	0	.000	3	0	2	13.50	0
2011 St. Louis	N.L.	3	2²/₃	1	0	1.000	4	0	0	0.00	0
2012 Detroit	A.L.	2	1	0	0	.000	2	1	0	0.00	0
Division Series Totals		12	8²/₃	1	0	1.000	14	3	8	6.23	0
Championship Series											
1999 New York	N.L.	1	3	1	0	1.000	5	2	4	3.00	0
2011 St. Louis	N.L.	4	4	1	0	1.000	5	1	2	2.25	0
2012 Detroit	A.L.	2	2¹/₃	0	0	.000	3	2	0	0.00	0
Championship Series Totals		7	9¹/₃	2	0	1.000	13	5	6	1.93	0
World Series Record											
2011 St. Louis	N.L.	5	3²/₃	0	1	.000	5	1	3	4.91	0
2012 Detroit	A.L.	2	1²/₃	0	0	.000	1	2	0	0.00	0
World Series Totals		7	5¹/₃	0	1	.000	6	3	3	3.38	0

a Traded with Roger Cedeno and Kyle Kessel to Houston for Mike Hampton and Derek Bell, December 23, 1999.
b Traded to Kansas City Royals with catcher John Buck for outfielder Carlos Beltran, June 24, 2004.
c Traded to Oakland Athletics with cash for pitcher Mike Wood and infielder Mark Teahen, June 24, 2004.
d On disabled list from May 19 to October 28, 2005.
e Filed for free agency, October 28, 2005. Signed with New York Yankees, December 29, 2005.
f On disabled list from March 24 to August 16, 2006.
g Filed for free agency, October 28, 2006. Signed with Kansas City Royals, December 8, 2006.
h On disabled list from March 30 to May 22, 2007 and August 8 to September 20, 2007.
i Traded to Atlanta Braves for pitcher Kyle Davies, July 31, 2007.
j Filed for free agency, November 6, 2007. Signed with Chicago White Sox, January 22, 2008.
k Filed for free agency, November 9, 2009. Signed with Pittsburgh Pirates, January 21, 2010.
l Traded to Los Angeles Dodgers for pitcher James McDonald and outfielder Andrew Lambo, July 31, 2010.
m Traded to Colorado Rockies for player to be named later, September 18, 2010. Los Angeles Dodgers received
   outfielder Anthony Jackson to complete trade, November 15, 2010.
n Filed for free agency, November 3, 2010. Signed with Toronto Blue Jays, January 4, 2011.
o On disabled list from March 22 to April 8, 2011.
p Traded to St. Louis Cardinals with pitcher Edwin Jackson, pitcher Marc Rzepczynski, outfielder Corey Patterson and
   cash for outfielder Colby Rasmus, pitcher Trever Miller, pitcher Brian Tallet and pitcher P.J. Walters, July 27, 2011.
q Filed for free agency, October 31, 2011. Signed with Detroit Tigers, December 9, 2011.
r On disabled list from June 3 to June 19, 2012.

DOUBRONT, FELIX ANTONIO
Born, Carabobo, Venezuela, October 23, 1987.
Bats Left. Throws Left. Height, 6 feet, 2 inches. Weight, 165 pounds.

Year	Club	Lea	G	IP	W	L	Pct	SO	BB	H	ERA	SAVES
2006 Red Sox	Gulf Coast	11	53²/₃	2	3	.400	36	13	41	2.52	0
2006 Lowell	N.Y.-Penn.	2	11	2	0	1.000	7	1	7	4.91	0
2007 Lowell	N.Y.-Penn.	8	35	1	3	.250	25	11	41	5.66	0
2007 Greenville	So.Atl.	11	42¹/₃	3	7	.300	22	17	63	8.93	0
2008 Lancaster	Calif.	3	14	1	1	.500	20	4	15	3.86	0
2008 Greenville	So.Atl.	23	115¹/₃	12	8	.600	118	24	115	3.67	0
2009 Portland	Eastern	26	121	8	6	.571	101	52	119	3.35	0

Year Club	Lea	G	IP	W	L	Pct	SO	BB	H	ERA	SAVES
2010 Portland	Eastern	8	43	4	0	1.000	38	17	39	2.51	0
2010 Pawtucket	Int.	9	37	4	3	.571	34	16	36	3.16	0
2010 Boston	A.L.	12	25	2	2	.500	23	10	27	4.32	2
2011 Portland	Eastern	1	5	1	0	1.000	9	0	4	1.80	0
2011 Lowell	N.Y.-Penn.	1	2	0	0	.000	4	0	0	0.00	0
2011 Pawtucket	Int.	18	70⅓	2	5	.286	61	26	65	4.22	0
2011 Boston a..............	A.L.	11	10⅓	0	0	.000	6	8	12	6.10	1
2012 Boston b	A.L.	29	161	11	10	.524	167	71	162	4.86	0
Major League Totals ....3 Yrs.		52	196⅓	13	12	.520	196	89	201	4.86	3

a On disabled list from March 22 to April 8, 2011.
b On disabled list from August 10 to August 25, 2012.

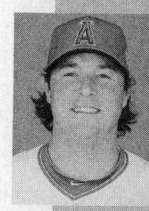

DOWNS, SCOTT JEREMY
Born, Louisville, Kentucky, March 17, 1976.
Bats Left. Throws Left. Height, 6 feet, 2 inches. Weight, 210 pounds.

Year Club	Lea	G	IP	W	L	Pct	SO	BB	H	ERA	SAVES
1997 Williamsprt.......	N.Y.-Penn.	5	23	0	2	.000	28	7	15	2.74	0
1997 Rockford	Midwest	5	36	3	0	1.000	43	8	17	1.25	0
1998 Daytona a..........	Fla.St.	27	161⅔	8	9	.471	117	55	179	3.90	0
1999 New Britain	Eastern	6	19⅔	0	0	.000	22	10	33	8.69	0
1999 Daytona	Fla.St.	7	48	5	0	1.000	41	11	41	1.88	0
1999 Fort Myers	Fla.St.	2	9⅔	0	1	.000	9	6	7	0.00	0
1999 West Tenn b.......	Southern	13	80	8	1	.889	101	28	56	1.35	0
2000 Chicago-Montreal c-d ...	N.L.	19	97	4	3	.571	63	40	122	5.29	0
2001 Montreal e	N.L.					INJURED—Did Not Play					
2002 Brevard County	Fla.St.	7	9	0	0	.000	7	2	7	3.00	1
2002 Ottawa f..............	Int.	17	23⅓	2	1	.667	15	3	31	5.79	0
2003 Edmonton	P.C.	21	121⅔	8	9	.471	54	39	119	4.29	0
2003 Montreal.............	N.L.	1	3	0	1	.000	4	3	5	15.00	0
2004 Edmonton	P.C.	22	135⅓	10	6	.625	67	26	143	3.52	0
2004 Montreal g...........	N.L.	12	63	3	6	.333	38	23	79	5.14	0
2005 Syracuse	Int.	7	39⅓	2	3	.400	35	3	45	4.81	0
2005 Toronto	A.L.	26	94	4	3	.571	75	34	93	4.31	0
2006 Toronto	A.L.	59	77	6	2	.750	61	30	73	4.09	1
2007 Toronto	A.L.	*81	58	4	2	.667	57	24	47	2.17	1
2008 Toronto h...........	A.L.	66	70⅔	0	3	.000	57	27	54	1.78	5
2009 Dunedin	Fla.St.	3	2⅓	0	0	.000	2	1	3	3.86	0
2009 Toronto i...........	A.L.	48	46⅔	1	3	.250	43	13	46	3.09	9
2010 Toronto j...........	A.L.	67	61⅓	5	5	.500	48	14	47	2.64	0
2011 Inland Empire........	Calif.	2	2	1	1	.500	1	1	5	9.00	0
2011 Los Angeles k.........	A.L.	60	53⅔	6	3	.667	35	15	39	1.34	1
2012 Los Angeles l.........	A.L.	57	45⅔	1	1	.500	32	17	43	3.15	9
Major League Totals ......11 Yrs.		496	670	34	32	.515	513	240	648	3.55	26

a Sent by Chicago Cubs to Minnesota Twins as player to be named later for pitcher Mike Morgan, November 3, 1998.
b Traded to Chicago Cubs with pitcher Rick Aguilera for pitcher Jason Ryan and pitcher Kyle Lohse, May 21, 1999.
c On disabled list from August 9 to October 1, 2000.
d Traded to Montreal Expos for outfielder Rondell White, July 31, 2000.
e On disabled list from March 23 to November 14, 2001.
f On disabled list from March 27 to June 10, 2002.
g Released by Montreal Expos, November 29, 2004. Signed with Toronto Blue Jays organization, December 16, 2004.
h On disabled list from September 20 to October 2, 2008.
i On disabled list from June 17 to July 8 and August 1 to August 24, 2009.
j Filed for free agency, November 1, 2010. Signed with Los Angeles Angels, December 10, 2010.
k On disabled list from March 22 to April 11 and April 14 to April 29, 2011.
l On disabled list from July 28 to August 18, 2012.

DRABEK, KYLE JORDAN
Born, The Woodlands, Texas, December 8, 1987.
Bats Right. Throws Right. Height, 6 feet, 1 inch. Weight, 190 pounds.

Year Club	Lea	G	IP	W	L	Pct	SO	BB	H	ERA	SAVES
2006 Phillies..........	Gulf Coast	6	23⅓	1	3	.250	14	11	33	7.71	0
2007 Lakewood...........	So.Atl.	11	54	5	1	.833	46	23	50	4.33	0
2008 Phillies...........	Gulf Coast	4	12	0	1	.000	6	6	6	2.25	0
2008 Williamsport......	N.Y.-Penn.	4	20⅓	1	2	.333	10	6	11	2.21	0
2009 Reading	Eastern	15	96⅓	8	2	.800	76	31	92	3.64	0
2009 Clearwater	Fla.St.	10	61⅔	4	1	.800	74	19	49	2.48	0
2010 New Hampshire	Eastern	27	162	14	9	.609	132	68	126	2.94	0
2010 Toronto	A.L.	3	17	0	3	.000	12	5	18	4.76	0

Year	Club	Lea	G	IP	W	L	Pct	SO	BB	H	ERA	SAVES
2011 Las Vegas.............	P.C.	15	75	5	4	.556	45	41	111	7.44	0
2011 Toronto	A.L.	18	78²/₃	4	5	.444	51	55	87	6.06	0
2012 Toronto b.............	A.L.	13	71¹/₃	4	7	.364	47	47	67	4.67	0
Major League Totals ....3 Yrs.		34	167	8	15	.348	110	107	172	5.34	0

a Traded by Philadelphia Phillies to Toronto Blue Jays with pitcher Michael Taylor and catcher Travis D'Arnaud for pitcher Roy Halladay, December 16, 2009.
b On disabled list from June 14 to October 31, 2012.

DUENSING, BRIAN MATTHEW
Born, Marysville, Kansas, February 22, 1983.
Bats Left. Throws Left. Height, 5 feet, 11 inches. Weight, 195 pounds.

Year	Club	Lea	G	IP	W	L	Pct	SO	BB	H	ERA	SAVES
2005 Elizabethton	Appal.	12	50¹/₃	4	3	.571	55	16	49	2.32	0
2006 New Britain	Eastern	10	49¹/₃	1	2	.333	30	18	51	3.65	0
2006 Fort Myers	Fla.St.	7	40¹/₃	2	5	.286	33	8	47	4.24	0
2006 Beloit.............	Midwest	11	70¹/₃	2	3	.400	55	14	68	2.94	0
2007 New Britain	Eastern	9	50²/₃	4	1	.800	38	7	47	2.66	0
2007 Rochester.............	Int.	19	116²/₃	11	5	.688	86	30	115	3.24	0
2008 Rochester.............	Int.	25	138²/₃	5	11	.313	77	34	150	4.28	0
2009 Rochester.............	Int.	13	75¹/₃	4	6	.400	44	19	87	4.66	0
2009 Minnesota	A.L.	24	84	5	2	.714	53	31	84	3.64	0
2010 Minnesota	A.L.	53	130²/₃	10	3	.769	78	35	122	2.62	0
2011 Minnesota	A.L.	32	161²/₃	9	14	.391	115	52	193	5.23	0
2012 Minnesota	A.L.	55	109	4	12	.250	69	27	126	5.12	0
Major League Totals ....4 Yrs.		164	485¹/₃	28	31	.475	315	145	525	4.23	0
Division Series											
2009 Minnesota	A.L.	1	4²/₃	0	1	.000	3	1	7	9.64	0
2010 Minnesota	A.L.	1	3¹/₃	0	1	.000	1	1	7	13.50	0
Division Series Totals		2	8	0	2	.000	4	2	14	11.25	0

DUNN, MICHAEL G.
Born, Farmington, New Mexico, May 23, 1985.
Bats Left. Throws Left. Height, 6 feet, 1 inch. Weight, 195 pounds.

Year	Club	Lea	G	IP	W	L	Pct	SO	BB	H	ERA	SAVES
2006 Yankees	Gulf Coast	11	24²/₃	3	0	1.000	26	9	13	0.73	4
2006 Staten Island	N.Y.-Penn.	3	6¹/₃	0	0	.000	7	7	3	5.68	0
2007 Charleston	So.Atl.	27	144²/₃	12	5	.706	138	45	136	3.42	0
2008 Trenton.............	Eastern	1	1²/₃	1	0	1.000	2	1	1	0.00	0
2008 Tampa	Fla.St.	30	124²/₃	4	7	.364	118	58	124	4.55	1
2009 Trenton.............	Eastern	26	53¹/₃	3	3	.500	76	32	41	3.71	2
2009 Scranton/WB	Int.	12	20	1	0	1.000	23	14	17	2.25	0
2009 New York a.............	A.L.	4	4	0	0	.000	5	5	3	6.75	0
2010 Gwinnett.............	Int.	38	47¹/₃	2	0	1.000	64	25	31	1.52	7
2010 Atlanta b.............	N.L.	25	19	2	0	1.000	27	17	15	1.89	0
2011 Florida	N.L.	72	63	5	6	.455	68	31	51	3.43	0
2012 New Orleans..........	P.C.	12	17²/₃	1	1	.500	24	7	19	4.58	0
2012 Miami.............	N.L.	60	44	0	3	.000	47	29	49	4.91	1
Major League Totals ....4 Yrs.		161	130	7	9	.438	147	82	118	3.81	1
Division Series											
2010 Atlanta	N.L.	3	1¹/₃	0	0	.000	2	0	2	0.00	0

a Traded to Atlanta Braves with outfielder Melky Cabrera, pitcher Arodys Vizcaino and cash for pitcher Javier Vazquez and pitcher Boone Logan, December 22, 2009.
b Traded to Florida Marlins with infielder Omar Infante for infielder Dan Uggla, November 16, 2010.

DURBIN, CHAD GRIFFIN
Born, Spring Valley, Illinois, December 3, 1977.
Bats Both. Throws Right. Height, 6 feet, 2 inches. Weight, 200 pounds.

Year	Club	Lea	G	IP	W	L	Pct	SO	BB	H	ERA	SAVES
1996 Royals	Gulf Coast	11	44¹/₃	3	2	.600	43	25	34	4.26	0
1997 Lansing	Midwest	26	144²/₃	5	8	.385	116	53	157	4.79	0
1998 Wilmington	Carolina	26	147²/₃	10	7	.588	162	59	126	2.93	0
1999 Wichita.............	Texas	28	157	8	10	.444	122	49	154	4.64	0
1999 Kansas City	A.L.	1	2¹/₃	0	0	.000	3	1	1	0.00	0
2000 Kansas City	A.L.	16	72¹/₃	2	5	.286	37	43	91	8.21	0
2000 Omaha	P.C.	12	72²/₃	4	4	.500	53	22	75	4.46	0

Year	Club	Lea	G	IP	W	L	Pct	SO	BB	H	ERA	SAVES
2001 Omaha	P.C.		5	27	2	2	.500	35	6	22	3.33	0
2001 Kansas City	A.L.		29	179	9	16	.360	95	58	201	4.93	0
2002 Omaha	P.C.		1	1²/₃	0	1	.000	2	0	4	10.80	0
2002 Royals	Gulf Coast		3	6	0	0	.000	5	1	4	0.00	0
2002 Wichita.	Texas		3	5¹/₃	0	0	.000	6	4	5	5.06	0
2002 Kansas City	A.L.		2	8¹/₃	0	1	.000	5	4	13	11.88	0
2003 Mahoning Valley. . .	N.Y.-Penn.		2	12	1	1	.500	8	3	9	2.25	0
2003 Akron	Eastern		3	12	2	0	1.000	11	1	7	1.50	0
2003 Buffalo	Int.		10	58²/₃	3	6	.333	64	16	51	4.60	0
2003 Cleveland a.	A.L.		3	8²/₃	0	1	.000	8	3	18	7.27	0
2004 Cleveland	A.L.		17	51¹/₃	5	6	.455	38	24	63	6.66	0
2004 Buffalo	Int.		9	52	3	3	.500	40	16	55	3.46	0
2004 Arizona b-c.	N.L.		7	9¹/₃	1	1	.500	10	11	9	8.68	0
2005 New Orleans.	P.C.		26	115¹/₃	4	5	.444	99	48	121	5.77	0
2006 Toledo	Int.		28	185	11	8	.579	149	46	169	3.11	0
2006 Detroit d.	A.L.		3	6	0	0	.000	3	0	6	1.50	0
2007 Detroit e	A.L.		36	127²/₃	8	7	.533	66	49	133	4.72	1
2008 Philadelphia	N.L.		71	87²/₃	5	4	.556	63	35	81	2.87	1
2009 Clearwater	Fla.St.		2	3	0	0	.000	4	1	3	0.00	0
2009 Lehigh Valley	Int.		1	1	0	0	.000	1	0	1	0.00	0
2009 Philadelphia f	N.L.		59	69²/₃	2	2	.500	62	47	56	4.39	2
2010 Clearwater	Fla.St.		2	3	1	0	1.000	3	0	0	0.00	0
2010 Philadelphia g-h	N.L.		64	68²/₃	4	1	.800	63	27	63	3.80	0
2011 Cleveland i	A.L.		56	68¹/₃	2	2	.500	59	26	86	5.53	0
2012 Atlanta j-k.	N.L.		76	61	4	1	.800	49	28	52	3.10	1
Major League Totals . . . . 13 Yrs.			440	820¹/₃	42	47	.472	561	356	873	4.95	5
Wild Card Playoff												
2012 Atlanta	N.L.		1	0	0	0	.000	0	0	0	—	0
Division Series												
2008 Philadelphia	N.L.		1	0²/₃	0	0	.000	1	0	3	0.00	0
2009 Philadelphia	N.L.		1	1	1	0	1.000	0	0	0	0.00	0
2010 Philadelphia	N.L.		1	0¹/₃	0	0	.000	0	1	0	0.00	0
Division Series Totals			3	2	1	0	1.000	1	1	3	0.00	0
Championship Series												
2008 Philadelphia	N.L.		3	2	0	0	.000	2	2	3	4.50	0
2009 Philadelphia	N.L.		4	3	1	0	1.000	1	0	0	0.00	0
2010 Philadelphia	N.L.		1	1	0	0	.000	1	2	2	18.00	0
Championship Series Totals			8	6	1	0	1.000	4	4	5	4.50	0
World Series Record												
2008 Philadelphia	N.L.		2	0²/₃	0	0	.000	0	1	1	0.00	0
2009 Philadelphia	N.L.		2	1¹/₃	0	0	.000	2	2	3	27.00	0
World Series Totals.			4	2	0	0	.000	2	3	4	18.00	0

a Not offered contract, December 20, 2002. Signed with Cleveland Indians organization, February 17, 2003.
b Claimed on waivers by Arizona Diamondbacks, August 13, 2004.
c Filed for free agency, October 11, 2004. Signed with Washington Nationals organization, December 23, 2004.
d Filed for free agency, October 28, 2005. Signed with Detroit Tigers organization, January 10, 2006.
e Not offered contract, December 12, 2007. Signed with Philadelphia Phillies, December 20, 2007.
f On disabled list from July 23 to August 10, 2009.
g On disabled list from June 24 to July 13, 2010.
h Filed for free agency, November 1, 2010. Signed with Cleveland Indians, March 1, 2011.
i Filed for free agency, October 30, 2011. Signed with Washington Nationals organization, February 1, 2012.
j Released by Washington Nationals, April 2, 2012. Signed with Atlanta Braves, April 3, 2012.
k Filed for free agency, November 3, 2012.

EDGIN, JOSHUA WAYNE (JOSH)

Born, Lewistown, Pennsylvania, December 17, 1986.
Bats Left. Throws Left. Height, 6 feet, 1 inch. Weight, 225 pounds.

Year	Club	Lea	G	IP	W	L	Pct	SO	BB	H	ERA	SAVES
2010 Kingsport	Appal.		18	31²/₃	0	1	.000	41	12	28	2.84	3
2010 Savannah	So.Atl.		2	3	0	0	.000	5	0	3	0.00	0
2011 St. Lucie.	Fla.St.		25	35	2	1	.667	35	13	30	2.06	11
2011 Savannah	So.Atl.		24	31	1	0	1.000	41	10	14	0.87	16
2012 Binghamton	Eastern		24	6¹/₃	0	0	.000	5	2	5	1.42	2
2012 Buffalo	Int.		35	37	3	2	.600	40	18	34	3.89	1
2012 New York	N.L.		34	25²/₃	1	2	.333	30	10	19	4.56	0

ELBERT, TIMOTHY SCOTT (SCOTT)
Born, Joplin, Missouri, August 13, 1985.
Bats Left. Throws Left. Height, 6 feet, 1 inch. Weight, 225 pounds.

Year Club	Lea	G	IP	W	L	Pct	SO	BB	H	ERA	SAVES
2004 Ogden	Pioneer	12	49²/₃	2	3	.400	45	30	47	5.26	0
2005 Columbus	So.Atl.	25	115	8	5	.615	128	57	83	2.66	0
2006 Vero Beach	Fla.St.	17	83²/₃	5	5	.500	97	41	57	2.37	0
2006 Jacksonville	Southern	11	62¹/₃	6	4	.600	76	44	40	3.61	0
2007 Jacksonville	Southern	3	14	0	1	.000	24	10	6	3.86	0
2008 Jacksonville	Southern	25	41¹/₃	4	1	.800	46	20	22	2.40	0
2008 Los Angeles	N.L.	10	6	0	1	.000	8	4	9	12.00	0
2009 Chattanooga	Southern	12	62¹/₃	2	3	.400	87	30	59	3.90	0
2009 Albuquerque	P.C.	8	33²/₃	2	1	.667	38	14	34	3.74	0
2009 Los Angeles	N.L.	19	19²/₃	2	0	1.000	21	7	19	5.03	0
2010 Los Angeles	N.L.	1	0²/₃	0	0	.000	0	3	1	13.50	0
2010 Albuquerque	P.C.	9	43¹/₃	1	1	.500	45	34	46	4.98	0
2011 Albuquerque	P.C.	13	14¹/₃	2	0	1.000	16	9	13	5.02	3
2011 Los Angeles	N.L.	47	33¹/₃	0	1	.000	34	14	27	2.43	2
2012 Chattanooga	Southern	3	2	0	0	.000	6	0	0	0.00	0
2012 Los Angeles a	N.L.	43	32²/₃	1	1	.500	29	13	27	2.20	0
Major League Totals 5 Yrs.		120	92¹/₃	3	3	.500	92	41	83	3.61	2
Championship Series											
2009 Los Angeles	N.L.	1	0¹/₃	0	0	.000	0	2	0	0.00	0

a On disabled list from July 26 to August 19 and August 27 to October 15, 2012.

EOVALDI, NATHAN EDWARD
Born, Houston, Texas, February 13, 1990.
Bats Right. Throws Right. Height, 6 feet, 3 inches. Weight, 195 pounds.

Year Club	Lea	G	IP	W	L	Pct	SO	BB	H	ERA	SAVES
2008 Dodgers	Gulf Coast	6	8	0	1	.000	9	3	6	1.13	1
2008 Ogden	Pioneer	1	2²/₃	0	0	.000	2	0	1	0.00	0
2009 Great Lakes	Midwest	26	96¹/₃	3	5	.375	71	41	95	3.27	1
2010 Dodgers	Arizona	3	8¹/₃	0	1	.000	10	4	6	4.32	0
2010 Inland Empire	Calif.	16	85	3	5	.375	58	33	99	4.45	0
2010 Ogden	Pioneer	1	5	1	0	1.000	4	0	3	1.80	0
2011 Chattanooga	Southern	20	103	6	5	.545	99	46	76	2.62	0
2011 Los Angeles	N.L.	10	34²/₃	1	2	.333	23	20	28	3.63	0
2012 Chattanooga	Southern	9	35	2	2	.500	30	13	30	3.09	0
2012 Los Angeles-Miami a	N.L.	22	119¹/₃	4	13	.235	78	47	133	4.30	0
Major League Totals 2 Yrs.		32	154	5	15	.250	101	67	161	4.15	0

a Traded to Miami Marlins with pitcher Scott McGough for infielder Hanley Ramirez and pitcher Randy Choate, July 25, 2012.

EPPLEY, CODY ALLEN
Born, Dillsburg, Pennsylvania, October 8, 1985.
Bats Right. Throws Right. Height, 6 feet, 5 inches. Weight, 205 pounds.

Year Club	Lea	G	IP	W	L	Pct	SO	BB	H	ERA	SAVES
2008 Rangers	Arizona	19	25²/₃	2	2	.500	34	5	19	2.10	7
2008 Clinton	Midwest	2	2	0	0	.000	3	0	2	9.00	0
2009 Hickory	So.Atl.	37	67²/₃	1	3	.250	76	6	65	2.93	6
2010 Bakersfield	Calif.	14	18	2	0	1.000	24	1	9	0.00	6
2010 Oklahoma	P.C.	18	28²/₃	2	1	.667	31	13	32	4.08	1
2010 Frisco	Texas	19	22²/₃	1	1	.500	27	9	12	1.19	9
2011 Texas	A.L.	10	9	1	1	.500	6	5	11	8.00	0
2011 Round Rock	P.C.	43	55¹/₃	4	2	.667	55	34	51	3.90	10
2012 Scranton-WB	Int.	7	9¹/₃	0	0	.000	13	1	3	0.00	2
2012 New York a	A.L.	59	46	1	2	.333	32	17	46	3.33	0
Major League Totals 2 Yrs.		69	55	2	3	.400	38	22	57	4.09	0
Championship Series											
2012 New York	A.L.	4	3²/₃	0	0	.000	4	1	4	0.00	0

a Claimed on waivers by New York Yankees, April 5, 2012.

ESTRADA, MARCO RENE

Born, Sonora, Mexico, July 5, 1983.
Bats Right. Throws Right. Height, 6 feet. Weight, 180 pounds.

Year	Club	Lea	G	IP	W	L	Pct	SO	BB	H	ERA	SAVES
2005	Vermont	N.Y.-Penn.	9	33²/₃	1	3	.250	37	16	31	5.08	1
2006	Nationals	Gulf Coast	5	23²/₃	2	0	1.000	27	6	14	1.52	0
2006	Savannah	So.Atl.	8	37	1	4	.200	29	14	44	5.59	0
2007	Hagerstown	So.Atl.	8	36	1	5	.167	35	17	39	5.25	0
2007	Nationals	Gulf Coast	4	11¹/₃	0	0	.000	13	3	19	3.18	0
2007	Potomac	Carolina	11	58¹/₃	5	3	.625	54	17	67	4.94	0
2008	Harrisburg	Eastern	13	74¹/₃	6	3	.667	67	32	62	2.66	0
2008	Columbus	Int.	12	65¹/₃	3	3	.500	52	21	73	3.58	0
2008	Washington	N.L.	11	12²/₃	0	0	.000	10	5	17	7.82	0
2009	Syracuse	Int.	27	136¹/₃	9	5	.643	98	33	133	3.63	0
2009	Washington	N.L.	4	7¹/₃	0	1	.000	9	4	6	6.14	0
2010	Nashville	P.C.	7	40	1	2	.333	33	11	30	3.15	0
2010	Milwaukee a-b	N.L.	7	11¹/₃	0	0	.000	13	6	14	9.53	0
2011	Milwaukee	N.L.	43	92²/₃	4	8	.333	88	29	83	4.08	0
2012	Nashville	P.C.	2	8	0	0	.000	5	5	7	1.13	0
2012	Milwaukee c	N.L.	29	138¹/₃	5	7	.417	143	29	129	3.64	0
Major League Totals		5 Yrs.	94	262¹/₃	9	16	.360	263	73	249	4.32	0
Division Series												
2011 Milwaukee		N.L.	2	3	0	0	.000	5	0	3	0.00	0
Championship Series												
2011 Milwaukee		N.L.	2	3	0	0	.000	4	2	4	12.00	0

a Claimed on waivers by Milwaukee Brewers, February 3, 2010.
b On disabled list from June 1 to October 5, 2010.
c On disabled list from May 24 to June 26, 2012.

FARNSWORTH, KYLE LYNN

Born, Wichita, Kansas, April 14, 1976.
Bats Right. Throws Right. Height, 6 feet, 4 inches. Weight, 230 pounds.

Year	Club	Lea	G	IP	W	L	Pct	SO	BB	H	ERA	SAVES
1995	Cubs	Gulf Coast	16	31	3	2	.600	18	11	22	0.87	1
1996	Rockford	Midwest	20	112	9	6	.600	82	35	122	3.70	0
1997	Daytona	Fla.St.	27	156¹/₃	10	10	.500	105	47	178	4.09	0
1998	West Tenn	Southern	13	81¹/₃	8	2	.800	73	21	70	2.77	0
1998	Iowa	P.C.	18	102²/₃	5	9	.357	79	36	129	6.93	0
1999	Iowa	P.C.	6	39¹/₃	2	2	.500	29	9	38	3.20	0
1999	Chicago	N.L.	27	130	5	9	.357	70	52	140	5.05	0
2000	Chicago	N.L.	46	77	2	9	.182	74	50	90	6.43	1
2000	Chicago	P.C.	22	25¹/₃	0	2	.000	22	18	24	3.20	9
2001	Chicago	N.L.	76	82	4	6	.400	107	29	65	2.74	2
2002	Iowa	P.C.	2	3	0	1	.000	2	0	3	6.00	0
2002	Chicago a	N.L.	45	46²/₃	4	6	.400	46	24	53	7.33	1
2003	Chicago	N.L.	77	76¹/₃	3	2	.600	92	36	53	3.30	0
2004	Chicago b	N.L.	72	66²/₃	4	5	.444	78	33	67	4.72	0
2005	Detroit	A.L.	46	42²/₃	1	1	.500	55	20	29	2.32	6
2005	Atlanta c-d-e	A.L.	26	27¹/₃	0	0	.000	32	7	15	1.98	10
2006	New York	A.L.	72	66	3	6	.333	75	28	60	4.36	6
2007	New York	A.L.	64	60	2	1	.667	48	27	60	4.80	0
2008	New York-Detroit f-g	A.L.	61	60¹/₃	2	3	.400	61	22	70	4.48	1
2009	Omaha	P.C.	2	2	0	0	.000	2	0	0	0.00	0
2009	NW Arkansas	Texas	3	3²/₃	0	0	.000	3	1	1	0.00	0
2009	Kansas City h	A.L.	41	37¹/₃	1	5	.167	42	14	43	4.58	0
2010	Kansas City	A.L.	37	44²/₃	3	0	1.000	36	12	40	2.42	0
2010	Atlanta i-j	N.L.	23	20	0	2	.000	25	7	15	5.40	0
2011	Tampa Bay	A.L.	63	57²/₃	5	1	.833	51	12	45	2.18	25
2012	Charlotte	Fla.St.	4	4	0	0	.000	2	0	3	2.25	0
2012	Durham	Int.	2	2	0	0	.000	4	0	2	0.00	0
2012	Tampa Bay k-l	A.L.	34	27	1	6	.143	25	14	22	4.00	0
Major League Totals		14 Yrs.	810	921²/₃	40	62	.392	917	387	869	4.24	52
Division Series												
2003 Chicago		N.L.	3	2²/₃	0	0	.000	2	1	1	0.00	0
2005 Atlanta		N.L.	2	3	0	0	.000	4	1	2	9.00	0
2006 New York		A.L.	2	2	0	0	.000	1	1	1	0.00	0
2007 New York		A.L.	1	1	0	0	.000	2	0	1	0.00	0
2010 Atlanta		N.L.	2	2	1	0	1.000	1	1	1	0.00	0
Division Series Totals			10	10²/₃	1	0	1.000	10	4	6	2.53	0

Year	Club	Lea	G	IP	W	L	Pct	SO	BB	H	ERA	SAVES
	Championship Series											
2003	Chicago	N.L.	5	5⅓	0	0	.000	7	2	6	10.13	0

a On disabled list from April 10 to June 4, 2002.
b On disabled list from August 28 to September 12, 2004.
c Traded to Detroit Tigers for pitcher Roberto Novoa, infielder Scott Moore and outfielder Clarence Flowers, February 9, 2005.
d Traded to Atlanta Braves for pitcher Roman Colon and pitcher Zach Miner, July 26, 2005.
e Filed for free agency, October 31, 2005. Signed with New York Yankees, December 5, 2005.
f Traded to Detroit Tigers for catcher Ivan Rodriguez, July 30, 2008.
g Filed for free agency, November 3, 2008. Signed with Kansas City Royals, December 13, 2008.
h On disabled list from June 25 to August 18, 2009.
i Traded to Atlanta Braves with outfielder Rick Ankiel and cash for outfielder Gregor Blanco, pitcher Jesse Chavez and pitcher Tim Collins, July 31, 2010.
j Filed for free agency, November 1, 2010. Signed with Tampa Bay Rays, January 15, 2011.
k On disabled list from April 1 to June 30, 2012.
l Filed for free agency, November 3, 2012.

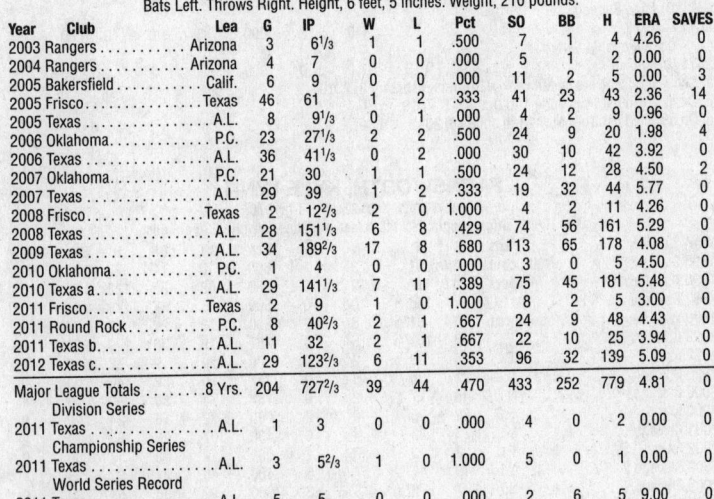

FELDMAN, SCOTT WAYNE

Born, Kailua, Hawaii, February 7, 1983.
Bats Left. Throws Right. Height, 6 feet, 5 inches. Weight, 210 pounds.

Year	Club	Lea	G	IP	W	L	Pct	SO	BB	H	ERA	SAVES
2003	Rangers	Arizona	3	6⅓	1	1	.500	7	1	4	4.26	0
2004	Rangers	Arizona	4	7	0	0	.000	5	1	2	0.00	0
2005	Bakersfield	Calif.	6	9	0	0	.000	11	2	5	0.00	3
2005	Frisco	Texas	46	61	1	2	.333	41	23	43	2.36	14
2005	Texas	A.L.	8	9⅓	0	1	.000	4	2	9	0.96	0
2006	Oklahoma	P.C.	23	27⅓	2	2	.500	24	9	20	1.98	4
2006	Texas	A.L.	36	41⅓	0	2	.000	30	10	42	3.92	0
2007	Oklahoma	P.C.	21	30	1	1	.500	24	12	28	4.50	2
2007	Texas	A.L.	29	39	1	2	.333	19	32	44	5.77	0
2008	Frisco	Texas	2	12⅔	2	0	1.000	4	2	11	4.26	0
2008	Texas	A.L.	28	151⅓	6	8	.429	74	56	161	5.29	0
2009	Texas	A.L.	34	189⅔	17	8	.680	113	65	178	4.08	0
2010	Oklahoma	P.C.	1	4	0	0	.000	3	0	5	4.50	0
2010	Texas a	A.L.	29	141⅓	7	11	.389	75	45	181	5.48	0
2011	Frisco	Texas	2	9	1	0	1.000	8	2	5	3.00	0
2011	Round Rock	P.C.	8	40⅔	2	1	.667	24	9	48	4.43	0
2011	Texas b	A.L.	11	32	2	1	.667	22	10	25	3.94	0
2012	Texas c	A.L.	29	123⅔	6	11	.353	96	32	139	5.09	0
Major League Totals	8 Yrs.		204	727⅔	39	44	.470	433	252	779	4.81	0
	Division Series											
2011	Texas	A.L.	1	3	0	0	.000	4	0	2	0.00	0
	Championship Series											
2011	Texas	A.L.	3	5⅔	1	0	1.000	5	0	1	0.00	0
	World Series Record											
2011	Texas	A.L.	5	5	0	0		2	6	5	9.00	0

a On disabled list from August 22 to September 7, 2010.
b On disabled list from March 22 to July 14, 2011.
c Filed for free agency, November 3, 2012. Signed with Chicago Cubs, November 27, 2012.

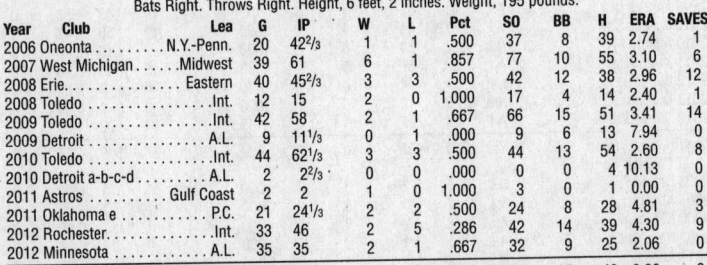

FIEN, CASEY M.

Born, Santa Rosa, California, October 21, 1983.
Bats Right. Throws Right. Height, 6 feet, 2 inches. Weight, 195 pounds.

Year	Club	Lea	G	IP	W	L	Pct	SO	BB	H	ERA	SAVES
2006	Oneonta	N.Y.-Penn.	20	42⅔	1	1	.500	37	8	39	2.74	1
2007	West Michigan	Midwest	39	61	6	1	.857	77	10	55	3.10	6
2008	Erie.	Eastern	40	45⅔	3	3	.500	42	12	38	2.96	12
2008	Toledo	Int.	12	15	2	0	1.000	17	4	14	2.40	1
2009	Toledo	Int.	42	58	2	1	.667	66	15	51	3.41	14
2009	Detroit	A.L.	9	11⅓	0	1	.000	9	6	13	7.94	0
2010	Toledo	Int.	44	62⅓	3	3	.500	44	13	54	2.60	8
2010	Detroit a-b-c-d	A.L.	2	2⅔	0	0	.000	0	0	4	10.13	0
2011	Astros	Gulf Coast	2	2	1	0	1.000	3	0	1	0.00	0
2011	Oklahoma e	P.C.	21	24⅓	2	2	.500	24	8	28	4.81	3
2012	Rochester.	Int.	33	46	2	5	.286	42	14	39	4.30	1
2012	Minnesota	A.L.	35	35	2	1	.667	32	9	25	2.06	0
Major League Totals	3 Yrs.		46	49	2	2	.500	41	15	42	3.86	0

a Claimed on waivers by Boston Red Sox, March 1, 2010.

b Claimed on waivers by Toronto Blue Jays, March 4, 2010.
c Released by Blue Jays, March 17, 2010. Signed with Detroit Tigers organization, March 19, 2010.
d Filed for free agency, October 5, 2010. Signed with Houston Astros organization, November 5, 2010.
e Released by Houston Astros, August 2, 2011. Signed with Minnesota Twins organization, January 3, 2012.

FIERS, MICHAEL BRUCE

Born, Hollywood, Florida, June 15, 1985.
Bats Right. Throws Right. Height, 6 feet, 3 inches. Weight, 195 pounds.

Year	Club	Lea	G	IP	W	L	Pct	SO	BB	H	ERA	SAVES
2009 Brevard County	Fla.St.	6	13²/₃	1	0	1.000	16	2	10	1.98	2
2009 Wisconsin	Midwest	3	6	0	0	.000	8	2	4	0.00	1
2009 Helena	Pioneer	13	21	1	0	1.000	35	1	10	1.29	8
2010 Brevard County	Fla.St.	17	93¹/₃	4	8	.333	94	23	78	3.47	0
2010 Huntsville	Southern	10	31²/₃	1	1	.500	36	9	28	3.69	1
2011 Huntsville	Southern	22	61¹/₃	5	3	.625	63	14	42	2.64	5
2011 Nashville	P.C.	12	64²/₃	8	0	1.000	69	22	41	1.11	0
2011 Milwaukee	N.L.	2	2	0	0	.000	2	3	2	0.00	0
2012 Nashville	P.C.	10	55	1	3	.250	49	18	49	4.42	0
2012 Milwaukee	N.L.	23	127²/₃	9	10	.474	135	36	125	3.74	0
Major League Totals	2 Yrs.	25	129²/₃	9	10	.474	137	39	127	3.68	0

FISTER, DOUGLAS WILDES (DOUG)

Born, Merced, California, February 4, 1984.
Bats Left. Throws Right. Height, 6 feet, 8 inches. Weight, 200 pounds.

Year	Club	Lea	G	IP	W	L	Pct	SO	BB	H	ERA	SAVES
2006 Everett	Northwest	20	40	3	5	.375	35	11	35	2.25	4
2007 West Tenn	Southern	24	131	7	8	.467	85	32	156	4.60	0
2008 West Tenn	Southern	31	134¹/₃	6	14	.300	104	45	155	5.43	0
2009 West Tenn	Southern	2	5²/₃	1	0	1.000	5	1	2	0.00	0
2009 Tacoma	P.C.	22	106¹/₃	6	4	.600	79	11	132	3.81	0
2009 Seattle	A.L.	11	61	3	4	.429	36	15	63	4.13	0
2010 Tacoma	P.C.	1	4	0	0	.000	3	0	4	4.50	0
2010 Seattle a	A.L.	28	171	6	14	.300	93	32	187	4.11	0
2011 Seattle-Detroit b	A.L.	32	216¹/₃	11	13	.458	146	37	193	2.83	0
2012 Toledo	Int.	1	4	0	0	.000	5	1	2	0.00	0
2012 Detroit c	A.L.	26	161²/₃	10	10	.500	137	37	156	3.45	0
Major League Totals	4 Yrs.	97	610	30	41	.423	412	121	599	3.48	0
Division Series											
2011 Detroit	A.L.	2	9²/₃	1	1	.500	10	4	12	6.52	0
2012 Detroit	A.L.	1	7	0	0	.000	8	2	6	2.57	0
Division Series Totals		3	16²/₃	1	1	.500	18	6	18	4.86	0
Championship Series											
2011 Detroit	A.L.	1	7¹/₃	1	0	1.000	3	0	7	2.45	0
2012 Detroit	A.L.	1	6¹/₃	0	0	.000	5	4	6	0.00	0
Championship Series Totals		2	13²/₃	1	0	1.000	8	4	13	1.32	0
World Series Record											
2012 Detroit	A.L.	1	6	0	1	.000	3	1	4	1.50	0

a On disabled list from June 1 to June 25, 2010.
b Traded to Detroit Tigers with pitcher David Pauley for pitcher Charlie Furbush, outfielder Casper Wells, infielder Francisco Martinez and player to be named later, July 30, 2011. Seattle Mariners received pitcher Chance Ruffin to complete trade, August 17, 2011.
c On disabled list from April 8 to May 7 and May 29 to June 16, 2012.

FLOYD, GAVIN CHRISTOPHER

Born, Annapolis, Maryland, January 27, 1983.
Bats Right. Throws Right. Height, 6 feet, 4 inches. Weight, 230 pounds.

Year	Club	Lea	G	IP	W	L	Pct	SO	BB	H	ERA	SAVES
2002 Lakewood	So.Atl.	27	166	11	10	.524	140	64	119	2.77	0
2003 Clearwater	Fla.St.	24	138	7	8	.467	115	45	128	3.00	0
2004 Reading	Eastern	20	119	6	6	.500	94	46	93	2.57	0
2004 Scranton-WB	Int.	5	30²/₃	1	3	.250	18	9	39	4.99	0
2004 Philadelphia	N.L.	6	28²/₃	2	0	1.000	24	16	25	3.49	0
2005 Scranton-WB	Int.	24	137¹/₃	6	9	.400	97	66	155	6.16	0
2005 Philadelphia	N.L.	7	26	1	2	.333	17	16	30	10.04	0
2006 Philadelphia	N.L.	11	54¹/₃	4	3	.571	34	32	70	7.29	0
2006 Scranton-WB a	Int.	17	115	7	4	.636	85	38	117	4.23	0

Year	Club	Lea	G	IP	W	L	Pct	SO	BB	H	ERA	SAVES
2007	Charlotte	Int.	17	$106^{2}/_{3}$	7	3	.700	96	35	93	3.12	0
2007	Chicago	A.L.	16	70	1	5	.167	49	19	85	5.27	0
2008	Chicago	A.L.	33	$206^{1}/_{3}$	17	8	.680	145	70	190	3.84	0
2009	Chicago	A.L.	30	193	11	11	.500	163	59	178	4.06	0
2010	Chicago	A.L.	31	$187^{1}/_{3}$	10	13	.435	151	58	199	4.08	0
2011	Chicago	A.L.	31	$193^{2}/_{3}$	12	13	.480	151	45	180	4.37	0
2012	Chicago b	A.L.	29	168	12	11	.522	144	63	166	4.29	0
Major League Totals ....9 Yrs.			194	1127	70	66	.515	878	378	1123	4.46	0
Division Series												
2008	Chicago	A.L.	1	3	0	1	.000	4	2	5	12.00	0

a Traded to Chicago White Sox with player to be named later for pitcher Freddy Garcia, December 6, 2006. Chicago White Sox received pitcher Gio Gonzalez to complete trade, December 7, 2006.

b On disabled list from July 8 to July 23 and August 27 to September 12, 2012.

FRANCIS, JEFFREY WILLIAM (JEFF)

Born, Vancouver, British Columbia, Canada, January 8, 1981.
Bats Left. Throws Left. Height, 6 feet, 5 inches. Weight, 220 pounds.

Year	Club	Lea	G	IP	W	L	Pct	SO	BB	H	ERA	SAVES
2002	Tri-City	Northwest	4	$10^{2}/_{3}$	0	0	.000	16	4	5	0.00	0
2002	Asheville............	So.Atl.	4	20	0	0	.000	23	4	16	1.80	0
2003	Visalia	Calif.	27	$160^{2}/_{3}$	12	9	.571	153	45	135	3.47	0
2004	Tulsa	Texas	17	$113^{2}/_{3}$	13	1	.929	147	22	73	1.98	0
2004	Colorado Springs.......	P.C.	7	41	3	2	.600	49	7	35	2.85	0
2004	Colorado	N.L.	7	$36^{2}/_{3}$	3	2	.600	32	13	42	5.15	0
2005	Colorado	N.L.	33	$183^{2}/_{3}$	14	12	.538	128	70	228	5.68	0
2006	Colorado	N.L.	32	199	13	11	.542	117	69	187	4.16	0
2007	Colorado	N.L.	34	$215^{1}/_{3}$	17	9	.654	165	63	234	4.22	0
2008	Tulsa	Texas	3	$14^{1}/_{3}$	1	0	1.000	19	2	12	0.63	0
2008	Colorado a	N.L.	24	$143^{2}/_{3}$	4	10	.286	94	49	164	5.01	0
2009	Colorado b............	N.L.		INJURED—Did Not Play								
2010	Tulsa	Texas	2	$11^{2}/_{3}$	0	0	.000	5	2	11	1.54	0
2010	Colorado Springs.......	P.C.	1	3	0	0	.000	3	1	1	0.00	0
2010	Colorado c-d	N.L.	20	$104^{1}/_{3}$	4	6	.400	67	23	119	5.00	0
2011	Kansas City e	A.L.	31	183	6	16	.273	91	39	224	4.82	0
2012	Louisville	Int.	12	$77^{1}/_{3}$	3	6	.333	65	18	84	3.72	0
2012	Colorado f-g..........	N.L.	24	113	6	7	.462	76	22	145	5.58	0
Major League Totals ....8 Yrs.			205	$1178^{2}/_{3}$	67	73	.479	770	348	1343	4.86	0
Division Series												
2007	Colorado	N.L.	1	6	1	0	1.000	8	2	4	3.00	0
Championship Series												
2007	Colorado	N.L.	1	$6^{2}/_{3}$	1	0	1.000	4	1	7	1.35	0
World Series Record												
2007	Colorado	N.L.	1	4	0	1	.000	3	3	10	13.50	0

a On disabled list from June 29 to August 6, 2008.

b On disabled list from March 27 to November 13, 2009.

c On disabled list from April 2 to May 16 and August 12 to September 7, 2010.

d Filed for free agency, November 3, 2010. Signed with Kansas City Royals, January 14, 2011.

e Filed for free agency, October 30, 2011. Signed with Cincinnati Reds organization, February 8, 2012.

f Released by Cincinnati Reds, June 4, 2012. Signed with Colorado Rockies, June 9, 2012.

g Filed for free agency, November 3, 2012, re-signed with Colorado Rockies, December 19, 2012.

FRANCISCO, FRANKLIN (FRANK)

Born, Santo Domingo, Dominican Republic, September 11, 1979.
Bats Right. Throws Right. Height, 6 feet, 2 inches. Weight, 235 pounds.

Year	Club	Lea	G	IP	W	L	Pct	SO	BB	H	ERA	SAVES
1997	....			INJURED—Did Not Play								
1998	Co-op..........	Dominican	16	48	0	5	.000	53	76	44	10.31	0
1999	Red Sox.........	Gulf Coast	12	$53^{1}/_{3}$	2	4	.333	48	35	58	4.56	0
2000	Red Sox.........	Gulf Coast	1	1	0	0	.000	1	2	2	18.00	0
2001	Augusta	So.Atl.	37	68	4	3	.571	90	30	40	2.91	2
2002	Winston-Salem	Carolina	6	$25^{2}/_{3}$	0	4	.000	25	18	31	8.06	0
2002	Trenton.............	Eastern	9	16	2	2	.500	18	16	10	5.63	0
2002	Sarasota a	Fla.St.	16	53	1	5	.167	58	27	33	2.55	0
2003	Winston-Salem	Carolina	16	$78^{1}/_{3}$	7	3	.700	67	36	59	3.56	0
2003	Frisco b	Texas	7	$35^{1}/_{3}$	2	3	.400	22	18	43	8.41	0
2004	Frisco...............	Texas	15	$17^{2}/_{3}$	1	3	.250	30	10	7	2.55	6
2004	Texas	A.L.	45	$51^{1}/_{3}$	5	1	.833	60	28	36	3.33	0
2005	Oklahoma............	P.C.	2	3	0	0	.000	4	2	2	3.00	1

Year	Club	Lea	G	IP	W	L	Pct	SO	BB	H	ERA	SAVES
2005 Frisco c	Texas	4	3⅓	0	1	.000	3	2	4	8.10	0
2006 Frisco	Texas	13	14⅔	0	0	.000	22	4	10	1.84	0
2006 Spokane	Northwest	4	4	0	0	.000	6	0	3	0.00	0
2006 Texas d	A.L.	8	7⅓	0	1	.000	6	2	8	4.91	0
2007 Oklahoma	P.C.	5	6	1	0	1.000	14	3	0	0.00	2
2007 Texas	A.L.	59	59⅓	1	1	.500	49	38	57	4.55	0
2008 Oklahoma	P.C.	8	9	0	0	.000	16	3	3	0.00	5
2008 Texas	A.L.	58	63⅓	3	5	.375	83	26	47	3.13	5
2009 Frisco	Texas	2	2	0	0	.000	1	0	1	0.00	0
2009 Texas e	A.L.	51	49⅓	2	3	.400	57	15	40	3.83	25
2010 Texas f-g	A.L.	56	52⅔	6	4	.600	60	18	49	3.76	2
2011 Dunedin	Fla.St.	5	5	0	1	.000	6	4	6	10.80	0
2011 Toronto h-i-j	A.L.	54	50⅔	1	4	.200	53	18	49	3.55	17
2012 Binghamton	Eastern	5	4⅔	0	0	.000	4	1	6	3.86	1
2012 New York k	N.L.	48	42⅓	1	3	.250	47	21	47	5.53	23
Major League Totals ....8 Yrs.		379	376⅓	19	22	.463	415	166	333	3.92	72

a Traded to Chicago White Sox by Boston Red Sox with pitcher Byeong An for pitcher Bob Howry, July 31, 2002.
b Sent to Texas Rangers as one of the players to be named later for outfielder Carl Everett, July 23, 2003.
c On disabled list from March 25 to October 12, 2005.
d On disabled list from March 24 to June 19, 2006.
e On disabled list from May 7 to May 22 and June 4 to June 20 and July 11 to August 2, 2009.
f On disabled list from August 28 to November 1, 2010.
g Filed for free agency, November 1, 2010, accepted arbitration to remain with Texas Rangers, November 30, 2010.
h Traded to Toronto Blue Jays for catcher Mike Napoli, January 25, 2011.
i On disabled list from March 22 to April 19, 2011.
j Filed for free agency, October 30, 2011. Signed with New York Mets, December 19, 2011.
k On disabled list from June 23 to August 3, 2012.

FRASOR, JASON ANDREW

Born, Chicago, Illinois, August 9, 1977.
Bats Right. Throws Right. Height, 5 feet, 10 inches. Weight, 170 pounds.

Year	Club	Lea	G	IP	W	L	Pct	SO	BB	H	ERA	SAVES
1999 Oneonta	N.Y.-Penn.	12	58⅔	3	3	.500	69	22	36	1.69	0
1999 West Michigan	Midwest	4	24	2	1	.667	33	9	17	2.63	0
2000 West Michigan	Midwest	14	71⅓	5	3	.625	65	29	55	3.28	0
2001 West Michigan a ...			INJURED—Did Not Play								
2002 Lakeland b	Fla.St.	24	117	5	6	.455	87	46	112	3.54	0
2003 Vero Beach..........	Fla.St.	15	24⅓	1	0	1.000	36	4	16	1.85	6
2003 Jacksonville	Southern	35	36⅔	1	0	1.000	50	14	33	2.95	17
2004 Syracuse	Int.	3	4	0	0	.000	6	5	1	2.25	0
2004 Toronto c	A.L.	63	68⅓	4	6	.400	54	36	64	4.08	17
2005 Toronto	A.L.	67	74⅔	3	5	.375	62	28	67	3.25	1
2006 Syracuse	Int.	18	20⅓	3	1	.750	33	13	21	3.98	1
2006 Toronto	A.L.	51	50	3	2	.600	51	17	47	4.32	0
2007 Toronto	A.L.	51	57	1	5	.167	59	23	47	4.58	3
2008 Toronto	A.L.	49	47⅓	1	2	.333	42	32	36	4.18	0
2009 Toronto	A.L.	61	57⅔	7	3	.700	56	16	43	2.50	11
2010 Toronto d	A.L.	69	63⅔	3	4	.429	65	27	61	3.68	4
2011 Toronto-Chicago e-f.....	A.L.	64	60	3	3	.500	57	26	58	3.60	0
2012 Dunedin	Fla.St.	2	2	0	0	.000	4	0	0	0.00	0
2012 Toronto g-h	A.L.	50	43⅔	1	1	.500	53	22	42	4.12	0
Major League Totals ....9 Yrs.		525	522⅓	26	31	.456	499	227	465	3.77	36

a On minor league disabled list, April 5 to September 14, 2001.
b Sent by Detroit Tigers to Los Angeles Dodgers as player to be named later for infielder Hiram Bocachica, September 18, 2002.
c Traded to Toronto Blue Jays for outfielder Jayson Werth, March 30, 2004.
d Filed for free agency, November 1, 2010, accepted arbitration to remain with Toronto Blue Jays, November 30, 2010.
e Traded to Chicago White Sox with pitcher Zach Stewart for pitcher Edwin Jackson and infielder Mark Teahen, July 27, 2011.
f Traded to Toronto Blue Jays for pitcher Daniel Webb and pitcher Myles Jaye, January 1, 2012.
g On disabled list from July 17 to September 3, 2012.
h Filed for free agency, November 3, 2012. Signed with Texas Rangers, January 3, 2013.

FRIEDRICH, CHRISTIAN LOUIS

Born, Evanston, Illinois, July 8, 1987.
Bats Right. Throws Left. Height, 6 feet, 4 inches. Weight, 215 pounds.

Year Club	Lea	G	IP	W	L	Pct	SO	BB	H	ERA	SAVES
2008 Tri-City	Northwest	8	36	2	1	.667	50	8	31	3.25	0
2008 Asheville	So.Atl.	3	12	0	1	.000	15	7	14	7.50	0
2009 Modesto	Calif.	14	74$\frac{1}{3}$	3	2	.600	93	28	59	2.54	0
2009 Asheville	So.Atl.	8	45$\frac{1}{3}$	3	3	.500	66	15	35	2.18	0
2010 Tulsa	Texas	18	87$\frac{1}{3}$	3	6	.333	78	35	100	5.05	0
2011 Tulsa	Texas	25	133$\frac{1}{3}$	6	10	.375	103	43	156	4.99	0
2012 Colorado Springs	P.C.	5	30	2	1	.667	27	4	23	3.00	0
2012 Colorado a	N.L.	16	84$\frac{2}{3}$	5	8	.385	74	30	102	6.17	0

a On disabled list from July 29 to November 2, 2012.

FRIERI (GUTIERREZ), ERNESTO

Born, Bolivar, Colombia, July 19, 1985.
Bats Right. Throws Right. Height, 6 feet, 2 inches. Weight, 200 pounds.

Year Club	Lea	G	IP	W	L	Pct	SO	BB	H	ERA	SAVES
2005 Lake Elsinore	Calif.	2	3$\frac{1}{3}$	0	0	.000	3	1	3	2.70	0
2005 Padres	Arizona	17	46$\frac{1}{3}$	7	1	.875	59	29	21	1.17	0
2006 Fort Wayne	Midwest	1	1	0	0	.000	1	5	1	9.00	0
2006 Lake Elsinore	Calif.	2	6	0	0	.000	4	3	8	6.00	0
2006 Eugene	Northwest	27	37$\frac{2}{3}$	3	3	.500	38	15	31	3.82	2
2007 Fort Wayne	Midwest	40	64$\frac{2}{3}$	1	2	.333	65	23	48	2.64	0
2007 Lake Elsinore	Calif.	13	21$\frac{2}{3}$	1	0	1.000	27	6	11	1.25	1
2008 Portland	P.C.	1	6	1	0	1.000	7	2	2	1.50	0
2008 Lake Elsinore	Calif.	33	123$\frac{2}{3}$	8	6	.571	108	32	125	4.00	0
2008 San Antonio	Texas	2	11	1	0	1.000	10	2	7	4.09	0
2009 San Antonio	Texas	27	140$\frac{1}{3}$	10	9	.526	118	62	125	3.59	0
2009 San Diego	N.L.	2	2	0	0	.000	2	1	0	0.00	0
2010 Portland	P.C.	34	37$\frac{2}{3}$	3	1	.750	49	18	14	1.43	17
2010 San Diego	N.L.	33	31$\frac{2}{3}$	1	1	.500	41	17	18	1.71	0
2011 Tucson	P.C.	4	3$\frac{1}{3}$	1	0	1.000	5	2	3	2.70	0
2011 San Diego a	N.L.	59	63	1	2	.333	76	34	51	2.71	0
2012 San Diego	N.L.	11	11$\frac{2}{3}$	1	0	1.000	18	4	9	2.31	0
2012 Los Angeles b	A.L.	56	54$\frac{1}{3}$	4	2	.667	80	26	26	2.32	23
Major League Totals ... 4 Yrs.		161	162$\frac{2}{3}$	7	5	.583	217	82	104	2.32	23

a On disabled list from August 8 to August 21, 2011.
b Traded to Los Angeles Angels for infielder Alexi Amarista and pitcher Donn Roach, May 3, 2012.

FURBUSH, CHARLES R. (CHARLIE)

Born, South Portland, Maine, April 11, 1986.
Bats Left. Throws Left. Height, 6 feet, 5 inches. Weight, 215 pounds.

Year Club	Lea	G	IP	W	L	Pct	SO	BB	H	ERA	SAVES
2007 Tigers	Gulf Coast	4	16	2	0	1.000	28	3	11	2.81	0
2007 West Michigan	Midwest	8	45$\frac{2}{3}$	4	1	.800	46	11	40	2.17	0
2008 a			INJURED—Did Not Play								
2009 Lakeland	Fla.St.	24	111$\frac{1}{3}$	6	7	.462	93	32	111	3.96	0
2010 Erie	Eastern	5	33$\frac{1}{3}$	1	0	1.000	37	10	31	3.24	0
2010 Lakeland	Fla.St.	13	77	4	5	.444	109	14	68	3.39	0
2010 Toledo	Int.	9	48$\frac{2}{3}$	3	4	.429	37	16	59	6.29	0
2011 Toledo	Int.	10	54	5	3	.625	61	16	35	3.17	0
2011 Detroit-Seattle b	A.L.	28	85$\frac{1}{3}$	4	10	.286	67	30	97	5.48	0
2012 Tacoma	P.C.	7	10	1	0	1.000	13	3	7	3.60	0
2012 Seattle c	A.L.	48	46$\frac{1}{3}$	5	2	.714	53	16	28	2.72	0
Major League Totals ... 2 Yrs.		76	131$\frac{2}{3}$	9	12	.429	120	46	125	4.51	0

a On minor league disabled list from April 3 to September 8, 2008.
b Traded to Seattle Mariners with outfielder Casper Wells, infielder Francisco Martinez and player to be named later for pitcher Doug Fister and pitcher David Pauley, July 30, 2011. Seattle Mariners received pitcher Chance Ruffin to complete trade, August 17, 2011.
c On disabled list from July 18 to August 17, 2012.

GALLARDO, YOVANI

Born, La Piedad, Mexico, February 27, 1986.
Bats Right. Throws Right. Height, 6 feet, 1 inch. Weight, 210 pounds.

Year Club	Lea	G	IP	W	L	Pct	SO	BB	H	ERA	SAVES
2004 Brewers	Arizona	6	19$\frac{1}{3}$	0	0	.000	23	4	14	0.47	0
2004 Beloit	Midwest	2	7$\frac{1}{3}$	0	1	.000	8	4	12	12.27	0

Year	Club	Lea	G	IP	W	L	Pct	SO	BB	H	ERA	SAVES
2005 West Virginia	So.Atl.	26	121⅓	8	3	.727	110	51	100	2.74	1	
2006 Brevard County	Fla.St.	13	77²/₃	6	3	.667	103	23	54	2.09	0	
2006 Huntsville	Southern	13	77⅓	5	2	.714	85	28	50	1.63	0	
2007 Nashville	P.C.	13	77²/₃	8	3	.727	110	28	53	2.90	0	
2007 Milwaukee	N.L.	20	110⅓	9	5	.643	101	37	103	3.67	0	
2008 Nashville	P.C.	3	15²/₃	0	1	.000	18	5	20	5.17	0	
2008 Milwaukee a	N.L.	4	24	0	0	.000	20	8	22	1.88	0	
2009 Milwaukee	N.L.	30	185²/₃	13	12	.520	204	94	150	3.73	0	
2010 Milwaukee b	N.L.	31	185	14	7	.667	200	75	178	3.84	0	
2011 Milwaukee	N.L.	33	207⅓	17	10	.630	207	59	193	3.52	0	
2012 Milwaukee	N.L.	33	204	16	9	.640	204	81	185	3.66	0	
Major League Totals	6 Yrs.	151	916⅓	69	43	.616	936	354	831	3.63	0	
Division Series												
2008 Milwaukee	N.L.	2	7	0	1	.000	4	5	4	0.00	0	
2011 Milwaukee	N.L.	2	14	1	0	1.000	14	3	10	1.29	0	
Division Series Totals		4	21	1	1	.500	18	8	14	0.86	0	
Championship Series												
2011 Milwaukee	N.L.	1	5	0	1	.000	2	5	8	7.20	0	

a On disabled list from March 21 to April 20 and May 2 to September 23, 2008.
b On disabled list from July 5 to July 22, 2010.

GARCIA, FREDDY ANTONIO

Born, Caracas, Venezuela, October 6, 1976.
Bats Right. Throws Right. Height, 6 feet, 4 inches. Weight, 250 pounds.

Year	Club	Lea	G	IP	W	L	Pct	SO	BB	H	ERA	SAVES
1994 Hou/Mil	Dominican	16	85	4	6	.400	68	38	80	5.29	0	
1995 Astros	Gulf Coast	11	58⅓	6	3	.667	58	14	60	4.47	0	
1996 Quad City	Midwest	13	60²/₃	5	4	.556	50	27	57	3.12	0	
1997 Kissimmee	Fla.St.	27	179	10	8	.556	131	49	165	2.56	0	
1998 Jackson	Texas	19	119⅓	6	7	.462	115	58	94	3.24	0	
1998 New Orleans	P.C.	2	14⅓	1	0	1.000	13	1	14	3.14	0	
1998 Tacoma a	P.C.	5	32²/₃	3	1	.750	30	13	30	3.86	0	
1999 Seattle	A.L.	33	201⅓	17	8	.680	170	90	205	4.07	0	
2000 Seattle	A.L.	21	124⅓	9	5	.643	79	64	112	3.91	0	
2000 Everett	Northwest	2	10	0	0	.000	15	2	11	4.50	0	
2000 Tacoma b	P.C.	1	7	1	0	1.000	11	2	5	2.57	0	
2001 Seattle	A.L.	34	*238²/₃	18	6	.750	163	69	199	*3.05	0	
2002 Seattle	A.L.	34	223²/₃	16	10	.615	181	63	227	4.39	0	
2003 Seattle	A.L.	33	201⅓	12	14	.462	144	71	196	4.51	0	
2004 Seattle-Chicago c	A.L.	31	210	13	11	.542	184	64	192	3.81	0	
2005 Chicago	N.L.	33	228	14	8	.636	146	60	225	3.87	0	
2006 Chicago d	A.L.	33	216⅓	17	9	.654	135	48	228	4.53	0	
2007 Philadelphia	N.L.	11	58	1	5	.167	50	19	74	5.90	0	
2007 Phillies	Gulf Coast	1	2	0	0	.000	2	0	2	4.50	0	
2007 Clearwater e	Fla.St.	2	6⅓	0	0	.000	8	1	5	0.00	0	
2008 Lakeland	Fla.St.	1	2	0	0	.000	1	1	3	0.00	0	
2008 Toledo	Int.	1	3	0	0	.000	4	0	2	0.00	0	
2008 Detroit f	A.L.	3	15	1	1	.500	12	6	11	4.20	0	
2009 Buffalo	Int.	2	11	0	2	.000	6	5	12	8.18	0	
2009 Kannapolis	So.Atl.	1	3	0	0	.000	3	1	2	0.00	0	
2009 Bristol	Appal.	2	11	0	0	.000	7	0	6	1.64	0	
2009 Charlotte	Int.	1	6	0	1	.000	9	0	8	3.00	0	
2009 Chicago g-h	A.L.	9	56	3	4	.429	37	12	56	4.34	0	
2010 Chicago i	A.L.	28	157	12	6	.667	89	45	171	4.64	0	
2011 Scranton-WB	Int.	1	4	1	0	1.000	0	1	8	4.50	0	
2011 New York j-k.	A.L.	26	146²/₃	12	8	.600	96	45	152	3.62	0	
2012 New York l	A.L.	30	107⅓	7	6	.538	89	35	112	5.20	0	
Major League Totals	14 Yrs.	359	2183²/₃	152	101	.601	1575	691	2160	4.15	0	
Division Series												
2000 Seattle	A.L.	1	3⅓	0	0	.000	2	3	6	10.80	0	
2001 Seattle	A.L.	2	11²/₃	1	1	.500	13	3	13	3.86	0	
2005 Chicago	A.L.	1	5	1	0	1.000	1	4	5	5.40	0	
2011 New York	A.L.	1	5⅓	0	1	.000	6	0	6	5.06	0	
Division Series Totals		5	25⅓	2	2	.500	22	10	30	5.33	0	
Championship Series												
2000 Seattle	A.L.	2	11²/₃	2	0	1.000	11	4	10	1.54	0	
2001 Seattle	A.L.	1	7⅓	0	1	.000	6	4	7	3.68	0	
2005 Chicago	A.L.	1	9	1	0	1.000	5	1	6	2.00	0	
Championship Series Totals		4	28	3	1	.750	22	9	23	2.25	0	

Year	Club	Lea	G	IP	W	L	Pct	SO	BB	H	ERA	SAVES

World Series Record

Year	Club	Lea	G	IP	W	L	Pct	SO	BB	H	ERA	SAVES
2005 Chicago		A.L.	1	7	1	0	1.000	7	3	4	0.00	0

a Traded by Houston Astros to Seattle Mariners with infielder Carlos Guillen and player to be named later for pitcher Randy Johnson, July 31, 1998. Seattle Mariners received pitcher John Halama to complete trade, October 1, 1998.
b On disabled list from April 22 to July 6, 2000.
c Traded to Chicago White Sox with catcher Ben Davis and cash for catcher Miguel Olivo, outfielder Jeremy Reed and infielder Michael Morse, June 27, 2004.
d Traded to Philadelphia Phillies for pitcher Gavin Floyd and player to be named later, December 6, 2006. Chicago White Sox received pitcher Gio Gonzalez to complete trade, December 7, 2006.
e On disabled list from March 23 to April 16 and June 9 to October 31, 2007.
f Filed for free agency, October 31, 2007. Signed with Detroit Tigers organization, August 12, 2008.
g Filed for free agency, October 30, 2008. Signed with New York Mets organization, January 22, 2009.
h Released by New York Mets, April 28, 2009. Signed with Chicago White Sox organization, June 9, 2009.
i Filed for free agency, November 1, 2010. Signed with New York Yankees organization, February 1, 2011.
j On disabled list from August 8 to August 29, 2011.
k Filed for free agency, October 30, 2011, re-signed with New York Yankees, December 9, 2011.
l Filed for free agency, November 3, 2012.

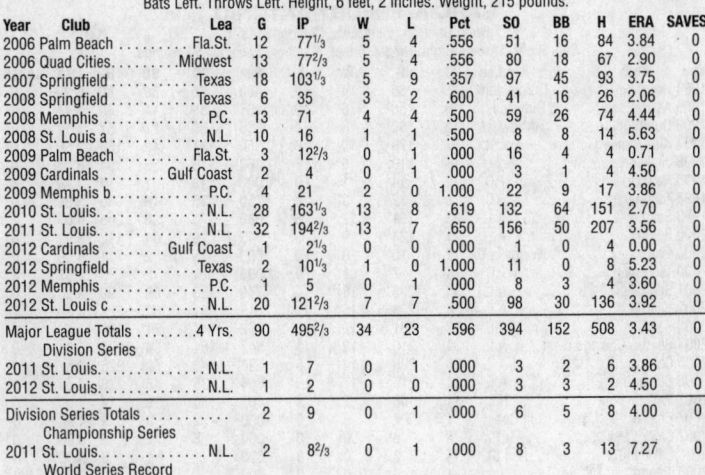

GARCIA, JAIME OMAR
Born, Reynosa, Mexico, July 8, 1986.
Bats Left. Throws Left. Height, 6 feet, 2 inches. Weight, 215 pounds.

Year	Club	Lea	G	IP	W	L	Pct	SO	BB	H	ERA	SAVES
2006 Palm Beach	Fla.St.	12	77⅓	5	4	.556	51	16	84	3.84	0
2006 Quad Cities	Midwest	13	77⅔	5	4	.556	80	18	67	2.90	0
2007 Springfield	Texas	18	103⅓	5	9	.357	97	45	93	3.75	0
2008 Springfield	Texas	6	35	3	2	.600	41	16	26	2.06	0
2008 Memphis	P.C.	13	71	4	4	.500	59	26	74	4.44	0
2008 St. Louis a	N.L.	10	16	1	1	.500	8	8	14	5.63	0
2009 Palm Beach	Fla.St.	3	12⅔	0	1	.000	16	4	4	0.71	0
2009 Cardinals	Gulf Coast	2	4	0	1	.000	3	1	4	4.50	0
2009 Memphis b	P.C.	4	21	2	0	1.000	22	9	17	3.86	0
2010 St. Louis	N.L.	28	163⅓	13	8	.619	132	64	151	2.70	0
2011 St. Louis	N.L.	32	194⅔	13	7	.650	156	50	207	3.56	0
2012 Cardinals	Gulf Coast	1	2⅓	0	0	.000	1	0	4	0.00	0
2012 Springfield	Texas	2	10⅓	1	0	1.000	11	0	8	5.23	0
2012 Memphis	P.C.	1	5	0	1	.000	8	3	4	3.60	0
2012 St. Louis c	N.L.	20	121⅔	7	7	.500	98	30	136	3.92	0
Major League Totals	4 Yrs.	90	495⅔	34	23	.596	394	152	508	3.43	0
Division Series											
2011 St. Louis	N.L.	1	7	0	1	.000	3	2	6	3.86	0
2012 St. Louis	N.L.	1	2	0	0	.000	3	3	2	4.50	0
Division Series Totals		2	9	0	1	.000	6	5	8	4.00	0
Championship Series											
2011 St. Louis	N.L.	2	8⅔	0	1	.000	8	3	13	7.27	0
World Series Record											
2011 St. Louis	N.L.	2	10	0	0	.000	10	3	8	1.80	0

a On disabled list from August 27 to October 8, 2008.
b On disabled list from March 27 to August 20, 2009.
c On disabled list from June 6 to August 19, 2012.

GARZA, MATTHEW SCOTT (MATT)
Born, Selma, California, November 11, 1983.
Bats Right. Throws Right. Height, 6 feet, 4 inches. Weight, 205 pounds.

Year	Club	Lea	G	IP	W	L	Pct	SO	BB	H	ERA	SAVES
2005 Elizabethton	Appal.	4	19⅔	1	1	.500	25	6	14	3.66	0
2006 Fort Myers	Fla.St.	8	44⅓	5	1	.833	53	11	27	1.42	0
2006 New Britain	Eastern	10	57⅓	6	2	.750	68	14	40	2.51	0
2006 Rochester	Int.	5	34	3	1	.750	33	7	20	1.85	0
2006 Minnesota	A.L.	10	50	3	6	.333	38	23	62	5.76	0
2007 Rochester	Int.	16	92	4	6	.400	95	31	93	3.62	0
2007 Minnesota a	A.L.	16	83	5	7	.417	67	32	96	3.69	0
2008 Vero Beach	Fla.St.	1	3⅔	0	0	.000	4	3	8	9.82	0
2008 Tampa Bay b	A.L.	30	184⅔	11	9	.550	128	59	170	3.70	0
2009 Tampa Bay	A.L.	32	203	8	12	.400	189	79	177	3.95	0
2010 Tampa Bay c-d	A.L.	33	204⅔	15	10	.600	150	63	193	3.91	1
2011 Chicago e	N.L.	31	198	10	10	.500	197	63	186	3.32	0

Year Club	Lea	G	IP	W	L	Pct	SO	BB	H	ERA	SAVES
2012 Chicago f	N.L.	18	103²/₃	5	7	.417	96	32	90	3.91	0
Major League Totals . . . . 7 Yrs.		170	1027	57	61	.483	865	351	974	3.84	1
Division Series											
2008 Tampa Bay	A.L.	1	6	0	1	.000	4	4	7	7.50	0
2010 Tampa Bay	A.L.	1	6	0	0	.000	4	2	5	1.50	0
Division Series Totals		2	12	0	1	.000	8	6	12	4.50	0
Championship Series											
2008 Tampa Bay	A.L.	2	13	2	0	1.000	14	6	8	1.38	0
World Series Record											
2008 Tampa Bay	A.L.	1	6	0	0	.000	7	2	6	6.00	0

a Traded to Tampa Bay Devil Rays with infielder Jason Bartlett and pitcher Eduardo Morlan for infielder Brendan Harris, outfielder Jason Pridie and outfielder Delmon Young, November 28, 2007.

b On disabled list from April 9 to April 25, 2008.

c Pitched no-hit, no-run game against Detroit Tigers, July 26, 2010.

d Traded to Chicago Cubs with outfielder Fernando Perez and pitcher Zachary Russcup for infielder Hak-Ju Lee, outfielder Brandon Guyer, pitcher Chris Archer, catcher Robinson Chirinos and outfielder Sam Fuld, January 8, 2011.

e On disabled list from May 24 to June 6, 2011.

f On disabled list from July 28 to November 2, 2012.

GAUDIN, CHAD EDWARD

Born, Metairie, Louisiana, March 24, 1983.
Bats Right. Throws Right. Height, 5 feet, 10 inches. Weight, 185 pounds.

Year Club	Lea	G	IP	W	L	Pct	SO	BB	H	ERA	SAVES
2002 Charleston-SC	So.Atl.	26	119¹/₃	4	6	.400	106	37	106	2.26	1
2003 Bakersfield	Calif.	14	80¹/₃	5	3	.625	70	23	63	2.13	0
2003 Orlando	Southern	3	19	2	0	1.000	23	3	8	0.47	0
2003 Tampa Bay	A.L.	15	40	2	0	1.000	23	16	37	3.60	0
2004 Tampa Bay	A.L.	26	42²/₃	1	2	.333	30	16	59	4.85	0
2004 Durham a	Int.	17	47²/₃	1	3	.250	52	17	48	4.72	2
2005 Toronto	A.L.	5	13	1	3	.250	12	6	31	13.15	0
2005 Syracuse b	Int.	23	150¹/₃	9	8	.529	113	35	140	3.35	0
2006 Sacramento	P.C.	4	24¹/₃	3	0	1.000	26	8	14	0.37	0
2006 Oakland . . . .`	A.L.	55	64	4	2	.667	36	42	51	3.09	2
2007 Oakland	A.L.	34	199¹/₃	11	13	.458	154	100	205	4.42	0
2008 Oakland	A.L.	26	62²/₃	5	3	.625	44	17	63	3.59	0
2008 Chicago c-d	N.L.	24	27¹/₃	4	2	.667	27	10	29	6.26	0
2009 Portland	P.C.	2	8²/₃	0	0	.000	10	2	4	0.00	0
2009 San Diego	N.L.	20	105¹/₃	4	10	.286	105	56	105	5.13	0
2009 New York e-f	A.L.	11	42	2	0	1.000	34	20	41	3.43	0
2010 Oakland-New York g-h-i k	A.L.	42	65¹/₃	1	4	.200	53	25	73	5.65	0
2011 Washington	N.L.	10	8¹/₃	1	1	.500	10	8	12	6.48	0
2011 Potomac	Carolina	1	1	0	0	.000	0	0	0	0.00	0
2011 Hagerstown	So.Atl.	1	2	0	0	.000	2	0	2	0.00	0
2011 Syracuse	Int.	6	12¹/₃	0	2	.000	14	3	17	4.38	0
2011 Las Vegas j	P.C.	6	29¹/₃	2	3	.400	13	9	37	6.14	0
2012 Miami l-m	N.L.	46	69¹/₃	4	2	.667	57	26	72	4.54	0
Major League Totals . . . . 10 Yrs.		314	739¹/₃	40	42	.488	585	342	778	4.63	2
Championship Series											
2006 Oakland	A.L.	3	3¹/₃	0	0	.000	1	3	2	0.00	0
2009 New York	A.L.	1	1	0	0	.000	0	0	0	0.00	0
Championship Series Totals		4	4¹/₃	0	0	.000	1	3	2	0.00	0

a Traded to Toronto Blue Jays for catcher Kevin Cash, December 13, 2004.

b Traded to Oakland Athletics for player to be named later, December 5, 2005. Toronto Blue Jays received outfielder Dustin Majewski to complete trade, December 8, 2005.

c On disabled list from March 19 to April 8, 2008.

d Traded to Chicago Cubs with pitcher Rich Harden for pitcher Sean Gallagher, outfielder Matt Murton, outfielder Eric Patterson and catcher Josh Donaldson, July 8, 2008.

e Released by Chicago Cubs, April 5, 2009. Signed with San Diego Padres organization, April 12, 2009.

f Sold to New York Yankees, August 6, 2009.

g Released by New York Yankees, March 25, 2010. Signed with Oakland Athletics, March 28, 2010.

h Released by Oakland Athletics, May 21, 2010. Signed with New York Yankees, May 26, 2010.

i Filed for free agency, November 2, 2010. Signed with Washington Nationals organization, December 17, 2010.

j On disabled list from April 26 to July 19, 2011.

k Released by Washington Nationals, July 21, 2011. Signed with Toronto Blue Jays organization, July 30, 2010.

l Filed for free agency, November 2, 2011. Signed with Miami Marlins organization, January 4, 2012.

m Filed for free agency, November 3, 2012. Signed with San Francisco Giants organization, December 13, 2012.

GEE, DILLON KYLE
Born, Cleburne, Texas, April 28, 1986.
Bats Right. Throws Right. Height, 6 feet, 1 inch. Weight, 205 pounds.

Year Club	Lea	G	IP	W	L	Pct	SO	BB	H	ERA	SAVES
2007 Brooklyn.........	N.Y.-Penn.	14	62	3	1	.750	56	9	57	2.47	0
2008 St. Lucie...........	Fla.St.	21	127¹/₃	8	6	.571	94	19	117	3.25	0
2008 Binghamton........	Eastern	4	27	2	0	1.000	20	5	18	1.33	0
2009 Buffalo...............	Int.	9	48¹/₃	1	3	.250	42	16	47	4.10	0
2010 Buffalo...............	Int.	28	161¹/₃	13	8	.619	165	41	174	4.96	0
2010 New York............	N.L.	5	33	2	2	.500	17	15	25	2.18	0
2011 Buffalo...............	Int.	2	11²/₃	1	1	.500	8	5	7	4.63	0
2011 New York...........	N.L.	30	160²/₃	13	6	.684	114	71	150	4.43	0
2012 New York a.........	N.L.	17	109²/₃	6	7	.462	97	29	108	4.10	0
Major League Totals.......3 Yrs.		52	303¹/₃	21	15	.583	228	115	283	4.06	0

a On disabled list from July 8 to October 29, 2012.

GOMEZ, JEANMAR ALEJANDRO
Born, Caracas, Venezuela, February 10, 1988.
Bats Right. Throws Right. Height, 6 feet, 3 inches. Weight, 200 pounds.

Year Club	Lea	G	IP	W	L	Pct	SO	BB	H	ERA	SAVES
2006 Indians..........	Gulf Coast	11	54¹/₃	4	3	.571	34	12	50	2.48	0
2007 Lake County.........	So.Atl.	27	140²/₃	11	7	.611	94	46	152	4.80	0
2008 Kinston............	Carolina	27	138¹/₃	5	9	.357	110	46	154	4.55	0
2009 Kinston............	Carolina	4	24	2	2	.500	15	5	17	2.63	0
2009 Akron.............	Eastern	22	123¹/₃	10	4	.714	109	40	117	3.43	0
2010 Columbus............	Int.	20	116	8	8	.500	78	42	129	5.20	0
2010 Cleveland............	A.L.	11	57²/₃	4	5	.444	34	22	73	4.68	0
2011 Mahoning Valley...	N.Y.-Penn.	1	4	0	0	.000	3	0	5	2.25	0
2011 Columbus............	Int.	21	137²/₃	10	7	.588	107	49	123	2.55	0
2011 Cleveland............	A.L.	11	58¹/₃	5	3	.625	31	15	73	4.47	0
2012 Columbus............	Int.	11	69¹/₃	6	5	.545	54	17	75	4.41	0
2012 Cleveland............	A.L.	20	90²/₃	5	8	.385	47	34	95	5.96	0
Major League Totals.......3 Yrs.		42	206²/₃	14	16	.467	112	71	241	5.18	0

GONZALEZ, GIOVANY A. (GIO)
Born, Hialeah, Florida, September 19, 1985.
Bats Right. Throws Left. Height, 5 feet, 11 inches. Weight, 195 pounds.

Year Club	Lea	G	IP	W	L	Pct	SO	BB	H	ERA	SAVES
2004 Bristol.............	Appal.	7	24	1	2	.333	36	8	17	2.25	0
2004 Kannapolis..........	So.Atl.	8	40²/₃	1	2	.333	34	20	39	3.76	0
2005 Winston-Salem.....	Carolina	13	73¹/₃	8	3	.727	79	25	61	3.56	0
2005 Kannapolis a........	So.Atl.	11	57²/₃	5	3	.625	84	22	36	1.87	0
2006 Reading b.........	Eastern	27	154²/₃	7	12	.368	166	81	140	4.66	0
2007 Birmingham.......	Southern	27	150	9	7	.563	185	57	116	3.18	0
2008 Sacramento..........	P.C.	23	123	8	7	.533	128	61	106	4.24	0
2008 Oakland c...........	A.L.	10	34	1	4	.200	34	25	32	7.68	0
2009 Sacramento...........	P.C.	12	61	4	1	.800	71	34	42	2.51	0
2009 Oakland.............	A.L.	20	98²/₃	6	7	.462	109	56	113	5.75	0
2010 Oakland.............	A.L.	33	200²/₃	15	9	.625	171	92	171	3.23	0
2011 Oakland d..........	A.L.	32	202	16	12	.571	197	*91	175	3.12	0
2012 Washington...........	N.L.	32	199¹/₃	*21	8	.724	207	76	149	2.89	0
Major League Totals........5 Yrs.		127	734²/₃	59	40	.596	718	340	640	3.65	0
Division Series											
2012 Washington...........	N.L.	2	10	0	0	.000	10	11	6	4.50	0

a Sent by Chicago White Sox to Philadelphia as player to be named later for infielder Jim Thome, December 8, 2005.
b Sent to Chicago White Sox as player to be named later for pitcher Freddy Garcia, December 7, 2006.
c Traded to Oakland Athletics with pitcher Fautino de los Santos and outfielder Ryan Sweeney for outfielder Nick Swisher, January 3, 2008.
d Traded to Washington Nationals with pitcher Robert Gilliam for pitcher A.J. Cole, pitcher Brad Peacock, catcher Derek Norris and pitcher Tom Milone, December 23, 2011.

GONZALEZ, MICHAEL VELA (MIKE)
Born, Corpus Christi, Texas, May 23, 1978.
Bats Right. Throws Left. Height, 6 feet, 2 inches. Weight, 215 pounds.

Year Club	Lea	G	IP	W	L	Pct	SO	BB	H	ERA	SAVES
1997 Pirates..........	Gulf Coast	7	29	2	0	1.000	33	8	21	2.48	0
1997 Augusta.............	So.Atl.	4	19¹/₃	1	1	.500	22	8	11	1.86	0

Year Club	Lea	G	IP	W	L	Pct	SO	BB	H	ERA	SAVES
1998 Lynchburg . . . . Carolina		7	28⅓	0	3	.000	22	13	40	6.67	0
1998 Augusta . . . . So.Atl.		11	50⅔	4	2	.667	72	26	43	2.84	0
1999 Lynchburg . . . . Carolina		20	112	10	4	.714	119	63	98	4.02	0
1999 Altoona. . . . . Eastern		7	26⅔	2	3	.400	31	19	34	8.10	0
2000 Pirates . . . . Gulf Coast		2	6	1	0	1.000	7	4	8	4.50	0
2000 Lynchburg . . . . Carolina		12	56	4	3	.571	53	34	57	4.66	0
2001 Lynchburg . . . . Carolina		14	30⅔	2	2	.500	32	7	28	2.93	0
2001 Altoona. . . . . Eastern		14	87⅓	5	4	.556	66	36	81	3.71	0
2002 Altoona. . . . . Eastern		16	85⅓	8	4	.667	82	47	77	3.80	0
2002 Pirates . . . . Gulf Coast		2	13⅓	2	0	1.000	14	3	5	0.00	0
2003 Lynchburg . . . . Carolina		5	7	0	1	.000	9	5	7	5.14	0
2003 Altoona. . . . . Eastern		5	7⅓	0	0	.000	10	2	4	1.23	1
2003 Pawtucket . . . . .Int.		2	1⅔	0	0	.000	2	1	2	0.00	1
2003 Nashville . . . . P.C.		7	10	0	0	.000	10	4	9	4.50	2
2003 Pittsburgh a-b . . . . N.L.		16	8⅓	0	1	.000	6	6	7	7.56	0
2004 Nashville . . . . P.C.		14	20	2	0	1.000	35	7	12	0.90	2
2004 Pittsburgh . . . . N.L.		47	43⅓	3	1	.750	55	6	32	1.25	1
2005 Indianapolis . . . . .Int.		2	3⅓	0	0	.000	5	0	0	0.00	0
2005 Pittsburgh c . . . . N.L.		51	50	1	3	.250	58	31	35	2.70	3
2006 Pittsburgh d . . . . N.L.		54	54	3	4	.429	64	31	42	2.17	24
2007 Atlanta e-f . . . . N.L.		18	17	2	0	1.000	13	8	15	1.59	2
2008 Mississippi . . . . Southern		4	5	0	0	.000	4	0	7	0.00	0
2008 Richmond . . . . .Int.		5	6	1	0	1.000	8	1	5	1.50	1
2008 Atlanta g. . . . . N.L.		36	33⅔	0	3	.000	44	14	26	4.28	14
2009 Atlanta h. . . . . N.L.		80	74⅓	5	4	.556	90	33	56	2.42	10
2010 Orioles . . . . Gulf Coast		2	2	0	0	.000	3	0	1	0.00	0
2010 Bowie. . . . . Eastern		4	4	1	0	1.000	4	1	2	2.25	0
2010 Aberdeen . . . . . . N.Y.-Penn.		4	5	0	1	.000	5	0	7	5.40	0
2010 Norfolk. . . . . .Int.		2	1⅔	0	0	.000	4	2	3	10.80	0
2010 Baltimore i . . . . A.L.		29	24⅔	1	3	.250	31	14	18	4.01	1
2011 Baltimore-Texas j-k . . . . . A.L.		56	53⅓	2	2	.500	51	21	51	4.39	1
2012 Syracuse . . . . .Int.		1	1⅓	0	0	.000	2	0	0	0.00	0
2012 Washington l . . . . N.L.		47	35⅔	0	0	.000	39	16	31	3.03	0
Major League Totals . . . . . . .10 Yrs.		434	394⅓	17	21	.447	451	180	313	2.94	56
Division Series											
2011 Texas . . . . A.L.		2	0⅔	0	0	.000	2	0	1	0.00	0
2012 Washington . . . . N.L.		1	1	0	0	.000	1	0	1	9.00	0
Division Series Totals		3	1⅔	0	0	.000	3	0	2	5.40	0
Championship Series											
2011 Texas . . . . A.L.		3	0⅔	0	0	.000	0	0	1	0.00	0
World Series Record											
2011 Texas . . . . A.L.		3	3	0	0	.000	2	1	1	6.00	0

a Traded to Boston Red Sox with pitcher Scott Sauerbeck for pitcher Brandon Lyon and pitcher Anastacio Martinez, July 22, 2003.

b Traded to Pittsburgh Pirates with infielder Freddy Sanchez and cash for pitcher Jeff Suppan, pitcher Brandon Lyon and pitcher Anastacio Martinez, July 31, 2003.

c On disabled list from June 23 to August 16, 2005.

d On disabled list from August 25 to October 3, 2006.

e Traded to Atlanta Braves with infielder Brent Lillibridge for infielder Adam LaRoche and outfielder Jamie Romak, January 17, 2007.

f On disabled list from May 16 to November 13, 2007.

g On disabled list from March 21 to June 18, 2008.

h Filed for free agency, November 5, 2009. Signed with Baltimore Orioles, December 18, 2009.

i On disabled list from April 10 to July 21, 2010.

j Traded to Texas Rangers for player to be named later, August 31, 2011. Baltimore Orioles received pitcher Pedro Strop to complete trade, September 1, 2011.

k Filed for free agency, October 30, 2011. Signed with Washington Nationals organization, May 8, 2012.

l Filed for free agency, November 3, 2012. Signed with Milwaukee Brewers, January 7, 2013.

GONZALEZ (MARTIN), MIGUEL ANGEL

Born, Guadalajara, Mexico, May 27, 1984.
Bats Right. Throws Right. Height, 6 feet, 1 inch. Weight, 170 pounds.

Year Club	Lea	G	IP	W	L	Pct	SO	BB	H	ERA	SAVES
2005 Angels . . . . Arizona		3	4	1	0	1.000	7	0	0	0.00	0
2005 Rancho Cucamonga . . . Calif.		2	4⅔	0	0	.000	3	2	0	0.00	0
2005 Cedar Rapids . . . . . . .Midwest		28	44	2	5	.286	42	8	47	4.70	8
2006 Rancho Cucamonga. . . . Calif.		14	26⅓	1	0	1.000	24	2	17	1.71	1
2006 Arkansas . . . . Texas		31	53⅓	0	2	.000	38	17	41	3.88	4
2007 Arkansas . . . . .Texas		30	130⅔	8	4	.667	81	42	128	3.38	1

Year Club	Lea	G	IP	W	L	Pct	SO	BB	H	ERA	SAVES
2008-2009 a-b-c...............			INJURED—Did Not Play								
2010 Salem ....Carolina		17	73⅓	6	4	.600	47	18	82	4.54	0
2011 Salem............Carolina		2	5	0	1	.000	4	2	5	1.80	0
2011 Portland.......... Eastern		15	46⅔	0	5	.000	45	19	55	6.17	0
2011 Pawtucket d...........Int.		1	5	0	1	.000	5	2	2	1.80	0
2012 Norfolk................Int.		14	44⅔	3	2	.600	53	10	22	1.61	1
2012 Baltimore.............A.L.		18	105⅓	9	4	.692	77	35	92	3.25	0
Division Series											
2012 Baltimore.............A.L.		1	7	0	0	.000	8	0	5	1.29	0

a On minor league disabled list from April 3 to September 22, 2008.
b Selected by Boston Red Sox from Baltimore Orioles in Rule V draft, December 11, 2008.
c On disabled list from March 27 to November 6, 2009.
d Released by Boston Red Sox, December 20, 2011. Signed with Baltimore Orioles organization, February 15, 2012.

GORZELANNY, THOMAS STEPHEN (TOM)
Born, Evergreen Park, Illinois, July 12, 1982.
Bats Left. Throws Left. Height, 6 feet, 2 inches. Weight, 205 pounds.

Year Club	Lea	G	IP	W	L	Pct	SO	BB	H	ERA	SAVES
2003 Williamsport......N.Y.-Penn.		8	30⅓	1	2	.333	22	10	23	1.78	0
2004 Lynchburg ....Carolina		10	55⅔	3	5	.375	61	19	54	4.85	0
2004 Hickory..............So.Atl.		16	93	7	2	.778	106	34	63	2.23	0
2005 Altoona............ Eastern		23	129⅔	8	5	.615	124	46	114	3.26	0
2005 Pittsburgh .............N.L.		3	6	0	1	.000	3	3	10	12.00	0
2006 Indianapolis ....Int.		16	99⅔	6	5	.545	94	27	67	2.35	0
2006 Pittsburgh a...........N.L.		11	61⅔	2	5	.286	40	31	50	3.79	0
2007 Pittsburgh .............N.L.		32	201⅔	14	10	.583	135	68	214	3.88	0
2008 Indianapolis ....Int.		7	35	3	1	.750	33	4	28	2.06	0
2008 Pittsburgh b...........N.L.		21	105⅓	6	9	.400	67	70	120	6.66	0
2009 Indianapolis ....Int.		15	87	4	3	.571	85	30	73	2.48	0
2009 Pittsburgh-Chicago c .....N.L.		22	47	7	3	.700	47	17	45	5.55	0
2010 Chicago d..............N.L.		29	136⅓	7	9	.438	119	68	136	4.09	1
2011 Syracuse ....Int.		1	4	0	1	.000	3	1	5	9.00	0
2011 Washington e...........N.L.		30	105	4	6	.400	95	33	102	4.03	0
2012 Washington f...........N.L.		45	72	4	2	.667	62	30	65	2.88	1
Major League Totals ....8 Yrs.		193	735	44	45	.494	568	320	742	4.41	2
Division Series											
2012 Washington ...........N.L.		1	0⅓	0	0	.000	0	0	1	0.00	0

a On disabled list from August 18 to September 16, 2006.
b On disabled list from September 24 to November 13, 2008.
c Traded to Chicago Cubs with pitcher John Grabow for pitcher Kevin Hart, pitcher Jose Ascanio and infielder Josh Harrison, July 30, 2009.
d Traded to Washington Nationals for outfielder Michael Burgess, pitcher Graham Hicks and pitcher A.J. Morris, January 19, 2011.
e On disabled list from May 24 to June 19, 2011.
f Not offered contract, November 30, 2012. Signed with Milwaukee Brewers, December 21, 2012.

GRAY, JEFFREY MICHAEL (JEFF)
Born, Texas City, Texas, November 19, 1981.
Bats Right. Throws Right. Height, 6 feet, 2 inches. Weight, 210 pounds.

Year Club	Lea	G	IP	W	L	Pct	SO	BB	H	ERA	SAVES
2004 Athletics........... Arizona		14	38	3	0	1.000	32	3	30	1.89	0
2005 Vancouver .... Northwest		12	46⅔	2	1	.667	24	5	33	2.51	0
2006 Stockton............. Calif.		19	31⅔	1	1	.500	26	6	32	3.41	1
2006 Kane County.......Midwest		22	78⅓	5	5	.500	62	19	77	4.71	0
2007 Sacramento ...........P.C.		46	55	2	4	.333	45	22	58	4.09	12
2007 Midland ....Texas		8	12⅓	2	0	1.000	12	2	7	0.00	3
2008 Sacramento ...........P.C.		54	67⅔	2	7	.222	50	23	86	4.39	4
2008 Oakland ..............A.L.		5	4⅔	0	0	.000	4	1	8	7.71	0
2009 Sacramento ...........P.C.		37	41	2	2	.500	22	6	30	1.54	16
2009 Oakland a.............A.L.		24	26⅓	0	1	.000	19	4	30	3.76	0
2010 Chicago ..............N.L.		7	9⅓	1	0	1.000	4	5	12	6.75	0
2010 Cubs............... Arizona		3	4	0	0	.000	3	0	3	2.25	0
2010 Iowa.................P.C.		25	35	3	1	.750	25	15	45	5.66	1
2011 Chicago-Seattle b-c-d-e....A.L.		30	48⅓	0	1	.000	23	21	52	4.28	1
2012 Minnesota ............A.L.		49	52	6	1	.857	26	22	58	5.71	0
Major League Totals ....5 Yrs.		115	140⅔	7	3	.700	76	53	160	4.99	1

a Traded to Chicago Cubs with pitcher Ronny Morla and outfielder Matt Spencer for infielder Jake Fox, infielder Aaron Miles and cash, December 3, 2009.

b Filed for free agency, November 6, 2010. Signed with Chicago White Sox organization, January 19, 2011.
c Claimed on waivers by Seattle Mariners, May 13, 2011.
d Claimed on waivers by Minnesota Twins, October 31, 2011.
e Filed for free agency, November 3, 2012. Signed with Chicago White Sox organization, December 12, 2012.

GREGERSON, LUKAS JOHN (LUKE)
Born, Park Ridge, Illinois, May 14, 1984.
Bats Left. Throws Right. Height, 6 feet, 3 inches. Weight, 200 pounds.

Year Club	Lea	G	IP	W	L	Pct	SO	BB	H	ERA	SAVES
2006 Johnson City . . . . Appal.	15	$16^{1}/_3$	0	1	.000	24	6	14	3.86	5
2006 State College . . . . . N.Y.-Penn.	12	$15^{2}/_3$	6	1	.857	22	9	9	1.72	4
2007 Palm Beach . . . . Fla.St.	53	64	3	4	.429	69	20	42	1.97	29
2007 Springfield . . . . Texas	1	1	0	0	.000	3	0	1	0.00	0
2008 Springfield . . . . Texas	57	$75^{1}/_3$	7	6	.538	78	26	62	3.35	10
2009 San Diego a-b . . . . N.L.	72	75	2	4	.333	93	31	62	3.24	1
2010 San Diego . . . . N.L.	80	$78^{1}/_3$	4	7	.364	89	18	47	3.22	2
2011 Tucson . . . . P.C.	2	$1^{1}/_3$	0	0	.000	2	2	3	20.25	0
2011 San Diego c . . . . N.L.	61	$55^{2}/_3$	3	3	.500	34	19	57	2.75	0
2012 San Diego . . . . N.L.	77	$71^{2}/_3$	2	0	1.000	72	21	57	2.39	9
Major League Totals . . . . 4 Yrs.	290	$280^{2}/_3$	11	14	.440	288	89	223	2.92	12

a Sent by St. Louis Cardinals to San Diego Padres as player to be named later for Khalil Greene, March 23, 2009.
b On disabled list from June 8 to July 6, 2009.
c On disabled list from June 9 to July 5, 2011.

GREINKE, DONALD ZACKARY (ZACK)
Born, Orlando, Florida, October 21, 1983.
Bats Right. Throws Right. Height, 6 feet, 2 inches. Weight, 185 pounds.

Year Club	Lea	G	IP	W	L	Pct	SO	BB	H	ERA	SAVES
2002 Wilmington . . . . Carolina	1	2	0	0	.000	0	0	1	0.00	0
2002 Royals . . . . Gulf Coast	3	$4^{2}/_3$	0	0	.000	4	3	3	1.93	0
2002 Spokane . . . . Northwest	2	$4^{2}/_3$	0	0	.000	5	0	9	7.71	0
2003 Wilmington . . . . Carolina	14	87	11	1	.917	78	13	56	1.14	0
2003 Wichita . . . . Texas	9	53	4	3	.571	34	5	58	3.23	0
2004 Omaha . . . . P.C.	6	$28^{2}/_3$	1	1	.500	23	6	25	2.51	0
2004 Kansas City . . . . A.L.	24	145	8	11	.421	100	26	143	3.97	0
2005 Kansas City . . . . A.L.	33	183	5	17	.227	114	53	233	5.80	0
2006 Wichita . . . . Texas	18	$105^{2}/_3$	8	3	.727	94	27	96	4.34	0
2006 Kansas City a . . . . A.L.	3	$6^{1}/_3$	1	0	1.000	5	3	7	4.26	0
2007 Kansas City . . . . A.L.	52	122	7	7	.500	106	36	122	3.69	1
2008 Kansas City . . . . A.L.	32	$202^{1}/_3$	13	10	.565	183	56	202	3.47	0
2009 Kansas City b . . . . A.L.	33	$229^{1}/_3$	16	8	.667	242	51	195	*2.16	0
2010 Kansas City c . . . . A.L.	33	220	10	14	.417	181	55	219	4.17	0
2011 Brevard County . . . . . . Fla.St.	1	3	0	0	.000	4	0	1	0.00	0
2011 Nashville . . . . P.C.	2	$7^{2}/_3$	0	1	.000	9	2	10	4.70	0
2011 Milwaukee d . . . . N.L.	28	$171^{2}/_3$	16	6	.727	201	45	161	3.83	0
2012 Milwaukee . . . . N.L.	21	123	9	3	.750	122	28	120	3.44	0
2012 Los Angeles e-f . . . . A.L.	13	$89^{1}/_3$	6	2	.750	78	26	80	3.53	0
Major League Totals . . . . 9 Yrs.	272	1492	91	78	.538	1332	379	1482	3.77	1
Division Series										
2011 Milwaukee . . . . N.L.	1	5	0	0	.000	7	0	8	7.20	0
Championship Series										
2011 Milwaukee . . . . N.L.	2	$11^{2}/_3$	1	1	.500	6	4	15	6.17	0

a On disabled list from April 1 to June 21, 2006.
b Selected Cy Young Award Winner in American League for 2009.
c Traded to Milwaukee Brewers with outfielder Yuniesky Betancourt for outfielder Lorenzo Cain, infielder Alcides Escobar, pitcher Jeremy Jeffress and pitcher Jake Odorizzi, December 19, 2010.
d On disabled list from March 26 to May 3, 2011.
e Traded to Los Angeles Angels for infielder Jean Segura, pitcher Ariel Pena and pitcher Johnny Hellweg, July 27, 2012.
f Filed for free agency, November 3, 2012. Signed with Los Angeles Dodgers, December 10, 2012.

GRIFFIN, ARTHUR JOSEPH (A.J.)
Born, El Cajon, California, January 28, 1988.
Bats Right. Throws Right. Height, 6 feet, 5 inches. Weight, 230 pounds.

Year Club	Lea	G	IP	W	L	Pct	SO	BB	H	ERA	SAVES
2010 Athletics . . . . Arizona	4	5	0	0	.000	6	0	1	0.00	0
2010 Vancouver . . . . Northwest	20	$21^{1}/_3$	1	1	.500	27	7	14	2.95	15
2011 Stockton . . . . Calif.	12	$70^{2}/_3$	5	3	.625	82	14	64	3.57	0

Year Club	Lea	G	IP	W	L	Pct	SO	BB	H	ERA	SAVES
2011 Burlington ....Midwest		8	52	4	0	1.000	46	5	36	1.56	0
2011 Sacramento ...........P.C.		1	6	0	1	.000	8	2	6	3.00	0
2011 Midland ....Texas		6	32	2	3	.400	20	11	39	6.47	0
2012 Midland ....Texas		7	43⅓	3	1	.750	44	7	31	2.49	0
2012 Sacramento ...........P.C.		10	58⅔	4	2	.667	47	11	48	3.07	0
2012 Oakland a.............A.L.		15	82⅓	7	1	.875	64	19	74	3.06	0
Division Series											
2012 Oakland ..............A.L.		1	5	0	0	.000	1	0	7	3.60	0

a On disabled list from August 5 to September 1, 2012.

GRILLI, JASON MICHAEL

Born, Royal Oak, Michigan, November 11, 1976.
Bats Right. Throws Right. Height, 6 feet, 4 inches. Weight, 225 pounds.

Year Club	Lea	G	IP	W	L	Pct	SO	BB	H	ERA	SAVES
1998 Shreveport...........Texas		21	123⅓	7	10	.412	100	37	113	3.79	0
1998 Fresno ...............P.C.		8	42	2	3	.400	37	18	49	5.14	0
1999 Calgary...............P.C.		8	41	1	5	.167	27	23	56	7.68	0
1999 Fresno a..............P.C.		19	100⅔	7	5	.583	76	39	124	5.54	0
2000 Calgary...............P.C.		8	41⅓	1	4	.200	21	23	58	7.19	0
2000 Florida ...............N.L.		1	6⅔	1	0	1.000	3	2	11	5.40	0
2001 Florida ...............N.L.		6	26⅔	2	2	.500	17	11	30	6.07	0
2001 Calgary...............P.C.		8	47	1	2	.333	35	20	46	4.02	0
2001 Marlins.........Gulf Coast		2	4	0	0	.000	6	0	2	0.00	0
2001 Brevard County ......Fla.St.		3	13⅔	2	0	1.000	14	5	12	1.98	0
2001 Portland ....Eastern		1	4	0	1	.000	3	0	3	2.25	0
2002 Calgary...............P.C.		1	5⅔	0	1	.000	8	3	3	1.59	0
2003 Jupiter ....Fla.St.		7	42⅔	4	2	.667	30	6	38	2.53	0
2003 Albuquerque b.........P.C.		12	66⅔	6	2	.750	38	30	64	3.38	0
2004 Charlotte ....Int.		25	152⅔	9	9	.500	101	58	163	4.83	0
2004 Chicago ..............A.L.		8	45	2	3	.400	26	20	52	7.40	0
2005 Toledo ....Int.		28	167⅓	12	9	.571	120	58	170	4.09	0
2005 Detroit c.............A.L.		3	16	1	1	.500	5	6	14	3.38	0
2006 Detroit ...............A.L.		51	62	2	3	.400	31	25	61	4.21	0
2007 Detroit ...............A.L.		57	79⅔	5	3	.625	62	32	81	4.74	0
2008 Detroit ...............A.L.		9	13⅔	0	1	.000	10	7	12	3.29	0
2008 Colorado d.............N.L.		51	61⅓	3	2	.600	59	31	55	2.93	1
2009 Colorado .............N.L.		22	19⅓	0	1	.000	22	13	29	6.05	1
2009 Frisco...............Texas		1	1	0	0	.000	1	1	0	0.00	0
2009 Texas e-f-g............A.L.		30	26⅓	2	2	.500	27	14	21	4.78	0
2010 h.................		INJURED—Did Not Play									
2011 Lehigh Valley ....Int.		28	32⅔	4	1	.800	43	12	26	1.93	3
2011 Pittsburgh i-j..........N.L.		28	32⅔	2	1	.667	37	15	24	2.48	1
2012 Pittsburgh k...........N.L.		64	58⅔	1	6	.143	90	22	45	2.91	2
Major League Totals ....10 Yrs.		330	448	21	25	.457	389	198	435	4.34	5
Division Series											
2006 Detroit ...............A.L.		1	0⅓	0	0	.000	0	0	0	0.00	0
Championship Series											
2006 Detroit ...............A.L.		2	1	0	0	.000	1	3	1	0.00	0
World Series Record											
2006 Detroit ...............A.L.		2	1⅔	0	0	.000	0	1	0	0.00	0

a Traded by San Francisco Giants to Florida Marlins with pitcher Nathan Bump for pitcher Livan Hernandez, July 24, 1999.
b Selected by Chicago White Sox in Rule V draft, December 15, 2003.
c Released by Chicago White Sox, January 28, 2005. Signed with Detroit Tigers organization, February 10, 2005.
d Traded to Colorado Rockies for pitcher Zachary Simons, April 30, 2008.
e Sold to Texas Rangers, June 9, 2009.
f On disabled list from August 2 to August 22, 2009.
g Filed for free agency, October 22, 2009. Signed with Cleveland Indians organization, December 2, 2009.
h On minor league disabled list from April 8 to September 19, 2010.
i Filed for free agency, November 6, 2010. Signed with Philadelphia Phillies organization, February 1, 2011.
j Released by Philadelphia Phillies, July 20, 2011. Signed with Pittsburgh Pirates, July 21, 2011.
k Filed for free agency, November 3, 2012, re-signed with Pittsburgh Pirates, December 12, 2012.

GUERRA, LUIS JAVIER (JAVY)

Born, Denton, Texas, October 31, 1985.
Bats Right. Throws Right. Height, 6 feet. Weight, 205 pounds.

Year	Club	Lea	G	IP	W	L	Pct	SO	BB	H	ERA	SAVES
2004	Dodgers	Gulf Coast	11	40	4	1	.800	36	19	31	3.38	0
2005	Columbus	So.Atl.	11	52²/₃	2	5	.286	40	23	51	4.96	0
2006	Dodgers	Gulf Coast	4	8²/₃	0	1	.000	11	4	10	4.15	0
2006	Ogden	Pioneer	7	28	1	3	.250	22	20	37	4.82	0
2007	Inland Empire	Calif.	27	117²/₃	6	9	.400	121	80	139	6.27	1
2008	Inland Empire	Calif.	31	66¹/₃	5	4	.556	63	44	68	4.07	2
2009	Great Lakes	Midwest	28	41	3	1	.750	55	15	23	1.54	16
2009	Chattanooga	Southern	23	28¹/₃	3	1	.750	29	16	32	4.13	0
2010	Dodgers	Arizona	2	2	0	1	.000	3	0	2	4.50	0
2010	Chattanooga	Southern	28	27	2	0	1.000	27	22	24	2.33	5
2011	Chattanooga	Southern	14	17	1	0	1.000	15	5	8	1.06	3
2011	Los Angeles	N.L.	47	46²/₃	2	2	.500	38	18	37	2.31	21
2012	Rancho Cucamonga	Calif.	2	2	0	0	.000	1	0	1	4.50	0
2012	Albuquerque	P.C.	3	4¹/₃	0	0	.000	3	1	7	8.31	0
2012	Los Angeles a	N.L.	45	45	2	3	.400	37	23	44	2.60	8
Major League Totals	2 Yrs.		92	91²/₃	4	5	.444	75	41	81	2.45	29

a On disabled list from June 3 to July 5 and September 3 to October 15, 2012.

GUTHRIE, JEREMY SHANE

Born, Roseburg, Oregon, April 8, 1979.
Bats Right. Throws Right. Height, 6 feet, 1 inch. Weight, 200 pounds.

Year	Club	Lea	G	IP	W	L	Pct	SO	BB	H	ERA	SAVES
2003	Akron	Eastern	10	62²/₃	6	2	.750	35	14	44	1.44	0
2003	Buffalo	Int.	18	96²/₃	4	9	.308	62	30	129	6.52	0
2004	Buffalo	Int.	4	19¹/₃	1	2	.333	10	18	23	7.91	0
2004	Akron	Eastern	23	130¹/₃	8	8	.500	94	42	145	4.21	0
2004	Cleveland	A.L.	6	11²/₃	0	0	.000	7	6	9	4.63	0
2005	Cleveland	A.L.	1	6	0	0	.000	3	2	9	6.00	0
2005	Buffalo	Int.	25	136¹/₃	12	10	.545	100	49	152	5.08	0
2006	Buffalo	Int.	21	123¹/₃	9	5	.643	88	48	104	3.14	0
2006	Cleveland	A.L.	9	19¹/₃	0	0	.000	14	15	24	6.98	0
2007	Baltimore a	A.L.	32	175¹/₃	7	5	.583	123	47	165	3.70	0
2008	Baltimore b	A.L.	30	190²/₃	10	12	.455	120	58	176	3.63	0
2009	Baltimore	A.L.	33	200	10	*17	.370	110	60	224	5.04	0
2010	Baltimore	A.L.	32	209¹/₃	11	14	.440	119	50	193	3.83	0
2011	Baltimore	A.L.	34	208	9	*17	.346	130	66	213	4.33	0
2012	Modesto	Calif.	1	4	0	0	.000	4	1	3	0.00	0
2012	Colorado	N.L.	19	90²/₃	3	9	.250	45	31	122	6.35	0
2012	Kansas City c-d-e-f	A.L.	14	91	5	3	.625	56	19	84	3.16	0
Major League Totals	9 Yrs.		210	1202	55	77	.417	727	354	1219	4.28	0

a Claimed on waivers by Baltimore Orioles, January 29, 2007.
b On disabled list from September 6 to September 27, 2008.
c Traded to Colorado Rockies for pitcher Jason Hammel and pitcher Matt Lindstrom, February 6, 2012.
d On disabled list from April 23 to May 15, 2012.
e Traded to Kansas City Royals for pitcher Jonathan Sanchez, July 20, 2012.
f Filed for free agency, November 3, 2012, re-signed with Kansas City Royals, November 20, 2012.

HALLADAY, HARRY LEROY (ROY)

Born, Denver, Colorado, May 14, 1977.
Bats Right. Throws Right. Height, 6 feet, 6 inches. Weight, 225 pounds.

Year	Club	Lea	G	IP	W	L	Pct	SO	BB	H	ERA	SAVES
1995	Blue Jays	Gulf Coast	10	50¹/₃	3	5	.375	48	16	35	3.40	0
1996	Dunedin	Fla.St.	27	164²/₃	15	7	.682	109	46	158	2.73	0
1997	Knoxville	Southern	7	36²/₃	2	3	.400	30	11	46	5.40	0
1997	Syracuse	Int.	22	125²/₃	7	10	.412	64	53	132	4.58	0
1998	Syracuse	Int.	21	116¹/₃	9	5	.643	71	53	107	3.79	0
1998	Toronto	A.L.	2	14	1	0	1.000	13	2	9	1.93	0
1999	Toronto	A.L.	36	149¹/₃	8	7	.533	82	79	156	3.92	1
2000	Syracuse	Int.	11	73²/₃	2	3	.400	38	21	85	5.50	0
2000	Toronto	A.L.	19	67²/₃	4	7	.364	44	42	107	10.64	0
2001	Dunedin	Fla.St.	13	22²/₃	0	1	.000	15	3	28	3.97	2
2001	Tennessee	Southern	5	34	2	1	.667	29	6	25	2.12	0
2001	Syracuse	Int.	2	14	1	0	1.000	13	0	12	3.21	0
2001	Toronto	A.L.	17	105¹/₃	5	3	.625	96	25	97	3.16	0

253

Year	Club	Lea	G	IP	W	L	Pct	SO	BB	H	ERA	SAVES
2002 Toronto	A.L.	34	*239⅓	19	7	.731	168	62	223	2.93	0
2003 Toronto a	A.L.	36	*266	*22	7	*.759	204	32	*253	3.25	0
2004 Toronto b	A.L.	21	133	8	8	.500	95	39	140	4.20	0
2005 Toronto c	A.L.	19	141⅔	12	4	.750	108	18	118	2.41	0
2006 Toronto	A.L.	32	220	16	5	*.762	132	34	208	3.19	0
2007 Toronto d	A.L.	31	225⅓	16	7	.696	139	48	232	3.71	0
2008 Toronto	A.L.	34	*246	20	11	.645	206	39	220	2.78	0
2009 Toronto e-f	A.L.	32	239	17	10	.630	208	35	234	2.79	0
2010 Philadelphia g-h-i	N.L.	33	*250⅔	*21	10	.677	219	30	*231	2.44	0
2011 Philadelphia	N.L.	32	233⅔	19	6	.760	220	35	208	2.35	0
2012 Clearwater	Fla.St.	1	3	0	0	.000	4	0	3	0.00	0
2012 Philadelphia j	N.L.	25	156⅓	11	8	.579	132	36	155	4.49	0
Major League Totals ...... 15 Yrs.		403	2687⅓	199	100	.666	2066	556	2591	3.31	1
Division Series											
2010 Philadelphia	N.L.	1	9	1	0	1.000	8	1	0	0.00	0
2011 Philadelphia	N.L.	2	16	1	1	.500	15	2	9	2.25	0
Division Series Totals		3	25	2	1	.667	23	3	9	1.44	0
Championship Series											
2010 Philadelphia	N.L.	2	13	1	1	.500	12	2	14	4.15	0

a Selected Cy Young Award Winner in American League for 2003.
b On disabled list from May 28 to June 12 and from July 17 to September 21, 2004.
c On disabled list from July 9 to October 3, 2005.
d On disabled list from May 11 to May 31, 2007.
e On disabled list from June 13 to June 28, 2009.
f Traded to Philadelphia Phillies for pitcher Kyle Drabek, pitcher Michael Taylor and catcher Travis D'Arnaud, December 16, 2009.
g Pitched no-hit, no-run perfect game against Florida Marlins, May 29, 2010.
h Pitched no-hit, no-run game against Cincinnati Reds in divisional playoff, October 6, 2010.
i Selected Cy Young Award Winner in National League for 2010.
j On disabled list from May 28 to July 17, 2012.

HAMELS, COLBERT RICHARD (COLE)

Born, San Diego, California, December 27, 1983.
Bats Left. Throws Left. Height, 6 feet, 4 inches. Weight, 195 pounds.

Year	Club	Lea	G	IP	W	L	Pct	SO	BB	H	ERA	SAVES
2003 Clearwater	Fla.St.	5	26⅓	0	2	.000	32	14	29	2.73	0
2003 Lakewood	So.Atl.	13	74⅔	6	1	.857	115	25	32	0.84	0
2004 Clearwater	Fla.St.	4	16	1	0	1.000	24	4	10	1.13	0
2005 Reading	Eastern	3	19	2	0	1.000	19	12	10	2.37	0
2005 Clearwater	Fla.St.	3	16	2	0	1.000	18	7	7	2.25	0
2006 Lakewood	So.Atl.	1	5⅔	0	0	.000	3	2	3	1.59	0
2006 Clearwater	Fla.St.	4	20⅓	1	1	.500	29	9	16	1.77	0
2006 Scranton/WB	Int.	3	23	2	0	1.000	36	1	10	0.39	0
2006 Philadelphia a	N.L.	23	132⅓	9	8	.529	145	48	117	4.08	0
2007 Philadelphia b	N.L.	28	183⅓	15	5	.750	177	43	163	3.39	0
2008 Philadelphia	N.L.	33	227⅓	14	10	.583	196	53	193	3.09	0
2009 Philadelphia	N.L.	32	193⅔	10	11	.476	168	43	206	4.32	0
2010 Philadelphia	N.L.	33	208⅔	12	11	.522	211	61	185	3.06	0
2011 Philadelphia c	N.L.	32	216	14	9	.609	194	44	169	2.79	0
2012 Philadelphia	N.L.	31	215⅓	17	6	.739	216	52	190	3.05	0
Major League Totals ...... 7 Yrs.		212	1376⅔	91	60	.603	1307	344	1223	3.34	0
Division Series											
2007 Philadelphia	N.L.	1	6⅔	0	1	.000	7	4	3	4.05	0
2008 Philadelphia	N.L.	1	8	1	0	1.000	9	1	2	0.00	0
2009 Philadelphia	N.L.	1	5	0	1	.000	5	0	7	7.20	0
2010 Philadelphia	N.L.	1	9	1	0	1.000	9	0	5	0.00	0
2011 Philadelphia	N.L.	1	6	1	0	1.000	8	3	5	0.00	0
Division Series Totals		5	34⅔	3	2	.600	38	8	22	1.82	0
Championship Series											
2008 Philadelphia	N.L.	2	14	2	0	1.000	13	5	11	1.93	0
2009 Philadelphia	N.L.	1	9⅔	1	0	1.000	7	2	13	6.52	0
2010 Philadelphia	N.L.	1	6	0	1	.000	8	1	5	4.50	0
Championship Series Totals		5	29⅔	3	1	.750	28	8	29	3.94	0
World Series Record											
2008 Philadelphia	N.L.	2	13	1	0	1.000	8	3	10	2.77	0
2009 Philadelphia	N.L.	1	4⅓	0	1	.000	3	2	5	10.38	0
World Series Totals		3	17⅓	1	1	.500	11	5	15	4.67	0

a On disabled list from May 19 to June 6, 2006.
b On disabled list from August 17 to September 18, 2007.
c On disabled list from August 13 to August 29, 2011.

HAMMEL, JASON AARON

Born, Greenville, South Carolina, September 2, 1982.
Bats Right. Throws Right. Height, 6 feet, 6 inches. Weight, 220 pounds.

Year Club	Lea	G	IP	W	L	Pct	SO	BB	H	ERA	SAVES
2002 Princeton . . . . Appal.		2	5¹/₃	0	0	.000	5	0	7	0.00	1
2002 Hudson Valley . . . . N.Y.-Penn.		13	51²/₃	1	5	.167	38	14	71	5.23	1
2003 Charleston . . . . So.Atl.		14	76²/₃	6	2	.750	50	27	70	3.40	0
2004 Bakersfield . . . . Calif.		11	71¹/₃	6	2	.750	65	20	52	1.89	0
2004 Charleston . . . . So.Atl.		18	94²/₃	4	7	.364	88	27	94	3.23	0
2005 Durham . . . . Int.		10	54²/₃	3	2	.600	48	27	57	4.12	0
2005 Montgomery . . . . . . Southern		12	81¹/₃	8	2	.800	76	19	70	2.66	0
2006 Durham . . . . Int.		24	127²/₃	5	9	.357	117	36	133	4.23	0
2006 Tampa Bay . . . . A.L.		9	44	0	6	.000	32	21	61	7.77	0
2007 Durham . . . . Int.		13	76¹/₃	4	5	.444	75	28	61	3.42	0
2007 Tampa Bay . . . . A.L.		24	85	3	5	.375	64	40	100	6.14	0
2008 Tampa Bay . . . . A.L.		40	78¹/₃	4	4	.500	44	35	83	4.60	2
2009 Colorado a . . . . N.L.		34	176²/₃	10	8	.556	133	42	203	4.33	0
2010 Colorado Springs . . . . P.C.		1	7	1	0	1.000	6	1	9	5.14	0
2010 Colorado b . . . . N.L.		30	177²/₃	10	9	.526	141	47	201	4.81	0
2011 Colorado . . . . N.L.		32	170¹/₃	7	13	.350	94	68	175	4.76	1
2012 Frederick . . . . Carolina		1	5	1	0	1.000	7	1	3	0.00	0
2012 Baltimore c-d . . . . A.L.		20	118	8	6	.571	113	42	104	3.43	0
Major League Totals . . . . .7 Yrs.		189	850	42	51	.452	621	295	927	4.78	3
Division Series											
2009 Colorado . . . . N.L.		1	3²/₃	0	0	.000	5	3	4	9.82	0
2012 Baltimore . . . . A.L.		2	11¹/₃	0	1	.000	11	6	8	3.18	0
Division Series Totals		3	15	0	1	.000	16	9	12	4.80	0

a Traded to Colorado Rockies for pitcher Aneury Rodriguez, April 4, 2009.
b On disabled list from April 27 to May 15, 2010.
c Traded to Baltimore Orioles with pitcher Matt Lindstrom for pitcher Jeremy Guthrie, February 6, 2012.
d On disabled list from July 15 to September 6, 2012.

HANRAHAN, JOEL RYAN

Born, Des Moines, Iowa, October 6, 1981.
Bats Right. Throws Right. Height, 6 feet, 3 inches. Weight, 250 pounds.

Year Club	Lea	G	IP	W	L	Pct	SO	BB	H	ERA	SAVES
2000 Great Falls . . . . Pioneer		12	55	3	1	.750	40	23	49	4.75	0
2001 Wilmington . . . . So.Atl.		27	144	9	11	.450	116	55	136	3.38	0
2002 Vero Beach . . . . Fla.St.		25	143²/₃	10	6	.625	139	51	129	4.20	0
2002 Jacksonville . . . . Southern		3	11	1	1	.500	10	7	15	10.64	0
2003 Las Vegas. . . . . P.C.		5	25	1	2	.333	13	20	36	10.08	0
2003 Jacksonville . . . . Southern		23	133¹/₃	10	4	.714	130	53	117	2.43	0
2004 Las Vegas . . . . P.C.		25	119¹/₃	7	7	.500	97	75	128	5.05	0
2005 Vero Beach. . . . . Fla.St.		5	21¹/₃	1	0	1.000	25	11	25	5.91	0
2005 Jacksonville . . . . Southern		23	111²/₃	9	8	.529	102	55	118	4.92	0
2006 Las Vegas . . . . P.C.		14	74¹/₃	4	3	.571	46	39	70	4.48	0
2006 Jacksonville a . . . . . Southern		12	66¹/₃	7	2	.778	67	38	49	2.58	0
2007 Columbus. . . . . Int.		15	75¹/₃	5	4	.556	71	36	65	3.70	0
2007 Washington . . . . N.L.		12	51	5	3	.625	43	38	59	6.00	0
2008 Washington . . . . N.L.		69	84¹/₃	6	3	.667	93	42	73	3.95	9
2009 Washington-Pittsburgh b N.L.		67	64	1	4	.200	72	34	73	4.78	5
2010 Bradenton . . . . Fla.St.		2	2	0	0	.000	3	0	0	0.00	0
2010 Pittsburgh c . . . . N.L.		72	69²/₃	4	1	.800	100	26	58	3.62	6
2011 Pittsburgh . . . . N.L.		70	68²/₃	1	4	.200	61	16	56	1.83	40
2012 Pittsburgh d . . . . N.L.		63	59²/₃	5	2	.714	67	36	40	2.72	36
Major League Totals . . . . .6 Yrs.		353	397¹/₃	22	17	.564	436	192	359	3.74	96

a Filed for free agency from Los Angeles Dodgers, October 15, 2006. Signed with Washington Nationals organization, November 6, 2006.
b Traded to Pittsburgh Pirates with outfielder Lastings Milledge for outfielder Nyjer Morgan and pitcher Sean Burnett, June 30, 2009.
c On disabled list from March 26 to April 12, 2010.
d Traded to Boston Red Sox with infielder Brock Holt for infielder Ivan DeJesus, pitcher Mark Melancon, pitcher Stolmy Pimentel and outfielder Jerry Sands, December 26, 2012.

HANSON, THOMAS J. (TOMMY)
Born, Tulsa, Oklahoma, August 28, 1986.
Bats Right. Throws Right. Height, 6 feet, 6 inches. Weight, 220 pounds.

Year	Club	Lea	G	IP	W	L	Pct	SO	BB	H	ERA	SAVES
2006 Danville		Appal.	13	51²/₃	4	1	.800	56	9	42	2.09	0
2007 Myrtle Beach		Carolina	11	60	3	3	.500	64	32	53	4.20	0
2007 Rome		So.Atl.	15	73	2	6	.250	90	26	51	2.59	0
2008 Myrtle Beach		Carolina	7	40	3	1	.750	49	11	15	0.90	0
2008 Mississippi		Southern	18	98	8	4	.667	114	41	70	3.03	0
2009 Gwinnett		Int.	11	66¹/₃	3	3	.500	90	17	40	1.49	0
2009 Atlanta		N.L.	21	127²/₃	11	4	.733	116	46	105	2.89	0
2010 Atlanta		N.L.	34	202²/₃	10	11	.476	173	56	182	3.33	0
2011 Atlanta a		N.L.	22	130	11	7	.611	142	46	106	3.60	0
2012 Gwinnett		Int.	1	5	1	0	1.000	5	2	3	0.00	0
2012 Atlanta b-c		N.L.	31	174²/₃	13	10	.565	161	71	183	4.48	0
Major League Totals	4 Yrs.		108	635	45	32	.584	592	219	576	3.61	0
Division Series												
2010 Atlanta		N.L.	1	4	0	0	.000	5	1	5	9.00	0

a On disabled list from June 13 to June 28 and August 7 to September 30, 2011.
b On disabled list from July 31 to August 17, 2012.
c Traded to Los Angeles Angels for pitcher Jordan Walden, November 30, 2012.

HAPP, JAMES ANTHONY (J.A.)
Born, Spring Valley, Illinois, October 19, 1982.
Bats Left. Throws Left. Height, 6 feet, 3 inches. Weight, 200 pounds.

Year	Club	Lea	G	IP	W	L	Pct	SO	BB	H	ERA	SAVES
2004 Batavia		N.Y.-Penn.	11	35²/₃	1	2	.333	37	18	22	2.02	0
2005 Reading		Eastern	1	6	1	0	1.000	8	2	3	1.50	0
2005 Lakewood		So.Atl.	14	72¹/₃	4	4	.500	70	26	57	2.36	0
2006 Reading		Eastern	12	74²/₃	6	2	.750	81	29	58	2.65	0
2006 Clearwater		Fla.St.	13	80	3	7	.300	77	19	63	2.81	0
2006 Scranton/WB		Int.	1	6	1	0	1.000	4	1	3	1.50	0
2007 Philadelphia		N.L.	1	4	0	1	.000	5	2	7	11.25	0
2007 Ottawa		Int.	24	118¹/₃	4	6	.400	117	62	118	5.02	0
2008 Lehigh Valley		Int.	24	135	8	7	.533	151	48	116	3.60	0
2008 Philadelphia		N.L.	8	31²/₃	1	0	1.000	26	14	28	3.69	0
2009 Philadelphia		N.L.	35	166	12	4	.750	119	56	149	2.93	0
2010 Clearwater		Fla.St.	1	3	0	1	.000	2	0	3	6.00	0
2010 Reading		Eastern	3	12¹/₃	1	0	1.000	10	4	18	8.03	0
2010 Lehigh Valley		Int.	5	22¹/₃	0	1	.000	22	15	26	4.84	0
2010 Philadelphia-Houston a-b		N.L.	16	87¹/₃	6	4	.600	70	47	73	3.40	0
2011 Oklahoma		P.C.	3	18	1	0	1.000	16	9	11	1.50	0
2011 Houston		N.L.	28	156¹/₃	6	15	.286	134	83	157	5.35	0
2012 Houston		N.L.	18	104¹/₃	7	9	.438	98	39	112	4.83	0
2012 Toronto c-d		A.L.	10	40¹/₃	3	2	.600	46	17	35	4.69	0
Major League Totals	6 Yrs.		116	590	35	35	.500	498	258	561	4.19	0
Division Series												
2009 Philadelphia		N.L.	2	3	0	0	.000	4	2	6	9.00	0
Championship Series												
2008 Philadelphia		N.L.	1	3	0	0	.000	2	2	4	3.00	0
2009 Philadelphia		N.L.	3	0²/₃	0	0	.000	0	3	0	0.00	0
Championship Series Totals			4	3²/₃	0	0	.000	2	5	4	2.45	0
World Series Record												
2009 Philadelphia		N.L.	2	2²/₃	0	0	.000	4	1	2	3.38	0

a On disabled list from April 16 to July 6, 2010.
b Traded to Houston Astros with outfielder Anthony Gose and infielder Jonathan Villar for pitcher Roy Oswalt and cash, July 29, 2010.
c Traded to Toronto Blue Jays with pitcher Brandon Lyon and pitcher David Carpenter for pitcher Francisco Cordero, outfielder Ben Francisco, pitcher Joseph Musgrove, pitcher Asher Wojciechowski, pitcher David Rollins, catcher Carlos Perez and player to be named later, July 20, 2012. Houston Astros received pitcher Kevin Comer to complete trade, August 16, 2012.
d On disabled list from September 4 to October 31, 2012.

HARANG, AARON MICHAEL
Born, San Diego, California, May 9, 1978.
Bats Right. Throws Right. Height, 6 feet, 7 inches. Weight, 270 pounds.

Year	Club	Lea	G	IP	W	L	Pct	SO	BB	H	ERA	SAVES
1999 Pulaski		Appal.	16	78¹/₃	9	2	.818	87	17	64	2.30	1
2000 Charlotte a		Fla.St.	28	157	13	5	.722	136	50	128	3.32	0

Year	Club	Lea	G	IP	W	L	Pct	SO	BB	H	ERA	SAVES
2001 Midland	Texas		27	150	10	8	.556	112	37	173	4.14	0
2002 Midland	Texas		3	16²/₃	2	0	1.000	21	7	12	1.08	0
2002 Sacramento	P.C.		8	38²/₃	3	3	.500	39	9	41	3.26	0
2002 Oakland	A.L.		16	78¹/₃	5	4	.556	64	45	78	4.83	0
2003 Louisville	Int.		1	3	0	1	.000	4	2	5	15.00	0
2003 Sacramento	P.C.		12	69²/₃	8	2	.800	60	17	62	2.71	0
2003 Oakland	A.L.		7	30¹/₃	1	3	.250	16	9	41	5.34	0
2003 Cincinnati b	N.L.		9	46	4	3	.571	26	10	48	5.28	0
2004 Louisville	Int.		1	3	0	1	.000	3	3	9	12.00	0
2004 Cincinnati c	N.L.		28	161	10	9	.526	125	53	177	4.86	0
2005 Cincinnati	N.L.		32	211²/₃	11	13	.458	163	51	217	3.83	0
2006 Cincinnati	N.L.		36	234¹/₃	*16	11	.593	*216	56	242	3.76	0
2007 Cincinnati	N.L.		34	231²/₃	16	6	.727	218	52	213	3.73	0
2008 Louisville	Int.		1	6	1	0	1.000	6	0	5	0.00	0
2008 Cincinnati d	N.L.		30	184¹/₃	6	*17	.261	153	50	205	4.78	0
2009 Cincinnati e	N.L.		26	162¹/₃	6	14	.300	142	43	186	4.21	0
2010 Louisville	Int.		2	16	0	2	.000	10	2	14	9.00	0
2010 Cincinnati f-g	N.L.		22	111²/₃	6	7	.462	82	38	139	5.32	0
2011 Lake Elsinore	Calif.		1	4	0	1	.000	7	1	5	6.75	0
2011 San Diego h-i	N.L.		28	170²/₃	14	7	.667	124	58	175	3.64	0
2012 Los Angeles	N.L.		31	179²/₃	10	10	.500	131	45	167	3.61	0
Major League Totals	11 Yrs.		299	1802	105	104	.502	1460	550	1888	4.19	0

a Traded by Texas Rangers to Oakland Athletics with pitcher Ryan Cullen for infielder Randy Velarde, November 17, 2000.

b Traded to Cincinnati Reds with pitcher Joe Valentine and pitcher Jeff Bruksch for outfielder Jose Guillen, July 30, 2003.

c On disabled list from June 2 to June 26, 2004.

d On disabled list from July 9 to August 10, 2008.

e On disabled list from August 21 to October 14, 2009.

f On disabled list from July 1 to August 31, 2010.

g Filed for free agency, November 3, 2010. Signed with San Diego Padres, December 6, 2010.

h On disabled list from June 10 to July 9, 2011.

i Filed for free agency, October 31, 2011. Signed with Los Angeles Dodgers, December 8, 2011.

HAREN, DANIEL JOHN (DAN)
Born, Monterey Park, California, September 17, 1980.
Bats Right. Throws Right. Height, 6 feet, 5 inches. Weight, 220 pounds.

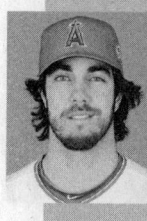

Year	Club	Lea	G	IP	W	L	Pct	SO	BB	H	ERA	SAVES
2001 New Jersey	N.Y.-Penn.		12	52¹/₃	3	3	.500	57	8	47	3.10	1
2002 Potomac	Carolina		14	92	3	6	.333	82	19	90	3.62	0
2002 Peoria	Midwest		14	101²/₃	7	3	.700	89	12	89	1.95	0
2003 Memphis	P.C.		8	45²/₃	2	1	.667	35	8	50	4.93	0
2003 Tennessee	Southern		8	55	6	0	1.000	49	6	36	0.82	0
2003 St. Louis	N.L.		14	72²/₃	3	7	.300	43	22	84	5.08	0
2004 Memphis	P.C.		21	128	11	4	.733	150	33	136	4.15	0
2004 St. Louis a	N.L.		14	46	3	3	.500	32	17	45	4.50	0
2005 Oakland	A.L.		34	217	14	12	.538	163	53	212	3.73	0
2006 Oakland	A.L.		34	223	14	13	.519	176	45	224	4.12	0
2007 Oakland b	A.L.		34	222²/₃	15	9	.625	192	55	214	3.07	0
2008 Arizona	N.L.		33	216	16	8	.667	206	40	204	3.33	0
2009 Arizona	N.L.		33	229¹/₃	14	10	.583	223	38	192	3.14	0
2010 Arizona	N.L.		21	141	7	8	.467	141	29	161	4.60	0
2010 Los Angeles c	A.L.		14	94	5	4	.556	75	25	84	2.87	0
2011 Los Angeles	A.L.		35	238¹/₃	16	10	.615	192	33	211	3.17	0
2012 Inland Empire	Calif.		1	5	0	0	.000	2	0	7	3.60	0
2012 Los Angeles d-e	A.L.		30	176²/₃	12	13	.480	142	38	190	4.33	0
Major League Totals	10 Yrs.		296	1876²/₃	119	97	.551	1585	395	1821	3.66	0
Division Series												
2004 St. Louis	N.L.		1	2	1	0	1.000	3	1	1	0.00	0
2006 Oakland	A.L.		1	6	1	0	1.000	2	1	9	3.00	0
Division Series Totals			2	8	2	0	1.000	5	2	10	2.25	0
Championship Series												
2004 St. Louis	N.L.		2	1²/₃	0	0	.000	2	0	3	10.80	0
2006 Oakland	A.L.		1	5	0	0	.000	7	2	7	5.40	0
Championship Series Totals			3	6²/₃	0	0	.000	9	2	10	6.75	0
World Series Record												
2004 St. Louis	N.L.		2	4²/₃	0	0	.000	2	3	4	0.00	0

a Traded to Oakland Athletics with pitcher Kiko Calero and catcher Daric Barton for pitcher Mark Mulder, December 18, 2004.

b Traded to Arizona Diamondbacks with pitcher Connor Robertson for pitcher Brett Anderson, pitcher Dana Eveland, pitcher Greg Smith, infielder Chris Carter, outfielder Aaron Cunningham and outfielder Carlos Gonzalez, December 14, 2007.

c Traded to Los Angeles Angels for pitcher Joe Saunders, pitcher Rafael Rodriguez, pitcher Patrick Corbin and player to be named later, July 25, 2010. Arizona Diamondbacks received pitcher Tyler Skaggs to complete trade, August 7, 2010.

d On disabled list from July 5 to July 22, 2012.

e Filed for free agency, November 3, 2012. Signed with Washington Nationals, December 7, 2012.

HARRELL, LUCAS WILLIAM BRADLEY

Born, Springfield, Missouri, June 3, 1985.
Bats Both. Throws Right. Height, 6 feet, 2 inches. Weight, 210 pounds.

Year Club	Lea	G	IP	W	L	Pct	SO	BB	H	ERA	SAVES
2004 Bristol	Appal.	13	48 1/3	3	5	.375	33	32	53	5.59	0
2005 Kannapolis	So.Atl.	26	133 1/3	7	11	.389	85	71	128	3.65	0
2006 Winston-Salem	Carolina	17	91 2/3	7	2	.778	70	44	58	2.45	0
2006 Birmingham	Southern	3	9 2/3	0	2	.000	4	14	12	10.24	0
2007 a					INJURED—Did Not Play						
2008 Bristol	Appal.	1	3	0	0	.000	5	1	3	3.00	0
2008 Kannapolis	So.Atl.	3	10 2/3	1	1	.500	7	4	13	5.91	0
2008 Birmingham	Southern	11	54 2/3	3	3	.500	34	19	56	3.46	0
2009 Charlotte	Int.	11	65 2/3	4	1	.800	42	37	58	3.29	0
2009 Birmingham	Southern	14	80 1/3	8	3	.727	51	32	78	3.25	0
2010 Charlotte	Int.	26	137 2/3	10	10	.500	84	61	141	4.58	0
2010 Chicago	A.L.	8	24	1	0	1.000	15	17	34	4.88	0
2011 Chicago	A.L.	3	5	0	0	.000	5	1	11	7.20	0
2011 Charlotte	Int.	13	74 1/3	7	3	.700	56	26	67	3.27	0
2011 Oklahoma	P.C.	9	52 1/3	5	2	.714	38	24	42	1.72	0
2011 Houston b	N.L.	6	13	0	2	.000	10	7	12	3.46	0
2012 Houston	N.L.	32	193 2/3	11	11	.500	140	78	185	3.76	0
Major League Totals	3 Yrs.	49	235 2/3	12	13	.480	170	103	242	3.93	0

a On minor league disabled list from April 5 to September 17, 2007.

b Claimed on waivers by Houston Astros, July 8, 2011.

HARRISON, MATTHEW REID (MATT)

Born, Durham, North Carolina, August 16, 1985.
Bats Left. Throws Left. Height, 6 feet, 4 inches. Weight, 225 pounds.

Year Club	Lea	G	IP	W	L	Pct	SO	BB	H	ERA	SAVES
2003 Braves	Gulf Coast	11	39	3	1	.750	33	9	40	3.69	1
2004 Danville	Appal.	13	66	4	4	.500	49	10	72	4.09	0
2005 Rome	So.Atl.	27	167	12	7	.632	118	30	151	3.23	0
2006 Myrtle Beach	Carolina	13	81 1/3	8	4	.667	60	16	77	3.10	0
2006 Mississippi	Southern	13	77 1/3	3	4	.429	54	17	83	3.61	0
2007 Mississippi a	Southern	20	116 2/3	5	7	.417	78	34	118	3.39	0
2008 Frisco	Texas	9	46	3	2	.600	35	14	49	3.33	0
2008 Oklahoma	P.C.	6	38	3	1	.750	20	14	40	3.55	0
2008 Texas	A.L.	15	83 2/3	9	3	.750	42	31	100	5.49	0
2009 Frisco	Texas	3	9	0	1	.000	7	4	9	3.00	0
2009 Texas b	A.L.	11	63 1/3	4	5	.444	34	23	81	6.11	0
2010 Frisco	Texas	2	3	0	0	.000	4	0	3	3.00	1
2010 Oklahoma	P.C.	1	4 1/3	0	1	.000	4	1	9	6.23	0
2010 Texas c	A.L.	37	78 1/3	3	2	.600	46	39	80	4.71	2
2011 Texas	A.L.	31	185 2/3	14	9	.609	126	57	180	3.39	0
2012 Texas	A.L.	32	213 1/3	18	11	.621	133	59	210	3.29	0
Major League Totals	5 Yrs.	126	624 1/3	48	30	.615	381	209	651	4.08	2
Division Series											
2011 Texas	A.L.	2	5 2/3	1	0	1.000	9	3	6	4.76	0
Championship Series											
2011 Texas	A.L.	1	5	0	0	.000	3	3	3	3.60	0
World Series Record											
2011 Texas	A.L.	2	7 2/3	0	2	.000	4	3	11	7.04	0

a Traded to Texas Rangers with catcher Jarrod Saltalamacchia, infielder Elvis Andrus, pitcher Neftali Feliz and pitcher Beau James for infielder Mark Teixeira and pitcher Ron Mahay, July 31, 2007.

b On disabled list from May 26 to June 17 and June 24 to November 13, 2009.

c On disabled list from May 7 to May 29, 2010.

HARVEY, MATTHEW EDWARD (MATT)

Born, New London, Connecticut, March 27, 1989.
Bats Right. Throws Right. Height, 6 feet, 4 inches. Weight, 225 pounds.

Year	Club	Lea	G	IP	W	L	Pct	SO	BB	H	ERA	SAVES
2011	Binghamton	Eastern	12	59²/₃	5	3	.625	64	23	58	4.53	0
2011	St. Lucie	Fla.St.	14	76	8	2	.800	92	24	67	2.37	0
2012	Buffalo	Int.	20	110	7	5	.583	112	48	97	3.68	0
2012	New York	N.L.	10	59¹/₃	3	5	.375	70	26	42	2.73	0

HAWKINS, LA TROY (LA TROY)

Born, Gary, Indiana, December 21, 1972.
Bats Right. Throws Right. Height, 6 feet, 5 inches. Weight, 220 pounds.

Year	Club	Lea	G	IP	W	L	Pct	SO	BB	H	ERA	SAVES
1991	Twins	Gulf Coast	11	55	4	3	.571	47	26	62	4.75	0
1992	Twins	Gulf Coast	6	36¹/₃	3	2	.600	35	10	36	3.22	0
1992	Elizabethtn	Appal.	5	26²/₃	0	1	.000	36	11	21	3.38	0
1993	Ft. Wayne	Midwest	26	157¹/₃	15	5	.750	179	41	110	2.06	0
1994	Ft. Myers	Fla.St.	6	38²/₃	4	0	1.000	36	6	32	2.33	0
1994	Nashville	Southern	11	73¹/₃	9	2	.818	53	28	50	2.33	0
1994	Salt Lake	P.C.	12	81²/₃	5	4	.556	37	33	92	4.08	0
1995	Salt Lake	P.C.	22	144¹/₃	9	7	.563	74	40	150	3.55	0
1995	Minnesota	A.L.	6	27	2	3	.400	9	12	39	8.67	0
1996	Minnesota	A.L.	7	26¹/₃	1	1	.500	24	9	42	8.20	0
1996	Salt Lake	P.C.	20	137²/₃	9	8	.529	99	31	138	3.92	0
1997	Salt Lake	P.C.	14	76	9	4	.692	53	16	100	5.45	0
1997	Minnesota	A.L.	20	103¹/₃	6	12	.333	58	47	134	5.84	0
1998	Minnesota	A.L.	33	190¹/₃	7	14	.333	105	61	227	5.25	0
1999	Minnesota	A.L.	33	174¹/₃	10	14	.417	103	60	238	6.66	0
2000	Minnesota	A.L.	66	87²/₃	2	5	.286	59	32	85	3.39	14
2001	Minnesota	A.L.	62	51¹/₃	1	5	.167	36	39	59	5.96	28
2002	Minnesota	A.L.	65	80¹/₃	6	0	1.000	63	15	63	2.13	0
2003	Minnesota a	A.L.	74	77¹/₃	9	3	.750	75	15	69	1.86	2
2004	Chicago	N.L.	77	82	5	4	.556	69	14	72	2.63	25
2005	Fresno	P.C.	2	2	0	0	.000	1	0	2	0.00	0
2005	Chicago-San Fran. b-c-d	A.L.	66	56¹/₃	2	8	.200	43	24	58	3.83	6
2006	Baltimore e	A.L.	60	60¹/₃	3	2	.600	27	15	73	4.48	0
2007	Colorado Springs	P.C.	4	4	1	0	1.000	5	2	2	2.25	0
2007	Colorado f-g	N.L.	62	55¹/₃	2	5	.286	29	16	52	3.42	0
2008	New York	A.L.	33	41	1	1	.500	23	17	42	5.71	0
2008	Houston h-i	N.L.	24	21	2	0	1.000	25	5	11	0.43	1
2009	Houston j-k	N.L.	65	63¹/₃	1	4	.200	45	16	60	2.13	11
2010	Brewers	Arizona	2	3²/₃	0	0	.000	5	0	4	2.45	0
2010	Nashville	P.C.	4	6¹/₃	0	0	.000	1	0	4	0.00	1
2010	Milwaukee l	N.L.	18	16	0	3	.000	18	6	21	8.44	0
2011	Brevard County	Fla.St.	3	3²/₃	0	0	.000	5	0	6	4.91	0
2011	Nashville	P.C.	2	1¹/₃	0	0	.000	1	2	1	0.00	0
2011	Milwaukee m-n	N.L.	52	48¹/₃	3	1	.750	28	10	50	2.42	0
2012	Inland Empire	Calif.	1	1	0	0	.000	2	0	2	9.00	0
2012	Salt Lake	P.C.	2	2	0	0	.000	1	1	1	0.00	0
2012	Los Angeles o-p	A.L.	48	42	2	3	.400	23	13	45	3.64	1
Major League Totals	18 Yrs.		871	1303²/₃	65	88	.425	862	426	1440	4.45	88
Division Series												
2002	Minnesota	A.L.	3	2¹/₃	0	0	.000	5	0	0	0.00	0
2003	Minnesota	A.L.	3	3	1	0	1.000	5	0	5	6.00	0
2007	Colorado	N.L.	1	1	0	0	.000	0	1	0	0.00	0
2011	Milwaukee	N.L.	1	1	0	0	.000	1	2	0	0.00	0
Division Series Totals			8	7¹/₃	1	0	1.000	11	3	5	2.45	0
Championship Series												
2002	Minnesota	A.L.	4	1¹/₃	0	0	.000	1	1	4	20.25	0
2007	Colorado	N.L.	2	2	0	0	.000	1	0	1	0.00	0
2011	Milwaukee	N.L.	3	3	0	0	.000	2	2	2	0.00	0
Championship Series Totals			9	6¹/₃	0	0	.000	4	3	7	4.26	0
World Series Record												
2007	Colorado	N.L.	2	2	0	0	.000	2	0	1	4.50	0

a Filed for free agency, October 27, 2003. Signed with Chicago Cubs, December 3, 2003.
b On disabled list from June 10 to July 4, 2005.
c Traded to San Francisco Giants for pitcher Jerome Williams and pitcher David Aardsma, May 28, 2005.
d Traded to Baltimore Orioles for pitcher Steve Kline, December 6, 2005.
e Filed for free agency, October 31, 2006. Signed with Colorado Rockies, December 5, 2006.

f On disabled list from April 21 to May 22, 2007.
g Filed for free agency, November 1, 2007. Signed with New York Yankees, December 21, 2007.
h Traded to Houston Astros for infielder Matt Cusick and cash, July 30, 2008.
i Filed for free agency, October 31, 2008, re-signed with Houston Astros, November 11, 2008.
j On disabled list from July 28 to August 12, 2009.
k Filed for free agency, November 6, 2009. Signed with Milwaukee Brewers, December 16, 2009.
l On disabled list from May 7 to July 29 and August 11 to October 5, 2010.
m On disabled list from March 22 to April 21, 2011.
n Filed for free agency, October 30, 2011. Signed with Los Angeles Angels, December 8, 2011.
o On disabled list from May 7 to June 9, 2012.
p Filed for free agency, November 3, 2012.

HEFNER, JEREMY SCOTT
Born, Perkins, Oklahoma, March 11, 1986.
Bats Right. Throws Right. Height, 6 feet, 4 inches. Weight, 215 pounds.

Year	Club	Lea	G	IP	W	L	Pct	SO	BB	H	ERA	SAVES
2007 Eugene	Northwest	17	62$^1/_3$	2	5	.286	74	20	51	3.90	0
2008 Lake Elsinore	Calif.	1	5	0	0	.000	6	2	3	3.60	0
2008 Fort Wayne	Midwest	29	140$^1/_3$	10	5	.667	144	41	117	3.33	0
2009 Lake Elsinore	Calif.	27	150$^2/_3$	14	9	.609	142	38	165	4.12	0
2009 Portland	P.C.	1	5$^1/_3$	0	0	.000	5	2	7	3.38	0
2010 San Antonio	Texas	28	167$^2/_3$	11	8	.579	115	51	156	2.95	0
2011 Tucson a-b	P.C.	28	157$^1/_3$	9	7	.563	120	61	178	4.98	0
2012 Buffalo	Int.	10	61$^2/_3$	5	2	.714	37	10	55	2.77	0
2012 New York	N.L.	26	93$^2/_3$	4	7	.364	62	18	110	5.09	0

a Claimed on waivers from San Diego Padres by Pittsburgh Pirates, November 18, 2011.
b Claimed on waivers by New York Mets, December 12, 2011.

HELLICKSON, JEREMY ROBERT
Born, Des Moines, Iowa, April 8, 1987.
Bats Right. Throws Right. Height, 6 feet, 1 inch. Weight, 185 pounds.

Year	Club	Lea	G	IP	W	L	Pct	SO	BB	H	ERA	SAVES
2005 Princeton	Appal.	4	6	0	0	.000	11	1	6	6.00	0
2006 Hudson Valley	N.Y.-Penn.	15	77$^2/_3$	3	3	.500	96	16	55	2.43	0
2007 Columbus	So.Atl.	21	111$^1/_3$	13	3	.813	106	34	87	2.67	0
2008 Vero Beach	Fla.St.	14	76$^2/_3$	7	1	.875	83	5	64	2.00	0
2008 Montgomery	Southern	13	75$^1/_3$	4	4	.500	79	15	84	3.94	0
2009 Durham	Int.	9	57$^1/_3$	6	1	.857	70	15	31	2.51	0
2009 Montgomery	Southern	11	56$^2/_3$	3	1	.750	62	14	41	2.38	0
2010 Charlotte	Fla.St.	1	1$^2/_3$	0	0	.000	4	2	4	21.60	0
2010 Durham	Int.	21	117$^2/_3$	12	3	.800	123	35	103	2.45	0
2010 Tampa Bay	A.L.	10	36$^1/_3$	4	0	1.000	33	8	32	3.47	0
2011 Tampa Bay a	A.L.	29	189	13	10	.565	117	72	146	2.95	0
2012 Tampa Bay b	A.L.	31	177	10	11	.476	124	59	163	3.10	0
Major League Totals	3 Yrs.	70	402$^1/_3$	27	21	.563	274	139	341	3.06	0
Division Series											
2011 Tampa Bay	A.L.	1	4	0	1	.000	1	1	4	6.75	0

a Selected Rookie of the Year in American League for 2011.
b On disabled list from June 15 to June 30, 2012.

HENDERSON, JAMES D. (JIM)
Born, Calgary, Alberta, Canada, October 21, 1982.
Bats Left. Throws Right. Height, 6 feet, 5 inches. Weight, 190 pounds.

Year	Club	Lea	G	IP	W	L	Pct	SO	BB	H	ERA	SAVES
2003 Expos	Gulf Coast	4	8	0	0	.000	3	1	6	2.25	1
2003 Vermont	N.Y.-Penn.	15	24$^2/_3$	1	1	.500	15	15	32	6.93	0
2004 Vermont	N.Y.-Penn.	14	76$^1/_3$	2	6	.250	39	27	61	2.59	0
2005 Savannah	So.Atl.	26	149$^2/_3$	9	11	.450	76	50	166	5.47	0
2006 Potomac	Carolina	25	52	2	2	.500	56	22	44	4.50	1
2006 Savannah a	So.Atl.	3	5$^1/_3$	0	1	.000	6	0	6	3.38	0
2007 Iowa	P.C.	8	13	3	0	1.000	6	6	16	5.54	0
2007 Tennessee	Southern	42	58	4	3	.571	49	25	50	1.86	10
2008 Iowa	P.C.	3	3	0	0	.000	4	5	2	15.00	0
2008 Tennessee	Southern	5	6$^1/_3$	0	1	.000	4	1	5	0.00	1
2009 Brevard County	Fla.St.	15	29$^1/_3$	3	0	1.000	20	14	16	2.76	4
2009 Wisconsin	Midwest	26	25$^1/_3$	0	0	.000	26	8	19	1.07	17
2009 Huntsville b	Southern	5	7	1	0	1.000	5	4	8	2.57	0
2010 Huntsville c	Southern	45	61	4	5	.444	60	35	49	5.46	7
2011 Nashville	P.C.	20	30$^1/_3$	3	1	.750	30	23	24	5.93	0

Year	Club	Lea	G	IP	W	L	Pct	SO	BB	H	ERA	SAVES
2011 Huntsville	Southern		22	$30^2/_3$	4	1	.800	39	8	22	2.64	5
2012 Nashville	P.C.		35	48	4	3	.571	56	22	36	1.69	15
2012 Milwaukee	N.L.		36	$30^2/_3$	1	3	.250	45	13	26	3.52	3

a Selected by Chicago Cubs from Washington Nationals in Rule V draft, December 7, 2006.
b Released by Chicago Cubs, March 13, 2009. Signed with Milwaukee Brewers organization, April 1, 2009.
c Filed for free agency, November 6, 2010, re-signed with Milwaukee Brewers organization, December 21, 2010.

HENDRIKS, LIAM JOHNSON

Born, Perth, Western Australia,Australia, February 10, 1989.
Bats Right. Throws Right. Height, 6 feet, 1 inch. Weight, 205 pounds.

Year	Club	Lea	G	IP	W	L	Pct	SO	BB	H	ERA	SAVES
2007 Twins	Gulf Coast		10	44	4	2	.667	52	11	41	2.05	0
2008 a							INJURED—Did Not Play					
2009 Elizabethton	Appal.		3	17	2	0	1.000	13	1	19	3.71	0
2009 Beloit	Midwest		11	$66^2/_3$	3	5	.375	62	15	73	3.51	0
2010 Fort Myers	Fla.St.		13	$74^2/_3$	6	3	.667	66	8	63	1.93	0
2010 Beloit	Midwest		6	34	2	1	.667	39	4	16	1.32	0
2011 New Britain	Eastern		16	90	8	2	.800	81	18	85	2.70	0
2011 Rochester	Int.		9	$49^1/_3$	4	4	.500	30	3	52	4.56	0
2011 Minnesota	A.L.		4	$23^1/_3$	0	2	.000	16	6	29	6.17	0
2012 Rochester	Int.		16	$106^1/_3$	9	3	.750	82	28	76	2.20	0
2012 Minnesota	A.L.		16	$85^1/_3$	1	8	.111	50	26	106	5.59	0
Major League Totals	2 Yrs.		20	$108^2/_3$	1	10	.091	66	32	135	5.71	

a On minor league disabled list from June 17 to September 25, 2008.

HENSLEY, CLAYTON ALLEN (CLAY)

Born, Tomball, Texas, August 31, 1979.
Bats Right. Throws Right. Height, 5 feet, 11 inches. Weight, 190 pounds.

Year	Club	Lea	G	IP	W	L	Pct	SO	BB	H	ERA	SAVES
2002 Salem-Keizer	Northwest		15	$81^2/_3$	7	0	1.000	84	25	72	2.53	0
2003 Hagerstown	So.Atl.		12	68	4	3	.571	74	20	56	3.18	0
2003 San Jose a	Calif.		5	$29^1/_3$	2	3	.400	25	9	38	5.83	0
2003 Lake Elsinore	Calif.		8	$44^1/_3$	3	4	.429	40	14	51	3.45	0
2004 Mobile	Southern		27	159	11	10	.524	125	48	167	4.30	0
2005 Portland	P.C.		15	$90^1/_3$	2	2	.500	71	22	63	2.99	0
2005 San Diego	N.L.		24	$47^2/_3$	1	1	.500	28	17	33	1.70	0
2006 San Diego	N.L.		37	187	11	12	.478	122	76	174	3.71	0
2007 Portland	P.C.		13	71	2	7	.222	50	34	102	6.72	0
2007 San Diego b	N.L.		13	50	2	3	.400	30	32	62	6.84	0
2008 Lake Elsinore	Calif.		1	1	1	0	1.000	1	0	1	0.00	0
2008 Portland	P.C.		16	48	1	1	.500	34	16	46	3.94	0
2008 San Diego c	N.L.		32	39	1	2	.333	26	25	36	5.31	0
2009 New Orleans	P.C.		19	114	8	4	.667	82	38	105	3.24	0
2009 Round Rock d-e-f	P.C.		6	10	1	0	1.000	5	7	12	7.20	0
2010 Jupiter	Fla.St.		2	$2^2/_3$	0	0	.000	2	1	1	0.00	0
2010 Florida g	N.L.		68	75	3	4	.429	77	29	54	2.16	7
2011 Marlins	Gulf Coast		1	$3^1/_3$	0	0	.000	6	0	2	2.70	0
2011 Jupiter	Fla.St.		1	4	0	1	.000	2	0	2	4.50	0
2011 Jacksonville	Southern		1	$4^1/_3$	0	0	.000	7	1	5	2.08	0
2011 Florida h-i	N.L.		37	$67^2/_3$	6	7	.462	46	30	62	5.19	0
2012 San Francisco j-k	N.L.		60	$50^2/_3$	4	5	.444	42	30	50	4.62	3
Major League Totals	7 Yrs.		271	517	28	34	.452	371	239	471	4.00	10
Division Series												
2005 San Diego	N.L.		3	$4^2/_3$	0	0	.000	1	3	4	3.86	0
2006 San Diego	N.L.		2	$2^2/_3$	0	0	.000	0	1	2	0.00	0
Division Series Totals			5	$7^1/_3$	0	0	.000	1	4	6	2.45	0

a Traded by San Francisco Giants to San Diego Padres with player to be named later for pitcher Matt Herges, July 13, 2003. San Diego Padres received pitcher R.D. Spiehs to complete trade, July 27, 2003.
b On disabled list from May 3 to June 1 and September 25 to November 1, 2007.
c On disabled list from March 21 to June 6, 2008.
d Not offered contract, December 12, 2008. Signed with Houston Astros organization, January 5, 2009.
e Released by Houston Astros, April 28, 2009. Signed with Florida Marlins organization, May 25, 2009.
f Filed for free agency, November 9, 2009, re-signed with Florida Marlins, December 14, 2009.
g On disabled list from June 12 to July 2, 2010.
h On disabled list from May 7 to May 22 and June 2 to July 17, 2011.
i Not offered contract, December 12, 2011. Signed with San Francisco Giants, February 8, 2012.
j On disabled list from August 27 to September 11, 2012.
k Filed for free agency, November 6, 2012.

HERNANDEZ, DAVID JESUS

Born, Sacramento, California, May 13, 1985.
Bats Right. Throws Right. Height, 6 feet, 3 inches. Weight, 215 pounds.

Year	Club	Lea	G	IP	W	L	Pct	SO	BB	H	ERA	SAVES
2005 Aberdeen	N.Y.-Penn.		12	41²/₃	1	2	.333	47	17	41	3.89	0
2006 Delmarva	So.Atl.		28	145¹/₃	7	8	.467	154	71	134	4.15	0
2007 Frederick	Carolina		28	145¹/₃	7	11	.389	168	47	139	4.95	0
2008 Bowie	Eastern		27	141	10	4	.714	166	71	112	2.68	0
2009 Bowie	Eastern		1	4	0	0	.000	4	1	2	2.25	0
2009 Norfolk	Int.		11	57¹/₃	3	2	.600	79	18	42	3.30	0
2009 Baltimore	A.L.		20	101¹/₃	4	10	.286	68	46	118	5.42	0
2010 Bowie	Eastern		2	2	0	0	.000	3	0	1	0.00	0
2010 Baltimore a-b	A.L.		41	79¹/₃	8	8	.500	72	42	72	4.31	2
2011 Arizona	N.L.		74	69¹/₃	5	3	.625	77	30	49	3.38	11
2012 Arizona	N.L.		72	68¹/₃	2	3	.400	98	22	48	2.50	4
Major League Totals	4 Yrs.		207	318¹/₃	19	24	.442	315	140	287	4.07	17
Division Series												
2011 Arizona	N.L.		4	5	0	0	.000	5	0	2	3.60	0

a On disabled list from August 5 to September 7, 2010.
b Traded to Baltimore Orioles with pitcher Kam Mickolio for infielder Mark Reynolds and player to be named later, December 6, 2010. Baltimore Orioles received catcher John Hester to complete trade, April 30, 2011.

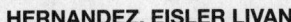

HERNANDEZ, EISLER LIVAN

Born, Villa Clara, Cuba, February 20, 1975.
Bats Right. Throws Right. Height, 6 feet, 2 inches. Weight, 245 pounds.

Year	Club	Lea	G	IP	W	L	Pct	SO	BB	H	ERA	SAVES
1996 Charlotte	Int.		10	49	2	4	.333	45	34	61	5.14	0
1996 Portland	Eastern		15	93¹/₃	9	2	.818	95	34	81	4.34	0
1996 Florida	N.L.		1	3	0	0	.000	2	2	3	0.00	0
1997 Portland	Eastern		1	4	0	0	.000	2	7	2	2.25	0
1997 Charlotte	Int.		14	81¹/₃	5	3	.625	58	38	76	3.98	0
1997 Florida	N.L.		17	96¹/₃	9	3	.750	72	38	81	3.18	0
1998 Florida	N.L.		33	234¹/₃	10	12	.455	162	104	*265	4.72	0
1999 Florida-San Francisco a	N.L.		30	199²/₃	8	12	.400	144	76	227	4.64	0
2000 San Francisco	N.L.		33	240	17	11	.607	165	73	*254	3.75	0
2001 San Francisco	N.L.		34	226²/₃	13	15	.464	138	85	*266	5.24	0
2002 San Francisco	N.L.		33	216	12	*16	.429	134	71	233	4.38	0
2003 Montreal b-c	N.L.		33	*233¹/₃	15	10	.600	178	57	225	3.20	0
2004 Montreal	N.L.		35	*255	11	15	.423	186	83	234	3.60	0
2005 Washington	N.L.		35	*246¹/₃	15	10	.600	147	84	*268	3.98	0
2006 Washington-Arizona d	N.L.		34	216	13	13	.500	128	78	246	4.83	0
2007 Arizona e	N.L.		33	204¹/₃	11	11	.500	90	79	*247	4.93	0
2008 Minnesota	A.L.		23	139²/₃	10	8	.556	54	29	199	5.48	0
2008 Colorado f-g	N.L.		8	40¹/₃	3	3	.500	13	14	58	8.03	0
2009 New York-Washington h-i	N.L.		31	183²/₃	9	12	.429	102	67	220	5.44	0
2010 Washington	N.L.		33	211²/₃	10	12	.455	114	64	216	3.66	0
2011 Washington j	N.L.		29	175¹/₃	8	13	.381	99	46	199	4.47	0
2012 Atlanta-Milwaukee k-l-m	N.L.		44	67¹/₃	4	1	.800	48	16	84	6.42	1
Major League Totals	17 Yrs.		519	3189	178	177	.501	1976	1066	3525	4.44	1
Division Series												
1997 Florida	N.L.		1	4	0	0	.000	3	0	3	2.25	0
2000 San Francisco	N.L.		1	7²/₃	1	0	1.000	5	5	5	1.17	0
2002 San Francisco	N.L.		1	8¹/₃	1	0	1.000	6	2	8	3.24	0
2007 Arizona	N.L.		1	6	1	0	1.000	2	5	5	1.50	0
Division Series Totals			4	26	3	0	1.000	16	12	21	2.08	0
Championship Series												
1997 Florida	N.L.		2	10²/₃	2	0	1.000	16	2	5	0.84	0
2002 San Francisco	N.L.		1	6¹/₃	0	0	.000	0	1	9	2.84	0
2007 Arizona	N.L.		1	5²/₃	0	1	.000	4	2	8	6.35	0
Championship Series Totals			4	22²/₃	2	1	.667	20	5	22	2.78	0
World Series Record												
1997 Florida	N.L.		2	13²/₃	2	0	1.000	7	10	15	5.27	0
2002 San Francisco	N.L.		2	5²/₃	0	2	.000	4	9	9	14.29	0
World Series Totals			4	19¹/₃	2	2	.500	11	19	24	7.91	0

a Traded to San Francisco Giants for pitcher Jason Grilli and pitcher Nathan Bump, July 24, 1999.
b Traded to Montreal Expos with catcher Edwards Guzman for pitcher Jim Brower and player to be named later, March 24, 2003.
c San Francisco Giants received pitcher Matt Blank to complete trade, April 30, 2003.
d Traded to Arizona Diamondbacks with cash for pitcher Garrett Mock and pitcher Matt Chico, August 7, 2006.

e Filed for free agency, October 29, 2007. Signed with Minnesota Twins, February 12, 2008.
f Claimed on waivers by Colorado Rockies, August 6, 2008.
g Filed for free agency, November 1, 2008. Signed with New York Mets organization, February 14, 2009.
h Released by New York Mets, August 20, 2009. Signed with Washington Nationals, August 26, 2009.
i Filed for free agency, November 5, 2009, re-signed with Washington Nationals organization, February 24, 2010.
j Filed for free agency, October 30, 2011. Signed with Houston Astros organization, January 31, 2012.
k Released by Houston Astros, March 30, 2012. Signed with Atlanta Braves, March 30, 2012.
l Released by Atlanta Braves, June 18, 2012. Signed with Milwaukee Brewers, June 22, 2012.
m Filed for free agency, October 17, 2012.

HERNANDEZ, FELIX ABRAHAM
Born, Valencia, Venezuela, April 8, 1986.
Bats Right. Throws Right. Height, 6 feet, 3 inches. Weight, 230 pounds.

Year	Club	Lea	G	IP	W	L	Pct	SO	BB	H	ERA	SAVES
2003 Wisconsin	Midwest		2	14	0	0	.000	18	3	9	1.93	0
2003 Everett	Northwest		11	55	7	2	.778	73	24	43	2.29	0
2004 Inland Empire	California		16	92	9	3	.750	114	26	85	2.74	0
2004 San Antonio	Texas		10	57⅓	5	1	.833	58	21	47	3.30	0
2005 Tacoma	P.C.		19	88	9	4	.692	100	48	62	2.25	0
2005 Seattle	A.L.		12	84⅓	4	4	.500	77	23	61	2.67	0
2006 Seattle	A.L.		31	191	12	14	.462	176	60	195	4.52	0
2007 Seattle a	A.L.		30	190⅓	14	7	.667	165	53	209	3.92	0
2008 Seattle b	A.L.		31	200⅔	9	11	.450	175	80	198	3.45	0
2009 Seattle	A.L.		34	238⅔	*19	5	*.792	217	71	200	2.49	0
2010 Seattle c	A.L.		34	*249⅔	13	12	.520	232	70	194	*2.27	0
2011 Seattle	A.L.		33	233⅔	14	14	.500	222	67	218	3.47	0
2012 Seattle d	A.L.		33	232	13	9	.591	223	56	209	3.06	0
Major League Totals	8 Yrs.		238	1620⅓	98	76	.563	1487	480	1484	3.22	0

a On disabled list from April 19 to May 15, 2007.
b On disabled list from June 24 to July 11, 2008.
c Selected Cy Young Award Winner in American League for 2010.
d Pitched no-hit, no-run perfect game against Tampa Bay Rays, August 15, 2012.

HERRERA, KELVIN DE JESUS
Born, Tenares, Dominican Republic, December 31, 1989.
Bats Right. Throws Right. Height, 5 feet, 10 inches. Weight, 190 pounds.

Year	Club	Lea	G	IP	W	L	Pct	SO	BB	H	ERA	SAVES
2008 Burlington	Appal.		11	50⅔	2	2	.500	45	5	48	1.42	0
2008 Burlington	Midwest		3	12⅔	2	0	1.000	7	2	13	2.13	0
2009 Burlington	Midwest		1	5	1	0	1.000	1	0	3	0.00	0
2010 Burlington	Midwest		8	41⅓	2	3	.400	40	15	38	4.35	0
2011 Wilmington	Carolina		8	14⅔	2	1	.667	12	2	8	0.61	1
2011 NW Arkansas	Texas		23	36	4	0	1.000	40	6	22	1.75	7
2011 Omaha	P.C.		14	17	1	0	1.000	18	7	12	2.12	6
2011 Kansas City	A.L.		2	2	0	1	.000	0	0	2	13.50	0
2012 Kansas City	A.L.		76	84⅓	4	3	.571	77	21	79	2.35	3
Major League Totals	2 Yrs.		78	86⅓	4	4	.500	77	21	81	2.61	3

HOCHEVAR, LUKE ANTHONY
Born, Denver, Colorado, September 15, 1983.
Bats Right. Throws Right. Height, 6 feet, 5 inches. Weight, 205 pounds.

Year	Club	Lea	G	IP	W	L	Pct	SO	BB	H	ERA	SAVES
2006 Burlington	Midwest		4	15⅓	0	1	.000	16	2	8	1.17	0
2007 Wichita	Texas		17	94	3	6	.333	94	26	110	4.69	0
2007 Omaha	P.C.		10	58	1	3	.250	44	21	53	5.12	0
2007 Kansas City	A.L.		4	12⅔	0	1	.000	5	4	11	2.13	0
2008 Omaha	P.C.		3	17⅓	1	1	.500	12	6	11	2.60	0
2008 Kansas City a	A.L.		22	129	6	12	.333	72	47	143	5.51	0
2009 Omaha	P.C.		8	48	5	1	.833	36	12	41	1.50	0
2009 Kansas City	A.L.		25	143	7	13	.350	106	46	167	6.55	0
2010 Omaha	P.C.		2	5	0	0	.000	4	1	3	1.80	0
2010 Kansas City b	A.L.		18	103	6	6	.500	76	37	110	4.81	0
2011 Kansas City	A.L.		31	198	11	11	.500	128	62	192	4.68	0
2012 Kansas City	A.L.		32	185⅓	8	16	.333	144	61	202	5.73	0
Major League Totals	6 Yrs.		132	771	38	59	.392	531	257	825	5.39	0

a On disabled list from August 20 to November 14, 2008.
b On disabled list from June 12 to September 3, 2010.

HOLLAND, DEREK LANE
Born, Newark, Ohio, October 9, 1986.
Bats Both. Throws Left. Height, 6 feet, 2 inches. Weight, 185 pounds.

Year	Club	Lea	G	IP	W	L	Pct	SO	BB	H	ERA	SAVES
2007	Spokane	Northwest	16	67	4	5	.444	83	21	57	3.22	0
2008	Bakersfield	Calif.	5	31	3	1	.750	37	5	20	3.19	0
2008	Clinton	Midwest	17	93²/₃	7	0	1.000	91	29	77	2.40	0
2008	Frisco	Texas	4	26	3	0	1.000	29	6	14	0.69	0
2009	Oklahoma	P.C.	1	4	0	1	.000	5	3	5	9.00	0
2009	Texas	A.L.	33	138¹/₃	8	13	.381	107	47	160	6.12	0
2010	Rangers	Arizona	1	3	0	0	.000	6	0	0	0.00	0
2010	Oklahoma	P.C.	11	62²/₃	6	2	.750	51	18	50	1.87	0
2010	Texas a	A.L.	14	57¹/₃	3	4	.429	54	24	55	4.08	0
2011	Texas	A.L.	32	198	16	5	.762	162	67	201	3.95	0
2012	Round Rock	P.C.	2	9	0	2	.000	5	2	11	6.00	0
2012	Texas b	A.L.	29	175¹/₃	12	7	.632	145	52	162	4.67	0
Major League Totals	4 Yrs.		108	569	39	29	.574	468	190	578	4.71	0
Wild Card Playoff												
2012	Texas	A.L.	1	0¹/₃	0	0	.000	1	0	1	0.00	0
Division Series												
2010	Texas	A.L.	2	4²/₃	0	0	.000	4	1	6	5.79	0
2011	Texas	A.L.	2	6¹/₃	1	0	1.000	2	2	7	1.42	0
Division Series Totals			4	11	1	0	1.000	6	3	13	3.27	0
Championship Series												
2010	Texas	A.L.	2	5²/₃	1	0	1.000	4	2	3	0.00	0
2011	Texas	A.L.	2	7¹/₃	0	0	.000	5	4	11	8.59	0
Championship Series Totals			4	13	1	0	1.000	9	6	14	4.85	0
World Series Record												
2010	Texas	A.L.	2	1	0	0	.000	1	4	0	27.00	0
2011	Texas	A.L.	2	10¹/₃	1	0	1.000	7	2	4	0.87	0
World Series Totals			4	11¹/₃	1	0	1.000	8	6	4	3.18	0

a On disabled list from May 31 to August 1, 2010.
b On disabled list from June 6 to July 7, 2012.

HOLLAND, GREGORY SCOTT (GREG)
Born, Morganton, North Carolina, November 20, 1985.
Bats Right. Throws Right. Height, 5 feet, 11 inches. Weight, 200 pounds.

Year	Club	Lea	G	IP	W	L	Pct	SO	BB	H	ERA	SAVES
2007	Idaho Falls	Pioneer	22	33²/₃	6	1	.857	37	15	28	3.48	6
2008	Wilmington	Carolina	32	84¹/₃	4	5	.444	96	35	70	3.42	4
2009	NW Arkansas	Texas	29	45¹/₃	3	2	.600	49	19	46	3.18	8
2009	Omaha	P.C.	6	9	1	1	.500	1	5	12	7.00	2
2010	Omaha	P.C.	36	56²/₃	3	3	.500	60	30	40	3.81	3
2010	Kansas City	A.L.	15	18²/₃	0	1	.000	23	8	23	6.75	0
2011	Omaha	P.C.	13	21²/₃	2	0	1.000	27	11	13	2.08	2
2011	Kansas City	A.L.	46	60	5	1	.833	74	19	37	1.80	4
2012	NW Arkansas	Texas	2	2	0	1	.000	3	0	1	0.00	0
2012	Kansas City a	A.L.	67	67	7	4	.636	91	34	58	2.96	16
Major League Totals	3 Yrs.		128	145²/₃	12	6	.667	188	61	118	2.97	20

a On disabled list from April 21 to May 12, 2012.

HOOVER, JAMES ALLEN (J.J.)
Born, Pittsburgh, Pennsylvania, August 13, 1987.
Bats Right. Throws Right. Height, 6 feet, 3 inches. Weight, 230 pounds.

Year	Club	Lea	G	IP	W	L	Pct	SO	BB	H	ERA	SAVES
2008	Danville	Appal.	2	4²/₃	1	0	1.000	6	1	4	0.00	0
2009	Myrtle Beach	Carolina	1	3	0	0	.000	2	5	3	9.00	0
2009	Rome	So.Atl.	25	134¹/₃	7	6	.538	148	25	135	3.35	1
2010	Myrtle Beach	Carolina	24	132²/₃	11	6	.647	118	35	126	3.26	0
2010	Mississippi	Southern	4	20²/₃	3	1	.750	34	15	15	3.48	0
2011	Gwinnett	Int.	12	18²/₃	1	1	.500	31	12	12	3.38	1
2011	Mississippi	Southern	31	87	2	5	.286	86	28	65	2.48	1
2012	Louisville	Int.	30	37	4	0	1.000	55	12	15	1.22	13
2012	Cincinnati	N.L.	28	30²/₃	1	0	1.000	31	13	17	2.05	1
Division Series												
2012	Cincinnati	N.L.	2	2²/₃	0	0	.000	2	2	0	0.00	0

HORST, JEREMY M.
Born, Cheyenne, Wyoming, October 1, 1985.
Bats Left. Throws Left. Height, 6 feet, 3 inches. Weight, 215 pounds.

Year	Club	Lea	G	IP	W	L	Pct	SO	BB	H	ERA	SAVES
2007	Reds............	Gulf Coast	1	2	0	0	.000	4	2	3	4.50	0
2007	Billings...........	Pioneer	16	39²/₃	3	2	.600	51	22	34	3.18	2
2008	Dayton..........	Midwest	36	102	8	2	.800	110	33	74	2.38	4
2009	Sarasota...........	Fla.St.	23	133	6	13	.316	101	41	136	3.25	0
2009	Carolina..........	Southern	5	29	1	4	.200	21	10	35	6.21	0
2010	Lynchburg.........	Carolina	11	14²/₃	0	2	.000	17	4	17	4.30	0
2010	Louisville............	Int.	6	14¹/₃	1	0	1.000	12	5	17	2.51	0
2010	Carolina.........	Southern	27	43	3	2	.600	46	9	35	2.09	0
2011	Louisville............	Int.	36	51¹/₃	1	4	.200	42	14	41	2.81	0
2011	Cincinnati............	N.L.	12	15¹/₃	0	0	.000	9	6	18	2.93	0
2012	Lehigh Valley..........	Int.	26	38¹/₃	2	1	.667	32	18	43	2.11	2
2012	Philadelphia a..........	N.L.	32	31¹/₃	1	0	1.000	40	14	21	1.15	0
Major League Totals........	2 Yrs.		44	46²/₃	2	0	1.000	49	20	39	1.74	0

a Traded to Philadelphia Phillies for infielder Wilson Valdez, January 25, 2012.

HOWELL, JAMES PHILLIP (J.P.)
Born, Modesto, California, April 25, 1983.
Bats Left. Throws Left. Height, 6 feet. Weight, 190 pounds.

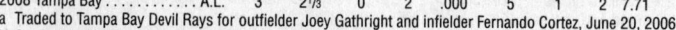

Year	Club	Lea	G	IP	W	L	Pct	SO	BB	H	ERA	SAVES
2004	Idaho Falls.........	Pioneer	6	26	3	1	.750	38	12	16	2.77	0
2005	High Desert..........	Calif.	8	46	3	1	.750	48	24	33	1.96	0
2005	Wichita............	Texas	3	18	2	0	1.000	23	5	12	2.50	0
2005	Omaha.............	P.C.	7	37²/₃	3	1	.750	29	19	40	4.06	0
2005	Kansas City..........	A.L.	15	72²/₃	3	5	.375	54	39	73	6.19	0
2006	Omaha.............	P.C.	8	36	3	2	.600	33	14	39	4.75	0
2006	Durham...........	Int.	10	55	5	3	.625	49	15	53	2.62	0
2006	Tampa Bay a..........	A.L.	8	42¹/₃	1	3	.250	33	14	52	5.10	0
2007	Durham...........	Int.	21	128	7	8	.467	145	34	110	3.38	0
2007	Tampa Bay..........	A.L.	10	51	1	6	.143	49	21	69	7.59	0
2008	Tampa Bay..........	A.L.	64	89¹/₃	6	1	.857	92	39	62	2.22	3
2009	Tampa Bay..........	A.L.	69	66²/₃	7	5	.583	79	33	47	2.83	17
2010	Tampa Bay b-c.........	A.L.					INJURED—Did Not Play					
2011	Durham............	Int.	4	3²/₃	0	0	.000	5	1	5	0.00	0
2011	Tampa Bay..........	A.L.	46	30²/₃	2	3	.400	26	18	30	6.16	1
2011	Charlotte d........	Fla.St.	3	3¹/₃	0	1	.000	4	1	3	2.70	0
2012	Tampa Bay e..........	A.L.	55	50¹/₃	1	0	1.000	42	22	39	3.04	0
Major League Totals........	7 Yrs.		267	403	21	23	.477	375	186	372	4.42	21
Division Series												
2008	Tampa Bay..........	A.L.	3	4¹/₃	0	0	.000	6	0	2	0.00	0
2011	Tampa Bay..........	A.L.	1	0	0	0	.000	0	0	1	—	0
Division Series Totals...........			4	4¹/₃	0	0	.000	6	0	3	0.00	0
Championship Series												
2008	Tampa Bay..........	A.L.	6	5¹/₃	0	1	.000	6	3	5	3.38	0
World Series Record												
2008	Tampa Bay............	A.L.	3	2¹/₃	0	2	.000	5	1	2	7.71	0

a Traded to Tampa Bay Devil Rays for outfielder Joey Gathright and infielder Fernando Cortez, June 20, 2006.
b On disabled list from March 26 to November 2, 2010.
c Not offered contract, December 2, 2010, re-signed with Tampa Bay Rays, December 13, 2010.
d On disabled list from March 22 to May 20, 2011.
e Filed for free agency, November 3, 2012. Signed with Los Angeles Dodgers, January 7, 2013

HUDSON, DANIEL CLAIRBORNE
Born, Lynchburg, Virginia, March 9, 1987.
Bats Right. Throws Right. Height, 6 feet, 4 inches. Weight, 220 pounds.

Year	Club	Lea	G	IP	W	L	Pct	SO	BB	H	ERA	SAVES
2008	Great Falls.........	Pioneer	14	69²/₃	5	4	.556	90	22	52	3.36	0
2009	Kannapolis..........	So.Atl.	4	22	1	2	.333	30	2	15	1.23	0
2009	Winston-Salem......	Carolina	8	45	4	3	.571	49	13	31	3.40	0
2009	Birmingham.......	Southern	9	56¹/₃	7	0	1.000	63	10	37	1.60	0
2009	Charlotte............	Int.	5	24	2	0	1.000	24	9	22	3.00	0
2009	Chicago............	A.L.	6	18²/₃	1	1	.500	14	9	16	3.38	0
2010	Charlotte............	Int.	17	93¹/₃	11	4	.733	108	31	81	3.47	0
2010	Chicago............	A.L.	3	15²/₃	1	1	.500	14	11	17	6.32	0
2010	Arizona a.........	N.L.	11	79²/₃	7	1	.875	70	16	51	1.69	0

Year	Club	Lea	G	IP	W	L	Pct	SO	BB	H	ERA	SAVES
2011 Arizona		N.L.	33	222	16	12	.571	169	50	217	3.49	0
2012 Reno		P.C.	1	5	1	0	1.000	2	1	5	3.60	0
2012 Arizona b		N.L.	9	$45\frac{1}{3}$	3	2	.600	37	12	62	7.35	0
Major League Totals	4 Yrs.		62	$381\frac{1}{3}$	28	17	.622	304	98	363	3.68	0
Division Series												
2011 Arizona		N.L.	1	$5\frac{1}{3}$	0	1	.000	6	0	9	8.44	0

a Traded to Arizona Diamondbacks with pitcher David Holmberg for pitcher Edwin Jackson, July 30, 2010.
b On disabled list from April 19 to May 27 and June 27 to October 25, 2012.

HUDSON, TIMOTHY ADAM (TIM)
Born, Columbus, Georgia, July 14, 1975.
Bats Right. Throws Right. Height, 6 feet, I Inch. Weight, 170 pounds.

Year	Club	Lea	G	IP	W	L	Pct	SO	BB	H	ERA	SAVES
1997 Sou Oregon	Northwest	8	$28\frac{2}{3}$	3	1	.750	37	15	12	2.51	0	
1998 Modesto	California	8	$37\frac{2}{3}$	4	0	1.000	48	18	19	1.67	0	
1998 Huntsville	Southern	22	$134\frac{2}{3}$	10	9	.526	104	71	136	4.54	0	
1999 Midland	Texas	3	18	3	0	1.000	18	3	9	0.50	0	
1999 Vancouver	P.C.	8	49	4	0	1.000	61	21	38	2.20	0	
1999 Oakland	A.L.	21	$136\frac{1}{3}$	11	2	.846	132	62	121	3.23	0	
2000 Oakland	A.L.	32	$202\frac{1}{3}$	*20	6	*.769	169	82	169	4.14	0	
2001 Oakland	A.L.	35	235	18	9	.667	181	71	216	3.37	0	
2002 Oakland	A.L.	34	$238\frac{1}{3}$	15	9	.625	152	62	237	2.98	0	
2003 Oakland	A.L.	34	240	16	7	.696	162	61	197	2.70	0	
2004 Sacramento	P.C.	1	3	0	0	.000	3	2	2	6.00	0	
2004 Oakland a-b	A.L.	27	$188\frac{2}{3}$	12	6	.667	103	44	194	3.53	0	
2005 Atlanta c	N.L.	29	192	14	9	.609	115	65	194	3.52	0	
2006 Atlanta	N.L.	35	$218\frac{1}{3}$	13	12	.520	141	79	235	4.86	0	
2007 Atlanta	N.L.	34	$224\frac{1}{3}$	16	10	.615	132	53	221	3.33	0	
2008 Atlanta d	N.L.	23	142	11	7	.611	85	40	125	3.17	0	
2009 Myrtle Beach	Carolina	2	$4\frac{2}{3}$	0	1	.000	3	2	5	5.79	0	
2009 Gwinnett	Int.	4	$18\frac{2}{3}$	1	0	1.000	11	2	24	3.38	0	
2009 Atlanta e	N.L.	7	$42\frac{1}{3}$	2	1	.667	30	13	49	3.61	0	
2010 Atlanta	N.L.	34	$228\frac{2}{3}$	17	9	.654	139	74	189	2.83	0	
2011 Atlanta	N.L.	33	215	16	10	.615	158	56	189	3.22	0	
2012 Rome	So.Atl.	2	7	0	2	.000	1	1	13	7.71	0	
2012 Gwinnett	Int.	2	$10\frac{2}{3}$	2	0	1.000	8	5	8	0.84	0	
2012 Atlanta f	N.L.	28	179	16	7	.696	102	48	168	3.62	0	
Major League Totals	14 Yrs.	406	$2682\frac{1}{3}$	197	104	.654	1801	810	2504	3.42	0	
Division Series												
2000 Oakland	A.L.	1	8	0	1	.000	5	4	6	3.38	0	
2001 Oakland	A.L.	2	$9\frac{2}{3}$	1	0	1.000	5	1	8	0.93	0	
2002 Oakland	A.L.	2	$8\frac{2}{3}$	0	1	.000	8	4	13	6.23	0	
2003 Oakland	A.L.	2	$7\frac{2}{3}$	0	0	.000	6	1	10	3.52	0	
2005 Atlanta	N.L.	2	$13\frac{2}{3}$	0	1	.000	8	6	13	5.27	0	
2010 Atlanta	N.L.	1	7	0	0	.000	5	4	4	0.00	0	
Division Series Totals		10	$54\frac{2}{3}$	1	3	.250	37	20	54	3.46	0	

a On disabled list from June 23 to August 7, 2004.
b Traded to Atlanta Braves for pitcher Juan Cruz, pitcher Dan Meyer and outfielder Charles Thomas, December 16, 2004.
c On disabled list from June 14 to July 16, 2005.
d On disabled list from July 27 to November 3, 2008.
e On disabled list from February 24 to September 1, 2009.
f On disabled list from April 3 to April 29, 2012.

HUGHES, PHILIP JOSEPH
Born, Mission Viejo, California, June 24, 1986.
Bats Right. Throws Right. Height, 6 feet, 5 inches. Weight, 220 pounds.

Year	Club	Lea	G	IP	W	L	Pct	SO	BB	H	ERA	SAVES
2004 Yankees	Gulf Coast	3	5	0	0	.000	8	0	4	0.00	0	
2005 Tampa	Fla.St.	5	$17\frac{2}{3}$	2	0	1.000	21	4	8	3.06	0	
2005 Charleston	So.Atl.	12	$68\frac{2}{3}$	7	1	.875	72	16	46	1.97	0	
2006 Trenton	Eastern	21	116	10	3	.769	138	32	73	2.25	0	
2006 Tampa	Fla.St.	5	30	2	3	.400	30	2	19	1.80	0	
2007 Tampa	Fla.St.	1	2	0	0	.000	3	2	0	0.00	0	
2007 Trenton	Eastern	2	7	0	0	.000	11	2	5	1.29	0	
2007 Scranton-WB	Int.	5	$28\frac{2}{3}$	4	1	.800	28	8	16	2.20	0	
2007 New York a	A.L.	13	$72\frac{2}{3}$	5	3	.625	58	29	64	4.46	0	
2008 Charleston	So.Atl.	2	$6\frac{2}{3}$	2	0	1.000	6	2	3	0.00	0	

Year	Club	Lea	G	IP	W	L	Pct	SO	BB	H	ERA	SAVES
2008 Scranton-WB	Int.		6	29	1	0	1.000	31	9	34	5.90	0
2008 New York b	A.L.		8	34	0	4	.000	23	15	43	6.62	0
2009 Scranton/WB	Int.		3	19⅓	3	0	1.000	19	3	17	1.86	0
2009 New York	A.L.		51	86	8	3	.727	96	28	68	3.03	3
2010 New York	A.L.		31	176⅓	18	8	.692	146	58	162	4.19	0
2011 Staten Island	N.Y.-Penn.		1	4⅓	0	0	.000	7	1	3	2.08	0
2011 Trenton	Eastern		2	9⅔	1	0	1.000	11	4	6	1.86	0
2011 New York c	A.L.		17	74⅔	5	5	.500	47	27	84	5.79	0
2012 New York	A.L.		32	191⅓	16	13	.552	165	46	196	4.23	0
Major League Totals	6 Yrs.		152	635	52	36	.591	535	203	617	4.39	3
Division Series												
2007 New York	A.L.		2	5⅔	1	0	1.000	6	0	3	1.59	0
2009 New York	A.L.		3	2	0	0	.000	3	1	5	9.00	0
2010 New York	A.L.		1	7	1	0	1.000	6	1	4	0.00	0
2011 New York	A.L.		2	2⅓	0	0	.000	4	0	2	0.00	0
2012 New York	A.L.		1	6⅔	0	0	.000	8	3	4	1.35	0
Division Series Totals			9	23⅔	2	0	1.000	27	5	18	1.52	0
Championship Series												
2009 New York	A.L.		3	2⅔	0	1	.000	3	1	4	3.38	0
2010 New York	A.L.		2	8⅔	0	2	.000	6	7	14	11.42	0
2012 New York	A.L.		1	3	0	1	.000	1	3	3	3.00	0
Championship Series Totals			6	14⅓	0	4	.000	10	11	21	8.16	0
World Series Record												
2009 New York	A.L.		3	1⅔	0	0	.000	1	2	2	16.20	0

a On disabled list from May 2 to August 4, 2007.
b On disabled list from April 30 to July 30, 2008.
c On disabled list from April 15 to July 6, 2011.

HUGHES, WILLIAM JARED (JARED)

Born, Stamford, Connecticut, July 4, 1985.
Bats Right. Throws Right. Height, 6 feet, 7 inches. Weight, 245 pounds.

Year	Club	Lea	G	IP	W	L	Pct	SO	BB	H	ERA	SAVES
2006 Williamsport	N.Y.-Penn.		5	23	1	2	.333	11	7	14	2.74	0
2006 Hickory	So.Atl.		10	48⅓	5	4	.556	25	31	46	5.77	0
2007 Hickory	So.Atl.		27	145⅓	8	9	.471	109	54	162	4.64	0
2008 Lynchburg	Carolina		21	105⅔	3	9	.250	54	50	108	4.60	0
2008 Altoona	Eastern		6	31	2	2	.500	18	16	35	4.94	0
2009 Altoona	Eastern		17	46⅓	1	6	.143	36	16	55	3.88	3
2009 Pirates	Gulf Coast		3	6	0	0	.000	5	1	3	1.50	0
2010 Altoona	Eastern		30	150⅔	12	8	.600	120	41	166	4.42	0
2011 Altoona	Eastern		13	61⅔	3	4	.429	33	18	62	4.09	0
2011 Indianapolis	Int.		35	42⅔	3	1	.750	45	18	35	2.11	0
2011 Pittsburgh	N.L.		12	11	0	1	.000	10	4	9	4.09	0
2012 Indianapolis	Int.		2	2	0	0	.000	3	1	1	0.00	0
2012 Pittsburgh	N.L.		66	75⅔	2	2	.500	50	22	65	2.85	2
Major League Totals	2 Yrs.		78	86⅔	2	3	.400	60	26	74	3.01	2

HUMBER, PHILIP GREGORY

Born, Nacogdoches, Texas, December 21, 1982.
Bats Right. Throws Right. Height, 6 feet, 4 inches. Weight, 210 pounds.

Year	Club	Lea	G	IP	W	L	Pct	SO	BB	H	ERA	SAVES
2005 St. Lucie	Fla.St.		14	70⅓	2	6	.250	65	18	74	4.99	0
2005 Binghamton	Eastern		1	4	0	1	.000	2	2	4	6.75	0
2006 Mets	Gulf Coast		1	4	0	0	.000	7	1	7	6.75	0
2006 St. Lucie	Fla.St.		7	38	3	1	.750	36	9	24	2.37	0
2006 Binghamton	Eastern		6	34⅓	2	2	.500	36	10	25	2.88	0
2006 New York	N.L.		2	2	0	0	.000	2	1	0	0.00	0
2007 New Orleans	P.C.		25	139	11	9	.550	120	44	129	4.27	0
2007 New York	N.L.		3	7	0	0	.000	2	2	9	7.71	0
2008 Rochester	Int.		31	136⅓	10	8	.556	106	49	145	4.56	0
2008 Minnesota a	A.L.		5	11⅔	0	0	.000	6	5	11	4.63	0
2009 Minnesota	A.L.		8	9	0	0	.000	9	9	17	8.00	0
2009 Rochester b	Int.		23	119⅔	7	9	.438	87	45	135	5.34	0
2010 Omaha	P.C.		21	118⅔	5	6	.455	80	20	131	4.47	0
2010 Kansas City c	A.L.		8	21⅔	2	1	.667	16	7	22	4.15	0
2011 Charlotte	Int.		1	5	0	0	.000	5	1	7	7.20	0

Year Club	Lea	G	IP	W	L	Pct	SO	BB	H	ERA	SAVES
2011 Chicago d-e	A.L.	28	163	9	9	.500	116	41	151	3.75	0
2012 Birmingham	Southern	1	6	1	0	1.000	5	0	2	1.50	0
2012 Charlotte	Int.	2	$6^{1/3}$	0	1	.000	4	4	8	5.68	0
2012 Chicago f-g-h	A.L.	26	102	5	5	.500	85	44	113	6.44	0
Major League Totals ....7 Yrs.		80	$316^{1/3}$	16	15	.516	236	109	323	4.87	0

a Traded to Minnesota Twins with outfielder Carlos Gomez, pitcher Kevin Mulvey and pitcher Deolis Garcia for pitcher Johan Santana, February 2, 2008.
b Filed for free agency, October 6, 2009. Signed with Kansas City Royals organization, December 15, 2009.
c Claimed on waivers by Oakland Athletics, December 17, 2010.
d Claimed on waivers by Chicago White Sox, January 18, 2011.
e On disabled list from August 19 to September 3, 2011.
f Pitched no-hit, no-run perfect game against Seattle Mariners, April 21, 2012.
g On disabled list from June 17 to July 17, 2012.
h Claimed on waivers by Houston Astros, November 30, 2012.

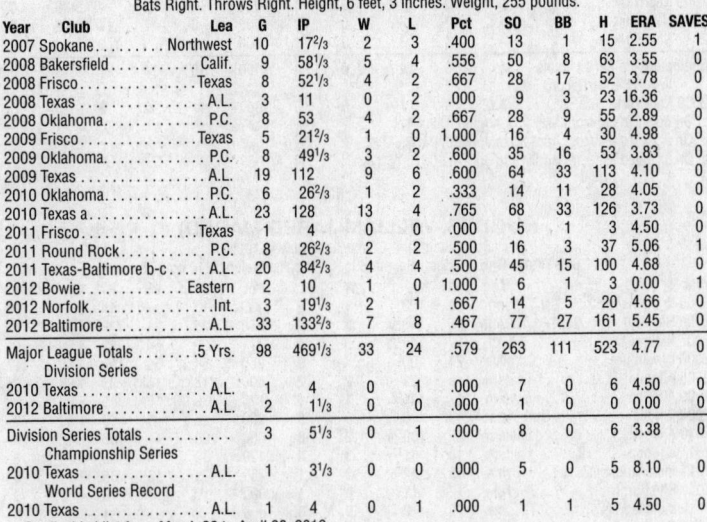

HUNTER, RAYMOND THOMAS (TOMMY)

Born, Tuscaloosa, Alabama, July 3, 1986.
Bats Right. Throws Right. Height, 6 feet, 3 inches. Weight, 255 pounds.

Year Club	Lea	G	IP	W	L	Pct	SO	BB	H	ERA	SAVES
2007 Spokane........	Northwest	10	$17^{2/3}$	2	3	.400	13	1	15	2.55	1
2008 Bakersfield	Calif.	9	$58^{1/3}$	5	4	.556	50	8	63	3.55	0
2008 Frisco..............	Texas	8	$52^{1/3}$	4	2	.667	28	17	52	3.78	0
2008 Texas	A.L.	3	11	0	2	.000	9	3	23	16.36	0
2008 Oklahoma.............	P.C.	8	53	4	2	.667	28	9	55	2.89	0
2009 Frisco..............	Texas	5	$21^{2/3}$	1	0	1.000	16	4	30	4.98	0
2009 Oklahoma.............	P.C.	8	$49^{1/3}$	3	2	.600	35	16	53	3.83	0
2009 Texas	A.L.	19	112	9	6	.600	64	33	113	4.10	0
2010 Oklahoma.............	P.C.	6	$26^{2/3}$	1	2	.333	14	11	28	4.05	0
2010 Texas a..............	A.L.	23	128	13	4	.765	68	33	126	3.73	0
2011 Frisco..............	Texas	1	4	0	0	.000	5	1	3	4.50	0
2011 Round Rock..........	P.C.	8	$26^{2/3}$	2	2	.500	16	3	37	5.06	1
2011 Texas-Baltimore b-c.....	A.L.	20	$84^{2/3}$	4	4	.500	45	15	100	4.68	0
2012 Bowie.............	Eastern	2	10	1	0	1.000	6	1	3	0.00	1
2012 Norfolk.............	Int.	3	$19^{1/3}$	2	1	.667	14	5	20	4.66	0
2012 Baltimore	A.L.	33	$133^{2/3}$	7	8	.467	77	27	161	5.45	0
Major League Totals ....5 Yrs.		98	$469^{1/3}$	33	24	.579	263	111	523	4.77	0
Division Series											
2010 Texas	A.L.	1	4	0	1	.000	7	0	6	4.50	0
2012 Baltimore	A.L.	2	$1^{1/3}$	0	0	.000	1	0	0	0.00	0
Division Series Totals		3	$5^{1/3}$	0	1	.000	8	0	6	3.38	0
Championship Series											
2010 Texas	A.L.	1	$3^{1/3}$	0	0	.000	5	0	5	8.10	0
World Series Record											
2010 Texas	A.L.	1	4	0	1	.000	1	1	5	4.50	0

a On disabled list from March 26 to April 28, 2010.
b On disabled list from March 25 to July 1, 2011.
c Traded to Baltimore Orioles with infielder Chris Davis for pitcher Koji Uehara and cash, July 30, 2011.

ISRINGHAUSEN, JASON DERIK

Born, Brighton, Illinois, September 7, 1972.
Bats Right. Throws Right. Height, 6 feet, 3 inches. Weight, 235 pounds.

Year Club	Lea	G	IP	W	L	Pct	SO	BB	H	ERA	SAVES
1992 Mets............	Gulf Coast	6	29	2	4	.333	25	17	26	4.34	0
1992 Kingsport..........	Appal.	7	36	4	1	.800	24	12	32	3.25	0
1993 Pittsfield........	N.Y.-Penn.	15	$90^{1/3}$	7	4	.636	104	28	68	3.29	0
1994 St. Lucie........	Fla.St.	14	101	6	4	.600	59	27	76	2.23	0
1994 Binghamton	Eastern	14	$92^{1/3}$	5	4	.556	69	23	78	3.02	0
1995 Binghamton	Eastern	6	41	2	1	.667	59	12	26	2.85	0
1995 Norfolk.............	Int.	12	87	9	1	.900	75	24	64	1.55	0
1995 New York	N.L.	14	93	9	2	.818	55	31	88	2.81	0
1996 New York a..........	N.L.	27	$171^{2/3}$	6	14	.300	114	73	190	4.77	0
1997 Mets.............	Gulf Coast	1	$4^{2/3}$	1	0	1.000	7	1	2	1.93	0
1997 St. Lucie...........	Fla.St.	2	12	1	0	1.000	15	5	8	0.00	0
1997 Norfolk.............	Int.	3	20	0	2	.000	17	8	20	4.05	0
1997 New York b..........	N.L.	6	$29^{2/3}$	2	2	.500	25	22	40	7.58	0
1998 c.....................			INJURED—Did Not Play								
1999 Norfolk.............	Int.	12	51	3	1	.750	51	20	33	2.29	0

Year	Club	Lea	G	IP	W	L	Pct	SO	BB	H	ERA	SAVES
1999 New York	N.L.		13	$39\frac{1}{3}$	1	3	.250	31	22	43	6.41	1
1999 Oakland d	A.L.		20	$25\frac{1}{3}$	0	1	.000	20	12	21	2.13	8
2000 Oakland	A.L.		66	69	6	4	.600	57	32	67	3.78	33
2001 Oakland e	A.L.		65	$71\frac{1}{3}$	4	3	.571	74	23	54	2.65	34
2002 St. Louis	N.L.		60	$65\frac{1}{3}$	3	2	.600	68	18	46	2.48	32
2003 Tennessee	Southern		2	2	0	0	.000	3	0	1	0.00	0
2003 St. Louis f	N.L.		40	42	0	1	.000	41	18	31	2.36	22
2004 St. Louis	N.L.		74	$75\frac{1}{3}$	4	2	.667	71	23	55	2.87	*47
2005 St. Louis g	N.L.		63	59	1	2	.333	51	27	43	2.14	39
2006 St. Louis	N.L.		59	$58\frac{1}{3}$	4	8	.333	52	38	47	3.55	33
2007 St. Louis	N.L.		63	$65\frac{1}{3}$	4	0	1.000	54	28	42	2.48	32
2008 Palm Beach	Fla.St.		1	2	0	0	.000	1	0	1	0.00	0
2008 Springfield	Texas		1	$1\frac{2}{3}$	0	0	.000	2	0	1	0.00	0
2008 St. Louis h	N.L.		42	$42\frac{2}{3}$	1	5	.167	36	22	48	5.70	12
2009 Montgomery	Southern		4	4	0	0	.000	3	4	2	2.25	0
2009 Durham	Int.		6	7	0	0	.000	0	2	7	5.14	0
2009 Tampa Bay i-j	A.L.		9	8	0	1	.000	6	5	6	2.25	0
2010 Louisville k	Int.		7	$5\frac{2}{3}$	1	0	1.000	5	7	4	9.53	0
2011 New York l-m	N.L.		53	$46\frac{2}{3}$	3	3	.500	44	24	36	4.05	7
2012 Los Angeles n	A.L.		50	$45\frac{2}{3}$	3	2	.600	31	19	44	4.14	0
Major League Totals ...... 16 Yrs.			724	$1007\frac{2}{3}$	51	55	.481	830	437	901	3.64	300
Division Series												
2000 Oakland	A.L.		2	2	0	0	.000	3	0	1	0.00	1
2001 Oakland	A.L.		2	2	0	0	.000	3	1	1	0.00	2
2002 St. Louis	N.L.		2	2	0	1	.000	1	0	0	0.00	2
2004 St. Louis	N.L.		2	2	0	0	.000	2	2	1	4.50	0
2005 St. Louis	N.L.		3	3	0	0	.000	4	1	5	3.00	1
Division Series Totals			11	11	0	0	.000	13	4	8	1.64	6
Championship Series												
2002 St. Louis	N.L.		2	2	0	0	.000	3	3	1	4.50	1
2004 St. Louis	N.L.		6	$7\frac{2}{3}$	0	1	.000	3	4	4	4.70	3
2005 St. Louis	N.L.		3	4	1	0	1.000	2	0	3	0.00	1
Championship Series Totals			11	$13\frac{2}{3}$	1	1	.500	8	7	8	3.29	5
World Series Record												
2004 St. Louis	N.L.		1	2	0	0	.000	2	1	1	0.00	0

a On disabled list from August 13 to September 1, 1996.
b On disabled list from April 1 to August 27, 1997.
c On disabled list from March 31 to September 28, 1998.
d Traded to Oakland Athletics with pitcher Greg McMichael for pitcher Billy Taylor, July 31, 1999.
e Filed for free agency, November 5, 2001. Signed with St. Louis Cardinals, December 10, 2001.
f On disabled list from March 21 to June 10, 2003.
g On disabled list from April 27 to May 13, 2005.
h On disabled list from May 16 to June 14 and August 17 to November 1, 2008.
i Filed for free agency, November 1, 2008. Signed with Tampa Bay Rays organization, February 20, 2009.
j On disabled list from March 31 to May 18 and June 14 to November 9, 2009.
k Filed for free agency, November 9, 2009. Signed with Cincinnati Reds organization, July 22, 2010.
l Filed for free agency, November 6, 2010. Signed with New York Mets organization, February 16, 2011.
m Filed for free agency, October 30, 2011. Signed with Los Angeles Angels organization, February 22, 2012.
n Filed for free agency, November 3, 2012.

IWAKUMA, HISASHI

Born, Tokyo, Japan, April 12, 1981.
Bats Right. Throws Right. Height, 6 feet, 3 inches. Weight, 190 pounds.

Year	Club	Lea	G	IP	W	L	Pct	SO	BB	H	ERA	SAVES
2001 Kintetsu	Japan Pac.		9	$43\frac{2}{3}$	4	2	.667	25	13	46	4.53	0
2002 Kintetsu	Japan Pac.		23	$141\frac{1}{3}$	8	7	.533	131	42	132	3.69	0
2003 Kintetsu	Japan Pac.		27	$195\frac{2}{3}$	15	10	.600	149	48	201	3.45	0
2004 Kintetsu	Japan Pac.		21	$158\frac{2}{3}$	15	2	.882	123	30	149	3.10	0
2005 Rakuten	Japan Pac.		27	$182\frac{1}{3}$	9	15	.375	124	40	218	4.99	0
2006 Rakuten	Japan Pac.		6	$38\frac{2}{3}$	1	2	.333	16	12	43	3.72	0
2007 Rakuten	Japan Pac.		16	90	5	5	.500	84	23	95	3.40	0
2008 Rakuten	Japan Pac.		28	$201\frac{2}{3}$	21	4	.840	159	36	161	1.87	0
2009 Rakuten	Japan Pac.		24	169	13	6	.684	121	43	179	3.25	0
2010 Rakuten	Japan Pac.		28	201	10	9	.526	153	36	184	2.82	0
2011 Rakuten	Japan Pac.		17	119	6	7	.462	90	19	106	2.42	0
2012 Seattle a	A.L.		30	$125\frac{1}{3}$	9	5	.643	101	43	117	3.16	2

a Signed with Seattle Mariners, January 5, 2012.

269

JACKSON, EDWIN

Born, Neu-Ulm, West Germany, September 9, 1983.
Bats Right. Throws Right. Height, 6 feet, 3 inches. Weight, 210 pounds.

Year	Club	Lea	G	IP	W	L	Pct	SO	BB	H	ERA	SAVES
2001 Dodgers	Gulf Coast		12	22	2	1	.667	23	19	14	2.45	0
2002 South Bend	So.Atl.		19	104²/₃	5	2	.714	85	33	79	1.98	0
2003 Jacksonville	Southern		27	148¹/₃	7	7	.500	157	53	121	3.70	0
2003 Los Angeles	N.L.		4	22	2	1	.667	19	11	17	2.45	0
2004 Las Vegas	P.C.		19	90²/₃	6	4	.600	70	55	90	5.86	0
2004 Los Angeles a	N.L.		8	24²/₃	2	1	.667	16	11	31	7.30	0
2005 Jacksonville	Southern		11	62	6	4	.600	44	18	52	3.48	0
2005 Las Vegas	P.C.		12	55¹/₃	3	7	.300	33	37	76	8.62	0
2005 Los Angeles	N.L.		7	28²/₃	2	2	.500	13	17	31	6.28	0
2006 Durham	Int.		22	73	3	7	.300	66	35	84	5.55	5
2006 Tampa Bay b	A.L.		23	36¹/₃	0	0	.000	27	25	42	5.45	0
2007 Tampa Bay	A.L.		32	161	5	15	.250	128	88	195	5.76	0
2008 Tampa Bay c	A.L.		32	183¹/₃	14	11	.560	108	77	199	4.42	0
2009 Detroit d	A.L.		33	214	13	9	.591	161	70	200	3.62	0
2010 Chicago	A.L.		11	75	4	2	.667	77	18	73	3.24	0
2010 Arizona e-f	N.L.		21	134¹/₃	6	10	.375	104	60	141	5.16	0
2011 Chicago	A.L.		19	121²/₃	7	7	.500	97	39	134	3.92	0
2011 St. Louis g-h-i	N.L.		13	78	5	2	.714	51	23	91	3.58	0
2012 Washington j	N.L.		31	189²/₃	10	11	.476	168	58	173	4.03	0
Major League Totals	10 Yrs.		234	1268²/₃	70	71	.496	969	497	1327	4.40	
Division Series												
2011 St. Louis	N.L.		1	6	1	0	1.000	4	1	5	3.00	0
2012 Washington	N.L.		2	6	0	1	.000	6	3	9	7.50	0
Division Series Totals			3	12	1	1	.500	10	4	14	5.25	0
Championship Series												
2008 Tampa Bay	N.L.		2	2¹/₃	0	0	.000	4	2	0	0.00	0
2011 St. Louis	N.L.		2	6¹/₃	0	0	.000	5	1	11	8.53	0
Championship Series Totals			4	8²/₃	0	0	.000	9	3	11	6.23	0
World Series Record												
2008 Tampa Bay c	N.L.		1	2	0	0	.000	1	1	2	4.50	0
2011 St. Louis	N.L.		1	5¹/₃	0	1	.000	3	7	3	5.06	0
World Series Totals			2	7¹/₃	0	1	.000	4	8	5	4.91	0

a On disabled list from July 9 to September 7, 2004.
b Traded to Tampa Bay Devil Rays with pitcher Chuck Tiffany for pitcher Danys Baez and pitcher Lance Carter, January 14, 2006.
c Traded to Detroit Tigers for outfielder Matt Joyce, December 10, 2008.
d Traded to Arizona Diamondbacks with pitcher Ian Kennedy for pitcher Daniel Schlereth and pitcher Max Scherzer, December 9, 2009.
e Pitched no-hit, no-run game against Tampa Bay Rays, June 25, 2010.
f Traded to Chicago White Sox for pitcher Daniel Hudson and pitcher David Holmberg, July 30, 2010.
g Traded to Toronto Blue Jays with infielder Mark Teahen for pitcher Jason Frasor and pitcher Zach Stewart, July 27, 2011.
h Traded to St. Louis Cardinals with pitcher Octavio Dotel, pitcher Marc Rzepczynski, outfielder Corey Patterson and cash for outfielder Colby Rasmus, pitcher Brian Tallet and pitcher P.J. Walters, July 27, 2011.
i Filed for free agency, October 30, 2011. Signed with Washington Nationals, February 2, 2012.
j Filed for free agency, November 3, 2012. Signed with Chicago Cubs, January 2, 2013.

JANSEN, KENLEY JERONIMO

Born, Curacao, Netherlands Antilles, September 30, 1987.
Bats Both. Throws Right. Height, 6 feet, 6 inches. Weight, 220 pounds.

Year	Club	Lea	G	IP	W	L	Pct	SO	BB	H	ERA	SAVES
2009 Inland Empire a	Calif.		12	11²/₃	0	0	.000	19	11	14	4.63	0
2010 Inland Empire	Calif.		11	18	1	1	.500	28	6	15	1.50	0
2010 Chattanooga	Southern		22	27	4	0	1.000	50	17	14	1.67	8
2010 Los Angeles	N.L.		25	27	1	0	1.000	41	15	12	0.67	4
2011 Rancho Cucamonga	Calif.		2	2	0	0	.000	4	0	0	0.00	0
2011 Chattanooga	Southern		5	6	0	1	.000	9	3	2	4.50	0
2011 Los Angeles b	N.L.		51	53²/₃	2	1	.667	96	26	30	2.85	5
2012 Los Angeles	N.L.		65	65	5	3	.625	99	22	33	2.35	25
Major League Totals	3 Yrs.		141	145²/₃	8	4	.667	236	63	75	2.22	34

a Played catcher in the Dodger organzation, 2005-2008.
b On disabled list from May 29 to June 17 and July 27 to August 25, 2011.

JANSSEN, ROBERT CASEY (CASEY)
Born, Orange, California, September 17, 1981.
Bats Right. Throws Right. Height, 6 feet, 4 inches. Weight, 205 pounds.

Year	Club	Lea	G	IP	W	L	Pct	SO	BB	H	ERA	SAVES
2004 Auburn	N.Y.-Penn.		10	50	3	1	.750	45	10	47	3.60	0
2005 New Hampshire	Eastern		9	43	3	3	.500	47	4	49	2.93	0
2005 Dunedin	Fla.St.		10	59²/₃	6	1	.857	51	12	46	2.26	0
2005 Lansing	Midwest		7	46	4	0	1.000	38	4	27	1.37	0
2006 Syracuse	Int.		9	42²/₃	1	5	.167	32	8	47	4.85	0
2006 Toronto	A.L.		19	94	6	10	.375	44	21	103	5.07	0
2007 Toronto	A.L.		70	72²/₃	2	3	.400	39	20	67	2.35	6
2008 Toronto a	A.L.			INJURED—Did Not Play								
2009 Blue Jays	Gulf Coast		1	1	0	0	.000	0	0	2	9.00	0
2009 Dunedin	Fla.St.		4	13	0	0	.000	10	2	6	0.69	0
2009 New Hampshire	Eastern		6	15	1	0	1.000	12	5	12	2.40	0
2009 Las Vegas	P.C.		7	6²/₃	0	0	.000	7	1	4	5.40	0
2009 Toronto b	A.L.		21	40	2	4	.333	24	14	59	5.85	1
2010 Toronto	A.L.		56	68²/₃	5	2	.714	63	21	74	3.67	0
2011 New Hampshire	Eastern		5	5	0	0	.000	7	1	1	0.00	0
2011 Las Vegas	P.C.		1	2	0	0	.000	3	0	1	0.00	0
2011 Toronto c	A.L.		55	55²/₃	6	0	1.000	53	14	47	2.26	2
2012 Toronto	A.L.		62	63²/₃	1	1	.500	67	11	44	2.54	22
Major League Totals	6 Yrs.		283	394²/₃	22	20	.524	290	101	394	3.60	31

a On disabled list from March 17 to November 14, 2008.
b On disabled list from March 27 to April 30 and June 14 to July 23, 2009.
c On disabled list from June 16 to July 19, 2011.

JEPSEN, KEVIN MARTIN
Born, Anaheim, California, July 26, 1984.
Bats Right. Throws Right. Height, 6 feet, 3 inches. Weight, 235 pounds.

Year	Club	Lea	G	IP	W	L	Pct	SO	BB	H	ERA	SAVES
2002 Angels	Arizona		8	26¹/₃	1	3	.250	19	12	29	6.84	0
2003 Cedar Rapids	Midwest		10	51	6	3	.667	42	28	32	2.65	0
2004 Cedar Rapids	Midwest		27	144¹/₃	8	10	.444	136	77	122	3.43	0
2005 Angels	Arizona		7	14²/₃	0	1	.000	17	11	8	5.52	0
2005 Rancho Cucamonga	Calif.		4	12¹/₃	0	1	.000	11	10	19	10.66	0
2006 Rancho Cucamonga	Calif.		47	54²/₃	4	4	.500	46	34	51	3.58	16
2007 Rancho Cucamonga	Calif.		44	53²/₃	1	5	.167	50	38	61	4.19	3
2008 Arkansas	Texas		25	31²/₃	2	1	.667	35	18	22	1.42	11
2008 Salt Lake	P.C.		15	23	1	3	.250	21	12	17	2.35	2
2008 Los Angeles	A.L.		9	8¹/₃	0	1	.000	7	4	8	4.32	0
2009 Salt Lake	P.C.		14	18	1	0	1.000	20	16	30	9.00	2
2009 Los Angeles a	A.L.		54	54²/₃	6	4	.600	48	19	63	4.94	1
2010 Los Angeles	A.L.		68	59	2	4	.333	61	29	54	3.97	0
2011 Los Angeles	A.L.		16	13	1	2	.333	6	9	21	7.62	0
2011 Salt Lake	P.C.		24	28¹/₃	1	3	.250	20	8	32	4.45	7
2012 Salt Lake	P.C.		23	25	2	2	.500	35	9	18	3.24	2
2012 Los Angeles	A.L.		49	44²/₃	3	2	.600	38	12	39	3.02	2
Major League Totals	5 Yrs.		196	179²/₃	12	13	.480	160	73	185	4.31	3
Division Series												
2009 Los Angeles	A.L.		2	1¹/₃	0	0	.000	1	0	3	6.75	0
Championship Series												
2009 Los Angeles	A.L.		3	3²/₃	1	0	1.000	2	2	5	2.45	0

a On disabled list from April 19 to May 4, 2009.

JIMENEZ, UBALDO
Born, Nagua, Dominican Republic, January 22, 1984.
Bats Right. Throws Right. Height, 6 feet, 4 inches. Weight, 200 pounds.

Year	Club	Lea	G	IP	W	L	Pct	SO	BB	H	ERA	SAVES
2002 Casper	Pioneer		14	62	3	5	.375	65	29	72	6.53	0
2003 Visalia	Calif.		1	5	1	0	1.000	7	1	3	0.00	0
2003 Asheville	So.Atl.		27	153²/₃	10	6	.625	138	67	129	3.46	0
2004 Visalia	Calif.		9	44¹/₃	4	1	.800	61	12	29	2.23	0
2005 Modesto	Calif.		14	72¹/₃	5	3	.625	78	40	61	3.98	0
2005 Tulsa	Texas		12	63	2	5	.286	53	31	58	5.43	0
2006 Tulsa	Texas		13	73¹/₃	9	2	.818	86	40	49	2.45	0
2006 Colorado Springs	P.C.		13	78¹/₃	5	2	.714	64	43	74	5.06	0
2006 Colorado	N.L.		2	7²/₃	0	0	.000	3	3	5	3.52	0

Year Club	Lea	G	IP	W	L	Pct	SO	BB	H	ERA	SAVES
2007 Colorado Springs	P.C.	19	103	8	5	.615	89	62	110	5.85	0
2007 Colorado	N.L.	15	82	4	4	.500	68	37	70	4.28	0
2008 Colorado	N.L.	34	198 2/3	12	12	.500	172	103	182	3.99	0
2009 Colorado	N.L.	33	218	15	12	.556	198	85	183	3.47	0
2010 Colorado	N.L.	33	221 2/3	19	8	*.704	214	92	164	2.88	0
2011 Colorado	N.L.	21	123	6	9	.400	118	51	118	4.46	0
2011 Cleveland a-b	A.L.	11	65 1/3	4	4	.500	62	27	68	5.10	0
2012 Cleveland	A.L.	31	176 2/3	9	*17	.346	143	95	190	5.40	0
Major League Totals 7 Yrs.		180	1093	69	66	.511	978	493	980	4.03	0
Division Series											
2007 Colorado	N.L.	1	6 1/3	0	0	.000	5	4	3	1.42	0
2009 Colorado	N.L.	2	12	0	1	.000	11	3	15	5.25	0
Division Series Totals		3	18 1/3	0	1	.000	16	7	18	3.93	0
Championship Series											
2007 Colorado	N.L.	1	5	0	0	.000	6	4	5	1.80	0
World Series Record											
2007 Colorado	N.L.	1	4 2/3	0	1	.000	2	5	3	3.86	0

a On disabled list from April 2 to April 19, 2011.
b Traded to Cleveland Indians for pitcher Alex White, pitcher Joseph Gardner, outfielder Matt McBride and player to be named later, July 31, 2011. Colorado Rockies received pitcher Drew Pomeranz to complete trade, August 17, 2011.

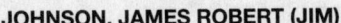

JOHNSON, JAMES ROBERT (JIM)
Born, Johnson City, New York, June 27, 1983.
Bats Right. Throws Right. Height, 6 feet, 5 inches. Weight, 230 pounds.

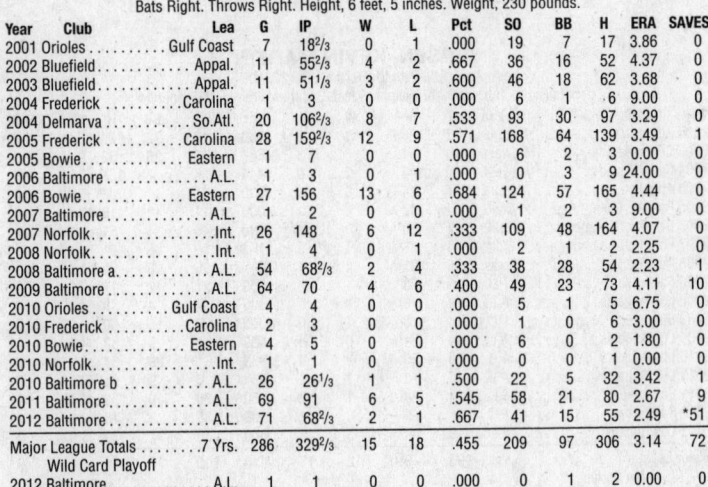

Year Club	Lea	G	IP	W	L	Pct	SO	BB	H	ERA	SAVES
2001 Orioles	Gulf Coast	7	18 2/3	0	1	.000	19	7	17	3.86	0
2002 Bluefield	Appal.	11	55 2/3	4	2	.667	36	16	52	4.37	0
2003 Bluefield	Appal.	11	51 1/3	3	2	.600	46	18	62	3.68	0
2004 Frederick	Carolina	1	3	0	0	.000	6	1	6	9.00	0
2004 Delmarva	So.Atl.	20	106 2/3	8	7	.533	93	30	97	3.29	0
2005 Frederick	Carolina	28	159 2/3	12	9	.571	168	64	139	3.49	1
2005 Bowie	Eastern	1	7	0	0	.000	6	2	3	0.00	0
2006 Baltimore	A.L.	1	3	0	1	.000	0	3	9	24.00	0
2006 Bowie	Eastern	27	156	13	6	.684	124	57	165	4.44	0
2007 Baltimore	A.L.	1	2	0	0	.000	1	2	3	9.00	0
2007 Norfolk	Int.	26	148	6	12	.333	109	48	164	4.07	0
2008 Norfolk	Int.	1	4	0	1	.000	2	1	2	2.25	0
2008 Baltimore a	A.L.	54	68 2/3	2	4	.333	38	28	54	2.23	1
2009 Baltimore	A.L.	64	70	4	6	.400	49	23	73	4.11	10
2010 Orioles	Gulf Coast	4	4	0	0	.000	5	1	5	6.75	0
2010 Frederick	Carolina	2	3	0	0	.000	1	0	6	3.00	0
2010 Bowie	Eastern	4	5	0	0	.000	6	0	2	1.80	0
2010 Norfolk	Int.	1	1	0	0	.000	0	0	1	0.00	0
2010 Baltimore b	A.L.	26	26 1/3	1	1	.500	22	5	32	3.42	1
2011 Baltimore	A.L.	69	91	6	5	.545	58	21	80	2.67	9
2012 Baltimore	A.L.	71	68 2/3	2	1	.667	41	15	55	2.49	*51
Major League Totals 7 Yrs.		286	329 2/3	15	18	.455	209	97	306	3.14	72
Wild Card Playoff											
2012 Baltimore	A.L.	1	1	0	0	.000	0	1	2	0.00	0
Division Series											
2012 Baltimore	A.L.	4	4 1/3	0	1	.000	4	0	6	10.38	2

a On disabled list from September 1 to October 2, 2008.
b On disabled list from May 28 to August 27, 2010.

JOHNSON, JOSHUA MICHAEL (JOSH)
Born, Minneapolis, Minnesota, January 31, 1984.
Bats Left. Throws Right. Height, 6 feet, 7 inches. Weight, 230 pounds.

Year Club	Lea	G	IP	W	L	Pct	SO	BB	H	ERA	SAVES
2002 Marlins	Gulf Coast	4	15	2	0	1.000	11	3	8	0.60	0
2003 Greensboro	So.Atl.	17	82 1/3	4	7	.364	59	29	69	3.61	0
2004 Jupiter	Fla.St.	23	114 1/3	5	12	.294	103	47	124	3.38	0
2005 Carolina	Southern	26	139 2/3	12	4	.750	113	50	139	3.87	0
2005 Florida	N.L.	4	12 1/3	0	0	.000	10	10	11	3.65	0
2006 Florida	N.L.	31	157	12	7	.632	133	68	136	3.10	0
2007 Carolina	Southern	2	10 1/3	0	0	.000	9	5	8	1.74	0
2007 Florida	N.L.	4	15 2/3	0	3	.000	14	12	26	7.47	0
2007 Jupiter a	Fla.St.	3	11 1/3	0	0	.000	13	0	9	0.79	0

Year	Club	Lea	G	IP	W	L	Pct	SO	BB	H	ERA	SAVES
2008	Greensboro	So.Atl.	1	5	0	1	.000	7	0	8	3.60	0
2008	Jupiter	Fla.St.	1	5⅓	0	0	.000	2		6	5.06	0
2008	Carolina	Southern	3	19	1	1	.500	14	3	22	3.32	0
2008	Florida b	N.L.	14	87⅓	7	1	.875	77	27	91	3.61	0
2009	Florida	N.L.	33	209	15	5	.750	191	58	184	3.23	0
2010	Florida	N.L.	28	182⅔	11	6	.647	186	48	155	*2.30	0
2011	Florida c	N.L.	9	60⅓	3	1	.750	56	20	39	1.64	0
2012	Miami d	N.L.	31	191⅓	8	14	.364	165	65	180	3.81	0
Major League Totals		8 Yrs.	154	916⅔	56	37	.602	832	308	822	3.15	0

a On disabled list from March 23 to June 18 and July 5 to November 12, 2007.
b On disabled list from March 21 to July 10, 2008.
c On disabled list from May 17 to October 31, 2011.
d Traded to Toronto Blue Jays with outfielder Emilio Bonifacio, catcher John Buck, pitcher Mark Buehrle and infielder Jose Reyes for pitcher Henderson Alvarez, infielder Yunel Escobar, infielder Adeiny Hechavarria, catcher Jeff Mathis, pitcher Anthony De Sclafani, outfielder Jake Marisnick and pitcher Justin Nicolino, November 19, 2012.

JONES, NATHAN ANDREW (NATE)

Born, Covington, Kentucky, January 28, 1986.
Bats Right. Throws Right. Height, 6 feet, 5 inches. Weight, 185 pounds.

Year	Club	Lea	G	IP	W	L	Pct	SO	BB	H	ERA	SAVES
2007	Bristol	Appal.	13	47⅓	0	4	.000	42	29	44	5.13	0
2008	Bristol	Appal.	4	6⅔	1	0	1.000	12	2	6	1.35	0
2008	Winston-Salem	Carolina	2	2⅔	0	0	.000	1	2	1	3.38	0
2008	Kannapolis	So.Atl.	18	56⅔	1	7	.125	71	35	63	6.83	0
2009	Winston-Salem	Carolina	32	49⅓	2	1	.667	43	13	44	3.65	0
2009	Kannapolis	So.Atl.	13	18⅔	2	0	1.000	25	9	8	2.41	1
2010	Winston-Salem	Carolina	28	152⅓	11	6	.647	109	56	176	4.08	0
2011	Birmingham	Southern	42	63⅓	2	3	.400	67	27	58	3.27	12
2012	Chicago	A.L.	65	71⅔	8	0	1.000	65	32	67	2.39	0

KARSTENS, JEFFREY WAYNE (JEFF)

Born, San Diego, California, September 24, 1982.
Bats Right. Throws Right. Height, 6 feet, 3 inches. Weight, 185 pounds.

Year	Club	Lea	G	IP	W	L	Pct	SO	BB	H	ERA	SAVES
2003	Staten Island	N.Y.-Penn.	14	67⅓	4	2	.667	53	16	63	2.54	0
2004	Tampa	Fla.St.	24	138⅔	6	9	.400	116	31	151	4.02	0
2005	Trenton	Eastern	28	169	12	11	.522	147	42	192	4.15	0
2006	Trenton	Eastern	11	74	6	0	1.000	67	14	54	2.31	0
2006	Columbus	Int.	14	73⅔	5	5	.500	48	30	80	4.28	0
2006	New York	A.L.	8	42⅔	2	1	.667	16	11	40	3.80	0
2007	Tampa	Fla.St.	1	4	0	0	.000	5	1	3	0.00	0
2007	Yankees	Gulf Coast	1	3⅓	0	0	.000	2	1	3	0.00	0
2007	Staten Island	N.Y.-Penn.	1	5	1	0	1.000	8	0	4	1.80	0
2007	Trenton	Eastern	1	5	1	0	1.000	5	2	4	1.80	0
2007	Scranton/WB	Int.	6	31	3	0	1.000	27	9	25	1.74	0
2007	New York a	A.L.	7	14⅔	1	4	.200	5	9	27	11.05	0
2008	Scranton/WB	Int.	12	68⅔	6	4	.600	55	15	66	3.80	0
2008	Pittsburgh b-c	N.L.	9	51⅓	2	6	.250	23	13	56	4.03	0
2009	Indianapolis	Int.	3	6	0	0	.000	7	0	4	0.00	0
2009	Pittsburgh d	N.L.	39	108	4	6	.400	52	45	115	5.42	0
2010	Indianapolis	Int.	5	16	1	2	.333	12	2	21	7.31	0
2010	Pittsburgh	N.L.	26	122⅔	3	10	.231	72	27	146	4.92	0
2011	Pittsburgh	N.L.	30	162⅓	9	9	.500	96	33	163	3.38	0
2012	Altoona	Eastern	2	10	1	0	1.000	6	1	8	0.90	0
2012	Indianapolis	Int.	3	13⅔	0	2	.000	13	3	11	4.61	0
2012	Pittsburgh e-f	N.L.	19	90⅔	5	4	.556	66	15	89	3.97	0
Major League Totals		7 Yrs.	138	592⅓	26	40	.394	330	153	636	4.44	0

a On disabled list from March 26 to April 21 and April 29 to August 1, 2007.
b On disabled list from March 28 to May 20, 2008.
c Traded to Pittsburgh Pirates with outfielder Jose Tabata, pitcher Ross Ohlendorf and pitcher Dan McCutchen for outfielder Xavier Nady and pitcher Damaso Marte, July 26, 2008.
d On disabled list from August 25 to September 9, 2009.
e On disabled list from April 18 to June 25, 2012.
f Not offered contract, November 30, 2012. Signed with Pittsburgh Pirates, January 15, 2013.

KELLEY, SHAWN ANDREW
Born, Louisville, Kentucky, April 26, 1984.
Bats Right. Throws Right. Height, 6 feet, 2 inches. Weight, 215 pounds.

Year	Club	Lea	G	IP	W	L	Pct	SO	BB	H	ERA	SAVES
2007	Wisconsin	Midwest	9	12	1	1	.500	14	4	16	2.25	0
2007	Everett	Northwest	3	3	1	0	1.000	4	0	2	3.00	0
2008	High Desert	Calif.	12	12	0	0	.000	12	3	8	0.00	3
2008	Wisconsin	Midwest	8	7²/₃	0	0	.000	12	2	10	3.52	3
2008	West Tenn	Southern	29	42²/₃	3	1	.750	44	17	31	2.11	9
2009	Mariners	Arizona	2	2	0	0	.000	3	0	0	0.00	0
2009	Tacoma	P.C.	1	1	0	0	.000	0	0	0	0.00	0
2009	Seattle a	A.L.	41	46	5	4	.556	41	9	45	4.50	0
2010	Tacoma	P.C.	3	3²/₃	0	0	.000	6	3	1	4.91	1
2010	Seattle b	A.L.	22	25	3	1	.750	26	12	26	3.96	0
2011	Jackson	Southern	3	3	0	1	.000	3	0	4	0.00	0
2011	Tacoma	P.C.	12	14²/₃	1	0	1.000	15	6	11	1.84	0
2011	Seattle c	A.L.	10	12²/₃	0	0	.000	10	3	7	0.00	0
2012	Tacoma	P.C.	14	20	2	0	1.000	25	4	9	0.90	6
2012	Seattle	A.L.	47	44¹/₃	2	4	.333	45	15	43	3.25	0

Major League Totals ....4 Yrs. 120 128 10 9 .526 122 39 121 3.52

a On disabled list from May 6 to July 3, 2009.
b On disabled list from June 16 to October 8, 2010.
c On disabled list from March 2 to August 9, 2011.

KELLY, JOSEPH WILLIAM (JOE)
Born, Anaheim, California, June 9, 1988.
Bats Right. Throws Right. Height, 6 feet, 1 inch. Weight, 185 pounds.

Year	Club	Lea	G	IP	W	L	Pct	SO	BB	H	ERA	SAVES
2009	Batavia	N.Y.-Penn.	16	30¹/₃	2	3	.400	30	11	33	4.75	1
2010	Quad Cities	Midwest	26	103¹/₃	6	8	.429	92	45	103	4.62	1
2011	Palm Beach	Fla.St.	12	72²/₃	5	2	.714	62	34	56	2.60	0
2011	Springfield	Texas	11	59¹/₃	6	4	.600	51	25	70	5.01	0
2012	Memphis	P.C.	12	72¹/₃	2	5	.286	45	21	75	2.86	0
2012	St. Louis	N.L.	24	107	5	7	.417	75	36	112	3.53	0
	Division Series											
2012	St. Louis	N.L.	3	3²/₃	0	0	.000	3	1	0	0.00	0
	Championship Series											
2012	St. Louis	N.L.	4	4	0	0	.000	2	3	6	4.50	0

KENDRICK, KYLE RODNEY
Born, Houston, Texas, August 26, 1984.
Bats Right. Throws Right. Height, 6 feet, 3 inches. Weight, 190 pounds.

Year	Club	Lea	G	IP	W	L	Pct	SO	BB	H	ERA	SAVES
2003	Phillies	Gulf Coast	9	31¹/₃	0	4	.000	26	12	40	5.46	0
2004	Batavia	N.Y.-Penn.	13	70²/₃	2	8	.200	53	18	94	5.48	0
2004	Lakewood	So.Atl.	15	66²/₃	3	8	.273	36	33	85	6.07	0
2005	Clearwater	Fla.St.	1	4	0	1	.000	1	2	5	0.00	0
2005	Batavia	N.Y.-Penn.	14	91¹/₃	5	4	.556	70	22	94	3.74	0
2005	Lakewood	So.Atl.	5	22²/₃	0	3	.000	11	10	38	9.13	0
2006	Clearwater	Fla.St.	21	130	9	7	.563	79	37	117	3.53	0
2006	Lakewood	So.Atl.	7	46	3	2	.600	54	15	34	2.15	0
2007	Reading	Eastern	12	81¹/₃	4	7	.364	50	18	82	3.21	0
2007	Philadelphia	N.L.	20	121	10	4	.714	49	25	129	3.87	0
2008	Philadelphia	N.L.	31	155²/₃	11	9	.550	68	57	194	5.49	0
2009	Lehigh Valley	Int.	24	143	9	7	.563	62	35	133	3.34	0
2009	Philadelphia	N.L.	9	26¹/₃	3	1	.750	15	9	27	3.42	0
2010	Philadelphia	N.L.	33	180²/₃	11	10	.524	84	49	199	4.73	0
2011	Philadelphia	N.L.	34	114²/₃	8	6	.571	59	30	110	3.22	0
2012	Philadelphia	N.L.	37	159¹/₃	11	12	.478	116	49	154	3.90	0

Major League Totals ....6 Yrs. 164 757²/₃ 54 42 .563 391 219 813 4.30

Division Series
| 2007 | Philadelphia | N.L. | 1 | 3²/₃ | 0 | 1 | .000 | 2 | 2 | 5 | 12.27 | 0 |

KENNEDY, IAN PATRICK

Born, Huntington Beach, California, December 19, 1984.
Bats Right. Throws Right. Height, 6 feet. Weight, 195 pounds.

Year	Club	Lea	G	IP	W	L	Pct	SO	BB	H	ERA	SAVES
2006 Staten Island	N.Y.-Penn.	1	2²/₃	0	0	.000	2	2	2	0.00	0
2007 Tampa	Fla.St.	11	63	6	1	.857	72	22	39	1.29	0
2007 Trenton	Eastern	9	48²/₃	5	1	.833	57	17	27	2.59	0
2007 Scranton/WB	Int.	6	34²/₃	1	1	.500	34	11	25	2.08	0
2007 New York	A.L.	3	19	1	0	1.000	15	9	13	1.89	0
2008 Yankees	Gulf Coast	1	3	1	0	1.000	7	0	3	3.00	0
2008 Tampa	Fla.St.	1	5	0	0	.000	4	1	2	0.00	0
2008 New York	A.L.	10	39²/₃	0	4	.000	27	26	50	8.17	0
2008 Scranton/WB a	Int.	13	69	5	3	.625	72	17	52	2.35	0
2009 Scranton/WB	Int.	4	22²/₃	1	0	1.000	25	7	18	1.59	0
2009 New York b-c	A.L.	1	1	0	0	.000	1	2	0	0.00	0
2010 Arizona	N.L.	32	194	9	10	.474	168	70	163	3.80	0
2011 Arizona	N.L.	33	222	*21	4	*.840	198	55	186	2.88	0
2012 Arizona	N.L.	33	208¹/₃	15	12	.556	187	55	216	4.02	0
Major League Totals	6 Yrs.	112	684	46	30	.605	596	217	628	3.76	0
Division Series											
2011 Arizona	N.L.	2	12²/₃	0	1	.000	8	3	13	4.26	0

a On disabled list from May 28 to June 24, 2008.
b Traded to Detroit Tigers with outfielder Austin Jackson and pitcher Phil Coke for outfielder Curtis Granderson, December 9, 2009.
c Traded to Arizona Diamondbacks with pitcher Edwin Jackson for pitcher Daniel Schlereth and pitcher Max Scherzer, December 9, 2009.

KERSHAW, CLAYTON EDWARD

Born, Dallas, Texas, March 19, 1988.
Bats Left. Throws Left. Height, 6 feet, 3 inches. Weight, 220 pounds.

Year	Club	Lea	G	IP	W	L	Pct	SO	BB	H	ERA	SAVES
2006 Dodgers	Gulf Coast	10	37	2	0	1.000	54	5	28	1.95	1
2007 Great Lakes	Midwest	20	97¹/₃	7	5	.583	134	50	72	2.77	0
2007 Jacksonville	Southern	5	24²/₃	1	2	.333	29	17	17	3.65	0
2008 Jacksonville	Southern	13	61¹/₃	2	3	.400	59	19	39	1.91	0
2008 Los Angeles	N.L.	22	107²/₃	5	5	.500	100	52	109	4.26	0
2009 Los Angeles	N.L.	31	171	8	8	.500	185	91	119	2.79	0
2010 Los Angeles	N.L.	32	204¹/₃	13	10	.565	212	81	160	2.91	0
2011 Los Angeles a	N.L.	33	233¹/₃	*21	5	.808	*248	54	174	*2.28	0
2012 Los Angeles	N.L.	33	227²/₃	14	9	.609	229	63	170	*2.53	0
Major League Totals	5 Yrs.	151	944	61	37	.622	974	341	732	2.79	0
Division Series											
2009 Los Angeles	N.L.	1	6²/₃	0	0	.000	4	1	9	2.70	0
Championship Series											
2008 Los Angeles	N.L.	2	2	0	0	.000	1	2	1	4.50	0
2009 Los Angeles	N.L.	2	6²/₃	0	1	.000	6	6	5	9.45	0
Championship Series Totals		4	8²/₃	0	1	.000	7	8	6	8.31	0

a Selected Cy Young Award Winner in National League for 2011.

KEUCHEL, DALLAS

Born, Tulsa, Oklahoma, January 1, 1988.
Bats Left. Throws Left. Height, 6 feet, 3 inches. Weight, 210 pounds.

Year	Club	Lea	G	IP	W	L	Pct	SO	BB	H	ERA	SAVES
2009 Tri-City	N.Y.-Penn.	11	56²/₃	2	3	.400	44	9	52	2.70	0
2010 Lancaster	Calif.	19	120¹/₃	5	8	.385	97	25	129	3.36	0
2010 Corpus Christi	Texas	9	53²/₃	2	6	.250	36	11	59	4.70	0
2011 Oklahoma	P.C.	7	36	1	1	.500	15	12	52	7.50	0
2011 Corpus Christi	Texas	20	127²/₃	9	7	.563	76	27	116	3.17	0
2012 Oklahoma	P.C.	16	92¹/₃	6	4	.600	50	20	92	3.90	0
2012 Houston	N.L.	16	85¹/₃	3	8	.273	38	39	93	5.27	0

KIMBREL, CRAIG MICHAEL

Born, Huntsville, Alabama, May 28, 1988.
Bats Right. Throws Right. Height, 5 feet, 11 inches. Weight, 205 pounds.

Year	Club	Lea	G	IP	W	L	Pct	SO	BB	H	ERA	SAVES
2008 Danville	Appal.	12	19	1	2	.333	27	10	5	0.47	6
2008 Myrtle Beach	Carolina	2	3²/₃	0	0	.000	3	1	5	0.00	0

Year	Club	Lea	G	IP	W	L	Pct	SO	BB	H	ERA	SAVES
2008 Rome	So.Atl.	10	12²/3	2	0	1.000	26	4	6	0.71	4	
2009 Myrtle Beach	Carolina	19	26¹/3	0	2	.000	45	28	18	5.47	2	
2009 Gwinnett	Int.	2	2	0	0	.000	3	4	0	0.00	0	
2009 Rome	So.Atl.	16	20	0	0	.000	38	6	9	0.90	10	
2009 Mississippi	Southern	12	11²/3	2	1	.667	17	7	3	0.77	6	
2010 Gwinnett	Int.	48	55²/3	3	2	.600	83	35	28	1.62	23	
2010 Atlanta	N.L.	21	20²/3	4	0	1.000	40	16	9	0.44	1	
2011 Atlanta a	N.L.	79	77	4	3	.571	127	32	48	2.10	*46	
2012 Atlanta	N.L.	63	62²/3	3	1	.750	116	14	27	1.01	*42	
Major League Totals	3 Yrs.	163	160¹/3	11	4	.733	283	62	84	1.46	89	
Wild Card Playoff												
2012 Atlanta	N.L.	1	1	0	0	.000	1	0	0	0.00	0	
Division Series												
2010 Atlanta	N.L.	4	4¹/3	0	1	.000	7	1	1	2.08	0	

a Selected Rookie of the Year in National League for 2011.

KONTOS, GEORGE NICHOLAS

Born, Lincolnwood, Illinois, June 12, 1985.
Bats Right. Throws Right. Height, 6 feet, 3 inches. Weight, 225 pounds.

Year	Club	Lea	G	IP	W	L	Pct	SO	BB	H	ERA	SAVES
2006 Staten Island	N.Y.-Penn.	14	78¹/3	7	3	.700	82	19	64	2.64	0
2007 Tampa	Fla.St.	19	94	4	6	.400	101	30	95	4.02	0
2008 Trenton	Eastern	27	151²/3	6	11	.353	152	57	134	3.68	0
2009 Trenton	Eastern	4	20¹/3	1	1	.500	24	9	19	2.66	0
2009 Scranton-WB	Int.	9	51	3	4	.429	39	21	44	3.35	0
2010 Trenton	Eastern	17	32	0	2	.000	28	11	30	3.38	0
2010 Tampa	Fla.St.	5	10¹/3	0	1	.000	8	3	7	2.61	0
2010 Scranton-WB	Int.	2	2²/3	0	1	.000	2	1	5	10.13	0
2011 Scranton-WB	Int.	40	89¹/3	4	4	.500	91	26	72	2.62	2
2011 New York a	A.L.	7	6	0	0	.000	6	3	4	3.00	0
2012 Fresno	P.C.	23	31²/3	2	0	1.000	26	7	24	1.71	1
2012 San Francisco b	N.L.	44	43²/3	2	1	.667	44	12	34	2.47	0
Major League Totals	2 Yrs.	51	49²/3	2	1	.667	50	15	38	2.54	0
Division Series												
2012 San Francisco	N.L.	4	3²/3	0	0	.000	2	0	2	0.00	0
Championship Series												
2012 San Francisco	N.L.	3	1¹/3	0	0	.000	0	0	2	13.50	0
World Series Record												
2012 San Francisco	N.L.	1	0¹/3	0	0	.000	0	1	2	54.00	0

a Selected by San Diego Padres from New York Yankees in Rule V draft, December 9, 2010. Returned by San Diego Padres, March 14, 2011.
b Traded to San Francisco Giants for catcher Chris Stewart, April 4, 2012.

KURODA, HIROKI

Born, Osaka, Japan, February 10, 1975.
Bats Right. Throws Right. Height, 6 feet, 1 inch. Weight, 210 pounds.

Year	Club	Lea	G	IP	W	L	Pct	SO	BB	H	ERA	SAVES
1997 Hiroshima	Japan Cent.	23	135	6	9	.400	64	63	147	4.40	0
1998 Hiroshima	Japan Cent.	18	45	1	4	.200	25	24	53	6.60	0
1999 Hiroshima	Japan Cent.	21	87²/3	5	8	.385	55	39	106	6.78	0
2000 Hiroshima	Japan Cent.	29	144	9	6	.600	116	61	147	4.31	0
2001 Hiroshima	Japan Cent.	27	190	12	8	.600	146	45	175	3.03	0
2002 Hiroshima	Japan Cent.	23	164¹/3	10	10	.500	144	34	166	3.67	0
2003 Hiroshima	Japan Cent.	28	205²/3	13	9	.591	137	45	197	3.11	0
2004 Hiroshima	Japan Cent.	21	147	7	9	.438	138	29	187	4.65	0
2005 Hiroshima	Japan Cent.	29	212²/3	15	12	.556	165	42	183	3.17	0
2006 Hiroshima	Japan Cent.	26	189¹/3	13	6	.684	144	21	169	1.85	1
2007 Hiroshima	Japan Cent.	26	179²/3	12	8	.600	123	42	176	3.56	0
2008 Los Angeles b	N.L.	31	183¹/3	9	10	.474	116	42	181	3.73	0
2009 Los Angeles c	N.L.	21	117¹/3	8	7	.533	87	24	110	3.76	0
2010 Los Angeles d	N.L.	31	196¹/3	11	13	.458	159	48	180	3.39	0
2011 Los Angeles e	N.L.	32	202	13	16	.448	161	49	196	3.07	0
2012 New York f	A.L.	33	219²/3	16	11	.593	167	51	205	3.32	0
Major League Totals	5 Yrs.	148	918²/3	57	57	.500	690	214	872	3.42	0
Division Series												
2008 Los Angeles	N.L.	1	6¹/3	1	0	1.000	4	2	6	0.00	0
2012 New York	A.L.	1	8¹/3	0	0	.000	3	1	5	2.16	0
Division Series Totals		2	14²/3	1	0	1.000	7	3	11	1.23	0

Year	Club	Lea	G	IP	W	L	Pct	SO	BB	H	ERA	SAVES
	Championship Series											
2008	Los Angeles	N.L.	1	6	1	0	1.000	3	1	5	3.00	0
2009	Los Angeles	N.L.	1	1⅓	0	1	.000	1	0	6	40.50	0
2012	New York	A.L.	1	7⅔	0	1	.000	11	0	5	3.52	0
	Championship Series Totals		3	15	1	2	.333	15	1	16	6.60	0

a Signed with Los Angeles Dodgers, December 16, 2007.
b On disabled list from June 13 to July 2, 2008.
c On disabled list from April 7 to June 1 and August 16 to September 6, 2009.
d Filed for free agency, November 1, 2010, re-signed with Los Angeles Dodgers, November 15, 2010.
e Filed for free agency, October 30, 2011. Signed with New York Yankees, January 26, 2012.
f Filed for free agency, November 3, 2012, re-signed with New York Yankees, November 20, 2012.

LAFFEY, AARON STEVEN

Born, Cumberland, Maryland, April 15, 1985.
Bats Left. Throws Left. Height, 6 feet. Weight, 185 pounds.

Year	Club	Lea	G	IP	W	L	Pct	SO	BB	H	ERA	SAVES
2003	Burlington	Appal.	9	34	3	1	.750	46	15	22	2.91	0
2004	Mahoning Valley	N.Y.-Penn.	8	43⅔	3	1	.750	30	10	38	1.24	0
2004	Lake County	So.Atl.	19	74	3	7	.300	69	44	79	6.45	1
2005	Akron	Eastern	1	5	1	0	1.000	6	2	8	3.60	0
2005	Lake County	Midwest	25	142⅓	7	7	.500	69	52	123	3.22	1
2006	Kinston	Carolina	10	41⅓	4	1	.800	24	6	38	2.18	1
2006	Akron	Eastern	19	112⅓	8	3	.727	61	33	121	3.53	0
2007	Akron	Eastern	6	35	4	1	.800	24	7	29	2.31	0
2007	Buffalo	Int.	16	96⅓	9	3	.750	75	23	89	3.08	0
2007	Cleveland	A.L.	9	49⅓	4	2	.667	25	12	54	4.56	0
2008	Buffalo	Int.	11	61⅔	6	2	.750	47	18	72	4.38	0
2008	Cleveland	A.L.	16	93⅔	5	7	.417	43	31	103	4.23	0
2009	Akron	Eastern	2	7⅓	0	0	.000	6	1	6	3.68	0
2009	Columbus	Int.	3	10⅓	0	2	.000	4	5	21	11.32	0
2009	Cleveland a	A.L.	25	121⅔	7	9	.438	59	57	140	4.44	1
2010	Lake County	Midwest	2	2	0	0	.000	3	0	2	4.50	0
2010	Akron	Eastern	1	1	0	0	.000	0	0	1	0.00	0
2010	Columbus	Int.	10	27	0	1	.000	12	16	29	3.67	0
2010	Cleveland b	A.L.	29	55⅔	2	3	.400	28	28	62	4.53	0
2011	Scranton-WB	Int.	2	33⅓	0	1	.000	1	2	5	7.36	0
2011	Seattle-New York c-d-e-f	A.L.	47	53⅓	3	2	.600	30	21	67	3.88	0
2012	Las Vegas	P.C.	11	63⅔	3	5	.375	38	20	77	4.52	0
2012	Toronto g	A.L.	22	100⅔	4	6	.400	48	37	100	4.56	0
	Major League Totals	6 Yrs.	148	474⅓	25	29	.463	233	186	526	4.38	1
	Championship Series											
2007	Cleveland	A.L.	1	4⅔	0	0	.000	3	1	1	0.00	0

a On disabled list from May 23 to July 8, 2009.
b On disabled list from July 20 to August 31, 2010.
c Traded to Seattle Mariners for infielder Matt Lawson, March 2, 2011.
d Claimed on waivers by New York Yankees, August 19, 2011.
e Claimed on waivers by Kansas City Royals, October 11, 2011.
f Not offered contract, December 12, 2011. Signed with Toronto Blue Jays organization, December 31, 2011.
g Filed for free agency, November 3, 2012. Signed with New York Mets organization, December 27, 2012.

LANNAN, JOHN EDWARD

Born, Long Beach, New York, September 27, 1984.
Bats Left. Throws Left. Height, 6 feet, 5 inches. Weight, 225 pounds.

Year	Club	Lea	G	IP	W	L	Pct	SO	BB	H	ERA	SAVES
2005	Vermont	N.Y.-Penn.	14	63⅓	3	5	.375	41	31	74	5.26	0
2006	Savannah	So.Atl.	27	138	6	8	.429	114	54	149	4.76	0
2007	Potomac	Carolina	8	50⅔	6	0	1.000	35	15	31	2.13	0
2007	Harrisburg	Eastern	6	36	3	2	.600	20	15	31	3.25	0
2007	Columbus	Int.	7	38	3	1	.750	19	12	30	1.66	0
2007	Washington	N.L.	6	34⅔	2	2	.500	10	17	36	4.15	0
2008	Washington	N.L.	31	182	9	15	.375	117	72	172	3.91	0
2009	Washington	N.L.	33	206⅓	9	13	.409	89	68	210	3.88	0
2010	Harrisburg	Eastern	7	40⅔	1	4	.200	28	10	49	4.20	0
2010	Washington	N.L.	25	143⅓	8	8	.500	71	49	175	4.65	0
2011	Washington	N.L.	33	184⅔	10	13	.435	106	76	194	3.70	0
2012	Syracuse	Int.	24	148⅔	9	11	.450	86	50	164	4.30	0
2012	Washington a	N.L.	6	32⅔	4	1	.800	17	14	33	4.13	0
	Major League Totals	6 Yrs.	134	783⅔	42	52	.447	410	296	820	4.01	0

a Not offered contract, November 30, 2012. Signed with Philadelphia Phillies, December 18, 2012.

LATOS, MATHEW ADAM (MAT)

Born, Alexandria, Virginia, December 9, 1987.
Bats Right. Throws Right. Height, 6 feet, 6 inches. Weight, 225 pounds.

Year	Club	Lea	G	IP	W	L	Pct	SO	BB	H	ERA	SAVES
2007 Eugene		Northwest	16	56¹/₃	1	4	.200	74	22	58	3.83	0
2008 Padres		Arizona	5	14	1	0	1.000	23	2	12	3.21	0
2008 Fort Wayne		Midwest	7	24²/₃	0	3	.000	23	8	24	3.28	0
2008 Eugene		Northwest	3	17¹/₃	2	0	1.000	23	3	13	1.04	0
2009 Fort Wayne		Midwest	4	25¹/₃	3	0	1.000	27	3	10	0.36	0
2009 San Antonio		Texas	9	47	5	1	.833	46	9	32	1.91	0
2009 San Diego		N.L.	10	50²/₃	4	5	.444	39	23	43	4.62	0
2010 San Diego a		N.L.	31	184²/₃	14	10	.583	189	50	150	2.92	0
2011 San Diego b-c		N.L.	31	194¹/₃	9	14	.391	185	62	168	3.47	0
2012 Cincinnati		N.L.	33	209¹/₃	14	4	.778	185	64	179	3.48	0
Major League Totals	4 Yrs.		105	639	41	33	.554	598	199	540	3.41	0
Division Series												
2012 Cincinnati		N.L.	2	8¹/₃	0	1	.000	5	2	11	6.48	0

a On disabled list from July 9 to July 24, 2010.
b On disabled list from March 22 to April 11, 2011.
c Traded to Cincinnati Reds for pitcher Edinson Volquez, pitcher Brad Boxberger, catcher Yasmani Grandal and infielder Yonder Alonso, December 17, 2011.

LEAGUE, BRANDON PAUL

Born, Sacramento, California, March 16, 1983.
Bats Right. Throws Right. Height, 6 feet, 3 inches. Weight, 200 pounds.

Year	Club	Lea	G	IP	W	L	Pct	SO	BB	H	ERA	SAVES
2001 Medicine Hat		Pioneer	9	38²/₃	2	2	.500	38	11	36	4.66	0
2002 Auburn		N.Y.-Penn.	16	85²/₃	7	2	.778	72	23	80	3.15	0
2003 Dunedin		Fla.St.	13	66¹/₃	4	3	.571	34	20	76	4.75	0
2003 Charleston		So.Atl.	12	70²/₃	2	3	.400	61	18	58	1.91	0
2004 New Hampshire		Eastern	41	104	6	4	.600	90	41	92	3.38	2
2004 Toronto		A.L.	3	4²/₃	1	0	1.000	2	1	3	0.00	0
2005 Syracuse		Int.	19	63	4	4	.500	35	18	78	5.71	0
2005 Toronto		A.L.	20	35²/₃	1	0	1.000	17	20	42	6.56	0
2006 Syracuse		Int.	31	54²/₃	3	2	.600	43	15	57	2.14	8
2006 Toronto		A.L.	33	42²/₃	1	2	.333	29	9	34	2.53	1
2007 Syracuse		Int.	11	12	0	0	.000	10	6	12	3.00	0
2007 Blue Jays		Gulf Coast	1	1	0	0	.000	1	0	1	0.00	0
2007 Dunedin		Fla.St.	4	6	0	0	.000	6	2	5	4.50	0
2007 New Hampshire		Eastern	6	7²/₃	1	1	.500	7	7	5	3.52	0
2007 Toronto a		A.L.	14	11²/₃	0	0	.000	7	7	19	6.17	0
2008 Syracuse		Int.	20	34¹/₃	2	3	.400	32	10	36	3.93	2
2008 Toronto		A.L.	31	33	1	2	.333	23	15	28	2.18	1
2009 Toronto b		A.L.	67	74²/₃	3	6	.333	76	21	72	4.58	0
2010 Seattle		A.L.	70	79	9	7	.563	56	27	67	3.42	6
2011 Seattle		A.L.	65	61¹/₃	1	5	.167	45	10	56	2.79	37
2012 Seattle		A.L.	46	44²/₃	0	5	.000	27	19	48	3.63	9
2012 Los Angeles c		N.L.	28	27¹/₃	2	1	.667	27	14	17	2.30	6
Major League Totals	377		414²/₃	19	28	.404	309	143	386	3.60	60	

a On disabled list from March 31 to July 15 and August 5 to September 4, 2007.
b Traded to Seattle Mariners with outfielder Johermyn Chavez for pitcher Brandon Morrow, December 23, 2009.
c Traded to Los Angeles Dodgers for pitcher Logan Bawcom and outfielder Leon Landry, July 31, 2012.

LEAKE, MICHAEL RAYMOND (MIKE)

Born, San Diego, California, November 12, 1987.
Bats Right. Throws Right. Height, 6 feet, 1 inch. Weight, 190 pounds.

Year	Club	Lea	G	IP	W	L	Pct	SO	BB	H	ERA	SAVES
2010 Cincinnati a		N.L.	24	138¹/₃	8	4	.667	91	49	158	4.23	0
2011 Louisville		Int.	2	7¹/₃	0	1	.000	5	0	12	9.82	0
2011 Cincinnati		N.L.	29	167²/₃	12	9	.571	118	38	159	3.86	0
2012 Cincinnati		N.L.	30	179	8	9	.471	116	41	201	4.58	0
Major League Totals	3 Yrs.		83	485	28	22	.560	325	128	518	4.23	0
Division Series												
2012 Cincinnati		N.L.	1	4¹/₃	0	1	.000	1	2	6	10.38	0

a On disabled list from August 25 to September 10, 2010.

LE BLANC, WADE MATTHEW

Born, Lake Charles, Louisiana, August 7, 1984.
Bats Left. Throws Left. Height, 6 feet, 3 inches. Weight, 215 pounds.

Year Club	Lea	G	IP	W	L	Pct	SO	BB	H	ERA	SAVES
2006 Fort Wayne	Midwest	7	32²/₃	4	1	.800	27	10	31	2.20	0
2006 Eugene	Northwest	7	21	1	0	1.000	20	6	19	4.29	0
2007 Lake Elsinore	Calif.	16	92	6	5	.545	90	17	72	2.64	0
2007 San Antonio	Texas	12	57¹/₃	7	3	.700	55	19	48	3.45	0
2008 Portland	P.C.	26	138²/₃	11	9	.550	139	42	136	5.32	0
2008 San Diego	N.L.	5	21¹/₃	1	3	.250	14	15	29	8.02	0
2009 Portland	P.C.	24	121	4	9	.308	95	31	109	3.87	0
2009 San Diego	N.L.	9	46¹/₃	3	1	.750	30	19	35	3.69	0
2010 Portland	P.C.	2	10	0	1	.000	15	1	13	7.20	0
2010 San Diego	N.L.	26	146	8	12	.400	110	51	157	4.25	0
2011 Tucson	P.C.	17	106²/₃	9	1	.900	92	28	108	4.30	0
2011 San Diego a	N.L.	14	79²/₃	5	6	.455	51	28	84	4.63	0
2012 New Orleans	P.C.	16	98²/₃	5	5	.500	91	20	91	3.74	0
2012 Miami	N.L.	25	68²/₃	2	5	.286	43	19	71	3.67	0
Major League Totals ...... 5 Yrs.		79	362	19	27	.413	248	132	376	4.38	0

a Traded to Miami Marlins for catcher Jon Baker, November 22, 2011.

LE CURE, SAMUEL R. (SAM)

Born, Jefferson City, Missouri, May 4, 1984.
Bats Right. Throws Right. Height, 6 feet, 1 inch. Weight, 205 pounds.

Year Club	Lea	G	IP	W	L	Pct	SO	BB	H	ERA	SAVES
2005 Billings	Pioneer	13	41¹/₃	5	1	.833	44	15	43	3.27	0
2006 Sarasota	Fla.St.	27	141²/₃	7	12	.368	115	46	130	3.43	0
2007 Sarasota	Fla.St.	1	5	1	0	1.000	8	0	2	1.80	0
2007 Chattanooga	Southern	21	110	7	5	.583	104	46	119	4.17	0
2008 Chattanooga	Southern	27	155¹/₃	9	7	.563	128	58	147	3.42	0
2009 Louisville	Int.	25	143¹/₃	10	8	.556	125	44	143	4.46	0
2010 Louisville	Int.	15	98	8	3	.727	87	23	98	3.67	0
2010 Cincinnati	N.L.	15	48	2	5	.286	37	25	50	4.50	0
2011 Louisville	Int.	4	6²/₃	0	1	.000	6	2	5	1.35	1
2011 Cincinnati a	N.L.	43	77²/₃	2	1	.667	73	21	57	3.71	0
2012 Cincinnati	N.L.	48	57¹/₃	3	3	.500	61	23	46	3.14	0
Major League Totals ...... 3 Yrs.		106	183	7	9	.438	171	69	153	3.74	0
Division Series											
2012 Cincinnati	N.L.	3	4	1	0	1.000	5	2	2	0.00	0

a On disabled list from May 29 to June 22, 2011.

LEE, CLIFTON PHIFER (CLIFF)

Born, Benton, Arkansas, August 30, 1978.
Bats Left. Throws Left. Height, 6 feet, 3 inches. Weight, 190 pounds.

Year Club	Lea	G	IP	W	L	Pct	SO	BB	H	ERA	SAVES
2000 Cape Fear	So.Atl.	11	44²/₃	1	4	.200	63	36	50	5.24	0
2001 Jupiter	Fla.St.	21	109²/₃	6	7	.462	179	46	78	2.79	0
2002 Harrisburg	Eastern	15	86¹/₃	7	2	.778	105	23	61	3.23	0
2002 Akron	Eastern	3	16²/₃	2	1	.667	18	10	11	5.40	0
2002 Buffalo	Int.	8	43	3	2	.600	30	22	36	3.77	0
2002 Cleveland a-b	A.L.	2	10¹/₃	0	1	.000	6	8	6	1.74	0
2003 Buffalo	Int.	11	63¹/₃	6	1	.857	61	31	62	3.27	0
2003 Kinston	Carolina	1	4¹/₃	0	0	.000	4	3	0	0.00	0
2003 Akron	Eastern	2	12	1	0	1.000	13	4	7	1.50	0
2003 Cleveland c	A.L.	9	52¹/₃	3	3	.500	44	20	41	3.61	0
2004 Cleveland	A.L.	33	179	14	8	.636	161	81	188	5.43	0
2005 Cleveland	A.L.	32	202	18	5	*.783	143	52	194	3.79	0
2006 Cleveland	A.L.	33	200²/₃	14	11	.560	129	58	224	4.40	0
2007 Kinston	Carolina	1	2	0	0	.000	4	0	1	0.00	0
2007 Akron	Eastern	1	5	1	0	1.000	7	1	2	0.00	0
2007 Buffalo	Int.	8	41	1	3	.250	50	25	32	3.51	0
2007 Cleveland d	A.L.	20	97¹/₃	5	8	.385	66	36	112	6.29	0
2008 Cleveland e	A.L.	31	223¹/₃	*22	3	*.880	170	34	214	*2.54	0
2009 Philadelphia	N.L.	12	79²/₃	7	4	.636	74	10	80	3.39	0
2009 Cleveland f-g	A.L.	22	152	7	9	.438	107	33	165	3.14	0
2010 Tacoma	P.C.	1	6	0	0	.000	4	0	3	0.00	0
2010 Seattle-Texas h-i-j	A.L.	28	212¹/₃	12	9	.571	185	18	195	3.18	0
2011 Philadelphia	N.L.	32	232²/₃	17	8	.680	238	42	197	2.40	0

Year Club	Lea	G	IP	W	L	Pct	SO	BB	H	ERA	SAVES
2012 Philadelphia k.........	N.L.	30	211	6	9	.400	207	28	207	3.16	0
Major League Totals ...... 11 Yrs.		284	1852²/₃	125	78	.616	1530	420	1823	3.59	0
Division Series											
2009 Philadelphia...........	N.L.	2	16¹/₃	1	0	1.000	10	3	11	1.10	0
2010 Texas	A.L.	2	16	2	0	1.000	21	0	11	1.13	0
2011 Philadelphia	N.L.	1	6	0	1	.000	9	2	12	7.50	0
Division Series Totals		5	38¹/₃	3	1	.750	40	5	34	2.11	0
Championship Series											
2009 Philadelphia...........	N.L.	1	8	1	0	1.000	10	0	3	0.00	0
2010 Texas	A.L.	1	8	1	0	1.000	13	1	2	0.00	0
Championship Series Totals		2	16	2	0	1.000	23	1	5	0.00	0
World Series Record											
2009 Philadelphia...........	N.L.	2	16	2	0	1.000	13	3	13	2.81	0
2010 Texas	A.L.	2	11²/₃	0	2	.000	13	1	14	6.94	0
World Series Totals...........		4	27²/₃	2	2	.500	26	4	27	4.55	0

a Traded to Cleveland Indians with infielder Lee Stevens, infielder Brandon Phillips and outfielder Grady Sizemore for pitcher Bartolo Colon and player to be named later, June 27, 2002.
b Montreal Expos received pitcher Tim Drew to complete trade, June 28, 2002.
c On disabled list from March 29 to May 30, 2003.
d On disabled list from March 23 to May 3, 2007.
e Selected Cy Young Award Winner in American League for 2008.
f Traded to Philadelphia Phillies with outfielder Ben Francisco for catcher Lou Marson, pitcher Jason Knapp, infielder Jason Donald and pitcher Carlos Carrasco, July 29, 2009.
g Traded to Seattle Mariners for outfielder J.C. Ramirez, pitcher Phillippe Aumont and outfielder Tyson Gillies, December 16, 2009.
h On disabled list from March 26 to April 30, 2010.
i Traded to Texas Rangers with pitcher Mark Lowe and cash for infielder Justin Smoak, pitcher Blake Beavan, pitcher Josh Lueke and infielder Matt Lawson, July 9, 2010.
j Filed for free agency, November 1, 2010. Signed with Philadelphia Phillies, December 15, 2010.
k On disabled list from April 19 to May 9, 2012.

LESTER, JONATHAN TYLER (JON)
Born, Tacoma, Washington, January 7, 1984.
Bats Left. Throws Left. Height, 6 feet, 2 inches. Weight, 190 pounds.

Year Club	Lea	G	IP	W	L	Pct	SO	BB	H	ERA	SAVES
2002 Red Sox	Gulf Coast	1	0²/₃	0	1	.000	1	1	5	13.50	0
2003 Augusta...........	So.Atl.	24	106	6	9	.400	71	44	102	3.65	0
2004 Sarasota...........	Fla.St.	21	90¹/₃	7	6	.538	97	37	82	4.28	0
2004 Red Sox	Gulf Coast	1	1	0	0	.000	1	2	0	0.00	0
2005 Portland...........	Eastern	26	148¹/₃	11	6	.647	163	57	114	2.61	0
2006 Pawtucket	Int.	11	46²/₃	3	4	.429	43	25	43	2.70	0
2006 Boston a.............	A.L.	15	81¹/₃	7	2	.778	60	43	91	4.76	0
2007 Greenville	So.Atl.	3	13	0	0	.000	15	2	11	2.08	0
2007 Portland...........	Eastern	1	6	1	0	1.000	4	4	5	1.50	0
2007 Pawtucket	Int.	14	71²/₃	4	5	.444	51	31	67	3.89	0
2007 Boston b.............	A.L.	12	63	4	0	1.000	50	31	61	4.57	0
2008 Boston c.............	A.L.	33	210¹/₃	16	6	.727	152	66	202	3.21	0
2009 Boston	A.L.	32	203¹/₃	15	8	.652	225	64	186	3.41	0
2010 Boston	A.L.	32	208	19	9	.679	225	83	167	3.25	0
2011 Boston d	A.L.	31	191²/₃	15	9	.625	182	75	166	3.47	0
2012 Boston	A.L.	33	205¹/₃	9	14	.391	166	68	216	4.82	0
Major League Totals .... 7 Yrs.		188	1163	85	48	.639	1060	430	1089	3.76	0
Division Series											
2008 Boston	A.L.	2	14	1	0	1.000	11	3	10	0.00	0
2009 Boston	A.L.	1	6	0	1	.000	5	4	4	4.50	0
Division Series Totals		3	20	1	1	.500	16	7	14	1.35	0
Championship Series											
2007 Boston	A.L.	2	3²/₃	0	0	.000	5	1	3	4.91	0
2008 Boston	A.L.	2	12²/₃	0	2	.000	15	2	14	4.97	0
Championship Series Totals		4	16¹/₃	0	2	.000	20	3	17	4.96	0
World Series Record											
2007 Boston	A.L.	1	5²/₃	1	0	1.000	3	3	3	0.00	0

a On disabled list from August 24 to November 6, 2006.
b On disabled list from March 23 to June 11, 2007.
c Pitched no-hit, no-run game against Kansas City Royals, May 19, 2008.
d On disabled list from July 6 to July 25, 2011.

LEWIS, COLBY PRESTON

Born, Bakersfield, California, August 2, 1979.
Bats Right. Throws Right. Height, 6 feet, 4 inches. Weight, 230 pounds.

Year Club	Lea	G	IP	W	L	Pct	SO	BB	H	ERA	SAVES
1999 Pulaski	Appal.	14	64²/₃	7	3	.700	84	27	46	1.95	0
2000 Charlotte	Fla.St.	28	163²/₃	11	10	.524	153	45	169	4.07	0
2001 Charlotte	Fla.St.	1	4¹/₃	1	0	1.000	8	0	0	0.00	0
2001 Tulsa	Texas	25	156	10	10	.500	162	62	150	4.50	0
2002 Texas	A.L.	15	34¹/₃	1	3	.250	28	26	42	6.29	0
2002 Oklahoma.	P.C.	20	106²/₃	5	6	.455	99	28	100	3.63	0
2003 Texas	A.L.	26	127	10	9	.526	88	70	163	7.30	0
2003 Oklahoma.	P.C.	7	47²/₃	5	1	.833	43	19	36	3.02	0
2004 Texas a-b	A.L.	3	15¹/₃	1	1	.500	11	13	13	4.11	0
2005 Detroit c	A.L.				INJURED—Did Not Play						
2006 Toledo	Int.	24	147²/₃	6	7	.462	104	36	154	3.96	0
2006 Detroit d	A.L.	2	3	0	0	.000	5	1	8	3.00	0
2007 Sacramento	P.C.	15	95²/₃	8	3	.727	97	23	70	1.88	0
2007 Oakland e-f.	A.L.	26	37²/₃	0	2	.000	23	14	44	6.45	0
2008 Hiroshima g	Japan Cent.	26	178	15	8	.652	183	27	151	2.68	0
2009 Hiroshima	Japan Cent.	29	176¹/₃	11	9	.550	186	19	156	2.96	0
2010 Texas h.	A.L.	32	201	12	13	.480	196	65	174	3.72	0
2011 Texas	A.L.	32	200¹/₃	14	10	.583	169	56	187	4.40	0
2012 Texas i	A.L.	16	105	6	6	.500	93	14	99	3.43	0
Major League Totals . . . . .8 Yrs.		152	723²/₃	44	44	.500	613	259	730	4.76	0
Division Series											
2010 Texas	A.L.	1	5	0	0	.000	5	5	2	0.00	0
2011 Texas	A.L.	1	6	1	0	1.000	6	2	1	1.50	0
Division Series Totals		2	11	1	0	1.000	11	7	3	0.82	0
Championship Series											
2010 Texas	A.L.	2	13²/₃	2	0	1.000	13	6	9	1.98	0
2011 Texas	A.L.	1	5²/₃	0	1	.000	6	2	8	6.35	0
Championship Series Totals		3	19¹/₃	2	1	.667	19	8	17	3.26	0
World Series Record											
2010 Texas	A.L.	1	7²/₃	1	0	1.000	6	2	5	2.35	0
2011 Texas	A.L.	2	12	0	0	.000	8	5	7	2.25	0
World Series Totals.		3	19²/₃	1	0	1.000	14	7	12	2.29	0

a On disabled list from April 18 to October 6, 2004.
b Claimed on waivers by Detroit Tigers, October 8, 2004.
c On disabled list from April 2 to October 31, 2005.
d Filed for free agency, October 2, 2006. Signed with Washington Nationals organization, November 6, 2006.
e Released by Washington Nationals, March 19, 2007. Signed with Oakland Athletics organization, March 29, 2007.
f Claimed on waivers by Kansas City Royals, November 2, 2007.
g Released by Kansas City Royals, December 4, 2007. Signed with Hiroshima (Japan) for 2008.
h Signed with Texas Rangers, January 14, 2010.
i On disabled list from June 24 to July 18 and July 19 to October 29, 2012.

LILLY, THEODORE ROOSEVELT (TED)

Born, Lamita, California, January 4, 1976.
Bats Left. Throws Left. Height, 6 feet, 1 inch. Weight, 190 pounds.

Year Club	Lea	G	IP	W	L	Pct	SO	BB	H	ERA	SAVES
1996 Yakima	Northwest	13	53²/₃	4	0	1.000	75	14	25	0.84	0
1997 San Bernardino	California	23	134²/₃	7	8	.467	158	32	116	2.81	0
1998 San Antonio	Texas	17	111²/₃	8	4	.667	96	37	114	3.30	0
1998 Albuquerque.	P.C.	5	31	1	3	.250	25	9	39	4.94	0
1998 Ottawa a	Int.	7	39	2	2	.500	49	19	45	4.85	0
1999 Ottawa	Int.	16	89	8	5	.615	78	23	81	3.84	0
1999 Montreal b-c	N.L.	9	23²/₃	0	1	.000	28	9	30	7.61	0
2000 Tampa	Fla.St.	1	6²/₃	0	0	.000	6	1	5	1.35	0
2000 Columbus.	Int.	22	137¹/₃	8	11	.421	127	48	157	4.19	0
2000 New York d-e	A.L.	7	8	0	0	.000	11	5	8	5.63	0
2001 Columbus	Int.	5	25¹/₃	0	0	.000	30	8	16	2.84	0
2001 New York	A.L.	26	120²/₃	5	6	.455	112	51	126	5.37	0
2002 New York-Oakland f-g . .	A.L.	22	100	5	7	.417	77	31	80	3.69	0
2003 Oakland h	A.L.	32	178¹/₃	12	10	.545	147	58	179	4.34	0
2004 Toronto	A.L.	32	197¹/₃	12	10	.545	168	89	171	4.06	0
2005 Syracuse	Int.	2	8²/₃	0	1	.000	9	5	5	3.12	0
2005 Toronto i	A.L.	25	126¹/₃	10	11	.476	96	58	135	5.56	0
2006 Toronto j.	A.L.	32	181²/₃	15	13	.536	160	81	179	4.31	0
2007 Chicago	N.L.	34	207	15	8	.652	174	55	181	3.83	0

Year	Club	Lea	G	IP	W	L	Pct	SO	BB	H	ERA	SAVES
2008 Chicago	N.L.	34	204²/₃	17	9	.654	184	64	187	4.09	0
2009 Peoria	Midwest	1	5	1	0	1.000	2	1	2	0.00	0
2009 Chicago k	N.L.	27	177	12	9	.571	151	36	151	3.10	0
2010 Peoria	Midwest	1	7	1	0	1.000	9	1	3	1.29	0
2010 Iowa	P.C.	1	4	0	0	.000	4	1	1	2.25	0
2010 Chicago-Los Angeles l-m	N.L.	30	193²/₃	10	12	.455	166	44	165	3.62	0
2011 Los Angeles	N.L.	33	192²/₃	12	14	.462	158	51	172	3.97	0
2012 Rancho Cucamonga	Calif.	4	11	0	1	.000	7	2	10	5.73	0
2012 Los Angeles n	N.L.	8	48²/₃	5	1	.833	31	19	36	3.14	0
Major League Totals ...14 Yrs.		351	1959²/₃	130	111	.539	1663	651	1800	4.13	0
Division Series											
2002 Oakland	A.L.	2	4	0	1	.000	3	1	10	13.50	0
2003 Oakland	A.L.	2	9	0	0	.000	7	2	2	0.00	0
2007 Chicago	N.L.	1	3¹/₃	0	1	.000	4	4	7	16.20	0
Division Series Totals		5	16¹/₃	0	2	.000	14	7	19	6.61	0

a Traded by Los Angeles Dodgers to Montreal Expos with infielder Wilton Guerrero, outfielder Peter Bergeron and infielder Jonathan Tucker for infielder Mark Grudzielanek, outfielder Hiram Bocachica and pitcher Carlos Perez, July 31, 1998.
b On disabled list from June 21 to September 30, 1999.
c Montreal Expos traded pitcher Jake Westbrook and two players to be named later to New York Yankees for pitcher Hideki Irabu, December 22, 1999.
d Sent to New York Yankees with pitcher Christian Parker as players to be named later for Jake Westbrook, March 17 and March 22, 2000.
e On disabled list from March 25 to May 22, 2000.
f Traded to Oakland Athletics with pitcher Jason Arnold and outfielder John-Ford Griffin for pitcher Jeff Weaver, July 5, 2002.
g On disabled list from July 23 to September 10, 2002.
h Traded to Toronto Blue Jays for outfielder Bobby Kielty and cash, November 18, 2003.
i On disabled list from March 25 to April 10 and July 25 to September 6, 2005.
j Filed for free agency, October 28, 2006. Signed with Chicago Cubs, December 15, 2006.
k On disabled list from July 21 to August 17, 2009.
l On disabled list from March 26 to April 24, 2010.
m Traded to Los Angeles Dodgers with infielder Ryan Theriot and cash for infielder Blake Dewitt, pitcher Kyle Smit and pitcher Brett Wallach, July 31, 2010.
n On disabled list from May 24 to October 29 and March 26 to April 14, 2012.

LINCECUM, TIMOTHY LEROY (TIM)

Born, Bellevue, Washington, June 15, 1984.
Bats Left. Throws Right. Height, 5 feet, 11 inches. Weight, 160 pounds.

Year	Club	Lea	G	IP	W	L	Pct	SO	BB	H	ERA	SAVES
2006 San Jose	Calif.	6	27²/₃	2	0	1.000	48	12	13	1.95	0
2006 Salem-Keizer	Northwest	2	4	0	0	.000	10	0	1	0.00	0
2007 Fresno	P.C.	5	31	4	0	1.000	46	11	12	0.29	0
2007 San Francisco	N.L.	24	146¹/₃	7	5	.583	150	65	122	4.00	0
2008 San Francisco a	N.L.	34	227	18	5	*.783	*265	84	182	2.62	0
2009 San Francisco b	N.L.	32	225¹/₃	15	7	.682	*261	68	168	2.48	0
2010 San Francisco	N.L.	33	212¹/₃	16	10	.615	*231	76	194	3.43	0
2011 San Francisco	N.L.	33	217	13	14	.481	220	86	176	2.74	0
2012 San Francisco	N.L.	33	186	10	*15	.400	190	90	183	5.18	0
Major League Totals ....6 Yrs.		189	1214	79	56	.585	1317	469	1025	3.31	0
Division Series											
2010 San Francisco	N.L.	1	9	1	0	1.000	14	1	2	0.00	0
2012 San Francisco	N.L.	2	6¹/₃	1	0	1.000	8	0	3	1.42	0
Division Series Totals		3	15¹/₃	2	0	1.000	22	1	5	0.59	0
Championship Series											
2010 San Francisco	N.L.	3	14¹/₃	1	1	.500	16	4	12	3.14	0
2012 San Francisco	N.L.	2	6²/₃	0	1	.000	4	4	6	5.40	0
Championship Series Totals		5	21	1	2	.333	20	8	18	3.86	0
World Series Record											
2010 San Francisco	N.L.	2	13²/₃	2	0	1.000	13	4	11	3.29	0
2012 San Francisco	N.L.	2	4²/₃	0	0	.000	8	1	0	0.00	0
World Series Totals		4	18¹/₃	2	0	1.000	21	5	11	2.45	0

a Selected Cy Young Award Winner in National League for 2008.
b Selected Cy Young Award Winner in National League for 2009.

LINCOLN, BRAD ERIC

Born, Lake Jackson, Texas, May 25, 1985.
Bats Left. Throws Right. Height, 6 feet. Weight, 210 pounds.

Year	Club	Lea	G	IP	W	L	Pct	SO	BB	H	ERA	SAVES
2006	Pirates	Gulf Coast	2	7²/₃	0	0	.000	9	1	6	0.00	0
2006	Hickory	So.Atl.	4	16	1	2	.333	10	6	25	6.75	0
2007	a					INJURED—Did Not Play						
2008	Hickory	So.Atl.	11	62	5	5	.500	46	6	72	4.65	0
2008	Lynchburg	Carolina	8	41²/₃	1	5	.167	29	11	42	4.75	0
2009	Altoona	Eastern	13	75	1	5	.167	65	18	63	2.28	0
2009	Indianapolis	Int.	12	61¹/₃	6	2	.750	42	10	72	4.70	0
2010	Indianapolis	Int.	17	94	7	5	.583	84	24	83	4.12	0
2010	Pittsburgh	N.L.	11	52²/₃	1	4	.200	25	15	66	6.66	0
2011	Indianapolis	Int.	19	111²/₃	7	8	.467	94	21	115	4.19	0
2011	Pittsburgh b	N.L.	12	47²/₃	2	3	.400	29	16	54	4.72	0
2012	Indianapolis	Int.	2	12	1	0	1.000	9	0	10	2.25	0
2012	Pittsburgh	N.L.	28	59¹/₃	4	2	.667	60	14	51	2.73	1
2012	Toronto c	A.L.	24	28²/₃	1	0	1.000	28	10	29	5.65	0
Major League Totals		3 Yrs.	75	188¹/₃	8	9	.471	142	55	200	4.78	1

a On minor league disabled list from April 5 to September 7, 2007.
b On disabled list from March 22 to April 11, 2011.
c Traded to Toronto Blue Jays for outfielder Travis Snider, July 31, 2012.

LINDBLOM, JOSHUA WILLIAM (JOSH)

Born, Lafayette, Indiana, June 15, 1987.
Bats Right. Throws Right. Height, 6 feet, 5 inches. Weight, 240 pounds.

Year	Club	Lea	G	IP	W	L	Pct	SO	BB	H	ERA	SAVES
2008	Great Lakes	Midwest	8	29	0	0	.000	33	4	14	1.86	0
2008	Jacksonville	Southern	1	5	0	0	.000	4	1	5	3.60	0
2009	Albuquerque	P.C.	20	39	3	0	1.000	36	12	34	2.54	1
2009	Chattanooga	Southern	14	57¹/₃	3	5	.375	46	14	55	4.71	0
2010	Albuquerque	P.C.	40	95	3	2	.600	84	32	143	6.54	0
2011	Chattanooga	Southern	34	42¹/₃	1	3	.250	54	14	30	2.13	17
2011	Los Angeles	N.L.	27	29²/₃	1	0	1.000	28	10	21	2.73	1
2012	Los Angeles-Phil. a-b	N.L.	74	71	3	5	.375	70	35	61	3.55	1
Major League Totals		2 Yrs.	101	100²/₃	4	5	.444	98	45	82	3.31	1

a Traded to Philadelphia Phillies with pitcher Ethan Martin and player to be named later for outfielder Shane Victorino, July 31, 2012.
b Traded to Texas Rangers with pitcher Lisalverto Bonilla for infielder Michael Young, December 9, 2012.

LINDSTROM, MATTHEW JAMES (MATT)

Born, Rexburg, Idaho, February 11, 1980.
Bats Right. Throws Right. Height, 6 feet, 4 inches. Weight, 210 pounds.

Year	Club	Lea	G	IP	W	L	Pct	SO	BB	H	ERA	SAVES
2002	Kingsport	Appal.	12	48¹/₃	0	6	.000	39	21	56	4.84	0
2003	Brooklyn	N.Y.-Penn.	14	65¹/₃	7	3	.700	52	27	61	3.44	0
2003	Capital City	So.Atl.	12	56²/₃	2	3	.400	50	33	46	2.86	0
2004	St. Lucie	Fla.St.	14	79²/₃	5	5	.500	50	20	83	3.73	0
2004	Capital City	So.Atl.	12	56	3	2	.600	64	10	47	3.21	0
2005	Binghamton	Eastern	35	73¹/₃	3	5	.286	58	55	90	5.40	0
2006	Binghamton	Eastern	35	40²/₃	2	4	.333	54	14	34	3.76	11
2006	St. Lucie a	Fla.St.	11	18	1	0	1.000	16	7	14	2.50	2
2007	Florida	N.L.	71	67	3	4	.429	62	21	66	3.09	0
2008	Albuquerque	P.C.	3	4	0	0	.000	4	1	5	9.00	0
2008	Florida	N.L.	66	57¹/₃	3	3	.500	43	26	57	3.14	5
2009	Jupiter	Fla.St.	2	2	0	0	.000	1	1	0	0.00	0
2009	Jacksonville	Southern	2	2	0	1	.000	3	0	2	9.00	0
2009	Florida b-c	N.L.	54	47¹/₃	2	1	.667	39	24	54	5.89	15
2010	Corpus Christi	Texas	1	1	0	0	.000	1	0	0	0.00	0
2010	Houston d-e	N.L.	58	53¹/₃	2	5	.286	43	20	68	4.39	23
2011	Colorado Springs	P.C.	2	2	0	0	.000	4	0	4	13.50	0
2011	Colorado f	N.L.	63	54	2	2	.500	36	14	52	3.06	2
2012	Orioles	Gulf Coast	2	2	0	0	.000	2	0	2	4.50	0
2012	Bowie	Eastern	2	2¹/₃	0	0	.000	1	1	4	3.86	0
2012	Baltimore	A.L.	34	36¹/₃	1	0	1.000	30	12	35	2.72	0
2012	Arizona g-h-i-j	N.L.	12	10²/₃	0	0	.000	10	2	10	2.53	0
Major League Totals		6 Yrs.	358	326	13	15	.464	263	119	342	3.64	45

a Traded to Florida Marlins by New York Mets with pitcher Henry Owens for pitcher Adam Bostick and pitcher Jason Vargas, November 20, 2006.
b On disabled list from June 24 to August 1, 2009.
c Traded to Houston Astros for infielder Luis Bryan and pitcher Robert Bono, December 9, 2009.
d On disabled list from August 17 to September 1, 2010.
e Traded to Colorado Rockies for pitcher Wes Musick and pitcher Jonnathan Aristil, December 23, 2010.
f On disabled list from August 10 to August 26, 2011.
g Traded to Baltimore Orioles with pitcher Jason Hammel for pitcher Jeremy Guthrie, February 6, 2012.
h On disabled list from May 11 to June 27, 2012.
i Traded to Arizona Diamondbacks with cash for pitcher Joe Saunders and cash, August 26, 2012.
j Filed for free agency, November 3, 2012.

LIRIANO, FRANCISCO CASILLAS

Born, San Cristobal, Dominican Republic, October 26, 1983.
Bats Left. Throws Left. Height, 6 feet, 2 inches. Weight, 225 pounds.

Year Club	Lea	G	IP	W	L	Pct	SO	BB	H	ERA	SAVES
2001 Giants............	Arizona	13	62	5	4	.556	67	24	51	3.63	0
2001 Salem-Keizer.....	Northwest	2	9	0	0	.000	12	1	7	5.00	0
2002 Hagerstown.........	So.Atl.	16	80	3	6	.333	85	31	61	3.49	0
2003 Giants............	Arizona	4	8¹/₃	0	1	.000	9	6	5	4.32	0
2003 San Jose a..........	Calif.	1	0²/₃	0	1	.000	0	2	5	54.00	0
2004 New Britain........	Eastern	7	39²/₃	3	2	.600	49	17	45	3.18	0
2004 Fort Myers.........	Fla.St.	21	117	6	7	.462	125	43	118	4.00	0
2005 New Britain........	Eastern	13	76²/₃	3	5	.375	92	26	70	3.64	0
2005 Rochester..........	.Int.	14	91	9	2	.818	112	24	56	1.78	0
2005 Minnesota..........	A.L.	6	23²/₃	1	2	.333	33	7	19	5.70	0
2006 Minnesota b........	A.L.	28	121	12	3	.800	144	32	89	2.16	1
2007 Minnesota c........	A.L.		INJURED—Did Not Play								
2008 Fort Myers.........	Fla.St.	1	5¹/₃	0	1	.000	8	2	6	6.75	0
2008 Rochester..........	.Int.	19	118	10	2	.833	113	31	102	3.28	0
2008 Minnesota.........	A.L.	14	76	6	4	.600	67	32	74	3.91	0
2009 Minnesota d........	A.L.	29	136²/₃	5	13	.278	122	65	147	5.80	0
2010 Minnesota.........	A.L.	31	191²/₃	14	10	.583	201	58	184	3.62	0
2011 Minnesota e-f......	A.L.	26	134¹/₃	9	10	.474	112	75	125	5.09	0
2012 Minnesota-Chicago g-h..	A.L.	34	156²/₃	6	12	.333	167	87	143	5.34	0
Major League Totals........7 Yrs.		168	840	53	54	.495	846	356	781	4.40	1
Division Series											
2009 Minnesota	A.L.	1	2	0	0	.000	1	1	1	4.50	0
2010 Minnesota............	A.L.	1	5²/₃	0	0	.000	7	3	6	6.35	0
Division Series Totals...........		2	7²/₃	0	0	.000	8	4	7	5.87	0

a Traded by San Francisco Giants to Minnesota Twins with pitcher Joe Nathan and pitcher Boof Bonser for catcher A.J. Pierzynski, November 14, 2003.
b On disabled list from August 8 to September 11, 2006.
c On disabled list from March 24 to October 10, 2007.
d On disabled list from August 18 to September 9, 2009.
e Pitched no-hit, no-run game against Chicago White Sox, May 3, 2011.
f On disabled list from August 26 to September 16 and May 30 to June 7, 2011.
g Traded to Chicago White Sox for infielder Eduardo Escobar and pitcher Pedro Hernandez, July 29, 2012.
h Filed for free agency, November 3, 2012.

LOCKE, JEFFREY ALAN (JEFF)

Born, Center Conway, New Hampshire, November 20, 1987.
Bats Left. Throws Left. Height, 6 feet, 1 inch. Weight, 215 pounds.

Year Club	Lea	G	IP	W	L	Pct	SO	BB	H	ERA	SAVES
2006 Braves..........	Gulf Coast	10	32	4	3	.571	38	5	38	4.22	0
2007 Danville.........	Appal.	13	61	7	1	.875	74	8	48	2.66	1
2008 Rome.............	So.Atl.	25	139²/₃	5	12	.294	113	38	150	4.06	0
2009 Lynchburg......	Carolina	17	81²/₃	4	4	.500	56	18	98	4.08	0
2009 Myrtle Beach a.....	Carolina	10	45²/₃	1	4	.200	43	26	47	5.52	0
2010 Altoona..........	Eastern	10	57²/₃	3	2	.600	56	12	57	3.59	0
2010 Bradenton.........	Fla.St.	17	86¹/₃	9	3	.750	83	14	82	3.54	0
2011 Altoona.........	Eastern	23	125	7	8	.467	114	46	118	4.03	0
2011 Indianapolis...........	.Int.	5	28¹/₃	1	2	.333	25	9	25	2.22	0
2011 Pittsburgh............	.N.L.	4	16²/₃	0	3	.000	5	10	21	6.48	0
2012 Indianapolis.........	.Int.	24	141²/₃	10	5	.667	131	43	126	2.48	0
2012 Pittsburgh............	.N.L.	8	34¹/₃	1	3	.250	34	11	36	5.50	0
Major League Totals........2 Yrs.		12	51	1	6	.143	39	21	57	5.82	0

a Traded by Atlanta Braves to Pittsburgh Pirates with outfielder Gorkys Hernandez and pitcher Charlie Morton for outfielder Nate McLouth, June 3, 2009.

LOE, KAMERON DAVID

Born, Simi Valley, California, September 10, 1981.
Bats Right. Throws Right. Height, 6 feet, 8 inches. Weight, 240 pounds.

Year	Club	Lea	G	IP	W	L	Pct	SO	BB	H	ERA	SAVES
2002 Pulaski	Appal.	14	58⅓	4	4	.500	55	17	64	4.47	1
2003 Stockton	Calif.	9	37⅔	3	0	1.000	31	6	26	0.96	1
2003 Clinton	Midwest	23	97	4	3	.571	94	19	78	1.95	2
2004 Frisco	Texas	19	113⅓	7	7	.500	97	29	122	3.10	0
2004 Oklahoma	P.C.	8	52⅓	5	2	.714	42	13	52	3.27	0
2004 Texas	A.L.	2	6⅔	0	0	.000	3	6	6	5.40	0
2005 Oklahoma	P.C.	5	28⅓	2	1	.667	23	10	32	5.08	0
2005 Texas	A.L.	48	92	9	6	.600	45	31	89	3.42	1
2006 Texas	A.L.	15	78⅓	3	6	.333	34	22	105	5.86	0
2006 Frisco	Texas	2	7	0	1	.000	4	4	8	5.14	0
2006 Oklahoma a	P.C.	13	22⅔	1	2	.333	21	13	32	9.13	1
2007 Frisco	Texas	1	3	0	0	.000	1	5	1	6.00	0
2007 Texas b	A.L.	28	136	6	11	.353	78	56	162	5.36	0
2008 Oklahoma	P.C.	26	58	3	5	.375	31	20	70	5.59	1
2008 Texas	A.L.	14	30⅔	1	0	1.000	20	8	36	3.23	0
2009 Fukuoka c-d	Japan Pac.	5	27	0	4	.000	18	12	36	6.33	0
2010 Nashville	P.C.	10	62⅔	4	3	.571	39	19	57	3.16	0
2010 Milwaukee	N.L.	53	58⅓	3	5	.375	46	15	54	2.78	0
2011 Milwaukee	N.L.	72	72	4	7	.364	61	16	65	3.50	1
2012 Milwaukee e	N.L.	70	68⅓	6	5	.545	55	20	78	4.61	2
Major League Totals	8 Yrs.	302	542⅓	32	40	.444	342	174	595	4.36	4
Division Series											
2011 Milwaukee	N.L.	2	2	0	0	.000	1	0	3	0.00	0
Championship Series											
2011 Milwaukee	N.L.	3	2⅓	0	0	.000	2	1	10	15.43	0

a On disabled list from June 19 to August 3, 2006.
b On disabled list from July 30 to August 18, 2007.
c Released by Texas Rangers, November 28, 2008. Signed with Fukuoka (Japan) for 2009.
d Signed with Milwaukee Brewers organization, December 18, 2009.
e Filed for free agency, November 2, 2012.

LOGAN, BOONE

Born, San Antonio, Texas, August 13, 1984.
Bats Right. Throws Left. Height, 6 feet, 5 inches. Weight, 215 pounds.

Year	Club	Lea	G	IP	W	L	Pct	SO	BB	H	ERA	SAVES
2003 Great Falls	Pioneer	16	67	3	3	.500	48	31	76	6.58	0
2004 Great Falls	Pioneer	18	64⅓	3	7	.300	48	14	74	5.60	1
2005 Winston-Salem	Carolina	4	5⅓	0	0	.000	5	4	7	5.06	0
2005 Great Falls	Pioneer	21	35⅓	1	1	.500	29	4	34	3.31	2
2006 Charlotte	Int.	38	42⅔	3	1	.750	57	12	35	3.38	11
2006 Chicago	A.L.	21	17⅓	0	0	.000	15	15	21	8.31	1
2007 Charlotte	Int.	4	8⅓	0	1	.000	11	4	8	2.16	1
2007 Chicago	A.L.	68	50⅔	2	1	.667	35	20	59	4.97	0
2008 Charlotte	Int.	5	9	0	1	.000	7	6	10	6.00	0
2008 Chicago a	A.L.	55	42⅓	2	3	.400	42	14	57	5.95	0
2009 Gwinnett	Int.	29	35⅔	4	2	.667	39	17	26	3.28	2
2009 Atlanta b	N.L.	20	17⅓	1	1	.500	10	9	21	5.19	0
2010 Scranton/WB	Int.	14	21⅓	0	1	.000	23	4	18	2.11	0
2010 New York	A.L.	51	40	2	0	1.000	38	20	34	2.93	0
2011 New York	A.L.	64	41⅔	5	3	.625	46	13	43	3.46	0
2012 New York	A.L.	*80	55⅓	7	2	.778	68	28	48	3.74	1
Major League Totals	7 Yrs.	359	264⅔	19	10	.655	254	119	283	4.56	2
Division Series											
2010 New York	A.L.	2	1	0	0	.000	0	0	1	0.00	0
2011 New York	A.L.	3	2⅓	0	0	.000	6	0	1	0.00	0
2012 New York	A.L.	2	0⅔	0	0	.000	1	0	0	0.00	0
Division Series Totals		7	4	0	0	.000	7	0	2	0.00	0
Championship Series											
2010 New York	A.L.	3	0⅔	0	0	.000	1	1	2	27.00	0
2012 New York	A.L.	3	3	0	0	.000	1	0	3	0.00	0
Championship Series Totals		6	3⅔	0	0	.000	2	1	5	4.91	0

a Traded to Atlanta Braves with pitcher Javier Vazquez for catcher Tyler Flowers, infielder Jonathan Gilmore, infielder Brent Lillibridge and pitcher Santos Rodriguez, December 4, 2008.
b Traded to New York Yankees with pitcher Javier Vazquez for outfielder Melky Cabrera, pitcher Arodys Vizcaino, pitcher Michael Dunn and cash, December 22, 2009.

LOHSE, KYLE MATTHEW
Born, Chico, California, October 4, 1978.
Bats Right. Throws Right. Height, 6 feet, 2 inches. Weight, 210 pounds.

Year Club	Lea	G	IP	W	L	Pct	SO	BB	H	ERA	SAVES
1997 Cubs	Arizona	12	47²/₃	2	2	.500	49	22	46	3.02	0
1998 Rockford	Midwest	28	170²/₃	13	8	.619	121	45	158	3.22	0
1999 New Britain	Eastern	11	70¹/₃	3	4	.429	41	23	87	5.89	0
1999 Daytona	Fla.St.	9	53	5	3	.625	41	16	48	2.89	0
1999 Fort Myers a	Fla.St.	7	41²/₃	2	3	.400	33	9	47	5.18	0
2000 New Britain	Eastern	28	167	3	18	.143	124	55	196	6.04	0
2001 New Britain	Eastern	6	38	3	1	.750	32	4	32	2.37	0
2001 Edmonton	P.C.	8	49	4	2	.667	48	13	50	3.12	0
2001 Minnesota	A.L.	19	90¹/₃	4	7	.364	64	29	102	5.68	0
2002 Minnesota	A.L.	32	180²/₃	13	8	.619	124	70	181	4.23	0
2003 Minnesota	A.L.	33	201	14	11	.560	130	45	211	4.61	0
2004 Minnesota	A.L.	35	194	9	13	.409	111	76	240	5.34	0
2005 Minnesota	A.L.	31	178²/₃	9	13	.409	86	44	211	4.18	0
2006 Rochester	Int.	4	24	2	1	.667	12	6	15	1.50	0
2006 Minnesota	A.L.	22	63²/₃	2	5	.286	46	25	80	7.07	0
2006 Cincinnati b	N.L.	12	63	3	5	.375	51	19	70	4.57	0
2007 Cincinnati-Philadelphia c-d	N.L.	34	192²/₃	9	12	.429	122	57	207	4.62	0
2008 St. Louis	N.L.	33	200	15	6	.714	119	49	211	3.78	0
2009 Springfield	Texas	1	4²/₃	0	0	.000	3	4	3	3.86	0
2009 Memphis	P.C.	1	6	1	0	1.000	6	2	2	0.00	0
2009 St. Louis e	N.L.	23	117²/₃	6	10	.375	77	36	125	4.74	0
2010 Springfield	Texas	1	5	0	1	.000	4	0	12	9.00	0
2010 Memphis	P.C.	3	14	1	0	1.000	14	2	9	3.21	0
2010 St. Louis f	N.L.	18	92	4	8	.333	54	35	129	6.55	0
2011 St. Louis	N.L.	30	188¹/₃	14	8	.636	111	42	178	3.39	0
2012 St. Louis g	N.L.	33	211	16	3	*.842	143	38	192	2.86	0
Major League Totals ... 12 Yrs.		355	1973	118	109	.520	1238	565	2137	4.45	0
Wild Card Playoff											
2012 St. Louis	N.L.	1	5²/₃	1	0	1.000	6	1	6	3.18	0
Division Series											
2002 Minnesota	A.L.	2	4	0	0	.000	5	0	2	0.00	0
2003 Minnesota	A.L.	1	5	0	1	.000	5	2	6	5.40	0
2004 Minnesota	A.L.	1	2	0	1	.000	3	0	1	4.50	0
2007 Philadelphia	N.L.	1	1²/₃	0	0	.000	1	0	1	6.75	0
2011 St. Louis	N.L.	1	5¹/₃	0	1	.000	4	1	7	8.44	0
2012 St. Louis	N.L.	1	7	0	0	.000	5	1	2	1.29	0
Division Series Totals		7	24²/₃	0	3	.000	23	4	19	4.01	0
Championship Series											
2002 Minnesota	A.L.	1	1	0	0	.000	1	0	0	0.00	0
2011 St. Louis	N.L.	1	4¹/₃	0	1	.000	3	0	6	6.23	0
2012 St. Louis	N.L.	2	7²/₃	1	1	.500	3	6	13	7.04	0
Championship Series Totals		4	13	1	2	.333	7	6	19	6.23	0
World Series Record											
2011 St. Louis	N.L.	1	3	0	0	.000	3	2	5	9.00	0

a Traded by Chicago Cubs to Minnesota Twins with pitcher Jason Ryan for pitcher Rick Aguilera and pitcher Scott Downs, May 21, 1999.
b Traded to Cincinnati Reds for pitcher Zach Ward, July 31, 2006.
c Traded to Philadelphia Phillies for pitcher Matt Maloney, July 30, 2007.
d Filed for free agency, October 31, 2007. Signed with St. Louis Cardinals, March 14, 2008.
e On disabled list from June 4 to July 12 and August 22 to September 6, 2009.
f On disabled list from May 23 to August 15, 2010.
g Filed for free agency, November 3, 2012.

LOPEZ, JAVIER ALFONSO
Born, San Juan, Puerto Rico, July 11, 1977.
Bats Left. Throws Left. Height, 6 feet, 4 inches. Weight, 225 pounds.

Year Club	Lea	G	IP	W	L	Pct	SO	BB	H	ERA	SAVES
1998 South Bend	Midwest	16	44	2	4	.333	31	30	60	6.55	0
1999 South Bend	Midwest	20	99	4	6	.400	70	43	122	6.00	0
2000 High Desert	Calif.	30	136¹/₃	4	8	.333	98	57	152	5.22	2
2001 Lancaster	Calif.	17	24	1	3	.250	18	5	30	2.63	1
2001 El Paso	Texas	22	40	1	0	1.000	21	14	64	7.43	0
2002 El Paso a	Texas	61	46¹/₃	2	2	.500	47	16	34	2.72	6
2003 Colorado b	N.L.	75	58¹/₃	4	1	.800	40	12	58	3.70	1
2004 Colorado Springs	P.C.	8	9	0	1	.000	9	2	10	4.00	0
2004 Colorado	N.L.	64	40²/₃	1	2	.333	20	26	45	7.52	0

Year	Club	Lea	G	IP	W	L	Pct	SO	BB	H	ERA	SAVES
2005 Tucson	P.C.	27	24¹/₃	0	1	.000	16	12	17	2.22	2	
2005 Colorado-Arizona c	N.L.	32	16¹/₃	1	1	.500	12	11	26	11.02	2	
2006 Charlotte	Int.	26	33	2	1	.667	26	6	28	0.55	12	
2006 Pawtucket	Int.	13	16²/₃	0	0	.000	12	8	20	4.86	4	
2006 Boston d-e	A.L.	27	16²/₃	1	0	1.000	11	10	13	2.70	1	
2007 Pawtucket	Int.	17	16²/₃	2	1	.667	15	8	19	3.78	0	
2007 Boston	A.L.	61	40²/₃	2	1	.667	26	18	36	3.10	0	
2008 Boston	A.L.	70	59¹/₃	2	0	1.000	38	27	53	2.43	0	
2009 Boston	A.L.	14	11²/₃	0	2	.000	5	9	20	9.26	0	
2009 Pawtucket f	Int.	38	39²/₃	1	1	.500	23	13	35	3.18	0	
2010 Pittsburgh-San Francisco g	N.L.	77	57²/₃	4	2	.667	38	20	50	2.34	0	
2011 San Francisco	N.L.	70	53	5	2	.714	40	26	42	2.72	1	
2012 San Francisco	N.L.	70	36	3	0	1.000	28	14	37	2.50	7	
Major League Totals	10 Yrs.	560	390¹/₃	23	11	.676	258	173	380	3.83	12	
Division Series												
2007 Boston	A.L.	1	0¹/₃	0	0	.000	0	0	0	0.00	0	
2008 Boston	A.L.	1	1	0	1	.000	1	0	3	9.00	0	
2010 San Francisco	N.L.	2	0²/₃	0	0	.000	2	0	0	0.00	0	
2012 San Francisco	N.L.	2	0²/₃	0	0	.000	0	0	0	0.00	0	
Division Series Totals		6	2²/₃	0	1	.000	3	0	3	3.38	0	
Championship Series												
2007 Boston	A.L.	3	2	0	0	.000	0	2	3	18.00	0	
2008 Boston	A.L.	2	1²/₃	0	0	.000	0	0	3	0.00	0	
2010 San Francisco	N.L.	5	4¹/₃	1	0	1.000	4	1	1	2.08	0	
2012 San Francisco	N.L.	3	2¹/₃	0	0	.000	4	2	0	0.00	0	
Championship Series Totals		13	10¹/₃	1	0	1.000	8	5	7	4.35	0	
World Series Record												
2007 Boston	A.L.	1	0	0	0	.000	0	0	2	INF	0	
2010 San Francisco	N.L.	2	0²/₃	0	0	.000	0	0	0	0.00	0	
World Series Totals		3	0²/₃	0	0	.000	0	0	2	27.00	0	

a Selected by Boston Red Sox from Arizona Diamondbacks in Rule V draft, December 16, 2002.
b Traded to Colorado Rockies for player to be named later, March 28, 2003. Boston Red Sox received pitcher Ryan Cameron to complete trade, March 29, 2003.
c Claimed on waivers by Arizona Diamondbacks, April 14, 2005.
d Filed for free agency, October 15, 2005. Signed with Chicago White Sox organization, January 19, 2006.
e Traded to Boston Red Sox for pitcher David Riske, June 15, 2006.
f Filed for free agency, October 5, 2009. Signed with Pittsburgh Pirates, December 18, 2009.
g Traded to San Francisco Giants for pitcher Joe Martinez and outfielder John Bowker, July 31, 2010.

LOPEZ, WILTON

Born, Leon, Nicaragua, July 19, 1983.
Bats Right. Throws Right. Height, 6 feet. Weight, 190 pounds.

Year	Club	Lea	G	IP	W	L	Pct	SO	BB	H	ERA	SAVES
2002-03							Did Not Play					
2004 Tampa	Fla.St.	1	2	0	0	.000	2	1	2	4.50	0	
2004 Yankees	Gulf Coast	4	5²/₃	1	0	1.000	6	0	2	0.00	1	
2004 Battle Creek	Midwest	2	1²/₃	0	1	.000	2	1	4	0.00	0	
2004 Staten Island	N.Y.-Penn.	2	3	0	0	.000	2	1	5	12.00	0	
2005-06							Did Not Play					
2007 Lake Elsinore	Calif.	22	20²/₃	2	1	.667	19	1	35	6.10	3	
2007 Fort Wayne a	Midwest	22	30	1	0	1.000	17	2	34	3.30	0	
2008 Lake Elsinore	Calif.	30	30²/₃	2	1	.667	26	4	34	2.64	12	
2008 Portland	P.C.	1	1	0	0	.000	1	2	1	9.00	0	
2008 San Antonio	Texas	27	38¹/₃	0	2	.000	24	9	41	4.93	0	
2009 Corpus Christi	Texas	29	110¹/₃	4	5	.444	69	13	133	4.73	0	
2009 Houston b	N.L.	8	19¹/₃	0	2	.000	9	8	32	8.38	0	
2010 Round Rock	P.C.	3	5	2	1	.667	2	0	8	5.40	0	
2010 Houston	N.L.	68	67	5	2	.714	50	5	66	2.96	1	
2011 Houston c	N.L.	73	71	2	6	.250	56	18	72	2.79	0	
2012 Oklahoma	P.C.	2	2	0	0	.000	1	0	4	13.50	0	
2012 Houston d-e	N.L.	64	66¹/₃	6	3	.667	54	8	61	2.17	10	
Major League Totals	4 Yrs.	213	223²/₃	13	13	.500	169	39	231	3.14	11	

a Released by New York Yankees, March 1, 2007. Signed with San Diego Padres organization, March 3, 2007.
b Claimed on waivers by Houston Astros, April 10, 2009.
c On disabled list from April 14 to May 3, 2011.
d On disabled list from June 11 to July 9, 2012.
e Traded to Colorado Rockies with player to be named later for pitcher Alex White and pitcher Alex Gillingham, December 4, 2012.

LOWE, DEREK CHRISTOPHER

Born, Dearborn, Michigan, June 1, 1973.
Bats Right. Throws Right. Height, 6 feet, 6 inches. Weight, 230 pounds.

Year Club	Lea	G	IP	W	L	Pct	SO	BB	H	ERA	SAVES
1991 Mariners...........	Arizona	12	71	5	3	.625	60	21	58	2.41	0
1992 Bellingham........	Northwest	14	85²/₃	7	3	.700	66	22	69	2.42	0
1993 Riverside	California	27	154	12	9	.571	80	60	189	5.26	0
1994 Jacksonville	Southern	26	151¹/₃	7	10	.412	75	50	177	4.94	0
1995 Mariners..........	Arizona	2	9²/₃	1	0	1.000	11	2	5	0.93	0
1995 Port City.........	Southern	10	53¹/₃	1	6	.143	30	22	70	6.07	0
1996 Port City.........	Southern	10	65	5	3	.625	33	17	56	3.05	0
1996 Tacoma	P.C.	17	105	6	9	.400	54	37	118	4.54	0
1997 Tacoma	P.C.	10	57¹/₃	3	4	.429	49	20	53	3.45	0
1997 Pawtucket	Int.	6	30¹/₃	4	0	1.000	21	11	23	2.37	0
1997 Seattle-Boston a........	A.L.	20	69	2	6	.250	52	23	74	6.13	0
1998 Boston	A.L.	63	123	3	9	.250	77	42	126	4.02	4
1999 Boston	A.L.	74	109¹/₃	6	3	.667	80	25	84	2.63	15
2000 Boston	A.L.	74	91¹/₃	4	4	.500	79	22	90	2.56	*42
2001 Boston	A.L.	67	91²/₃	5	10	.333	82	29	103	3.53	24
2002 Boston b	A.L.	32	219²/₃	21	8	.724	127	48	166	2.58	0
2003 Boston	A.L.	33	203¹/₃	17	7	.708	110	72	216	4.47	0
2004 Boston c...........	A.L.	33	182²/₃	14	12	.538	105	71	224	5.42	0
2005 Los Angeles	N.L.	35	222	12	15	.444	146	55	223	3.61	0
2006 Los Angeles	N.L.	35	218	*16	8	.667	123	55	221	3.63	0
2007 Los Angeles	N.L.	33	199¹/₃	12	14	.462	147	59	194	3.88	0
2008 Los Angeles d	N.L.	34	211	14	11	.560	147	45	194	3.24	0
2009 Atlanta	N.L.	34	194²/₃	15	10	.600	111	63	*232	4.67	0
2010 Atlanta	N.L.	33	193²/₃	16	12	.571	136	61	204	4.00	0
2011 Atlanta e..............	N.L.	34	187	9	*17	.346	137	70	212	5.05	0
2012 Cleveland-New York f-g ..	A.L.	38	142²/₃	9	11	.450	55	51	180	5.11	1
Major League Totals ....16 Yrs.		672	2658¹/₃	175	157	.527	1714	791	2743	4.00	86
Division Series											
1998 Boston ...............A.L.	A.L.	2	4¹/₃	0	0	.000	2	1	3	2.08	0
1999 Boston	A.L.	3	8¹/₃	1	1	.500	7	1	6	4.32	0
2003 Boston	A.L.	3	9²/₃	0	1	.000	6	7	7	0.93	1
2004 Boston	A.L.	1	1	1	0	1.000	0	1	1	0.00	0
2006 Los Angeles	N.L.	1	5¹/₃	0	0	.000	6	2	6	6.75	0
2008 Los Angeles	N.L.	1	6	1	0	1.000	6	1	7	3.00	0
2010 Atlanta	N.L.	2	11²/₃	0	2	.000	14	6	6	2.31	0
2012 New York	A.L.	1	0¹/₃	0	0	.000	0	0	0	0.00	0
Division Series Totals		14	46²/₃	3	4	.429	41	19	36	2.89	1
Championship Series											
1999 Boston	A.L.	3	6¹/₃	0	0	.000	7	2	6	1.42	0
2003 Boston	A.L.	2	14	0	2	.000	5	7	14	6.43	0
2004 Boston	A.L.	2	11¹/₃	1	0	1.000	6	1	7	3.18	0
2008 Los Angeles	N.L.	2	10¹/₃	0	1	.000	6	2	12	3.48	0
2012 New York	A.L.	2	1²/₃	0	0	.000	1	0	3	16.20	0
Championship Series Totals		11	43²/₃	1	3	.250	25	12	42	4.53	0
World Series Record											
2004 Boston	A.L.	1	7	1	0	1.000	4	1	3	0.00	0

a Traded to Boston Red Sox with catcher Jason Varitek for pitcher Heathcliff Slocumb, July 31, 1997.
b Pitched no-hit, no-run game against Tampa Bay Devil Rays, April 27, 2002.
c Filed for free agency, November 1, 2004. Signed with Los Angeles Dodgers, January 11, 2005.
d Filed for free agency, October 30, 2008. Signed with Atlanta Braves, January 13, 2009.
e Traded to Cleveland Indians for pitcher Chris Jones, October 31, 2011.
f Released by Cleveland Indians, August 10, 2012. Signed with New York Yankees, August 13, 2012.
g Filed for free agency, November 3, 2012.

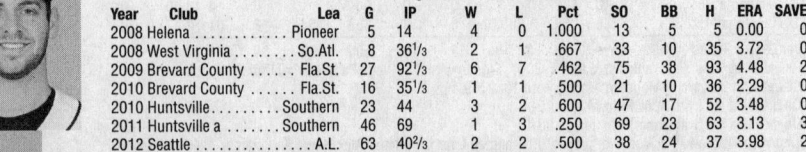

LUETGE, LUCAS LESTER

Born, Brenham, Texas, March 24, 1987.
Bats Left. Throws Left. Height, 6 feet, 4 inches. Weight, 205 pounds.

Year Club	Lea	G	IP	W	L	Pct	SO	BB	H	ERA	SAVES
2008 Helena	Pioneer	5	14	4	0	1.000	13	5	5	0.00	0
2008 West Virginia	So.Atl.	8	36¹/₃	2	1	.667	33	10	35	3.72	0
2009 Brevard County	Fla.St.	27	92¹/₃	6	7	.462	75	38	93	4.48	2
2010 Brevard County	Fla.St.	16	35¹/₃	1	1	.500	21	10	36	2.29	0
2010 Huntsville.........	Southern	23	44	3	2	.600	47	17	52	3.48	0
2011 Huntsville a	Southern	46	69	1	3	.250	69	23	63	3.13	3
2012 Seattle	A.L.	63	40²/₃	2	2	.500	38	24	37	3.98	2

a Selected by Seattle Mariners from Milwaukee Brewers in Rule V draft, December 8, 2011.

LYLES, JORDAN HORTON

Born, Florence, North Carolina, October 19, 1990.
Bats Right. Throws Right. Height, 6 feet, 4 inches. Weight, 210 pounds.

Year	Club	Lea	G	IP	W	L	Pct	SO	BB	H	ERA	SAVES
2008	Greeneville	Appal.	13	49²/₃	3	3	.500	64	10	44	3.99	0
2008	Tri-City	N.Y.-Penn.	2	5²/₃	0	0	.000	4	7	7	6.35	0
2009	Lexington	So.Atl.	26	144²/₃	7	11	.389	167	38	134	3.24	0
2010	Round Rock	P.C.	6	31²/₃	0	3	.000	22	11	48	5.40	0
2010	Corpus Christi	Texas	21	127	7	9	.438	115	35	133	3.12	0
2011	Oklahoma	P.C.	12	62¹/₃	3	3	.500	42	17	64	3.61	0
2011	Houston	N.L.	20	94	2	8	.200	67	26	107	5.36	0
2012	Oklahoma	P.C.	7	40²/₃	5	0	1.000	33	8	41	3.54	0
2012	Houston	N.L.	25	141¹/₃	5	12	.294	99	42	159	5.09	0
Major League Totals	2 Yrs.		45	235¹/₃	7	20	.259	166	68	266	5.20	0

LYNN, MICHAEL LANCE (LANCE)

Born, Indianapolis, Indiana, May 12, 1987.
Bats Right. Throws Right. Height, 6 feet, 5 inches. Weight, 250 pounds.

Year	Club	Lea	G	IP	W	L	Pct	SO	BB	H	ERA	SAVES
2008	Quad Cities	Midwest	2	8	0	1	.000	7	2	8	2.25	0
2008	Batavia	N.Y.-Penn.	6	18²/₃	1	0	1.000	22	4	12	0.96	0
2009	Palm Beach	Fla.St.	5	15²/₃	0	0	.000	17	3	16	2.30	0
2009	Memphis	P.C.	1	6²/₃	0	0	.000	9	3	5	2.70	0
2009	Springfield	Texas	22	126¹/₃	11	4	.733	98	51	117	2.92	0
2010	Memphis	P.C.	29	164	13	10	.565	141	62	164	4.77	0
2011	Memphis	P.C.	12	75	7	3	.700	64	25	79	3.84	0
2011	St. Louis a	N.L.	18	34²/₃	1	1	.500	40	11	25	3.12	1
2012	St. Louis	N.L.	35	176	18	7	.720	180	64	168	3.78	0
Major League Totals	2 Yrs.		53	210²/₃	19	8	.704	220	75	193	3.67	1
Wild Card Playoff												
2012 St. Louis	N.L.		1	0¹/₃	0	0	.000	0	0	0	0.00	0
Division Series												
2012 St. Louis	N.L.		3	3¹/₃	1	1	.500	6	2	4	8.10	0
Championship Series												
2011 St. Louis	N.L.		5	5¹/₃	1	0	1.000	1	2	3	0.00	0
2012 St. Louis	N.L.		2	7¹/₃	0	1	.000	9	4	9	4.91	0
Championship Series Totals			7	12²/₃	1	1	.500	10	6	12	2.84	0
World Series Record												
2011 St. Louis	N.L.		5	5²/₃	1	0	1.000	4	3	7	6.35	0

a On disabled list from August 10 to October 9, 2011.

LYON, BRANDON JAMES

Born, Salt Lake City, Utah, August 10, 1979.
Bats Right. Throws Right. Height, 6 feet, 1 inch. Weight, 200 pounds.

Year	Club	Lea	G	IP	W	L	Pct	SO	BB	H	ERA	SAVES
2000	Queens	N.Y.-Penn.	15	60¹/₃	5	3	.625	55	6	43	2.39	0
2001	Tennessee	Southern	9	58²/₃	5	0	1.000	45	9	57	3.68	0
2001	Syracuse	Int.	11	68¹/₃	5	3	.625	53	10	68	3.69	0
2001	Toronto	A.L.	11	63	5	4	.556	35	15	63	4.29	0
2002	Toronto	A.L.	15	62	1	4	.200	30	19	78	6.53	0
2002	Syracuse a	Int.	14	75²/₃	4	9	.308	35	19	99	5.11	0
2003	Boston	A.L.	49	59	4	6	.400	50	19	73	4.12	9
2003	Pawtucket b-c-d-e	Int.	5	8¹/₃	0	0	.000	7	2	7	3.24	0
2004	Tucson f	P.C.	6	8¹/₃	2	3	.400	4	4	15	15.12	0
2005	Tucson	P.C.	5	5	0	1	.000	4	0	5	5.40	0
2005	Arizona g	N.L.	32	29¹/₃	0	2	.000	17	10	44	6.44	14
2006	Arizona	N.L.	68	69¹/₃	2	4	.333	46	22	68	3.89	0
2007	Arizona	N.L.	73	74	6	4	.600	40	22	70	2.68	2
2008	Arizona	N.L.	61	59¹/₃	3	5	.375	44	13	75	4.70	26
2009	Detroit h-i	A.L.	65	78²/₃	6	5	.545	57	31	56	2.86	3
2010	Houston	N.L.	79	78	6	6	.500	54	31	68	3.12	20
2011	Oklahoma	P.C.	2	2	0	0	.000	0	0	2	0.00	0
2011	Houston j	N.L.	15	13¹/₃	3	3	.500	6	5	27	11.48	4
2012	Houston	N.L.	37	36	0	2	.000	35	11	37	3.25	0
2012	Toronto k-l	A.L.	30	25	4	0	1.000	28	9	19	2.88	1
Major League Totals	11 Yrs.		535	647	40	45	.471	442	207	678	4.12	79
Division Series												
2007 Arizona	N.L.		3	3	0	0	.000	1	1	1	0.00	0

Year	Club	Lea	G	IP	W	L	Pct	SO	BB	H	ERA	SAVES
	Championship Series											
2007 Arizona.............		N.L.	2	3	0	0	.000	4	0	0	0.00	0

a Claimed on waivers by Boston Red Sox, October 9, 2002.
b Traded to Pittsburgh Pirates with pitcher Anastacio Martinez for pitcher Scott Sauerbeck and pitcher Mike Gonzalez, July 22, 2003.
c On disabled list from July 24 to September 1, 2003.
d Traded to Boston Red Sox with pitcher Jeff Suppan and pitcher Anastacio Martinez for infielder Freddy Sanchez, pitcher Mike Gonzalez and cash, July 31, 2003.
e Traded to Arizona Diamondbacks with pitcher Casey Fossum, pitcher Jorge DeRosa and outfielder Michael Goss for pitcher Curt Schilling, November 28, 2003.
f On disabled list from April 3 to October 4, 2004.
g On disabled list from May 13 to August 13, 2005.
h Filed for free agency, November 3, 2008. Signed with Detroit Tigers, January 24, 2009.
i Filed for free agency, November 9, 2009. Signed with Houston Astros, December 12, 2009.
j On disabled list from May 5 to June 9 and June 15 to October 31, 2011.
k Traded to Toronto Blue Jays with pitcher J.A. Happ and pitcher David Carpenter for pitcher Francisco Cordero, outfielder Ben Francisco, pitcher Joseph Musgrove, pitcher Asher Wojciechowski, pitcher David Rollins, catcher Carlos Perez and player to be named later, July 20, 2012. Houston Astros received pitcher Kevin Comer to complete trade, August 16, 2012.
l Filed for free agency, November 3, 2012.

MAHOLM, PAUL GURNER

Born, Greenwood, Mississippi, June 25, 1982.
Bats Left. Throws Left. Height, 6 feet, 2 inches. Weight, 230 pounds.

Year	Club	Lea	G	IP	W	L	Pct	SO	BB	H	ERA	SAVES
2003 Williamsport......	N.Y.-Penn.	8	34⅓	2	1	.667	32	10	25	1.83	0	
2004 Lynchburg........	Carolina	8	44	1	3	.250	28	15	39	1.84	0	
2004 Pirates.........	Gulf Coast	1	4	0	0	.000	2	1	5	2.25	0	
2004 Hickory.........	So.Atl.	3	12⅓	0	2	.000	12	10	17	9.49	0	
2005 Altoona..........	Eastern	16	81⅔	6	2	.750	75	26	73	3.20	0	
2005 Indianapolis......	Int.	6	35⅔	1	1	.500	21	12	40	3.53	0	
2005 Pittsburgh.......	N.L.	6	41⅓	3	1	.750	26	17	31	2.18	0	
2006 Pittsburgh.......	N.L.	30	176	8	10	.444	117	81	202	4.76	0	
2007 Pittsburgh.......	N.L.	29	177⅔	10	15	.400	105	49	204	5.02	0	
2008 Pittsburgh.......	N.L.	31	206⅓	9	9	.500	139	63	201	3.71	0	
2009 Pittsburgh.......	N.L.	31	194⅔	8	9	.471	119	60	221	4.44	0	
2010 Pittsburgh.......	N.L.	32	185⅓	9	15	.375	102	62	228	5.10	0	
2011 Pittsburgh a-b.....	N.L.	26	162⅓	6	14	.300	97	50	160	3.66	0	
2012 Chicago-Atlanta c...	N.L.	32	189	13	11	.542	140	53	178	3.67	0	
Major League Totals.......8 Yrs.			217	1332⅔	66	84	.440	845	435	1425	4.26	0

a On disabled list from August 18 to October 31, 2011.
b Filed for free agency, October 31, 2011. Signed with Chicago Cubs organization, January 10, 2012.
c Traded to Atlanta Braves with outfielder Reed Johnson and cash for pitcher Jaye Chapman and pitcher Arodys Vizcaino, July 31, 2012.

MARCUM, SHAUN MICHAL

Born, Kansas City, Missouri, December 14, 1981.
Bats Right. Throws Right. Height, 6 feet. Weight, 195 pounds.

Year	Club	Lea	G	IP	W	L	Pct	SO	BB	H	ERA	SAVES
2003 Auburn.........	N.Y.-Penn.	21	34	1	0	1.000	47	7	15	1.32	8
2004 Dunedin..........	Fla.St.	12	69⅓	3	2	.600	72	4	74	3.12	0
2004 Charleston.......	So.Atl.	13	79	7	4	.636	83	16	64	3.19	0
2005 New Hampshire.....	Eastern	9	53⅓	7	1	.875	40	10	44	2.53	0
2005 Syracuse..........	Int.	18	103⅔	6	4	.600	90	18	112	4.95	0
2005 Toronto..........	A.L.	5	8	0	0	.000	4	6	0.00	0	
2006 Syracuse..........	Int.	18	52⅔	4	0	1.000	60	9	48	3.42	0
2006 Toronto..........	A.L.	21	78⅓	3	4	.429	65	38	87	5.06	0
2007 Toronto..........	A.L.	38	159	12	6	.667	122	49	149	4.13	1
2008 Dunedin..........	Fla.St.	1	4	0	0	.000	6	0	0	0.00	0
2008 Syracuse..........	Int.	2	13	0	1	.000	15	3	10	2.77	0
2008 Toronto a........	A.L.	25	151⅓	9	7	.563	123	50	126	3.39	0
2009 New Hampshire.....	Eastern	2	7⅔	0	1	.000	8	2	8	1.17	0
2009 Dunedin..........	Fla.St.	2	6	0	1	.000	5	0	7	3.00	0
2009 Las Vegas b......	P.C.	1	2	0	0	.000	0	1	2	4.50	0
2010 Toronto c-d......	A.L.	31	195⅓	13	8	.619	165	43	181	3.64	0
2011 Milwaukee.........	N.L.	33	200⅔	13	7	.650	158	57	175	3.54	0
2012 Wisconsin.........	Midwest	3	12⅔	1	0	1.000	10	3	9	2.84	0
2012 Milwaukee e-f.....	N.L.	21	124	7	4	.636	109	41	116	3.70	0
Major League Totals........7 Yrs.			174	916⅔	57	36	.613	746	282	840	3.76	1

Year	Club	Lea	G	IP	W	L	Pct	SO	BB	H	ERA	SAVES
	Division Series											
2011	Milwaukee	N.L.	1	4²/₃	0	1	.000	3	3	7	13.50	0
	Championship Series											
2011	Milwaukee	N.L.	2	5	0	2	.000	2	2	10	16.20	0

a On disabled list from June 19 to July 22, 2008.
b On disabled list from March 27 to November 13, 2009.
c On disabled list from July 2 to July 18, 2010.
d Traded to Milwaukee Brewers for infielder Brett Lawrie, December 6, 2010.
e On disabled list from June 15 to August 24, 2012.
f Filed for free agency, November 3, 2012.

MARMOL, CARLOS AGUSTIN

Born, Bonao, Dominican Republic, October 14, 1982.
Bats Right. Throws Right. Height, 6 feet, 2 inches. Weight, 180 pounds.

Year	Club	Lea	G	IP	W	L	Pct	SO	BB	H	ERA	SAVES
2002	Cubs.............	Arizona	1	1	0	0	.000	1	1	1	0.00	0
2003	Cubs.............	Arizona	15	64¹/₃	3	5	.375	74	37	59	4.76	0
2004	Lansing	Midwest	26	154²/₃	14	8	.636	154	53	131	3.20	0
2005	Daytona	Fla.St.	13	72¹/₃	6	2	.750	71	37	60	2.99	0
2005	West Tenn	Southern	14	81¹/₃	3	4	.429	70	40	70	3.65	0
2006	West Tenn	Southern	11	58	3	2	.600	67	25	42	2.33	0
2006	Iowa................	P.C.	2	3	0	0	.000	1	1	4	9.00	0
2006	Chicago a	N.L.	19	77	5	7	.417	59	59	71	6.08	0
2007	Iowa................	P.C.	8	41	4	1	.800	48	12	30	3.95	0
2007	Chicago	N.L.	59	69¹/₃	5	1	.833	96	35	41	1.43	1
2008	Chicago	N.L.	82	87¹/₃	2	4	.333	114	41	40	2.68	7
2009	Chicago	N.L.	79	74	2	4	.333	93	65	43	3.41	15
2010	Chicago	N.L.	77	77²/₃	2	3	.400	138	52	40	2.55	38
2011	Chicago	N.L.	75	74	2	6	.250	99	48	54	4.01	34
2012	Iowa................	P.C.	2	2	0	0	.000	4	2	1	0.00	0
2012	Chicago b	N.L.	61	55¹/₃	3	3	.500	72	45	40	3.42	20
Major League Totals		7 Yrs.	452	514²/₃	21	28	.429	671	345	329	3.38	115
	Division Series											
2007	Chicago	N.L.	2	3	0	1	.000	6	3	3	9.00	0
2008	Chicago	N.L.	2	2²/₃	0	0	.000	3	0	3	6.75	0
Division Series Totals			4	5²/₃	0	1	.000	9	3	6	7.94	0

a On disabled list from August 19 to September 4, 2006.
b On disabled list from May 12 to May 28, 2012.

MARQUIS, JASON SCOTT

Born, Manhasset, New York, August 21, 1978.
Bats Left. Throws Right. Height, 6 feet, 1 inch. Weight, 210 pounds.

Year	Club	Lea	G	IP	W	L	Pct	SO	BB	H	ERA	SAVES
1996	Danville	Appal.	7	23¹/₃	1	1	.500	24	7	30	4.63	0
1997	Macon	So.Atl.	28	141²/₃	14	10	.583	121	55	156	4.38	0
1998	Danville	Carolina	22	114²/₃	2	12	.143	135	41	120	4.87	0
1999	Myrtle Beach	Carolina	6	32	3	0	1.000	41	17	22	0.28	0
1999	Greenville a	Southern	12	55	3	4	.429	35	29	52	4.58	0
2000	Greenville........	Southern	11	68	4	2	.667	49	23	68	3.57	0
2000	Atlanta	N.L.	15	23¹/₃	1	0	1.000	17	12	23	5.01	0
2000	Richmond	Int.	6	20	0	3	.000	18	13	26	9.00	0
2001	Atlanta	N.L.	38	129¹/₃	5	6	.455	98	59	113	3.48	0
2002	Richmond	Int.	1	5	0	1	.000	6	1	5	3.60	0
2002	Atlanta b.............	N.L.	22	114¹/₃	8	9	.471	84	49	127	5.04	0
2003	Richmond	Int.	15	94	8	4	.667	75	34	93	3.35	0
2003	Atlanta c...........	N.L.	21	40²/₃	0	0	.000	19	18	43	5.53	1
2004	St. Louis.............	N.L.	32	201¹/₃	15	7	.682	138	70	215	3.71	0
2005	St. Louis.............	N.L.	33	207	13	14	.481	100	69	206	4.13	0
2006	St. Louis d	N.L.	33	194¹/₃	14	*16	.467	96	75	221	6.02	0
2007	Chicago	N.L.	34	191²/₃	12	9	.571	109	76	190	4.60	0
2008	Chicago e	N.L.	29	167	11	9	.550	91	70	172	4.53	0
2009	Colorado f	N.L.	33	216	15	13	.536	115	80	218	4.04	0
2010	Nationals	Gulf Coast	1	3	0	0	.000	4	0	2	0.00	0
2010	Potomac..........	Carolina	1	3²/₃	0	0	.000	3	1	6	7.36	0
2010	Harrisburg	Eastern	1	3¹/₃	0	0	.000	3	1	5	8.10	0
2010	Syracuse	Int.	2	11	0	0	.000	11	3	7	4.09	0
2010	Washington g..........	N.L.	13	58²/₃	2	9	.182	31	24	76	6.60	0
2011	Washington-Arizona h-i-j..	N.L.	23	132	8	6	.571	76	43	154	4.43	0

Year Club	Lea	G	IP	W	L	Pct	SO	BB	H	ERA	SAVES
2012 San Antonio ....Texas	1	7	1	0	1.000	5	2	5	1.29	0
2012 New Britain .... Eastern	2	14	1	0	1.000	11	0	12	1.93	0
2012 Minnesota .... A.L.	7	34	2	4	.333	12	14	52	8.47	0
2012 San Diego k-l-m........N.L.	15	93⅔	6	7	.462	79	28	94	4.04	0
Major League Totals ....13 Yrs.	348	1803⅓	112	109	.507	1065	687	1904	4.60	1
Division Series										
2004 St. Louis.............. N.L.	1	3⅓	0	0	.000	0	4	4	8.10	0
2008 Chicago .... N.L.	1	1	0	0	.000	1	0	1	9.00	0
2009 Colorado .... N.L.	1	1	0	0	.000	0	0	1	0.00	0
Division Series Totals	3	5⅓	0	0	.000	1	4	6	6.75	0
Championship Series										
2001 Atlanta .... N.L.	2	2	0	0	.000	3	2	2	0.00	0
2004 St. Louis.............. N.L.	1	4	0	0	.000	2	2	5	6.75	0
2005 St. Louis.............. N.L.	3	5⅓	0	1	.000	4	3	6	3.38	0
Championship Series Totals	6	11⅓	0	1	.000	9	7	13	3.97	0
World Series Record										
2004 St. Louis.............. N.L.	2	7	0	1	.000	4	7	6	3.86	0

a On disabled list from July 5 to 31, 1999.
b On disabled list from April 15 to May 11, 2002.
c Traded to St. Louis Cardinals with pitcher Ray King and pitcher Adam Wainwright for catcher Eli Marrero and outfielder J.D. Drew, December 13, 2003.
d Filed for free agency, October 30, 2006. Signed with Chicago Cubs, December 19, 2006.
e Traded to Colorado Rockies for pitcher Luis Vizcaino, January 6, 2009.
f Filed for free agency, November 5, 2009. Signed with Washington Nationals, December 22, 2009.
g On disabled list from April 19 to August 8, 2010.
h Traded to Arizona Diamondbacks for infielder Zachary Walters, July 30, 2011. .
i On disabled list from August 15 to October 30, 2011.
j Filed for free agency, October 31, 2011. Signed with Minnesota Twins, December 22, 2011.
k Released by Minnesota Twins, May 26, 2012. Signed with San Diego Padres organization, May 29, 2012.
l On disabled list from August 23 to October 15, 2012.
m Filed for free agency, November 3, 2012, re-signed with San Diego Padres, December 3, 2012.

MARSHALL, SEAN CHRISTOPHER
Born, Richmond, Virginia, August 30, 1982.
Bats Left. Throws Left. Height, 6 feet, 7 inches. Weight, 220 pounds.

Year Club	Lea	G	IP	W	L	Pct	SO	BB	H	ERA	SAVES
2003 Lansing .... Midwest	1	7	1	0	1.000	11	0	5	0.00	0
2003 Boise .... Northwest	14	73⅔	5	6	.455	88	23	66	2.57	0
2004 Lansing .... Midwest	7	48⅔	2	0	1.000	51	4	29	1.11	0
2004 West Tenn .... Southern	6	29	2	2	.500	23	12	36	5.90	0
2005 Daytona .... Fla.St.	12	69	4	4	.500	61	26	63	2.74	0
2005 West Tenn .... Southern	4	25	0	1	.000	24	5	16	2.52	0
2006 Iowa................. P.C.	4	21⅔	0	2	.000	21	14	17	3.32	0
2006 Chicago a............. N.L.	24	125⅔	6	9	.400	77	59	132	5.59	0
2007 Daytona .... Fla.St.	1	6	1	0	1.000	4	1	7	3.00	0
2007 Iowa................. P.C.	4	24⅔	2	0	1.000	15	8	17	1.82	0
2007 Chicago .... N.L.	21	103⅓	7	8	.467	67	35	107	3.92	0
2008 Iowa................. P.C.	7	31⅔	1	1	.500	25	6	26	3.41	0
2008 Chicago .... N.L.	34	65⅓	3	5	.375	58	23	60	3.86	1
2009 Chicago .... N.L.	55	85⅓	3	7	.300	68	32	91	4.32	0
2010 Chicago .... N.L.	80	74⅔	7	5	.583	90	25	58	2.65	1
2011 Chicago b............. N.L.	78	75⅔	6	6	.500	79	17	66	2.26	5
2012 Cincinnati............. N.L.	73	61	5	5	.500	74	16	55	2.51	9
Major League Totals ....7 Yrs.	365	591	37	45	.451	513	207	569	3.81	16
Division Series										
2008 Chicago .... N.L.	2	3⅓	0	0	.000	5	1	2	2.70	0
2012 Cincinnati............. N.L.	3	4	0	0	.000	3	0	0	0.00	0
Division Series Totals	5	7⅓	0	0	.000	8	1	2	1.23	0

a On disabled list from July 23 to September 1, 2006.
b Traded to Cincinnati Reds for pitcher Travis Wood, outfielder Dave Sappelt and infielder Ronald Torreyes, December 23, 2011.

MARTINEZ (MERCEDES), CRISTHIAN A.

Born, Santo Domingo, Dominican Republic, March 6, 1982.
Bats Right. Throws Right. Height, 6 feet, 1 inch. Weight, 185 pounds.

Year	Club	Lea	G	IP	W	L	Pct	SO	BB	H	ERA	SAVES
2003	Tigers	Gulf Coast	9	36²/₃	4	2	.667	39	13	35	5.65	0
2004	Oneonta	N.Y.-Penn.	2	13	1	0	1.000	12	1	9	2.08	0
2004	West Michigan	Midwest	12	73²/₃	5	2	.714	45	20	59	2.44	0
2005	Lakeland	Fla.St.	3	11	2	0	1.000	9	4	11	4.91	0
2006	Lakeland	Fla.St.	5	21²/₃	1	1	.500	15	5	27	4.98	0
2006	Tigers	Gulf Coast	7	35	3	2	.600	27	4	30	1.54	0
2006	Oneonta a	N.Y.-Penn.	7	41²/₃	1	2	.333	30	5	38	2.16	0
2007	Greensboro	So.Atl.	18	97	9	5	.643	74	18	97	4.08	0
2008	Greensboro	So.Atl.	8	44¹/₃	4	1	.800	14	9	44	4.67	0
2008	Jupiter	Fla.St.	20	109¹/₃	2	7	.222	78	16	117	3.79	0
2009	Jacksonville	Southern	17	104	9	3	.750	62	22	96	2.94	0
2009	Florida	N.L.	15	26¹/₃	1	1	.500	18	8	27	5.13	0
2010	Gwinnett	Int.	23	52²/₃	5	1	.833	49	8	45	3.08	0
2010	Atlanta b	N.L.	18	26	0	0	.000	22	6	28	4.85	0
2011	Gwinnett	Int.	4	22	2	1	.667	18	2	26	2.86	0
2011	Atlanta	N.L.	46	77²/₃	1	3	.250	58	19	56	3.36	0
2012	Atlanta	N.L.	54	73²/₃	5	4	.556	65	19	80	3.91	1
Major League Totals		4 Yrs.	133	203²/₃	7	8	.467	163	52	191	3.98	1

a Selected by Florida Marlin from Detroit Tigers in Rule V draft, December 7, 2006.

b Claimed on waivers by Atlanta Braves, April 8, 2010.

MASTERSON, JUSTIN DANIEL

Born, Kingston, Jamaica, March 22, 1985.
Bats Right. Throws Right. Height, 6 feet, 6 inches. Weight, 250 pounds.

Year	Club	Lea	G	IP	W	L	Pct	SO	BB	H	ERA	SAVES
2006	Lowell	N.Y.-Penn.	14	31²/₃	3	1	.750	33	2	20	0.85	0
2007	Lancaster	Calif.	17	95²/₃	8	5	.615	56	22	103	4.33	0
2007	Portland	Eastern	10	58	4	3	.571	59	18	49	4.34	0
2008	Portland	Eastern	8	38¹/₃	1	3	.250	37	16	37	4.23	0
2008	Pawtucket	Int.	4	9	1	0	1.000	8	1	6	2.89	0
2008	Boston	A.L.	36	88¹/₃	6	5	.545	68	40	68	3.16	0
2009	Boston-Cleveland a	A.L.	42	129¹/₃	4	10	.286	119	60	128	4.52	0
2010	Cleveland	A.L.	34	180	6	13	.316	140	73	197	4.70	0
2011	Cleveland	A.L.	34	216	12	10	.545	158	65	211	3.21	0
2012	Cleveland	A.L.	34	206¹/₃	11	15	.423	159	88	212	4.93	0
Major League Totals		5 Yrs.	180	820	39	53	.424	644	326	816	4.17	0
Division Series												
2008	Boston	A.L.	4	4	0	0	.000	3	3	6	2.25	0
Championship Series												
2008	Boston	A.L.	5	5²/₃	1	0	1.000	6	2	4	1.59	0

a Traded to Cleveland Indians with pitcher Nick Hagadone and pitcher Bryan Price for catcher Victor Martinez, July 31, 2009.

MATTHEUS, RYAN BRENT

Born, Galt, California, November 10, 1983.
Bats Right. Throws Right. Height, 6 feet, 3 inches. Weight, 205 pounds.

Year	Club	Lea	G	IP	W	L	Pct	SO	BB	H	ERA	SAVES
2004	Casper	Pioneer	7	27¹/₃	3	3	.500	16	14	27	4.94	0
2005	Asheville	So.Atl.	23	128¹/₃	7	6	.538	102	52	142	5.82	0
2006	Modesto	Calif.	28	156	7	12	.368	131	65	198	5.19	0
2007	Tulsa	Texas	26	158²/₃	9	11	.450	102	55	182	5.56	0
2008	Tulsa	Texas	58	57²/₃	2	5	.286	56	27	50	3.28	17
2009	Modesto	Calif.	3	4¹/₃	0	1	.000	2	2	2	2.08	0
2009	Colorado Springs	P.C.	13	16²/₃	1	1	.500	20	8	19	4.32	0
2009	Tulsa a	Texas	3	5	0	1	.000	5	1	3	3.60	0
2010	Nationals	Gulf Coast	6	6	0	1	.000	6	1	5	1.50	0
2010	Vermont	N.Y.-Penn.	4	5¹/₃	1	0	1.000	5	2	3	0.00	0
2011	Harrisburg	Eastern	13	14²/₃	2	1	.667	18	5	9	2.45	4
2011	Syracuse	Int.	9	10	0	0	.000	10	3	3	0.00	2
2011	Washington b	N.L.	35	32	2	2	.500	12	15	26	2.81	0
2012	Potomac	Carolina	1	1	0	1	.000	0	0	2	18.00	0
2012	Harrisburg	Eastern	2	2	0	0	.000	3	1	4	4.50	0
2012	Washington c	N.L.	66	66¹/₃	5	3	.625	41	19	57	2.85	0
Major League Totals		2 Yrs.	101	98¹/₃	7	5	.583	53	34	83	2.84	0

Year	Club	Lea	G	IP	W	L	Pct	SO	BB	H	ERA	SAVES
	Division Series											
2012 Washington	N.L.	3	3	1	0	1.000	0	1	3	6.00	0

a Traded by Colorado Rockies to Washington Nationals with pitcher Robinson Fabian for pitcher Joe Beimel, July 31, 2009.
b On disabled list from August 26 to September 20, 2011.
c On disabled list from May 21 to June 17, 2012.

MATUSZ, BRIAN ROBERT
Born, Grand Junction, Colorado, February 11, 1987.
Bats Left. Throws Left. Height, 6 feet, 5 inches. Weight, 200 pounds.

Year	Club	Lea	G	IP	W	L	Pct	SO	BB	H	ERA	SAVES
2009 Frederick	Carolina	11	66²/₃	4	2	.667	75	21	56	2.16	0
2009 Bowie	Eastern	8	46¹/₃	7	0	1.000	46	11	31	1.55	0
2009 Baltimore	A.L.	8	44²/₃	5	2	.714	38	14	52	4.63	0
2010 Baltimore	A.L.	32	175²/₃	10	12	.455	143	63	173	4.30	0
2011 Frederick	Carolina	1	4	0	0	.000	2	2	2	2.25	0
2011 Bowie	Eastern	1	6	0	0	.000	1	1	3	0.00	0
2011 Norfolk.	Int.	9	54²/₃	2	3	.400	41	19	51	3.46	0
2011 Baltimore a.	A.L.	12	49²/₃	1	9	.100	38	24	81	10.69	0
2012 Norfolk.	Int.	10	47	2	1	.667	32	15	43	4.21	1
2012 Baltimore	A.L.	34	98	6	10	.375	81	41	112	4.87	0
Major League Totals	4 Yrs.	86	368	22	33	.400	300	142	418	5.36	0
	Wild Card Playoff											
2012 Baltimore	A.L.	1	0¹/₃	0	0	.000	1	0	0	0.00	0
	Division Series											
2012 Baltimore	A.L.	5	4¹/₃	0	0	.000	5	2	2	2.08	0

a On disabled list from April 3 to June 1, 2011.

MC ALLISTER, ZACHARY TAYLOR (ZACH)
Born, Chillicothe, Illinois, December 8, 1987.
Bats Right. Throws Right. Height, 6 feet, 6 inches. Weight, 240 pounds.

Year	Club	Lea	G	IP	W	L	Pct	SO	BB	H	ERA	SAVES
2006 Yankees	Gulf Coast	11	35	5	2	.714	28	12	35	3.09	0
2007 Staten Island	N.Y.-Penn.	16	71¹/₃	4	6	.400	75	28	80	5.17	0
2008 Tampa	Fla.St.	15	88²/₃	8	6	.571	62	13	74	1.83	1
2008 Charleston	So.Atl.	10	62¹/₃	6	3	.667	53	8	59	2.45	0
2009 Trenton.	Eastern	22	121	7	5	.583	96	33	98	2.23	0
2010 Columbus.	Int.	3	17	1	2	.333	11	7	20	6.88	0
2010 Scranton-WB a.	Int.	24	132²/₃	8	10	.444	88	38	165	5.09	0
2011 Columbus.	Int.	25	154²/₃	12	3	.800	128	31	155	3.32	0
2011 Cleveland	A.L.	4	17²/₃	0	1	.000	14	7	26	6.11	0
2012 Columbus.	Int.	11	63¹/₃	5	2	.714	52	19	59	2.98	0
2012 Cleveland	A.L.	22	125¹/₃	6	8	.429	110	38	133	4.24	0
Major League Totals	2 Yrs.	26	143	6	9	.400	124	45	159	4.47	0

a Sent by New York Yankees to Cleveland Indians as player to be named later for outfielder Austin Kearns, August 20, 2010.

MC CARTHY, BRANDON PATRICK
Born, Glendale, California, July 7, 1983.
Bats Right. Throws Right. Height, 6 feet, 7 inches. Weight, 200 pounds.

Year	Club	Lea	G	IP	W	L	Pct	SO	BB	H	ERA	SAVES
2002 White Sox	Arizona	14	78¹/₃	4	4	.500	79	15	78	2.76	0
2003 Great Falls	Pioneer	16	101	9	4	.692	125	15	105	3.65	0
2004 Kannapolis	So.Atl.	15	94	8	5	.615	113	21	80	3.64	0
2004 Winston-Salem	Carolina	8	52	6	0	1.000	60	3	31	2.08	0
2004 Birmingham	Southern	4	26	3	1	.750	29	6	23	3.46	0
2005 Charlotte	Int.	20	119¹/₃	7	7	.500	130	32	104	3.92	0
2005 Chicago	A.L.	12	67	3	2	.600	48	17	62	4.03	0
2006 Chicago a	A.L.	53	84²/₃	4	7	.364	69	33	77	4.68	0
2007 Oklahoma	P.C.	1	4¹/₃	0	0	.000	6	0	3	0.00	0
2007 Texas b	A.L.	23	101²/₃	5	10	.333	59	48	111	4.87	0
2008 Rangers	Arizona	2	5	0	0	.000	5	1	7	3.60	0
2008 Oklahoma	P.C.	5	26²/₃	1	1	.500	23	8	21	3.38	0
2008 Texas c	A.L.	5	22	1	1	.500	10	8	20	4.09	0
2009 Oklahoma	P.C.	5	21²/₃	0	1	.000	22	9	20	4.15	0
2009 Texas d.	A.L.	17	97¹/₃	7	4	.636	65	36	96	4.62	0
2010 Oklahoma e-f	P.C.	11	56¹/₃	4	2	.667	44	11	51	3.36	0

Year	Club	Lea	G	IP	W	L	Pct	SO	BB	H	ERA	SAVES
2011 Stockton............	Calif.	2	10	1	0	1.000	8	0	7	0.00	0
2011 Oakland g.......	A.L.	25	170²/₃	9	9	.500	123	25	168	3.32	0
2012 Sacramento..........	P.C.	2	9²/₃	0	1	.000	11	3	9	5.59	0
2012 Oakland h-i............	A.L.	18	111	8	6	.571	73	24	115	3.24	0
Major League Totals........7 Yrs.		153	654¹/₃	37	39	.487	447	191	649	4.02	0

a Traded to Texas Rangers with outfielder David Paisano for pitcher John Danks, pitcher Jacob Rasner and pitcher Nick Massett, December 23, 2006.
b On disabled list from June 10 to July 2 and August 11 to September 11, 2007.
c On disabled list from March 30 to August 7, 2008.
d On disabled list from June 5 to September 1, 2009.
e On disabled list from July 29 to November 3, 2010.
f Filed for free agency, November 5, 2010. Signed with Oakland Athletics, December 14, 2010.
g On disabled list from May 19 to July 3, 2011.
h On disabled list from May 18 to June 2 and June 20 to August 10, 2012.
i Filed for free agency, November 3, 2012. Signed with Arizona Diamondbacks, December 11, 2012.

MC DONALD, JAMES ZELL

Born, Long Beach, California, October 19, 1984.
Bats Left. Throws Right. Height, 6 feet, 5 inches. Weight, 195 pounds.

Year	Club	Lea	G	IP	W	L	Pct	SO	BB	H	ERA	SAVES
2003 Dodgers........	Gulf Coast	12	48²/₃	2	4	.333	47	15	39	3.33	0
2004 a......................			Did Not Pitch								
2005 Ogden............	Pioneer	4	6	0	0	.000	9	2	4	1.50	0
2006 Columbus.........	So.Atl.	30	142¹/₃	5	10	.333	146	65	119	3.98	0
2007 Inland Empire........	Calif.	16	82	6	7	.462	104	21	79	3.95	0
2007 Jacksonville......	Southern	10	52²/₃	7	2	.778	64	16	42	1.71	0
2008 Jacksonville......	Southern	22	118²/₃	5	3	.625	113	46	98	3.19	0
2008 Las Vegas............	P.C.	5	22¹/₃	2	1	.667	28	7	17	3.63	0
2008 Los Angeles........	N.L.	4	6	0	0	.000	2	1	5	0.00	0
2009 Albuquerque........	P.C.	6	30¹/₃	1	0	1.000	40	14	21	3.26	0
2009 Los Angeles...........	N.L.	45	63	5	5	.500	54	34	60	4.00	0
2010 Dodgers...........	Arizona	2	5²/₃	0	0	.000	8	3	3	1.59	0
2010 Albuquerque..........	P.C.	12	63¹/₃	6	1	.857	57	24	64	4.41	0
2010 Los Angeles-Pittsburgh b	N.L.	15	71²/₃	4	6	.400	68	29	70	4.02	0
2011 Pittsburgh.............	N.L.	31	171	9	9	.500	142	78	176	4.21	0
2012 Pittsburgh............	N.L.	30	171	12	8	.600	151	69	147	4.21	0
Major League Totals........5 Yrs.		125	482²/₃	30	28	.517	417	211	458	4.10	0
Championship Series											
2008 Los Angeles...........	N.L.	2	5¹/₃	0	0	.000	7	2	3	0.00	0

a Played outfield for Dodgers in the Gulf Coast League.
b Traded to Pittsburgh Pirates with outfielder Andrew Lambo for pitcher Octavio Dotel, July 31, 2010.

MC GEE, JACOB DANIEL (JAKE)

Born, San Jose, California, August 6, 1986.
Bats Left. Throws Left. Height, 6 feet, 3 inches. Weight, 230 pounds.

Year	Club	Lea	G	IP	W	L	Pct	SO	BB	H	ERA	SAVES
2004 Princeton...........	Appal.	12	56²/₃	4	1	.800	53	25	49	3.97	0
2005 Hudson Valley....	N.Y.-Penn.	15	76²/₃	5	4	.556	89	23	64	3.64	0
2006 SW Michigan......	Midwest	26	134	7	9	.438	171	65	103	2.96	0
2007 Vero Beach.........	Fla.St.	21	116²/₃	5	4	.556	145	39	86	2.93	0
2007 Montgomery......	Southern	5	23¹/₃	3	2	.600	30	13	19	4.24	0
2008 Montgomery......	Southern	15	77²/₃	6	4	.600	65	37	65	3.94	0
2009 Charlotte...........	Fla.St.	11	22¹/₃	0	2	.000	26	9	26	6.45	0
2009 Rays............	Gulf Coast	5	7²/₃	0	2	.000	14	3	5	3.52	0
2010 Montgomery......	Southern	19	88¹/₃	3	7	.300	100	33	81	3.57	0
2010 Durham..............	Int.	11	17¹/₃	1	1	.500	27	3	9	0.52	1
2010 Tampa Bay............	A.L.	8	5	0	0	.000	6	3	2	1.80	0
2011 Durham..............	Int.	24	33¹/₃	4	2	.667	38	8	30	2.70	9
2011 Tampa Bay............	A.L.	37	28	5	2	.714	27	12	30	4.50	0
2012 Tampa Bay............	A.L.	69	55¹/₃	5	2	.714	73	11	33	1.95	0
Major League Totals........3 Yrs.		114	88¹/₃	10	4	.714	106	26	65	2.75	0
Division Series											
2011 Tampa Bay............	A.L.	1	0¹/₃	0	0	.000	0	0	0	0.00	0

MC PHERSON, KYLE LANDON

Born, Mobile, Alabama, November 11, 1987.
Bats Both. Throws Right. Height, 6 feet, 4 inches. Weight, 220 pounds.

Year	Club	Lea	G	IP	W	L	Pct	SO	BB	H	ERA	SAVES
2007	Pirates	Gulf Coast	12	51⅔	4	2	.667	35	10	47	2.61	0
2007	State College	N.Y.-Penn.	3	14⅓	0	1	.000	6	3	20	6.28	0
2008	State College	N.Y.-Penn.	15	55⅔	1	3	.250	41	5	52	4.37	1
2009	State College	N.Y.-Penn.	13	75⅓	4	3	.571	57	11	70	2.99	0
2009	West Virginia	So.Atl.	13	51	5	2	.714	32	6	53	4.94	0
2010	Bradenton	Fla.St.	2	4	0	0	.000	7	0	2	0.00	0
2010	West Virginia	So.Atl.	26	117⅔	9	9	.500	124	31	96	3.59	0
2011	Altoona	Eastern	16	89⅓	8	5	.615	82	21	75	3.02	0
2011	Bradenton	Fla.St.	12	71⅔	4	1	.800	60	6	62	2.89	0
2012	Altoona	Eastern	9	48⅔	3	5	.375	46	5	54	4.07	0
2012	Indianapolis	Int.	3	18⅓	0	1	.000	17	4	11	0.98	0
2012	Pittsburgh	N.L.	10	26⅓	0	2	.000	21	7	24	2.73	0

MEDLEN, KRISTOPHER ALLEN (KRIS)

Born, Artesia, California, October 7, 1985.
Bats Both. Throws Right. Height, 5 feet, 10 inches. Weight, 190 pounds.

Year	Club	Lea	G	IP	W	L	Pct	SO	BB	H	ERA	SAVES
2006	Danville	Appal.	20	22	1	0	1.000	36	2	14	0.41	10
2007	Myrtle Beach	Carolina	18	24	2	0	1.000	28	7	22	1.13	2
2007	Rome	So.Atl.	17	20⅔	0	1	.000	33	3	13	0.87	8
2007	Mississippi	Southern	3	2⅓	0	0	.000	2	2	4	11.57	1
2008	Mississippi	Southern	36	120⅓	7	8	.467	120	27	121	3.52	1
2009	Gwinnett	Int.	8	37⅔	5	0	1.000	44	10	20	1.19	0
2009	Atlanta	N.L.	37	67⅔	3	5	.375	72	30	65	4.26	0
2010	Atlanta a	N.L.	31	107⅔	6	2	.750	83	21	108	3.68	0
2011	Atlanta b	N.L.	2	2⅓	0	0	.000	2	0	1	0.00	0
2012	Gwinnett	Int.	3	13⅓	0	2	.000	12	6	15	4.72	0
2012	Atlanta	N.L.	50	138	10	1	.909	120	23	103	1.57	1
Major League Totals	4 Yrs.		120	315⅔	19	8	.704	277	74	277	2.85	2
Wild Card Playoff												
2012	Atlanta	N.L.	1	6⅓	0	1	.000	4	0	3	2.84	0

a On disabled list from August 5 to November 4, 2010.
b On disabled list from March 27 to September 24, 2011.

MELANCON, MARK DAVID

Born, Wheat Ridge, Colorado, March 28, 1985.
Bats Right. Throws Right. Height, 6 feet, 2 inches. Weight, 215 pounds.

Year	Club	Lea	G	IP	W	L	Pct	SO	BB	H	ERA	SAVES
2006	Staten Island	N.Y.-Penn.	7	7⅔	0	1	.000	8	2	9	3.52	2
2007 a					INJURED—Did Not Play							
2008	Trenton	Eastern	19	49⅔	6	0	1.000	47	12	32	1.81	2
2008	Tampa	Fla.St.	13	25⅓	1	0	1.000	20	6	26	2.84	0
2008	Scranton/WB	Int.	12	20	1	1	.500	22	4	11	2.70	1
2009	Scranton/WB	Int.	32	53	4	0	1.000	54	11	37	2.89	3
2009	New York	A.L.	13	16⅓	0	1	.000	10	10	13	3.86	0
2010	Round Rock	P.C.	3	4⅓	1	0	1.000	2	1	5	0.00	1
2010	Scranton/WB	Int.	40	56⅓	6	1	.857	58	31	63	3.67	6
2010	New York b	A.L.	2	4	0	0	.000	3	0	7	9.00	0
2010	Houston b	N.L.	20	17⅓	2	0	1.000	19	8	12	3.12	0
2011	Houston c	N.L.	71	74⅓	8	4	.667	66	26	65	2.78	20
2012	Pawtucket	Int.	21	21⅔	0	0	.000	27	3	15	0.83	11
2012	Boston d	A.L.	41	45	0	2	.000	41	12	45	6.20	1
Major League Totals	4 Yrs.		147	157	10	7	.588	139	56	142	4.07	21

a On minor league disabled list from April 5 to September 16, 2007.
b Traded to Houston Astros with infielder Jimmy Paredes for infielder Lance Berkman and cash, July 31, 2010.
c Traded to Boston Red Sox for infielder Jed Lowrie and pitcher Kyle Weiland, December 14, 2011.
d Traded to Pittsburgh Pirates with infielder Ivan DeJesus, pitcher Stolmy Pimentel and outfielder Jerry Sands for pitcher Joel Hanrahan and infielder Brock Holt, December 26, 2012.

MENDOZA (RODRIGUEZ), LUIS ALONSO

Born, Veracruz, Mexico, October 31, 1983.
Bats Right. Throws Right. Height, 6 feet, 3 inches. Weight, 240 pounds.

Year	Club	Lea	G	IP	W	L	Pct	SO	BB	H	ERA	SAVES
2002	Red Sox	Gulf Coast	13	57²/₃	3	4	.429	21	8	76	4.21	1
2003	Red Sox	Gulf Coast	2	5	0	0	.000	3	0	4	0.00	0
2003	Augusta	So.Atl.	13	59²/₃	3	3	.500	29	14	46	2.26	0
2004	Sarasota	Fla.St.	25	137	8	7	.533	51	54	133	3.74	0
2005	Lake Elsinore	Calif.	2	10²/₃	0	1	.000	3	4	18	9.28	0
2005	Wilmington a-b	Carolina	23	119¹/₃	4	9	.308	60	36	145	6.34	0
2006	Wilmington	Carolina	13	63	5	4	.556	46	14	67	3.14	0
2006	Portland	Eastern	9	48	1	5	.167	29	14	73	6.38	0
2006	Frisco c	Texas	7	38¹/₃	2	4	.333	21	11	55	7.75	0
2007	Frisco	Texas	26	148²/₃	15	4	.789	93	48	145	3.93	0
2007	Texas	A.L.	6	16	1	0	1.000	7	4	13	2.25	0
2008	Frisco	Texas	1	1¹/₃	0	0	.000	1	2	1	6.75	0
2008	Oklahoma	P.C.	8	35	2	3	.400	19	8	43	5.14	0
2008	Texas d	A.L.	25	63¹/₃	3	8	.273	35	25	97	8.67	1
2009	Texas	A.L.	1	1	0	0	.000	0	1	2	36.00	0
2009	Oklahoma	P.C.	25	111¹/₃	6	7	.462	78	50	130	4.53	0
2010	Kansas City	A.L.	4	4	0	1	.000	1	3	10	22.50	0
2010	Omaha e	P.C.	24	131²/₃	10	9	.526	59	32	145	4.10	0
2011	Omaha	P.C.	33	144¹/₃	12	5	.706	81	54	126	2.18	2
2011	Kansas City	A.L.	2	14²/₃	2	0	1.000	7	5	11	1.23	0
2012	Kansas City	A.L.	30	166	8	10	.444	104	59	176	4.23	0
Major League Totals		6 Yrs.	68	265	14	19	.424	154	97	309	5.40	1

a Claimed on waivers by San Diego Padres from Boston Red Sox, July 8, 2005.
b Claimed on waivers by Boston Red Sox, July 27, 2005.
c Traded to Texas Rangers for pitcher Bryan Corey, July 30, 2006.
d On disabled list from March 24 to April 12 and from April 24 to June 9, 2008.
e Sold to Kansas City Royals, April 2, 2010.

MIJARES, JOSE MANUEL

Born, Caracas, Venezuela, October 29, 1984.
Bats Left. Throws Left. Height, 6 feet. Weight, 230 pounds.

Year	Club	Lea	G	IP	W	L	Pct	SO	BB	H	ERA	SAVES
2004	Twins	Gulf Coast	19	29²/₃	4	0	1.000	25	15	22	2.43	5
2005	Fort Myers	Fla.St.	5	12	0	0	.000	17	5	5	1.50	0
2005	Beloit	Midwest	20	54¹/₃	6	3	.667	78	40	43	4.31	2
2006	Fort Myers	Fla.St.	27	63	3	5	.375	77	27	52	3.57	0
2007	New Britain	Eastern	46	61	5	3	.625	75	48	40	3.54	9
2007	Rochester	Int.	5	8²/₃	0	1	.000	6	5	9	6.23	0
2008	Twins	Gulf Coast	7	11	2	1	.667	16	1	10	2.45	0
2008	Fort Myers	Fla.St.	5	10¹/₃	0	0	.000	8	3	7	2.61	0
2008	New Britain	Eastern	11	15¹/₃	1	1	.500	17	7	16	2.93	2
2008	Minnesota	A.L.	10	10¹/₃	0	1	.000	5	0	3	0.87	0
2009	Rochester	Int.	5	6¹/₃	1	0	1.000	4	1	2	0.00	1
2009	Minnesota	A.L.	71	61²/₃	2	2	.500	55	23	50	2.34	0
2010	Rochester	Int.	2	1²/₃	0	0	.000	2	1	6	27.00	0
2010	Minnesota a	A.L.	47	32²/₃	1	1	.500	28	9	34	3.31	0
2011	Minnesota b-c	A.L.	58	49	0	2	.000	30	30	53	4.59	0
2012	Kansas City	A.L.	51	38²/₃	2	2	.500	37	13	36	2.56	0
2012	San Francisco d	N.L.	27	17²/₃	1	0	1.000	20	8	14	2.55	0
Major League Totals		5 Yrs.	264	210	6	8	.429	175	83	190	3.00	0
Division Series												
2009	Minnesota	A.L.	2	0²/₃	0	1	.000	0	1	1	13.50	0
2010	Minnesota	A.L.	3	1¹/₃	0	0	.000	0	1	0	0.00	0
2012	San Francisco	N.L.	2	0¹/₃	0	0	.000	1	1	2	81.00	0
Division Series Totals			7	2¹/₃	0	1	.000	1	3	3	15.43	0
Championship Series												
2012	San Francisco	N.L.	3	2	0	0	.000	3	1	1	0.00	0
World Series Record												
2012	San Francisco	N.L.	1	0¹/₃	0	0	.000	0	0	0	0.00	0

a On disabled list from April 16 to May 14 and August 12 to September 11, 2010.
b On disabled list from May 15 to May 30, 2011.
c Not offered contract, December 12, 2011. Signed with Kansas City Royals, December 21, 2011.
d Claimed on waivers by San Francisco Giants, August 6, 2012.

MILEY, WADE A.
Born, Hammond, Louisiana, November 13, 1986.
Bats Left. Throws Left. Height, 6 feet, 1 inch. Weight, 220 pounds.

Year	Club	Lea	G	IP	W	L	Pct	SO	BB	H	ERA	SAVES
2008 Yakima	. . . .	Northwest	7	11	1	1	.500	11	5	11	4.91	0
2009 Visalia	. . . .	Calif.	3	15	1	1	.500	11	4	18	4.80	0
2009 South Bend	. . . .	Midwest	21	113²/₃	5	9	.357	91	29	127	4.12	0
2010 Visalia	. . . .	Calif.	14	80¹/₃	4	5	.444	50	37	81	3.25	0
2010 Mobile	. . . .	Southern	13	72²/₃	5	2	.714	63	28	60	1.98	0
2011 Mobile	. . . .	Southern	14	75¹/₃	4	2	.667	46	28	74	4.78	0
2011 Reno	. . . .	P.C.	8	54¹/₃	4	1	.800	56	16	53	3.64	0
2011 Arizona	. . . .	N.L.	8	40	4	2	.667	25	18	48	4.50	0
2012 Arizona	. . . .	N.L.	32	194²/₃	16	11	.593	144	37	193	3.33	0
Major League Totals	. . . .	.2 Yrs.	40	234²/₃	20	13	.606	169	55	241	3.53	0

MILLER, ANDREW MARK
Born, Gainesville, Florida, May 21, 1985.
Bats Left. Throws Left. Height, 6 feet, 6 inches. Weight, 210 pounds.

Year	Club	Lea	G	IP	W	L	Pct	SO	BB	H	ERA	SAVES
2006 Lakeland	. . . .	Fla.St.	3	5	0	0	.000	9	1	2	0.00	0
2006 Detroit	. . . .	A.L.	8	10¹/₃	0	1	.000	6	10	8	6.10	0
2007 Lakeland	. . . .	Fla.St.	7	41¹/₃	1	4	.200	28	15	43	3.48	0
2007 Erie	. . . .	Eastern	4	30²/₃	2	0	1.000	24	5	22	0.59	0
2007 Toledo	. . . .	Int.	2	6	0	0	.000	9	5	6	9.00	0
2007 Detroit a-b	. . . .	A.L.	13	64	5	5	.500	56	39	73	5.63	0
2008 Marlins	. . . .	Gulf Coast	1	1	0	1	.000	0	1	2	18.00	0
2008 Carolina	. . . .	Southern	1	5²/₃	0	0	.000	6	4	2	3.18	0
2008 Jupiter	. . . .	Fla.St.	4	12²/₃	1	0	1.000	11	1	10	0.71	0
2008 Florida c	. . . .	N.L.	29	107¹/₃	6	10	.375	89	56	120	5.87	0
2009 Jupiter	. . . .	Fla.St.	1	4	0	0	.000	5	1	3	2.25	0
2009 Jacksonville	. . . . . .	Southern	1	6	0	0	.000	5	2	5	1.50	0
2009 Marlins	. . . .	Gulf Coast	2	7	0	0	.000	10	4	8	2.57	0
2009 New Orleans	. . . .	P.C.	3	11²/₃	1	2	.333	16	13	9	7.71	0
2009 Florida d	. . . .	N.L.	20	80	3	5	.375	59	43	85	4.84	0
2010 Jupiter	. . . .	Fla.St.	3	15²/₃	1	1	.500	23	15	8	1.72	0
2010 Jacksonville	. . . . . .	Southern	18	85¹/₃	1	8	.111	66	61	98	6.01	0
2010 Florida e	. . . .	N.L.	9	32²/₃	1	5	.167	28	26	51	8.54	0
2011 Pawtucket	. . . .	Int.	13	65²/₃	3	3	.500	61	35	42	2.47	0
2011 Boston f	. . . .	A.L.	17	65	6	3	.667	50	41	77	5.54	0
2012 Greenville	. . . .	So.Atl.	2	2	0	0	.000	3	0	2	0.00	0
2012 Pawtucket	. . . .	Int.	10	11	0	0	.000	23	14	4	5.73	1
2012 Boston g	. . . .	A.L.	53	40¹/₃	3	2	.600	51	20	28	3.35	0
Major League Totals	. . . .	.7 Yrs.	149	399²/₃	24	31	.436	339	235	442	5.54	0

a On disabled list from August 4 to August 24, 2007.

b Traded to Florida Marlins with pitcher Burke Badenhop, pitcher Eulogio De La Cruz, catcher Mike Rabelo and outfielder Cameron Maybin for pitcher Dontrelle Willis and infielder Miguel Cabrera, December 5, 2007.

c On disabled list from July 14 to September 1, 2008.

d On disabled list from April 21 to May 16, 2009.

e Traded to Boston Red Sox for pitcher Dustin Richardson, November 12, 2010.

f Not offered contract, December 2, 2010, re-signed with Boston Red Sox organization, December 16, 2010.

g On disabled list from March 26 to May 6, 2012.

MILLWOOD, KEVIN AUSTIN
Born, Gastonia, North Carolina, December 24, 1974.
Bats Right. Throws Right. Height, 6 feet, 4 inches. Weight, 230 pounds.

Year	Club	Lea	G	IP	W	L	Pct	SO	BB	H	ERA	SAVES
1993 Braves	. . . .	Gulf Coast	12	50	3	3	.500	49	28	36	3.06	0
1994 Macon	. . . .	So.Atl.	12	32²/₃	0	5	.000	24	32	31	5.79	1
1994 Danville	. . . .	Appal.	13	46	3	3	.500	56	34	42	3.72	1
1995 Macon	. . . .	So.Atl.	29	103	5	6	.455	89	57	86	4.63	0
1996 Durham	. . . .	Carolina	33	149¹/₃	6	9	.400	139	58	138	4.28	1
1997 Greenville	. . . .	Southern	11	61¹/₃	3	5	.375	61	24	59	4.11	0
1997 Richmond	. . . .	Int.	9	60²/₃	7	0	1.000	46	16	38	1.93	0
1997 Atlanta	. . . .	N.L.	12	51¹/₃	5	3	.625	42	21	55	4.03	0
1998 Atlanta	. . . .	N.L.	31	174¹/₃	17	8	.680	163	56	175	4.08	0
1999 Atlanta	. . . .	N.L.	33	228	18	7	.720	205	59	168	2.68	0
2000 Atlanta	. . . .	N.L.	36	212²/₃	10	13	.435	168	62	213	4.66	0
2001 Macon	. . . .	So.Atl.	1	3	0	0	.000	5	0	0	0.00	0
2001 Greenville	. . . .	Southern	2	10	0	1	.000	10	3	9	4.50	0

Year	Club	Lea	G	IP	W	L	Pct	SO	BB	H	ERA	SAVES
2001 Atlanta a...............	N.L.	21	121	7	7	.500	84	40	121	4.31	0	
2002 Atlanta b...............	N.L.	35	217	18	8	.692	178	65	186	3.24	0	
2003 Philadelphia c.........	N.L.	35	222	14	12	.538	169	68	210	4.01	0	
2004 Philadelphia d	N.L.	25	141	9	6	.600	125	51	155	4.85	0	
2005 Cleveland e-f-g........	A.L.	30	192	9	11	.450	146	52	182	*2.86	0	
2006 Texas	A.L.	34	215	16	12	.571	157	53	228	4.52	0	
2007 Frisco................	Texas	1	5	0	0	.000	3	1	1	0.00	0	
2007 Texas h...............	A.L.	31	172²/₃	10	14	.417	123	67	213	5.16	0	
2008 Frisco................	Texas	1	4	0	1	.000	6	2	5	2.25	0	
2008 Texas i	A.L.	29	168²/₃	9	10	.474	125	49	220	5.07	0	
2009 Texas j	A.L.	31	198²/₃	13	10	.565	123	71	195	3.67	0	
2010 Baltimore k...........	A.L.	31	190²/₃	4	*16	.200	132	65	223	5.10	0	
2011 Trenton............	Eastern	1	7	1	0	1.000	3	4	1	0.00	0	
2011 Scranton-WB	Int.	2	9	1	1	.500	7	2	14	8.00	0	
2011 Pawtucket	Int.	13	73²/₃	5	1	.833	66	25	79	4.28	0	
2011 Colorado l-m-n-o	N.L.	9	54¹/₃	4	3	.571	36	8	58	3.98	0	
2012 Seattle p.............	A.L.	28	161	6	12	.333	107	56	168	4.25	0	
Major League Totals ....16 Yrs.		451	2720¹/₃	169	152	.526	2083	843	2770	4.11	0	
Division Series												
1999 Atlanta	N.L.	2	10	1	0	1.000	9	0	1	0.90	1	
2000 Atlanta	N.L.	1	4²/₃	0	1	.000	3	3	4	7.71	0	
2002 Atlanta	N.L.	2	11	1	1	.500	14	0	7	3.27	0	
Division Series Totals		5	25²/₃	2	2	.500	26	3	12	3.16	1	
Championship Series												
1999 Atlanta	N.L.	2	12²/₃	1	0	1.000	9	1	13	3.55	0	
2001 Atlanta	N.L.	1	1	0	0	.000	1	0	0	0.00	0	
Championship Series Totals		3	13²/₃	1	0	1.000	10	1	13	3.29	0	
World Series Record												
1999 Atlanta	N.L.	1	2	0	1	.000	2	2	8	18.00	0	

a On disabled list from May 7 to July 20, 2001.
b Traded to Philadelphia Phillies for catcher Johnny Estrada, December 20, 2002.
c Filed for free agency, October 29, 2003, re-signed with Philadelphia Phillies, December 19, 2003.
d On disabled list from August 6 to September 12, 2004.
e Filed for free agency, October 28, 2004. Signed with Cleveland Indians, January 7, 2005.
f On disabled list from May 26 to June 16, 2005.
g Filed for free agency, October 28, 2005. Signed with Texas Rangers, December 29, 2005.
h On disabled list from April 29 to May 14 and May 15 to June 1, 2007.
i On disabled list from May 11 to May 28 and from July 24 to August 15, 2008.
j Traded to Baltimore Orioles with cash for pitcher Chris Ray and pitcher Ben Snyder, December 9, 2009.
k On disabled list from July 6 to July 22, 2010.
l Filed for free agency, November 1, 2010. Signed with New York Yankees organization, March 25, 2011.
m Released by New York Yankees, March 25, 2011. Signed with Boston Red Sox organization, May 19, 2011.
n Released by Boston Red Sox, August 7, 2011. Signed with Colorado Rockies, August 10, 2011.
o Filed for free agency, October 30, 2011. Signed with Seattle Mariners organization, January 24, 2012.
p Filed for free agency, November 3, 2012.

MILONE, TOM

Born, Saugas, California, February 16, 1987.
Bats Left. Throws Left. Height, 6 feet, 1 inch. Weight, 205 pounds.

Year	Club	Lea	G	IP	W	L	Pct	SO	BB	H	ERA	SAVES
2008 Vermont.........	N.Y.-Penn.	6	21²/₃	1	3	.250	22	3	27	4.57	0	
2008 Hagerstown	So.Atl.	7	37¹/₃	0	3	.000	27	6	36	2.89	0	
2009 Potomac.........	Carolina	27	151¹/₃	12	5	.706	106	36	144	2.91	0	
2010 Harrisburg	Eastern	27	158	12	5	.706	155	23	161	2.85	0	
2011 Syracuse	Int.	24	148¹/₃	12	6	.667	155	16	137	3.22	0	
2011 Washington a..........	N.L.	5	26	1	0	1.000	15	4	28	3.81	0	
2012 Oakland	A.L.	31	190	13	10	.565	137	36	207	3.74	0	
Major League Totals ....2 Yrs.		36	216	14	10	.583	152	40	235	3.75	0	
Division Series												
2012 Oakland	A.L.	1	6	0	0	.000	6	1	5	1.50	0	

a Traded to Oakland Athletics with pitcher A.J. Cole, pitcher Brad Peacock and catcher Derek Norris for pitcher Gio Gonzalez and pitcher Robert Gilliam, December 23, 2011.

MINOR, MICHAEL DAVID (MIKE)

Born, Chapel Hill, Tennessee, December 26, 1987.
Bats Right. Throws Left. Height, 6 feet, 3 inches. Weight, 205 pounds.

Year	Club	Lea	G	IP	W	L	Pct	SO	BB	H	ERA	SAVES
2009 Rome...............	So.Atl.	4	14	0	1	.000	17	0	10	0.64	0	
2010 Mississippi........	Southern	15	87	2	6	.250	109	34	74	4.03	0	

Year Club	Lea	G	IP	W	L	Pct	SO	BB	H	ERA	SAVES
2010 Gwinnett............Int.		6	33⅓	4	1	.800	37	12	19	1.89	0
2010 Atlanta..............N.L.		9	40⅔	3	2	.600	43	11	53	5.98	0
2011 Gwinnett............Int.		16	100⅔	4	5	.444	99	27	93	3.13	0
2011 Atlanta..............N.L.		15	82⅔	5	3	.625	77	30	93	4.14	0
2012 Atlanta..............N.L.		30	179⅓	11	10	.524	145	56	151	4.12	0
Major League Totals.......3 Yrs.		54	302⅔	19	15	.559	265	97	297	4.37	0

MOORE, MATTHEW CODY (MATT)
Born, Fort Walton Beach, Florida, June 18, 1989.
Bats Left. Throws Left. Height, 6 feet, 2 inches. Weight, 205 pounds.

Year Club	Lea	G	IP	W	L	Pct	SO	BB	H	ERA	SAVES
2007 Princeton...........Appal.		8	20⅓	0	0	.000	29	16	12	2.66	0
2008 Princeton...........Appal.		12	54⅓	2	2	.500	77	19	30	1.66	0
2009 Bowling Green.......So.Atl.		26	123	8	5	.615	176	70	86	3.15	0
2010 Charlotte...........Fla.St.		26	144⅔	6	11	.353	208	61	109	3.36	0
2011 Montgomery......Southern		18	102⅓	8	3	.727	131	28	68	2.20	0
2011 Durham..............Int.		9	52⅔	4	0	1.000	79	18	33	1.37	0
2011 Tampa Bay...........A.L.		3	9⅓	1	0	1.000	15	3	9	2.89	0
2012 Tampa Bay...........A.L.		31	177⅓	11	11	.500	175	81	158	3.81	0
Major League Totals.......2 Yrs.		34	186⅔	12	11	.522	190	84	167	3.76	0
Division Series											
2011 Tampa Bay...........A.L.		2	10	1	0	1.000	8	3	3	0.90	0

MORALES, FRANKLIN MIGUEL
Born, San Juan de Los Morros, Venezuela, January 24, 1986.
Bats Left. Throws Left. Height, 6 feet. Weight, 210 pounds.

Year Club	Lea	G	IP	W	L	Pct	SO	BB	H	ERA	SAVES
2004 Casper.............Pioneer		15	65	6	4	.600	82	39	92	7.62	0
2005 Asheville............So.Atl.		21	96⅓	8	4	.667	108	48	73	3.08	1
2006 Modesto............Calif.		27	154	10	9	.526	179	89	126	3.68	0
2007 Tulsa..............Texas		17	95⅔	3	4	.429	77	45	77	3.48	0
2007 Colorado Springs......P.C.		3	17	2	0	1.000	16	13	20	3.71	0
2007 Colorado...........N.L.		8	39⅓	3	2	.600	26	14	34	3.43	0
2008 Colorado...........N.L.		5	25⅓	1	2	.333	9	17	28	6.39	0
2008 Colorado Springs......P.C.		21	110⅓	10	5	.667	83	82	108	5.47	0
2009 Colorado Springs......P.C.		8	41⅓	2	2	.500	37	19	39	3.48	0
2009 Colorado a...........N.L.		40	40	3	2	.600	41	23	38	4.50	7
2010 Colorado Springs......P.C.		24	30⅓	3	0	1.000	34	19	20	2.67	1
2010 Colorado b...........N.L.		35	28⅔	0	4	.000	27	24	28	6.28	3
2011 Pawtucket...........Int.		6	6⅓	0	0	.000	6	3	3	1.42	0
2011 Colorado...........N.L.		14	14	0	1	.000	11	8	10	3.86	0
2011 Boston c-d...........A.L.		36	32⅓	1	1	.500	31	11	30	3.62	0
2012 Boston e...........A.L.		37	76⅓	3	4	.429	76	30	64	3.77	1
Major League Totals.......6 Yrs.		175	256	11	16	.407	221	127	232	4.36	11
Division Series											
2009 Colorado...........N.L.		4	2⅔	0	0	.000	1	3	0	0.00	0

a On disabled list from April 22 to June 12, 2009.
b On disabled list from May 6 to June 2, 2010.
c Sold to Boston Red Sox, May 20, 2011.
d On disabled list from May 26 to June 28, 2011.
e On disabled list from August 24 to November 2, 2012.

MORROW, BRANDON JOHN
Born, Santa Rosa, California, July 26, 1984.
Bats Right. Throws Right. Height, 6 feet, 3 inches. Weight, 190 pounds.

Year Club	Lea	G	IP	W	L	Pct	SO	BB	H	ERA	SAVES
2006 Mariners...........Arizona		7	13	0	2	.000	13	9	10	2.77	0
2006 Inland Empire........Calif.		1	3	0	0	.000	4	0	0	0.00	0
2007 Seattle.............A.L.		60	63⅓	3	4	.429	66	50	56	4.12	0
2008 West Tenn........Southern		6	7⅓	0	0	.000	8	6	3	0.00	0
2008 Tacoma.............P.C.		6	23⅓	1	2	.333	26	11	17	5.01	0
2008 Seattle.............A.L.		45	64⅔	3	4	.429	75	34	40	3.34	10
2009 Tacoma.............P.C.		10	55	5	3	.625	40	23	50	3.60	0
2009 Seattle a-b.........A.L.		26	69⅔	2	4	.333	63	44	66	4.39	6
2010 Toronto.............A.L.		26	146⅓	10	7	.588	178	66	136	4.49	0
2011 Dunedin............Fla.St.		3	9⅓	0	2	.000	11	6	13	7.71	0

Year Club	Lea	G	IP	W	L	Pct	SO	BB	H	ERA	SAVES
2011 Toronto c	A.L.	30	179$\frac{1}{3}$	11	11	.500	203	69	162	4.72	0
2012 Dunedin	Fla.St.	2	6	0	0	.000	6	3	8	1.50	0
2012 New Hampshire	Eastern	3	14$\frac{1}{3}$	1	0	1.000	12	3	10	2.51	0
2012 Toronto d	A.L.	21	124$\frac{2}{3}$	10	7	.588	108	41	98	2.96	0
Major League Totals . . . . . . .6 Yrs.		208	648	39	37	.513	693	304	558	4.10	16

a On disabled list from April 24 to May 9, 2009.
b Traded to Toronto Blue Jays for pitcher Brandon League and outfielder Johermyn Chavez, December 23, 2009.
c On disabled list from March 22 to April 21, 2011.
d On disabled list from June 12 to August 25, 2012.

MOSELEY, DUSTIN AARON
Born, Texarkana, Texas, December 26, 1981.
Bats Right. Throws Right. Height, 6 feet, 4 inches. Weight, 215 pounds.

Year Club	Lea	G	IP	W	L	Pct	SO	BB	H	ERA	SAVES
2001 Dayton	Midwest	25	148	10	8	.556	108	42	158	4.20	0
2002 Stockton.	Calif.	14	88$\frac{2}{3}$	6	3	.667	80	21	60	2.74	0
2002 Chattanooga	Southern	13	80$\frac{2}{3}$	5	6	.455	52	37	91	4.13	0
2003 Louisville	Int.	8	50	2	3	.400	27	14	46	2.70	0
2003 Chattanooga	Southern	18	112$\frac{2}{3}$	5	6	.455	73	28	116	3.83	0
2004 Louisville	Int.	12	71$\frac{2}{3}$	2	4	.333	48	34	78	4.65	0
2004 Chattanooga a	Southern	8	47$\frac{1}{3}$	3	2	.600	40	10	33	2.66	0
2005 Salt Lake	P.C.	17	82$\frac{1}{3}$	4	6	.400	38	30	102	5.03	0
2006 Salt Lake	P.C.	26	149$\frac{2}{3}$	13	8	.619	114	51	164	4.69	0
2006 Los Angeles	A.L.	3	11	1	0	1.000	3	2	22	9.00	0
2007 Los Angeles	A.L.	46	92	4	3	.571	50	27	97	4.40	0
2008 Rancho Cucamonga	Calif.	1	3$\frac{2}{3}$	0	0	.000	6	2	3	0.00	0
2008 Salt Lake	P.C.	20	116$\frac{2}{3}$	7	10	.412	83	34	150	6.94	0
2008 Los Angeles b	A.L.	12	50$\frac{1}{3}$	2	4	.333	37	20	70	6.79	0
2009 Los Angeles c.	A.L.	3	14$\frac{2}{3}$	1	0	1.000	8	3	20	4.30	0
2010 Scranton-WB	Int.	12	72$\frac{2}{3}$	4	4	.500	55	18	83	4.21	0
2010 New York d-e	A.L.	16	65$\frac{1}{3}$	4	4	.500	33	27	66	4.96	0
2011 San Diego f	N.L.	20	120	3	10	.231	64	36	117	3.30	0
2012 San Diego g-h	N.L.	1	5	0	0	.000	4	2	5	9.00	0
Major League Totals . . . . .7 Yrs.		101	358$\frac{1}{3}$	15	21	.417	199	117	397	4.67	0
Division Series											
2007 Los Angeles	A.L.	1	1	0	0	.000	1	0	1	0.00	0
Championship Series											
2010 New York	A.L.	1	2	1	0	1.000	4	0	0	0.00	0

a Traded by Cincinnati Reds to Anaheim Angels for pitcher Ramon Ortiz, December 14, 2004.
b On disabled list from May 2 to May 30, 2008.
c On disabled list from April 18 to November 12, 2009.
d Not offered contract, December 12, 2009. Signed with New York Yankees organization, February 16, 2010.
e Not offered contract, December 2, 2010. Signed with San Diego Padres, December 13, 2010.
f On disabled list from July 31 to October 28, 2011.
g On disabled list from April 8 to October 26, 2012.
h Filed for free agency, October 26, 2012.

MOTTE, JASON LOUIS
Born, Port Huron, Michigan, June 22, 1982.
Bats Right. Throws Right. Height, 6 feet. Weight, 195 pounds.

Year Club	Lea	G	IP	W	L	Pct	SO	BB	H	ERA	SAVES
2006 Quad Cities.	Midwest	8	12$\frac{2}{3}$	1	1	.500	13	16	16	4.97	0
2006 State College a . .	N.Y.-Penn.	21	26$\frac{1}{3}$	1	2	.333	25	4	30	3.08	8
2007 Palm Beach	Fla.St.	9	10	1	0	1.000	6	1	7	0.90	3
2007 Springfield	Texas	44	49	3	3	.500	63	22	36	2.20	8
2008 Memphis	P.C.	63	66$\frac{2}{3}$	4	3	.571	110	26	64	3.24	9
2008 St. Louis.	N.L.	12	11	0	0	.000	16	3	5	0.82	1
2009 St. Louis.	N.L.	69	56$\frac{2}{3}$	4	4	.500	54	23	57	4.76	0
2010 Memphis	P.C.	2	2$\frac{2}{3}$	0	0	.000	2	1	2	3.38	0
2010 St. Louis b	N.L.	56	52$\frac{1}{3}$	4	2	.667	54	18	41	2.24	2
2011 St. Louis.	N.L.	78	68	5	2	.714	63	16	49	2.25	9
2012 St. Louis.	N.L.	67	72	4	5	.444	86	17	49	2.75	*42
Major League Totals . . . . .5 Yrs.		282	260	17	13	.567	273	77	201	2.87	54
Wild Card Playoff											
2012 St. Louis.	N.L.	1	1$\frac{1}{3}$	0	0	.000	1	1	2	0.00	1
Division Series											
2009 St. Louis.	N.L.	1	1	0	0	.000	0	0	0	0.00	0

Year Club	Lea	G	IP	W	L	Pct	SO	BB	H	ERA	SAVES
2011 St. Louis	N.L.	3	3$\frac{1}{3}$	0	0	.000	3	0	1	0.00	2
2012 St. Louis	N.L.	2	3	1	0	1.000	1	0	3	3.00	0
Division Series Totals		6	7$\frac{1}{3}$	1	0	1.000	4	0	4	1.23	2
Championship Series											
2011 St. Louis	N.L.	4	4$\frac{2}{3}$	0	0	.000	4	0	0	0.00	2
2012 St. Louis	N.L.	3	4	0	0	.000	0	0	2	2.25	2
Championship Series Totals		7	8$\frac{2}{3}$	0	0	.000	4	0	2	1.04	4
World Series Record											
2011 St. Louis	N.L.	5	4$\frac{1}{3}$	0	1	.000	1	1	4	6.23	1

a Played catcher 2003-2006.
b On disabled list from August 3 to August 30, 2010.

MUJICA, EDWARD JOSE

Born, Valencia, Venezuela, May 10, 1984.
Bats Right. Throws Right. Height, 6 feet, 2 inches. Weight, 215 pounds.

Year Club	Lea	G	IP	W	L	Pct	SO	BB	H	ERA	SAVES
2003 Burlington	Appal.	14	55$\frac{2}{3}$	2	6	.250	41	20	57	4.37	0
2004 Lake County	So.Atl.	26	124	7	7	.500	89	32	130	4.65	2
2005 Kinston	Carolina	25	26	1	0	1.000	32	2	17	2.08	14
2005 Akron	Eastern	27	34$\frac{1}{3}$	2	1	.667	33	5	36	2.88	10
2006 Akron	Eastern	12	19	1	0	1.000	17	9	11	0.00	8
2006 Buffalo	Int.	22	32$\frac{2}{3}$	3	1	.750	29	5	31	2.48	5
2006 Cleveland	A.L.	10	18$\frac{1}{3}$	0	1	.000	12	0	25	2.95	0
2007 Buffalo	Int.	34	37$\frac{2}{3}$	2	1	.667	44	9	35	5.02	14
2007 Cleveland	A.L.	10	13	0	0	.000	7	2	19	8.31	0
2008 Buffalo	Int.	18	26	0	2	.000	27	10	29	4.15	4
2008 Cleveland	A.L.	33	38$\frac{2}{3}$	3	2	.600	27	10	46	6.75	0
2009 San Diego a	N.L.	67	93$\frac{2}{3}$	3	5	.375	76	19	101	3.94	2
2010 San Diego b	N.L.	59	69$\frac{2}{3}$	2	1	.667	72	6	59	3.62	0
2011 Florida	N.L.	67	76	9	6	.600	63	14	64	2.96	0
2012 Jupiter	Fla.St.	2	3	0	0	.000	2	0	0	0.00	0
2012 Miami-St. Louis c-d	N.L.	70	65$\frac{1}{3}$	0	3	.000	47	12	56	3.03	2
Major League Totals	7 Yrs.	316	374$\frac{2}{3}$	17	18	.486	304	63	370	3.92	4
Wild Card Playoff											
2012 St. Louis	N.L.	1	0$\frac{2}{3}$	0	0	.000	0	0	2	13.50	0
Division Series											
2012 St. Louis	N.L.	3	3	0	0	.000	1	1	3	3.00	0
Championship Series											
2012 St. Louis	N.L.	5	4	1	0	1.000	3	0	4	0.00	0

a Sold to San Diego Padres, April 1, 2009.
b Traded to Florida Marlins with pitcher Ryan Webb for outfielder Cameron Maybin, November 13, 2010.
c On disabled list from June 30 to July 18, 2012.
d Traded to St. Louis Cardinals for infielder Zack Cox, July 31, 2012.

MYERS, BRETT ALLEN

Born, Jacksonville, Florida, August 17, 1980.
Bats Right. Throws Right. Height, 6 feet, 4 inches. Weight, 240 pounds.

Year Club	Lea	G	IP	W	L	Pct	SO	BB	H	ERA	SAVES
1999 Phillies	Gulf Coast	7	27	2	1	.667	30	7	17	2.33	0
2000 Piedmont	So.Atl.	27	175$\frac{1}{3}$	13	7	.650	140	69	165	3.18	0
2001 Reading	Eastern	26	156	13	4	.765	130	43	156	3.87	0
2002 Scranton-WB	Int.	19	128	9	6	.600	97	20	121	3.59	0
2002 Philadelphia	N.L.	12	72	4	5	.444	34	29	73	4.25	0
2003 Philadelphia	N.L.	32	193	14	9	.609	143	76	205	4.43	0
2004 Philadelphia	N.L.	32	176	11	11	.500	116	62	196	5.52	0
2005 Philadelphia	N.L.	34	215$\frac{1}{3}$	13	8	.619	208	68	193	3.72	0
2006 Philadelphia	N.L.	31	198	12	7	.632	189	63	194	3.91	0
2007 Clearwater	Fla.St.	3	3$\frac{1}{3}$	0	0	.000	4	1	2	0.00	0
2007 Philadelphia a	N.L.	51	68$\frac{2}{3}$	5	7	.417	83	27	61	4.33	21
2008 Clearwater	Fla.St.	1	6$\frac{2}{3}$	0	1	.000	6	1	7	2.70	0
2008 Reading	Eastern	1	8	0	1	.000	10	2	5	2.25	0
2008 Lehigh	Int.	2	12$\frac{1}{3}$	1	1	.500	12	4	12	3.65	0
2008 Philadelphia	N.L.	30	190	10	13	.435	163	65	197	4.55	0
2009 Lakewood	So.Atl.	1	1	0	0	.000	1	1	0	0.00	0
2009 Clearwater	Fla.St.	1	1	0	0	.000	3	0	2	0.00	0
2009 Reading	Eastern	2	4	0	1	.000	7	1	2	2.25	0
2009 Lehigh Valley	Int.	2	2	0	0	.000	3	0	0	0.00	1

Year Club	Lea	G	IP	W	L	Pct	SO	BB	H	ERA	SAVES
2009 Philadelphia b-c	N.L.	18	70²/₃	4	3	.571	50	23	74	4.84	0
2010 Houston	N.L.	33	223²/₃	14	8	.636	180	66	212	3.14	0
2011 Houston	N.L.	34	216	7	14	.333	160	57	226	4.46	0
2012 Houston	N.L.	35	30²/₃	0	4	.000	20	6	35	3.52	19
2012 Chicago d-e	A.L.	35	34²/₃	3	4	.429	21	9	30	3.12	0
Major League Totals ..... 11 Yrs.		377	1688²/₃	97	93	.511	1367	551	1696	4.20	40
Division Series											
2007 Philadelphia	N.L.	2	1¹/₃	0	0	.000	3	0	2	0.00	0
2008 Philadelphia	N.L.	1	7	1	0	1.000	4	3	2	2.57	0
2009 Philadelphia	N.L.	1	0²/₃	0	0	.000	0	2	0	0.00	0
Division Series Totals		4	9	1	0	1.000	7	5	4	2.00	0
Championship Series											
2008 Philadelphia	N.L.	1	5	1	0	1.000	6	4	6	9.00	0
World Series Record											
2008 Philadelphia	N.L.	1	7	0	1	.000	2	3	7	3.86	0
2009 Philadelphia	N.L.	1	1	0	0	.000	2	0	1	9.00	0
World Series Totals		2	8	0	1	.000	4	3	8	4.50	0

a On disabled list from May 24 to July 27, 2007.

b On disabled list from May 28 to September 4, 2009.

c Filed for free agency, November 6, 2009. Signed with Houston Astros, January 9, 2010.

d Traded to Chicago White Sox with cash for pitcher Matthew Heidenreich, pitcher Blair Walters and player to be named later, July 21, 2012.

e Filed for free agency, November 3, 2012. Signed with Cleveland Indians. January 4, 2013.

NARVESON, CHRISTOPHER GREGG (CHRIS)

Born, Englewood, Colorado, December 20, 1981.
Bats Left. Throws Left. Height, 6 feet, 3 inches. Weight, 205 pounds.

Year Club	Lea	G	IP	W	L	Pct	SO	BB	H	ERA	SAVES
2000 Johnson City	Appal.	12	55	2	4	.333	63	25	57	3.27	0
2001 Potomac	Carolina	11	66²/₃	4	3	.571	53	13	52	2.57	0
2001 Peoria	Midwest	8	50	3	3	.500	53	11	32	1.98	0
2002 Johnson City	Appal.	6	18¹/₃	0	2	.000	16	6	23	4.91	0
2002 Peoria	Midwest	9	42¹/₃	2	1	.667	36	8	49	4.46	0
2003 Palm Beach	Fla.St.	15	91¹/₃	7	7	.500	65	19	83	2.86	0
2003 Tennessee	Southern	10	57	4	3	.571	34	26	56	3.00	0
2004 Tennessee	Southern	23	127²/₃	5	10	.333	121	51	114	4.16	0
2004 Tulsa a	Texas	4	20	0	3	.000	14	13	16	3.15	0
2005 Pawtucket	Int.	21	111¹/₃	4	5	.444	66	46	109	4.77	0
2005 Memphis b-c	P.C.	2	6²/₃	0	1	.000	8	7	11	12.15	0
2006 Palm Beach	Fla.St.	3	17	0	0	.000	13	1	9	2.12	0
2006 Memphis	P.C.	15	80	8	5	.615	58	33	70	2.81	0
2006 St. Louis	N.L.	5	9¹/₃	0	0	.000	12	5	6	4.82	0
2007 Palm Beach	Fla.St.	3	10	0	0	.000	6	3	10	2.70	0
2007 Memphis d	P.C.	9	45²/₃	3	2	.600	35	21	41	5.72	0
2008 Nashville	P.C.	28	136	6	13	.316	125	57	140	5.43	0
2009 Nashville	P.C.	26	75¹/₃	4	4	.500	76	26	59	3.70	5
2009 Milwaukee	N.L.	21	47	2	0	1.000	46	16	45	3.83	0
2010 Milwaukee	N.L.	37	167²/₃	12	9	.571	137	59	172	4.99	0
2011 Milwaukee e	N.L.	30	161²/₃	11	8	.579	126	65	160	4.45	0
2012 Milwaukee f	N.L.	2	9	1	1	.500	5	4	10	7.00	0
Major League Totals ..... 5 Yrs.		95	394²/₃	26	18	.591	326	149	393	4.67	0
Division Series											
2011 Milwaukee	N.L.	2	2¹/₃	0	0	.000	5	1	2	11.57	0
Championship Series											
2011 Milwaukee	N.L.	4	5	0	0	.000	8	1	5	10.80	0

a Sent by St. Louis Cardinals to Colorado Rockies as player to be named later for outfielder Larry Walker, August 11, 2004.

b Traded to Boston Red Sox with catcher Charles Johnson and cash for pitcher Byung-Hyun Kim, March 30, 2005.

c Claimed on waivers by St. Louis Cardinals, August 9, 2005.

d Filed for free agency, October 29, 2007. Signed with Milwaukee Brewers organization, December 4, 2007.

e On disabled list from August 7 to August 22, 2011.

f On disabled list from April 16 to October 29, 2012.

NATHAN, JOSEPH MICHAEL (JOE)
Born, Houston, Texas, November 22, 1974.
Bats Right. Throws Right. Height, 6 feet, 4 inches. Weight, 220 pounds.

Year	Club	Lea	G	IP	W	L	Pct	SO	BB	H	ERA	SAVES
1995 San Francisco a		N.L.					Did Not Pitch					
1996							Did Not Play					
1997 Salem-Keizer		Northwest	18	62	2	1	.667	44	26	53	2.47	2
1998 Shreveport		Texas	4	15$\frac{1}{3}$	1	3	.250	10	9	20	8.80	0
1998 San Jose		California	22	122	8	6	.571	118	48	100	3.32	0
1999 Shreveport		Texas	2	8$\frac{2}{3}$	0	1	.000	7	7	5	3.12	0
1999 San Francisco		N.L.	19	90$\frac{1}{3}$	7	4	.636	54	46	84	4.18	1
1999 Fresno		P.C.	13	74$\frac{2}{3}$	6	4	.600	82	36	68	4.46	0
2000 San Francisco		N.L.	20	93$\frac{1}{3}$	5	2	.714	61	63	89	5.21	0
2000 San Jose		California	1	5	0	1	.000	2	1	4	3.60	0
2000 Bakersfield		California	1	5$\frac{1}{3}$	1	0	1.000	6	7	2	5.06	0
2000 Fresno b		P.C.	3	14$\frac{1}{3}$	0	2	.000	9	7	15	4.40	0
2001 Fresno		P.C.	10	46$\frac{1}{3}$	0	5	.000	21	33	63	7.77	0
2001 Shreveport		Texas	21	62$\frac{1}{3}$	3	6	.333	33	37	73	6.93	0
2002 Fresno		P.C.	31	146$\frac{1}{3}$	6	12	.333	117	74	167	5.60	0
2002 San Francisco		N.L.	4	3$\frac{2}{3}$	0	0	.000	2	0	1	0.00	0
2003 San Francisco c		N.L.	78	79	12	4	.750	83	33	51	2.96	0
2004 Minnesota		A.L.	73	72$\frac{1}{3}$	1	2	.333	89	23	48	1.62	44
2005 Minnesota		A.L.	69	70	7	4	.636	94	22	46	2.70	43
2006 Minnesota		A.L.	64	68$\frac{1}{3}$	7	0	1.000	95	16	38	1.58	36
2007 Minnesota		A.L.	68	71$\frac{2}{3}$	4	2	.667	77	19	54	1.88	37
2008 Minnesota		A.L.	68	67$\frac{2}{3}$	1	2	.333	74	18	43	1.33	39
2009 Minnesota		A.L.	70	68$\frac{2}{3}$	2	2	.500	89	22	42	2.10	47
2010 Minnesota d		A.L.					INJURED—Did Not Play					
2011 Rochester		Int.	3	3	0	0	.000	5	1	2	0.00	0
2011 Minnesota e-f		A.L.	48	44$\frac{2}{3}$	2	1	.667	43	14	38	4.84	14
2012 Texas		A.L.	66	64$\frac{1}{3}$	3	5	.375	78	13	55	2.80	37
Major League Totals	12 Yrs.		647	794	51	28	.646	839	289	589	2.87	298
Wild Card Playoff												
2012 Texas		A.L.	1	1	0	0	.000	1	1	2	18.00	0
Division Series												
2003 San Francisco		N.L.	2	0$\frac{1}{3}$	0	1	.000	1	1	4	81.00	0
2004 Minnesota		A.L.	3	5	0	1	.000	6	5	2	3.60	1
2006 Minnesota		A.L.	1	0$\frac{2}{3}$	0	0	.000	1	0	1	0.00	0
2009 Minnesota		A.L.	2	2	0	0	.000	2	1	5	9.00	0
Division Series Totals			8	8	0	2	.000	10	7	12	7.88	1

a Played shortstop in 1995.
b On disabled list from May 13 to June 5 and July 14 to August 18, 2000.
c Traded to Minnesota Twins with pitcher Boof Bonser and pitcher Francisco Liriano for catcher A.J. Pierzynski, November 14, 2003.
d On disabled list from March 26 to November 3, 2010.
e On disabled list from May 28 to June 24, 2011.
f Filed for free agency, October 30, 2011. Signed with Texas Rangers, November 21, 2011.

NICASIO, JUAN RAMON
Born, San Francisco de Macoris, Dominican Republic, August 31, 1986.
Bats Right. Throws Right. Height, 6 feet, 3 inches. Weight, 230 pounds.

Year	Club	Lea	G	IP	W	L	Pct	SO	BB	H	ERA	SAVES
2007 Casper		Pioneer	13	43$\frac{1}{3}$	0	3	.000	33	13	48	4.36	0
2008 Tri-City		Northwest	12	54	2	4	.333	61	19	46	4.50	0
2009 Asheville		So.Atl.	18	112	9	3	.750	115	23	110	2.41	0
2010 Modesto		Calif.	28	177$\frac{1}{3}$	12	10	.545	171	31	186	3.91	0
2011 Tulsa		Texas	9	56$\frac{2}{3}$	5	1	.833	63	10	48	2.22	0
2011 Colorado a		N.L.	13	71$\frac{2}{3}$	4	4	.500	58	18	73	4.14	0
2012 Colorado b		N.L.	11	58	2	3	.400	54	22	72	5.28	0
Major League Totals	2 Yrs.		24	129$\frac{2}{3}$	6	7	.462	112	40	145	4.65	0

a On disabled list from August 6 to October 31, 2011.
b On disabled list from June 3 to November 2, 2012.

NIEMANN, JEFFREY WARREN (JEFF)
Born, Houston, Texas, February 28, 1983.
Bats Right. Throws Right. Height, 6 feet, 9 inches. Weight, 280 pounds.

Year	Club	Lea	G	IP	W	L	Pct	SO	BB	H	ERA	SAVES
2005 Visalia		Calif.	5	20$\frac{1}{3}$	0	1	.000	28	10	12	3.98	0
2005 Montgomery		Southern	6	10$\frac{1}{3}$	0	1	.000	14	5	7	4.35	0

Year	Club	Lea	G	IP	W	L	Pct	SO	BB	H	ERA	SAVES
2006 Montgomery	Southern	14	77$^{1}/_{3}$	5	5	.500	84	29	56	2.68	0
2007 Durham	Int.	25	131	12	6	.667	123	46	144	3.98	0
2008 Durham	Int.	24	133	9	5	.643	128	50	101	3.59	0
2008 Tampa Bay	A.L.	5	16	2	2	.500	14	8	18	5.06	0
2009 Tampa Bay	A.L.	31	180$^{2}/_{3}$	13	6	.684	125	59	185	3.94	0
2010 Tampa Bay a	A.L.	30	174$^{1}/_{3}$	12	8	.600	131	61	159	4.39	0
2011 Charlotte	Fla.St.	1	4	0	0	.000	2	0	1	0.00	0
2011 Durham	Int.	2	9$^{1}/_{3}$	1	1	.500	8	3	10	3.86	0
2011 Tampa Bay b	A.L.	23	135$^{1}/_{3}$	11	7	.611	105	37	131	4.06	0
2012 Charlotte	Fla.St.	2	6	0	0	.000	6	3	9	6.00	0
2012 Durham	Int.	2	8$^{1}/_{3}$	0	0	.000	4	2	17	7.56	0
2012 Tampa Bay c	A.L.	8	38	2	3	.400	34	12	30	3.08	0
Major League Totals ....5 Yrs.		97	544$^{1}/_{3}$	40	26	.606	409	177	523	4.08	0
Division Series											
2010 Tampa Bay	A.L.	1	3	0	0	.000	4	1	1	0.00	0

a On disabled list from August 4 to August 25, 2010.
b On disabled list from May 6 to June 19, 2011.
c On disabled list from May 15 to September 1, 2012.

NIESE, JONATHON JOSEPH
Born, Lima, Ohio, October 27, 1986.
Bats Left. Throws Left. Height, 6 feet, 4 inches. Weight, 215 pounds.

Year	Club	Lea	G	IP	W	L	Pct	SO	BB	H	ERA	SAVES
2005 Mets	Gulf Coast	7	24$^{2}/_{3}$	1	0	1.000	24	10	23	3.65	0
2006 St. Lucie	Fla.St.	2	10	0	2	.000	10	5	8	4.50	0
2006 Hagerstown	So.Atl.	25	123$^{2}/_{3}$	11	9	.550	132	62	121	3.93	0
2007 St. Lucie	Fla.St.	27	134$^{1}/_{3}$	11	7	.611	110	31	151	4.29	0
2008 Binghamton	Eastern	22	124$^{1}/_{3}$	6	7	.462	112	44	118	3.04	0
2008 New Orleans	P.C.	7	39$^{2}/_{3}$	5	1	.833	32	14	34	3.40	0
2008 New York	N.L.	3	14	1	1	.500	11	8	20	7.07	0
2009 Buffalo	Int.	16	94$^{1}/_{3}$	5	6	.455	82	26	95	3.82	0
2009 New York a	N.L.	5	25$^{2}/_{3}$	1	1	.500	18	9	27	4.21	0
2010 Buffalo	Int.	1	6	0	0	.000	3	0	8	3.00	0
2010 New York b	N.L.	30	173$^{2}/_{3}$	9	10	.474	148	62	192	4.20	0
2011 New York c	N.L.	27	157$^{1}/_{3}$	11	11	.500	138	44	178	4.40	0
2012 New York	N.L.	30	190$^{1}/_{3}$	13	9	.591	155	49	174	3.40	0
Major League Totals ......5 Yrs.		95	561	35	32	.522	470	172	591	4.06	0

a On disabled list from August 6 to November 12, 2009.
b On disabled list from May 17 to June 5, 2010.
c On disabled list from August 24 to September 30, 2011.

NOESI, HECTOR
Born, Esperanza, Dominican Republic, January 26, 1987.
Bats Right. Throws Right. Height, 6 feet, 3 inches. Weight, 200 pounds.

Year	Club	Lea	G	IP	W	L	Pct	SO	BB	H	ERA	SAVES
2006 Yankees	Gulf Coast	5	7	0	0	.000	11	1	5	1.29	1
2007 Charleston	So.Atl.	5	20	1	1	.500	11	8	25	4.50	0
2008 Yankees	Gulf Coast	9	24$^{2}/_{3}$	2	1	.667	24	3	23	3.65	0
2008 Staten Island	N.Y.-Penn.	5	24	1	1	.500	31	7	20	3.00	0
2009 Charleston	So.Atl.	17	75$^{2}/_{3}$	3	4	.429	78	11	62	2.38	0
2009 Tampa	Fla.St.	9	41$^{1}/_{3}$	3	0	1.000	40	4	34	3.92	0
2010 Trenton	Eastern	17	98$^{2}/_{3}$	8	4	.667	86	18	90	3.10	0
2010 Tampa	Fla.St.	8	43	5	2	.714	53	6	35	2.72	0
2010 Scranton-WB	Int.	3	18$^{2}/_{3}$	1	1	.500	14	4	23	4.82	0
2011 Scranton-WB	Int.	6	24$^{2}/_{3}$	1	1	.500	17	9	28	3.28	0
2011 New York a	A.L.	30	56$^{1}/_{3}$	2	2	.500	45	22	63	4.47	0
2012 Tacoma	P.C.	11	64$^{1}/_{3}$	2	6	.250	55	22	80	5.74	0
2012 Seattle	A.L.	22	106$^{2}/_{3}$	2	12	.143	68	39	107	5.82	0
Major League Totals ......2 Yrs.		52	163	4	14	.222	113	61	170	5.36	0

a Traded to Seattle Mariners with catcher Jesus Montero for pitcher Michael Pineda and pitcher Jose Campos, January 17, 2012.

NOLASCO, CARLOS ENRIQUE (RICKY)
Born, Corona, California, December 13, 1982.
Bats Right. Throws Right. Height, 6 feet, 2 inches. Weight, 220 pounds.

Year	Club	Lea	G	IP	W	L	Pct	SO	BB	H	ERA	SAVES
2001 Cubs.	Arizona	5	18	1	0	1.000	23	5	11	1.50	0
2002 Boise	Northwest	15	90²/₃	7	2	.778	92	25	72	2.48	0
2003 Daytona	Fla.St.	26	149	11	5	.688	136	48	129	2.96	0
2004 Iowa	P.C.	9	40²/₃	2	3	.400	28	16	68	9.30	0
2004 West Tenn	Southern	19	107	6	4	.600	115	37	104	3.70	0
2005 West Tenn a	Southern	27	161²/₃	14	3	.824	173	46	151	2.89	0
2006 Florida	N.L.	35	140	11	11	.500	99	41	157	4.82	0
2007 Florida	N.L.	5	21¹/₃	1	2	.333	11	9	26	5.48	0
2007 Florida	Gulf Coast	2	3¹/₃	0	0	.000	8	0	4	2.70	0
2007 Jupiter	Fla.St.	5	12	1	1	.500	9	1	10	0.75	0
2007 Carolina	Southern	1	3	0	1	.000	2	1	2	6.00	0
2007 Albuquerque b	P.C.	4	15¹/₃	0	2	.000	15	4	29	14.09	0
2008 Florida	N.L.	34	212¹/₃	15	8	.652	186	42	192	3.52	0
2009 New Orleans	P.C.	2	15	1	1	.500	12	3	12	2.40	0
2009 Florida	N.L.	31	185	13	9	.591	195	44	188	5.06	0
2010 Florida c	N.L.	26	157²/₃	14	9	.609	147	33	169	4.51	0
2011 Florida	N.L.	33	206	10	12	.455	148	44	*244	4.67	0
2012 Miami	N.L.	31	191	12	13	.480	125	47	214	4.48	0
Major League Totals	7 Yrs.	195	1113¹/₃	76	64	.543	911	260	1190	4.49	0

a Traded by Chicago Cubs to Florida Marlins with pitcher Sergio Mitre and pitcher Renyel Pinto for outfielder Juan Pierre, December 7, 2005.
b On disabled list from April 7 to May 1 and May 18 to August 20, 2007.
c On disabled list from September 1 to November 5, 2010.

NORBERTO, JORDAN
Born, Nagua, Dominican Republic, December 8, 1986.
Bats Left. Throws Left. Height, 6 feet. Weight, 195 pounds.

Year	Club	Lea	G	IP	W	L	Pct	SO	BB	H	ERA	SAVES
2006 Missoula	Pioneer	16	75²/₃	3	2	.600	64	40	59	3.09	0
2007 South Bend	Midwest	21	102¹/₃	6	7	.462	111	46	102	5.28	0
2008 South Bend	Midwest	31	101²/₃	5	7	.417	109	56	108	5.31	0
2009 Visalia	Calif.	29	44²/₃	4	1	.800	59	22	36	1.61	2
2009 Mobile	Southern	19	23²/₃	0	2	.000	30	18	29	7.99	2
2010 Reno	P.C.	21	29¹/₃	3	0	1.000	38	19	25	3.07	4
2010 Arizona	N.L.	33	20	0	2	.000	15	22	16	5.85	0
2011 Reno	P.C.	41	48²/₃	6	2	.750	54	26	46	4.25	1
2011 Oakland	A.L.	6	6²/₃	0	0	.000	4	7	8	8.10	0
2011 Sacramento a	P.C.	6	8¹/₃	0	0	.000	10	4	6	1.08	1
2012 Sacramento	P.C.	1	1	0	0	.000	2	0	0	0.00	0
2012 Oakland b	A.L.	39	52	4	1	.800	46	22	37	2.77	1
Major League Totals	3 Yrs.	78	78²/₃	4	3	.571	65	51	61	4.00	1

a Traded to Oakland Athletics with infielder Brandon Allen for pitcher Brad Ziegler, July 31, 2011.
b On disabled list from May 31 to June 21 and August 18 to October 15, 2012.

NORRIS, DAVID STEFAN (BUD)
Born, Greenbrae, California, March 2, 1985.
Bats Right. Throws Right. Height, 6 feet. Weight, 225 pounds.

Year	Club	Lea	G	IP	W	L	Pct	SO	BB	H	ERA	SAVES
2006 Tri-City	N.Y.-Penn.	15	38	2	0	1.000	46	13	28	3.79	2
2007 Salem	Carolina	1	6	1	0	1.000	2	1	4	1.50	0
2007 Lexington	So.Atl.	22	96²/₃	2	8	.200	117	41	85	4.75	0
2008 Corpus Christi	Texas	19	80	3	8	.273	84	31	89	4.05	0
2009 Round Rock	P.C.	19	120	4	9	.308	112	53	104	2.63	0
2009 Houston	N.L.	11	55²/₃	6	3	.667	54	25	59	4.53	0
2010 Round Rock	P.C.	3	14²/₃	1	0	1.000	14	6	16	3.07	0
2010 Houston a	N.L.	27	153²/₃	9	10	.474	158	77	151	4.92	0
2011 Houston	N.L.	31	186	6	11	.353	176	70	177	3.77	0
2012 Oklahoma	P.C.	1	5	1	0	1.000	7	3	3	3.60	0
2012 Houston b	N.L.	29	168¹/₃	7	13	.350	165	66	165	4.65	0
Major League Totals	4 Yrs.	98	563²/₃	28	37	.431	553	238	552	4.42	0

a On disabled list from May 24 to June 27, 2010.
b On disabled list from June 13 to June 29, 2012.

NOVA (GUANCE), IVAN MANUEL

Born, San Cristobal, Dominican Republic, January 12, 1987.
Bats Right. Throws Right. Height, 6 feet, 4 inches. Weight, 225 pounds.

Year	Club	Lea	G	IP	W	L	Pct	SO	BB	H	ERA	SAVES
2006	Yankees	Gulf Coast	10	43	3	0	1.000	36	7	36	2.72	1
2007	Charleston	So.Atl.	21	99$\frac{1}{3}$	6	8	.429	54	31	121	4.98	0
2008	Tampa	Fla.St.	26	148$\frac{2}{3}$	8	13	.381	109	46	168	4.36	0
2009	Trenton	Eastern	12	72$\frac{1}{3}$	5	4	.556	47	31	65	2.36	0
2009	Scranton-WB	Int.	12	67	1	4	.200	43	28	72	5.10	0
2010	Scranton-WB	Int.	23	145	12	3	.800	115	48	135	2.86	0
2010	New York	A.L.	10	42	1	2	.333	26	17	44	4.50	0
2011	Scranton-WB	Int.	3	16	1	2	.333	18	2	16	3.38	0
2011	New York	A.L.	28	165$\frac{1}{3}$	16	4	.800	98	57	163	3.70	0
2012	New York b	A.L.	28	170$\frac{1}{3}$	12	8	.600	153	56	194	5.02	0
Major League Totals		3 Yrs.	66	377$\frac{2}{3}$	29	14	.674	277	130	401	4.38	0
Division Series												
2011	New York	A.L.	2	8$\frac{1}{3}$	1	1	.500	8	4	7	4.32	0

a Selected by San Diego Padres from New York Yankees in Rule V draft, December 11, 2008. Returned to New York Yankees, March 25, 2009.
b On disabled list from August 22 to September 15, 2012.

O'DAY, DARREN CHRISTOPHER

Born, Jacksonville, Florida, October 22, 1982.
Bats Right. Throws Right. Height, 6 feet, 4 inches. Weight, 225 pounds.

Year	Club	Lea	G	IP	W	L	Pct	SO	BB	H	ERA	SAVES
2006	Cedar Rapids	Midwest	17	23$\frac{1}{3}$	3	1	.750	14	2	20	2.70	1
2006	Orem	Pioneer	14	14$\frac{1}{3}$	0	1	.000	15	5	11	2.51	7
2007	Rancho Cucamonga	Calif.	24	24	4	0	1.000	26	6	10	0.75	11
2007	Arkansas	Texas	29	29$\frac{1}{3}$	3	4	.429	22	14	27	3.99	10
2008	Salt Lake	P.C.	21	33	2	2	.500	30	7	29	3.27	7
2008	Los Angeles a	A.L.	30	43$\frac{1}{3}$	0	1	.000	29	14	49	4.57	0
2009	New York	N.L.	4	3	0	0	.000	2	1	5	0.00	0
2009	Texas b	A.L.	64	55$\frac{2}{3}$	2	1	.667	54	17	36	1.94	2
2010	Texas	A.L.	72	62	6	2	.750	45	12	43	2.03	0
2011	Frisco	Texas	1	1	0	0	.000	1	0	1	9.00	0
2011	Round Rock	P.C.	17	20$\frac{1}{3}$	1	0	1.000	26	4	16	2.21	1
2011	Texas c-d	A.L.	16	16$\frac{2}{3}$	0	*	.000	18	5	17	5.40	0
2012	Baltimore	A.L.	69	67	7	1	.875	69	14	49	2.28	0
Major League Totals		5 Yrs.	255	247$\frac{2}{3}$	15	6	.714	217	63	199	2.73	2
Wild Card Playoff												
2012	Baltimore	A.L.	1	2	0	0	.000	1	0	1	0.00	0
Division Series												
2010	Texas	A.L.	4	2	0	0	.000	4	0	2	0.00	0
2012	Baltimore	A.L.	4	5	0	0	.000	4	1	0	0.00	0
Division Series Totals			8	7	0	0	.000	8	1	2	0.00	0
Championship Series												
2010	Texas	A.L.	3	0$\frac{2}{3}$	0	1	.000	1	1	1	13.50	0
World Series Record												
2010	Texas	A.L.	4	2	0	0	.000	3	0	3	13.50	0

a Selected by New York Mets in Rule V draft, December 11, 2008.
b Claimed on waivers by Texas Rangers, April 22, 2009.
c On disabled list from April 27 to July 2 and August 25 to September 13, 2011.
d Claimed on waivers by Baltimore Orioles, November 2, 2011.

O'FLAHERTY, ERIC GEORGE

Born, Walla Walla, Washington, February 5, 1985.
Bats Left. Throws Left. Height, 6 feet, 2 inches. Weight, 220 pounds.

Year	Club	Lea	G	IP	W	L	Pct	SO	BB	H	ERA	SAVES
2003	Mariners	Arizona	13	27$\frac{2}{3}$	3	0	1.000	20	7	17	1.95	0
2003	Everett	Northwest	3	10$\frac{2}{3}$	1	0	1.000	7	3	8	3.38	0
2004	Wisconsin	Midwest	12	57$\frac{1}{3}$	3	3	.500	38	23	83	6.12	0
2005	Wisconsin	Midwest	45	69$\frac{2}{3}$	4	4	.500	51	30	73	3.75	13
2006	Inland Empire	Calif.	16	28$\frac{2}{3}$	0	1	.000	33	6	31	3.45	1
2006	San Antonio	Texas	25	39$\frac{1}{3}$	2	2	.500	36	15	45	1.14	7
2006	Tacoma	P.C.	2	3$\frac{2}{3}$	1	0	1.000	4	1	3	0.00	0
2006	Seattle	A.L.	15	11	0	0	.000	6	6	18	4.09	0
2007	Tacoma	P.C.	6	8	0	0	.000	8	4	5	1.13	3
2007	Seattle	A.L.	56	52$\frac{1}{3}$	7	1	.875	36	20	45	4.47	0

Year	Club	Lea	G	IP	W	L	Pct	SO	BB	H	ERA	SAVES
2008 Seattle	A.L.	7	6²/₃	0	1	.000	4	4	16	20.25	0
2008 West Tenn	Southern	1	2	0	0	.000	2	0	1	0.00	0
2008 Tacoma a	P.C.	14	16¹/₃	1	0	1.000	19	9	23	4.96	2
2009 Atlanta	N.L.	78	56¹/₃	2	1	.667	39	18	52	3.04	0
2010 Gwinnett	Int.	3	4	0	0	.000	5	1	1	0.00	0
2010 Atlanta b	N.L.	56	44	3	2	.600	36	18	37	2.45	0
2011 Atlanta	N.L.	78	73²/₃	2	4	.333	67	21	59	0.98	0
2012 Atlanta	N.L.	64	57¹/₃	3	0	1.000	46	19	47	1.73	0

Major League Totals 7 Yrs.		354	301¹/₃	17	9	.654	234	106	274	2.87	0
Wild Card Playoff											
2012 Atlanta	N.L.	1	1	0	0	.000	0	0	2	0.00	0

a Claimed on waivers by Atlanta Braves, November 20, 2008.
b On disabled list from July 10 to August 20, 2010.

OGANDO, ALEXI

Born, San Pedro de Macoris, Dominican Republic, October 5, 1983.
Bats Right. Throws Right. Height, 6 feet, 4 inches. Weight, 185 pounds.

Year	Club	Lea	G	IP	W	L	Pct	SO	BB	H	ERA	SAVES
2010 Texas a-b-c	A.L.	44	41²/₃	4	1	.800	39	16	31	1.30	0
2011 Texas	A.L.	31	169	13	8	.619	126	43	149	3.51	0
2012 Round Rock	P.C.	2	3	0	0	.000	5	0	1	0.00	0
2012 Texas d	A.L.	58	66	2	0	1.000	66	17	49	3.27	3

Major League Totals 3 Yrs.		133	276²/₃	19	9	.679	231	76	229	3.12	3
Division Series											
2010 Texas	A.L.	1	0¹/₃	0	0	.000	0	0	1	0.00	0
2011 Texas	A.L.	3	2²/₃	0	0	.000	2	0	1	0.00	0

Division Series Totals		4	3	0	0	.000	2	0	2	0.00	0
Championship Series											
2010 Texas	A.L.	2	2	0	0	.000	2	1	3	4.50	0
2011 Texas	A.L.	4	7²/₃	2	0	1.000	10	2	3	1.17	0

Championship Series Totals		6	9¹/₃	2	0	1.000	12	3	6	1.86	0
World Series Record											
2010 Texas	A.L.	2	3²/₃	0	0	.000	6	0	1	0.00	0
2011 Texas	A.L.	6	2²/₃	0	0	.000	3	7	7	10.13	0

| World Series Totals | | 8 | 6¹/₃ | 0 | 0 | .000 | 9 | 7 | 8 | 4.26 | 0 |

a Played as an outfielder in the Arizona and Northern Leagues in 2003-2004.
b Confined to the Dominican Republic with visa problems 2005-2009.
c Selected by Texas Rangers from Oakland Athletics in Rule V draft. December 8, 2005.
d On disabled list from June 11 to July 17, 2012.

OLIVER, DARREN CHRISTOPHER

Born, Rio Linda, California, October 6, 1970.
Bats Right. Throws Left. Height, 6 feet, 2 inches. Weight, 200 pounds.

Year	Club	Lea	G	IP	W	L	Pct	SO	BB	H	ERA	SAVES
1988 Rangers	Gulf Coast	12	54¹/₃	5	1	.833	59	18	39	2.15	0
1989 Gastonia	So.Atl.	24	122¹/₃	8	7	.533	108	82	86	3.16	0
1990 Rangers	Gulf Coast	3	6	0	0	.000	7	1	1	0.00	0
1990 Gastonia	So.Atl.	1	2	0	0	.000	2	4	1	13.50	0
1991 Charlotte	Fla.St.	2	8	0	1	.000	12	3	6	4.50	0
1992 Charlotte	Fla.St.	8	25	1	0	1.000	33	10	11	0.72	2
1992 Tulsa	Texas	3	14¹/₃	0	1	.000	14	4	15	3.14	0
1993 Tulsa	Texas	46	73¹/₃	7	5	.583	77	41	51	1.96	6
1993 Texas	A.L.	2	3¹/₃	0	0	.000	4	1	2	2.70	0
1994 Okla City	A.A.	6	7¹/₃	0	0	.000	6	3	1	0.00	1
1994 Texas	A.L.	43	50	4	0	1.000	50	35	40	3.42	2
1995 Texas a	A.L.	17	49	4	2	.667	39	32	47	4.22	0
1996 Charlotte	Fla.St.	2	12	0	1	.000	9	3	8	3.00	0
1996 Texas	A.L.	30	173²/₃	14	6	.700	112	76	190	4.66	0
1997 Texas	A.L.	32	201¹/₃	13	12	.520	104	82	213	4.20	0
1998 Oklahoma	P.C.	1	5	0	0	.000	1	1	2	0.00	0
1998 Texas b	A.L.	19	103¹/₃	6	7	.462	58	43	140	6.53	0
1998 St. Louis c	N.L.	10	57	4	4	.500	29	23	64	4.26	0
1999 St. Louis	N.L.	30	196¹/₃	9	9	.500	119	74	197	4.26	0
2000 Texas	A.L.	21	108	2	9	.182	49	42	151	7.42	0
2000 Oklahoma	P.C.	7	32	2	1	.667	28	14	22	1.97	0
2000 Tulsa d-e	Texas	1	4²/₃	0	1	.000	5	2	10	11.57	0
2001 Texas	A.L.	28	154	11	11	.500	104	65	189	6.02	0

Year	Club	Lea	G	IP	W	L	Pct	SO	BB	H	ERA	SAVES
2001	Oklahoma............	P.C.	1	3	0	0	.000	3	0	3	0.00	0
2001	Tulsa f-g...........	Texas	1	5	0	1	.000	5	2	4	5.40	0
2002	Memphis	P.C.	5	16	0	2	.000	9	17	17	7.87	0
2002	Boston h	A.L.	14	58	4	5	.444	32	27	70	4.66	0
2003	Colorado i	N.L.	33	$180^{1}/_3$	13	11	.542	88	61	201	5.04	0
2004	Florida-Houston j-k-l	N.L.	27	$72^{2}/_3$	3	3	.500	46	21	87	5.94	0
2005	Iowa................	P.C.	3	$13^{1}/_3$	0	3	.000	10	5	28	13.50	0
2005	Tucson m-n-o-p	P.C.	4	$18^{1}/_3$	1	0	1.000	8	3	33	6.38	0
2006	New York q...........	N.L.	45	81	4	1	.800	60	21	70	3.44	0
2007	Los Angeles	A.L.	61	$64^{1}/_3$	3	1	.750	51	23	58	3.78	0
2008	Los Angeles r.........	A.L.	54	72	7	1	.875	48	16	67	2.88	0
2009	Los Angeles s-t	A.L.	63	73	5	1	.833	65	22	61	2.71	0
2010	Texas	A.L.	64	$61^{2}/_3$	1	2	.333	65	15	53	2.48	1
2011	Texas u.............	A.L.	61	51	5	5	.500	44	11	47	2.29	2
2012	Toronto	A.L.	62	$56^{2}/_3$	3	4	.429	52	15	43	2.06	2
Major League Totals		19 Yrs.	716	$1866^{2}/_3$	115	94	.550	1219	705	1990	4.53	7
Division Series												
1996	Texas	A.L.	1	8	0	1	.000	3	2	6	3.38	0
2006	New York	N.L.	1	$1^{1}/_3$	0	0	.000	0	0	3	20.25	0
2007	Los Angeles	A.L.	1	$0^{2}/_3$	0	0	.000	0	0	2	27.00	0
2008	Los Angeles	A.L.	2	$1^{1}/_3$	0	0	.000	1	1	0	0.00	0
2009	Los Angeles	A.L.	3	$2^{1}/_3$	1	0	1.000	2	0	1	0.00	0
2010	Texas	A.L.	3	$4^{1}/_3$	0	1	.000	5	1	3	4.15	0
2011	Texas	A.L.	2	$1^{1}/_3$	0	0	.000	1	0	3	6.75	0
Division Series Totals			13	$19^{1}/_3$	1	2	.333	12	4	18	5.12	0
Championship Series												
2006	New York	N.L.	1	6	0	0	.000	3	1	3	0.00	0
2009	Los Angeles	A.L.	5	$6^{1}/_3$	0	0	.000	6	4	6	4.26	0
2010	Texas	A.L.	3	$2^{1}/_3$	0	0	.000	1	3	1	7.71	1
2011	Texas	A.L.	3	$2^{1}/_3$	0	0	.000	2	0	0	0.00	0
Championship Series Totals			12	$17^{1}/_3$	0	0	.000	12	8	10	2.60	1
World Series Record												
2010	Texas	A.L.	2	$2^{2}/_3$	0	0	.000	4	0	3	3.38	0
2011	Texas	A.L.	3	$2^{1}/_3$	1	0	1.000	3	0	3	11.57	0
World Series Totals.............			5	5	1	0	1.000	7	0	6	7.20	0

a On disabled list from June 27 to October 2, 1995.

b On disabled list from June 11 to June 26, 1998.

c Traded to St. Louis Cardinals with infielder Fernando Tatis and player to be named later for infielder Royce Clayton and pitcher Todd Stottlemyre, July 31, 1998. St. Louis Cardinals received infielder Mark Little to complete trade, August 9, 1998.

d Filed for free agency, October 29, 1999. Signed with Texas Rangers, January 27, 2000.

e On disabled list from June 17 to July 19 and July 31 to August 31, 2000.

f On disabled list from May 8 to June 6, 2001.

g Traded to Boston Red Sox for outfielder Carl Everett, December 12, 2001.

h Released by Boston Red Sox, July 2, 2002. Signed with St. Louis Cardinals organization, July 20, 2002.

i Released by St. Louis Cardinals, August 13, 2002. Signed with Colorado Rockies organization, January 29, 2003.

j Filed for free agency, October 26, 2003. Signed with Florida Marlins, January 28, 2004.

k Sold to Houston Astros, July 22, 2004.

l On disabled list from August 6 to September 6, 2004.

m Filed for free agency, November 8, 2004. Signed with Colorado Rockies organization, January 22, 2005.

n Released by Colorado Rockies, March 31, 2005. Signed with Arizona Diamondbacks organization, April 12, 2005.

o Released by Arizona Diamondbacks, May 3, 2005. Signed with Chicago Cubs organization, May 7, 2005.

p Released by Chicago Cubs, May 20, 2005. Signed with New York Mets organization, December 16, 2005.

q Filed for free agency, October 31, 2006. Signed with Los Angeles Angels, December 11, 2006.

r Filed for free agency, October 31, 2008, re-signed with Los Angeles Angels, January 17, 2009.

s On disabled list from April 19 to May 4, 2009.

t Filed for free agency, November 5, 2009. Signed with Texas Rangers, December 22, 2009.

u Filed for free agency, October 30, 2011. Signed with Toronto Blue Jays, January 9, 2012.

ONDRUSEK, LOGAN JARED

Born, Hallettsville, Texas, February 13, 1985.
Bats Right. Throws Right. Height, 6 feet, 8 inches. Weight, 225 pounds.

Year	Club	Lea	G	IP	W	L	Pct	SO	BB	H	ERA	SAVES
2005	Billings...........	Pioneer	15	$55^{1}/_3$	1	6	.143	46	19	72	6.02	0
2006	Dayton............	Midwest	27	$52^{2}/_3$	4	5	.444	47	19	48	3.42	0
2006	Billings...........	Pioneer	1	1	0	1	.000	3	1	4	27.00	0
2006	Chattanooga.......	Southern	1	4	0	0	.000	7	3	0	0.00	0
2007	Sarasota...........	Fla.St.	31	124	7	10	.412	86	48	131	4.43	1

Year Club	Lea	G	IP	W	L	Pct	SO	BB	H	ERA	SAVES
2008 Sarasota............	Fla.St.	40	79²/₃	1	7	.125	58	32	93	4.97	1
2008 Louisville.............	Int.	1	1¹/₃	0	0	.000	1	2	1	0.00	0
2009 Sarasota...........	Fla.St.	13	18²/₃	2	0	1.000	12	7	7	0.96	0
2009 Louisville.............	Int.	19	20²/₃	0	0	.000	11	2	16	1.74	12
2009 Carolina.........	Southern	24	32²/₃	2	1	.667	24	12	21	1.65	7
2010 Louisville.............	Int.	14	19²/₃	0	1	.000	14	3	21	4.12	1
2010 Cincinnati.............	N.L.	60	58²/₃	5	0	1.000	39	20	49	3.68	0
2011 Cincinnati a...........	N.L.	66	61¹/₃	5	5	.500	41	28	55	3.23	0
2012 Louisville.............	Int.	3	4	0	1	.000	5	4	8	9.00	0
2012 Cincinnati.............	N.L.	63	54²/₃	5	2	.714	39	31	51	3.46	2
Major League Totals........3 Yrs.		189	174²/₃	15	7	.682	119	79	155	3.45	2
Division Series											
2010 Cincinnati.............	N.L.	2	2	0	0	.000	0	1	0	0.00	0

a On disabled list from August 8 to August 26, 2011.

OTTAVINO, ADAM ROBERT
Born, New York, New York, November 22, 1985.
Bats Left. Throws Right. Height, 6 feet, 5 inches. Weight, 230 pounds.

Year Club	Lea	G	IP	W	L	Pct	SO	BB	H	ERA	SAVES
2006 Quad Cities........	Midwest	8	36²/₃	2	3	.400	38	19	28	3.44	0
2006 State College.....	N.Y.-Penn.	6	28²/₃	2	2	.500	26	13	23	3.14	0
2007 Palm Beach.........	Fla.St.	27	143¹/₃	12	8	.600	128	63	130	3.08	0
2008 Springfield...........	Texas	24	115¹/₃	3	7	.300	96	52	133	5.23	0
2009 Memphis.............	P.C.	27	144	7	12	.368	119	82	141	4.75	0
2010 Memphis.............	P.C.	9	47²/₃	5	3	.625	43	12	43	3.97	0
2010 St. Louis a.............	N.L.	5	22¹/₃	0	2	.000	12	9	37	8.46	0
2011 Memphis.............	P.C.	26	141	7	8	.467	120	71	154	4.85	0
2012 Colorado Springs.......	P.C.	13	19²/₃	0	0	.000	25	7	22	3.20	0
2012 Colorado b............	N.L.	53	79	5	1	.833	81	34	76	4.56	0
Major League Totals........2 Yrs.		58	101¹/₃	5	3	.625	93	43	113	5.42	0

a On disabled list from July 4 to September 29, 2010.
b Claimed on waivers by Colorado Rockies, April 3, 2012.

PADILLA, VICENTE DE LA CRUZ
Born, Chinandega, Nicaragua, September 27, 1977.
Bats Right. Throws Right. Height, 6 feet, 2 inches. Weight, 220 pounds.

Year Club	Lea	G	IP	W	L	Pct	SO	BB	H	ERA	SAVES
1999 High Desert........	California	9	50²/₃	4	1	.800	55	17	50	3.73	0
1999 Tucson..............	P.C.	18	93²/₃	7	4	.636	58	24	107	3.75	0
1999 Arizona..............	N.L.	5	2²/₃	0	1	.000	0	3	7	16.88	0
2000 Tucson..............	P.C.	12	18¹/₃	0	1	.000	22	8	22	4.42	1
2000 Arizona-Philadelphia a...	N.L.	55	65¹/₃	4	7	.364	51	28	72	3.72	2
2001 Scranton-WB...........	Int.	16	81²/₃	7	0	1.000	75	11	64	2.42	0
2001 Philadelphia b.........	N.L.	23	34	3	1	.750	29	12	36	4.24	0
2002 Philadelphia...........	N.L.	32	206	14	11	.560	128	53	198	3.28	0
2003 Philadelphia...........	N.L.	32	208²/₃	14	12	.538	133	62	196	3.62	0
2004 Clearwater..........	Fla.St.	1	2	0	1	.000	1	1	3	9.00	0
2004 Scranton/WB...........	Int.	2	4²/₃	0	0	.000	6	5	6	13.50	0
2004 Philadelphia c..........	N.L.	20	115¹/₃	7	7	.500	82	36	119	4.53	0
2005 Clearwater..........	Fla.St.	1	5	0	1	.000	3	1	4	1.80	0
2005 Scranton/WB...........	Int.	1	5	1	0	1.000	4	2	6	3.60	0
2005 Philadelphia d-e........	N.L.	27	147	9	12	.429	103	74	146	4.71	0
2006 Texas f..............	A.L.	33	200	15	10	.600	156	70	206	4.50	0
2007 Frisco..............	Texas	6	12	0	1	.000	12	9	14	8.25	0
2007 Texas g..............	A.L.	23	120¹/₃	6	10	.375	71	50	146	5.76	0
2008 Texas h..............	A.L.	29	171	14	8	.636	127	65	185	4.74	0
2009 Albuquerque..........	P.C.	1	5	1	0	1.000	5	3	3	3.60	0
2009 Texas................	A.L.	18	108	8	6	.571	59	42	120	4.92	0
2009 Los Angeles i-j-k.......	N.L.	8	39¹/₃	4	0	1.000	38	12	36	3.20	0
2010 Inland Empire..........	Calif.	3	10²/₃	0	0	.000	10	1	6	0.84	0
2010 Albuquerque..........	P.C.	1	5²/₃	0	1	.000	5	0	8	6.35	0
2010 Los Angeles l-m........	N.L.	16	95	6	5	.545	84	24	79	4.07	0
2011 Rancho Cucamonga....	Calif.	4	6¹/₃	0	0	.000	5	1	4	1.42	0
2011 Los Angeles n-o........	N.L.	9	8²/₃	0	0	.000	9	5	7	4.15	3
2012 Boston p-q............	A.L.	56	50	4	1	.800	51	15	59	4.50	1
Major League Totals........14 Yrs.		386	1571¹/₃	108	91	.543	1121	551	1612	4.32	6
Division Series											
2009 Los Angeles...........	N.L.	1	7	1	0	1.000	4	1	4	0.00	0

Year	Club	Lea	G	IP	W	L	Pct	SO	BB	H	ERA	SAVES
Championship Series												
2009 Los Angeles	N.L.	2	10$\frac{1}{3}$	0	1	.000	9	3	8	6.10	0	

a Traded to Philadelphia Phillies with infielder Travis Lee, pitcher Omar Daal and pitcher Nelson Figueroa for pitcher Curt Schilling, July 26, 2000.
b On disabled list from May 4 to May 30, 2001.
c On disabled list from May 30 to August 10, 2004.
d On disabled list from March 25 to April 19, 2005.
e Traded to Texas Rangers for player to be named later, December 12, 2005. Philadelphia Phillies received pitcher Ricardo Rodriguez to complete trade, December 19, 2005.
f Filed for free agency, October 30, 2006, re-signed with Texas Rangers, December 9, 2006.
g On disabled list from June 22 to August 15, 2007.
h On disabled list from July 5 to July 20 and August 25 to September 9, 2008.
i On disabled list from May 17 to June 2, 2009.
j Released by Texas Rangers, August 17, 2009. Signed with Los Angeles Dodgers organization, August 19, 2009.
k Filed for free agency, November 6, 2009, Re-signed with Los Angeles Dodgers, January 21, 2010.
l On disabled list from April 23 to June 19 and August 16 to September 3, 2010.
m Filed for free agency, November 1, 2010, re-signed with Los Angeles Dodgers, December 9, 2010.
n Filed for free agency, October 30, 2011. Signed with Boston Red Sox organization, January 16, 2012.
o On disabled list from March 22 to April 22 and May 14 to October 30, 2011.
p On disabled list from August 6 to August 21, 2012.
q Filed for free agency, November 3, 2012. Signed with Fukuoka Softbank Hawks (Japan), January 16, 2013.

PAPELBON, JONATHAN ROBERT

Born, Baton Rouge, Louisiana, November 23, 1980.
Bats Right. Throws Right. Height, 6 feet, 4 inches. Weight, 230 pounds.

Year	Club	Lea	G	IP	W	L	Pct	SO	BB	H	ERA	SAVES
2003 Lowell	N.Y.-Penn.	13	32$\frac{2}{3}$	1	2	.333	36	9	43	6.34	0	
2004 Sarasota	Fla.St.	24	129$\frac{2}{3}$	12	7	.632	153	43	97	2.64	0	
2005 Portland	Eastern	14	87	5	2	.714	83	23	59	2.48	0	
2005 Pawtucket	Int.	7	27$\frac{2}{3}$	1	2	.333	27	3	21	2.93	1	
2005 Boston	A.L.	17	34	3	1	.750	34	17	33	2.65	0	
2006 Boston	A.L.	59	68$\frac{1}{3}$	4	2	.667	75	13	40	0.92	35	
2007 Boston	A.L.	59	58$\frac{1}{3}$	1	3	.250	84	15	30	1.85	37	
2008 Boston	A.L.	67	69$\frac{1}{3}$	5	4	.556	77	8	58	2.34	41	
2009 Boston	A.L.	66	68	1	1	.500	76	24	54	1.85	38	
2010 Boston	A.L.	65	67	5	7	.417	76	28	57	3.90	37	
2011 Boston a	A.L.	63	64$\frac{1}{3}$	4	1	.800	87	10	50	2.94	31	
2012 Philadelphia	N.L.	70	70	5	6	.455	92	18	56	2.44	38	
Major League Totals . . . . 8 Yrs.		466	499$\frac{1}{3}$	28	25	.528	601	133	378	2.34	257	
Division Series												
2005 Boston	A.L.	2	4	0	0	.000	2	0	2	0.00	0	
2007 Boston	A.L.	1	1$\frac{1}{3}$	1	0	1.000	1	2	0	0.00	0	
2008 Boston	A.L.	3	5	1	0	1.000	7	1	2	0.00	1	
2009 Boston	A.L.	2	2	0	1	.000	1	2	4	13.50	0	
Division Series Totals		8	12$\frac{1}{3}$	2	1	.667	11	5	8	2.19	1	
Championship Series												
2007 Boston	A.L.	3	5	0	0	.000	3	2	3	0.00	1	
2008 Boston	A.L.	4	5$\frac{1}{3}$	0	0	.000	6	1	1	0.00	2	
Championship Series Totals		7	10$\frac{1}{3}$	0	0	.000	9	3	4	0.00	3	
World Series Record												
2007 Boston	A.L.	3	4$\frac{1}{3}$	0	0	.000	3	0	2	0.00	3	

a Filed for free agency, October 30, 2011. Signed with Philadelphia Phillies, November 14, 2011.

PARKER, JARROD BRENT

Born, Fort Wayne, Indiana, November 24, 1988.
Bats Right. Throws Right. Height, 6 feet, 1 inch. Weight, 195 pounds.

Year	Club	Lea	G	IP	W	L	Pct	SO	BB	H	ERA	SAVES
2008 South Bend	Midwest	24	117$\frac{2}{3}$	12	5	.706	117	33	113	3.44	0	
2009 Visalia	Calif.	4	19	1	0	1.000	21	4	12	0.95	0	
2009 Mobile	Southern	16	78$\frac{1}{3}$	4	6	.400	74	34	82	3.68	0	
2010 a					INJURED—Did Not Play								
2011 Mobile b	Southern	26	130$\frac{2}{3}$	11	8	.579	112	55	112	3.79	0	
2011 Arizona	N.L.	1	5$\frac{2}{3}$	0	0	.000	1	1	4	0.00	0	
2012 Sacramento	P.C.	4	20$\frac{2}{3}$	1	0	1.000	21	6	22	2.18	0	
2012 Oakland	A.L.	29	181$\frac{1}{3}$	13	8	.619	140	63	166	3.47	0	
Major League Totals . . . . 2 Yrs.		30	187	13	8	.619	141	64	170	3.37	0	

Year Club	Lea	G	IP	W	L	Pct	SO	BB	H	ERA	SAVES
Division Series											
2011 Arizona	N.L.	1	0$\frac{1}{3}$	0	0	.000	0	1	2	27.00	0
2012 Oakland	A.L.	2	12$\frac{2}{3}$	0	2	.000	11	2	14	4.26	0
Division Series Totals		3	13	0	2	.000	11	3	16	4.85	0

a On minor league disabled list from April 8 to September 7, 2010.
b Traded to Oakland Athletics with outfielder Collin Cowgill and pitcher Ryan Cook for pitcher Craig Breslow and pitcher Trevor Cahill, December 9, 2011.

PARNELL, ROBERT ALLEN (BOBBY)
Born, Salisbury, North Carolina, September 8, 1984.
Bats Right. Throws Right. Height, 6 feet, 4 inches. Weight, 200 pounds.

Year Club	Lea	G	IP	W	L	Pct	SO	BB	H	ERA	SAVES
2005 Brooklyn.........	N.Y.-Penn.	15	73	2	3	.400	67	29	48	1.73	0
2006 St. Lucie...........	Fla.St.	3	11$\frac{2}{3}$	0	1	.000	13	9	16	9.26	0
2006 Hagerstown.......	So.Atl.	18	93$\frac{2}{3}$	5	10	.333	84	40	44	4.04	0
2007 Binghamton.......	Eastern	17	88$\frac{2}{3}$	5	5	.500	74	38	98	4.77	0
2007 St. Lucie...........	Fla.St.	12	55$\frac{1}{3}$	3	3	.500	62	22	56	3.25	0
2008 Binghamton.......	Eastern	24	127$\frac{2}{3}$	10	6	.625	91	57	126	4.30	0
2008 New Orleans.......	P.C.	5	20$\frac{1}{3}$	2	2	.500	23	9	25	6.64	0
2008 New York..........	N.L.	6	5	0	0	.000	3	2	3	5.40	0
2009 New York..........	N.L.	68	88$\frac{1}{3}$	4	8	.333	74	46	101	5.30	1
2010 Buffalo.............	Int.	24	41$\frac{1}{3}$	1	1	.500	42	17	36	4.14	4
2010 New York..........	N.L.	41	35	0	1	.000	33	8	41	2.83	0
2011 St. Lucie...........	Fla.St.	1	1	0	0	.000	0	1	0	0.00	0
2011 Buffalo.............	Int.	8	8	0	0	.000	11	2	7	3.38	1
2011 New York a...........	N.L.	60	59$\frac{1}{3}$	4	6	.400	64	27	60	3.64	6
2012 New York..........	N.L.	74	68$\frac{2}{3}$	5	4	.556	61	20	65	2.49	7

| Major League Totals .... | 5 Yrs. | 249 | 256$\frac{1}{3}$ | 13 | 19 | .406 | 235 | 103 | 270 | 3.83 | 14 |

a On disabled list from April 20 to May 30, 2011.

PARRA, MANUEL ALEX (MANNY)
Born, Carmichael, California, October 30, 1982.
Bats Left. Throws Left. Height, 6 feet, 3 inches. Weight, 205 pounds.

Year Club	Lea	G	IP	W	L	Pct	SO	BB	H	ERA	SAVES
2002 Brewers...........	Arizona	1	2	0	0	.000	4	0	1	4.50	0
2002 Ogden............	Pioneer	11	47$\frac{2}{3}$	3	1	.750	51	10	59	3.21	0
2003 Beloit.............	Midwest	23	138$\frac{2}{3}$	11	2	.846	117	24	127	2.73	0
2004 High Desert.........	Calif.	13	67$\frac{1}{3}$	5	2	.714	64	19	76	3.48	0
2004 Huntsville.........	Southern	3	6	0	1	.000	10	0	5	3.00	0
2005 Huntsville.........	Southern	16	91	5	6	.455	86	21	111	3.96	0
2006 Brevard County	Fla.St.	15	54$\frac{2}{3}$	1	3	.250	61	32	47	2.96	0
2006 Huntsville.........	Southern	6	31$\frac{1}{3}$	3	0	1.000	29	8	26	2.87	0
2007 Huntsville.........	Southern	13	80$\frac{2}{3}$	7	3	.700	81	26	70	2.68	0
2007 Nashville.........	P.C.	4	26	3	1	.750	25	7	15	1.73	0
2007 Milwaukee a...........	N.L.	9	26$\frac{1}{3}$	0	1	.000	26	12	25	3.76	0
2008 Milwaukee	N.L.	32	166	10	8	.556	147	75	181	4.39	0
2009 Nashville.........	P.C.	4	24$\frac{2}{3}$	1	2	.333	19	13	16	2.92	0
2009 Milwaukee	N.L.	27	140	11	11	.500	116	77	179	6.36	0
2010 Milwaukee	N.L.	42	122	3	10	.231	129	63	135	5.02	0
2011 Wisconsin	Midwest	1	2	1	0	1.000	4	0	0	0.00	0
2011 Nashville b...........	P.C.	7	10$\frac{1}{3}$	0	1	.000	8	5	12	6.10	0
2012 Milwaukee c...........	N.L.	62	58$\frac{2}{3}$	2	3	.400	61	35	62	5.06	0

Major League Totals	5 Yrs.	172	513	26	33	.441	479	262	582	5.12	0
Division Series											
2008 Milwaukee	N.L.	2	2$\frac{1}{3}$	0	0	.000	3	1	2	0.00	0

a On disabled list from August 31 to September 21, 2007.
b On disabled list from March 26 to October 25, 2011.
c Not offered contract, November 30, 2012.

PATTON, TROY JAMIESON
Born, Spring, Texas, September 3, 1985.
Bats Both. Throws Left. Height, 6 feet, 1 inch. Weight, 180 pounds.

Year Club	Lea	G	IP	W	L	Pct	SO	BB	H	ERA	SAVES
2004 Greeneville.........	Appal.	6	28	2	2	.500	32	5	23	1.93	0
2005 Salem.............	Carolina	10	41	1	4	.200	38	8	34	2.63	0
2005 Lexington.........	So.Atl.	15	78$\frac{2}{3}$	5	2	.714	94	20	59	1.94	0

Year	Club	Lea	G	IP	W	L	Pct	SO	BB	H	ERA	SAVES
2006	Salem............Carolina		19	101⅓	7	7	.500	102	37	92	2.93	0
2006	Corpus Christi........	Texas	8	45⅓	2	5	.286	37	13	48	4.37	0
2007	Corpus Christi........	Texas	16	102⅓	6	6	.500	69	33	96	2.99	0
2007	Round Rock..........	P.C.	8	49	4	2	.667	25	11	44	4.59	0
2007	Houston a	N.L.	3	12⅔	0	2	.000	8	4	10	3.55	0
2008 b				INJURED—Did Not Play								
2009	Bowie.............	Eastern	11	63⅓	6	2	.750	47	18	50	1.99	0
2009	Norfolk..............	Int.	9	44⅔	1	3	.250	26	14	62	6.45	0
2010	Norfolk..............	Int.	25	136	8	11	.421	89	43	144	4.43	0
2010	Baltimore	A.L.	1	0⅔	0	0	.000	1	1	1	0.00	0
2011	Norfolk..............	Int.	17	44⅓	4	1	.800	30	12	44	1.83	0
2011	Baltimore	A.L.	20	30	2	1	.667	22	5	25	3.00	0
2012	Baltimore c...........	A.L.	54	55⅔	1	0	1.000	49	12	45	2.43	0
Major League Totals ....4 Yrs.			78	99	3	3	.500	80	22	81	2.73	0
Division Series												
2012	Baltimore	A.L.	3	2	0	0	.000	3	2	3	4.50	0

a Traded to Baltimore Orioles with outfielder Luke Scott, pitcher Matt Albers, pitcher Dennis Sarfate and infielder Michael Costanzo for infielder Miguel Tejada, December 12, 2007.

b On disabled list from March 21 to October 21, 2008.

c On disabled list from August 13 to September 21, 2012.

PAVANO, CARL ANTHONY

Born, New Britain, Connecticut, January 8, 1976.
Bats Right. Throws Right. Height, 6 feet, 5 inches. Weight, 240 pounds.

Year	Club	Lea	G	IP	W	L	Pct	SO	BB	H	ERA	SAVES
1994	Red Sox........	Gulf Coast	9	44	4	3	.571	47	7	31	1.84	0
1995	Michigan	Midwest	22	141⅓	6	6	.500	138	52	118	3.44	0
1996	Trenton...........	Eastern	27	185	16	5	.762	146	47	154	2.63	0
1997	Pawtucket a	Int.	23	161⅔	11	6	.647	147	34	148	3.12	0
1998	Jupiter	Fla.St.	4	15	0	0	.000	14	3	20	6.60	0
1998	Ottawa	Int.	3	18⅔	1	0	1.000	14	7	12	2.41	0
1998	Montreal..............	N.L.	24	134⅔	6	9	.400	83	43	130	4.21	0
1999	Montreal.............	N.L.	19	104	6	8	.429	70	35	117	5.63	0
1999	Ottawa b.............	Int.	2	5	0	1	.000	3	0	7	9.00	0
2000	Montreal c	N.L.	15	97	8	4	.667	64	34	89	3.06	0
2001	Jupiter	Fla.St.	3	12⅓	1	1	.500	11	2	10	2.19	0
2001	Ottawa	Int.	4	27⅔	2	1	.667	19	5	27	3.58	0
2001	Montreal d	N.L.	8	42⅔	1	6	.143	36	16	59	6.33	0
2002	Ottawa	Int.	3	20⅓	3	0	1.000	9	2	23	3.10	0
2002	Montreal-Florida e	N.L.	37	136	6	10	.375	92	45	174	5.16	0
2003	Florida	N.L.	33	201	12	13	.480	133	49	204	4.30	0
2004	Florida f	N.L.	31	222⅓	18	8	.692	139	49	212	3.00	0
2005	Yankees	Gulf Coast	1	5	0	0	.000	5	0	2	1.80	0
2005	Tampa	Fla.St.	1	6	0	1	.000	3	0	6	4.50	0
2005	New York g...........	A.L.	17	100	4	6	.400	56	18	129	4.77	0
2006	Trenton...........	Eastern	3	11	1	0	1.000	12	0	6	1.64	0
2006	Tampa	Fla.St.	3	11⅔	0	2	.000	10	3	10	2.31	0
2006	Columbus h	Int.	1	6	1	0	1.000	5	1	8	3.00	0
2007	New York i	A.L.	2	11⅓	1	0	1.000	4	2	12	4.76	0
2008	Charleston	So.Atl.	2	5	0	0	.000	6	1	6	1.80	0
2008	Trenton...........	Eastern	3	14	1	1	.500	13	3	14	3.86	0
2008	New York j-k...........	A.L.	7	34⅓	4	2	.667	15	10	41	5.77	0
2009	Cleveland-Minnesota l-m ..	A.L.	33	199⅓	14	12	.538	147	39	235	5.10	0
2010	Minnesota n...........	A.L.	32	221	17	11	.607	117	37	227	3.75	0
2011	Minnesota	A.L.	33	222	9	13	.409	102	40	*262	4.30	0
2012	Fort Myers	Fla.St.	2	5	0	0	.000	3	0	4	1.80	0
2012	Minnesota o-p	A.L.	11	63	2	5	.286	33	8	80	6.00	0
Major League Totals ....14 Yrs.			302	1788⅔	108	107	.502	1091	425	1971	4.39	0
Division Series												
2003	Florida	N.L.	3	2⅔	2	0	1.000	1	1	1	0.00	0
2009	Minnesota	A.L.	1	7	0	1	.000	9	0	5	2.57	0
2010	Minnesota	A.L.	1	6	0	1	.000	3	1	10	6.00	0
Division Series Totals			5	15⅔	2	2	.500	13	2	16	3.45	0
Championship Series												
2003	Florida	N.L.	3	7⅔	0	0	.000	8	1	8	2.35	0
World Series Record												
2003	Florida	N.L.	2	9	0	0	.000	6	1	8	1.00	0

a Traded by Boston Red Sox to Montreal Expos with player to be named later for pitcher Pedro Martinez, November 18, 1997. Montreal Expos received pitcher Tony Armas to complete trade, December 18, 1997.

b On disabled list from July 12 to September 11, 1999.
c On disabled list from June 25 to November 13, 2000.
d On disabled list from March 23 to August 15, 2001.
e Traded to Florida Marlins with pitcher Graeme Lloyd, infielder Mike Mordecai and pitcher Justin Wayne for outfielder Cliff Floyd, infielder Wilton Guerrero and cash, July 11, 2002.
f Filed for free agency, November 3, 2004. Signed with New York Yankees, December 22, 2004.
g On disabled list from June 28 to October 31, 2005.
h On disabled list from March 29 to October 31, 2006.
i On disabled list from April 10 to October 31, 2007.
j On disabled list from March 21 to August 23, 2008.
k Filed for free agency, November 5, 2008. Signed with Cleveland Indians, January 6, 2009.
l Traded to Minnesota Twins for player to be named later, August 7, 2009. Cleveland Indians received pitcher Yohan Pinto to complete trade, August 28, 2009.
m Filed for free agency, November 7, 2009. Accepted arbitration, December 7, 2009.
n Filed for free agency, November 1, 2010, re-signed with Minnesota Twins, January 19, 2011.
o On disabled list from June 2 to October 24, 2012.
p Filed for free agency, November 3, 2012.

PEAVY, JACOB EDWARD (JAKE)
Born, Mobile, Alabama, May 3, 1981.
Bats Right. Throws Right. Height, 6 feet, 1 inch. Weight, 195 pounds.

Year	Club	Lea	G	IP	W	L	Pct	SO	BB	H	ERA	SAVES
1999 Padres	Arizona		13	73²/₃	7	1	.875	90	23	52	1.34	0
1999 Idaho Falls	Pioneer		2	11	2	0	1.000	13	1	5	0.00	0
2000 Fort Wayne	Midwest		26	133²/₃	13	8	.619	164	53	107	2.90	0
2001 Mobile	Southern		5	28	2	1	.667	44	12	19	2.57	0
2002 Mobile	Southern		14	80¹/₃	4	5	.444	89	30	65	2.80	0
2002 San Diego		N.L.	17	97²/₃	6	7	.462	90	33	106	4.52	0
2003 San Diego		N.L.	32	194²/₃	12	11	.522	156	82	173	4.11	0
2004 Mobile	Southern		1	4²/₃	0	1	.000	4	2	7	5.79	0
2004 San Diego a		N.L.	27	166¹/₃	15	6	.714	173	53	146	*2.27	0
2005 San Diego		N.L.	30	203	13	7	.650	*216	50	162	2.88	0
2006 San Diego		N.L.	32	202¹/₃	11	14	.440	215	62	187	4.09	0
2007 San Diego b		N.L.	34	223¹/₃	*19	6	.760	*240	68	169	*2.54	0
2008 San Diego c		N.L.	27	173²/₃	10	11	.476	166	59	146	2.85	0
2009 Charlotte		Int.	4	15¹/₃	1	1	.500	17	4	14	2.93	0
2009 San Diego		N.L.	13	81²/₃	6	6	.500	92	28	69	3.97	0
2009 Chicago d-e		A.L.	3	20	3	0	1.000	18	6	11	1.35	0
2010 Chicago f		A.L.	17	107	7	6	.538	93	34	98	4.63	0
2011 Birmingham	Southern		2	4¹/₃	0	0	.000	4	1	9	6.23	0
2011 Charlotte		Int.	4	24²/₃	1	1	.500	26	1	21	3.65	0
2011 Chicago g		A.L.	19	111²/₃	7	7	.500	95	24	117	4.92	0
2012 Chicago		A.L.	32	219	11	12	.478	194	49	191	3.37	0
Major League Totals	11 Yrs.		283	1800¹/₃	120	93	.563	1748	548	1575	3.46	0
Division Series												
2005 San Diego		N.L.	1	4¹/₃	0	1	.000	3	3	8	16.62	0
2006 San Diego		N.L.	1	5¹/₃	0	1	.000	2	1	11	8.44	0
Division Series Totals			2	9²/₃	0	2	.000	5	4	19	12.10	0

a On disabled list from May 20 to July 2, 2004.
b Selected Cy Young Award Winner in National League for 2007.
c On disabled list from May 15 to June 12, 2008.
d Traded to Chicago White Sox for pitcher Aaron Poreda, pitcher Clayton Richard, pitcher Adam Russell and pitcher Dexter Carter, July 31, 2009.
e On disabled list from June 9 to September 19, 2009.
f On disabled list from July 7 to November 2, 2010.
g On disabled list from March 22 to May 11, 2011.

PERALTA (GUTIERREZ), JOEL
Born, Bonao, Dominican Republic, March 23, 1976.
Bats Right. Throws Right. Height, 5 feet, 11 inches. Weight, 195 pounds.

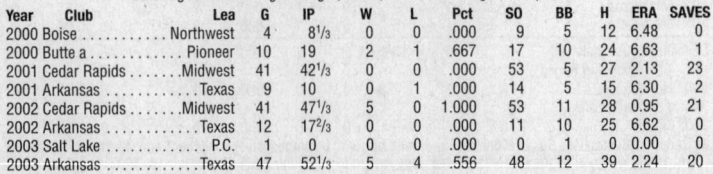

Year	Club	Lea	G	IP	W	L	Pct	SO	BB	H	ERA	SAVES
2000 Boise	Northwest		4	8¹/₃	0	0	.000	9	5	12	6.48	0
2000 Butte a	Pioneer		10	19	2	1	.667	17	10	24	6.63	1
2001 Cedar Rapids	Midwest		41	42¹/₃	0	0	.000	53	5	27	2.13	23
2001 Arkansas	Texas		9	10	0	1	.000	14	5	15	6.30	2
2002 Cedar Rapids	Midwest		41	47¹/₃	5	0	1.000	53	11	28	0.95	21
2002 Arkansas	Texas		12	17²/₃	0	0	.000	11	10	25	6.62	0
2003 Salt Lake	P.C.		1	0	0	0	.000	0	1	0	0.00	0
2003 Arkansas	Texas		47	52¹/₃	5	4	.556	48	12	39	2.24	20

Year	Club	Lea	G	IP	W	L	Pct	SO	BB	H	ERA	SAVES
2004	Angels	Arizona	2	4⅓	0	0	.000	9	0	1	2.08	0
2004	Rancho Cucamonga	Calif.	1	2	0	0	.000	1	1	5	9.00	0
2004	Salt Lake	P.C.	39	56	4	2	.667	68	18	64	4.98	1
2005	Los Angeles	A.L.	28	34⅔	1	0	1.000	30	14	28	3.89	0
2005	Salt Lake b	P.C.	19	20	4	1	.800	18	6	11	2.70	10
2006	Omaha	P.C.	6	7⅔	1	0	1.000	8	3	8	2.35	2
2006	Kansas City	A.L.	64	73⅔	1	3	.250	57	17	74	4.40	1
2007	Kansas City	A.L.	62	87⅔	1	3	.250	66	19	93	3.80	1
2008	Omaha	P.C.	10	18⅔	1	0	1.000	19	6	9	0.00	2
2008	Kansas City	A.L.	40	52⅔	1	2	.333	38	14	56	5.98	0
2009	Colorado Springs	P.C.	31	36⅔	6	0	1.000	32	11	31	2.45	4
2009	Colorado c-d	N.L.	27	24⅔	0	3	.000	22	12	27	6.20	0
2010	Syracuse	Int.	28	33⅓	2	0	1.000	38	7	24	1.08	20
2010	Washington e	N.L.	39	49	1	0	1.000	49	9	30	2.02	0
2011	Tampa Bay	A.L.	71	67⅔	3	4	.429	61	18	44	2.93	6
2012	Tampa Bay f	A.L.	76	67	2	6	.250	84	17	49	3.63	2
Major League Totals		8 Yrs.	407	457	10	21	.323	407	120	401	3.94	10
Division Series												
2011	Tampa Bay	A.L.	3	2⅓	0	0	.000	0	2	1	0.00	0

a Released by Oakland Athletics, July 4, 1998. Signed with Anaheim Angels organization, February 25, 1999.
b Claimed on waivers by Kansas City Royals, October 7, 2005.
c Released by Kansas City Royals, March 31, 2009. Signed with Colorado Rockies organization, April 8, 2009.
d Filed for free agency, October 26, 2009. Signed with Washington Nationals organization, December 15, 2009.
e Not offered contract, December 2, 2010. Signed with Tampa Bay Rays, December 17, 2010.
f Filed for free agency, November 3, 2012, re-signed with Tampa Bay Rays, November 19, 2012.

PEREZ, CHRISTOPHER RALPH (CHRIS)

Born, Bradenton, Florida, July 1, 1985.
Bats Right. Throws Right. Height, 6 feet, 4 inches. Weight, 225 pounds.

Year	Club	Lea	G	IP	W	L	Pct	SO	BB	H	ERA	SAVES
2006	Quad Cities	Midwest	25	29⅓	2	0	1.000	32	19	20	1.84	12
2007	Memphis	P.C.	15	14	0	1	.000	15	13	6	4.50	8
2007	Springfield	Texas	39	40⅔	2	0	1.000	62	28	17	2.43	27
2008	Memphis	P.C.	26	25⅓	1	1	.500	38	12	18	3.20	11
2008	St. Louis	N.L.	41	41⅔	3	3	.500	42	22	34	3.46	7
2009	Memphis	P.C.	3	4	1	0	1.000	4	3	0	0.00	2
2009	St. Louis	N.L.	29	23⅔	1	1	.500	30	15	17	4.18	1
2009	Cleveland a	A.L.	32	33⅓	0	1	.000	38	12	24	4.32	1
2010	Cleveland	A.L.	63	63	2	2	.500	61	28	40	1.71	23
2011	Cleveland	A.L.	64	59⅔	4	7	.364	39	26	46	3.32	36
2012	Cleveland	A.L.	61	57⅔	0	4	.000	59	16	49	3.59	39
Major League Totals		5 Yrs.	290	279	10	18	.357	269	119	210	3.23	107

a Traded to Cleveland Indians with player to be named later for infielder Mark DeRosa, June 27, 2009. Cleveland Indians received pitcher Jess Todd to complete trade, July 26, 2009.

PEREZ (JIMENEZ), MARTIN

Born, Guanare, Venezuela, April 4, 1991.
Bats Left. Throws Left. Height, 6 feet. Weight, 180 pounds.

Year	Club	Lea	G	IP	W	L	Pct	SO	BB	H	ERA	SAVES
2008	Spokane	Northwest	15	61⅔	1	2	.333	53	28	66	3.65	0
2009	Hickory	So.Atl.	22	93⅔	5	5	.500	105	33	82	2.31	1
2009	Frisco	Texas	5	21	1	3	.250	14	5	29	5.57	0
2010	Frisco	Texas	24	99⅔	5	8	.385	101	50	117	5.96	0
2011	Round Rock	P.C.	10	49	4	4	.500	37	20	72	6.43	0
2011	Frisco	Texas	17	88⅓	4	2	.667	83	36	80	3.16	0
2012	Round Rock	P.C.	22	127	7	6	.538	69	56	122	4.25	0
2012	Texas	A.L.	12	38	1	4	.200	25	15	47	5.45	0

PERKINS, GLEN WESTON

Born, St.Paul, Minnesota, March 2, 1983.
Bats Left. Throws Left. Height, 5 feet, 11 inches. Weight, 210 pounds.

Year	Club	Lea	G	IP	W	L	Pct	SO	BB	H	ERA	SAVES
2004	Elizabethton	Appal.	3	12	1	0	1.000	22	4	8	2.25	0
2004	Quad Cities	Midwest	9	48⅓	2	1	.667	49	12	33	1.30	0
2005	Fort Myers	Fla.St.	10	55	3	2	.600	66	13	41	2.13	0
2005	New Britain	Eastern	14	79	4	4	.500	67	35	80	4.90	0

315

Year	Club	Lea	G	IP	W	L	Pct	SO	BB	H	ERA	SAVES
2006 New Britain	Eastern	23	117$\frac{1}{3}$	4	11	.267	131	45	109	3.91	0
2006 Rochester	Int.	1	4$\frac{1}{3}$	0	1	.000	3	5	6	2.08	0
2006 Minnesota	A.L.	4	5$\frac{2}{3}$	0	0	.000	6	0	3	1.59	0
2007 Rochester	Int.	1	6	0	0	.000	2	1	2	1.50	0
2007 Fort Myers	Fla.St.	1	1	0	0	.000	0	0	3	27.00	0
2007 Twins	Gulf Coast	3	5	0	0	.000	6	2	3	1.80	0
2007 New Britain	Eastern	3	7$\frac{1}{3}$	0	2	.000	7	7	11	11.05	0
2007 Minnesota a	A.L.	19	28$\frac{2}{3}$	0	0	.000	20	12	23	3.14	0
2008 Rochester	Int.	7	33$\frac{1}{3}$	2	1	.667	27	19	28	2.97	0
2008 Minnesota	A.L.	26	151	12	4	.750	74	39	183	4.41	0
2009 Fort Myers	Fla.St.	2	11	1	0	1.000	9	1	8	2.45	0
2009 Minnesota	A.L.	18	96$\frac{1}{3}$	6	7	.462	45	23	120	5.89	0
2009 Twins	Gulf Coast	1	1	0	0	.000	0	0	0	0.00	0
2010 Rochester	Int.	26	124	4	9	.308	98	36	160	5.81	0
2010 Minnesota b	A.L.	13	21$\frac{2}{3}$	1	1	.500	14	5	29	5.82	0
2011 Rochester	Int.	2	3	0	0	.000	2	0	4	0.00	0
2011 Minnesota c	A.L.	65	61$\frac{2}{3}$	4	4	.500	65	21	55	2.48	2
2012 Minnesota	A.L.	70	70$\frac{1}{3}$	3	1	.750	78	16	57	2.56	16
Major League Totals	7 Yrs.	215	435$\frac{1}{3}$	26	17	.605	302	116	470	4.11	18
Division Series											
2006 Minnesota	A.L.	1	0$\frac{1}{3}$	0	0	.000	0	0	2	0.00	0

a On disabled list from May 22 to September 11, 2007.
b On disabled list from May 19 to June 16 and August 9 to August 30, 2009.
c On disabled list from May 22 to June 17, 2011.

PESTANO, VINCENT WILLIAM (VINNIE)
Born, Huntington Beach, California, February 20, 1985.
Bats Right. Throws Right. Height, 6 feet, 1 inch. Weight, 200 pounds.

Year	Club	Lea	G	IP	W	L	Pct	SO	BB	H	ERA	SAVES
2007 Mahoning Valley	N.Y.-Penn.	21	22$\frac{2}{3}$	1	1	.500	27	7	17	3.57	6
2008 Lake County	So.Atl.	29	29	1	1	.500	23	13	25	1.55	15
2008 Kinston	Carolina	25	27	1	2	.333	27	11	23	4.00	9
2009 Akron	Eastern	34	34$\frac{2}{3}$	2	3	.400	31	13	30	2.86	24
2010 Akron	Eastern	14	13$\frac{1}{3}$	1	1	.500	18	2	12	2.70	3
2010 Columbus	Int.	43	46$\frac{1}{3}$	1	2	.333	59	14	35	1.55	14
2010 Cleveland	A.L.	5	5	0	0	.000	8	5	4	3.60	1
2011 Cleveland	A.L.	67	62	1	2	.333	84	24	41	2.32	2
2012 Cleveland	A.L.	70	70	3	3	.500	76	24	53	2.57	2
Major League Totals	3 Yrs.	142	137	4	5	.444	168	53	98	2.50	5

PETTITTE, ANDREW EUGENE (ANDY)
Born, Baton Rouge, Louisiana, June 15, 1972.
Bats Left. Throws Left. Height, 6 feet, 5 inches. Weight, 225 pounds.

Year	Club	Lea	G	IP	W	L	Pct	SO	BB	H	ERA	SAVES
1991 Yankees	Gulf Coast	6	36$\frac{2}{3}$	4	1	.800	51	8	16	0.98	0
1991 Oneonta	N.Y.-Penn.	6	33	2	2	.500	32	16	33	2.18	0
1992 Greensboro	So.Atl.	27	168	10	4	.714	130	55	141	2.20	0
1993 Pr William	Carolina	26	159$\frac{2}{3}$	11	9	.550	129	47	146	3.04	0
1993 Albany	Eastern	1	5	1	0	1.000	6	2	5	3.60	0
1994 Albany	Eastern	11	73	7	2	.778	50	18	60	2.71	0
1994 Columbus	Int.	16	96$\frac{2}{3}$	7	2	.778	61	21	101	2.98	0
1995 Columbus	Int.	2	11$\frac{2}{3}$	0	0	.000	8	0	7	0.00	0
1995 New York	A.L.	31	175	12	9	.571	114	63	183	4.17	0
1996 New York	A.L.	35	221	*21	8	.724	162	72	229	3.87	0
1997 New York	A.L.	35	240$\frac{1}{3}$	18	7	.720	166	65	233	2.88	0
1998 New York	A.L.	33	216$\frac{1}{3}$	16	11	.593	146	87	226	4.24	0
1999 Tampa	Fla.St.	1	5	1	0	1.000	8	2	4	0.00	0
1999 New York a	A.L.	31	191$\frac{2}{3}$	14	11	.560	121	89	216	4.70	0
2000 New York b	A.L.	32	204$\frac{2}{3}$	19	9	.679	125	80	219	4.35	0
2001 New York c	A.L.	31	200$\frac{2}{3}$	15	10	.600	164	41	224	3.99	0
2002 Tampa	Fla.St.	2	5	0	0	.000	4	0	3	0.00	0
2002 Norwich	Eastern	1	6$\frac{1}{3}$	0	0	.000	5	0	2	1.42	0
2002 New York d	A.L.	22	134$\frac{2}{3}$	13	5	.722	97	32	144	3.27	0
2003 New York e	A.L.	33	208$\frac{1}{3}$	21	8	.724	180	50	227	4.02	0
2004 Round Rock	Texas	2	8	0	0	.000	9	2	4	2.25	0
2004 Houston f	N.L.	15	83	6	4	.600	79	31	71	3.90	0
2005 Houston	N.L.	33	222$\frac{1}{3}$	17	9	.654	171	41	188	2.39	0
2006 Houston g	N.L.	36	214$\frac{1}{3}$	14	13	.519	178	70	238	4.20	0

Year	Club	Lea	G	IP	W	L	Pct	SO	BB	H	ERA	SAVES
2007 New York		A.L.	36	215⅓	15	9	.625	141	69	238	4.05	0
2008 New York h		A.L.	33	204	14	14	.500	158	55	233	4.54	0
2009 New York		A.L.	32	194⅔	14	8	.636	148	76	193	4.16	0
2010 New York i		A.L.	21	129	11	3	.786	101	41	123	3.28	0
2011 j					RETIRED—Did Not Play							
2012 Tampa		Fla.St.	2	7	0	0	.000	5	0	4	1.29	0
2012 Trenton		Eastern	1	5	0	1	.000	3	1	7	5.40	0
2012 Scranton-WB		Int.	1	5	0	1	.000	5	2	8	5.40	0
2012 New York k-l-m		A.L.	12	75⅓	5	4	.556	69	21	65	2.87	0
Major League Totals	17 Yrs.		501	3130⅔	245	142	.633	2320	983	3250	3.86	0
Division Series												
1995 New York		A.L.	1	7	0	0	.000	0	3	9	5.14	0
1996 New York		A.L.	1	6⅓	0	0	.000	3	6	4	5.68	0
1997 New York		A.L.	2	11⅔	0	2	.000	5	1	15	8.49	0
1998 New York		A.L.	1	7	1	0	1.000	8	0	3	1.29	0
1999 New York		A.L.	1	7⅓	1	0	1.000	5	0	7	1.23	0
2000 New York		A.L.	2	11⅓	1	0	1.000	7	3	15	3.97	0
2001 New York		A.L.	1	6⅓	0	1	.000	4	2	7	1.42	0
2002 New York		A.L.	1	3	0	0	.000	1	0	8	12.00	0
2003 New York		A.L.	1	7	1	0	1.000	10	3	4	1.29	0
2005 Houston		N.L.	1	7	1	0	1.000	6	2	4	3.86	0
2007 New York		A.L.	1	6⅓	0	0	.000	5	2	7	0.00	0
2009 New York		A.L.	1	6⅓	1	0	1.000	7	1	3	1.42	0
2010 New York		A.L.	1	7	1	0	1.000	4	1	5	2.57	0
2012 New York		A.L.	1	7	0	1	.000	5	1	7	3.86	0
Division Series Totals			16	100⅔	7	4	.636	70	25	98	3.67	0
Championship Series												
1996 New York		A.L.	2	15	1	0	1.000	7	5	10	3.60	0
1998 New York		A.L.	1	4⅔	0	1	.000	1	3	8	11.57	0
1999 New York		A.L.	1	7⅓	1	0	1.000	5	1	8	2.45	0
2000 New York		A.L.	1	6⅔	1	0	1.000	2	1	9	2.70	0
2001 New York		A.L.	2	14⅓	2	0	1.000	8	2	11	2.51	0
2003 New York		A.L.	2	11⅔	1	0	1.000	10	4	17	4.63	0
2005 Houston		N.L.	2	12⅓	0	1	.000	6	4	15	5.11	0
2009 New York		A.L.	2	12⅔	1	0	1.000	8	2	14	2.84	0
2010 New York		A.L.	1	7	0	1	.000	5	0	5	2.57	0
2012 New York		A.L.	1	6⅔	0	0	.000	5	3	7	2.70	0
Championship Series Totals			15	98⅓	7	3	.700	57	25	104	3.75	0
World Series Record												
1996 New York		A.L.	2	10⅔	1	1	.500	5	4	11	5.91	0
1998 New York		A.L.	1	7⅓	1	0	1.000	4	3	5	0.00	0
1999 New York		A.L.	1	3⅔	0	0	.000	1	1	10	12.27	0
2000 New York		A.L.	2	13⅔	0	0	.000	9	4	16	1.98	0
2001 New York		A.L.	2	9	0	2	.000	9	2	12	10.00	0
2003 New York		A.L.	2	15⅔	1	1	.500	14	4	12	0.57	0
2005 Houston		N.L.	1	6	0	0	.000	4	0	8	3.00	0
2009 New York		A.L.	2	11⅔	2	0	1.000	10	8	9	5.40	0
World Series Totals			13	77⅔	5	4	.556	56	26	83	4.06	0

a On disabled list from March 26 to April 17, 1999.
b On disabled list from April 8 to April 25, 2000.
c On disabled list from June 16 to July 1, 2001.
d On disabled list from April 16 to June 14, 2002.
e Filed for free agency, November 6, 2003. Signed with Houston Astros, December 11, 2003.
f On disabled list from April 7 to April 29 and from May 27 to June 29 and from August 18 to October 28, 2004.
g Filed for free agency, November 6, 2006. Signed with New York Yankees, December 8, 2006.
h On disabled list from March 21 to April 5, 2008.
i On disabled list from July 19 to September 17, 2010.
j Announced retirement, February 4, 2011.
k Signed with New York Yankees organization, March 16, 2012.
l On disabled list from June 28 to September 19, 2012.
m Filed for free agency, November 3, 2012, re-signed with New York Yankees, November 28, 2012.

PHELPS, DAVID EDWARD

Born, St.Louis, Missouri, October 9, 1986.
Bats Right. Throws Right. Height, 6 feet, 2 inches. Weight, 200 pounds.

Year	Club	Lea	G	IP	W	L	Pct	SO	BB	H	ERA	SAVES
2008 Staten Island	N.Y.-Penn.	15	72⅔	8	2	.800	52	18	67	2.72	0
2009 Tampa	Fla.St.	7	38⅓	3	1	.750	32	6	34	1.17	0
2009 Charleston	So.Atl.	19	112⅔	10	3	.769	90	25	117	2.80	0

Year	Club	Lea	G	IP	W	L	Pct	SO	BB	H	ERA	SAVES
2010 Trenton	Eastern	14	88¹/₃	6	0	1.000	84	23	63	2.04	0
2010 Scranton-WB	Int.	12	70¹/₃	4	2	.667	57	13	76	3.07	0
2011 Yankees	Gulf Coast	2	7	1	1	.500	5	1	4	0.00	0
2011 Scranton-WB	Int.	18	107¹/₃	6	6	.500	90	26	115	3.19	0
2012 Tampa	Fla.St.	2	5¹/₃	0	0	.000	5	1	7	0.00	0
2012 Trenton	Eastern	1	6²/₃	1	0	1.000	11	1	1	0.00	0
2012 Scranton-WB	Int.	1	6²/₃	1	0	1.000	7	3	4	0.00	0
2012 New York	A.L.	33	99²/₃	4	4	.500	96	38	81	3.34	0
Division Series											
2012 New York	A.L.	1	1¹/₃	0	1	.000	1	0	2	6.75	0
Championship Series											
2012 New York	A.L.	2	2	0	1	.000	1	1	5	9.00	0

POMERANZ, THOMAS ANDREW (DREW)
Born, Collierville, Tennessee, November 22, 1988.
Bats Right. Throws Left. Height, 6 feet, 5 inches. Weight, 230 pounds.

Year	Club	Lea	G	IP	W	L	Pct	SO	BB	H	ERA	SAVES
2011 Kinston	Carolina	15	77	3	2	.600	95	32	56	1.87	0
2011 Tulsa	Texas	2	10	1	0	1.000	7	0	2	0.00	0
2011 Akron	Eastern	3	14	0	1	.000	17	6	10	2.57	0
2011 Colorado a	N.L.	4	18¹/₃	2	1	.667	13	5	19	5.40	0
2012 Tulsa	Texas	1	4	0	0	.000	4	1	4	0.00	0
2012 Colorado Springs	P.C.	9	46²/₃	4	4	.500	46	20	52	2.51	0
2012 Colorado	N.L.	22	96²/₃	2	9	.182	83	46	97	4.93	0
Major League Totals	2 Yrs.	26	115	4	10	.286	96	51	116	5.01	0

a Sent to Colorado Rockies as player to be named later for pitcher Ubaldo Jimenez, August 17, 2011.

PORCELLO, FREDERICK ALFRED (RICK)
Born, Morristown, New Jersey, December 27, 1988.
Bats Right. Throws Right. Height, 6 feet, 5 inches. Weight, 200 pounds.

Year	Club	Lea	G	IP	W	L	Pct	SO	BB	H	ERA	SAVES
2008 Lakeland	Fla.St.	24	125	8	6	.571	72	33	116	2.66	0
2009 Detroit	A.L.	31	170²/₃	14	9	.609	89	52	176	3.96	0
2010 Toledo	Int.	4	28	1	2	.333	19	10	24	3.21	0
2010 Detroit	A.L.	27	162²/₃	10	12	.455	84	38	188	4.92	0
2011 Detroit	A.L.	31	182	14	9	.609	104	46	210	4.75	0
2012 Detroit	A.L.	31	176¹/₃	10	12	.455	107	44	*226	4.59	0
Major League Totals	4 Yrs.	120	691²/₃	48	42	.533	384	180	800	4.55	0
Division Series											
2011 Detroit	A.L.	1	6	0	1	.000	5	1	5	6.00	0
2012 Detroit	A.L.	1	0¹/₃	0	0	.000	0	0	0	0.00	0
Division Series Totals		2	6¹/₃	0	1	.000	5	1	5	5.68	0
Championship Series											
2011 Detroit	A.L.	3	9	0	0	.000	7	1	10	4.00	0
World Series Record											
2012 Detroit	A.L.	1	1	0	0	.000	1	0	0	0.00	0

PRICE, DAVID TAYLOR
Born, Murfreesboro, Tennessee, August 26, 1985.
Bats Left. Throws Left. Height, 6 feet, 6 inches. Weight, 225 pounds.

Year	Club	Lea	G	IP	W	L	Pct	SO	BB	H	ERA	SAVES
2008 Vero Beach	Fla.St.	6	34²/₃	4	0	1.000	37	7	28	1.82	0
2008 Montgomery	Southern	9	57	7	4	.636	55	16	42	1.89	0
2008 Durham	Int.	4	18	1	1	.500	17	9	22	4.50	0
2008 Tampa Bay	A.L.	5	14	0	0	.000	12	4	9	1.93	0
2009 Durham	Int.	8	34¹/₃	1	4	.200	35	18	28	3.93	0
2009 Tampa Bay	A.L.	23	128¹/₃	10	7	.588	102	54	119	4.42	0
2010 Tampa Bay	A.L.	32	208²/₃	19	6	.760	188	79	170	2.72	0
2011 Tampa Bay	A.L.	34	224¹/₃	12	13	.480	218	63	192	3.49	0
2012 Tampa Bay a	A.L.	31	211	*20	5	*.800	205	59	173	*2.56	0
Major League Totals	5 Yrs.	125	786¹/₃	61	31	.663	725	259	663	3.16	0
Division Series											
2010 Tampa Bay	A.L.	2	12²/₃	0	2	.000	14	0	17	4.97	0
2011 Tampa Bay	A.L.	1	6²/₃	0	1	.000	3	1	7	4.05	0
Division Series Totals		3	19¹/₃	0	3	.000	17	1	24	4.66	0

Year	Club	Lea	G	IP	W	L	Pct	SO	BB	H	ERA	SAVES
	Championship Series											
2008	Tampa Bay	A.L.	3	2⅓	1	0	1.000	4	2	0	0.00	1
	World Series Record											
2008	Tampa Bay	A.L.	2	3⅓	0	0	.000	4	2	2	2.70	0

a Selected Cy Young Award Winner in American League for 2012.

PRYOR, STEPHEN MICHAEL

Born, Donelson, Tennessee, July 23, 1989.
Bats Right. Throws Right. Height, 6 feet, 4 inches. Weight, 245 pounds.

Year	Club	Lea	G	IP	W	L	Pct	SO	BB	H	ERA	SAVES
2010	Clinton	Midwest	12	17	0	2	.000	29	6	17	3.71	1
2010	Everett	Northwest	11	18⅓	0	0	.000	26	7	7	0.49	4
2011	High Desert	Calif.	22	27	1	0	1.000	34	26	28	7.67	4
2011	Jackson	Southern	17	22⅔	2	1	.667	27	7	9	1.19	6
2012	High Desert	Calif.	2	2⅔	0	0	.000	3	3	0	6.75	0
2012	Jackson	Southern	11	16	1	0	1.000	24	5	7	1.13	7
2012	Tacoma	P.C.	16	20	0	0	.000	20	11	11	0.00	3
2012	Seattle a............	A.L.	26	23	3	1	.750	27	13	22	3.91	0

a On disabled list from June 13 to July 21, 2012.

PUTZ, JOSEPH JASON (J.J.)

Born, Trenton, Michigan, February 2, 1977.
Bats Right. Throws Right. Height, 6 feet, 5 inches. Weight, 250 pounds.

Year	Club	Lea	G	IP	W	L	Pct	SO	BB	H	ERA	SAVES
1999	Everett	Northwest	10	22⅓	0	0	.000	17	11	23	4.84	2
2000	Wisconsin	Midwest	26	142⅔	12	6	.667	105	63	130	3.15	0
2001	San Antonio	Texas	27	148	7	9	.438	135	59	145	3.83	0
2002	San Antonio	Texas	15	84	3	10	.231	60	28	84	3.64	0
2002	Tacoma	P.C.	9	54	2	4	.333	39	21	51	3.83	0
2003	Tacoma	P.C.	41	86	0	3	.000	60	34	69	2.51	11
2003	Seattle	A.L.	3	3⅔	0	0	.000	3	3	4	4.91	0
2004	Tacoma	P.C.	7	8⅓	0	0	.000	13	3	10	4.32	3
2004	Seattle	A.L.	54	63	0	3	.000	47	24	66	4.71	9
2005	Seattle	A.L.	64	60	6	5	.545	45	23	58	3.60	1
2006	Seattle	A.L.	72	78⅓	4	1	.800	104	13	59	2.30	36
2007	Seattle	A.L.	68	71⅔	6	1	.857	82	13	37	1.38	40
2008	Mariners..........	Arizona	2	3	0	0	.000	4	0	2	0.00	0
2008	Tacoma	P.C.	1	1⅔	0	0	.000	1	0	0	0.00	0
2008	Seattle a-b........	A.L.	47	46⅓	6	5	.545	56	28	46	3.88	15
2009	New York c-d..........	N.L.	29	29⅓	1	4	.200	19	19	29	5.22	2
2010	Chicago e-f...........	A.L.	60	54	7	5	.583	65	15	41	2.83	3
2011	Diamondbacks......	Arizona	2	2	0	0	.000	0	0	1	0.00	0
2011	Reno	P.C.	2	2	0	0	.000	3	0	1	0.00	0
2011	Arizona g	N.L.	60	58	2	2	.500	61	12	41	2.17	45
2012	Arizona..............	N.L.	57	54⅓	1	5	.167	65	11	45	2.82	32
Major League Totals .... 10 Yrs.			514	518⅔	33	31	.516	547	161	426	3.04	183
	Division Series											
2011	Arizona...............	N.L.	3	2⅓	0	1	.000	0	1	3	3.86	0

a On disabled list from April 2 to April 22 and June 12 to July 20, 2008.
b Traded to New York Mets with pitcher Sean Green and outfielder Jeremy Reed for pitcher Aaron Heilman, outfielder Endy Chavez, pitcher Jason Vargas, infielder Mike Carp, outfielder Ezequiel Carrera and pitcher Maikel Cleto, December 10, 2008.
c On disabled list from June 5 to November 7, 2009.
d Filed for free agency, November 7, 2009. Signed with Chicago White Sox, December 11, 2009.
e On disabled list from August 25 to September 9, 2010.
f Filed for free agency, November 1, 2010. Signed with Arizona Diamondbacks, December 7, 2010.
g On disabled list from June 29 to July 26, 2011.

QUALLS, CHAD MICHAEL

Born, Lomita, California, August 17, 1978.
Bats Right. Throws Right. Height, 6 feet, 5 inches. Weight, 220 pounds.

Year	Club	Lea	G	IP	W	L	Pct	SO	BB	H	ERA	SAVES
2001	Michigan	Midwest	26	162	15	6	.714	125	31	149	3.72	0
2002	Round Rock........	Texas	29	163	6	13	.316	142	67	174	4.36	0
2003	Round Rock........	Texas	28	175⅓	8	11	.421	132	61	174	3.85	0
2004	New Orleans.......	P.C.	32	106⅔	3	6	.333	72	30	134	5.57	1
2004	Houston..............	N.L.	25	33	4	0	1.000	24	8	34	3.55	1

Year	Club	Lea	G	IP	W	L	Pct	SO	BB	H	ERA	SAVES
2005 Houston	N.L.	77	79²/₃	6	4	.600	60	23	73	3.28	0
2006 Houston	N.L.	81	88²/₃	7	3	.700	56	28	76	3.76	0
2007 Houston a	N.L.	79	82²/₃	6	5	.545	78	25	84	3.05	5
2008 Arizona	N.L.	77	73²/₃	4	8	.333	71	18	61	2.81	9
2009 Arizona b	N.L.	51	52	2	2	.500	45	7	53	3.63	24
2010 Arizona	N.L.	43	38	1	4	.200	34	15	61	8.29	12
2010 Tampa Bay c-d-e	A.L.	27	21	2	0	1.000	15	6	24	5.57	0
2011 San Diego f	N.L.	77	74¹/₃	6	8	.429	43	20	73	3.51	0
2012 Indianapolis	Int.	1	1	0	0	.000	3	0	0	0.00	0
2012 New York	A.L.	8	7¹/₃	1	0	1.000	2	3	10	6.14	0
2012 Phil.-Pittsburgh g-h-i-j	N.L.	52	45	1	1	.500	25	11	53	5.20	0
Major League Totals	9 Yrs.	597	595¹/₃	40	35	.533	453	164	602	3.92	51
Division Series											
2004 Houston	N.L.	4	4	0	0	.000	3	1	4	6.75	0
2005 Houston	N.L.	2	3	0	0	.000	1	2	5	6.00	0
2010 Tampa Bay	A.L.	2	1²/₃	0	0	.000	0	0	4	10.80	0
Division Series Totals		8	8²/₃	0	0	.000	4	3	13	7.27	0
Championship Series											
2004 Houston	N.L.	2	4	0	1	.000	4	2	8	11.25	0
2005 Houston	N.L.	4	4²/₃	1	0	1.000	4	0	0	0.00	0
Championship Series Totals		6	8²/₃	1	1	.500	8	2	8	5.19	0
World Series Record											
2005 Houston	N.L.	3	5¹/₃	0	0	.000	5	2	3	1.69	0

a Traded to Arizona Diamondbacks with pitcher Juan Gutierrez and outfielder Chris Burke for pitcher Jose Valverde, December 14, 2007.
b On disabled list from August 31 to November 20, 2009.
c Traded to Tampa Bay Rays for player to be named later, July 31, 2010.
d Arizona Diamondbacks received pitcher Matt Gorgen to complete trade, September 9, 2010.
e Filed for free agency, November 1, 2010. Signed with San Diego Padres, January 19, 2011.
f Filed for free agency, October 31, 2011. Signed with Philadelphia Phillies, January 31, 2012.
g Sold to New York Yankees, July 1, 2012.
h Traded to Pittsburgh Pirates for outfielder Casey McGehee and cash, July 31, 2012.
i On disabled list from August 25 to September 9, 2012.
j Filed for free agency, November 3, 2012.

QUINTANA, JOSE GUILLERMO
Born, Arjona, Colombia, January 24, 1989.
Bats Right. Throws Left. Height, 6 feet. Weight, 215 pounds.

Year	Club	Lea	G	IP	W	L	Pct	SO	BB	H	ERA	SAVES
2010 Yankees	Gulf Coast	15	23²/₃	3	1	.750	32	8	14	2.31	1
2010 Charleston a-b	So.Atl.	5	15¹/₃	0	1	.000	12	10	11	4.70	0
2011 Tampa c	Fla.St.	30	102	10	2	.833	88	28	86	2.91	1
2012 Birmingham	Southern	9	48²/₃	1	3	.250	41	14	43	2.77	0
2012 Chicago	A.L.	25	136¹/₃	6	6	.500	81	42	142	3.76	0

a Released by New York Mets, July 11, 2007. Signed with New York Yankees organization, March 10, 2008.
b Filed for free agency, November 6, 2010, re-signed with New York Yankees organization, December 14, 2010.
c Filed for free agency, November 2, 2011. Signed with Chicago White Sox organization, November 9, 2011.

RAMIREZ, ERASMO JOSE
Born, Rivas, Nicaragua, May 2, 1990.
Bats Right. Throws Right. Height, 5 feet, 11 inches. Weight, 205 pounds.

Year	Club	Lea	G	IP	W	L	Pct	SO	BB	H	ERA	SAVES
2010 Clinton	Midwest	26	151²/₃	10	4	.714	117	21	142	2.97	1
2011 Tacoma	P.C.	7	42¹/₃	3	2	.600	35	13	51	5.10	0
2011 Jackson	Southern	19	110¹/₃	7	6	.538	81	14	127	4.73	0
2012 Tacoma	P.C.	15	77¹/₃	6	3	.667	58	18	81	3.72	0
2012 Seattle a	A.L.	16	59	1	3	.250	48	12	47	3.36	0

a On disabled list from July 1 to August 5, 2012.

RAMIREZ, RAMON SANTO
Born, Puerto Plata, Dominican Republic, August 31, 1981.
Bats Right. Throws Right. Height, 5 feet, 11 inches. Weight, 190 pounds.

Year	Club	Lea	G	IP	W	L	Pct	SO	BB	H	ERA	SAVES
2002 Hiroshima a-b	Japan Cent.	2	3	0	0	.000	3	2	3	3.00	0
2003 Tampa	Fla.St.	14	74¹/₃	2	8	.200	70	20	88	5.21	0
2003 Trenton	Eastern	4	21¹/₃	1	1	.500	21	8	18	1.69	0

Year Club	Lea	G	IP	W	L	Pct	SO	BB	H	ERA	SAVES
2003 Columbus c	Int.	2	6	0	1	.000	5	1	5	4.50	0
2004 Trenton	Eastern	18	114	4	6	.400	128	32	116	4.66	0
2004 Columbus	Int.	4	18	0	3	.000	17	8	25	8.50	0
2005 Columbus	Int.	6	27	1	3	.250	26	9	32	5.33	0
2005 Trenton	Eastern	15	89	6	5	.545	82	35	79	3.84	0
2005 Tulsa d	Texas	9	25^1/3	2	1	.667	23	8	27	5.33	0
2006 Colorado Springs	P.C.	1	1	0	0	.000	1	0	0	0.00	0
2006 Colorado	N.L.	61	67^2/3	4	3	.571	61	27	58	3.46	0
2007 Colorado Springs	P.C.	25	27^2/3	4	0	1.000	35	16	18	2.28	0
2007 Colorado e	N.L.	22	17^1/3	2	2	.500	15	6	21	8.31	0
2008 Kansas City f-g	A.L.	71	71^2/3	3	2	.600	70	31	57	2.64	1
2009 Boston	A.L.	70	69^2/3	7	4	.636	52	32	61	2.84	0
2010 Boston	A.L.	44	42^1/3	0	3	.000	31	16	39	4.46	2
2010 San Francisco h	N.L.	25	27	1	0	1.000	15	11	13	0.67	1
2011 San Francisco i	N.L.	66	68^2/3	3	3	.500	66	26	54	2.62	4
2012 St. Lucie	Fla.St.	2	2	0	0	.000	0	0	5	13.50	0
2012 Buffalo	Int.	1	0^2/3	0	1	.000	0	1	4	40.50	0
2012 New York j-k	N.L.	58	63^1/3	3	4	.429	52	35	58	4.24	1
Major League Totals ..... 7 Yrs.		417	428	23	21	.523	362	184	361	3.32	9
Division Series											
2009 Boston	A.L.	1	0	0	0	.000	0	1	1	INF	0
2010 San Francisco	N.L.	1	2	0	1	.000	1	0	1	4.50	0
Division Series Totals		2	2	0	1	.000	1	1	2	13.50	0
Championship Series											
2010 San Francisco	N.L.	2	1	0	0	.000	0	1	3	27.00	0
World Series Record											
2010 San Francisco	N.L.	2	1	0	0	.000	1	1	1	18.00	0

a Played for Texas Rangers in the Dominican Summer League as an infielder 1997. Did not play 1998 through 2001.
b Released by Texas Rangers, June 4, 1998. Signed with Hiroshima (Japan) 2002.
c Signed with New York Yankees organization, March 5, 2003.
d Traded to Colorado Rockies with pitcher Eduardo Sierra for pitcher Shawn Chacon, July 28, 2005.
e On disabled list from April 18 to May 15 and September 8 to October 31, 2007.
f Traded to Kansas City Royals for player to be named later, March 26, 2008. Colorado Rockies received pitcher Jorge De La Rosa to complete trade, April 30, 2008.
g Traded to Boston Red Sox for outfielder Coco Crisp, November 19, 2008.
h Traded to San Francisco Giants for pitcher Daniel Turpen, July 31, 2010.
i Traded to New York Mets with outfielder Andres Torres for outfielder Angel Pagan, December 7, 2011.
j On disabled list from May 31 to June 24, 2012.
k Filed for free agency, November 3, 2012.

RAPADA, CLAYTON ANTHONY
Born, Portsmouth, Virginia, March 9, 1981.
Bats Right. Throws Left. Height, 6 feet, 5 inches. Weight, 200 pounds.

Year Club	Lea	G	IP	W	L	Pct	SO	BB	H	ERA	SAVES
2002 Boise	Northwest	12	18	0	0	.000	12	8	18	1.50	1
2003 Lansing	Midwest	21	42^1/3	1	2	.333	24	19	46	5.31	0
2003 Boise	Northwest	1	3	0	0	.000	3	1	2	0.00	0
2004 Lansing	Midwest	57	85	6	6	.500	91	30	65	2.33	3
2005 Daytona	Fla.St.	27	42^1/3	1	3	.250	61	16	40	3.83	5
2006 Iowa	P.C.	28	23^2/3	3	2	.600	21	15	27	3.04	0
2006 West Tenn	Southern	33	43^2/3	3	2	.600	45	10	30	0.82	21
2007 Iowa	P.C.	55	55^1/3	7	2	.778	50	25	55	3.58	17
2007 Toledo	Int.	2	2^1/3	0	0	.000	3	1	5	11.57	0
2007 Chicago	N.L.	1	0^1/3	0	0	.000	0	0	0	0.00	0
2007 Detroit a	A.L.	4	2^1/3	0	0	.000	4	2	3	11.57	0
2008 Toledo	Int.	28	35	0	1	.000	45	14	32	2.31	2
2008 Detroit b	A.L.	25	21^1/3	3	0	1.000	15	14	19	4.22	0
2009 Toledo	Int.	42	45^2/3	4	2	.667	47	17	50	2.76	5
2009 Detroit c	A.L.	3	3^1/3	0	0	.000	2	2	4	5.40	0
2010 Oklahoma	P.C.	50	59^1/3	1	2	.333	61	21	32	1.82	2
2010 Texas	A.L.	13	9	0	0	.000	5	7	6	4.00	0
2011 Norfolk	Int.	26	20^2/3	0	1	.000	20	4	24	3.92	1
2011 Baltimore d	A.L.	32	16^1/3	2	0	1.000	18	7	14	6.06	0
2012 New York e	A.L.	70	38^1/3	3	0	1.000	38	17	29	2.82	0
Major League Totals ..... 6 Yrs.		148	91	8	0	1.000	82	49	75	4.15	0
Division Series											
2012 New York	A.L.	1	0^1/3	0	0	.000	0	0	0	0.00	0

e Released by Baltimore Orioles, February 14, 2012. Signed with New York Yankees organization, February 20, 2012.

Year	Club	Lea	G	IP	W	L	Pct	SO	BB	H	ERA	SAVES
	Championship Series											
2010 Texas	....	A.L.	3	0⅓	0	0	.000	1	1	1	0.00	0
2012 New York	....	A.L.	4	1⅓	0	0	.000	1	2	0	0.00	0
Championship Series Totals	......		7	1⅔	0	0	.000	2	3	1	0.00	0

a Sent to Detroit Tigers as player to be named later for outfielder Craig Monroe, August 30, 2007.
b On disabled list from May 21 to June 8, 2008.
c Sold to Texas Rangers, December 7, 2009.
d Released by Texas Rangers, January 14, 2011. Signed with Baltimore Orioles organization, February 3, 2011.

RAUCH, JON ERICH

Born, Louisville, Kentucky, September 27, 1978.
Bats Right. Throws Right. Height, 6 feet, 11 inches. Weight, 290 pounds.

Year	Club	Lea	G	IP	W	L	Pct	SO	BB	H	ERA	SAVES
1999 Bristol	....	Appal.	14	56⅔	4	4	.500	66	16	65	4.45	2
1999 Winston-Salem	.....	Carolina	1	6	0	0	.000	7	3	4	3.00	0
2000 Winston-Salem	.....	Carolina	18	110	11	3	.786	124	33	102	2.86	0
2000 Birmingham	....	Southern	8	56	5	1	.833	63	16	36	2.25	0
2001 Charlotte	....	Int.	6	28	1	3	.250	27	7	28	5.79	0
2002 Chicago	....	A.L.	8	28⅔	2	1	.667	19	14	28	6.59	0
2002 Charlotte	....	Int.	19	109⅓	7	8	.467	97	42	91	4.28	0
2003 Charlotte	....	Int.	24	124⅔	7	1	.875	94	35	121	4.11	0
2004 Charlotte	....	Int.	14	72⅓	6	3	.667	61	25	57	3.11	0
2004 Chicago	....	A.L.	2	8⅔	1	1	.500	4	4	16	6.23	0
2004 Edmonton	....	P.C.	3	18	1	1	.500	13	2	17	4.50	0
2004 Montreal a-b	....	N.L.	9	23⅓	3	0	1.000	18	7	14	1.54	0
2005 New Orleans	....	P.C.	7	21⅓	1	1	.500	25	2	19	2.53	0
2005 Washington c	....	N.L.	15	30	2	4	.333	23	11	24	3.60	0
2006 Washington	....	N.L.	85	91⅓	4	5	.444	86	36	78	3.35	2
2007 Washington	....	N.L.	*88	87⅓	8	4	.667	71	21	75	3.61	4
2008 Washington-Arizona d	...	N.L.	74	71⅔	4	8	.333	66	16	69	4.14	18
2009 Arizona	....	N.L.	58	54⅓	2	2	.500	35	17	57	4.14	2
2009 Minnesota e	....	A.L.	17	15⅔	5	1	.833	14	6	13	1.72	0
2010 Minnesota f	....	A.L.	59	57⅔	3	1	.750	46	14	61	3.12	21
2011 Toronto g-h	....	A.L.	53	52	5	4	.556	36	14	56	4.85	11
2012 New York i	....	N.L.	73	57⅔	3	7	.300	42	12	45	3.59	4
Major League Totals	....	10 Yrs.	541	578⅓	42	38	.525	460	172	536	3.80	62
	Division Series											
2009 Minnesota	....	A.L.	3	1⅓	0	0	.000	0	2	1	6.75	0
2010 Minnesota	....	A.L.	2	1⅔	0	0	.000	1	0	0	0.00	0
Division Series Totals	....		5	3	0	0	.000	1	2	1	3.00	0

a Traded to Montreal Expos with pitcher Gary Majewski for outfielder Carl Everett, July 18, 2004.
b On disabled list from August 14 to September 14, 2004.
c On disabled list from May 26 to September 6, 2005.
d Traded to Arizona Diamondbacks for infielder Emilio Bonifacio, July 22, 2008.
e Traded to Minnesota Twins for player to be named later, August 28, 2009. Arizona Diamondbacks received pitcher Kevin Mulvey to complete trade, September 1, 2009.
f Filed for free agency, November 1, 2010. Signed with Toronto Blue Jays, January 17, 2011.
g On disabled list from September 5 to September 29 and August 16 to September 1, 2011.
h Filed for free agency, October 31, 2011. Signed with New York Mets, December 14, 2011.
i Filed for free agency, November 3, 2012.

REED, ADDISON DEVON

Born, Montclair, California, December 27, 1988.
Bats Left. Throws Right. Height, 6 feet, 4 inches. Weight, 220 pounds.

Year	Club	Lea	G	IP	W	L	Pct	SO	BB	H	ERA	SAVES
2010 Great Falls	....	Pioneer	13	30	1	0	1.000	44	6	17	1.80	1
2011 Kannapolis	....	So.Atl.	4	8	0	0	.000	11	1	4	1.13	0
2011 Winston-Salem	.....	Carolina	15	28⅓	2	0	1.000	39	4	21	1.59	1
2011 Birmingham	....	Southern	13	20⅔	0	1	.000	33	6	10	0.87	2
2011 Charlotte	....	Int.	11	21⅓	0	0	.000	28	3	8	1.27	2
2011 Chicago	....	A.L.	6	7⅓	0	0	.000	12	1	10	3.68	0
2012 Chicago	....	A.L.	62	55	3	2	.600	54	18	57	4.75	29
Major League Totals	....	2 Yrs.	68	62⅓	3	2	.600	66	19	67	4.62	29

RESOP, CHRISTOPHER PAUL (CHRIS)

Born, Naples, Florida, November 4, 1982.
Bats Right. Throws Right. Height, 6 feet, 3 inches. Weight, 225 pounds.

Year	Club	Lea	G	IP	W	L	Pct	SO	BB	H	ERA	SAVES
2003 Greensboro	So.Atl.	11	12²/₃	0	1	.000	15	5	11	4.97	0
2004 Greensboro	So.Atl.	42	42²/₃	3	1	.750	71	8	28	2.11	13
2005 Carolina	Southern	43	49	3	2	.600	56	16	47	2.57	24
2005 Florida	N.L.	15	17	2	0	1.000	15	9	22	8.47	0
2006 Albuquerque	P.C.	40	49²/₃	4	0	1.000	43	15	49	3.81	2
2006 Florida a	N.L.	22	21¹/₃	1	2	.333	10	16	26	3.38	0
2007 Salt Lake	P.C.	27	45¹/₃	1	3	.250	39	16	50	4.57	0
2007 Los Angeles b-c	A.L.	4	4¹/₃	0	0	.000	2	1	4	4.15	0
2008 Atlanta	N.L.	16	18¹/₃	0	1	.000	13	10	16	5.89	0
2008 Richmond d	Int.	9	18	2	0	1.000	22	12	14	1.50	0
2009 Hanshin	Japan Pac.	8	21¹/₃	0	2	.000	6	7	29	6.75	0
2010 Mississippi	Southern	2	4¹/₃	0	0	.000	2	1	5	4.15	0
2010 Gwinnett	Int.	15	82	6	3	.667	91	32	53	2.09	0
2010 Atlanta-Pittsburgh e-f	N.L.	23	21	0	0	.000	26	13	15	3.86	0
2011 Pittsburgh	N.L.	76	69²/₃	5	4	.556	79	30	73	4.39	1
2012 Pittsburgh g	N.L.	61	73²/₃	1	4	.200	46	24	81	3.91	1
Major League Totals .... 7 Yrs.		217	225¹/₃	9	11	.450	191	103	237	4.51	2

a Traded to Los Angeles Angels for pitcher Kevin Gregg, November 20, 2006.
b On disabled list from July 9 to October 25, 2007.
c Claimed on waivers by Atlanta Braves, October 25, 2007.
d Sold to Hanshin Tigers (Japan), July 7, 2009. Signed with Atlanta Braves organization, February 17, 2010.
e On disabled list from June 16 to August 5, 2010.
f Claimed on waivers by Pittsburgh Pirates, August 4, 2010.
g Traded to Oakland Athletics for pitcher Zach Thornton, November 30, 2012.

REYNOLDS, MATTHEW PAUL (MATT)

Born, Knoxville, Tennessee, October 2, 1984.
Bats Left. Throws Left. Height, 6 feet, 5 inches. Weight, 240 pounds.

Year	Club	Lea	G	IP	W	L	Pct	SO	BB	H	ERA	SAVES
2007 Tri-City	Northwest	20	35	1	4	.200	27	4	37	3.60	0
2008 Asheville	So.Atl.	42	57	6	2	.750	53	14	49	2.53	2
2009 Modesto	Calif.	39	49	5	3	.625	58	8	32	1.29	3
2009 Tulsa	Texas	21	25²/₃	1	2	.333	29	9	23	4.21	1
2010 Colorado Springs	P.C.	50	55	1	3	.250	67	16	49	2.62	7
2010 Colorado	N.L.	21	18	1	0	1.000	17	5	10	2.00	0
2011 Colorado	N.L.	73	50²/₃	1	2	.333	50	18	48	4.09	0
2012 Colorado a	N.L.	71	57¹/₃	3	1	.750	51	17	65	4.40	0
Major League Totals .... 3 Yrs.		165	126	5	3	.625	118	40	123	3.93	0

a Traded to Arizona Diamondbacks for infielder Ryan Wheeler, November 20, 2012.

RICHARD, CLAYTON COLBY

Born, Lafayette, Indiana, September 12, 1983.
Bats Left. Throws Left. Height, 6 feet, 5 inches. Weight, 240 pounds.

Year	Club	Lea	G	IP	W	L	Pct	SO	BB	H	ERA	SAVES
2005 Great Falls	Pioneer	10	41	2	1	.667	39	12	37	2.85	0
2005 Kannapolis	So.Atl.	3	10¹/₃	0	1	.000	8	1	14	5.23	0
2006 Winston-Salem	Carolina	4	23²/₃	1	3	.250	12	6	29	4.56	0
2006 Kannapolis	So.Atl.	18	95²/₃	6	6	.500	54	28	117	3.67	0
2007 Winston-Salem	Carolina	28	161¹/₃	8	12	.400	99	59	159	3.63	0
2008 Birmingham	Southern	13	83²/₃	6	6	.500	53	16	66	2.47	0
2008 Charlotte	Int.	7	44	6	0	1.000	33	4	33	2.45	0
2008 Chicago a	A.L.	13	47²/₃	2	5	.286	29	13	61	6.04	0
2009 Chicago	A.L.	26	89	4	3	.571	66	37	94	4.65	0
2009 San Diego b	N.L.	12	64	5	2	.714	48	34	60	4.08	0
2010 San Diego	N.L.	33	201²/₃	14	9	.609	153	78	206	3.75	0
2011 San Diego c	N.L.	18	99²/₃	5	9	.357	53	38	104	3.88	0
2012 San Diego	N.L.	33	218²/₃	14	14	.500	107	42	*228	3.99	0
Major League Totals .... 5 Yrs.		135	720²/₃	44	42	.512	456	242	753	4.13	0
Division Series											
2008 Chicago	A.L.	2	6¹/₃	0	0	.000	6	3	5	1.42	0

a On disabled list from March 22 to May 29, 2008.
b Traded to San Diego Padres with pitcher Aaron Poreda, pitcher Adam Russell and pitcher Dexter Carter for pitcher Jake Peavy, July 31, 2009.
c On disabled list from July 5 to October 28, 2011.

RICHARDS, GARRETT THOMAS
Born, Riverside, California, May 27, 1988.
Bats Right. Throws Right. Height, 6 feet, 3 inches. Weight, 215 pounds.

Year Club	Lea	G	IP	W	L	Pct	SO	BB	H	ERA	SAVES
2009 Orem . . . . Pioneer		8	35⅓	3	1	.750	30	4	37	1.53	0
2010 Rancho Cucamonga. . . . Calif.		7	34⅔	4	1	.800	41	9	38	3.89	0
2010 Cedar Rapids . . . . . . .Midwest		19	108⅓	8	4	.667	108	34	92	3.41	0
2011 Arkansas . . . . .Texas		22	143	12	2	.857	103	40	123	3.15	0
2011 Los Angeles a. . . . . A.L.		7	14	0	2	.000	9	7	16	5.79	0
2012 Salt Lake . . . . P.C.		14	77	7	3	.700	65	35	87	4.21	0
2012 Los Angeles. . . . . A.L.		30	71	4	3	.571	47	34	77	4.69	1
Major League Totals . . . . .2 Yrs.		37	85	4	5	.444	56	41	93	4.87	1

a On disabled list from August 16 to September 6, 2011.

RIVERA, MARIANO
Born, Panama City, Panama, November 29, 1969.
Bats Right. Throws Right. Height, 6 feet, 2 inches. Weight, 195 pounds.

Year Club	Lea	G	IP	W	L	Pct	SO	BB	H	ERA	SAVES
1990 Yankees . . . . Gulf Coast		22	52	5	1	.833	58	7	17	0.17	1
1991 Greensboro . . . . So. Atl.		29	114⅔	4	9	.308	123	36	103	2.75	0
1992 Ft. Lauderdale . . . . . . .Fla. St.		10	59⅓	5	3	.625	42	5	40	2.28	0
1993 Yankees . . . . Gulf Coast		.2	4	0	1	.000	6	1	2	2.25	0
1993 Greensboro . . . . So. Atl.		10	39⅓	1	0	1.000	32	15	31	2.06	0
1994 Tampa . . . . .Fla. St.		7	36⅔	3	0	1.000	27	12	34	2.21	0
1994 Albany . . . . Eastern		9	63⅓	3	0	1.000	39	8	58	2.27	0
1994 Columbus. . . . . .Int.		6	31	4	2	.667	23	10	34	5.81	0
1995 Columbus. . . . . .Int.		7	30	2	2	.500	30	3	25	2.10	0
1995 New York . . . . A.L.		19	67	5	3	.625	51	30	71	5.51	0
1996 New York . . . . A.L.		61	107⅔	8	3	.727	130	34	73	2.09	5
1997 New York . . . . A.L.		66	71⅔	6	4	.600	68	20	65	1.88	43
1998 New York a. . . . . A.L.		54	61⅓	3	0	1.000	36	17	48	1.91	36
1999 New York . . . . A.L.		66	69	4	3	.571	52	18	43	1.83	*45
2000 New York . . . . A.L.		66	75⅔	7	4	.636	58	25	58	2.85	36
2001 New York . . . . A.L.		71	80⅔	4	6	.400	83	12	61	2.34	*50
2002 Yankees . . . . Gulf Coast		1	2	0	0	.000	2	1	2	0.00	0
2002 New York b. . . . . A.L.		45	46	1	4	.200	41	11	35	2.74	28
2003 New York c. . . . . A.L.		64	70⅔	5	2	.714	63	10	61	1.66	40
2004 New York . . . . A.L.		74	78⅔	4	2	.667	66	20	65	1.94	*53
2005 New York . . . . A.L.		71	78⅓	7	4	.636	80	18	50	1.38	43
2006 New York . . . . A.L.		63	75	5	5	.500	55	11	61	1.80	34
2007 New York d. . . . . A.L.		67	71⅓	3	4	.429	74	12	68	3.15	30
2008 New York . . . . A.L.		64	70⅔	6	5	.545	77	6	41	1.40	39
2009 New York . . . . A.L.		66	66⅓	3	3	.500	72	12	48	1.76	44
2010 New York e. . . . . A.L.		61	60	3	3	.500	45	11	39	1.80	33
2011 New York . . . . A.L.		64	61⅓	1	2	.333	60	8	47	1.91	44
2012 New York f-g . . . . A.L.		9	8⅓	1	1	.500	8	2	6	2.16	5
Major League Totals . . . . . . .18 Yrs.		1051	1219⅔	76	58	.567	1119	277	940	2.21	608
Division Series											
1995 New York . . . . A.L.		3	5⅓	1	0	1.000	8	1	3	0.00	0
1996 New York . . . . A.L.		2	4⅔	0	0	.000	1	1	0	0.00	0
1997 New York . . . . A.L.		2	2	0	0	.000	1	0	2	4.50	1
1998 New York . . . . A.L.		3	3⅓	0	0	.000	2	1	1	0.00	2
1999 New York . . . . A.L.		2	3	0	0	.000	3	0	1	0.00	2
2000 New York . . . . A.L.		3	5	0	0	.000	2	0	2	0.00	3
2001 New York . . . . A.L.		3	5	0	0	.000	4	0	4	0.00	2
2002 New York . . . . A.L.		1	1	0	0	.000	0	0	1	0.00	1
2003 New York . . . . A.L.		2	4	0	0	.000	4	0	0	0.00	2
2004 New York . . . . A.L.		4	5⅔	1	0	1.000	2	0	2	0.00	0
2005 New York . . . . A.L.		2	3	0	0	.000	2	1	1	3.00	2
2006 New York . . . . A.L.		1	1	0	0	.000	0	0	1	0.00	0
2007 New York . . . . A.L.		3	4⅔	0	0	.000	6	1	2	0.00	0
2009 New York . . . . A.L.		3	3⅔	0	0	.000	7	1	4	0.00	1
2010 New York . . . . A.L.		3	3⅓	0	0	.000	1	0	2	0.00	2
2011 New York . . . . A.L.		2	1⅓	0	0	.000	1	0	0	0.00	0
Division Series Totals		39	56	2	0	1.000	44	6	26	0.32	18
Championship Series											
1996 New York . . . . A.L.		2	4	1	0	1.000	5	1	6	0.00	0
1998 New York . . . . A.L.		4	5⅔	0	0	.000	5	1	0	0.00	1
1999 New York . . . . A.L.		3	4⅔	1	0	1.000	3	0	5	0.00	2

Year	Club	Lea	G	IP	W	L	Pct	SO	BB	H	ERA	SAVES
2000 New York	A.L.	3	4²/₃	0	0	.000	1	0	4	1.93	1
2001 New York	A.L.	4	4²/₃	1	0	1.000	3	1	2	1.93	2
2003 New York	A.L.	4	8	1	0	1.000	6	0	5	1.13	2
2004 New York	A.L.	5	7	0	0	.000	6	2	6	1.29	2
2009 New York	A.L.	5	7	0	0	.000	4	2	3	1.29	2
2010 New York	A.L.	3	3	0	0	.000	1	0	2	0.00	1
Championship Series Totals		33	48²/₃	4	0	1.000	34	7	33	0.92	13
World Series Record											
1996 New York	A.L.	4	5²/₃	0	0	.000	4	3	4	1.59	0
1998 New York	A.L.	3	4¹/₃	0	0	.000	4	0	5	0.00	3
1999 New York	A.L.	3	4²/₃	1	0	1.000	3	1	3	0.00	2
2000 New York	A.L.	4	6	0	0	.000	7	1	4	3.00	2
2001 New York	A.L.	4	6¹/₃	1	1	.500	7	1	6	1.42	0
2003 New York	A.L.	2	4	0	0	.000	4	0	2	0.00	1
2009 New York	A.L.	4	5¹/₃	0	0	.000	3	2	3	0.00	2
World Series Totals		24	36¹/₃	2	1	.667	32	8	27	0.99	11

a On disabled list from April 6 to April 24, 1998.
b On disabled list from June 9 to June 25 and July 21 to August 8 and August 18 to September 20, 2002.
c On disabled list from March 25 to April 29, 2003.
d Filed for free agency, October 30, 2007, re-signed with New York Yankees, December 17, 2007.
e Filed for free agency, November 1, 2010, re-signed with New York Yankees, December 14, 2010.
f On disabled list from May 4 to October 29, 2012.
g Filed for free agency, November 3, 2012, re-signed with New York Yankees, November 30, 2012.

ROBERTSON, DAVID

Born, Birmingham, Alabama, April 9, 1985.
Bats Right. Throws Right. Height, 5 feet, 11 inches. Weight, 190 pounds.

Year	Club	Lea	G	IP	W	L	Pct	SO	BB	H	ERA	SAVES
2007 Trenton	Eastern	2	4	0	0	.000	9	2	2	2.25	0
2007 Tampa	Fla.St.	18	33¹/₃	3	1	.750	37	15	18	1.08	1
2007 Charleston	So.Atl.	24	47	5	2	.714	67	15	25	0.77	3
2008 Trenton	Eastern	9	18²/₃	0	0	.000	26	6	8	0.96	2
2008 Scranton/WB	Int.	21	35	4	0	1.000	51	17	20	2.06	1
2008 New York	A.L.	25	30¹/₃	4	0	1.000	36	15	29	5.34	0
2009 Scranton/WB	Int.	8	14²/₃	0	3	.000	25	6	10	1.84	2
2009 New York	A.L.	45	43²/₃	2	1	.667	63	23	36	3.30	1
2010 New York	A.L.	64	61¹/₃	4	5	.444	71	33	59	3.82	1
2011 New York	A.L.	70	66²/₃	4	0	1.000	100	35	40	1.08	1
2012 Scranton-WB	Int.	2	2	0	0	.000	2	0	0	0.00	0
2012 New York a	A.L.	65	60²/₃	2	7	.222	81	19	52	2.67	2
Major League Totals	5 Yrs.	269	262²/₃	16	13	.552	351	125	216	2.95	5
Division Series											
2009 New York	A.L.	1	1	1	0	1.000	0	0	1	0.00	0
2010 New York	A.L.	2	0²/₃	0	0	.000	1	1	0	0.00	0
2011 New York	A.L.	2	2	0	0	.000	2	0	0	0.00	0
2012 New York	A.L.	4	4¹/₃	1	0	1.000	5	0	1	0.00	0
Division Series Totals		9	8	2	0	1.000	8	1	2	0.00	0
Championship Series											
2009 New York	A.L.	2	2	1	0	1.000	1	2	1	0.00	0
2010 New York	A.L.	4	2²/₃	0	0	.000	4	1	8	20.25	0
2012 New York	A.L.	2	2	0	0	.000	2	0	2	4.50	0
Championship Series Totals		8	6²/₃	1	0	1.000	7	3	11	9.45	0
World Series Record											
2009 New York	A.L.	2	2¹/₃	0	0	.000	2	1	2	0.00	0

a On disabled list from May 14 to June 14, 2012.

RODNEY, FERNANDO

Born, Samana, Dominican Republic, March 17, 1977.
Bats Right. Throws Right. Height, 5 feet, 11 inches. Weight, 220 pounds.

Year	Club	Lea	G	IP	W	L	Pct	SO	BB	H	ERA	SAVES
1998 Detroit	Dominican	11	32	1	3	.250	37	19	25	3.38	1
1999 Lakeland	Fla.St.	4	6¹/₃	1	0	1.000	5	1	7	1.42	2
1999 Tigers	Gulf Coast	22	30	3	3	.500	39	21	20	2.40	9
2000 West Michigan	Midwest	22	82²/₃	6	4	.600	56	35	74	2.94	0
2001 Erie	Eastern	4	6	0	0	.000	8	3	7	4.26	1
2001 Lakeland	Fla.St.	16	55¹/₃	4	2	.667	44	19	53	3.42	0
2001 Tigers	Gulf Coast	1	1	0	0	.000	1	1	0	0.00	0

Year	Club	Lea	G	IP	W	L	Pct	SO	BB	H	ERA	SAVES
2002 Erie	Eastern	21	20⅓	1	0	1.000	18	5	14	1.33	11
2002 Detroit	A.L.	20	18	1	3	.250	10	10	25	6.00	0
2002 Toledo	Int.	20	22⅓	1	1	.500	25	9	13	0.81	4
2003 Toledo	Int.	38	40⅔	1	1	.500	58	13	22	1.33	23
2003 Toledo	A.L.	27	29⅔	1	3	.250	33	17	35	6.07	3
2004 Detroit a	A.L.		INJURED—Did Not Play								
2005 Toledo	Int.	3	3	0	0	.000	4	1	2	3.00	0
2005 Detroit b	A.L.	39	44	2	3	.400	42	17	39	2.86	9
2006 Detroit	A.L.	63	71⅔	7	4	.636	65	34	51	3.52	7
2007 Toledo	Int.	4	3	0	0	.000	4	2	4	0.00	0
2007 Detroit c	A.L.	48	50⅔	2	6	.250	54	21	46	4.26	1
2008 Toledo	Int.	4	5⅓	1	0	1.000	8	5	3	6.75	0
2008 Detroit d	A.L.	38	40⅓	0	6	.000	49	30	34	4.91	13
2009 Detroit e	A.L.	73	75⅔	2	5	.286	61	41	70	4.40	37
2010 Los Angeles	A.L.	72	68	4	3	.571	53	35	70	4.24	14
2011 Inland Empire	Calif.	2	2	0	0	.000	3	1	2	9.00	0
2011 Los Angeles f-g	A.L.	39	32	3	5	.375	26	28	26	4.50	3
2012 Tampa Bay	A.L.	76	74⅔	2	2	.500	76	15	43	0.60	48
Major League Totals	10 Yrs.	495	504⅔	24	40	.375	469	248	439	3.75	135
Championship Series												
2006 Detroit	A.L.	3	3⅔	0	0	.000	4	1	1	0.00	0
World Series Record												
2006 Detroit	A.L.	4	4	0	0	.000	5	4	5	4.50	0

a On disabled list from March 26 to October 4, 2004.
b On disabled list from March 29 to June 9, 2005.
c On disabled list from May 21 to June 5 and June 24 to August 4, 2007.
d On disabled list from March 30 to June 16, 2008.
e Filed for free agency, November 5, 2009. Signed with Los Angeles Angels, December 24, 2009.
f On disabled list from June 9 to July 22, 2011.
g Filed for free agency, October 30, 2011. Signed with Tampa Bay Rays, January 4, 2012.

RODRIGUEZ, FERNANDO
Born, El Paso, Texas, June 18, 1984.
Bats Right. Throws Right. Height, 6 feet, 3 inches. Weight, 215 pounds.

Year	Club	Lea	G	IP	W	L	Pct	SO	BB	H	ERA	SAVES
2003 Angels	Arizona	15	25	0	2	.000	27	14	29	6.48	0
2003 Provo	Pioneer	4	6	0	0	.000	9	1	9	1.50	1
2004 Provo	Pioneer	14	58⅔	4	3	.571	54	18	64	4.14	0
2005 Cedar Rapids	Midwest	28	157⅓	8	10	.444	128	49	161	4.18	0
2006 Rancho Cucamonga	Calif.	28	163⅓	11	8	.579	112	49	188	4.57	0
2007 Arkansas	Texas	22	125⅓	8	4	.667	61	46	138	4.52	0
2008 Arkansas	Texas	33	136⅔	7	11	.389	85	62	153	5.53	0
2009 Los Angeles	A.L.	1	0⅔	0	0	.000	1	2	1	27.00	0
2009 Salt Lake	P.C.	23	37	1	1	.500	25	23	44	7.54	0
2009 Arkansas	Texas	26	42⅓	3	1	.750	52	22	20	1.28	4
2010 Salt Lake a	P.C.	31	97⅓	4	6	.400	84	42	134	5.92	0
2011 Oklahoma	P.C.	16	24	2	3	.400	33	11	16	1.50	2
2011 Houston	N.L.	47	52⅓	2	3	.400	57	30	51	3.96	0
2012 Houston	N.L.	71	70⅓	2	10	.167	78	34	68	5.37	0
Major League Totals	3 Yrs.	119	123⅓	4	13	.235	136	66	120	4.89	0

a Filed for free agency, November 6, 2010. Signed with Houston Astros organization, November 10, 2010.

RODRIGUEZ, FRANCISCO JOSE
Born, Caracas, Venezuela, January 7, 1982.
Bats Right. Throws Right. Height, 6 feet. Weight, 195 pounds.

Year	Club	Lea	G	IP	W	L	Pct	SO	BB	H	ERA	SAVES
1999 Boise	Northwest	1	5	1	0	1.000	6	1	3	5.40	0
1999 Butte	Pioneer	12	51⅔	1	1	.500	69	21	33	3.31	0
2000 Lake Elsinore	California	13	64	4	4	.500	79	32	43	2.81	0
2001 Rancho Cucamonga	California	20	113⅔	5	7	.417	147	55	127	5.38	0
2002 Arkansas	Texas	23	41⅓	3	3	.500	61	15	32	1.96	9
2002 Salt Lake	P.C.	27	42	2	3	.400	59	13	30	2.57	6
2002 Anaheim	A.L.	5	5⅔	0	0	.000	13	2	3	0.00	0
2003 Anaheim	A.L.	59	86	8	3	.727	95	35	50	3.03	2
2004 Anaheim	A.L.	69	84	4	1	.800	123	33	51	1.82	12
2005 Los Angeles a	A.L.	66	67⅓	2	5	.286	91	32	45	2.67	*45
2006 Los Angeles	A.L.	69	73	2	3	.400	98	28	52	1.73	*47
2007 Los Angeles	A.L.	64	67⅓	5	2	.714	90	34	50	2.81	40

Year	Club	Lea	G	IP	W	L	Pct	SO	BB	H	ERA	SAVES
2008 Los Angeles b	A.L.	*76	68⅓	2	3	.400	77	34	54	2.24	*62
2009 New York	N.L.	70	68	3	6	.333	73	38	51	3.71	35
2010 New York	N.L.	53	57⅓	4	2	.667	67	21	45	2.20	25
2011 New York-Milwaukee	N.L.	73	71⅔	6	2	.750	79	26	67	2.64	23
2012 Milwaukee c	N.L.	78	72	2	7	.222	72	31	65	4.38	3
Major League Totals ....11 Yrs.		682	720⅔	38	34	.528	878	314	533	2.70	294

Division Series

Year	Club	Lea	G	IP	W	L	Pct	SO	BB	H	ERA	SAVES
2002 Anaheim	A.L.	3	5⅔	2	0	1.000	8	2	2	3.18	0
2004 Anaheim	A.L.	2	4⅔	0	0	.000	5	3	4	3.86	0
2005 Los Angeles	A.L.	3	3⅓	0	0	.000	2	0	5	2.70	2
2007 Los Angeles	A.L.	1	0⅓	0	0	.000	1	1	1	54.00	0
2008 Los Angeles	A.L.	2	2⅓	0	1	.000	2	2	5	7.71	0
2011 Milwaukee	N.L.	2	2	0	0	.000	4	3	2	0.00	0
Division Series Totals		13	18⅓	2	3	.400	22	11	19	4.42	2

Championship Series

Year	Club	Lea	G	IP	W	L	Pct	SO	BB	H	ERA	SAVES
2002 Anaheim	A.L.	4	4⅓	2	0	1.000	7	2	2	0.00	0
2005 Los Angeles	A.L.	2	2⅓	0	0	.000	3	3	2	0.00	1
2011 Milwaukee	N.L.	3	3	0	0	.000	4	1	3	3.00	0
Championship Series Totals		9	9⅔	2	0	1.000	14	6	7	0.93	1

World Series Record

Year	Club	Lea	G	IP	W	L	Pct	SO	BB	H	ERA	SAVES
2002 Anaheim	A.L.	4	8⅔	1	1	.500	13	1	6	2.08	0

a On disabled list from May 15 to June 1, 2005.
b Filed for free agency, November 3, 2008. Signed with New York Mets, December 10, 2008.
c Filed for free agency, November 3, 2012.

RODRIGUEZ, WANDY FULTON

Born, Santiago Rodriguez, Dominican Republic, January 18, 1979.
Bats Both. Throws Left. Height, 5 feet, 11 inches. Weight, 160 pounds.

Year	Club	Lea	G	IP	W	L	Pct	SO	BB	H	ERA	SAVES
2001 Martinsville	Appal.	12	74	4	3	.571	67	20	54	1.58	0
2002 Lexington	So.Atl.	28	159⅓	11	4	.733	137	44	167	3.78	0
2003 Salem	Carolina	20	111	8	7	.533	72	41	102	3.49	0
2004 Round Rock	Texas	26	142⅓	11	6	.647	115	57	159	4.48	0
2005 Corpus Christi	Texas	1	3⅓	0	0	.000	3	2	3	2.70	0
2005 Round Rock	P.C.	8	46⅓	4	2	.667	48	16	43	3.69	0
2005 Houston	N.L.	25	128⅔	10	10	.500	80	53	135	5.53	0
2006 Round Rock	P.C.	5	26	2	2	.500	13	13	32	6.92	0
2006 Houston	N.L.	30	135⅔	9	10	.474	98	63	154	5.64	0
2007 Houston	N.L.	31	182⅔	9	13	.409	158	62	179	4.58	0
2008 Corpus Christi	Texas	1	6	0	0	.000	0	1	4	1.50	0
2008 Houston a	N.L.	25	137⅓	9	7	.563	131	44	136	3.54	0
2009 Houston	N.L.	33	205⅔	14	12	.538	193	63	192	3.02	0
2010 Houston	N.L.	32	195	11	12	.478	178	68	183	3.60	0
2011 Corpus Christi	Texas	1	4	0	0	.000	2	1	6	2.25	0
2011 Houston b	N.L.	30	191	11	11	.500	166	69	182	3.49	0
2012 Houston-Pittsburgh c	N.L.	34	205⅔	12	13	.480	139	56	205	3.76	0
Major League Totals ....8 Yrs.		240	1381⅔	85	88	.491	1143	478	1366	4.03	0

Division Series

Year	Club	Lea	G	IP	W	L	Pct	SO	BB	H	ERA	SAVES
2005 Houston	N.L.	1	1	0	0	.000	2	0	1	9.00	0

World Series Record

Year	Club	Lea	G	IP	W	L	Pct	SO	BB	H	ERA	SAVES
2005 Houston	N.L.	2	3⅔	0	1	.000	2	5	4	2.45	0

a On disabled list from April 20 to May 28, 2008.
b On disabled list from May 23 to June 13, 2011.
c Traded to Pittsburgh Pirates with cash for pitcher Rudy Owens, pitcher Colton Cain and outfielder Robbie Grossman, July 25, 2012.

ROENICKE, JOSHUA JAMES (JOSH)

Born, Baltimore, Maryland, August 4, 1982.
Bats Right. Throws Right. Height, 6 feet, 3 inches. Weight, 200 pounds.

Year	Club	Lea	G	IP	W	L	Pct	SO	BB	H	ERA	SAVES
2006 Reds	Gulf Coast	7	7⅔	1	0	1.000	9	3	8	1.17	0
2006 Billings	Pioneer	14	15⅔	1	0	1.000	24	12	10	6.32	6
2007 Sarasota	Fla.St.	27	27⅔	2	1	.667	41	15	23	3.25	16
2007 Chattanooga	Southern	19	19	1	1	.500	15	6	12	0.95	8
2008 Chattanooga	Southern	22	22	4	2	.667	28	12	21	3.27	10
2008 Louisville	Int.	35	39	2	0	1.000	43	14	34	2.54	3
2008 Cincinnati	N.L.	5	3	0	0	.000	6	2	6	9.00	0

Year	Club	Lea	G	IP	W	L	Pct	SO	BB	H	ERA	SAVES
2009 Louisville	Int.	27	28	1	0	1.000	32	6	30	2.57	12
2009 Cincinnati	N.L.	11	13⅓	0	0	.000	14	4	13	2.70	0
2009 Toronto a	A.L.	13	17⅔	0	0	.000	19	12	19	7.13	0
2010 Las Vegas	P.C.	36	59⅓	9	1	.900	54	25	61	3.64	1
2010 Toronto	A.L.	16	19	1	0	1.000	18	13	18	5.68	0
2011 Las Vegas	P.C.	16	22⅓	1	3	.250	20	15	25	6.04	0
2011 Colorado Springs	P.C.	23	30⅔	0	1	.000	22	7	30	3.52	0
2011 Colorado b	N.L.	19	16⅔	0	0	.000	12	7	14	3.78	0
2012 Colorado c	N.L.	63	88⅔	4	2	.667	54	43	85	3.25	1
Major League Totals ....5 Yrs.		127	158⅓	5	2	.714	123	81	155	4.09	1

a Traded to Toronto Blue Jays with infielder Edwin Encarnacion and pitcher Zach Stewart for infielder Scott Rolen, July 31, 2009.

b Claimed on waivers by Colorado Rockies, June 2, 2011.

c Claimed on waivers by Minnesota Twins, November 2, 2012.

ROGERS, ESMIL ANTONIO
Born, Santo Domingo, Dominican Republic, August 14, 1985.
Bats Right. Throws Right. Height, 6 feet, 1 inch. Weight, 190 pounds.

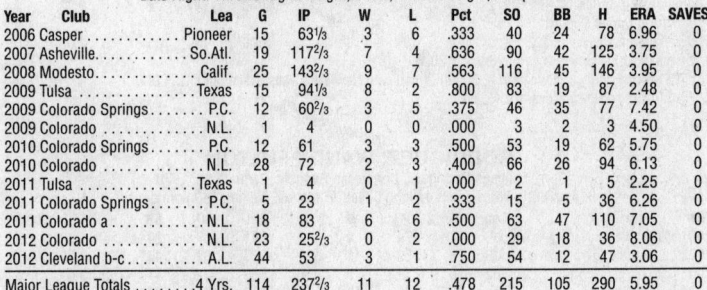

Year	Club	Lea	G	IP	W	L	Pct	SO	BB	H	ERA	SAVES
2006 Casper	Pioneer	15	63⅓	3	6	.333	40	24	78	6.96	0
2007 Asheville	So.Atl.	19	117⅔	7	4	.636	90	42	125	3.75	0
2008 Modesto	Calif.	25	143⅔	9	7	.563	116	45	146	3.95	0
2009 Tulsa	Texas	15	94⅓	8	2	.800	83	19	87	2.48	0
2009 Colorado Springs	P.C.	12	60⅔	3	5	.375	46	35	77	7.42	0
2009 Colorado	N.L.	1	4	0	0	.000	3	2	3	4.50	0
2010 Colorado Springs	P.C.	12	61	3	3	.500	53	19	62	5.75	0
2010 Colorado	N.L.	28	72	2	3	.400	66	26	94	6.13	0
2011 Tulsa	Texas	1	4	0	1	.000	2	1	5	2.25	0
2011 Colorado Springs	P.C.	5	23	1	2	.333	15	5	36	6.26	0
2011 Colorado a	N.L.	18	83	6	6	.500	63	47	110	7.05	0
2012 Colorado	N.L.	23	25⅔	0	2	.000	29	18	36	8.06	0
2012 Cleveland b-c	A.L.	44	53	3	1	.750	54	12	47	3.06	0
Major League Totals ....4 Yrs.		114	237⅔	11	12	.478	215	105	290	5.95	0

a On disabled list from May 2 to July 25, 2011.

b Sold to Cleveland Indians, June 12, 2012.

c Traded to Toronto Blue Jays for infielder Mike Aviles and catcher Yan Gomes, November 3, 2012.

ROGERS, MARK ELLIOT
Born, Brunswick, Maine, January 30, 1986.
Bats Right. Throws Right. Height, 6 feet, 3 inches. Weight, 225 pounds.

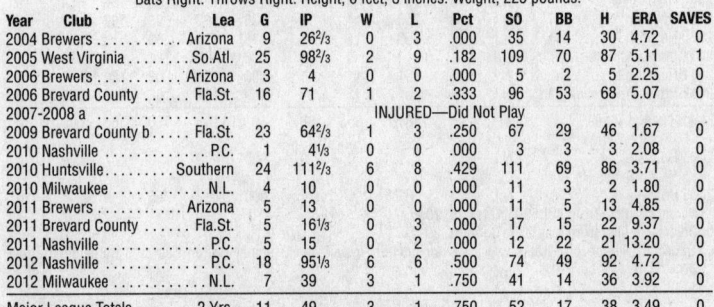

Year	Club	Lea	G	IP	W	L	Pct	SO	BB	H	ERA	SAVES
2004 Brewers	Arizona	9	26⅔	0	3	.000	35	14	30	4.72	0
2005 West Virginia	So.Atl.	25	98⅔	2	9	.182	109	70	87	5.11	1
2006 Brewers	Arizona	3	4	0	0	.000	5	2	5	2.25	0
2006 Brevard County	Fla.St.	16	71	1	2	.333	96	53	68	5.07	0
2007-2008 a						INJURED—Did Not Play					
2009 Brevard County b	Fla.St.	23	64⅔	1	3	.250	67	29	46	1.67	0
2010 Nashville	P.C.	1	4⅓	0	0	.000	3	3	3	2.08	0
2010 Huntsville	Southern	24	111⅔	6	8	.429	111	69	86	3.71	0
2010 Milwaukee	N.L.	4	10	0	0	.000	11	3	2	1.80	0
2011 Brewers	Arizona	5	13	0	0	.000	11	5	13	4.85	0
2011 Brevard County	Fla.St.	5	16⅓	0	3	.000	17	15	22	9.37	0
2011 Nashville	P.C.	5	15	0	2	.000	12	22	21	13.20	0
2012 Nashville	P.C.	18	95⅓	6	6	.500	74	49	92	4.72	0
2012 Milwaukee	N.L.	7	39	3	1	.750	41	14	36	3.92	0
Major League Totals ....2 Yrs.		11	49	3	1	.750	52	17	38	3.49	0

a On minor league disabled list from April 5 to September 12, 2007.

b On minor league disabled list from April 3 to September 1, 2008.

ROMERO, RICARDO (RICKY)
Born, Los Angeles, California, November 6, 1984.
Bats Right. Throws Left. Height, 6 feet. Weight, 215 pounds.

Year	Club	Lea	G	IP	W	L	Pct	SO	BB	H	ERA	SAVES
2005 Dunedin	Fla.St.	8	30⅔	1	0	1.000	22	7	36	3.82	0
2005 Auburn	N.Y.-Penn.	1	2	0	0	.000	2	1	2	0.00	0
2006 New Hampshire	Eastern	12	67⅓	2	7	.222	41	26	65	5.08	0

Year	Club	Lea	G	IP	W	L	Pct	SO	BB	H	ERA	SAVES
2006 Dunedin	Fla.St.	10	58 1/3	2	1	.667	61	14	48	2.47	0	
2007 New Hampshire	Eastern	18	88 1/3	3	6	.333	80	51	98	4.89	0	
2007 Dunedin	Fla.St.	1	4 2/3	0	0	.000	2	1	4	3.86	0	
2008 New Hampshire	Eastern	21	121 2/3	5	5	.500	78	55	139	4.96	0	
2008 Syracuse	Int.	7	42 2/3	3	3	.500	38	20	42	3.38	0	
2009 Dunedin	Fla.St.	1	4	0	1	.000	5	1	6	13.50	0	
2009 New Hampshire	Eastern	1	5 1/3	0	0	.000	4	5	3	1.69	0	
2009 Las Vegas	P.C.	1	5	0	0	.000	3	2	8	7.20	0	
2009 Toronto a	A.L.	29	178	13	9	.591	141	79	192	4.30	0	
2010 Toronto	A.L.	32	210	14	9	.609	174	82	189	3.73	0	
2011 Toronto	A.L.	32	225	15	11	.577	178	80	176	2.92	0	
2012 Toronto	A.L.	32	181	9	14	.391	124	*105	198	5.77	0	
Major League Totals	4 Yrs.	125	794	51	43	.543	617	346	755	4.09	0	

a On disabled list from April 20 to May 15, 2009.

ROMO, SERGIO FRANCISCO

Born, Brawley, California, March 4, 1983.
Bats Right. Throws Right. Height, 5 feet, 11 inches. Weight, 190 pounds.

Year	Club	Lea	G	IP	W	L	Pct	SO	BB	H	ERA	SAVES
2005 Salem-Keizer	Northwest	15	68 2/3	7	1	.875	65	9	70	2.75	0	
2006 Augusta	So.Atl.	31	103 1/3	10	2	.833	95	19	78	2.53	4	
2007 San Jose	Calif.	41	66 1/3	6	2	.750	106	15	35	1.36	9	
2008 Connecticut	Eastern	24	27	1	3	.250	30	7	22	4.00	11	
2008 Fresno	P.C.	3	6	0	0	.000	7	2	3	0.00	0	
2008 San Francisco	N.L.	29	34	3	1	.750	33	8	16	2.12	0	
2009 San Jose	Calif.	3	4 2/3	0	0	.000	6	2	2	0.00	0	
2009 Fresno	P.C.	3	3	0	0	.000	3	0	2	0.00	0	
2009 San Francisco a	N.L.	45	34	5	2	.714	41	11	30	3.97	2	
2010 San Francisco	N.L.	68	62	5	3	.625	70	14	46	2.18	0	
2011 Giants	Arizona	1	1	0	0	.000	3	0	1	0.00	0	
2011 San Francisco b	N.L.	65	48	3	1	.750	70	5	29	1.50	1	
2012 San Francisco	N.L.	69	55 1/3	4	2	.667	63	10	37	1.79	14	
Major League Totals	5 Yrs.	276	233 1/3	20	9	.690	277	48	158	2.20	17	
Division Series												
2010 San Francisco	N.L.	2	0 2/3	1	0	1.000	0	0	3	40.50	0	
2012 San Francisco	N.L.	3	4 1/3	1	0	1.000	1	1	2	2.08	1	
Division Series Totals		5	5	2	0	1.000	1	1	5	7.20	1	
Championship Series												
2010 San Francisco	N.L.	3	2 1/3	0	0	.000	3	1	2	0.00	0	
2012 San Francisco	N.L.	4	3 1/3	0	0	.000	3	0	2	0.00	0	
Championship Series Totals		7	5 2/3	0	0	.000	6	1	4	0.00	0	
World Series Record												
2010 San Francisco	N.L.	1	0 2/3	0	0	.000	1	0	1	0.00	0	
2012 San Francisco	N.L.	3	3	0	0	.000	5	0	0	0.00	3	
World Series Totals		4	3 2/3	0	0	.000	6	0	1	0.00	3	

a On disabled list from March 26 to May 30, 2009.
b On disabled list from August 10 to August 28, 2011.

ROSENTHAL, TREVOR JORDAN

Born, Lees Summit, Missouri, May 29, 1990.
Bats Right. Throws Right. Height, 6 feet, 2 inches. Weight, 190 pounds.

Year	Club	Lea	G	IP	W	L	Pct	SO	BB	H	ERA	SAVES
2009 Cardinals	Gulf Coast	14	24	4	1	.800	26	10	25	4.88	0	
2010 Johnson City	Appal.	10	32	3	0	1.000	30	7	23	2.25	1	
2011 Quad Cities	Midwest	22	120 1/3	7	7	.500	133	39	111	4.11	0	
2012 Springfield	Texas	17	94	8	6	.571	83	37	67	2.78	0	
2012 Memphis	P.C.	3	15	0	0	.000	21	5	11	4.20	0	
2012 St. Louis	N.L.	19	22 2/3	0	2	.000	25	7	14	2.78	0	
Division Series												
2012 St. Louis	N.L.	3	3 1/3	0	0	.000	6	0	1	0.00	0	
Championship Series												
2012 St. Louis	N.L.	4	5 1/3	0	0	.000	9	2	1	0.00	0	

ROSS, ROBERT CHARLES (ROBBIE)
Born, Lexington, Kentucky, June 24, 1989.
Bats Left. Throws Left. Height, 5 feet, 11 inches. Weight, 185 pounds.

Year Club	Lea	G	IP	W	L	Pct	SO	BB	H	ERA	SAVES
2009 Spokane........	Northwest	15	74⅓	4	4	.500	76	17	68	2.66	0
2010 Bakersfield..........	Calif.	11	52	4	4	.500	49	17	67	5.37	0
2010 Hickory.............	So.Atl.	16	94	8	7	.533	62	20	89	2.59	0
2011 Myrtle Beach	Carolina	21	123⅓	9	4	.692	98	28	102	2.26	0
2011 Frisco..............	Texas	6	38	1	1	.500	36	5	33	2.61	0
2012 Texas a.............	A.L.	58	65	6	0	1.000	47	23	55	2.22	0

a On disabled list from August 30 to September 15, 2012.

ROSS, TYSON WILLIAM
Born, Berkeley, California, April 22, 1987.
Bats Right. Throws Right. Height, 6 feet, 6 inches. Weight, 230 pounds.

Year Club	Lea	G	IP	W	L	Pct	SO	BB	H	ERA	SAVES
2008 Kane County........	Midwest	6	19⅓	0	1	.000	16	5	16	4.66	0
2009 Stockton............	Calif.	18	86⅓	5	6	.455	82	33	78	4.17	0
2009 Midland	Texas	9	50	5	4	.556	31	20	40	3.96	0
2010 Oakland	A.L.	26	39⅓	1	4	.200	32	20	39	5.49	1
2010 Sacramento	P.C.	6	25⅓	2	1	.667	30	13	22	3.55	0
2011 Oakland	A.L.	9	36	3	3	.500	24	13	33	2.75	0
2011 Stockton............	Calif.	1	1	0	0	.000	1	1	2	9.00	0
2011 Sacramento a..........	P.C.	9	36⅔	3	2	.600	34	22	52	7.61	0
2012 Sacramento	P.C.	15	78⅓	6	2	.750	64	29	69	2.99	0
2012 Oakland b............	A.L.	18	73⅓	2	11	.154	46	37	96	6.50	0
Major League Totals	3 Yrs.	53	148⅔	6	18	.250	102	70	168	5.33	1

a On disabled list from May 20 to July 24, 2011.
b Traded to San Diego Padres with infielder A.J. Kirby-Jones for infielder Andy Parrino and pitcher Andrew Werner, November 16, 2012.

RUSIN, CHRISTOPHER PATRICK (CHRIS)
Born, Detroit, Michigan, October 22, 1986.
Bats Left. Throws Left. Height, 6 feet, 2 inches. Weight, 195 pounds.

Year Club	Lea	G	IP	W	L	Pct	SO	BB	H	ERA	SAVES
2009 Cubs.............	Arizona	2	5	0	0	.000	2	3	1	0.00	0
2009 Boise	Northwest	8	31	0	4	.000	27	9	33	3.48	0
2010 Daytona	Fla.St.	20	91	4	3	.571	84	15	79	3.36	0
2010 Tennessee	Southern	4	19	2	1	.667	15	4	21	1.89	0
2011 Iowa.................	P.C.	11	62⅔	5	2	.714	46	14	70	4.02	0
2011 Tennessee	Southern	15	76	3	2	.600	49	16	80	3.91	0
2012 Tennessee	Southern	1	3	0	0	.000	1	0	0	0.00	0
2012 Iowa.................	P.C.	25	140⅓	8	9	.471	94	53	146	4.55	0
2012 Chicago	N.L.	7	29⅔	2	3	.400	21	11	38	6.37	0

RUSSELL, JAMES CLAYTON
Born, Cincinnati, Ohio, January 8, 1986.
Bats Left. Throws Left. Height, 6 feet, 4 inches. Weight, 205 pounds.

Year Club	Lea	G	IP	W	L	Pct	SO	BB	H	ERA	SAVES
2007 Cubs.............	Arizona	1	2	0	0	.000	2	0	0	0.00	0
2007 Peoria............	Midwest	2	7	0	0	.000	9	4	3	0.00	0
2008 Daytona	Fla.St.	8	41	2	2	.500	24	13	36	3.51	0
2008 Tennessee	Southern	18	86⅓	4	8	.333	62	25	111	6.36	0
2009 Iowa.................	P.C.	26	65⅔	3	3	.500	46	19	71	3.43	0
2009 Tennessee	Southern	11	37	2	3	.400	26	9	45	5.11	0
2010 Iowa.................	P.C.	5	11	0	0	.000	10	4	11	5.73	0
2010 Chicago	N.L.	57	49	1	1	.500	42	11	55	4.96	0
2011 Chicago	N.L.	64	67⅔	1	6	.143	43	14	76	4.12	0
2012 Chicago	N.L.	77	69⅓	7	1	.875	55	23	67	3.25	2
Major League Totals	3 Yrs.	198	186	9	8	.529	140	48	198	4.02	2

RYU, HYUN-JIN
Born, Incheon, Korea, March 25, 1987.
Bats Left. Throws Left. Height, 6 feet, 2 inches. Weight, 215 pounds.

Year Club	Lea	G	IP	W	L	Pct	SO	BB	H	ERA	SAVES
2006 Hanwha	Korea	30	201⅔	18	6	.750	204	52	159	2.23	1
2007 Hanwha	Korea	30	211	17	7	.708	178	68	195	2.94	0

Year Club	Lea	G	IP	W	L	Pct	SO	BB	H	ERA	SAVES
2008 Hanwha . . . . .Korea		26	165²/₃	14	7	.667	143	67	144	3.31	0
2009 Hanwha . . . . .Korea		28	189¹/₃	13	12	.520	188	67	180	3.57	0
2010 Hanwha . . . . .Korea		25	192²/₃	16	4	.800	187	45	149	1.82	0
2011 Hanwha . . . . .Korea		24	126	11	7	.611	128	38	101	3.36	0
2012 Hanwha a . . . . .Korea		27	182²/₃	9	9	.500	210	46	153	2.66	0

a Signed with Los Angeles Dodgers, December 9, 2012.

RZEPCZYNSKI, MARC WALTER

Born, Yorba Linda, California, August 29, 1985.
Bats Left. Throws Left. Height, 6 feet, 1 inch. Weight, 205 pounds.

Year Club	Lea	G	IP	W	L	Pct	SO	BB	H	ERA	SAVES
2007 Auburn . . . . N.Y.-Penn.		11	45²/₃	5	0	1.000	49	17	33	2.76	0
2008 Lansing . . . . .Midwest		22	121	7	6	.538	124	42	100	2.83	0
2009 New Hampshire . . . . . Eastern		14	76²/₃	7	5	.583	88	36	80	2.93	0
2009 Las Vegas. . . . . P.C.		2	11¹/₃	2	0	1.000	16	4	7	0.79	0
2009 Toronto . . . . A.L.		11	61¹/₃	2	4	.333	60	30	51	3.67	0
2010 Las Vegas. . . . . P.C.		12	67	5	5	.500	61	27	81	6.04	0
2010 Toronto a . . . . A.L.		14	63²/₃	4	4	.500	57	30	72	4.95	0
2011 Toronto . . . . A.L.		43	39¹/₃	2	3	.400	33	15	28	2.97	0
2011 St. Louis b . . . . N.L.		28	22²/₃	0	3	.000	28	11	22	3.97	0
2012 St. Louis. . . . . N.L.		70	46²/₃	1	3	.250	33	17	46	4.24	0
Major League Totals . . . . .4 Yrs.		166	233²/₃	9	17	.346	211	103	219	4.04	0
Wild Card Playoff											
2012 St. Louis. . . . . N.L.		1	0¹/₃	0	0	.000	0	0	1	0.00	0
Division Series											
2011 St. Louis. . . . . N.L.		3	1	0	0	.000	1	0	4	27.00	0
2012 St. Louis. . . . . N.L.		1	0¹/₃	0	0	.000	1	0	1	0.00	0
Division Series Totals		4	1¹/₃	0	0	.000	2	0	5	20.25	0
Championship Series											
2011 St. Louis. . . . . N.L.		5	4²/₃	1	0	1.000	4	1	1	1.93	0
2012 St. Louis. . . . . N.L.		3	1¹/₃	0	0	.000	2	1	1	6.75	0
Championship Series Totals		8	6	1	0	1.000	6	2	2	3.00	0
World Series Record											
2011 St. Louis. . . . . N.L.		4	2²/₃	0	0	.000	4	0	2	0.00	0

a On disabled list from March 31 to May 19, 2010.

b Traded to St. Louis Cardinals with pitcher Edwin Jackson, pitcher Octavio Dotel, outfielder Corey Patterson and cash for outfielder Colby Rasmus, pitcher Trever Miller, pitcher Brian Tallet and pitcher P.J. Walters, July 27, 2011.

SABATHIA, CARSTEN CHARLES (CC)

Born, Vallejo, California, July 21, 1980.
Bats Left. Throws Left. Height, 6 feet, 7 inches. Weight, 290 pounds.

Year Club	Lea	G	IP	W	L	Pct	SO	BB	H	ERA	SAVES
1998 Burlington . . . . Appal.		5	18	1	0	1.000	35	8	20	4.50	0
1999 Kinston. . . . . .Carolina		7	32	3	3	.500	29	19	30	5.34	0
1999 Mahoning Valley. . . N.Y.-Penn.		6	19²/₃	0	0	.000	27	12	9	1.83	0
1999 Columbus a . . . . So.Atl.		3	16²/₃	2	0	1.000	20	5	8	1.08	0
2000 Kinston. . . . . .Carolina		10	56	3	2	.600	69	24	48	3.54	0
2000 Akron . . . . Eastern		17	90¹/₃	3	7	.300	90	48	75	3.59	0
2001 Cleveland . . . . A.L.		33	180¹/₃	17	5	.773	171	95	149	4.39	0
2002 Cleveland . . . . A.L.		33	210	13	11	.542	149	88	198	4.37	0
2003 Cleveland . . . . A.L.		30	197²/₃	13	9	.591	141	66	190	3.60	0
2004 Cleveland . . . . A.L.		30	188	11	10	.524	139	72	176	4.12	0
2005 Akron . . . . Eastern		2	9	0	1	.000	9	2	4	1.00	0
2005 Cleveland b . . . . A.L.		31	196²/₃	15	10	.600	161	62	185	4.03	0
2006 Buffalo . . . . .Int.		1	5	1	0	1.000	5	1	6	1.80	0
2006 Cleveland c. . . . . A.L.		28	192²/₃	12	11	.522	172	44	182	3.22	0
2007 Cleveland d . . . . A.L.		34	*241	19	7	.731	209	37	238	3.21	0
2008 Cleveland . . . . A.L.		18	122¹/₃	6	8	.429	123	34	117	3.83	0
2008 Milwaukee e-f. . . . . N.L.		17	130²/₃	11	2	.846	128	25	106	1.65	0
2009 New York . . . . A.L.		34	230	*19	8	.704	197	67	197	3.37	0
2010 New York . . . . A.L.		34	237²/₃	*21	7	.750	197	74	209	3.18	0
2011 New York . . . . A.L.		33	237¹/₃	19	8	.704	230	61	230	3.00	0
2012 New York g. . . . . A.L.		28	200	15	6	.714	197	44	184	3.38	0
Major League Totals . . . . . . .12 Yrs.		383	2564¹/₃	191	102	.652	2214	769	2361	3.50	0
Division Series											
2001 Cleveland . . . . A.L.		1	6	1	0	1.000	5	5	6	3.00	0
2007 Cleveland . . . . A.L.		1	5	1	0	1.000	5	6	4	5.40	0

Year Club	Lea	G	IP	W	L	Pct	SO	BB	H	ERA	SAVES
2008 Milwaukee	N.L.	1	3²/₃	0	1	.000	5	4	6	12.27	0
2009 New York	A.L.	1	6²/₃	1	0	1.000	8	0	8	1.35	0
2010 New York	A.L.	1	6	1	0	1.000	5	3	5	4.50	0
2011 New York	A.L.	3	8²/₃	0	0	.000	11	8	10	6.23	0
2012 New York	A.L.	2	17²/₃	2	0	1.000	16	3	12	1.53	0
Division Series Totals		10	53²/₃	6	1	.857	55	29	51	3.86	0
Championship Series											
2007 Cleveland	A.L.	2	10¹/₃	0	2	.000	9	7	17	10.45	0
2009 New York	A.L.	2	16	2	0	1.000	12	3	9	1.13	0
2010 New York	A.L.	2	10	1	0	1.000	10	4	17	6.30	0
2012 New York	A.L.	1	3²/₃	0	1	.000	3	2	11	12.27	0
Championship Series Totals		7	40	3	3	.500	34	16	54	5.85	0
World Series Record											
2009 New York	A.L.	2	13²/₃	0	1	.000	12	6	11	3.29	0

a On disabled list from April 1 through June 20, 1999.
b On disabled list from March 25 to April 17, 2005.
c On disabled list from April 3 to May 2, 2006.
d Selected Cy Young Award Winner in American League for 2007.
e Traded to Milwaukee Brewers for outfielder Matt LaPorta, pitcher Zach Jackson, pitcher Rob Bryson and player to be named later, July 7, 2008. Cleveland Indians received outfielder Michael Brantley to complete trade, October 3, 2008.
f Filed for free agency, November 1, 2008. Signed with New York Yankees, December 18, 2008.
g On disabled list from June 28 to July 17 and August 9 to August 24, 2012.

SALAS, NOEL FERNANDO (FERNANDO)
Born, Huatabampo, Mexico, May 30, 1985.
Bats Right. Throws Right. Height, 6 feet, 2 inches. Weight, 200 pounds.

Year Club	Lea	G	IP	W	L	Pct	SO	BB	H	ERA	SAVES
2005 Saltillo	Mexican	14	16²/₃	0	0	.000	12	10	21	2.08	0
2006 Saltillo	Mexican	29	47²/₃	8	2	.800	38	20	40	3.02	0
2007 Palm Beach	Fla.St.	16	39¹/₃	2	3	.400	25	10	39	5.26	0
2007 Saltillo a	Mexican	3	2²/₃	0	0	.000	2	2	5	6.75	0
2008 Springfield	Texas	60	74	7	3	.700	100	16	65	3.65	25
2009 Cardinals	Gulf Coast	1	1	0	0	.000	1	0	0	0.00	0
2009 Springfield	Texas	10	11¹/₃	1	0	1.000	7	2	10	3.18	0
2009 Memphis	P.C.	24	27	3	2	.600	24	10	22	3.67	0
2010 Memphis	P.C.	34	35²/₃	1	0	1.000	44	9	26	3.79	19
2010 St. Louis.............	N.L.	27	30²/₃	0	0	.000	29	15	28	3.52	0
2011 Memphis	P.C.	3	3	0	0	.000	4	0	2	0.00	2
2011 St. Louis.............	N.L.	68	75	5	6	.455	75	21	50	2.28	24
2012 Memphis	P.C.	4	4	1	0	1.000	5	0	6	9.00	1
2012 St. Louis.............	N.L.	65	58²/₃	1	4	.200	60	27	56	4.30	0
Major League Totals	3 Yrs.	160	164¹/₃	6	10	.375	164	63	134	3.23	24
Division Series											
2011 St. Louis.............	N.L.	3	3²/₃	0	0	.000	2	0	2	2.45	0
2012 St. Louis.............	N.L.	1	1	0	0	.000	1	0	0	0.00	0
Division Series Totals		4	4²/₃	0	0	.000	3	0	2	1.93	0
Championship Series											
2011 St. Louis.............	N.L.	4	6	0	0	.000	6	1	3	1.50	0
2012 St. Louis.............	N.L.	4	4²/₃	0	0	.000	4	0	3	3.86	0
Championship Series Totals		8	10²/₃	0	0	.000	10	1	6	2.53	0
World Series Record											
2011 St. Louis.............	N.L.	4	3²/₃	0	0	.000	4	3	7	7.36	0

a Sold to St. Louis Cardinals, April 5, 2007. Loaned back to Saltillo (Mexican), July 29, 2007.

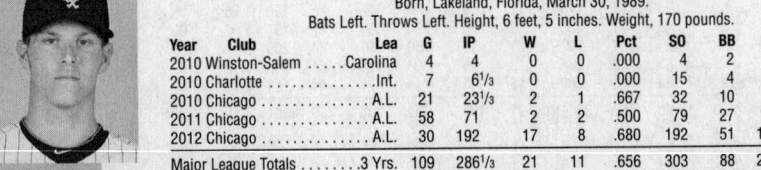

SALE, CHRISTOPHER (CHRIS)
Born, Lakeland, Florida, March 30, 1989.
Bats Left. Throws Left. Height, 6 feet, 5 inches. Weight, 170 pounds.

Year Club	Lea	G	IP	W	L	Pct	SO	BB	H	ERA	SAVES
2010 Winston-Salem	Carolina	4	4	0	0	.000	4	2	3	2.25	0
2010 Charlotte	Int.	7	6¹/₃	0	0	.000	15	4	3	2.84	0
2010 Chicago	A.L.	21	23¹/₃	2	1	.667	32	10	15	1.93	4
2011 Chicago	A.L.	58	71	2	2	.500	79	27	52	2.79	8
2012 Chicago	A.L.	30	192	17	8	.680	192	51	167	3.05	0
Major League Totals	3 Yrs.	109	286¹/₃	21	11	.656	303	88	234	2.89	12

SAMARDZIJA, JEFFREY ALAN (JEFF)

Born, Merrillville, Indiana, January 23, 1985.
Bats Right. Throws Right. Height, 6 feet, 5 inches. Weight, 225 pounds.

Year	Club	Lea	G	IP	W	L	Pct	SO	BB	H	ERA	SAVES
2006 Boise	Northwest		5	19	1	1	.500	13	6	18	2.37	0
2006 Peoria	Midwest		2	11	0	1	.000	4	6	6	3.27	0
2007 Daytona	Fla.St.		24	107$\frac{1}{3}$	3	8	.273	45	35	142	4.95	0
2007 Tennessee	Southern		6	34$\frac{1}{3}$	3	3	.500	20	9	33	3.41	0
2008 Tennessee	Southern		16	76	3	5	.375	44	42	71	4.86	0
2008 Iowa	P.C.		6	37$\frac{1}{3}$	4	1	.800	40	16	32	3.13	0
2008 Chicago	N.L.		26	27$\frac{2}{3}$	1	0	1.000	25	15	24	2.28	1
2009 Iowa	P.C.		18	89	6	6	.500	71	27	98	4.35	0
2009 Chicago	N.L.		20	34$\frac{2}{3}$	1	3	.250	21	15	46	7.53	0
2010 Iowa	P.C.		35	111$\frac{1}{3}$	11	3	.786	102	67	86	4.37	0
2010 Chicago	N.L.		7	19$\frac{1}{3}$	2	2	.500	9	20	21	8.38	0
2011 Chicago	N.L.		75	88	8	4	.667	87	50	64	2.97	0
2012 Chicago	N.L.		28	174$\frac{2}{3}$	9	13	.409	180	56	157	3.81	0
Major League Totals	5 Yrs.		156	344$\frac{1}{3}$	21	22	.488	322	156	312	4.10	1
Division Series												
2008 Chicago	N.L.		1	1	0	0	.000	0	0	2	9.00	0

SANCHEZ, ANIBAL ALEJANDRO

Born, Maracay, Venezuela, February 27, 1984.
Bats Right. Throws Right. Height, 6 feet. Weight, 180 pounds.

Year	Club	Lea	G	IP	W	L	Pct	SO	BB	H	ERA	SAVES
2004 Lowell a	N.Y.-Penn.		15	76$\frac{1}{3}$	4	4	.500	101	29	43	1.77	0
2005 Wilmington	Carolina		14	78$\frac{2}{3}$	6	1	.857	95	24	53	2.40	0
2005 Portland b	Eastern		11	57$\frac{1}{3}$	3	5	.375	63	16	53	3.45	0
2006 Carolina	Southern		15	85$\frac{2}{3}$	3	6	.333	92	27	82	3.15	0
2006 Florida	N.L.		18	114$\frac{1}{3}$	10	3	.769	72	46	90	2.83	0
2007 Florida d	N.L.		6	30	2	1	.667	14	19	43	4.80	0
2008 Marlins	Gulf Coast		1	5	1	0	1.000	4	1	4	3.60	0
2008 Jupiter	Fla.St.		2	10	0	0	.000	9	4	7	1.80	0
2008 Carolina	Southern		2	13	1	0	1.000	12	5	12	3.46	0
2008 Florida e	N.L.		10	51$\frac{2}{3}$	2	5	.286	50	27	54	5.57	0
2009 Marlins	Gulf Coast		1	2$\frac{2}{3}$	0	0	.000	2	3	3	3.38	0
2009 Jupiter	Fla.St.		3	13$\frac{1}{3}$	1	0	1.000	12	3	7	0.68	0
2009 Jacksonville	Southern		2	10$\frac{1}{3}$	1	0	1.000	8	3	5	2.61	0
2009 Florida f	N.L.		16	86	4	8	.333	71	46	84	3.87	0
2010 Florida	N.L.		32	195	13	12	.520	157	70	192	3.55	0
2011 Florida	N.L.		32	196$\frac{1}{3}$	8	9	.471	202	64	187	3.67	0
2012 Miami	N.L.		19	121	5	7	.417	110	33	119	3.94	0
2012 Detroit g-h	A.L.		12	74$\frac{2}{3}$	4	6	.400	57	15	81	3.74	0
Major League Totals	7 Yrs.		145	869	48	51	.485	733	320	850	3.75	0
Division Series												
2012 Detroit	A.L.		1	6$\frac{1}{3}$	0	1	.000	3	2	5	2.84	0
Championship Series												
2012 Detroit	A.L.		1	7	1	0	1.000	7	3	3	0.00	0
World Series Record												
2012 Detroit	A.L.		1	7	0	1	.000	8	1	6	2.57	0

a On minor league disabled list July 1 to September 16, 2003.
b Traded by Boston Red Sox to Florida Marlins with infielder Hanley Ramirez and pitcher Jesus Delgado for pitcher Josh Beckett, infielder Mike Lowell and pitcher Guillermo Mota, November 24, 2005.
c Pitched no-hit, no-run game against Arizona Diamondbacks, September 6, 2006.
d On minor league disabled list May 7 to September 30, 2007.
e On disabled list from March 21 to July 31, 2008.
f On disabled list from May 8 to June 2 and June 3 to August 21, 2009.
g Traded to Detroit Tigers with infielder Omar Infante for pitcher Jacob Turner, catcher Rob Brantley and pitcher Brian Flynn, July 23, 2012.
h Filed for free agency, November 3, 2012, re-signed with Detroit Tigers, December 17, 2012.

SANTANA, ERVIN RAMON

Born, La Romana, Dominican Republic, January 10, 1983.
Bats Right. Throws Right. Height, 6 feet, 2 inches. Weight, 185 pounds.

Year	Club	Lea	G	IP	W	L	Pct	SO	BB	H	ERA	SAVES
2001 Angels	Arizona		10	58$\frac{2}{3}$	3	2	.600	69	35	40	3.22	0
2001 Provo	Pioneer		4	18$\frac{2}{3}$	2	1	.667	22	12	19	7.71	0
2002 Cedar Rapids	Midwest		27	147	14	8	.636	146	48	133	4.16	0

Year	Club	Lea	G	IP	W	L	Pct	SO	BB	H	ERA	SAVES
2003	Rancho Cucamonga	California	20	124 2/3	10	2	.833	130	36	98	2.53	0
2003	Arkansas	Texas	6	29 2/3	1	1	.500	23	12	23	3.94	0
2004	Arkansas	Texas	8	43 2/3	2	1	.667	48	18	41	3.30	0
2005	Arkansas	Texas	7	39	5	1	.833	32	15	34	2.31	0
2005	Salt Lake	P.C.	3	19 1/3	1	0	1.000	17	2	19	4.19	0
2005	Los Angeles	A.L.	23	133 2/3	12	8	.600	99	47	139	4.65	0
2006	Los Angeles	A.L.	33	204	16	8	.667	141	70	181	4.28	0
2007	Salt Lake	P.C.	5	32 1/3	2	1	.667	32	10	39	5.01	0
2007	Los Angeles	A.L.	28	150	7	14	.333	126	58	174	5.76	0
2008	Los Angeles	A.L.	32	219	16	7	.696	214	47	198	3.49	0
2009	Angels	Arizona	1	3 1/3	0	0	.000	7	0	3	0.00	0
2009	Rancho Cucamonga	Calif.	1	4 2/3	0	0	.000	3	0	4	5.79	0
2009	Salt Lake	P.C.	1	5	1	0	1.000	4	1	3	3.60	0
2009	Los Angeles a	A.L.	24	139 2/3	8	8	.500	107	47	159	5.03	0
2010	Los Angeles	A.L.	33	222 2/3	17	10	.630	169	73	221	3.92	0
2011	Los Angeles b	A.L.	33	228 2/3	11	12	.478	178	72	207	3.38	0
2012	Los Angeles c	A.L.	30	178	9	13	.409	133	61	165	5.16	0
Major League Totals		8 Yrs.	236	1475 2/3	96	80	.545	1167	475	1444	4.33	0
	Division Series											
2005	Los Angeles	A.L.	1	5 1/3	1	0	1.000	2	3	5	5.06	0
2007	Los Angeles	A.L.	1	2	0	0	.000	2	0	0	0.00	0
2008	Los Angeles	A.L.	1	5 1/3	0	0	.000	3	0	8	8.44	0
Division Series Totals			3	12 2/3	1	0	1.000	7	3	13	5.68	0
	Championship Series											
2005	Los Angeles	A.L.	1	4 1/3	0	1	.000	2	3	3	10.38	0
2009	Los Angeles	A.L.	4	5 2/3	1	1	.500	5	4	5	1.59	0
Championship Series Totals			5	10	1	2	.333	7	7	8	5.40	0

a On disabled list from March 27 to May 14 and June 17 to July 3, 2009.

b Pitched no-hit, no-run game against Cleveland Indians, July 27, 2011.

c Traded to Kansas City Royals with cash for pitcher Brandon Sisk, October 31, 2012.

SANTANA, JOHAN ALEXANDER

Born, Tovar, Venezuela, March 13, 1979.

Bats Left. Throws Left. Height, 6 feet. Weight, 210 pounds.

Year	Club	Lea	G	IP	W	L	Pct	SO	BB	H	ERA	SAVES
1996	Houston/Bos	Dominican	23	40	4	3	.571	51	22	26	2.70	3
1997	Auburn	N.Y.-Penn.	1	4	0	0	.000	5	6	1	2.25	0
1997	Astros	Gulf Coast	9	36 1/3	0	4	.000	25	18	49	7.93	0
1998	Quad City	Midwest	2	6 2/3	0	1	.000	6	3	14	9.45	0
1998	Auburn	N.Y.-Penn.	15	86 2/3	7	5	.583	88	21	81	4.36	0
1999	Michigan a-b	Midwest	27	160 1/3	8	8	.500	150	55	162	4.66	0
2000	Minnesota	A.L.	30	86	2	3	.400	64	54	102	6.49	0
2001	Minnesota	A.L.	15	43 2/3	1	0	1.000	28	16	50	4.74	0
2002	Edmonton	P.C.	11	48 2/3	5	2	.714	75	27	37	3.14	0
2002	Minnesota	A.L.	27	108 1/3	8	6	.571	137	49	84	2.99	1
2003	Minnesota	A.L.	45	158 1/3	12	3	.800	169	47	127	3.07	0
2004	Minnesota c	A.L.	34	228	20	6	.769	*265	54	156	*2.61	0
2005	Minnesota	A.L.	33	231 2/3	16	7	.696	*238	45	180	2.87	0
2006	Minnesota d	A.L.	34	*233 2/3	*19	6	.760	*245	47	186	*2.77	0
2007	Minnesota	A.L.	33	219	15	13	.536	235	52	183	3.33	0
2008	New York e	N.L.	34	*234 1/3	16	7	.696	206	63	206	*2.53	0
2009	New York f	N.L.	25	166 2/3	13	9	.591	146	46	156	3.13	0
2010	New York	N.L.	29	199	11	9	.550	144	55	179	2.98	0
2011	New York g	N.L.	INJURED—Did Not Play									
2012	Brooklyn	N.Y.-Penn.	1	3	0	0	.000	3	1	1	0.00	0
2012	New York h-i	N.L.	21	117	6	9	.400	111	39	117	4.85	0
Major League Totals		12 Yrs.	360	2025 2/3	139	78	.641	1988	567	1726	3.20	1
	Division Series											
2002	Minnesota	A.L.	2	3	0	0	.000	2	2	3	6.00	0
2003	Minnesota	A.L.	2	7 2/3	0	1	.000	6	3	9	7.04	0
2004	Minnesota	A.L.	2	12	1	0	1.000	12	4	14	0.75	0
2006	Minnesota	A.L.	1	8	0	1	.000	8	1	5	2.25	0
Division Series Totals			7	30 2/3	1	2	.333	28	10	31	3.23	0
	Championship Series											
2002	Minnesota	A.L.	4	3 1/3	0	1	.000	4	0	4	10.80	0

a Selected by Florida Marlins from Houston Astros in Rule V draft, December 13, 1999.

b Traded to Minnesota Twins with cash for pitcher Jared Camp, December 13, 1999.

c Selected Cy Young Award Winner in American League for 2004.

d Selected Cy Young Award Winner in American League for 2006.
e Traded to New York Mets for outfielder Carlos Gomez, pitcher Philip Humber, pitcher Kevin Mulvey and pitcher Deolis Garcia, February 2, 2008.
f On disabled list from August 25 to October 14, 2009.
g On disabled list from March 22 to October 24, 2011.
h Pitched no-hit, no-run game against St. Louis Cardinals, June 1, 2012.
i On disabled list from July 21 to August 11 and August 18 to October 16, 2012.

SANTIAGO, HECTOR FELIPE

Born, Newark, New Jersey, December 16, 1987.
Bats Right. Throws Left. Height, 6 feet. Weight, 210 pounds.

Year	Club	Lea	G	IP	W	L	Pct	SO	BB	H	ERA	SAVES
2007	Bristol	Appal.	17	32⅔	1	1	.500	38	16	19	1.65	0
2008	Kannapolis	So.Atl.	38	64⅓	5	1	.833	83	44	57	4.06	1
2009	Winston-Salem	Carolina	38	58	4	4	.500	66	25	54	3.88	1
2010	Winston-Salem	Carolina	37	60⅔	4	5	.444	61	19	63	4.15	2
2011	Winston-Salem	Carolina	8	44	2	3	.400	43	14	38	3.68	0
2011	Chicago	A.L.	2	5⅓	0	0	.000	2	1	1	0.00	0
2011	Birmingham	Southern	15	83⅓	7	5	.583	74	39	71	3.56	0
2012	Charlotte	Int.	3	14⅔	1	0	1.000	13	6	9	0.00	0
2012	Chicago	A.L.	42	70⅓	4	1	.800	79	40	54	3.33	4
Major League Totals	2 Yrs.		44	75⅔	4	1	.800	81	41	55	3.09	4

SAUNDERS, JOSEPH FRANCIS (JOE)

Born, Falls Church, Virginia, June 16, 1981.
Bats Left. Throws Left. Height, 6 feet, 3 inches. Weight, 210 pounds.

Year	Club	Lea	G	IP	W	L	Pct	SO	BB	H	ERA	SAVES
2002	Cedar Rapids	Midwest	5	28⅔	3	1	.750	27	9	16	1.88	0
2002	Provo	Pioneer	8	32⅓	2	1	.667	21	11	40	3.62	0
2003	Provo a	Pioneer				INJURED—Did Not Play						
2004	Rancho Cucamonga	Calif.	19	105⅔	9	7	.563	76	23	106	3.41	0
2004	Arkansas	Texas	8	39	4	3	.571	25	14	51	5.77	0
2005	Arkansas	Texas	18	105⅔	7	4	.636	80	32	107	3.49	0
2005	Salt Lake	P.C.	9	55	3	3	.500	29	21	65	4.58	0
2005	Los Angeles	A.L.	2	9⅓	0	0	.000	4	4	10	7.71	0
2006	Salt Lake	P.C.	21	135	10	4	.714	97	38	117	2.67	0
2006	Los Angeles	A.L.	13	70⅔	7	3	.700	51	29	71	4.71	0
2007	Salt Lake	P.C.	14	86⅓	4	7	.364	84	20	89	5.11	0
2007	Los Angeles	A.L.	18	107⅓	8	5	.615	69	34	129	4.44	0
2008	Los Angeles	A.L.	31	198	17	7	.708	103	53	187	3.41	0
2009	Los Angeles b	A.L.	31	186	16	7	.696	101	64	202	4.60	0
2010	Los Angeles	A.L.	20	120⅔	6	10	.375	64	45	135	4.62	0
2010	Arizona c	N.L.	13	82⅔	3	7	.300	50	19	97	4.25	0
2011	Arizona d	N.L.	33	212	12	13	.480	108	67	210	3.69	0
2012	D-Backs	Arizona	1	4⅓	0	1	.000	7	5	3	6.23	0
2012	Arizona	N.L.	21	130	6	10	.375	89	31	146	4.22	0
2012	Baltimore e-f-g	A.L.	7	44⅔	3	3	.500	23	8	49	3.63	0
Major League Totals	8 Yrs.		189	1161⅓	78	65	.545	662	354	1236	4.15	0
Wild Card Playoff												
2012	Baltimore	A.L.	1	5⅔	1	0	1.000	4	1	6	1.59	0
Division Series												
2008	Los Angeles	A.L.	1	4⅔	0	0	.000	2	4	5	7.71	0
2011	Arizona	N.L.	1	3	0	0	.000	1	2	5	9.00	0
2012	Baltimore	A.L.	1	5⅔	0	0	.000	5	4	3	1.59	0
Division Series Totals			3	13⅓	0	0	.000	8	10	13	5.40	0
Championship Series												
2009	Los Angeles	A.L.	2	10⅓	0	1	.000	5	6	13	4.35	0

a On minor league disabled list from April 3 to September 18, 2003.
b On disabled list from August 8 to August 26, 2009.
c Traded to Arizona Diamondbacks with pitcher Rafael Rodriguez, pitcher Patrick Corbin and player to be named later for pitcher Danny Haren, July 25, 2010. Arizona Diamondbacks received pitcher Tyler Skaggs to complete trade, August 7, 2010.
d Not offered contract, December 12, 2011, re-signed with Arizona Diamondbacks, January 17, 2012.
e On disabled list from June 17 to July 14, 2012.
f Traded to Baltimore Orioles with cash for pitcher Matt Lindstrom and cash, August 26, 2012.
g Filed for free agency, November 3, 2012.

SCHEPPERS, TANNER ROSS
Born, Mission Viejo, California, January 17, 1987.
Bats Right. Throws Right. Height, 6 feet, 4 inches. Weight, 220 pounds.

Year Club	Lea	G	IP	W	L	Pct	SO	BB	H	ERA	SAVES
2009 St. Paul	Amer. Assoc.	4	19	1	1	.500	20	11	17	3.32	0
2010 Oklahoma	P.C.	30	69	1	3	.250	71	30	82	5.48	4
2010 Frisco	Texas	6	11	0	0	.000	19	0	3	0.82	2
2011 Round Rock	P.C.	11	20²/₃	2	0	1.000	20	12	23	4.35	2
2011 Frisco	Texas	17	23	2	1	.667	24	9	18	3.13	0
2012 Round Rock	P.C.	27	31	1	2	.333	31	4	30	3.48	11
2012 Texas	A.L.	39	32¹/₃	1	1	.500	30	9	47	4.45	1

SCHERZER, MAXWELL M. (MAX)
Born, St. Louis, Missouri, July 27, 1984.
Bats Right. Throws Right. Height, 6 feet, 3 inches. Weight, 215 pounds.

Year Club	Lea	G	IP	W	L	Pct	SO	BB	H	ERA	SAVES
2007 Fort Worth	Amer. Assoc.	3	16	1	0	1.000	25	4	9	0.56	0
2007 Visalia	Calif.	3	17	2	0	1.000	30	2	5	0.53	0
2007 Mobile a-b	Southern	14	73²/₃	4	4	.500	76	40	64	3.91	0
2008 Tucson	P.C.	13	53	1	1	.500	79	22	35	2.72	0
2008 Arizona	N.L.	16	56	0	4	.000	66	21	48	3.05	0
2009 Visalia	Calif.	1	4²/₃	0	0	.000	5	4	1	1.93	0
2009 Arizona c-d	N.L.	30	170¹/₃	9	11	.450	174	63	166	4.12	0
2010 Toledo	Int.	2	15	2	0	1.000	17	2	4	0.60	0
2010 Detroit	A.L.	31	195²/₃	12	11	.522	184	70	174	3.50	0
2011 Detroit	A.L.	33	195	15	9	.625	174	56	207	4.43	0
2012 Detroit	A.L.	32	187²/₃	16	7	.696	231	60	179	3.74	0
Major League Totals	5 Yrs.	142	804²/₃	52	42	.553	829	270	774	3.88	0
Division Series											
2011 Detroit	A.L.	2	7¹/₃	1	0	1.000	7	4	4	1.23	0
2012 Detroit	A.L.	1	5¹/₃	0	0	.000	8	1	3	0.00	0
Division Series Totals		3	12²/₃	1	0	1.000	15	5	7	0.71	0
Championship Series											
2011 Detroit	A.L.	2	8¹/₃	0	1	.000	7	5	11	9.72	0
2012 Detroit	A.L.	1	5²/₃	1	0	1.000	10	2	2	1.59	0
Championship Series Totals		3	14	1	1	.500	17	7	13	6.43	0
World Series Record											
2012 Detroit	A.L.	1	6¹/₃	0	0	.000	8	1	7	4.26	0

a Signed by independent Fort Worth (American Association), 2007.
b Signed by Arizona Diamondbacks, May 31, 2007.
c On disabled list from March 29 to April 14, 2009.
d Traded to Detroit Tigers with pitcher Daniel Schlereth for pitcher Edwin Jackson and pitcher Ian Kennedy, December 9, 2009.

SHAW, BRYAN ANTHONY
Born, Livermore, California, November 8, 1987.
Bats Both. Throws Right. Height, 6 feet, 1 inch. Weight, 210 pounds.

Year Club	Lea	G	IP	W	L	Pct	SO	BB	H	ERA	SAVES
2008 South Bend	Midwest	11	22¹/₃	0	1	.000	16	6	18	4.03	0
2008 Missoula	Pioneer	10	17¹/₃	0	1	.000	17	7	24	6.75	2
2009 Visalia	Calif.	30	107¹/₃	3	7	.300	95	40	96	4.70	0
2010 Mobile	Southern	33	101¹/₃	4	9	.308	75	43	102	4.26	2
2011 Mobile	Southern	15	20²/₃	3	1	.750	15	8	15	0.87	7
2011 Reno	P.C.	16	17²/₃	1	0	1.000	15	4	14	4.58	9
2011 Arizona	N.L.	33	28¹/₃	1	0	1.000	24	8	30	2.54	0
2012 Reno	P.C.	8	8	0	0	.000	10	2	6	2.25	2
2012 Arizona a	N.L.	64	59¹/₃	1	6	.143	41	24	60	3.49	2
Major League Totals	2 Yrs.	97	87²/₃	2	6	.250	65	32	90	3.18	2
Division Series											
2011 Arizona	N.L.	4	4	0	0	.000	3	1	0	0.00	0

a Traded to Cleveland Indians with pitcher Matt Albers and pitcher Trevor Bauer for infielder Lars Anderson, infielder Didi Gregorius and pitcher Tony Sipp, December 11, 2012.

SHIELDS, JAMES ANTHONY (JAMIE)

Born, Newhall, California, December 20, 1981.
Bats Right. Throws Right. Height, 6 feet, 4 inches. Weight, 215 pounds.

Year	Club	Lea	G	IP	W	L	Pct	SO	BB	H	ERA	SAVES
2001	Hudson Valley	N.Y.-Penn.	5	27¹/₃	2	1	.667	25	5	27	2.30	0
2001	Charleston-SC	So.Atl.	10	71¹/₃	4	5	.444	60	10	63	2.65	0
2002	Charleston-SC a						INJURED—Did Not Play					
2003	Bakersfield	Calif.	26	143²/₃	10	10	.500	119	38	161	4.45	1
2004	Bakersfield	Calif.	20	117	8	5	.615	92	33	119	4.23	0
2004	Montgomery	Southern	4	18¹/₃	0	3	.000	14	8	24	7.85	0
2005	Durham	Int.	1	6	1	0	1.000	6	3	9	6.00	0
2005	Montgomery	Southern	17	109¹/₃	7	5	.583	104	31	95	2.80	0
2006	Durham	Int.	10	61¹/₃	3	2	.600	64	6	60	2.64	0
2006	Tampa Bay	A.L.	21	124²/₃	6	8	.429	104	38	141	4.84	0
2007	Tampa Bay	A.L.	31	215	12	8	.600	184	36	202	3.85	0
2008	Tampa Bay	A.L.	33	215	14	8	.636	160	40	208	3.56	0
2009	Tampa Bay	A.L.	33	219²/₃	11	12	.478	167	52	239	4.14	0
2010	Tampa Bay	A.L.	34	203¹/₃	13	15	.464	187	51	*246	5.18	0
2011	Tampa Bay	A.L.	33	249¹/₃	16	12	.571	225	65	195	2.82	0
2012	Tampa Bay b	A.L.	33	227²/₃	15	10	.600	223	58	208	3.52	0
Major League Totals		7 Yrs.	218	1454²/₃	87	73	.544	1250	340	1439	3.89	0
Division Series												
2008	Tampa Bay	A.L.	1	6¹/₃	1	0	1.000	4	1	6	4.26	0
2010	Tampa Bay	A.L.	1	4¹/₃	0	1	.000	2	0	4	8.31	0
2011	Tampa Bay	A.L.	1	5	0	1	.000	6	0	8	12.60	0
Division Series Totals			3	15²/₃	1	2	.333	12	1	18	8.04	0
Championship Series												
2008	Tampa Bay	A.L.	2	13	0	2	.000	9	5	15	3.46	0
World Series Record												
2008	Tampa Bay	A.L.	1	5²/₃	1	0	1.000	4	2	7	0.00	0

a On minor league disabled list April 4 to September 10, 2002.
b Traded to Kansas City Royals with pitcher Wade Davis and player to be named later for pitcher Mike Montgomery, pitcher Jake Odorizzi, infielder Patrick Leonard and outfielder Wil Myers, December 9, 2012.

SIMON (CABRERA), ALFREDO

Born, Santiago, Dominican Republic, May 8, 1981.
Bats Right. Throws Right. Height, 6 feet, 4 inches. Weight, 230 pounds.

Year	Club	Lea	G	IP	W	L	Pct	SO	BB	H	ERA	SAVES
2001	Phillies	Gulf Coast	10	43¹/₃	2	2	.500	40	23	35	2.91	0
2002	Batavia	N.Y.-Penn.	15	90¹/₃	9	2	.818	77	46	79	3.59	0
2003	Lakewood	So.Atl.	14	71¹/₃	5	0	1.000	66	25	59	3.79	2
2004	San Jose	Calif.	6	31²/₃	1	2	.333	21	12	44	5.68	0
2004	Clearwater a	Fla.St.	22	134²/₃	7	9	.438	107	38	121	3.27	0
2005	Norwich	Eastern	43	91¹/₃	3	8	.273	60	24	104	5.03	19
2006	San Jose	Calif.	18	36¹/₃	2	4	.333	35	14	43	6.44	0
2006	Fresno b-c-d	P.C.	10	52	0	6	.000	35	19	76	6.75	0
2007	Oklahoma e	P.C.	22	119	5	10	.333	73	46	152	6.43	0
2008	Monterrey	Mexican	15	81	7	2	.778	61	20	66	2.67	0
2008	Norfolk f-g-h	Int.	1	4²/₃	0	1	.000	5	2	9	7.71	0
2008	Baltimore	A.L.	4	13	0	0	.000	8	2	16	6.23	0
2009	Baltimore i-j	A.L.	2	6¹/₃	0	1	.000	3	2	8	9.95	0
2010	Norfolk	Int.	4	17	1	1	.500	14	5	15	1.59	0
2010	Baltimore k	A.L.	49	91¹/₃	4	2	.667	37	22	54	4.93	17
2011	Bowie	Eastern	4	18	1	0	1.000	20	6	15	3.00	0
2011	Baltimore l	A.L.	23	115²/₃	4	9	.308	83	40	128	4.90	0
2012	Cincinnati m	N.L.	36	61	3	2	.600	52	22	65	2.66	1
Major League Totals		5 Yrs.	114	245¹/₃	11	14	.440	183	88	271	4.55	18
Division Series												
2012	Cincinnati	N.L.	1	1	0	0	.000	1	1	1	0.00	0

a Traded by Philadelphia Phillies to San Francisco Giants with outfielder Ricky Ledee for pitcher Felix Rodriguez, July 30, 2004.
b Filed for free agency, October 15, 2006. Signed with Texas Rangers organization, November 3, 2006.
c Selected by Baltimore Orioles in Rule V draft, December 7, 2006.
d Traded to Philadelphia Phillies for catcher Adam Donachie and cash, December 7, 2006.
e Returned to Texas Rangers, March 17, 2007.
f Filed for free agency, October 29, 2007. Signed with Los Angeles Dodgers organization, January 20, 2008.
g Released by Los Angeles Dodgers, March 30, 2008. Signed with Monterrey (Mexican) for 2008.
h Signed with Baltimore Orioles organization, September 5, 2008.
i On disabled list from April 15 to October 30, 2009.

j Filed for free agency, November 9, 2009, re-signed with Baltimore Orioles, December 2, 2009.
k On disabled list from May 25 to June 14, 2010.
l On disabled list from June 13 to June 29, 2011.
m Claimed on waivers by Cincinnati Reds, April 3, 2012.

SIPP, TONY MARCEL
Born, Pascagoula, Mississippi, July 12, 1983.
Bats Left. Throws Left. Height, 6 feet. Weight, 190 pounds.

Year	Club	Lea	G	IP	W	L	Pct	SO	BB	H	ERA	SAVES
2004 Mahoning Valley...	N.Y.-Penn.		10	42²/₃	3	1	.750	74	13	33	3.16	0
2005 Kinston...........	Carolina		22	47¹/₃	2	2	.500	59	23	34	2.66	2
2005 Lake County........	So.Atl.		13	69	4	1	.800	71	19	47	2.22	0
2006 Akron............	Eastern		29	60¹/₃	4	2	.667	80	21	44	3.13	3
2007 a...................				INJURED—Did Not Play								
2008 Kinston...........	Carolina		5	8	0	0	.000	10	3	4	1.13	0
2008 Akron............	Eastern		16	21²/₃	0	3	.000	32	7	19	3.74	1
2008 Indians..........	Gulf Coast		3	4	0	0	.000	4	1	0	0.00	0
2009 Columbus..........	Int.		12	17	1	0	1.000	22	6	17	3.71	1
2009 Cleveland........	A.L.		46	40	2	0	1.000	48	25	27	2.93	0
2010 Cleveland........	A.L.		70	63	2	2	.500	69	39	48	4.14	1
2011 Cleveland........	A.L.		69	62¹/₃	6	3	.667	57	24	45	3.03	0
2012 Cleveland b......	A.L.		63	55	1	2	.333	51	23	47	4.42	1
Major League Totals........4 Yrs.			248	220¹/₃	11	7	.611	225	111	167	3.68	2

a On minor league disabled list from April 5 to September 21, 2007.
b Traded to Arizona Diamondbacks with infielder Lars Anderson and infielder Didi Gregorius for pitcher Matt Albers, pitcher Trevor Bauer and pitcher Bryan Shaw, December 11, 2012.

SMITH, JOSEPH MICHAEL (JOE)
Born, Cincinnati, Ohio, March 22, 1984.
Bats Right. Throws Right. Height, 6 feet, 2 inches. Weight, 205 pounds.

Year	Club	Lea	G	IP	W	L	Pct	SO	BB	H	ERA	SAVES
2006 Binghamton........	Eastern		10	12²/₃	0	2	.000	12	11	12	5.68	0
2006 Brooklyn.........	N.Y.-Penn.		17	20	0	1	.000	28	3	10	0.45	9
2007 New Orleans........	P.C.		8	9	0	0	.000	5	4	7	2.00	2
2007 New York........	N.L.		54	44¹/₃	3	2	.600	45	21	48	3.45	0
2008 New York a-b........	N.L.		82	63¹/₃	6	3	.667	52	31	51	3.55	0
2009 Columbus..........	Int.		5	5	0	0	.000	6	1	4	0.00	0
2009 Cleveland c.......	A.L.		37	34	0	0	.000	30	13	30	3.44	0
2010 Columbus..........	Int.		20	23	2	1	.667	19	10	17	1.96	2
2010 Cleveland........	A.L.		53	40	2	2	.500	32	24	30	3.83	0
2011 Akron...........	Eastern		4	3²/₃	0	0	.000	7	2	1	2.45	0
2011 Cleveland d........	A.L.		71	67	3	3	.500	45	21	52	2.01	0
2012 Cleveland........	A.L.		72	67	7	4	.636	53	25	53	2.96	0
Major League Totals........6 Yrs.			369	315²/₃	21	14	.600	257	135	264	3.11	0

a Traded to Seattle Mariners with pitcher Aaron Heilman, outfielder Endy Chavez, pitcher Jason Vargas, infielder Mike Carp, outfielder Ezequiel Carrera and pitcher Maikel Cleto for pitcher J.J. Putz, pitcher Sean Green and outfielder Jeremy Reed, December 10, 2008.
b Traded to Cleveland Indians with pitcher Luis Valbuena for outfielder Franklin Gutierrez, December 10, 2008.
c On disabled list from April 29 to June 9 and September 1 to October 14, 2009.
d On disabled list from March 22 to April 15, 2011.

SMITH, WILLIAM MICHAEL (WILL)
Born, Newnan, Georgia, July 10, 1989.
Bats Right. Throws Left. Height, 6 feet, 5 inches. Weight, 240 pounds.

Year	Club	Lea	G	IP	W	L	Pct	SO	BB	H	ERA	SAVES
2008 Orem............	Pioneer		16	73	8	2	.800	76	6	73	3.08	0
2009 Cedar Rapids.......	Midwest		20	115	10	5	.667	95	24	109	3.76	0
2010 Rancho Cucamonga....	Calif.		6	37¹/₃	2	2	.500	31	13	36	4.58	0
2010 Wilmington........	Carolina		8	54²/₃	4	1	.800	51	4	48	2.80	0
2010 Salt Lake............	P.C.		9	53	2	4	.333	40	20	65	5.60	0
2010 Arkansas a........	Texas		4	18²/₃	1	2	.333	8	9	33	7.23	0
2011 NW Arkansas........	Texas		27	161¹/₃	13	9	.591	108	45	171	3.85	0
2012 Omaha............	P.C.		15	89²/₃	4	4	.500	74	22	104	3.61	0
2012 Kansas City........	A.L.		16	89²/₃	6	9	.400	59	33	111	5.32	0

a Traded by Los Angeles Angels to Kansas City Royals with pitcher Sean O'Sullivan for infielder Alberto Callaspo, July 22, 2010.

SMYLY, TODD ANDREW (DREW)

Born, Maumelle, Arkansas, June 13, 1989.
Bats Left. Throws Left. Height, 6 feet, 3 inches. Weight, 190 pounds.

Year Club	Lea	G	IP	W	L	Pct	SO	BB	H	ERA	SAVES
2011 Erie..............	Eastern	8	45⅔	4	3	.571	53	15	32	1.18	0
2011 Lakeland...........	Fla.St.	14	80⅓	7	3	.700	77	21	71	2.58	0
2012 Toledo............	Int.	7	17⅔	0	2	.000	25	8	22	6.11	0
2012 Detroit a..........	A.L.	23	99⅓	4	3	.571	94	33	93	3.99	0
Championship Series											
2012 Detroit.............	A.L.	2	2⅓	1	0	1.000	2	0	1	0.00	0
World Series Record											
2012 Detroit.............	A.L.	2	1⅔	0	0	.000	2	3	1	5.40	0

a On disabled list from June 11 to June 26 and July 7 to July 29, 2012.

SORIANO, RAFAEL

Born, San Jose, Dominican Republic, December 19, 1979.
Bats Right. Throws Right. Height, 6 feet, 1 inch. Weight, 220 pounds.

Year Club	Lea	G	IP	W	L	Pct	SO	BB	H	ERA	SAVES
1999 Everett	Northwest	14	75⅓	5	4	.556	83	49	56	3.11	0
2000 Wisconsin	Midwest	21	122⅓	8	4	.667	90	50	97	2.87	0
2001 San Bernardino	Calif.	15	89	6	3	.667	98	39	49	2.53	0
2001 San Antonio	Texas	8	48⅓	2	2	.500	53	14	34	3.35	0
2002 San Antonio	Texas	10	46⅔	2	3	.400	52	15	32	2.31	0
2002 Seattle a.............	A.L.	10	47⅓	0	3	.000	32	16	45	4.56	1
2003 Tacoma	P.C.	11	62	4	3	.571	63	12	43	3.19	0
2003 Seattle	A.L.	40	53	3	0	1.000	68	12	30	1.53	1
2004 Seattle	A.L.	6	3⅓	0	3	.000	3	3	9	13.50	0
2004 Inland Empire........	Calif.	2	8	0	0	.000	9	1	7	2.25	0
2004 San Antonio	Texas	2	8	1	0	1.000	10	0	4	1.13	0
2004 Tacoma b............	P.C.	3	3⅔	0	0	.000	5	2	2	2.45	0
2005 Inland Empire........	Calif.	3	4	0	0	.000	5	0	2	0.00	0
2005 San Antonio	Texas	1	1	0	0	.000	0	0	0	0.00	0
2005 Everett	Northwest	4	6	0	0	.000	8	2	6	3.00	0
2005 Tacoma	P.C.	5	5⅓	1	0	1.000	11	1	3	0.00	0
2005 Seattle c.............	A.L.	7	7⅓	0	0	.000	9	1	6	2.45	0
2006 Seattle d-e...........	A.L.	53	60	1	2	.333	65	21	44	2.25	2
2007 Atlanta	N.L.	71	72	3	3	.500	70	15	47	3.00	.9
2008 Mississippi	Southern	2	2	0	0	.000	2	1	1	0.00	0
2008 Atlanta f.............	N.L.	14	14	0	1	.000	16	9	7	2.57	3
2009 Atlanta g.............	N.L.	77	75⅔	1	6	.143	102	27	53	2.97	27
2010 Tampa Bay h.........	A.L.	64	62⅓	3	2	.600	57	14	36	1.73	*45
2011 Tampa	Fla.St.	2	2⅓	0	1	.000	1	0	4	11.57	0
2011 Scranton-WB...........	Int.	2	2	1	0	1.000	2	0	1	4.50	0
2011 New York i...........	A.L.	42	39⅓	2	3	.400	36	18	33	4.12	2
2012 New York j...........	A.L.	69	67⅔	2	1	.667	69	24	55	2.26	42
Major League Totals ....11 Yrs.		453	502	15	24	.385	527	160	365	2.78	132
Division Series											
2010 Tampa Bay	A.L.	3	3	0	0	.000	1	0	4	9.00	1
2011 New York.............	A.L.	3	4⅔	0	1	.000	4	0	1	1.93	0
2012 New York.............	A.L.	2	3⅓	0	0	.000	2	0	2	0.00	0
Division Series Totals		8	11	0	1	.000	7	0	7	3.27	1
Championship Series											
2012 New York.............	A.L.	1	1	0	0	.000	0	0	0	0.00	0

a On disabled list from July 3 to August 2, 2002.
b On disabled list from May 10 to November 1, 2004.
c On disabled list from April 1 to September 5, 2005.
d On disabled list from July 20 to August 4, 2006.
e Traded to Atlanta Braves for pitcher Horacio Ramirez, December 7, 2006.
f On disabled list from April 7 to May 28 and June 6 to July 21 and August 3 to November 3, 2008.
g Traded to Tampa Bay Rays for pitcher Jesse Chavez, December 11, 2009.
h Filed for free agency, November 1, 2010. Signed with New York Yankees, January 18, 2011.
i On disabled list from May 17 to July 29, 2011.
j Filed for free agency, November 3, 2012. Signed with Washington Nationals, January 15, 2013.

STAMMEN, CRAIG N.

Born, Coldwater, Ohio, March 9, 1984.
Bats Right. Throws Right. Height, 6 feet, 3 inches. Weight, 225 pounds.

Year Club	Lea	G	IP	W	L	Pct	SO	BB	H	ERA	SAVES
2005 Vermont..........	N.Y.-Penn.	13	51	4	5	.444	32	12	62	4.06	0
2006 Potomac..........	Carolina	7	29⅔	0	2	.000	16	7	34	5.76	0

Year	Club	Lea	G	IP	W	L	Pct	SO	BB	H	ERA	SAVES
2006 Savannah	So.Atl.	21	113	6	9	.400	93	29	110	3.58	0
2007 Potomac	Carolina	28	125	8	6	.571	96	54	156	4.18	0
2007 Columbus	Int.	1	3²/₃	0	1	.000	2	3	4	12.27	0
2008 Potomac	Carolina	15	69¹/₃	4	2	.667	62	17	59	2.21	1
2008 Harrisburg	Eastern	6	38¹/₃	3	1	.750	31	11	22	1.64	0
2008 Columbus	Int.	9	43	1	4	.200	35	16	62	7.33	0
2009 Syracuse	Int.	7	40	4	2	.667	14	8	33	1.80	0
2009 Washington	N.L.	19	105²/₃	4	7	.364	48	24	112	5.11	0
2010 Syracuse	Int.	3	20	2	0	1.000	10	3	18	2.25	0
2010 Washington	N.L.	35	128	4	4	.500	85	41	151	5.13	0
2011 Syracuse	Int.	25	142	10	7	.588	127	40	163	4.75	0
2011 Washington	N.L.	7	10¹/₃	1	1	.500	12	4	3	0.87	0
2012 Washington	N.L.	59	88¹/₃	6	1	.857	87	36	70	2.34	1
Major League Totals 4 Yrs.		120	332¹/₃	15	13	.536	232	105	336	4.25	1
Division Series											
2012 Washington	N.L.	4	3	0	0	.000	3	2	5	9.00	0

STAUFFER, TIMOTHY JAMES (TIM)

Born, Portland, Maine, June 2, 1982.
Bats Right. Throws Right. Height, 6 feet, 1 inch. Weight, 205 pounds.

Year	Club	Lea	G	IP	W	L	Pct	SO	BB	H	ERA	SAVES
2004 Lake Elsinore	Calif.	6	35¹/₃	2	0	1.000	30	9	28	1.78	0
2004 Portland	P.C.	14	81¹/₃	6	3	.667	50	26	83	3.54	0
2004 Mobile	Southern	8	51¹/₃	3	2	.600	33	13	56	2.63	0
2005 San Diego	N.L.	15	81	3	6	.333	49	29	92	5.33	0
2005 Portland	P.C.	13	75¹/₃	3	5	.375	64	17	90	5.14	0
2006 San Diego	N.L.	1	6	1	0	1.000	2	1	3	1.50	0
2006 Portland	P.C.	28	153	7	12	.368	89	52	199	5.53	0
2007 San Diego	N.L.	2	7²/₃	0	1	.000	6	6	15	21.13	0
2007 Portland	P.C.	25	130²/₃	8	5	.615	96	36	147	4.34	0
2008 San Diego a	N.L.					INJURED—Did Not Play					
2009 San Antonio	Texas	12	19	1	0	1.000	12	4	13	1.89	1
2009 Portland	P.C.	4	23	2	1	.667	16	4	16	2.35	0
2009 San Diego	N.L.	14	73	4	7	.364	53	34	71	3.58	0
2010 Portland	P.C.	6	17²/₃	0	0	.000	8	7	24	4.58	0
2010 San Diego b	N.L.	32	82²/₃	6	5	.545	61	24	65	1.85	0
2011 San Diego	N.L.	31	185²/₃	9	12	.429	128	53	180	3.73	0
2012 Padres	Arizona	1	1	0	0	.000	1	0	1	0.00	0
2012 Lake Elsinore	Calif.	4	13¹/₃	0	1	.000	11	2	15	3.38	0
2012 Tucson	P.C.	2	8	0	1	.000	2	1	10	3.38	0
2012 San Diego c-d	N.L.	1	5	0	0	.000	5	3	7	5.40	0
Major League Totals 7 Yrs.		96	441	23	31	.426	304	150	433	3.94	0

a On disabled list from March 26 to October 8, 2008.
b On disabled list from May 11 to July 1, 2010.
c On disabled list from April 4 to May 14 and May 15 to October 26, 2012.
d Filed for free agency, October 26, 2012.

STOREN, DREW PATRICK

Born, Brownsburg, Indiana, August 11, 1987.
Bats Both. Throws Right. Height, 6 feet, 2 inches. Weight, 180 pounds.

Year	Club	Lea	G	IP	W	L	Pct	SO	BB	H	ERA	SAVES
2009 Potomac	Carolina	7	10	1	0	1.000	11	2	7	1.80	2
2009 Harrisburg	Eastern	10	12¹/₃	1	0	1.000	12	6	3	0.00	9
2009 Hagerstown	So.Atl.	11	14²/₃	0	1	.000	26	0	11	3.68	0
2010 Harrisburg	Eastern	7	9¹/₃	0	0	.000	11	1	5	0.96	4
2010 Syracuse	Int.	6	7¹/₃	0	0	.000	4	2	7	1.23	0
2010 Washington	N.L.	54	55¹/₃	4	4	.500	52	22	48	3.58	5
2011 Washington	N.L.	73	75¹/₃	6	3	.667	74	20	57	2.75	43
2012 Potomac	Carolina	5	6	1	0	1.000	8	1	4	3.00	0
2012 Harrisburg	Eastern	1	0²/₃	0	0	.000	0	1	3	54.00	0
2012 Washington a	N.L.	37	30¹/₃	3	1	.750	24	8	22	2.37	4
Major League Totals 3 Yrs.		164	161	13	8	.619	150	50	127	2.96	52
Division Series											
2012 Washington	N.L.	4	4	1	1	.500	6	3	3	9.00	1

a On disabled list from March 26 to July 19, 2012.

STRAILY, DANIEL STEVEN (DAN)

Born, Redlands, California, December 1, 1988.
Bats Right. Throws Right. Height, 6 feet, 2 inches. Weight, 220 pounds.

Year Club	Lea	G	IP	W	L	Pct	SO	BB	H	ERA	SAVES
2009 Vancouver	Northwest	16	59	5	3	.625	66	18	66	4.12	0
2010 Kane County	Midwest	28	148	10	7	.588	149	61	138	4.32	0
2011 Stockton	Calif.	28	160²/₃	11	9	.550	154	40	160	3.87	0
2012 Midland	Texas	14	85¹/₃	3	4	.429	108	23	70	3.38	0
2012 Sacramento	P.C.	11	66²/₃	6	3	.667	82	19	40	2.03	0
2012 Oakland	A.L.	7	39¹/₃	2	1	.667	32	16	36	3.89	0

STRASBURG, STEPHEN JAMES

Born, San Diego, California, July 20, 1988.
Bats Right. Throws Right. Height, 6 feet, 4 inches. Weight, 220 pounds.

Year Club	Lea	G	IP	W	L	Pct	SO	BB	H	ERA	SAVES
2010 Harrisburg	Eastern	5	22	3	1	.750	27	6	13	1.64	0
2010 Syracuse	Int.	6	33¹/₃	4	1	.800	38	7	18	1.08	0
2010 Washington a	N.L.	12	68	5	3	.625	92	17	56	2.91	0
2011 Hagerstown	So.Atl.	3	6¹/₃	1	0	1.000	13	3	9	9.95	0
2011 Potomac	Carolina	1	3	0	0	.000	5	0	2	0.00	0
2011 Harrisburg	Eastern	1	6	1	0	1.000	4	0	1	0.00	0
2011 Syracuse	Int.	1	5	0	0	.000	7	0	2	1.80	0
2011 Washington b	N.L.	5	24	1	1	.500	24	2	15	1.50	0
2012 Washington	N.L.	28	159¹/₃	15	6	.714	197	48	136	3.16	0
Major League Totals	3 Yrs.	45	251¹/₃	21	10	.677	313	67	207	2.94	0

a On disabled list from July 22 to August 7 and August 24 to November 10, 2010.
b On disabled list from March 23 to September 6, 2011.

STREET, HUSTON LOWELL

Born, Austin, Texas, August 2, 1983.
Bats Right. Throws Right. Height, 6 feet. Weight, 190 pounds.

Year Club	Lea	G	IP	W	L	Pct	SO	BB	H	ERA	SAVES
2004 Kane County	Midwest	9	10²/₃	0	1	.000	14	5	9	1.69	4
2004 Sacramento	P.C.	2	2	0	0	.000	2	0	2	0.00	1
2004 Midland	Texas	10	13¹/₃	1	0	1.000	14	3	10	1.35	3
2005 Oakland a	A.L.	67	78¹/₃	5	1	.833	72	26	53	1.72	23
2006 Oakland b	A.L.	69	70²/₃	4	4	.500	67	13	64	3.31	37
2007 Sacramento	P.C.	1	1	0	0	.000	2	0	1	0.00	0
2007 Oakland c	A.L.	48	50	5	2	.714	63	12	35	2.88	16
2008 Oakland d	A.L.	63	70	7	5	.583	69	27	58	3.73	18
2009 Colorado	N.L.	64	61²/₃	4	1	.800	70	13	43	3.06	35
2010 Tulsa	Texas	2	1¹/₃	0	0	.000	2	1	1	0.00	0
2010 Colorado Springs	P.C.	7	7	1	1	.500	9	2	11	10.29	0
2010 Colorado e	N.L.	44	47¹/₃	4	4	.500	45	11	39	3.61	20
2011 Colorado Springs	P.C.	2	2	0	0	.000	2	0	0	0.00	0
2011 Colorado f-g	N.L.	62	58¹/₃	1	4	.200	55	9	62	3.86	29
2012 Lake Elsinore	Calif.	2	2	0	0	.000	1	1	9	9.00	0
2012 San Diego h	N.L.	40	39	2	1	.667	47	11	17	1.85	23
Major League Totals	8 Yrs.	457	475¹/₃	32	22	.593	488	122	371	3.01	201
Division Series											
2006 Oakland	A.L.	3	3	0	0	.000	1	1	4	3.00	2
2009 Colorado	N.L.	3	2²/₃	0	2	.000	1	3	6	13.50	1
Division Series Totals		6	5²/₃	0	2	.000	2	4	10	7.94	3
Championship Series											
2006 Oakland	A.L.	2	3¹/₃	0	1	.000	3	0	4	10.80	0

a Selected Rookie of the Year in American League for 2005.
b On disabled list from August 19 to September 8, 2006.
c On disabled list from May 13 to July 23, 2007.
d Traded to Colorado Rockies with outfielder Carlos Gonzalez and pitcher Greg Smith for outfielder Matt Holliday, November 12, 2008.
e On disabled list from March 26 to June 22, 2010.
f On disabled list from August 9 to August 26, 2011.
g Traded to San Diego Padres with cash for pitcher Nick Schmidt, December 7, 2011.
h On disabled list from May 5 to June 5 and August 11 to September 21, 2012.

STROP, PEDRO ANGEL
Born, San Cristobal, Dominican Republic, June 13, 1985.
Bats Right. Throws Right. Height, 6 feet. Weight, 215 pounds.

Year	Club	Lea	G	IP	W	L	Pct	SO	BB	H	ERA	SAVES
2006 Casper	Pioneer	11	13	1	0	1.000	22	2	9	2.08	0
2006 Asheville	So.Atl.	11	13⅓	2	1	.667	13	5	10	4.72	0
2007 Modesto	Calif.	48	54⅔	5	2	.714	75	29	43	4.28	7
2008 Tulsa a	Texas	7	7	0	0	.000	7	4	6	2.57	3
2009 Frisco	Texas	36	51⅓	5	5	.500	48	29	48	4.38	4
2009 Oklahoma	P.C.	11	12⅔	1	1	.500	13	4	13	7.82	1
2009 Texas	A.L.	7	7	0	0	.000	9	4	6	7.71	0
2010 Oklahoma	P.C.	39	42⅓	1	2	.333	57	14	32	1.91	13
2010 Texas	A.L.	15	10⅔	0	0	.000	11	11	17	10.13	0
2011 Round Rock	P.C.	39	47⅔	4	4	.500	55	24	53	3.59	11
2011 Texas-Baltimore b	A.L.	23	22	2	1	.667	21	10	15	2.05	0
2012 Baltimore	A.L.	70	66⅓	5	2	.714	58	37	52	2.44	3
Major League Totals	4 Yrs.	115	106	7	3	.700	99	62	90	3.48	3
Division Series											
2012 Baltimore	A.L.	2	2⅓	1	0	1.000	2	1	1	0.00	0

a Released by Colorado Rockies, September 19, 2008. Signed with Texas Rangers organization, November 7, 2008.
b Sent to Baltimore Orioles as player to be named later for pitcher Mike Gonzalez, September 1, 2011.

STULTS, ERIC WILLIAM
Born, Plymouth, Indiana, December 9, 1979.
Bats Left. Throws Left. Height, 6 feet. Weight, 225 pounds.

Year	Club	Lea	G	IP	W	L	Pct	SO	BB	H	ERA	SAVES
2002 Vero Beach	Fla.St.	13	42	3	1	.750	40	20	39	3.00	0
2002 Great Falls	Pioneer	5	8	1	0	1.000	9	3	6	2.25	1
2002 Jacksonville	Southern	1	1	0	0	.000	0	0	0	0.00	0
2003 Vero Beach	Fla.St.	1	3	0	1	.000	1	1	6	6.00	0
2003 Jacksonville	Southern	9	38	3	4	.429	14	13	44	4.97	1
2004 Vero Beach	Fla.St.	7	10	2	1	.667	6	4	11	2.70	1
2004 Columbus	So.Atl.	12	21⅔	1	2	.333	16	6	18	2.49	3
2005 Las Vegas	P.C.	15	78	3	7	.300	60	24	107	6.58	0
2005 Jacksonville	Southern	12	68	4	3	.571	58	14	73	3.31	0
2006 Las Vegas	P.C.	26	153⅓	10	11	.476	128	68	153	4.23	0
2006 Los Angeles	N.L.	6	17⅔	1	0	1.000	5	7	17	5.60	0
2007 Las Vegas	P.C.	21	89⅓	5	7	.417	81	36	134	7.56	0
2007 Los Angeles	N.L.	12	38⅔	1	4	.200	30	17	50	5.82	0
2008 Las Vegas	P.C.	20	117⅔	7	7	.500	102	35	118	3.82	0
2008 Los Angeles	N.L.	7	38⅔	2	3	.400	30	13	38	3.49	0
2009 Inland Empire	Calif.	2	7⅓	0	0	.000	5	0	5	1.23	0
2009 Los Angeles	N.L.	10	50	4	3	.571	33	26	51	4.86	0
2009 Albuquerque a	P.C.	12	64	5	4	.556	40	24	86	5.20	0
2010 Hiroshima b	Japan Cent.	21	124⅓	6	10	.375	87	46	149	5.07	0
2011 Colorado	N.L.	6	12	0	0	.000	7	4	11	6.00	0
2011 Colorado Springs c	P.C.	52	68	4	4	.500	69	16	76	4.63	1
2012 Tucson	P.C.	2	6⅔	0	0	.000	10	4	7	5.40	0
2012 Charlotte	Int.	5	28⅔	1	1	.500	26	10	25	2.20	0
2012 Chicago	A.L.	2	6⅔	0	0	.000	4	4	6	2.70	0
2012 San Diego d-e	N.L.	18	92⅓	8	3	.727	51	23	86	2.92	0
Major League Totals	6 Yrs.	61	256	16	13	.552	160	94	259	4.15	0

a On disabled list from May 31 to July 1, 2009.
b Sold to Hiroshima, March 31, 2010. Signed with Colorado Rockies organization, November 30, 2010.
c Filed for free agency, November 2, 2011. Signed with Chicago White Sox organization, December 11, 2011.
d Claimed on waivers by San Diego Padres, May 17, 2012.
e On disabled list from June 4 to July 22, 2012.

STUTES, MICHAEL CHRISTOPHER
Born, Metairie, Louisiana, September 4, 1986.
Bats Right. Throws Right. Height, 6 feet, 1 inch. Weight, 185 pounds.

Year	Club	Lea	G	IP	W	L	Pct	SO	BB	H	ERA	SAVES
2008 Williamsport	N.Y.-Penn.	6	27	2	1	.667	31	11	16	1.33	0
2008 Lakewood	So.Atl.	7	42⅔	5	1	.833	53	18	20	1.48	0
2009 Reading	Eastern	27	145⅔	8	8	.500	109	58	147	4.26	0
2010 Reading	Eastern	25	35⅔	3	0	1.000	37	14	28	3.79	2
2010 Lehigh Valley	Int.	28	40⅔	4	1	.800	42	23	29	3.10	4
2011 Lehigh Valley	Int.	7	10	2	1	.667	14	4	9	1.80	1
2011 Philadelphia	N.L.	57	62	6	2	.750	58	28	49	3.63	0

Year Club	Lea	G	IP	W	L	Pct	SO	BB	H	ERA	SAVES
2012 Philadelphia a.........	N.L.	6	5⅔	0	0	.000	5	4	7	6.35	0
Major League Totals.......2 Yrs.		63	67⅔	6	2	.750	63	32	56	3.86	0
Division Series											
2011 Philadelphia..........	N.L.	1	0⅓	0	0	.000	0	1	3	81.00	0

a On disabled list from April 22 to October 29, 2012.

SWARZAK, ANTHONY RAY
Born, Ft.Lauderdale, Florida, September 10, 1985.
Bats Right. Throws Right. Height, 6 feet, 4 inches. Weight, 225 pounds.

Year Club	Lea	G	IP	W	L	Pct	SO	BB	H	ERA	SAVES
2004 Twins	Gulf Coast	11	48	5	3	.625	42	6	46	2.63	1
2005 Beloit	Midwest	18	91⅓	9	5	.643	101	32	81	4.04	0
2005 Fort Myers	Fla.St.	10	59	3	4	.429	55	11	72	3.66	0
2006 Fort Myers	Fla.St.	27	145⅔	11	7	.611	131	60	131	3.27	0
2007 New Britain	Eastern	15	86⅓	5	4	.556	76	23	78	3.23	0
2007 Fort Myers	Fla.St.	3	15⅔	0	0	.000	18	5	14	2.30	0
2008 New Britain	Eastern	20	101⅔	3	8	.273	76	37	126	5.67	0
2008 Rochester..........	Int.	7	45	5	0	1.000	26	14	41	1.80	0
2009 Minnesota	A.L.	12	59	3	7	.300	34	20	76	6.25	0
2009 Rochester..........	Int.	13	79⅔	4	5	.444	45	21	79	3.28	0
2010 Rochester..........	Int.	22	111⅔	5	12	.294	69	38	143	6.21	0
2011 Rochester..........	Int.	6	32⅓	2	1	.667	25	7	35	3.90	0
2011 Minnesota	A.L.	27	102	4	7	.364	55	26	111	4.32	0
2012 Minnesota a.........	A.L.	44	96⅔	3	6	.333	62	31	106	5.03	0
Major League Totals.......3 Yrs.		83	257⅔	10	20	.333	151	77	293	5.03	0

a On disabled list from July 25 to August 15, 2012.

TAZAWA, JUNICHI
Born, Yokohama, Japan, June 6, 1986.
Bats Right. Throws Right. Height, 5 feet, 11 inches. Weight, 180 pounds.

Year Club	Lea	G	IP	W	L	Pct	SO	BB	H	ERA	SAVES
2009 Portland	Eastern	18	98	9	5	.643	88	26	80	2.57	0
2009 Pawtucket	Int.	2	11⅓	0	2	.000	6	1	7	2.38	0
2009 Boston a..............	A.L.	6	25⅓	2	3	.400	13	9	43	7.46	0
2010 Boston b	A.L.		INJURED—Did Not Play								
2011 Salem............	Carolina	6	19⅓	0	1	.000	13	6	20	6.05	0
2011 Portland	Eastern	8	23	3	2	.600	27	7	20	4.70	0
2011 Pawtucket	Int.	8	14⅓	1	1	.500	19	3	14	2.51	0
2011 Boston c.............	A.L.	3	3	0	0	.000	4	1	3	6.00	0
2012 Pawtucket	Int.	25	42⅓	3	2	.600	56	17	34	2.55	4
2012 Boston	A.L.	37	44	1	1	.500	45	5	37	1.43	1
Major League Totals.......3 Yrs.		46	72⅓	3	4	.429	62	15	83	3.73	1

a On disabled list from September 21 to November 13, 2009.
b On disabled list from April 3 to November 8, 2010.
c On disabled list from March 26 to June 27, 2011.

THATCHER, JOSEPH (JOE)
Born, Indianapolis, Indiana, October 4, 1981.
Bats Left. Throws Left. Height, 6 feet, 2 inches. Weight, 230 pounds.

Year Club	Lea	G	IP	W	L	Pct	SO	BB	H	ERA	SAVES
2004 River City	Frontier	29	41⅓	2	3	.400	55	15	38	2.98	5
2005 River City	Frontier	18	21⅓	4	2	.667	27	4	18	1.27	5
2005 Brevard County a	Fla.St.	7	9	0	0	.000	14	0	6	0.00	2
2005 Helena	Pioneer	6	7⅔	2	0	1.000	10	1	8	3.52	2
2006 Brevard County	Fla.St.	16	30⅔	3	1	.750	32	9	12	0.29	2
2006 West Virginia	So.Atl.	26	29⅔	1	3	.250	42	6	28	2.43	10
2006 Huntsville..........	Southern	4	5⅓	1	0	1.000	6	2	2	1.69	0
2007 Huntsville..........	Southern	14	16⅓	1	0	1.000	20	2	11	0.55	0
2007 Nashville	P.C.	24	21⅔	2	1	.667	33	7	19	2.08	1
2007 Portland	P.C.	8	8⅔	1	0	1.000	11	1	10	1.04	0
2007 San Diego b	N.L.	22	21	2	2	.500	16	6	13	1.29	0
2008 San Diego	N.L.	25	25⅔	0	4	.000	17	13	42	8.42	0
2008 Portland..............	P.C.	37	39	5	2	.714	44	11	38	2.77	3
2009 Portland.............	P.C.	19	19	1	2	.333	22	5	18	1.89	1
2009 San Diego	N.L.	52	45	1	0	1.000	55	18	37	2.80	0
2010 Portland.............	P.C.	6	5	0	1	.000	3	3	6	3.60	0

Year Club	Lea	G	IP	W	L	Pct	SO	BB	H	ERA	SAVES
2010 San Diego c	N.L.	65	35	1	0	1.000	45	7	23	1.29	0
2011 Lake Elsinore	Calif.	1	1	0	0	.000	2	0	0	0.00	0
2011 Tucson	P.C.	8	7⅓	0	0	.000	10	3	3	1.23	0
2011 San Diego d	N.L.	18	10	0	0	.000	9	7	8	4.50	0
2012 Lake Elsinore	Calif.	1	1	0	0	.000	1	0	0	0.00	0
2012 San Diego e	N.L.	55	31⅔	1	4	.200	39	14	30	3.41	1
Major League Totals .... 6 Yrs.		237	168⅓	5	10	.333	181	65	153	3.37	1

a Signed by Milwaukee Brewers, July 19, 2005.
b Traded to San Diego Padres with pitcher Will Inman and pitcher Steve Garrison for pitcher Scott Linebrink, July 25, 2007.
c On disabled list from March 26 to April 22, 2010.
d On disabled list from March 22 to August 4, 2011.
e On disabled list from July 26 to September 1, 2012.

THAYER, DALE SCOTT

Born, Fountain Valley, California, December 17, 1980.
Bats Right. Throws Right. Height, 6 feet. Weight, 195 pounds.

Year Club	Lea	G	IP	W	L	Pct	SO	BB	H	ERA	SAVES
2003 Fort Wayne	Midwest	45	48	1	3	.250	72	15	31	2.06	25
2004 Lake Elsinore	Calif.	50	55⅓	2	1	.667	54	11	36	1.63	23
2004 Mobile	Southern	8	7⅓	1	1	.500	7	1	8	3.68	0
2005 Mobile	Southern	56	57⅔	3	5	.375	59	26	60	2.34	27
2006 Portland	P.C.	2	3	0	0	.000	4	1	2	3.00	0
2006 Mobile a	Southern	57	65⅓	7	4	.636	57	22	59	2.48	27
2007 Durham	Int.	8	9⅓	0	0	.000	9	4	5	2.89	0
2007 Montgomery	Southern	47	5⅔	9	0	1.000	54	20	40	2.26	21
2008 Durham	Int.	52	68⅓	3	1	.750	76	24	73	2.77	9
2009 Durham	Int.	51	63⅓	2	5	.286	44	15	59	2.27	17
2009 Tampa Bay	A.L.	11	13⅔	0	0	.000	8	1	18	4.61	1
2010 Tampa Bay	A.L.	1	2	0	0	.000	2	0	7	27.00	0
2010 Durham	Int.	46	60	4	1	.800	55	25	68	3.45	3
2011 Durham	Int.	54	71	4	3	.571	66	15	54	2.66	21
2011 New York b-c	N.L.	11	10⅓	0	3	.000	5	0	12	3.48	0
2012 Tucson	P.C.	7	8⅓	0	0	.000	5	2	2	0.00	0
2012 San Diego	N.L.	64	57⅔	2	2	.500	47	12	53	3.43	7
Major League Totals .... 4 Yrs.		87	83⅔	2	5	.286	62	13	90	4.20	8

a Sent by San Diego Padres to Tampa Bay Devil Rays as player to be named later for infielder Russell Branyan, September 15, 2006.
b Filed for free agency, November 6, 2010. Signed with New York Mets organization, February 8, 2011.
c Filed for free agency, November 2, 2011. Signed with San Diego Padres organization, December 6, 2011.

THORNTON, MATTHEW J. (MATT)

Born, Three Rivers, Michigan, September 15, 1976.
Bats Left. Throws Left. Height, 6 feet, 6 inches. Weight, 235 pounds.

Year Club	Lea	G	IP	W	L	Pct	SO	BB	H	ERA	SAVES
1998 Everett	Northwest	2	1⅓	0	0	.000	0	3	1	27.00	0
1999 Wisconsin	Midwest	25	62	0	0	.000	34	25	39	4.91	1
2000 Wisconsin	Midwest	26	103⅓	6	9	.400	88	72	94	4.01	0
2001 San Bernardino	California	27	157	14	7	.667	192	60	126	2.52	0
2002 San Antonio	Texas	12	62	1	5	.167	44	29	52	3.63	0
2003 Inland Empire	California	2	9	0	0	.000	14	4	9	4.00	0
2003 Tacoma	P.C.	2	9	0	2	.000	5	3	14	8.00	0
2003 San Antonio	Texas	4	25⅓	3	0	1.000	18	9	8	0.36	0
2004 Tacoma	P.C.	16	83	7	5	.583	74	63	85	5.20	0
2004 Seattle	A.L.	19	32⅔	1	2	.333	30	25	30	4.13	0
2005 Seattle	A.L.	55	57	0	4	.000	57	42	54	5.21	0
2006 Chicago a	A.L.	63	54	5	3	.625	49	21	46	3.33	2
2007 Chicago	A.L.	68	56⅓	4	4	.500	55	26	59	4.79	2
2008 Chicago	A.L.	74	67⅓	5	3	.625	77	19	48	2.67	1
2009 Chicago	A.L.	70	72⅓	6	3	.667	87	20	58	2.74	4
2010 Chicago b	A.L.	61	60⅔	5	4	.556	81	20	41	2.67	8
2011 Chicago	A.L.	62	59⅔	2	5	.286	60	21	60	3.32	3
2012 Chicago	A.L.	74	65	4	10	.286	53	17	63	3.46	3
Major League Totals .... 9 Yrs.		546	525	32	38	.457	552	211	459	3.51	23
Division Series											
2008 Chicago	A.L.	3	3⅓	0	0	.000	2	2	2	0.00	0

a Traded to Chicago White Sox for outfielder Joe Borchard, March 20, 2006.
b On disabled list from August 18 to September 3, 2010.

TILLMAN, CHRISTOPHER STEVEN (CHRIS)
Born, Anaheim, California, April 15, 1988.
Bats Right. Throws Right. Height, 6 feet, 5 inches. Weight, 195 pounds.

Year	Club	Lea	G	IP	W	L	Pct	SO	BB	H	ERA	SAVES
2006 Mariners		Arizona	5	11	2	0	1.000	16	5	9	0.82	1
2006 Everett		Northwest	5	19²/₃	1	3	.250	29	15	25	7.78	0
2007 High Desert		Calif.	20	102²/₃	6	7	.462	105	48	107	5.26	0
2007 Wisconsin		Midwest	8	33	1	4	.200	34	13	31	3.55	0
2008 Bowie a		Eastern	28	135²/₃	11	4	.733	154	65	115	3.18	0
2009 Norfolk		Int.	18	96²/₃	8	6	.571	99	26	85	2.70	0
2009 Baltimore		A.L.	12	65	2	5	.286	39	24	77	5.40	0
2010 Norfolk		Int.	21	121¹/₃	11	7	.611	94	30	120	3.34	0
2010 Baltimore		A.L.	11	53²/₃	2	5	.286	31	31	51	5.87	0
2011 Norfolk		Int.	15	76¹/₃	3	6	.333	54	38	77	5.19	0
2011 Baltimore		A.L.	13	62	3	5	.375	46	25	77	5.52	0
2012 Bowie		Eastern	1	3¹/₃	0	1	.000	2	2	4	8.10	0
2012 Norfolk		Int.	16	89¹/₃	8	8	.500	92	30	85	3.63	0
2012 Baltimore		A.L.	15	86	9	3	.750	66	24	66	2.93	0
Major League Totals	4 Yrs.		51	266²/₃	16	18	.471	182	104	271	4.72	0

a Traded by Seattle Mariners to Baltimore Orioles with pitcher Tony Butler, outfielder Adam Jones, pitcher Kam Mickolio and pitcher George Sherrill for pitcher Erik Bedard, February 8, 2008.

TOMLIN, JOSHUA AUBRY (JOSH)
Born, Tyler, Texas, October 19, 1984.
Bats Right. Throws Right. Height, 6 feet, 1 inch. Weight, 195 pounds.

Year	Club	Lea	G	IP	W	L	Pct	SO	BB	H	ERA	SAVES
2006 Mahoning Valley		N.Y.-Penn.	15	77¹/₃	8	2	.800	69	15	56	2.09	0
2007 Kinston		Carolina	6	27²/₃	1	1	.500	20	12	24	3.58	0
2007 Lake County		So.Atl.	26	103²/₃	10	3	.769	89	19	103	3.30	0
2008 Kinston		Carolina	40	102²/₃	9	5	.643	109	16	82	2.98	3
2008 Buffalo		Int.	1	7	1	0	1.000	3	1	6	3.86	0
2009 Akron		Eastern	26	145	14	9	.609	125	27	149	4.16	0
2010 Columbus		Int.	20	107¹/₃	8	4	.667	80	33	83	2.68	0
2010 Cleveland		A.L.	12	73	6	4	.600	43	19	72	4.56	0
2011 Cleveland a		A.L.	26	165¹/₃	12	7	.632	89	21	157	4.25	0
2012 Cleveland b		A.L.	21	103¹/₃	5	8	.385	56	25	126	6.36	0
Major League Totals	3 Yrs.		59	341²/₃	23	19	.548	188	65	355	4.95	0

a On disabled list from August 25 to November 2, 2011.
b On disabled list from May 8 to May 28 and August 13 to November 2, 2012.

TURNER, JACOB EDWARD
Born, St.Charles, Missouri, May 21, 1991.
Bats Right. Throws Right. Height, 6 feet, 5 inches. Weight, 210 pounds.

Year	Club	Lea	G	IP	W	L	Pct	SO	BB	H	ERA	SAVES
2010 West Michigan		Midwest	11	54	2	3	.400	51	9	53	3.67	0
2010 Lakeland		Fla.St.	13	61¹/₃	4	2	.667	51	14	53	2.93	0
2011 Erie		Eastern	17	113²/₃	3	5	.375	90	32	102	3.48	0
2011 Toledo		Int.	3	17¹/₃	1	0	1.000	20	3	15	3.12	0
2011 Detroit		A.L.	3	12²/₃	0	1	.000	8	4	17	8.53	0
2012 Lakeland		Fla.St.	4	21²/₃	1	2	.333	17	7	17	1.66	0
2012 New Orleans		P.C.	5	27¹/₃	2	0	1.000	12	12	27	1.98	0
2012 Toledo		Int.	10	62²/₃	4	2	.667	40	24	52	3.16	0
2012 Detroit		A.L.	3	12¹/₃	1	1	.500	7	7	17	8.03	0
2012 Miami a		N.L.	7	42²/₃	1	4	.200	29	9	33	3.38	0
Major League Totals	2 Yrs.		13	67²/₃	2	6	.250	44	20	67	5.19	0

a Traded to Miami Marlins with catcher Rob Brantley and pitcher Brian Flynn for infielder Omar Infante and pitcher Anibal Sanchez, July 23, 2012.

UEHARA, KOJI
Born, Osaka, Japan, April 3, 1975.
Bats Right. Throws Right. Height, 6 feet, 1 inch. Weight, 190 pounds.

Year	Club	Lea	G	IP	W	L	Pct	SO	BB	H	ERA	SAVES
1999 Yomiuri		Japan Cent.	25	197²/₃	20	4	.833	179	24	153	2.09	0
2000 Yomiuri		Japan Cent.	20	131	9	7	.562	126	22	112	3.57	0
2001 Yomiuri		Japan Cent.	24	138²/₃	10	7	.588	108	28	133	4.02	0
2002 Yomiuri		Japan Cent.	26	204	17	5	.773	182	23	173	2.60	0
2003 Yomiuri		Japan Cent.	27	207¹/₃	16	5	.762	194	28	190	3.17	0

Year	Club	Lea	G	IP	W	L	Pct	SO	BB	H	ERA	SAVES
2004 Yomiuri	Japan	Cent.	22	163	13	5	.722	153	23	135	2.60	0
2005 Yomiuri	Japan	Cent.	27	187⅓	9	12	.429	145	22	164	3.31	0
2006 Yomiuri	Japan	Cent.	24	168⅓	8	9	.471	151	21	157	3.21	0
2007 Yomiuri	Japan	Cent.	55	62	4	3	.571	66	4	47	1.74	32
2008 Yomiuri	Japan	Cent.	26	89⅔	6	5	.545	72	16	90	3.81	1
2009 Baltimore a-b	A.L.		12	66⅔	2	4	.333	48	12	71	4.05	0
2010 Bowie	Eastern		2	2	0	0	.000	1	1	1	0.00	0
2010 Norfolk	Int.		2	2	0	0	.000	1	0	2	0.00	0
2010 Baltimore c-d	A.L.		43	44	1	2	.333	55	5	37	2.86	13
2011 Baltimore-Texas e	A.L.		65	65	2	3	.400	85	9	38	2.35	0
2012 Texas f-g	A.L.		37	36	0	0	.000	43	3	20	1.75	1
Major League Totals . . . . .4 Yrs.			157	211⅔	5	9	.357	231	29	166	2.89	14
Wild Card Playoff												
2012 Texas	A.L.		1	1	0	0	.000	3	0	0	0.00	0
Division Series												
2011 Texas	A.L.		1	0	0	0	.000	0	1	2	INF	0
Championship Series												
2011 Texas	A.L.		2	1⅓	0	0	.000	1	1	3	13.50	0

a Signed with Baltimore Orioles, January 13, 2009.
b On disabled list from May 24 to June 11 and June 24 to November 6, 2009.
c On disabled list from March 26 to May 6 and May 20 to June 27, 2010.
d Filed for free agency, November 1, 2010, re-signed with Baltimore Orioles, December 9, 2010.
e Traded to Texas Rangers with cash for pitcher Tommy Hunter and infielder Chris Davis, July 30, 2011.
f On disabled list from June 10 to August 26, 2012.
g Filed for free agency, November 3, 2012. Signed with Boston Red Sox, December 18, 2012.

VALVERDE, JOSE RAFAEL

Born, San Pedro de Macoris, Dominican Republic, July 24, 1979.
Bats Right. Throws Right. Height, 6 feet, 4 inches. Weight, 255 pounds.

Year	Club	Lea	G	IP	W	L	Pct	SO	BB	H	ERA	SAVES
1997 Arizona	Dominican		14	18⅔	0	0	.000	19	13	20	5.30	0
1998 Arizona	Dominican		23	51⅓	1	3	.250	56	22	31	1.75	7
1999 Diamondbacks	Arizona		20	28⅔	1	2	.333	47	10	34	4.08	8
1999 South Bend	Midwest		2	2⅔	0	0	.000	3	2	2	0.00	0
2000 South Bend	Midwest		31	31⅔	0	5	.000	39	25	31	5.40	14
2000 Missoula	Pioneer		12	11⅔	1	0	1.000	24	4	3	0.00	4
2001 El Paso	Texas		39	41⅓	2	2	.500	72	27	36	3.92	13
2002 Tucson	P.C.		49	47⅔	2	4	.333	65	23	45	5.85	5
2003 Tucson	P.C.		22	29	1	1	.500	26	14	26	3.10	5
2003 Arizona	N.L.		54	50⅓	2	1	.667	71	26	24	2.15	10
2004 Arizona	N.L.		29	29⅔	1	2	.333	38	17	23	4.25	8
2004 Tucson a	P.C.		10	10⅔	1	1	.500	5	5	9	4.22	3
2005 Tucson	P.C.		2	2	0	0	.000	3	1	1	0.00	0
2005 Arizona b	N.L.		61	66⅓	3	4	.429	75	20	51	2.44	15
2006 Tucson	P.C.		15	17⅔	1	0	1.000	18	10	13	3.06	3
2006 Arizona	N.L.		44	49⅓	2	3	.400	69	22	50	5.84	18
2007 Arizona c	N.L.		65	64⅓	1	4	.200	78	26	46	2.66	*47
2008 Houston	N.L.		74	72	6	3	.667	83	23	62	3.38	*44
2009 Corpus Christi	Texas		2	2	0	0	.000	2	2	0	0.00	0
2009 Houston d-e	N.L.		52	54	4	2	.667	56	21	40	2.33	25
2010 Detroit	A.L.		60	63	2	4	.333	63	32	41	3.00	26
2011 Detroit	A.L.		*75	72⅓	2	4	.333	69	34	52	2.24	*49
2012 Detroit f	A.L.		71	69	3	4	.429	48	27	59	3.78	35
Major League Totals . . . . . . .10 Yrs.			585	590⅓	26	31	.456	650	248	448	3.11	277
Division Series												
2007 Arizona	N.L.		3	3	0	0	.000	6	1	1	0.00	1
2011 Detroit	A.L.		3	3	0	0	.000	3	4	2	6.00	2
2012 Detroit	A.L.		2	1⅔	0	1	.000	3	0	4	16.20	1
Division Series Totals			8	7⅔	0	1	.000	12	5	7	5.87	4
Championship Series												
2007 Arizona	N.L.		1	1⅔	0	1	.000	2	3	1	5.40	0
2011 Detroit	A.L.		3	4⅓	0	1	.000	3	2	5	8.31	1
2012 Detroit	A.L.		1	0⅔	0	0	.000	2	1	3	54.00	0
Championship Series Totals			5	6⅔	0	2	.000	7	6	9	12.15	0
World Series Record												
2012 Detroit	A.L.		1	0⅓	0	0	.000	1	0	4	54.00	0

a On disabled list from June 14 to October 4, 2004.
b On disabled list from March 25 to May 2, 2005.

c Traded to Houston Astros for pitcher Chad Qualls, pitcher Juan Gutierrez and outfielder Chris Burke, December 14, 2007.
d On disabled list from April 27 to June 13, 2009.
e Filed for free agency, November 9, 2009. Signed with Detroit Tigers, January 19, 2010.
f Filed for free agency, November 3, 2012.

VARGAS, JASON MATTHEW

Born, Apple Valley, California, February 2, 1983.
Bats Left. Throws Left. Height, 6 feet. Weight, 215 pounds.

Year	Club	Lea	G	IP	W	L	Pct	SO	BB	H	ERA	SAVES
2004 Jamestown	N.Y.-Penn.	8	41⅓	3	1	.750	41	13	35	1.96	0
2004 Greensboro	So.Atl.	3	19	2	1	.667	17	2	9	2.37	0
2005 Greensboro	So.Atl.	5	33⅔	4	1	.800	33	10	16	0.80	0
2005 Jupiter	Fla.St.	9	55⅓	2	3	.400	60	14	47	3.42	0
2005 Carolina	Southern	3	19	1	0	1.000	25	7	13	2.84	0
2005 Florida	N.L.	17	73⅔	5	5	.500	59	31	71	4.03	0
2006 Florida	N.L.	12	43	1	2	.333	25	30	50	7.33	0
2006 Albuquerque a	P.C.	13	69	3	6	.333	51	28	98	7.43	0
2007 New York	N.L.	2	10⅓	0	1	.000	4	2	17	12.19	0
2007 New Orleans b	P.C.	24	125	9	7	.563	108	44	141	4.97	0
2008 New York c-d	N.L.		INJURED—Did Not Play								
2009 Tacoma	P.C.	9	51⅔	4	3	.571	46	15	48	3.14	0
2009 Seattle	A.L.	23	91⅔	3	6	.333	54	24	98	4.91	0
2010 Seattle	A.L.	31	192⅔	9	12	.429	116	54	187	3.78	0
2011 Seattle	A.L.	32	201	10	13	.435	131	55	205	4.25	0
2012 Seattle e	A.L.	33	217⅓	14	11	.560	141	55	201	3.85	0
Major League Totals	7 Yrs.	150	829⅔	42	50	.457	530	255	829	4.35	0

a Traded to New York Mets with pitcher Adam Bostick for pitcher Matt Lindstrom and pitcher Henry Owens, November 20, 2006.
b On disabled list from September 21 to November 6, 2007.
c On disabled list from March 21 to November 3, 2008.
d Traded to Seattle Mariners with pitcher Aaron Heilman, outfielder Endy Chavez, infielder Mike Carp, outfielder Ezequiel Carrera, pitcher Maikel Cleto and pitcher Joe Smith for pitcher J.J. Putz, pitcher Sean Green and outfielder Jeremy Reed, December 10, 2008.
e Traded to Los Angeles Angels for infielder Kendrys Morales, December 19, 2012.

VENTERS, JONATHAN WILLIAM (JONNY)

Born, Pikeville, Kentucky, March 20, 1985.
Bats Left. Throws Left. Height, 6 feet, 3 inches. Weight, 195 pounds.

Year	Club	Lea	G	IP	W	L	Pct	SO	BB	H	ERA	SAVES
2004 Braves	Gulf Coast	11	42⅓	1	6	.143	54	12	53	5.74	0
2005 Rome	So.Atl.	23	103	8	6	.571	66	52	100	3.93	3
2006 a			INJURED—Did Not Play								
2007 Myrtle Beach	Carolina	17	79⅔	3	3	.500	64	38	60	3.39	1
2008 Myrtle Beach	Carolina	5	17⅔	1	2	.333	7	7	21	4.08	1
2008 Braves	Gulf Coast	4	7⅔	0	0	.000	10	2	10	4.70	0
2008 Mississippi	Southern	3	9	1	0	1.000	7	5	10	1.00	0
2009 Gwinnett	Int.	17	91⅓	4	7	.364	58	42	103	5.62	0
2009 Mississippi	Southern	12	65⅓	4	4	.500	40	35	60	2.76	0
2010 Gwinnett	Int.	2	6⅔	1	0	1.000	6	1	4	1.35	0
2010 Atlanta	N.L.	79	83	4	4	.500	93	39	61	1.95	1
2011 Atlanta	N.L.	*85	88	6	2	.750	96	43	53	1.84	5
2012 Gwinnett	Int.	1	1	0	0	.000	0	0	0	0.00	0
2012 Atlanta b	N.L.	66	58⅔	5	4	.556	69	28	61	3.22	0
Major League Totals	3 Yrs.	230	229⅔	15	10	.600	258	110	175	2.23	6

Wild Card Playoff

Year	Club	Lea	G	IP	W	L	Pct	SO	BB	H	ERA	SAVES
2012 Atlanta	N.L.	1	0⅔	0	0	.000	0	0	1	0.00	0

Division Series

Year	Club	Lea	G	IP	W	L	Pct	SO	BB	H	ERA	SAVES
2010 Atlanta	N.L.	4	5⅓	0	0	.000	8	0	7	0.00	0

a On minor league disabled list from April 6 to September 9, 2006.
b On disabled list from July 5 to July 21, 2012.

VERAS, JOSE ENGER

Born, Santo Domingo, Dominican Republic, October 20, 1980.
Bats Right. Throws Right. Height, 6 feet, 5 inches. Weight, 235 pounds.

Year	Club	Lea	G	IP	W	L	Pct	SO	BB	H	ERA	SAVES
1998 Devil Rays	Gulf Coast	5	16	1	1	.500	19	12	19	6.75	0
1999 Princeton	Appal.	14	60⅔	3	5	.375	48	50	74	7.12	0
2000 Charleston-SC	So.Atl.	20	106⅔	8	8	.500	102	41	125	4.81	0

Year Club	Lea	G	IP	W	L	Pct	SO	BB	H	ERA	SAVES
2001 Bakersfield	Calif.	27	153	9	8	.529	138	55	163	4.53	0
2002 Bakersfield	Calif.	11	59	3	4	.429	57	30	77	5.34	0
2002 Hudson Valley	N.Y.-Penn.	2	7	0	0	.000	7	5	2	0.00	0
2003 Durham	Int.	3	5$\frac{1}{3}$	0	0	.000	3	1	9	8.44	0
2003 Orlando	Southern	27	130$\frac{1}{3}$	6	9	.400	118	53	108	3.45	0
2004 Durham	Int.	30	84$\frac{1}{3}$	6	5	.545	63	33	101	5.23	0
2004 Montgomery a	Southern	3	10	1	0	1.000	6	7	10	6.30	0
2005 Oklahoma b	P.C.	57	61$\frac{2}{3}$	3	5	.375	72	33	63	3.79	24
2006 Columbus	Int.	50	59$\frac{2}{3}$	5	3	.625	68	19	49	2.41	21
2006 New York	A.L.	12	11	0	0	.000	6	5	8	4.09	1
2007 Yankees	Gulf Coast	2	2	0	0	.000	1	0	2	0.00	0
2007 Tampa	Fla.St.	2	3	0	0	.000	5	2	0	0.00	0
2007 Scranton-WB	Int.	12	16	2	0	1.000	17	7	17	4.50	4
2007 New York c	A.L.	9	9$\frac{1}{3}$	0	0	.000	7	7	6	5.79	2
2008 Scranton-WB	Int.	13	13	0	0	.000	21	4	8	1.38	9
2008 New York	A.L.	60	57$\frac{2}{3}$	5	3	.625	63	29	52	3.59	0
2009 Columbus	Int.	7	7	0	1	.000	9	2	3	1.29	0
2009 New York-Cleveland d-e	A.L.	47	50$\frac{1}{3}$	4	3	.571	40	28	42	5.19	0
2010 New Orleans	P.C.	24	29$\frac{1}{3}$	1	1	.500	37	15	34	4.60	2
2010 Florida f	N.L.	48	48	3	3	.500	54	29	32	3.75	0
2011 Pittsburgh g	N.L.	79	71	2	4	.333	79	34	54	3.80	1
2012 Milwaukee h	N.L.	72	67	5	4	.556	79	40	61	3.63	1
Major League Totals ....7 Yrs.		327	314$\frac{1}{3}$	19	17	.528	328	172	255	4.01	5
Division Series											
2007 New York	A.L.	2	0$\frac{2}{3}$	0	0	.000	1	1	1	0.00	0

a Filed for free agency from Tampa Bay Devil Rays, October 15, 2004. Signed with Texas Rangers organization, November 15, 2004.

b Filed for free agency, October 15, 2005. Signed with New York Yankees organization, December 12, 2005.

c On disabled list from March 23 to August 14, 2007.

d Sold to Cleveland Indians, June 24, 2009.

e Not offered contract, December 12, 2009. Signed with Florida Marlins organization, January 29, 2010.

f Not offered contract, December 2, 2010. Signed with Pittsburgh Pirates organization, January 18, 2011.

g Traded to Milwaukee Brewers for infielder Casey McGehee, December 13, 2011.

h Filed for free agency, November 1, 2012. Signed with Houston Astros, December 21, 2012.

VERLANDER, JUSTIN BROOKS

Born, Manakin Sabot, Virginia, February 20, 1983.
Bats Right. Throws Right. Height, 6 feet, 5 inches. Weight, 200 pounds.

Year Club	Lea	G	IP	W	L	Pct	SO	BB	H	ERA	SAVES
2005 Lakeland	Fla.St.	13	86	9	2	.818	104	19	70	1.67	0
2005 Erie	Eastern	7	32$\frac{2}{3}$	2	0	1.000	32	7	11	0.28	0
2005 Detroit	A.L.	2	11$\frac{1}{3}$	0	2	.000	7	5	15	7.15	0
2006 Detroit a	A.L.	30	186	17	9	.654	124	60	187	3.63	0
2007 Detroit b	A.L.	32	201$\frac{2}{3}$	18	6	*.750	183	67	181	3.66	0
2008 Detroit	A.L.	33	201	11	*17	.393	163	87	195	4.84	0
2009 Detroit	A.L.	35	*240	*19	9	.679	*269	63	219	3.45	0
2010 Detroit	A.L.	33	224$\frac{1}{3}$	18	9	.667	219	71	190	3.37	0
2011 Detroit c-d-e	A.L.	34	*251	*24	5	*.828	*250	57	174	*2.40	0
2012 Detroit	A.L.	33	*238$\frac{1}{3}$	17	8	.680	*239	60	192	2.64	0
Major League Totals ....8 Yrs.		232	1553$\frac{2}{3}$	124	65	.656	1454	470	1353	3.40	0
Division Series											
2006 Detroit	A.L.	1	5$\frac{1}{3}$	0	0	.000	5	4	7	5.06	0
2011 Detroit	A.L.	2	9	1	0	1.000	12	5	6	5.00	0
2012 Detroit	A.L.	2	16	2	0	1.000	22	5	7	0.56	0
Division Series Totals		5	30$\frac{1}{3}$	3	0	1.000	39	14	20	2.67	0
Championship Series											
2006 Detroit	A.L.	1	5$\frac{1}{3}$	1	0	1.000	6	1	7	6.75	0
2011 Detroit	A.L.	2	11$\frac{1}{3}$	1	1	.500	13	5	13	5.56	0
2012 Detroit	A.L.	1	8$\frac{1}{3}$	1	0	1.000	3	0	3	1.08	0
Championship Series Totals		4	25	3	1	.750	22	6	23	4.32	0
World Series Record											
2006 Detroit	A.L.	2	11	0	2	.000	12	5	12	5.73	0
2012 Detroit	A.L.	1	4	0	1	.000	4	1	6	11.25	0
World Series Totals		3	15	0	3	.000	16	6	18	7.20	0

a Selected Rookie of the Year in American League for 2006.

b Pitched no-hit, no-run game against Milwaukee Brewers, June 12, 2007.

c Pitched no-hit, no-run game against Toronto Blue Jays, May 7, 2011.

d Selected Cy Young Award Winner in American League for 2011.

e Selected Most Valuable Player in American League for 2011.

VILLANUEVA, CARLOS MANUEL

Born, Santiago, Dominican Republic, November 28, 1983.
Bats Right. Throws Right. Height, 6 feet, 2 inches. Weight, 215 pounds.

Year Club	Lea	G	IP	W	L	Pct	SO	BB	H	ERA	SAVES
2002 Giants............	Arizona	19	30⅓	4	0	1.000	23	3	24	0.59	3
2003 Giants............	Arizona	12	59	3	6	.333	67	13	64	3.97	0
2004 Beloit a..........	Midwest	25	114⅔	8	8	.500	113	30	102	3.77	1
2005 Brevard County	Fla.St.	21	112⅓	8	1	.889	124	32	78	2.32	0
2005 Huntsville.........	Southern	4	20⅔	1	3	.250	14	9	21	7.40	0
2006 Huntsville........	Southern	11	62⅓	4	5	.444	59	14	60	3.75	0
2006 Nashville	P.C.	11	66⅓	7	1	.875	61	26	42	2.71	0
2006 Milwaukee	N.L.	10	53⅔	2	2	.500	39	11	43	3.69	0
2007 Nashville	P.C.	2	8⅓	0	0	.000	9	1	3	3.24	0
2007 Milwaukee	N.L.	59	114⅓	8	5	.615	99	53	101	3.94	1
2008 Milwaukee	N.L.	47	108⅓	4	7	.364	93	30	112	4.07	1
2009 Milwaukee	N.L.	64	96	4	10	.286	83	35	102	5.34	3
2010 Nashville	P.C.	11	14⅓	0	0	.000	14	7	13	3.77	0
2010 Milwaukee b..........	N.L.	50	52⅔	2	0	1.000	67	22	48	4.61	1
2011 Dunedin	Fla.St.	1	1	0	0	.000	0	0	1	0.00	0
2011 Toronto c.............	A.L.	33	107	6	4	.600	68	32	103	4.04	0
2012 Toronto d.............	A.L.	38	125⅓	7	7	.500	122	46	113	4.16	0
Major League Totals	7 Yrs.	301	657⅓	33	35	.485	571	229	622	4.26	6
Division Series											
2008 Milwaukee	N.L.	2	3⅔	0	0	.000	3	0	0	0.00	0

a Traded to Milwaukee Brewers by San Francisco Giants with pitcher Glenn Woolard for pitcher Wayne Franklin and pitcher Leo Estrella, March 30, 2004.
b Traded to Toronto Blue Jays for player to be named later, December 3, 2010. Milwaukee Brewers received cash to complete the transaction, April 8, 2011.
c On disabled list from August 4 to August 31, 2011.
d Filed for free agency, November 3, 2012.

VILLARREAL, BRAYAN RENE

Born, LaGuaira, Venezuela, May 10, 1987.
Bats Right. Throws Right. Height, 6 feet. Weight, 170 pounds.

Year Club	Lea	G	IP	W	L	Pct	SO	BB	H	ERA	SAVES
2007 Tigers..........	Gulf Coast	1	4⅓	0	0	.000	5	3	4	6.23	0
2008 Tigers..........	Gulf Coast	11	37	1	5	.167	37	11	26	3.65	0
2008 West Michigan......	Midwest	1	3⅓	0	1	.000	0	1	7	16.20	0
2009 West Michigan......	Midwest	26	103⅓	5	5	.500	118	34	85	2.87	2
2010 Erie.............	Eastern	8	43⅔	0	4	.000	46	16	37	3.71	0
2010 Lakeland...........	Fla.St.	16	85⅔	7	4	.636	90	23	73	3.47	0
2011 Detroit	A.L.	16	16	1	1	.500	14	10	21	6.75	0
2011 Toledo	Int.	17	66	3	5	.375	40	29	65	5.05	0
2012 Toledo	Int.	8	14	0	0	.000	22	7	5	1.29	1
2012 Detroit	A.L.	50	54⅔	3	5	.375	66	28	38	2.63	0
Major League Totals	2 Yrs.	66	70⅔	4	6	.400	80	38	59	3.57	0

VOGELSONG, RYAN ANDREW

Born, Charlotte, North Carolina, July 22, 1977.
Bats Right. Throws Right. Height, 6 feet, 3 inches. Weight, 215 pounds.

Year Club	Lea	G	IP	W	L	Pct	SO	BB	H	ERA	SAVES
1998 Salem-Keizr	Northwest	10	56	6	1	.857	66	16	37	1.77	0
1998 San Jose	Calif.	4	19	0	0	.000	26	4	23	7.58	0
1999 San Jose	Calif.	13	69⅔	4	4	.500	86	27	37	2.45	0
1999 Shreveport..........	Texas	6	28⅓	0	2	.000	23	15	40	7.31	0
2000 Shreveport..........	Texas	27	155⅓	6	10	.375	147	69	153	4.23	0
2000 San Francisco	N.L.	4	6	0	0	.000	6	2	4	0.00	0
2001 Fresno	P.C.	10	58	3	3	.500	53	18	35	2.79	0
2001 Nashville	P.C.	6	31⅔	2	3	.400	33	15	26	3.98	0
2001 San Fran.-Pittsburgh a...	N.L.	15	34⅔	0	5	.000	24	20	39	6.75	0
2002 Lynchburg	Carolina	4	15⅔	1	1	.500	20	7	19	8.04	0
2002 Altoona b	Eastern	8	43⅔	1	5	.167	35	10	47	5.56	0
2003 Nashville	P.C.	26	149	12	8	.600	146	54	142	4.29	0
2003 Pittsburgh	N.L.	6	22	2	2	.500	15	9	30	6.55	0
2004 Pittsburgh	N.L.	31	133	6	13	.316	92	67	148	6.50	0
2005 Pittsburgh	N.L.	44	81⅓	2	2	.500	52	40	82	4.43	0
2006 Pittsburgh	N.L.	20	38	0	0	.000	27	16	44	6.39	0
2006 Indianapolis c.......	Int.	11	67⅔	4	5	.444	43	12	54	2.66	0
2007 Hanshin	Japan Pac.	20	106⅔	7	6	.538	91	41	113	4.13	0
2008 Hanshin	Japan Pac.	12	65⅓	3	4	.429	50	19	65	3.99	0

Year Club	Lea	G	IP	W	L	Pct	SO	BB	H	ERA	SAVES
2009 Orix . . . . Japan Pac.	30	42 1/3	1	4	.200	56	16	39	4.54	0
2010 Salt Lake . . . . P.C.	8	36 2/3	1	3	.250	37	22	47	4.66	0
2010 Lehigh Valley d-e-f . . . . . . Int.	25	58 2/3	2	5	.286	73	40	60	4.91	1
2011 Fresno . . . . P.C.	2	11 1/3	2	0	1.000	17	5	8	1.59	0
2011 San Francisco h . . . . N.L.	30	179 2/3	13	7	.650	139	61	164	2.71	0
2012 Fresno . . . . P.C.	2	10	1	0	1.000	12	4	9	1.80	0
2012 San Francisco g . . . . N.L.	31	189 2/3	14	9	.609	158	62	171	3.37	0
Major League Totals . . . . .8 Yrs.	181	684 1/3	37	38	.493	513	277	682	4.34	0
Division Series										
2012 San Francisco . . . . N.L.	1	5	0	0	.000	5	3	3	1.80	0
Championship Series										
2012 San Francisco . . . . N.L.	2	14	2	0	1.000	13	3	8	1.29	0
World Series Record										
2012 San Francisco . . . . N.L.	1	5 2/3	1	0	1.000	3	4	5	0.00	0

a Traded to Pittsburgh Pirates with outfielder Armando Rios for pitcher Jason Schmidt and outfielder John Vander Wal, July 30, 2001.
b On disabled list from March 30 to August 1, 2002.
c Filed for free agency, October 2, 2006. Signed with Hanshin Tigers for 2007.
d Signed with Philadelphia Phillies organization, January 5, 2010.
e Released by Philadelphia Phillies, July 16, 2010. Signed with Los Angeles Angels organization, July 27, 2010.
f Filed for free agency, November 6, 2010. Signed with San Francisco Giants organization, January 15, 2011.
g On disabled list from March 27 to April 15, 2012.

VOLQUEZ, EDINSON

Born, Santo Domingo, Dominican Republic, July 3, 1983.
Bats Right. Throws Right. Height, 6 feet, 1 inch. Weight, 200 pounds.

Year Club	Lea	G	IP	W	L	Pct	SO	BB	H	ERA	SAVES
2003 Rangers . . . . Arizona	10	27	2	1	.667	28	11	24	4.00	1
2004 Stockton . . . . Calif.	8	39 2/3	4	1	.800	34	14	31	2.95	0
2004 Clinton . . . . .Midwest	22	91	4	4	.500	77	30	83	4.05	3
2005 Bakersfield . . . . Calif.	11	66 2/3	5	4	.556	77	12	64	4.18	0
2005 Rangers . . . . Arizona	1	2	0	0	.000	2	0	2	0.00	0
2005 Frisco . . . . Texas	10	58 2/3	1	5	.167	49	17	58	4.14	0
2005 Texas . . . . A.L.	6	12 2/3	0	4	.000	11	10	25	14.21	0
2006 Oklahoma . . . . P.C.	21	120 2/3	6	6	.500	130	72	86	3.21	0
2006 Texas . . . . A.L.	8	33 1/3	1	6	.143	15	17	52	7.29	0
2007 Bakersfield . . . . Calif.	7	35 1/3	0	0	.000	38	20	27	7.13	0
2007 Frisco . . . . : . . . . Texas	11	58 1/3	8	1	.889	62	19	46	3.55	0
2007 Oklahoma . . . . P.C.	8	51	6	1	.857	66	21	25	1.41	0
2007 Texas a . . . . A.L.	6	34	2	1	.667	29	15	34	4.50	0
2008 Cincinnati . . . . N.L.	33	196	17	6	.739	206	93	167	3.21	0
2009 Cincinnati b . . . . N.L.	9	49 2/3	4	2	.667	47	32	34	4.35	0
2010 Dayton . . . . .Midwest	2	13	0	0	.000	19	4	11	1.38	0
2010 Lynchburg . . . . .Carolina	2	8	1	0	1.000	7	0	3	0.00	0
2010 Louisville . . . . .Int.	4	23	3	0	1.000	21	8	11	1.96	0
2010 Cincinnati c . . . . N.L.	12	62 2/3	4	3	.571	67	35	59	4.31	0
2011 Louisville . . . . .Int.	13	87 1/3	4	2	.667	83	29	72	2.37	0
2011 Cincinnati d . . . . N.L.	20	108 2/3	5	7	.417	104	65	106	5.71	0
2012 San Diego . . . . N.L.	32	182 2/3	11	11	.500	174	*105	160	4.14	0
Major League Totals . . . . .8 Yrs.	126	679 2/3	44	40	.524	653	372	637	4.52	0
Division Series										
2010 Cincinnati . . . . N.L.	1	1 2/3	0	1	.000	0	2	4	21.60	0

a Traded to Cincinnati Reds with pitcher Danny Herrera for outfielder Josh Hamilton, December 21, 2007.
b On disabled list from May 17 to June 1 and June 2 to November 16, 2009.
c On disabled list from February 24 to July 17, 2010.
d Traded to San Diego Padres with pitcher Brad Boxberger, catcher Yasmani Grandal and infielder Yonder Alonso for pitcher Mat Latos, December 17, 2011.

VOLSTAD, CHRISTOPHER KENNETH (CHRIS)

Born, Palm Beach Gardens, Florida, September 23, 1986.
Bats Right. Throws Right. Height, 6 feet, 8 inches. Weight, 225 pounds.

Year Club	Lea	G	IP	W	L	Pct	SO	BB	H	ERA	SAVES
2005 Marlins . . . . Gulf Coast	6	27	1	1	.500	26	4	25	2.33	0
2005 Jamestown . . . . N.Y.-Penn.	7	38	3	2	.600	29	11	43	2.13	0
2006 Greensboro . . . . So.Atl.	26	152	11	8	.579	99	36	161	3.08	0
2007 Jupiter . . . . Fla.St.	21	126	8	9	.471	93	37	152	4.50	0
2007 Carolina . . . . Southern	7	42 2/3	4	2	.667	25	10	41	3.16	0
2008 Carolina . . . . Southern	15	91	4	4	.500	56	30	86	3.36	0
2008 Florida . . . . N.L.	15	84 1/3	6	4	.600	52	36	76	2.88	0

Year	Club	Lea	G	IP	W	L	Pct	SO	BB	H	ERA	SAVES
2009 New Orleans	P.C.	1	4	0	1	.000	7	2	5	6.75	0
2009 Florida	N.L.	29	159	9	13	.409	107	59	169	5.21	0
2010 New Orleans	P.C.	3	17	1	0	1.000	13	9	13	3.18	0
2010 Florida	N.L.	30	175	12	9	.571	102	60	187	4.58	0
2011 New Orleans	P.C.	3	18$^{1}/_{3}$	1	1	.500	14	9	20	4.42	0
2011 Florida a	N.L.	29	165$^{2}/_{3}$	5	13	.278	117	49	187	4.89	0
2012 Iowa	P.C.	12	71$^{1}/_{3}$	3	5	.375	52	19	86	5.17	0
2012 Chicago b-c	N.L.	21	111$^{1}/_{3}$	3	12	.200	61	43	137	6.31	0
Major League Totals ....5 Yrs.	124	695$^{1}/_{3}$	35	51	.407	439	247	756	4.87	0	

a Traded to Chicago Cubs for pitcher Carlos Zambrano and cash, January 5, 2012.
b Claimed on waivers by Kansas City Royals, October 26, 2012.
c Filed for free agency, November 28, 2012.

WAINWRIGHT, ADAM PARRISH

Born, Brunswick, Georgia, August 30, 1981.
Bats Right. Throws Right. Height, 6 feet, 7 inches. Weight, 205 pounds.

Year	Club	Lea	G	IP	W	L	Pct	SO	BB	H	ERA	SAVES
2000 Danville	Appal.	6	29$^{1}/_{3}$	2	2	.500	39	2	28	3.68	0
2000 Braves	Gulf Coast	7	32	4	0	1.000	42	10	15	1.13	0
2001 Macon	So.Atl.	28	164$^{2}/_{3}$	10	10	.500	184	48	144	3.77	0
2002 Myrtle Beach	Carolina	28	163$^{1}/_{3}$	9	6	.600	167	66	149	3.31	0
2003 Greenville a	Southern	27	149$^{2}/_{3}$	10	8	.556	128	37	133	3.37	0
2004 Memphis	P.C.	12	63$^{2}/_{3}$	4	4	.500	64	28	68	5.37	0
2005 Memphis	P.C.	29	182	10	10	.500	147	51	204	4.40	0
2005 St. Louis	N.L.	2	2	0	0	.000	0	1	2	13.50	0
2006 St. Louis	N.L.	61	75	2	1	.667	72	22	64	3.12	3
2007 St. Louis	N.L.	32	202	14	12	.538	136	70	212	3.70	0
2008 Springfield	Texas	1	4$^{2}/_{3}$	0	0	.000	7	0	4	0.00	0
2008 Memphis	P.C.	2	3$^{2}/_{3}$	0	1	.000	3	2	8	12.27	0
2008 St. Louis b	N.L.	20	132	11	3	.786	91	34	122	3.20	0
2009 St. Louis	N.L.	34	*233	*19	8	.704	212	66	216	2.63	0
2010 St. Louis	N.L.	33	230$^{1}/_{3}$	20	11	.645	213	56	186	2.42	0
2011 St. Louis c	N.L.			INJURED—Did Not Play							
2012 St. Louis	N.L.	32	198$^{2}/_{3}$	14	13	.519	184	52	196	3.94	0
Major League Totals ....7 Yrs.	214	1073	80	48	.625	908	301	998	3.15	3	
Division Series												
2006 St. Louis	N.L.	3	3$^{2}/_{3}$	0	0	.000	6	0	3	0.00	1
2009 St. Louis	N.L.	1	8	0	0	.000	7	1	3	1.13	0
2012 St. Louis	N.L.	2	8	0	0	.000	15	3	13	7.88	0
Division Series Totals		6	19$^{2}/_{3}$	0	0	.000	28	4	19	3.66	1
Championship Series												
2006 St. Louis	N.L.	3	3	0	0	.000	4	1	2	0.00	2
2012 St. Louis	N.L.	1	7	1	0	1.000	5	0	4	1.29	0
Championship Series Totals		4	10	1	0	1.000	9	1	6	0.90	2
World Series Record												
2006 St. Louis	N.L.	3	3	1	0	1.000	5	1	2	0.00	1

a Traded by Atlanta Braves to St. Louis Cardinals with pitcher Jason Marquis and pitcher Ray King for catcher Eli Marrero and outfielder J.D. Drew, December 13, 2003.
b On disabled list from June 8 to August 22, 2008.
c On disabled list from March 25 to November 1, 2011.

WALDEN, JORDAN CRAIG

Born, Fort Worth, Texas, November 16, 1987.
Bats Right. Throws Right. Height, 6 feet, 5 inches. Weight, 235 pounds.

Year	Club	Lea	G	IP	W	L	Pct	SO	BB	H	ERA	SAVES
2007 Orem	Pioneer	15	64$^{1}/_{3}$	1	1	.500	63	17	49	3.08	0
2008 Cedar Rapids	Midwest	18	107$^{1}/_{3}$	4	6	.400	91	32	80	2.18	0
2008 Rancho Cucamonga	Calif.	9	49	5	2	.714	50	24	42	4.04	0
2009 Arkansas	Texas	13	60	1	5	.167	57	29	72	5.25	0
2010 Arkansas	Texas	38	43	1	1	.500	38	22	44	3.35	8
2010 Salt Lake	P.C.	6	6$^{2}/_{3}$	0	0	.000	3	2	8	4.05	0
2010 Los Angeles	A.L.	16	15$^{1}/_{3}$	0	1	.000	23	7	13	2.35	1
2011 Los Angeles	A.L.	62	60$^{1}/_{3}$	5	5	.500	67	26	49	2.98	32
2012 Salt Lake	P.C.	3	2$^{2}/_{3}$	0	1	.000	3	0	3	6.75	0
2012 Los Angeles a-b	A.L.	45	39	3	2	.600	48	18	35	3.46	1
Major League Totals ....3 Yrs.	123	114$^{2}/_{3}$	8	8	.500	138	51	97	3.06	34	

a On disabled list from July 15 to August 19, 2012.
b Traded to Atlanta Braves for pitcher Tommy Hanson, November 30, 2012.

WATSON, ANTHONY M. (TONY)

Born, Sioux City, Iowa, May 30, 1985.
Bats Left. Throws Left. Height, 6 feet, 4 inches. Weight, 220 pounds.

Year	Club	Lea	G	IP	W	L	Pct	SO	BB	H	ERA	SAVES
2007 State College	N.Y.-Penn.	10	53²/₃	6	1	.857	40	7	47	2.52	0
2007 Hickory	So.Atl.	3	14	1	1	.500	18	1	14	3.86	0
2008 Lynchburg	Carolina	28	151²/₃	8	12	.400	104	36	149	3.56	0
2009 Altoona	Eastern	5	15¹/₃	0	3	.000	14	11	22	8.22	0
2010 Altoona	Eastern	34	111¹/₃	6	4	.600	105	24	82	2.67	2
2011 Indianapolis	Int.	26	34¹/₃	3	3	.500	35	11	24	2.36	0
2011 Pittsburgh	N.L.	43	41	2	2	.500	37	20	34	3.95	0
2012 Pittsburgh	N.L.	68	53¹/₃	5	2	.714	53	23	37	3.38	0
Major League Totals	2 Yrs.	111	94¹/₃	7	4	.636	90	43	71	3.63	0

WEAVER, JERED DAVID

Born, Northridge, California, October 4, 1982.
Bats Right. Throws Right. Height, 6 feet, 7 inches. Weight, 205 pounds.

Year	Club	Lea	G	IP	W	L	Pct	SO	BB	H	ERA	SAVES
2005 Arkansas	Texas	8	43	3	3	.500	46	19	43	3.98	0
2006 Salt Lake	P.C.	12	77	6	1	.857	93	10	63	2.10	0
2006 Los Angeles	A.L.	19	123	11	2	.846	105	33	94	2.56	0
2007 Rancho Cucamonga	Calif.	2	11	1	0	1.000	12	3	5	0.82	0
2007 Los Angeles a	A.L.	28	161	13	7	.650	115	45	178	3.91	0
2008 Los Angeles	A.L.	30	176²/₃	11	10	.524	152	54	173	4.33	0
2009 Los Angeles	A.L.	33	211	16	8	.667	174	66	196	3.75	0
2010 Inland Empire	Calif.	1	3	0	0	.000	3	1	2	0.00	0
2010 Los Angeles	A.L.	34	224¹/₃	13	12	.520	*233	54	187	3.01	0
2011 Los Angeles	A.L.	33	235²/₃	18	8	.692	198	56	182	2.41	0
2012 Los Angeles b-c	A.L.	30	188²/₃	*20	5	*.800	142	45	147	2.81	0
Major League Totals	7 Yrs.	207	1320¹/₃	102	52	.662	1119	353	1157	3.24	0
Division Series											
2007 Los Angeles	A.L.	1	5	0	1	.000	5	3	4	3.60	0
2008 Los Angeles	A.L.	1	2	1	0	1.000	3	1	1	0.00	0
2009 Los Angeles	A.L.	1	7¹/₃	1	0	1.000	7	2	2	1.23	0
Division Series Totals		3	14¹/₃	2	1	.667	15	6	7	1.88	0
Championship Series											
2009 Los Angeles	A.L.	3	6¹/₃	0	0	.000	7	4	5	4.26	0

a On disabled list from March 23 to April 17, 2007.
b Pitched no-hit, no-run game against Minnesota Twins, May 2, 2012.
c On disabled list from May 29 to June 20, 2012.

WEBB, RYAN CHRISTOPHER

Born, Clearwater, Florida, February 5, 1986.
Bats Right. Throws Right. Height, 6 feet, 6 inches. Weight, 215 pounds.

Year	Club	Lea	G	IP	W	L	Pct	SO	BB	H	ERA	SAVES
2004 Athletics	Arizona	8	20¹/₃	1	1	.500	23	1	18	4.87	0
2005 Kane County	Midwest	24	128²/₃	5	11	.313	84	41	139	4.76	0
2006 Stockton	Calif.	23	117²/₃	8	9	.471	96	37	160	5.28	0
2007 Stockton	Calif.	15	83	4	7	.364	71	22	83	5.75	0
2007 Midland	Texas	5	25²/₃	0	4	.000	16	10	34	9.12	0
2008 Midland	Texas	25	130	9	8	.529	94	44	165	5.19	0
2009 Sacramento	P.C.	31	45²/₃	7	1	.875	39	15	57	4.34	2
2009 Portland	P.C.	3	3	0	0	.000	0	1	3	3.00	0
2009 San Diego a	N.L.	28	25²/₃	2	1	.667	19	11	27	3.86	0
2010 Portland	P.C.	17	20²/₃	1	0	1.000	23	5	12	0.87	1
2010 San Diego b	N.L.	54	59	3	1	.750	44	19	64	2.90	0
2011 Marlins	Gulf Coast	1	2	0	0	.000	2	0	2	0.00	0
2011 Jupiter	Fla.St.	3	3¹/₃	1	0	1.000	3	3	4	2.70	0
2011 Florida c	N.L.	53	50²/₃	2	4	.333	31	20	48	3.20	0
2012 New Orleans	P.C.	3	5²/₃	2	0	1.000	1	1	3	1.59	0
2012 Miami	N.L.	65	60¹/₃	4	3	.571	44	20	72	4.03	0
Major League Totals	4 Yrs.	200	195²/₃	11	9	.550	138	70	211	3.45	0

a Traded by Oakland Athletics to San Diego Padres with pitcher Craig Italiano and player to be named later for outfielder Scott Hairston, July 5, 2009. San Diego Padres received pitcher Sean Gallagher to complete trade, July 28, 2009.
b Traded to Florida Marlins with pitcher Edward Mujica for outfielder Cameron Maybin, November 13, 2010.
c On disabled list from June 27 to August 17, 2011.

WESTBROOK, JACOB CAUTHEN (JAKE)

Born, Athens, Georgia, September 29, 1977.
Bats Right. Throws Right. Height, 6 feet, 3 inches. Weight, 215 pounds.

Year	Club	Lea	G	IP	W	L	Pct	SO	BB	H	ERA	SAVES
1996 Rockies	Arizona		11	62²/₃	4	2	.667	57	14	66	2.87	0
1996 Portland	Northwest		4	24²/₃	1	1	.500	19	5	22	2.55	0
1997 Asheville a	So.Atl.		28	170	14	11	.560	92	55	176	4.29	0
1998 Jupiter	Fla.St.		27	171	11	6	.647	79	60	169	3.26	0
1999 Harrisburg b	Eastern		27	174²/₃	11	5	.688	90	63	180	3.92	0
2000 Columbus	Int.		16	89	5	7	.417	61	38	94	4.65	0
2000 New York c-d-e-f	A.L.		3	6²/₃	0	2	.000	1	4	15	13.50	0
2001 Buffalo	Int.		12	64²/₃	8	1	.889	45	23	60	3.20	0
2001 Cleveland	A.L.		23	64²/₃	4	4	.500	48	22	79	5.85	0
2002 Akron	Eastern		3	15	0	1	.000	8	1	13	4.80	0
2002 Buffalo	Int.		1	6	1	0	1.000	2	0	8	6.00	0
2002 Cleveland g	A.L.		11	41²/₃	1	3	.250	20	12	50	5.83	0
2003 Buffalo	Int.		2	10	1	0	1.000	7	4	0	0.00	0
2003 Cleveland	A.L.		34	133	7	10	.412	58	56	142	4.33	0
2004 Cleveland	A.L.		33	215²/₃	14	9	.609	116	61	208	3.38	0
2005 Cleveland	A.L.		34	210²/₃	15	15	.500	119	56	218	4.49	0
2006 Cleveland	A.L.		32	211¹/₃	15	10	.600	109	55	*247	4.17	0
2007 Lake County	So.Atl.		1	5	0	1	.000	5	0	6	7.20	0
2007 Akron	Eastern		1	2¹/₃	0	1	.000	1	3	5	15.43	0
2007 Buffalo	Int.		2	5¹/₃	0	1	.000	5	5	9	8.44	0
2007 Cleveland h	A.L.		25	152	6	9	.400	93	55	159	4.32	0
2008 Lake County	So.Atl.		1	3²/₃	0	0	.000	4	1	3	2.45	0
2008 Akron	Eastern		1	6	0	0	.000	2	4	3	0.00	0
2008 Cleveland i	A.L.		5	34²/₃	1	2	.333	19	7	33	3.12	0
2009 Akron	Eastern		3	9	0	1	.000	8	6	1	2.00	0
2009 Cleveland j	A.L.		INJURED—Did Not Play									
2010 Cleveland	A.L.		21	127²/₃	6	7	.462	73	44	133	4.65	0
2010 St. Louis k-l	N.L.		12	75	4	4	.500	55	24	70	3.48	0
2011 St. Louis	N.L.		33	183¹/₃	12	9	.571	104	73	208	4.66	0
2012 St. Louis	N.L.		28	174²/₃	13	11	.542	106	52	191	3.97	0
Major League Totals	12 Yrs.		294	1631	98	95	.508	921	521	1753	4.30	0
Division Series												
2007 Cleveland	A.L.		1	5	0	1	.000	1	0	9	10.80	0
Championship Series												
2007 Cleveland	A.L.		2	12²/₃	1	1	.500	7	4	16	3.55	0
World Series Record												
2011 St. Louis	N.L.		2	2	1	0	1.000	0	1	2	0.00	0

a Traded to Montreal Expos by Colorado Rockies with pitcher John Nicholson and outfielder Mike Hamlin for infielder Mike Lansing, November 18, 1997.
b Traded to New York Yankees with two players to be named later for pitcher Hideki Irabu, December 22, 1999. Pitchers Ted Lilly and Christian Parker were sent to New York Yankees to complete trade, March 17 and March 22, 2000.
c On disabled list from May 5 to 23, 2000.
d Sent to Cleveland Indians by New York Yankees with pitcher Zach Day to complete trade for outfielder David Justice, July 24, 2000.
e On disabled list from July 25 to September 1, 2000.
f On disabled list from September 1 to October 31, 2000.
g On disabled list from March 30 to July 11 and August 26 to November 4, 2002.
h On disabled list from May 3 to June 24, 2007.
i On disabled list from April 20 to May 28 and May 29 to November 13, 2008.
j On disabled list from March 26 to November 18, 2009.
k Traded to St. Louis Cardinals with cash for pitcher Corey Kluber, July 31, 2010.
l Filed for free agency, November 1, 2010, re-signed with St. Louis Cardinals, November 16, 2010.

WHITE, ALEX BRUCE

Born, Greenville, North Carolina, August 29, 1988.
Bats Right. Throws Right. Height, 6 feet, 3 inches. Weight, 215 pounds.

Year	Club	Lea	G	IP	W	L	Pct	SO	BB	H	ERA	SAVES
2010 Kinston	Carolina		8	44	2	3	.400	41	19	32	2.86	0
2010 Akron	Eastern		18	106²/₃	8	7	.533	76	27	91	2.28	0
2011 Tulsa	Texas		4	16¹/₃	1	1	.500	10	1	10	1.65	0
2011 Columbus	Int.		4	23²/₃	1	0	1.000	28	5	19	1.90	0
2011 Cleveland	A.L.		3	15	1	0	1.000	13	9	14	3.60	0
2011 Colorado a-b	N.L.		7	36¹/₃	2	4	.333	24	16	48	8.42	0
2012 Colorado Springs	P.C.		11	60²/₃	3	4	.429	45	23	54	3.71	0
2012 Colorado c	N.L.		23	98	2	9	.182	64	51	114	5.51	0
Major League Totals	2 Yrs.		33	149¹/₃	5	13	.278	101	76	176	6.03	0

a Traded to Colorado Rockies with pitcher Joseph Gardner, outfielder Matt McBride and player to be named later for pitcher Ubaldo Jimenez, July 31, 2011. Colorado Rockies received pitcher Drew Pomeranz to complete trade, August 17, 2011.

b On disabled list from May 21 to August 23, 2011.

c Traded to Houston Astros with pitcher Alex Gillingham for pitcher Wilton Lopez and player to be named later, December 4, 2012.

WILHELMSEN, THOMAS MARK (TOM)

Born, Tucson, Arizona, December 16, 1983.
Bats Right. Throws Right. Height, 6 feet, 6 inches. Weight, 230 pounds.

Year	Club	Lea	G	IP	W	L	Pct	SO	BB	H	ERA	SAVES
2003	Brewers	Arizona	2	4	0	1	.000	4	4	5	4.50	0
2003	Beloit	Midwest	15	88	5	5	.500	63	27	78	2.76	0
2004-2008							Did Not Play					
2009	Tucson	Golden	11	12	0	0	.000	15	4	15	6.00	2
2010	Mariners	Arizona	5	15	0	0	.000	22	2	4	0.60	0
2010	Clinton	Midwest	7	44 1/3	6	1	.857	37	15	33	2.23	0
2010	Everett a	Northwest	3	14 2/3	1	0	1.000	14	2	14	3.68	0
2011	Jackson	Southern	14	60 2/3	4	5	.444	40	26	66	5.49	0
2011	Seattle	A.L.	25	32 2/3	2	0	1.000	30	13	25	3.31	0
2012	Seattle	A.L.	73	79 1/3	4	3	.571	87	29	59	2.50	29
Major League Totals	2 Yrs.		98	112	6	3	.667	117	42	84	2.73	29

a Released by Milwaukee Brewers, August 22, 2009. Signed with Seattle Mariners organization, March 3, 2010.

WILLIAMS, JEROME LEE

Born, Honolulu, Hawaii, December 4, 1981.
Bats Right. Throws Right. Height, 6 feet, 3 inches. Weight, 240 pounds.

Year	Club	Lea	G	IP	W	L	Pct	SO	BB	H	ERA	SAVES
1999	Salem-Keizer	Northwest	7	37	1	1	.500	34	11	29	2.19	0
2000	San Jose	Calif.	23	125 2/3	7	6	.538	115	48	89	2.94	0
2001	Shreveport	Texas	23	130	9	7	.563	84	34	116	3.95	0
2002	Fresno	P.C.	28	160 2/3	6	11	.353	130	50	140	3.59	0
2003	Fresno	P.C.	10	57	4	2	.667	40	16	52	2.68	0
2003	San Francisco	N.L.	21	131	7	5	.583	88	49	116	3.30	0
2004	San Francisco a	N.L.	22	129 1/3	10	7	.588	80	44	123	4.24	0
2005	Fresno	P.C.	6	30 2/3	1	4	.200	15	17	47	9.39	0
2005	Iowa	P.C.	4	24 1/3	1	1	.500	17	6	27	2.22	0
2005	San Francisco-Chicago b	N.L.	22	122 2/3	6	10	.375	70	49	119	4.26	0
2006	Chicago	N.L.	5	12 1/3	0	2	.000	5	11	15	7.30	0
2006	Iowa c	P.C.	29	111 2/3	5	7	.417	52	35	145	4.76	0
2007	Columbus	Int.	1	6	0	0	.000	5	2	4	1.50	0
2007	Washington	N.L.	6	30	0	5	.000	15	18	34	7.20	0
2007	Harrisburg	Eastern	14	35 2/3	0	3	.000	26	16	53	9.08	0
2007	Rochester d-e-f	Int.	8	11	0	1	.000	6	7	18	9.00	1
2008	Long Beach	Golden	6	40	3	2	.600	28	8	48	4.95	0
2008	Inland Empire	Calif.	3	10	0	1	.000	8	6	13	6.30	0
2008	Las Vegas g-h-i	P.C.	10	26	2	2	.500	21	9	23	2.08	0
2009	Sacramento	P.C.	27	101 2/3	5	6	.455	52	41	116	5.58	0
2010	Uni-President	Taiwan					No Data Available					
2011	Lancaster	Atlantic	8	52 2/3	7	1	.875	40	12	43	2.91	0
2011	Salt Lake	P.C.	11	73 2/3	7	2	.778	60	15	78	3.91	0
2011	Los Angeles j	A.L.	10	44	4	0	1.000	28	15	45	3.68	0
2012	Inland Empire	Calif.	2	11	1	0	1.000	9	1	11	3.27	0
2012	Salt Lake	P.C.	2	8	0	1	.000	8	0	13	7.87	0
2012	Los Angeles k	A.L.	32	137 2/3	6	8	.429	98	35	139	4.58	1
Major League Totals	7 Yrs.		118	607	33	37	.471	384	221	591	4.29	1
Division Series												
2003	San Francisco	N.L.	1	2	0	0	.000	1	1	5	13.50	0

a On disabled list from July 31 to September 16, 2004.

b Traded to Chicago Cubs with pitcher David Aardsma for pitcher La Troy Hawkins, May 28, 2005.

c Claimed on waivers by Oakland Athletics, September 5, 2006.

d Filed for free agency, December 12, 2006. Signed with Washington Nationals organization, January 12, 2007.

e On disabled list from April 29 to May 15 and May 16 to June 20, 2007.

f Released by Washington Nationals, August 5, 2007. Signed with Minnesota Twins organization, August 9, 2007.

g Filed for free agency, October 29, 2007. Signed with Long Beach (Golden) for 2008.

h Signed with Los Angeles Dodgers organization, June 25, 2008.

i Filed for free agency, November 3, 2008. Signed with Oakland Athletics organization, December 1, 2008.

j Filed for free agency, November 9, 2009. Signed with Los Angeles Angels organization, June 17, 2011.

k On disabled list from March 26 to April 15 and June 20 to July 14, 2012.

WILSON, BRIAN PATRICK

Born, Londonderry, New Hampshire, March 16, 1982.
Bats Right. Throws Right. Height, 6 feet, 1 inch. Weight, 205 pounds.

Year	Club	Lea	G	IP	W	L	Pct	SO	BB	H	ERA	SAVES
2004 Hagerstown	So.Atl.	23	57⅓	2	5	.286	41	22	63	5.34	3
2005 Norwich	Eastern	15	15⅔	0	0	.000	22	5	6	0.57	8
2005 Fresno	P.C.	9	11⅓	1	1	.500	13	8	8	3.97	0
2005 Augusta	So.Atl.	26	33	5	1	.833	30	7	23	0.82	13
2006 San Jose	Calif.	1	1	0	0	.000	1	1	1	9.00	0
2006 Fresno	P.C.	24	28	1	3	.250	30	14	20	2.89	7
2006 San Francisco	N.L.	31	30	2	3	.400	23	21	32	5.40	1
2007 San Jose	Calif.	3	3	0	0	.000	6	0	1	0.00	2
2007 Fresno	P.C.	31	34⅓	1	2	.333	37	24	24	2.10	11
2007 San Francisco	N.L.	24	23⅔	1	2	.333	18	7	16	2.28	6
2008 San Francisco	N.L.	63	62⅓	3	2	.600	67	28	62	4.62	41
2009 San Francisco	N.L.	68	72⅓	5	6	.455	83	27	60	2.74	38
2010 San Francisco	N.L.	70	74⅔	3	3	.500	93	26	62	1.81	*48
2011 San Francisco a	N.L.	57	55	6	4	.600	54	31	50	3.11	36
2012 San Francisco b-c	N.L.	2	2	0	0	.000	2	2	4	9.00	1
Major League Totals	7 Yrs.	315	320	20	20	.500	340	142	286	3.21	171

Division Series

Year	Club	Lea	G	IP	W	L	Pct	SO	BB	H	ERA	SAVES
2010 San Francisco	N.L.	3	4	0	0	.000	5	2	2	0.00	2

Championship Series

Year	Club	Lea	G	IP	W	L	Pct	SO	BB	H	ERA	SAVES
2010 San Francisco	N.L.	4	5	1	0	1.000	7	2	2	0.00	3

World Series Record

Year	Club	Lea	G	IP	W	L	Pct	SO	BB	H	ERA	SAVES
2010 San Francisco	N.L.	3	2⅔	0	0	.000	4	0	1	0.00	1

a On disabled list from March 22 to April 6 and August 16 to September 18, 2011.
b On disabled list from April 13 to November 1, 2012.
c Not offered contract, November 30, 2012.

WILSON, CHRISTOPHER JOHN (C.J.)

Born, Newport Beach, California, November 18, 1980.
Bats Left. Throws Left. Height, 6 feet, 2 inches. Weight, 215 pounds.

Year	Club	Lea	G	IP	W	L	Pct	SO	BB	H	ERA	SAVES
2001 Pulaski	Appal.	8	37⅓	1	0	1.000	49	9	24	0.96	0
2001 Savannah	So.Atl.	5	34	1	2	.333	26	9	30	3.18	0
2002 Charlotte	Fla.St.	26	106	10	2	.833	76	41	86	3.06	1
2002 Tulsa	Texas	5	30	1	0	1.000	17	12	23	1.80	0
2003 Frisco	Texas	22	123	6	9	.400	89	38	135	5.05	0
2004				INJURED—Did Not Play								
2005 Bakersfield	Calif.	4	13⅔	0	1	.000	14	4	10	3.29	0
2005 Frisco	Texas	12	44⅔	0	4	.000	43	14	51	4.43	0
2005 Texas	A.L.	24	48	1	7	.125	30	18	63	6.94	1
2006 Frisco	Texas	4	3⅓	0	0	.000	6	2	3	2.70	0
2006 Oklahoma	P.C.	9	11	1	0	1.000	17	5	10	2.45	2
2006 Texas a	A.L.	44	44⅓	2	4	.333	43	18	39	4.06	1
2007 Texas	A.L.	66	68⅓	2	1	.667	63	33	50	3.03	12
2008 Texas b	A.L.	50	46⅓	2	2	.500	41	27	49	6.02	24
2009 Texas	A.L.	74	73⅔	5	6	.455	84	32	66	2.81	14
2010 Texas	A.L.	33	204	15	8	.652	170	*93	161	3.35	0
2011 Texas c	A.L.	34	223⅓	16	7	.696	206	74	191	2.94	0
2012 Los Angeles	A.L.	34	202⅓	13	10	.565	173	91	181	3.83	0
Major League Totals	8 Yrs.	359	910⅓	56	45	.554	810	386	800	3.65	52

Division Series

Year	Club	Lea	G	IP	W	L	Pct	SO	BB	H	ERA	SAVES
2010 Texas	A.L.	1	6⅓	1	0	1.000	7	2	2	0.00	0
2011 Texas	A.L.	1	5	0	1	.000	6	1	7	10.80	0
Division Series Totals		2	11⅓	1	1	.500	13	3	9	4.76	0

Championship Series

Year	Club	Lea	G	IP	W	L	Pct	SO	BB	H	ERA	SAVES
2010 Texas	A.L.	2	12	0	1	.000	6	6	12	6.00	0
2011 Texas	A.L.	2	10⅔	0	1	.000	11	7	14	6.75	0
Championship Series Totals		4	22⅔	0	2	.000	17	13	26	6.35	0

World Series Record

Year	Club	Lea	G	IP	W	L	Pct	SO	BB	H	ERA	SAVES
2010 Texas	A.L.	1	6	0	1	.000	4	2	3	3.00	0
2011 Texas	A.L.	3	12⅓	0	1	.000	9	11	8	2.92	0
World Series Totals		4	18⅓	0	2	.000	13	13	11	2.95	0

a On disabled list from March 24 to April 14, 2006.
b On disabled list from August 6 to October 2, 2008.
c Filed for free agency, October 30, 2011. Signed with Los Angeles Angels, December 10, 2011.

WOOD, TRAVIS ALAN
Born, Little Rock, Arkansas, February 6, 1987.
Bats Right. Throws Left. Height, 5 feet, 11 inches. Weight, 165 pounds.

Year	Club	Lea	G	IP	W	L	Pct	SO	BB	H	ERA	SAVES
2005 Reds	Gulf Coast	8	24	0	0	.000	45	7	13	0.75	0
2005 Billings	Pioneer	6	24²/₃	2	0	1.000	22	13	15	1.82	0
2006 Dayton	Midwest	27	140	10	5	.667	133	56	108	3.66	0
2007 Sarasota	Fla.St.	12	46¹/₃	3	2	.600	54	27	49	4.86	0
2008 Sarasota	Fla.St.	9	46²/₃	3	4	.429	41	21	39	2.70	0
2008 Chattanooga	Southern	17	80	4	9	.308	58	48	91	7.09	0
2009 Louisville	Int.	8	48²/₃	4	2	.667	32	16	43	3.14	0
2009 Carolina	Southern	19	119	9	3	.750	103	37	78	1.21	0
2010 Louisville	Int.	16	100	5	6	.455	99	24	86	3.06	0
2010 Cincinnati	N.L.	17	102²/₃	5	4	.556	86	26	85	3.51	0
2011 Louisville	Int.	10	52¹/₃	2	3	.400	47	17	64	5.33	0
2011 Cincinnati a	N.L.	22	106	6	6	.500	76	40	118	4.84	0
2012 Iowa	P.C.	7	41¹/₃	3	3	.500	39	11	48	4.57	0
2012 Chicago	N.L.	26	156	6	13	.316	119	54	133	4.27	0
Major League Totals	3 Yrs.	65	364²/₃	17	23	.425	281	120	336	4.22	0
Division Series											
2010 Cincinnati	N.L.	1	3¹/₃	0	0	.000	3	1	1	0.00	0

a Traded to Chicago Cubs with outfielder Dave Sappelt and infielder Ronald Torreyes for pitcher Sean Marshall, December 23, 2011.

WORLEY, VANCE RICHARD
Born, Sacramento, California, September 25, 1987.
Bats Right. Throws Right. Height, 6 feet, 2 inches. Weight, 230 pounds.

Year	Club	Lea	G	IP	W	L	Pct	SO	BB	H	ERA	SAVES
2008 Williamsport	N.Y.-Penn.	2	8	0	0	.000	8	1	3	1.13	0
2008 Lakewood	So.Atl.	11	61	3	2	.600	53	7	58	2.66	0
2009 Reading	Eastern	27	153¹/₃	7	12	.368	100	49	163	5.34	0
2010 Reading	Eastern	19	112²/₃	9	4	.692	83	36	114	3.20	0
2010 Lehigh Valley	Int.	8	45¹/₃	1	3	.250	36	10	46	3.77	0
2010 Philadelphia	N.L.	5	13	1	1	.500	12	4	8	1.38	0
2011 Lehigh Valley	Int.	9	50²/₃	5	2	.714	50	12	41	2.31	0
2011 Philadelphia	N.L.	25	131²/₃	11	3	.786	119	46	116	3.01	0
2012 Philadelphia a-b	N.L.	23	133	6	9	.400	107	47	154	4.20	0
Major League Totals	3 Yrs.	53	277²/₃	18	13	.581	238	97	278	3.50	0
Division Series											
2011 Philadelphia	N.L.	2	1¹/₃	0	0	.000	0	1	3	6.75	0

a On disabled list from May 13 to June 4 and August 29 to October 5, 2012.
b Traded to Minnesota Twins with pitcher Trevor May for outfielder Ben Revere, December 6, 2012.

WRIGHT, DEQUAM LA WESLEY (WESLEY)
Born, Montgomery, Alabama, January 28, 1985.
Bats Right. Throws Left. Height, 5 feet, 11 inches. Weight, 180 pounds.

Year	Club	Lea	G	IP	W	L	Pct	SO	BB	H	ERA	SAVES
2003 Dodgers	Gulf Coast	14	37²/₃	3	1	.750	26	19	37	3.58	0
2004 Ogden	Pioneer	17	44¹/₃	3	3	.500	66	23	56	6.29	0
2005 Vero Beach	Fla.St.	6	6²/₃	0	0	.000	8	10	8	9.45	0
2005 Columbus	So.Atl.	30	60²/₃	1	5	.167	68	33	38	1.93	1
2006 Vero Beach	Fla.St.	26	42¹/₃	3	3	.500	51	23	29	1.49	0
2006 Jacksonville	Southern	15	21¹/₃	1	1	.500	28	11	14	4.64	1
2007 Las Vegas	P.C.	14	16²/₃	1	2	.333	18	18	28	9.18	0
2007 Jacksonville a	Southern	30	61¹/₃	6	2	.750	68	31	45	2.49	2
2008 Houston	N.L.	71	55²/₃	4	3	.571	57	34	45	5.01	1
2009 Round Rock	P.C.	13	19	2	1	.667	18	10	13	3.32	0
2009 Houston b	N.L.	49	44²/₃	3	4	.429	47	25	53	5.44	0
2010 Round Rock	P.C.	15	69²/₃	4	1	.800	41	33	76	4.65	0
2010 Houston	N.L.	14	33	1	2	.333	29	13	37	5.73	0
2011 Oklahoma	P.C.	39	65¹/₃	3	1	.750	52	23	49	2.07	2
2011 Houston	N.L.	21	12	0	0	.000	11	5	6	1.50	0
2012 Houston	N.L.	77	52¹/₃	2	2	.500	54	17	45	3.27	1
Major League Totals	5 Yrs.	232	197²/₃	10	11	.476	198	94	186	4.55	2

a Selected by Houston Astros from Los Angeles Dodgers in Rule V draft, December 6, 2007.
b On disabled list from August 12 to September 1, 2009.

WRIGHT, JAMEY ALAN

Born, Oklahoma City, Oklahoma, December 24, 1974.
Bats Right. Throws Right. Height, 6 feet, 6 inches. Weight, 235 pounds.

Year	Club	Lea	G	IP	W	L	Pct	SO	BB	H	ERA	SAVES
1993 Rockies	....	Arizona	8	36	1	3	.250	26	9	35	4.00	0
1994 Asheville	....	So.Atl.	28	143⅓	7	14	.333	103	59	188	5.97	0
1995 Salem	....	Carolina	26	171	10	8	.556	95	72	160	2.47	0
1995 New Haven	....	Eastern	1	3	0	1	.000	0	3	6	9.00	0
1996 New Haven	....	Eastern	7	44⅔	5	1	.833	54	12	27	0.81	0
1996 Colorado Springs	....	P.C.	9	59⅔	4	2	.667	40	22	53	2.72	0
1996 Colorado	....	N.L.	16	91⅓	4	4	.500	45	41	105	4.93	0
1997 Salem	....	Carolina	1	1	0	1	.000	1	1	1	9.00	0
1997 Colorado Springs	....	P.C.	2	11	1	0	1.000	11	5	9	1.64	0
1997 Colorado a	....	N.L.	26	149⅔	8	12	.400	59	71	198	6.25	0
1998 Colorado	....	N.L.	34	206⅓	9	14	.391	86	95	235	5.67	0
1999 Colorado	....	N.L.	16	94⅓	4	3	.571	49	54	110	4.87	0
1999 Colorado Springs b	......	P.C.	17	100⅓	5	7	.417	75	38	133	6.46	0
2000 Huntsville	....	Southern	2	12⅓	2	0	1.000	10	5	7	0.00	0
2000 Indianapolis	....	Int.	1	5	0	0	.000	7	3	8	1.80	0
2000 Milwaukee c	....	N.L.	26	164⅔	7	9	.438	96	88	157	4.10	0
2001 Milwaukee d	....	N.L.	33	194⅔	11	12	.478	129	98	201	4.90	0
2002 Indianapolis	....	Int.	3	15⅓	1	1	.500	13	5	16	4.11	0
2002 Milwaukee-St. Louis e-f-g		N.L.	23	129⅓	7	13	.350	77	75	130	5.29	0
2003 Indianapolis	....	Int.	7	22	1	3	.250	17	10	32	7.36	0
2003 Oklahoma	....	P.C.	7	39⅓	2	1	.667	40	21	38	4.12	0
2003 Omaha	....	P.C.	13	76⅔	3	5	.375	65	38	70	3.64	0
2003 Kansas City h-i-j-k	......	A.L.	4	25⅓	1	2	.333	19	11	23	4.26	0
2004 Omaha	....	P.C.	18	104⅔	8	6	.571	70	35	111	4.21	0
2004 Colorado l-m	....	N.L.	14	78⅔	2	3	.400	41	45	82	4.12	0
2005 Colorado n	....	N.L.	34	171⅓	8	16	.333	101	81	201	5.46	0
2006 San Francisco o	....	N.L.	34	156	6	10	.375	79	64	167	5.19	0
2007 Frisco	....	Texas	1	4	0	0	.000	2	0	6	4.50	0
2007 Oklahoma	....	P.C.	3	16⅓	2	1	.667	11	3	21	4.41	0
2007 Texas p-q	....	A.L.	20	77	4	5	.444	39	41	72	3.62	0
2008 Texas r	....	A.L.	75	84⅓	8	7	.533	60	35	93	5.12	0
2009 Kansas City s	....	A.L.	65	79	3	5	.375	60	44	73	4.33	0
2010 Sacramento	....	P.C.	10	14	1	0	1.000	16	9	23	9.00	1
2010 Cleveland-Seattle t-u	.....	A.L.	46	58⅓	1	3	.250	28	25	55	4.17	0
2011 Seattle v	....	A.L.	60	68⅓	2	3	.400	48	30	61	3.16	1
2012 Los Angeles w	....	N.L.	66	67⅔	5	3	.625	54	30	72	3.72	0
Major League Totals	....	17 Yrs.	592	1896⅓	90	124	.421	1070	928	2035	4.89	1

a On disabled list from May 15 to June 8, 1997.

b Traded to Milwaukee Brewers with catcher Henry Blanco and pitcher Justin Miller for infielder Jeff Cirillo and pitcher Scott Karl, December 13, 1999.

c On disabled list from March 28 to May 22, 2000.

d On disabled list from May 21 to June 10, 2001.

e On disabled list from April 5 to May 24, 2002.

f Traded to St. Louis Cardinals with cash for outfielder Chris Morris and player to be named later, August 29, 2002. Milwaukee Brewers received pitcher Mike Matthews to complete trade, September 11, 2002.

g Filed for free agency, November 1, 2002. Signed with Seattle Mariners organization, January 24, 2003.

h Released by Seattle Mariners, March 18, 2003. Signed with Milwaukee Brewers organization, March 23, 2003.

i Released by Milwaukee Brewers, April 28, 2003. Signed with Texas Rangers organization, May 5, 2003.

j Released by Texas Rangers, June 16, 2003. Signed with Kansas City Royals organization, June 24, 2003.

k Filed for free agency, October 30, 2003, re-signed with Kansas City Royals organization, March 29, 2004.

l Released by Kansas City Royals, July 21, 2004. Signed with Colorado Rockies organization, July 22, 2004.

m Filed for free agency, November 1, 2004, re-signed with Colorado Rockies, December 21, 2004.

n Filed for free agency, November 2, 2005. Signed with San Francisco Giants organization, January 17, 2006.

o Filed for free agency, November 2, 2006. Signed with Texas Rangers organization, January 25, 2007.

p On disabled list from April 11 to June 16, 2007.

q Filed for free agency, November 12, 2007, re-signed with Texas Rangers organization, January 11, 2008.

r Filed for free agency, October 30, 2008. Signed with Kansas City Royals organization, February 10, 2009.

s Filed for free agency, November 5, 2009. Signed with Cleveland Indians organization, February 9, 2010.

t Released by Cleveland Indians, June 10, 2010. Signed with Seattle Mariners, July 15, 2010.

u Filed for free agency, November 1, 2010, re-signed with Seattle Mariners organization, February 1, 2011.

v Filed for free agency, October 30, 2011. Signed with Los Angeles Dodgers organization, February 15, 2012.

w Filed for free agency, November 3, 2012.

YOUNG, CHRISTOPHER RYAN (CHRIS)
Born, Dallas, Texas, May 25, 1979.
Bats Right. Throws Right. Height, 6 feet, 10 inches. Weight, 280 pounds.

Year Club	Lea	G	IP	W	L	Pct	SO	BB	H	ERA	SAVES
2001 Hickory.............	So.Atl.	12	74¹/₃	5	3	.625	72	20	79	4.12	0
2002 Hickory a...........	So.Atl.	26	142²/₃	11	9	.550	136	34	127	3.11	0
2003 Harrisburg.........	Eastern	15	83	4	4	.500	64	22	83	4.01	0
2003 Brevard County......	Fla.St.	8	50	5	2	.714	39	5	26	1.62	0
2004 Frisco..............	Texas	18	88¹/₃	6	5	.545	75	31	94	4.48	0
2004 Oklahoma............	P.C.	5	30¹/₃	3	0	1.000	34	9	20	1.48	0
2004 Texas b............	A.L.	7	36¹/₃	3	2	.600	27	10	36	4.71	0
2005 Lynchburg.........	Carolina	10	15	0	1	.000	14	5	9	3.00	2
2005 Tulsa..............	Texas	35	53	3	2	.600	35	17	63	4.75	1
2005 Texas c-d...........	A.L.	31	164²/₃	12	7	.632	137	45	162	4.26	0
2006 San Diego..........	N.L.	31	179¹/₃	11	5	.688	164	69	134	3.46	0
2007 San Diego e.........	N.L.	30	173	9	8	.529	167	72	118	3.12	0
2008 Lake Elsinore.......	Calif.	2	8²/₃	0	1	.000	7	1	5	3.12	0
2008 San Diego f.........	N.L.	18	102¹/₃	7	6	.538	93	48	84	3.96	0
2009 San Diego g.........	N.L.	14	76	4	6	.400	50	40	70	5.21	0
2010 San Antonio.........	Texas	1	0²/₃	0	1	.000	1	4	2	67.50	0
2010 Portland............	P.C.	2	6¹/₃	0	0	.000	4	2	2	1.42	0
2010 San Diego h-i.......	N.L.	4	20	2	0	1.000	15	11	10	0.90	0
2011 New York k-l........	N.L.	4	24	1	0	1.000	22	11	12	1.88	0
2012 St. Lucie..........	Fla.St.	3	17	1	0	1.000	7	2	17	3.18	0
2012 Buffalo.............	Int.	1	6	0	0	.000	2	3	2	0.00	0
2012 New York m.........	N.L.	20	115	4	9	.308	80	36	119	4.15	0
Major League Totals........9 Yrs.		159	890²/₃	53	43	.552	755	342	745	3.79	0
Division Series											
2006 San Diego..........	N.L.	1	6²/₃	1	0	1.000	9	2	4	0.00	0

a Traded by Pittsburgh Pirates to Montreal Expos with pitcher Jon Searles for pitcher Matt Herges, December 20, 2002.
b Traded to Texas Rangers with catcher Josh McKinley for catcher Einar Diaz, April 3, 2004.
c Traded to Arizona Diamondbacks with pitcher Orlando Hernandez and pitcher Luis Vizcaino for pitcher Javier Vazquez, December 20, 2005.
d Traded to San Diego Padres with infielder Adrian Gonzalez and outfielder Terrmel Sledge for pitcher Adam Eaton, pitcher Akinori Otsuka and catcher Billy Killian, January 4, 2006.
e On disabled list from July 25 to August 9, 2007.
f On disabled list from May 22 to July 29 and August 11 to September 1, 2008.
g On disabled list from June 15 to October 28, 2009.
h On disabled list from April 7 to September 18, 2010.
i Filed for free agency, November 3, 2010. Signed with New York Mets, January 20, 2011.
k On disabled list from April 11 to April 26 and May 2 to October 30, 2011.
l Filed for free agency, October 30, 2011, re-signed with New York Mets organization, March 27, 2012.
m Filed for free agency, November 3, 2012.

ZAMBRANO, CARLOS ALBERTO
Born, Puerto Cabello, Venezuela, June 1, 1981.
Bats Both. Throws Right. Height, 6 feet, 5 inches. Weight, 255 pounds.

Year Club	Lea	G	IP	W	L	Pct	SO	BB	H	ERA	SAVES
1998 Cubs.............	Arizona	14	40	0	1	.000	36	25	39	3.15	1
1999 Lansing..........	Midwest	27	153¹/₃	13	7	.650	98	62	150	4.17	0
2000 Iowa..............	P.C.	34	56²/₃	2	5	.286	46	40	54	3.97	6
2000 West Tenn........	Southern	9	60¹/₃	3	1	.750	43	21	39	1.34	0
2001 Iowa..............	P.C.	26	150²/₃	10	5	.667	155	68	124	3.88	0
2001 Chicago...........	N.L.	6	7²/₃	1	2	.333	4	8	11	15.26	0
2002 Iowa..............	P.C.	3	9	0	0	.000	11	6	2	0.00	0
2002 Chicago a.........	N.L.	32	108¹/₃	4	8	.333	93	63	94	3.66	0
2003 Chicago..........	N.L.	32	214	13	11	.542	168	94	188	3.11	0
2004 Chicago..........	N.L.	31	209²/₃	16	8	.667	188	81	174	2.75	0
2005 Chicago..........	N.L.	33	223¹/₃	14	6	.700	202	86	170	3.26	0
2006 Chicago..........	N.L.	33	214	*16	7	.696	210	*115	162	3.41	0
2007 Chicago..........	N.L.	34	216¹/₃	18	13	.581	177	*101	187	3.95	0
2008 Chicago b-c......	N.L.	30	188²/₃	14	6	.700	130	72	172	3.91	0
2009 Peoria...........	Midwest	1	5	0	0	.000	5	0	4	0.00	0
2009 Daytona..........	Fla.St.	1	3²/₃	0	1	.000	1	3	5	9.82	0
2009 Chicago d........	N.L.	28	169¹/₃	9	7	.563	152	78	155	3.77	0
2010 Cubs.............	Arizona	1	1	0	0	.000	1	0	0	0.00	0
2010 Iowa.............	P.C.	3	4	0	0	.000	4	1	6	6.75	0
2010 Chicago..........	N.L.	36	129²/₃	11	6	.647	117	69	119	3.33	0
2011 Peoria...........	Midwest	1	4	0	0	.000	4	3	3	0.00	0
2011 Chicago e........	N.L.	24	145²/₃	9	7	.563	101	56	154	4.82	0

Year Club	Lea	G	IP	W	L	Pct	SO	BB	H	ERA	SAVES
2012 Miami f-g	N.L.	35	132¹/₃	7	10	.412	95	75	123	4.49	0
Major League Totals . . . . . . .12 Yrs.		354	1959	132	91	.592	1637	898	1709	3.66	0
Division Series											
2003 Chicago	N.L.	1	5²/₃	0	0	.000	4	0	11	4.76	0
2007 Chicago	N.L.	1	6	0	0	.000	8	1	4	1.50	0
2008 Chicago	N.L.	1	6¹/₃	0	1	.000	7	2	6	4.26	0
Division Series Totals		3	18	0	1	.000	19	3	21	3.50	0
Championship Series											
2003 Chicago	N.L.	2	11	0	1	.000	8	5	14	5.73	0

a On disabled list from May 10 to June 7, 2002.
b On disabled list from June 19 to July 4, 2008.
c Pitched no-hit, no-run game against Houston Astros, September 14, 2008.
d On disabled list from May 4 to May 22 and August 6 to August 25, 2009.
e On disabled list from July 1 to July 16, 2011.
f Traded to Florida Marlins with cash for pitcher Chris Volstad, January 5, 2012.
g Filed for free agency, November 3, 2012.

ZIEGLER, BRAD GREGORY

Born, Pratt, Kansas, October 10, 1979.
Bats Right. Throws Right. Height, 6 feet, 4 inches. Weight, 200 pounds.

Year Club	Lea	G	IP	W	L	Pct	SO	BB	H	ERA	SAVES
2003 Batavia	N.Y.-Penn.	3	6	1	0	1.000	6	1	5	1.50	0
2004 Schaumburg	Northern	4	24	3	0	1.000	26	1	12	1.50	0
2004 Modesto a-b	Calif.	16	92¹/₃	9	2	.818	77	22	94	3.90	0
2005 Stockton	Calif.	24	141	9	7	.563	144	20	166	4.66	0
2005 Midland	Texas	4	21	2	1	.667	20	4	27	6.86	0
2006 Sacramento	P.C.	4	21	0	1	.000	11	5	32	6.00	0
2006 Midland	Texas	23	141²/₃	9	6	.600	88	37	151	3.37	0
2007 Sacramento	P.C.	35	54²/₃	8	3	.727	44	14	46	2.96	1
2007 Midland	Texas	15	23²/₃	4	0	1.000	18	4	19	1.14	1
2008 Sacramento	P.C.	19	24¹/₃	2	0	1.000	20	4	15	0.37	8
2008 Oakland	A.L.	47	59²/₃	3	0	1.000	30	22	47	1.06	11
2009 Oakland	A.L.	69	73¹/₃	2	4	.333	54	28	82	3.07	7
2010 Oakland	A.L.	64	60²/₃	3	7	.300	41	28	54	3.26	0
2011 Oakland	A.L.	43	37²/₃	3	2	.600	29	13	38	2.39	1
2011 Arizona c	N.L.	23	20²/₃	0	0	.000	15	6	15	1.74	0
2012 Arizona	N.L.	77	68²/₃	6	1	.857	42	21	54	2.49	0
Major League Totals . . . . .5 Yrs.		323	320²/₃	17	14	.548	211	118	290	2.44	19
Division Series											
2011 Arizona	N.L.	2	0¹/₃	0	0	.000	0	2	4	108.00	0

a Released by Philadelphia Phillies, March 28, 2004. Signed with independent Schaumburg (Northern), April 18, 2004.
b Sold to Oakland Athletics organization, June 16, 2004.
c Traded to Arizona Diamondbacks for infielder Brandon Allen and pitcher Jordan Norberto, July 31, 2011.

ZIMMERMANN, JORDAN M.

Born, Auburndale, Wisconsin, May 23, 1986.
Bats Right. Throws Right. Height, 6 feet, 2 inches. Weight, 220 pounds.

Year Club	Lea	G	IP	W	L	Pct	SO	BB	H	ERA	SAVES
2007 Vermont	N.Y.-Penn.	13	53	5	2	.714	71	18	45	2.38	0
2008 Potomac	Carolina	5	27¹/₃	3	1	.750	31	8	15	1.65	1
2008 Harrisburg	Eastern	20	106²/₃	7	2	.778	103	39	89	3.21	0
2009 Potomac	Carolina	1	3¹/₃	0	0	.000	6	1	2	2.70	0
2009 Syracuse	Int.	1	5¹/₃	0	0	.000	4	1	4	5.06	0
2009 Washington a	N.L.	16	91¹/₃	3	5	.375	92	29	95	4.63	0
2010 Hagerstown	So.Atl.	1	5	0	1	.000	3	1	7	10.80	0
2010 Potomac	Carolina	4	13	0	1	.000	13	0	11	0.00	0
2010 Harrisburg	Eastern	1	4²/₃	0	0	.000	3	2	1	0.00	0
2010 Syracuse	Int.	4	17	1	0	1.000	12	3	8	0.53	0
2010 Washington b	N.L.	7	31	1	2	.333	27	10	31	4.94	0
2011 Washington	N.L.	26	161¹/₃	8	11	.421	124	31	154	3.18	0
2012 Washington	N.L.	32	195²/₃	12	8	.600	153	43	186	2.94	0
Major League Totals . . . . .4 Yrs.		81	479¹/₃	24	26	.480	396	113	466	3.47	0
Division Series											
2012 Washington	N.L.	2	4	0	1	.000	5	0	7	11.25	0

a On disabled list from July 19 to November 8, 2009.
b On disabled list from February 19 to July 31, 2010.

ZITO, BARRY WILLIAM

Born, Las Vegas, Nevada, May 13, 1978.
Bats Left. Throws Left. Height, 6 feet, 4 inches. Weight, 210 pounds.

Year	Club	Lea	G	IP	W	L	Pct	SO	BB	H	ERA	SAVES
1999	Vancouver	P.C.	1	6	1	0	1.000	6	2	5	1.50	0
1999	Midland	Texas	4	22	2	1	.667	29	11	22	4.91	0
1999	Visalia	California	8	40$\frac{1}{3}$	3	0	1.000	62	22	21	2.45	0
2000	Sacramento	P.C.	18	101$\frac{2}{3}$	8	5	.615	91	45	88	3.19	0
2000	Oakland	A.L.	14	92$\frac{2}{3}$	7	4	.636	78	45	64	2.72	0
2001	Oakland	A.L.	35	214$\frac{1}{3}$	17	8	.680	205	80	184	3.49	0
2002	Oakland a	A.L.	35	229$\frac{1}{3}$	*23	5	.821	182	78	182	2.75	0
2003	Oakland	A.L.	35	231$\frac{2}{3}$	14	12	.538	146	88	186	3.30	0
2004	Oakland	A.L.	34	213	11	11	.500	163	81	216	4.48	0
2005	Oakland	A.L.	35	228$\frac{1}{3}$	14	13	.519	171	89	185	3.86	0
2006	Oakland b	A.L.	34	221	16	10	.615	151	99	211	3.83	0
2007	San Francisco	N.L.	34	196$\frac{2}{3}$	11	13	.458	131	83	182	4.53	0
2008	San Francisco	N.L.	32	180	10	*17	.370	120	102	186	5.15	0
2009	San Francisco	N.L.	33	192	10	13	.435	154	81	179	4.03	0
2010	San Francisco	N.L.	34	199$\frac{1}{3}$	9	14	.391	150	84	184	4.15	0
2011	San Jose	Calif.	3	21$\frac{1}{3}$	2	1	.667	19	5	15	2.53	0
2011	Fresno	P.C.	3	17$\frac{2}{3}$	2	0	1.000	17	5	10	2.55	0
2011	San Francisco c	N.L.	13	53$\frac{2}{3}$	3	4	.429	32	24	51	5.87	0
2012	San Francisco	N.L.	32	184$\frac{1}{3}$	15	8	.652	114	70	186	4.15	0
Major League Totals	13 Yrs.		400	2436$\frac{1}{3}$	160	132	.548	1797	1004	2196	3.93	0
Division Series												
2000	Oakland	A.L.	1	5$\frac{2}{3}$	1	0	1.000	5	2	7	1.59	0
2001	Oakland	A.L.	1	8	0	1	.000	6	1	2	1.13	0
2002	Oakland	A.L.	1	6	1	0	1.000	8	4	5	4.50	0
2003	Oakland	A.L.	2	13	1	1	.500	13	4	9	3.46	0
2006	Oakland	A.L.	1	8	1	0	1.000	1	3	4	1.13	0
2012	San Francisco	N.L.	1	2$\frac{2}{3}$	0	0	.000	4	4	4	6.75	0
Division Series Totals			7	43$\frac{1}{3}$	4	2	.667	37	18	31	2.70	0
Championship Series												
2006	Oakland	A.L.	1	3$\frac{2}{3}$	0	1	.000	0	3	7	12.27	0
2012	San Francisco	N.L.	1	7$\frac{2}{3}$	1	0	1.000	6	1	6	0.00	0
Championship Series Totals			2	11$\frac{1}{3}$	1	1	.500	6	4	13	3.97	0
World Series Record												
2012	San Francisco	N.L.	1	5$\frac{2}{3}$	1	0	1.000	3	1	6	1.59	0

a Selected Cy Young Award Winner in American League for 2002.
b Filed for free agency, October 31, 2006. Signed with San Francisco Giants, December 29, 2006.
c On disabled list from April 17 to June 25 and August 1 to September 11, 2011.